Engineering Mathematics

Third Edition

We work with leading authors to develop the strongest
educational materials in mathematics,
bringing cutting-edge thinking and best learning
practice to a global market.

Under a range of well-known imprints, including
Prentice Hall, we craft high quality print and electronic
publications which help readers to understand and apply
their content, whether studying or at work.

To find out more about the complete range of our
publishing, please visit us on the World Wide Web at:
www.pearsoned.co.uk

Engineering Mathematics

A Foundation for Electronic, Electrical, Communications and Systems Engineers

Third Edition

Anthony Croft *Loughborough University*
Robert Davison *De Montfort University*
Martin Hargreaves *De Montfort University*

PEARSON
Prentice
Hall

Harlow, England • London • New York • Boston • San Francisco • Toronto • Sydney • Singapore • Hong Kong
Tokyo • Seoul • Taipei • New Delhi • Cape Town • Madrid • Mexico City • Amsterdam • Munich • Paris • Milan

Pearson Education Limited
Edinburgh Gate
Harlow
Essex, CM20 2JE
England

and Associated Companies throughout the world

Visit us on the World Wide Web at:
www.pearsoned.co.uk

First published under the Addison-Wesley imprint 1992
Second edition under the Addison-Wesley imprint 1996
Third Edition published 2001

© Addison-Wesley Publishers Limited 1992, 1996
This Edition © Pearson Education Limited 2001

ISBN 0 130 26858 5

British Library Cataloguing in Publication Data
A catalogue record for this book is available from the British Library.

Library of Congress Cataloging in Publication Data
Croft, Tony, 1957–
    Engineering mathematics : a foundation for electronic, electrical, communications, and
    systems engineers / Anthony Croft, Robert Davison, Martin Hargreaves. — 3rd ed.
        p.   cm.
    Includes index.
    ISBN 0–13–026858–5
    1. Engineering mathematics.   2. Electric engineering—Mathematics.
    3. Electronics—Mathematics.   I. Davison, Robert.   II. Hargreaves, Martin.   III. Title.

TA330 .C76 2000
510'.2462—dc21

                                                                        00-065272

10
10

Typeset by 56 in 10/12pt Times
Printed and bound in Italy by G.Canale & C. S.p.A.

A.C. To Jan and Thomas
R.D. To Charlie and Wikki
M.H. To the memory of my dear father, George Frederick Hargreaves

Contents

Preface   xxi
Acknowledgements   xxv

Chapter 1   **Review of algebraic techniques**   **1**

1.1   Introduction   2

1.2   Laws of indices   2

1.3   Polynomial equations   8

1.4   Algebraic fractions   14

1.5   Solution of inequalities   21

1.6   Partial fractions   27

      Review exercises   34

Chapter 2   **Engineering functions**   **39**

2.1   Introduction   40

2.2   Numbers and intervals   40

2.3   Basic concepts of functions   42

2.4   Review of some common engineering functions and techniques   54

      Review exercises   92

Chapter 3   **The trigonometric functions**   **95**

3.1   Introduction   96

3.2	Degrees and radians	96
3.3	The trigonometric ratios	97
3.4	The sine, cosine and tangent functions	101
3.5	Trigonometric identities	104
3.6	Modelling waves using $\sin t$ and $\cos t$	110
3.7	Trigonometric equations	120
	Review exercises	127

Chapter 4	**Coordinate systems**	**131**
4.1	Introduction	132
4.2	Cartesian coordinate system – two dimensions	132
4.3	Cartesian coordinate system – three dimensions	134
4.4	Polar coordinates	136
4.5	Some simple polar curves	140
4.6	Cylindrical polar coordinates	142
4.7	Spherical polar coordinates	145
	Review exercises	147

Chapter 5	**Discrete mathematics**	**149**
5.1	Introduction	150
5.2	Set theory	150
5.3	Logic	158
5.4	Boolean algebra	160
	Review exercises	171

Chapter 6	**Sequences and series**	**175**
6.1	Introduction	176
6.2	Sequences	176
6.3	Series	185
6.4	The binomial theorem	190
6.5	Power series	194
6.6	Sequences arising from the iterative solution of non-linear equations	196
	Review exercises	199

Chapter 7	**Vectors**	**201**
7.1	Introduction	202
7.2	Vectors and scalars: basic concepts	202
7.3	Cartesian components	210
7.4	Scalar fields and vector fields	217
7.5	The scalar product	219
7.6	The vector product	224
7.7	Vectors of n dimensions	230
	Review exercises	232

Chapter 8	**Matrix algebra**	**235**
8.1	Introduction	236
8.2	Basic definitions	236
8.3	Addition, subtraction and multiplication	237
8.4	Robot coordinate frames	244

8.5	Some special matrices	248
8.6	The inverse of a 2×2 matrix	251
8.7	Determinants	255
8.8	The inverse of a 3×3 matrix	259
8.9	Application to the solution of simultaneous equations	261
8.10	Gaussian elimination	264
8.11	Eigenvalues and eigenvectors	271
8.12	Analysis of electrical networks	285
8.13	Iterative techniques for the solution of simultaneous equations	291
8.14	Computer solutions of matrix problems	297
	Review exercises	298

Chapter 9	**Complex numbers**	**301**
9.1	Introduction	302
9.2	Complex numbers	302
9.3	Operations with complex numbers	306
9.4	Graphical representation of complex numbers	310
9.5	Polar form of a complex number	311
9.6	Vectors and complex numbers	315
9.7	The exponential form of a complex number	316
9.8	Phasors	318
9.9	De Moivre's theorem	322
9.10	Loci and regions of the complex plane	328
	Review exercises	332

Chapter 10	**Differentiation**	**333**
10.1	Introduction	334
10.2	Graphical approach to differentiation	334
10.3	Limits and continuity	336
10.4	Rate of change at a specific point	339
10.5	Rate of change at a general point	342
10.6	Existence of derivatives	348
10.7	Common derivatives	350
10.8	Differentiation as a linear operator	353
	Review exercises	362

Chapter 11	**Techniques of differentiation**	**365**
11.1	Introduction	366
11.2	Rules of differentiation	366
11.3	Parametric, implicit and logarithmic differentiation	372
11.4	Higher derivatives	380
	Review exercises	384

Chapter 12	**Applications of differentiation**	**387**
12.1	Introduction	388
12.2	Maximum points and minimum points	388
12.3	Points of inflexion	397
12.4	The Newton–Raphson method for solving equations	400
12.5	Differentiation of vectors	405
	Review exercises	409

Chapter 13	**Integration**	**411**
13.1	Introduction	412
13.2	Elementary integration	412
13.3	Definite and indefinite integrals	425
	Review exercises	435

Chapter 14	**Techniques of integration**	**439**
14.1	Introduction	440
14.2	Integration by parts	440
14.3	Integration by substitution	446
14.4	Integration using partial fractions	449
	Review exercises	452

Chapter 15	**Applications of integration**	**455**
15.1	Introduction	456
15.2	Average value of a function	456
15.3	Root mean square value of a function	459
	Review exercises	463

Chapter 16	**Further topics in integration**	**465**
16.1	Introduction	466
16.2	Orthogonal functions	466
16.3	Improper integrals	469
16.4	Integral properties of the delta function	474
16.5	Integration of piecewise continuous functions	477

16.6	Integration of vectors	478
	Review exercises	479

Chapter 17	**Numerical integration**	**483**
17.1	Introduction	484
17.2	Trapezium rule	484
17.3	Simpson's rule	488
	Review exercises	493

Chapter 18	**Taylor polynomials, Taylor series and Maclaurin series**	**495**
18.1	Introduction	496
18.2	Linearization using first order Taylor polynomials	496
18.3	Second order Taylor polynomials	501
18.4	Taylor polynomials of the nth order	506
18.5	Taylor's formula and the remainder term	510
18.6	Taylor and Maclaurin series	513
	Review exercises	519

Chapter 19	**Ordinary differential equations I**	**521**
19.1	Introduction	522
19.2	Basic definitions	522
19.3	First order equations: simple equations and separation of variables	528
19.4	First order linear equations: use of an integrating factor	535
19.5	Second order linear equations	547
	Review exercises	568

Chapter 20	**Ordinary differential equations II**	**571**
20.1	Introduction	572
20.2	Analog simulation	572
20.3	Higher order equations	574
20.4	State-space models	578
20.5	Numerical methods	584
20.6	Euler's method	584
20.7	Improved Euler method	589
20.8	Runge–Kutta method of order 4	592
	Review exercises	595

Chapter 21	**The Laplace transform**	**597**
21.1	Introduction	598
21.2	Definition of the Laplace transform	598
21.3	Laplace transforms of some common functions	599
21.4	Properties of the Laplace transform	601
21.5	Laplace transform of derivatives and integrals	606
21.6	Inverse Laplace transforms	608
21.7	Using partial fractions to find the inverse Laplace transform	612
21.8	Finding the inverse Laplace transform using complex numbers	614
21.9	The convolution theorem	618
21.10	Solving linear constant coefficient differential equations using the Laplace transform	621
21.11	Transfer functions	631
21.12	Poles, zeros and the s plane	640

| 21.13 | Laplace transforms of some special functions | 644 |
| | Review exercises | 648 |

Chapter 22 — Difference equations and the z transform — 651

22.1	Introduction	652
22.2	Basic definitions	652
22.3	Rewriting difference equations	657
22.4	Block diagram representation of difference equations	659
22.5	Design of a discrete-time controller	663
22.6	Numerical solution of difference equations	665
22.7	Definition of the z transform	668
22.8	Sampling a continuous signal	672
22.9	The relationship between the z transform and the Laplace transform	674
22.10	Properties of the z transform	680
22.11	Inversion of z transforms	686
22.12	The z transform and difference equations	690
	Review exercises	692

Chapter 23 — Fourier series — 695

23.1	Introduction	696
23.2	Periodic waveforms	696
23.3	Odd and even functions	700
23.4	Orthogonality relations and other useful identities	705
23.5	Fourier series	706
23.6	Half-range series	717

23.7	Parseval's theorem	721
23.8	Complex notation	721
23.9	Frequency response of a linear system	724
	Review exercises	728

Chapter 24 The Fourier transform **731**

24.1	Introduction	732
24.2	The Fourier transform – definitions	732
24.3	Some properties of the Fourier transform	736
24.4	Spectra	741
24.5	The t–ω duality principle	743
24.6	Fourier transforms of some special functions	744
24.7	The relationship between the Fourier transform and the Laplace transform	747
24.8	Convolution and correlation	749
24.9	The discrete Fourier transform	759
24.10	Derivation of the d.f.t.	762
24.11	Using the d.f.t. to estimate a Fourier transform	765
24.12	Matrix representation of the d.f.t.	767
24.13	Some properties of the d.f.t.	769
24.14	Discrete convolution and correlation	770
	Review exercises	785

Chapter 25 Functions of several variables **787**

25.1	Introduction	788

25.2	Functions of more than one variable	788
25.3	Partial derivatives	789
25.4	Higher order derivatives	794
25.5	Partial differential equations	797
25.6	Taylor polynomials and Taylor series in two variables	800
25.7	Maximum and minimum points of a function of two variables	808
	Review exercises	813

Chapter 26	**Vector calculus**	**817**
26.1	Introduction	818
26.2	Partial differentiation of vectors	818
26.3	The gradient of a scalar field	820
26.4	The divergence of a vector field	824
26.5	The curl of a vector field	828
26.6	Combining the operators grad, div and curl	830
26.7	Vector calculus and electromagnetism	833
	Review exercises	834

Chapter 27	**Line integrals and multiple integrals**	**837**
27.1	Introduction	838
27.2	Line integrals	838
27.3	Evaluation of line integrals in two dimensions	841
27.4	Evaluation of line integrals in three dimensions	844
27.5	Conservative fields and potential functions	845
27.6	Double and triple integrals	851

27.7	Some simple volume and surface integrals	860
27.8	The divergence theorem and Stokes' theorem	866
27.9	Maxwell's equations in integral form	871
	Review exercises	872

Chapter 28	**Probability**	**875**
28.1	Introduction	876
28.2	Introducing probability	876
28.3	Mutually exclusive events: the addition law of probability	882
28.4	Complementary events	886
28.5	Concepts from communication theory	887
28.6	Conditional probability: the multiplication law	892
28.7	Independent events	897
	Review exercises	902

Chapter 29	**Statistics and probability distributions**	**905**
29.1	Introduction	906
29.2	Random variables	906
29.3	Probability distributions – discrete variable	907
29.4	Probability density functions – continuous variable	908
29.5	Mean value	911
29.6	Standard deviation	913
29.7	Expected value of a random variable	916
29.8	Standard deviation of a random variable	919
29.9	Permutations and combinations	921

29.10	The binomial distribution	927
29.11	The Poisson distribution	931
29.12	The uniform distribution	934
29.13	The exponential distribution	935
29.14	The normal distribution	937
29.15	Reliability engineering	944
	Review exercises	951

Appendix I	Representing a continuous function and a sequence as a sum of weighted impulses	954
Appendix II	The Greek alphabet	956
Appendix III	SI units and prefixes	956
Appendix IV	The binomial expansion of $\left(\frac{n-N}{n}\right)^n$	957

Index		959

Preface

Audience

This book has been written to serve the mathematical needs of students engaged in a first course in engineering at degree level. It is primarily aimed at students of electronic, electrical, communications and systems engineering. Systems engineering typically encompasses areas such as manufacturing, control and production engineering. The book will also be useful for engineers who wish to engage in self-study and continuing education.

Motivation

Engineers are called upon to analyse a variety of engineering systems, which can be anything from a few electronic components connected together through to a complete factory. The analysis of these systems benefits from the intelligent application of mathematics. Indeed, many cannot be analysed without the use of mathematics. Mathematics is the language of engineering. It is essential to understand how mathematics works in order to master the complex relationships present in modern engineering systems and products.

Aims

There are two main aims of the book. Firstly, we wish to provide an accessible, readable introduction to engineering mathematics at degree level. The second aim is to encourage the integration of engineering and mathematics.

Content

The first three chapters include a review of some important functions and techniques that the reader may have met in previous courses. This material ensures that the book is self-contained and provides a convenient reference. The reader who is unfamiliar with this material is referred to our companion text *Introduction to Engineering Mathematics*, also published by Pearson Education.

Traditional topics in algebra and calculus have been covered. However, the changing needs of engineers require emphasis to be placed on more up-to-date techniques.

The growing importance of computers is reflected in the increasing use of discrete mathematics by the modern engineer. Thus we have included set theory, sequences and series, Boolean algebra, logic, difference equations and the z transform. The increased use of signal processing techniques is reflected by a greater emphasis on integral transform methods. Thus the Laplace, z and Fourier transforms have been given greater coverage than is normally found.

In the light of feedback from readers, several new topics have been included in the Third Edition. A complete chapter on Coordinate Systems has been added. The material on matrix algebra has been expanded to include eigenvalues and eigenvectors. To reflect the growing importance of digital signal processing and communications engineering, the Fourier transform chapter has been amplified by sections on correlation, convolution and the discrete Fourier transform. Finally, Stokes' theorem and the Divergence theorem are now included in the chapter on line and multiple integrals.

Style

The style of the book is to develop and illustrate mathematical concepts through examples. We have tried throughout to adopt an informal approach and to describe mathematical processes using everyday language. Mathematical ideas are often developed by examples rather than by using abstract proof, which has been kept to a minimum. This reflects the authors' experience that engineering students learn better from practical examples, rather than from formal abstract development. We have included many engineering examples and have tried to make them as free-standing as possible to keep the necessary engineering prerequisites to a minimum. Consequently, the engineering examples are not central to the mathematical development and so can be missed out if desired. This provides the flexibility necessary to tailor a course to the needs of different types of engineer. However, we feel that at this level it is desirable for an engineer to be exposed to as wide a range of different engineering examples as possible. This has the obvious benefit of illustrating the reason for learning a particular piece of mathematics. The engineering examples, which have been carefully selected to be relevant, informative and modern, range from short illustrative examples through to complete sections which can be regarded as case studies. A further benefit is the development of the link between mathematics and the physical world. An appreciation of this link is essential if engineers are to take full advantage of engineering mathematics. The engineering examples make the book more colourful and, more importantly, they help develop the ability to see an engineering problem and translate it into a mathematical form so that a solution can be obtained. This is one of the most difficult skills that an engineer needs to acquire. The ability to manipulate mathematical equations is of itself insufficient. It is sometimes necessary to derive the equations corresponding to an engineering problem. Interpretation of mathematical solutions in terms of the physical variables is also essential. Engineers cannot afford to get lost in mathematical symbolism.

Use of modern computer aids

One of the main developments in the teaching of engineering mathematics in recent years has been the widespread availability of sophisticated computer software and its adoption by many educational institutions. We would encourage its use and so we have made general references at several points in the text. Two packages that we have found to be of particular value are the symbolic mathematics processor and graph plotter, DERIVE®, and the general-purpose mathematics package, MATLAB®. The latter is extremely useful for engineering subjects such as control, signal processing and systems. In fact, the widening availability of such software makes the learning of basic mathematical techniques more important than ever before because of the sophistication of the packages. Many features available in software packages can also be found in graphics calculators.

Format

Important results are highlighted for easy reference. Exercises and solutions are provided at the end of most sections; it is essential to attempt these as the only way to develop competence and understanding is through practice. A further set of review exercises is provided at the end of each chapter. In addition some sections include computer and calculator exercises. All engineering examples have headings and computer and

calculator exercises are denoted by the use of the icon.

Supplements

Available with this text is an interactive CD testing and assessment package, with multi-choice and hot-spot questions that allow students to test their understanding of the key topics. Ideal for reinforcing learning during the course or pre-examination revision, all questions provide detailed student feedback on-screen, and also direct students back to the relevant section or page in the text for further study.

A comprehensive Solutions Manual is obtainable free of charge to lecturers using this textbook. It is also available for download via the web at *www.booksites.net/croft*.

Finally we hope you will come to share our enthusiasm for engineering mathematics and enjoy the book.

Anthony Croft
Robert Davison
Martin Hargreaves
July 2000

Acknowledgements

Authors' acknowledgements

We wish to thank all of the staff at Pearson Education who have been involved in the production of this book: Alex Seabrook for having the vision to include the CD, Joe Ward and Duncan Lawson for writing the test questions on the CD, Dylan Reisenberger for coordinating this aspect of the project, and the desk editor for this project, Lorna Sharrock.

We also wish to thank the following colleagues who have read and commented upon various drafts of the book: Dr Eric Chowanietz, Professor Don Conway, Professor Bryan Coulbeck, Dr Martin Crane, Jane Fudge, Derek Hart, Mike Howkins, Cyril Lander, Andrejs Ozolins, Brian Riches, Dr Harry Sharma, Dr Roy Smith, Dr David Storry, John Taylor, Don Thatcher and Bill Thompson. A particular mention must go to John Royle for his thorough appraisal of the manuscript and valuable comments.

Finally, the comments of unknown referees were most useful and are gratefully acknowledged.

Publisher's acknowledgements

We are grateful to the following for permission to reproduce copyright material:
Table 29.7 condensed from Table 1 of the *Biometrika Tables for Statisticians*, Vol. 1 (1st ed.), edited by E.S. Pearson and H.O. Hartley, by permission of Oxford University Press.

Whilst every effort has been made to trace the owners of copyright material, in a few cases this has proved impossible and we take this opportunity to offer our apologies to any copyright holders whose rights we may have unwittingly infringed.

1 Review of algebraic techniques

Chapter 1	Contents	

	1.1	Introduction	2
	1.2	Laws of indices	2
	1.3	Polynomial equations	8
	1.4	Algebraic fractions	14
	1.5	Solution of inequalities	21
	1.6	Partial fractions	27
		Review exercises	34

1.1 Introduction

This chapter introduces some algebraic techniques which are commonly used in engineering mathematics. For some readers, this may be revision. Section 1.2 examines the laws of indices. These laws are used throughout engineering mathematics. Section 1.3 looks at methods of solving quadratic equations. Section 1.4 examines algebraic fractions, while Section 1.5 examines the solution of inequalities. The chapter closes with a study of partial fractions.

1.2 Laws of indices

Consider the product $6 \times 6 \times 6 \times 6 \times 6$. This may be written more compactly as 6^5. We call 5 the **index** or **power**. The **base** is 6. Similarly, $y \times y \times y \times y$ may be written as y^4. Here the base is y and the index is 4.

Example 1.1 Write the following using index notation.

(a) $(-2)(-2)(-2)$ (b) $4.4.4.5.5$ (c) $\dfrac{yyy}{xxxx}$ (d) $\dfrac{aa(-a)(-a)}{bb(-b)}$

Solution (a) $(-2)(-2)(-2)$ may be written as $(-2)^3$.

(b) $4.4.4.5.5$ may be written as $4^3 5^2$.

(c) $\dfrac{yyy}{xxxx}$ may be written as $\dfrac{y^3}{x^4}$.

(d) Note that $(-a)(-a) = aa$ since the product of two negative quantities is positive. So $aa(-a)(-a) = aaaa = a^4$. Also $bb(-b) = -bbb = -b^3$. Hence

$$\frac{aa(-a)(-a)}{bb(-b)} = \frac{a^4}{-b^3} = -\frac{a^4}{b^3}$$

Example 1.2 Evaluate

(a) 7^3 (b) $(-3)^3$ (c) $2^3(-3)^4$

Solution (a) $7^3 = 7.7.7 = 343$

(b) $(-3)^3 = (-3)(-3)(-3) = -27$

(c) $2^3(-3)^4 = 8(81) = 648$

Most scientific calculators have an x^y button to enable easy calculation of expressions of a similar form to those in Example 1.2.

1.2.1 Multiplying expressions involving indices

Consider the product $(6^2)(6^3)$. We may write this as

$$(6^2)(6^3) = (6.6)(6.6.6) = 6^5$$

So

$$6^2 6^3 = 6^5$$

This illustrates the **first law of indices** which is

$$a^m a^n = a^{m+n}$$

When expressions with the same base are multiplied, the indices are added.

Example 1.3 Simplify each of the following expressions:

(a) $3^9 3^{10}$ (b) $4^3 4^4 4^6$ (c) $x^3 x^6$ (d) $y^4 y^2 y^3$

Solution (a) $3^9 3^{10} = 3^{9+10} = 3^{19}$

(b) $4^3 4^4 4^6 = 4^{3+4+6} = 4^{13}$

(c) $x^3 x^6 = x^{3+6} = x^9$

(d) $y^4 y^2 y^3 = y^{4+2+3} = y^9$

Consider the product $3(3^3)$. Now

$$3(3^3) = 3(3.3.3) = 3^4$$

Also, using the first law of indices we see $3^1 3^3 = 3^4$. This suggests that 3 is the same as 3^1. This illustrates the general rule:

$$a = a^1$$

Raising a number to the power 1 leaves the number unchanged.

Example 1.4 Simplify (a) $5^6 5$ (b) $x^3 x x^2$

Solution (a) $5^6 5 = 5^{6+1} = 5^7$

(b) $x^3 x x^2 = x^{3+1+2} = x^6$

1.2.2 Dividing expressions involving indices

Consider the expression $\dfrac{4^5}{4^3}$:

$$\frac{4^5}{4^3} = \frac{4.4.4.4.4}{4.4.4}$$
$$= 4.4 \qquad \text{by cancelling 4s}$$
$$= 4^2$$

This serves to illustrate the **second law of indices** which is

$$\frac{a^m}{a^n} = a^{m-n}$$

When expressions with the same base are divided, the indices are subtracted.

Example 1.5 Simplify

(a) $\dfrac{5^9}{5^7}$ (b) $\dfrac{(-2)^{16}}{(-2)^{13}}$ (c) $\dfrac{x^9}{x^5}$ (d) $\dfrac{y^6}{y}$

Solution (a) $\dfrac{5^9}{5^7} = 5^{9-7} = 5^2$

(b) $\dfrac{(-2)^{16}}{(-2)^{13}} = (-2)^{16-13} = (-2)^3$

(c) $\dfrac{x^9}{x^5} = x^{9-5} = x^4$

(d) $\dfrac{y^6}{y} = y^{6-1} = y^5$

Consider the expression $\dfrac{2^3}{2^3}$. Using the second law of indices we may write

$$\frac{2^3}{2^3} = 2^{3-3} = 2^0$$

But, clearly, $\dfrac{2^3}{2^3} = 1$, and so $2^0 = 1$. This illustrates the general rule:

$$a^0 = 1$$

Any expression raised to the power 0 is 1.

1.2.3 Negative indices

Consider the expression $\dfrac{4^3}{4^5}$. We can write this as

$$\frac{4^3}{4^5} = \frac{4.4.4}{4.4.4.4.4} = \frac{1}{4.4} = \frac{1}{4^2}$$

Alternatively, using the second law of indices we have

$$\frac{4^3}{4^5} = 4^{3-5} = 4^{-2}$$

So we see that

$$4^{-2} = \frac{1}{4^2}$$

Thus we are able to interpret negative indices. The sign of an index changes when the expression is inverted. In general we can state

$$a^{-m} = \frac{1}{a^m} \qquad a^m = \frac{1}{a^{-m}}$$

Example 1.6   Evaluate the following:

(a) 3^{-2} (b) $\dfrac{2}{4^{-3}}$ (c) 3^{-1} (d) $(-3)^{-2}$ (e) $\dfrac{6^{-3}}{6^{-2}}$

Solution   (a) $3^{-2} = \dfrac{1}{3^2} = \dfrac{1}{9}$

(b) $\dfrac{2}{4^{-3}} = 2(4^3) = 2(64) = 128$

(c) $3^{-1} = \dfrac{1}{3^1} = \dfrac{1}{3}$

(d) $(-3)^{-2} = \dfrac{1}{(-3)^2} = \dfrac{1}{9}$

(e) $\dfrac{6^{-3}}{6^{-2}} = 6^{-3-(-2)} = 6^{-1} = \dfrac{1}{6^1} = \dfrac{1}{6}$

Example 1.7   Write the following expressions using only positive indices.

(a) x^{-4} (b) $3x^{-4}$ (c) $\dfrac{x^{-2}}{y^{-2}}$ (d) $3x^{-2}y^{-3}$

Solution   (a) $x^{-4} = \dfrac{1}{x^4}$

(b) $3x^{-4} = \dfrac{3}{x^4}$

(c) $\dfrac{x^{-2}}{y^{-2}} = x^{-2}y^2 = \dfrac{y^2}{x^2}$

(d) $3x^{-2}y^{-3} = \dfrac{3}{x^2y^3}$

1.2.4 Multiple indices

Consider the expression $(4^3)^2$. This may be written as

$$(4^3)^2 = 4^3.4^3 = 4^{3+3} = 4^6$$

This illustrates the **third law of indices** which is

$$(a^m)^n = a^{mn}$$

Note that the indices m and n have been multiplied.

Example 1.8 Write the following expressions using a single index.

(a) $(3^2)^4$ (b) $(7^{-2})^3$ (c) $(x^2)^{-3}$ (d) $(x^{-2})^{-3}$

Solution (a) $(3^2)^4 = 3^{2\times4} = 3^8$

(b) $(7^{-2})^3 = 7^{-2\times3} = 7^{-6}$

(c) $(x^2)^{-3} = x^{2\times(-3)} = x^{-6}$

(d) $(x^{-2})^{-3} = x^{-2\times-3} = x^6$

Consider the expression $(2^4 5^2)^3$. We see that

$$(2^4 5^2)^3 = (2^4 5^2)(2^4 5^2)(2^4 5^2)$$
$$= 2^4 2^4 2^4 5^2 5^2 5^2$$
$$= 2^{12} 5^6$$

This illustrates a generalization of the third law of indices which is

$$(a^m b^n)^k = a^{mk} b^{nk}$$

Example 1.9 Remove the brackets from

(a) $(2x^2)^3$ (b) $(-3y^4)^2$ (c) $(x^{-2}y)^3$

Solution (a) $(2x^2)^3 = (2^1 x^2)^3 = 2^3 x^6 = 8x^6$

(b) $(-3y^4)^2 = (-3)^2 y^8 = 9y^8$

(c) $(x^{-2}y)^3 = x^{-6}y^3$

1.2.5 Fractional indices

The third law of indices states that $(a^m)^n = a^{mn}$. If we take $a = 2$, $m = \frac{1}{2}$ and $n = 2$ we obtain

$$(2^{1/2})^2 = 2^1 = 2$$

So when $2^{1/2}$ is squared, the result is 2. Thus, $2^{1/2}$ is a square root of 2. Each positive number has two square roots and so

$$2^{1/2} = \sqrt{2} = \pm 1.4142\ldots$$

Similarly

$$(2^{1/3})^3 = 2^1 = 2$$

so that $2^{1/3}$ is a cube root of 2:

$$2^{1/3} = \sqrt[3]{2} = 1.2599\ldots$$

In general $2^{1/n}$ is an nth root of 2. The general law states

$$x^{1/n} \text{ is an } n\text{th root of } x$$

Example 1.10   Write the following using a single positive index.

(a) $(3^{-2})^{1/4}$ (b) $x^{2/3}x^{5/3}$ (c) $yy^{-2/5}$ (d) $\sqrt{k^3}$

Solution   (a) $(3^{-2})^{1/4} = 3^{-2\times\frac{1}{4}} = 3^{-1/2} = \dfrac{1}{3^{1/2}}$

(b) $x^{2/3}x^{5/3} = x^{2/3+5/3} = x^{7/3}$

(c) $yy^{-2/5} = y^1 y^{-2/5} = y^{1-2/5} = y^{3/5}$

(d) $\sqrt{k^3} = (k^3)^{1/2} = k^{3\times\frac{1}{2}} = k^{3/2}$

Example 1.11   Evaluate

(a) $8^{1/3}$ (b) $8^{2/3}$ (c) $8^{-1/3}$ (d) $8^{-2/3}$ (e) $8^{4/3}$

Solution   We note that 8 may be written as 2^3.

(a) $8^{1/3} = (2^3)^{1/3} = 2^1 = 2$

(b) $8^{2/3} = (8^{1/3})^2 = 2^2 = 4$

(c) $8^{-1/3} = \dfrac{1}{8^{1/3}} = \dfrac{1}{2}$

(d) $8^{-2/3} = \dfrac{1}{8^{2/3}} = \dfrac{1}{4}$

(e) $8^{4/3} = (8^{1/3})^4 = 2^4 = 16$

Exercises 1.2

1 Evaluate

(a) 2^3

(b) 3^2

(c) $\dfrac{5^{13}}{5^{12}}$

(d) $\dfrac{19^{-11}}{19^{-13}}$

(e) $(2^{1/4})^8$

(f) $(-4)^{-2}$

(g) $4^{-1/2}$

(h) $(9^{1/3})^{3/2}$

(i) $\sqrt{32}\sqrt{2}$

(j) $\sqrt{0.01}$

(k) $81^{3/4}$

2 Use a scientific calculator to evaluate

(a) $10^{1.2}$

(b) $6^{-0.7}$

(c) $6^{2.5}$

(d) $(3^{-1}4^2)^{0.8}$

3 Express each of the following expressions using a single positive index.

(a) $x^4 x^7$

(b) $x^2(-x)$

(c) $\dfrac{x^2}{x}$

(d) $\dfrac{x^{-2}}{x^{-1}}$

(e) $(x^{-2})^4$

(f) $(x^{-2.5}x^{-3.5})^2$

4 Simplify as much as possible

(a) $\dfrac{x^{1/2}}{x^{1/3}}$

(b) $(16x^4)^{0.25}$

(c) $\left(\dfrac{27}{y^3}\right)^{1/3}$

(d) $\dfrac{2xy^2}{(2xy)^2}$

(e) $\sqrt{a^2 b^6 c^4}$

(f) $(64t^3)^{2/3}$

Solutions

1 (a) 8   (b) 9   (c) 5   (d) 361

(e) 4   (f) $\dfrac{1}{16}$ (g) $\dfrac{1}{2}$ (h) 3

(i) 8   (j) 0.1   (k) 27

2 (a) 15.8489   (b) 0.2853
    (c) 88.1816   (d) 3.8159

3 (a) x^{11} (b) $-x^3$ (c) x

(d) $\dfrac{1}{x}$ (e) $\dfrac{1}{x^8}$ (f) $\dfrac{1}{x^{12}}$

4 (a) $x^{1/6}$ (b) $2x$ (c) $\dfrac{3}{y}$

(d) $\dfrac{1}{2x}$ (e) $ab^3 c^2$ (f) $16t^2$

1.3 Polynomial equations

A **polynomial equation** has the form

$$P(x) = a_n x^n + a_{n-1}x^{n-1} + a_{n-2}x^{n-2} + \cdots + a_2 x^2 + a_1 x + a_0 = 0 \qquad (1.1)$$

where n is a positive whole number, $a_n, a_{n-1}, \ldots, a_0$ are constants and x is a variable. The constants $a_n, a_{n-1}, \ldots, a_2, a_1, a_0$ are called the **coefficients** of the polynomial.

The **roots** of an equation are those values of x which satisfy $P(x) = 0$. So if $x = x_1$ is a root then $P(x_1) = 0$.

Examples of polynomial equations are

$$7x^2 + 4x - 1 = 0 \qquad (1.2)$$

$$2x - 3 = 0 \qquad (1.3)$$

$$x^3 - 20 = 0 \qquad (1.4)$$

The **degree** of an equation is the value of the highest power. Equation (1.2) has degree 2, Equation (1.3) has degree 1 and Equation (1.4) has degree 3. A polynomial equation of degree n has n roots.

There are some special names for polynomial equations of low degree (see Table 1.1).

Table 1.1

Equation	Degree	Name
$ax + b = 0$	1	Linear
$ax^2 + bx + c = 0$	2	Quadratic
$ax^3 + bx^2 + cx + d = 0$	3	Cubic
$ax^4 + bx^3 + cx^2 + dx + e = 0$	4	Quartic

1.3.1 Quadratic equations

We now focus attention on quadratic equations. The standard form of a quadratic equation is $ax^2 + bx + c = 0$. We look at three methods of solving quadratic equations:

(1) factorization,

(2) use of a formula,

(3) completing the square.

Example 1.12 illustrates solution by factorization.

Example 1.12   Solve

$$6x^2 + 11x - 10 = 0$$

Solution   The left-hand side (l.h.s.) is factorized:

$$(3x - 2)(2x + 5) = 0$$

So either

$$3x - 2 = 0 \quad \text{or} \quad 2x + 5 = 0$$

Hence

$$x = \frac{2}{3}, -\frac{5}{2}$$

When roots cannot be found by factorization we can make use of a formula.

> The formula for finding the roots of $ax^2 + bx + c = 0$ is
> $$x = \frac{-b \pm \sqrt{b^2 - 4ac}}{2a}$$

Example 1.13

Use the quadratic formula to solve

$$3x^2 - x - 6 = 0$$

Solution

Comparing $3x^2 - x - 6$ with $ax^2 + bx + c$ we see that $a = 3$, $b = -1$ and $c = -6$. So

$$x = \frac{-(-1) \pm \sqrt{(-1)^2 - 4(3)(-6)}}{2(3)}$$

$$= \frac{1 \pm \sqrt{73}}{6}$$

$$= -1.2573, \ 1.5907$$

We now introduce the method of **completing the square**. The idea behind completing the square is to absorb both the x^2 and the x term into a single squared term. Note that this is possible since

$$x^2 + 2kx + k^2 = (x + k)^2$$

and so

$$x^2 + 2kx = (x + k)^2 - k^2$$

and finally

$$x^2 + 2kx + A = (x + k)^2 + A - k^2$$

The x^2 and the x terms are both contained in the $(x + k)^2$ term. The coefficient of x on the l.h.s. is $2k$. The squared term on the right-hand side (r.h.s.) has the form $(x + k)^2$, that is $\left(x + \dfrac{\text{coefficient of } x}{2}\right)^2$. The following example illustrates the idea.

Example 1.14

Solve the following quadratic equations by completing the square.

(a) $x^2 + 8x + 2 = 0$

(b) $2x^2 - 4x + 1 = 0$

Solution (a) By comparing $x^2 + 8x + 2$ with $x^2 + 2kx + A$ we see $k = 4$. Thus the squared term must be $(x + 4)^2$. Now

$$(x + 4)^2 = x^2 + 8x + 16$$

and so

$$x^2 + 8x = (x + 4)^2 - 16$$

Therefore

$$x^2 + 8x + 2 = (x + 4)^2 - 16 + 2$$
$$= (x + 4)^2 - 14$$

At this stage we have completed the square. Finally, solving $x^2 + 8x + 2 = 0$ we have

$$x^2 + 8x + 2 = 0$$
$$(x + 4)^2 - 14 = 0$$
$$(x + 4)^2 = 14$$
$$x + 4 = \pm\sqrt{14}$$
$$x = -4 \pm \sqrt{14} = -7.7417, -0.2583$$

(b) $2x^2 - 4x + 1 = 0$ may be expressed as $x^2 - 2x + 0.5 = 0$. Comparing $x^2 - 2x + 0.5$ with $x^2 + 2kx + A$ we see that $k = -1$. Thus the required squared term must be $(x - 1)^2$. Now

$$(x - 1)^2 = x^2 - 2x + 1$$

and so

$$x^2 - 2x = (x - 1)^2 - 1$$

and

$$x^2 - 2x + 0.5 = (x - 1)^2 - 1 + 0.5$$
$$= (x - 1)^2 - 0.5$$

Finally, solving $x^2 - 2x + 0.5 = 0$ we have

$$(x - 1)^2 - 0.5 = 0$$
$$(x - 1)^2 = 0.5$$
$$x - 1 = \pm\sqrt{0.5}$$
$$x = 1 \pm \sqrt{0.5} = 0.2929, 1.7071$$

1.3.2 Polynomial equations of higher degree

Example 1.15   Verify that $x = 1$ and $x = 2$ are roots of

$$P(x) = x^4 - 2x^3 - x + 2 = 0$$

Solution

$$P(x) = x^4 - 2x^3 - x + 2$$
$$P(1) = 1 - 2 - 1 + 2 = 0$$
$$P(2) = 2^4 - 2(2^3) - 2 + 2 = 16 - 16 - 2 + 2 = 0$$

Since $P(1) = 0$ and $P(2) = 0$, then $x = 1$ and $x = 2$ are roots of the given polynomial equation and are sometimes referred to as **real roots**. Further knowledge is required to find the two remaining roots, which are known as **complex roots**. This topic is covered in Chapter 9.

Example 1.16   Solve the equation

$$P(x) = x^3 + 2x^2 - 37x + 52 = 0$$

Solution   As seen in Example 1.13 a formula can be used to solve quadratic equations. For higher degree polynomial equations such simple formulae do not always exist. However, if one of the roots can be found by inspection we can proceed as follows. By inspection $P(4) = 4^3 + 2(4)^2 - 37(4) + 52 = 0$ so that $x = 4$ is a root. Hence $x - 4$ is a factor of $P(x)$. Therefore $P(x)$ can be written as

$$P(x) = x^3 + 2x^2 - 37x + 52 = (x - 4)(x^2 + \alpha x + \beta)$$

where α and β must now be found. Expanding the r.h.s. gives

$$P(x) = x^3 + \alpha x^2 + \beta x - 4x^2 - 4\alpha x - 4\beta$$

Hence

$$x^3 + 2x^2 - 37x + 52 = x^3 + (\alpha - 4)x^2 + (\beta - 4\alpha)x - 4\beta$$

By comparing constant terms on the l.h.s. and r.h.s. we see that

$$52 = -4\beta$$

so that

$$\beta = -13$$

By comparing coefficients of x^2 we see that

$$2 = \alpha - 4$$

Therefore,

$$\alpha = 6$$

Hence, $P(x) = (x - 4)(x^2 + 6x - 13)$. The quadratic equation $x^2 + 6x - 13 = 0$ can be solved using the formula

$$x = \frac{-6 \pm \sqrt{36 - 4(-13)}}{2}$$

$$= \frac{-6 \pm \sqrt{88}}{2}$$

$$= 1.690, -7.690$$

We conclude that $P(x) = 0$ has roots at $x = 4$, $x = 1.690$ and $x = -7.690$.

Exercises 1.3

1 Calculate the roots of the following linear equations.

(a) $4x - 12 = 0$

(b) $5t + 20 = 0$

(c) $t + 10 = 2t$

(d) $\frac{y}{2} - 1 = 3$

(e) $0.5t - 6 = 0$

(f) $2x + 3 = 5x - 6$

(g) $\frac{3x}{2} - 17 = 0$

(h) $\frac{x}{2} + \frac{x}{3} = 1$

(i) $2x - 1 = \frac{x}{2} + 2$

(j) $2(y + 1) = 6$

(k) $3(2y - 1) = 2(y + 2)$

(l) $\frac{3}{2}(t + 3) = \frac{2}{3}(4t - 1)$

2 Solve the following quadratic equations by factorization.

(a) $t^2 - 5t + 6 = 0$

(b) $x^2 + x - 12 = 0$

(c) $t^2 = 10t - 25$

(d) $x^2 + 4x - 21 = 0$

(e) $x^2 - 9x + 18 = 0$

(f) $x^2 = 1$

(g) $y^2 - 10y + 9 = 0$

(h) $2z^2 - z - 1 = 0$

(i) $2x^2 + 3x - 2 = 0$

(j) $3t^2 + 4t + 1 = 0$

(k) $4y^2 + 12y + 5 = 0$

(l) $4r^2 - 9r + 2 = 0$

(m) $6d^2 - d - 2 = 0$

(n) $6x^2 - 13x + 2 = 0$

3 Complete the square for the following quadratic equations and hence find their roots.

(a) $x^2 + 2x - 8 = 0$

(b) $x^2 - 6x - 5 = 0$

(c) $x^2 + 4x - 6 = 0$

(d) $x^2 - 14x - 10 = 0$

(e) $x^2 + 5x - 49 = 0$

4 Solve the following quadratic equations using the quadratic formula.

(a) $x^2 + x - 1 = 0$

(b) $t^2 - 3t - 2 = 0$

(c) $h^2 + 5h + 1 = 0$

(d) $0.5x^2 + 3x - 2 = 0$

(e) $2k^2 - k - 3 = 0$

(f) $-y^2 + 3y + 1 = 0$

(g) $3r^2 = 7r + 2$

(h) $x^2 - 70 = 0$

(i) $4s^2 - 2 = s$

(j) $2t^2 + 5t + 2 = 0$

(k) $3x^2 = 50$

5. Calculate the roots of the following polynomial equations.

(a) $x^3 - 6x^2 + 11x - 6 = 0$ given $x = 1$ is a root

(b) $t^3 - 2t^2 - 5t + 6 = 0$ given $t = 3$ is a root

(c) $v^3 - v^2 - 30v + 72 = 0$ given $v = 4$ is a root

(d) $2y^3 + 3y^2 - 11y + 3 = 0$ given $y = 1.5$ is a root

(e) $2x^3 + 3x^2 - 7x - 5 = 0$ given $x = -\dfrac{5}{2}$ is a root.

6. Check that the given values are roots of the following polynomial equations.

(a) $x^2 + x - 2 = 0$ $x = -2, 1$

(b) $2t^3 - 3t^2 - 3t + 2 = 0$ $t = -1, 0.5$

(c) $y^3 + y^2 + y + 1 = 0$ $y = -1$

(d) $v^4 + 4v^3 + 6v^2 + 3v = 0$ $v = -1, 0$

Solutions

1. (a) 3   (b) −4   (c) 10   (d) 8

(e) 12   (f) 3   (g) $\dfrac{34}{3}$ (h) $\dfrac{6}{5}$

(i) 2   (j) 2   (k) $\dfrac{7}{4}$ (l) $\dfrac{31}{7}$

2. (a) 2, 3   (b) −4, 3   (c) 5
   (d) −7, 3   (e) 3, 6   (f) −1, 1
   (g) 1, 9   (h) −0.5, 1   (i) −2, 0.5

   (j) $-1, -\dfrac{1}{3}$ (k) −2.5, −0.5   (l) 0.25, 2

   (m) $-\dfrac{1}{2}, \dfrac{2}{3}$ (n) $\dfrac{1}{6}, 2$

3. (a) $(x+1)^2 - 9 = 0, x = -4, 2$
   (b) $(x-3)^2 - 14 = 0, x = -0.7417, 6.7417$
   (c) $(x+2)^2 - 10 = 0, x = -5.1623, 1.1623$
   (d) $(x-7)^2 - 59 = 0, x = -0.6811, 14.6811$
   (e) $\left(x+\dfrac{5}{2}\right)^2 - \dfrac{221}{4} = 0, x = -9.9330, 4.9330$

4. (a) −1.6180, 0.6180

(b) −0.5616, 3.5616

(c) −4.7913, −0.2087

(d) −6.6056, 0.6056

(e) −1, 1.5

(f) −0.3028, 3.3028

(g) −0.2573, 2.5907

(h) −8.3666, 8.3666

(i) −0.5931, 0.8431

(j) −2, −0.5

(k) −4.0825, 4.0825

5. (a) 1, 2, 3   (b) −2, 1, 3
   (c) −6, 3, 4   (d) −3.3028, 0.3028, 1.5
   (e) −2.5, −0.6180, 1.6180

1.4 Algebraic fractions

An algebraic fraction has the form

$$\text{algebraic fraction} = \frac{\text{numerator}}{\text{denominator}} = \frac{\text{polynomial expression}}{\text{polynomial expression}}$$

For example,

$$\frac{3t+1}{t^2+t+4}, \quad \frac{x^3}{x^2+1} \quad \text{and} \quad \frac{y^2+1}{y^2+2y+3}$$

are all algebraic fractions.

1.4.1 Proper and improper fractions

When presented with a fraction, we can note the degree of the numerator, say n, and the degree of the denominator, say d.

A fraction is **proper** if $d > n$, that is the degree of the denominator is greater than the degree of the numerator. If $d \leqslant n$ then the fraction is **improper**.

Example 1.17 Classify the following fractions as either proper or improper. In each case, state the degree of both numerator and denominator.

(a) $\dfrac{x^2 + 9x - 6}{3x^3 + x^2 + 100}$

(b) $\dfrac{t^3 + t^2 + 9t - 6}{t^5 + 9}$

(c) $\dfrac{(v + 1)(v - 6)}{v^2 + 3v + 6}$

(d) $\dfrac{(z + 2)^3}{5z^2 + 10z + 16}$

Solution (a) The degree of the numerator, n, is 2. The degree of the denominator, d, is 3. Since $d > n$ the fraction is proper.

(b) Here $n = 3$ and $d = 5$. The fraction is proper since $d > n$.

(c) Here $n = 2$ and $d = 2$, so $d = n$ and the fraction is improper.

(d) Here $n = 3$ and $d = 2$, so $d < n$ and the fraction is improper.

1.4.2 Equivalent fractions

Consider the numerical fractions $\dfrac{1}{2}$ and $\dfrac{2}{4}$. These fractions have the same value. Similarly, $\dfrac{2}{3}$, $\dfrac{6}{9}$ and $\dfrac{20}{30}$ all have the same value. The algebraic fractions $\dfrac{x}{y}$, $\dfrac{2x}{2y}$ and $\dfrac{xt}{yt}$ all have the same value. Fractions with the same value are called **equivalent fractions**.

The value of a fraction remains unchanged if both numerator and denominator are multiplied or divided by the same quantity. This fact can be used to write a fraction in many equivalent forms. Consider for example the fractions

(a) $\dfrac{2}{x}$ (b) $\dfrac{2(x + 1)}{x(x + 1)}$ (c) $\dfrac{2xt}{x^2 t}$

These are all equivalent fractions. Fraction (b) can be obtained by multiplying both numerator and denominator of fraction (a) by $(x + 1)$, so they are equivalent. Fraction (a) can be obtained by dividing numerator and denominator of fraction (c) by xt and so they are also equivalent.

Example 1.18   Show that

$$\frac{x+1}{x+7} \quad \text{and} \quad \frac{x^2+4x+3}{x^2+10x+21}$$

are equivalent.

Solution   We factorize the numerator and denominator of the second fraction:

$$\frac{x^2+4x+3}{x^2+10x+21} = \frac{(x+1)(x+3)}{(x+7)(x+3)}$$

Dividing both numerator and denominator by $(x+3)$ results in $\dfrac{x+1}{x+7}$. So the two given fractions are equivalent.

Dividing both numerator and denominator by $x+3$ is often referred to as 'cancelling $x+3$'.

1.4.3 Expressing a fraction in its simplest form

Consider the numerical fraction $\dfrac{6}{10}$. To simplify this we factorize both numerator and denominator and then cancel any common factors. Thus

$$\frac{6}{10} = \frac{2 \times 3}{2 \times 5} = \frac{3}{5}$$

The fractions $\dfrac{6}{10}$ and $\dfrac{3}{5}$ have identical values but $\dfrac{3}{5}$ is in a simpler form than $\dfrac{6}{10}$. It is important to stress that only factors which are common to both numerator and denominator can be cancelled.

Example 1.19   Simplify

(a) $\dfrac{6x}{18x^2}$

(b) $\dfrac{12x^3y^2}{4x^2yz}$

Solution   (a) Note that 18 can be factorized to 6×3 and so 6 is a factor common to both numerator and denominator. Also x^2 is $x \times x$ and so x is also a common factor. Cancelling the common factors, 6 and x, produces

$$\frac{6x}{18x^2} = \frac{6x}{(6)(3)(x)(x)} = \frac{1}{3x}$$

(b) The common factors are 4, x^2 and y. Cancelling these factors gives

$$\frac{12x^3y^2}{4x^2yz} = \frac{3xy}{z}$$

Example 1.20 Simplify (a) $\dfrac{4}{6x+4}$ (b) $\dfrac{6t^3 + 3t^2 + 6t}{3t^2 + 3t}$

Solution (a) Factorizing both numerator and denominator and cancelling common factors yields

$$\frac{4}{6x+4} = \frac{(2)(2)}{2(3x+2)} = \frac{2}{3x+2}$$

(b) Factorizing and cancelling common factors yields

$$\frac{6t^3 + 3t^2 + 6t}{3t^2 + 3t} = \frac{3t(2t^2 + t + 2)}{3t(t+1)} = \frac{2t^2 + t + 2}{t+1}$$

Note that the common factor, $3t$, has been cancelled.

Example 1.21 Simplify (a) $\dfrac{4t+8}{t^2 + 3t + 2}$ (b) $\dfrac{2y^2 - y - 1}{y^2 - 2y + 1}$

Solution The numerator and denominator are factorized and common factors are cancelled.

(a) $\dfrac{4t+8}{t^2 + 3t + 2} = \dfrac{4(t+2)}{(t+2)(t+1)} = \dfrac{4}{t+1}$

The common factor, $t+2$, has been cancelled.

(b) $\dfrac{2y^2 - y - 1}{y^2 - 2y + 1} = \dfrac{(2y+1)(y-1)}{(y-1)^2} = \dfrac{2y+1}{y-1}$

The common factor, $y-1$, has been cancelled.

1.4.4 Multiplication and division of algebraic fractions

To multiply two algebraic fractions together, we multiply their numerators together, and multiply their denominators together, that is

$$\frac{a}{b} \times \frac{c}{d} = \frac{a \times c}{b \times d} = \frac{ac}{bd}$$

Division is performed by inverting the second fraction and then multiplying, that is

$$\frac{a}{b} \div \frac{c}{d} = \frac{a}{b} \times \frac{d}{c} = \frac{ad}{bc}$$

Before multiplying or dividing fractions it is advisable to express each fraction in its simplest form.

Example 1.22 Simplify

$$\frac{x^2 + 5x + 6}{2x - 2} \times \frac{x^2 - x}{x^2 + 3x + 2}$$

Solution Factorizing numerators and denominators produces

$$\frac{x^2+5x+6}{2x-2} \times \frac{x^2-x}{x^2+3x+2} = \frac{(x+2)(x+3)}{2(x-1)} \times \frac{x(x-1)}{(x+1)(x+2)}$$

$$= \frac{(x+2)(x+3)x(x-1)}{2(x-1)(x+1)(x+2)}$$

Common factors $(x+2)$ and $(x-1)$ can be cancelled from numerator and denominator to give

$$\frac{(x+2)(x+3)x(x-1)}{2(x-1)(x+1)(x+2)} = \frac{(x+3)x}{2(x+1)}$$

Hence

$$\frac{x^2+5x+6}{2x-2} \times \frac{x^2-x}{x^2+3x+2} = \frac{x(x+3)}{2(x+1)}$$

Example 1.23 Simplify

$$\frac{x^2+8x+7}{x^2-6x} \div \frac{x+7}{x^3+x^2}$$

Solution The second fraction is inverted to give

$$\frac{x^2+8x+7}{x^2-6x} \times \frac{x^3+x^2}{x+7}$$

Factorizing numerators and denominators yields

$$\frac{(x+1)(x+7)}{x(x-6)} \times \frac{x^2(x+1)}{(x+7)} = \frac{(x+1)(x+7)x^2(x+1)}{x(x-6)(x+7)}$$

Common factors of x and $(x+7)$ are cancelled leaving

$$\frac{(x+1)x(x+1)}{x-6}$$

which may be written as

$$\frac{x(x+1)^2}{x-6}$$

1.4.5 Addition and subtraction of algebraic fractions

The method of adding and subtracting algebraic fractions is identical to that for numerical fractions.

Each fraction is written in its simplest form. The denominators of the fractions are then examined and the **lowest common denominator** (l.c.d.) is found. This is the simplest expression that has the given denominators as factors. All fractions are then written in an equivalent form with the l.c.d. as denominator. Finally the numerators are added/subtracted and placed over the l.c.d. Consider the following examples.

Example 1.24   Express as a single fraction

$$\frac{2}{x+1} + \frac{4}{x+2}$$

Solution   Both fractions are already in their simplest form. The l.c.d. of the denominators, $(x+1)$ and $(x+2)$, is found. This is $(x+1)(x+2)$. Note that this is the simplest expression that has both $x+1$ and $x+2$ as factors.

Each fraction is written in an equivalent form with the l.c.d. as denominator. So

$$\frac{2}{x+1} \text{ is written as } \frac{2(x+2)}{(x+1)(x+2)}$$

and

$$\frac{4}{x+2} \text{ is written as } \frac{4(x+1)}{(x+1)(x+2)}$$

Finally the numerators are added. Hence we have

$$\frac{2}{x+1} + \frac{4}{x+2} = \frac{2(x+2)}{(x+1)(x+2)} + \frac{4(x+1)}{(x+1)(x+2)}$$

$$= \frac{2(x+2) + 4(x+1)}{(x+1)(x+2)}$$

$$= \frac{6x+8}{(x+1)(x+2)}$$

$$= \frac{6x+8}{x^2 + 3x + 2}$$

Example 1.25   Express as a single fraction

$$\frac{x^2 + 3x + 2}{x^2 - 1} - \frac{2}{2x+6}$$

Solution   Each fraction is written in its simplest form:

$$\frac{x^2 + 3x + 2}{x^2 - 1} = \frac{(x+1)(x+2)}{(x-1)(x+1)} = \frac{x+2}{x-1}$$

$$\frac{2}{2x+6} = \frac{2}{2(x+3)} = \frac{1}{x+3}$$

The l.c.d. is $(x-1)(x+3)$. Each fraction is written in an equivalent form with l.c.d. as denominator:

$$\frac{x+2}{x-1} = \frac{(x+2)(x+3)}{(x-1)(x+3)}, \qquad \frac{1}{x+3} = \frac{x-1}{(x-1)(x+3)}$$

So

$$\frac{x^2 + 3x + 2}{x^2 - 1} - \frac{2}{2x + 6} = \frac{x + 2}{x - 1} - \frac{1}{x + 3}$$

$$= \frac{(x + 2)(x + 3)}{(x - 1)(x + 3)} - \frac{(x - 1)}{(x - 1)(x + 3)}$$

$$= \frac{(x + 2)(x + 3) - (x - 1)}{(x - 1)(x + 3)}$$

$$= \frac{x^2 + 5x + 6 - x + 1}{(x - 1)(x + 3)}$$

$$= \frac{x^2 + 4x + 7}{(x - 1)(x + 3)}$$

Exercises 1.4

1 Classify each fraction as either proper or improper.

(a) $\dfrac{x + 2}{x^2 + 2}$ (b) $\dfrac{2}{x + 2}$ (c) $\dfrac{2 + x}{2}$

(d) $\dfrac{x^2 + 2}{x + 2}$ (e) $\dfrac{x^2 + 2}{x^2 + 1}$ (f) $\dfrac{x^2 + 1}{x^2 + 2}$

2 Classify each of the following algebraic fractions as proper or improper.

(a) $\dfrac{3t + 1}{t^2 - 1}$

(b) $\dfrac{10v^2 + 4v - 6}{3v^2 + v - 1}$

(c) $\dfrac{6 - 4t + t^3}{6t^2 + 1}$

(d) $\dfrac{9t + 1}{t + 1}$

(e) $\dfrac{100f^2 + 1}{f^3 - 1}$

(f) $\dfrac{(x + 1)(x + 2)}{(x + 3)^3}$

(g) $\dfrac{(y + 1)(y + 2)(y + 3)}{(y + 4)^3}$

(h) $\dfrac{(z + 1)^{10}}{(2z + 1)^{10}}$

(i) $\dfrac{(q + 1)^{10}}{(q^2 + 1)^6}$

(j) $\dfrac{3k^2 + 2k - 1}{k^3 + k^2 - 4k + 1}$

3 Express each fraction in its simplest form.

(a) $\dfrac{y^3 + 2y}{2y - y^2}$ (b) $\dfrac{5x^2 + 5}{10x - 10}$

(c) $\dfrac{t^2 + 7t + 12}{t^2 + 5t + 4}$ (d) $\dfrac{x^2 - 1}{x^3 - 2x^2 + x}$

(e) $\dfrac{x^2 + 2x + 1}{x^2 - 2x + 1}$

4 Simplify the following:

(a) $\dfrac{x + 1}{x + 3} \times \dfrac{x + 3}{x + 2}$

(b) $\dfrac{4}{x^2 - 1} \times \dfrac{x + 1}{6}$

(c) $\dfrac{x^2 + 3x}{x^3 + 2x^2} \times \dfrac{x^2 + 4x + 4}{4x}$

(d) $\dfrac{4xt + 4t}{xt^2 - t^2} \times \dfrac{4x^2 - 4}{8x + 8}$

(e) $\dfrac{x^2 + 2x - 15}{x^2 + 4x - 5} \times \dfrac{x^2 + 3x - 4}{x^2 - 4x + 3}$

5 Express as a single fraction

(a) $\dfrac{3}{x + 6} + \dfrac{2}{x + 1}$

(b) $\dfrac{4}{x + 2} - \dfrac{2}{(x + 2)^2}$

(c) $\dfrac{2x + 1}{x^2 + x + 1} + \dfrac{4}{x - 1}$

(d) $\dfrac{x^2 + 3x - 18}{x^2 + 7x + 6} - \dfrac{2x^2 + 7x - 4}{x^2 + 9x + 20}$

(e) $\dfrac{3(x+1)}{x^2 + 4x + 4} + \dfrac{2(x-1)}{x^2 - 4}$

Solutions

1 (a) proper   (b) proper   (c) improper
   (d) improper (e) improper (f) improper

2 (a) proper   (b) improper (c) improper
   (d) improper (e) proper   (f) proper
   (g) improper (h) improper (i) proper
   (j) proper

3 (a) $\dfrac{y^2 + 2}{2 - y}$ (b) $\dfrac{x^2 + 1}{2x - 2}$ (c) $\dfrac{t + 3}{t + 1}$

   (d) $\dfrac{x + 1}{x(x - 1)}$ (e) $\dfrac{x^2 + 2x + 1}{x^2 - 2x + 1}$

4 (a) $\dfrac{x + 1}{x + 2}$ (b) $\dfrac{2}{3(x - 1)}$

   (c) $\dfrac{(x + 2)(x + 3)}{4x^2}$ (d) $\dfrac{2(x + 1)}{t}$

   (e) $\dfrac{x + 4}{x - 1}$

5 (a) $\dfrac{5x + 15}{(x + 1)(x + 6)}$ (b) $\dfrac{4x + 6}{(x + 2)^2}$

   (c) $\dfrac{6x^2 + 3x + 3}{(x - 1)(x^2 + x + 1)}$

   (d) $\dfrac{-x^2 + x - 14}{(x + 1)(x + 5)}$

   (e) $\dfrac{5x^2 - x - 10}{(x + 2)^2(x - 2)}$

1.5 Solution of inequalities

An **inequality** is any expression involving one of the symbols $>, \geqslant, <, \leqslant$.

> $a > b$ means a is greater than b
> $a < b$ means a is less than b
> $a \geqslant b$ means a is greater than or equal to b
> $a \leqslant b$ means a is less than or equal to b

Just as with an equation, when we add or subtract the same quantity to both sides of an inequality the inequality still remains. Mathematically we have
If $a > b$ then

$$a + k > b + k \qquad \text{adding } k \text{ to both sides}$$
$$a - k > b - k \qquad \text{subtracting } k \text{ from both sides}$$

We can make similar statements for $a \geqslant b$, $a < b$ and $a \leqslant b$.

When multiplying or dividing both sides of an inequality extra care must be taken. Suppose we wish to multiply or divide an inequality by a quantity k. If k is positive the inequality remains the same; if k is negative then the inequality is reversed.
If $a > b$ then

$$\left.\begin{array}{c} ka > kb \\ \dfrac{a}{k} > \dfrac{b}{k} \end{array}\right\} \quad \text{if } k \text{ is positive} \qquad\qquad \left.\begin{array}{c} ka < kb \\ \dfrac{a}{k} < \dfrac{b}{k} \end{array}\right\} \quad \text{if } k \text{ is negative}$$

Note that when k is negative the inequality changes from $>$ to $<$. Similar statements can be made for $a \geqslant b$, $a < b$ and $a \leqslant b$. When asked to solve an inequality we need to state all the values of the variable for which the inequality is true.

Example 1.26   Solve the following inequalities.

(a) $3t + 1 > t + 7$ (b) $2 - 3z \leqslant 6 + z$

Solution   (a) $3t + 1 > t + 7$

$\quad\quad 2t + 1 > 7$ subtracting t from both sides
$\quad\quad\quad 2t > 6$ subtracting 1 from both sides
$\quad\quad\quad\quad t > 3$ dividing both sides by 2

Hence all values of t greater than 3 satisfy the inequality.

(b) $2 - 3z \leqslant 6 + z$

$\quad\quad -3z \leqslant 4 + z$ subtracting 2 from both sides
$\quad\quad -4z \leqslant 4$ subtracting z from both sides
$\quad\quad\quad z \geqslant -1$ dividing both sides by -4, remembering to reverse the inequality

Hence all values of z greater than or equal to -1 satisfy the inequality.

We often have inequalities of the form $\dfrac{\alpha}{\beta} > 0$, $\dfrac{\alpha}{\beta} < 0$, $\alpha\beta > 0$ and $\alpha\beta < 0$ to solve. It is useful to note that if

$\dfrac{\alpha}{\beta} > 0$ then either $\alpha > 0$ and $\beta > 0$ or $\alpha < 0$ and $\beta < 0$

$\dfrac{\alpha}{\beta} < 0$ then either $\alpha > 0$ and $\beta < 0$ or $\alpha < 0$ and $\beta > 0$

$\alpha\beta > 0$ then either $\alpha > 0$ and $\beta > 0$ or $\alpha < 0$ and $\beta < 0$

$\alpha\beta < 0$ then either $\alpha > 0$ and $\beta < 0$ or $\alpha < 0$ and $\beta > 0$

The following examples illustrate this.

Example 1.27   Solve the following inequalities.

(a) $\dfrac{x + 1}{2x - 6} > 0$ (b) $\dfrac{2t + 3}{t + 2} \leqslant 1$

Solution   (a) Consider the fraction $\dfrac{x + 1}{2x - 6}$. For the fraction to be positive requires either of the following:

(i) $x + 1 > 0$ and $2x - 6 > 0$.
(ii) $x + 1 < 0$ and $2x - 6 < 0$.

We consider both cases.

Case (i) $x + 1 > 0$ and so $x > -1$.

$2x - 6 > 0$ and so $x > 3$.

Both of these inequalities are true only when $x > 3$. Hence the fraction is positive when $x > 3$.

Case (ii) $x + 1 < 0$ and so $x < -1$.

$2x - 6 < 0$ and so $x < 3$.

Both of these inequalities are true only when $x < -1$. Hence the fraction is positive when $x < -1$.

In summary, $\dfrac{x+1}{2x-6} > 0$ when $x > 3$ or $x < -1$.

(b) $\dfrac{2t+3}{t+2} \leqslant 1$

$\dfrac{2t+3}{t+2} - 1 \leqslant 0$

$\dfrac{t+1}{t+2} \leqslant 0$

We now consider the fraction $\dfrac{t+1}{t+2}$. For the fraction to be negative or zero requires either of the following:

(i) $t + 1 \leqslant 0$ and $t + 2 > 0$.
(ii) $t + 1 \geqslant 0$ and $t + 2 < 0$.

We consider each case in turn.

Case (i) $t + 1 \leqslant 0$ and so $t \leqslant -1$.

$t + 2 > 0$ and so $t > -2$.

Hence the inequality is true when t is greater than -2 and less than or equal to -1. We write this as $-2 < t \leqslant -1$.

Case (ii) $t + 1 \geqslant 0$ and so $t \geqslant -1$.

$t + 2 < 0$ and so $t < -2$.

It is impossible to satisfy both $t \geqslant -1$ and $t < -2$ and so this case yields no values of t.

In summary, $\dfrac{2t+3}{t+2} \leqslant 1$ when $-2 < t \leqslant -1$.

Example 1.28   Solve the following inequalities:

(a) $x^2 > 4$ (b) $x^2 < 4$

Solution   (a) $x^2 > 4$

$x^2 - 4 > 0$

$(x-2)(x+2) > 0$

For the product $(x - 2)(x + 2)$ to be positive requires either

(i) $x - 2 > 0$ and $x + 2 > 0$

or

(ii) $x - 2 < 0$ and $x + 2 < 0$.

We examine each case in turn.

Case (i) $x - 2 > 0$ and so $x > 2$.

$x + 2 > 0$ and so $x > -2$.

Both of these are true only when $x > 2$.

Case (ii) $x - 2 < 0$ and so $x < 2$.

$x + 2 < 0$ and so $x < -2$.

Both of these are true only when $x < -2$.

In summary, $x^2 > 4$ when $x > 2$ or $x < -2$.

(b) $$x^2 < 4$$
$$x^2 - 4 < 0$$
$$(x - 2)(x + 2) < 0$$

For the product $(x - 2)(x + 2)$ to be negative requires either

(i) $x - 2 > 0$ and $x + 2 < 0$

or

(ii) $x - 2 < 0$ and $x + 2 > 0$.

We examine each case in turn.

Case (i) $x - 2 > 0$ and so $x > 2$.

$x + 2 < 0$ and so $x < -2$.

No values of x are possible.

Case (ii) $x - 2 < 0$ and so $x < 2$.

$x + 2 > 0$ and so $x > -2$.

Here we have $x < 2$ and $x > -2$. This is usually written as $-2 < x < 2$. Thus all values of x between -2 and 2 will ensure that $x^2 < 4$.

In summary, $x^2 < 4$ when $-2 < x < 2$.

The previous example illustrates a general rule.

> If $x^2 > k$ then $x > \sqrt{k}$ or $x < -\sqrt{k}$.
>
> If $x^2 < k$ then $-\sqrt{k} < x < \sqrt{k}$.

Example 1.29 Solve the following inequalities.

(a) $x^2 + x - 6 > 0$ (b) $x^2 + 8x + 1 < 0$

Solution (a) $x^2 + x - 6 > 0$

$$(x - 2)(x + 3) \; > \; 0$$

For the product $(x - 2)(x + 3)$ to be positive requires either

(i) $x - 2 > 0$ and $x + 3 > 0$

or

(ii) $x - 2 < 0$ and $x + 3 < 0$.

Case (i) $x - 2 > 0$ and so $x > 2$.

$x + 3 > 0$ and so $x > -3$.

Both of these inequalities are satisfied only when $x > 2$.

Case (ii) $x - 2 < 0$ and so $x < 2$.

$x + 3 < 0$ and so $x < -3$.

Both of these inequalities are satisfied only when $x < -3$.

In summary, $x^2 + x - 6 > 0$ when either $x > 2$ or $x < -3$.

(b) The quadratic expression $x^2 + 8x + 1$ does not factorize and so the technique of completing the square is used.

$$x^2 + 8x + 1 = (x + 4)^2 - 15$$

Hence

$$(x + 4)^2 - 15 < 0$$
$$(x + 4)^2 < 15$$

Using the result after Example 1.28 we may write

$$-\sqrt{15} < x + 4 < \sqrt{15}$$
$$-\sqrt{15} - 4 < x < \sqrt{15} - 4$$
$$-7.873 < x < -0.127$$

Exercises 1.5

1 Solve the following inequalities:

(a) $2x > 6$

(b) $\dfrac{y}{4} > 0.6$

(c) $3t < 12$

(d) $z + 1 \geqslant 4$

(e) $3v - 2 \leqslant 4$

(f) $6 - k \geqslant -1$

(g) $\dfrac{6 - 2v}{3} < 1$

(h) $m^2 \geqslant 2$

(i) $x^2 < 9$

(j) $v^2 + 1 \leqslant 10$

(k) $x^2 + 10 < 6$

(l) $2k^2 - 3 \geqslant 1$

(m) $10 - 2v^2 \leqslant 6$

(n) $5 + 4k^2 > 21$

(o) $(v - 2)^2 \leqslant 25$

(p) $(3t + 1)^2 > 16$

(h) $4t^2 + 4t + 9 \leqslant 12$

(i) $\dfrac{x + 4}{x - 5} > 1$

(j) $\dfrac{2t - 3}{t + 6} \leqslant 6$

(k) $\dfrac{3v + 12}{6 - 2v} \geqslant 0$

(l) $\dfrac{x^2}{x + 1} > 0$

(m) $\dfrac{x}{x^2 + 1} < 0$

(n) $\dfrac{3y + 1}{y - 2} \leqslant 2$

(o) $k^3 > 0$

(p) $x^3 > 8$

(q) $\dfrac{t^2 + 6t + 9}{t + 5} < 0$

(r) $(x + 1)(x - 2)(x + 3) > 0$

2 Solve the following inequalities:

(a) $x^2 - 6x + 8 > 0$

(b) $x^2 + 6x + 8 \leqslant 0$

(c) $2t^2 + 3t - 2 < 0$

(d) $y^2 - 2y - 24 \geqslant 0$

(e) $h^2 + 6h + 9 \leqslant 1$

(f) $r^2 + 6r + 7 \geqslant 0$

(g) $x^2 + 4x - 6 < 0$

Solutions

1 (a) $x > 3$

(b) $y > 2.4$

(c) $t < 4$

(d) $z \geqslant 3$

(e) $v \leqslant 2$

(f) $k \leqslant 7$

(g) $v > \dfrac{3}{2}$

(h) $m \geqslant \sqrt{2}$ or $m \leqslant -\sqrt{2}$

(i) $-3 < x < 3$

(j) $-3 \leqslant v \leqslant 3$

(k) no solution

(l) $k \geqslant \sqrt{2}$ or $k \leqslant -\sqrt{2}$

(m) $v \geqslant \sqrt{2}$ or $v \leqslant -\sqrt{2}$

(n) $k > 2$ or $k < -2$

(o) $-3 \leqslant v \leqslant 7$

(p) $t > 1$ or $t < -\dfrac{5}{3}$

2 (a) $x > 4$ or $x < 2$

(b) $-4 \leqslant x \leqslant -2$

(c) $-2 < t < \dfrac{1}{2}$

(d) $y \geqslant 6$ or $y \leqslant -4$

(e) $-4 \leqslant h \leqslant -2$

(f) $r \geqslant \sqrt{2} - 3$ or $r \leqslant -\sqrt{2} - 3$

(g) $-\sqrt{10} - 2 < x < \sqrt{10} - 2$

(h) $-\dfrac{3}{2} \leqslant t \leqslant \dfrac{1}{2}$

(i) $x > 5$

(j) $t \leqslant -\dfrac{39}{4}$ or $t > -6$

(k) $-4 \leqslant v < 3$

(l) $x > -1$ with $x \neq 0$

(m) $x < 0$

(n) $-5 \leqslant y < 2$

(o) $k > 0$

(p) $x > 2$

(q) $t < -5$

(r) $x > 2$ or $-3 < x < -1$

1.6 Partial fractions

Given a set of fractions, we can add them together to form a single fraction. For example, in Example 1.24 we saw

$$\frac{2}{x+1} + \frac{4}{x+2} = \frac{2(x+2)+4(x+1)}{(x+1)(x+2)}$$

$$= \frac{6x+8}{x^2+3x+2}$$

Alternatively, if we are given a single fraction, we can break it down into the sum of easier fractions. These simple fractions, which when added together form the given fraction, are called **partial fractions**. The partial fractions of $\frac{6x+8}{x^2+3x+2}$ are $\frac{2}{x+1}$ and $\frac{4}{x+2}$.

When expressing a given fraction as a sum of partial fractions it is important to classify the fraction as proper or improper. The denominator is then factorized into a product of factors which can be linear and/or quadratic. **Linear factors** are those of the form $ax+b$, for example $2x-1$, $\frac{x}{2}+6$. **Repeated linear factors** are those of the form $(ax+b)^2$, $(ax+b)^3$ and so on, for example $(3x-2)^2$ and $(2x+1)^3$ are repeated linear factors. **Quadratic factors** are those of the form ax^2+bx+c, for example $2x^2-6x+1$.

1.6.1 Linear factors

We can calculate the partial fractions of proper fractions whose denominator can be factorized into linear factors. The following steps are used:

(1) Factorize the denominator.

(2) Each factor of the denominator produces a partial fraction. A factor $ax+b$ produces a partial fraction of the form $\frac{A}{ax+b}$ where A is an unknown constant.

(3) Evaluate the unknown constants of the partial fractions. This is done by evaluation using a specific value of x or by equating coefficients.

A linear factor $ax+b$ in the denominator produces a partial fraction of the form $\frac{A}{ax+b}$.

Example 1.30   Express

$$\frac{6x+8}{x^2+3x+2}$$

as its partial fractions.

Solution The denominator is factorized as

$$x^2 + 3x + 2 = (x + 1)(x + 2)$$

The linear factor, $x + 1$, produces a partial fraction of the form $\dfrac{A}{x + 1}$. The linear factor, $x + 2$, produces a partial fraction of the form $\dfrac{B}{x + 2}$. A and B are unknown constants whose values have to be found. So we have

$$\frac{6x + 8}{x^2 + 3x + 2} = \frac{6x + 8}{(x + 1)(x + 2)} = \frac{A}{x + 1} + \frac{B}{x + 2} \tag{1.5}$$

Multiplying both sides of Equation (1.5) by $(x + 1)$ and $(x + 2)$ we obtain

$$6x + 8 = A(x + 2) + B(x + 1) \tag{1.6}$$

We now evaluate A and B. There are two techniques which enable us to do this: **evaluation using a specific value of x** and **equating coefficients**. Each is illustrated in turn.

Evaluation using a specific value of x

We examine Equation (1.6). We will substitute a specific value of x into this equation. Although any value can be substituted for x we will choose a value which simplifies the equation as much as possible. We note that substituting $x = -2$ will simplify the r.h.s. of the equation since the term $A(x + 2)$ will then be zero. Similarly, substituting in $x = -1$ will simplify the r.h.s. because the term $B(x + 1)$ will then be zero. So $x = -1$ and $x = -2$ are two convenient values to substitute into Equation (1.6). We substitute each in turn.

Evaluating Equation (1.6) with $x = -1$ gives

$$-6 + 8 = A(-1 + 2)$$
$$2 = A$$

Evaluating Equation (1.6) with $x = -2$ gives

$$-4 = B(-1)$$
$$B = 4$$

Substituting $A = 2$, $B = 4$ into Equation (1.5) yields

$$\frac{6x + 8}{x^2 + 3x + 2} = \frac{2}{x + 1} + \frac{4}{x + 2}$$

Thus the required partial fractions are $\dfrac{2}{x + 1}$ and $\dfrac{4}{x + 2}$.

The constants A and B could have been found by equating coefficients.

Equating coefficients

Equation (1.6) may be written as

$$6x + 8 = (A + B)x + 2A + B$$

Equating the coefficients of x on both sides gives

$$6 = A + B$$

Equating the constant terms on both sides gives

$$8 = 2A + B$$

Thus we have two simultaneous equations in A and B, which may be solved to give $A = 2$ and $B = 4$ as before.

1.6.2 Repeated linear factor

We now examine proper fractions whose denominators factorize into linear factors, where one or more of the linear factors is repeated.

A repeated linear factor, $(ax + b)^2$, produces two partial fractions of the form

$$\frac{A}{ax + b} + \frac{B}{(ax + b)^2}$$

A repeated linear factor, $(ax + b)^2$, leads to partial fractions

$$\frac{A}{ax + b} + \frac{B}{(ax + b)^2}$$

Example 1.31 Express

$$\frac{2x + 5}{x^2 + 2x + 1}$$

as partial fractions.

Solution The denominator is factorized to give $(x + 1)^2$. Here we have a case of a repeated factor. This repeated factor generates partial fractions $\dfrac{A}{x + 1} + \dfrac{B}{(x + 1)^2}$. Thus

$$\frac{2x + 5}{x^2 + 2x + 1} = \frac{2x + 5}{(x + 1)^2} = \frac{A}{x + 1} + \frac{B}{(x + 1)^2}$$

Multiplying by $(x + 1)^2$ gives

$$2x + 5 = A(x + 1) + B = Ax + A + B$$

Equating coefficients of x gives $A = 2$. Evaluation with $x = -1$ gives $B = 3$. So

$$\frac{2x + 5}{x^2 + 2x + 1} = \frac{2}{x + 1} + \frac{3}{(x + 1)^2}$$

Example 1.32   Express

$$\frac{14x^2 + 13x}{(4x^2 + 4x + 1)(x - 1)}$$

as partial fractions.

Solution   The denominator is factorized to $(2x + 1)^2(x - 1)$. The repeated factor, $(2x + 1)^2$, produces partial fractions of the form

$$\frac{A}{2x + 1} + \frac{B}{(2x + 1)^2}$$

The factor, $(x - 1)$, produces a partial fraction of the form $\dfrac{C}{x - 1}$. So

$$\frac{14x^2 + 13x}{(4x^2 + 4x + 1)(x - 1)} = \frac{14x^2 + 13x}{(2x + 1)^2(x - 1)} = \frac{A}{2x + 1} + \frac{B}{(2x + 1)^2} + \frac{C}{x - 1}$$

Multiplying both sides by $(2x + 1)^2(x - 1)$ gives

$$14x^2 + 13x = A(2x + 1)(x - 1) + B(x - 1) + C(2x + 1)^2 \tag{1.7}$$

The unknown constants A, B and C can now be found.
  Evaluating Equation (1.7) with $x = 1$ gives

$$27 = C(3)^2$$

from which

$$C = 3$$

Evaluating Equation (1.7) with $x = -0.5$ gives

$$14(-0.5)^2 + 13(-0.5) = B(-0.5 - 1)$$

from which

$$B = 2$$

Finally, comparing the coefficients of x^2 on both sides of Equation (1.7) we have

$$14 = 2A + 4C$$

Since we already have $C = 3$ then

$$A = 1$$

Hence we see that

$$\frac{14x^2 + 13x}{(4x^2 + 4x + 1)(x - 1)} = \frac{1}{2x + 1} + \frac{2}{(2x + 1)^2} + \frac{3}{x - 1}$$

1.6.3 Quadratic factors

We now look at proper fractions whose denominator contains a quadratic factor, that is a factor of the form $ax^2 + bx + c$.

> A quadratic factor, $ax^2 + bx + c$, produces a partial fraction of the form
>
> $$\frac{Ax + B}{ax^2 + bx + c}$$

Example 1.33   Noting that $x^3 + 2x^2 - 11x - 52 = (x - 4)(x^2 + 6x + 13)$, express

$$\frac{3x^2 + 11x + 14}{x^3 + 2x^2 - 11x - 52}$$

as partial fractions.

Solution   The denominator has already been factorized. The linear factor, $x - 4$, produces a partial fraction of the form $\dfrac{A}{x - 4}$.

The quadratic factor, $x^2 + 6x + 13$, will not factorize further into two linear factors. Thus this factor generates a partial fraction of the form $\dfrac{Bx + C}{x^2 + 6x + 13}$. Hence

$$\frac{3x^2 + 11x + 14}{(x - 4)(x^2 + 6x + 13)} = \frac{A}{x - 4} + \frac{Bx + C}{x^2 + 6x + 13}$$

Multiplying by $(x - 4)$ and $(x^2 + 6x + 13)$ produces

$$3x^2 + 11x + 14 = A(x^2 + 6x + 13) + (Bx + C)(x - 4) \tag{1.8}$$

The constants A, B and C can now be found.
Putting $x = 4$ into Equation (1.8) gives

$$106 = A(53)$$
$$A = 2$$

Equating the coefficients of x^2 gives

$$3 = A + B$$
$$B = 1$$

Equating the constant term on both sides gives

$$14 = A(13) - 4C$$
$$C = 3$$

Hence

$$\frac{3x^2 + 11x + 14}{x^3 + 2x^2 - 11x - 52} = \frac{2}{x - 4} + \frac{x + 3}{x^2 + 6x + 13}$$

1.6.4 Improper fractions

The techniques of calculating partial fractions in Sections 1.6.1 to 1.6.3 have all been applied to proper fractions. We now look at the calculation of partial fractions of improper fractions. The techniques described in Sections 1.6.1 to 1.6.3 are all applicable to improper fractions. However, when calculating the partial fractions of an improper fraction, an extra term needs to be included. The extra term is a polynomial of degree $n - d$, where n is the degree of the numerator and d is the degree of the denominator. A polynomial of degree 0 is a constant, a polynomial of degree 1 has the form $Ax + B$, a polynomial of degree 2 has the form $Ax^2 + Bx + C$, and so on. For example, if the numerator has degree 3 and the denominator has degree 2, the partial fractions will include a polynomial of degree $n - d = 3 - 2 = 1$, that is a term of the form $Ax + B$. If the numerator and denominator are of the same degree, the fraction is improper. The partial fractions will include a polynomial of degree $n - d = 0$, that is a constant term.

> Let the degree of the numerator be n and the degree of the denominator be d. If $n \geqslant d$ then the fraction is improper. Improper fractions have partial fractions in addition to those generated by the factors of the denominator. These additional partial fractions take the form of a polynomial of degree $n - d$.

Example 1.34 Express as partial fractions

$$\frac{4x^3 + 10x + 4}{2x^2 + x}$$

Solution The degree of the numerator is 3, that is $n = 3$. The degree of the denominator is 2, that is $d = 2$. Thus, the fraction is improper.

Now $n - d = 1$ and this is a measure of the extent to which the fraction is improper. The partial fractions will include a polynomial of degree 1, that is $Ax + B$, in addition to the partial fractions generated by the factors of the denominator.

The denominator factorizes to $x(2x + 1)$. These factors generate partial fractions of the form $\dfrac{C}{x} + \dfrac{D}{2x + 1}$. Hence

$$\frac{4x^3 + 10x + 4}{2x^2 + x} = \frac{4x^3 + 10x + 4}{x(2x + 1)} = Ax + B + \frac{C}{x} + \frac{D}{2x + 1}$$

Multiplying by x and $2x + 1$ yields

$$4x^3 + 10x + 4 = (Ax + B)x(2x + 1) + C(2x + 1) + Dx \tag{1.9}$$

The constants A, B, C and D can now be evaluated.

Putting $x = 0$ into Equation (1.9) gives

$$4 = C$$

Putting $x = -0.5$ into Equation (1.9) gives

$$-1.5 = -\frac{D}{2}$$

$$D = 3$$

Equating coefficients of x^3 gives

$$4 = 2A$$
$$A = 2$$

Equating coefficients of x gives

$$10 = B + 2C + D$$
$$B = -1$$

Hence

$$\frac{4x^3 + 10x + 4}{2x^2 + x} = 2x - 1 + \frac{4}{x} + \frac{3}{2x + 1}$$

Exercises 1.6

1 Calculate the partial fractions of the following fractions.

(a) $\dfrac{6x + 14}{x^2 + 4x + 3}$

(b) $\dfrac{7 - 2x}{x^2 - x - 2}$

(c) $\dfrac{3x + 6}{2x^2 + 3x}$

(d) $\dfrac{8 - x}{6x^2 - x - 1}$

(e) $\dfrac{13x^2 + 11x + 2}{(x + 1)(2x + 1)(3x + 1)}$

2 Calculate the partial fractions of the following fractions.

(a) $\dfrac{2x + 7}{x^2 + 6x + 9}$

(b) $\dfrac{4x - 5}{x^2 - 2x + 1}$

(c) $\dfrac{3x^2 + 8x + 6}{(x^2 + 2x + 1)(x + 2)}$

(d) $\dfrac{3x^2 - 3x - 2}{(x^2 - 1)(x - 1)}$

(e) $\dfrac{3x^2 + 7x + 6}{x^3 + 2x^2}$

3 Express the following as partial fractions.

(a) $\dfrac{x^2 + x + 2}{(x^2 + 1)(x + 1)}$

(b) $\dfrac{5x^2 + 11x + 5}{(2x + 3)(x^2 + 5x + 5)}$

(c) $\dfrac{4x^2 + 5}{(x^2 + 1)(x^2 + 2)}$

(d) $\dfrac{18x^2 + 7x + 44}{(2x - 3)(2x^2 + 5x + 7)}$

(e) $\dfrac{2x}{(x^2 - x + 1)(x^2 + x + 1)}$

4 Express the following fractions as partial fractions.

(a) $\dfrac{x^2 + 7x + 13}{x + 4}$

(b) $\dfrac{12x - 4}{2x - 1}$

(c) $\dfrac{x^2 + 8x + 2}{x^2 + 6x + 1}$

(d) $\dfrac{x^3 - 2x^2 + 3x - 3}{x^2 - 2x + 1}$

(e) $\dfrac{2x^3 + 2x^2 - 2x - 1}{x^2 + x}$

Solutions

1 (a) $\dfrac{2}{x+3} + \dfrac{4}{x+1}$ (b) $\dfrac{1}{x-2} - \dfrac{3}{x+1}$

(c) $\dfrac{2}{x} - \dfrac{1}{2x+3}$ (d) $\dfrac{3}{2x-1} - \dfrac{5}{3x+1}$

(e) $\dfrac{2}{x+1} + \dfrac{1}{2x+1} - \dfrac{1}{3x+1}$

2 (a) $\dfrac{2}{x+3} + \dfrac{1}{(x+3)^2}$

(b) $\dfrac{4}{x-1} - \dfrac{1}{(x-1)^2}$

(c) $\dfrac{1}{x+1} + \dfrac{1}{(x+1)^2} + \dfrac{2}{x+2}$

(d) $\dfrac{2}{x-1} - \dfrac{1}{(x-1)^2} + \dfrac{1}{x+1}$

(e) $\dfrac{2}{x} + \dfrac{3}{x^2} + \dfrac{1}{x+2}$

3 (a) $\dfrac{1}{x+1} + \dfrac{1}{x^2+1}$

(b) $\dfrac{2x}{x^2+5x+5} + \dfrac{1}{2x+3}$

(c) $\dfrac{1}{x^2+1} + \dfrac{3}{x^2+2}$

(d) $\dfrac{5}{2x-3} + \dfrac{4x-3}{2x^2+5x+7}$

(e) $\dfrac{1}{x^2-x+1} - \dfrac{1}{x^2+x+1}$

4 (a) $x+3+\dfrac{1}{x+4}$

(b) $6+\dfrac{2}{2x-1}$

(c) $1+\dfrac{2x+1}{x^2+6x+1}$

(d) $x+\dfrac{2}{x-1} - \dfrac{1}{(x-1)^2}$

(e) $2x-\dfrac{1}{x} - \dfrac{1}{x+1}$

Review exercises 1

1 Simplify each of the following as far as possible:

(a) $7^6 7^4$

(b) $\dfrac{6^3}{6^{-2}}$

(c) $(3^4)^{-2}$

(d) $\sqrt{3^4 6^2}$

(e) $(3^{2/3} 4^{1/3})^6$

(f) $\dfrac{10^{-3}}{10^{-4}}$

2 Simplify as far as possible:

(a) $x^7 x^{-3}$

(b) $(x^2)^4$

(c) $\left(\dfrac{\sqrt{x}}{x}\right)^{-1}$

(d) $(y^{-2})^{-1}$

(e) $y^{1/3} y y^2$

3 Remove the brackets and simplify:

(a) $(2x^2 y)^3$

(b) $(6a^2 b^3 \sqrt{c})^2$

(c) $\left(\dfrac{y^{-2}}{2}\right)^{-1}$

(d) $(x^2 y^{-1})^{0.5}$

(e) $\left(\dfrac{3^{-1} x^{-2}}{y^{-3}}\right)^{-2}$

4 Express the following as their partial fractions:

(a) $\dfrac{3x+11}{(x-3)(x+7)}$

(b) $\dfrac{-3-x}{x^2-x}$

(c) $\dfrac{6x^2-2}{2x^2-x}$

(d) $\dfrac{2x^2-x-7}{(x+1)(x-1)(x+2)}$

(e) $\dfrac{4x-11}{2x^2+15x+7}$

5 Convert the following into a single fraction:

(a) $\dfrac{1}{x} + \dfrac{3}{x+2} + \dfrac{6}{8x+4}$

(b) $\dfrac{1}{s} + \dfrac{2}{s^2} + \dfrac{3s+4}{8s+6}$

(c) $\dfrac{6}{s} + \dfrac{10}{s^2} - \dfrac{s+1}{(s+2)(s+3)} + \dfrac{s-1}{(s+4)(s+3)}$

6 Express the following as partial fractions:

(a) $\dfrac{5x}{(x+1)(2x-3)}$

(b) $\dfrac{3x+2}{x^2+5x+6}$

(c) $\dfrac{y+3}{y^2+3y+2}$

(d) $\dfrac{1}{t^2+3t+2}$

(e) $\dfrac{2z^2+15z+30}{(z+2)(z+3)(z+6)}$

(f) $\dfrac{24x^2+33x+11}{(2x+1)(3x+2)(4x+3)}$

(g) $\dfrac{s+3}{(s+1)^2}$

(h) $\dfrac{2k^2+k+1}{k^3-k}$

(i) $\dfrac{x^3}{x^2+1}$

(j) $\dfrac{t+5}{(t+3)^2}$

(k) $\dfrac{s^2}{s^2+1}$

(l) $\dfrac{8x-15}{4x^2-12x+9}$

(m) $\dfrac{6d^2+15d+8}{(d+1)^2(d+2)}$

(n) $\dfrac{2x^2+x+3}{x^2+2x+1}$

(o) $\dfrac{-y-1}{(y^2+1)(y-1)}$

(p) $\dfrac{s^2-8s-5}{(s^2+s+1)(s-4)}$

(q) $\dfrac{t^2+t-2}{(t-2)^2(t+1)}$

(r) $\dfrac{2s^3+3s^2-s-4}{s^2+s-1}$

(s) $\dfrac{x^3+4x^2+7x+5}{x^2+3x+2}$

7 Solve the following quadratic equations using the quadratic formula:

(a) $x^2+10x+2=0$

(b) $y^2-6y-3=0$

(c) $2t^2+2t-9=0$

(d) $3z^2-9z-1=0$

(e) $5v^2+v-6=0$

8 Solve the quadratic equations in Question 7 by completing the square.

9 Solve

$$x^3-4x^2-25x+28=0$$

given $x=7$ is a root.

10 Solve the following inequalities:

(a) $6t-1 \leqslant 4$

(b) $-6 \leqslant 3r \leqslant 6$

(c) $1-2v < v+4$

(d) $2 \leqslant \dfrac{x-2}{3}$

(e) $(x-2)^2 \geqslant 36$

(f) $x^2-2x-3 < 0$

(g) $\dfrac{x-3}{x+1} \geqslant 0$

(h) $x^2-8x+5 \leqslant 0$

(i) $\dfrac{x}{2} \leqslant \dfrac{3}{x}$

(j) $\dfrac{x^2-2x-3}{x-5} > 0$

11 Express each fraction in its simplest form.

(a) $\dfrac{3ab^2}{12ab}$

(b) $\dfrac{6x^2y^2z}{3xy^3z}$

(c) $\dfrac{9t+6}{12-3t}$

(d) $\dfrac{3x^2+3x}{6x^2-3x}$

(e) $\dfrac{xyz-2x^2y^2z}{x^2y^2-2x^3y^3}$

12 Express each fraction in its simplest form.

(a) $\dfrac{x^2 + 2x - 15}{x^2 - 2x - 3}$

(b) $\dfrac{y^2 + 4y - 12}{y^2 + 13y + 42}$

(c) $\dfrac{2x^2 + 7x - 4}{2x^2 - 3x + 1}$

(d) $\dfrac{3x^2 t + 3xt - 3t}{4x^2 z + 4xz - 4z}$

(e) $\dfrac{x^3 - 2x^2 + x - 2}{x^3 + x^2 + x + 1}$

13 Express as a single fraction in its simplest form

(a) $\dfrac{x+1}{x+6} \times \dfrac{x+6}{x+2}$

(b) $\dfrac{3x-6}{xy+2y} \times \dfrac{xy+3y}{4x-8}$

(c) $\dfrac{x^2 - 1}{4} \div \dfrac{x-1}{6}$

(d) $\dfrac{x^2 - 9x}{x+1} \div \dfrac{x-9}{x^3 + x^2}$

(e) $\dfrac{x^2 - 5x - 6}{x^2 + x - 42} \div \dfrac{x^2 - 1}{x^2 + 6x - 7}$

14 Express as a single fraction:

(a) $\dfrac{5}{x+6} + \dfrac{3}{x+1}$

(b) $\dfrac{3x}{2x-1} - \dfrac{4}{x+5}$

(c) $\dfrac{x+1}{x^2 - 5x - 6} + \dfrac{5x}{x+3}$

(d) $x+1+\dfrac{2}{x-3}$

(e) $2x - 3 + \dfrac{1}{x+1} - \dfrac{x}{x^2 + 1}$

Solutions

1 (a) 7^{10} (b) 6^5 (c) 3^{-8}
(d) $3^2 6$ (e) $3^4 4^2$ (f) 10

2 (a) x^4 (b) x^8 (c) $\sqrt{x}$
(d) y^2 (e) $y^{10/3}$

3 (a) $8x^6 y^3$ (b) $36a^4 b^6 c$ (c) $2y^2$
(d) $xy^{-0.5}$ (e) $\dfrac{9x^4}{y^6}$

4 (a) $\dfrac{2}{x-3} + \dfrac{1}{x+7}$

(b) $\dfrac{3}{x} - \dfrac{4}{x-1}$

(c) $3 + \dfrac{2}{x} - \dfrac{1}{2x-1}$

(d) $\dfrac{2}{x+1} - \dfrac{1}{x-1} + \dfrac{1}{x+2}$

(e) $\dfrac{3}{x+7} - \dfrac{2}{2x+1}$

5 (a) $\dfrac{19x^2 + 22x + 4}{2x(x+2)(2x+1)}$

(b) $\dfrac{3s^3 + 12s^2 + 22s + 12}{2s^2(4s+3)}$

(c) $\dfrac{2(3s^4 + 30s^3 + 120s^2 + 202s + 120)}{s^2(s+2)(s+3)(s+4)}$

6 (a) $\dfrac{1}{x+1} + \dfrac{3}{2x-3}$

(b) $\dfrac{7}{x+3} - \dfrac{4}{x+2}$

(c) $\dfrac{2}{y+1} - \dfrac{1}{y+2}$

(d) $\dfrac{1}{t+1} - \dfrac{1}{t+2}$

(e) $\dfrac{2}{z+2} - \dfrac{1}{z+3} + \dfrac{1}{z+6}$

(f) $\dfrac{1}{2x+1} + \dfrac{3}{3x+2} - \dfrac{2}{4x+3}$

(g) $\dfrac{1}{s+1} + \dfrac{2}{(s+1)^2}$

(h) $\dfrac{1}{k+1} + \dfrac{2}{k-1} - \dfrac{1}{k}$

(i) $x - \dfrac{x}{x^2 + 1}$

(j) $\dfrac{1}{t+3} + \dfrac{2}{(t+3)^2}$

(k) $1 - \dfrac{1}{s^2 + 1}$

(l) $\dfrac{4}{2x-3} - \dfrac{3}{(2x-3)^2}$

(m) $\dfrac{4}{d+1} - \dfrac{1}{(d+1)^2} + \dfrac{2}{d+2}$

(n) $2 - \dfrac{3}{x+1} + \dfrac{4}{(x+1)^2}$

(o) $\dfrac{y}{y^2+1} - \dfrac{1}{y-1}$

(p) $\dfrac{2s+1}{s^2+s+1} - \dfrac{1}{s-4}$

(q) $\dfrac{11}{9(t-2)} + \dfrac{4}{3(t-2)^2} - \dfrac{2}{9(t+1)}$

(r) $2s+1 - \dfrac{3}{s^2+s-1}$

(s) $x+1 + \dfrac{1}{x+1} + \dfrac{1}{x+2}$

7 (a) $-9.7958, -0.2042$

(b) $-0.4641, 6.4641$

(c) $-2.6794, 1.6794$

(d) $-0.1073, 3.1073$

(e) $-1.2, 1$

8 (a) $(x+5)^2 - 23 = 0$

(b) $(y-3)^2 - 12 = 0$

(c) $2\left[\left(t+\dfrac{1}{2}\right)^2 - \dfrac{19}{4}\right] = 0$

(d) $3\left[\left(z-\dfrac{3}{2}\right)^2 - \dfrac{31}{12}\right] = 0$

(e) $5\left[\left(v+\dfrac{1}{10}\right)^2 - \dfrac{121}{100}\right] = 0$

Solutions same as for Question 7

9 $x = -4, 1, 7$

10 (a) $t \leqslant \dfrac{5}{6}$ (b) $-2 \leqslant r \leqslant 2$

(c) $v > -1$ (d) $x \geqslant 8$

(e) $x \leqslant -4$ or $x \geqslant 8$

(f) $-1 < x < 3$

(g) $x < -1$ or $x \geqslant 3$

(h) $4 - \sqrt{11} \leqslant x \leqslant 4 + \sqrt{11}$

(i) $0 < x \leqslant \sqrt{6}, x \leqslant -\sqrt{6}$

(j) $x > 5$ or $-1 < x < 3$

11 (a) $\dfrac{b}{4}$ (b) $\dfrac{2x}{y}$ (c) $\dfrac{3t+2}{4-t}$

(d) $\dfrac{x+1}{2x-1}$ (e) $\dfrac{z}{xy}$

12 (a) $\dfrac{x+5}{x+1}$ (b) $\dfrac{y-2}{y+7}$ (c) $\dfrac{x+4}{x-1}$

(d) $\dfrac{3t}{4z}$ (e) $\dfrac{x-2}{x+1}$

13 (a) $\dfrac{x+1}{x+2}$ (b) $\dfrac{3(x+3)}{4(x+2)}$

(c) $\dfrac{3(x+1)}{2}$ (d) x^3 (e) 1

14 (a) $\dfrac{8x+23}{(x+1)(x+6)}$

(b) $\dfrac{3x^2+7x+4}{(2x-1)(x+5)}$

(c) $\dfrac{5x^2-29x+3}{(x-6)(x+3)}$

(d) $\dfrac{x^2-2x-1}{x-3}$

(e) $\dfrac{2x^4-x^3-x^2-2x-2}{(x+1)(x^2+1)}$

2 Engineering functions

Chapter 2 Contents

2.1	Introduction	40
2.2	Numbers and intervals	40
2.3	Basic concepts of functions	42
2.4	Review of some common engineering functions and techniques	54
	Review exercises	92

2.1 Introduction

The study of functions is central to engineering mathematics. Functions can be used to describe the way quantities change: for example, the variation in the voltage across an electronic component with time, the variation in position of an electric motor with time and the variation in the strength of a signal with both position and time.

In this chapter we introduce several concepts associated with functions before going on to catalogue a number of engineering functions in Section 2.4. Much of the material of Section 2.4 will already be familiar to the reader and so this section should be treated as a reference section to be dipped into whenever necessary. A number of mathematical methods are also included in Section 2.4, most of which will be familiar but they have been collected together in order to make the book complete.

When trying to understand a mathematical function it is always useful to sketch a graph in order to obtain an idea of its behaviour. The reader is encouraged to sketch such graphs whenever a new function is met. Graphics calculators are now readily available and they make this task relatively easy. If you possess such a calculator then it would be useful to make use of it whenever a new function is introduced. Software packages are also available to allow such plots to be carried out on a computer. These can be useful for plotting more complicated functions and ones that depend on more than one variable. We examine functions of more than one variable in Chapter 25.

Throughout the book we make use of the term **mathematical model**. When doing so we mean an idealization of an engineering system or a physical situation so that it can be described by mathematical equations. To reflect an engineering system very accurately, a sophisticated model, consisting of many interrelated equations, may be needed. Although accurate, such a model may be cumbersome to use. Accuracy can be sacrificed in order to achieve a simple, easy-to-use model. A judgement is made as to when the right blend of accuracy and conciseness is achieved. For example, the most common mathematical model for a resistor uses Ohm's law which states that the voltage across a resistor equals the current through the resistor multiplied by the resistance value of the resistor, that is $V = IR$. However, this model is based on a number of simplifications. It ignores any variation in current density across the cross-section of the resistor and assumes a single current value is acceptable. It also ignores the fact that if a large enough voltage is placed across the resistor then the resistor will break down. In most cases it is worth accepting these simplifications in order to obtain a concise model.

Having obtained a mathematical model, it is then used to predict the effect of changing elements or conditions within the actual system. Using the model to examine these effects is often cheaper, safer and more convenient than using the actual system.

2.2 Numbers and intervals

Numbers can be grouped into various classes, or **sets**. The **integers** are the set of numbers

$$\{\ldots, -3, -2, -1, 0, 1, 2, 3, \ldots\}$$

Figure 2.1
Both rational and
irrational numbers are
represented on the real
line.

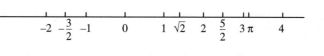

denoted by $\mathbb{Z}$. The **natural numbers** are $\{0, 1, 2, 3, \ldots\}$ and this set is denoted by $\mathbb{N}$. The **positive integers**, denoted by $\mathbb{N}^+$, are given by $\{1, 2, 3, \ldots\}$. Note that some numbers occur in more than one set, that is the sets overlap.

A **rational number** has the form p/q, where p and q are integers with $q \neq 0$. For example, $5/2$, $7/118$, $-1/9$ and $3/1$ are all rational numbers. The set of rational numbers is denoted by $\mathbb{Q}$. When rational numbers are expressed as a decimal fraction they either terminate or recur infinitely.

$\frac{5}{2}$ can be expressed as 2.5 $\left.\right\}$ These decimal fractions terminate,
$\frac{1}{8}$ can be expressed as 0.125   that is they are of finite length.

$\frac{1}{9}$ can be expressed as $0.111\,111\ldots$ $\left.\right\}$ These are infinitely
$\frac{1}{11}$ can be expressed as $0.090\,909\ldots$ recurring decimal fractions.

A number which cannot be expressed in the form p/q is called **irrational**. When written as a decimal fraction, an irrational number is infinite in length and non-recurring. The numbers π and $\sqrt{2}$ are both irrational.

It is useful to introduce the **factorial notation**. We write 3! to represent the product $3 \times 2 \times 1$. The expression 3! is read as 'factorial 3'. Similarly 4! is a shorthand way of writing $4 \times 3 \times 2 \times 1$. In general, for any positive integer, n, we can write

$$n! = n(n-1)(n-2)(n-3)\ldots(3)(2)(1)$$

It is useful to represent numbers by points on the **real line**. Figure 2.1 illustrates some rational and irrational numbers marked on the real line. Numbers which can be represented by points on the real line are known as **real numbers**. The set of real numbers is denoted by $\mathbb{R}$. This set comprises all the rational and all the irrational numbers. In Chapter 9 we shall meet complex numbers which cannot be represented as points on the real line. The real line extends indefinitely to the left and to the right so that any real number can be represented.

Sometimes we are interested in only a small section, or **interval**, of the real line. We write [1, 3] to denote all the real numbers between 1 and 3 inclusive, that is 1 and 3 are included in the interval. Thus the interval [1, 3] consists of all real numbers x, such that $1 \leqslant x \leqslant 3$. The square brackets, [ ], are used to denote that the end-points are included in the interval and such an interval is said to be **closed**. The interval (1, 3) consists of all real numbers x, such that $1 < x < 3$. In this case the end-points are not included and the interval is said to be **open**. Parentheses, (), denote open intervals. An interval may be open at one end and closed at the other. For example, (1, 3] is open at the left and closed at the right. It consists of all real numbers x, such that $1 < x \leqslant 3$, and is known as a **semi-open** interval. Open and closed intervals can be represented on the real line. A closed end-point is denoted by ●; an open end-point is denoted by ○. The intervals $(-6, -4)$, $[-1, 2]$ and $(3, 4]$ are illustrated in Figure 2.2.

Figure 2.2
The intervals
$(-6, -4), [-1, 2],$
$(3, 4]$ depicted on the
real line.

An **upper bound** of a set of numbers is any number which is greater than every number in the given set. So, for example, 7, is an upper bound for the set [3, 6]. Clearly, 7 is greater than every number in the interval [3, 6].

A **lower bound** of a set of numbers is any number which is smaller than every number in the given set. For example, 3 is a lower bound for the set (3.7, 5).

Note that upper and lower bounds are not unique. Both 3 and 10 are upper bounds for (1, 2). Both -1 and -3 are lower bounds for [0, 6].

2.3 Basic concepts of functions

Loosely speaking, we can think of a function as a rule which, when given an input, produces a single output. If more than one output is produced, the rule is not a function. Consider the function given by the rule: 'double the input'. If 3 is the input then 6 is the output. If x is the input then $2x$ is the output, as shown in Figure 2.3.

Figure 2.3
The function: 'double
the input'.

If the doubling function has the symbol f we write

$$f : x \rightarrow 2x$$

or more compactly,

$$f(x) = 2x$$

The last form is often written simply as $f = 2x$. If $f(x)$ is a function of x, then the value of the function when $x = 3$, for example, is written as $f(x = 3)$ or simply as $f(3)$.

Example 2.1   Given $f(x) = 2x + 1$ find

(a) $f(3)$ (e) $f(2\alpha)$

(b) $f(0)$ (f) $f(t)$

(c) $f(-1)$ (g) $f(t + 1)$

(d) $f(\alpha)$

Solution   (a) $f(3) = 2(3) + 1 = 7$

(b) $f(0) = 2(0) + 1 = 1$

(c) $f(-1) = 2(-1) + 1 = -1$

(d) $f(\alpha)$ is the value of $f(x)$ when x has a value of α, hence $f(\alpha) = 2\alpha + 1$

(e) $f(2\alpha) = 2(2\alpha) + 1 = 4\alpha + 1$

(f) $f(t) = 2t + 1$

(g) $f(t + 1) = 2(t + 1) + 1 = 2t + 3$

Observe from Example 2.1 that it is the rule that is important and not the letter being used. Both $f(t) = 2t + 1$ and $f(x) = 2x + 1$ instruct us to double the input and then add 1.

2.3.1 Argument of a function

The input to a function is often called the **argument**. In Example 2.1(d) the argument is α, while in Example 2.1(e) the argument is 2α.

Example 2.2   Given $f(x) = \dfrac{x}{5}$, write down

(a) $f(5x)$ (c) $f(x+2)$

(b) $f(-x)$ (d) $f(x^2)$

Solution   (a) $f(5x) = \dfrac{5x}{5} = x$ (c) $f(x + 2) = \dfrac{x + 2}{5}$

(b) $f(-x) = -\dfrac{x}{5}$ (d) $f(x^2) = \dfrac{x^2}{5}$

Example 2.3   Given $y(t) = t^2 + t$, write down

(a) $y(t + 2)$ (b) $y\left(\dfrac{t}{2}\right)$

Solution   (a) $y(t + 2) = (t + 2)^2 + (t + 2) = t^2 + 5t + 6$

(b) $y\left(\dfrac{t}{2}\right) = \left(\dfrac{t}{2}\right)^2 + \left(\dfrac{t}{2}\right) = \dfrac{t^2}{4} + \dfrac{t}{2}$

2.3.2 Graph of a function

A function may be represented in graphical form. The function $f(x) = 2x$ is shown in Figure 2.4. Note that the function values are plotted vertically and the x values horizontally. The horizontal axis is then called the x axis. The vertical axis is commonly referred to as the y axis, so that we often write

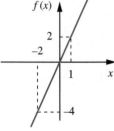

Figure 2.4 The function: $f(x) = 2x$.

$$y = f(x) = 2x$$

Since x and y can have a number of possible values, they are called **variables**: x is the **independent variable** and y is the **dependent variable**. Knowing a value of the independent variable, x, allows us to calculate the corresponding value of the dependent variable, y. To show this dependence we often write $y(x)$. The set of values that x is allowed to take is called the **domain** of the function. A domain is often an interval on the x axis. For example, if

$$f(x) = 3x + 1 \qquad -5 \leqslant x \leqslant 10 \tag{2.1}$$

the domain of the function, f, is the closed interval $[-5, 10]$. If the domain of a function is not explicitly given it is taken to be the largest set possible. For example,

$$g(x) = x^2 - 4 \tag{2.2}$$

has a domain of $(-\infty, \infty)$ since g is defined for every value of x and the domain has not been given otherwise. The set of values that the function takes on is called the **range**. The range of $f(x)$ in Equation (2.1) is $[-14, 31]$; the range of $g(x)$ in Equation (2.2) is $[-4, \infty)$.

Example 2.4   Consider the function, f, given by the rule: 'square the input'. This can be written as

$$f(x) = x^2$$

The rule and the graph of f are shown in Figure 2.5. The domain of f is $(-\infty, \infty)$ and the range is $[0, \infty)$.

Figure 2.5
The function: 'square the input'.

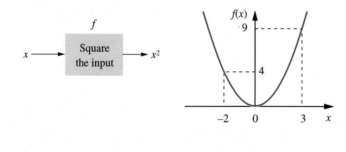

Many variables of interest to engineers, for example voltage, resistance and current, can be related by means of functions. We try to choose an appropriate letter for a particular variable; so, for example, t is used for time and P for power.

Example 2.5 | **Power dissipated in a resistor**

The power, P, dissipated in a resistor depends on the current, I, flowing through the resistor and the resistance, R. The relationship is given by

$$P = I^2R$$

The power dissipated in the resistor depends on the square of the current passing through it. In this case I is the independent variable and P is the dependent variable, assuming R remains constant. The function is given by the rule: 'square the input and multiply by the constant R', and the input to the function is I. The output from the function is P. This is illustrated in Figure 2.6, for the cases $R = 4$ and $R = 2$.

Figure 2.6
The function:
$P = I^2R$.

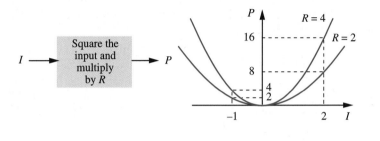

2.3.3 One-to-many

Some rules relating input to output are not functions. Consider the rule: 'take plus or minus the square root of the input', that is

$$x \rightarrow \pm\sqrt{x}$$

Now, for example, if 4 is the input, the output is $\pm\sqrt{4}$ which can be 2 or -2. Thus a single input has produced more than one output. The rule is said to be **one-to-many**, meaning that one input has produced many outputs. Rules with this property are not functions. For a rule to be a function there must be a single output for any given input.

By defining a rule more specifically, it may become a function. For example, consider the rule: 'take the positive square root of the input'. This rule is a function because there is a single output for a given input. Note that the domain of this function is $[0, \infty)$ and the range is also $[0, \infty)$.

2.3.4 Many-to-one and one-to-one functions

Consider again the function $f(x) = x^2$ given in Example 2.4. The inputs 2 and -2 both produce the same output, 4, and the function is said to be **many-to-one**. This means that many inputs produce the same output. A many-to-one function can be recognized from its graph. If a horizontal line intersects the graph in more than one place, the function is many-to-one. Figure 2.7 illustrates a many-to-one function, $g(x)$. The inputs x_1, x_2, x_3 and x_4 all produce the same output.

A function is **one-to-one** if different inputs always produce different outputs. A horizontal line will intersect the graph of a one-to-one function in only one place. Figure 2.8 illustrates a one-to-one function, $h(x)$.

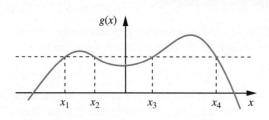

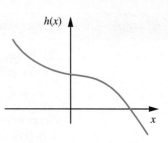

Figure 2.7 The inputs x_1, x_2, x_3 and x_4 all produce the same output, therefore $g(x)$ is a many-to-one function.

Figure 2.8 Each input produces a different output and so $h(x)$ is a one-to-one function.

2.3.5 Parametric definition of a function

Functions are often expressed in the form $y(x)$. For every value of x the corresponding value of y can be found and the point with coordinates (x, y) can then be plotted. Sometimes it is useful to express x and y coordinates in terms of a third variable known as a **parameter**. Commonly we use t or θ to denote a parameter. Thus the coordinates (x, y) of the points on a curve can be expressed in the form

$$x = f(t) \qquad y = g(t)$$

For example, given the parametric equations

$$x = t^2 \qquad y = 2t \qquad 0 \leqslant t \leqslant 5$$

we can calculate x and y for various values of the parameter t. Plotting the points (x, y) produces part of a curve known as a parabola.

2.3.6 Composition of functions

Consider the function $y(x) = 2x^2$. We can think of $y(x)$ as being composed of two functions. One function is described by the rule: 'square the input', while the other function is described by the rule: 'double the input'. This is shown in Figure 2.9.

Figure 2.9
The function:
$y(x) = h(g(x))$.

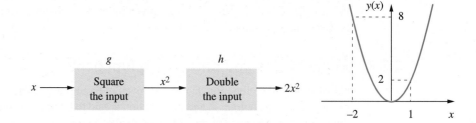

Mathematically, if $h(x) = 2x$ and $g(x) = x^2$ then

$$y(x) = 2x^2 = 2(g(x)) = h(g(x))$$

The form $h(g(x))$ is known as a **composition** of the functions h and g. Note that the composition $h(g(x))$ is different from $g(h(x))$ as Example 2.6 illustrates.

Example 2.6 If $f(t) = 2t + 3$ and $g(t) = \dfrac{t+1}{2}$ write expressions for the compositions

(a) $f(g(t))$ (b) $g(f(t))$

Solution (a) $f(g(t)) = f\left(\dfrac{t+1}{2}\right)$

The rule describing the function f is: 'double the input and then add 3'. Hence,

$$f\left(\frac{t+1}{2}\right) = 2\left(\frac{t+1}{2}\right) + 3 = t + 4$$

So

$$f(g(t)) = t + 4$$

(b) $g(f(t)) = g(2t + 3)$

The rule for g is: 'add 1 to the input and then divide everything by 2'. So,

$$g(2t + 3) = \frac{2t + 3 + 1}{2} = t + 2$$

Hence

$$g(f(t)) = t + 2$$

Clearly $f(g(t)) \neq g(f(t))$.

2.3.7 Inverse of a function

Consider a function $f(x)$. It can be thought of as accepting an input x, and producing an output $f(x)$. Suppose now that this output becomes the input to the function $g(x)$, and the output from $g(x)$ is x, that is

$$g(f(x)) = x$$

We can think of $g(x)$ as undoing the work of $f(x)$. Figure 2.10 illustrates this situation. Then $g(x)$ is the **inverse** of f, and is written as $f^{-1}(x)$. Since $f^{-1}(x)$ undoes the work of $f(x)$ we have

$$f(f^{-1}(x)) = f^{-1}(f(x)) = x$$

Figure 2.10
The function g is the inverse of f.

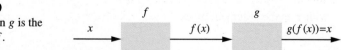

Example 2.7   If $f(x) = 5x$ verify that the inverse of f is given by $f^{-1}(x) = \dfrac{x}{5}$.

Solution   The function f receives an input of x, and produces an output of $5x$. Hence when the inverse function, f^{-1}, receives an input of $5x$, it produces an output of x, that is

$$f^{-1}(5x) = x$$

We introduce a new variable, z, given by

$$z = 5x$$

so

$$x = \frac{z}{5}$$

Then

$$f^{-1}(z) = x = \frac{z}{5}$$

Writing f^{-1} with x as the argument gives

$$f^{-1}(x) = \frac{x}{5}$$

Example 2.8   If $f(x) = 2x + 1$, find $f^{-1}(x)$.

Solution   The function f receives an input of x and produces an output of $2x + 1$. So when the inverse function, f^{-1}, receives an input of $2x + 1$ it produces an output of x, that is

$$f^{-1}(2x + 1) = x$$

We introduce a new variable, z, defined by

$$z = 2x + 1$$

Rearranging gives

$$x = \frac{z - 1}{2}$$

So

$$f^{-1}(z) = x = \frac{z - 1}{2}$$

Writing f^{-1} with x as the argument gives

$$f^{-1}(x) = \frac{x - 1}{2}$$

Example 2.9   Given $g(x) = \dfrac{x-1}{2}$ find the inverse of g.

Solution   We know $g(x) = \dfrac{x-1}{2}$, and so $g^{-1}\left(\dfrac{x-1}{2}\right) = x$. Let $y = \dfrac{x-1}{2}$ so that

$$g^{-1}(y) = x$$

But,

$$x = 2y + 1$$

and so

$$g^{-1}(y) = 2y + 1$$

Using the same independent variable as for the function g, we obtain

$$g^{-1}(x) = 2x + 1$$

We note that the inverses of the functions in Examples 2.8 and 2.9 are themselves functions. They are called **inverse functions**. The inverse of $f(x) = 2x+1$ is $f^{-1}(x) = \dfrac{x-1}{2}$, and the inverse of $g(x) = \dfrac{x-1}{2}$ is $g^{-1}(x) = 2x + 1$. This illustrates the important point that if $f(x)$ and $g(x)$ are two functions and $f(x)$ is the inverse of $g(x)$, then $g(x)$ is the inverse of $f(x)$. It is important to point out that not all functions possess an inverse function. Consider $f(x) = x^2$, for $-\infty < x < \infty$.

The function, f, is given by the rule: 'square the input'. Since both a positive and negative value of x will yield the output x^2, the inverse rule is given by: 'take plus or minus the square root of the input'. As discussed earlier, this is a one-to-many rule and so is not a function. Clearly not all functions have an inverse function. In fact, only one-to-one functions have an inverse function. Suppose we restrict the domain of $f(x) = x^2$ such that $x \geqslant 0$. Then f is a one-to-one function and so there is an inverse function. The inverse function is $f^{-1}(x)$ given by

$$f^{-1}(x) = +\sqrt{x}$$

Clearly,

$$f^{-1}(f(x)) = f^{-1}(x^2) = x$$

where x is the positive square root of x^2. Restricting the domain of a many-to-one function so that a one-to-one function results is a common technique of ensuring an inverse function can be found.

2.3.8   Continuous and piecewise continuous functions

We now introduce in an informal way the concept of continuous and piecewise continuous functions. A more rigorous treatment follows in Chapter 10 after we have discussed limits. Figure 2.11 shows a graph of $f(x) = \dfrac{1}{x}$. Note that there is a break, or discontinuity, in the graph at $x = 0$. The function $f(x) = \dfrac{1}{x}$ is said to be **discontinuous** at $x = 0$.

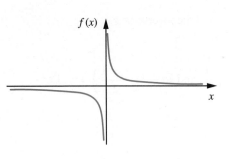

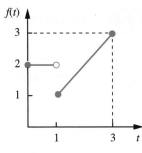

Figure 2.11 The function $f(x) = \dfrac{1}{x}$ has a discontinuity at $x = 0$.

Figure 2.12 The function $f(t)$ is a piecewise continuous function with a discontinuity at $t = 1$.

If the graph of a function, $f(x)$, contains a break, then $f(x)$ is discontinuous.

A function whose graph has no breaks is a **continuous** function.

Sometimes a function is defined by different rules on different intervals of the domain. For example, consider

$$f(t) = \begin{cases} 2 & 0 \leqslant t < 1 \\ t & 1 \leqslant t \leqslant 3 \end{cases}$$

The domain is $[0, 3]$ but the rule on $[0, 1)$ is different to that on $[1, 3]$. The graph of $f(t)$ is shown in Figure 2.12. Recall the convention of using ● to denote that the end-point is included and ○ to denote the end-point is excluded. Note that $f(t)$ has a discontinuity at $t = 1$. Each component, or piece, of the graph is continuous and $f(t)$ is said to be **piecewise continuous**.

A piecewise continuous function has a finite number of discontinuities in any given interval.

Not all functions defined differently on different intervals are discontinuous. For example,

$$g(t) = \begin{cases} 2 & 0 < t < 1 \\ 2t & 1 \leqslant t < 3 \end{cases}$$

is a continuous function on the interval $(0, 3)$, as shown in Figure 2.13.

2.3.9 Periodic functions

A **periodic function** is a function which has a definite pattern which is repeated at regular intervals. More formally we say a function, $f(t)$, is periodic if

$$f(t) = f(t + T)$$

for all values of t. The constant, T, is known as the **period** of the function.

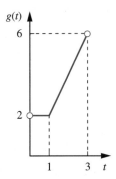

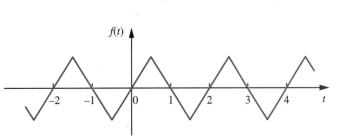

Figure 2.13 The function $g(t)$ is a continuous function on $(0, 3)$.

Figure 2.14 The triangular waveform is a periodic function.

| Example 2.10 | **Triangular waveform** |

Figure 2.14 illustrates a triangular waveform. The form of the function is repeated every two seconds, that is

$$f(t) = f(t + 2)$$

and so the function is periodic. The period is 2 seconds, that is $T = 2$. Note that this function is continuous.

| Example 2.11 | **Square waveform** |

Periodic functions may be piecewise continuous. Consider the function $g(t)$ defined by

$$g(t) = \begin{cases} 1 & 0 \leqslant t < 1 \\ 0 & 1 \leqslant t < 2 \end{cases} \qquad \text{period} = 2$$

The function $g(t)$ is periodic with period 2. A graph of $g(t)$ is shown in Figure 2.15. This function is commonly referred to as a square waveform by engineers. In Figure 2.15 the open and closed end-points have been shown for mathematical correctness. Note, however, that engineers tend to omit these when sketching functions with discontinuities and usually they use a vertical line to show the discontinuity. This reflects the fact that no practical waveform can ever change its level instantaneously: even very fast rising waveforms still have a finite **risetime**. The function has discontinuities at $t = \ldots, -3, -2, -1, 0, 1, 2, 3, 4, 5, \ldots$.

Figure 2.15
The function $g(t)$ is both piecewise continuous and periodic.

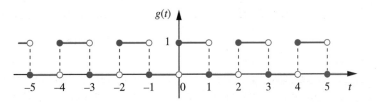

Exercises 2.3

1 Represent the following intervals on the real line.
(a) $[1, 3]$ (b) $[2, 4)$
(c) $(0, 3.5)$ (d) $[-2, 0)$
(e) $(-1, 1]$ (f) $2 \leqslant x < 4$
(g) $0 < x < 2$ (h) $-3 \leqslant x \leqslant -1$
(i) $0 \leqslant x < 3$

2 Describe the rule associated with the following functions, sketch their graphs and state their domains and ranges.

(a) $f(x) = 2x^2$

(b) $f(x) = x^2 - 1$ $0 \leqslant x$

(c) $g(t) = 3t - 4$ $0 \leqslant t$

(d) $y(x) = x^3$

(e) $f(t) = 0.5t + 2$ $-2 \leqslant t \leqslant 10$

(f) $z(x) = 3x - 2$ $3 \leqslant x \leqslant 8$

3 If $f(x) = 5x + 4$, find

(a) $f(3)$

(b) $f(-3)$

(c) $f(\alpha)$

(d) $f(x + 1)$

(e) $f(3\alpha)$

(f) $f(x^2)$

4 If $g(t) = 5t^2 - 4$, find

(a) $g(0)$

(b) $g(2)$

(c) $g(-3)$

(d) $g(x)$

(e) $g(2t - 1)$

5 The reactance, X_C, offered by a capacitor is given by $X_C = \dfrac{1}{2\pi f C}$, where f is the frequency of the applied alternating current, and C is the capacitance of the capacitor. If $C = 10^{-6}$ F, find X_C when $f = 50$ Hz.

6 Classify the functions in Question 2 as one-to-one or many-to-one.

7 Find the inverse of the following functions:

(a) $f(x) = x + 4$

(b) $g(t) = 3t + 1$

(c) $y(x) = x^3$

(d) $h(t) = \dfrac{t - 8}{3}$

(e) $f(t) = \dfrac{t - 1}{3}$

(f) $h(x) = x^3 - 1$

(g) $k(v) = 7 - v$

(h) $m(n) = \frac{1}{3}(1 - 2n)$

8 Given $f(t) = 2t$, $g(t) = t - 1$ and $h(t) = t^2$ write expressions for
(a) $f(g(t))$ (b) $f(h(t))$
(c) $g(h(t))$ (d) $g(f(t))$
(e) $h(g(t))$ (f) $h(f(t))$
(g) $f(f(t))$ (h) $g(g(t))$
(i) $h(h(t))$ (j) $f(g(h(t)))$
(k) $g(f(h(t)))$ (l) $h(g(f(t)))$

9 Given $f(t) = t^2 + 1$, $g(t) = 3t + 2$ and $h(t) = \dfrac{1}{t}$, write expressions for

(a) $f(g(t))$

(b) $f(h(t))$

(c) $g(h(t))$

(d) $h(f(t))$

(e) $f(g(h(t)))$

10 Given $f(t) = 2t$, $g(t) = 2t + 1$, $h(t) = 1 - 3t$, write expressions for the following:
(a) $f^{-1}(t)$ (b) $g^{-1}(t)$ (c) $h^{-1}(t)$

11 Given $a(x) = 3x - 2$, $b(x) = \dfrac{2}{x}$, $c(x) = 1 + \dfrac{1}{x}$ write expressions for
(a) $a^{-1}(x)$ (b) $b^{-1}(x)$ (c) $c^{-1}(x)$

12 Given $f(t) = 2t + 3$, $g(t) = 3t$ and $h(t) = f(g(t))$ write expressions for

(a) $h(t)$

(b) $f^{-1}(t)$

(c) $g^{-1}(t)$

(d) $h^{-1}(t)$

(e) $g^{-1}(f^{-1}(t))$

What do you notice about (d) and (e)?

13 Sketch the following functions:

(a) $f(t) = \begin{cases} t & 0 \leqslant t \leqslant 3 \\ 3 & 3 < t \leqslant 4 \end{cases}$

(b) $g(x) = \begin{cases} 2 - x & 0 \leqslant x < 1 \\ 2 & 1 \leqslant x \leqslant 3 \end{cases}$

(c) $a(t) = \begin{cases} 1 - t & 0 \leqslant t \leqslant 1 \\ t - 1 & 1 < t \leqslant 2 \end{cases}$

(d) $b(x) = \begin{cases} 2 & 0 \leqslant x \leqslant 1 \\ 1 & 1 < x \leqslant 2 \\ 3 - x & 2 < x \leqslant 3 \end{cases}$

14 Sketch

$$f(t) = \begin{cases} t & 0 \leqslant t < 2 \\ 5 - 2t & 2 \leqslant t < 3 \end{cases}$$

Is the function piecewise continuous or continuous? State, if they exist, the position of any discontinuities.

15 The function $h(t)$ is defined by

$$h(t) = \begin{cases} 2 - t & 0 \leqslant t < 2 \\ 2t - 4 & 2 \leqslant t \leqslant 3 \end{cases}$$

and $h(t)$ has period 3. Sketch $h(t)$ on the interval $[0, 6]$.

16 The function $g(t)$ is defined by

$$g(t) = \begin{cases} 1 & 0 \leqslant t \leqslant 1 \\ 2 - t & 1 < t < 2 \end{cases}$$

and $g(t)$ has period 2. Sketch $g(t)$ on the interval $[-1, 4]$. State any points of discontinuity.

Solutions

2 (a) Square the input and then multiply by 2; domain $(-\infty, \infty)$, range $[0, \infty)$

(b) Square the input, then subtract 1; domain $[0, \infty)$, range $[-1, \infty)$

(c) Multiply input by 3 and subtract 4; domain $[0, \infty)$, range $[-4, \infty)$

(d) Cube the input; domain $(-\infty, \infty)$, range $(-\infty, \infty)$

(e) Multiply input by 0.5 and then add 2; domain $[-2, 10]$, range $[1, 7]$

(f) Multiply input by 3 and then subtract 2; domain $[3, 8]$, range $[7, 22]$

3 (a) 19   (b) -11 (c) $5\alpha + 4$
(d) $5x + 9$ (e) $15\alpha + 4$ (f) $5x^2 + 4$

4 (a) -4 (b) 16   (c) 41
(d) $5x^2 - 4$ (e) $20t^2 - 20t + 1$

5 3183 ohms

6 (a) many-to-one   (b) one-to-one
(c) one-to-one   (d) one-to-one
(e) one-to-one   (f) one-to-one

7 (a) $f^{-1}(x) = x - 4$

(b) $g^{-1}(t) = \dfrac{t - 1}{3}$

(c) $y^{-1}(x) = x^{1/3}$

(d) $h^{-1}(t) = 3t + 8$

(e) $f^{-1}(t) = 3t + 1$

(f) $h^{-1}(x) = (x + 1)^{1/3}$

(g) $k^{-1}(v) = 7 - v$

(h) $m^{-1}(n) = \dfrac{1 - 3n}{2}$

8 (a) $2(t - 1)$ (b) $2t^2$
(c) $t^2 - 1$ (d) $2t - 1$
(e) $(t - 1)^2$ (f) $4t^2$
(g) $4t$ (h) $t - 2$
(i) t^4 (j) $2(t^2 - 1)$
(k) $2t^2 - 1$ (l) $(2t - 1)^2$

9 (a) $9t^2 + 12t + 5$ (b) $\dfrac{1}{t^2} + 1$

(c) $\dfrac{3}{t} + 2$ (d) $\dfrac{1}{t^2 + 1}$

(e) $\dfrac{9}{t^2} + \dfrac{12}{t} + 5$

10 (a) $\dfrac{t}{2}$ (b) $\dfrac{t - 1}{2}$ (c) $\dfrac{1 - t}{3}$

11 (a) $\dfrac{x + 2}{3}$ (b) $\dfrac{2}{x}$ (c) $\dfrac{1}{x - 1}$

12 (a) $6t + 3$ (b) $\dfrac{t - 3}{2}$ (c) $\dfrac{t}{3}$

(d) $\dfrac{t - 3}{6}$ (e) $\dfrac{t - 3}{6}$

13   See Figure S.1.

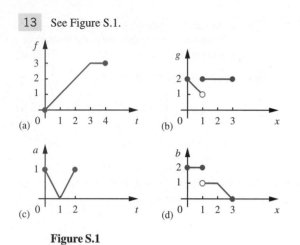

Figure S.1

14   Piecewise continuous; discontinuity at $t = 2$.
See Figure S.2.

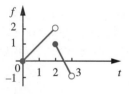

Figure S.2

15   See Figure S.3.

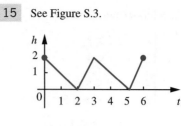

Figure S.3

16   Discontinuities at $t = 0, 2$. See Figure S.4.

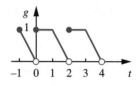

Figure S.4

2.4   Review of some common engineering functions and techniques

This section provides a catalogue of the more common engineering functions. The important properties and definitions are included together with some techniques. It is intended that readers will refer to this section for revision purposes and as the need arises throughout the rest of the book.

2.4.1   Polynomial functions

A **polynomial expression** has the form

$$a_n x^n + a_{n-1} x^{n-1} + a_{n-2} x^{n-2} + \cdots + a_2 x^2 + a_1 x + a_0$$

where n is a non-negative integer, $a_n, a_{n-1}, \ldots, a_1, a_0$ are constants and x is a variable. A **polynomial function**, $P(x)$, has the form

$$P(x) = a_n x^n + a_{n-1} x^{n-1} + a_{n-2} x^{n-2} + \cdots + a_2 x^2 + a_1 x + a_0 \tag{2.3}$$

Examples of polynomial functions include

$$P_1(x) = 3x^2 - x + 2 \tag{2.4}$$

$$P_2(z) = 7z^4 + z^2 - 1 \tag{2.5}$$

$$P_3(t) = 3t + 9 \tag{2.6}$$

$$P_4(t) = 6 \tag{2.7}$$

where x, z and t are independent variables. It is common practice to contract the term polynomial expression to **polynomial**. By convention, a polynomial is usually written with the powers either increasing or decreasing. For example,

$$3x + 9x^2 - x^3 + 2$$

would be written as either

$$-x^3 + 9x^2 + 3x + 2 \qquad \text{or} \qquad 2 + 3x + 9x^2 - x^3$$

The **degree** of a polynomial or polynomial function is the value of the highest power. Equation (2.4) has degree 2, Equation (2.5) has degree 4, Equation (2.6) has degree 1 and Equation (2.7) has degree 0. Equation (2.3) has degree n. Polynomials with low degrees have special names (see Table 2.1).

Table 2.1

Polynomial	Degree	Name
$ax^4 + bx^3 + cx^2 + dx + e$	4	Quartic
$ax^3 + bx^2 + cx + d$	3	Cubic
$ax^2 + bx + c$	2	Quadratic
$ax + b$	1	Linear
a	0	Constant

Typical graphs of some polynomial functions are shown in Figure 2.16.

Figure 2.16
Some typical
polynomials.

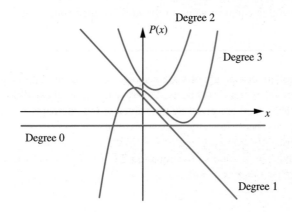

Example 2.12   **Ohm's Law**

Ohm's law relates the current through a resistor to the voltage applied across it. The equation is

$$V = IR$$

where $V =$ voltage across the resistor;

$\quad I =$ current through the resistor;

$\quad R =$ resistance value of the resistor, which is a constant for a given temperature.

Note that the voltage is a linear polynomial function with I as the independent variable.

Example 2.13   **A non-ideal voltage source**

An ideal voltage source has zero internal resistance and its output voltage, V, is independent of the load applied to it; that is, V remains constant, independent of the current it supplies. Figure 2.17 shows a non-ideal voltage source. It is modelled as an ideal voltage source in series with an internal resistor with resistance R_s. The output voltage of the non-ideal voltage source is v_o while v_R is the voltage drop across the internal resistor and i is the load current. Using Kirchhoff's voltage law,

$$V = v_R + v_o$$

and hence by Ohm's law,

$$V = iR_s + v_o$$
$$v_o = V - iR_s$$

Note that V and R_s are constants and so the output voltage is a linear polynomial function with independent variable i. The equation gives the output voltage across the load as a function of the current through the load. The output characteristic for the non-ideal voltage source is obtained by varying the load resistor R_L and is plotted in Figure 2.18. Notice that the output voltage of the source decreases as the load current increases and is equal in value to the ideal voltage source only when there is no load current.

Many excellent computer software packages exist for plotting graphs and these, as well as graphics calculators, may be used to solve polynomial equations. The real roots of the equation $P(x) = 0$ are given by the values of the intercepts of the function $y = P(x)$ and the x axis, because on the x axis y is zero.

Figure 2.19 shows a graph of $y = P(x)$. The graph intersects the x axis at $x = x_1$, $x = x_2$ and $x = x_3$, and so the equation $P(x) = 0$ has real roots x_1, x_2 and x_3, that is $P(x_1) = P(x_2) = P(x_3) = 0$.

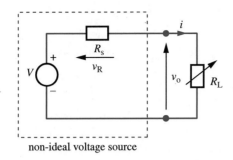

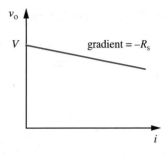

Figure 2.17 A non-ideal voltage source connected to a load resistor, R_L.

Figure 2.18 Output characteristic of a non-ideal voltage source.

Figure 2.19
A polynomial function which cuts the x axis at points x_1, x_2 and x_3.

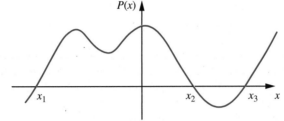

Exercises 2.4.1

1. State the degree of the following polynomial expressions.

   (a) $z^3 + 2z^2 - 8 + 13z$

   (b) $t^2 - 5t^5 + 2 - 8t^3$

   (c) $3w - 5w^2 + 12w^4$

   (d) $7x - x^2$

   (e) $3(2t^2 - 9t + 1)$

   (f) $2z(2z + 1)(2z - 1)$

Solutions

1. (a) 3   (b) 5   (c) 4   (d) 2   (e) 2   (f) 3

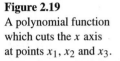 Computer and calculator exercises 2.4.1

1. (a) Draw $y = x^3$ and $y = 4 - 2x$ using the same axes. Note the x coordinate of the point of intersection.

   (b) Draw $y = x^3 + 2x - 4$. Note the coordinate of the point where the curve cuts the x axis. Compare your answer with that from (a). Explain your findings.

2. Obtain graphs of the following functions using a graphics calculator or software package.

   (a) $y = 3x^3 - x^2 + 2x + 1$ $-2 \leqslant x \leqslant 2$

   (b) $y = x^4 + \dfrac{x^3}{3} - \dfrac{5x^2}{2} + x - 1$ $-3 \leqslant x \leqslant 2$

   (c) $y = x^5 - x^2 + 2$ $-2 \leqslant x \leqslant 2$

Hence estimate the real roots of

$$0 = 3x^3 - x^2 + 2x + 1 \qquad -2 \leqslant x \leqslant 2$$

$$0 = x^4 + \frac{x^3}{3} - \frac{5x^2}{2} + x - 1$$

$$-3 \leqslant x \leqslant 2$$

$$0 = x^5 - x^2 + 2 \qquad -2 \leqslant x \leqslant 2$$

3 (a) Draw $y = 2x^2$ and $y = x^3 + 6$ using the same axes. Use your graphs to find approximate solutions to $x^3 - 2x^2 + 6 = 0$.

(b) Add the line $y = -3x + 5$ to your graph. State approximate solutions to

(i) $x^3 + 3x + 1 = 0$

(ii) $2x^2 + 3x - 5 = 0$

2.4.2 Rational functions

A **rational function**, $R(x)$, has the form

$$R(x) = \frac{P(x)}{Q(x)}$$

where P and Q are polynomial functions; P is the **numerator** and Q is the **denominator**.

The functions

$$R_1(x) = \frac{x + 6}{x^2 + 1} \qquad R_2(t) = \frac{t^3 - 1}{2t + 3} \qquad R_3(z) = \frac{2z^2 + z - 1}{z^2 + 3z - 2}$$

are all rational. When sketching the graph of a rational function, $y = f(x)$, it is usual to draw up a table of x and y values. Indeed this has been common practice when sketching any graph although the use of graphics calculators is now replacing this custom. It is still useful to answer questions such as:

'How does the function behave as x becomes large positively?'
'How does the function behave as x becomes large negatively?'
'What is the value of the function when $x = 0$?'
'At what values of x is the denominator zero?'

Figure 2.20 shows a graph of the function $y = \frac{1 + 2x}{x} = \frac{1}{x} + 2$. As x increases, the value of y approaches 2. We write this as

$$y \to 2 \quad \text{as} \quad x \to \infty$$

and say 'y tends to 2 as x tends to infinity'. Also from Figure 2.20, we see that

$$y \to \pm\infty \quad \text{as} \quad x \to 0$$

As $x \to \infty$, the graph gets nearer and nearer to the straight line $y = 2$. We say that $y = 2$ is an **asymptote** of the graph. Similarly, $x = 0$, that is the y axis, is an asymptote since the graph approaches the line $x = 0$ as $x \to 0$.

If the graph of any function gets closer and closer to a straight line then that line is called an asymptote. Figure 2.21 illustrates some rational functions with their asymptotes indicated by dashed lines. In Figure 2.21(a) the asymptotes are the horizontal line $y = 3$ and the y axis, that is $x = 0$. In Figure 2.21(b) the asymptotes are the horizontal line $y = 1$ and the vertical line $x = -2$; in Figure 2.21(c) they are $y = x + 3$ and the

Figure 2.20
The function:
$$y = \frac{1 + 2x}{x} = \frac{1}{x} + 2.$$

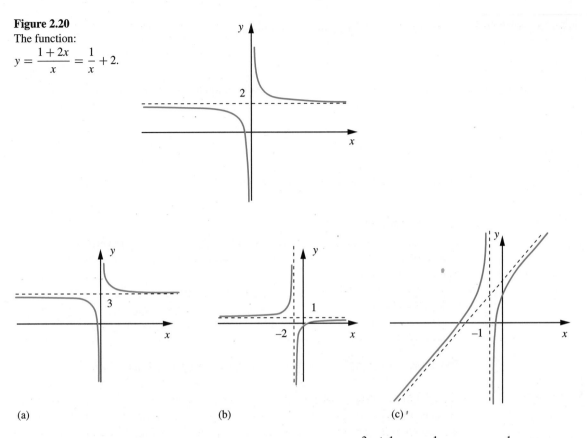

(a)   (b)   (c)

Figure 2.21 Some examples of functions with their asymptotes: (a) $y = \dfrac{3x + 1}{x} = 3 + \dfrac{1}{x}$; (b) $y = \dfrac{x - 1}{x + 2}$;

(c) $y = \dfrac{x^2 + 4x + 2}{x + 1} = x + 3 - \dfrac{1}{x + 1}$.

vertical line $x = -1$. The asymptote $y = x + 3$, being neither horizontal nor vertical, is called an **oblique asymptote**. Oblique asymptotes occur only when the degree of the numerator exceeds the degree of the denominator by one.

We see that the vertical asymptotes occur at values of x which make the denominator zero. These values are particularly important to engineers and are known as the **poles** of the function. The function shown in Figure 2.21(a) has a pole at $x = 0$; the function shown in Figure 2.21(b) has a pole at $x = -2$ and the function shown in Figure 2.21(c) has a pole at $x = -1$.

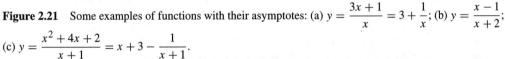

If the graph of a function approaches a straight line, the line is known as an asymptote. Asymptotes may be horizontal, vertical or oblique.

Values of the independent variable where the denominator is zero are called poles of the function.

Example 2.14   Sketch the rational function $y = \dfrac{x}{x^2 + x - 2}$.

Solution   For large values of x, the x^2 term in the denominator has a much greater value than the x in the numerator. Hence,

$$y \to 0 \qquad \text{as} \qquad x \to \infty$$
$$y \to 0 \qquad \text{as} \qquad x \to -\infty$$

Therefore the x axis, that is $y = 0$, is an asymptote. Writing y as

$$y = \frac{x}{(x-1)(x+2)}$$

we see the function has poles at $x = 1$ and $x = -2$; that is, there are vertical asymptotes at $x = 1$ and $x = -2$. Substitution into the function of a number of values of x allows a table to be drawn up:

x	−3	−2.5	−2.1	−1.9	−1.5	−1	0	0.5	0.9	1.1	1.5	2	3
y	−0.75	−1.43	−6.77	6.55	1.20	0.50	0	−0.40	−3.10	3.55	0.86	0.50	0.30

The graph of the function can then be sketched as shown in Figure 2.22.

Figure 2.22
The function:
$y = \dfrac{x}{x^2 + x - 2}$.

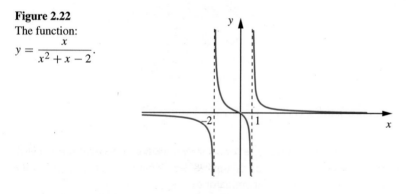

Example 2.15   **Equivalent resistance**

Consider a circuit consisting of two resistors in parallel as shown in Figure 2.23. One has a known resistance of $1\ \Omega$ and the other has a variable resistance, $R\ \Omega$. The equivalent resistance, $R_E\ \Omega$, satisfies

$$\frac{1}{R_E} = \frac{1}{R} + \frac{1}{1} = \frac{1+R}{R}$$

Hence,

$$R_E = \frac{R}{1+R}$$

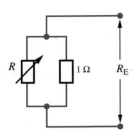

Figure 2.23 Two resistors in parallel.

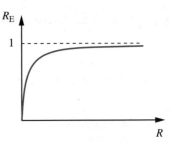

Figure 2.24 The equivalent resistance, R_E, increases as R increases.

Thus the equivalent resistance is a rational function of R, with domain $R \geqslant 0$. The graph of this function is shown in Figure 2.24. When $R = 0$ we note that $R_E = 0$, corresponding to a short circuit. As the value of R increases, that is $R \to \infty$, the equivalent resistance R_E approaches 1 so that $R_E = 1$ is an asymptote.

Exercises 2.4.2

1 State the poles of the following rational functions.

(a) $y(x) = \dfrac{x+3}{x-2}$

(b) $y(x) = \dfrac{2x+1}{x+7}$

(c) $y(t) = \dfrac{t^2+t+1}{2t+3}$

(d) $X(s) = \dfrac{s+1}{s^2-4}$

(e) $H(s) = \dfrac{3}{s^2+6s+5}$

(f) $G(s) = \dfrac{2s+7}{s^2+3s-18}$

(g) $x(t) = \dfrac{9}{t^3-t}$

(h) $p(t) = \dfrac{2t-6}{t^2+10t+25}$

2 Describe the horizontal asymptote of each of the following functions.

(a) $y(x) = 6 + \dfrac{1}{x}$

(b) $h(t) = \dfrac{2}{t} - 1$

(c) $y(r) = 3 - \dfrac{2}{5r}$

(d) $v(t) = \dfrac{6+t}{t}$

(e) $r(v) = \dfrac{2v-5}{3v}$

(f) $a(t) = \dfrac{t^2+2t+1}{t^2}$

(g) $m(s) = \dfrac{10-2s-3s^2}{2s^2}$

3 Describe the vertical asymptotes of each of the following functions.

(a) $y(x) = \dfrac{3x+1}{x-2}$

(b) $y(t) = \dfrac{6t-3}{4t+4}$

(c) $h(s) = \dfrac{9}{(s+2)(s-1)}$

(d) $G(t) = \dfrac{1}{t^2-1}$

(e) $H(s) = \dfrac{s}{s^2-1}$

(f) $y(x) = \dfrac{2x}{x^2-1}$

(g) $w(f) = \dfrac{f+2}{f^2+f-6}$

(h) $P(t) = \dfrac{t^2 + t + 1}{t^2 + 6t + 9}$

(i) $T(x) = \dfrac{x^3}{2x - 1}$

(j) $Q(r) = \dfrac{6 + r}{r^2 - r - 12}$

4 Describe the oblique asymptote of each of the following functions.

(a) $y(x) = x + 3 + \dfrac{1}{x - 1}$

(b) $y(x) = 2x - 1 + \dfrac{3}{x + 2}$

(c) $y(x) = \dfrac{x}{2} - \dfrac{3}{4} + \dfrac{1}{2x + 7}$

(d) $y(x) = 3x - 1 + \dfrac{5}{2x + 2}$

(e) $y(x) = 2x - 1 + \dfrac{x + 2}{x^2 - 1}$

(f) $y(x) = 3x - 2 + \dfrac{4}{2x - 1}$

(g) $y(x) = 4 - 2x + \dfrac{3}{2x + 3}$

5 Show that

$$I(x) = \dfrac{2x}{3} - \dfrac{7}{9} + \dfrac{23}{9(3x + 2)}$$

can be expressed in the equivalent form

$$\dfrac{2x^2 - x + 1}{3x + 2}$$

Sketch the rational function $I(x)$ and state any asymptotes.

6 Show that

$$p(x) = 2x + \dfrac{1}{2} + \dfrac{9}{2(2x + 3)}$$

can be written in the equivalent form

$$\dfrac{4x^2 + 7x + 6}{2x + 3}$$

Sketch the rational function $p(x)$ and state any asymptotes.

7 Show that the function

$$y(x) = x + \dfrac{7 - x}{x^2 + 3}$$

can be expressed in the equivalent form

$$\dfrac{x^3 + 2x + 7}{x^2 + 3}$$

Sketch the rational function $y(x)$ and state any asymptotes.

Solutions

1 (a) 2   (b) −7   (c) $-\dfrac{3}{2}$

(d) −2, 2   (e) −5, −1   (f) −6, 3
(g) −1, 0, 1   (h) −5

2 (a) $y = 6$ (b) $h = -1$
(c) $y = 3$ (d) $v = 1$
(e) $r = \dfrac{2}{3}$ (f) $a = 1$

(g) $m = -\dfrac{3}{2}$

3 (a) $x = 2$ (b) $t = -1$
(c) $s = -2, 1$ (d) $t = -1, 1$
(e) $s = -1, 1$ (f) $x = -1, 1$
(g) $f = -3, 2$ (h) $t = -3$
(i) $x = 0.5$ (j) $r = -3, 4$

4 (a) $y = x + 3$ (b) $y = 2x - 1$
(c) $y = \dfrac{x}{2} - \dfrac{3}{4}$ (d) $y = 3x - 1$
(e) $y = 2x - 1$ (f) $y = 3x - 2$
(g) $y = 4 - 2x$

5 $x = -\dfrac{2}{3}$, $I = \dfrac{2x}{3} - \dfrac{7}{9}$

6 $x = -\dfrac{3}{2}$, $p = 2x + \dfrac{1}{2}$

7 $y = x$

💻 Computer and calculator exercises 2.4.2

1 Draw the following rational functions. State any asymptotes.

(a) $f(x) = \dfrac{(2x+1)}{(x-3)}$ $-4 \leqslant x \leqslant 4$

(b) $g(s) = \dfrac{s}{(s+1)}$ $-3 \leqslant s \leqslant 3$

(c) $h(z) = \dfrac{z}{(z^2+1)}$ $-3 \leqslant z \leqslant 3$

(d) $y(x) = \dfrac{(x+1)}{x}$ $-3 \leqslant x \leqslant 3$

(e) $r(x) = \dfrac{2x}{(x-1)(x-2)}$ $-3 \leqslant x \leqslant 3$

2 Plot the functions given in Question 4 in Exercises 2.4.2 for $-10 \leqslant x \leqslant 10$.

2.4.3 Exponential functions

An **exponent** is another name for a power or index. Expressions involving exponents are called **exponential expressions**, for example 3^4, a^b, m^n. In the exponential expression a^x, a is called the **base**; x is the exponent. Exponential expressions can be simplified and manipulated using the laws of indices. These laws are summarized here.

$$a^m a^n = a^{m+n} \qquad \frac{a^m}{a^n} = a^{m-n} \qquad a^0 = 1 \qquad a^{-m} = \frac{1}{a^m} \qquad (a^m)^n = a^{mn}$$

Example 2.16   Simplify

(a) $\dfrac{a^{3x} a^{2x}}{a^{4x}}$

(b) $a^{2t}(1 - a^t) + a^{3t}$

(c) $\dfrac{(a^y)^2}{2a^y}$

(d) $\dfrac{a^{-6z}}{a^{-2z}}$

(e) $\dfrac{(2a^{3r})^2 a^{2r}}{3a^{-5r}}$

(f) $\dfrac{a^{x+y} a^y}{a^{2x}}$

(g) $\dfrac{3a^{(x/y)} a^x}{a^y}$

Solution

(a) $\dfrac{a^{3x} a^{2x}}{a^{4x}} = \dfrac{a^{5x}}{a^{4x}} = a^x$

(b) $a^{2t}(1 - a^t) + a^{3t} = a^{2t} - a^{3t} + a^{3t} = a^{2t}$

(c) $\dfrac{(a^y)^2}{2a^y} = \dfrac{a^{2y}}{2a^y} = \dfrac{a^y}{2}$

(d) $\dfrac{a^{-6z}}{a^{-2z}} = a^{-6z-(-2z)} = a^{-4z}$

(e) $\dfrac{(2a^{3r})^2 a^{2r}}{3a^{-5r}} = \dfrac{4a^{6r} a^{2r}}{3a^{-5r}} = \dfrac{4a^{8r}}{3a^{-5r}} = \dfrac{4a^{13r}}{3}$

(f) $\dfrac{a^{x+y} a^y}{a^{2x}} = a^{x+2y-2x} = a^{2y-x}$

(g) $\dfrac{3a^{(x/y)} a^x}{a^y} = 3a^{(x/y)+x-y}$

Exponential functions

An **exponential function**, $f(x)$, has the form

$$f(x) = a^x$$

where a is a positive constant called the base.

Some typical exponential functions are tabulated in Table 2.2 and are shown in Figure 2.25. Note from the graphs that these are one-to-one functions.

An exponential function is not a polynomial function. The powers of a polynomial function are constants; the power of an exponential function, that is the exponent, is the variable x.

Table 2.2   Values of a^x for $a = 0.5, 2$ and 3.

x	0.5^x	2^x	3^x
−3	8	0.125	0.037
−2	4	0.25	0.111
−1	2	0.5	0.333
0	1	1	1
1	0.5	2	3
2	0.25	4	9
3	0.125	8	27

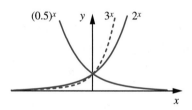

Figure 2.25   Some typical exponential functions.

The most widely used exponential function, commonly called **the** exponential function, is

$$f(x) = e^x$$

where e is an irrational constant (e $= 2.718\,281\,828\ldots$).

Most scientific calculators have values of e^x available. The function is tabulated in Table 2.3. The graph is shown in Figure 2.26. This particular exponential function so dominates engineering applications that whenever an engineer refers to the exponential function it almost invariably means this one. We will see later why it is so important.

As x increases positively, e^x increases very rapidly; that is, as $x \to \infty$, $e^x \to \infty$. This situation is known as **exponential growth**. As x increases negatively, e^x approaches zero; that is, as $x \to -\infty$, $e^x \to 0$. Thus $y = 0$ is an asymptote. Note that the exponential function is never negative.

Figure 2.27 shows a graph of e^{-x}. As x increases positively, e^{-x} decreases to zero; that is, as $x \to \infty$, $e^{-x} \to 0$. This is known as **exponential decay**. The function is tabulated in Table 2.4.

Table 2.3   The values of the exponential function $f(x) = e^x$ for various values of x.

x	e^x
-3	0.050
-2	0.135
-1	0.368
0	1
1	2.718
2	7.389
3	20.086

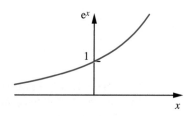

Figure 2.26   Graph of $y = e^x$ showing exponential growth.

Table 2.4   The values of the exponential function $f(x) = e^{-x}$ for various values of x.

x	e^{-x}
-3	20.086
-2	7.389
-1	2.718
0	1
1	0.368
2	0.135
3	0.050

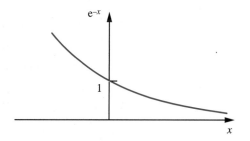

Figure 2.27   Graph of $y = e^{-x}$ showing exponential decay.

Example 2.17   **Discharge of a capacitor**

Consider the circuit of Figure 2.28. Before the switch is closed, the capacitor has a voltage V across it. Suppose the switch is closed at time $t = 0$. A current then flows in the circuit and the voltage, v, across the capacitor decays with time. The voltage across the capacitor is given by

$$v = \begin{cases} V & t < 0 \\ Ve^{-t/(RC)} & t \geqslant 0 \end{cases}$$

The quantity RC is known as the **time constant** of the circuit and is usually denoted by τ. So

$$v = \begin{cases} V & t < 0 \\ Ve^{-t/\tau} & t \geqslant 0 \end{cases}$$

If τ is small, then the capacitor voltage decays more quickly than if τ is large. This is illustrated in Figure 2.29.

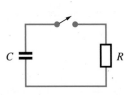
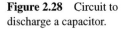

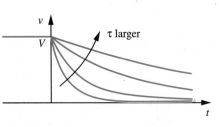

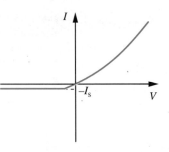

Figure 2.28 Circuit to discharge a capacitor.

Figure 2.29 The capacitor takes longer to discharge for a larger circuit time constant, τ.

Figure 2.30 A typical diode characteristic.

Example 2.18

The diode equation

A semiconductor diode can be modelled by the equation

$$I = I_s(e^{qV/(kT)} - 1)$$

where $V =$ applied voltage (V);

$I =$ diode current (A);

$I_s =$ reverse saturation current (A);

$k = 1.38 \times 10^{-23}$ J K^{-1};

$q = 1.60 \times 10^{-19}$ C;

$T =$ temperature (K).

This equation relates the current through the diode to the voltage across it. This is a good model for germanium diodes but only an approximate model for silicon diodes. At room temperature $q/(kT) \approx 40$ and so the equation can be written as

$$I = I_s(e^{40V} - 1)$$

Figure 2.30 shows a graph of I against V. Notice that for negative values of V, the equation may be approximated by

$$I \approx -I_s$$

since $e^{40V} \approx 0$. The diode is said to be **reverse saturated** in this case. In reality, I_s is usually quite small for a practical device, although its size has been exaggerated in Figure 2.30. This model does not cater for the breakdown of the diode. According to the model it would be possible to apply a very large reverse voltage to a diode and yet only a small saturation current would flow. This illustrates an important point that no mathematical model covers every facet of the physical device or system it is modelling. A different model would be needed to deal with breakdown characteristics.

Exercises 2.4.3

1 Simplify

(a) $\dfrac{e^{2x}}{3e^{3x}}$

(b) $\dfrac{e^{2t-3}}{e^2}$

(c) $\dfrac{e^x(e^x + e^{2x})}{e^{2x}}$

(d) $\dfrac{e^{-3}e^{-7}}{e^6 e^{-2}}$

(e) $\dfrac{(e^{2t})^3 (e^{3t})^4}{e^{10t}}$

2 Consider the RC circuit of Figure 2.28. Given an initial capacitor voltage of 10 V plot the variation in capacitor voltage with time, using the same axes, for the following pairs of component values.

(a) $R = 1\ \Omega,\ C = 1\ \mu F$

(b) $R = 10\ \Omega,\ C = 1\ \mu F$

(c) $R = 3.3\ \Omega,\ C = 1\ \mu F$

(d) $R = 56\ \Omega,\ C = 0.1\ \mu F$

Calculate the time constant, τ, in each case.

3 Sketch the following functions, using the same axes:

$$y = e^{2x} \quad y = e^{x/2} \quad y = e^{-2x}$$
$$\text{for} \quad -3 \leqslant x \leqslant 3$$

4 Sketch a graph of the function $y = 1 - e^{-x}$ for $x \geqslant 0$.

Solutions

1 (a) $\dfrac{e^{-x}}{3}$ (b) e^{2t-5} (c) $1 + e^x$

(d) e^{-14} (e) e^{8t}

2 (a) 10^{-6} (b) 10^{-5} (c) 3.3×10^{-6}

(d) 5.6×10^{-6}

 Computer and calculator exercises 2.4.3

1 Plot $y = e^{kx}$ for $k = -3, -2, -1, 0, 1, 2, 3$, for $-3 \leqslant x \leqslant 3$.

2 Plot $y = ke^x$ for $k = -3, -2, -1, 0, 1, 2, 3$, for $-3 \leqslant x \leqslant 3$.

3 Plot $y = 5 - x^2$ and $y = e^x$ for $-3 \leqslant x \leqslant 3$. For which values of x is $e^x < 5 - x^2$?

4 Plot $y = x^4$ and $y = e^x$ for $-1 \leqslant x \leqslant 9$. For which values of x is (a) $e^x < x^4$, (b) $e^x > x^4$?

2.4.4 Logarithm functions

Logarithms

The equation $16 = 2^4$ may be expressed in an alternative form using **logarithms**. In logarithmic form we write

$$\log_2 16 = 4$$

and say 'log to the base 2 of 16 equals 4'. Hence logarithms are nothing other than powers. The logarithmic form is illustrated by more examples:

$$125 = 5^3 \quad \text{so} \quad \log_5 125 = 3$$
$$64 = 8^2 \quad \text{so} \quad \log_8 64 = 2$$
$$16 = 4^2 \quad \text{so} \quad \log_4 16 = 2$$
$$1000 = 10^3 \quad \text{so} \quad \log_{10} 1000 = 3$$

In general,

$$\text{if } c = a^b, \text{ then } b = \log_a c$$

In practice, most logarithms use base 10 or base e. Logarithms using base e are called **natural logarithms**. $\log_{10} x$ and $\log_e x$ are usually abbreviated to $\log x$ and $\ln x$, respectively. Most scientific calculators have both logs to base 10 and logs to base e as preprogrammed functions, usually denoted as log and ln, respectively. Some calculations in communications engineering use base 2. Your calculator will probably not calculate base 2 logarithms directly. We shall see how to overcome this shortly.

Logarithmic expressions can be manipulated using the laws of logarithms. These laws are identical for any base, but it is essential when applying the laws that bases are not mixed.

$$\log_a A + \log_a B = \log_a (AB)$$
$$\log_a A - \log_a B = \log_a \left(\frac{A}{B}\right)$$
$$n \log_a A = \log_a (A^n)$$
$$\log_a a = 1$$

We sometimes need to change from one base to another. This can be achieved using the following rule.

$$\log_a X = \frac{\log_b X}{\log_b a}$$

In particular,

$$\log_2 X = \frac{\log_{10} X}{\log_{10} 2} = \frac{\log_{10} X}{0.3010}$$

Example 2.19 Simplify

(a) $\log x + \log x^3$

(b) $3 \log x + \log x^2$

(c) $5 \ln x + \ln \left(\frac{1}{x}\right)$

(d) $\log(xy) + \log x - 2\log y$

(e) $\ln(2x^3) - \ln\left(\dfrac{4}{x^2}\right) + \dfrac{1}{3}\ln 27$

Solution   (a) Using the laws of logarithms we find
$$\log x + \log x^3 = \log x^4$$

(b) $3\log x + \log x^2 = \log x^3 + \log x^2 = \log x^5$

(c) $5\ln x + \ln\left(\dfrac{1}{x}\right) = \ln x^5 + \ln\left(\dfrac{1}{x}\right) = \ln\left(\dfrac{x^5}{x}\right) = \ln x^4$

(d) $\log xy + \log x - 2\log y = \log xy + \log x - \log y^2$
$$= \log\left(\dfrac{xyx}{y^2}\right) = \log\left(\dfrac{x^2}{y}\right)$$

(e) $\ln(2x^3) - \ln\left(\dfrac{4}{x^2}\right) + \dfrac{\ln 27}{3} = \ln\left(\dfrac{2x^3}{4/x^2}\right) + \ln 27^{1/3}$
$$= \ln\left(\dfrac{2x^3 x^2}{4}\right) + \ln 3$$
$$= \ln\left(\dfrac{x^5}{2}\right) + \ln 3 = \ln\left(\dfrac{3x^5}{2}\right)$$

Example 2.20   Find $\log_2 14$.

Solution   Using the formula for change of base we have
$$\log_2 14 = \dfrac{\log_{10} 14}{\log_{10} 2} = \dfrac{1.146}{0.301} = 3.807$$

Example 2.21   **Signal ratios and decibels**

The ratio between two signal levels is often of interest to engineers. For example, the output and input signals of an electronic system can be compared to see if the system has increased the level of a signal. A common case is an amplifier, where the output signal is usually much larger than the input signal. This signal ratio is often expressed in decibels (dB) given by

$$\text{power gain (dB)} = 10\log\left(\dfrac{P_o}{P_i}\right)$$

where P_o is the power of the output signal and P_i is the power of the input signal. The term **gain** is used because if $P_o > P_i$, then the logarithm function is positive corresponding to an increase in power. If $P_o < P_i$ then the gain is negative, corresponding to a decrease in power. A negative gain is often termed an **attenuation**.

The advantage of using decibels as a measure of gain is that if several electronic systems are connected together then it is possible to obtain the overall system gain in decibels by adding together the individual system gains. We will show this for three systems connected together, but the development is easily generalized to more systems. Let the power input to the first system be P_{i1}, and the power output from the third system be P_{o3}. Suppose the three are connected so that the power output from system 1, P_{o1}, is used as input to system 2, that is $P_{i2} = P_{o1}$. The power output from system 2, P_{o2}, is then used as input to system 3, that is $P_{i3} = P_{o2}$. We wish to find the overall power gain, $10\log(P_{o3}/P_{i1})$. Now

$$\frac{P_{o3}}{P_{i1}} = \frac{P_{o3}}{P_{i3}}\frac{P_{o2}}{P_{i2}}\frac{P_{o1}}{P_{i1}}$$

because $P_{i3} = P_{o2}$ and $P_{i2} = P_{o1}$. Therefore,

$$10\log\left(\frac{P_{o3}}{P_{i1}}\right) = 10\log\left(\frac{P_{o3}}{P_{i3}}\frac{P_{o2}}{P_{i2}}\frac{P_{o1}}{P_{i1}}\right)$$

that is

$$10\log\left(\frac{P_{o3}}{P_{i1}}\right) = 10\log\left(\frac{P_{o3}}{P_{i3}}\right) + 10\log\left(\frac{P_{o2}}{P_{i2}}\right) + 10\log\left(\frac{P_{o1}}{P_{i1}}\right)$$

using the laws of logarithms.

It follows that the overall power gain is equal to the sum of the individual power gains. Often engineers are more interested in voltage gain rather than power gain. The power of a signal is proportional to the square of its voltage. We define **voltage gain** (dB) by

$$\text{voltage gain (dB)} = 10\log\left(\frac{V_o^2}{V_i^2}\right) = 20\log\left(\frac{V_o}{V_i}\right)$$

Logarithm functions

The **logarithm functions** are defined by

$$f(x) = \log_a x \qquad x > 0$$

where a is a positive constant called the base.

In particular the logarithm functions $f(x) = \log x$ and $f(x) = \ln x$ are shown in Figure 2.31 and some values are given in Table 2.5. The domain of both of these functions is $(0, \infty)$ and their ranges are $(-\infty, \infty)$. We observe from the graphs that these functions are one-to-one. It is important to stress that the logarithm functions, $\log_a x$, are only defined for positive values of x. The following properties should be noted.

$$\left.\begin{matrix} \log x \to \infty \\ \ln x \to \infty \end{matrix}\right\} \text{ as } x \to \infty \qquad\qquad \left.\begin{matrix} \log x \to -\infty \\ \ln x \to -\infty \end{matrix}\right\} \text{ as } x \to 0$$

$$\log 1 = \ln 1 = 0 \qquad\qquad\qquad \log 10 = 1 \qquad \ln e = 1$$

Table 2.5 Some values for logarithm functions $\log x$ and $\ln x$.

x	$\log x$	$\ln x$
0.1	-1	-2.303
0.5	-0.301	-0.693
1	0	0
2	0.301	0.693
5	0.699	1.609
10	1	2.303
50	1.699	3.912

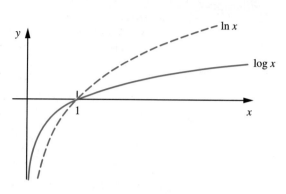

Figure 2.31 Graphs of $\ln x$ and $\log x$.

Connection between exponential and logarithm functions

The exponential function, $f(x) = a^x$, is a one-to-one function and so an inverse function, $f^{-1}(x)$, exists. Recall

$$f^{-1}(f(x)) = x$$

So

$$f^{-1}(a^x) = x$$

Now

$$\log_a(a^x) = x \log_a a \qquad \text{using laws of logarithms}$$
$$= x \qquad \text{since } \log_a a = 1$$

Hence the inverse of $f(x) = a^x$ is $f^{-1}(x) = \log_a x$. By similar analysis the inverse of $f(x) = \log_a x$ is $f^{-1}(x) = a^x$.

> The inverse of the exponential function, $f(x) = a^x$, is the logarithm function, that is $f^{-1}(x) = \log_a x$.
> The inverse of the logarithm function, $f(x) = \log_a x$, is the exponential function, that is $f^{-1}(x) = a^x$.

In particular:

> If $f(x) = e^x$, then $f^{-1}(x) = \ln x$.
> If $f(x) = \ln x$, then $f^{-1}(x) = e^x$.
> If $f(x) = 10^x$, then $f^{-1}(x) = \log x$.
> If $f(x) = \log x$, then $f^{-1}(x) = 10^x$.

Example 2.22   Solve the equations

(a) $16 = 10^x$ (e) $e^{3x} = 2e^x$

(b) $30 = e^x$ (f) $3e^{-(2x+1)} = 10$

(c) $19 = 3e^x$ (g) $\dfrac{17}{2 - 10^{-(x/2)}} = 60$

(d) $50 = 9(10^{2x})$

Solution (a) $16 = 10^x$ (b) $30 = e^x$ (c) $19 = 3e^x$

$\log 16 = x$ $\ln 30 = x$ $e^x = \dfrac{19}{3}$

$x = 1.204$ $x = 3.401$ $x = \ln\left(\dfrac{19}{3}\right) = 1.846$

(d) $50 = 9(10^{2x})$ (e) $e^{3x} = 2e^x$

$10^{2x} = \dfrac{50}{9}$ $\dfrac{e^{3x}}{e^x} = 2$

$2x = \log\left(\dfrac{50}{9}\right)$ $e^{2x} = 2$

$x = \dfrac{\log(50/9)}{2}$ $2x = \ln 2$

$x = 0.372$ $x = \dfrac{\ln 2}{2} = 0.347$

(f) $3e^{-(2x+1)} = 10$ (g) $\dfrac{17}{2 - 10^{-(x/2)}} = 60$

$e^{-(2x+1)} = \dfrac{10}{3}$ $2 - 10^{-x/2} = \dfrac{17}{60}$

$-(2x + 1) = \ln\left(\dfrac{10}{3}\right)$ $10^{-x/2} = 2 - \dfrac{17}{60} = \dfrac{103}{60}$

$2x = -\ln\left(\dfrac{10}{3}\right) - 1$ $-\dfrac{x}{2} = \log\left(\dfrac{103}{60}\right)$

$2x = -2.204$ $x = -2\log\left(\dfrac{103}{60}\right) = -0.469$

$x = -1.102$

Use of log–log and log–linear scales

Suppose we wish to plot

$$y(x) = x^6 \qquad 1 \leqslant x \leqslant 10$$

This may appear a straightforward exercise but consider the variation in the x and y values. As x varies from 1 to 10, then y varies from 1 to 1 000 000, as tabulated below. Several of these points would not be discernible on a graph and so information would be lost. This can be overcome by using a **log scale** which accommodates the large variation

x	y
1	1
2	64
3	729
4	4096
5	15625
6	46656
7	117649
8	262144
9	531441
10	1000000

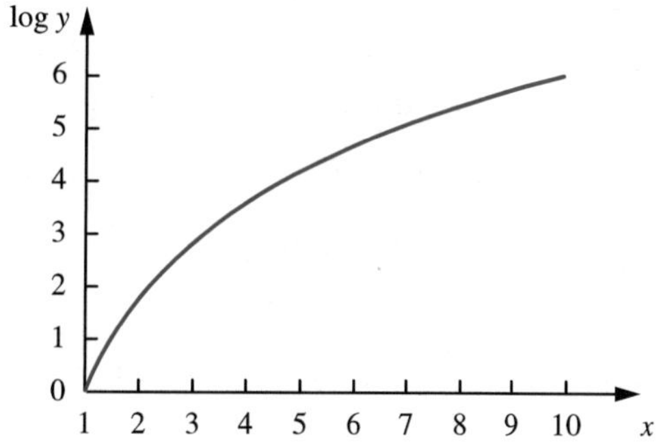

Figure 2.32   The function $y = x^6$ plotted on a log–linear graph.

in y. Thus $\log y$ is plotted against x, rather than y against x. Note that in this example

$$\log y = \log x^6 = 6\log x$$

so as x varies from 1 to 10, $\log y$ varies from 0 to 6. A plot in which one scale is logarithmic and the other is linear is known as a **log–linear** graph. Figure 2.32 shows $\log y$ plotted against x. In effect, use of the log scale has compressed a large variation into one which is much smaller and easier to observe.

Example 2.23   Consider $y = 7^x$ for $-3 \leqslant x \leqslant 3$. Plot a log–linear graph of this function.

Solution   We have

$$y = 7^x$$

and so

$$\log y = \log(7^x) = x\log 7 = 0.8451x$$

Putting $Y = \log y$ we have $Y = 0.8451x$ which is the equation of a straight line passing through the origin with gradient $\log 7$. Hence when $\log y$ is plotted against x a straight line graph is produced. This is shown in Figure 2.33. Note that by taking logs, the range on the vertical axis has been greatly reduced.

A plot in which both scales are logarithmic is known as a **log–log plot**. Here $\log y$ is plotted against $\log x$.

Example 2.24   Consider $y = x^7$ for $1 \leqslant x \leqslant 10$. Plot a log–log graph of this function.

Solution   We have

$$y = x^7$$

x	y	$Y = \log y$
-3	0.003	-2.54
-2	0.020	-1.69
-1	0.143	-0.85
0	1	0
1	7	0.85
2	49	1.69
3	343	2.54

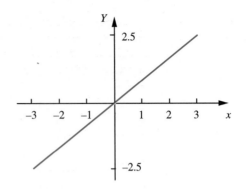

Figure 2.33 A log–linear plot of $y = 7^x$ produces a straight line graph.

x	y	$X = \log x$	$Y = \log y$
1	1	0	0
2	128	0.301	2.107
3	2 187	0.477	3.340
4	16 384	0.602	4.214
5	78 125	0.699	4.893
6	279 936	0.778	5.447
7	823 543	0.845	5.916
8	2 097 152	0.903	6.322
9	4 782 969	0.954	6.680
10	10 000 000	1	7

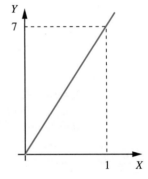

Figure 2.34 A log–log plot of $y = x^7$ produces a straight line graph.

and so

$$\log y = \log(x^7) = 7 \log x$$

We plot $\log y$ against $\log x$ in Figure 2.34 for a log–log plot. Putting $Y = \log y$ and $X = \log x$ we have $Y = 7X$ which is a straight line through the origin with gradient 7.

Examples 2.23 and 2.24 illustrate the following general points.

A log–linear plot of $y = a^x$ produces a straight line with a gradient of $\log a$.
A log–log plot of $y = x^n$ produces a straight line with a gradient of n.

Use of log–linear and log–log graph paper

The requirement to take logarithms is a tedious process which can be avoided by using special graph papers called log–linear graph paper and log–log graph paper. An example of log–linear graph paper is shown in Figure 2.35.

Figure 2.35
Two-cycle log–linear
graph paper.

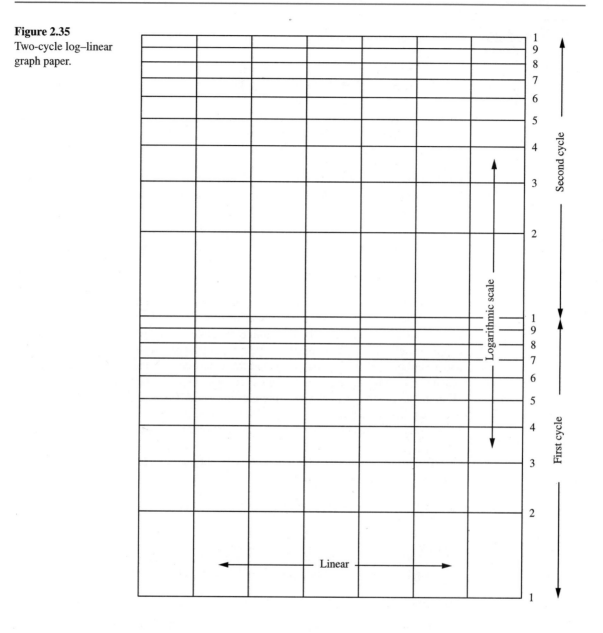

Note that on one axis the scale is uniform; this is the linear scale. On the other, the scale is not uniform and is marked in **cycles** from 1 to 9. This is the logarithmic scale. On this scale values of y are plotted directly, without first taking logarithms. On the graph paper shown in Figure 2.35 there are two cycles but papers are also available with three or more cycles. To decide which sort of graph paper is appropriate it is necessary to examine the variation in size of the variable to be plotted measured in powers of 10. If, for example, y varies from 1 to 10, then paper with one cycle is appropriate. If y varies from 1 to 10^2, two-cycle paper is necessary. If y varies from 10^{-1} to 10^4, then paper with $4 - (-1) = 5$ cycles would be appropriate. To see how log–linear paper is used in practice, consider the following example.

Example 2.25   Following an experiment the following pairs of data values were recorded.

	A	B	C	D
x	0	1	5	12
y	4.00	5.20	14.85	93.19

It is believed that y and x are related by the equation $y = ab^x$. By plotting a log–linear graph verify the relationship is of this form and determine a and b.

Solution   If the relationship is given by $y = ab^x$, then taking logarithms yields

$$\log y = \log a + x \log b$$

So, plotting $\log y$ against x should produce a straight line graph with gradient $\log b$ and vertical intercept $\log a$. The need to find $\log y$ is eliminated by plotting the y values directly on a logarithmic scale. Examining the table of data we see that y varies from approximately 10^0 to 10^2 so that two-cycle paper is appropriate. Values of y between 1 and 10 are plotted on the first cycle, and those between 10 and 100 are plotted on the second. The points are plotted in Figure 2.36. Note in particular that in this example the '1' at the start of the second cycle represents the value 10, the '2' represents the value 20 and so on. From the graph, the straight line relationship between $\log y$ and x is evident. It is therefore reasonable to assume that the relationship between y and x is of the form $y = ab^x$.

To find the gradient of the graph we can choose any two points on the line, for example C and B. The gradient is then

$$\frac{\log 14.85 - \log 5.20}{5 - 1} = \frac{\log(14.85/5.20)}{4} = 0.1139$$

Recall that $\log b$ is the gradient of the line and so

$$\log b = 0.1139, \qquad \text{that is } b = 10^{0.1139} = 1.2999$$

The vertical intercept is $\log a$. From the graph the vertical intercept is $\log 4$ so that

$$\log a = \log 4, \qquad \text{that is } a = 4$$

We conclude that the relationship between y and x is given by $y = 4(1.3)^x$.

Example 2.26   **Bode plot of a linear circuit**

Engineers are often interested in how a circuit will respond to a sinusoidal signal. In Section 23.9 we will see that if the circuit is **linear** then, after it has settled down, the output signal is also a sinusoidal signal of the same frequency but with a different amplitude and phase (see Section 3.6 for details of these terms).

Figure 2.36
The log–linear graph is
a straight line.

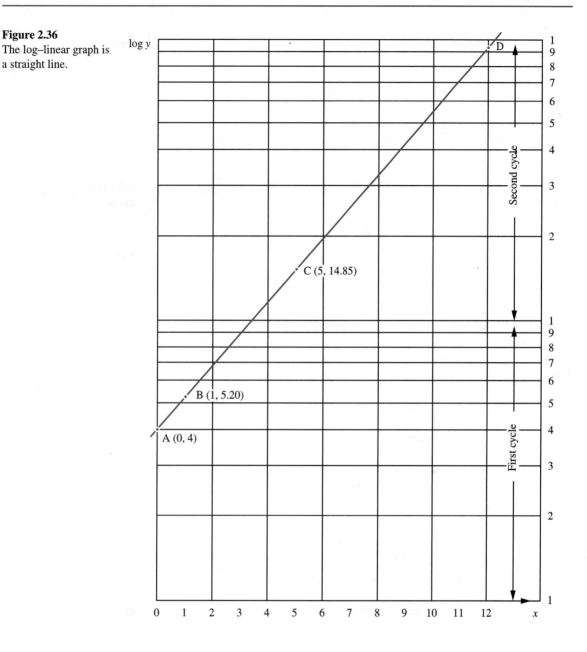

A **Bode plot** consists of two components:

(1) The ratio of the amplitudes of the output signal and the input signal is plotted against frequency.

(2) The phase shift between the input and output signals is plotted against frequency.

A log scale is used for the frequency in order to compress its length; for example, a typical frequency range is 0.1 Hz to 10^6 Hz which corresponds to a range of -1 to 6 on a log scale. A log scale is also used for the ratio of the signal amplitudes as this is calculated in decibels. Phase shift is plotted on a linear scale. So the signal amplitude ratio versus frequency is a log–log graph and the phase shift versus frequency is a linear–log graph.

Exercises 2.4.4

1 Evaluate

(a) $\log_2 8$

(b) $\log_2 15$

(c) $\log_{16} 50$

(d) $\log_{16} 123$

(e) $\log_8 23$

(f) $\log_8 47$

2 Simplify each of the following to a single log term:

(a) $\log 7 + \log x$

(b) $\log x + \log y + \log z$

(c) $\ln y - \ln 3$

(d) $2 \log y + \log x$

(e) $\ln(xy) + \ln(y^2)$

(f) $\ln(x + y) - \ln y$

(g) $\log(2x^2) + \log(4x)$

(h) $3 \log y + 2 \log x$

(i) $\frac{1}{2} \log x^4 - 2 \log x$

(j) $3 \ln x + 2 \ln y + 4 \ln z$

(k) $\log z - 2 \log x + 3 \log y$

(l) $\log t^3 - \log(2t) + 2 \log t$

3 Simplify each of the following to a single log term:

(a) $3 \ln t - \ln t$

(b) $6 \log t^2 + 4 \log t$

(c) $\ln(3y^6) - 2 \ln 3 + \ln y$

(d) $\ln(6x + 4) - \ln(3x + 2)$

(e) $\frac{\log(9x)}{2} - \log\left(\frac{2}{3x}\right)$

4 Sketch graphs of the following functions, using the same axes.

$$y = \ln(2x), \qquad y = \ln x \quad 0 < x \leqslant 10$$

Measure the vertical distance between the graphs for $x = 1$, $x = 2$ and $x = 8$. Can you explain your findings using the laws of logarithms?

5 Solve the following equations.

(a) $e^x = 70$

(b) $e^x = \frac{1}{3}$

(c) $e^{-x} = 1$

(d) $3e^x = 50$

(e) $e^{3x} = 50$

(f) $e^{2x+3} = 300$

(g) $e^{-x+1} = 0.75$

(h) $2ee^{2x} = 50$

(i) $\frac{3}{e^x + 1} = 0.6$

(j) $\frac{3}{e^{x+1}} = 0.6$

(k) $(e^x)^3 = 200$

(l) $\sqrt{e^{2x}} = 2$

(m) $\sqrt{e^{2x} + 4} = 6$

(n) $\frac{e^x}{e^x + 2} = 0.7$

(o) $e^{2x} = 7e^x$

(p) $2e^{-x} = 9$

(q) $(e^x + 3)^2 = 25$

(r) $(3e^{-x} - 6)^3 = 8$

(s) $e^{2x} - 3e^x + 2 = 0$

(t) $2e^{2x} - 7e^x + 3 = 0$

(u) $e^x(5 - e^x) = 6$

(v) $e^x - 7 + \frac{12}{e^x} = 0$

6 Solve the following equations.

(a) $10^x = 30$

(b) $10^x = 0.25$

(c) $4(10^x) = 20$

(d) $10^{2x} = 90$

(e) $10^{3x-2} = 20$

(f) $3(10^{x+3}) = 36$

(g) $10^{-3x} = 0.02$

(h) $7(10^{-2x}) = 1.4$

(i) $10^{x-2} = 20$

(j) $10^{3x+1} = 75$

(k) $\dfrac{4}{10^x} = 6$

(l) $(10^{-x})^2 = 40$

(m) $\sqrt{10^{4x}} = 3$

(n) $\dfrac{10^{-x}}{2 + 10^{-x}} = \dfrac{1}{2}$

(o) $\sqrt{10^{2x} + 6} = 5$

(p) $10^{6x} = 30(10^{3x})$

(q) $(10^{-x} + 2)^2 = 6$

(r) $6(10^{-3x}) = 10$

(s) $10^{2x} - 7(10^x) + 10 = 0$

(t) $10^{4x} - 8(10^{2x}) + 16 = 0$

(u) $10^x - 5 + 6(10^{-x}) = 0$

(v) $4(10^{2x}) - 8(10^x) + 3 = 0$

7 Solve

(a) $e^{3x} = 21$

(b) $10^{-2x} = 6.7$

(c) $\dfrac{1}{e^{-x} + 2} = 0.3$

(d) $2e^{(x/2)} - 1 = 0$

(e) $3(10^{(-4x+6)}) = 17$

(f) $(e^{x-1})^3 + e^{3x} = 500$

(g) $\sqrt{10^{2x} + 100} = 3(10^x)$

8 Calculate the voltage gain in decibels of the following amplifiers:

(a) input signal $= 0.1$ V, output signal $= 1$ V;

(b) input signal $= 1$ mV, output signal $= 10$ V;

(c) input signal $= 5$ mV, output signal $= 8$ V;

(d) input signal $= 60$ mV, output signal $= 2$ V.

9 An audio amplifier consists of two stages: a preamplifier and a main amplifier. Given the following data, calculate the voltage gain in decibels of the individual stages and the overall gain in decibels of the audio amplifier:

| preamplifier: | input signal $= 10$ mV, output signal $= 200$ mV |
| main amplifier: | input signal $= 400$ mV, output signal $= 3$ V |

10 By using log–linear paper find the relationship between x and y given the following table of values.

x	1.5	1.7	3.2	3.9	4.3	4.9
y	8.5	9.7	27.6	44.8	59.1	89.6

11 By using log–log paper find the relationship between x and y given the following table of values.

x	2.0	2.5	3.0	3.5	4.0	4.5
y	13.0	19.0	25.9	33.6	42.2	51.6

Solutions

1 (a) 3   (b) 3.9069   (c) 1.4110
      (d) 1.7356   (e) 1.5079   (f) 1.8515

2 (a) $\log 7x$ (b) $\log xyz$

(c) $\ln\left(\dfrac{y}{3}\right)$ (d) $\log xy^2$

(e) $\ln(xy^3)$ (f) $\ln\left(\dfrac{x+y}{y}\right)$

(g) $\log 8x^3$ (h) $\log x^2 y^3$

(i) $\log 1 = 0$ (j) $\ln x^3 y^2 z^4$

(k) $\log\left(\dfrac{y^3 z}{x^2}\right)$ (l) $\log\left(\dfrac{t^4}{2}\right)$

3 (a) $2\ln t$ or $\ln t^2$ (b) $16\log t$

(c) $\ln\left(\dfrac{y^7}{3}\right)$ (d) $\ln 2$

(e) $\log\left(\dfrac{9x^{3/2}}{2}\right)$

5 (a) 4.2485   (b) −1.0986

(c) 0   (d) 2.8134

(e) 1.3040   (f) 1.3519

(g) 1.2877   (h) 1.1094

(i) 1.3863   (j) 0.6094

(k) 1.7661   (l) 0.6931

(m) 1.7329   (n) 1.5404

(o) 1.9459   (p) −1.5041

(q) 0.6931   (r) −0.9808

(s) 0, 0.6931   (t) −0.6931, 1.0986

(u) 0.6931, 1.0986   (v) 1.0986, 1.3863

6 (a) 1.4771   (b) −0.6021

(c) 0.6990   (d) 0.9771

(e) 1.1003   (f) −1.9208

(g) 0.5663   (h) 0.3495

(i) 3.3010   (j) 0.2917

(k) −0.1761   (l) −0.8010

(m) 0.2386   (n) −0.3010

(o) 0.6395   (p) 0.4924

(q) 0.3473   (r) −0.0739

(s) 0.3010, 0.6990   (t) 0.3010

(u) 0.3010, 0.4771   (v) −0.3010, 0.1761

7 (a) 1.0148   (b) −0.4130

(c) −0.2877   (d) −1.3863

(e) 1.3117   (f) 2.0553

(g) 0.5485

8 (a) 20 dB   (b) 80 dB   (c) 64.1 dB

(d) 30.46 dB

9 Preamplifier gain = 26.02 dB, main amplifier gain = 17.50 dB, total gain = 43.52 dB

10 $y = 3(2^x)$

11 $y = 4x^{1.7}$

🖥 Computer and calculator exercises 2.4.4

1 Draw $y = \log(kx)$ for $0.5 \leqslant x \leqslant 50$ for $k = 1$, 2, 3 and 4.

2 Draw $y = \ln x$ and $y = \ln\left(\dfrac{1}{x}\right)$ for

$0.5 \leqslant x \leqslant 20$. What do you observe? Can you explain your observation using the laws of logarithms?

3 Draw $y = \ln x$ and $y = 1 - \dfrac{x}{3}$ for

$0.5 \leqslant x \leqslant 4$. From your graphs state an approximate solution to

$$\ln x = 1 - \frac{x}{3}$$

2.4.5 The hyperbolic functions

The **hyperbolic functions** are $y(x) = \cosh x$, $y(x) = \sinh x$, $y(x) = \tanh x$, $y(x) = \operatorname{sech} x$, $y(x) = \operatorname{cosech} x$ and $y(x) = \coth x$. Cosh is a contracted form of 'hyperbolic cosine', sinh of 'hyperbolic sine' and so on. We define $\cosh x$ and $\sinh x$ by

$$y(x) = \cosh x = \frac{e^x + e^{-x}}{2} \qquad y(x) = \sinh x = \frac{e^x - e^{-x}}{2}.$$

Note:

$$\cosh(-x) = \frac{e^{-x} + e^x}{2} = \cosh x$$

$$\sinh(-x) = \frac{e^{-x} - e^x}{2} = -\sinh x$$

so, for example, $\cosh 1.7 = \cosh(-1.7)$ and $\sinh(-1.7) = -\sinh 1.7$. Clearly, hyperbolic functions are nothing other than combinations of the exponential functions e^x and e^{-x}. However, these particular combinations occur so frequently in engineering that it is worth introducing the $\cosh x$ and $\sinh x$ functions. The remaining hyperbolic functions are defined in terms of $\cosh x$ and $\sinh x$.

$$y(x) = \tanh x = \frac{\sinh x}{\cosh x} = \frac{e^x - e^{-x}}{e^x + e^{-x}}$$

$$y(x) = \operatorname{sech} x = \frac{1}{\cosh x} = \frac{2}{e^x + e^{-x}}$$

$$y(x) = \operatorname{cosech} x = \frac{1}{\sinh x} = \frac{2}{e^x - e^{-x}}$$

$$y(x) = \coth x = \frac{\cosh x}{\sinh x} = \frac{1}{\tanh x} = \frac{e^x + e^{-x}}{e^x - e^{-x}}$$

Values of the hyperbolic functions for various x values can be found from a scientific calculator. Usually a Hyp button followed by a Sin, Cos or Tan button is used.

Example 2.27   Evaluate

(a) $\cosh 3$

(b) $\sinh(-2)$

(c) $\tanh 1.6$

(d) $\operatorname{sech}(-2.5)$

(e) $\coth 1$

(f) $\operatorname{cosech}(-1)$

Solution   (a) $\cosh 3 = 10.07$

(b) $\sinh(-2) = -3.627$

(c) $\tanh(1.6) = 0.9217$

(d) $\operatorname{sech}(-2.5) = 1/\cosh(-2.5) = 0.1631$

(e) $\coth 1 = 1/\tanh 1 = 1.313$

(f) $\operatorname{cosech}(-1) = 1/\sinh(-1) = -0.8509$

Graphs of the functions $\sinh x$, $\cosh x$ and $\tanh x$ can be obtained using a graphics calculator.

Hyperbolic identities

Several identities involving hyperbolic functions exist. They can be verified algebraically using the definitions given, and are listed for reference.

$$\cosh^2 x - \sinh^2 x = 1$$
$$1 - \tanh^2 x = \operatorname{sech}^2 x$$
$$\coth^2 x - 1 = \operatorname{cosech}^2 x$$
$$\sinh(x \pm y) = \sinh x \cosh y \pm \cosh x \sinh y$$
$$\cosh(x \pm y) = \cosh x \cosh y \pm \sinh x \sinh y$$
$$\sinh 2x = 2 \sinh x \cosh x$$
$$\cosh 2x = \cosh^2 x + \sinh^2 x$$
$$\cosh^2 x = \frac{\cosh 2x + 1}{2}$$
$$\sinh^2 x = \frac{\cosh 2x - 1}{2}$$

Note also that

$$e^x = \cosh x + \sinh x \qquad e^{-x} = \cosh x - \sinh x$$

Hence any combination of exponential terms may be expressed as a combination of $\cosh x$ and $\sinh x$, and vice versa.

Example 2.28   Express

(a) $3e^x - 2e^{-x}$ in terms of $\cosh x$ and $\sinh x$,

(b) $2 \sinh x + \cosh x$ in terms of e^x and e^{-x}.

Solution   (a) $3e^x - 2e^{-x} = 3(\cosh x + \sinh x) - 2(\cosh x - \sinh x) = \cosh x + 5 \sinh x$.

(b) $2 \sinh x + \cosh x = e^x - e^{-x} + \dfrac{e^x + e^{-x}}{2} = \dfrac{3e^x - e^{-x}}{2}$.

Inverse hyperbolic functions

The inverse hyperbolic functions use the familiar notation. Both $y = \sinh x$ and $y = \tanh x$ are one-to-one functions and no domain restriction is needed for an inverse to be defined. However, on $(-\infty, \infty)$, $y = \cosh x$ is a many-to-one function. If the domain is restricted to $[0, \infty)$ the resulting function is one-to-one and an inverse function can be defined.

The inverse of the function $\sinh x$ is denoted by $\sinh^{-1} x$. Here the -1 must not be interpreted as a power but rather the notation we use for the inverse function. Similarly the inverses of $\cosh x$ and $\tanh x$ are denoted by $\cosh^{-1} x$ and $\tanh^{-1} x$ respectively.

Values of $\sinh^{-1} x$, $\cosh^{-1} x$ and $\tanh^{-1} x$ can be obtained using a scientific calculator.

Example 2.29 Evaluate

(a) $\cosh^{-1}(3.7)$ (b) $\sinh^{-1}(-2)$ (c) $\tanh^{-1}(0.5)$

Solution Using a calculator we get

(a) 1.9827 (b) -1.4436 (c) 0.5493

A word of warning about the inverse of $\cosh x$ is needed. The calculator returns a value of 1.9827 for $\cosh^{-1}(3.7)$. Note, however, that $\cosh(-1.9827) = 3.7$. The value -1.9827 is not returned by the calculator; only values on $[0, \infty)$ will be returned. This is because the domain of $y = \cosh x$ is restricted to ensure it has an inverse function.

Exercises 2.4.5

1 Evaluate the following:
(a) $\sinh 3$ (b) $\cosh 1.6$
(c) $\tanh 0.95$ (d) $\operatorname{sech} 1$
(e) $\operatorname{cosech} 2$ (f) $\coth 1.5$
(g) $\cosh(-3)$ (h) $\operatorname{cosech}(-1.6)$
(i) $\sinh(-2)$ (j) $\coth(-2.7)$
(k) $\tanh(-1.4)$ (l) $\operatorname{sech}(-0.5)$

2 Evaluate

(a) $\sinh^{-1} 3$

(b) $\cosh^{-1} 2$

(c) $\tanh^{-1}(-0.25)$

3 Express

(a) $6e^x + 5e^{-x}$ in terms of $\sinh x$ and $\cosh x$,

(b) $4e^{2x} - 3e^{-2x}$ in terms of $\sinh 2x$ and $\cosh 2x$,

(c) $2e^{-3x} - 5e^{3x}$ in terms of $\sinh 3x$ and $\cosh 3x$.

4 Express

(a) $4 \sinh x + 3 \cosh x$ in terms of e^x and e^{-x},

(b) $3 \sinh 2x - \cosh 2x$ in terms of e^{2x} and e^{-2x},

(c) $3 \cosh 3x - 0.5 \sinh 3x$ in terms of e^{3x} and e^{-3x}.

5 Express $ae^x + be^{-x}$, where a and b are constants, in terms of $\cosh x$ and $\sinh x$.

6 Express $a \cosh x + b \sinh x$, where a and b are constants, in terms of e^x and e^{-x}.

7 Show that the point $x = \cosh u$, $y = \sinh u$ lies on the curve

$$x^2 - y^2 = 1$$

8 Prove the hyperbolic identities listed in the box earlier in this section.

Solutions

1 (a) 10.0179 (b) 2.5775 (c) 0.7398
(d) 0.6481 (e) 0.2757 (f) 1.1048
(g) 10.0677 (h) -0.4210 (i) -3.6269
(j) -1.0091 (k) -0.8854 (l) 0.8868

2 (a) 1.8184 (b) 1.3170 (c) -0.2554

3 (a) $11 \cosh x + \sinh x$
(b) $\cosh 2x + 7 \sinh 2x$
(c) $-3 \cosh 3x - 7 \sinh 3x$

4   (a) $3.5e^x - 0.5e^{-x}$
   (b) $e^{2x} - 2e^{-2x}$
   (c) $1.25e^{3x} + 1.75e^{-3x}$

5    $(a + b)\cosh x + (a - b)\sinh x$

6    $\dfrac{a+b}{2}e^x + \dfrac{a-b}{2}e^{-x}$

🖥 Computer and calculator exercises 2.4.5

1   Draw (a) $y = \sinh x$ (b) $y = \cosh x$
   (c) $y = \tanh x$ for $-5 \leqslant x \leqslant 5$.

2   Draw graphs of $y = \sinh x$, $y = \cosh x$ and
$y = \dfrac{e^x}{2}$ for $0 \leqslant x \leqslant 5$. What happens to the
three graphs as x increases? Can you explain
this algebraically?

3   Draw

   (a) $y = \sinh^{-1} x$ $-5 \leqslant x \leqslant 5$

   (b) $y = \cosh^{-1} x$ $1 \leqslant x \leqslant 5$

   (c) $y = \tanh^{-1} x$ $-1 < x < 1$

2.4.6   The modulus function

The modulus of a positive number is simply the number itself. The modulus of a negative number is a positive number of the same magnitude. For example, the modulus of 3 is 3; the modulus of -3 is also 3. We enclose the number in vertical lines to show we are finding its modulus, thus

$$|3| = 3 \qquad |-3| = 3$$

Mathematically we define the modulus function as follows:

> The **modulus function** is defined by
> $$f(x) = |x| = \begin{cases} x & x \geqslant 0 \\ -x & x < 0 \end{cases}$$

Figure 2.37 illustrates a graph of $f(x) = |x|$. The modulus of a quantity is never negative.

Consider two points on the x axis, a and b, as shown in Figure 2.38. Then

$$|a - b| = |b - a| = \text{distance from } a \text{ to } b$$

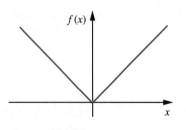

Figure 2.37   The function: $f(x) = |x|$.

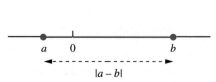
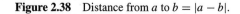

Figure 2.38   Distance from a to $b = |a - b|$.

Example 2.30

Find the distance from

(a) $x = 2$ to $x = 9$ (b) $x = -2$ to $x = 9$ (c) $x = -2$ to $x = -9$

Solution

(a) Distance $= |2 - 9| = |-7| = 7$

(b) Distance $= |-2 - 9| = |-11| = 11$

(c) Distance $= |-2 - (-9)| = |7| = 7$

, From the definition of the modulus function it follows:

> If $|x| = a$, then either $x = a$ or $x = -a$.
> If $|x| < a$, then $-a < x < a$.
> If $|x| > a$, then either $x > a$ or $x < -a$.

For example, if $|x| = 4$ then either $x = 4$ or $x = -4$. If $|x| < 4$ then $-4 < x < 4$; that is, x lies between -4 and 4. If $|x| > 4$, then either $x > 4$ or $x < -4$; that is, x is either greater than 4 or less than -4.

Example 2.31

Describe the interval on the x axis defined by

(a) $|x| < 2$

(b) $|x| \geqslant 3$

(c) $|x - 1| < 3$

(d) $|x + 2| > 1$

Solution

(a) $|x| < 2$ is the same statement as $-2 < x < 2$; that is, x is numerically less than 2. Figure 2.39 illustrates this region. Note that the region is an open interval. Since the points $x = -2$ and $x = 2$ are not included, they are shown on the graph as ○.

(b) If $|x| \geqslant 3$ then either $x \geqslant 3$ or $x \leqslant -3$. This is shown in Figure 2.40. The required region of the x axis has two distinct parts. Since the points $x = 3$ and $x = -3$ are included in the interval of interest, they are shown on the graph as ●.

(c) $|x - 1| < 3$ is equivalent to $-3 < x - 1 < 3$, that is $-2 < x < 4$.

(d) $|x + 2| > 1$ is equivalent to $x + 2 > 1$ or $x + 2 < -1$, that is $x > -1$ or $x < -3$.

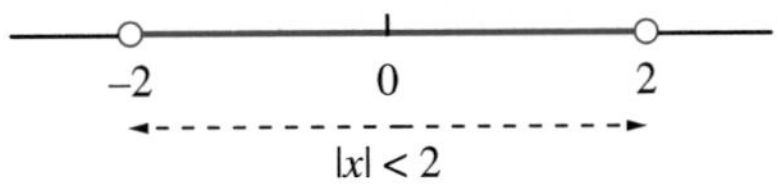

Figure 2.39   The quantity $|x| < 2$ is equivalent to $-2 < x < 2$.

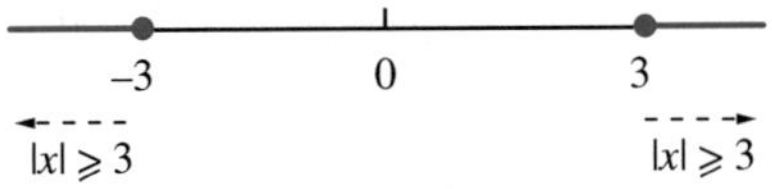

Figure 2.40   The quantity $|x| \geqslant 3$ is equivalent to $x \geqslant 3$ or $x \leqslant -3$.

The modulus function can be used to describe regions in the x–y plane.

Example 2.32

Sketch the region defined by

(a) $|x| < 2$ and $|y| < 1$

(b) $|x^2 + y^2| \leqslant 9$

Solution

(a) The region is a rectangle as shown in Figure 2.41. The boundary is not part of the region as strict inequalities were used to define it. The region $|x| \leqslant 2$, $|y| \leqslant 1$ is the same as that in Figure 2.41 with the boundary included.

(b) $|x^2 + y^2| \leqslant 9$ is equivalent to $-9 \leqslant x^2 + y^2 \leqslant 9$. Note, however, that $x^2 + y^2$ is never negative and so the region is given by $0 \leqslant x^2 + y^2 \leqslant 9$.

Let $P(x, y)$ be a general point as shown in Figure 2.42. Then from Pythagoras's theorem, the distance of P to the origin is $\sqrt{x^2 + y^2}$. So,

$$(\text{distance from origin})^2 = x^2 + y^2 \leqslant 9$$

Then,

$$(\text{distance from origin}) \leqslant 3$$

This describes a disc, centre the origin, of radius 3 (see Figure 2.43).

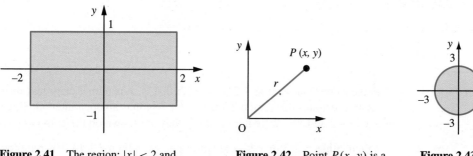

Figure 2.41 The region: $|x| < 2$ and $|y| < 1$.

Figure 2.42 Point $P(x, y)$ is a general point.

Figure 2.43 The region: $|x^2 + y^2| \leqslant 9$.

Example 2.33

Full-wave rectifier

A fully rectified sine wave is the modulus of the sine wave. The circuit for a full-wave rectifier is shown in Figure 2.44 together with the input and output waveforms. The input signal is v_{in} and the output signal is v_o. Ignoring the voltage drops across the diodes gives

$$v_o = |v_{in}|$$

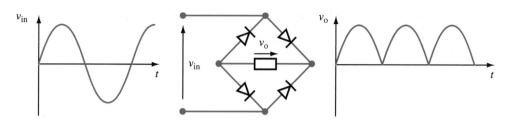

Figure 2.44   A full-wave rectifier.

Exercises   2.4.6

1 Sketch the interval defined by

(a) $|x| > 4$

(b) $|y - 1| \leqslant 3$

(c) $|t + 6| \geqslant 3$

(d) $|t^2 - 2| < 7$

(e) $|t| < -1$

Also, state the intervals without using the modulus signs.

2 Sketch the regions defined by

(a) $|x| > 2, |y| < 3$

(b) $|x + 2| < 4, |y + 1| < 3$

(c) $|x^2 + y^2 - 1| \leqslant 4$

(d) $|(x - 1)^2 + (y + 2)^2| \geqslant 1$

3 Express the following intervals using modulus notation.

(a) $-2 \leqslant x \leqslant 2$

(b) $-4 < t < 4$

(c) $1 < y < 3$

(d) $-6 \leqslant t \leqslant 0$

Solutions

1 (a) $x > 4$ or $x < -4$

(b) $-2 \leqslant y \leqslant 4$

(c) $t \geqslant -3$ or $t \leqslant -9$

(d) $-3 < t < 3$

(e) no value of t satisfies this

3 (a) $|x| \leqslant 2$

(b) $|t| < 4$

(c) $|y - 2| < 1$

(d) $|t + 3| \leqslant 3$

2.4.7   The ramp function

The **ramp function** is defined by

$$f(t) = \begin{cases} ct & t \geqslant 0 \\ 0 & t < 0 \end{cases} \qquad c \text{ constant}$$

Its graph is shown in Figure 2.45.

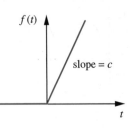

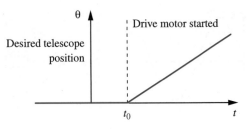

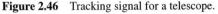

Figure 2.45 The ramp function. **Figure 2.46** Tracking signal for a telescope.

Example 2.34 | **Telescope drive signal**

In order to track the motion of the stars large telescopes are usually driven by an electric motor. The speed of this motor is controlled in order that the angular position of the telescope follows a specified trajectory with time. The whole assembly, including telescope, gears, motor, controller and sensors, forms a **position control system** or **servo-system**. This servo-system must be fed a signal corresponding to the desired trajectory of the system. Often this trajectory is a ramp function as illustrated in Figure 2.46. The drive motor is started at time $t = t_0$ and the desired angular position of the telescope is θ.

2.4.8 The unit step function, $u(t)$

The **unit step function** is defined by
$$u(t) = \begin{cases} 1 & t \geq 0 \\ 0 & t < 0 \end{cases}$$

Its graph is shown in Figure 2.47. Note that $u(t)$ has a discontinuity at $t = 0$. The point $(0,1)$ is part of the function defined on $t \geq 0$. This is depicted by ●. The point $(0,0)$ is not part of the function defined on $t < 0$. We use ○ to illustrate this.

The position of the discontinuity may be shifted.
$$u(t - d) = \begin{cases} 1 & t \geq d \\ 0 & t < d \end{cases}$$

The graph of $u(t - d)$ is shown in Figure 2.48.

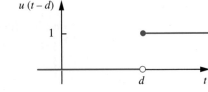

Figure 2.47 The unit step function. **Figure 2.48** Graph of $u(t - d)$.

Figure 2.49
RLC circuit.

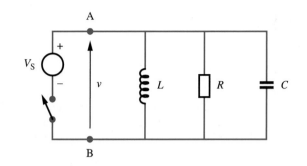

Example 2.35 **RLC circuit**

Consider the circuit shown in Figure 2.49. When the switch is open the voltage v across terminals A and B is zero. If the switch is closed at $t = 0$ the voltage across A and B is V_S, where V_S is the supply voltage. Thus v can be modelled by the function

$$v = \begin{cases} 0 & t < 0 \\ V_S & t \geqslant 0 \end{cases}$$

This can be written, using the unit step function, as

$$v = V_S u(t)$$

Example 2.36 Sketch the following functions:

(a) $f = u(t - 3)$

(b) $f = u(t - 1)$

(c) $f = u(t - 1) - u(t - 3)$

(d) $f = u(t - 3) - u(t - 1)$

(e) $f = e^t u(t)$

Solution (a) See Figure 2.50.

(b) See Figure 2.51.

(c) See Figure 2.52.

(d) See Figure 2.53.

(e) See Figure 2.54.

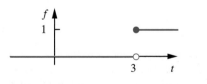

Figure 2.50 The function: $f = u(t - 3)$.

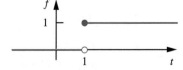

Figure 2.51 The function: $f = u(t - 1)$.

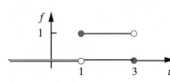

Figure 2.52 The function:
$f = u(t-1) - u(t-3)$.

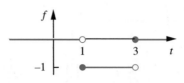

Figure 2.53 The function:
$f = u(t-3) - u(t-1)$.

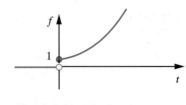

Figure 2.54 The function:
$f = e^t u(t)$.

Exercises 2.4.8

1 Sketch the following functions.

(a) $f(t) = u(t-1)$

(b) $f(t) = u(t+1)$

(c) $f(t) = u(t-2) - u(t-6)$

(d) $f(t) = 3u(t-1)$

(e) $f(t) = u(t+1) - u(t-1)$

(f) $f(t) = u(t-1) - u(t+1)$

(g) $f(t) = u(t+1) - 2u(t-1)$

(h) $f(t) = 2u(t+1) - u(t-1)$

(i) $f(t) = 3u(t-1) - 2u(t-2)$

2 A ramp function, $f(t)$, is defined by

$$f(t) = \begin{cases} 2t & t \geqslant 0 \\ 0 & t < 0 \end{cases}$$

Sketch the following for $-1 \leqslant t \leqslant 3$.

(a) $f(t)$

(b) $u(t)f(t)$

(c) $u(t-1)f(t)$

(d) $u(t-1)f(t) - u(t-2)f(t)$

Solutions

2 See Figure S.5.

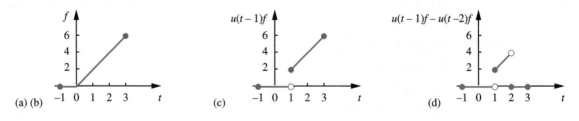

(a) (b)   (c)   (d)

Figure S.5

2.4.9 The delta function or unit impulse function, $\delta(t)$

Consider the rectangle function, $R(t)$, shown in Figure 2.55. The base of the rectangle is h, the height is $1/h$ and so the area is 1. For $t > h/2$ and $t < -h/2$, the function is 0. As h decreases, the base diminishes and the height increases; the area remains constant at 1.

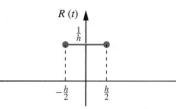

Figure 2.55 The rectangle function, $R(t)$.

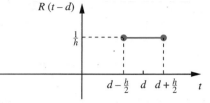

Figure 2.56 The delayed rectangle function, $R(t - d)$.

As h approaches 0, the base becomes infinitesimally small and the height infinitely large. The area remains at unity. The rectangle function is then called a **delta function** or **unit impulse function**. It has a value of 0 everywhere except at the origin.

$$\delta(t) = \text{rectangle function as } h \text{ approaches } 0$$

We write this concisely as

$$\delta(t) = R(t) \qquad \text{as} \qquad h \to 0$$

The position of the delta function may be changed from the origin to $t = d$. Consider a rectangle function, $R(t - d)$, shown in Figure 2.56. $R(t - d)$ is obtained by translating $R(t)$ an amount d to the right. Again, letting h approach 0 produces a delta function, this time centred on $t = d$.

$$\delta(t - d) = R(t - d) \qquad \text{as} \qquad h \to 0$$

We have seen that the delta function can be regarded as bounding an area 1 between itself and the horizontal axis. More generally the area bounded by the function

$$f(t) = k\delta(t)$$

is k. We say that $k\delta(t)$ represents an impulse of strength k at the origin, and $k\delta(t - d)$ is an impulse of strength k at $t = d$. It is often useful to depict such an impulse by an arrow where the height of the arrow gives the strength of the impulse. A series of impulses is often termed an **impulse train**.

Example 2.37   A train of impulses is given by

$$f(t) = \delta(t) + 3\delta(t - 1) + 2\delta(t - 2)$$

Depict the train graphically.

Solution   Figure 2.57 shows the representation. In Section 22.8 we shall call such a function a series of **weighted impulses** where the weights are 1, 3 and 2, respectively.

Example 2.38   **Impulse response of a system**

It is not possible to produce an impulse function electronically as no practical signal can have an infinite height. However, an approximation to an impulse function is often used, consisting of a pulse with a large voltage, V, and short duration, T. The strength

Figure 2.57
A train of impulses
given by $f(t) = \delta(t) + 3\delta(t-1) + 2\delta(t-2)$.

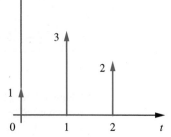

of such an impulse is VT. When this pulse signal is injected into a system the output obtained is known as the **impulse response** of the system.

The approximation is valid provided the width of the pulse is an order of magnitude less than the fastest time constant in the system. If the value of T required is small in order to satisfy this constraint, then the value of V may need to be large to achieve the correct impulse strength, VT. Often this can rule out its use for many systems as the value of V is large enough to distort the system characteristics.

Exercises 2.4.9

1 Sketch the impulse train given by

(a) $f(t) = \delta(t-1) + 2\delta(t-2)$

(b) $f(t) = 3\delta(t) + 4\delta(t-2) + \delta(t-3)$

Review exercises 2

1 State the rule and sketch the graph of each of the following functions:

(a) $f(x) = 7x - 2$
(b) $f(t) = t^2 - 2 \quad 0 \leqslant t \leqslant 5$
(c) $g(x) = 3e^x + 4 \quad 0 \leqslant x \leqslant 2$
(d) $y(t) = (e^{2t} - 1)/2 \quad t \geqslant 0$
(e) $f(x) = x^3 + 2x + 5 \quad -2 \leqslant x \leqslant 2$

2 State the domain and range of the functions in Question 1.

3 Determine the inverse of each of the following functions.

(a) $y(x) = 2x$
(b) $f(t) = 8t - 3$
(c) $h(x) = \dfrac{2x}{3} + 1$

(d) $m(r) = 1 - 3r$
(e) $H(s) = \dfrac{3}{s} + 2$
(f) $f(v) = \ln v$
(g) $f(t) = e^{2t}$
(h) $g(v) = \ln v + 1$
(i) $g(v) = \ln(v + 1)$
(j) $y(t) = 3e^{t-2}$

4 If $f(t) = e^t$ find

(a) $f(2t)$
(b) $f(x)$
(c) $f(\lambda)$
(d) $f(t - \lambda)$

5 If $g(t) = \ln(t^2 + 1)$ find (a) $g(\lambda)$, (b) $g(t - \lambda)$.

6 Sketch the following functions.

(a) $f(t) = \begin{cases} 0 & t < 0 \\ 0.5t & t \geqslant 0 \end{cases}$

(b) $f(t) = \begin{cases} 4 & t < 0 \\ t & 0 \leqslant t < 3 \\ 2t & 3 \leqslant t \leqslant 4 \end{cases}$

(c) $f(t) = |e^t| \quad -3 \leqslant t \leqslant 3$

7 The function $f(x)$ is periodic with a period of 2, and $f(x) = |x|, -1 \leqslant x \leqslant 1$. Sketch f for $-3 \leqslant x \leqslant 3$.

8 Given $a(t) = 3t, b(t) = t + 3$ and $c(t) = t^2 - 3$ write expressions

(a) $b(c(t))$

(b) $c(b(t))$

(c) $a(b(t))$

(d) $a(c(t))$

(e) $a(b(c(t)))$

(f) $c(b(a(t)))$

9 Sketch the following functions, stating any asymptotes.

(a) $y(x) = \dfrac{3 + x}{x}$

(b) $y(x) = \dfrac{2x}{x^2 - 1}$

(c) $y(x) = 3 - e^{-x}$

(d) $y(x) = \dfrac{e^x + 1}{e^x}$

10 Simplify each expression as far as possible.

(a) $e^{2x}e^{3x}$ (b) $e^x e^{2x}e^{-3x}$

(c) $e^4 e^3 e$ (d) $\dfrac{e^x}{e^{-x}}$

(e) $\left(\dfrac{e^x}{e^{-x}}\right)^2$ (f) $\ln 3x + \ln\left(\dfrac{2}{x}\right)$

(g) $3 \ln t + 2 \ln t^2$ (h) $e^{\ln x}$

(i) $\ln(e^x)$ (j) $e^{\ln x^2}$

(k) $e^{0.5 \ln x^2}$ (l) $\ln(e^{2x})$

(m) $e^{2 \ln x}$ (n) $\ln(e^3) + \ln(e^{2x})$

11 Solve the following:

(a) $e^{4x} = 200$

(b) $e^{3x-6} = 150$

(c) $9e^{-x} = 54$

(d) $e^{(x^2)} = 60$

(e) $\dfrac{1}{6 + e^{-x}} = 0.1$

12 Solve the following:

(a) $0.5 \ln t = 1.2$

(b) $\ln(3t + 2) = 1.4$

(c) $3 \ln(t - 1) = 6$

(d) $\log_{10}(t^2 - 1) = 1.5$

(e) $\log_{10}(\ln t) = 0.5$

(f) $\ln(\log_{10} t) = 0.5$

13 Express each of the following in terms of $\sinh x$ and $\cosh x$.

(a) $7e^x + 3e^{-x}$

(b) $6e^x - 5e^{-x}$

(c) $\dfrac{3e^x - 2e^{-x}}{2}$

(d) $\dfrac{1}{e^x + e^{-x}}$

(e) $\dfrac{e^x}{1 + e^x}$

14 Express each of the following in terms of e^x and e^{-x}.

(a) $2 \sinh x + 5 \cosh x$

(b) $\tanh x + \operatorname{sech} x$

(c) $2 \cosh x - \dfrac{3}{4} \sinh x$

(d) $\dfrac{1}{\sinh x - 2 \cosh x}$

(e) $(\sinh x)^2$

15 Describe the interval on the x axis defined by

(a) $|x| < 1.5$

(b) $|x| > 2$

(c) $|x + 3| < 7$

(d) $|2x| \geqslant 6$

(e) $|2x - 1| \leqslant 5$

16 Sketch

(a) $f = |-2t| \qquad -3 \leqslant t \leqslant 3$

(b) $f = -|2t| \qquad -3 \leqslant t \leqslant 3$

(c) $2\delta(t) - \delta(t - 1) + 3\delta(t + 1)$

Solutions

1 (a) Multiply input by 7, then subtract 2

   (b) Square the input, then subtract 2

   (c) Calculate e^x, where x is the input, multiply by 3 and then add 4

   (d) Multiply by 2, calculate exponential, subtract 1 and then divide by 2

   (e) Cube input, add to twice the input and add 5

2 (a) Domain $(-\infty, \infty)$ range $(-\infty, \infty)$

   (b) Domain $[0, 5]$ range $[-2, 23]$

   (c) Domain $[0, 2]$ range $[7, 3e^2 + 4]$

   (d) Domain $[0, \infty)$ range $[0, \infty)$

   (e) Domain $[-2, 2]$ range $[-7, 17]$

3 (a) $y^{-1}(x) = \dfrac{x}{2}$

   (b) $f^{-1}(t) = \dfrac{t+3}{8}$

   (c) $h^{-1}(x) = \dfrac{3}{2}(x-1)$

   (d) $m^{-1}(r) = \dfrac{1-r}{3}$

   (e) $H^{-1}(s) = \dfrac{3}{s-2}$

   (f) $f^{-1}(v) = e^v$

   (g) $f^{-1}(t) = \frac{1}{2}\ln t$

   (h) $g^{-1}(v) = e^{v-1}$

   (i) $g^{-1}(v) = e^v - 1$

   (j) $y^{-1}(t) = \ln\left(\dfrac{t}{3}\right) + 2$

4 (a) e^{2t} (b) e^x (c) e^λ (d) $e^{t-\lambda}$

5 (a) $\ln(\lambda^2 + 1)$ (b) $\ln((t-\lambda)^2 + 1)$

8 (a) t^2

   (b) $(t+3)^2 - 3$ or $t^2 + 6t + 6$

   (c) $3(t+3)$

   (d) $3(t^2 - 3)$

   (e) $3t^2$

   (f) $(3t+3)^2 - 3$ or $9t^2 + 18t + 6$

10 (a) e^{5x} (b) 1   (c) e^8
    (d) e^{2x} (e) e^{4x} (f) $\ln 6$
    (g) $\ln t^7$ (h) x (i) x
    (j) x^2 (k) x (l) $2x$
    (m) x^2 (n) $3 + 2x$

11 (a) 1.3246   (b) 3.6702
    (c) -1.7918 (d) ±2.0234
    (e) -1.3863

12 (a) 11.0232   (b) 0.6851
    (c) 8.3891   (d) ±5.7116
    (e) 23.6243   (f) 44.5370

13 (a) $10\cosh x + 4\sinh x$

    (b) $\cosh x + 11\sinh x$

    (c) $\dfrac{\cosh x + 5\sinh x}{2}$

    (d) $\dfrac{1}{2\cosh x}$

    (e) $\dfrac{\cosh x + \sinh x}{1 + \cosh x + \sinh x}$

14 (a) $\dfrac{7}{2}e^x + \dfrac{3}{2}e^{-x}$

    (b) $\dfrac{e^x - e^{-x} + 2}{e^x + e^{-x}}$

    (c) $\dfrac{5e^x + 11e^{-x}}{8}$

    (d) $\dfrac{-2}{e^x + 3e^{-x}}$

    (e) $\left(\dfrac{e^x - e^{-x}}{2}\right)^2$

15 (a) $-1.5 < x < 1.5$

    (b) $x > 2$ and $x < -2$

    (c) $-10 < x < 4$

    (d) $x \geqslant 3$ and $x \leqslant -3$

    (e) $-2 \leqslant x \leqslant 3$

3 The trigonometric functions

Chapter 3 Contents

3.1	Introduction	96
3.2	Degrees and radians	96
3.3	The trigonometric ratios	97
3.4	The sine, cosine and tangent functions	101
3.5	Trigonometric identities	104
3.6	Modelling waves using $\sin t$ and $\cos t$	110
3.7	Trigonometric equations	120
	Review exercises	127

3.1 Introduction

Many common engineering functions were studied in Section 2.4. However, the trigonometric functions are so important that they deserve separate treatment. Often alternating currents and voltages can be described using trigonometric functions, and they occur frequently in the solution of various kinds of equations.

Section 3.3 introduces the three trigonometric ratios: $\sin \theta$, $\cos \theta$ and $\tan \theta$. These are defined as ratios of the sides of a right-angled triangle. The definitions are then extended so that angles of any magnitude may be considered. Trigonometric identities are introduced, the most common ones being tabulated. These identities are useful in simplifying trigonometric expressions. Graphs of the trigonometric functions are illustrated. The application of these functions to the modelling of waveforms is an important section. The chapter closes with the solution of trigonometric equations.

3.2 Degrees and radians

Angles can be measured in units of either degrees or radians. The symbol for degree is °. Usually no symbol is used to denote radians and this is the convention adopted in this book.

A complete revolution is defined as $360°$ or 2π radians. It is easy to use this fact to convert between the two measures. We have

$$360° = 2\pi \text{ radians}$$

$$1° = \frac{2\pi}{360} = \frac{\pi}{180} \text{ radians}$$

$$1 \text{ radian} = \frac{180}{\pi} \text{ degrees} \approx 57.3°$$

Note that

$$\frac{\pi}{2} \text{ radians} = 90°$$

$$\pi \text{ radians} = 180°$$

$$\frac{3\pi}{2} \text{ radians} = 270°$$

Your calculator should be able to work with angles measured in both radians and degrees. Usually the Mode button allows you to select the appropriate measure.

Figure 3.1
A right-angled
triangle, ABC.

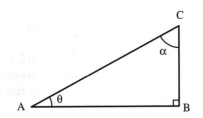

3.3 The trigonometric ratios

Consider the angle θ in the right-angled triangle ABC, as shown in Figure 3.1. We define the trigonometric ratios **sine**, **cosine** and **tangent** as follows:

$$\sin\theta = \frac{\text{side opposite to angle}}{\text{hypotenuse}} = \frac{BC}{AC}$$

$$\cos\theta = \frac{\text{side adjacent to angle}}{\text{hypotenuse}} = \frac{AB}{AC}$$

$$\tan\theta = \frac{\text{side opposite to angle}}{\text{side adjacent to angle}} = \frac{BC}{AB}$$

Note that

$$\tan\theta = \frac{BC}{AB} = \frac{BC}{AC} \times \frac{AC}{AB} = \frac{\sin\theta}{\cos\theta}$$

Note that when θ reduces to $0°$ the length of the side BC reduces to zero and so

$$\sin 0° = 0, \qquad \tan 0° = 0$$

Also when θ reduces to $0°$ the lengths of AB and AC become equal and so

$$\cos 0° = 1$$

Similarly when θ approaches $90°$, the lengths of BC and AC become equal and the length of AB shrinks to zero. Hence

$$\sin 90° = 1, \qquad \cos 90° = 0$$

Note also that the length of AB shrinks to zero as θ approaches $90°$, and so $\tan\theta$ approaches infinity. We write this as

$$\tan\theta \to \infty \qquad \text{as } \theta \to 90°$$

The trigonometric ratios of $30°$, $45°$ and $60°$ occur frequently in calculations. They can be calculated exactly by considering the right-angled triangles shown in Figure 3.2.

$$\sin 45° = \frac{1}{\sqrt{2}}, \qquad \cos 45° = \frac{1}{\sqrt{2}}, \qquad \tan 45° = 1$$

$$\sin 30° = \frac{1}{2}, \qquad \cos 30° = \frac{\sqrt{3}}{2}, \qquad \tan 30° = \frac{1}{\sqrt{3}}$$

$$\sin 60° = \frac{\sqrt{3}}{2}, \qquad \cos 60° = \frac{1}{2}, \qquad \tan 60° = \sqrt{3}$$

Figure 3.2
The trigonometric ratios for 30°, 45° and 60° can be found exactly from these triangles.

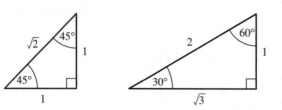

Most scientific calculators have pre-programmed values of $\sin\theta$, $\cos\theta$ and $\tan\theta$. Angles can be measured in degrees or radians. We will use radians unless stated otherwise. If we let $\angle ACB = \alpha$ (see Figure 3.1), then

$$\sin\alpha = \frac{AB}{AC} = \cos\theta$$

and

$$\cos\alpha = \frac{BC}{AC} = \sin\theta$$

But

$$\alpha + \theta = \frac{\pi}{2}$$

Hence,

$$\sin\theta = \cos\left(\frac{\pi}{2} - \theta\right)$$

$$\cos\theta = \sin\left(\frac{\pi}{2} - \theta\right)$$

Since θ is an angle in a right-angled triangle it cannot exceed $\pi/2$. In order to define the sine, cosine and tangent ratios for angles larger than $\pi/2$ we introduce an extended definition which is applicable to angles of any size.

Consider an arm, OP, fixed at O, which can rotate (see Figure 3.3). The angle, θ, in radians, between the arm and the positive x axis is measured anticlockwise. The arm can be projected onto both the x and y axes. These projections are OA and OB, respectively. Whether the arm projects onto the positive or negative x and y axes depends upon which quadrant the arm is situated in. The length of the arm OP is always positive. Then,

$$\sin\theta = \frac{\text{projection of } OP \text{ onto } y \text{ axis}}{OP} = \frac{OB}{OP}$$

$$\cos\theta = \frac{\text{projection of } OP \text{ onto } x \text{ axis}}{OP} = \frac{OA}{OP}$$

$$\tan\theta = \frac{\text{projection of } OP \text{ onto } y \text{ axis}}{\text{projection of } OP \text{ onto } x \text{ axis}} = \frac{OB}{OA}$$

In the first quadrant, that is $0 \leqslant \theta < \pi/2$, both the x and y projections are positive, so $\sin\theta$, $\cos\theta$ and $\tan\theta$ are positive. In the second quadrant, that is $\pi/2 \leqslant \theta < \pi$, the x

Figure 3.3
An arm, OP, fixed at
O, which can rotate.

Figure 3.4
Evaluating the
trigonometric ratios in
each of the four
quadrants.

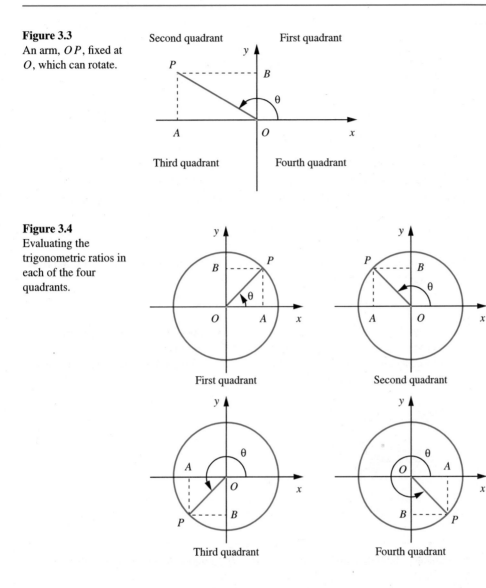

projection, OA, is negative and the y projection, OB, positive. Hence $\sin\theta$ is positive,
and $\cos\theta$ and $\tan\theta$ are negative. Both the x and y projections are negative for the third
quadrant and so $\sin\theta$ and $\cos\theta$ are negative while $\tan\theta$ is positive. Finally, in the fourth
quadrant, the x projection is positive and the y projection is negative. Hence, $\sin\theta$ and
$\tan\theta$ are negative, and $\cos\theta$ is positive (see Figure 3.4). The sign of the trigonometric
ratios can be summarized by Figure 3.5.

For angles greater than 2π, the arm OP simply rotates more than one revolution
before coming to rest. Each complete revolution brings OP back to its original position.
So, for example,

$$\sin(8.76) = \sin(8.76 - 2\pi) = \sin(2.477) = 0.617$$
$$\cos(14.5) = \cos(14.5 - 4\pi) = \cos(1.934) = -0.355$$

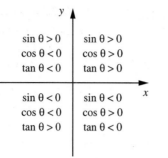

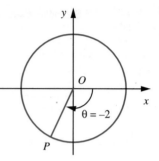

Figure 3.5 Sign of the trigonometric ratios in each of the four quadrants.

Figure 3.6 Illustration of the angle $\theta = -2$.

Negative angles are interpreted as a clockwise movement of the arm. Figure 3.6 illustrates an angle of -2. Note that

$$\sin(-2) = \sin(2\pi - 2) = \sin(4.283) = -0.909$$

since an anticlockwise movement of OP of 4.283 radians would result in the arm being in the same position as a clockwise movement of 2 radians.

The **cosecant**, **secant** and **cotangent** ratios are defined as the reciprocals of the sine, cosine and tangent ratios.

$$\operatorname{cosec} \theta = \frac{1}{\sin \theta}$$

$$\sec \theta = \frac{1}{\cos \theta}$$

$$\cot \theta = \frac{1}{\tan \theta}$$

Example 3.1 An angle θ is such that $\sin \theta > 0$ and $\cos \theta < 0$. In which quadrant does θ lie?

Solution From Figure 3.5 we see that $\sin \theta > 0$ when θ is in the first and second quadrants. Also, $\cos \theta < 0$ when θ is in the second and third quadrants. For both $\sin \theta > 0$ and $\cos \theta < 0$ thus requires θ to be in the second quadrant. Hence $\sin \theta > 0$ and $\cos \theta < 0$ when θ is in the second quadrant.

Exercises 3.3

1   Verify using a scientific calculator that

(a) $\sin 30° = \sin 390° = \sin 750°$

(b) $\cos 100° = \cos 460° = \cos 820°$

(c) $\tan 40° = \tan 220° = \tan 400°$

(d) $\sin 70° = \sin(-290°) = \sin(-650°)$

(e) $\cos 200° = \cos(-160°) = \cos(-520°)$

(f) $\tan 150° = \tan(-30°) = \tan(-210°)$

2 Verify the following using a scientific calculator. All angles are in radians.

(a) $\sin 0.7 = \sin(0.7 + 2\pi) = \sin(0.7 + 4\pi)$

(b) $\cos 1.4 = \cos(1.4 + 8\pi) = \cos(1.4 - 6\pi)$

(c) $\tan 1 = \tan(1 + \pi) = \tan(1 + 2\pi) = \tan(1 + 3\pi)$

(d) $\sin 2.3 = \sin(2.3 - 2\pi) = \sin(2.3 - 4\pi)$

(e) $\cos 2 = \cos(2 - 2\pi) = \cos(2 - 4\pi)$

(f) $\tan 4 = \tan(4 - \pi) = \tan(4 - 2\pi) = \tan(4 - 3\pi)$

3 An angle θ is such that $\cos \theta > 0$ and $\tan \theta < 0$. In which quadrant does θ lie?

4 An angle α is such that $\tan \alpha > 0$ and $\sin \alpha < 0$. In which quadrant does α lie?

Solutions

3 4th quadrant

4 3rd quadrant

3.4 The sine, cosine and tangent functions

The sine, cosine and tangent functions follow directly from the trigonometric ratios. These are defined to be $f(x) = \sin x$, $f(x) = \cos x$ and $f(x) = \tan x$. Graphs can be constructed from a table of values found using a scientific calculator. They are shown in Figures 3.7, 3.8 and 3.9. Note that these functions are many-to-one.

By shifting the cosine function to the right by an amount $\pi/2$ the sine function is obtained. Similarly, shifting the sine function to the left by $\pi/2$ results in the cosine function. This interchangeability between the sine and cosine functions is reflected in them being commonly referred to as **sinusoidal** functions. Notice also from the graphs two important properties of $\sin x$ and $\cos x$:

$$\sin x = -\sin(-x)$$
$$\cos x = \cos(-x)$$

For example,

$$\sin \frac{\pi}{3} = -\sin\left(-\frac{\pi}{3}\right) \quad \text{and} \quad \cos \frac{\pi}{3} = \cos\left(-\frac{\pi}{3}\right)$$

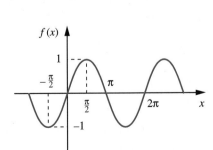

Figure 3.7 Graph of $f(x) = \sin x$.

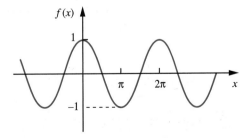

Figure 3.8 Graph of $f(x) = \cos x$.

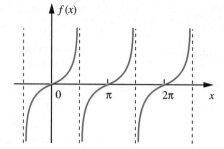

3.4.1 Inverse trigonometric functions

All six trigonometric functions have an inverse but we will only examine those of $\sin x$, $\cos x$ and $\tan x$. The inverse functions of $\sin x$, $\cos x$ and $\tan x$ are denoted $\sin^{-1} x$, $\cos^{-1} x$ and $\tan^{-1} x$. This notation can and does cause confusion. The '-1' in $\sin^{-1} x$ is sometimes mistakenly interpreted as a power. We write $(\sin x)^{-1}$ to denote $1/\sin x$. Values of $\sin^{-1} x$, $\cos^{-1} x$ and $\tan^{-1} x$ can be found using a scientific calculator. If $y = \sin x$, then $x = \sin^{-1} y$, as in

$$\sin x = 0.7654 \qquad x = \sin^{-1}(0.7654) = 0.8717$$

Note that $y = \sin x$ is a many-to-one function. If the domain is restricted to $[-\pi/2, \pi/2]$ then the resulting function is one-to-one. This is shown in Figure 3.10.

Recall from Section 2.3 that a one-to-one function has a corresponding inverse. So if the domain of $y = \sin x$ is restricted to $[-\pi/2, \pi/2]$, then an inverse function exists. A graph of $y = \sin^{-1} x$ is shown in Figure 3.11. Without the domain restriction, a one-to-many graph would result as shown in Figure 3.12. To denote the inverse sine function clearly, we write

$$y = \sin^{-1} x \qquad -\frac{\pi}{2} \leqslant y \leqslant \frac{\pi}{2}$$

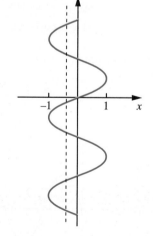

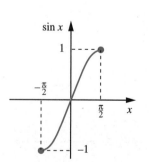

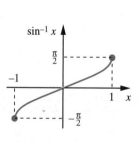

Figure 3.10   The function $\sin x$ is one-to-one if the domain is restricted to $\left[-\dfrac{\pi}{2}, \dfrac{\pi}{2}\right]$.

Figure 3.11   The inverse sine function, $\sin^{-1} x$.

Figure 3.12   A single input produces many output values. This is not a function.

Example 3.2   Use a scientific calculator to evaluate

(a) $\sin^{-1}(0.3169)$

(b) $\sin^{-1}(-0.8061)$

Solution   (a) $\sin^{-1}(0.3169) = 0.3225$

(b) $\sin^{-1}(-0.8061) = -0.9375$

A word of warning about inverse trigonometric functions is needed. The calculator returns a value of 0.3225 for $\sin^{-1}(0.3169)$. Note, however, that $\sin(0.3225 \pm 2n\pi) = 0.3169$, $n = 0, 1, 2, 3, \ldots$, so there are an infinite number of values of x such that $\sin x = 0.3169$. Only one of these values is returned by the calculator. This is because the domain of $y = \sin x$ is restricted to ensure it has an inverse function. To ensure the inverse functions $y = \cos^{-1} x$ and $y = \tan^{-1} x$ can be obtained, restrictions are placed on the domains of $y = \cos x$ and $y = \tan x$. By convention, $y = \cos x$ has its domain restricted to $[0, \pi]$ whereas with $y = \tan x$ the restriction is $(-\pi/2, \pi/2)$.

Exercises 3.4

1   Evaluate the following:

(a) $\sin^{-1}(0.75)$

(b) $\cos^{-1}(0.625)$

(c) $\tan^{-1} 3$

(d) $\sin^{-1}(-0.9)$

(e) $\cos^{-1}(-0.75)$

(f) $\tan^{-1}(-3)$

2   Show that

$$\sin^{-1} x + \cos^{-1} x = \frac{\pi}{2}$$

3   Sketch $y = \sin x$ and $y = \cos x$ for x in the interval $[-2\pi, 2\pi]$. Mark on the graphs the points where $x = 1$, $x = 1.5$, $x = -3$ and $x = 2.3$.

Solutions

1   (a) 0.8481   (b) 0.8957   (c) 1.2490   (d) -1.1198 (e) 2.4189   (f) -1.2490

Computer and calculator exercises 3.4

1   Draw $y = \sin x$ and $y = \cos x$ for $0 \leqslant x \leqslant 4\pi$ using the same axes. Use your graphs to find approximate solutions to the equation $\sin x = \cos x$.

2   Draw the graphs of $y = \cos^{-1} x$ and $y = \tan^{-1} x$.

3.5 Trigonometric identities

We have seen that $\tan\theta = \dfrac{\sin\theta}{\cos\theta}$ for all values of θ. We call this an **identity**. In an identity, the l.h.s. and the r.h.s. are always equal, unlike in an equation where the l.h.s. and the r.h.s. are equal only for particular values of the variable concerned. Table 3.1 lists some common trigonometric identities.

Table 3.1
Common trigonometric identities.

$$\tan A = \frac{\sin A}{\cos A}$$

$$\sin(A \pm B) = \sin A \cos B \pm \sin B \cos A$$

$$\cos(A \pm B) = \cos A \cos B \mp \sin A \sin B$$

$$\tan(A \pm B) = \frac{\tan A \pm \tan B}{1 \mp \tan A \tan B}$$

$$2 \sin A \cos B = \sin(A + B) + \sin(A - B)$$

$$2 \cos A \cos B = \cos(A + B) + \cos(A - B)$$

$$2 \sin A \sin B = \cos(A - B) - \cos(A + B)$$

$$\sin^2 A + \cos^2 A = 1$$

$$1 + \cot^2 A = \operatorname{cosec}^2 A$$

$$\tan^2 A + 1 = \sec^2 A$$

$$\cos 2A = 1 - 2\sin^2 A = 2\cos^2 A - 1 = \cos^2 A - \sin^2 A$$

$$\sin 2A = 2 \sin A \cos A$$

$$\sin^2 A = \frac{1 - \cos 2A}{2}$$

$$\cos^2 A = \frac{1 + \cos 2A}{2}$$

Note: $\sin^2 A$ is the notation used for $(\sin A)^2$. Similarly $\cos^2 A$ means $(\cos A)^2$.

Example 3.3   Simplify

$$\frac{\cot A}{\cos A}$$

Solution   We know that

$$\tan A = \frac{\sin A}{\cos A}$$

and so

$$\cot A = \frac{1}{\tan A} = \frac{\cos A}{\sin A}$$

Hence

$$\frac{\cot A}{\cos A} = \cot A \times \frac{1}{\cos A}$$

$$= \frac{\cos A}{\sin A} \times \frac{1}{\cos A}$$

$$= \frac{1}{\sin A}$$

This may also be written as cosec A.

Example 3.4 Show that

$$\tan A + \cot A$$

may be written as

$$\frac{2}{\sin 2A}$$

Solution We have

$$\tan A = \frac{\sin A}{\cos A}, \qquad \cot A = \frac{\cos A}{\sin A}$$

and so

$$\tan A + \cot A = \frac{\sin A}{\cos A} + \frac{\cos A}{\sin A}$$

$$= \frac{\sin^2 A + \cos^2 A}{\sin A \cos A}$$

$$= \frac{1}{\sin A \cos A} \qquad \text{using the identity } \sin^2 A + \cos^2 A = 1$$

$$= \frac{2}{2\sin A \cos A}$$

$$= \frac{2}{\sin 2A} \qquad \text{using the identity } \sin 2A = 2\sin A \cos A$$

Example 3.5 Use the identities in Table 3.1 to simplify the following expressions.

(a) $\sin\left(\dfrac{\pi}{2} + \theta\right)$ (b) $\cos\left(\dfrac{3\pi}{2} - \theta\right)$

(c) $\tan(2\pi - \theta)$ (d) $\sin(\pi - \theta)$

Solution (a) The expression $\sin\left(\dfrac{\pi}{2} + \theta\right)$ is of the form $\sin(A + B)$ and so we use the identity

$$\sin(A + B) = \sin A \cos B + \sin B \cos A$$

Putting $A = \dfrac{\pi}{2}$ and $B = \theta$ we obtain

$$\sin\left(\frac{\pi}{2} + \theta\right) = \sin\frac{\pi}{2}\cos\theta + \sin\theta\cos\frac{\pi}{2}$$

We note that $\sin\dfrac{\pi}{2} = 1$, $\cos\dfrac{\pi}{2} = 0$ and so

$$\sin\left(\frac{\pi}{2} + \theta\right) = 1\cos\theta + \sin\theta\,(0)$$
$$= \cos\theta$$

(b) The expression $\cos\left(\dfrac{3\pi}{2} - \theta\right)$ has the form $\cos(A - B)$; hence we use the identity

$$\cos(A - B) = \cos A\cos B + \sin A\sin B$$

Putting $A = \dfrac{3\pi}{2}$, $B = \theta$ we obtain

$$\cos\left(\frac{3\pi}{2} - \theta\right) = \cos\frac{3\pi}{2}\cos\theta + \sin\frac{3\pi}{2}\sin\theta$$

Now $\cos\dfrac{3\pi}{2} = 0$, $\sin\dfrac{3\pi}{2} = -1$ and so

$$\cos\left(\frac{3\pi}{2} - \theta\right) = 0\cos\theta + (-1)\sin\theta$$
$$= -\sin\theta$$

(c) We use the identity

$$\tan(A - B) = \frac{\tan A - \tan B}{1 + \tan A\tan B}$$

Substituting $A = 2\pi$, $B = \theta$ we obtain

$$\tan(2\pi - \theta) = \frac{\tan 2\pi - \tan\theta}{1 + \tan 2\pi\tan\theta}$$

Since $\tan 2\pi = 0$ this simplifies to

$$\tan(2\pi - \theta) = \frac{-\tan\theta}{1} = -\tan\theta$$

(d) We use the identity

$$\sin(A - B) = \sin A\cos B - \sin B\cos A$$

Substituting $A = \pi$, $B = \theta$, this then becomes

$$\sin(\pi - \theta) = \sin\pi\cos\theta - \sin\theta\cos\pi$$

Now $\sin\pi = 0$, $\cos\pi = -1$ and so we obtain

$$\sin(\pi - \theta) = 0\cos\theta - \sin\theta(-1) = \sin\theta$$

Example 3.6   Simplify

(a) $\cos(\pi + \theta)$

(b) $\tan(\pi - \theta)$

(c) $\sin^3 B + \sin B \cos^2 B$

(d) $\tan A(1 + \cos 2A)$

Solution   (a) Using the identity for $\cos(A + B)$ with $A = \pi$, $B = \theta$ we obtain

$$
\begin{aligned}
\cos(\pi + \theta) &= \cos \pi \cos \theta - \sin \pi \sin \theta \\
&= (-1) \cos \theta - (0) \sin \theta \\
&= - \cos \theta
\end{aligned}
$$

(b) Using the identity for $\tan(A - B)$ with $A = \pi$, $B = \theta$ we obtain

$$
\begin{aligned}
\tan(\pi - \theta) &= \frac{\tan \pi - \tan \theta}{1 + \tan \pi \tan \theta} \\[2mm]
&= \frac{0 - \tan \theta}{1 + (0) \tan \theta} \\[2mm]
&= - \tan \theta
\end{aligned}
$$

(c)
$$
\begin{aligned}
\sin^3 B + \sin B \cos^2 B &= \sin B(\sin^2 B + \cos^2 B) \\
&= \sin B \qquad \text{since } \sin^2 B + \cos^2 B = 1
\end{aligned}
$$

(d) Firstly we note that $\tan A = \dfrac{\sin A}{\cos A}$. Also we have from Table 3.1

$$
\cos^2 A = \frac{1 + \cos 2A}{2}
$$

from which

$$
1 + \cos 2A = 2 \cos^2 A
$$

Hence

$$
\begin{aligned}
\tan A(1 + \cos 2A) &= \frac{\sin A}{\cos A} 2 \cos^2 A \\
&= 2 \sin A \cos A \\
&= \sin 2A
\end{aligned}
$$

Example 3.7   Show that

$$\sin A + \sin B = 2 \sin \left(\frac{A + B}{2} \right) \cos \left(\frac{A - B}{2} \right)$$

Solution   Consider the identities

$$\sin(C + D) = \sin C \cos D + \sin D \cos C$$
$$\sin(C - D) = \sin C \cos D - \sin D \cos C$$

By adding these identities we obtain

$$\sin(C + D) + \sin(C - D) = 2 \sin C \cos D$$

We now make the substitutions $C + D = A$, $C - D = B$ from which

$$C = \frac{A + B}{2}, \qquad D = \frac{A - B}{2}$$

Hence

$$\sin A + \sin B = 2 \sin \left(\frac{A + B}{2} \right) \cos \left(\frac{A - B}{2} \right)$$

   The result of Example 3.7 is one of many similar results. These are listed in Table 3.2.

Table 3.2
Further trigonometric
identities

$$\sin A + \sin B = 2 \sin \left(\frac{A + B}{2} \right) \cos \left(\frac{A - B}{2} \right)$$

$$\sin A - \sin B = 2 \sin \left(\frac{A - B}{2} \right) \cos \left(\frac{A + B}{2} \right)$$

$$\cos A + \cos B = 2 \cos \left(\frac{A + B}{2} \right) \cos \left(\frac{A - B}{2} \right)$$

$$\cos A - \cos B = -2 \sin \left(\frac{A + B}{2} \right) \sin \left(\frac{A - B}{2} \right)$$

Example 3.8   Simplify

$$\frac{\sin 70° - \sin 30°}{\cos 50°}$$

Solution   We note that the numerator, $\sin 70° - \sin 30°$, has the form $\sin A - \sin B$. Using the identity for $\sin A - \sin B$ with $A = 70°$ and $B = 30°$ we see

$$\sin 70° - \sin 30° = 2 \sin \left(\frac{70° - 30°}{2} \right) \cos \left(\frac{70° + 30°}{2} \right)$$

$$= 2 \sin 20° \cos 50°$$

Hence

$$\frac{\sin 70° - \sin 30°}{\cos 50°} = \frac{2 \sin 20° \cos 50°}{\cos 50°}$$
$$= 2 \sin 20°$$

Exercises 3.5

1 Use the identities for $\sin(A \pm B)$, $\cos(A \pm B)$ and $\tan(A \pm B)$ to simplify the following.

(a) $\sin\left(\theta - \dfrac{\pi}{2}\right)$

(b) $\cos\left(\theta - \dfrac{\pi}{2}\right)$

(c) $\tan(\theta + \pi)$

(d) $\sin(\theta - \pi)$

(e) $\cos(\theta - \pi)$

(f) $\tan(\theta - 3\pi)$

(g) $\sin(\theta + \pi)$

(h) $\cos\left(\theta + \dfrac{3\pi}{2}\right)$

(i) $\sin\left(2\theta + \dfrac{3\pi}{2}\right)$

(j) $\cos\left(\theta - \dfrac{3\pi}{2}\right)$

(k) $\cos\left(\dfrac{\pi}{2} + \theta\right)$

(d) $\cot 2x \sec 2x$

(e) $\tan \theta \tan\left(\dfrac{\pi}{2} + \theta\right)$

[*Hint:* see Question 2.]

(f) $\dfrac{\sin 2t}{\cos t}$

(g) $\sin^2 A + 2 \cos^2 A$

(h) $2 \cos^2 B - 1$

(i) $(1 + \cot^2 X) \tan^2 X$

(j) $(\sin^2 A + \cos^2 A)^2$

(k) $\dfrac{1}{2} \sin 2A \tan A$

(l) $(\sec^2 t - 1) \cos^2 t$

(m) $\dfrac{\sin 2A}{\cos 2A}$

(n) $\dfrac{\sin A}{\sin 2A}$

(o) $(\tan^2 \theta + 1) \cot^2 \theta$

(p) $\cos 2A + 2 \sin^2 A$

2 Write down the trigonometric identity for $\tan(A + \theta)$. By letting $A \to \dfrac{\pi}{2}$ show that $\tan\left(\dfrac{\pi}{2} + \theta\right)$ can be simplified to $- \cot \theta$.

3 (a) By dividing the identity $\sin^2 A + \cos^2 A = 1$ by $\cos^2 A$ show that $\tan^2 A + 1 = \sec^2 A$.

(b) By dividing the identity $\sin^2 A + \cos^2 A = 1$ by $\sin^2 A$ show that $1 + \cot^2 A = \operatorname{cosec}^2 A$.

4 Simplify the following expressions.

(a) $\cos A \tan A$

(b) $\sin \theta \cot \theta$

(c) $\tan B \operatorname{cosec} B$

5 Simplify

(a) $\sin 110° - \sin 70°$

(b) $\cos 20° - \cos 80°$

(c) $\sin 40° + \sin 20°$

(d) $\dfrac{\cos 50° + \cos 40°}{\sqrt{2}}$

6 Show that

$$\frac{\sin 60° + \sin 30°}{\sin 50° - \sin 40°}$$

is equivalent to

$$\frac{\cos 15°}{\sin 5°}$$

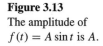

Solutions

1 (a) $-\cos\theta$ (b) $\sin\theta$ (c) $\tan\theta$
   (d) $-\sin\theta$ (e) $-\cos\theta$ (f) $\tan\theta$
   (g) $-\sin\theta$ (h) $\sin\theta$ (i) $-\cos 2\theta$
   (j) $-\sin\theta$ (k) $-\sin\theta$

   (g) $1+\cos^2 A$ (h) $\cos 2B$ (i) $\sec^2 X$
   (j) 1 (k) $\sin^2 A$ (l) $\sin^2 t$
   (m) $\tan 2A$ (n) $\frac{1}{2}\sec A$ (o) $\operatorname{cosec}^2\theta$
   (p) 1

4 (a) $\sin A$ (b) $\cos\theta$ (c) $\sec B$
   (d) $\operatorname{cosec} 2x$ (e) -1 (f) $2\sin t$

5 (a) 0 (b) $\sin 50°$ (c) $\cos 10°$
   (d) $\cos 5°$

3.6 Modelling waves using sin *t* and cos *t*

Examining the graphs of $\sin x$ and $\cos x$ reveals that they have a similar shape to waves. In fact, sine and cosine functions are often used to model waves and we will see in Chapter 23 that almost any wave can be broken down into a combination of sine and cosine functions. The main waves found in engineering are ones that vary with time and so t is often the independent variable.

The **amplitude** of a wave is the maximum displacement of the wave from its mean position. So, for example, $\sin t$ and $\cos t$ have an amplitude of 1, the amplitude of $2\sin t$ is 2, and the amplitude of $A\sin t$ is A (see Figure 3.13).

> The amplitude of $A\sin t$ is A. The amplitude of $A\cos t$ is A.

A more general wave is defined by $A\cos\omega t$ or $A\sin\omega t$. The symbol ω represents the **angular frequency** of the wave. It is measured in radians per second. For example, $\sin 3t$ has an angular frequency of 3 rad s^{-1}. As t increases by 1 second the angle, $3t$, increases by 3 radians. Note that $\sin t$ has an angular frequency of 1 rad s^{-1}.

> The angular frequency of $y = A\sin\omega t$ and $y = A\cos\omega t$ is ω radians per second.

The sine and cosine functions repeat themselves at regular intervals and so are **periodic** functions. Looking at Figure 3.7 we see that one complete **cycle** of $\sin t$ is

Figure 3.13
The amplitude of
$f(t) = A\sin t$ is A.

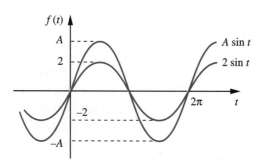

completed every 2π seconds. The time taken to complete one full cycle is called the **period** and is denoted by T. Hence the period of $y = \sin t$ is 2π seconds. Similarly the period of $y = \cos t$ is 2π seconds. Mathematically this means that adding or subtracting multiples of 2π to t does not change the sine or cosine of that angle.

$$\sin t = \sin(t \pm 2n\pi) \qquad n = 0, 1, 2, 3, \ldots$$
$$\cos t = \cos(t \pm 2n\pi) \qquad n = 0, 1, 2, 3, \ldots$$

In particular we note that

$$\sin t = \sin(t + 2\pi)$$
$$\cos t = \cos(t + 2\pi)$$

We now consider $y = A \sin \omega t$ and $y = A \cos \omega t$. When $t = 0$ seconds, $\omega t = 0$ radians. When $t = \dfrac{2\pi}{\omega}$ seconds, $\omega t = \omega \dfrac{2\pi}{\omega} = 2\pi$ radians. We can see that as t increases from 0 to $\dfrac{2\pi}{\omega}$ seconds, the angle ωt increases from 0 to 2π radians. We know that as the angle ωt increases by 2π radians then $A \sin \omega t$ completes a full cycle. Hence a full cycle is completed in $\dfrac{2\pi}{\omega}$ seconds, that is the period of $y = A \sin \omega t$ is $\dfrac{2\pi}{\omega}$ seconds.

If $y = A \sin \omega t$ or $y = A \cos \omega t$, then the period T is $\dfrac{2\pi}{\omega}$.

In particular we note that the period of $y = A \sin t$ and $y = A \cos t$ is 2π.

Closely related to the period is the frequency of a wave. The **frequency** is the number of cycles completed in 1 second. Frequency is measured in units called hertz (Hz). One hertz is one cycle per second. We have seen that $y = A \sin \omega t$ takes

$$\dfrac{2\pi}{\omega} \text{ seconds to complete one cycle}$$

and so it will take

$$1 \text{ second to complete } \dfrac{\omega}{2\pi} \text{ cycles}$$

We use f as the symbol for frequency and so

frequency, $f = \dfrac{\omega}{2\pi}$

For example, $\sin 3t$ has a frequency of $\left(\dfrac{3}{2\pi}\right)$ Hz.

Note that by rearrangement we may write

$$\omega = 2\pi f$$

and so the wave $y = A \sin \omega t$ may also be written as $y = A \sin 2\pi f t$.

From the definitions of period and frequency we can see that

$$\text{period} = \dfrac{1}{\text{frequency}}$$

Figure 3.14
The generalized wave
$A \sin(\omega t + \phi)$.

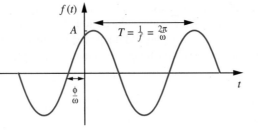

that is

$$T = \frac{1}{f}$$

We see that the period is the reciprocal of the frequency. Identical results apply for the wave $y = A \cos \omega t$.

A final generalization is to introduce a **phase angle**, ϕ. This allows the wave to be shifted along the time axis. It also means that either a sine function or a cosine function can be used to represent the same wave. So the general forms are

$$A \cos(\omega t + \phi), \qquad A \sin(\omega t + \phi)$$

Figure 3.14 depicts $A \sin(\omega t + \phi)$. Note from Figure 3.14 that the actual movement of the wave along the time axis is ϕ/ω. It is easy to show this mathematically:

$$A \sin(\omega t + \phi) = A \sin \omega \left(t + \frac{\phi}{\omega} \right)$$

The quantity $\dfrac{\phi}{\omega}$ is called the **time displacement**.

The waves met in engineering are often termed **signals** or **waveforms**. There are no rigid rules concerning the use of the words wave, signal and waveform, and often engineers use them interchangeably. We will follow this convention.

Example 3.9   State the amplitude, angular frequency and period of each of the following waves.

(a) $2 \sin 3t$

(b) $\dfrac{1}{2} \cos \left(2t + \dfrac{\pi}{6} \right)$

Solution   (a) Amplitude, $A = 2$, angular frequency, $\omega = 3$, period, $T = \dfrac{2\pi}{\omega} = \dfrac{2\pi}{3}$.

(b) Amplitude, $A = 0.5$, angular frequency, $\omega = 2$, period, $T = \dfrac{2\pi}{\omega} = \dfrac{2\pi}{2} = \pi$.

Example 3.10   State the amplitude, period, phase angle and time displacement of

(a) $2 \sin(4t + 1)$

(b) $\dfrac{2\cos(t-0.7)}{3}$

(c) $4\cos\left(\dfrac{2t+1}{3}\right)$

(d) $\dfrac{3}{4}\sin\left(\dfrac{4t}{3}\right)$

Solution   (a) Amplitude $= 2$, period $= \dfrac{2\pi}{4} = \dfrac{\pi}{2}$, phase angle $= 1$ relative to $2\sin 4t$, time displacement $= 0.25$.

(b) Amplitude $= \dfrac{2}{3}$, period $= 2\pi$, phase angle $= -0.7$ relative to $\dfrac{2}{3}\cos t$, time displacement $= -0.7$.

(c) Amplitude $= 4$, period $= \dfrac{2\pi}{2/3} = 3\pi$, phase angle $= \dfrac{1}{3}$ relative to $4\cos\left(\dfrac{2t}{3}\right)$, time displacement $= 0.5$.

(d) Amplitude $= \dfrac{3}{4}$, period $= \dfrac{2\pi}{4/3} = \dfrac{3\pi}{2}$, phase angle $= 0$ relative to $\dfrac{3}{4}\sin\left(\dfrac{4t}{3}\right)$, time displacement $= 0$.

Example 3.11   **Alternating current waveforms**

Sine and cosine functions are often used to model alternating current (a.c.) wave forms. The equations for an a.c. current waveform are

$$I = I_m \sin(\omega t + \phi) \qquad \text{or} \qquad I = I_m \cos(\omega t + \phi)$$

where $I_m = $ maximum current, $\omega = $ angular frequency and $\phi = $ phase angle. In practice the functions can be shifted along the time axis by giving ϕ a non-zero value and so both the sine and the cosine function can be used to model any a.c. waveform; which one is used is usually a matter of convenience.

3.6.1 Combining waves

There are many situations in which engineers need to combine two or more waves together to form a single wave. It is possible to make use of trigonometric identities to calculate the resulting waveform when several waves are combined. Consider the following example.

Example 3.12   Two voltage signals, $v_1(t)$ and $v_2(t)$, have the following mathematical expressions:

$$v_1(t) = 3\sin t$$
$$v_2(t) = 2\cos t$$

(a) State the amplitude and angular frequency of the two signals.

(b) Obtain an expression for the signal, $v_3(t)$, given by

$$v_3(t) = v_1(t) + 2v_2(t)$$

(c) Reduce the expression obtained in part (b) to a single sinusoid and hence state its amplitude and phase.

Solution   (a) $v_1(t)$ has an amplitude of 3 volts and an angular frequency $\omega = 1$ rad s^{-1}. $v_2(t)$ has an amplitude of 2 volts and an angular frequency $\omega = 1$ rad s^{-1}. Note that both of these signals have the same angular frequency.

(b) $v_3(t) = v_1(t) + 2v_2(t)$
$$= 3\sin t + 2(2\cos t)$$
$$= 3\sin t + 4\cos t$$

(c) We wish to write $v_3(t)$ in the form $R\sin(t + \phi)$. The choice of sine is arbitrary. We could have chosen cosine instead. R is the amplitude of the single sinusoid and ϕ is its phase angle.

Using the trigonometric identity $\sin(t + \phi) = \sin t \cos \phi + \sin \phi \cos t$ found in Table 3.1 we can write

$$R\sin(t + \phi) = R(\sin t \cos \phi + \sin \phi \cos t)$$
$$= (R\cos \phi)\sin t + (R\sin \phi)\cos t$$

Comparing this expression with that for $v_3(t)$ we note that, in order to make the expressions identical,

$$R\cos \phi = 3 \tag{3.1}$$
$$R\sin \phi = 4 \tag{3.2}$$

We need to solve (3.1) and (3.2) to obtain R and ϕ. Squaring each equation gives

$$R^2 \cos^2 \phi = 9$$
$$R^2 \sin^2 \phi = 16$$

Adding these equations together we obtain

$$R^2 \cos^2 \phi + R^2 \sin^2 \phi = 9 + 16$$
$$R^2(\cos^2 \phi + \sin^2 \phi) = 25$$

Using the identity $\cos^2 \phi + \sin^2 \phi = 1$ this simplifies to

$$R^2 = 25$$
$$R = 5$$

Next we determine ϕ. Dividing (3.2) by (3.1) we find

$$\frac{R\sin\phi}{R\cos\phi} = \frac{4}{3}$$

$$\tan\phi = \frac{4}{3}$$

$$\phi = \tan^{-1}\left(\frac{4}{3}\right)$$

From (3.1) and (3.2) we can see that both $\sin\phi$ and $\cos\phi$ are positive, and so ϕ must lie in the first quadrant. Calculating $\tan^{-1}\left(\frac{4}{3}\right)$ using a calculator gives $\phi = 0.927$ radians. So we can express $v_3(t)$ as

$$v_3(t) = 3\sin t + 4\cos t = 5\sin(t + 0.927)$$

Finally $v_3(t)$ has amplitude 5 volts and phase 0.927 radians.

Example 3.12 illustrates an important property when combining together two sinusoidal waves of the same angular frequency.

If two waves of equal angular frequency, ω, are added the result is a wave of the same angular frequency, ω.

In fact this result holds true when combining any number of waves of the same angular frequency.

Example 3.13   Two current signals $i_1(t)$ and $i_2(t)$, have the following mathematical expressions:

$$i_1(t) = 10\sin 4t$$
$$i_2(t) = 5\cos 4t$$

(a) State the amplitude and angular frequency of the two signals.

(b) Obtain an expression for the signal, $i_3(t)$, given by $i_3(t) = 0.3i_1(t) - 0.4i_2(t)$

(c) Reduce the expression obtained in part (b) to a single sinusoid in the form $R\cos(4t + \phi)$ and hence state its amplitude and phase.

Solution   (a) $i_1(t)$ has an amplitude of 10 amps and an angular frequency $\omega = 4$ rad s^{-1}. $i_2(t)$ has an amplitude of 5 amps and an angular frequency $\omega = 4$ rad s^{-1}. Note that both signals have the same angular frequency.

(b) $i_3(t) = 0.3i_1(t) - 0.4i_2(t)$
$$= 0.3 \times 10\sin 4t - 0.4 \times 5\cos 4t$$
$$= 3\sin 4t - 2\cos 4t$$

(c) Let

$$3 \sin 4t - 2 \cos 4t = R \cos(4t + \phi)$$

Then using the trigonometric identity given in Table 3.1

$$\cos(A + B) = \cos A \cos B - \sin A \sin B$$

with $A = 4t$ and $B = \phi$ we find

$$3 \sin 4t - 2 \cos 4t = R \cos(4t + \phi)$$
$$= R(\cos 4t \cos \phi - \sin 4t \sin \phi)$$
$$= (R \cos \phi) \cos 4t - (R \sin \phi) \sin 4t$$

Hence

$$3 = -R \sin \phi \qquad\qquad (3.3)$$
$$-2 = R \cos \phi \qquad\qquad (3.4)$$

By squaring each equation and adding we obtain

$$9 + 4 = R^2(\sin^2 \phi + \cos^2 \phi) = R^2$$

so that $R = \sqrt{13}$.

From (3.3) and (3.4), both $\sin \phi$ and $\cos \phi$ are negative and so ϕ lies in the third quadrant. Division of (3.3) by (3.4) gives

$$\frac{3}{-2} = \frac{-R \sin \phi}{R \cos \phi} = -\tan \phi$$
$$\tan \phi = 1.5$$

Using a calculator and noting that ϕ lies in the third quadrant we find $\phi = 4.124$. Finally

$$3 \sin 4t - 2 \cos 4t = \sqrt{13} \cos(4t + 4.124)$$

So $i_3(t) = \sqrt{13} \cos(4t + 4.124)$. Therefore $i_3(t)$ has an amplitude of $\sqrt{13}$ amps and a phase of 4.124 radians.

Example 3.14   Express $0.5 \cos 3t + \sin 3t$ as a single cosine wave.

Solution   Let

$$0.5 \cos 3t + \sin 3t = R \cos(3t + \phi)$$
$$= R(\cos 3t \cos \phi - \sin 3t \sin \phi)$$
$$= (R \cos \phi) \cos 3t - (R \sin \phi) \sin 3t$$

Hence

$$0.5 = R\cos\phi \qquad (3.5)$$
$$1 = -R\sin\phi \qquad (3.6)$$

By squaring and adding we obtain

$$1.25 = R^2$$
$$R = \sqrt{1.25} = 1.1180 \qquad \text{(4 d.p.)}$$

Division of (3.6) by (3.5) yields

$$2 = -\tan\phi$$

From (3.5), $\cos\phi$ is positive; from (3.6), $\sin\phi$ is negative, and so ϕ lies in the fourth quadrant. Hence, using a calculator, $\phi = 5.1760$. So

$$0.5\cos 3t + \sin 3t = 1.1180\cos(3t + 5.1760)$$

Example 3.15   If $a\cos\omega t + b\sin\omega t$ is expressed in the form $R\cos(\omega t - \theta)$ show that $R = \sqrt{a^2 + b^2}$ and $\tan\theta = \dfrac{b}{a}$.

Solution   Let

$$a\cos\omega t + b\sin\omega t = R\cos(\omega t - \theta)$$

Then, using the trigonometric identity for $\cos(A - B)$, we can write

$$a\cos\omega t + b\sin\omega t = R\cos(\omega t - \theta)$$
$$= R(\cos\omega t \cos\theta + \sin\omega t \sin\theta)$$
$$= (R\cos\theta)\cos\omega t + (R\sin\theta)\sin\omega t$$

Equating coefficients of $\cos\omega t$ and then $\sin\omega t$ gives

$$a = R\cos\theta \qquad (3.7)$$
$$b = R\sin\theta \qquad (3.8)$$

Squaring these equations and adding gives

$$a^2 + b^2 = R^2$$

that is

$$R = \sqrt{a^2 + b^2}$$

Division of (3.8) by (3.7) gives

$$\frac{b}{a} = \tan\theta$$

as required.

Note that this example demonstrates that adding two waves of angular frequency ω forms another wave having the same angular frequency but with a modified amplitude and phase.

Exercises 3.6

1 State the amplitude, angular frequency, frequency, phase angle and time displacement of the following waves:

(a) $3 \sin 2t$

(b) $\dfrac{1}{2} \sin 4t$

(c) $\sin(t + 1)$

(d) $4 \cos 3t$

(e) $2 \sin(t - 3)$

(f) $5 \cos(0.4t)$

(g) $\sin(100\pi t)$

(h) $6 \cos(5t + 2)$

(i) $\dfrac{2}{3} \sin(0.5t)$

(j) $4 \cos(\pi t - 20)$

2 State the period of

(a) $2 \sin 7t$

(b) $7 \sin(2t + 3)$

(c) $\tan \dfrac{t}{2}$

(d) $\sec 3t$

(e) $\operatorname{cosec}(2t - 1)$

(f) $\cot\left(\dfrac{2t}{3} + 2\right)$

3 A voltage source produces a time-varying voltage, $v(t)$, given by

$$v(t) = 15 \sin(20\pi t + 4) \qquad t \geqslant 0$$

(a) State the amplitude of $v(t)$.

(b) State the angular frequency of $v(t)$.

(c) State the period of $v(t)$.

(d) State the phase of $v(t)$.

(e) State the time displacement of $v(t)$.

(f) State the minimum value of $v(t)$.

4 A sinusoidal function has an amplitude of $\frac{2}{3}$ and a period of 2. State a possible form of the function. ·

5 State the phase angle and time displacement of

(a) $2 \sin(t + 3)$ relative to $2 \sin t$

(b) $\sin(2t - 3)$ relative to $\sin 2t$

(c) $\cos\left(\dfrac{t}{2} + 0.2\right)$ relative to $\cos \dfrac{t}{2}$

(d) $\cos(2 - t)$ relative to $\cos t$

(e) $\sin\left(\dfrac{3t + 4}{5}\right)$ relative to $\sin \dfrac{3t}{5}$

(f) $\sin(4 - 3t)$ relative to $\sin 3t$

(g) $\sin(2\pi t + \pi)$ relative to $\sin 2\pi t$

(h) $3 \cos(5\pi t - 3)$ relative to $3 \cos 5\pi t$

(i) $\sin\left(\dfrac{\pi t}{3} + 2\right)$ relative to $\sin \dfrac{\pi t}{3}$

(j) $\cos(3\pi - t)$ relative to $\cos t$

6 Write each of the following in the form $A \sin(3t + \theta)$, $\theta \geqslant 0$:

(a) $2 \sin 3t + 3 \cos 3t$

(b) $\cos 3t - 2 \sin 3t$

(c) $\sin 3t - 4 \cos 3t$

(d) $-\cos 3t - 4 \sin 3t$

7 Write each of the following in the form $A \cos(t - \theta)$, $\theta \geqslant 0$:

(a) $2 \sin t - 3 \cos t$

(b) $9 \sin t + 6 \cos t$

(c) $4 \cos t - \sin t$

(d) $3 \sin t$

8 Write each of the following expressions in the form (i) $A \sin(\omega t + \theta)$, (ii) $A \sin(\omega t - \theta)$, (iii) $A \cos(\omega t + \theta)$, (iv) $A \cos(\omega t - \theta)$ where $\theta \geqslant 0$:

(a) $5 \sin t + 4 \cos t$

(b) $-2 \sin 3t + 2 \cos 3t$

(c) $4 \sin 2t - 6 \cos 2t$

(d) $-\sin 5t - 3 \cos 5t$

Solutions

1 (a) $3, 2, \dfrac{1}{\pi}, 0, 0$ (b) $\dfrac{1}{2}, 4, \dfrac{2}{\pi}, 0, 0$

   (c) $1, 1, \dfrac{1}{2\pi}, 1, 1$ (d) $4, 3, \dfrac{3}{2\pi}, 0, 0$

   (e) $2, 1, \dfrac{1}{2\pi}, -3, -3$ (f) $5, 0.4, \dfrac{1}{5\pi}, 0, 0$

   (g) $1, 100\pi, 50, 0, 0$ (h) $6, 5, \dfrac{5}{2\pi}, 2, 0.4$

   (i) $\dfrac{2}{3}, 0.5, \dfrac{1}{4\pi}, 0, 0$ (j) $4, \pi, \dfrac{1}{2}, -20, -\dfrac{20}{\pi}$

2 (a) $\dfrac{2\pi}{7}$ (b) π (c) 2π

   (d) $\dfrac{2\pi}{3}$ (e) π (f) $\dfrac{3\pi}{2}$

3 (a) 15   (b) 20π (c) 0.1

   (d) 4   (e) $\dfrac{1}{5\pi}$ (f) -15

4 $\dfrac{2}{3}\sin(\pi t + k)$ or $\dfrac{2}{3}\cos(\pi t + k)$

5 (a) $3, 3$ (b) $-3, -\dfrac{3}{2}$

   (c) $0.2, 0.4$ (d) $-2, -2$

   (e) $\dfrac{4}{5}, \dfrac{4}{3}$ (f) $-0.858, -0.286$

   (g) $\pi, \dfrac{1}{2}$ (h) $-3, -\dfrac{3}{5\pi}$

   (i) $2, \dfrac{6}{\pi}$ (j) $-3\pi, -3\pi$

6 (a) $\sqrt{13}\sin(3t + 0.9828)$

   (b) $\sqrt{5}\sin(3t + 2.6779)$

   (c) $\sqrt{17}\sin(3t + 4.9574)$

   (d) $\sqrt{17}\sin(3t + 3.3866)$

7 (a) $\sqrt{13}\cos(t - 2.5536)$

   (b) $\sqrt{117}\cos(t - 0.9828)$

   (c) $\sqrt{17}\cos(t - 6.0382)$

   (d) $3\cos\left(t - \dfrac{\pi}{2}\right)$

8 (a) (i) $\sqrt{41}\sin(t + 0.675)$

      (ii) $\sqrt{41}\sin(t - 5.608)$

      (iii) $\sqrt{41}\cos(t + 5.387)$

      (iv) $\sqrt{41}\cos(t - 0.896)$

   (b) (i) $\sqrt{8}\sin\left(3t + \dfrac{3\pi}{4}\right)$

      (ii) $\sqrt{8}\sin\left(3t - \dfrac{5\pi}{4}\right)$

      (iii) $\sqrt{8}\cos\left(3t + \dfrac{\pi}{4}\right)$

      (iv) $\sqrt{8}\cos\left(3t - \dfrac{7\pi}{4}\right)$

   (c) (i) $\sqrt{52}\sin(2t + 5.300)$

      (ii) $\sqrt{52}\sin(2t - 0.983)$

      (iii) $\sqrt{52}\cos(2t + 3.730)$

      (iv) $\sqrt{52}\cos(2t - 2.554)$

   (d) (i) $\sqrt{10}\sin(5t + 4.391)$

      (ii) $\sqrt{10}\sin(5t - 1.893)$

      (iii) $\sqrt{10}\cos(5t + 2.820)$

      (iv) $\sqrt{10}\cos(5t - 3.463)$

Computer and calculator exercises 3.6

1 Plot $y = \sin 2t$ for $0 \leqslant t \leqslant 2\pi$.

2 Plot $y = \cos 3t$ for $0 \leqslant t \leqslant 3\pi$.

3 Plot $y = \sin\left(\dfrac{t}{2}\right)$ for $0 \leqslant t \leqslant 4\pi$.

4 Plot $y = \cos\left(\dfrac{2t}{3}\right)$ for $0 \leqslant t \leqslant 6\pi$.

5 Plot $y = \sin t + 3\cos t$ for $0 \leqslant t \leqslant 3\pi$. By

reading from your graph, state the maximum value of $\sin t + 3\cos t$.

6 (a) Plot $y = 2\sin 3t - \cos 3t$ for $0 \leqslant t \leqslant 2\pi$. Use your graph to state the amplitude of $2\sin 3t - \cos 3t$.

   (b) On the same axes plot $y = \sin 3t$. Estimate the time displacement of $2\sin 3t - \cos 3t$.

3.7 Trigonometric equations

We examine trigonometric equations which can be written in one of the forms $\sin z = k$, $\cos z = k$ or $\tan z = k$, where z is the independent variable and k is a constant. These equations all have an infinite number of solutions. This is a consequence of the trigonometric functions being periodic. For example, $\sin z = 1$ has solutions $z = \ldots, \dfrac{-7\pi}{2}, \dfrac{-3\pi}{2}, \dfrac{\pi}{2}, \dfrac{5\pi}{2}, \ldots$ These solutions could be expressed as $z = \dfrac{\pi}{2} \pm 2n\pi$, $n = 0, 1, 2, \ldots$. Sometimes it is useful, indeed necessary, to state all the solutions. At other times we are interested only in solutions in some specified interval, for example solving $\sin z = 1$ for $0 \leqslant z \leqslant 2\pi$. The following examples illustrate the method of solution.

Example 3.16

Solve

(a) $\sin t = 0.6105$ for $0 \leqslant t \leqslant 2\pi$ (b) $\sin t = -0.6105$ for $0 \leqslant t \leqslant 2\pi$.

Solution

Figure 3.15 shows a graph of $y = \sin t$, with horizontal lines drawn at $y = 0.6105$ and $y = -0.6105$.

(a) From Figure 3.15 we see that there are two solutions in the interval $0 \leqslant t \leqslant 2\pi$. These are given by points A and B. We have

$$\sin t = 0.6105$$

and so, using a scientific calculator, we have

$$t = \sin^{-1}(0.6105) = 0.6567$$

This is the solution at point A. From the symmetry of the graph, the second solution is

$$t = \pi - 0.6567 = 2.4849$$

This is the solution at point B. The required solutions are $t = 0.6567, 2.4849$.

Figure 3.15
A and B are solution points for $\sin t = 0.6105$. C and D are solution points for $\sin t = -0.6105$.

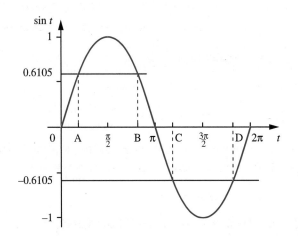

(b) Again from Figure 3.15 we see that the equation has two solutions in the interval $0 \leqslant t \leqslant 2\pi$. These are given by the points C and D. One solution lies in the interval π to $\dfrac{3\pi}{2}$; the other solution lies in the interval $\dfrac{3\pi}{2}$ to 2π. We have

$$\sin t = -0.6105$$

and so, using a calculator, we see

$$t = \sin^{-1}(-0.6105) = -0.6567$$

Although this value of t is a solution of $\sin t = -0.6105$ it is outside the range of values of interest. Recall that

$$\sin t = \sin(t + 2\pi)$$

that is, adding 2π to an angle does not change the sine of the angle. Hence

$$t = -0.6567 + 2\pi = 5.6265$$

is a required solution. This is the solution given by point D. From the symmetry of Figure 3.15 the other solution is

$$t = \pi + 0.6567 = 3.7983$$

This is the solution at point C. The required solutions are $t = 3.7983, 5.6265$.

Example 3.17   Solve

(a) $\cos t = 0.3685$ for $0 \leqslant t \leqslant 2\pi$

(b) $\cos t = -0.3685$ for $0 \leqslant t \leqslant 2\pi$

Solution   Figure 3.16 shows a graph of $y = \cos t$ between $t = 0$ and $t = 2\pi$ together with horizontal lines at $y = 0.3685$ and $y = -0.3685$.

(a) From Figure 3.16 we see that there is a solution of $\cos t = 0.3685$ between 0 and $\dfrac{\pi}{2}$ and a solution between $\dfrac{3\pi}{2}$ and 2π. These are given by points A and D. Now

$$\cos t = 0.3685$$

and so, using a scientific calculator, we see

$$t = \cos^{-1}(0.3685) = 1.1934$$

This is the solution between 0 and $\dfrac{\pi}{2}$, that is at point A. Using the symmetry of Figure 3.16 the other solution at point D is

$$t = 2\pi - 1.1934 = 5.0898$$

The required solutions are $t = 1.1934$ and 5.0898.

Figure 3.16
A and D are solution
points for
$\cos t = 0.3685$. B and
C are solution points
for $\cos t = -0.3685$.

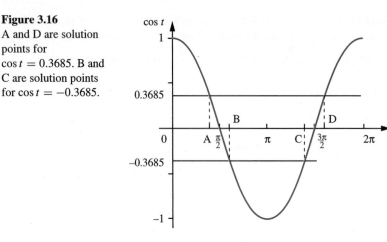

(b) The graph in Figure 3.16 shows there are two solutions of $\cos t = -0.3685$. These solutions are at points B and C. Given

$$\cos t = -0.3685$$

then using a scientific calculator we have

$$t = \cos^{-1}(-0.3685) = 1.9482$$

This is the solution given by point B. By symmetry the other solution at point C is

$$t = 2\pi - 1.9482 = 4.3350$$

The required solutions are $t = 1.9482$ and 4.3350.

Example 3.18 Solve

(a) $\tan t = 1.3100$ for $0 \leqslant t \leqslant 2\pi$

(b) $\tan t = -1.3100$ for $0 \leqslant t \leqslant 2\pi$

Solution Figure 3.17 shows a graph of $y = \tan t$ for $t = 0$ to $t = 2\pi$ together with horizontal lines $y = 1.3100$ and $y = -1.3100$.

(a) There is a solution of $\tan t = 1.3100$ between 0 and $\dfrac{\pi}{2}$ and a solution between π and $\dfrac{3\pi}{2}$. These are given by points A and C.

$$\tan t = 1.3100$$
$$t = \tan^{-1}(1.3100) = 0.9188$$

Figure 3.17
A and C are solution
points for
$\tan t = 1.3100$. B and
D are solution points
for $\tan t = -1.3100$.

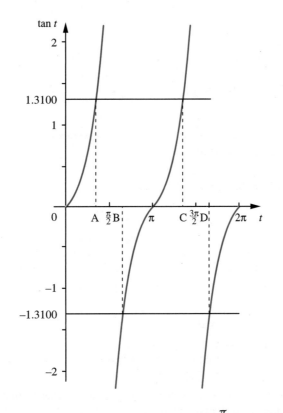

This is the solution between 0 and $\dfrac{\pi}{2}$ given by point A. Using Figure 3.17 we can see that the second solution is given by

$$t = \pi + 0.9188 = 4.0604$$

This is given by point C.

(b) Figure 3.17 shows that there are two solutions of $\tan t = -1.3100$, one between $\dfrac{\pi}{2}$ and π, the other between $\dfrac{3\pi}{2}$ and 2π. Points B and D represent these solutions. Using a scientific calculator we have

$$t = \tan^{-1}(-1.3100) = -0.9188$$

This solution is outside the range of interest. Noting that the period of $\tan t$ is π we see that

$$t = -0.9188 + \pi = 2.2228$$

is a solution between $\dfrac{\pi}{2}$ and π. This is given by point B. The second solution is

$$t = -0.9188 + 2\pi = 5.3644$$

This is the solution given by point D. The required solutions are $t = 2.2228$ and 5.3644.

Example 3.19   Solve

(a) $\sin 2t = 0.6105$ for $0 \leqslant t \leqslant 2\pi$

(b) $\cos(3t + 2) = -0.3685$ for $0 \leqslant t \leqslant 2\pi$

Solution   (a) Let $z = 2t$. As t varies from 0 to 2π then z varies from 0 to 4π. Thus the problem is equivalent to solving

$$\sin z = 0.6105 \qquad 0 \leqslant z \leqslant 4\pi$$

From Example 3.16 the solutions between 0 and 2π are 0.6567 and 2.4849. Since $\sin z$ has period 2π, then the solutions in the next cycle, that is between 2π and 4π, are $z = 0.6567 + 2\pi = 6.9399$ and $z = 2.4849 + 2\pi = 8.7681$. Hence

$$z = 2t = 0.6567, 2.4849, 6.9399, 8.7681$$

and so, to four decimal places,

$$t = 0.3284, 1.2425, 3.4700, 4.3840$$

(b) Let $z = 3t + 2$. As t varies from 0 to 2π then z varies from 2 to $6\pi + 2$. Hence the problem is equivalent to solving

$$\cos z = -0.3685 \qquad 2 \leqslant z \leqslant 6\pi + 2$$

Solutions between 0 and 2π are given in Example 3.17 as $z = 1.9482, 4.3350$. Noting that $\cos z$ has period 2π, then solutions between 2π and 4π are $z = 1.9482 + 2\pi = 8.2314$ and $z = 4.3350 + 2\pi = 10.6182$, solutions between 4π and 6π are $z = 1.9482 + 4\pi = 14.5146$ and $z = 4.3350 + 4\pi = 16.9014$ and solutions between 6π and 8π are $z = 1.9482 + 6\pi = 20.7978$ and $z = 4.3350 + 6\pi = 23.1846$. The solutions between $z = 0$ and $z = 8\pi$ are thus

$$z = 1.9482, 4.3350, 8.2314, 10.6182, 14.5146, 16.9014, 20.7978, 23.1846$$

Noting that $6\pi + 2 = 20.8496$ we require values of z between 2 and 20.8496, that is

$$z = 4.3350, 8.2314, 10.6182, 14.5146, 16.9014, 20.7978$$

Finally

$$t = \frac{z - 2}{3} = 0.7783, 2.0771, 2.8727, 4.1715, 4.9671, 6.2659$$

Example 3.20 A voltage, $v(t)$, is given by

$$v(t) = 3\sin(t + 1) \qquad t \geqslant 0$$

Find the first time that the voltage has a value of 1.5 volts.

Solution We need to solve $3\sin(t + 1) = 1.5$, that is

$$\sin(t + 1) = 0.5 \qquad t \geqslant 0$$

Let $z = t + 1$. Since $t \geqslant 0$ then $z \geqslant 1$. The problem is thus equivalent to

$$\sin z = 0.5 \qquad z \geqslant 1$$

Using a scientific calculator we have

$$z = \sin^{-1}(0.5) = 0.5236$$

This solution is outside the range of interest. By reference to Figure 3.7 the next solution is

$$z = \pi - 0.5236 = 2.6180$$

This is the first value of z greater than 1 such that $\sin z = 0.5$. Finally

$$t = z - 1 = 1.6180$$

The voltage first has a value of 1.5 volts when $t = 1.618$ seconds.

Exercises 3.7

1 Solve the following equations for $0 \leqslant t \leqslant 2\pi$:

(a) $\sin t = 0.8426$

(b) $\sin t = 0.2146$

(c) $\sin t = 0.5681$

(d) $\sin t = -0.4316$

(e) $\sin t = -0.9042$

(f) $\sin t = -0.2491$

2 Solve the following equations for $0 \leqslant t \leqslant 2\pi$:

(a) $\cos t = 0.4243$

(b) $\cos t = 0.8040$

(c) $\cos t = 0.3500$

(d) $\cos t = -0.5618$

(e) $\cos t = -0.7423$

(f) $\cos t = -0.3658$

3 Solve the following equations for $0 \leqslant t \leqslant 2\pi$:

(a) $\tan t = 0.8493$

(b) $\tan t = 1.5326$

(c) $\tan t = 1.2500$

(d) $\tan t = -0.8437$

(e) $\tan t = -2.0612$

(f) $\tan t = -1.5731$

4 Solve the following equations for $0 \leqslant t \leqslant 2\pi$:

(a) $\sin 2t = 0.6347$

(b) $\sin 3t = -0.2516$

(c) $\sin\left(\dfrac{t}{2}\right) = 0.4250$

(d) $\sin(2t + 1) = -0.6230$

(e) $\sin(2t - 3) = 0.1684$

(f) $\sin\left(\dfrac{t+2}{3}\right) = -0.4681$

5 Solve the following equations for $0 \leqslant t \leqslant 2\pi$:

(a) $\cos 2t = 0.4234$

(b) $\cos\left(\dfrac{t}{3}\right) = -0.5618$

(c) $\cos\left(\dfrac{2t}{3}\right) = 0.6214$

(d) $\cos(2t + 0.5) = -0.8300$

(e) $\cos(t - 2) = 0.7431$

(f) $\cos(\pi t - 1) = -0.5325$

6 Solve the following equations for $0 \leqslant t \leqslant 2\pi$:

(a) $\tan 2t = 1.5234$

(b) $\tan\left(\dfrac{t}{3}\right) = -0.8439$

(c) $\tan(3t - 2) = 1.0641$

(d) $\tan(1.5t - 1) = -1.7300$

(e) $\tan\left(\dfrac{2t+1}{3}\right) = 1.0000$

(f) $\tan(5t - 6) = -1.2323$

7 A time-varying voltage, $v(t)$, has the form

$$v(t) = 20\sin(50\pi t + 20) \qquad t \geqslant 0$$

Calculate the first time that the voltage has a value of
(a) 2 volts   (b) 10 volts   (c) 15 volts

Solutions

1 (a) 1.0021, 2.1395   (b) 0.2163, 2.9253
(c) 0.6042, 2.5374   (d) 3.5879, 5.8369
(e) 4.2711, 5.1537   (f) 3.3933, 6.0314

2 (a) 1.1326, 5.1506   (b) 0.6368, 5.6464
(c) 1.2132, 5.0700   (d) 2.1674, 4.1158
(e) 2.4073, 3.8759   (f) 1.9453, 4.3379

3 (a) 0.7041, 3.8457   (b) 0.9927, 4.1343
(c) 0.8961, 4.0376   (d) 2.4408, 5.5824
(e) 2.0225, 5.1641   (f) 2.1370, 5.2786

4 (a) 0.3438, 1.2270, 3.4854, 4.3686

(b) 1.1320, 2.0096, 3.2264, 4.1040, 5.3208, 6.1984

(c) 0.8779, 5.4053

(d) 1.4071, 2.3053, 4.5487, 5.4469

(e) 1.5846, 2.9862, 4.7262, 6.1278

(f) no solutions

5 (a) 0.5668, 2.5748, 3.7084, 5.7164

(b) no solutions

(c) 1.3504

(d) 1.0250, 1.6166, 4.1665, 4.7582

(e) 1.2669, 2.7331

(f) 0.9971, 1.6396, 2.9971, 3.6396, 4.9971, 5.6396

6 (a) 0.4950, 2.0658, 3.6366, 5.2073

(b) no solutions

(c) 0.9388, 1.9860, 3.0332, 4.0804, 5.1276, 6.1748

(d) 2.0633, 4.1577, 6.2521

(e) 0.6781, 5.3905

(f) 0.3939, 1.0222, 1.6505, 2.2788, 2.9071, 3.5355, 4.1638, 4.7921, 5.4204, 6.0487

7 (a) 1.2038×10^{-2}

(b) 9.3427×10^{-3}

(c) 7.2771×10^{-3}

Computer and calculator exercises 3.7

1 Plot $y = \sin t$ for $0 \leqslant t \leqslant 2\pi$ and $y = 0.3500$ using the same axes. Use your graphs to find approximate solutions to

$$\sin t = 0.3500 \qquad 0 \leqslant t \leqslant 2\pi$$

2 Plot $y = \cos t$ for $0 \leqslant t \leqslant 2\pi$ and $y = -0.5500$ using the same axes. Use your graphs to find approximate solutions to

$$\cos t + 0.5500 = 0 \qquad 0 \leqslant t \leqslant 2\pi$$

3 Plot $y = \sin(2t + 1)$ and $y = 2 \sin t$ for $0 \leqslant t \leqslant 2\pi$. Use your graphs to state approximate solutions to

$$\sin(2t + 1) = 2 \sin t \qquad 0 \leqslant t \leqslant 2\pi$$

4 Plot $y = 2 \sin 3t$ and $y = 3 \cos 2t$ for $0 \leqslant t \leqslant 2\pi$. Hence state approximate solutions of

$$2 \sin 3t = 3 \cos 2t \qquad 0 \leqslant t \leqslant 2\pi$$

Review exercises 3

1 Express the following angles in radians:
(a) $45°$ (b) $72°$ (c) $100°$
(d) $300°$ (e) $440°$

2 The following angles are in radians. Express them in degrees.

(a) $\dfrac{\pi}{3}$ (b) 3π (c) $\dfrac{3\pi}{4}$ (d) 2

(e) 3.62

3 State the quadrant in which the angle α lies given

(a) $\sin \alpha > 0$ and $\tan \alpha > 0$

(b) $\cos \alpha > 0$ and $\sin \alpha < 0$

(c) $\tan \alpha > 0$ and $\cos \alpha < 0$

(d) $\sin \alpha < 0$ and $\cos \alpha < 0$

(e) $\tan \alpha < 0$ and $\cos \alpha < 0$

4 Simplify the following expressions:

(a) $\sin t \operatorname{cosec} t$

(b) $\dfrac{\sin x}{\tan x}$

(c) $\dfrac{\cot A}{\cos A}$

(d) $\dfrac{\sec A}{\operatorname{cosec} A}$

(e) $\cot x \tan x$

5 Simplify the following expressions:

(a) $\cos^2 A + 1 + \sin^2 A$

(b) $\dfrac{2 \sin A \cos A}{\cos^2 A - \sin^2 A}$

(c) $\sqrt{\sec^2 x - 1}$

(d) $\sin t \cos t + \dfrac{1}{\sec t \operatorname{cosec} t}$

(e) $\dfrac{1}{\operatorname{cosec}^2 A - 1}$

6 Simplify the following expressions:

(a) $(\sin x + \cos x)^2 - 1$

(b) $\tan A \sin 2A + 1 + \cos 2A$

(c) $\dfrac{\sin 4\theta + \sin 2\theta}{\cos 2\theta - \cos 4\theta}$

(d) $4 \sin A \cos A \cos 2A$

(e) $\dfrac{\sin t}{\cos\left(\dfrac{t}{2}\right)}$

7 State the amplitude, angular frequency, period, frequency, phase and time displacement of the following waves.

(a) $2 \sin 3t$

(b) $4 \cos 6t$

(c) $0.7 \sin(2t + 3)$

(d) $0.1 \cos \pi t$

(e) $\sin(50\pi t + 20)$

(f) $6 \cos(100\pi t - 30)$

(g) $\dfrac{1}{2} \sin\left(\dfrac{t}{2}\right)$

(h) $0.25 \cos(2\pi t + 1)$

8 Express the following in the form $A \sin(\omega t + \phi)$, $\phi \geqslant 0$.

(a) $6 \sin 5t + 5 \cos 5t$

(b) $0.1 \sin t - 0.2 \cos t$

(c) $7 \sin 3t + 6 \cos 3t$

(d) $9 \cos\left(\dfrac{t}{2}\right) - 4 \sin\left(\dfrac{t}{2}\right)$

(e) $3 \sin 2t + 15 \cos 2t$

9 Express the following in the form $A \sin(\omega t - \phi)$, $\phi \geqslant 0$.

(a) $3 \sin 4t + 7 \cos 4t$

(b) $3 \cos 2t - 5 \sin 2t$

(c) $4 \sin 6t - 7 \cos 6t$

(d) $\dfrac{1}{2}\cos t + \dfrac{2}{3}\sin t$

(e) $0.75\sin(0.5t) - 1.25\cos(0.5t)$

10 Express the following in the form
$A\cos(\omega t + \phi), \phi \geqslant 0.$

(a) $10\sin 3t + 16\cos 3t$

(b) $-6\sin 2t - 3\cos 2t$

(c) $\sin t - 2\cos t$

(d) $0.6\cos 4t + 1.3\sin 4t$

(e) $\cos 7t - 5\sin 7t$

11 Express each of the following in the form
$A\cos(\omega t - \phi), \phi \geqslant 0.$

(a) $2.3\sin 3t + 6.4\cos 3t$

(b) $-\sin 2t - 2\cos 2t$

(c) $2\cos 9t + 9\sin 9t$

(d) $4\sin 4t + 5\cos 4t$

(e) $-6\cos\left(\dfrac{t}{2}\right) - 2\sin\left(\dfrac{t}{2}\right)$

12 Express each of the following in the form
$A\sin(\omega t + \phi), \phi \geqslant 0.$

(a) $\sin(t+1) + \cos(t+1)$

(b) $2\sin(2t+3) - 3\cos(2t+1)$

(c) $\cos(3t-1) - 2\sin(3t+4)$

(d) $\sin(t+1) + \sin(t+3)$

(e) $\cos(2t-1) + 3\cos(2t+3)$

13 Reduce each of the following expressions to a
single wave and in each case state the amplitude
and phase angle of the resultant wave.

(a) $2\cos\omega t + 3\sin\omega t$

(b) $\cos\left(\omega t + \dfrac{\pi}{4}\right) + \sin\omega t$

(c) $2\sin\left(\omega t + \dfrac{\pi}{2}\right) + 4\cos\left(\omega t + \dfrac{\pi}{4}\right)$

(d) $0.5\sin\left(\omega t - \dfrac{\pi}{4}\right) + 1.5\sin\left(\omega t + \dfrac{\pi}{4}\right)$

(e) $3\sin\omega t + 4\sin(\omega t + \pi) - 2\cos\left(\omega t - \dfrac{\pi}{2}\right)$

14 Solve the following equations, stating all
solutions between 0 and 2π.

(a) $\sin t = 0.5216$

(b) $\sin t = -0.3724$

(c) $\cos t = 0.9231$

(d) $\cos t = -1$

(e) $\tan t = 0.1437$

(f) $\tan t = -1$

15 Solve the following equations, stating all
solutions between 0 and 2π.

(a) $\sin 2t = 0.5421$

(b) $\cos 2t = -0.4687$

(c) $\tan\left(\dfrac{t}{2}\right) = -1.6235$

(d) $2\sin 4t = 1.5$

(e) $5\cos 2t = 2$

(f) $4\tan 2t = 5$

16 A voltage, $v(t)$, varies with time, t, according to

$$v(t) = 240\sin(100\pi t + 30) \qquad t \geqslant 0$$

Find the first time that $v(t)$ has a value of
(a) 240   (b) 0
(c) -240 (d) 100

17 Simplify as far as possible

(a) $\cos 100° + \cos 80°$

(b) $\cos 100° - \cos 80°$

(c) $\dfrac{\sin 50° + \sin 40°}{\cos 5°}$

(d) $\dfrac{\sin 80° - \sin 60°}{2\sin 10°}$

Solutions

1 (a) $\dfrac{\pi}{4}$ (b) $\dfrac{2\pi}{5}$ (c) 1.7453

(d) 5.2360   (e) 7.6794

2 (a) 60°   (b) 540°   (c) 135°

(d) 114.6°   (e) 207.4°

3   (a)   1st   (b)   4th   (c)   3rd
     (d)   3rd   (e)   2nd

4   (a)   1   (b) $\cos x$ (c) $\operatorname{cosec} A$
     (d) $\tan A$ (e)   1

5   (a)   2   (b) $\tan 2A$ (c) $\tan x$
     (d) $\sin 2t$ (e) $\tan^2 A$

6   (a) $\sin 2x$ (b)   2   (c) $\cot \theta$
     (d) $\sin 4A$ (e) $2 \sin\left(\dfrac{t}{2}\right)$

7   (a) $2, 3, \dfrac{2\pi}{3}, \dfrac{3}{2\pi}, 0, 0$

     (b) $4, 6, \dfrac{\pi}{3}, \dfrac{3}{\pi}, 0, 0$

     (c) $0.7, 2, \pi, \dfrac{1}{\pi}, 3, \dfrac{3}{2}$

     (d) $0.1, \pi, 2, \dfrac{1}{2}, 0, 0$

     (e) $1, 50\pi, 0.04, 25, 20, \dfrac{2}{5\pi}$

     (f) $6, 100\pi, 0.02, 50, -30, -\dfrac{3}{10\pi}$

     (g) $\dfrac{1}{2}, \dfrac{1}{2}, 4\pi, \dfrac{1}{4\pi}, 0, 0$

     (h) $0.25, 2\pi, 1, 1, 1, \dfrac{1}{2\pi}$

8   (a) $\sqrt{61} \sin(5t + 0.6947)$

     (b) $\sqrt{0.05} \sin(t + 5.1760)$

     (c) $\sqrt{85} \sin(3t + 0.7086)$

     (d) $\sqrt{97} \sin\left(\dfrac{t}{2} + 1.9890\right)$

     (e) $\sqrt{234} \sin(2t + 1.3734)$

9   (a) $\sqrt{58} \sin(4t - 5.1173)$

     (b) $\sqrt{34} \sin(2t - 3.6820)$

     (c) $\sqrt{65} \sin(6t - 1.0517)$

     (d) $\dfrac{5}{6} \sin(t - 5.6397)$

     (e) $1.4577 \sin(0.5t - 1.0304)$

10   (a) $\sqrt{356} \cos(3t + 5.7246)$

     (b) $\sqrt{45} \cos(2t + 2.0344)$

     (c) $\sqrt{5} \cos(t + 3.6052)$

     (d) $\sqrt{2.05} \cos(4t + 5.1448)$

     (e) $\sqrt{26} \cos(7t + 1.3734)$

11   (a) $6.8007 \cos(3t - 0.3450)$

     (b) $\sqrt{5} \cos(2t - 3.6052)$

     (c) $\sqrt{85} \cos(9t - 1.3521)$

     (d) $\sqrt{41} \cos(4t - 0.6747)$

     (e) $\sqrt{40} \cos\left(\dfrac{t}{2} - 3.4633\right)$

12   (a) $\sqrt{2} \sin(t + 1.7854)$

     (b) $1.4451 \sin(2t + 5.0987)$

     (c) $2.9725 \sin(3t + 0.7628)$

     (d) $1.0806 \sin(t + 2)$

     (e) $2.4654 \sin(2t + 4.8828)$

13   (a) $\sqrt{13} \sin(\omega t + 0.5880)$, amplitude $= \sqrt{13}$, phase angle $= 0.5880$

     (b) $0.765 \sin(\omega t + 1.1781)$, amplitude $= 0.765$, phase angle $= 1.1781$

     (c) $5.596 \sin(\omega t + 2.10)$, amplitude $= 5.596$, phase angle $= 2.10$

     (d) $1.581 \sin(\omega t + 0.4636)$, amplitude $= 1.581$, phase angle $= 0.4636$

     (e) $-3 \sin \omega t$, amplitude $= 3$, phase angle $= \pi$

14   (a) $0.5487, 2.5929$ (b) $3.5232, 5.9016$
     (c) $0.3947, 5.8885$ (d) 3.1416, i.e. π

     (e) $0.1427, 3.2843$ (f) $\dfrac{3\pi}{4}, \dfrac{7\pi}{4}$

15   (a) $0.2865, 1.2843, 3.4281, 4.4259$

     (b) $1.0293, 2.1123, 4.1709, 5.2539$

     (c) 4.2457

     (d) $0.2120, 0.5734, 1.7828, 2.1442, 3.3536,$
         $3.7150, 4.9244, 5.2858$

     (e) $0.5796, 2.5620, 3.7212, 5.7035$

     (f) $0.4480, 2.0188, 3.5896, 5.1604$

16   (a) 9.5070×10^{-3} (b) 4.5070×10^{-3}
     (c) 1.9507×10^{-2} (d) 5.8751×10^{-3}

17   (a) 0 (b) $-2 \sin 10°$ (c) $\sqrt{2}$
     (d) $\cos 70°$

4 Coordinate systems

Chapter 4	Contents	
4.1	Introduction	132
4.2	Cartesian coordinate system – two dimensions	132
4.3	Cartesian coordinate system – three dimensions	134
4.4	Polar coordinates	136
4.5	Some simple polar curves	140
4.6	Cylindrical polar coordinates	142
4.7	Spherical polar coordinates	145
	Review exercises	147

4.1 Introduction

The coordinates of a point describe its position. The most common coordinate system is the x–y system: the first number, x, gives the distance along the x axis, the second number, y, gives the distance along the y axis. However, this is not the only way to describe the position of a point. This chapter outlines several ways in which the position of a point can be described.

4.2 Cartesian coordinate system – two dimensions

The Cartesian coordinate system is named after the French mathematician Descartes. The system comprises two axes – the x axis and the y axis – which intersect at right angles at the point O. The point O is called the **origin**. Figure 4.1 shows the Cartesian coordinate system. By convention the x axis is drawn horizontally. The positive x axis lies to the right of the origin, the negative x axis lies to the left of the origin, the positive y axis lies above the origin and the negative y axis lies below the origin.

Figure 4.1
Cartesian coordinate
system in two
dimensions.

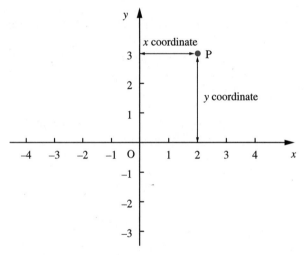

Note that this coordinate system can be used only for locating points in a plane, that is it has two dimensions.

Consider any point, P, in the plane. The horizontal distance of P from the y axis is called the x **coordinate**. The vertical distance of P from the x axis is called the y **coordinate**. Either coordinate can be positive or negative.

When stating the coordinates of a point, by convention we always state the x coordinate first. Thus (3, 1) means that the x coordinate is 3 and the y coordinate is 1. We also write, for example, A(3, 1) to mean that the point whose coordinates are (3, 1) is labelled A. In Figure 4.1 P has coordinates (x, y).

Example 4.1

Plot the points whose Cartesian coordinates are

(a) (4, 2)   (b) (−1, −3)   (c) (−2, 1)

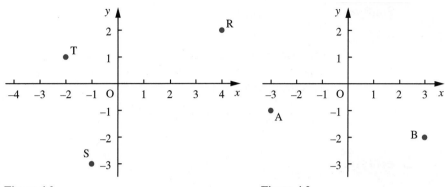

Figure 4.2   **Figure 4.3**

Solution   As plotted in Figure 4.2

(a) R has coordinates $(4, 2)$.

(b) S has coordinates $(-1, -3)$.

(c) T has coordinates $(-2, 1)$.

Example 4.2   State the coordinates of the points A and B as shown in Figure 4.3.

Solution   A has coordinates $(-3, -1)$; B has coordinates $(3, -2)$.

Example 4.3   **Electrode coordinates**

Figure 4.4 shows two electrodes inside an evacuated glass envelope. State the coordinates of the four points A, B, C and D.

Figure 4.4
Electrode coordinates.

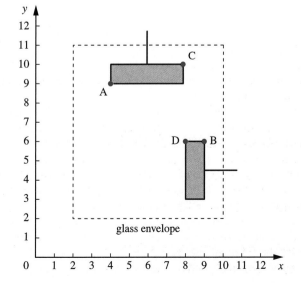

Solution   A has coordinates (4, 9).

B has coordinates (9, 6).

C has coordinates (8, 10).

D has coordinates (8, 6).

Exercises 4.2

1 Plot the following points: A(2, −2), B(−2, 1), C(−1, 0), D(0, −2).

2 State the coordinates of the points U, V and W as shown in Figure 4.5.

3 A point P lies on the *x* axis. State the *y* coordinate of P.

4 A point Q lies on the *y* axis. State the *x* coordinate of Q.

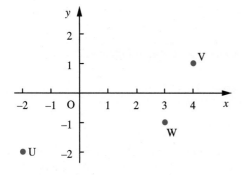

Figure 4.5

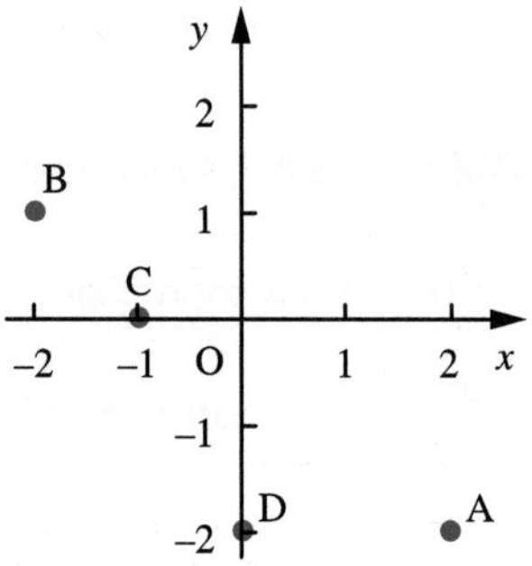

Figure 4.6

Solutions

1 Figure 4.6 shows the points A, B, C and D.

2 U(−2, −2), V(4, 1), W(3, −1)

3 0

4 0

4.3 Cartesian coordinate system – three dimensions

Many engineering problems require the use of three dimensions. Figure 4.7 illustrates a three-dimensional coordinate system. It comprises three axes, *x*, *y* and *z*. The axes are all at right angles to one another and intersect at the origin, O.

The position of any point in three-dimensional space is given by specifying its *x*, *y* and *z* coordinates. By convention the *x* coordinate is stated first, then the *y* coordinate and finally the *z* coordinate. For example, P(2, 3, 4) has an *x* coordinate of 2, a *y* coordinate of 3 and a *z* coordinate of 4. It is illustrated in Figure 4.7. From the origin, P

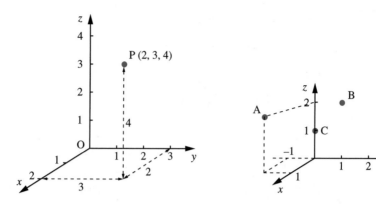

Figure 4.7 Cartesian coordinate system in three dimensions.

Figure 4.8 The points A, B and C are plotted in three dimensions.

is located by travelling 2 units in the x direction, followed by 3 units in the y direction, followed by 4 units in the z direction.

Note that, as with a two-dimensional system, coordinates can be negative.

Example 4.4 Plot the following points: A(1, −1, 2), B(0, 1, 2), C(0, 0, 1).

Solution Figure 4.8 illustrates the points A, B and C.

We now consider the equation of a plane. Any point on the x–y plane has a z coordinate of 0. Hence the equation of the x–y plane is $z = 0$. Similarly $z = 1$ represents a plane parallel to the x–y plane but 1 unit above it. Point C in Figure 4.8 lies in the plane $z = 1$. All points in this plane have a z coordinate of 1.

A and B in Figure 4.8 lie in the plane $z = 2$. All points in this plane have a z coordinate of 2.

Exercises 4.3

1 Plot the points A(2, 0, −1), B(1, −1, 1) and C(−1, 1, 2).

2 State the equation of the plane passing through (4, 7, −1), (3, 0, −1) and (1, 2, −1).

3 State the equation of the plane passing through (3, 1, 7), (−1, 1, 0) and (6, 1, −3).

Solutions

1 Figure 4.9 illustrates the points A, B and C.

2 $z = -1$

3 $y = 1$

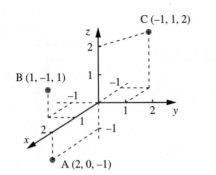

Figure 4.9

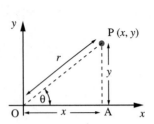

Figure 4.10 P has polar coordinates r and θ.

4.4 Polar coordinates

We have seen how the x and y coordinates of a point describe its location in the x–y plane. There is an alternative way to describe the location of a point. Figure 4.10 illustrates a point P in the x–y plane.

P has Cartesian coordinates (x, y). Hence

$$OA = x, \qquad AP = y$$

Consider the arm OP. The length of OP is the distance of P from the origin. We denote this by r, that is

$$\text{length of OP} = r$$

Clearly, r is never negative, that is $r \geqslant 0$.

We note that the angle between the positive x axis and OP is θ. The value of θ lies between 0 and 2π radians or 0° to 360° if degrees are used.

The values of r and θ are known as the **polar coordinates** of P. Conventionally, the value of r is stated first, then the value of θ. We commonly write these polar coordinates as $r \angle \theta$.

The values of r and θ specify the position of a point. Conventionally, positive values of θ are measured anticlockwise from the positive x axis.

The polar coordinates of a point, P, are $r \angle \theta$. The value of r is the distance of P from the origin; the value of θ is the angle between the positive x axis and the arm OP.

$$r \geqslant 0 \qquad 0 \leqslant \theta < 2\pi \ (0° \leqslant \theta < 360°)$$

Example 4.5 | **Pick and place robot**

Figure 4.11 shows a pick and place robot. It consists of a rotating arm the length of which can be extended and contracted. On the end of the arm is a hand which can be closed to pick up a component and opened to release it.

Figure 4.11
A pick and place robot.

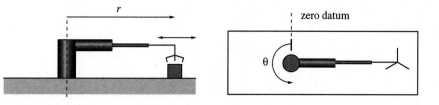

It is necessary for a computer to carry out calculations in order to find where a component is located and where to place a component. Decide upon a suitable coordinate system to use when carrying out these calculations.

Solution If we examine the geometry of the robot then we see that a polar coordinate system would be the most suitable. The centre of the coordinate system should be on the axis of rotation. The length of the arm is then given by r and the orientation of the arm is given by θ relative to an agreed zero datum mark.

Example 4.6 Plot the points P, Q and R whose polar coordinates are

(a) 2, 70°

(b) 4, 160°

(c) 3, 300°

Solution Figure 4.12 shows the three points plotted.

Figure 4.12
A point can be located by the values of its polar coordinates.

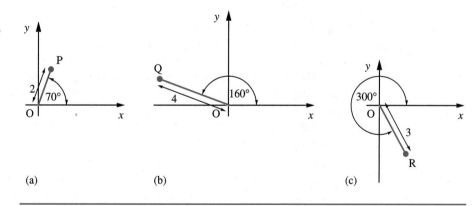

(a)   (b)   (c)

Consider, in each case, the arm from the origin to the point. The value of r gives the length of this arm. The value of θ gives the angle between the positive x axis and the arm, measuring anticlockwise from the positive x axis.

By studying $\triangle$OPA, shown in Figure 4.14, we can see that

$$\cos\theta = \frac{x}{r} \qquad \text{and so } x = r\cos\theta \qquad (4.1)$$

$$\sin\theta = \frac{y}{r} \qquad \text{and so } y = r\sin\theta \qquad (4.2)$$

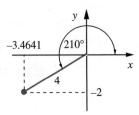

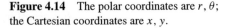

Figure 4.13 The Cartesian coordinates can be calculated from the polar coordinates.

Figure 4.14 The polar coordinates are r, θ; the Cartesian coordinates are x, y.

Hence if we know the values of r and θ, that is the polar coordinates of a point, we can use Equations (4.1) and (4.2) to calculate x and y, the Cartesian coordinates of the point.

Example 4.7 A point has polar coordinates $r = 4$, $\theta = 210°$. Calculate the Cartesian coordinates of the point. Plot the point.

Solution The Cartesian coordinates are given by

$$x = r\cos\theta = 4\cos 210° = -3.4641$$
$$y = r\sin\theta = 4\sin 210° = -2$$

Figure 4.13 illustrates the point.

We now look at the problem of calculating the polar coordinates given the Cartesian coordinates. Equations (4.1) and (4.2) can be arranged so that r and θ can be found from the values of x and y. Consider a typical point P as shown in Figure 4.14.

The Cartesian coordinates are (x, y). Suppose that the values of x and y are known. The polar coordinates are r, θ; these values are unknown. By applying Pythagoras's theorem to $\triangle OPA$ we see that

$$r^2 = x^2 + y^2$$

and so

$$r = \sqrt{x^2 + y^2}$$

Note that since r is the distance from O to P it is always positive and so the positive square root is taken.

We now express θ in terms of the Cartesian coordinates x and y. From Figure 4.14 we see that

$$\tan\theta = \frac{y}{x}$$

and hence

$$\theta = \tan^{-1}\left(\frac{y}{x}\right)$$

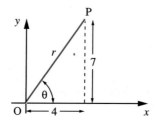

Figure 4.15 P is in the first quadrant.

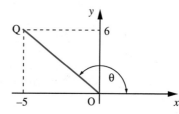

Figure 4.16 Q lies in the second quadrant.

In summary we have

$$r = \sqrt{x^2 + y^2} \qquad \theta = \tan^{-1}\left(\frac{y}{x}\right)$$

However, we need to exercise a little extra care before calculating $\tan^{-1}\left(\frac{y}{x}\right)$ and reading the result from a calculator. As an illustration note that

$$\tan 40° = 0.8391 \qquad \text{and} \qquad \tan 220° = 0.8391$$

and so $\tan^{-1}(0.8391)$ could be $40°$ or $220°$. Similarly $\tan 105° = -3.7321$ and $\tan 285° = -3.7321$ and so $\tan^{-1}(-3.7321)$ could be $105°$ or $285°$. The value given on your calculator when calculating $\tan^{-1}\left(\frac{y}{x}\right)$ may not be the actual value of θ we require. In order to clarify the situation it is always useful to sketch the Cartesian coordinates and the angle θ before embarking on the calculation.

Example 4.8 The Cartesian coordinates of P are (4, 7); those of Q are (−5, 6). Calculate the polar coordinates of P and Q.

Solution Figure 4.15 illustrates the situation for P.
Then

$$r = \sqrt{4^2 + 7^2} = \sqrt{65} = 8.0623$$

Note from Figure 4.15 that P is in the first quadrant, that is θ lies between $0°$ and $90°$. Now

$$\tan^{-1}\left(\frac{y}{x}\right) = \tan^{-1}\left(\frac{7}{4}\right)$$

From a calculator, $\tan^{-1}\left(\frac{7}{4}\right) = 60.26°$. Since we know that θ lies between $0°$ and $90°$ then clearly $60.26°$ is the required value.
The polar coordinates of P are $r = 8.0623$, $\theta = 60.26°$.
Figure 4.16 illustrates the situation for Q.
We have

$$r = \sqrt{(-5)^2 + 6^2} = \sqrt{61} = 7.8102$$

From Figure 4.16 we see that θ lies between 90° and 180°. Now

$$\tan^{-1}\left(\frac{y}{x}\right) = \tan^{-1}\left(\frac{6}{-5}\right) = \tan^{-1}(-1.2)$$

A calculator returns the value of $-50.19°$ which is clearly not the required value. Recall that $\tan\theta$ is periodic with period 180°. Hence the required angle is

$$180° + (-50.19°) = 129.81°$$

The polar coordinates of Q are $r = 7.8102, \theta = 129.81°$.

Exercises 4.4

1 Given the polar coordinates, calculate the Cartesian coordinates of each point.

   (a) $r = 7, \theta = 36°$

   (b) $r = 10, \theta = 101°$

   (c) $r = 15.7, \theta = 3.7$ radians

   (d) $r = 1, \theta = \dfrac{\pi}{2}$ radians

2 Given the Cartesian coordinates, calculate the polar coordinates of each point.

   (a) (7, 11)   (b) (−6, −12)   (c) (0, 15)
   (d) (−4, 6)   (e) (4, 0)   (f) (−4, 0)

Solutions

1 (a) 5.6631, 4.1145

   (b) −1.9081, 9.8163

   (c) −13.3152, −8.3184

   (d) 0, 1

2 (a) $r = 13.0384, \theta = 57.53°$

   (b) 13.4164, 243.43°

   (c) 15, 90°

   (d) 7.2111, 123.69°

   (e) 4, 0°

   (f) 4, 180°

4.5 Some simple polar curves

Using Cartesian coordinates the equation $y = mx$ describes the equation of a line passing through the origin. The equation of a line through the origin can also be stated using polar coordinates. In addition, it is easy to state the equation of a circle using polar coordinates.

Equation of a line

Consider all points whose polar coordinates are of the form $r\angle45°$. Note that the angle θ is fixed at 45° but that r, the distance from the origin, can vary. As r increases, a line at 45° to the positive x axis is traced out. Figure 4.17 illustrates this.

  Thus, $\theta = 45°$ is the equation of a line starting at the origin, at 45° to the positive x axis.

  In general, $\theta = \theta_c$, where θ_c is a fixed value, is the equation of a line inclined at θ_c to the positive x axis, starting at the origin.

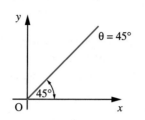

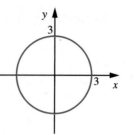

Figure 4.17 When θ is fixed and r varies, a straight line from the origin is traced out.

Figure 4.18 When r is fixed and θ varies, a circle is swept out.

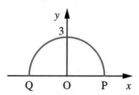

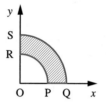

Figure 4.19 As θ varies from $0°$ to $180°$ a semicircle is traced out.

Figure 4.20 Surface for Example 4.10.

Equation of a circle, centre on the origin

Consider all points with polar coordinates $3\angle\theta$. Here r, the distance from the origin, is fixed at 3 and θ can vary. As θ varies from $0°$ to $360°$ a circle, radius 3, centre on the origin, is swept out. Figure 4.18 illustrates this.

In general $r = r_c$ where r_c is a fixed value, $0° \leqslant \theta \leqslant 360°$ describes a circle of radius r_c, centred on the origin.

Example 4.9 Draw the curve traced out by $r = 3, 0° \leqslant \theta \leqslant 180°$.

Solution Here r is fixed at 3 and θ varies from $0°$ to $180°$. As θ varies a semicircle is traced out. Figure 4.19 illustrates this.

At P, $\theta = 0°$, while at Q, $\theta = 180°$.

Example 4.10 Describe the surface defined by $1 \leqslant r \leqslant 2, 0° \leqslant \theta \leqslant 90°$.

Solution Here r varies from 1 to 2 and θ varies from $0°$ to $90°$. Figure 4.20 illustrates the surface so formed.

At P, $r = 1$, $\theta = 0°$; at Q, $r = 2$, $\theta = 0°$; at R, $r = 1$, $\theta = 90°$; at S, $r = 2$, $\theta = 90°$.

Exercises 4.5

1 Describe the curve defined by $r = 2, 0° \leqslant \theta \leqslant 90°$.

2 Describe the surface defined by $0 \leqslant r \leqslant 2$, $30° \leqslant \theta \leqslant 45°$.

Solutions

1 This is a quarter circle of radius 2 as shown in Figure 4.21.

2 Figure 4.22 illustrates the surface. OP is set at 30° to the x axis; OQ is at 45° to the x axis. OP = OQ = 2.

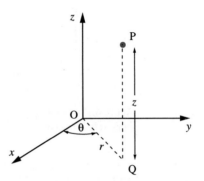

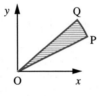

Figure 4.21

Figure 4.22

Figure 4.23 The cylindrical polar coordinates of P are (r, θ, z).

4.6 Cylindrical polar coordinates

Consider the problem of studying the flow of water around a cylinder. Such a problem would be studied by engineers when investigating the forces exerted by the sea on the cylindrical supports of oil-rigs. Because the cylinder is the key shape in such a problem it makes sense to use a coordinate system specifically designed for such situations; such a system is cylindrical polar coordinates.

Cylindrical polar coordinates comprise polar coordinates with the addition of a vertical, or z, axis. Figure 4.23 illustrates a typical point, P, and its cylindrical polar coordinates.

The point Q is in the x–y plane and lies directly below P. Q is the **projection** of P onto the x–y plane.

Consider a point P in three-dimensional space, with Cartesian coordinates (x, y, z). We can also describe the position of P using cylindrical polar coordinates. To do this, the x and y coordinates are expressed as their equivalent polar coordinates, while the z coordinate remains unaltered. Hence the cylindrical polar coordinates of a point have the form (r, θ, z).

Recall that r is the length of the arm OQ (see Figure 4.23); that is, it is the distance of a point in the x–y plane from the origin, and so $r \geqslant 0$. The angle θ is measured from the positive x axis to the arm OQ and so θ has values between $0°$ and $360°$ or 2π radians. Finally, z is positive for points above the x–y plane and negative for points below the x–y plane. In summary

$$r \geqslant 0, \qquad 0 \leqslant \theta < 2\pi, \qquad -\infty < z < \infty$$

We can relate the Cartesian coordinates, (x, y, z), to the cylindrical polar coordinates, (r, θ, z). The following key point does this.

$$x = r \cos \theta \qquad r \geqslant 0$$
$$y = r \sin \theta \qquad 0 \leqslant \theta < 2\pi$$
$$z = z$$

Example 4.11 Fluid flow along a pipe

Cylindrical polar coordinates provide a convenient framework for analyzing liquid flow down a pipe. The radial symmetry of a pipe makes it the natural choice. The distance along the pipe is defined using z. In order to utilize the radial symmetry of the pipe it is necessary to align the z axis with the centre axis of the pipe. Figure 4.24 illustrates the arrangement. Distance from the centre of the pipe is defined by r. The angle θ is used in conjunction with z and r to fix the position within the pipe. A typical problem that may be analyzed is the variation in fluid velocity with distance from the centre of the pipe. For smooth flow, liquid tends to travel faster at the centre of a pipe than it does near the edge.

Figure 4.24
Fluid flow along a pipe.

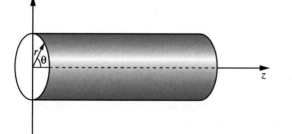

Example 4.12

The Cartesian coordinates of P are $(4, 7, -6)$. State the cylindrical polar coordinates of P.

Solution

We have

$$x = 4, \qquad y = 7, \qquad z = -6$$

Using $x = 4$ and $y = 7$ the values of r and θ are found to be $r = 8.0623$, $\theta = 60.26°$ (see Example 4.8). The z coordinate remains unchanged. Hence the cylindrical polar coordinates are $(8.0623, 60.26°, -6)$.

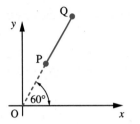

Figure 4.25 At P, $r = 1$; at Q, $r = 2$.

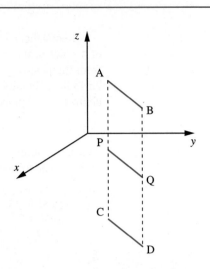

Figure 4.26 On the line AB, $z = 1$; on the line CD, $z = -1$.

Example 4.13   Describe the figure defined by

(a) $1 \leqslant r \leqslant 2, \theta = 60°, -1 \leqslant z \leqslant 1$

(b) $r = 1, 0° \leqslant \theta \leqslant 90°, 0 \leqslant z \leqslant 2$

Solution   (a) Consider the r and θ coordinates first. The r coordinate varies from 1 to 2 while θ is fixed at 60°. This represents the line PQ as shown in Figure 4.25. At P the value of r is 1; at Q the value of r is 2. The length of PQ is 1 and it is inclined at 60° to the x axis.

Now, we note that z varies from -1 to 1. We imagine the line PQ moving in the z direction from $z = -1$ to $z = 1$. This movement sweeps out a plane. Figure 4.26 illustrates this.

(b) The r coordinate is fixed at $r = 1$. The θ coordinate varies from 0° to 90°. This produces the quarter circle, AB, as shown in Figure 4.27. At A, $r = 1$, $\theta = 0°$; at B, $r = 1, \theta = 90°$.

Examining the z coordinate, we see that z varies from 0 to 2. As z varies from 0 to 2, we imagine the curve AB sweeping out the curved surface as shown in Figure 4.28. At C, $r = 1, \theta = 0°, z = 2$; at D, $r = 1, \theta = 90°, z = 2$. This surface is part of a cylinder.

If the range of values of a coordinate is not given it is understood that that variable varies across all its possible values. For example, a curve may be described by $r = 1, z = -2$. Here there is no mention of the values that θ can have. It is assumed that θ can have its full range of values, that is 0° to 360°.

Figure 4.27 As θ varies from $0°$ to $90°$, a quarter circle is swept out.

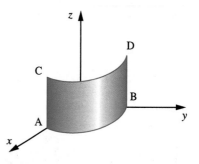

Figure 4.28 As z varies from 0 to 2, the curve AB sweeps out the curved surface.

Exercises 4.6

1 Express the following Cartesian coordinates as cylindrical polar coordinates.
(a) $(-2, -1, 4)$ (b) $(0, 3, -1)$
(c) $(-4, 5, 0)$

2 Express the following cylindrical polar coordinates as Cartesian coordinates.
(a) $(3, 70°, 7)$ (b) $(1, 200°, 6)$
(c) $(5, 180°, 0)$

3 Describe the surface defined by
(a) $z = 0$
(b) $z = -1$
(c) $r = 2, z = 1$
(d) $\theta = 90°, z = 3$
(e) $r = 2, 0 \leqslant z \leqslant 4$

Solutions

1 (a) $(\sqrt{5}, 206.57°, 4)$
(b) $(3, 90°, -1)$
(c) $(\sqrt{41}, 128.66°, 0)$

2 (a) $(1.0261, 2.8191, 7)$
(b) $(-0.9397, -0.3420, 6)$
(c) $(-5, 0, 0)$

3 (a) the $x-y$ plane

(b) a plane parallel to the $x-y$ plane and 1 unit below it
(c) a circle, radius 2, parallel to the $x-y$ plane and with centre at $(0, 0, 1)$
(d) a line 3 units above the positive y axis and parallel to it
(e) the curved surface of a cylinder, radius 2, height 4

4.7 Spherical polar coordinates

When problems involve spheres, for example modelling the flow of oil around a ball bearing, it may be useful to use **spherical polar coordinates**. The position of a point is given by three coordinates, (R, θ, ϕ). These are illustrated in Figure 4.29.

Consider a typical point, P. We look at each of the three coordinates in turn.

The value of R is the distance of the point from the origin; that is, R is the length of OP. Note that $R \geqslant 0$.

Figure 4.29
Spherical polar
coordinates are
(R, θ, ϕ).

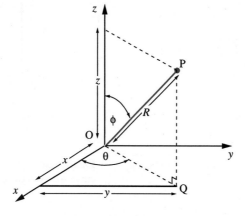

Let Q be the projection of P onto the x–y plane. Then θ is the angle between the positive x axis and OQ. Thus, θ has the same definition as for polar and cylindrical polar coordinates. Note that θ can have any value from $0°$ to $360°$.

Consider the line OP. Then ϕ is the angle between the positive z axis and OP. The angle ϕ can have values between $0°$ and $180°$. When P is above the x–y plane, then ϕ lies between $0°$ and $90°$; when P lies below the x–y plane, then ϕ is between $90°$ and $180°$. When $\phi = 0°$, then P is on the positive z axis; when $\phi = 90°$, P lies in the x–y plane; when $\phi = 180°$, P lies on the negative z axis.

We can determine equations which relate the Cartesian coordinates, (x, y, z), and the spherical polar coordinates, (R, θ, ϕ).

Note that some books describe spherical polar coordinates as (R, ϕ, θ), that is the definitions of θ and ϕ are interchanged. Be aware of this when reading other texts.

Consider $\triangle$OPQ. Note that $\angle$OQP is a right angle and so

$$OQ = OP \sin \phi = R \sin \phi$$

OQ lies in the x–y plane and so

$$x = OQ \, \cos \theta = R \sin \phi \cos \theta$$
$$y = OQ \, \sin \theta = R \sin \phi \sin \theta$$

We also note that

$$z = OP \, \cos \phi = R \cos \phi$$

In summary we have

$$x = R \sin \phi \cos \theta$$
$$y = R \sin \phi \sin \theta$$
$$z = R \cos \phi$$

and

$$R \geqslant 0, \qquad 0 \leqslant \phi \leqslant \pi \ (180°) \qquad 0 \leqslant \theta < 2\pi \ (360°)$$

Example 4.14   Show that

$$R = \sqrt{x^2 + y^2 + z^2}$$

Solution   From Figure 4.29

$$x^2 + y^2 = OQ^2$$

From $\triangle OPQ$

$$OP^2 = OQ^2 + PQ^2$$

But OP = R and PQ = z, so

$$R^2 = x^2 + y^2 + z^2$$

and so

$$R = \sqrt{x^2 + y^2 + z^2}$$

Example 4.15   Describe the surface $R = 4$.

Solution   We have $R = 4$ and θ and ϕ can vary across their full range of values. Such points generate a sphere of radius 4, centred on the origin.

Exercises 4.7

1 A point has spherical polar coordinates $(3, 40°, 70°)$. Determine the Cartesian coordinates.

2 A point has Cartesian coordinates $(1, 2, 3)$.

Determine the spherical polar coordinates.

3 Describe the surface $R = 1, 0° \leqslant \theta \leqslant 360°$, $0° \leqslant \phi \leqslant 90°$.

Solutions

1 $(2.1595, 1.8121, 1.0261)$

2 $R = 3.7417, \theta = 63.43°, \phi = 36.70°$

3 A hemisphere of radius 1. The flat side is on the x–y plane.

Review exercises 4

1 P has Cartesian coordinates $(6, -3, -2)$. Calculate the distance of P from the origin.

2 P has Cartesian coordinates $(-4, -3)$. Calculate the polar coordinates of P.

3 P has polar coordinates $(5, 240°)$. Calculate the Cartesian coordinates of P.

4 Describe the surface defined by $1 \leqslant r \leqslant 4, 0° \leqslant \theta \leqslant 90°$.

5 Calculate the cylindrical polar coordinates of a point with Cartesian coordinates $(-1, 4, 1)$.

6 Describe the surface $x = 0$ in three dimensions.

7 A point has Cartesian coordinates $(-1, -1, 2)$. Calculate the spherical polar coordinates of the point.

8 Describe the surface $R = 2, 0° \leqslant \theta \leqslant 180°$, $0° \leqslant \phi \leqslant 180°$.

9 Describe the three-dimensional surface defined by $x = y$.

10 The sphere defined by $R = 2$ intersects the plane defined by $z = 1$. Describe the curve of intersection.

Solutions

1 7

2 $5, 216.87°$

3 $-2.5, -4.3301$

4 Figure 4.30 illustrates the surface.

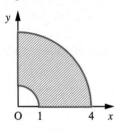

Figure 4.30

5 $(4.1231, 104.04°, 1)$

6 y–z plane

7 $R = \sqrt{6}, \theta = 225°, \phi = 35.26°$

8 A hemisphere of radius 2. The flat surface is on the x–z plane.

9 The surface is a plane generated by moving the line $y = x$ up and down the z axis.

10 A circle of radius $\sqrt{3}$, centre $(0, 0, 1)$, in the plane $z = 1$.

5 Discrete mathematics

Chapter 5 Contents

5.1	Introduction	150
5.2	Set theory	150
5.3	Logic	158
5.4	Boolean algebra	160
	Review exercises	171

5.1 Introduction

The term **discrete** is used to describe a growing number of modern branches of mathematics involving topics such as set theory, logic, Boolean algebra, difference equations and z transforms. These topics are particularly relevant to the needs of electrical and electronic engineers. **Set theory** provides us with a language for precisely specifying a great deal of mathematical work. Over the next few years this language will become particularly important as more and more emphasis is placed upon verification of software. **Boolean algebra** finds its main use in the design of digital electronic circuits. Given that an increasing proportion of electronic circuits are digital rather than analog, this is an important area of study. Digital electronic circuits confine themselves to two effective voltage levels rather than the range of voltage levels used by analog electronic circuits. These make them easier to design and manufacture as tolerances are not so critical. Digital circuits are becoming more complex each year and one of the few ways of dealing with this complexity is to use mathematics. One of the likely trends for the future is that more and more circuit designs will be proved to be correct using mathematics before they are implemented. **Difference equations** and z **transforms** are of increasing importance in fields such as digital control and digital signal processing. We shall deal with these in Chapter 22.

5.2 Set theory

A **set** is any collection of objects, things or states.

The objects may be numbers, letters, days of the week, or, in fact, anything under discussion. One way of describing a set is to list the whole collection of members or **elements** and enclose them in braces { }. Consider the following examples.

$A = \{1, 0\}$ the set of binary digits, one and zero

$B = \{\text{off, on}\}$ the set of possible states of a two-state system

$C = \{\text{high, low}\}$ the set of effective voltage levels in a digital electronic circuit

$D = \{0, 1, 2, 3, 4, 5, 6, 7, 8, 9\}$ the set of digits used in the decimal system

Notice that we usually use a capital letter to represent a set. To state that a particular object belongs to a particular set we use the symbol $\in$ which means 'is a member of'. So, for example, we can write

off $\in B$ $3 \in D$

Likewise, $\notin$ means 'is not a member of' so that

low $\notin B$ $5 \notin A$

are sensible statements.

Listing members of a set is fine when there are relatively few but is useless if we are dealing with very large sets. Clearly, we could not possibly write down all the members of the set of whole numbers because there is an infinite number. To assist us special symbols have been introduced to stand for some commonly used sets. These are

$\mathbb{N}$	the set of non-negative whole numbers, $0, 1, 2, 3, \ldots$
$\mathbb{N}^+$	the set of positive whole numbers, $1, 2, 3, \ldots$
$\mathbb{Z}$	the set of whole numbers, positive, negative and zero, $\ldots - 3, -2, -1, 0, 1, 2, 3 \ldots$
$\mathbb{R}$	the set of all real numbers
$\mathbb{R}^+$	the set of positive real numbers
$\mathbb{R}^-$	the set of negative real numbers
$\mathbb{Q}$	the set of rational numbers

Note that a real number is any number in the interval $(-\infty, \infty)$.

Another way of defining a set is to give a rule by which all members can be found. Consider the following notation:

$$A = \{x : x \in \mathbb{R} \text{ and } x < 2\}$$

This reads 'A is the set of values of x such that x is a member of the set of real numbers and x is less than 2'. Thus A corresponds to the interval $(-\infty, 2)$. Using this notation other sets can be defined.

Note that

$$\mathbb{R}^+ = \{x : x \in \mathbb{R} \text{ and } x > 0\}$$
$$\mathbb{R}^- = \{x : x \in \mathbb{R} \text{ and } x < 0\}$$

Example 5.1

Use set notation to describe the intervals on the x axis given by

(a) $[0, 2]$ (b) $[0, 2)$ (c) $[-9, 9]$

Solution

(a) $\{x : x \in \mathbb{R} \text{ and } 0 \leqslant x \leqslant 2\}$

(b) $\{x : x \in \mathbb{R} \text{ and } 0 \leqslant x < 2\}$

(c) $\{x : x \in \mathbb{R} \text{ and } -9 \leqslant x \leqslant 9\}$

Sometimes we shall be content to use an English description of a set of objects, such as

M is the set of capacitors made by machine M
N is the set of capacitors made by machine N
Q is the set of faulty capacitors

5.2.1 Equal sets

Two sets are said to be equal if they contain exactly the same members. For example, the sets $\{9, 5, 2\}$ and $\{5, 9, 2\}$ are identical. The order in which we write down the members is immaterial. The sets $\{2, 2, 5, 9\}$ and $\{2, 5, 9\}$ are equal since repetition of elements is ignored.

Figure 5.1
Venn diagram for
Example 5.2.

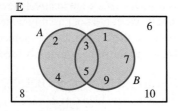

5.2.2 Venn diagrams

Venn diagrams provide a graphical way of picturing sets which often aids understanding. The sets are drawn as regions, usually circles, from which various properties can be observed.

Example 5.2

Suppose we are interested in discussing the set of positive whole numbers between 1 and 10. Let $A = \{2, 3, 4, 5\}$ and $B = \{1, 3, 5, 7, 9\}$. The Venn diagram representing these sets is shown in Figure 5.1. The set containing all the numbers of interest is called the **universal set**, $\mathbb{E}$. $\mathbb{E}$ is represented by the rectangular region. Sets A and B are represented by the interiors of the circles and it is evident that 2, 3, 4 and 5 are members of A while 1, 3, 5, 7 and 9 are members of B. It is also clear that $6 \notin A$, $6 \notin B$, $8 \notin A$, $8 \notin B$. The elements 3 and 5 are common to both sets.

The set containing all the members of interest is called the universal set $\mathbb{E}$.

It is useful to ask whether two or more sets have elements in common. This leads to the following definition.

5.2.3 Intersection

Given sets A and B, a new set which contains the elements common to both A and B is called the **intersection** of A and B, written as

$$A \cap B = \{x : x \in A \text{ and } x \in B\}$$

In Example 5.2, we see that $A \cap B = \{3, 5\}$, that is $3 \in A \cap B$ and $5 \in A \cap B$. If the set $A \cap B$ has no elements we say the sets A and B are **disjoint** and write $A \cap B = \varnothing$, where $\varnothing$ denotes the **empty set**.

A set with no elements is called an empty set and is denoted by $\varnothing$.
If $A \cap B = \varnothing$, then A and B are disjoint sets.

5.2.4 Union

Given two sets A and B, the set which contains all the elements of A and those of B is called the **union** of A and B, written as

$$A \cup B = \{x : x \in A \text{ or } x \in B \text{ or both}\}$$

In Example 5.2, $A \cup B = \{1, 2, 3, 4, 5, 7, 9\}$. We note that although the elements 3 and 5 are common to both sets they are listed only once.

5.2.5 Subsets

If all the members of a set A are also members of a set B we say A is a **subset** of B and write $A \subset B$. We have already met a number of subsets. Convince yourself that

$$\mathbb{N} \subset \mathbb{Z} \text{ and } \mathbb{Z} \subset \mathbb{R}$$

Example 5.3

If M represents the set of all capacitors manufactured by machine M, and M_f represents the faulty capacitors made by machine M, then clearly $M_f \subset M$.

5.2.6 Complement

If we are given a well-defined universal set $\mathbb{E}$ and a set A with $A \subset \mathbb{E}$, then the set of members of $\mathbb{E}$ that are not in A is called the **complement** of A and is written as $\overline{A}$. Clearly $A \cup \overline{A} = \mathbb{E}$. There are no members in the set $A \cap \overline{A}$, that is $A \cap \overline{A} = \varnothing$.

Example 5.4

A company has a number of machines which manufacture thyristors. We consider only two machines, M and N. A small proportion made by each is faulty. Denoting the sets of faulty thyristors made by M and N by M_f and N_f, respectively, depict this situation on a Venn diagram. Describe the sets $M_f \cup N_f$ and $\overline{M \cup N}$.

Solution

Let $\mathbb{E}$ be the universal set of all thyristors manufactured by the company. The Venn diagram is shown in Figure 5.2. Note in particular that $M \cap N = \varnothing$. There can be no thyristors in the intersection since if a thyristor is made by machine M it cannot be made by machine N and vice versa. Thus M and N are disjoint sets. Also note $M_f \subset M$, $N_f \subset N$. The set $M_f \cup N_f$ is the set of faulty thyristors manufactured by either machine M or N. The set $\overline{M \cup N}$ is the set of thyristors made by machines other than M or N.

We have seen how the operations $\cap$, $\cup$ can be used to define new sets. It is not difficult to show that a number of laws hold, most of which are obvious from the inspection of an appropriate Venn diagram.

Figure 5.2
Venn diagram for
Example 5.4.

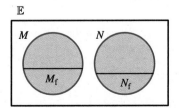

Table 5.1
The laws of set
algebra.

$$A \cup B = B \cup A$$
$$A \cap B = B \cap A$$
} Commutative laws

$$A \cup (B \cup C) = (A \cup B) \cup C$$
$$A \cap (B \cap C) = (A \cap B) \cap C$$
} Associative laws

$$A \cap (B \cup C) = (A \cap B) \cup (A \cap C)$$
$$A \cup (B \cap C) = (A \cup B) \cap (A \cup C)$$
} Distributive laws

$$A \cup \varnothing = A$$
$$A \cap \mathbb{E} = A$$
} Identity laws

$$A \cup \overline{A} = \mathbb{E}$$
$$A \cap \overline{A} = \varnothing$$
$$\overline{\overline{A}} = A$$
} Complement laws

Table 5.2
Laws derivable from
Table 5.1.

$$A \cup (A \cap B) = A$$
$$A \cap (A \cup B) = A$$
} Absorption laws

$$(A \cap B) \cup (A \cap \overline{B}) = A$$
$$(A \cup B) \cap (A \cup \overline{B}) = A$$
} Minimization laws

$$\overline{A \cup B} = \overline{A} \cap \overline{B}$$
$$\overline{A \cap B} = \overline{A} \cup \overline{B}$$
} De Morgan's laws

5.2.7 Laws of set algebra

For any sets A, B, C and a universal set $\mathbb{E}$, we have the laws in Table 5.1. From these it is possible to prove the laws given in Table 5.2.

5.2.8 Sets and functions

If we are given two sets, A and B, a useful exercise is to examine relationships, given by rules, between the elements of A and the elements of B. For example, if $A = \{0, 1, 4, 9\}$ and $B = \{-3, -2, -1, 0, 1, 2, 3\}$ then each element of B is plus or minus the square root of some element of A. We can depict this as in Figure 5.3.

The rule, which when given an element of A, produces an element of B, is called a **relation**. If the rule of the relation is given the symbol r we write

$$r : A \to B$$

and say 'the relation r **maps** elements of the set A to elements of the set B'. For the example above, we can write $r : 1 \to \pm 1$, $r : 4 \to \pm 2$, and generally $r : x \to \pm\sqrt{x}$. The set from which we choose our input is called the **domain**; the set to which we map is called the **co-domain**; the subset of the co-domain actually used is called the **range**. As we shall see this need not be the whole of the co-domain.

A relation r maps elements of a set D, called the domain, to one or more elements of a set C called the co-domain. We write

$$r : D \to C$$

$r : A \rightarrow B$

'take plus or minus the square root of'

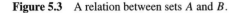

$s : D \rightarrow E$

$s : m \rightarrow 3m + 1$

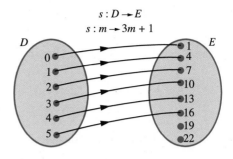

Figure 5.3   A relation between sets A and B.

Figure 5.4   The relation s maps elements of D to E.

Example 5.5   If $D = \{0, 1, 2, 3, 4, 5\}$ and $E = \{1, 4, 7, 10, 13, 16, 19, 22\}$ and the relation with symbol s is defined by $s : D \rightarrow E$, $s : m \rightarrow 3m + 1$, identify the domain and co-domain of s. Draw a mapping diagram to illustrate the relation. What is the range of s?

Solution   The domain of s is the set of values from which we choose our input, that is $D = \{0, 1, 2, 3, 4, 5\}$. The co-domain of s is the set to which we map, that is $E = \{1, 4, 7, 10, 13, 16, 19, 22\}$. The rule $s : m \rightarrow 3m + 1$ enables us to draw the mapping diagram. For example, $s : 3 \rightarrow 10$ and so on. The diagram is shown in Figure 5.4. The range of s is the subset of E actually used, in this case $\{1, 4, 7, 10, 13, 16\}$. We note that not all the elements of the co-domain are actually used.

The notation introduced is very similar to that for functions described in Section 2.3. This is no accident. In fact, a function is a very special form of a relation. Let us recall the definition of a function:

'A function is a rule which when given an input produces a single output'.

If we study the two relations r and s, we note that when relation r received input, it could produce two outputs. On the mapping diagram this shows up as two arrows leaving some elements in A. When relation s received an input, it produced a single output. This shows up as a single arrow leaving each element in D. Hence the relation r is not a function, whereas the relation s is. This leads to the following more rigorous definition of a function.

A function f is a relation which maps each element of a set D, called the domain, to a single element of a set C called the co-domain. We write

$$f : D \rightarrow C$$

Example 5.6   If $M = \{\text{off, on}\}$, $N = \{0, 1\}$ and we define a relation r by

$$r : M \rightarrow N$$

$$r : \text{off} \rightarrow 0 \qquad r : \text{on} \rightarrow 1$$

then the relation r is a function since each element in M is mapped to a single element in N.

Example 5.7   If $P = \{0, 1\}$ and $Q = \{high\}$ and we define a relation r by

$$r : P \rightarrow Q$$
$$r : 1 \rightarrow high$$

then r is not a function since each element in P is not mapped to an element in Q.

All of the functions described in Chapter 2 have domains which are subsets of the real numbers $\mathbb{R}$. The input to each function is the particular value of the independent variable chosen from the domain and the output is the value of the dependent variable. When dealing with continuous domains the graphs we have already considered replace the mapping diagrams.

Example 5.8   Find the domain, D, of the rational function $f : D \rightarrow \mathbb{R}$ given by

$$f : x \rightarrow \frac{3x}{x - 2}$$

Solution   Since no domain is given, we choose it to be the largest set possible. This is the set of all real numbers except the value $x = 2$ at which point f is not defined. We have $D = \{x : x \in \mathbb{R}, x \neq 2\}$.

Exercises 5.2

1   Use set notation to describe the intervals on the x axis given by

(a) $(-3, 2)$

(b) $[0, 2]$

(c) $[-2, -1)$

(d) $(3, 6]$

(e) $|x| < 1$

2   Sketch the following sets. [*Hint*: see Section 2.2 on open and closed intervals.]

(a) $\{x : x \in \mathbb{R} \text{ and } 2 < x \leqslant 4\}$

(b) $\{x : x \in \mathbb{R} \text{ and } -1 \leqslant x \leqslant 0\}$

(c) $\{x : x \in \mathbb{R} \text{ and } 0 \leqslant x < 2\}$

(d) $\{x : x \in \mathbb{R} \text{ and } 1 < x < 3\}$

3   Using the definitions given in Section 5.2, state whether each of the following is true or false.

(a) $7 \in \mathbb{Z}$

(b) $\mathbb{R}^- \cap \mathbb{Q} = \varnothing$

(c) $0.7 \notin \mathbb{Q}$

(d) $\mathbb{N}^+ \cup \mathbb{Q} = \mathbb{R}^+$

(e) $\mathbb{R}^- \cap \mathbb{N} = \varnothing$

(f) $\mathbb{R} \cap \mathbb{Z} = \mathbb{Z}$

(g) $5 \in \mathbb{Q}$

(h) $\mathbb{N} \subset \mathbb{Q}$

4   If $A = \{1, 3, 5, 7, 9, 11\}$ and $B = \{3, 4, 5, 6\}$ find

(a) $A \cap B$

(b) $A \cup B$

5 Given $A = \{1, 2, 3, 4, 5, 6\}$, $B = \{2, 4, 6, 8, 10\}$ and $C = \{3, 6, 9\}$ state the elements of each of the following:

(a) $A \cap B$

(b) $B \cap C$

(c) $A \cap C$

(d) $A \cap B \cap C$

(e) $A \cap (B \cup C)$

(f) $B \cup (A \cap C)$

6 Write out all the members of the following sets.

(a) $A = \{x : x \in \mathbb{N} \text{ and } x < 10\}$

(b) $B = \{x : x \in \mathbb{R} \text{ and } 0 \leqslant x \leqslant 10 \text{ and } x \text{ is divisible by } 3\}$

7 The sets A, B and C are given by $A = \{1, 3, 5, 7, 9\}$, $B = \{0, 2, 4, 6\}$ and $C = \{1, 5, 9\}$ and the universal set, $\mathbb{E} = \{0, 1, 2, \dots, 9\}$.

(a) Represent the sets on a Venn diagram.

(b) State $A \cup B$.

(c) State $B \cap C$.

(d) State $\mathbb{E} \cap C$.

(e) State $\overline{A}$.

(f) State $\overline{B} \cap \overline{C}$.

(g) State $\overline{B \cup C}$.

8 Use Venn diagrams to illustrate the following for general sets C and D:

(a) $C \cap D$ (b) $C \cup D$ (c) $C \cap \overline{D}$

(d) $\overline{C \cup D}$ (e) $\overline{C \cap D}$.

9 By drawing Venn diagrams verify De Morgan's laws

$$\overline{A \cap B} = \overline{A} \cup \overline{B} \quad \text{and} \quad \overline{A \cup B} = \overline{A} \cap \overline{B}$$

10 For sets $A = \{0, 1, 2\}$ and $B = \{3, 4\}$, draw a mapping diagram to illustrate the following relations. Determine which relations are functions. For those that are not functions, give reasons for your decision.

(a) $r : A \to B, r : 0 \to 3, r : 1 \to 4,$
$r : 2 \to 4$

(b) $s : A \to B, s : 0 \to 3, s : 0 \to 4,$
$s : 1 \to 3, s : 2 \to 3$

(c) $t : A \to B, t : 0 \to 3, t : 1 \to 4$

11 If $A = \{1, 3, 5, 7\}$ and $B = \{1, 2, 3, 4\}$, draw a mapping diagram to illustrate the relation $r : A \to B$, where r is the relation 'is bigger than'. Is r a function?

Solutions

1 (a) $\{x : x \in \mathbb{R} \text{ and } -3 < x < 2\}$

(b) $\{x : x \in \mathbb{R} \text{ and } 0 \leqslant x \leqslant 2\}$

(c) $\{x : x \in \mathbb{R} \text{ and } -2 \leqslant x < -1\}$

(d) $\{x : x \in \mathbb{R} \text{ and } 3 < x \leqslant 6\}$

(e) $\{x : x \in \mathbb{R} \text{ and } -1 < x < 1\}$

2 See Figure S.6.

(a) 0 1 2 3 4 5 x (b) −1 0 1 x

(c) 0 1 2 3 x (d) 0 1 2 3 4 x

Figure S.6

3 (a) T   (b) F   (c) F   (d) F

(e) T   (f) T   (g) T   (h) T

4 (a) $\{3, 5\}$ (b) $\{1, 3, 4, 5, 6, 7, 9, 11\}$

5 (a) $\{2, 4, 6\}$

(b) $\{6\}$

(c) $\{3, 6\}$

(d) $\{6\}$

(e) $\{2, 3, 4, 6\}$

(f) $\{2, 3, 4, 6, 8, 10\}$

6 (a) $\{0, 1, 2, 3, 4, 5, 6, 7, 8, 9\}$

(b) $\{0, 3, 6, 9\}$

7 (a) See Figure S.7.

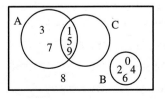

Figure S.7

(b) $\{0, 1, 2, 3, 4, 5, 6, 7, 9\}$

(c) $\varnothing$

(d) $\{1, 5, 9\}$

(e) $\{0, 2, 4, 6, 8\}$

(f) $\{3, 7, 8\}$

(g) $\{3, 7, 8\}$

8 See Figure S.8.

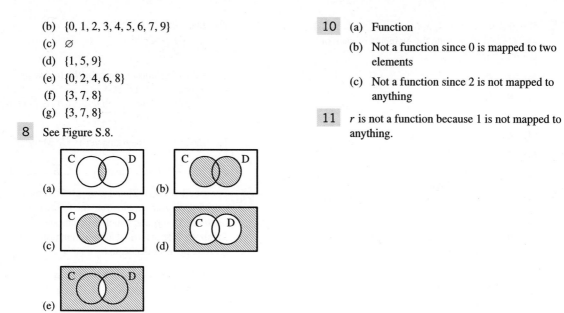

Figure S.8

10 (a) Function

(b) Not a function since 0 is mapped to two elements

(c) Not a function since 2 is not mapped to anything

11 r is not a function because 1 is not mapped to anything.

5.3 Logic

In Section 5.4 we will examine Boolean algebra. This concerns itself with the manipulation of logic statements and so is suitable for analysing digital logic circuits. In this section we introduce the basic concepts of logic by means of logic gates as these form the usual starting point for engineers studying this topic.

5.3.1 The OR gate

The OR gate is an electronic device which receives two inputs each in the form of a binary digit, that is 0 or 1, and produces a binary digit as output, depending upon the values of the two inputs. It is represented by the symbol shown in Figure 5.5.

A and B are the two inputs, and F is the single output. As high (1) or low (0)

Table 5.3 The truth table for an OR gate with inputs A and B.

A	B	$F = A + B$
1	1	1
1	0	1
0	1	1
0	0	0

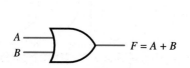

Figure 5.5 Symbol for an OR gate.

Table 5.4 The truth table for an AND gate with inputs A and B.

A	B	$F = A \cdot B$
1	1	1
1	0	0
0	1	0
0	0	0

Figure 5.6 Symbol for an AND gate.

Table 5.5 The truth table for a NOT gate.

A	$F = \overline{A}$
1	0
0	1

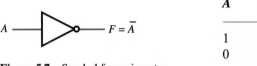

Figure 5.7 Symbol for an inverter.

voltages are applied to A and B various possible outputs are achieved, these being defined by means of a **truth table** as shown in Table 5.3. So, for example, if a low (0) voltage is applied to A and a high (1) voltage is applied to B, the output is a high (1) voltage at F. We note that a '1' appears in the right-hand column of the truth table whenever A or B takes the value 1, hence the name OR gate. We use the symbol $+$ to represent OR. Because it connects the variables A and B, OR is known as a **logical connective**. We shall meet other logical connectives shortly. This connective is also known as a **disjunction**, so that $A + B$ is said to be the disjunction of A and B.

5.3.2 The AND gate

It is possible to construct another electronic device called an AND gate which works in a similar way except that the output only takes the value 1 when both inputs are 1. The symbol for this gate is shown in Figure 5.6 and the complete truth table is shown in Table 5.4. The logical connective AND is given the symbol $\cdot$ and is known as a **conjunction** so that $A \cdot B$ is said to be the conjunction of A and B.

5.3.3 The inverter or NOT gate

The inverter is a device with one input and one output and has the symbol shown in Figure 5.7. It has a truth table defined by Table 5.5. If the input is A, then the output is represented by the symbol $\overline{A}$, known as the complement of A.

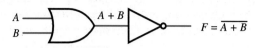

Figure 5.8 A NOT gate in series with an OR gate.

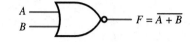

Figure 5.9 Symbol for a NOR gate.

Table 5.6 The truth table for a NOR gate.

A	B	$F = \overline{A + B}$
1	1	0
1	0	0
0	1	0
0	0	1

5.3.4 The NOR gate

This gate is logically equivalent to a NOT gate in series with an OR gate as shown in Figure 5.8. It is represented by the symbol shown in Figure 5.9 and has its truth table defined in Table 5.6.

5.3.5 The NAND gate

This gate is logically equivalent to a NOT gate in series with an AND gate as shown in Figure 5.10. It is represented by the symbol shown in Figure 5.11 and has the truth table defined by Table 5.7.

Although we have only examined gates with two inputs it is possible for a gate to have more than two. For example, the Boolean expression for a four-input NAND gate would be $F = \overline{A \cdot B \cdot C \cdot D}$ while that of a four-input OR gate would be $F = A + B + C + D$, where A, B, C and D are the inputs, and F is the output. Logic gates form the building blocks for more complicated digital electronic circuits.

5.4	Boolean algebra

Suppose A and B are binary digits, that is 1 or 0. These, together with the logical connectives $+$ and $\cdot$ and also the complement NOT, form what is known as a Boolean algebra. The quantities A and B are known as **Boolean variables**. Expressions such

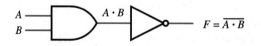

Figure 5.10 A NOT gate in series with an AND gate.

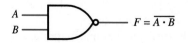

Figure 5.11 Symbol for a NAND gate.

Table 5.7 The truth table for a NAND gate.

A	B	$F = \overline{A \cdot B}$
1	1	0
1	0	1
0	1	1
0	0	1

as $A + B$, $A \cdot B$ and $\overline{A}$ are known as **Boolean expressions**. More complex Boolean expressions can be built up using more Boolean variables together with combinations of $+$, $\cdot$ and NOT; for example, we can draw up a truth table for expressions such as $(A \cdot B) + (C \cdot \overline{D})$.

We shall restrict our attention to the logic gates described in the last section although the techniques of Boolean algebra are more widely applicable. A Boolean variable can only take the values 0 or 1. For our purposes a **Boolean algebra** is a set of Boolean variables with the two operations $\cdot$ and $+$, together with the operation of taking the complement, for which certain laws hold.

5.4.1 Laws of Boolean algebra

For any Boolean variables A, B, C, we have the laws in Table 5.8. From these it is possible to prove the laws given in Table 5.9. You will notice that these laws are analogous to those of set algebra if we interpret $+$ as $\cup$, $\cdot$ as $\cap$, 1 as the universal set $\mathbb{E}$, and 0 as the empty set $\varnothing$. In ordinary algebra, multiplication takes precedence over addition. In Boolean algebra $\cdot$ takes precedence over $+$. So, for example, we can write the first absorption law without brackets, that is

$$A + A \cdot B = A$$

Similarly, the first minimization law becomes

$$A \cdot B + A \cdot \overline{B} = A$$

We shall follow this rule of precedence from now on.

Table 5.8
Laws of Boolean algebra.

$$
\left.\begin{aligned}
A + B &= B + A \\
A \cdot B &= B \cdot A
\end{aligned}\right\} \quad \text{Commutative laws}
$$

$$
\left.\begin{aligned}
A + (B + C) &= (A + B) + C \\
A \cdot (B \cdot C) &= (A \cdot B) \cdot C
\end{aligned}\right\} \quad \text{Associative laws}
$$

$$
\left.\begin{aligned}
A \cdot (B + C) &= (A \cdot B) + (A \cdot C) \\
A + (B \cdot C) &= (A + B) \cdot (A + C)
\end{aligned}\right\} \quad \text{Distributive laws}
$$

$$
\left.\begin{aligned}
A + 0 &= A \\
A \cdot 1 &= A
\end{aligned}\right\} \quad \text{Identity laws}
$$

$$
\left.\begin{aligned}
A + \overline{A} &= 1 \\
A \cdot \overline{A} &= 0 \\
\overline{\overline{A}} &= A
\end{aligned}\right\} \quad \text{Complement laws}
$$

Table 5.9
Laws derived from the laws of Table 5.8.

$$
\left.\begin{aligned}
A + (A \cdot B) &= A \\
A \cdot (A + B) &= A
\end{aligned}\right\} \quad \text{Absorption laws}
$$

$$
\left.\begin{aligned}
(A \cdot B) + (A \cdot \overline{B}) &= A \\
(A + B) \cdot (A + \overline{B}) &= A
\end{aligned}\right\} \quad \text{Minimization laws}
$$

$$
\left.\begin{aligned}
\overline{A + B} &= \overline{A} \cdot \overline{B} \\
\overline{A \cdot B} &= \overline{A} + \overline{B}
\end{aligned}\right\} \quad \text{De Morgan's laws}
$$

$$
\begin{aligned}
A + 1 &= 1 \\
A \cdot 0 &= 0
\end{aligned}
$$

Table 5.10 The possible combinations for three variables, A, B and C.

A	B	C
1	1	1
1	1	0
1	0	1
1	0	0
0	1	1
0	1	0
0	0	1
0	0	0

Table 5.11 The truth table for $A + B \cdot \overline{C}$.

A	B	C	$\overline{C}$	$B \cdot \overline{C}$	$A + B \cdot \overline{C}$
1	1	1	0	0	1
1	1	0	1	1	1
1	0	1	0	0	1
1	0	0	1	0	1
0	1	1	0	0	0
0	1	0	1	1	1
0	0	1	0	0	0
0	0	0	1	0	0

Example 5.9   Find the truth table for the Boolean expression $A + B \cdot \overline{C}$.

Solution   We construct the table by noting that A, B and C are Boolean variables; that is, they can take the values 0 or 1. The first stage in the process is to form all possible combinations of A, B and C, as shown in Table 5.10. Then we complete the table by forming $\overline{C}$, then $B \cdot \overline{C}$ and finally $A + B \cdot \overline{C}$, using the truth tables defined earlier. So, for example, whenever $C = 1$, $\overline{C} = 0$. The complete process is shown in Table 5.11. Work through the table to ensure you understand how it was constructed.

5.4.2   Logical equivalence

We know from the distributive laws of Boolean algebra that

$$A + (B \cdot \overline{C}) = (A + B) \cdot (A + \overline{C})$$

Let us construct the truth table for the r.h.s. of this expression (Table 5.12). If we now observe the final column of Table 5.12 we see it is the same as that of Table 5.11. We say

Table 5.12 Truth table for $(A + B) \cdot (A + \overline{C})$.

A	B	C	$\overline{C}$	$A + B$	$A + \overline{C}$	$(A + B) \cdot (A + \overline{C})$
1	1	1	0	1	1	1
1	1	0	1	1	1	1
1	0	1	0	1	1	1
1	0	0	1	1	1	1
0	1	1	0	1	0	0
0	1	0	1	1	1	1
0	0	1	0	0	0	0
0	0	0	1	0	1	0

Figure 5.12
Circuit to implement
$A + (B \cdot \overline{C})$.

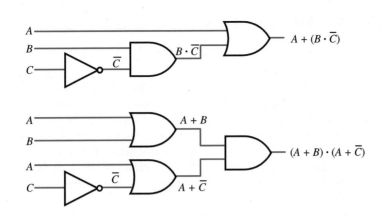

Figure 5.13
Circuit to implement
$(A + B) \cdot (A + \overline{C})$.

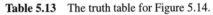

that $A+(B\cdot\overline{C})$ is **logically equivalent** to $(A+B)\cdot(A+\overline{C})$. Figures 5.12 and 5.13 show the two ways in which these logically equivalent circuits could be constructed using OR gates, AND gates and inverters. Clearly different electronic circuits can be constructed to perform the same logical task. We shall shortly explore a way of simplifying circuits to reduce the number of components required.

Example 5.10   Find the Boolean expression and truth table for the electronic circuit shown in Figure 5.14.

Solution   By labelling intermediate points in the circuit we see that $X = A \cdot B + \overline{C}$. In order to obtain the truth table we form all possible combinations of A, B and C, followed by $A \cdot B$, $\overline{C}$ and finally $X = A \cdot B + \overline{C}$. The complete calculation is shown in Table 5.13.

Table 5.13   The truth table for Figure 5.14.

A	B	C	$A \cdot B$	$\overline{C}$	$X = A \cdot B + \overline{C}$
1	1	1	1	0	1
1	1	0	1	1	1
1	0	1	0	0	0
1	0	0	0	1	1
0	1	1	0	0	0
0	1	0	0	1	1
0	0	1	0	0	0
0	0	0	0	1	1

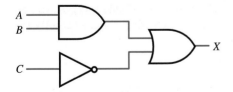

Figure 5.14   Circuit for Example 5.10.

What we would now like to be able to do is carry out the reverse process: that is, start with a truth table and find an appropriate Boolean expression so that the required electronic device can be constructed.

Example 5.11

Given inputs A, B and C, find a Boolean expression for X as given by the truth table in Table 5.14.

Solution

To find an equivalent Boolean expression the procedure is as follows. Look down the rows of the truth table and select those with an r.h.s. equal to 1. In this example, there are five such rows: 1, 2, 4, 6 and 8. Each of these rows gives rise to a term in the required Boolean expression. Each term is constructed so that it has a value 1 for the input values of that row. For example, for the input values of row 1, that is 1, 1, 1, we find $A \cdot B \cdot C$ has the value 1, whereas for the input values of row 2, that is 1, 1, 0, we find $A \cdot B \cdot \overline{C}$ has the value 1. Carrying out this process for the other rows we find that the required expression is

Table 5.14 The truth table for a system with inputs A, B and C and an output X.

A	B	C	X
1	1	1	1
1	1	0	1
1	0	1	0
1	0	0	1
0	1	1	0
0	1	0	1
0	0	1	0
0	0	0	1

$$X = A \cdot B \cdot C + A \cdot B \cdot \overline{C} + A \cdot \overline{B} \cdot \overline{C} + \overline{A} \cdot B \cdot \overline{C} + \overline{A} \cdot \overline{B} \cdot \overline{C} \qquad (5.1)$$

that is, a disjunction of terms, each term corresponding to one of the selected rows. This important expression is known as a **disjunctive normal form** (d.n.f.). We note that the truth table is the same as that of Example 5.10 which had Boolean expression $(A \cdot B) + \overline{C}$. The d.n.f. we have just calculated, while correct, is not the simplest.

More generally, to find the required d.n.f. from a truth table we write down an expression of the form

$$(\quad) + (\quad) + \cdots + (\quad)$$

where each term has the value 1 for the input values of that row. We could now construct an electronic circuit corresponding to Equation (5.1) using a number of AND and OR gates together with inverters, and it would do the required job in the sense that the desired truth table would be achieved.

However, we know from Example 5.10 that the much simpler expression $(A \cdot B) + \overline{C}$ has the same truth table and if a circuit were to be built corresponding to this it would require fewer components. Clearly what we need is a technique for finding the simplest expression which does the desired job since the d.n.f. is not in general the simplest. It is not obvious what is meant by 'simplest expression'. In what follows we shall be concerned with finding the simplest d.n.f. It is nevertheless possible that a logically equivalent statement exists which would give a simpler circuit. Simplification can be achieved using the laws of Boolean algebra as we shall see in Examples 5.13 and 5.14.

Example 5.12

The exclusive OR gate

We have already looked at the OR gate in Section 5.3. The full name for this type of OR gate is the **inclusive** OR gate. It is so called because it gives an output of 1 when either or both inputs are 1. The **exclusive** OR gate only gives an output of 1 when either but not both inputs are 1. The truth table for this gate is given in Table 5.15 and its symbol is shown in Figure 5.15. Using the truth table, the d.n.f. for the gate is

$$F = A \cdot \overline{B} + \overline{A} \cdot B$$

The exclusive OR often arises in the design of digital logic circuits. In fact, it is possible to buy integrated circuits that contain exclusive OR gates as basic units.

Table 5.15 The truth table for an exclusive OR gate.

A	B	F
1	1	0
1	0	1
0	1	1
0	0	0

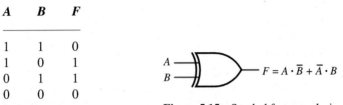

$$F = A \cdot \overline{B} + \overline{A} \cdot B$$

Figure 5.15 Symbol for an exclusive OR gate.

Example 5.13 Use the laws of Boolean algebra given in Table 5.8 to simplify the following expressions.

(a) $A \cdot B + A \cdot \overline{B}$

(b) $A + \overline{A} \cdot \overline{B}$

(c) $A + \overline{A} \cdot \overline{B} \cdot C$

(d) $A \cdot B \cdot C + A \cdot \overline{B} \cdot C + A \cdot B \cdot \overline{C} + A \cdot \overline{B} \cdot \overline{C} + \overline{A} \cdot \overline{B} \cdot C$

Solution (a) Using the distributive law we can write

$$A \cdot B + A \cdot \overline{B} = A \cdot (B + \overline{B})$$

Using the complement law, $B + \overline{B} = 1$ and hence

$$A \cdot B + A \cdot \overline{B} = A \cdot 1$$
$$= A \qquad \text{using the identity law}$$

Hence $A \cdot B + A \cdot \overline{B}$ simplifies to A. Note that this is the first minimization law given in Table 5.9.

(b) $\qquad A + \overline{A} \cdot \overline{B} = (A + \overline{A}) \cdot (A + \overline{B}) \qquad$ by the distributive law
$$= 1 \cdot (A + \overline{B}) \qquad\qquad \text{by the complement law}$$
$$= A + \overline{B} \qquad\qquad\quad \text{using the identity law}$$

(c) Note that $A + \overline{A} \cdot \overline{B} \cdot C$ can be written as $A + (\overline{A} \cdot \overline{B}) \cdot C$ using the associative laws. Then

$$A + (\overline{A} \cdot \overline{B}) \cdot C = (A + \overline{A} \cdot \overline{B}) \cdot (A + C) \qquad \text{by the distributive law}$$
$$= (A + \overline{B}) \cdot (A + C) \qquad\quad \text{using part (b)}$$
$$= A + \overline{B} \cdot C \qquad\qquad\quad\;\; \text{by the distributive law}$$

(d) $A \cdot B \cdot C + A \cdot \overline{B} \cdot C + A \cdot B \cdot \overline{C} + A \cdot \overline{B} \cdot \overline{C} + \overline{A} \cdot \overline{B} \cdot C$

can be rearranged using the commutative law to give

$$A \cdot B \cdot C + A \cdot B \cdot \overline{C} + A \cdot \overline{B} \cdot C + A \cdot \overline{B} \cdot \overline{C} + \overline{A} \cdot \overline{B} \cdot C$$

This equals

$$A \cdot B \cdot (C + \overline{C}) + A \cdot \overline{B} \cdot (C + \overline{C}) + \overline{A} \cdot \overline{B} \cdot C \qquad \text{by the distributive law}$$
$$= A \cdot B \cdot 1 + A \cdot \overline{B} \cdot 1 + \overline{A} \cdot \overline{B} \cdot C \qquad \text{using the complement law}$$
$$= A \cdot B + A \cdot \overline{B} + \overline{A} \cdot \overline{B} \cdot C \qquad \text{using the identity law}$$
$$= A \cdot (B + \overline{B}) + \overline{A} \cdot \overline{B} \cdot C \qquad \text{using the distributive law}$$
$$= A + \overline{A} \cdot \overline{B} \cdot C \qquad \text{using the complement and identity laws}$$

Using the result of part (c) this can be further simplified to $A + \overline{B} \cdot C$

Example 5.14   Design of a binary full-adder circuit

The binary adder circuit is a common type of digital logic circuit. For example, the accumulator of a microprocessor is essentially a binary adder. The term **full-adder** is used to describe a circuit which can add together two binary digits and also add the carry-out digit from a previous stage. The outputs from the full-adder consist of the sum value and the carry-out value. By connecting together a series of full-adders it is possible to add together two binary words. (A binary word is a group of binary digits, such as 0111 1010.) For example, adding together two 4-bit binary words would require four full-adder circuits. This is shown in Figure 5.16.

The inputs A0–A3 and B0–B3 hold the two binary words that are to be added. The outputs S0–S3 hold the result of carrying out the addition. The lines C0–C3 hold the carry-out values from each of the stages. Sometimes there will be a carry-in to stage 0 as a result of a previous calculation. Let us consider the design of stage 2 in more detail. The design of the other stages will be identical. First of all a truth table for the circuit is derived. This is shown in Table 5.16.

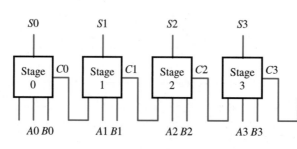

Figure 5.16   Four full-adders connected to allow two 4-bit binary words to be added.

Table 5.16   Truth table for a full-adder.

C1	A2	B2	S2	C2
0	0	0	0	0
0	0	1	1	0
0	1	0	1	0
0	1	1	0	1
1	0	0	1	0
1	0	1	0	1
1	1	0	0	1
1	1	1	1	1

Notice that there are three inputs to the circuit, $C1$, $A2$ and $B2$. There are also two outputs from the circuit, $S2$ and $C2$. Writing expressions for the outputs in d.n.f. yields

$$S2 = \overline{C1} \cdot \overline{A2} \cdot B2 + \overline{C1} \cdot A2 \cdot \overline{B2} + C1 \cdot \overline{A2} \cdot \overline{B2} + C1 \cdot A2 \cdot B2$$

$$C2 = \overline{C1} \cdot A2 \cdot B2 + C1 \cdot \overline{A2} \cdot B2 + C1 \cdot A2 \cdot \overline{B2} + C1 \cdot A2 \cdot B2$$

It is important to reduce these expressions to as simple a form as possible in order to minimize the number of electronic gates needed to implement the expressions. So, starting with $S2$,

$$
\begin{aligned}
S2 &= \overline{C1} \cdot \overline{A2} \cdot B2 + \overline{C1} \cdot A2 \cdot \overline{B2} + C1 \cdot \overline{A2} \cdot \overline{B2} + C1 \cdot A2 \cdot B2 \\
&= C1 \cdot (A2 \cdot B2 + \overline{A2} \cdot \overline{B2}) + \overline{C1} \cdot (A2 \cdot \overline{B2} + \overline{A2} \cdot B2)
\end{aligned}
$$

by the distributive law   (5.2)

Let

$$X = A2 \cdot \overline{B2} + \overline{A2} \cdot B2 \qquad (5.3)$$

Notice this is an equation for an exclusive OR gate with inputs $A2$ and $B2$.

Using Equation (5.3) we have

$$
\begin{aligned}
\overline{X} &= \overline{A2 \cdot \overline{B2} + \overline{A2} \cdot B2} & \\
&= (\overline{A2 \cdot \overline{B2}}) \cdot (\overline{\overline{A2} \cdot B2}) & \text{by De Morgan's law} \\
&= (\overline{A2} + \overline{\overline{B2}}) \cdot (\overline{\overline{A2}} + \overline{B2}) & \text{by De Morgan's law} \\
&= (\overline{A2} + B2) \cdot (A2 + \overline{B2}) & \text{by the complement law} \\
&= \overline{A2} \cdot A2 + \overline{A2} \cdot \overline{B2} + B2 \cdot A2 + B2 \cdot \overline{B2} & \text{by the distributive law} \\
&= 0 + \overline{A2} \cdot \overline{B2} + B2 \cdot A2 + 0 & \text{by the complement law} \\
&= \overline{A2} \cdot \overline{B2} + B2 \cdot A2 & \text{by the identity law} \\
&= A2 \cdot B2 + \overline{A2} \cdot \overline{B2} & \text{by the commutative law}
\end{aligned}
$$

It is now possible to write Equation (5.2) as

$$S2 = C1 \cdot \overline{X} + \overline{C1} \cdot X$$

This is the expression for an exclusive OR gate with inputs $C1$ and X. It is therefore possible to obtain $S2$ with two exclusive OR gates which are usually available as a basic building block on an integrated circuit. The circuit for $S2$ is shown in Figure 5.17. Turning to $C2$, we have

$$
\begin{aligned}
C2 &= \overline{C1} \cdot A2 \cdot B2 + C1 \cdot \overline{A2} \cdot B2 + C1 \cdot A2 \cdot \overline{B2} + C1 \cdot A2 \cdot B2 \\
&= A2 \cdot B2 \cdot (\overline{C1} + C1) + C1 \cdot (\overline{A2} \cdot B2 + A2 \cdot \overline{B2}) & \text{by the distributive law} \\
&= A2 \cdot B2 + C1 \cdot X & \text{by the complement law}
\end{aligned}
$$

since $\overline{C1} + C1 = 1$, where X is given by Equation (5.3). The output, X, has already been generated to produce $S2$ but can be used again provided the exclusive OR gate can stand feeding two inputs. Assuming this is so then the final circuit for the full-adder is shown in Figure 5.18.

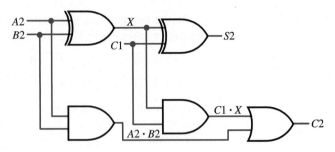

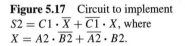

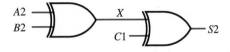

Figure 5.17 Circuit to implement
$S2 = C1 \cdot \overline{X} + \overline{C1} \cdot X$, where
$X = A2 \cdot \overline{B2} + \overline{A2} \cdot B2$.

Figure 5.18 Circuit to implement the stage 2 full-adder.

Exercises 5.4

1 Write Boolean expressions for the output, F, from the electronic devices shown in Figure 5.19.

2 Write Boolean expressions for the output from the devices shown in Figure 5.20.

3 Design electronic devices which produce the following outputs.

    (a) $\overline{A + \overline{B}}$

    (b) $\overline{A \cdot (B \cdot C)}$

    (c) $(C + D) \cdot (A + \overline{B})$

    (d) $\overline{\overline{A} + \overline{B}}$

    (e) $A \cdot B + \overline{A} \cdot \overline{B} + B \cdot \overline{C}$

4 Draw up the truth tables for the expressions given in Question 3.

Figure 5.19

    (a)

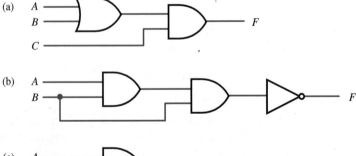

    (b)

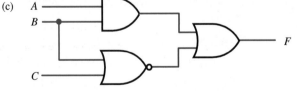

    (c)

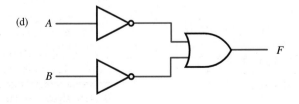

    (d)

Figure 5.20

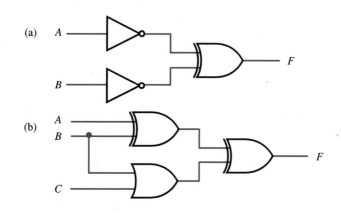

(a)

(b)

---

5 Use truth tables to verify that the following pairs of expressions are logically equivalent.

(a) $p + p \cdot q \cdot r + \overline{p} \cdot \overline{q}$ and $p + \overline{q}$

(b) $(A + \overline{B}) \cdot (A + \overline{C})$ and $A + \overline{B} \cdot \overline{C}$

(c) $p \cdot q \cdot r + p \cdot q \cdot \overline{r} + p \cdot \overline{q} \cdot r$ and $p \cdot (r + q)$

6 Simplify the following Boolean expressions using the laws of Boolean algebra.

(a) $A \cdot A \cdot A$

(b) $A \cdot A \cdot \overline{A}$

(c) $A \cdot \overline{A} \cdot \overline{A}$

(d) $(A + A) \cdot (A + \overline{A})$

(e) $\overline{A + 0}$

(f) $(A + 1) \cdot (\overline{A} + 1)$

(g) $\overline{A + 1}$

7 Simplify the following Boolean expressions using the laws of Boolean algebra.

(a) $(A + A) \cdot (B + B)$

(b) $A \cdot (A + B + A \cdot B)$

(c) $(A + A) \cdot (A + C)$

(d) $\overline{A} \cdot \overline{B} \cdot (A + B)$

(e) $A \cdot (\overline{A} + \overline{B}) \cdot B$

(f) $A \cdot B \cdot \overline{C} + A \cdot B \cdot C$

(g) $\overline{A \cdot B \cdot C} + \overline{A} + \overline{B} + \overline{C}$

8 Construct a truth table showing $\overline{A \cdot B}$ and $\overline{A} + \overline{B}$ in order to verify the logical equivalence expressed in De Morgan's law $\overline{A \cdot B} = \overline{A} + \overline{B}$. Carry out a similar exercise to verify $\overline{A + B} = \overline{A} \cdot \overline{B}$.

9 Let $B = 1$ and then $B = 0$ in the absorption laws, and use the identity laws to obtain(a) $A + A = A$ and (b) $A \cdot A = A$. Verify your results using truth tables.

10 Derive Boolean expressions and truth tables for the circuits shown in Figure 5.21.

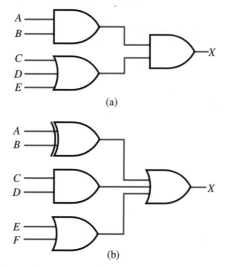

(a)

(b)

Figure 5.21

11 Simplify the following Boolean expressions using Boolean algebra.

(a) $A \cdot B + A \cdot \overline{B} + B \cdot C + A \cdot B \cdot C$

(b) $A \cdot (C + A) + C \cdot B + D + C + B \cdot \overline{C} + C \cdot A$

(c) $A \cdot B \cdot C \cdot D + A \cdot B \cdot \overline{C} + A \cdot B \cdot C \cdot \overline{D} + A \cdot \overline{B} \cdot C \cdot D + A \cdot \overline{B} \cdot \overline{C} \cdot D$

12 The truth values of the Boolean expression, X, are given in the following tables. Write X in disjunctive normal form. Use the laws of Boolean algebra to simplify your expressions.

(a)

A	B	X
0	0	1
0	1	0
1	0	1
1	1	1

(b)

A	B	X
0	0	1
0	1	1
1	0	0
1	1	0

(d)

A	B	C	X
0	0	0	0
0	0	1	0
0	1	0	0
0	1	1	1
1	0	0	0
1	0	1	1
1	1	0	1
1	1	1	0

(c)

A	B	C	X
0	0	0	1
0	0	1	1
0	1	0	0
0	1	1	0
1	0	0	0
1	0	1	0
1	1	0	1
1	1	1	1

13 Express $A \cdot \overline{B} + \overline{A} \cdot B$ using only conjunction (AND gate) and negation (NOT gate).

Solutions

1 (a) $(A + B) \cdot C$ (b) $\overline{(A \cdot B) \cdot B}$
(c) $(A \cdot B) + \overline{B + C}$ (d) $\overline{A} + \overline{B}$

2 (a) $\overline{A} \cdot \overline{B} + \overline{\overline{A}} \cdot \overline{B}$ which is the same as $\overline{A} \cdot B + A \cdot \overline{B}$

(b) $(A \cdot \overline{B} + \overline{A} \cdot B) \cdot (\overline{B + C}) + (A \cdot \overline{B} + \overline{A} \cdot B) \cdot (B + C)$

3 See Figure S.9.

4 (a)

A	B	$\overline{A + B}$
1	1	0
1	0	0
0	1	1
0	0	0

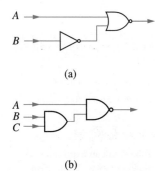

(a)

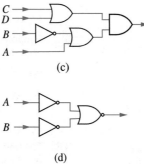

(c)

(b)

(d)

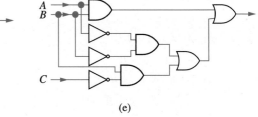

(e)

Figure S.9

(b)

A	B	C	$\overline{A \cdot (B \cdot C)}$
1	1	1	0
1	1	0	1
1	0	1	1
1	0	0	1
0	1	1	1
0	1	0	1
0	0	1	1
0	0	0	1

(c)

A	B	C	D	$(C + D) \cdot (A + \overline{B})$
1	1	1	1	1
1	1	1	0	1
1	1	0	1	1
1	1	0	0	0
1	0	1	1	1
1	0	1	0	1
1	0	0	1	1
1	0	0	0	0
0	1	1	1	0
0	1	1	0	0
0	1	0	1	0
0	1	0	0	0
0	0	1	1	1
0	0	1	0	1
0	0	0	1	1
0	0	0	0	0

(d)

A	B	$\overline{\overline{A} + \overline{B}}$
1	1	1
1	0	0
0	1	0
0	0	0

(e)

A	B	C	$A \cdot B + \overline{A} \cdot \overline{B} + B \cdot \overline{C}$
1	1	1	1
1	1	0	1
1	0	1	0
1	0	0	0
0	1	1	0
0	1	0	1
0	0	0	1

6 (a) A (b) 0   (c) 0   (d) A
   (e) $\overline{A}$ (f) 1   (g) 0

7 (a) $A \cdot B$ (b) A (c) A
   (d) 0   (e) 0   (f) $A \cdot B$
   (g) $\overline{A \cdot B \cdot C}$

10 (a) $X = (A \cdot B) \cdot (C + D + E)$

   (b) $X = A \cdot \overline{B} + \overline{A} \cdot B + C \cdot D + E + F$

11 (a) $A + B \cdot C$

   (b) $A + B + C + D$

   (c) $(A \cdot B) + (A \cdot \overline{B} \cdot D)$ which can be further simplified to $A \cdot (B + D)$

12 (a) $\overline{A} \cdot \overline{B} + A \cdot \overline{B} + A \cdot B$

   (b) $\overline{A} \cdot \overline{B} + \overline{A} \cdot B$

   (c) $\overline{A} \cdot \overline{B} \cdot \overline{C} + \overline{A} \cdot \overline{B} \cdot C + A \cdot B \cdot \overline{C} + A \cdot B \cdot C$

   (d) $\overline{A} \cdot B \cdot C + A \cdot \overline{B} \cdot C + A \cdot B \cdot \overline{C}$

13 $\overline{(A \cdot \overline{B}) \cdot (\overline{A} \cdot B)}$

Review exercises 5

1 Classify the following as true or false.

   (a) $\mathbb{R}^+ \subset \mathbb{R}$

   (b) $0.667 \in \mathbb{R}^-$

   (c) $0.667 \in \mathbb{Q}$

   (d) $\mathbb{N} \cup \mathbb{Z} = \mathbb{R}$

   (e) $-6 \in \mathbb{Q}$

   (f) $9 \notin \mathbb{R}$

   (g) $\mathbb{N} \cap \mathbb{Q} = \mathbb{N}$

   (h) $\mathbb{R}^- \cap \mathbb{Q} = \emptyset$

2 Use set notation to describe the following intervals on the x axis.
   (a) $[-6, 9]$ (b) $(-1, 1)$
   (c) $|x| < 1.7$ (d) $(0, 2]$
   (e) $|x| > 1$ (f) $|x| \geqslant 2$

Figure 5.22

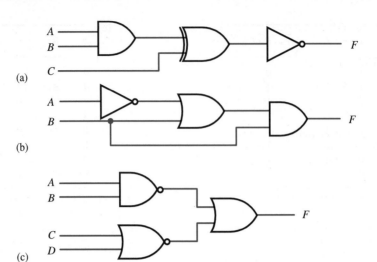

(a)

(b)

(c)

3 The sets A, B and C are given by
$A = \{1, 2, 6, 7, 10, 11, 12, 13\}$,
$B = \{3, 4, 7, 8, 11\}$, $C = \{4, 5, 6, 7, 9, 13\}$ and
the universal set
$\mathbb{E} = \{x : x \in \mathbb{N}^+, 1 \leqslant x \leqslant 13\}$. List the
elements of the following sets.

(a) $A \cup B$

(b) $B \cup C$

(c) $A \cap B$

(d) $A \cap (B \cup C)$

(e) $A \cap B \cap C$

(f) $A \cup (B \cap C)$

(g) $C \cup (B \cap A)$

4 Represent the sets A, B and C described in
Question 3 on a Venn diagram.

5 List all the elements of the following sets:

(a) $S = \{n : n \in \mathbb{Z}, 5 \leqslant n^2 \leqslant 50\}$

(b) $S = \{m : m \in \mathbb{N}, 5 \leqslant m^2 \leqslant 50\}$

(c) $S = \{m : m \in \mathbb{N}, m^2 + 2m - 15 = 0\}$

6 If $A = \{n : n \in \mathbb{Z}, -10 \leqslant n \leqslant 20\}$,
$B = \{m : m \in \mathbb{N}, m > 15\}$ list the members of
$A \cap B$ and write down an expression for $A \cup B$.

7 Write Boolean expressions for the output, F,
from the electronic devices shown in
Figure 5.22.

8 Simplify the following Boolean expressions
using the laws of Boolean algebra.

(a) $A \cdot B \cdot 1$

(b) $A + A \cdot B + B$

(c) $1 + 0$

(d) $D \cdot (C + B) + C \cdot D$

(e) $(A + C) \cdot (C + \overline{A})$

(f) $\overline{A \cdot B} + \overline{A} + \overline{B}$

(g) $\overline{\overline{A \cdot B}}$

(h) $\overline{\overline{A + B}}$

(i) $\overline{A \cdot (B + C)} \cdot C$

(j) $(\overline{C} + A + \overline{D}) \cdot (C \cdot D + A)$

9 Draw up truth tables to verify that $A \cdot B + \overline{B}$
and $\overline{A} \cdot B + A$ are logically equivalent.

10 Express $A + B + C + D$ using the Boolean
connectives AND ($\cdot$) and negation.

11 Simplify the following expressions using the
laws of Boolean algebra.

(a) $(A + \overline{A}) \cdot (B + \overline{B})$

(b) $A \cdot B \cdot \overline{A}$

(c) $(A + B) \cdot (A + B)$

(d) $\overline{\overline{A}} \cdot A$

(e) $A \cdot B \cdot C \cdot D \cdot 1 \cdot 0$

(f) $A \cdot B \cdot C \cdot \overline{B}$

(g) $B \cdot C \cdot 1$

12 Reduce the following expressions using Boolean algebra:

(a) $\overline{A + C} + \overline{A} \cdot B \cdot (B + C)$

(b) $\overline{(\overline{A} + B)} \cdot B \cdot C + (A + \overline{C}) \cdot (B + A \cdot C)$

(c) $\overline{(\overline{A} + \overline{B}) \cdot (\overline{A} + \overline{C})}$

13 The truth tables of the Boolean expression, X, are given in the following tables. Write the disjunctive normal form of X in each case.

(a)

A	B	X
0	0	0
0	1	1
1	0	0
1	1	0

(b)

A	B	X
0	0	0
0	1	0
1	0	1
1	1	0

(c)

A	B	C	X
0	0	0	1
0	0	1	0
0	1	0	0
0	1	1	1
1	0	0	0
1	0	1	1
1	1	0	0
1	1	1	1

(d)

A	B	C	X
0	0	0	0
0	0	1	1
0	1	0	0
0	1	1	1
1	0	0	1
1	0	1	1
1	1	0	0
1	1	1	0

Solutions

1 (a) T (b) F (c) T (d) F
(e) T (f) F (g) T (h) F

2 (a) $\{x : x \in \mathbb{R}, -6 \leqslant x \leqslant 9\}$

(b) $\{x : x \in \mathbb{R}, -1 < x < 1\}$

(c) $\{x : x \in \mathbb{R}, -1.7 < x < 1.7\}$

(d) $\{x : x \in \mathbb{R}, 0 < x \leqslant 2\}$

(e) $\{x : x \in \mathbb{R}, x > 1 \text{ or } x < -1\}$

(f) $\{x : x \in \mathbb{R}, x \geqslant 2 \text{ or } x \leqslant -2\}$

3 (a) $\{1, 2, 3, 4, 6, 7, 8, 10, 11, 12, 13\}$

(b) $\{3, 4, 5, 6, 7, 8, 9, 11, 13\}$

(c) $\{7, 11\}$

(d) $\{6, 7, 11, 13\}$

(e) $\{7\}$

(f) $\{1, 2, 4, 6, 7, 10, 11, 12, 13\}$

(g) $\{4, 5, 6, 7, 9, 11, 13\}$

4 See Figure S.10.

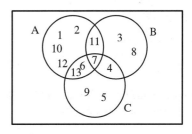

Figure S.10

5 (a) $S = \{-7, -6, -5, -4, -3, 3, 4, 5, 6, 7\}$

(b) $S = \{3, 4, 5, 6, 7\}$

(c) $S = \{3\}$

6 $A \cap B = \{16, 17, 18, 19, 20\}$
$A \cup B = \{m : m \in \mathbb{Z}, m \geqslant -10\}$

7 (a) $\overline{(A \cdot B) \cdot \overline{C} + (\overline{A} \cdot B) \cdot C}$

(b) $\overline{(\overline{A} + B) \cdot B}$

(c) $\overline{(A \cdot B) + (\overline{C + D})}$

8 (a) $A \cdot B$ (b) $A + B$ (c) 1
   (d) $D \cdot (C + B)$ (e) C (f) $\overline{A \cdot B}$
   (g) $A + B$ (h) $A \cdot B$ (i) $\overline{A} \cdot C$
   (j) A

10 $\overline{\overline{A} \cdot \overline{B} \cdot \overline{C} \cdot \overline{D}}$

11 (a) 1   (b) 0   (c) $A + B$ (d) A
    (e) 0   (f) 0   (g) $B \cdot C$

12 (a) $\overline{A} + \overline{B} \cdot C$
    (b) $A \cdot B + A \cdot C + B \cdot \overline{C}$
    (c) $A \cdot (B + C)$

13 (a) $\overline{A} \cdot B$
    (b) $A \cdot \overline{B}$
    (c) $\overline{A} \cdot \overline{B} \cdot \overline{C} + \overline{A} \cdot B \cdot C + A \cdot \overline{B} \cdot C + A \cdot B \cdot C$
    (d) $\overline{A} \cdot \overline{B} \cdot C + \overline{A} \cdot B \cdot C + A \cdot \overline{B} \cdot \overline{C} + A \cdot \overline{B} \cdot C$

6 Sequences and series

Chapter 6	Contents	

6.1	Introduction	176
6.2	Sequences	176
6.3	Series	185
6.4	The binomial theorem	190
6.5	Power series	194
6.6	Sequences arising from the iterative solution of non-linear equations	196
	Review exercises	199

6.1 Introduction

Much of the material in this chapter is of a fundamental nature and is applicable to many different areas of engineering. For example, if continuous signals or waveforms, such as those described in Chapter 2, are sampled at periodic intervals we obtain a sequence of measured values. Sequences also arise when we attempt to obtain approximate solutions of equations which model physical phenomena. Such approximations are necessary if a solution is to be obtained using a digital computer. For many problems of practical interest to engineers a computer solution is the only possibility. The z transform is an example of an infinite series which is particularly important in the field of digital signal processing. Signal processing is concerned with modifying signals in order to improve them in some way. For example, the signals received from space satellites have to undergo extensive processing in order to counteract the effects of noise, and to filter out unwanted frequencies before they can provide, say, acceptable visual images. Digital signal processing is signal processing carried out using a computer. So, skill in manipulating sequences and series is crucial. Later chapters will develop these concepts and show examples of their use in solving real engineering problems.

6.2 Sequences

A **sequence** is a set of numbers or terms, not necessarily distinct, written down in a definite order.

For example,

$$1, 3, 5, 7, 9 \qquad \text{and} \qquad 1, \tfrac{1}{2}, \tfrac{1}{4}, \tfrac{1}{8}, \tfrac{1}{16}$$

are both sequences. Sometimes we use the notation '...' to indicate that the sequence continues. For example, the sequence $1, 2, 3, \ldots, 20$ is the sequence of integers from 1 to 20 inclusive. These sequences have a finite number of terms but we shall frequently deal with ones involving an infinite number of terms. To indicate that a sequence might go on for ever we can use the ... notation. Thus

$$2, 4, 6, 8, \ldots$$

and

$$1, -1, 1, -1, \ldots$$

can be assumed to continue indefinitely.

In general situations we shall write a sequence as

$$x[1], x[2], x[3], \ldots$$

or more compactly,

$$x[k] \qquad k = 1, 2, 3, \ldots$$

An alternative notation is

$$x_1, x_2, x_3, \ldots$$

The former notation is usually used in signal processing where the terms in the sequence represent the values of the signal. The latter notation arises in the numerical solution of equations. Hence both forms will be required. Often $x[1]$ will be the first term of the sequence although this is not always the case. The sequence

$$\ldots, x[-3], x[-2], x[-1], x[0], x[1], x[2], x[3], \ldots$$

is usually written as

$$x[k] \qquad k = \ldots, -3, -2, -1, 0, 1, 2, 3, \ldots$$

A complete sequence, as opposed to a specific term of a sequence, is often written using braces, for example

$$\{x[k]\} = x[1], x[2], \ldots$$

although it is common to write $x[k]$ for both the complete sequence and a general term in the sequence when there is no confusion, and this is the convention we shall adopt in this book.

A sequence can also be regarded as a function whose domain is a subset of the set of integers. For example, the function defined by

$$x: \mathbb{N} \to \mathbb{R} \qquad x: k \to \frac{3k}{2}$$

is the sequence

$$x[0] = 0 \qquad x[1] = \tfrac{3}{2} \qquad x[2] = 3 \qquad x[3] = \tfrac{9}{2} \ldots$$

The values in the range of the function are the terms of the sequence. The independent variable is k. Functions of this sort differ from those described in Chapter 2 because the independent variable is not selected from a continuous interval but rather is **discrete**. It is, nevertheless, possible to represent $x[k]$ graphically as illustrated in Examples 6.1–6.3, but instead of a piecewise continuous curve, we now have a collection of isolated points.

Example 6.1 Graph the sequences given by

(a) $\qquad x[k] = \begin{cases} 0 & k < 0 \\ 1 & k \geqslant 0 \end{cases} \qquad k = \ldots, -3, -2, -1, 0, 1, 2, \ldots, \text{ that is } k \in \mathbb{Z}$

(b) $\qquad x[k] = \begin{cases} 1 & k \text{ even} \\ -1 & k \text{ odd} \end{cases} \qquad k \in \mathbb{Z}$

Solution (a) From the definition of this sequence, the term $x[k]$ is zero if $k < 0$ and 1 if $k \geqslant 0$. The graph is obtained by plotting the terms of the sequence against k (see Figure 6.1). This sequence is known as the **unit step sequence**. We shall denote this by $u[k]$.

(b) The sequence $x[k]$ is shown in Figure 6.2.

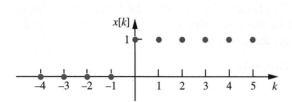

Figure 6.1   The unit step sequence.

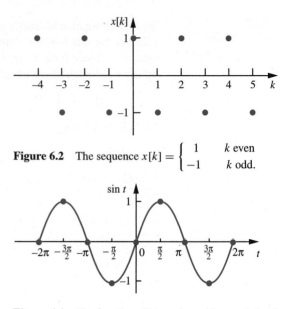

Figure 6.2   The sequence $x[k] = \begin{cases} 1 & k \text{ even} \\ -1 & k \text{ odd.} \end{cases}$

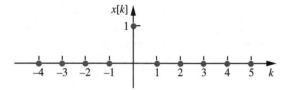

Figure 6.3   The Kronecker delta sequence.

Figure 6.4   The function $f(t) = \sin t$ with sampled points shown.

Example 6.2   Graph the sequence defined by

$$x[k] = \begin{cases} 1 & k = 0 \\ 0 & k \neq 0 \end{cases} \qquad k = \dots, -3, -2, -1, 0, 1, 2, 3, \dots$$

Solution   From the definition, if $k = 0$ then $x[k] = 1$. If k is not equal to zero the corresponding term in the sequence equals zero. Figure 6.3 shows the graph of this sequence which is commonly called the **Kronecker delta sequence**.

Example 6.3   The sequence $x[k]$ is obtained by measuring or **sampling** the continuous function $f(t) = \sin t$, $t \in \mathbb{R}$, at $t = -2\pi, -3\pi/2, -\pi, -\pi/2, 0, \pi/2, \pi, 3\pi/2$ and 2π. Write down the terms of this sequence and show them on a graph.

Solution   The function $f(t) = \sin t$, for $-2\pi \leqslant t \leqslant 2\pi$, is shown in Figure 6.4. We sample the continuous function at the required points. The sample values are shown as ●. From the graph we see that

$$x[k] = 0, 1, 0, -1, 0, 1, 0, -1, 0 \qquad k = -4, -3, \dots, 3, 4$$

The graph of $x[k]$ is shown in Figure 6.5.

Figure 6.5
Sequence formed from
sampling $f(t) = \sin t$.

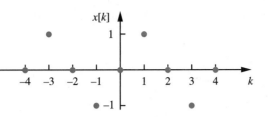

Sometimes it is possible to describe a sequence by a rule giving the kth term. For example, the sequence for which $x[k] = 2^k$, $k = 0, 1, 2, \ldots$, is given by $1, 2, 4, 8 \ldots$. On occasions, a rule gives $x[k]$ in terms of earlier members of the sequence. For example, the previous sequence could have been defined by $x[k] = 2x[k-1]$, $x[0] = 1$. The sequence is then said to be defined **recursively** and the defining formula is called a **recurrence relation** or **difference equation**. Difference equations are particularly important in digital signal processing and are dealt with in Chapter 22.

Example 6.4   Write down the terms $x[k]$ for $k = 0, \ldots, 7$ of the sequence defined recursively as

$$x[k] = x[k-2] + x[k-1]$$

where $x[0] = 1$ and $x[1] = 1$.

Solution   The values of $x[0]$ and $x[1]$ are given. Using the given recurrence relation we find

$$x[2] = x[0] + x[1] = 2$$
$$x[3] = x[1] + x[2] = 3$$

Continuing in this fashion we find the first eight terms of the sequence are

$$1, 1, 2, 3, 5, 8, 13, 21$$

This sequence is known as the Fibonacci sequence.

6.2.1 Arithmetic progressions

An arithmetic progression is a sequence where each term is found by adding a fixed quantity, called the **common difference**, to the previous term.

Example 6.5   Write down the first five terms of the arithmetic progression where the first term is 1 and the common difference is 3.

Solution   The second term is found by adding the common difference, 3, to the first term, 1, and so the second term is 4. Continuing in this way we can construct the sequence

$$1, 4, 7, 10, 13, \ldots$$

A more general arithmetic progression has first term a and common difference d, that is

$$a, a+d, a+2d, a+3d, \ldots$$

It is easy to see that the kth term is

$$a + (k-1)d$$

All arithmetic progressions can be written recursively as $x[k] = x[k-1] + d$.

> Arithmetic progression: $a, a+d, a+2d, \ldots$
> $a =$ first term, $d =$ common difference, kth term $= a + (k-1)d$

Example 6.6   Find the 10th and 20th terms of the arithmetic progression with a first term 5 and common difference -4.

Solution   Here $a = 5$ and $d = -4$. The kth term is $5 - 4(k-1)$. Therefore the 10th term is $5 - 4(9) = -31$ and the 20th term is $5 - 4(19) = -71$.

6.2.2 Geometric progressions

A geometric progression is a sequence where each term is found by multiplying the previous term by a fixed quantity called the **common ratio**.

Example 6.7   Write down the geometric progression whose first term is 1 and whose common ratio is $\frac{1}{2}$.

Solution   The second term is found by multiplying the first by the common ratio, $\frac{1}{2}$, that is $\frac{1}{2} \times 1 = \frac{1}{2}$. Continuing in this way we obtain the sequence

$$1, \tfrac{1}{2}, \tfrac{1}{4}, \tfrac{1}{8}, \ldots$$

A general geometric progression has first term a and common ratio r and can therefore be written as

$$a, ar, ar^2, ar^3, \ldots$$

and it is easy to see that the kth term is ar^{k-1}. All geometric progressions can be written recursively as $x[k] = rx[k-1]$.

> Geometric progression: $a, ar, ar^2, \ldots$
> $a =$ first term, $r =$ common ratio, kth term $= ar^{k-1}$

6.2.3 More general sequences

We have already met a number of infinite sequences. For example,

(1) $x[k] = 2, 4, 6, 8, \ldots$

(2) $x[k] = 1, \frac{1}{2}, \frac{1}{4}, \ldots$

In case (1) the terms of the sequence go on increasing without bound. We say the sequence is **unbounded**. On the other hand, in case (2) it is clear that successive terms get smaller and smaller and as $k \to \infty$, $x[k] \to 0$. The notion of getting closer and closer to a fixed value is very important in mathematics and gives rise to the concept of a **limit**. In case (2) we say 'the limit of $x[k]$ as k tends to infinity is 0' and we write this concisely as

$$\lim_{k \to \infty} x[k] = 0$$

We say that the sequence converges to 0, and because its terms do not increase without bound we say it is **bounded**.

More formally, we say that a sequence $x[k]$ **converges** to a limit l if, by proceeding far enough along the sequence, all subsequent terms can be made to lie as close to l as we wish. Whenever a sequence is not convergent it is said to be **divergent**.

It is possible to have sequences which are bounded but nevertheless do not converge to a limit. The sequence

$$x[k] = -1, 1, -1, 1, -1, 1, \ldots$$

clearly fails to have a limit as $k \to \infty$ although it is bounded, that is its values all lie within a given range. This particular sequence is said to **oscillate**.

It is possible to evaluate the limit of a sequence, when such a limit exists, from knowledge of its general term. To be able to do this we can make use of certain rules, the proofs of which are beyond the scope of this book, but which we now state:

If $x[k]$ and $y[k]$ are two sequences such that $\lim_{k \to \infty} x[k] = l_1$, and $\lim_{k \to \infty} y[k] = l_2$, where l_1 and l_2 are finite, then:

(1) The sequence given by $x[k] \pm y[k]$ has limit $l_1 \pm l_2$.

(2) The sequence given by $cx[k]$, where c is a constant, has limit, cl_1.

(3) The sequence $x[k]y[k]$ has limit $l_1 l_2$.

(4) The sequence $\dfrac{x[k]}{y[k]}$ has limit $\dfrac{l_1}{l_2}$ provided $l_2 \neq 0$.

Furthermore, we can always assume that

$$\lim_{k \to \infty} \frac{1}{k^m} = 0 \qquad \text{for any constant } m > 0$$

Example 6.8 Find, if possible, the limit of each of the following sequences, $x[k]$.

(a) $x[k] = \dfrac{1}{k}$ $k = 1, 2, 3, 4, \ldots$

(b) $x[k] = 5$ $k = 1, 2, 3, 4, \ldots$

(c) $x[k] = 3 + \dfrac{1}{k}$ $k = 1, 2, 3, 4, \ldots$

(d) $x[k] = \dfrac{1}{k+1}$ $k = 1, 2, 3, 4, \ldots$

(e) $x[k] = k^2$ $k = 1, 2, 3, 4, \ldots$

Solution (a) The sequence $x[k]$ is given by

$$1, \tfrac{1}{2}, \tfrac{1}{3}, \tfrac{1}{4}, \ldots$$

Successive terms get smaller and smaller, and as $k \to \infty$, $x[k] \to 0$. By proceeding far enough along the sequence we can get as close to the limit 0 as we wish. Hence

$$\lim_{k \to \infty} x[k] = \lim_{k \to \infty} \frac{1}{k} = 0$$

(b) The sequence $x[k]$ is given by $5, 5, 5, 5, \ldots$. This sequence has limit 5.

(c) The sequence $3, 3, 3, 3, \ldots$ has limit 3. The sequence $1, \tfrac{1}{2}, \tfrac{1}{3}, \ldots$ has limit 0. Therefore, using rule (1) we have

$$\lim_{k \to \infty} 3 + \frac{1}{k} = 3 + 0 = 3$$

The terms of the sequence $x[k] = 3 + \dfrac{1}{k}$ are given by $4, 3\tfrac{1}{2}, 3\tfrac{1}{3}, \ldots$, and by proceeding far enough along we can make all subsequent terms lie as close to the limit 3 as we wish.

(d) The sequence $x[k] = \dfrac{1}{k+1}, k = 1, 2, 3, 4, \ldots$, is given by

$$\tfrac{1}{2}, \tfrac{1}{3}, \tfrac{1}{4}, \ldots$$

and has limit 0.

(e) The sequence $x[k] = k^2, k = 1, 2, 3, 4, \ldots$, is given by $1, 4, 9, 16, \ldots$, and increases without bound. This sequence has no limit – it is divergent.

Example 6.9   Given a sequence with general term $x[k] = \dfrac{k-1}{k+1}$, find $\lim_{k \to \infty} x[k]$.

Solution   It is meaningless simply to write $k = \infty$ to obtain $\lim_{k \to \infty} x[k] = \dfrac{\infty - 1}{\infty + 1}$, since such a quantity is undefined. What we should do is try to rewrite $x[k]$ in a form in which we can sensibly let $k \to \infty$. Dividing both numerator and denominator by k, we write

$$\frac{k-1}{k+1} = \frac{1 - (1/k)}{1 + (1/k)}$$

Then, as $k \to \infty$, $1/k \to 0$ so that

$$\lim_{k \to \infty} \left(\frac{1 - (1/k)}{1 + (1/k)} \right) = \frac{\lim_{k \to \infty}(1 - (1/k))}{\lim_{k \to \infty}(1 + (1/k))} \qquad \text{by rule (4)}$$

$$= \frac{1}{1}$$

$$= 1$$

Example 6.10   Given a sequence with general term

$$x[k] = \frac{3k^2 - 5k + 6}{k^2 + 2k + 1}$$

find $\lim_{k \to \infty} x[k]$.

Solution   Dividing the numerator and denominator by k^2 introduces terms which tend to zero as $k \to \infty$, that is

$$\frac{3k^2 - 5k + 6}{k^2 + 2k + 1} = \frac{3 - (5/k) + (6/k^2)}{1 + (2/k) + (1/k^2)}$$

Then as $k \to \infty$, we find

$$\lim_{k \to \infty} x[k] = \frac{3}{1} = 3$$

Example 6.11   Examine the behaviour of $\dfrac{k^2}{3k+1}$ as $k \to \infty$.

Solution $$\frac{k^2}{3k+1} = \frac{k}{3 + (1/k)}$$

As $k \to \infty$, $1/k \to 0$ so that the denominator approaches 3. On the other hand, as $k \to \infty$ the numerator tends to infinity so that this sequence diverges to infinity.

Exercises 6.2

1 Graph the sequences given by

(a) $x[k] = k, k = 0, 1, 2, 3, \ldots$

(b) $x[k] = \begin{cases} 3 & k = 2 \\ 0 & \text{otherwise} \end{cases}$ $k = 0, 1, 2, 3, \ldots$

(c) $x[k] = e^{-k}, k = 0, 1, 2, 3, \ldots$

2 The sequence $x[k]$ is obtained by sampling $f(t) = \cos(t + 2), t \in \mathbb{R}$. The sampling begins at $t = 0$ and thereafter at $t = 1, 2, 3, \ldots$. Write down the first six terms of the sequence.

3 A sequence, $x[k]$, is defined by

$$x[k] = \frac{k^2}{2} + k, k = 0, 1, 2, 3, \ldots$$

State the first five terms of the sequence.

4 Write down the first five terms, and plot graphs, of the sequences given recursively by

(a) $x[k] = \frac{x[k-1]}{2}$, $x[0] = 1$

(b) $x[k] = 3x[k-1] - 2x[k-2]$, $x[0] = 2$, $x[1] = 1$

5 A recurrence relation is defined by
$x[n+1] = x[n] + 10$, $x[0] = 1$,
$n = 0, 1, 2, 3, \ldots$

Find $x[1], x[2], x[3]$ and $x[4]$.

6 A sequence is defined by means of the recurrence relation
$x[n+1] = x[n] + n^2$, $x[0] = 1$,
$n = 0, 1, 2, 3, \ldots$
Write down the first five terms.

7 Consider the difference equation
$x[n+2] - x[n+1] = 3x[n]$,
$n = 0, 1, 2, 3, \ldots$
If $x[0] = 1$ and $x[1] = 2$, find the terms
$x[2], x[3], \ldots, x[6]$.

8 Write down the 10th and 19th terms of the arithmetic progressions

(a) $8, 11, 14, \ldots$

(b) $8, 5, 2, \ldots$

9 An arithmetic progression is given by

$$b, \frac{2b}{3}, \frac{b}{3}, 0, \ldots$$

(a) State the sixth term.

(b) State the kth term.

(c) If the 20th term has a value of 15, find b.

10 Write down the 5th and 10th terms of the geometric progression $8, 4, 2, \ldots$.

11 Find the 10th and 20th terms of the geometric progression with first term 3 and common ratio 2.

12 A geometric progression is given by

$$a, ar, ar^2, ar^3, \ldots$$

If $|(k+1)\text{th term}| > |k\text{th term}|$ and $(k+1)\text{th}$ term $\times$ kth term < 0, which of the following, if any, must be true?

(a) $r > 1$ (b) $a > 1$

(c) $r < -1$ (d) a is negative

(e) $-1 < r < 1$

13 A geometric progression has first term $a = 1$. The ninth term exceeds the fifth term by 240. Find possible values for the eighth term.

14 If $x[k] = \dfrac{3k+2}{k}$ find $\lim_{k \to \infty} x[k]$.

15 Find $\lim_{k \to \infty} \dfrac{3k+2}{k^2+7}$.

16 Find the limits as k tends to infinity, if they exist, of the following sequences:

(a) $x[k] = k^3$

(b) $x[k] = \dfrac{2k+3}{4k+2}$

(c) $x[k] = \dfrac{k^2 + k}{k^2 + k + 1}$

17 Find $\lim_{k \to \infty} \left(\dfrac{6k+7}{3k-2} \right)^4$.

18 Find $\lim_{k \to \infty} x[k]$, if it exists, when

(a) $x[k] = (-1)^k$

(b) $x[k] = 2 - \dfrac{k}{10}$

(c) $x[k] = \left(\dfrac{1}{3} \right)^k$

(d) $x[k] = \dfrac{3k^3 - 2k^2 + 4}{5k^3 + 2k^2 + 4}$

(e) $x[k] = \left(\dfrac{1}{5} \right)^{2k}$

Solutions

2 $\cos 2, \cos 3, \cos 4, \cos 5, \cos 6, \cos 7$

3 $0, \frac{3}{2}, 4, \frac{15}{2}, 12$

4 (a) $1, \frac{1}{2}, \frac{1}{4}, \frac{1}{8}, \frac{1}{16}$ (b) $2, 1, -1, -5, -13$

5 $11, 21, 31, 41$

6 $1, 1, 2, 6, 15$

7 $5, 11, 26, 59, 137$

8 (a) 10th term $= 35$, 19th term $= 62$
      (b) 10th term $= -19$, 19th term $= -46$

9 (a) $-\dfrac{2b}{3}$ (b) $\dfrac{b(4-k)}{3}$ (c) $-\frac{45}{16}$

10 $\frac{1}{2}, \frac{1}{64}$

11 $1536, 1572\,864$

12 Only (c) must be true

13 ± 128

14 3

15 0

16 (a) Limit does not exist   (b) $\frac{1}{2}$ (c) 1

17 16

18 (a) Limit does not exist
       (b) Limit does not exist
       (c) 0   (d) $\frac{3}{5}$ (e) 0

6.3 Series

Whenever the terms of a sequence are added together we obtain what is known as a **series**. For example, if we add the terms of the sequence $1, \frac{1}{2}, \frac{1}{4}, \frac{1}{8}$, we obtain the series S, where

$$S = 1 + \tfrac{1}{2} + \tfrac{1}{4} + \tfrac{1}{8}$$

This series ends after the fourth term and is said to be a **finite series**. Other series we shall meet continue indefinitely and are said to be **infinite series**.

Given an arbitrary sequence $x[k]$, we introduce the **sigma** notation

$$S_n = \sum_{k=1}^{n} x[k]$$

to mean the sum $x[1] + x[2] + \cdots + x[n]$, the first and last values of k being shown below and above the Greek letter Σ, which is pronounced 'sigma'. If the first term of the sequence is $x[0]$ rather than $x[1]$ we would write $\sum_{k=0}^{n} x[k]$.

6.3.1 Sum of a finite arithmetic series

An arithmetic series is the sum of an arithmetic progression. Consider the sum

$$S = 1 + 2 + 3 + 4 + 5$$

Clearly this sums to 15. When there are many more terms it is necessary to find a more efficient way of adding them up. The equation for S can be written in two ways:

$$S = 1 + 2 + 3 + 4 + 5$$

and

$$S = 5 + 4 + 3 + 2 + 1$$

If we add these two equations together we get

$$2S = 6 + 6 + 6 + 6 + 6$$

There are five terms so that

$$2S = 5 \times 6 = 30$$

that is

$$S = 15$$

Now a general arithmetic series with k terms can be written as

$$S_k = a + (a + d) + (a + 2d) + \cdots + (a + (k - 1)d)$$

but rewriting this back to front, we have

$$S_k = (a + (k - 1)d) + (a + (k - 2)d) + \cdots + (a + d) + a$$

Adding together the first term in each series produces $2a + (k - 1)d$. Adding the second terms together produces $2a + (k - 1)d$. Indeed adding together the ith terms yields $2a + (k - 1)d$. Hence,

$$2S_k = \underbrace{(2a + (k - 1)d) + (2a + (k - 1)d) + \cdots + (2a + (k - 1)d)}_{k \text{ times}}$$

that is

$$2S_k = k(2a + (k - 1)d)$$

so that

$$S_k = \frac{k}{2}(2a + (k - 1)d)$$

This formula tells us the sum to k terms of the arithmetic series with first term a and common difference d.

Sum of an arithmetic series: $S_k = \frac{k}{2}(2a + (k - 1)d)$

Example 6.12   Find the sum of the arithmetic series containing 30 terms, with first term 1 and common difference 4.

Solution   We wish to find S_k:

$$S_k = \underbrace{1 + 5 + 9 + \cdots}_{30 \text{ terms}}$$

Using $S_k = \frac{k}{2}(2a + (k - 1)d)$ we find $S_{30} = \frac{30}{2}(2 + 29 \times 4) = 1770$.

Example 6.13 Find the sum of the arithmetic series with first term 1, common difference 3 and with last term 100.

Solution We already know that the kth term of an arithmetic progression is given by $a + (k-1)d$. In this case the last term is 100. We can use this fact to find the number of terms. Thus,

$$100 = 1 + 3(k-1)$$

that is

$$3(k-1) = 99$$
$$k - 1 = 33$$
$$k = 34$$

So there are 34 terms in this series. Therefore the sum, S_{34}, is given by

$$S_{34} = \tfrac{34}{2}\{2(1) + (33)(3)\}$$
$$= 17(101)$$
$$= 1717$$

6.3.2 Sum of a finite geometric series

A geometric series is the sum of the terms of a geometric progression. If we sum the geometric progression $1, \frac{1}{2}, \frac{1}{4}, \frac{1}{8}, \frac{1}{16}$ we find

$$S = 1 + \tfrac{1}{2} + \tfrac{1}{4} + \tfrac{1}{8} + \tfrac{1}{16} \tag{6.1}$$

If there had been a large number of terms it would have been impractical to add them all directly. However, let us multiply Equation (6.1) by the common ratio, $\frac{1}{2}$:

$$\tfrac{1}{2}S = \tfrac{1}{2} + \tfrac{1}{4} + \tfrac{1}{8} + \tfrac{1}{16} + \tfrac{1}{32} \tag{6.2}$$

so that, subtracting Equation (6.2) from Equation (6.1), we find

$$S - \tfrac{1}{2}S = 1 - \tfrac{1}{32}$$

since most terms cancel out. Therefore $\frac{1}{2}S = \frac{31}{32}$ and so $S = \frac{31}{16} = 1\frac{15}{16}$.

We can apply this approach more generally: when we have a geometric progression with first term a and common ratio r, the sum to k terms is

$$S_k = a + ar + ar^2 + ar^3 + \cdots + ar^{k-1}$$

Multiplying by r gives

$$rS_k = ar + ar^2 + ar^3 + \cdots + ar^{k-1} + ar^k$$

Subtraction gives $S_k - rS_k = a - ar^k$, so that

$$S_k = \frac{a(1 - r^k)}{1 - r} \qquad \text{provided } r \neq 1$$

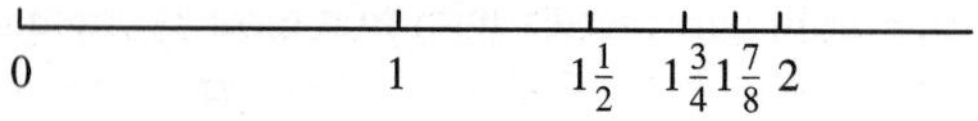

Figure 6.6
Graphical
interpretation of the
series
$1 + \frac{1}{2} + \frac{1}{4} + \frac{1}{8} + \cdots$.

This formula gives the sum to k terms of the geometric series with first term a and common ratio r.

$$\text{Sum of a geometric series: } S_k = \frac{a(1 - r^k)}{1 - r} \qquad r \neq 1$$

6.3.3 Sum of an infinite series

When dealing with infinite series the situation is more complicated. Nevertheless, it is frequently the case that the answer to many problems can be expressed as an infinite series. In certain circumstances, the sum of a series tends to a finite answer as more and more terms are included and we say the series has **converged**. To illustrate this idea, consider the graphical interpretation of the series $1 + \frac{1}{2} + \frac{1}{4} + \frac{1}{8} + \ldots$, as given in Figure 6.6.

Start at 0 and move a length 1: total distance moved $= 1$

Move further, a length $\frac{1}{2}$: total distance moved $= 1\frac{1}{2}$

Move further, a length $\frac{1}{4}$: total distance moved $= 1\frac{3}{4}$

At each stage the extra distance moved is half the distance remaining up to the point $x = 2$. It is obvious that the total distance we move cannot exceed 2 although we can get as close to 2 as we like by adding on more and more terms. We say that the series $1 + \frac{1}{2} + \frac{1}{4} + \ldots$ converges to 2. The sequence of total distances moved, given previously,

$$1, 1\frac{1}{2}, 1\frac{3}{4}, 1\frac{7}{8}, \ldots$$

is called the **sequence of partial sums** of the series.

For any given infinite series $\sum_{k=1}^{\infty} x[k]$, we can form the sequence of partial sums,

$$S_1 = \sum_{k=1}^{1} x[k] = x[1]$$

$$S_2 = \sum_{k=1}^{2} x[k] = x[1] + x[2]$$

$$S_3 = \sum_{k=1}^{3} x[k] = x[1] + x[2] + x[3]$$

$$\vdots$$

If the sequence $\{S_n\}$ converges to a limit S, we say that the infinite series has a sum S or that it has converged to S. Clearly not all infinite series will converge. For example, consider the series

$$1 + 2 + 3 + 4 + 5 + \ldots$$

The sequence of partial sums is $1, 3, 6, 10, 15, \dots$. This sequence diverges to infinity and so the series $1 + 2 + 3 + 4 + 5 + \dots$ is divergent.

It is possible to establish tests or **convergence criteria** to help us to decide whether or not a given series converges or diverges, but for these you must refer to a more advanced text.

6.3.4 Sum of an infinite geometric series

In the case of an infinite geometric series, it is possible to derive a simple formula for its sum when convergence takes place. We have already seen that the sum to k terms is given by

$$S_k = \frac{a(1 - r^k)}{1 - r} \qquad r \neq 1$$

What we must do is allow k to become large so that more and more terms are included in the sum. Provided that $-1 < r < 1$, then $r^k \to 0$ as $k \to \infty$. Then $S_k \to \dfrac{a}{1 - r}$. When this happens we write

$$S_\infty = \frac{a}{1 - r}$$

where S_∞ is known as the 'sum to infinity'. If $r > 1$ or $r < -1$, r^k fails to approach a finite limit as $k \to \infty$ and the geometric series diverges.

> Sum of an infinite geometric series: $S_\infty = \dfrac{a}{1 - r}$ $-1 < r < 1$

Example 6.14 Find the sum to k terms of the following series and deduce their sums to infinity:

(a) $1 + \frac{1}{3} + \frac{1}{9} + \frac{1}{27} + \dots$ (b) $12 + 6 + 3 + 1\frac{1}{2} + \dots$

Solution (a) This is a geometric series with first term 1 and common ratio $1/3$. Therefore,

$$S_k = \frac{a(1 - r^k)}{1 - r} = \frac{1(1 - (1/3)^k)}{2/3} = \frac{3}{2}\left(1 - \left(\frac{1}{3}\right)^k\right)$$

As $k \to \infty$, $(1/3)^k \to 0$ so that $S_\infty = 3/2$.

(b) This is a geometric series with first term 12 and common ratio $\frac{1}{2}$. Therefore,

$$S_k = 24(1 - (1/2)^k)$$

As $k \to \infty$, $(1/2)^k \to 0$ so that $S_\infty = 24$. This could, of course, have been obtained directly from the formula for the sum to infinity.

Exercises 6.3

1 An arithmetic series has a first term of 4 and its 30th term is 1000. Find the sum to 30 terms.

2 Find the sum to 20 terms of the arithmetic series with first term a, and common difference d, given by
(a) $a = 4, d = 3$ (b) $a = 4, d = -3$

3 If the sum to 10 terms of an arithmetic series is 100 and its common difference, d, is -3, find its first term.

4 The sum to 20 terms of an arithmetic series is identical to the sum to 22 terms. If the common difference is -2, find the first term.

5 Find the sum to five terms of the geometric series with first term 1 and common ratio $1/3$. Find the sum to infinity.

6 Find the sum of the first 20 terms of the geometric series with first term 3 and common ratio 1.5.

7 Find the sum of the arithmetic series with first term 2, common difference 2, and last term 50.

8 The sum to infinity of a geometric series is four times the first term. Find the common ratio.

9 The sum to infinity of a geometric series is twice the sum of the first two terms. Find possible values of the common ratio.

10 Express the alternating harmonic series $1 - \frac{1}{2} + \frac{1}{3} - \frac{1}{4} + \ldots$ in sigma notation.

11 Write down the first six terms of the series $\sum_{k=0}^{\infty} z^{-k}$.

12 Explain why $\sum_{k=1}^{\infty} x[k]$ is the same as $\sum_{n=1}^{\infty} x[n]$. Further, explain why both can be written as $\sum_{k=0}^{\infty} x[k+1]$.

Solutions

1 15 060

2 (a) 650   (b) −490

3 23.5

4 41

5 1.494

6 19 946

7 650

8 $\frac{3}{4}$

9 $\pm\dfrac{1}{\sqrt{2}}$

10 $\sum_{1}^{\infty} \dfrac{(-1)^{n+1}}{n}$

11 $1 + \dfrac{1}{z} + \dfrac{1}{z^2} + \dfrac{1}{z^3} + \dfrac{1}{z^4} + \dfrac{1}{z^5}$

6.4 The binomial theorem

It is straightforward to show that the expression $(a + b)^2$ can be written as $a^2 + 2ab + b^2$. It is slightly more complicated to expand the expression $(a + b)^3$ to $a^3 + 3a^2b + 3ab^2 + b^3$. However, it is often necessary to expand quantities such as $(a + b)^6$ or $(a + b)^{10}$, say, and then the algebra becomes extremely lengthy. A simple technique for expanding expressions of the form $(a + b)^n$, where n is a positive integer, is given by Pascal's triangle.

Pascal's triangle is the triangle of numbers shown in Figure 6.7, where it is observed that every entry is obtained by adding the two entries on either side in the preceeding row, always starting and finishing a row with a '1'. You will note that the third row down, 1   2   1, gives the coefficients in the expansion of $(a + b)^2 =$

Figure 6.7
Pascal's triangle.

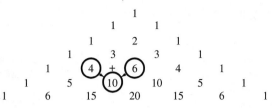

$1a^2 + 2ab + 1b^2$, while the fourth row, 1   3   3   1, gives the coefficients in the expansion of $(a + b)^3 = 1a^3 + 3a^2b + 3ab^2 + 1b^3$. Furthermore, the terms in these expansions are composed of decreasing powers of a and increasing powers of b. When we come to expand the quantity $(a + b)^4$ the row beginning '1   4' in the triangle will provide us with the necessary coefficients in the expansion and we must simply take care to put in place the appropriate powers of a and b. Thus $(a + b)^4 = 1a^4 + 4a^3b + 6a^2b^2 + 4ab^3 + 1b^4$.

Example 6.15 Use Pascal's triangle to expand $(a + b)^6$.

Solution We look to the row commencing '1   6', that is 1   6   15   20   15   6   1, because $a + b$ is raised to the power 6. This row provides the necessary coefficients. Thus,

$$(a + b)^6 = a^6 + 6a^5b + 15a^4b^2 + 20a^3b^3 + 15a^2b^4 + 6ab^5 + b^6$$

Example 6.16 Expand $(1 + x)^7$ using Pascal's triangle.

Solution Forming the row commencing '1   7' we select the coefficients

1   7   21   35   35   21   7   1

In this example, $a = 1$ and $b = x$ so that

$$(1 + x)^7 = 1 + 7x + 21x^2 + 35x^3 + 35x^4 + 21x^5 + 7x^6 + x^7$$

When it is necessary to expand the quantity $(a + b)^n$ for large n, it is clearly inappropriate to use Pascal's triangle since an extremely large triangle would have to be constructed. However, it is frequently the case that in such situations only the first few terms in the expansion are required. This is where the **binomial theorem** is useful.

The binomial theorem states that when n is a positive integer

$$(a + b)^n = a^n + na^{n-1}b + \frac{n(n - 1)}{2!}a^{n-2}b^2 + \frac{n(n - 1)(n - 2)}{3!}a^{n-3}b^3 + \cdots + b^n$$

It is also frequently quoted for the case when $a = 1$ and $b = x$, so that

$$(1+x)^n = 1 + nx + \frac{n(n-1)}{2!}x^2 + \frac{n(n-1)(n-2)}{3!}x^3 + \cdots + x^n \qquad (6.3)$$

Example 6.17   Expand $(1+x)^{10}$ up to the term in x^3.

Solution   We could use Pascal's triangle to answer this question and look to the row commencing '1   10' but to find this row considerable calculations would be needed. We shall use the binomial theorem in the form of Equation (6.3). Taking $n = 10$, we find

$$(1+x)^{10} = 1 + 10x + \frac{10(9)}{2!}x^2 + \frac{(10)(9)(8)}{3!}x^3 + \cdots$$

$$= 1 + 10x + 45x^2 + 120x^3 + \ldots$$

so that, up to and including x^3, the expansion is

$$1 + 10x + 45x^2 + 120x^3$$

We have assumed in the foregoing discussion that n is a positive integer in which case the expansion given by Equation (6.3) will eventually terminate. In Example 6.17 this would occur when we reached the term in x^{10}. It can be shown, however, that when n is not a positive integer the function $(1+x)^n$ and the expansion given by

$$(1+x)^n = 1 + nx + \frac{n(n-1)}{2!}x^2 + \frac{n(n-1)(n-2)}{3!}x^3 + \ldots \qquad (6.4)$$

have the same value provided $-1 < x < 1$. However, when n is not a positive integer the series does not terminate and we must deal with an infinite series. This series converges when $-1 < x < 1$ and the expansion is then said to be valid. When x lies outside this interval the infinite series diverges and so bears no relation to the value of $(1+x)^n$. The expansion is then said to be invalid.

The binomial theorem:

$$(1+x)^n = 1 + nx + \frac{n(n-1)}{2!}x^2 + \frac{n(n-1)(n-2)}{3!}x^3 + \ldots \qquad -1 < x < 1$$

Example 6.18   Use the binomial theorem to expand $\dfrac{1}{1+x}$ in ascending powers of x up to and including the term in x^3.

Solution $\dfrac{1}{1+x}$ can be written as $(1+x)^{-1}$. Using the binomial theorem given by Equation (6.4) with $n = -1$, we find

$$(1+x)^{-1} = 1 + (-1)x + \frac{(-1)(-2)}{2!}x^2 + \frac{(-1)(-2)(-3)}{3!}x^3 + \dots$$

$$= 1 - x + x^2 - x^3 + \dots$$

provided $-1 < x < 1$. Consequently, if in future applications we come across the series $1 - x + x^2 - x^3 + \dots$, we shall be able to write it in the form $(1+x)^{-1}$. This **closed form** avoids the use of an infinite series and so it is easier to handle. We shall make use of this technique in Chapter 22 when we meet the z transform.

Example 6.19 Obtain a quadratic approximation to $(1 - 2x)^{1/2}$ using the binomial theorem.

Solution Using Equation (6.4) with x replaced by $-2x$ and $n = \frac{1}{2}$ we have

$$(1 - 2x)^{1/2} = 1 + \left(\tfrac{1}{2}\right)(-2x) + \frac{(1/2)(-1/2)}{2!}(-2x)^2 + \dots$$

$$= 1 - x - \tfrac{1}{2}x^2 + \dots$$

provided that $-1 < -2x < 1$, that is $-\frac{1}{2} < x < \frac{1}{2}$. A quadratic approximation is therefore $1 - x - \frac{1}{2}x^2$.

Exercises 6.4

1 Use the binomial theorem to expand

(a) $(1+x)^3$

(b) $(1+x)^4$

(c) $\left(1 + \dfrac{x}{3}\right)^4$

(d) $\left(1 - \dfrac{x}{2}\right)^5$

(e) $\left(2 + \dfrac{x}{2}\right)^5$

(f) $\left(3 - \dfrac{x}{4}\right)^4$

2 Use Pascal's triangle to expand $(a + b)^8$.

3 Use Pascal's triangle to expand $(2x + 3y)^4$.

4 Expand $(a - 2b)^5$.

5 Use the binomial theorem to find the expansion of $(3 - 2x)^6$ up to and including the term in x^3.

6 Obtain the first four terms in the expansion of $\left(1 + \tfrac{1}{2}x\right)^{10}$.

7 Obtain the first five terms in the expansion of $(1 + 2x)^{1/2}$. State the range of values of x for which the expansion is valid. Choose a value of x within the range of validity and compute values of your expansion for comparison with the true function values.

8 Expand $\left(1 + \tfrac{1}{2}x\right)^{-4}$ in ascending powers of x up to the term in x^4, stating the range of values of x for which the expansion is valid.

9 Expand $\left(1 + \tfrac{1}{x}\right)^{-1/2}$ in descending powers up to the fourth term.

10 (a) Expand $(1 + x^2)^4$.

(b) Expand $(1 + 1/x^2)^4$.

11 A function, $f(x)$, is given by

$$f(x) = \left(1 + \frac{1}{x}\right)^{1/2}$$

(a) Obtain the first four terms in the expansion of $f(x)$ in descending powers of x. State the range of values of x for which the expansion is valid.

(b) By writing $f(x)$ in the form

$$f(x) = x^{-1/2}(1 + x)^{1/2}$$

obtain the first four terms in the expansion of $f(x)$ in ascending powers of x. State the range of values of x for which the expansion is valid.

12 The function, $g(x)$, is defined by

$$g(x) = \frac{1}{(1 + x^2)^4}$$

(a) Obtain the first four terms in the expansion of $g(x)$ in ascending powers of x. State the range of values of x for which the expansion is valid.

(b) By rewriting $g(x)$ in an appropriate form, obtain the first four terms in the expansion of $g(x)$ in descending powers of x. State the range of values of x for which the expansion is valid.

Solutions

1 (a) $1 + 3x + 3x^2 + x^3$

(b) $1 + 4x + 6x^2 + 4x^3 + x^4$

(c) $1 + \frac{4x}{3} + \frac{2x^2}{3} + \frac{4x^3}{27} + \frac{x^4}{81}$

(d) $1 - \frac{5x}{2} + \frac{5x^2}{2} - \frac{5x^3}{4} + \frac{5x^4}{16} - \frac{x^5}{32}$

(e) $32 + 40x + 20x^2 + 5x^3 + \frac{5x^4}{8} + \frac{x^5}{32}$

(f) $81 - 27x + \frac{27x^2}{8} - \frac{3x^3}{16} + \frac{x^4}{256}$

2 $a^8 + 8a^7b + 28a^6b^2 + 56a^5b^3 + 70a^4b^4 + 56a^3b^5 + 28a^2b^6 + 8ab^7 + b^8$

3 $16x^4 + 96x^3y + 216x^2y^2 + 216xy^3 + 81y^4$

4 $a^5 - 10a^4b + 40a^3b^2 - 80a^2b^3 + 80ab^4 - 32b^5$

5 $729 - 2916x + 4860x^2 - 4320x^3$

6 $1 + 5x + \frac{45x^2}{4} + 15x^3$

7 $1 + x - \frac{x^2}{2} + \frac{x^3}{2} - \frac{5x^4}{8}$ valid for $-\frac{1}{2} < x < \frac{1}{2}$

8 $1 - 2x + \frac{5x^2}{2} - \frac{5x^3}{2} + \frac{35x^4}{16}$ valid for $-2 < x < 2$

9 $1 - \frac{1}{2x} + \frac{3}{8x^2} - \frac{5}{16x^3}$

10 (a) $1 + 4x^2 + 6x^4 + 4x^6 + x^8$

(b) $1 + \frac{4}{x^2} + \frac{6}{x^4} + \frac{4}{x^6} + \frac{1}{x^8}$

11 (a) $1 + \frac{1}{2x} - \frac{1}{8x^2} + \frac{1}{16x^3}$ valid for $|x| > 1$

(b) $x^{-1/2}\left(1 + \frac{x}{2} - \frac{x^2}{8} + \frac{x^3}{16}\right)$ valid for $|x| < 1$

12 (a) $1 - 4x^2 + 10x^4 - 20x^6$ valid for $|x| < 1$

(b) $x^{-8}\left(1 - \frac{4}{x^2} + \frac{10}{x^4} - \frac{20}{x^6} \cdots\right)$ valid for $|x| > 1$

6.5 ## Power series

A particularly important class of series are known as **power series** and these are infinite series involving integer powers of the variable x. For example,

$$1 + x + x^2 + x^3 + \ldots$$

and

$$1 + x + \frac{x^2}{2} + \frac{x^3}{6} + \dots$$

are both power series. Note that a power series can be regarded as an infinite polynomial. Many common functions can be expressed in terms of a power series, for example

$$\sin x = x - \frac{x^3}{3!} + \frac{x^5}{5!} - \dots \qquad x \text{ in radians}$$

which converges for any value of x. For example,

$$\sin(0.5) = 0.5 - \frac{(0.5)^3}{6} + \frac{(0.5)^5}{120} - \dots$$

Taking just the first three terms, we find

$$\sin(0.5) \approx 0.5 - 0.020\,833\,3 + 0.000\,260\,4 = 0.479\,427\,1$$

as compared with the true value, $\sin 0.5 = 0.479\,425\,5$.

More generally, a power series is only meaningful if the series converges for the particular value of x chosen. We define an important quantity known as the **radius of convergence**, R, as the largest value for which an x chosen in the interval $-R < x < R$ causes the series to converge.

The open interval $(-R, R)$ is known as the **interval of convergence**. Tests for convergence of a power series are the subject of more advanced texts. Further consideration will be given to power series in Chapter 18, but for future reference we give some common expansions now:

$$\sin x = x - \frac{x^3}{3!} + \frac{x^5}{5!} - \dots \qquad x \text{ in radians}$$

$$\cos x = 1 - \frac{x^2}{2!} + \frac{x^4}{4!} - \dots \qquad x \text{ in radians}$$

$$e^x = 1 + x + \frac{x^2}{2!} + \frac{x^3}{3!} + \frac{x^4}{4!} + \dots$$

all of which converge for any value of x.

Each of these series converges rapidly when x is small, and so can be used to obtain useful approximations. In particular, we note that

If x is small and measured in radians

$$\sin x \approx x \qquad \text{and} \qquad \cos x \approx 1 - \frac{x^2}{2!}$$

These formulae are known as the **small-angle approximations**.

Exercises 6.5

1 The power series expansion of e^x is given by

$$e^x = 1 + x + \frac{x^2}{2!} + \frac{x^3}{3!} + \ldots$$

and is valid for any x. Take four terms of the series when $x = 0, 0.1, 0.5$ and 1, to compare the sum to four terms with the value of e^x obtained from your calculator. Comment upon the result.

2 Using the power series expansion for $\cos x$:

(a) Write down the power series expansion for $\cos 2x$.

(b) Write down the power series expansion for $\cos(x/2)$.

By considering the power series expansion for $\cos(-x)$ show that $\cos x = \cos(-x)$.

3 By considering the power series expansion of e^x find $\sum_{k=0}^{\infty} 1/k!$.

4 Obtain a cubic approximation to $e^x \sin x$.

5 (a) State the power series expansion for e^{-x}.

(b) By using your solution to (a) and the expansion for e^x, deduce the power series expansions of $\cosh x$ and $\sinh x$.

Solutions

1

x	e^x	Sum to 4 terms
0	1	1
0.1	1.1052	1.1052
0.5	1.6487	1.6458
1	2.7183	2.6667

Values are in close agreement when x is small

2 (a) $1 - 2x^2 + \frac{2x^4}{3} - \ldots$

(b) $1 - \frac{x^2}{8} + \frac{x^4}{384} - \ldots$

3 e

4 $x + x^2 + \frac{x^3}{3}$

5 (a) $1 - x + \frac{x^2}{2!} - \frac{x^3}{3!} + \ldots$

(b) $\cosh x = 1 + \frac{x^2}{2!} + \frac{x^4}{4!} + \ldots,$

$\sinh x = x + \frac{x^3}{3!} + \frac{x^5}{5!} + \ldots$

6.6 Sequences arising from the iterative solution of non-linear equations

It is often necessary to solve equations of the form $f(x) = 0$. For example,

$$f(x) = x^3 - 3x^2 + 7 = 0, \qquad f(x) = \ln x - \frac{1}{x} = 0$$

To **solve** means to find values of x which satisfy the given equation. These values are known as **roots**. For example, the roots of $x^2 - 3x + 2 = 0$ are $x = 1$ and $x = 2$ because when these values are substituted into the equation both sides are equal. Equations where the unknown quantity, x, occurs only to the first power are called **linear equations**. Otherwise an equation is **non-linear**. A simple way of finding the roots of an equation $f(x) = 0$ is to sketch a graph of $y = f(x)$ as shown in Figure 6.8.

The roots are those values of x where the graph cuts or touches the x axis. Generally, there is no analytical way of solving the equation $f(x) = 0$ and so it is often necessary to resort to approximate or **numerical** techniques of solution. An

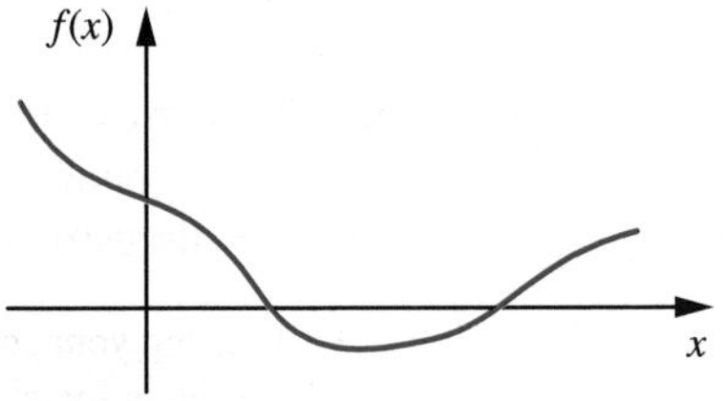

Table 6.1 Iterative solution of $e^{-x} - x = 0$.

n	x_n
0	0
1	1
2	0.368
3	0.692
4	0.501
5	0.606
6	0.546
$\vdots$	$\vdots$
$\vdots$	0.567

Figure 6.8 A root of $f(x) = 0$ occurs where the graph touches or crosses the x axis.

iterative technique is one which produces a sequence of approximate solutions which may converge to a root. Iterative techniques can fail in that the sequence produced can diverge. Whether or not this happens depends upon the equation to be solved and the availability of a good estimate of the root. Such an estimate could be obtained by sketching a graph. The technique we shall describe here is known as **simple iteration**. It requires that the equation be rewritten in the form $x = g(x)$. An estimate of the root is made, say x_0, and this value is substituted into the r.h.s. of $x = g(x)$. This yields another estimate, x_1. The process is then repeated. Formally we express this as

$$x_{n+1} = g(x_n)$$

This is a recurrence relation which produces a sequence of estimates $x_0, x_1, x_2, \ldots$. Under certain circumstances the sequence will converge to a root of the equation. It is particularly simple to program this technique on a computer. A check would be built into the program to test whether or not successive estimates are converging.

Example 6.20 Solve the equation $f(x) = e^{-x} - x = 0$ by simple iteration.

Solution The equation must first be arranged into the form $x = g(x)$, and so we write $e^{-x} - x = 0$ as

$$x = e^{-x}$$

In this example we see that $g(x) = e^{-x}$. The recurrence relation which will produce estimates of the root is

$$x_{n+1} = e^{-x_n}$$

Suppose we estimate $x_0 = 0$. Then

$$x_1 = e^{-x_0} = e^{-0} = 1$$

Then

$$x_2 = e^{-x_1} = e^{-1} = 0.368$$

The process is continued. The calculation is shown in Table 6.1 from which we see that the sequence eventually converges to 0.567 (3 d.p.). We conclude that $x = 0.567$ is a root of $e^{-x} - x = 0$.

Note that if the equation to be solved involves trigonometric functions, angles will usually be measured in radians and not degrees.

It is possible to devise a test to check whether any given rearrangement will converge. For details of this you should refer to a textbook on numerical analysis. There are other more sophisticated iterative methods for the solution of non-linear equations. One such method, the Newton–Raphson method, is discussed in Chapter 12.

Exercises 6.6

1 Show that the quadratic equation $x^2 - 5x - 7 = 0$ can be written in the form $x = \sqrt{7 + 5x}$. With $x_0 = 6$ locate a root of this equation.

2 For the quadratic equation of Question 1 show that an alternative rearrangement is $x = \dfrac{x^2 - 7}{5}$. With $x_0 = 0.6$ find the second solution of this equation.

3 For the quadratic equation of Question 1 show that another rearrangement is $x = \dfrac{7}{x} + 5$. Try to solve the equation using various initial estimates. Investigate further alternative arrangements of the original equation.

4 Show that one recurrence relation for the solution of the equation
$$e^x + 10x - 3 = 0$$

is

$$x_{n+1} = \frac{3 - e^{x_n}}{10}$$

With $x_0 = 0$ locate a root of the given equation.

5 (a) Show that the cubic equation $x^3 + 3x - 5 = 0$ can be written as

(i) $x = \dfrac{5 - x^3}{3}$,

(ii) $x = \dfrac{5}{x^2 + 3}$.

(b) By sketching a graph for values of x between 0 and 3 obtain a rough estimate of the root of the equation given in part (a).

(c) Determine which, if either, of the arrangements in part (a) converges more rapidly to the root.

Solutions

1 6.14

2 −1.14

4 0.18

5 (b) 1.15

(c) Arrangement (ii) converges more rapidly

Computer and calculator exercises 6.6

1 Write a computer program to implement the simple iteration method. By comparing successive estimates the program should check whether convergence is taking place.

Review exercises 6

1 Write down and graph the first five terms of the sequences $x[k]$ defined by

(a) $x[k] = (-1)^k$, $k = 0, 1, 2, 3, \ldots$

(b) $x[k] = \dfrac{(-1)^k}{2k+1}$, $k = 0, 1, 2, 3, \ldots$

2 Find expressions for the kth terms of the sequences whose first five terms are

(a) $1, 9, 17, 25, 33$

(b) $-1, 1, -1, 1, -1$

3 For the Fibonacci sequence

$$1, 1, 2, 3, 5, 8, \ldots$$

show that

$$\lim_{k \to \infty} \frac{x[k+1]}{x[k]} = \frac{1}{2}(1 + \sqrt{5})$$

[Hint: write $x[k+1] = x[k] + x[k-1]$, form $x[k+1]/x[k]$ and take limits.]

4 Use the binomial theorem to expand $(1 + x + x^2)^5$ as far as the term in x^3.

5 Use the binomial theorem to expand $\dfrac{1}{(3+x)^3}$ in ascending powers of x as far as the term in x^3.

6 The power series expansion for $\ln(1+x)$ is given by

$$\ln(1+x) = x - \frac{x^2}{2} + \frac{x^3}{3} - \frac{x^4}{4} + \ldots$$

and is valid for $-1 < x \leqslant 1$. Take a number of values of x in this interval and obtain an approximate value of $\ln(1+x)$ by means of this series. Compare your answers with the values obtained from your calculator.

7 By multiplying both numerator and denominator of $\dfrac{\sqrt{k+1} - \sqrt{k}}{2}$ by $\sqrt{k+1} + \sqrt{k}$ find

$$\lim_{k \to \infty} \frac{\sqrt{k+1} - \sqrt{k}}{2}$$

8 Find $\displaystyle\lim_{k \to \infty} \left(\frac{3k-1}{2k+7}\right)^3$

9 Find $\displaystyle\lim_{k \to \infty} \frac{2k^5 - 3k^2}{7k^7 + 2k}$.

10 Write down the first eight terms of the series $\sum_{k=1}^{n} k$. By noting that this is an arithmetic series show that

$$\sum_{k=1}^{n} k = \frac{n(n+1)}{2}$$

11 Write down the first six terms of the sequence defined by the recurrence relation

$$x[n+3] = x[n+2] - 2x[n]$$
$$x[0] = 0 \qquad x[1] = 2 \qquad x[2] = 3$$

12 Find the limit, if it exists, as $k \to \infty$ of the geometric progression

$$a, ar, ar^2, \ldots, ar^{k-1}, \ldots$$

when

(a) $-1 < r < 1$

(b) $r > 1$

(c) $r < -1$

(d) $r = 1$

(e) $r = -1$

13 An arithmetic series has a first term of 4 and the 10th term is 0.

(a) Find S_{20}.

(b) If $S_n = 0$, find n.

14 A geometric series has

$$S_3 = \frac{37}{8} \qquad S_6 = \frac{3367}{512}$$

Find the first term and the common ratio.

15 (a) Write down the series given by $\sum_{r=1}^{5} r^2$.

(b) The sum of the squares of the first n whole numbers can be found from the formula

$$\sum_{r=1}^{n} r^2 = \frac{n(n+1)(2n+1)}{6}$$

Use this formula to find

(i) $\sum_{r=1}^{5} r^2$,

(ii) $\sum_{r=1}^{10} r^2$,

(iii) $\sum_{r=6}^{10} r^2$.

16 (a) Write down the series given by $\sum_{r=1}^{6} r^3$.

(b) The sum of the cubes of the first n whole numbers can be found from the formula

$$\sum_{r=1}^{n} r^3 = \left(\frac{n(n+1)}{2}\right)^2$$

Use this formula to find

(i) $\sum_{r=1}^{6} r^3$,

(ii) $\sum_{r=1}^{12} r^3$,

(iii) $\sum_{r=7}^{12} r^3$.

17 The third term of an arithmetic progression is 18. The fifth term is 28. Find the sum of 20 terms.

18 (a) Find an expression for the general term in the sequence

$$2, 5, 10, 17, \ldots$$

(b) Define the sequence in terms of a recurrence relation.

19 (a) Show that the equation $x^3 + 2x - 14 = 0$ can be rearranged into the form $x = \sqrt[3]{14 - 2x}$. With $x_0 = 2$ use simple iteration to find a root of the equation.

(b) Rearrange the equation $0.8 \sin x - 0.5x = 0$ into the form $x = g(x)$. With $x_0 = 2$ use simple iteration to find a root of the equation.

(c) Rearrange the equation $x^3 = 2e^{-x}$ into the form $x = g(x)$. With $x_0 = 0$ use simple iteration to find a root of the equation.

Solutions

1 (a) $1, -1, 1, -1, 1$ (b) $1, -\frac{1}{3}, \frac{1}{5}, -\frac{1}{7}, \frac{1}{9}$

2 (a) $8k - 7$ $k \geqslant 1$ (b) $(-1)^k$ $k \geqslant 1$

4 $1 + 5x + 15x^2 + 30x^3$

5 $\frac{1}{27}\left(1 - x + \frac{2x^2}{3} - \frac{10x^3}{27} + \ldots\right)$

7 0

8 $\frac{27}{8}$

9 0

11 $0, 2, 3, 3, -1, -7$

12 (a) 0 (b) no limit   (c) no limit
(d) a (e) no limit

13 (a) $-\frac{40}{9}$ (b) 19

14 $2, \frac{3}{4}$

15 (a) $1 + 4 + 9 + 16 + 25$
(b) (i) 55 (ii) 385 (iii) 330

16 (a) $1 + 8 + 27 + 64 + 125 + 216$
(b) (i) 441 (ii) 6084 (iii) 5643

17 1110

18 (a) $x[k] = k^2 + 1, k = 1, 2, 3, \ldots$
(b) $x[k+1] = x[k] + 2k + 1$

19 (a) 2.13
(b) $x = 1.6 \sin x, 1.6$
(c) $x = \sqrt[3]{2e^{-x}}, 0.93$

7 Vectors

Chapter 7 Contents

7.1	Introduction	202
7.2	Vectors and scalars: basic concepts	202
7.3	Cartesian components	210
7.4	Scalar fields and vector fields	217
7.5	The scalar product	219
7.6	The vector product	224
7.7	Vectors of n dimensions	230
	Review exercises	232

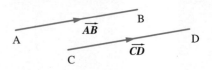

Figure 7.1 A vector, $\overrightarrow{AB}$, of length 4.   **Figure 7.2** Two equal vectors.

7.1 Introduction

Certain physical quantities are fully described by a single number: for example, the mass of a stone, the speed of a car. Such quantities are called **scalars**. On the other hand, some quantities are not fully described until a direction is specified in addition to the number. For example, a velocity of 30 metres per second due east is different from a velocity of 30 metres per second due north. These quantities are called **vectors** and it is important to distinguish them from scalars. There are many engineering applications in which vector and scalar quantities play important roles. For example, speed, potential, work and energy are scalar quantities, while velocity, electric and magnetic forces, the position of a robot and the state-space representation of a system can all be described by vectors. A variety of mathematical techniques have been developed to enable useful calculations to be carried out using vectors and in this chapter these will be discussed.

7.2 Vectors and scalars: basic concepts

Scalars are the simplest quantities with which to deal; the specification of a single number is all that is required. Vectors also have a direction and it is useful to consider a graphical representation. Thus the line segment AB of length 4 in Figure 7.1 can represent a vector in the direction shown by the arrow on AB. This vector is denoted by $\overrightarrow{AB}$. Note that $\overrightarrow{AB} \neq \overrightarrow{BA}$. The vector $\overrightarrow{AB}$ is directed from A to B, but $\overrightarrow{BA}$ is directed from B to A.

An alternative notation is frequently used: we denote $\overrightarrow{AB}$ by **a**. This bold notation is commonly used in textbooks but the notation $\underline{a}$ is preferable for handwritten work. We now need to refer to the diagram to appreciate the intended direction. The length of the line segment represents the **magnitude**, or **modulus**, of the vector and we use the notation $|\overrightarrow{AB}|$, $|\mathbf{a}|$ or simply a to denote this. Note that whereas **a** is a vector, $|\mathbf{a}|$ is a scalar.

7.2.1 Negative vectors

The vector $-\mathbf{a}$ is a vector in the opposite direction to, but with the same magnitude as, a. Geometrically it will be $\overrightarrow{BA}$. Thus $-\mathbf{a}$ is the same as $\overrightarrow{BA}$.

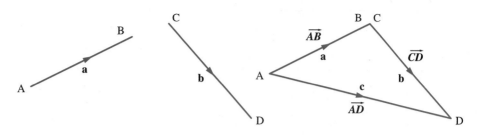

Figure 7.3 Two vectors, $\overrightarrow{AB}$ and $\overrightarrow{CD}$.

Figure 7.4 Addition of the two vectors of Figure 7.3 using the triangle law.

7.2.2 Equal vectors

Two vectors are equal if they have the same magnitude and direction. In Figure 7.2 vectors $\overrightarrow{CD}$ and $\overrightarrow{AB}$ are equal even though their locations differ. This is a useful property of vectors: a vector can be translated, maintaining its length and direction without changing the vector itself. There are exceptions to this property. For example, we shall soon meet position vectors which are used to locate specific fixed points in space. They clearly cannot be moved around freely. Nevertheless most of the vectors we shall meet can be translated freely, and as such are often called **free vectors**.

7.2.3 Vector addition

It is frequently useful to add two or more vectors together and the addition of vectors is defined by the **triangle law**. Referring to Figure 7.3, if we wish to add $\overrightarrow{AB}$ to $\overrightarrow{CD}$, $\overrightarrow{CD}$ is translated until C and B coincide. As mentioned earlier, this translation does not change the vector $\overrightarrow{CD}$. Then the sum, $\overrightarrow{AB} + \overrightarrow{CD}$, is defined by the vector represented by the third side of the completed triangle, that is $\overrightarrow{AD}$ (Figure 7.4). Thus,

$$\overrightarrow{AB} + \overrightarrow{CD} = \overrightarrow{AD}$$

Similarly, if $\overrightarrow{AB}$ is denoted by $\mathbf{a}$, $\overrightarrow{CD}$ is denoted by $\mathbf{b}$, $\overrightarrow{AD}$ is denoted by $\mathbf{c}$, then we have

$$\mathbf{c} = \mathbf{a} + \mathbf{b}$$

We note that to add $\mathbf{a}$ and $\mathbf{b}$ a triangle is formed using $\mathbf{a}$ and $\mathbf{b}$ as two of the sides in such a way that the head of one vector touches the tail of the other as shown in Figure 7.4. The sum $\mathbf{a} + \mathbf{b}$ is then represented by the third side.

It is possible to prove the following rules:

$\mathbf{a} + \mathbf{b} = \mathbf{b} + \mathbf{a}$	vector addition is commutative
$\mathbf{a} + (\mathbf{b} + \mathbf{c}) = (\mathbf{a} + \mathbf{b}) + \mathbf{c}$	vector addition is associative

To see why it is appropriate to add vectors using the triangle law consider Examples 7.1 and 7.2.

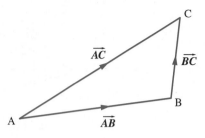
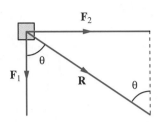

Figure 7.5 Routing of an automated vehicle from stores at A to workers at C.

Figure 7.6 Resultant force, **R**, produced by a vertical force, **F**$_1$, and a horizontal force, **F**$_2$.

Example 7.1

Routing of an automated vehicle

An automated vehicle moves on tracks around a factory floor carrying electrical components from stores at A to workers at C as illustrated in Figure 7.5. The vehicle may arrive at C either directly, or via point B. The movement from A to B can be represented by a vector $\vec{AB}$ known as a **displacement vector**, whose magnitude is the distance between points A and B. Similarly, movement from B to C is represented by $\vec{BC}$, and movement directly from A to C is represented by $\vec{AC}$. Clearly, since A, B and C are fixed points, these displacement vectors are fixed too. Since the head of the vector $\vec{AB}$ touches the tail of the vector $\vec{BC}$ we are ready to use the triangle law of vector addition to find the combined effect of the two displacements:

$$\vec{AB} + \vec{BC} = \vec{AC}$$

This means that the combined effect of displacements $\vec{AB}$ and $\vec{BC}$ is the displacement $\vec{AC}$. We say that $\vec{AC}$ is the **resultant** of $\vec{AB}$ and $\vec{BC}$.

In considering motion from point A to point B, the vector $\vec{AB}$ is called a displacement vector.

Example 7.2

Resultant of two forces acting on a body

A force **F**$_1$ of 2 N acts vertically downwards, and a force **F**$_2$ of 3 N acts horizontally to the right, upon the body shown in Figure 7.6. Translating **F**$_1$ until its tail touches the head of **F**$_2$ we can apply the triangle law to find the combined effect of the two forces. This is a single force **R** known as the resultant of **F**$_2$ and **F**$_1$. We write

$$\mathbf{R} = \mathbf{F}_2 + \mathbf{F}_1$$

and say that **R** is the vector sum of **F**$_2$ and **F**$_1$. The resultant force, **R**, acts at an angle of θ to the vertical, where $\tan\theta = 3/2$, and has a magnitude given by Pythagoras's theorem as $\sqrt{2^2 + 3^2} = \sqrt{13}$ N.

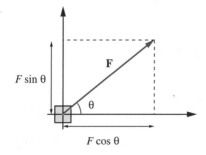

Figure 7.7 A force **F** can be resolved into two perpendicular components.

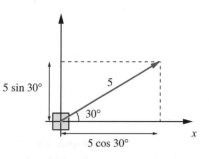

Figure 7.8 The 5 N force can be resolved into two perpendicular components.

Example 7.3 Resolving a force into two perpendicular directions

In the previous example we saw that two forces acting upon a body can be replaced by a single force which has the same effect. Equivalently we can consider a single force as two forces acting at right angles to each other. Consider the force **F** in Figure 7.7. It can be replaced by two forces, one of magnitude $|\mathbf{F}|\cos\theta$ and one of magnitude $|\mathbf{F}|\sin\theta$ as shown. We say that the force **F** has been **resolved into two perpendicular components**.

For example, Figure 7.8 shows a force of 5 N acting at an angle of 30° to the x axis. It can be resolved into two components. The first component is directed along the x axis and has magnitude $5\cos 30°$ N. The second component is perpendicular to the first and has magnitude $5\sin 30°$ N. These two components combine to have the same effect as the original 5 N force.

Example 7.4

Vectors **p**, **q**, **r** and **s** form the sides of the square shown in Figure 7.9. Express

(a) **p** in terms of **r**

(b) **s** in terms of **q**

(c) diagonal $\overrightarrow{BD}$ in terms of **q** and **r**

Solution

(a) The vector **p** has the same length as **r** but has the opposite direction. Therefore $\mathbf{p} = -\mathbf{r}$.

(b) Vector **s** has the same length as **q** but has the opposite direction. Therefore $\mathbf{s} = -\mathbf{q}$.

(c) The head of $\overrightarrow{BC}$ coincides with the tail of $\overrightarrow{CD}$. Therefore, by the triangle law of addition, the third side of triangle BCD represents the sum of $\overrightarrow{BC}$ and $\overrightarrow{CD}$, that is

$$\overrightarrow{BD} = \overrightarrow{BC} + \overrightarrow{CD}$$
$$= \mathbf{q} + \mathbf{r}$$

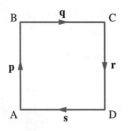
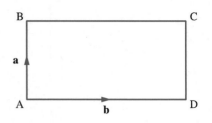

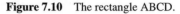

Figure 7.9 The vectors **p**, **q**, **r** and **s** form the sides of a square.

Figure 7.10 The rectangle ABCD.

7.2.4 Vector subtraction

Subtraction of one vector from another is performed by adding the corresponding negative vector; that is, if we seek $\mathbf{a} - \mathbf{b}$, we form $\mathbf{a} + (-\mathbf{b})$.

Example 7.5

Consider the rectangle illustrated in Figure 7.10 with **a** and **b** as shown. Express in terms of A, B, C or D the vectors $\mathbf{a} - \mathbf{b}$ and $\mathbf{b} - \mathbf{a}$.

Solution

We have

$$\mathbf{b} = \overrightarrow{AD}$$

hence

$$-\mathbf{b} = \overrightarrow{DA}$$

Then

$$\mathbf{a} - \mathbf{b} = \mathbf{a} + (-\mathbf{b})$$
$$= \overrightarrow{AB} + \overrightarrow{DA}$$
$$= \overrightarrow{DA} + \overrightarrow{AB} \qquad \text{by commutativity}$$

$\overrightarrow{DA}$ and $\overrightarrow{AB}$ are shown in Figure 7.11. Their sum is given by the triangle law, that is

$$\mathbf{a} - \mathbf{b} = \overrightarrow{DA} + \overrightarrow{AB} = \overrightarrow{DB}$$

Similarly,

$$\mathbf{a} = \overrightarrow{AB}$$

hence

$$-\mathbf{a} = \overrightarrow{BA}$$

Then

$$\mathbf{b} - \mathbf{a} = \mathbf{b} + (-\mathbf{a})$$
$$= \overrightarrow{AD} + \overrightarrow{BA}$$
$$= \overrightarrow{BA} + \overrightarrow{AD}$$

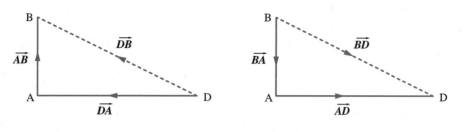

Figure 7.11 The vectors $\vec{AB}$ and $\vec{DA}$. **Figure 7.12** The vectors $\vec{BA}$ and $\vec{AD}$.

$\vec{BA}$ and $\vec{AD}$ are shown in Figure 7.12. Again their sum is given by the triangle law, that is

$$\mathbf{b} - \mathbf{a} = \vec{BA} + \vec{AD} = \vec{BD}$$

Example 7.6   Referring to Figure 7.13, if $\mathbf{r}_1$ and $\mathbf{r}_2$ are as shown, find the vector $\mathbf{b} = \vec{QP}$ represented by the third side of the triangle OPQ.

Solution   From Figure 7.13 we note from the triangle law that

$$\vec{QP} = \vec{QO} + \vec{OP} = \vec{OP} + \vec{QO} \text{ by commutativity.}$$

But $\vec{QO} = -\mathbf{r}_2$ and $\vec{QP} = \mathbf{b}$, and so

$$\mathbf{b} = \mathbf{r}_1 - \mathbf{r}_2$$

Vectors do not necessarily lie in a two-dimensional plane. Three-dimensional vectors are commonly used as is illustrated in the following example.

Example 7.7   OPQR is the tetrahedron shown in Figure 7.14. Let $\vec{OP} = \mathbf{p}, \vec{OQ} = \mathbf{q}$ and $\vec{OR} = \mathbf{r}$. Express $\vec{PQ}, \vec{QR}$ and $\vec{RP}$ in terms of $\mathbf{p}, \mathbf{q}$ and $\mathbf{r}$.

Solution   Consider the triangle OPQ shown in Figure 7.15. We note that $\vec{OQ}$ represents the third side of the triangle formed when $\mathbf{p}$ and $\vec{PQ}$ are placed head to tail. Using the triangle law we find

$$\vec{OP} + \vec{PQ} = \vec{OQ}$$

Therefore,

$$\vec{PQ} = \vec{OQ} - \vec{OP}$$
$$= \mathbf{q} - \mathbf{p}$$

Similarly, $\vec{QR} = \mathbf{r} - \mathbf{q}$ and $\vec{RP} = \mathbf{p} - \mathbf{r}$.

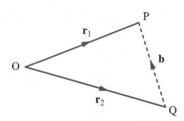

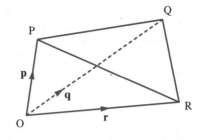

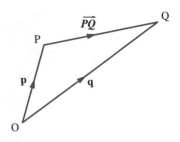

Figure 7.13 The two vectors $\mathbf{r}_1$ and $\mathbf{r}_2$.

Figure 7.14 The tetrahedron OPQR.

Figure 7.15 The triangle OPQ.

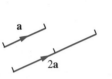

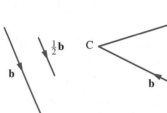

Figure 7.16 Scalar multiplication of a vector.

Figure 7.17 The triangle ABC, with midpoint M of side AB.

7.2.5 Multiplication of a vector by a scalar

If k is any positive scalar and $\mathbf{a}$ is a vector then $k\mathbf{a}$ is a vector in the same direction as $\mathbf{a}$ but k times as long. If k is any negative scalar, $k\mathbf{a}$ is a vector in the opposite direction to $\mathbf{a}$, and k times as long. By way of example, study the vectors in Figure 7.16. Clearly $2\mathbf{a}$ is twice as long as $\mathbf{a}$ but has the same direction. The vector $\frac{1}{2}\mathbf{b}$ is half as long as $\mathbf{b}$ but has the same direction as $\mathbf{b}$. It is possible to prove the following rules.

> For any scalars k and l, and any vectors $\mathbf{a}$ and $\mathbf{b}$:
>
> $$k(\mathbf{a} + \mathbf{b}) = k\mathbf{a} + k\mathbf{b}$$
> $$(k + l)\mathbf{a} = k\mathbf{a} + l\mathbf{a}$$
> $$k(l\mathbf{a}) = (kl)\mathbf{a}$$

The vector $k\mathbf{a}$ is said to be a **scalar multiple** of $\mathbf{a}$.

Example 7.8 In a triangle ABC, M is the midpoint of AB. Let $\vec{AB}$ be denoted by $\mathbf{a}$, and $\vec{BC}$ by $\mathbf{b}$. Express $\vec{AC}$, $\vec{CA}$ and $\vec{CM}$ in terms of $\mathbf{a}$ and $\mathbf{b}$.

Solution The situation is sketched in Figure 7.17. Using the triangle rule for addition we find

$$\vec{AB} + \vec{BC} = \vec{AC}$$

Therefore,

$$\vec{AC} = \mathbf{a} + \mathbf{b}$$

It follows that $\vec{CA} = -\vec{AC} = -(\mathbf{a} + \mathbf{b})$.

Again by the triangle rule applied to triangle CMB we find

$$\vec{CM} = \vec{CB} + \vec{BM}$$

Now $\vec{BM} = \frac{1}{2}\vec{BA} = -\frac{1}{2}\mathbf{a}$ and so

$$\vec{CM} = -\mathbf{b} + \left(-\frac{1}{2}\mathbf{a}\right)$$
$$= -\left(\mathbf{b} + \frac{1}{2}\mathbf{a}\right)$$

7.2.6 Unit vectors

Vectors which have length 1 are called **unit vectors**. If $\mathbf{a}$ has length 3, for example, then a unit vector in the direction of $\mathbf{a}$ is clearly $\frac{1}{3}\mathbf{a}$. More generally we denote the unit vector in the direction $\mathbf{a}$ by $\hat{\mathbf{a}}$. Recall that the length or modulus of $\mathbf{a}$ is $|\mathbf{a}|$ and so we can write

$$\hat{\mathbf{a}} = \frac{\mathbf{a}}{|\mathbf{a}|}$$

Note that $|\mathbf{a}|$ and hence $\frac{1}{|\mathbf{a}|}$ are scalars.

7.2.7 Orthogonal vectors

If the angle between two vectors $\mathbf{a}$ and $\mathbf{b}$ is $90°$, that is $\mathbf{a}$ and $\mathbf{b}$ are perpendicular, then $\mathbf{a}$ and $\mathbf{b}$ are said to be **orthogonal**.

Exercises 7.2

1 For the arbitrary points A, B, C, D and E, find a single vector which is equivalent to
   (a) $\vec{DC} + \vec{CB}$ (b) $\vec{CE} + \vec{DC}$

2 Figure 7.18 shows a cube. Let $\mathbf{p} = \vec{AB}$, $\mathbf{q} = \vec{AD}$ and $\mathbf{r} = \vec{AE}$. Express the vectors representing $\vec{BD}$, $\vec{AC}$ and $\vec{AG}$ in terms of $\mathbf{p}$, $\mathbf{q}$ and $\mathbf{r}$.

3 In a triangle ABC, M is the midpoint of BC, and N is the midpoint of AC. Show that
$$\vec{NM} = \frac{1}{2}\vec{AB}.$$

4 Consider a rectangle with vertices at E, F, G and H. Suppose $\vec{EF} = \mathbf{p}$ and $\vec{FG} = \mathbf{q}$. Express each of the vectors $\vec{EH}$, $\vec{GH}$, $\vec{FH}$ and $\vec{GE}$ in terms of $\mathbf{p}$ and $\mathbf{q}$.

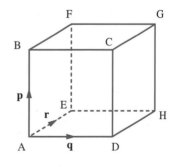

Figure 7.18

5 If $\mathbf{a}$ is an arbitrary vector, represent on a diagram the vectors $\mathbf{a}$, $\frac{1}{2}\mathbf{a}$, $-\frac{\mathbf{a}}{4}$, $3\mathbf{a}$, $-3\mathbf{a}$ and $\hat{\mathbf{a}}$.

6   A particle is positioned at the origin. Two forces act on the particle. The first force has magnitude 7 N and acts in the negative x direction. The second force has magnitude 12 N and acts in the y direction. Calculate the magnitude and direction of the resultant force.

7   A force of 15 N acts at an angle of 65° to the x axis. Resolve this force into two forces, one directed along the x axis and the other directed along the y axis.

Solutions

1   (a) $\overrightarrow{DB}$ (b) $\overrightarrow{DE}$

2   $\mathbf{q} - \mathbf{p}, \mathbf{q} + \mathbf{p}, \mathbf{q} + \mathbf{r} + \mathbf{p}$

4   $\mathbf{q}, -\mathbf{p}, \mathbf{q} - \mathbf{p}, -\mathbf{p} - \mathbf{q}$

5   See Figure S.11.

6   13.9 N at an angle of 59.7° to the negative x axis

7   6.34 N, 13.59 N

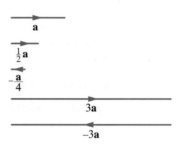

Figure S.11

Cartesian components

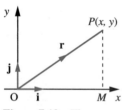

Figure 7.19   The x–y plane with point P.

Consider the x–y plane in Figure 7.19. The general point P has coordinates (x, y). We can join the origin to P by a vector $\overrightarrow{OP}$, which is called the position vector of P, which we often denote by $\mathbf{r}$. The modulus of $\mathbf{r}$ is $|\mathbf{r}| = r$, and is the length of $\overrightarrow{OP}$. It is possible to express $\mathbf{r}$ in terms of the numbers of x and y. If we denote a unit vector along the x axis by $\mathbf{i}$, and a unit vector along the y axis by $\mathbf{j}$ (we usually omit the ^ here), then it is clear from the definition of scalar multiplication that $\overrightarrow{OM} = x\mathbf{i}$, and $\overrightarrow{MP} = y\mathbf{j}$. It follows from the triangle law of addition that

$$\mathbf{r} = \overrightarrow{OP} = \overrightarrow{OM} + \overrightarrow{MP} = x\mathbf{i} + y\mathbf{j}$$

Clearly the vectors $\mathbf{i}$ and $\mathbf{j}$ are orthogonal. The numbers x and y are the $\mathbf{i}$ and $\mathbf{j}$ components of $\mathbf{r}$. Furthermore, using Pythagoras's theorem we can deduce that

$$r = \sqrt{x^2 + y^2}$$

Alternative notations which are sometimes useful are

$$\mathbf{r} = \overrightarrow{OP} = \begin{pmatrix} x \\ y \end{pmatrix}$$

and

$$\mathbf{r} = \overrightarrow{OP} = (x, y)$$

When written in these forms $\begin{pmatrix} x \\ y \end{pmatrix}$ is called a **column vector** and (x, y) is called a **row vector**. To avoid confusion with the coordinates (x, y) we shall not use row vectors here but they will be needed in Chapter 26. We will also use the column vector notation for more general vectors, thus,

$$a\mathbf{i} + b\mathbf{j} = \begin{pmatrix} a \\ b \end{pmatrix}$$

We said earlier that a vector can be translated, maintaining its length and direction without changing the vector itself. While this is true generally, position vectors form an important exception. Position vectors are constrained to their specific position and must always remain tied to the origin.

Example 7.9   If A is the point with coordinates $(5, 4)$ and B is the point with coordinates $(-3, 2)$ find the position vectors of A and B, and the vector $\overrightarrow{AB}$. Further, find $|\overrightarrow{AB}|$.

Solution   The position vector of A is $5\mathbf{i} + 4\mathbf{j} = \begin{pmatrix} 5 \\ 4 \end{pmatrix}$, which we shall denote by **a**. The position vector of B is $-3\mathbf{i}+2\mathbf{j} = \begin{pmatrix} -3 \\ 2 \end{pmatrix}$, which we shall denote by **b**. Application of the triangle law to triangle OAB (Figure 7.20) gives

$$\overrightarrow{OA} + \overrightarrow{AB} = \overrightarrow{OB}$$

that is

$$\mathbf{a} + \overrightarrow{AB} = \mathbf{b}$$

Therefore,

$$\begin{aligned} \overrightarrow{AB} &= \mathbf{b} - \mathbf{a} \\ &= (-3\mathbf{i} + 2\mathbf{j}) - (5\mathbf{i} + 4\mathbf{j}) \\ &= -8\mathbf{i} - 2\mathbf{j} \end{aligned}$$

Alternatively, in terms of column vectors

$$\begin{aligned} \mathbf{b} - \mathbf{a} &= \begin{pmatrix} -3 \\ 2 \end{pmatrix} - \begin{pmatrix} 5 \\ 4 \end{pmatrix} \\ &= \begin{pmatrix} -8 \\ -2 \end{pmatrix} \end{aligned}$$

Figure 7.20
Points A and B in the
x–y plane.

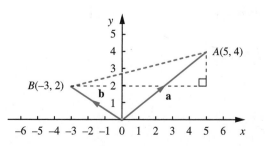

We note that subtraction (and likewise addition) of column vectors is carried out component by component. To find $|\overrightarrow{AB}|$ we must obtain the length of the vector $\overrightarrow{AB}$. Referring to Figure 7.20, we note that this quantity is the length of the hypotenuse of a right-angled triangle with perpendicular sides 8 and 2. That is, $|\overrightarrow{AB}| = \sqrt{8^2 + 2^2} = \sqrt{68} = 8.25$.

More generally we have the following result:

Given vectors $\mathbf{a} = \overrightarrow{OA} = a_1\mathbf{i} + a_2\mathbf{j}$ and $\mathbf{b} = \overrightarrow{OB} = b_1\mathbf{i} + b_2\mathbf{j}$ (Figure 7.21), then

$$\overrightarrow{AB} = \mathbf{b} - \mathbf{a} = (b_1 - a_1)\mathbf{i} + (b_2 - a_2)\mathbf{j}$$

and

$$|\overrightarrow{AB}| = |\mathbf{b} - \mathbf{a}| = |(b_1 - a_1)\mathbf{i} + (b_2 - a_2)\mathbf{j}|$$
$$= \sqrt{(b_1 - a_1)^2 + (b_2 - a_2)^2}$$

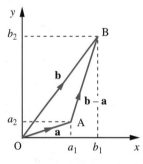

Figure 7.21 The quantity $|\mathbf{b} - \mathbf{a}| = \sqrt{(b_1 - a_1)^2 + (b_2 - a_2)^2}$.

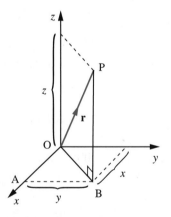

Figure 7.22 The quantity $|\mathbf{r}| = \sqrt{x^2 + y^2 + z^2}$.

Example 7.10   If $\mathbf{a} = \begin{pmatrix} 7 \\ 3 \end{pmatrix}$ and $\mathbf{b} = \begin{pmatrix} -2 \\ 5 \end{pmatrix}$,

(a) find $\mathbf{a} + \mathbf{b}$, $\mathbf{a} - \mathbf{b}$, $\mathbf{b} + \mathbf{a}$ and $\mathbf{b} - \mathbf{a}$, commenting upon the results

(b) find $2\mathbf{a} - 3\mathbf{b}$

(c) find $|\mathbf{a} - \mathbf{b}|$.

Solution (a) $\mathbf{a} + \mathbf{b} = \begin{pmatrix} 7 \\ 3 \end{pmatrix} + \begin{pmatrix} -2 \\ 5 \end{pmatrix} = \begin{pmatrix} 5 \\ 8 \end{pmatrix}$

$\mathbf{a} - \mathbf{b} = \begin{pmatrix} 7 \\ 3 \end{pmatrix} - \begin{pmatrix} -2 \\ 5 \end{pmatrix} = \begin{pmatrix} 9 \\ -2 \end{pmatrix}$

$\mathbf{b} + \mathbf{a} = \begin{pmatrix} -2 \\ 5 \end{pmatrix} + \begin{pmatrix} 7 \\ 3 \end{pmatrix} = \begin{pmatrix} 5 \\ 8 \end{pmatrix}$

$\mathbf{b} - \mathbf{a} = \begin{pmatrix} -2 \\ 5 \end{pmatrix} - \begin{pmatrix} 7 \\ 3 \end{pmatrix} = \begin{pmatrix} -9 \\ 2 \end{pmatrix}$

We note that addition is commutative whereas subtraction is not.

(b) $2\mathbf{a} - 3\mathbf{b} = 2\begin{pmatrix} 7 \\ 3 \end{pmatrix} - 3\begin{pmatrix} -2 \\ 5 \end{pmatrix} = \begin{pmatrix} 14 \\ 6 \end{pmatrix} - \begin{pmatrix} -6 \\ 15 \end{pmatrix} = \begin{pmatrix} 20 \\ -9 \end{pmatrix}$

(c) $|\mathbf{a} - \mathbf{b}| = |9\mathbf{i} - 2\mathbf{j}| = \sqrt{9^2 + (-2)^2} = \sqrt{85}$

The previous development readily generalizes to the three-dimensional case. Taking Cartesian axes x, y and z, any point in three-dimensional space can be represented by giving x, y and z coordinates (Figure 7.22). Denoting unit vectors along these axes by $\mathbf{i}$, $\mathbf{j}$ and $\mathbf{k}$, respectively, we can write the vector from O to $P(x, y, z)$ as

$$\overrightarrow{OP} = \mathbf{r} = x\mathbf{i} + y\mathbf{j} + z\mathbf{k} = \begin{pmatrix} x \\ y \\ z \end{pmatrix}$$

The vectors $\mathbf{i}$, $\mathbf{j}$ and $\mathbf{k}$ are orthogonal.

Example 7.11 If $\mathbf{r} = x\mathbf{i} + y\mathbf{j} + z\mathbf{k}$ show that the modulus of $\mathbf{r}$ is $r = \sqrt{x^2 + y^2 + z^2}$.

Solution Recalling Figure 7.22 we first calculate the length of OB. Now OAB is a right-angled triangle with perpendicular sides OA $= x$ and AB $= y$. Therefore by Pythagoras's theorem OB has length $\sqrt{x^2 + y^2}$. Then, applying Pythagoras's theorem to right-angled triangle OBP which has perpendicular sides OB and BP $= z$, we find

$$|\mathbf{r}| = \text{OP} = \sqrt{\text{OB}^2 + \text{BP}^2}$$

$$= \sqrt{(x^2 + y^2) + z^2}$$

$$= \sqrt{x^2 + y^2 + z^2}$$

as required.

If $\mathbf{r} = x\mathbf{i} + y\mathbf{j} + z\mathbf{k}$ then $|\mathbf{r}| = \sqrt{x^2 + y^2 + z^2}$

In three dimensions we have the following general result:

Given vectors $\mathbf{a} = \vec{OA} = a_1\mathbf{i} + a_2\mathbf{j} + a_3\mathbf{k}$ and $\mathbf{b} = \vec{OB} = b_1\mathbf{i} + b_2\mathbf{j} + b_3\mathbf{k}$, then

$$\vec{AB} = \mathbf{b} - \mathbf{a} = (b_1 - a_1)\mathbf{i} + (b_2 - a_2)\mathbf{j} + (b_3 - a_3)\mathbf{k}$$

and

$$|\vec{AB}| = |\mathbf{b} - \mathbf{a}| = |(b_1 - a_1)\mathbf{i} + (b_2 - a_2)\mathbf{j} + (b_3 - a_3)\mathbf{k}|$$
$$= \sqrt{(b_1 - a_1)^2 + (b_2 - a_2)^2 + (b_3 - a_3)^2}$$

Example 7.12

If $\mathbf{a} = 3\mathbf{i} - 2\mathbf{j} + \mathbf{k}$ and $\mathbf{b} = -2\mathbf{i} + \mathbf{j} - 5\mathbf{k}$, find

(a) $|\mathbf{a}|$ (b) $\hat{\mathbf{a}}$ (c) $|\mathbf{b}|$ (d) $\hat{\mathbf{b}}$ (e) $\mathbf{b} - \mathbf{a}$ (f) $|\mathbf{b} - \mathbf{a}|$

Solution

(a) $|\mathbf{a}| = \sqrt{3^2 + (-2)^2 + 1^2} = \sqrt{14}$

(b) $\hat{\mathbf{a}} = \dfrac{\mathbf{a}}{|\mathbf{a}|} = \dfrac{1}{\sqrt{14}}(3\mathbf{i} - 2\mathbf{j} + \mathbf{k}) = \dfrac{3}{\sqrt{14}}\mathbf{i} - \dfrac{2}{\sqrt{14}}\mathbf{j} + \dfrac{1}{\sqrt{14}}\mathbf{k}$

(c) $|\mathbf{b}| = \sqrt{(-2)^2 + 1^2 + (-5)^2} = \sqrt{30}$

(d) $\hat{\mathbf{b}} = \dfrac{\mathbf{b}}{|\mathbf{b}|} = \dfrac{1}{\sqrt{30}}(-2\mathbf{i} + \mathbf{j} - 5\mathbf{k}) = \dfrac{-2}{\sqrt{30}}\mathbf{i} + \dfrac{1}{\sqrt{30}}\mathbf{j} - \dfrac{5}{\sqrt{30}}\mathbf{k}$

(e) $\mathbf{b} - \mathbf{a} = -5\mathbf{i} + 3\mathbf{j} - 6\mathbf{k}$

(f) $|\mathbf{b} - \mathbf{a}| = \sqrt{(-5)^2 + 3^2 + (-6)^2} = \sqrt{70}$

7.3.1 The zero vector

A vector, all the components of which are zero, is called a **zero vector** and is denoted by **0** to distinguish it from the scalar 0. Clearly the zero vector has a length of 0; it is unusual in that it has arbitrary direction.

Example 7.13

Robot positions

Position vectors provide a useful means of determining the position of a robot. There are many different types of robot but a common type uses a series of rigid links connected together by flexible joints. Usually the mechanism is anchored at one point. A typical example is illustrated in Figure 7.23.

The anchor point is X and the tip of the robot is situated at point Y. The final link is sometimes called the hand of the robot. The hand often has rotating and gripping

Figure 7.23
A typical robot configuration with vectors representing the robot links.

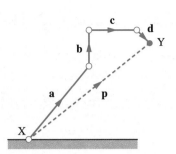

facilities and its size relative to the rest of the robot is usually quite small. Each of the robot links can be represented by a vector (see Figure 7.23). The vector **d** corresponds to the hand. A common requirement in robotics is to be able to calculate the position of the tip of the hand to ensure it does not collide with other objects. This can be achieved by defining a set of Cartesian coordinates with origin at the anchor point of the robot, X. Each of the link vectors can then be represented in terms of these coordinates. For example, in the case of the robot in Figure 7.23:

$$\mathbf{a} = a_1\mathbf{i} + a_2\mathbf{j} + a_3\mathbf{k} \qquad \mathbf{c} = c_1\mathbf{i} + c_2\mathbf{j} + c_3\mathbf{k}$$
$$\mathbf{b} = b_1\mathbf{i} + b_2\mathbf{j} + b_3\mathbf{k} \qquad \mathbf{d} = d_1\mathbf{i} + d_2\mathbf{j} + d_3\mathbf{k}$$

The position of the tip of the hand can be calculated by adding together these vectors. So,

$$\mathbf{p} = \mathbf{a} + \mathbf{b} + \mathbf{c} + \mathbf{d}$$
$$= (a_1 + b_1 + c_1 + d_1)\mathbf{i} + (a_2 + b_2 + c_2 + d_2)\mathbf{j} + (a_3 + b_3 + c_3 + d_3)\mathbf{k}$$

7.3.2 Linear combinations, dependence and independence

Suppose we have two vectors **a** and **b**. If we form arbitrary scalar multiples of these, that is $k_1\mathbf{a}$ and $k_2\mathbf{b}$, and add these together, we obtain a new vector **c** where $\mathbf{c} = k_1\mathbf{a} + k_2\mathbf{b}$. The vector **c** is said to be a **linear combination** of **a** and **b**. Note that scalar multiplication and addition of vectors are the only operations allowed when forming a linear combination. Vector **c** is said to **depend linearly** on **a** and **b**. Of course we could also write

$$\mathbf{a} = \frac{1}{k_1}\mathbf{c} - \frac{k_2}{k_1}\mathbf{b} \qquad \text{provided } k_1 \neq 0$$

so that **a** depends linearly on **c** and **b**. Provided $k_2 \neq 0$, then

$$\mathbf{b} = \frac{1}{k_2}\mathbf{c} - \frac{k_1}{k_2}\mathbf{a}$$

so that **b** depends linearly on **c** and **a**. The set of vectors $\{\mathbf{a}, \mathbf{b}, \mathbf{c}\}$ is said to be **linearly dependent** and any one of the set can be written as a linear combination of the other two. In general, we have the following definition:

A set of n vectors $\{\mathbf{a}_1, \mathbf{a}_2, \ldots, \mathbf{a}_n\}$ is linearly dependent if the expression

$$k_1\mathbf{a}_1 + k_2\mathbf{a}_2 + \cdots + k_n\mathbf{a}_n = \mathbf{0}$$

can be satisfied by finding scalar constants $k_1, k_2, \ldots, k_n$, not all of which are zero. If the only way we can make the combination zero is by choosing all the k_is to be zero, then the given set of vectors is said to be **linearly independent**.

Example 7.14   Show that the vectors $\mathbf{i}$ and $\mathbf{j}$ are linearly independent.

Solution   We form the expression $k_1\mathbf{i} + k_2\mathbf{j} = \mathbf{0}$ and try to choose k_1 and k_2 so that the equation is satisfied. Using column vectors we have

$$k_1 \begin{pmatrix} 1 \\ 0 \end{pmatrix} + k_2 \begin{pmatrix} 0 \\ 1 \end{pmatrix} = \begin{pmatrix} 0 \\ 0 \end{pmatrix}$$

that is

$$\begin{pmatrix} k_1 \\ 0 \end{pmatrix} + \begin{pmatrix} 0 \\ k_2 \end{pmatrix} = \begin{pmatrix} k_1 \\ k_2 \end{pmatrix} = \begin{pmatrix} 0 \\ 0 \end{pmatrix}$$

The only way we can satisfy the equation is by choosing $k_1 = 0$ and $k_2 = 0$ and hence we conclude that the vectors $\mathbf{i}$ and $\mathbf{j}$ are linearly independent. Geometrically, we note that since they are perpendicular, no scalar multiple of $\mathbf{i}$ can give $\mathbf{j}$ and vice versa.

Example 7.15   The vectors

$$\begin{pmatrix} 1 \\ 2 \\ 3 \end{pmatrix} \quad \begin{pmatrix} 5 \\ 1 \\ 9 \end{pmatrix} \quad \begin{pmatrix} 13 \\ -1 \\ 21 \end{pmatrix}$$

are linearly dependent because, for example,

$$3 \begin{pmatrix} 5 \\ 1 \\ 9 \end{pmatrix} - 2 \begin{pmatrix} 1 \\ 2 \\ 3 \end{pmatrix} - 1 \begin{pmatrix} 13 \\ -1 \\ 21 \end{pmatrix} = \begin{pmatrix} 0 \\ 0 \\ 0 \end{pmatrix}$$

Exercises 7.3

1 P and Q lie in the x–y plane. Find $\overrightarrow{PQ}$, where P is the point with coordinates $(5, 1)$ and Q is the point with coordinates $(-1, 4)$. Find $|\overrightarrow{PQ}|$.

2 A and B lie in the x–y plane. If A is the point $(3, 4)$ and **B** is the point $(1, -5)$ write down the vectors $\overrightarrow{OA}$, $\overrightarrow{OB}$ and $\overrightarrow{AB}$. Find a unit vector in the direction of $\overrightarrow{AB}$.

3 If $\mathbf{a} = 4\mathbf{i} - \mathbf{j} + 3\mathbf{k}$ and $\mathbf{b} = -2\mathbf{i} + 2\mathbf{j} - \mathbf{k}$, find unit vectors in the directions of $\mathbf{a}$, $\mathbf{b}$ and $\mathbf{b} - \mathbf{a}$.

4 If $\mathbf{a} = 5\mathbf{i} - 2\mathbf{j}$, $\mathbf{b} = 3\mathbf{i} - 7\mathbf{j}$ and $\mathbf{c} = -3\mathbf{i} + 4\mathbf{j}$, express, in terms of $\mathbf{i}$ and $\mathbf{j}$,

$$\mathbf{a} + \mathbf{b} \qquad \mathbf{a} + \mathbf{c} \qquad \mathbf{c} - \mathbf{b} \qquad 3\mathbf{c} - 4\mathbf{b}$$

Draw diagrams to illustrate your results. Repeat the calculations using column vector notation.

5 Write down a unit vector which is parallel to the line $y = 7x - 3$.

6 Find $\vec{PQ}$ where P is the point in three-dimensional space with coordinates $(4, 1, 3)$ and Q is the point with coordinates $(1, 2, 4)$. Find the distance between P and Q. Further, find the position vector of the point dividing PQ in the ratio 1 : 3.

7 If P, Q and R have coordinates $(3, 2, 1)$, $(2, 1, 2)$ and $(1, 3, 3)$, respectively, use vectors to determine which pair of points are closest to each other.

8 Consider the robot of Example 7.13. The link vectors have the following values:

$$\mathbf{a} = 12\mathbf{i} + 18\mathbf{j} + \mathbf{k}$$
$$\mathbf{b} = 6\mathbf{i} - 3\mathbf{j} + 8\mathbf{k}$$
$$\mathbf{c} = 3\mathbf{i} + 2\mathbf{j} - 4\mathbf{k}$$
$$\mathbf{d} = 0.5\mathbf{i} - 0.2\mathbf{j} + 0.6\mathbf{k}$$

Calculate the length of each of the links and the position vector of the tip of the robot.

9 Show that the vectors $\mathbf{a} = \mathbf{i} + \mathbf{j}$ and $\mathbf{b} = -\mathbf{i} + \mathbf{j}$ are linearly independent.

10 Show that the vectors $\mathbf{i}$, $\mathbf{j}$ and $\mathbf{k}$ are linearly independent.

Solutions

1 $\vec{PQ} = -6\mathbf{i} + 3\mathbf{j}$ $|\vec{PQ}| = 6.71$

2 $3\mathbf{i} + 4\mathbf{j}, \mathbf{i} - 5\mathbf{j}, -2\mathbf{i} - 9\mathbf{j}$

unit vector: $\dfrac{-1}{\sqrt{85}}(2\mathbf{i} + 9\mathbf{j})$

3 $\dfrac{1}{\sqrt{26}}(4\mathbf{i} - \mathbf{j} + 3\mathbf{k}), \dfrac{1}{3}(-2\mathbf{i} + 2\mathbf{j} - \mathbf{k}),$

$\dfrac{1}{\sqrt{61}}(-6\mathbf{i} + 3\mathbf{j} - 4\mathbf{k})$

4 $8\mathbf{i} - 9\mathbf{j}, 2\mathbf{i} + 2\mathbf{j}, -6\mathbf{i} + 11\mathbf{j}, -21\mathbf{i} + 40\mathbf{j}$

5 $\dfrac{1}{\sqrt{50}}(\mathbf{i} + 7\mathbf{j})$

6 $\vec{PQ} = -3\mathbf{i} + \mathbf{j} + \mathbf{k}$, distance from P to Q

$= 3.32, \dfrac{1}{4}(13\mathbf{i} + 5\mathbf{j} + 13\mathbf{k})$

7 P and Q

8 $21.66, 10.44, 5.39, 0.81, 21.5\mathbf{i} + 16.8\mathbf{j} + 5.6\mathbf{k}$

7.4   Scalar fields and vector fields

Imagine a large room filled with air. At any point, P, we can measure the temperature, ϕ, say. The temperature will depend upon whereabouts in the room we take the measurement. Perhaps, close to a radiator the temperature will be higher than near to an open window. Clearly the temperature ϕ is a function of the position of the point. If we label the point by its Cartesian coordinates (x, y, z), then ϕ will be a function of x, y and z, that is

$$\phi = \phi(x, y, z)$$

Additionally, ϕ may be a function of time but for now we will leave this additional complication aside. Since temperature is a scalar what we have done is define a scalar at each point $P(x, y, z)$ in a region. This is an example of a **scalar field**.

Alternatively, suppose we consider the motion of a large body of fluid. At each point, fluid will be moving with a certain speed in a certain direction; that is, each small fluid element has a particular velocity, $\mathbf{v}$, depending upon whereabouts in the fluid it is. Since velocity is a vector, what we have done is define a vector at each point $P(x, y, z)$.

Figure 7.24
A charge at O gives
rise to an electric field
E.

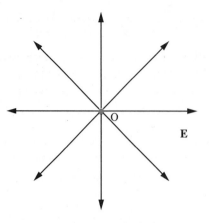

We now have a vector function of x, y and z, known as a **vector field**. Let us write

$$\mathbf{v} = (v_x, v_y, v_z)$$

so that v_x, v_y and v_z are the $\mathbf{i}$, $\mathbf{j}$ and $\mathbf{k}$ components respectively of $\mathbf{v}$, that is

$$\mathbf{v} = v_x\mathbf{i} + v_y\mathbf{j} + v_z\mathbf{k}$$

We note that v_x, v_y and v_z will each be scalar functions of x, y and z.

Example 7.16	**Electric field strength E and electric displacement D**

Electrostatics is the study of the forces which stationary positive and negative electric charges exert upon one another. Consider Figure 7.24 which shows a single charge placed at O. The presence of this charge gives rise to an electric force field around it. Faraday introduced the idea of **lines of force** to help visualize the field. At any point, P, there exists a vector which gives the direction and magnitude of the electrostatic force at P. Because all the lines of force emerge radially from O, the direction of the electrostatic force is radially outwards. It can be shown that the magnitude of the force is inversely proportional to the square of the distance from O.

If a second charge is placed in this field it experiences a force. An important quantity is the **electric field strength**, **E**. This is a vector field which describes the force experienced by a unit charge.

A related quantity is the **electric displacement**, **D**, also called the electric flux density, defined as $\mathbf{D} = \varepsilon\mathbf{E}$, where ε is called the permittivity of the medium in which the field is located. Note that **D** is a scalar multiple of **E**.

Example 7.17	**Electrostatic potential V**

An important electrostatic field is the electrostatic potential V. This is an example of a scalar field. The difference between the potential measured at any two points in the field is equal to the work which needs to be done to move a unit charge from one point to the other. Later, in Chapter 26, we will see that the scalar field V is closely related to the vector field **E**.

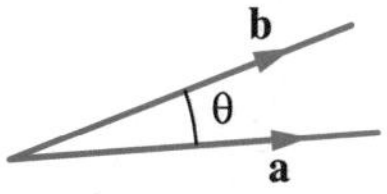

Figure 7.25 Two vectors **a** and **b** separated by angle θ.

7.5 The scalar product

Given any two vectors **a** and **b**, there are two ways in which we can define their product. These are known as the scalar product and the vector product. As the names suggest, the result of finding a scalar product is a scalar whereas the result of finding a vector product is a vector. The **scalar product** of **a** and **b** is written as

$$\mathbf{a} \cdot \mathbf{b}$$

This notation gives rise to the alternative name **dot product**. It is defined by the formula

$$\mathbf{a} \cdot \mathbf{b} = |\mathbf{a}||\mathbf{b}| \cos \theta$$

where θ is the angle between the two vectors as shown in Figure 7.25.

From the definition of the scalar product, it is possible to show that the following rules hold.

$\mathbf{a} \cdot \mathbf{b} = \mathbf{b} \cdot \mathbf{a}$	the scalar product is commutative
$k(\mathbf{a} \cdot \mathbf{b}) = (k\mathbf{a} \cdot \mathbf{b})$	where k is a scalar
$(\mathbf{a} + \mathbf{b}) \cdot \mathbf{c} = (\mathbf{a} \cdot \mathbf{c}) + (\mathbf{b} \cdot \mathbf{c})$	the distributive rule

It is important at this stage to realize that notation is very important in vector work. You should not use a $\times$ to denote the scalar product because this is the symbol we shall use for the vector product.

Example 7.18

If **a** and **b** are parallel vectors, show that $\mathbf{a} \cdot \mathbf{b} = |\mathbf{a}||\mathbf{b}|$. If **a** and **b** are orthogonal show that their scalar product is zero.

Solution

If **a** and **b** are parallel then the angle between them is zero. Therefore $\mathbf{a} \cdot \mathbf{b} = |\mathbf{a}||\mathbf{b}| \cos 0° = |\mathbf{a}||\mathbf{b}|$. If **a** and **b** are orthogonal, then the angle between them is 90° and $\mathbf{a} \cdot \mathbf{b} = |\mathbf{a}||\mathbf{b}| \cos 90° = 0$.

Similarly we can show that if **a** and **b** are two non-zero vectors for which $\mathbf{a} \cdot \mathbf{b} = 0$, then **a** and **b** must be orthogonal.

If **a** and **b** are parallel vectors, $\mathbf{a} \cdot \mathbf{b} = |\mathbf{a}||\mathbf{b}|$.
If **a** and **b** are orthogonal vectors, $\mathbf{a} \cdot \mathbf{b} = 0$.

An immediate consequence of the previous result is the following useful set of formulae:

$$\mathbf{i} \cdot \mathbf{i} = \mathbf{j} \cdot \mathbf{j} = \mathbf{k} \cdot \mathbf{k} = 1$$
$$\mathbf{i} \cdot \mathbf{j} = \mathbf{j} \cdot \mathbf{k} = \mathbf{k} \cdot \mathbf{i} = 0$$

Example 7.19

If $\mathbf{a} = a_1\mathbf{i} + a_2\mathbf{j} + a_3\mathbf{k}$ and $\mathbf{b} = b_1\mathbf{i} + b_2\mathbf{j} + b_3\mathbf{k}$ show that $\mathbf{a} \cdot \mathbf{b} = a_1b_1 + a_2b_2 + a_3b_3$.

Solution   We have

$$\mathbf{a} \cdot \mathbf{b} = (a_1\mathbf{i} + a_2\mathbf{j} + a_3\mathbf{k}) \cdot (b_1\mathbf{i} + b_2\mathbf{j} + b_3\mathbf{k})$$
$$= a_1\mathbf{i} \cdot (b_1\mathbf{i} + b_2\mathbf{j} + b_3\mathbf{k}) + a_2\mathbf{j}{\cdot}(b_1\mathbf{i} + b_2\mathbf{j} + b_3\mathbf{k})$$
$$\qquad + a_3\mathbf{k} \cdot (b_1\mathbf{i} + b_2\mathbf{j} + b_3\mathbf{k})$$
$$= a_1b_1\mathbf{i} \cdot \mathbf{i} + a_1b_2\mathbf{i} \cdot \mathbf{j} + a_1b_3\mathbf{i} \cdot \mathbf{k} + a_2b_1\mathbf{j} \cdot \mathbf{i} + a_2b_2\mathbf{j} \cdot \mathbf{j} + a_2b_3\mathbf{j} \cdot \mathbf{k}$$
$$\qquad + a_3b_1\mathbf{k} \cdot \mathbf{i} + a_3b_2\mathbf{k} \cdot \mathbf{j} + a_3b_3\mathbf{k} \cdot \mathbf{k}$$
$$= a_1b_1 + a_2b_2 + a_3b_3$$

as required. Thus, given two vectors in component form their scalar product is the sum of the products of corresponding components.

The result developed in Example 7.19 is important and should be memorized:

> If $\mathbf{a} = a_1\mathbf{i} + a_2\mathbf{j} + a_3\mathbf{k}$ and $\mathbf{b} = b_1\mathbf{i} + b_2\mathbf{j} + b_3\mathbf{k}$,
> then $\mathbf{a} \cdot \mathbf{b} = a_1b_1 + a_2b_2 + a_3b_3$.

Example 7.20   If $\mathbf{a} = 5\mathbf{i} - 3\mathbf{j} + 2\mathbf{k}$ and $\mathbf{b} = -2\mathbf{i} + 4\mathbf{j} + \mathbf{k}$ find the scalar product $\mathbf{a} \cdot \mathbf{b}$.

Solution   Using the previous result we find

$$\mathbf{a} \cdot \mathbf{b} = (5\mathbf{i} - 3\mathbf{j} + 2\mathbf{k}) \cdot (-2\mathbf{i} + 4\mathbf{j} + \mathbf{k})$$
$$= (5)(-2) + (-3)(4) + (2)(1)$$
$$= -10 - 12 + 2$$
$$= -20$$

Example 7.21   If $\mathbf{a} = a_1\mathbf{i} + a_2\mathbf{j} + a_3\mathbf{k}$, find

(a) $\mathbf{a} \cdot \mathbf{a}$

(b) $|\mathbf{a}|^2$

Solution   (a) Using the previous result we find

$$\mathbf{a} \cdot \mathbf{a} = (a_1\mathbf{i} + a_2\mathbf{j} + a_3\mathbf{k}) \cdot (a_1\mathbf{i} + a_2\mathbf{j} + a_3\mathbf{k})$$
$$= a_1^2 + a_2^2 + a_3^2$$

(b) From Example 7.11 we know that the modulus of $\mathbf{r} = x\mathbf{i} + y\mathbf{j} + z\mathbf{k}$ is $\sqrt{x^2 + y^2 + z^2}$ and therefore

$$|\mathbf{a}| = \sqrt{a_1^2 + a_2^2 + a_3^2}$$

so that

$$|\mathbf{a}|^2 = a_1^2 + a_2^2 + a_3^2$$

We note the general result that

$$\mathbf{a} \cdot \mathbf{a} = |\mathbf{a}|^2$$

Example 7.22   If $\mathbf{a} = 3\mathbf{i} + \mathbf{j} - \mathbf{k}$ and $\mathbf{b} = 2\mathbf{i} + \mathbf{j} + 2\mathbf{k}$ find $\mathbf{a} \cdot \mathbf{b}$ and the angle between $\mathbf{a}$ and $\mathbf{b}$.

Solution   We have

$$\begin{aligned}\mathbf{a} \cdot \mathbf{b} &= (3)(2) + (1)(1) + (-1)(2) \\ &= 6 + 1 - 2 \\ &= 5\end{aligned}$$

Furthermore, from the definition of the scalar product $\mathbf{a} \cdot \mathbf{b} = |\mathbf{a}||\mathbf{b}| \cos \theta$. Now,

$$|\mathbf{a}| = \sqrt{9 + 1 + 1} = \sqrt{11} \qquad \text{and} \qquad |\mathbf{b}| = \sqrt{4 + 1 + 4} = 3$$

Therefore,

$$\cos \theta = \frac{\mathbf{a} \cdot \mathbf{b}}{|\mathbf{a}||\mathbf{b}|} = \frac{5}{3\sqrt{11}}$$

from which we deduce that $\theta = 59.8°$ or 1.04 radians.

Example 7.23   ### Work done by a force

Suppose a constant force $\mathbf{F}$ is applied to an object and as a consequence the object moves from A to B, represented by the displacement vector $\mathbf{s}$, as shown in Figure 7.26.

We can resolve the force into two perpendicular components, one parallel to $\mathbf{s}$ and one perpendicular to $\mathbf{s}$. The **work done** by each component is equal to the product of its magnitude and the distance moved in its direction. The component perpendicular to $\mathbf{s}$ will not do any work because there is no movement in this direction. For the component along $\mathbf{s}$, that is $|\mathbf{F}| \cos \theta$, we find

$$\text{work done} = |\mathbf{F}| \cos \theta |\mathbf{s}|$$

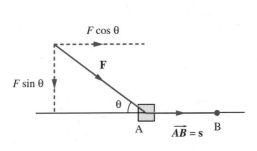

Figure 7.26   The component of $\mathbf{F}$ in the direction of $\mathbf{s}$ is $F \cos \theta$.

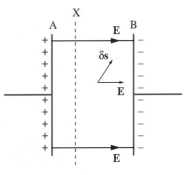

Figure 7.27   Two charged plates situated in a vacuum.

From the definition of the scalar product we see that the r.h.s. of this expression is the scalar product of **F** and **s**.

The work done by a constant force **F** which moves an object along the vector **s** is equal to the scalar product **F** · **s**.

Example 7.24

A force $\mathbf{F} = 3\mathbf{i} + 2\mathbf{j} - \mathbf{k}$ is applied to an object which moves through a displacement $\mathbf{s} = 2\mathbf{i} + 2\mathbf{j} + \mathbf{k}$. Find the work done by the force.

Solution

The work done is equal to

$$\mathbf{F} \cdot \mathbf{s} = (3\mathbf{i} + 2\mathbf{j} - \mathbf{k}) \cdot (2\mathbf{i} + 2\mathbf{j} + \mathbf{k})$$
$$= 6 + 4 - 1$$
$$= 9 \text{ joules}$$

Example 7.25

Movement of a charged particle in an electric field

Figure 7.27 shows two charged plates situated in a vacuum. Plate A has an excess of positive charge, while plate B has an excess of negative charge. Such an arrangement gives rise to an electric field. An electric field is an example of a **vector field**.

In Figure 7.27 the electric field vector **E** in the region of space between the charged plates has a direction perpendicular to the plates pointing from A to B. The magnitude of the electric field vector is constant in this region if end effects are ignored. If a charged particle is required to move against an electric field, then work must be done to achieve this. For example, to transport a positively charged particle from the surface of plate B to the surface of plate A would require work to be done. This would lead to an increase in potential of the charged particle.

If **s** represents the displacement and V the potential it is conventional to write $\delta \mathbf{s}$ to represent a very small change in displacement, and δV to represent a very small change in potential.

If a unit charge is moved a small displacement $\delta \mathbf{s}$ in an electric field (Figure 7.27) then the change in potential δV is given by

$$\delta V = -\mathbf{E} \cdot \delta \mathbf{s} \tag{7.1}$$

This is an example of the use of a scalar product. Notice that although **E** and $\delta \mathbf{s}$ are vector quantities the change in potential, δV, is a scalar.

Consider again the charged plates of Figure 7.27. If a unit charge is moved a small displacement along the plane X, then $\delta \mathbf{s}$ is perpendicular to **E**. So,

$$\delta V = -\mathbf{E} \cdot \delta \mathbf{s} = -|\mathbf{E}||\delta \mathbf{s}| \cos \theta$$

With $\theta = 90°$, we find $\delta V = 0$. The surface X is known as an **equipotential surface** because movement of a charged particle along this surface does not give rise to a change in its potential. Movement of a charge in a direction parallel to the electric field gives rise to the maximum change in potential, as for this case $\theta = 0°$.

Exercises 7.5

1 If $\mathbf{a} = 3\mathbf{i} - 7\mathbf{j}$ and $\mathbf{b} = 2\mathbf{i} + 4\mathbf{j}$ find
$\mathbf{a} \cdot \mathbf{b}, \mathbf{b} \cdot \mathbf{a}, \mathbf{a} \cdot \mathbf{a}$ and $\mathbf{b} \cdot \mathbf{b}$.

2 If $\mathbf{a} = 4\mathbf{i} + 2\mathbf{j} - \mathbf{k}, \mathbf{b} = 3\mathbf{i} - 3\mathbf{j} + 3\mathbf{k}$ and
$\mathbf{c} = 2\mathbf{i} - \mathbf{j} - \mathbf{k}$, find
(a) $\mathbf{a} \cdot \mathbf{a}$ (b) $\mathbf{a} \cdot \mathbf{b}$
(c) $\mathbf{a} \cdot \mathbf{c}$ (d) $\mathbf{b} \cdot \mathbf{c}$

3 Evaluate $(-13\mathbf{i} - 5\mathbf{j}) \cdot (-3\mathbf{i} + 4\mathbf{j})$.

4 Find the angle between the vectors
$\mathbf{p} = 7\mathbf{i} + 3\mathbf{j} + 2\mathbf{k}$ and $\mathbf{q} = 2\mathbf{i} - \mathbf{j} + \mathbf{k}$.

5 Find the angle between the vectors $7\mathbf{i} + \mathbf{j}$ and
$4\mathbf{j} - \mathbf{k}$.

6 Find the angle between the vectors $4\mathbf{i} - 2\mathbf{j}$ and
$3\mathbf{i} - 3\mathbf{j}$.

7 If $\mathbf{a} = 7\mathbf{i} + 8\mathbf{j}$ and $\mathbf{b} = 5\mathbf{i}$ find $\mathbf{a} \cdot \hat{\mathbf{b}}$.

8 If $\mathbf{r}_1 = \begin{pmatrix} 3 \\ 1 \\ 2 \end{pmatrix}$ and $\mathbf{r}_2 = \begin{pmatrix} 5 \\ 1 \\ 0 \end{pmatrix}$ find $\mathbf{r}_1 \cdot \mathbf{r}_1, \mathbf{r}_1 \cdot \mathbf{r}_2$
and $\mathbf{r}_2 \cdot \mathbf{r}_2$.

9 Given that $\mathbf{p} = 2\mathbf{q}$ simplify $\mathbf{p} \cdot \mathbf{q}, (\mathbf{p} + 5\mathbf{q}) \cdot \mathbf{q}$,
and $(\mathbf{q} - \mathbf{p}) \cdot \mathbf{p}$.

10 Find the modulus of $\mathbf{a} = \mathbf{i} - \mathbf{j} - \mathbf{k}$, the modulus
of $\mathbf{b} = 2\mathbf{i} + \mathbf{j} + 2\mathbf{k}$ and the scalar product $\mathbf{a} \cdot \mathbf{b}$.
Deduce the angle between $\mathbf{a}$ and $\mathbf{b}$.

11 If $\mathbf{a} = 2\mathbf{i} + 2\mathbf{j} - \mathbf{k}$ and $\mathbf{b} = 3\mathbf{i} - 6\mathbf{j} + 2\mathbf{k}$, find
$|\mathbf{a}|, |\mathbf{b}|, \mathbf{a} \cdot \mathbf{b}$ and the angle between $\mathbf{a}$ and $\mathbf{b}$.

12 Use a vector method to show that the diagonals
of the rhombus shown in Figure 7.28 intersect at
$90°$.

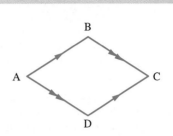

Figure 7.28   The rhombus ABCD.

13 Use the scalar product to find a two-dimensional
vector $\mathbf{a} = a_1\mathbf{i} + a_2\mathbf{j}$ perpendicular to the vector
$4\mathbf{i} - 2\mathbf{j}$.

14 If $\mathbf{a} = 3\mathbf{i} - 2\mathbf{j}, \mathbf{b} = 7\mathbf{i} + 5\mathbf{j}$ and $\mathbf{c} = 9\mathbf{i} - \mathbf{j}$, show
that $\mathbf{a} \cdot (\mathbf{b} - \mathbf{c}) = (\mathbf{a} \cdot \mathbf{b}) - (\mathbf{a} \cdot \mathbf{c})$.

15 Find the work done by the force $\mathbf{F} = 3\mathbf{i} - \mathbf{j} + \mathbf{k}$
in moving an object through a displacement
$\mathbf{s} = 3\mathbf{i} + 5\mathbf{j}$.

16 A force of magnitude 14 N acts in the direction
$\mathbf{i} + \mathbf{j} + \mathbf{k}$ upon an object. It causes the object to
move from point $A(2, 1, 0)$ to point $B(3, 3, 3)$.
Find the work done by the force.

17 (a) Use the scalar product to show that the
component of $\mathbf{a}$ in the direction of $\mathbf{b}$ is
$\mathbf{a} \cdot \hat{\mathbf{b}}$, where $\hat{\mathbf{b}}$ is a unit vector in the
direction of $\mathbf{b}$.

   (b) Find the component of $2\mathbf{i} + 3\mathbf{j}$ in the
direction of $\mathbf{i} + 5\mathbf{j}$.

Solutions

1 $-22, -22, 58, 20$

2 (a) 21   (b) 3   (c) 7   (d) 6

3 19

4 $47.62°$

5 $82.11°$

6 $18.4°$

7 7

8 14, 16, 26

9 $2|\mathbf{q}|^2, 7|\mathbf{q}|^2, -2|\mathbf{q}|^2$

10 $\sqrt{3}, 3, -1, 101.1°$

11 $3, 7, -8, 112.4°$

13 $c(\mathbf{i} + 2\mathbf{j}), c$ constant

15 4 J

16 48.5 J

17 $17/\sqrt{26}$

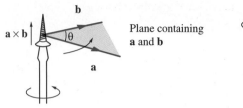

Figure 7.29 $\mathbf{a} \times \mathbf{b}$ is perpendicular to the plane containing $\mathbf{a}$ and $\mathbf{b}$. The right-handed screw rule allows the direction of $\mathbf{a} \times \mathbf{b}$ to be found.

Figure 7.30 Right-handed screw rule allows the direction of $\mathbf{b} \times \mathbf{a}$ to be found.

7.6 The vector product

The result of finding the vector product of $\mathbf{a}$ and $\mathbf{b}$ is a vector of length $|\mathbf{a}||\mathbf{b}| \sin \theta$, where θ is the angle between $\mathbf{a}$ and $\mathbf{b}$. The direction of this vector is such that it is perpendicular to $\mathbf{a}$ and to $\mathbf{b}$, and so it is perpendicular to the plane containing $\mathbf{a}$ and $\mathbf{b}$ (Figure 7.29). There are, however, two possible directions for this vector, but it is conventional to choose the one associated with the application of the right-handed screw rule. Imagine turning a right-handed screw in the sense from $\mathbf{a}$ towards $\mathbf{b}$ as shown. A right-handed screw is one which, when turned clockwise, enters the material into which it is being screwed. The direction in which the screw advances is the direction of the required vector product. The symbol we shall use to denote the vector product is $\times$. Formally, we write

$$\mathbf{a} \times \mathbf{b} = |\mathbf{a}||\mathbf{b}| \sin \theta \hat{\mathbf{e}}$$

where $\hat{\mathbf{e}}$ is the unit vector required to define the appropriate direction, that is $\hat{\mathbf{e}}$ is a unit vector perpendicular to $\mathbf{a}$ and to $\mathbf{b}$ in a sense defined by the right-handed screw rule. To evaluate $\mathbf{b} \times \mathbf{a}$ we must imagine turning the screw from the direction of $\mathbf{b}$ towards that of $\mathbf{a}$. The screw will advance as shown in Figure 7.30.

We notice immediately that $\mathbf{a} \times \mathbf{b} \neq \mathbf{b} \times \mathbf{a}$ since their directions are different. From the definition of the vector product, it is possible to show that the following rules hold:

$\mathbf{a} \times \mathbf{b} = -(\mathbf{b} \times \mathbf{a})$	the vector product is not commutative
$\mathbf{a} \times (\mathbf{b} + \mathbf{c}) = (\mathbf{a} \times \mathbf{b}) + (\mathbf{a} \times \mathbf{c})$	the distributive rule
$k(\mathbf{a} \times \mathbf{b}) = (k\mathbf{a}) \times \mathbf{b} = \mathbf{a} \times (k\mathbf{b})$	where k is a scalar

Example 7.26

If $\mathbf{a}$ and $\mathbf{b}$ are parallel show that $\mathbf{a} \times \mathbf{b} = \mathbf{0}$.

Solution

If $\mathbf{a}$ and $\mathbf{b}$ are parallel then the angle between $\mathbf{a}$ and $\mathbf{b}$ is zero. Therefore, $\mathbf{a} \times \mathbf{b} = |\mathbf{a}||\mathbf{b}| \sin 0 \, \hat{\mathbf{e}} = \mathbf{0}$. Note that the answer is still a vector, and that we denote the zero vector $0\mathbf{i} + 0\mathbf{j} + 0\mathbf{k}$ by $\mathbf{0}$, to distinguish it from the scalar 0. In particular, we note that

$$\mathbf{i} \times \mathbf{i} = \mathbf{j} \times \mathbf{j} = \mathbf{k} \times \mathbf{k} = \mathbf{0}$$

> If $\mathbf{a}$ and $\mathbf{b}$ are parallel, then $\mathbf{a} \times \mathbf{b} = \mathbf{0}$.

In particular:

> $$\mathbf{i} \times \mathbf{i} = \mathbf{j} \times \mathbf{j} = \mathbf{k} \times \mathbf{k} = \mathbf{0}$$

Example 7.27   Show that $\mathbf{i} \times \mathbf{j} = \mathbf{k}$ and find expressions for $\mathbf{j} \times \mathbf{k}$ and $\mathbf{k} \times \mathbf{i}$.

Solution   We note that $\mathbf{i}$ and $\mathbf{j}$ are perpendicular so that $|\mathbf{i} \times \mathbf{j}| = |\mathbf{i}||\mathbf{j}| \sin 90° = 1$. Furthermore, the unit vector perpendicular to $\mathbf{i}$ and to $\mathbf{j}$ in the sense defined by the right-handed screw rule is $\mathbf{k}$. Therefore, $\mathbf{i} \times \mathbf{j} = \mathbf{k}$ as required. Similarly you should be able to show that $\mathbf{j} \times \mathbf{k} = \mathbf{i}$ and $\mathbf{k} \times \mathbf{i} = \mathbf{j}$.

> $$\mathbf{i} \times \mathbf{j} = \mathbf{k} \qquad \mathbf{j} \times \mathbf{k} = \mathbf{i} \qquad \mathbf{k} \times \mathbf{i} = \mathbf{j}$$
> $$\mathbf{j} \times \mathbf{i} = -\mathbf{k} \qquad \mathbf{k} \times \mathbf{j} = -\mathbf{i} \qquad \mathbf{i} \times \mathbf{k} = -\mathbf{j}$$

Example 7.28   Simplify $(\mathbf{a} \times \mathbf{b}) - (\mathbf{b} \times \mathbf{a})$.

Solution   Use the result $\mathbf{a} \times \mathbf{b} = -(\mathbf{b} \times \mathbf{a})$ to obtain

$$(\mathbf{a} \times \mathbf{b}) - (\mathbf{b} \times \mathbf{a}) = (\mathbf{a} \times \mathbf{b}) - (-(\mathbf{a} \times \mathbf{b}))$$
$$= (\mathbf{a} \times \mathbf{b}) + (\mathbf{a} \times \mathbf{b})$$
$$= 2(\mathbf{a} \times \mathbf{b})$$

Example 7.29   (a) If $\mathbf{a} = a_1\mathbf{i} + a_2\mathbf{j} + a_3\mathbf{k}$ and $\mathbf{b} = b_1\mathbf{i} + b_2\mathbf{j} + b_3\mathbf{k}$, show that

$$\mathbf{a} \times \mathbf{b} = (a_2 b_3 - a_3 b_2)\mathbf{i} - (a_1 b_3 - a_3 b_1)\mathbf{j} + (a_1 b_2 - a_2 b_1)\mathbf{k}$$

(b) If $\mathbf{a} = 2\mathbf{i} + \mathbf{j} + 3\mathbf{k}$ and $\mathbf{b} = 3\mathbf{i} + 2\mathbf{j} + \mathbf{k}$ find $\mathbf{a} \times \mathbf{b}$.

Solution   (a) $\mathbf{a} \times \mathbf{b} = (a_1\mathbf{i} + a_2\mathbf{j} + a_3\mathbf{k}) \times (b_1\mathbf{i} + b_2\mathbf{j} + b_3\mathbf{k})$
$\qquad = a_1\mathbf{i} \times (b_1\mathbf{i} + b_2\mathbf{j} + b_3\mathbf{k}) + a_2\mathbf{j} \times (b_1\mathbf{i} + b_2\mathbf{j} + b_3\mathbf{k})$
$\qquad \quad + a_3\mathbf{k} \times (b_1\mathbf{i} + b_2\mathbf{j} + b_3\mathbf{k})$
$\qquad = a_1 b_1 (\mathbf{i} \times \mathbf{i}) + a_1 b_2 (\mathbf{i} \times \mathbf{j}) + a_1 b_3 (\mathbf{i} \times \mathbf{k}) + a_2 b_1 (\mathbf{j} \times \mathbf{i}) + a_2 b_2 (\mathbf{j} \times \mathbf{j})$
$\qquad \quad + a_2 b_3 (\mathbf{j} \times \mathbf{k}) + a_3 b_1 (\mathbf{k} \times \mathbf{i}) + a_3 b_2 (\mathbf{k} \times \mathbf{j}) + a_3 b_3 (\mathbf{k} \times \mathbf{k})$

Using the results of Examples 7.26 and 7.27, we find that the expression for $\mathbf{a} \times \mathbf{b}$ simplifies to

$$\mathbf{a} \times \mathbf{b} = (a_2 b_3 - a_3 b_2)\mathbf{i} - (a_1 b_3 - a_3 b_1)\mathbf{j} + (a_1 b_2 - a_2 b_1)\mathbf{k}$$

(b) Using the result of part (a) we have

$$\mathbf{a} \times \mathbf{b} = ((1)(1) - (3)(2))\mathbf{i} - ((2)(1) - (3)(3))\mathbf{j} + ((2)(2) - (1)(3))\mathbf{k}$$
$$= -5\mathbf{i} + 7\mathbf{j} + \mathbf{k}$$

Verify for yourself that $\mathbf{b} \times \mathbf{a} = 5\mathbf{i} - 7\mathbf{j} - \mathbf{k}$.

7.6.1 Using determinants to evaluate vector products

Evaluation of a vector product using the previous formula is very cumbersome. A more convenient and easily remembered method is now described. The vectors $\mathbf{a}$ and $\mathbf{b}$ are written in the following pattern.

$$\begin{vmatrix} \mathbf{i} & \mathbf{j} & \mathbf{k} \\ a_1 & a_2 & a_3 \\ b_1 & b_2 & b_3 \end{vmatrix}$$

This quantity is called a **determinant**. A more thorough treatment of determinants is given in Section 8.7. To find the $\mathbf{i}$ component of the vector product, imagine crossing out the row and column containing $\mathbf{i}$ and performing the following calculation on what is left, that is

$$a_2 b_3 - a_3 b_2$$

The resulting number is the $\mathbf{i}$ component of the vector product. The $\mathbf{j}$ component is found by crossing out the row and column containing $\mathbf{j}$, performing a similar calculation, but now changing the sign of the result. Thus the $\mathbf{j}$ component equals

$$-(a_1 b_3 - a_3 b_1)$$

The $\mathbf{k}$ component is found by crossing out the row and column containing $\mathbf{k}$ and performing the calculation

$$a_1 b_2 - a_2 b_1$$

We have

If $\mathbf{a} = a_1\mathbf{i} + a_2\mathbf{j} + a_3\mathbf{k}$ and $\mathbf{b} = b_1\mathbf{i} + b_2\mathbf{j} + b_3\mathbf{k}$, then

$$\mathbf{a} \times \mathbf{b} = \begin{vmatrix} \mathbf{i} & \mathbf{j} & \mathbf{k} \\ a_1 & a_2 & a_3 \\ b_1 & b_2 & b_3 \end{vmatrix}$$

$$= (a_2 b_3 - a_3 b_2)\mathbf{i} - (a_1 b_3 - a_3 b_1)\mathbf{j} + (a_1 b_2 - a_2 b_1)\mathbf{k}$$

Example 7.30 Find the vector product of $\mathbf{a} = 2\mathbf{i} + 3\mathbf{j} + 7\mathbf{k}$ and $\mathbf{b} = \mathbf{i} + 2\mathbf{j} + \mathbf{k}$.

Solution The two given vectors are represented in the following determinant:

$$\begin{vmatrix} \mathbf{i} & \mathbf{j} & \mathbf{k} \\ 2 & 3 & 7 \\ 1 & 2 & 1 \end{vmatrix}$$

Evaluating this determinant we obtain

$$\mathbf{a} \times \mathbf{b} = (3 - 14)\mathbf{i} - (2 - 7)\mathbf{j} + (4 - 3)\mathbf{k} = -11\mathbf{i} + 5\mathbf{j} + \mathbf{k}$$

You will find that, with practice, this method of evaluating a vector product is simple to apply.

7.6.2 Applications of the vector product

The following three examples illustrate applications of the vector product.

Example 7.31

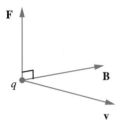

Figure 7.31 Force, **F**, exerted on a particle with charge, q, when moving with velocity, **v**, in a magnetic field, **B**.

Magnetic flux density B and magnetic field strength H

It is possible to model the effect of magnetism by means of a vector field. A magnetic field with magnetic flux density **B** is a vector field which is defined in relation to the force it exerts on a moving charged particle placed in the field. Consider Figure 7.31. If a charge q moves with velocity **v** in a magnetic field **B** it experiences a force **F** given by

$$\mathbf{F} = q\mathbf{v} \times \mathbf{B}$$

Note that this force is defined using a vector product. The unit of magnetic flux density is the weber per square metre (Wb m^{-2}), or tesla (T). The direction of this force is at right angles to both **v** and **B**, in a sense defined by the right-handed screw rule. Its magnitude, or modulus, is

$$F = qvB \sin \theta$$

where θ is the angle between **v** and **B**, v is the modulus of **v** and B is the modulus of **B**.

Note that if $\theta = 90°$, $\sin \theta = 1$, then $B = \dfrac{F}{qv}$.

These formulae are useful because they can be used to calculate the forces exerted on a conductor in an electric motor. They are also used to analyse electricity generators in which the motion of a conductor in a magnetic field leads to movement of charges within the conductor, thus generating electricity.

A related quantity is the **magnetic field strength**, or the **magnetic field intensity**, **H**, defined from

$$\mathbf{B} = \mu\mathbf{H}$$

μ is called the permeability of a material and has units of webers per ampere per metre (Wb A^{-1}m^{-1}). The units of **H** are amperes per metre (A m^{-1}). Confirm for yourself that the units match on both sides of the equation.

Example 7.32

Magnetic field due to a moving charge

A charge q moving with velocity **v** gives rise to a magnetic field with magnetic flux density **B** in its vicinity. As a result of this, another moving charge placed in this field will experience a magnetic force. The magnetic flux density is given by

$$\mathbf{B} = \frac{q\mu_0}{4\pi r^2}(\mathbf{v} \times \hat{\mathbf{r}})$$

where **r** is a vector from the charge to the point at which **B** is measured, and μ_0 is a constant called the permeability of free space.

This equation can be used to find the magnetic field due to a current in a wire. Suppose a small portion of wire has length δs and contains a current I. By writing $\delta\mathbf{s}$ as a vector of length δs in the direction of the wire, it can be shown that the corresponding contribution to the magnetic flux density is given by

$$\delta\mathbf{B} = \frac{\mu_0 I}{4\pi r^2}(\delta\mathbf{s} \times \hat{\mathbf{r}})$$

This is the Biot–Savart law. Techniques of integration are required in order to complete the calculation, but using this it is possible to show, for example, that the magnetic flux density a distance r from a long straight wire has magnitude $B = \dfrac{\mu_0 I}{2\pi r}$.

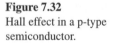

Example 7.33　The Hall effect in a semiconductor

A frequent requirement in the semiconductor industry is to be able to measure the density of holes in a p-type semiconductor and the density of electrons in an n-type semiconductor. This can be achieved by using the **Hall effect**. We will consider the case of a p-type semiconductor but the derivation for an n-type semiconductor is similar.

Consider the piece of semiconductor shown in Figure 7.32. A d.c. voltage, V, is applied to the ends of the semiconductor. This gives rise to a flow of current composed mainly of holes as they are the majority carriers for a p-type semiconductor. This current can be represented by a vector pointing in the x direction and denoted by **I**. A magnetic field, **B**, is applied to the semiconductor in the y direction. The moving holes experience a force, $\mathbf{F}_B$, per unit volume, caused by the magnetic field given by

$$\mathbf{F}_B = \frac{1}{A}\mathbf{I} \times \mathbf{B}$$

where A is the cross-sectional area of the semiconductor. This causes the holes to drift in the z direction and so causes an excess of positive charge to appear on one side of the semiconductor. This gives rise to a voltage known as the Hall voltage, V_H. As this excess

Figure 7.32
Hall effect in a p-type semiconductor.

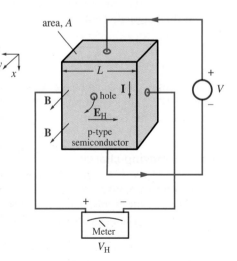

charge builds up it creates an electric field, $\mathbf{E}_H$, in the negative z direction, which in turn exerts an opposing force on the holes. This force is given by $\mathbf{F}_E = qp_0\mathbf{E}_H$ where $q =$ elementary charge $= 1.60 \times 10^{-19}$ C, and $p_0 =$ density of holes (holes per cubic metre). Equilibrium is reached when the two forces are equal in magnitude, that is $|\mathbf{F}_B| = |\mathbf{F}_E|$. Now,

$$|\mathbf{F}_E| = qp_0|\mathbf{E}_H| \qquad |\mathbf{F}_B| = \frac{|\mathbf{I} \times \mathbf{B}|}{A} = \frac{IB}{A}$$

In equilibrium the magnitude of the electric field, $|\mathbf{E}_H|$, is constant and so we can write $|\mathbf{E}_H| = \dfrac{V_H}{L}$, where L is the width of the semiconductor. Hence,

$$\frac{IB}{A} = qp_0\frac{V_H}{L}$$

so that

$$p_0 = \frac{BIL}{V_H q A}$$

So, by measuring the value of the Hall voltage, it is possible to calculate the density of the holes, p_0, in the semiconductor.

Exercises 7.6

1   Evaluate

(a) $\begin{vmatrix} \mathbf{i} & \mathbf{j} & \mathbf{k} \\ 3 & 1 & 2 \\ 2 & 1 & 4 \end{vmatrix}$

(b) $\begin{vmatrix} \mathbf{i} & \mathbf{j} & \mathbf{k} \\ -1 & 2 & -3 \\ -4 & 0 & 1 \end{vmatrix}$

(c) $\begin{vmatrix} \mathbf{i} & \mathbf{j} & \mathbf{k} \\ 0 & 1 & 0 \\ 1 & 0 & 4 \end{vmatrix}$

(d) $\begin{vmatrix} \mathbf{i} & \mathbf{j} & \mathbf{k} \\ 3 & 5 & 2 \\ -3 & -1 & 4 \end{vmatrix}$

2   If $\mathbf{a} = \mathbf{i} - 2\mathbf{j} + 3\mathbf{k}$ and $\mathbf{b} = 2\mathbf{i} - \mathbf{j} - \mathbf{k}$, find

(a) $\mathbf{a} \times \mathbf{b}$

(b) $\mathbf{b} \times \mathbf{a}$

3   If $\mathbf{a} = \mathbf{i} - 2\mathbf{j}$ and $\mathbf{b} = 5\mathbf{i} + 5\mathbf{k}$ find $\mathbf{a} \times \mathbf{b}$.

4   If $\mathbf{a} = \mathbf{i} + \mathbf{j} - \mathbf{k}, \mathbf{b} = \mathbf{i} - \mathbf{j}$ and $\mathbf{c} = 2\mathbf{i} + \mathbf{k}$ find

(a) $(\mathbf{a} \times \mathbf{b}) \times \mathbf{c}$

(b) $\mathbf{a} \times (\mathbf{b} \times \mathbf{c})$

5   If $\mathbf{p} = 6\mathbf{i} + 7\mathbf{j} - 2\mathbf{k}$ and $\mathbf{q} = 3\mathbf{i} - \mathbf{j} + 4\mathbf{k}$ find $|\mathbf{p}|, |\mathbf{q}|$ and $|\mathbf{p} \times \mathbf{q}|$. Deduce the sine of the angle between $\mathbf{p}$ and $\mathbf{q}$.

6   For arbitrary vectors $\mathbf{p}$ and $\mathbf{q}$ simplify

(a) $(\mathbf{p} + \mathbf{q}) \times \mathbf{p}$

(b) $(\mathbf{p} + \mathbf{q}) \times (\mathbf{p} - \mathbf{q})$

7   If $\mathbf{c} = \mathbf{i} + \mathbf{j}$ and $\mathbf{d} = 2\mathbf{i} + \mathbf{k}$, find a unit vector perpendicular to both $\mathbf{c}$ and $\mathbf{d}$. Further, find the sine of the angle between $\mathbf{c}$ and $\mathbf{d}$.

8   A, B, C are points with coordinates $(1, 2, 3)$, $(3, 2, 1)$ and $(-1, 1, 0)$, respectively. Find a unit vector perpendicular to the plane containing A, B and C.

9   If $\mathbf{a} = 7\mathbf{i} - 2\mathbf{j} - 5\mathbf{k}$ and $\mathbf{b} = 5\mathbf{i} + \mathbf{j} + 3\mathbf{k}$, find a vector perpendicular to $\mathbf{a}$ and $\mathbf{b}$.

10 If $\mathbf{a} = 7\mathbf{i} - \mathbf{j} + \mathbf{k}$, $\mathbf{b} = 3\mathbf{i} - \mathbf{j} - 2\mathbf{k}$ and $\mathbf{c} = 9\mathbf{i} + \mathbf{j} - 3\mathbf{k}$, show that

$$\mathbf{a} \times (\mathbf{b} + \mathbf{c}) = (\mathbf{a} \times \mathbf{b}) + (\mathbf{a} \times \mathbf{c})$$

11 (a) The area, A, of a parallelogram with base b and perpendicular height h is given by $A = bh$. Show that if the two non-parallel sides of the parallelogram are represented by the vectors $\mathbf{a}$ and $\mathbf{b}$, then the area is also given by $A = |\mathbf{a} \times \mathbf{b}|$.

  (b) Find the area of the parallelogram with sides represented by $2\mathbf{i} + 3\mathbf{j} + \mathbf{k}$ and $3\mathbf{i} + \mathbf{j} - \mathbf{k}$.

12 The volume, V, of a parallelepiped with sides $\mathbf{a}$, $\mathbf{b}$ and $\mathbf{c}$ is given by $V = |\mathbf{a} \cdot (\mathbf{b} \times \mathbf{c})|$. Find the volume of the parallelepiped with sides $3\mathbf{i} + 2\mathbf{j} + \mathbf{k}$, $2\mathbf{i} + \mathbf{j} + \mathbf{k}$ and $\mathbf{i} + 2\mathbf{j} + 4\mathbf{k}$.

13 Suppose a force $\mathbf{F}$ acts through the point P with position vector $\mathbf{r}$. The **moment about the origin**, $\mathbf{M}$, of the force is a measure of the turning effect of the force and is given by $\mathbf{M} = \mathbf{r} \times \mathbf{F}$. A force of 4 N acts in the direction $\mathbf{i} + \mathbf{j} + \mathbf{k}$, and through the point with coordinates $(7, 1, 3)$. Find the moment of the force about the origin.

14 In the theory of electromagnetic waves an important quantity associated with the flow of electromagnetic energy is the Poynting vector $\mathbf{S}$. This is defined as $\mathbf{S} = \mathbf{E} \times \mathbf{H}$ where $\mathbf{E}$ is the electric field strength and $\mathbf{H}$ the magnetic field strength. Suppose that in a plane electromagnetic wave

$$\mathbf{E} = E_0 \cos\left(\frac{2\pi z}{\lambda} - \omega t\right)\mathbf{j}$$

and

$$\mathbf{H} = -\frac{2\pi E_0}{\lambda \omega \mu_0} \cos\left(\frac{2\pi z}{\lambda} - \omega t\right)\mathbf{i}$$

where λ, ω, μ_0 and E_0 are constants. Find the Poynting vector and confirm that the direction of energy flow is the z direction.

Solutions

1 (a) $2\mathbf{i} - 8\mathbf{j} + \mathbf{k}$ (b) $2\mathbf{i} + 13\mathbf{j} + 8\mathbf{k}$
    (c) $4\mathbf{i} - \mathbf{k}$ (d) $22\mathbf{i} - 18\mathbf{j} + 12\mathbf{k}$

2 (a) $5\mathbf{i} + 7\mathbf{j} + 3\mathbf{k}$ (b) $-5\mathbf{i} - 7\mathbf{j} - 3\mathbf{k}$

3 $-10\mathbf{i} - 5\mathbf{j} + 10\mathbf{k}$

4 (a) $-\mathbf{i} - 3\mathbf{j} + 2\mathbf{k}$ (b) $\mathbf{i} - \mathbf{j}$

5 $\sqrt{89}, \sqrt{26}, 48.01, 0.9980$

6 (a) $\mathbf{q} \times \mathbf{p}$ (b) $2\mathbf{q} \times \mathbf{p}$

7 $\dfrac{1}{\sqrt{6}}(\mathbf{i} - \mathbf{j} - 2\mathbf{k}), 0.775$

8 $\dfrac{1}{\sqrt{27}}(\mathbf{i} - 5\mathbf{j} + \mathbf{k})$

9 $-\mathbf{i} - 46\mathbf{j} + 17\mathbf{k}$

11 (b) $\sqrt{90} = 9.49$

12 5

13 $\dfrac{4}{\sqrt{3}}(-2\mathbf{i} - 4\mathbf{j} + 6\mathbf{k})$

14 $\dfrac{2\pi E_0^2}{\lambda \omega \mu_0} \cos^2\left(\frac{2\pi z}{\lambda} - \omega t\right)\mathbf{k}$,

  which is a vector in the z direction.

7.7 Vectors of n dimensions

The examples we have discussed have all concerned two- and three-dimensional vectors. Our understanding has been helped by the fact that two-dimensional vectors can be drawn in the plane of the paper and three-dimensional vectors can be visualized in the three-dimensional space in which we live. However, there are some situations when the generalization to higher dimensions is appropriate, but no convenient geometrical interpretation is available. Nevertheless, many of the concepts we have discussed are still applicable. For example, we can introduce the four-dimensional vectors

$$\mathbf{a} = \begin{pmatrix} 3 \\ 1 \\ 2 \\ 4 \end{pmatrix} \quad \text{and} \quad \mathbf{b} = \begin{pmatrix} 1 \\ 0 \\ 3 \\ 1 \end{pmatrix}$$

It is natural to define the magnitude, or **norm**, of $\mathbf{a}$ as $\sqrt{3^2 + 1^2 + 2^2 + 4^2} = \sqrt{30}$ and the scalar product of $\mathbf{a}$ and $\mathbf{b}$ as $\mathbf{a} \cdot \mathbf{b} = (3)(1) + (1)(0) + (2)(3) + (4)(1) = 13$. An n-dimensional vector will have n components. Operations such as addition, subtraction and scalar multiplication are defined in an obvious way.

It is also possible to define a set of variables as a vector. This turns out to be a useful way of modelling a physical system. The system is described by means of a vector which consists of an ordered set of variables sufficient to describe the state of the system. Such a vector is called a **state vector**. This concept is explored in more detail in Chapter 20.

Example 7.34 **Mesh current vector**

A circuit has a set of mesh currents $\{I_1, I_2, I_3, I_4\}$ from which we can form a current vector

$$\mathbf{I} = \begin{pmatrix} I_1 \\ I_2 \\ I_3 \\ I_4 \end{pmatrix}$$

No geometrical interpretation is possible but nevertheless this vector provides a useful mathematical way of handling the mesh currents. We shall see how vectors such as these can be manipulated in Section 8.12.

Exercises 7.7

1 If the following are mutually orthogonal.

$$\mathbf{a} = \begin{pmatrix} 1 \\ 1 \\ 0 \\ 1 \\ 1 \end{pmatrix} \quad \text{and} \quad \mathbf{b} = \begin{pmatrix} 3 \\ 2 \\ 1 \\ 0 \\ 1 \end{pmatrix} \qquad\qquad \mathbf{a} = \begin{pmatrix} 1 \\ 2 \\ 4 \\ -1 \end{pmatrix} \quad \mathbf{b} = \begin{pmatrix} 2 \\ 1 \\ 0 \\ 0 \end{pmatrix} \quad \mathbf{c} = \begin{pmatrix} 3 \\ 0 \\ 1 \\ 0 \end{pmatrix}$$

find the norm of $\mathbf{a}$, the norm of $\mathbf{b}$ and $\mathbf{a} \cdot \mathbf{b}$.
Further, find the norm of $\mathbf{a} - \mathbf{b}$.

$$\mathbf{d} = \begin{pmatrix} 0 \\ 0 \\ 7 \\ 2 \end{pmatrix} \quad \mathbf{e} = \begin{pmatrix} 3 \\ 0 \\ -2 \\ -5 \end{pmatrix}$$

2 Two non-zero vectors are mutually orthogonal if their scalar product is zero. Determine which of

Solutions

1 $2, \sqrt{15}, 6, \sqrt{7}$

2 **a** and **e**, **b** and **d**

Review exercises 7

1 Find $\mathbf{a} \cdot \mathbf{b}$ and $\mathbf{a} \times \mathbf{b}$ when
   (a) $\mathbf{a} = 7\mathbf{i} - \mathbf{j} + \mathbf{k}, \mathbf{b} = 3\mathbf{i} + 2\mathbf{j} + 5\mathbf{k}$
   (b) $\mathbf{a} = 6\mathbf{i} - 6\mathbf{j} - 6\mathbf{k}, \mathbf{b} = \mathbf{i} - \mathbf{j} - \mathbf{k}$.

2 For a triangle ABC, express as simply as possible the vector $\overrightarrow{AB} + \overrightarrow{BC} + \overrightarrow{CA}$.

3 If $\mathbf{a} = 7\mathbf{i} - \mathbf{j} + 2\mathbf{k}$ and $\mathbf{b} = 8\mathbf{i} + \mathbf{j} + \mathbf{k}$, find $|\mathbf{a}|, |\mathbf{b}|$ and $\mathbf{a} \cdot \mathbf{b}$. Deduce the cosine of the angle between $\mathbf{a}$ and $\mathbf{b}$.

4 If $\mathbf{a} = 6\mathbf{i} - \mathbf{j} + 2\mathbf{k}$ and $\mathbf{b} = 3\mathbf{i} - \mathbf{j} + 3\mathbf{k}$, find $|\mathbf{a}|, |\mathbf{b}|, |\mathbf{a} \times \mathbf{b}|$. Deduce the sine of the angle between $\mathbf{a}$ and $\mathbf{b}$.

5 If $\mathbf{a} = 7\mathbf{i} + 9\mathbf{j} - 3\mathbf{k}$ and $\mathbf{b} = 2\mathbf{i} - 4\mathbf{j}$, find $\hat{\mathbf{a}}$, $\hat{\mathbf{b}}, \widehat{\mathbf{a} \times \mathbf{b}}$.

6 By combining the scalar and vector products other types of products can be defined. The **triple scalar product** for three vectors is defined as $(\mathbf{a} \times \mathbf{b}) \cdot \mathbf{c}$ which is a scalar. If $\mathbf{a} = 3\mathbf{i} - \mathbf{j} + 2\mathbf{k}, \mathbf{b} = 2\mathbf{i} - 2\mathbf{j} - \mathbf{k}, \mathbf{c} = 3\mathbf{i} + \mathbf{j}$, find $\mathbf{a} \times \mathbf{b}$ and $(\mathbf{a} \times \mathbf{b}) \cdot \mathbf{c}$. Show that $(\mathbf{a} \times \mathbf{b}) \cdot \mathbf{c} = \mathbf{a} \cdot (\mathbf{b} \times \mathbf{c})$.

7 The **triple vector product** is defined by $(\mathbf{a} \times \mathbf{b}) \times \mathbf{c}$. Find the triple vector product of the vectors given in Question 6. Also find $\mathbf{a} \cdot \mathbf{c}, \mathbf{b} \cdot \mathbf{c}$ and verify that

   $$(\mathbf{a} \cdot \mathbf{c})\mathbf{b} - (\mathbf{b} \cdot \mathbf{c})\mathbf{a} = (\mathbf{a} \times \mathbf{b}) \times \mathbf{c}$$

   Further, find $\mathbf{a} \times (\mathbf{b} \times \mathbf{c})$ and confirm that $\mathbf{a} \times (\mathbf{b} \times \mathbf{c}) \neq (\mathbf{a} \times \mathbf{b}) \times \mathbf{c}$.

8 Show that the vectors $\mathbf{p} = 3\mathbf{i} - 2\mathbf{j} + \mathbf{k}$, $\mathbf{q} = 2\mathbf{i} + \mathbf{j} - 4\mathbf{k}$ and $\mathbf{r} = \mathbf{i} - 3\mathbf{j} + 5\mathbf{k}$ form the three sides of a right-angled triangle.

9 Find a unit vector parallel to the line $y = 7x - 3$. Find a unit vector parallel to $y = 2x + 7$. Use the scalar product to find the angle between these two lines.

10 An electric charge q which moves with a velocity $\mathbf{v}$ produces a magnetic field $\mathbf{B}$ given by

   $$\mathbf{B} = \frac{\mu q}{4\pi} \frac{\mathbf{v} \times \hat{\mathbf{r}}}{|\mathbf{r}|^2} \text{ where } \mu = \text{constant}$$

   Find $\mathbf{B}$ if $\mathbf{r} = 3\mathbf{i} + \mathbf{j} - 2\mathbf{k}$ and $\mathbf{v} = \mathbf{i} - 2\mathbf{j} + 3\mathbf{k}$.

11 In a triangle ABC, denote $\overrightarrow{AB}$ by $\mathbf{c}$, $\overrightarrow{AC}$ by $\mathbf{b}$ and $\overrightarrow{CB}$ by $\mathbf{a}$. Use the scalar product to prove the cosine rule:
   $$a^2 = b^2 + c^2 - 2bc \cos A.$$

12 Evaluate

   (a) $\begin{vmatrix} \mathbf{i} & \mathbf{j} & \mathbf{k} \\ -4 & 0 & -3 \\ 7 & 1 & 4 \end{vmatrix}$

   (b) $\begin{vmatrix} \mathbf{i} & \mathbf{j} & \mathbf{k} \\ 8 & 2 & 5 \\ 1 & 0 & 0 \end{vmatrix}$

13 Find the area of the parallelogram with sides represented by $3\mathbf{i} + 5\mathbf{j} - \mathbf{k}$ and $\mathbf{i} + 3\mathbf{j} - \mathbf{k}$.

14 Find the angle between the vectors $7\mathbf{i} + 2\mathbf{j}$ and $\mathbf{i} - 3\mathbf{j}$.

15 Find a unit vector in the direction of the line joining the points $(2, 3, 4)$ and $(7, 17, 1)$.

16 Show that the vectors $\mathbf{i} - \mathbf{j}$ and $-3\mathbf{i} - 3\mathbf{j}$ are perpendicular.

17 Find the norm of each of the vectors

   $$\begin{pmatrix} 7 \\ 2 \\ -1 \\ 2 \end{pmatrix} \text{ and } \begin{pmatrix} 2 \\ 1 \\ 0 \\ -4 \end{pmatrix}$$

18 (a) Use the scalar product to find the value of the scalar μ so that $\mathbf{i} + \mathbf{j} + \mu\mathbf{k}$ is perpendicular to the vector $\mathbf{i} + \mathbf{j} + \mathbf{k}$.

   (b) Use the vector product and the results from part (a) to find a mutually perpendicular set of unit vectors $\hat{\mathbf{v}}_1, \hat{\mathbf{v}}_2$ and $\hat{\mathbf{v}}_3$, where $\hat{\mathbf{v}}_1$ is inclined equally to the vectors $\mathbf{i}, \mathbf{j}$ and $\mathbf{k}$.

19 The points A, B and C have coordinates $(2, -1, -2), (4, -1, -3)$ and $(1, 3, -1)$.

   (a) Write down the vectors $\overrightarrow{AB}$ and $\overrightarrow{AC}$.

(b) Using the vector product find a unit vector which is perpendicular to the plane containing A, B and C.

(c) If D is the point with coordinates $(3, 0, 1)$, use the scalar product to find the perpendicular distance from D to the plane ABC.

20 The condition for vectors **a**, **b** and **c** to be coplanar (i.e. they lie in the same plane) is $\mathbf{a} \cdot (\mathbf{b} \times \mathbf{c}) = 0$.

(a) Show that the vectors $\mathbf{a} = 4\mathbf{i} + 5\mathbf{j} + 6\mathbf{k}$, $\mathbf{b} = 6\mathbf{i} - 3\mathbf{j} - 3\mathbf{k}$, and $\mathbf{c} = -\mathbf{i} + 2\mathbf{j} + 2\mathbf{k}$ are not coplanar.

(b) Given $\mathbf{d} = -\mathbf{i} + 2\mathbf{j} + \lambda\mathbf{k}$, find the value of λ so that **a**, **b** and **d** are coplanar.

21 Points A and B have position vectors **a** and **b** respectively. Show that the position vector of an arbitrary point on the line AB is given by $\mathbf{r} = \mathbf{a} + \lambda(\mathbf{b} - \mathbf{a})$ for some scalar λ. This is the **vector equation of the line**.

22 Use vector methods to show that the three medians of any triangle intersect at a common point (called the centroid).

23 Use the vector product to find the area of a triangle with vertices at the points with coordinates $(1, 2, 3)$, $(4, -3, 2)$, and $(8, 1, 1)$.

Solutions

1 (a) $24, -7\mathbf{i} - 32\mathbf{j} + 17\mathbf{k}$ (b) $18, \mathbf{0}$

2 $\mathbf{0}$

3 $\sqrt{54}, \sqrt{66}, 57, 0.9548$

4 $\sqrt{41}, \sqrt{19}, \sqrt{154}, 0.4446$

5 $\frac{1}{\sqrt{139}}\mathbf{a}, \frac{1}{\sqrt{20}}\mathbf{b}, \frac{1}{\sqrt{2296}}(-12\mathbf{i} - 6\mathbf{j} - 46\mathbf{k})$

6 $5\mathbf{i} + 7\mathbf{j} - 4\mathbf{k}, 22$

7 $(\mathbf{a} \times \mathbf{b}) \times \mathbf{c} = 4\mathbf{i} - 12\mathbf{j} - 16\mathbf{k}$
$\mathbf{a} \cdot \mathbf{c} = 8, \mathbf{b} \cdot \mathbf{c} = 4$
$\mathbf{a} \times (\mathbf{b} \times \mathbf{c}) = -2\mathbf{i} - 22\mathbf{j} - 8\mathbf{k}$

9 $\frac{1}{\sqrt{50}}(\mathbf{i} + 7\mathbf{j}), \frac{1}{\sqrt{5}}(\mathbf{i} + 2\mathbf{j}), 18.4°$

10 $\frac{\mu q}{56\sqrt{14}\pi}(\mathbf{i} + 11\mathbf{j} + 7\mathbf{k})$

12 (a) $3\mathbf{i} - 5\mathbf{j} - 4\mathbf{k}$ (b) $5\mathbf{j} - 2\mathbf{k}$

13 $\sqrt{24} = 4.90$

14 $87.5°$

15 $\frac{1}{\sqrt{230}}(5\mathbf{i} + 14\mathbf{j} - 3\mathbf{k})$

17 $\sqrt{58}, \sqrt{21}$

18 (a) $\mu = -2$
(b) $\widehat{\mathbf{v_1}} = \frac{1}{\sqrt{3}}(1, 1, 1), \widehat{\mathbf{v_2}} = \frac{1}{\sqrt{6}}(1, 1, -2),$
$\widehat{\mathbf{v_3}} = \frac{1}{\sqrt{2}}(-1, 1, 0)$

19 (a) $(2, 0, -1), (-1, 4, 1)$ (b) $\frac{1}{9}(4, -1, 8)$
(c) 3

20 (a) $\mathbf{a} \cdot (\mathbf{b} \times \mathbf{c}) = 9 \neq 0$ and hence the vectors are not coplanar
(b) $\lambda = 31/14$

23 $\frac{1}{2}\sqrt{1106}$

8 Matrix algebra

Chapter 8   Contents

8.1	Introduction	236
8.2	Basic definitions	236
8.3	Addition, subtraction and multiplication	237
8.4	Robot coordinate frames	244
8.5	Some special matrices	248
8.6	The inverse of a 2×2 matrix	251
8.7	Determinants	255
8.8	The inverse of a 3×3 matrix	259
8.9	Application to the solution of simultaneous equations	261
8.10	Gaussian elimination	264
8.11	Eigenvalues and eigenvectors	271
8.12	Analysis of electrical networks	285
8.13	Iterative techniques for the solution of simultaneous equations	291
8.14	Computer solutions of matrix problems	297
	Review exercises	298

8.1 Introduction

Matrices provide a means of storing large quantities of information in such a way that each piece can be easily identified and manipulated. They permit the solution of large systems of linear equations to be carried out in a logical and formal way so that computer implementation follows naturally. Applications of matrices extend over many areas of engineering including electrical network analysis and robotics.

An example of an extremely large electrical network is the national grid in Britain. The equations governing this network are expressed in matrix form for analysis by computer because solutions are required at regular intervals throughout the day and night in order to make decisions such as whether or not a power station should be connected to, or removed from, the grid.

To obtain the trajectory of a robot it is necessary to perform matrix calculations to find the speed at which various motors within the robot should operate. This is a complicated problem as it is necessary to ensure that a robot reaches its required destination and does not collide with another object during its movement.

8.2 Basic definitions

A **matrix** is a rectangular pattern or array of numbers.

For example,

$$A = \begin{pmatrix} 1 & 2 & 3 \\ 4 & 5 & 6 \\ -1 & 2 & 4 \end{pmatrix} \qquad B = \begin{pmatrix} 1 & 2 & -2 \\ 3 & 4 & 0.5 \end{pmatrix} \qquad C = \begin{pmatrix} 1 & -1 & 1 \end{pmatrix}$$

are all matrices. Note that we usually use a capital letter to denote a matrix, and enclose the array of numbers in brackets. To describe the size of a matrix we quote its number of rows and columns in that order so, for example, an $r \times s$ matrix has r rows and s columns. We say the matrix has **order** $r \times s$.

An $r \times s$ matrix has r rows and s columns.

Example 8.1 Describe the sizes of the matrices A, B and C at the start of this section, and give examples of matrices of order 3×1, 3×2 and 4×2.

Solution A has order 3×3, B has order 2×3 and C has order 1×3.

$$\begin{pmatrix} -1 \\ -2 \\ 3 \end{pmatrix} \text{ is a } 3 \times 1 \text{ matrix} \qquad \begin{pmatrix} 1 & 2 \\ 3 & 4 \\ 5 & 6 \end{pmatrix} \text{ is a } 3 \times 2 \text{ matrix}$$

and

$$\begin{pmatrix} -1 & -1 \\ -1 & 2 \\ 2 & -0.5 \\ 1 & 0 \end{pmatrix} \text{ is a } 4 \times 2 \text{ matrix}$$

More generally, if the matrix A has m rows and n columns we can write

$$A = \begin{pmatrix} a_{11} & a_{12} & \cdots & a_{1n} \\ a_{21} & a_{22} & \cdots & a_{2n} \\ \vdots & \vdots & \ddots & \vdots \\ a_{m1} & a_{m2} & \cdots & a_{mn} \end{pmatrix}$$

where a_{ij} represents the number or **element** in the ith row and jth column. A matrix with a single column can also be regarded as a column vector.

The operations of addition, subtraction and multiplication are defined upon matrices and these are explained in Section 8.3.

8.3 Addition, subtraction and multiplication

8.3.1 Matrix addition and subtraction

Two matrices can be added (or subtracted) if they have the same shape and size, that is the same order. Their sum (or difference) is found by adding (or subtracting) corresponding elements as the following example shows.

Example 8.2 If

$$A = \begin{pmatrix} 1 & 5 & -2 \\ 3 & 1 & 1 \end{pmatrix} \quad \text{and} \quad B = \begin{pmatrix} 1 & 2 & 0 \\ -1 & 1 & 4 \end{pmatrix}$$

find $A + B$ and $A - B$.

Solution

$$A + B = \begin{pmatrix} 1 & 5 & -2 \\ 3 & 1 & 1 \end{pmatrix} + \begin{pmatrix} 1 & 2 & 0 \\ -1 & 1 & 4 \end{pmatrix} = \begin{pmatrix} 2 & 7 & -2 \\ 2 & 2 & 5 \end{pmatrix}$$

$$A - B = \begin{pmatrix} 1 & 5 & -2 \\ 3 & 1 & 1 \end{pmatrix} - \begin{pmatrix} 1 & 2 & 0 \\ -1 & 1 & 4 \end{pmatrix} = \begin{pmatrix} 0 & 3 & -2 \\ 4 & 0 & -3 \end{pmatrix}$$

On the other hand, the matrices $\begin{pmatrix} 1 & 2 \\ 0 & 1 \end{pmatrix}$ and $\begin{pmatrix} 3 \\ 1 \end{pmatrix}$ cannot be added or subtracted because they have different orders.

Example 8.3 If $C = \begin{pmatrix} a & b \\ c & d \end{pmatrix}$ and $D = \begin{pmatrix} e & f \\ g & h \end{pmatrix}$ show that $C + D = D + C$.

Solution

$$C + D = \begin{pmatrix} a & b \\ c & d \end{pmatrix} + \begin{pmatrix} e & f \\ g & h \end{pmatrix} = \begin{pmatrix} a+e & b+f \\ c+g & d+h \end{pmatrix}$$

$$D + C = \begin{pmatrix} e & f \\ g & h \end{pmatrix} + \begin{pmatrix} a & b \\ c & d \end{pmatrix} = \begin{pmatrix} e+a & f+b \\ g+c & h+d \end{pmatrix}$$

Now $a + e$ is exactly the same as $e + a$ because addition of numbers is **commutative**. The same observation can be made of $b + f$, $c + g$ and $d + h$. Hence $C + D = D + C$. The addition of these matrices is therefore commutative. This may seem an obvious statement but we shall shortly meet matrix multiplication which is not commutative, so in general commutativity should not be simply assumed.

The result obtained in Example 8.3 is true more generally:

> Matrix addition is commutative, that is
>
> $$A + B = B + A$$

It is also easy to show that

> Matrix addition is **associative**, that is
>
> $$A + (B + C) = (A + B) + C$$

8.3.2 Scalar multiplication

Given any matrix A, we can multiply it by a number, that is a scalar, to form a new matrix of the same order as A. This multiplication is performed by multiplying every element of A by the number.

Example 8.4 If

$$A = \begin{pmatrix} 1 & 3 \\ -2 & 1 \\ 0 & 1 \end{pmatrix}$$

find $2A$, $-3A$ and $\frac{1}{2}A$.

Solution
$$2A = 2 \begin{pmatrix} 1 & 3 \\ -2 & 1 \\ 0 & 1 \end{pmatrix} = \begin{pmatrix} 2 & 6 \\ -4 & 2 \\ 0 & 2 \end{pmatrix}$$

$$-3A = -3 \begin{pmatrix} 1 & 3 \\ -2 & 1 \\ 0 & 1 \end{pmatrix} = \begin{pmatrix} -3 & -9 \\ 6 & -3 \\ 0 & -3 \end{pmatrix}$$

and

$$\frac{1}{2}A = \frac{1}{2} \begin{pmatrix} 1 & 3 \\ -2 & 1 \\ 0 & 1 \end{pmatrix} = \begin{pmatrix} \frac{1}{2} & \frac{3}{2} \\ -1 & \frac{1}{2} \\ 0 & \frac{1}{2} \end{pmatrix}$$

In general we have

$$\text{If } A = \begin{pmatrix} a_{11} & a_{12} & \cdots & a_{1n} \\ a_{21} & a_{22} & \cdots & a_{2n} \\ \vdots & \vdots & \ddots & \vdots \\ a_{m1} & a_{m2} & \cdots & a_{mn} \end{pmatrix} \text{ then } kA = \begin{pmatrix} ka_{11} & ka_{12} & \cdots & ka_{1n} \\ ka_{21} & ka_{22} & \cdots & ka_{2n} \\ \vdots & \vdots & \ddots & \vdots \\ ka_{m1} & ka_{m2} & \cdots & ka_{mn} \end{pmatrix}$$

8.3.3 Matrix multiplication

Matrix multiplication is defined in a special way which at first seems strange but is in fact very useful. If A is a $p \times q$ matrix and B is an $r \times s$ matrix we can form the product AB only if $q = r$; that is, only if the number of columns in A is the same as the number of rows in B. The product is then a $p \times s$ matrix C, that is

$$C = AB \qquad \text{where} \qquad A \text{ is } p \times q$$
$$B \text{ is } q \times s$$
$$C \text{ is } p \times s$$

Example 8.5   Given $A = \begin{pmatrix} 4 & 2 \end{pmatrix}$ and $B = \begin{pmatrix} 3 & 7 & 6 \\ 5 & 2 & -1 \end{pmatrix}$ can the product AB be formed?

Solution A has size 1×2
B has size 2×3

Because the number of columns in A is the same as the number of rows in B, we can form the product AB. The resulting matrix will have size 1×3 because there is one row in A and three columns in B.

Suppose we wish to find AB when $A = \begin{pmatrix} 4 & 2 \end{pmatrix}$ and $B = \begin{pmatrix} 3 \\ 7 \end{pmatrix}$. A has size 1×2 and B has size 2×1 and so we can form the product AB. The result will be a 1×1 matrix, that is a single number. We perform the calculation as follows:

$$AB = \begin{pmatrix} 4 & 2 \end{pmatrix} \begin{pmatrix} 3 \\ 7 \end{pmatrix} = 4 \times 3 + 2 \times 7 = 12 + 14 = 26$$

Note that we have multiplied elements in the row of A with corresponding elements in the column of B, and added the results together.

Example 8.6   Find CD when $C = \begin{pmatrix} 1 & 9 & 2 \end{pmatrix}$ and $D = \begin{pmatrix} 2 \\ 6 \\ 8 \end{pmatrix}$.

Solution $$CD = \begin{pmatrix} 1 & 9 & 2 \end{pmatrix} \begin{pmatrix} 2 \\ 6 \\ 8 \end{pmatrix} = 1 \times 2 + 9 \times 6 + 2 \times 8 = 2 + 54 + 16 = 72$$

Let us now extend this idea to general matrices A and B. Suppose we wish to find C where $C = AB$. The element c_{11} is found by pairing each element in row 1 of A with the corresponding element in column 1 of B. The pairs are multiplied together and then the results are added to give c_{11}. Similarly, to find the element c_{12}, each element in row 1 of A is paired with the corresponding element in column 2 of B. Again, the paired elements are multiplied together and the results are added to form c_{12}. Other elements of C are found in a similar way. In general the element c_{ij} is found by pairing elements in the ith row of A with those in the jth column of B. These are multiplied together and the results are added to give c_{ij}. Consider the following example.

Example 8.7 If $A = \begin{pmatrix} 1 & 2 \\ 4 & 3 \end{pmatrix}$ and $B = \begin{pmatrix} 5 \\ -3 \end{pmatrix}$ find, if possible, the matrix C where $C = AB$.

Solution We can form the product

$$C = AB = \begin{pmatrix} 1 & 2 \\ 4 & 3 \end{pmatrix} \begin{pmatrix} 5 \\ -3 \end{pmatrix}$$
$$\begin{matrix} \uparrow & \uparrow \\ 2 \times 2 & 2 \times 1 \end{matrix}$$

because the number of columns in A, that is 2, is the same as the number of rows in B. The size of the product is found by inspecting the number of rows in the first matrix, which is 2, and the number of columns in the second, which is 1. These numbers give the number of rows and columns respectively in C. Therefore C will be a 2×1 matrix.

To find the element c_{11} we pair the elements in the first row of A with those in the first column of B, multiply and then add these together. Thus

$$c_{11} = 1 \times 5 + 2 \times -3 = 5 - 6 = -1$$

Similarly to find the element c_{21} we pair the elements in the second row of A with those in the first column of B, multiply and then add these together. Thus

$$c_{21} = 4 \times 5 + 3 \times -3 = 20 - 9 = 11$$

The complete calculation is written as

$$AB = \begin{pmatrix} 1 & 2 \\ 4 & 3 \end{pmatrix} \begin{pmatrix} 5 \\ -3 \end{pmatrix} = \begin{pmatrix} 1 \times 5 + 2 \times -3 \\ 4 \times 5 + 3 \times -3 \end{pmatrix}$$
$$= \begin{pmatrix} 5 - 6 \\ 20 - 9 \end{pmatrix}$$
$$= \begin{pmatrix} -1 \\ 11 \end{pmatrix}$$

If A is a $p \times q$ matrix and B is a $q \times s$ matrix, then the product $C = AB$ will be a $p \times s$ matrix. To find c_{ij} we take the ith row of A and pair its elements with the jth column of B. The paired elements are multiplied together and added to form c_{ij}.

Example 8.8 If $B = \begin{pmatrix} 1 & 2 & 3 \\ 4 & 5 & 6 \end{pmatrix}$ and $C = \begin{pmatrix} 1 \\ 2 \\ 4 \end{pmatrix}$ find BC.

Solution B has order 2×3 and C has order 3×1 so clearly the product BC exists and will have order 2×1. BC is formed as follows:

$$BC = \begin{pmatrix} 1 & 2 & 3 \\ 4 & 5 & 6 \end{pmatrix} \begin{pmatrix} 1 \\ 2 \\ 4 \end{pmatrix} = \begin{pmatrix} 1 \times 1 + 2 \times 2 + 3 \times 4 \\ 4 \times 1 + 5 \times 2 + 6 \times 4 \end{pmatrix} = \begin{pmatrix} 17 \\ 38 \end{pmatrix}$$

Note the order of the product, 2×1, can be determined at the start by considering the orders of B and C.

Example 8.9 Find AB where

$$A = \begin{pmatrix} 1 & 2 \\ 3 & 4 \\ -1 & 0 \end{pmatrix} \quad \text{and} \quad B = \begin{pmatrix} -1 \\ 2 \\ -1 \end{pmatrix}$$

Solution A and B have orders 3×2 and 3×1, respectively, and consequently the product, AB, cannot be formed.

Example 8.10 Given

$$A = \begin{pmatrix} 1 & 1 & 1 \\ 2 & 1 & 0 \\ 3 & -1 & 2 \end{pmatrix} \quad \text{and} \quad B = \begin{pmatrix} 0 & 3 & 1 \\ 4 & -1 & 0 \\ 2 & 2 & 1 \end{pmatrix}$$

find, if possible, AB and BA, and comment upon the result.

Solution A and B both have order 3×3 and the products AB and BA can both be formed. Both will have order 3×3.

$$AB = \begin{pmatrix} 1 & 1 & 1 \\ 2 & 1 & 0 \\ 3 & -1 & 2 \end{pmatrix} \begin{pmatrix} 0 & 3 & 1 \\ 4 & -1 & 0 \\ 2 & 2 & 1 \end{pmatrix} = \begin{pmatrix} 6 & 4 & 2 \\ 4 & 5 & 2 \\ 0 & 14 & 5 \end{pmatrix}$$

$$BA = \begin{pmatrix} 0 & 3 & 1 \\ 4 & -1 & 0 \\ 2 & 2 & 1 \end{pmatrix} \begin{pmatrix} 1 & 1 & 1 \\ 2 & 1 & 0 \\ 3 & -1 & 2 \end{pmatrix} = \begin{pmatrix} 9 & 2 & 2 \\ 2 & 3 & 4 \\ 9 & 3 & 4 \end{pmatrix}$$

Clearly AB and BA are not the same. Matrix multiplication is not usually commutative and we must pay particular attention to this detail when we are working with matrices.

In general $AB \neq BA$ and so matrix multiplication is not commutative.

In the product AB we say that B has been **premultiplied** by A, or alternatively A has been **postmultiplied** by B.

Example 8.11   Given

$$A = \begin{pmatrix} 1 & -1 & 2 \\ 3 & 0 & 2 \\ -1 & 3 & 5 \end{pmatrix} \qquad B = \begin{pmatrix} -1 & 2 & 9 \\ 1 & 0 & 0 \\ 3 & -2 & 1 \end{pmatrix} \qquad C = \begin{pmatrix} 4 & 1 & 5 \\ 2 & 3 & 1 \\ 0 & 1 & 5 \end{pmatrix}$$

find BC, $A(BC)$, AB and $(AB)C$, commenting upon the result.

Solution $$BC = \begin{pmatrix} -1 & 2 & 9 \\ 1 & 0 & 0 \\ 3 & -2 & 1 \end{pmatrix} \begin{pmatrix} 4 & 1 & 5 \\ 2 & 3 & 1 \\ 0 & 1 & 5 \end{pmatrix} = \begin{pmatrix} 0 & 14 & 42 \\ 4 & 1 & 5 \\ 8 & -2 & 18 \end{pmatrix}$$

$$A(BC) = \begin{pmatrix} 1 & -1 & 2 \\ 3 & 0 & 2 \\ -1 & 3 & 5 \end{pmatrix} \begin{pmatrix} 0 & 14 & 42 \\ 4 & 1 & 5 \\ 8 & -2 & 18 \end{pmatrix} = \begin{pmatrix} 12 & 9 & 73 \\ 16 & 38 & 162 \\ 52 & -21 & 63 \end{pmatrix}$$

$$AB = \begin{pmatrix} 1 & -1 & 2 \\ 3 & 0 & 2 \\ -1 & 3 & 5 \end{pmatrix} \begin{pmatrix} -1 & 2 & 9 \\ 1 & 0 & 0 \\ 3 & -2 & 1 \end{pmatrix} = \begin{pmatrix} 4 & -2 & 11 \\ 3 & 2 & 29 \\ 19 & -12 & -4 \end{pmatrix}$$

$$(AB)C = \begin{pmatrix} 4 & -2 & 11 \\ 3 & 2 & 29 \\ 19 & -12 & -4 \end{pmatrix} \begin{pmatrix} 4 & 1 & 5 \\ 2 & 3 & 1 \\ 0 & 1 & 5 \end{pmatrix} = \begin{pmatrix} 12 & 9 & 73 \\ 16 & 38 & 162 \\ 52 & -21 & 63 \end{pmatrix}$$

We note that $A(BC) = (AB)C$ so that in this case matrix multiplication is associative.

The result obtained in Example 8.11 is also true in general:

Matrix multiplication is associative:

$$(AB)C = A(BC)$$

Exercises 8.3

1   Evaluate

(a) $(1 \ \ 4) \begin{pmatrix} -1 \\ 4 \end{pmatrix}$

(c) $\begin{pmatrix} 5 & 2 \\ 1 & 3 \end{pmatrix} \begin{pmatrix} 9 \\ 1 \end{pmatrix}$

(b) $(3 \ \ 7) \begin{pmatrix} 3 \\ -4 \end{pmatrix}$

(d) $\begin{pmatrix} 1 & 4 \\ -1 & 3 \end{pmatrix} \begin{pmatrix} 5 & 2 \\ -3 & 4 \end{pmatrix}$

(e) $\begin{pmatrix} 5 & 1 \\ 29 & 6 \end{pmatrix} \begin{pmatrix} 6 & -1 \\ -29 & 5 \end{pmatrix}$

(f) $(1 \ \ 2 \ \ 4) \begin{pmatrix} 1 \\ 3 \\ 2 \end{pmatrix}$

(g) $(5 \ \ -1 \ \ 3) \begin{pmatrix} 3 & 3 \\ 2 & 6 \\ 4 & 1 \end{pmatrix}$

(h) $(1 \ \ 9) \begin{pmatrix} 1 & 1 & 1 \\ 2 & 2 & 2 \end{pmatrix}$

(i) $\begin{pmatrix} 1 & 3 \\ -1 & 0 \end{pmatrix} \begin{pmatrix} 2 & 1 \\ 5 & 0 \end{pmatrix}$

(j) $\begin{pmatrix} 3 & 0 \\ 0 & 1 \end{pmatrix} \begin{pmatrix} 0 & 3 \\ 9 & 0 \end{pmatrix}$

2 If $A = \begin{pmatrix} 1 & 1 \\ 3 & 4 \end{pmatrix}$, $B = \begin{pmatrix} 2 \\ 1 \end{pmatrix}$, $C = \begin{pmatrix} -7 & 1 \\ 0 & 4 \end{pmatrix}$,

   $D = (3 \ \ 2 \ \ 1)$ and $E = \begin{pmatrix} 2 & 3 & 4 \\ 1 & 2 & -1 \end{pmatrix}$ find, if possible,

   (a) $A + D$, $C - A$ and $D - E$
   (b) AB, BA, CA, AC, DA, DB, BD, EB, BE and AE
   (c) $7C$, $-3D$ and kE, where k is a scalar.

3 Plot the points A, B, C with position vectors given by

$$\mathbf{v}_1 = \begin{pmatrix} 1 \\ 0 \end{pmatrix} \qquad \mathbf{v}_2 = \begin{pmatrix} 2 \\ 0 \end{pmatrix} \qquad \mathbf{v}_3 = \begin{pmatrix} 2 \\ 3 \end{pmatrix}$$

respectively. Treating these vectors as matrices of order 2×1 find the products $M\mathbf{v}_1$, $M\mathbf{v}_2$, $M\mathbf{v}_3$ when

   (a) $M = \begin{pmatrix} 1 & 0 \\ 0 & -1 \end{pmatrix}$

   (b) $M = \begin{pmatrix} 0 & 1 \\ 1 & 0 \end{pmatrix}$

   (c) $M = \begin{pmatrix} 0 & -1 \\ 1 & 0 \end{pmatrix}$

In each case draw a diagram to illustrate the effect upon the vectors of multiplication by the matrix.

4 Find AB and BA where

$$A = \begin{pmatrix} 1 & 3 & 2 \\ -1 & 0 & 4 \\ 5 & 1 & -1 \end{pmatrix}$$

$$B = \begin{pmatrix} 5 & 2 & 1 \\ 0 & 3 & 4 \\ 1 & 3 & 5 \end{pmatrix}$$

5 Given that A^2 means the product of a matrix A with itself, find A^2 when $A = \begin{pmatrix} 4 & 2 \\ 1 & 3 \end{pmatrix}$. Find A^3.

6 If $A = \begin{pmatrix} 1 & 3 \\ -2 & 4 \end{pmatrix}$, $B = \begin{pmatrix} 2 & 1 \\ -4 & 5 \end{pmatrix}$ find AB, BA, $A + B$ and $(A + B)^2$. Show that

$$(A + B)^2 = A^2 + AB + BA + B^2$$

Why is $(A + B)^2$ not equal to $A^2 + 2AB + B^2$?

7 Find, if possible,

   (a) $\begin{pmatrix} 1 & 0 & 0 & 0 \\ 0 & 0 & -1 & 0 \\ 0 & 1 & 0 & 0 \\ 0 & 0 & 0 & 1 \end{pmatrix} \begin{pmatrix} 1 \\ 1 \\ 2 \\ 1 \end{pmatrix}$

   (b) $\begin{pmatrix} 0 & 0 & 1 & 0 \\ 0 & 1 & 0 & 0 \\ -1 & 0 & 0 & 0 \\ 0 & 0 & 0 & 1 \end{pmatrix} \begin{pmatrix} 2 \\ 5 \\ 5 \\ 1 \end{pmatrix}$

8 Find $\begin{pmatrix} 1 & 3 & 6 \\ 2 & -5 & 7 \end{pmatrix} \begin{pmatrix} 1 & 2 \\ 3 & -5 \\ 6 & 7 \end{pmatrix}$.

9 Given the vector $\mathbf{v} = \begin{pmatrix} 1 \\ 2 \\ 3 \end{pmatrix}$ calculate the vectors obtained when $\mathbf{v}$ is premultiplied by the following matrices.

   (a) $\begin{pmatrix} 6 & 2 & 9 \\ 1 & 3 & 2 \\ -1 & 2 & -3 \end{pmatrix}$

   (b) $\begin{pmatrix} -1 & 0 & 3 \\ 7 & 1 & 9 \\ 1 & 3 & 4 \end{pmatrix}$

   (c) $\begin{pmatrix} 1 & 3 & 1 \\ 9 & 2 & 6 \\ 2 & 8 & 0 \end{pmatrix}$

   (d) $\begin{pmatrix} 3 & 1 & 2 \\ 6 & 5 & 4 \end{pmatrix}$

   (e) $\begin{pmatrix} 6 & 8 & 3 \\ 9 & 6 & 4 \\ 5 & 3 & 9 \\ 2 & 5 & 2 \end{pmatrix}$

Solutions

1 (a) 15   (b) −19

(c) $\begin{pmatrix} 47 \\ 12 \end{pmatrix}$ (d) $\begin{pmatrix} -7 & 18 \\ -14 & 10 \end{pmatrix}$

(e) $\begin{pmatrix} 1 & 0 \\ 0 & 1 \end{pmatrix}$ (f) 15

(g) $(25 \ \ 12)$ (h) $(19 \ \ 19 \ \ 19)$

(i) $\begin{pmatrix} 17 & 1 \\ -2 & -1 \end{pmatrix}$ (j) $\begin{pmatrix} 0 & 9 \\ 9 & 0 \end{pmatrix}$

2 (a) $A + D$ does not exist, $\begin{pmatrix} -8 & 0 \\ -3 & 0 \end{pmatrix}$,

$D - E$ does not exist

(b) $\begin{pmatrix} 3 \\ 10 \end{pmatrix}$, BA does not exist,

$\begin{pmatrix} -4 & -3 \\ 12 & 16 \end{pmatrix}, \begin{pmatrix} -7 & 5 \\ -21 & 19 \end{pmatrix}$,

DA does not exist, DB does not exist,

$\begin{pmatrix} 6 & 4 & 2 \\ 3 & 2 & 1 \end{pmatrix}$,

EB does not exist, BE does not exist,

$\begin{pmatrix} 3 & 5 & 3 \\ 10 & 17 & 8 \end{pmatrix}$

(c) $\begin{pmatrix} -49 & 7 \\ 0 & 28 \end{pmatrix}, (-9, -6, -3), \begin{pmatrix} 2k & 3k & 4k \\ k & 2k & -k \end{pmatrix}$

3 (a) $\begin{pmatrix} 1 \\ 0 \end{pmatrix}, \begin{pmatrix} 2 \\ 0 \end{pmatrix}, \begin{pmatrix} 2 \\ -3 \end{pmatrix}$

(b) $\begin{pmatrix} 0 \\ 1 \end{pmatrix}, \begin{pmatrix} 0 \\ 2 \end{pmatrix}, \begin{pmatrix} 3 \\ 2 \end{pmatrix}$

(c) $\begin{pmatrix} 0 \\ 1 \end{pmatrix}, \begin{pmatrix} 0 \\ 2 \end{pmatrix}, \begin{pmatrix} -3 \\ 2 \end{pmatrix}$

4 $\begin{pmatrix} 7 & 17 & 23 \\ -1 & 10 & 19 \\ 24 & 10 & 4 \end{pmatrix}, \begin{pmatrix} 8 & 16 & 17 \\ 17 & 4 & 8 \\ 23 & 8 & 9 \end{pmatrix}$

5 $\begin{pmatrix} 18 & 14 \\ 7 & 11 \end{pmatrix}, \begin{pmatrix} 86 & 78 \\ 39 & 47 \end{pmatrix}$

6 $\begin{pmatrix} -10 & 16 \\ -20 & 18 \end{pmatrix}, \begin{pmatrix} 0 & 10 \\ -14 & 8 \end{pmatrix}$,

$\begin{pmatrix} 3 & 4 \\ -6 & 9 \end{pmatrix}, \begin{pmatrix} -15 & 48 \\ -72 & 57 \end{pmatrix}$

7 (a) $\begin{pmatrix} 1 \\ -2 \\ 1 \\ 1 \end{pmatrix}$ (b) $\begin{pmatrix} 5 \\ 5 \\ -2 \\ 1 \end{pmatrix}$

8 $\begin{pmatrix} 46 & 29 \\ 29 & 78 \end{pmatrix}$

9 (a) $\begin{pmatrix} 37 \\ 13 \\ -6 \end{pmatrix}$ (b) $\begin{pmatrix} 8 \\ 36 \\ 19 \end{pmatrix}$ (c) $\begin{pmatrix} 10 \\ 31 \\ 18 \end{pmatrix}$

(d) $\begin{pmatrix} 11 \\ 28 \end{pmatrix}$ (e) $\begin{pmatrix} 31 \\ 33 \\ 38 \\ 18 \end{pmatrix}$

8.4 Robot coordinate frames

In Chapter 7 we saw that vectors provide a useful tool for the analysis of the position of robots. By assigning a vector to each of the links the position vector corresponding to the tip of the robot can be calculated (Figure 8.1). In practice the inverse problem is more likely: calculate the link vectors to achieve a particular position vector. Usually a desired position for the tip of the robot is known and link positions to achieve this are required. The problem is made more complicated because the position of a link depends upon the movements of all the joints between it and the anchor point. The solution of this problem can be quite complicated, especially when the robot has several links. One way forward is to define the position of a link by its own local set of coordinates. This is usually termed a **coordinate frame** because it provides a frame of reference for the link. Matrix operations can then be used to relate the coordinate frames, thus allowing

Figure 8.1
A robot with links
represented by vectors
a, **b**, **c** and **d**.

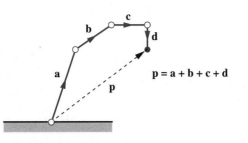

a link position to be defined with respect to a convenient coordinate frame. A common
requirement is to be able to relate the link positions to a **world coordinate frame**. If a
robot is being used in conjunction with other machines then the world coordinate frame
may have an origin some distance away from the robot. The advantage of defining link
coordinate frames is that the position of a link is easily defined within its own coordinate
frame and the movement of coordinate frames relative to each other can be expressed
by means of matrix equations.

8.4.1 Translation and rotation of vectors

An introduction to the mathematics involved in analysing the movement of robots can
be obtained by examining the way in which vectors can be translated and rotated using
matrix operations.

Consider the point **P** with position vector given by

$$\mathbf{r} = \begin{pmatrix} x \\ y \\ z \end{pmatrix}$$

In order to translate and rotate this vector it is useful to introduce an augmented vector
V given by

$$\mathbf{V} = \begin{pmatrix} x \\ y \\ z \\ 1 \end{pmatrix} \tag{8.1}$$

It is then possible to define several matrices:

$$\mathrm{Rot}(x, \theta) = \begin{pmatrix} 1 & 0 & 0 & 0 \\ 0 & \cos\theta & -\sin\theta & 0 \\ 0 & \sin\theta & \cos\theta & 0 \\ 0 & 0 & 0 & 1 \end{pmatrix} \tag{8.2}$$

$$\mathrm{Rot}(y, \theta) = \begin{pmatrix} \cos\theta & 0 & \sin\theta & 0 \\ 0 & 1 & 0 & 0 \\ -\sin\theta & 0 & \cos\theta & 0 \\ 0 & 0 & 0 & 1 \end{pmatrix} \tag{8.3}$$

$$\text{Rot}(z, \theta) = \begin{pmatrix} \cos\theta & -\sin\theta & 0 & 0 \\ \sin\theta & \cos\theta & 0 & 0 \\ 0 & 0 & 1 & 0 \\ 0 & 0 & 0 & 1 \end{pmatrix} \tag{8.4}$$

$$\text{Trans}(a, b, c) = \begin{pmatrix} 1 & 0 & 0 & a \\ 0 & 1 & 0 & b \\ 0 & 0 & 1 & c \\ 0 & 0 & 0 & 1 \end{pmatrix} \tag{8.5}$$

Matrices (8.2)–(8.4) allow vectors to be rotated by an angle θ around axes x, y and z, respectively. For example, the product $\text{Rot}(x, \theta)\, \mathbf{V}$ has the effect of rotating $\mathbf{r}$ through an angle θ about the x axis. Matrix (8.5) allows a vector to be translated a units in the x direction, b units in the y direction and c units in the z direction.

It is possible to combine these matrices to calculate the effect of several operations on a vector. In doing so, it is important to maintain the correct order of operations as matrix multiplication is non-commutative.

For example, the position of a vector that has first been translated and then rotated about the x axis can be defined by

$$\mathbf{V}_{\text{new}} = \text{Rot}(x, \theta)\, \text{Trans}(a, b, c)\, \mathbf{V}_{\text{old}}$$

A few examples will help to clarify these ideas.

Example 8.12   Rotate the vector

$$\mathbf{r} = \begin{pmatrix} 1 \\ 1 \\ 2 \end{pmatrix}$$

through 90° about the x axis.

Solution
$$\mathbf{r}_{\text{old}} = \begin{pmatrix} 1 \\ 1 \\ 2 \end{pmatrix} \qquad \mathbf{V}_{\text{old}} = \begin{pmatrix} 1 \\ 1 \\ 2 \\ 1 \end{pmatrix}$$

$$\text{Rot}(x, 90°) = \begin{pmatrix} 1 & 0 & 0 & 0 \\ 0 & \cos 90° & -\sin 90° & 0 \\ 0 & \sin 90° & \cos 90° & 0 \\ 0 & 0 & 0 & 1 \end{pmatrix} = \begin{pmatrix} 1 & 0 & 0 & 0 \\ 0 & 0 & -1 & 0 \\ 0 & 1 & 0 & 0 \\ 0 & 0 & 0 & 1 \end{pmatrix}$$

$$\mathbf{V}_{\text{new}} = \begin{pmatrix} 1 & 0 & 0 & 0 \\ 0 & 0 & -1 & 0 \\ 0 & 1 & 0 & 0 \\ 0 & 0 & 0 & 1 \end{pmatrix} \begin{pmatrix} 1 \\ 1 \\ 2 \\ 1 \end{pmatrix} = \begin{pmatrix} 1 \\ -2 \\ 1 \\ 1 \end{pmatrix}$$

So,

$$\mathbf{r}_{\text{new}} = \begin{pmatrix} 1 \\ -2 \\ 1 \end{pmatrix}$$

Example 8.13   Translate the vector

$$\mathbf{r} = \begin{pmatrix} 1 \\ 3 \\ 2 \end{pmatrix}$$

by

$$\begin{pmatrix} 1 \\ 2 \\ 3 \end{pmatrix}$$

and then rotate by 90° about the y axis.

Solution $\mathbf{r}_{old} = \begin{pmatrix} 1 \\ 3 \\ 2 \end{pmatrix}$ $\mathbf{V}_{old} = \begin{pmatrix} 1 \\ 3 \\ 2 \\ 1 \end{pmatrix}$

To translate $\mathbf{r}_{old}$, we form

$$\text{Trans}(1, 2, 3) = \begin{pmatrix} 1 & 0 & 0 & 1 \\ 0 & 1 & 0 & 2 \\ 0 & 0 & 1 & 3 \\ 0 & 0 & 0 & 1 \end{pmatrix}$$

Then

$$\text{Trans}(1, 2, 3)\mathbf{V}_{old} = \begin{pmatrix} 1 & 0 & 0 & 1 \\ 0 & 1 & 0 & 2 \\ 0 & 0 & 1 & 3 \\ 0 & 0 & 0 & 1 \end{pmatrix} \begin{pmatrix} 1 \\ 3 \\ 2 \\ 1 \end{pmatrix} = \begin{pmatrix} 2 \\ 5 \\ 5 \\ 1 \end{pmatrix}$$

To rotate by 90° about the y axis we require

$$\text{Rot}(y, 90°) = \begin{pmatrix} \cos 90° & 0 & \sin 90° & 0 \\ 0 & 1 & 0 & 0 \\ -\sin 90° & 0 & \cos 90° & 0 \\ 0 & 0 & 0 & 1 \end{pmatrix} = \begin{pmatrix} 0 & 0 & 1 & 0 \\ 0 & 1 & 0 & 0 \\ -1 & 0 & 0 & 0 \\ 0 & 0 & 0 & 1 \end{pmatrix}$$

The vector $\begin{pmatrix} 2 \\ 5 \\ 5 \\ 1 \end{pmatrix}$ is premultiplied by this matrix to give

$$\mathbf{V}_{new} = \text{Rot}(y, 90°)\text{Trans}(1, 2, 3)\mathbf{V}_{old}$$

$$= \begin{pmatrix} 0 & 0 & 1 & 0 \\ 0 & 1 & 0 & 0 \\ -1 & 0 & 0 & 0 \\ 0 & 0 & 0 & 1 \end{pmatrix} \begin{pmatrix} 2 \\ 5 \\ 5 \\ 1 \end{pmatrix} = \begin{pmatrix} 5 \\ 5 \\ -2 \\ 1 \end{pmatrix}$$

Hence

$$\mathbf{r}_{new} = \begin{pmatrix} 5 \\ 5 \\ -2 \end{pmatrix}$$

8.5 Some special matrices

8.5.1 Square matrices

A matrix which has the same number of rows as columns is called a **square** matrix. Thus

$$\begin{pmatrix} 1 & 2 & 3 \\ -1 & 0 & 1 \\ 3 & 2 & 1 \end{pmatrix} \text{ is a square matrix, while } \begin{pmatrix} -1 & 3 & 0 \\ 2 & 4 & 1 \end{pmatrix} \text{ is not}$$

8.5.2 Diagonal matrices

Some square matrices have elements which are zero everywhere except on the leading diagonal (top-left to bottom-right). Such matrices are said to be **diagonal**. Thus

$$\begin{pmatrix} 1 & 0 & 0 \\ 0 & 2 & 0 \\ 0 & 0 & -1 \end{pmatrix} \quad \begin{pmatrix} 1 & 0 \\ 0 & b \end{pmatrix} \quad \begin{pmatrix} 3 & 0 & 0 & 0 \\ 0 & 2 & 0 & 0 \\ 0 & 0 & 1 & 0 \\ 0 & 0 & 0 & 0 \end{pmatrix}.$$

are all diagonal matrices, whereas

$$\begin{pmatrix} 1 & 2 & 4 \\ 0 & 1 & 0 \\ 3 & 0 & 1 \end{pmatrix}$$

is not.

8.5.3 Identity matrices

Diagonal matrices which have only ones on their leading diagonals, for example

$$\begin{pmatrix} 1 & 0 \\ 0 & 1 \end{pmatrix} \quad \text{and} \quad \begin{pmatrix} 1 & 0 & 0 \\ 0 & 1 & 0 \\ 0 & 0 & 1 \end{pmatrix}$$

are called **identity** matrices and are denoted by the letter I.

Example 8.14   Find IA where $I = \begin{pmatrix} 1 & 0 \\ 0 & 1 \end{pmatrix}$ and $A = \begin{pmatrix} 2 & 4 & 4 \\ 3 & -1 & 0 \end{pmatrix}$ and comment upon the result.

Solution $IA = \begin{pmatrix} 1 & 0 \\ 0 & 1 \end{pmatrix}\begin{pmatrix} 2 & 4 & 4 \\ 3 & -1 & 0 \end{pmatrix} = \begin{pmatrix} 2 & 4 & 4 \\ 3 & -1 & 0 \end{pmatrix}$

The effect of premultiplying A by I has been to leave A unaltered. The product is identical to the original matrix A, and this is why I is called an identity matrix.

In general, if A is an arbitrary matrix and I is an identity matrix of the appropriate size, then

$$IA = A$$

> If A is a square matrix then $IA = AI = A$.

8.5.4 The transpose of a matrix

If A is an arbitrary $m \times n$ matrix, a related matrix is the **transpose** of A, written A^T, found by interchanging the rows and columns of A. Thus the first row of A becomes the first column of A^T and so on. A^T is an $n \times m$ matrix.

Example 8.15   If $A = \begin{pmatrix} 1 & -1 \\ 2 & 4 \end{pmatrix}$ find A^T.

Solution $A^T = \begin{pmatrix} 1 & 2 \\ -1 & 4 \end{pmatrix}$

Example 8.16   If $A = \begin{pmatrix} 4 & 2 & 6 \\ 1 & 8 & 7 \end{pmatrix}$ find A^T and evaluate AA^T.

Solution $A^T = \begin{pmatrix} 4 & 1 \\ 2 & 8 \\ 6 & 7 \end{pmatrix}$ $AA^T = \begin{pmatrix} 4 & 2 & 6 \\ 1 & 8 & 7 \end{pmatrix} \begin{pmatrix} 4 & 1 \\ 2 & 8 \\ 6 & 7 \end{pmatrix} = \begin{pmatrix} 56 & 62 \\ 62 & 114 \end{pmatrix}$

8.5.5 Symmetric matrices

If a square matrix A and its transpose A^T are identical, then A is said to be a **symmetric** matrix.

Example 8.17   If $A = \begin{pmatrix} 5 & -4 & 2 \\ -4 & 6 & 9 \\ 2 & 9 & 13 \end{pmatrix}$ find A^T.

Solution $A^T = \begin{pmatrix} 5 & -4 & 2 \\ -4 & 6 & 9 \\ 2 & 9 & 13 \end{pmatrix}$

which is clearly equal to A. Hence A is a symmetric matrix. Note that a symmetric matrix is symmetrical about its leading diagonal.

8.5.6 Skew symmetric matrices

If a square matrix A is such that $A^T = -A$ then A is said to be **skew symmetric**.

Example 8.18 If $A = \begin{pmatrix} 0 & 5 \\ -5 & 0 \end{pmatrix}$, find A^T and deduce that A is skew symmetric.

Solution We have $A^T = \begin{pmatrix} 0 & -5 \\ 5 & 0 \end{pmatrix}$ which is clearly equal to $-A$. Hence A is skew symmetric.

Exercises 8.5

1 If $A = \begin{pmatrix} 3 & 1 \\ 2 & 6 \end{pmatrix}$ and $B = \begin{pmatrix} -1 & 4 \\ 3 & 8 \end{pmatrix}$

  (a) find A^T,
  (b) find B^T,
  (c) find AB,
  (d) find $(AB)^T$,
  (e) deduce that $(AB)^T = B^T A^T$.

2 Treating the column vector $\mathbf{x} = \begin{pmatrix} x \\ y \\ z \end{pmatrix}$ as a 3×1

matrix, find $I\mathbf{x}$ where I is the 3×3 identity matrix.

3 If $A = \begin{pmatrix} a & b \\ c & d \end{pmatrix}$ show that AA^T is a symmetric

matrix.

4 If $A = \begin{pmatrix} 2 & 1 & 3 \\ 4 & 2 & 1 \\ -1 & 3 & 2 \end{pmatrix}$ and $B = \begin{pmatrix} 1 & -7 & 0 \\ 0 & 2 & 5 \\ 3 & 4 & 5 \end{pmatrix}$

find A^T, B^T, AB and $(AB)^T$.
Deduce that $(AB)^T = B^T A^T$.

5 Determine the type of matrix obtained when two diagonal matrices are multiplied together.

6 If $A = \begin{pmatrix} a & b \\ c & d \end{pmatrix}$ is skew symmetric, show that

$a = d = 0$, that is the diagonal elements are zero.

7 If $A = \begin{pmatrix} 1 & 13 \\ 15 & 7 \end{pmatrix}$

  (a) find A^T,
  (b) find $(A^T)^T$,
  (c) deduce that $(A^T)^T$ is equal to A.

8 If $A = \begin{pmatrix} 9 & 4 \\ 3 & 2 \end{pmatrix}$

  (a) find $A + A^T$ and show that this is a symmetric matrix,
  (b) find $A - A^T$ and show that this is a skew symmetric matrix.

9 The sum of the elements on the leading diagonal of a square matrix is known as its **trace**. Find the trace of

  (a) $\begin{pmatrix} 7 & 2 \\ -1 & 5 \end{pmatrix}$

  (b) $\begin{pmatrix} 0 & 9 \\ -1 & 0 \end{pmatrix}$

  (c) $\begin{pmatrix} 1 & 0 & 0 \\ 0 & 1 & 0 \\ 0 & 0 & 1 \end{pmatrix}$

  (d) $\begin{pmatrix} 7 & 2 & 1 \\ 8 & 2 & 3 \\ 9 & -1 & -4 \end{pmatrix}$

Solutions

1 (a) $\begin{pmatrix} 3 & 2 \\ 1 & 6 \end{pmatrix}$ (b) $\begin{pmatrix} -1 & 3 \\ 4 & 8 \end{pmatrix}$ (c) $\begin{pmatrix} 0 & 20 \\ 16 & 56 \end{pmatrix}$ (d) $\begin{pmatrix} 0 & 16 \\ 20 & 56 \end{pmatrix}$

2 $\begin{pmatrix} x \\ y \\ z \end{pmatrix}$

4 $\begin{pmatrix} 2 & 4 & -1 \\ 1 & 2 & 3 \\ 3 & 1 & 2 \end{pmatrix}, \begin{pmatrix} 1 & 0 & 3 \\ -7 & 2 & 4 \\ 0 & 5 & 5 \end{pmatrix},$

$\begin{pmatrix} 11 & 0 & 20 \\ 7 & -20 & 15 \\ 5 & 21 & 25 \end{pmatrix}, \begin{pmatrix} 11 & 7 & 5 \\ 0 & -20 & 21 \\ 20 & 15 & 25 \end{pmatrix}$

5 Diagonal matrix

7 (a) $\begin{pmatrix} 1 & 15 \\ 13 & 7 \end{pmatrix}$ (b) $\begin{pmatrix} 1 & 13 \\ 15 & 7 \end{pmatrix}$

8 (a) $\begin{pmatrix} 18 & 7 \\ 7 & 4 \end{pmatrix}$ (b) $\begin{pmatrix} 0 & 1 \\ -1 & 0 \end{pmatrix}$

9 (a) 12 (b) 0 (c) 3 (d) 5

8.6 The inverse of a 2×2 matrix

When we are dealing with ordinary numbers it is often necessary to carry out the operation of division. Thus, for example, if we know that $3x = 4$, then clearly $x = 4/3$. If we are given matrices A and C and know that

$$AB = C$$

how do we find B? It might be tempting to write

$$B = \frac{C}{A}$$

Unfortunately, this would be entirely wrong since division of matrices is not defined. However, given expressions like $AB = C$ it is often necessary to be able to find the appropriate expression for B. This is where we need to introduce the concept of an inverse matrix.

If A is a square matrix and we can find another matrix B with the property that

$$AB = BA = I$$

then B is said to be the **inverse** of A and is written A^{-1}, that is

$$AA^{-1} = A^{-1}A = I$$

If B is the inverse of A, then A is also the inverse of B. Note that A^{-1} does not mean a reciprocal; there is no such thing as matrix division. A^{-1} is the notation we use for the inverse of A.

Multiplying a matrix by its inverse yields the identity matrix I, that is

$$AA^{-1} = A^{-1}A = I$$

Since A is a square matrix, A^{-1} is also square and of the same order, so that the products AA^{-1} and $A^{-1}A$ can be formed. The term 'inverse' cannot be applied to a matrix which is not square.

Example 8.19 If $A = \begin{pmatrix} 2 & 1 \\ 3 & 2 \end{pmatrix}$ show that the matrix $\begin{pmatrix} 2 & -1 \\ -3 & 2 \end{pmatrix}$ is the inverse of A.

Solution Forming the products

$$\begin{pmatrix} 2 & 1 \\ 3 & 2 \end{pmatrix} \begin{pmatrix} 2 & -1 \\ -3 & 2 \end{pmatrix} = \begin{pmatrix} 1 & 0 \\ 0 & 1 \end{pmatrix}$$

$$\begin{pmatrix} 2 & -1 \\ -3 & 2 \end{pmatrix} \begin{pmatrix} 2 & 1 \\ 3 & 2 \end{pmatrix} = \begin{pmatrix} 1 & 0 \\ 0 & 1 \end{pmatrix}$$

we see that $\begin{pmatrix} 2 & -1 \\ -3 & 2 \end{pmatrix}$ is the inverse of A.

8.6.1 Finding the inverse of a matrix

For 2×2 matrices a simple formula exists to find the inverse of

$$A = \begin{pmatrix} a & b \\ c & d \end{pmatrix}$$

This formula states

$$\text{If } A = \begin{pmatrix} a & b \\ c & d \end{pmatrix} \text{ then } A^{-1} = \frac{1}{ad - bc} \begin{pmatrix} d & -b \\ -c & a \end{pmatrix}.$$

Example 8.20 If $A = \begin{pmatrix} 3 & 5 \\ 1 & 2 \end{pmatrix}$ find A^{-1}.

Solution Clearly $ad - bc = 6 - 5 = 1$, so that

$$A^{-1} = \frac{1}{1} \begin{pmatrix} 2 & -5 \\ -1 & 3 \end{pmatrix} = \begin{pmatrix} 2 & -5 \\ -1 & 3 \end{pmatrix}$$

The solution should always be checked by forming AA^{-1}.

Example 8.21 If $A = \begin{pmatrix} 1 & 5 \\ 2 & 4 \end{pmatrix}$ find A^{-1}.

Solution Here we have $ad - bc = 4 - 10 = -6$. Therefore

$$A^{-1} = \frac{1}{-6} \begin{pmatrix} 4 & -5 \\ -2 & 1 \end{pmatrix} = \begin{pmatrix} -\frac{2}{3} & \frac{5}{6} \\ \frac{1}{3} & -\frac{1}{6} \end{pmatrix}$$

Example 8.22 If $A = \begin{pmatrix} 2 & 4 \\ 1 & 2 \end{pmatrix}$ find A^{-1}.

Solution This time, $ad - bc = 4 - 4 = 0$, so when we come to form $\dfrac{1}{ad - bc}$ we find 1/0 which is not defined. We cannot form the inverse of A in this case; it does not exist.

Clearly not all square matrices have inverses. The quantity $ad - bc$ is obviously the important determining factor since only if $ad - bc \neq 0$ can we find A^{-1}. This quantity is therefore given a special name: the **determinant** of A, denoted by $|A|$, or det A. Given any 2×2 matrix A, its determinant, $|A|$, is the scalar $ad - bc$. This is easily remembered as

$$[\text{product of} \searrow \text{diagonal}] - [\text{product of} \nearrow \text{diagonal}]$$

If A is the matrix $\begin{pmatrix} a & b \\ c & d \end{pmatrix}$, we write its determinant as $\begin{vmatrix} a & b \\ c & d \end{vmatrix}$. Note that the straight lines $||$ indicate that we are discussing the determinant, which is a scalar, rather than the matrix itself. If the matrix A is such that $|A| = 0$, then it has no inverse and is said to be **singular**. If $|A| \neq 0$ then A^{-1} exists and A is said to be **non-singular**.

> A singular matrix A has $|A| = 0$.
>
> A non-singular matrix A has $|A| \neq 0$.

Example 8.23 If $A = \begin{pmatrix} 1 & 2 \\ 5 & 0 \end{pmatrix}$ and $B = \begin{pmatrix} -1 & 2 \\ -3 & 1 \end{pmatrix}$ find $|A|$, $|B|$ and $|AB|$.

Solution

$$|A| = \begin{vmatrix} 1 & 2 \\ 5 & 0 \end{vmatrix} = (1)(0) - (2)(5) = -10$$

$$|B| = \begin{vmatrix} -1 & 2 \\ -3 & 1 \end{vmatrix} = (-1)(1) - (2)(-3) = 5$$

$$AB = \begin{pmatrix} 1 & 2 \\ 5 & 0 \end{pmatrix} \begin{pmatrix} -1 & 2 \\ -3 & 1 \end{pmatrix} = \begin{pmatrix} -7 & 4 \\ -5 & 10 \end{pmatrix}$$

$$|AB| = (-7)(10) - (4)(-5) = -50$$

We note that $|A||B| = |AB|$.

The result obtained in Example 8.23 is true more generally:

> If A and B are square matrices of the same order, $|A||B| = |AB|$.

8.6.2 Orthogonal matrices

A non-singular square matrix A such that $A^T = A^{-1}$ is said to be **orthogonal**. Consequently, if A is orthogonal $AA^T = A^T A = I$.

Example 8.24 Find the inverse of $A = \begin{pmatrix} 0 & -1 \\ 1 & 0 \end{pmatrix}$. Deduce that A is an orthogonal matrix.

Solution From the formula for the inverse of a 2×2 matrix we find

$$A^{-1} = \frac{1}{1} \begin{pmatrix} 0 & 1 \\ -1 & 0 \end{pmatrix} = \begin{pmatrix} 0 & 1 \\ -1 & 0 \end{pmatrix}$$

This is clearly equal to the transpose of A. Hence A is an orthogonal matrix.

To find the inverses of larger matrices we shall need to study determinants further. This is done in Section 8.7.

Exercises 8.6

1 If $A = \begin{pmatrix} 5 & 6 \\ -4 & 8 \end{pmatrix}$ find A^{-1}.

2 Find the inverse, if it exists, of each of the following matrices:

(a) $\begin{pmatrix} 1 & 0 \\ 0 & 1 \end{pmatrix}$

(b) $\begin{pmatrix} -1 & 0 \\ 0 & -1 \end{pmatrix}$

(c) $\begin{pmatrix} 2 & 3 \\ 4 & 1 \end{pmatrix}$

(d) $\begin{pmatrix} -1 & 0 \\ -1 & 7 \end{pmatrix}$

(e) $\begin{pmatrix} 6 & 2 \\ 9 & 3 \end{pmatrix}$

(f) $\begin{pmatrix} -6 & 2 \\ 9 & 3 \end{pmatrix}$

(g) $\begin{pmatrix} \frac{1}{2} & \frac{1}{2} \\ 0 & \frac{1}{2} \end{pmatrix}$

3 If $A = \begin{pmatrix} 3 & 0 \\ -1 & 4 \end{pmatrix}$ and $B = \begin{pmatrix} 7 & 8 \\ 4 & 3 \end{pmatrix}$ find $|AB|$, $|BA|$.

4 If $A = \begin{pmatrix} a & b \\ c & d \end{pmatrix}$, $B = \begin{pmatrix} e & f \\ g & h \end{pmatrix}$ find AB, $|A|$, $|B|$, $|AB|$.

Verify that $|AB| = |A||B|$.

5 If $A = \begin{pmatrix} 1 & 2 \\ 3 & 4 \end{pmatrix}$ find A^{-1}.

Find values of the constants a and b such that $A + aA^{-1} = bI$.

6 If $A = \begin{pmatrix} 1 & 1 \\ 0 & 3 \end{pmatrix}$ and $B = \begin{pmatrix} 2 & 1 \\ -1 & 3 \end{pmatrix}$ find AB, $(AB)^{-1}$, B^{-1}, A^{-1} and $B^{-1}A^{-1}$.

Deduce that $(AB)^{-1} = B^{-1}A^{-1}$.

7 Given that the matrix

$$M = \begin{pmatrix} \cos \omega t & -\sin \omega t & 0 \\ \sin \omega t & \cos \omega t & 0 \\ 0 & 0 & 1 \end{pmatrix}$$

is orthogonal, find M^{-1}.

8 (a) If $A = \begin{pmatrix} a & b \\ c & d \end{pmatrix}$ and k is a scalar constant, show that the inverse of the matrix kA is $\frac{1}{k}A^{-1}$.

(b) Find the inverse of $\begin{pmatrix} 1 & 1 \\ 1 & 0 \end{pmatrix}$ and hence write down the inverse of $\begin{pmatrix} \frac{1}{3} & \frac{1}{3} \\ \frac{1}{3} & 0 \end{pmatrix}$.

Solutions

1 $\frac{1}{64}\begin{pmatrix} 8 & -6 \\ 4 & 5 \end{pmatrix}$

2 (a) $\begin{pmatrix} 1 & 0 \\ 0 & 1 \end{pmatrix}$

(b) $\begin{pmatrix} -1 & 0 \\ 0 & -1 \end{pmatrix}$

(c) $\begin{pmatrix} -\frac{1}{10} & \frac{3}{10} \\ \frac{2}{5} & -\frac{1}{5} \end{pmatrix}$

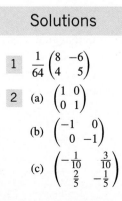

(d) $\begin{pmatrix} -1 & 0 \\ -\frac{1}{7} & \frac{1}{7} \end{pmatrix}$

(e) No inverse

(f) $\begin{pmatrix} -\frac{1}{12} & \frac{1}{18} \\ \frac{1}{4} & \frac{1}{6} \end{pmatrix}$

(g) $\begin{pmatrix} 2 & -2 \\ 0 & 2 \end{pmatrix}$

3 $-132, -132$

4 $\begin{pmatrix} ae + bg & af + bh \\ ce + dg & cf + dh \end{pmatrix}$,

   $ad - bc, eh - fg$,

   $(ad - bc)(eh - fg)$

5 $\begin{pmatrix} -2 & 1 \\ \frac{3}{2} & -\frac{1}{2} \end{pmatrix}$ $a = -2, b = 5$

6 $AB = \begin{pmatrix} 1 & 4 \\ -3 & 9 \end{pmatrix}, (AB)^{-1} = \frac{1}{21}\begin{pmatrix} 9 & -4 \\ 3 & 1 \end{pmatrix},$

   $B^{-1} = \frac{1}{7}\begin{pmatrix} 3 & -1 \\ 1 & 2 \end{pmatrix}, A^{-1} = \frac{1}{3}\begin{pmatrix} 3 & -1 \\ 0 & 1 \end{pmatrix}$

7 $\begin{pmatrix} \cos \omega t & \sin \omega t & 0 \\ -\sin \omega t & \cos \omega t & 0 \\ 0 & 0 & 1 \end{pmatrix}$

8 (b) $\begin{pmatrix} 0 & 1 \\ 1 & -1 \end{pmatrix}, \begin{pmatrix} 0 & 3 \\ 3 & -3 \end{pmatrix}$

8.7 Determinants

If $A = \begin{pmatrix} a_{11} & a_{12} & a_{13} \\ a_{21} & a_{22} & a_{23} \\ a_{31} & a_{32} & a_{33} \end{pmatrix}$, the value of its determinant, $|A|$, is given by

$$|A| = a_{11}\begin{vmatrix} a_{22} & a_{23} \\ a_{32} & a_{33} \end{vmatrix} - a_{12}\begin{vmatrix} a_{21} & a_{23} \\ a_{31} & a_{33} \end{vmatrix} + a_{13}\begin{vmatrix} a_{21} & a_{22} \\ a_{31} & a_{32} \end{vmatrix}$$

If we choose an element of A, a_{ij} say, and cross out its row and column and form the determinant of the four remaining elements, this determinant is known as the **minor** of the element a_{ij}.

A moment's study will therefore reveal that the determinant of A is given by

$$|A| = (a_{11} \times \text{its minor}) - (a_{12} \times \text{its minor}) + (a_{13} \times \text{its minor})$$

This method of evaluating a determinant is known as **expansion along the first row**.

Example 8.25 Find the determinant of the matrix

$$A = \begin{pmatrix} 1 & 2 & 1 \\ -1 & 3 & 4 \\ 5 & 1 & 2 \end{pmatrix}$$

Solution The determinant of A, written as

$$\begin{vmatrix} 1 & 2 & 1 \\ -1 & 3 & 4 \\ 5 & 1 & 2 \end{vmatrix}$$

is found by expanding along its first row:

$$|A| = 1\begin{vmatrix} 3 & 4 \\ 1 & 2 \end{vmatrix} - 2\begin{vmatrix} -1 & 4 \\ 5 & 2 \end{vmatrix} + 1\begin{vmatrix} -1 & 3 \\ 5 & 1 \end{vmatrix}$$

$$= 1(2) - 2(-22) + 1(-16)$$

$$= 2 + 44 - 16$$

$$= 30$$

Example 8.26   Find the minors of the elements 1 and 4 in the matrix

$$B = \begin{pmatrix} 7 & 2 & 3 \\ 1 & 0 & 3 \\ 0 & 4 & 2 \end{pmatrix}$$

Solution   To find the minor of 1 delete its row and column to form the determinant $\begin{vmatrix} 2 & 3 \\ 4 & 2 \end{vmatrix}$. The required minor is therefore $4 - 12 = -8$.

Similarly, the minor of 4 is $\begin{vmatrix} 7 & 3 \\ 1 & 3 \end{vmatrix} = 21 - 3 = 18$.

In addition to finding the minor of each element in a matrix, it is often useful to find a related quantity – the **cofactor** of each element. The cofactor is found by imposing on the minor a positive or negative sign depending upon its position that is, a **place sign**, according to the following rule:

$$\begin{array}{ccc} + & - & + \\ - & + & - \\ + & - & + \end{array}$$

Example 8.27   If

$$A = \begin{pmatrix} 3 & 2 & 7 \\ 9 & 1 & 0 \\ 3 & -1 & 2 \end{pmatrix}$$

find the cofactors of 9 and 7.

Solution   The minor of 9 is $\begin{vmatrix} 2 & 7 \\ -1 & 2 \end{vmatrix} = 4 - (-7) = 11$, but since its place sign is negative, the required cofactor is -11.

The minor of 7 is $\begin{vmatrix} 9 & 1 \\ 3 & -1 \end{vmatrix} = -9 - 3 = -12$. Its place sign is positive, so that the required cofactor is simply -12.

8.7.1 Using determinants to find vector products

Determinants can also be used to evaluate the vector product of two vectors. If $\mathbf{a} = a_1\mathbf{i} + a_2\mathbf{j} + a_3\mathbf{k}$ and $\mathbf{b} = b_1\mathbf{i} + b_2\mathbf{j} + b_3\mathbf{k}$, we showed in Section 7.6 that $\mathbf{a} \times \mathbf{b}$ is the vector defined by

$$\mathbf{a} \times \mathbf{b} = (a_2b_3 - a_3b_2)\mathbf{i} + (a_3b_1 - a_1b_3)\mathbf{j} + (a_1b_2 - a_2b_1)\mathbf{k}$$

If we consider the expansion of the determinant given by

$$\begin{vmatrix} \mathbf{i} & \mathbf{j} & \mathbf{k} \\ a_1 & a_2 & a_3 \\ b_1 & b_2 & b_3 \end{vmatrix}$$

we find the same result. This definition is therefore a convenient mechanism for evaluating a vector product.

If $\mathbf{a} = a_1\mathbf{i} + a_2\mathbf{j} + a_3\mathbf{k}$ and $\mathbf{b} = b_1\mathbf{i} + b_2\mathbf{j} + b_3\mathbf{k}$, then

$$\mathbf{a} \times \mathbf{b} = \begin{vmatrix} \mathbf{i} & \mathbf{j} & \mathbf{k} \\ a_1 & a_2 & a_3 \\ b_1 & b_2 & b_3 \end{vmatrix}$$

Example 8.28   If $\mathbf{a} = 3\mathbf{i} + \mathbf{j} - 2\mathbf{k}$ and $\mathbf{b} = 4\mathbf{i} + 5\mathbf{k}$ find $\mathbf{a} \times \mathbf{b}$.

Solution   We have

$$\mathbf{a} \times \mathbf{b} = \begin{vmatrix} \mathbf{i} & \mathbf{j} & \mathbf{k} \\ 3 & 1 & -2 \\ 4 & 0 & 5 \end{vmatrix}$$
$$= 5\mathbf{i} - 23\mathbf{j} - 4\mathbf{k}$$

8.7.2 Cramer's rule

A useful application of determinants is to the solution of simultaneous equations. Consider the case of three simultaneous equations in three unknowns:

$$a_{11}x + a_{12}y + a_{13}z = b_1$$
$$a_{21}x + a_{22}y + a_{23}z = b_2$$
$$a_{31}x + a_{32}y + a_{33}z = b_3$$

Cramer's rule states that x, y and z are given by the following ratios of determinants.

Cramer's rule:

$$x = \frac{\begin{vmatrix} b_1 & a_{12} & a_{13} \\ b_2 & a_{22} & a_{23} \\ b_3 & a_{32} & a_{33} \end{vmatrix}}{\begin{vmatrix} a_{11} & a_{12} & a_{13} \\ a_{21} & a_{22} & a_{23} \\ a_{31} & a_{32} & a_{33} \end{vmatrix}} \qquad y = \frac{\begin{vmatrix} a_{11} & b_1 & a_{13} \\ a_{21} & b_2 & a_{23} \\ a_{31} & b_3 & a_{33} \end{vmatrix}}{\begin{vmatrix} a_{11} & a_{12} & a_{13} \\ a_{21} & a_{22} & a_{23} \\ a_{31} & a_{32} & a_{33} \end{vmatrix}} \qquad z = \frac{\begin{vmatrix} a_{11} & a_{12} & b_1 \\ a_{21} & a_{22} & b_2 \\ a_{31} & a_{32} & b_3 \end{vmatrix}}{\begin{vmatrix} a_{11} & a_{12} & a_{13} \\ a_{21} & a_{22} & a_{23} \\ a_{31} & a_{32} & a_{33} \end{vmatrix}}$$

Note that in all cases the determinant in the denominator is identical and its elements are the coefficients on the l.h.s. of the simultaneous equations. When this determinant is zero, Cramer's method will clearly fail.

Example 8.29   Solve

$$3x + 2y - z = 4$$
$$2x - y + 2z = 10$$
$$x - 3y - 4z = 5$$

Solution   We find

$$x = \frac{\begin{vmatrix} 4 & 2 & -1 \\ 10 & -1 & 2 \\ 5 & -3 & -4 \end{vmatrix}}{\begin{vmatrix} 3 & 2 & -1 \\ 2 & -1 & 2 \\ 1 & -3 & -4 \end{vmatrix}} = \frac{165}{55} = 3$$

Verify for yourself that $y = -2$ and $z = 1$.

Exercises   8.7

1 Find $\begin{vmatrix} 4 & 6 \\ 2 & 8 \end{vmatrix}$, $\begin{vmatrix} 1 & 3 & 4 \\ 2 & 1 & 0 \\ 3 & 5 & -1 \end{vmatrix}$ and $\begin{vmatrix} 6 & 7 & 2 \\ 1 & 4 & 3 \\ -1 & 1 & 4 \end{vmatrix}$.

2 Find $\begin{vmatrix} \cos \omega t & \sin \omega t \\ -\sin \omega t & \cos \omega t \end{vmatrix}$.

3 Evaluate $\begin{vmatrix} 5 & 0 & 0 \\ 6 & 3 & 2 \\ 4 & 5 & 7 \end{vmatrix}$ and $\begin{vmatrix} 9 & 0 & 0 \\ 0 & 7 & 0 \\ 0 & 0 & 8 \end{vmatrix}$.

4 If $A = \begin{pmatrix} 2 & -1 & 7 \\ 0 & 8 & 4 \\ 3 & 6 & 4 \end{pmatrix}$, find $|A|$ and $|A^T|$.

Comment upon your result.

5 Use Cramer's rule to solve

(a) $2x - 3y + z = 0$
$5x + 4y + z = 10$
$2x - 2y - z = -1$

(b) $3x + y = -1$
$2x - y + z = -1$
$5x + 5y - 7z = -16$

(c) $4x + y + z = 13$
$2x - y = 4$
$x + y - z = -3$

(d) $3x + 2y = 1$
$x + y - z = 1$
$2x + 3z = -1$

6 Given

$$A = \begin{pmatrix} 3 & 7 & 6 \\ -2 & 1 & 0 \\ 4 & 2 & -5 \end{pmatrix}$$

(a) find $|A|$

(b) find the cofactors of the elements of row 2, that is $-2, 1, 0$

(c) calculate

$$-2 \times (\text{cofactor of } -2)$$
$$+1 \times (\text{cofactor of } 1)$$
$$+0 \times (\text{cofactor of } 0).$$

What do you deduce?

7 If $\mathbf{a} = 7\mathbf{i} + 11\mathbf{j} - 2\mathbf{k}$ and $\mathbf{b} = 6\mathbf{i} - 3\mathbf{j} + \mathbf{k}$ find $\mathbf{a} \times \mathbf{b}$.

8 Find $\mathbf{a} \times \mathbf{b}$ when

(a) $\mathbf{a} = 3\mathbf{i} - \mathbf{j}, \mathbf{b} = \mathbf{i} + \mathbf{j} + \mathbf{k}$

(b) $\mathbf{a} = 2\mathbf{i} + \mathbf{j} + \mathbf{k}, \mathbf{b} = 7\mathbf{k}$

(c) $\mathbf{a} = -7\mathbf{j} - \mathbf{k}, \mathbf{b} = -3\mathbf{i} + \mathbf{j}$

Solutions

1 20, 33, 39

2 1

3 55, 504

4 −164, −164   Note $|A| = |A^T|$

5 (a) $x = y = z = 1$

   (b) $x = -1, y = 2, z = 3$

   (c) $x = 2, y = 0, z = 5$

(d) $x = 1, y = -1, z = -1$

6 (a) −133   (b) 47, −39, 22   (c) −133

7 $5\mathbf{i} - 19\mathbf{j} - 87\mathbf{k}$

8 (a) $-\mathbf{i} - 3\mathbf{j} + 4\mathbf{k}$

   (b) $7\mathbf{i} - 14\mathbf{j}$

   (c) $\mathbf{i} + 3\mathbf{j} - 21\mathbf{k}$

8.8 The inverse of a 3×3 matrix

Given a 3×3 matrix, A, its inverse is found as follows:

(1) Find the transpose of A, by interchanging the rows and columns of A.

(2) Replace each element of A^T by its cofactor; by its minor together with its associated place sign. The resulting matrix is known as the **adjoint** of A, denoted adj (A).

(3) Finally, the inverse of A is given by

$$A^{-1} = \frac{\text{adj}(A)}{|A|}$$

Example 8.30 Find the inverse of

$$A = \begin{pmatrix} 1 & -2 & 0 \\ 3 & 1 & 5 \\ -1 & 2 & 3 \end{pmatrix}$$

Solution

$$A^T = \begin{pmatrix} 1 & 3 & -1 \\ -2 & 1 & 2 \\ 0 & 5 & 3 \end{pmatrix}$$

Replacing each element of A^T by its cofactor, we find

$$\text{adj}(A) = \begin{pmatrix} -7 & 6 & -10 \\ -14 & 3 & -5 \\ 7 & 0 & 7 \end{pmatrix}$$

The determinant of A is given by

$$|A| = 1 \begin{vmatrix} 1 & 5 \\ 2 & 3 \end{vmatrix} - (-2) \begin{vmatrix} 3 & 5 \\ -1 & 3 \end{vmatrix} + 0 \begin{vmatrix} 3 & 1 \\ -1 & 2 \end{vmatrix}$$

$$= (1)(-7) + (2)(14)$$

$$= 21$$

Therefore,

$$A^{-1} = \frac{\text{adj}(A)}{|A|} = \frac{1}{21} \begin{pmatrix} -7 & 6 & -10 \\ -14 & 3 & -5 \\ 7 & 0 & 7 \end{pmatrix}$$

Note that this solution should be checked by forming AA^{-1} to give I.

It is clear that should $|A| = 0$ then no inverse will exist since then the quantity $1/|A|$ is undefined. Recall that such a matrix is said to be singular.

> For any square matrix A, the following statements are equivalent:
>
> $|A| = 0$
> A is singular
> A has no inverse

Exercises 8.8

1 Find adj(A), $|A|$ and, if it exists, A^{-1}, if

(a) $A = \begin{pmatrix} 2 & -3 & 1 \\ 5 & 4 & 1 \\ 2 & -2 & -1 \end{pmatrix}$

(b) $A = \begin{pmatrix} 3 & 1 & 0 \\ 2 & -1 & 1 \\ 5 & 5 & -7 \end{pmatrix}$

(c) $A = \begin{pmatrix} 2 & -1 & 4 \\ 5 & -2 & 9 \\ 3 & 2 & -1 \end{pmatrix}$

2 If $P = \begin{pmatrix} 10 & -5 & -4 \\ -5 & 10 & -3 \\ -4 & -3 & 8 \end{pmatrix}$, find adj($P$) and $|P|$.

Deduce P^{-1}.

Solutions

1 (a) $|A| = -43$

$$\text{adj}(A) = \begin{pmatrix} -2 & -5 & -7 \\ 7 & -4 & 3 \\ -18 & -2 & 23 \end{pmatrix},$$

$$A^{-1} = \frac{1}{43} \begin{pmatrix} 2 & 5 & 7 \\ -7 & 4 & -3 \\ 18 & 2 & -23 \end{pmatrix}$$

(b) $|A| = 25$

$$\text{adj}(A) = \begin{pmatrix} 2 & 7 & 1 \\ 19 & -21 & -3 \\ 15 & -10 & -5 \end{pmatrix},$$

$$A^{-1} = \frac{1}{25} \begin{pmatrix} 2 & 7 & 1 \\ 19 & -21 & -3 \\ 15 & -10 & -5 \end{pmatrix}$$

(c) $|A| = 0$

$$\text{adj}(A) = \begin{pmatrix} -16 & 7 & -1 \\ 32 & -14 & 2 \\ 16 & -7 & 1 \end{pmatrix}$$

A^{-1} does not exist

2 $|P| = 230$

$$\text{adj}(P) = \begin{pmatrix} 71 & 52 & 55 \\ 52 & 64 & 50 \\ 55 & 50 & 75 \end{pmatrix}$$

$$P^{-1} = \frac{1}{230} \begin{pmatrix} 71 & 52 & 55 \\ 52 & 64 & 50 \\ 55 & 50 & 75 \end{pmatrix}$$

8.9 Application to the solution of simultaneous equations

The matrix techniques we have developed allow the solution of simultaneous equations to be found in a systematic way.

Example 8.31 Use a matrix method to solve the simultaneous equations

$$
\begin{aligned}
2x + 4y &= 14 \\
x - 3y &= -8
\end{aligned}
\tag{8.6}
$$

Solution We first note that the system of equations can be written in matrix form as follows:

$$
\begin{pmatrix} 2 & 4 \\ 1 & -3 \end{pmatrix} \begin{pmatrix} x \\ y \end{pmatrix} = \begin{pmatrix} 14 \\ -8 \end{pmatrix}
\tag{8.7}
$$

To understand this expression it is necessary that matrix multiplication has been fully mastered, for, by multiplying out the l.h.s. we find

$$
\begin{pmatrix} 2 & 4 \\ 1 & -3 \end{pmatrix} \begin{pmatrix} x \\ y \end{pmatrix} = \begin{pmatrix} 2x + 4y \\ 1x - 3y \end{pmatrix}
$$

and the form (8.7) follows immediately.

We can write Equation (8.7) as

$$
AX = B
\tag{8.8}
$$

where A is the matrix $\begin{pmatrix} 2 & 4 \\ 1 & -3 \end{pmatrix}$, X is the matrix $\begin{pmatrix} x \\ y \end{pmatrix}$ and B is the matrix $\begin{pmatrix} 14 \\ -8 \end{pmatrix}$.

In order to find $X = \begin{pmatrix} x \\ y \end{pmatrix}$ it is now necessary to make X the subject of the equation $AX = B$. We can premultiply Equation (8.8) by A^{-1}, the inverse of A, provided such an inverse exists, to give

$$
A^{-1}AX = A^{-1}B
$$

Then, noting that $A^{-1}A = I$, we find

$$
IX = A^{-1}B
$$

that is

$$
X = A^{-1}B
$$

using the properties of the identity matrix. We have now made X the subject of the equation as required and we see that to find X we must premultiply the r.h.s. of Equation (8.8) by the inverse of A.

In this case

$$
A^{-1} = \frac{1}{-10} \begin{pmatrix} -3 & -4 \\ -1 & 2 \end{pmatrix}
$$

$$
= \begin{pmatrix} 3/10 & 2/5 \\ 1/10 & -1/5 \end{pmatrix}
$$

and

$$A^{-1}B = \begin{pmatrix} 3/10 & 2/5 \\ 1/10 & -1/5 \end{pmatrix} \begin{pmatrix} 14 \\ -8 \end{pmatrix}$$

$$= \begin{pmatrix} 1 \\ 3 \end{pmatrix}$$

that is, $X = \begin{pmatrix} x \\ y \end{pmatrix} = \begin{pmatrix} 1 \\ 3 \end{pmatrix}$, so that $x = 1$ and $y = 3$ is the required solution.

If $AX = B$ then $X = A^{-1}B$ provided A^{-1} exists.

This technique can be applied to three equations in three unknowns in an analogous way.

Example 8.32   Express the following equations in the form $AX = B$ and hence solve them:

$$3x + 2y - z = 4$$
$$2x - y + 2z = 10$$
$$x - 3y - 4z = 5$$

Solution   Using the rules of matrix multiplication, we find

$$\begin{pmatrix} 3 & 2 & -1 \\ 2 & -1 & 2 \\ 1 & -3 & -4 \end{pmatrix} \begin{pmatrix} x \\ y \\ z \end{pmatrix} = \begin{pmatrix} 4 \\ 10 \\ 5 \end{pmatrix}$$

which is in the form $AX = B$. The matrix A is called the **coefficient matrix** and is simply the coefficients of x, y and z in the equations. As before,

$$AX = B$$
$$A^{-1}AX = A^{-1}B$$
$$IX = X = A^{-1}B$$

We must therefore find the inverse of A in order to solve the equations.
To invert A we use the adjoint. If

$$A = \begin{pmatrix} 3 & 2 & -1 \\ 2 & -1 & 2 \\ 1 & -3 & -4 \end{pmatrix}$$

then

$$A^T = \begin{pmatrix} 3 & 2 & 1 \\ 2 & -1 & -3 \\ -1 & 2 & -4 \end{pmatrix}$$

and you should verify that adj(A) is given by

$$\text{adj}(A) = \begin{pmatrix} 10 & 11 & 3 \\ 10 & -11 & -8 \\ -5 & 11 & -7 \end{pmatrix}$$

The determinant of A is found by expanding along the first row:

$$|A| = 3\begin{vmatrix} -1 & 2 \\ -3 & -4 \end{vmatrix} - 2\begin{vmatrix} 2 & 2 \\ 1 & -4 \end{vmatrix} - 1\begin{vmatrix} 2 & -1 \\ 1 & -3 \end{vmatrix}$$

$$= (3)(10) - (2)(-10) - (1)(-5)$$

$$= 30 + 20 + 5$$

$$= 55$$

Therefore,

$$A^{-1} = \frac{\text{adj}(A)}{|A|} = \frac{1}{55}\begin{pmatrix} 10 & 11 & 3 \\ 10 & -11 & -8 \\ -5 & 11 & -7 \end{pmatrix}$$

Finally, the solution X is given by

$$X = \begin{pmatrix} x \\ y \\ z \end{pmatrix} = A^{-1}B = \frac{1}{55}\begin{pmatrix} 10 & 11 & 3 \\ 10 & -11 & -8 \\ -5 & 11 & -7 \end{pmatrix}\begin{pmatrix} 4 \\ 10 \\ 5 \end{pmatrix}$$

$$= \begin{pmatrix} 3 \\ -2 \\ 1 \end{pmatrix}$$

that is, the solution is $x = 3$, $y = -2$ and $z = 1$.

Exercises 8.9

1 By expressing the following equations in matrix form and finding an inverse matrix, solve

(a) $4x - 2y = 14$
  $2x + y = 5$

(b) $2x - 2y = 0$
  $x + 3y = -8$

(c) $8x + 3y = 59$
  $-2x + y = -13$

2 Solve the following equations $AX = B$ by finding A^{-1}, if it exists.

(a) $\begin{pmatrix} 6 & 3 \\ 5 & 2 \end{pmatrix}\begin{pmatrix} x \\ y \end{pmatrix} = \begin{pmatrix} 12 \\ 9 \end{pmatrix}$

(b) $\begin{pmatrix} 4 & 4 \\ 1 & 3 \end{pmatrix}\begin{pmatrix} x \\ y \end{pmatrix} = \begin{pmatrix} 20 \\ 11 \end{pmatrix}$

(c) $\begin{pmatrix} 2 & -1 \\ 3 & 2 \end{pmatrix}\begin{pmatrix} x \\ y \end{pmatrix} = \begin{pmatrix} -4 \\ 1 \end{pmatrix}$

(d) $\begin{pmatrix} 4 & 1 & 3 \\ 2 & -1 & 4 \\ 0 & 1 & 5 \end{pmatrix}\begin{pmatrix} x \\ y \\ z \end{pmatrix} = \begin{pmatrix} 20 \\ 20 \\ 20 \end{pmatrix}$

(e) $\begin{pmatrix} 4 & 1 & 3 \\ 2 & -1 & 4 \\ 0 & 1 & 5 \end{pmatrix} \begin{pmatrix} x \\ y \\ z \end{pmatrix} = \begin{pmatrix} 15 \\ 12 \\ 17 \end{pmatrix}$ (f) $\begin{pmatrix} 4 & 1 & 3 \\ 2 & -1 & 4 \\ 0 & 1 & 5 \end{pmatrix} \begin{pmatrix} x \\ y \\ z \end{pmatrix} = \begin{pmatrix} 0 \\ 0 \\ 0 \end{pmatrix}$

Solutions

1 (a) $x = 3, y = -1$ (c) $x = -1, y = 2$

   (b) $x = -2, y = -2$

   (c) $x = 7, y = 1$ (d) $x = 2, y = 0, z = 4$

2 (a) $x = 1, y = 2$ (e) $x = 1, y = 2, z = 3$

   (b) $x = 2, y = 3$ (f) $x = y = z = 0$

8.10 Gaussian elimination

An alternative technique for the solution of simultaneous equations is that of Gaussian elimination which we introduce by means of the following trivial example.

Example 8.33 Use Gaussian elimination to solve

$$2x + 3y = 1$$
$$x + y = 3$$

Solution First consider the equations with a step pattern imposed as follows:

$\quad x \lfloor + \; y \; = 3$ (2)

Our aim will be to perform various operations on these equations to remove or eliminate all the values underneath the step. You will probably remember from your early work on simultaneous equations that in order to eliminate a variable from an equation, that equation can be multiplied by any suitable number and then added to or subtracted from another equation. In this example we can eliminate the x term from below the step by multiplying the second equation by 2 and subtracting the first equation. Since the first equation is entirely above the step we shall leave it as it stands. This whole process will be written as follows:

$$\begin{array}{ll} R_1 & \lfloor 2x \; + \; 3y \; = \; 1 \\ R_2 \to 2R_2 - R_1 & \overline{0x \lfloor - \; y \; = \; 5} \end{array} \qquad (8.9)$$

where the symbol R_1 means that Equation (1) is unaltered, and $R_2 \to 2R_2 - R_1$ means that Equation (2) has been replaced by $2 \times$ Equation (2) – Equation (1). All this may seem to be overcomplicating a simple problem but a moment's study of Equation (8.9) will reveal why this 'stepped' form is useful. Because the value under the step is zero we can read off y from the last line, that is $-y = 5$, so that

$$y = -5$$

Knowing y we can then move up to the first equation and substitute for y to find x.

$$2x + 3(-5) = 1$$
$$x = 8$$

This last stage is known as **back substitution**.

Before we consider another example, let us note some important points.

(1) It is necessary to write down the operations used as indicated previously. This aids checking and provides a record of the working used.

(2) The operations allowed to eliminate unwanted variables are:

    (a) any equation can be multiplied by any non-zero constant;

    (b) any equation can be added to or subtracted from any other equation;

    (c) equations can be interchanged.

It is often convenient to use matrices to carry out this method, in which case the operations allowed are referred to as **row operations**. The advantage of using matrices is that it is unnecessary to write down x, y (and later z) each time. To do this, we first form the **augmented matrix**:

$$\begin{pmatrix} 2 & 3 & 1 \\ 1 & 1 & 3 \end{pmatrix}$$

so called because the coefficient matrix $\begin{pmatrix} 2 & 3 \\ 1 & 1 \end{pmatrix}$ is augmented by the r.h.s. matrix $\begin{pmatrix} 1 \\ 3 \end{pmatrix}$.

It is to be understood that this notation means $2x + 3y = 1$, and so on, so that we no longer write down x and y. Each row of the augmented matrix corresponds to one equation. The aim, as before, is to carry out row operations on the stepped form

$$\begin{pmatrix} 2 & 3 & 1 \\ 1 & 1 & 3 \end{pmatrix}$$

in order to obtain values of zero under the step. Clearly to achieve the required form, the row operations we performed earlier are required, that is

$$\begin{matrix} R_1 \\ R_2 \to 2R_2 - R_1 \end{matrix} \qquad \begin{pmatrix} 2 & 3 & 1 \\ 0 & -1 & 5 \end{pmatrix}$$

The last line means $0x - 1y = 5$, that is $y = -5$, and finally back substitution yields x, as before.

This technique has other advantages in that it allows us to observe other forms of behaviour. We shall see that some equations have a unique solution, some have no solutions, while others have an infinite number.

Example 8.34   Use Gaussian elimination to solve

$$2x + 3y = 4$$
$$4x + 6y = 7$$

Solution   In augmented matrix form we have

$$\left(\begin{array}{cc|c} 2 & 3 & 4 \\ 4 & 6 & 7 \end{array}\right)$$

We proceed to eliminate entries under the step:

$$\begin{array}{c} R_1 \\ R_2 \to R_2 - 2R_1 \end{array} \quad \left(\begin{array}{cc|c} 2 & 3 & 4 \\ 0 & 0 & -1 \end{array}\right)$$

Study of the last line seems to imply that $0x + 0y = -1$, which is clearly nonsense. When this happens the equations have no solutions and we say that the simultaneous equations are **inconsistent**.

Example 8.35   Use Gaussian elimination to solve

$$x + y = 0$$
$$2x + 2y = 0$$

Solution   In augmented matrix form we have

$$\left(\begin{array}{cc|c} 1 & 1 & 0 \\ 2 & 2 & 0 \end{array}\right)$$

Eliminating entries under the step we find

$$\begin{array}{c} R_1 \\ R_2 \to R_2 - 2R_1 \end{array} \quad \left(\begin{array}{cc|c} 1 & 1 & 0 \\ 0 & 0 & 0 \end{array}\right)$$

This last line implies that $0x + 0y = 0$. This is not an inconsistency, but we are now observing a third type of behaviour. Whenever this happens we need to introduce what are called **free variables**. The first row starts off with a non-zero x. There is now no row which starts off with a non-zero y. We therefore say y is free and choose it to be anything we please, that is

$$y = \lambda \qquad \lambda \text{ is our free choice}$$

Then back substitution occurs as before.

$$x + \lambda = 0$$
$$x = -\lambda$$

The solution is therefore $x = -\lambda$, $y = \lambda$, where λ is any number. There are thus an infinite number of solutions, for example

$$x = -1 \qquad y = 1$$

or

$$x = \frac{1}{2} \qquad y = -\frac{1}{2}$$

and so on.

Observation of the coefficient matrices in the last two examples shows that they have a determinant of zero. Whenever this happens we shall find the equations are either inconsistent or have an infinite number of solutions. We shall next consider the generalization of this method to three equations in three unknowns.

Example 8.36 Solve by Gaussian elimination

$$x - 4y - 2z = 21$$
$$2x + y + 2z = 3$$
$$3x + 2y - z = -2$$

Solution We first form the augmented matrix and add the stepped pattern as indicated:

$$\begin{pmatrix} 1 & -4 & -2 & 21 \\ 2 & 1 & 2 & 3 \\ 3 & 2 & -1 & -2 \end{pmatrix}$$

The aim is to eliminate all numbers underneath the steps by carrying out appropriate row operations. This should be carried out by eliminating unwanted numbers in the first column first. We find

$$\begin{array}{c} R_1 \\ R_2 \to R_2 - 2R_1 \\ R_3 \to R_3 - 3R_1 \end{array} \qquad \begin{pmatrix} 1 & -4 & -2 & 21 \\ 0 & 9 & 6 & -39 \\ 0 & 14 & 5 & -65 \end{pmatrix}$$

We have combined the elimination of unwanted numbers in the first column into one stage. We now remove unwanted numbers in the second column:

$$\begin{array}{c} R_1 \\ R_2 \\ R_3 \to R_3 - \frac{14}{9} R_2 \end{array} \qquad \begin{pmatrix} 1 & -4 & -2 & 21 \\ 0 & 9 & 6 & -39 \\ 0 & 0 & -\frac{13}{3} & -\frac{13}{3} \end{pmatrix}$$

and the elimination is complete. Although $R_3 \to R_3 + \frac{14}{4} R_1$ would eliminate the 14, it would reintroduce a non-zero term into the first column. It is therefore essential to use the second row and not the first to eliminate this element. We can now read off z since the last equation states $0x + 0y - \frac{13}{3}z = -\frac{13}{3}$, that is $z = 1$. Back substitution of $z = 1$ in the second equation gives $y = -5$ and finally, substitution of z and y into the first equation gives $x = 3$.

Example 8.37 Solve the following equations by Gaussian elimination:

$$x - y + z = 3$$
$$x + 5y - 5z = 2$$
$$2x + y - z = 1$$

Solution Forming the augmented matrix, we find

$$\left(\begin{array}{ccc|c} 1 & -1 & 1 & 3 \\ 1 & 5 & -5 & 2 \\ 2 & 1 & -1 & 1 \end{array}\right)$$

Then, as before, we aim to eliminate all non-zero entries under the step. Starting with those in the first column, we find

$$
\begin{array}{c}
R_1 \\
R_2 \rightarrow R_2 - R_1 \\
R_3 \rightarrow R_3 - 2R_1
\end{array}
\qquad
\left(\begin{array}{ccc|c} 1 & -1 & 1 & 3 \\ 0 & 6 & -6 & -1 \\ 0 & 3 & -3 & -5 \end{array}\right)
$$

Then,

$$
\begin{array}{c}
R_1 \\
R_2 \\
R_3 \rightarrow 2R_3 - R_2
\end{array}
\qquad
\left(\begin{array}{ccc|c} 1 & -1 & 1 & 3 \\ 0 & 6 & -6 & -1 \\ 0 & 0 & 0 & -9 \end{array}\right)
$$

This last line implies that $0x + 0y + 0z = -9$, which is clearly inconsistent. We conclude that there are no solutions.

You will see from Examples 8.36 and 8.37 that not only have all entries under the step been reduced to zero, but also each successive row contains more leading zeros than the previous one. We say the system has been reduced to **echelon** form. More generally the system has been reduced to echelon form if for $i < j$ the number of leading zeros in row j is larger than the number in row i. Consider Example 8.38.

Example 8.38 Solve the following equations by Gaussian elimination:

$$
\begin{aligned}
2x - y + z &= 2 \\
-2x + y + z &= 4 \\
6x - 3y - 2z &= -9
\end{aligned}
$$

Solution Forming the augmented matrix, we have

$$\left(\begin{array}{ccc|c} 2 & -1 & 1 & 2 \\ -2 & 1 & 1 & 4 \\ 6 & -3 & -2 & -9 \end{array}\right)$$

Eliminating the unwanted values in the first column, we find

$$
\begin{array}{c}
R_1 \\
R_2 \rightarrow R_2 + R_1 \\
R_3 \rightarrow R_3 - 3R_1
\end{array}
\qquad
\left(\begin{array}{ccc|c} 2 & -1 & 1 & 2 \\ 0 & 0 & 2 & 6 \\ 0 & 0 & -5 & -15 \end{array}\right)
$$

Entries under the step are now zero. To reduce the matrix to echelon form we must ensure each successive row has more leading zeros than the row before. We continue:

$$
\begin{array}{c}
R_1 \\
R_2 \\
R_3 \rightarrow 2R_3 + 5R_2
\end{array}
\qquad
\left(\begin{array}{ccc|c} 2 & -1 & 1 & 2 \\ 0 & 0 & 2 & 6 \\ 0 & 0 & 0 & 0 \end{array}\right)
$$

which is now in echelon form.

In this form there is a row which starts off with a non-zero x value, that is the first row, there is a row which starts off with a non-zero z value, but no row which starts off with a non-zero y value. Therefore, we choose y to be the free variable, $y = \lambda$ say. From the second row we have $z = 3$ and from the first $2x - y + z = 2$, so that $2x = \lambda - 1$, that is $x = (\lambda - 1)/2$.

Example 8.39 | **Signal analysis and the Vandermonde matrix**

In signal analysis it is often necessary to approximate a signal by a polynomial. For example, to approximate a signal $f(t)$ by a second-degree polynomial we write

$$f(t) \approx a_0 + a_1 t + a_2 t^2$$

where a_0, a_1 and a_2 are coefficients of the polynomial which must be found. These are found by forcing the original signal $f(t)$ and its polynomial approximation to agree at three different values of t, say t_0, t_1 and t_2. This gives rise to the following system of equations:

$$\begin{pmatrix} 1 & t_0 & t_0^2 \\ 1 & t_1 & t_1^2 \\ 1 & t_2 & t_2^2 \end{pmatrix} \begin{pmatrix} a_0 \\ a_1 \\ a_2 \end{pmatrix} = \begin{pmatrix} f(t_0) \\ f(t_1) \\ f(t_2) \end{pmatrix}$$

The coefficient matrix is known as a **Vandermonde matrix**. Suppose we wish to find a second-degree polynomial approximation to the signal $f(t) = \cos\dfrac{\pi t}{2}$ for values of t between -1 and 1. We can do this by making the approximating polynomial and the original signal equal at three points, say $t = -1$, $t = 0$ and $t = 1$. The equations to be solved are then

$$\begin{pmatrix} 1 & -1 & 1 \\ 1 & 0 & 0 \\ 1 & 1 & 1 \end{pmatrix} \begin{pmatrix} a_0 \\ a_1 \\ a_2 \end{pmatrix} = \begin{pmatrix} f(-1) \\ f(0) \\ f(1) \end{pmatrix} = \begin{pmatrix} 0 \\ 1 \\ 0 \end{pmatrix}$$

It is straightforward to solve this system of equations by Gaussian elimination and obtain $a_0 = 1$, $a_1 = 0$ and $a_2 = -1$. Therefore the second-degree polynomial which approximates $f(t) = \cos\dfrac{\pi t}{2}$ is $1 - t^2$.

8.10.1 Finding the inverse matrix using row operations

A similar technique can be used to find the inverse of a square matrix A where this exists. Suppose we are given the matrix A and wish to find its inverse B. Then we know

$$AB = I$$

that is,

$$\begin{pmatrix} a_{11} & a_{12} & a_{13} \\ a_{21} & a_{22} & a_{23} \\ a_{31} & a_{32} & a_{33} \end{pmatrix} \begin{pmatrix} b_{11} & b_{12} & b_{13} \\ b_{21} & b_{22} & b_{23} \\ b_{31} & b_{32} & b_{33} \end{pmatrix} = \begin{pmatrix} 1 & 0 & 0 \\ 0 & 1 & 0 \\ 0 & 0 & 1 \end{pmatrix}$$

We form the augmented matrix

$$\begin{pmatrix} a_{11} & a_{12} & a_{13} & 1 & 0 & 0 \\ a_{21} & a_{22} & a_{23} & 0 & 1 & 0 \\ a_{31} & a_{32} & a_{33} & 0 & 0 & 1 \end{pmatrix}$$

Now carry out row operations on this matrix in such a way that the l.h.s. is reduced to a 3×3 identity matrix. The matrix which then remains on the r.h.s. is the required inverse.

Example 8.40   Find the inverse of

$$A = \begin{pmatrix} -1 & 8 & -2 \\ -6 & 49 & -10 \\ -4 & 34 & -5 \end{pmatrix}$$

by row reduction to the identity.

Solution   We form the augmented matrix

$$\begin{pmatrix} -1 & 8 & -2 & 1 & 0 & 0 \\ -6 & 49 & -10 & 0 & 1 & 0 \\ -4 & 34 & -5 & 0 & 0 & 1 \end{pmatrix}$$

We now carry out row operations on the whole matrix to reduce the l.h.s. to an identity matrix. This means we must eliminate all the elements off the diagonal. Work through the following calculation yourself:

$$\begin{matrix} R_1 \\ R_2 \to R_2 - 6R_1 \\ R_3 \to R_3 - 4R_1 \end{matrix} \begin{pmatrix} -1 & 8 & -2 & 1 & 0 & 0 \\ 0 & 1 & 2 & -6 & 1 & 0 \\ 0 & 2 & 3 & -4 & 0 & 1 \end{pmatrix}$$

This has removed all the off-diagonal entries in column 1. To remove those in column 2:

$$\begin{matrix} R_1 \to R_1 - 8R_2 \\ R_2 \\ R_3 \to R_3 - 2R_2 \end{matrix} \begin{pmatrix} -1 & 0 & -18 & 49 & -8 & 0 \\ 0 & 1 & 2 & -6 & 1 & 0 \\ 0 & 0 & -1 & 8 & -2 & 1 \end{pmatrix}$$

To remove those in column 3:

$$\begin{matrix} R_1 \to R_1 - 18R_3 \\ R_2 \to R_2 + 2R_3 \\ R_3 \end{matrix} \begin{pmatrix} -1 & 0 & 0 & -95 & 28 & -18 \\ 0 & 1 & 0 & 10 & -3 & 2 \\ 0 & 0 & -1 & 8 & -2 & 1 \end{pmatrix}$$

We must now adjust the '-1' entries to obtain the identity matrix:

$$\begin{matrix} R_1 \to -R_1 \\ R_2 \\ R_3 \to -R_3 \end{matrix} \begin{pmatrix} 1 & 0 & 0 & 95 & -28 & 18 \\ 0 & 1 & 0 & 10 & -3 & 2 \\ 0 & 0 & 1 & -8 & 2 & -1 \end{pmatrix}$$

Finally, the required inverse is the matrix remaining on the r.h.s.:

$$\begin{pmatrix} 95 & -28 & 18 \\ 10 & -3 & 2 \\ -8 & 2 & -1 \end{pmatrix}$$

You should check this result by evaluating AA^{-1}.

Exercises 8.10

1 Solve the following equations by Gaussian elimination:

(a) $2x - 3y = 32$
$3x + 7y = -21$

(b) $2x + y - 3z = -5$
$x - y + 2z = 12$
$7x - 2y + 3z = 37$

(c) $x + y - z = 1$
$3x - y + 5z = 3$
$7x + 2y + 3z = 7$

(d) $2x + y - z = -9$
$3x - 2y + 4z = 5$
$-2x - y + 7z = 33$

(e) $4x + 7y + 8z = 2$
$5x + 8y + 13z = 0$
$3x + 5y + 7z = 1$

2 Use Gaussian elimination to solve

$x + y + z = 7$
$x - y + 2z = 9$
$2x + y - z = 1$

3 Find the inverses of the following matrices using the technique of Example 8.40:

(a) $\begin{pmatrix} 4 & 1 \\ 3 & 2 \end{pmatrix}$

(b) $\begin{pmatrix} 4 & 2 & 1 \\ 0 & 3 & 4 \\ -1 & 1 & 3 \end{pmatrix}$

(c) $\begin{pmatrix} 1 & 0 & 3 \\ 2 & 1 & 5 \\ -7 & 2 & 1 \end{pmatrix}$

Solutions

1 (a) $x = 7, y = -6$

(b) $x = 3, y = -5, z = 2$

(c) $x = 1 - \mu, y = 2\mu, z = \mu$

(d) $x = -3, y = 1, z = 4$

(e) Inconsistent

2 $x = 2, y = 1, z = 4$

3 (a) $\dfrac{1}{5}\begin{pmatrix} 2 & -1 \\ -3 & 4 \end{pmatrix}$

(b) $\dfrac{1}{15}\begin{pmatrix} 5 & -5 & 5 \\ -4 & 13 & -16 \\ 3 & -6 & 12 \end{pmatrix}$

(c) $\dfrac{1}{24}\begin{pmatrix} -9 & 6 & -3 \\ -37 & 22 & 1 \\ 11 & -2 & 1 \end{pmatrix}$

8.11 Eigenvalues and eigenvectors

We are now in a position to examine the meaning and calculation of eigenvalues and their corresponding eigenvectors.

8.11.1 Solution to systems of linear homogeneous equations

Recall that an equation is linear when the variables occur only to the first power. For example,

$$2x + 3y = 1 \qquad (1)$$

is a linear equation but

$$2x^2 + 3y = 1 \qquad (2)$$

is a non-linear equation due to the term $2x^2$.

Equations such as (1) and (2) are called inhomogeneous. When the r.h.s. is 0, then the equation is homogeneous. For example,

$$2x + 3y = 0 \qquad \text{and} \qquad 7x - 3y = 0$$

are both homogeneous. This section looks at the solution of systems of linear homogeneous equations.

Consider the simultaneous linear homogeneous equations

$$ax + by = 0$$
$$cx + dy = 0$$

where a, b, c and d are constants. Clearly $x = 0$, $y = 0$ is a solution. It is called the **trivial solution**. Non-trivial solutions are solutions other than $x = 0$, $y = 0$. We now study the system to find conditions on a, b, c and d under which non-trivial solutions exist.

For definiteness we consider two cases with values of a, b, c and d given.

Case 1

$$3x - 5y = 0$$
$$6x - 7y = 0$$

Solving Case 1, for example by Gaussian elimination, leads to $x = 0$, $y = 0$ as the only possible solution. Thus, the only solution is the trivial solution.

Case 2

$$x + y = 0$$
$$2x + 2y = 0$$

This system was solved in Example 8.35 using Gaussian elimination to yield

$$x = -\lambda, \qquad y = \lambda$$

where λ is any number and y is a free variable. Thus there is an infinite number of solutions. Note that in this system the second equation, $2x + 2y = 0$, is a multiple of the first equation, $x + y = 0$. The second equation is twice the first equation.

We now return to the system

$$ax + by = 0$$
$$cx + dy = 0$$

As seen, depending upon the values of a, b, c and d the system has either only the trivial solution or an infinite number of non-trivial solutions. For there to be non-trivial solutions the second equation must be a multiple of the first. When this is the case, then c is a multiple of a and d is the same multiple of b, that is

$$c = \alpha a, \qquad d = \alpha b \qquad \text{for some value of } \alpha$$

In this case, consider the quantity $ad - bc$:

$$ad - bc = a(\alpha b) - b(\alpha a)$$
$$= \alpha ab - \alpha ab$$
$$= 0$$

Hence the condition for non-trivial solutions to exist is that $ad - bc = 0$. Writing the system in matrix form gives

$$\begin{pmatrix} a & b \\ c & d \end{pmatrix} \begin{pmatrix} x \\ y \end{pmatrix} = \begin{pmatrix} 0 \\ 0 \end{pmatrix}$$

or

$$AX = \mathbf{0}$$

where

$$A = \begin{pmatrix} a & b \\ c & d \end{pmatrix}, \qquad X = \begin{pmatrix} x \\ y \end{pmatrix}, \qquad \mathbf{0} = \begin{pmatrix} 0 \\ 0 \end{pmatrix}$$

We note that $ad - bc$ is the determinant of A, so non-trivial solutions exist when the determinant of A is zero; that is, when A is a singular matrix.

In summary

> Consider the system
>
> $$AX = \mathbf{0}$$
>
> If $|A| = 0$, the system has non-trivial solutions.
> If $|A| \neq 0$, the system has only the trivial solution.

Example 8.41 Decide which of the following systems of equations has non-trivial solutions.

(a) $3x + 7y = 0$
     $2x - y = 0$

(b) $2x + y = 0$
     $6x + 3y = 0$

Solution (a) We write the system as

$$\begin{pmatrix} 3 & 7 \\ 2 & -1 \end{pmatrix} \begin{pmatrix} x \\ y \end{pmatrix} = \begin{pmatrix} 0 \\ 0 \end{pmatrix}$$

Let

$$A = \begin{pmatrix} 3 & 7 \\ 2 & -1 \end{pmatrix}$$

Then

$$|A| = 3(-1) - 2(7) = -17$$

Since the determinant of A is non-zero, the system has only the trivial solution.

(b) We write the system as

$$\begin{pmatrix} 2 & 1 \\ 6 & 3 \end{pmatrix} \begin{pmatrix} x \\ y \end{pmatrix} = \begin{pmatrix} 0 \\ 0 \end{pmatrix}$$

Let

$$A = \begin{pmatrix} 2 & 1 \\ 6 & 3 \end{pmatrix}$$

from which $|A| = 2(3) - 1(6) = 0$. Since the determinant of A is 0, the system has non-trivial solutions.

Example 8.42   Determine which of the following systems of equations has non-trivial solutions.

(a) $2x + y - 3z = 0$
     $x - 3y + 2z = 0$
     $5x - 8y + 3z = 0$

(b) $2x + y - 3z = 0$
     $x - 3y + 2z = 0$
     $5x - 7y + 3z = 0$

Solution   (a) We have

$$AX = \mathbf{0}$$

where

$$A = \begin{pmatrix} 2 & 1 & -3 \\ 1 & -3 & 2 \\ 5 & -8 & 3 \end{pmatrix} \qquad X = \begin{pmatrix} x \\ y \\ z \end{pmatrix}$$

Evaluation of $|A|$ shows that $|A| = 0$ and so the system has non-trivial solutions.

(b) Here

$$A = \begin{pmatrix} 2 & 1 & -3 \\ 1 & -3 & 2 \\ 5 & -7 & 3 \end{pmatrix}$$

from which $|A| = -7$. Since $|A| \neq 0$ the system has only the trivial solution.

Exercises 8.11.1

1 Explain what is meant by the trivial solution of a system of linear equations and what is meant by a non-trivial solution.

2 Determine which of the following systems has non-trivial solutions:

(a) $x - 2y = 0$
$3x - 6y = 0$

(b) $3x + y = 0$
$9x + 2y = 0$

(c) $4x - 3y = 0$
$-4x + 3y = 0$

(d) $6x - 2y = 0$
$2x - \frac{2}{3}y = 0$

(e) $y = 2x$
$x = 3y$

3 Determine which of the following systems have non-trivial solutions:

(a) $x + 2y - z = 0$
$3x + y + 2z = 0$
$x + y \quad\quad = 0$

(b) $2x - 3y - 2z = 0$
$3x + y - 3z = 0$
$x - 7y - z = 0$

(c) $x + 2y + 3z = 0$
$4x - 3y - z = 0$
$6x + y + 3z = 0$

(d) $x + \quad 3z = 0$
$x - y \quad\quad = 0$
$y + 2z = 0$

Solutions

2 (a), (c) and (d) have non-trivial solutions.

3 (a) and (b) have non-trivial solutions.

8.11.2 Eigenvalues

We will explain the meaning of the term eigenvalue by means of an example. Consider the system

$$2x + y = \lambda x$$
$$3x + 4y = \lambda y$$

where λ is some unknown constant. Clearly these equations have the trivial solution $x = 0$, $y = 0$. The equations may be written in matrix form as

$$\begin{pmatrix} 2 & 1 \\ 3 & 4 \end{pmatrix} \begin{pmatrix} x \\ y \end{pmatrix} = \lambda \begin{pmatrix} x \\ y \end{pmatrix}$$

or, using the usual notation,

$$AX = \lambda X$$

We now seek values of λ so that the system has non-trivial solutions. Although it is tempting to write $(A - \lambda)X = \mathbf{0}$ this would be incorrect since $A - \lambda$ is not defined: A is a matrix and λ is constant. Hence to progress we need to write the r.h.s. in a slightly different way. To help us do this we use the 2×2 identity matrix, I. Now $\lambda \begin{pmatrix} x \\ y \end{pmatrix}$ may be expressed as

$$\lambda \begin{pmatrix} 1 & 0 \\ 0 & 1 \end{pmatrix} \begin{pmatrix} x \\ y \end{pmatrix}$$

since multiplying $\begin{pmatrix} x \\ y \end{pmatrix}$ by the identity matrix leaves it unaltered. So λX may be written as $\lambda I X$. Hence we have

$$AX = \lambda I X$$

which can be written as

$$AX - \lambda I X = \mathbf{0}$$
$$(A - \lambda I)X = \mathbf{0}$$

Note that the expression $(A - \lambda I)$ is defined since both A and λI are square matrices of the same size.

We have seen in Section 8.11.1 that for $AX = \mathbf{0}$ to have non-trivial solutions requires $|A| = 0$. Hence for

$$(A - \lambda I)X = \mathbf{0}$$

to have non-trivial solutions requires

$$|A - \lambda I| = 0$$

Now

$$A - \lambda I = \begin{pmatrix} 2 & 1 \\ 3 & 4 \end{pmatrix} - \lambda \begin{pmatrix} 1 & 0 \\ 0 & 1 \end{pmatrix}$$

$$= \begin{pmatrix} 2 & 1 \\ 3 & 4 \end{pmatrix} - \begin{pmatrix} \lambda & 0 \\ 0 & \lambda \end{pmatrix}$$

$$= \begin{pmatrix} 2 - \lambda & 1 \\ 3 & 4 - \lambda \end{pmatrix}$$

So the condition $|A - \lambda I| = 0$ gives

$$\begin{vmatrix} 2 - \lambda & 1 \\ 3 & 4 - \lambda \end{vmatrix} = 0$$

It follows that

$$(2 - \lambda)(4 - \lambda) - 3 = 0$$
$$\lambda^2 - 6\lambda + 5 = 0$$
$$(\lambda - 1)(\lambda - 5) = 0$$

so that

$$\lambda = 1 \quad \text{or} \quad 5$$

These are the values of λ which cause the system $AX = \lambda X$ to have non-trivial solutions. They are called **eigenvalues**.

The equation

$$|A - \lambda I| = 0$$

which when written out explicitly is the quadratic equation in λ, is called the **characteristic equation**.

Example 8.43 Find values of λ for which

$$x + 4y = \lambda x$$
$$2x + 3y = \lambda y$$

has non-trivial solutions.

Solution We write the system as

$$AX = \lambda X$$

where

$$A = \begin{pmatrix} 1 & 4 \\ 2 & 3 \end{pmatrix}, \qquad X = \begin{pmatrix} x \\ y \end{pmatrix}$$

To have non-trivial solutions we require

$$|A - \lambda I| = 0$$

Now

$$A - \lambda I = \begin{pmatrix} 1 & 4 \\ 2 & 3 \end{pmatrix} - \lambda \begin{pmatrix} 1 & 0 \\ 0 & 1 \end{pmatrix}$$

$$= \begin{pmatrix} 1 & 4 \\ 2 & 3 \end{pmatrix} - \begin{pmatrix} \lambda & 0 \\ 0 & \lambda \end{pmatrix}$$

$$= \begin{pmatrix} 1 - \lambda & 4 \\ 2 & 3 - \lambda \end{pmatrix}$$

Hence

$$|A - \lambda I| = (1 - \lambda)(3 - \lambda) - 8$$
$$= \lambda^2 - 4\lambda - 5$$

To have non-trivial solutions we require

$$\lambda^2 - 4\lambda - 5 = 0$$
$$(\lambda + 1)(\lambda - 5) = 0$$

which yields

$$\lambda = -1 \qquad \text{or} \qquad 5$$

The given system has non-trivial solutions when $\lambda = -1$ and $\lambda = 5$. These are the eigenvalues.

If A is a 2×2 matrix, the characteristic equation will be a polynomial of degree 2, that is a quadratic equation in λ, leading to two eigenvalues. If A is a 3×3 matrix, the characteristic equation will be a polynomial of degree 3, that is a cubic, leading to three eigenvalues. In general an $n \times n$ matrix gives rise to a characteristic equation of degree n and hence to n eigenvalues.

The characteristic equation of a square matrix A is given by

$$|A - \lambda I| = 0$$

Solutions of this equation are the eigenvalues of A. These are the values of λ for which $AX = \lambda X$ has non-trivial solutions.

Example 8.44 Determine the characteristic equation and eigenvalues, λ, in the system

$$\begin{pmatrix} 3 & 1 \\ -1 & 5 \end{pmatrix} \begin{pmatrix} x \\ y \end{pmatrix} = \lambda \begin{pmatrix} x \\ y \end{pmatrix}$$

Solution In this example the equations have been written in matrix form with $A = \begin{pmatrix} 3 & 1 \\ -1 & 5 \end{pmatrix}$. The characteristic equation is given by

$$|A - \lambda I| = 0$$

$$\left| \begin{pmatrix} 3 & 1 \\ -1 & 5 \end{pmatrix} - \lambda \begin{pmatrix} 1 & 0 \\ 0 & 1 \end{pmatrix} \right| = 0$$

$$\begin{vmatrix} 3 - \lambda & 1 \\ -1 & 5 - \lambda \end{vmatrix} = 0$$

$$(3 - \lambda)(5 - \lambda) + 1 = 0$$

$$\lambda^2 - 8\lambda + 16 = 0$$

The characteristic equation is $\lambda^2 - 8\lambda + 16 = 0$. Solving the characteristic equation gives

$$\lambda^2 - 8\lambda + 16 = 0$$

$$(\lambda - 4)(\lambda - 4) = 0$$

$$\lambda = 4 \quad \text{(twice)}$$

There is one repeated eigenvalue, $\lambda = 4$.

Example 8.45 Find the eigenvalues λ in the system

$$\begin{pmatrix} 4 & 1 \\ 3 & 2 \end{pmatrix} \begin{pmatrix} x \\ y \end{pmatrix} = \lambda \begin{pmatrix} x \\ y \end{pmatrix}$$

Solution We form the characteristic equation, $|A - \lambda I| = 0$. Now

$$A - \lambda I = \begin{pmatrix} 4 - \lambda & 1 \\ 3 & 2 - \lambda \end{pmatrix}$$

Then

$$|A - \lambda I| = (4 - \lambda)(2 - \lambda) - 3 = \lambda^2 - 6\lambda + 5$$

Solving the characteristic equation, $\lambda^2 - 6\lambda + 5 = 0$, gives

$$\lambda = 1 \quad \text{or} \quad 5$$

There are two eigenvalues, $\lambda = 1, \lambda = 5$.

The process of finding the characteristic equation and eigenvalues of a matrix has been illustrated using 2×2 matrices. This same process can be applied to a square matrix of any size.

Example 8.46 Find (a) the characteristic equation (b) the eigenvalues of A where

$$A = \begin{pmatrix} 1 & 2 & 0 \\ -1 & -1 & 1 \\ 3 & 2 & -2 \end{pmatrix}$$

Solution (a) We need to calculate $|A - \lambda I|$. Now

$$A - \lambda I = \begin{pmatrix} 1 - \lambda & 2 & 0 \\ -1 & -1 - \lambda & 1 \\ 3 & 2 & -2 - \lambda \end{pmatrix}$$

and

$$\begin{vmatrix} 1 - \lambda & 2 & 0 \\ -1 & -1 - \lambda & 1 \\ 3 & 2 & -2 - \lambda \end{vmatrix} = (1 - \lambda) \begin{vmatrix} -1 - \lambda & 1 \\ 2 & -2 - \lambda \end{vmatrix} - 2 \begin{vmatrix} -1 & 1 \\ 3 & -2 - \lambda \end{vmatrix}$$

$$= (1 - \lambda)[(-1 - \lambda)(-2 - \lambda) - 2]$$
$$- 2[-1(-2 - \lambda) - 3]$$

Upon simplification this reduces to $-\lambda^3 - 2\lambda^2 + \lambda + 2$. Hence

$$|A - \lambda I| = 0$$

yields

$$-\lambda^3 - 2\lambda^2 + \lambda + 2 = 0$$

which may be written as

$$\lambda^3 + 2\lambda^2 - \lambda - 2 = 0$$

The characteristic equation is $\lambda^3 + 2\lambda^2 - \lambda - 2 = 0$.

(b) The characteristic equation is solved to yield the eigenvalues:

$$\lambda^3 + 2\lambda^2 - \lambda - 2 = 0$$

Factorizing yields

$$(\lambda + 2)(\lambda + 1)(\lambda - 1) = 0$$

from which $\lambda = -2, -1, 1$.

The eigenvalues are $\lambda = -2, -1, 1$.

Exercises 8.11.2

1. Calculate (i) the characteristic equation (ii) the eigenvalues of the system $AX = \lambda X$ where A is given by

(a) $\begin{pmatrix} 5 & 6 \\ 2 & 1 \end{pmatrix}$

(b) $\begin{pmatrix} -3 & 4 \\ -4 & 5 \end{pmatrix}$

(c) $\begin{pmatrix} 7 & -2 \\ 1 & 4 \end{pmatrix}$

(d) $\begin{pmatrix} 1 & 3 \\ 4 & -1 \end{pmatrix}$

2. Calculate (i) the characteristic equation (ii) the eigenvalues of the following 3×3 matrices:

(a) $\begin{pmatrix} 1 & -1 & 2 \\ -3 & -2 & 3 \\ 2 & -1 & 1 \end{pmatrix}$

(b) $\begin{pmatrix} 1 & 0 & -1 \\ 3 & 1 & 4 \\ 0 & 2 & 2 \end{pmatrix}$

(c) $\begin{pmatrix} 2 & 1 & 2 \\ -1 & 1 & -1 \\ 8 & 3 & 0 \end{pmatrix}$

(d) $\begin{pmatrix} -2 & 6 & 2 \\ 0 & 3 & 4 \\ 3 & -3 & 5 \end{pmatrix}$

(e) $\begin{pmatrix} 3 & -2 & 1 \\ 2 & -4 & 3 \\ 16 & -4 & 1 \end{pmatrix}$

Solutions

1. (a) (i) $\lambda^2 - 6\lambda - 7 = 0$
       (ii) $\lambda = -1, 7$
   (b) (i) $\lambda^2 - 2\lambda + 1 = 0$
       (ii) $\lambda = 1$ (twice)
   (c) (i) $\lambda^2 - 11\lambda + 30 = 0$
       (ii) $\lambda = 5, 6$
   (d) (i) $\lambda^2 - 13 = 0$
       (ii) $\lambda = -\sqrt{13}, \sqrt{13}$
2. (a) (i) $-\lambda^3 + 7\lambda + 6 = 0$

       (ii) $\lambda = -2, -1, 3$
   (b) (i) $\lambda^3 - 4\lambda^2 - 3\lambda + 12 = 0$
       (ii) $\lambda = -\sqrt{3}, \sqrt{3}, 4$
   (c) (i) $\lambda^3 - 3\lambda^2 - 10\lambda + 24 = 0$
       (ii) $\lambda = -3, 2, 4$
   (d) (i) $\lambda^3 - 6\lambda^2 + 5\lambda = 0$
       (ii) $\lambda = 0, 1, 5$
   (e) (i) $\lambda^3 - 13\lambda + 12 = 0$
       (ii) $\lambda = -4, 1, 3$

8.11.3 Eigenvectors

We have studied the system

$$AX = \lambda X$$

and determined the values of λ for which non-trivial solutions exist. These values of λ are called eigenvalues of the system, or more simply, eigenvalues of A. For each eigenvalue there is a non-trivial solution of the system. This solution is called an **eigenvector**.

Example 8.47   Find the eigenvectors of

$$AX = \lambda X$$

where

$$A = \begin{pmatrix} 4 & 1 \\ 3 & 2 \end{pmatrix} \text{ and } X = \begin{pmatrix} x \\ y \end{pmatrix}$$

Solution   We seek solutions of $AX = \lambda X$ which may be written as

$$(A - \lambda I)X = \mathbf{0}$$

The eigenvalues were found in Example 8.45 to be $\lambda = 1, 5$.

Firstly we consider $\lambda = 1$. The system equation becomes

$$(A - \lambda I)X = \mathbf{0}$$

$$(A - I)X = \mathbf{0}$$

$$\left[\begin{pmatrix} 4 & 1 \\ 3 & 2 \end{pmatrix} - \begin{pmatrix} 1 & 0 \\ 0 & 1 \end{pmatrix} \right] \begin{pmatrix} x \\ y \end{pmatrix} = \begin{pmatrix} 0 \\ 0 \end{pmatrix}$$

$$\begin{pmatrix} 3 & 1 \\ 3 & 1 \end{pmatrix} \begin{pmatrix} x \\ y \end{pmatrix} = \begin{pmatrix} 0 \\ 0 \end{pmatrix}$$

Written as individual equations we have

$$3x + y = 0$$
$$3x + y = 0$$

Clearly there is only one equation which is repeated. As long as $y = -3x$ the equation is satisfied. Thus there is an infinite number of solutions such as $x = 1$, $y = -3$; $x = -5$, $y = 15$ and so on. Generally we write

$$x = t, \ y = -3t$$

for any number t. Thus the eigenvector corresponding to $\lambda = 1$ is

$$X = \begin{pmatrix} x \\ y \end{pmatrix} = \begin{pmatrix} t \\ -3t \end{pmatrix} = t \begin{pmatrix} 1 \\ -3 \end{pmatrix}$$

Note that the eigenvector has been determined to within an arbitrary scalar, t. Thus there is an infinity of solutions corresponding to $\lambda = 1$.

We now consider $\lambda = 5$ and seek solutions of the system equation.

$$(A - \lambda I)X = 0$$

$$\left[\begin{pmatrix} 4 & 1 \\ 3 & 2 \end{pmatrix} - 5 \begin{pmatrix} 1 & 0 \\ 0 & 1 \end{pmatrix} \right] \begin{pmatrix} x \\ y \end{pmatrix} = \begin{pmatrix} 0 \\ 0 \end{pmatrix}$$

$$\begin{pmatrix} -1 & 1 \\ 3 & -3 \end{pmatrix} \begin{pmatrix} x \\ y \end{pmatrix} = \begin{pmatrix} 0 \\ 0 \end{pmatrix}$$

Written as individual equations we have

$$-x + y = 0$$
$$3x - 3y = 0$$

We note that the second equation is simply a multiple of the first so that in essence there is only one equation. Solving $-x + y = 0$ gives $y = x$ for any x. So we write $x = t$, $y = t$. Hence the eigenvector corresponding to $\lambda = 5$ is $X = t \begin{pmatrix} 1 \\ 1 \end{pmatrix}$. Again the eigenvector has been determined to within an arbitrary scaling constant.

Sometimes the arbitrary scaling constants are not written down; it is understood that they are there. In such a case we say the eigenvectors of the system are

$$X = \begin{pmatrix} 1 \\ -3 \end{pmatrix} \qquad \text{and} \qquad X = \begin{pmatrix} 1 \\ 1 \end{pmatrix}$$

Example 8.48 Determine the eigenvectors of

$$\begin{pmatrix} 3 & 1 \\ -1 & 5 \end{pmatrix} \begin{pmatrix} x \\ y \end{pmatrix} = \lambda \begin{pmatrix} x \\ y \end{pmatrix}$$

Solution In Example 8.44 we found that there is only one eigenvalue, $\lambda = 4$. We seek the solution of $(A - \lambda I)X = 0$. With $\lambda = 4$ we have

$$A - \lambda I = \begin{pmatrix} 3 & 1 \\ -1 & 5 \end{pmatrix} - 4 \begin{pmatrix} 1 & 0 \\ 0 & 1 \end{pmatrix} = \begin{pmatrix} -1 & 1 \\ -1 & 1 \end{pmatrix}$$

Hence $(A - \lambda I)X = 0$ is the same as

$$\begin{pmatrix} -1 & 1 \\ -1 & 1 \end{pmatrix} \begin{pmatrix} x \\ y \end{pmatrix} = \begin{pmatrix} 0 \\ 0 \end{pmatrix}$$

Thus there is only one equation, namely

$$-x + y = 0$$

which has an infinity of solutions: $x = t$, $y = t$. Hence there is one eigenvector:

$$X = t \begin{pmatrix} 1 \\ 1 \end{pmatrix}$$

The concept of eigenvectors is easily extended to matrices of higher order.

Example 8.49   Determine the eigenvectors of

$$\begin{pmatrix} 1 & 2 & 0 \\ -1 & -1 & 1 \\ 3 & 2 & -2 \end{pmatrix} \begin{pmatrix} x \\ y \\ z \end{pmatrix} = \lambda \begin{pmatrix} x \\ y \\ z \end{pmatrix}$$

The eigenvalues were found in Example 8.46.

Solution   From Example 8.46 the eigenvalues are $\lambda = -2, -1, 1$. We consider each eigenvalue in turn.

$\lambda = -2$

$$\begin{pmatrix} 1 & 2 & 0 \\ -1 & -1 & 1 \\ 3 & 2 & -2 \end{pmatrix} \begin{pmatrix} x \\ y \\ z \end{pmatrix} = -2 \begin{pmatrix} x \\ y \\ z \end{pmatrix}$$

$$\left[\begin{pmatrix} 1 & 2 & 0 \\ -1 & -1 & 1 \\ 3 & 2 & -2 \end{pmatrix} + 2 \begin{pmatrix} 1 & 0 & 0 \\ 0 & 1 & 0 \\ 0 & 0 & 1 \end{pmatrix} \right] \begin{pmatrix} x \\ y \\ z \end{pmatrix} = \begin{pmatrix} 0 \\ 0 \\ 0 \end{pmatrix}$$

$$\begin{pmatrix} 3 & 2 & 0 \\ -1 & 1 & 1 \\ 3 & 2 & 0 \end{pmatrix} \begin{pmatrix} x \\ y \\ z \end{pmatrix} = \begin{pmatrix} 0 \\ 0 \\ 0 \end{pmatrix}$$

We note that the first and last rows are identical. So we have

$$3x + 2y \quad = 0$$
$$-x + y + z = 0$$

Solving these equations gives

$$x = t, \quad y = -\tfrac{3}{2}t, \quad z = \tfrac{5}{2}t$$

Hence the corresponding eigenvector is

$$X = t \begin{pmatrix} 1 \\ -\tfrac{3}{2} \\ \tfrac{5}{2} \end{pmatrix}$$

$\lambda = -1$

We have

$$\left[\begin{pmatrix} 1 & 2 & 0 \\ -1 & -1 & 1 \\ 3 & 2 & -2 \end{pmatrix} + \begin{pmatrix} 1 & 0 & 0 \\ 0 & 1 & 0 \\ 0 & 0 & 1 \end{pmatrix} \right] \begin{pmatrix} x \\ y \\ z \end{pmatrix} = \begin{pmatrix} 0 \\ 0 \\ 0 \end{pmatrix}$$

$$\begin{pmatrix} 2 & 2 & 0 \\ -1 & 0 & 1 \\ 3 & 2 & -1 \end{pmatrix} \begin{pmatrix} x \\ y \\ z \end{pmatrix} = \begin{pmatrix} 0 \\ 0 \\ 0 \end{pmatrix}$$

Thus we have

$$2x + 2y \quad\quad = 0$$
$$-x \quad\quad +z = 0$$
$$3x + 2y - z = 0$$

We note that the third equation can be derived from the first two equations, by subtracting the second equation from the first. If you cannot spot this the equations should be solved by Gaussian elimination. In effect we have only two equations:

$$2x + 2y = 0$$
$$-x + z = 0$$

Solving these gives $x = t$, $y = -t$, $z = t$. The eigenvector is

$$X = t \begin{pmatrix} 1 \\ -1 \\ 1 \end{pmatrix}$$

$\lambda = 1$

We have

$$\left[\begin{pmatrix} 1 & 2 & 0 \\ -1 & -1 & 1 \\ 3 & 2 & -2 \end{pmatrix} - \begin{pmatrix} 1 & 0 & 0 \\ 0 & 1 & 0 \\ 0 & 0 & 1 \end{pmatrix} \right] \begin{pmatrix} x \\ y \\ z \end{pmatrix} = \begin{pmatrix} 0 \\ 0 \\ 0 \end{pmatrix}$$

$$\begin{pmatrix} 0 & 2 & 0 \\ -1 & -2 & 1 \\ 3 & 2 & -3 \end{pmatrix} \begin{pmatrix} x \\ y \\ z \end{pmatrix} = \begin{pmatrix} 0 \\ 0 \\ 0 \end{pmatrix}$$

Thus we have

$$2y \quad\quad = 0$$
$$-x - 2y + \quad z = 0$$
$$3x + 2y - 3z = 0$$

From the first equation, $y = 0$; putting $y = 0$ into the other equations yields

$$-x + z = 0$$
$$3x - 3z = 0$$

Here the second equation can be derived from the first by multiplying the first by -3. Solving, we have $x = t$, $z = t$. So the eigenvector is

$$X = t \begin{pmatrix} 1 \\ 0 \\ 1 \end{pmatrix}$$

Exercises 8.11.3

1 Calculate the eigenvectors of the matrices given in Question 1 of Exercises 8.11.2.

2 Calculate the eigenvectors of the matrices given in Question 2 of Exercises 8.11.2.

Solutions

1 (a) $t\begin{pmatrix} 1 \\ -1 \end{pmatrix}, t\begin{pmatrix} 1 \\ \frac{1}{3} \end{pmatrix}$

(b) $t\begin{pmatrix} 1 \\ 1 \end{pmatrix}$

(c) $t\begin{pmatrix} 1 \\ 1 \end{pmatrix}, t\begin{pmatrix} 1 \\ \frac{1}{2} \end{pmatrix}$

(d) $t\begin{pmatrix} 1 \\ -(1+\sqrt{13})/3 \end{pmatrix}, t\begin{pmatrix} 1 \\ (\sqrt{13}-1)/3 \end{pmatrix}$

2 (a) $t\begin{pmatrix} 1 \\ 5 \\ 1 \end{pmatrix}, t\begin{pmatrix} 1 \\ 12 \\ 5 \end{pmatrix}, t\begin{pmatrix} 1 \\ 0 \\ 1 \end{pmatrix}$

(b) $t\begin{pmatrix} 1 \\ -5.0981 \\ 2.7321 \end{pmatrix}, t\begin{pmatrix} 1 \\ 0.0981 \\ -0.7321 \end{pmatrix}, t\begin{pmatrix} 1 \\ -3 \\ -3 \end{pmatrix}$

(c) $t\begin{pmatrix} 1 \\ -\frac{1}{3} \\ -\frac{7}{3} \end{pmatrix}, t\begin{pmatrix} 1 \\ -2 \\ 1 \end{pmatrix}, t\begin{pmatrix} 1 \\ -0.8 \\ 1.4 \end{pmatrix}$

(d) $t\begin{pmatrix} 1 \\ \frac{4}{9} \\ -\frac{1}{3} \end{pmatrix}, t\begin{pmatrix} 1 \\ 0.6 \\ -0.3 \end{pmatrix}, t\begin{pmatrix} 1 \\ 1 \\ 0.5 \end{pmatrix}$

(e) $t\begin{pmatrix} 1 \\ \frac{19}{6} \\ -\frac{2}{3} \end{pmatrix}, t\begin{pmatrix} 1 \\ 4 \\ 6 \end{pmatrix}, t\begin{pmatrix} 1 \\ 2 \\ 4 \end{pmatrix}$

8.12 Analysis of electrical networks

Matrix algebra is very useful for the analysis of certain types of electrical network. For such networks it is possible to produce a mathematical model consisting of simultaneous equations which can be solved using Gaussian elimination. We will consider the case when the network consists of resistors and voltage sources. The technique is similar for other types of network.

In order to develop this approach, it is necessary to develop a systematic method for writing the circuit equations. The method adopted depends on what the unknown variables are. A common problem is that the voltage sources and the resistor values are known and it is desired to know the current values in each part of the network. This can be formulated as a matrix equation. Given

$$V = RI'$$

where

$$V = \text{ voltage vector for the network}$$
$$I' = \text{current vector for the network}$$
$$R = \text{matrix of resistor values}$$

the problem is to calculate I' when V and R are known. I' is used to avoid confusion with the identity matrix.

Any size of electrical network can be analysed using this approach. We will limit the discussion to the case where I' has three components, for simplicity. The extension

Figure 8.2
An electrical network
with mesh currents
shown.

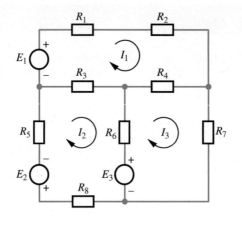

to larger networks is straightforward. Consider the electrical network of Figure 8.2. Mesh currents have been drawn for each of the loops in the circuit. A **mesh** is defined as a loop that cannot contain a smaller closed current path. For convenience, each mesh current is drawn in a clockwise direction even though it may turn out to be in the opposite direction when the calculations have been performed. The net current in each branch of the circuit can be obtained by combining the mesh currents. These are termed the **branch currents**. The concept of a mesh current may appear slightly abstract but it does provide a convenient mechanism for analysing electrical networks. We will examine an approach that avoids the use of mesh currents later in this section.

The next stage is to make use of Kirchhoff's voltage law for each of the meshes in the network. This states that the algebraic sum of the voltages around any closed loop in an electrical network is zero. Therefore the sum of the voltage rises must equal the sum of voltage drops. When applying Kirchhoff's voltage law it is important to use the correct sign for a voltage source depending on whether or not it is 'aiding' a mesh current.

For mesh 1

$$E_1 = I_1 R_1 + I_1 R_2 + (I_1 - I_3)R_4 + (I_1 - I_2)R_3$$
$$E_1 = I_1(R_1 + R_2 + R_4 + R_3) + I_2(-R_3) + I_3(-R_4)$$

For mesh 2

$$-E_2 - E_3 = I_2 R_5 + (I_2 - I_1)R_3 + (I_2 - I_3)R_6 + I_2 R_8$$
$$-E_2 - E_3 = I_1(-R_3) + I_2(R_5 + R_3 + R_6 + R_8) + I_3(-R_6)$$

For mesh 3

$$E_3 = (I_3 - I_2)R_6 + (I_3 - I_1)R_4 + I_3 R_7$$
$$E_3 = I_1(-R_4) + I_2(-R_6) + I_3(R_6 + R_4 + R_7)$$

These equations can be written in matrix form as

$$\begin{pmatrix} E_1 \\ -E_2 - E_3 \\ E_3 \end{pmatrix} = \begin{pmatrix} R_1 + R_2 + R_4 + R_3 & -R_3 & -R_4 \\ -R_3 & R_5 + R_3 + R_6 + R_8 & -R_6 \\ -R_4 & -R_6 & R_6 + R_4 + R_7 \end{pmatrix} \begin{pmatrix} I_1 \\ I_2 \\ I_3 \end{pmatrix}$$

Figure 8.3
The electrical network
of Figure 8.2 with
values for the source
voltages and resistors
added.

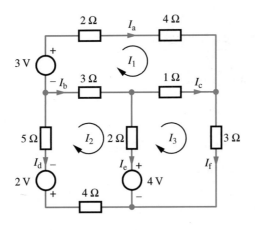

Example 8.50 Consider the electrical network of Figure 8.3. It has the same structure as that of Figure 8.2 but with actual values for the voltage sources and resistors. Branch currents as well as mesh currents have been shown. Calculate the mesh currents and hence the branch currents for the network.

Solution We have already obtained the equations for this network. Substituting actual values for the resistors and voltage sources gives

$$\begin{pmatrix} 3 \\ -2-4 \\ 4 \end{pmatrix} = \begin{pmatrix} 10 & -3 & -1 \\ -3 & 14 & -2 \\ -1 & -2 & 6 \end{pmatrix} \begin{pmatrix} I_1 \\ I_2 \\ I_3 \end{pmatrix}$$

This is now in the form $V = RI'$. We shall solve these equations by Gaussian elimination. Forming the augmented matrix, we have

$$\begin{pmatrix} 10 & -3 & -1 & 3 \\ -3 & 14 & -2 & -6 \\ -1 & -2 & 6 & 4 \end{pmatrix}$$

Then

$$\begin{matrix} R_1 \\ R_2 \to 10R_2 + 3R_1 \\ R_3 \to 10R_3 + R_1 \end{matrix} \qquad \begin{pmatrix} 10 & -3 & -1 & 3 \\ 0 & 131 & -23 & -51 \\ 0 & -23 & 59 & 43 \end{pmatrix}$$

and

$$\begin{matrix} R_1 \\ R_2 \\ R_3 \to 131R_3 + 23R_2 \end{matrix} \qquad \begin{pmatrix} 10 & -3 & -1 & 3 \\ 0 & 131 & -23 & -51 \\ 0 & 0 & 7200 & 4460 \end{pmatrix}$$

Hence,

$$I_3 = \frac{4460}{7200} = 0.619 \text{ A}$$

Similarly,

$$I_2 = \frac{-51 + 23(0.619)}{131} = -0.281 \text{ A}$$

Finally,

$$I_1 = \frac{3 + 0.619 + 3(-0.281)}{10} = 0.278 \text{ A}$$

The branch currents are then

$$I_a = I_1 = 278 \text{ mA}$$
$$I_b = I_2 - I_1 = -281 - 278 = -559 \text{ mA}$$
$$I_c = I_3 - I_1 = 619 - 278 = 341 \text{ mA}$$
$$I_d = -I_2 = 281 \text{ mA}$$
$$I_e = I_2 - I_3 = -281 - 619 = -900 \text{ mA}$$
$$I_f = I_3 = 619 \text{ mA}$$

An alternative approach to analysing an electrical network is to use the **node voltage method**. For our purposes the nodes of an electrical network can be thought of as the 'islands' of equal potential that lie between electrical components and sources. The procedure is as follows:

(1) Pick a reference node. In order to simplify the equations this is usually chosen to be the node which is common to the largest number of voltage sources and/or the largest number of branches.

(2) Assign a node voltage variable to all of the other nodes. If two nodes are separated solely by a voltage source then only one of the nodes need be assigned a voltage variable. The node voltages are all measured with respect to the reference node.

(3) At each node, write Kirchhoff's current law in terms of the node voltages. Note that once the node voltages have been calculated it is easy to obtain the branch currents.

We will again examine the network of Figure 8.2, but this time use the node voltage method. The network is shown in Figure 8.4 with node voltages assigned and branch currents labelled. The reference node is indicated by using the earth symbol. Writing Kirchhoff's current law for each node, we obtain:

node a

$$I_a = I_a$$
$$\frac{V_b + E_1 - V_a}{R_1} = \frac{V_a - V_d}{R_2}$$
$$V_b R_2 + E_1 R_2 - V_a R_2 = V_a R_1 - V_d R_1$$
$$V_a(R_1 + R_2) - V_b R_2 - V_d R_1 = E_1 R_2$$

node b

$$I_a + I_b + I_d = 0$$
$$\frac{V_b + E_1 - V_a}{R_1} + \frac{V_b - V_c}{R_3} + \frac{V_b + E_2 - V_e}{R_5} = 0$$

Figure 8.4
The network of
Figure 8.2 with node
voltages labelled.

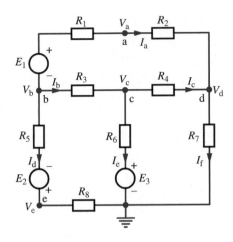

Rearrangement yields

$$V_b R_3 R_5 + E_1 R_3 R_5 - V_a R_3 R_5 + V_b R_1 R_5 - V_c R_1 R_5 + V_b R_1 R_3$$
$$+ E_2 R_1 R_3 - V_e R_1 R_3 = 0$$

that is,

$$V_a R_3 R_5 - V_b(R_1 R_3 + R_1 R_5 + R_3 R_5) + V_c R_1 R_5 + V_e R_1 R_3$$
$$= E_1 R_3 R_5 + E_2 R_1 R_3$$

node c

$$I_b = I_c + I_e$$
$$\frac{V_b - V_c}{R_3} = \frac{V_c - V_d}{R_4} + \frac{V_c - E_3}{R_6}$$

so that

$$V_b R_4 R_6 - V_c R_4 R_6 = V_c R_3 R_6 - V_d R_3 R_6 + V_c R_3 R_4 - E_3 R_3 R_4$$

that is,

$$V_b R_4 R_6 - V_c(R_4 R_6 + R_3 R_6 + R_3 R_4) + V_d R_3 R_6 = -E_3 R_3 R_4$$

node d

$$I_a + I_c = I_f$$
$$\frac{V_a - V_d}{R_2} + \frac{V_c - V_d}{R_4} = \frac{V_d}{R_7}$$
$$V_a R_4 R_7 - V_d R_4 R_7 + V_c R_2 R_7 - V_d R_2 R_7 = V_d R_2 R_4$$
$$V_a R_4 R_7 + V_c R_2 R_7 - V_d(R_4 R_7 + R_2 R_7 + R_2 R_4) = 0$$

node e

$$I_d = I_d$$
$$\frac{V_b + E_2 - V_e}{R_5} = \frac{V_e}{R_8}$$
$$V_b R_8 - V_e(R_5 + R_8) = -E_2 R_8$$

These equations can be written in the matrix form $AV = B$, where A is the matrix

$$\begin{pmatrix} R_1 + R_2 & -R_2 & 0 & -R_1 & 0 \\ R_3 R_5 & -R_1 R_3 - R_1 R_5 - R_3 R_5 & R_1 R_5 & 0 & R_1 R_3 \\ 0 & R_4 R_6 & -R_4 R_6 - R_3 R_6 - R_3 R_4 & R_3 R_6 & 0 \\ R_4 R_7 & 0 & R_2 R_7 & -R_4 R_7 - R_2 R_7 - R_2 R_4 & 0 \\ 0 & R_8 & 0 & 0 & -R_5 - R_8 \end{pmatrix}$$

and

$$V = \begin{pmatrix} V_a \\ V_b \\ V_c \\ V_d \\ V_e \end{pmatrix} \quad \text{and} \quad B = \begin{pmatrix} E_1 R_2 \\ E_1 R_3 R_5 + E_2 R_1 R_3 \\ -E_3 R_3 R_4 \\ 0 \\ -E_2 R_8 \end{pmatrix}$$

The equations would generally be solved by Gaussian elimination to obtain the node voltages and hence the branch currents.

Using the component values from Example 8.50, these equations become

$$\begin{pmatrix} 6 & -4 & 0 & -2 & 0 \\ 15 & -31 & 10 & 0 & 6 \\ 0 & 2 & -11 & 6 & 0 \\ 3 & 0 & 12 & -19 & 0 \\ 0 & 4 & 0 & 0 & -9 \end{pmatrix} \begin{pmatrix} V_a \\ V_b \\ V_c \\ V_d \\ V_e \end{pmatrix} = \begin{pmatrix} 12 \\ 57 \\ -12 \\ 0 \\ -8 \end{pmatrix}$$

Use of a computer package avoids the tedious arithmetic associated with Gaussian elimination and yields

$$V_a = 2.969 \qquad V_b = 0.5250 \qquad V_c = 2.200 \qquad V_d = 1.858 \qquad V_e = 1.122$$

It is then straightforward to calculate the branch currents:

$$I_a = \frac{V_a - V_d}{R_2} = 278 \text{ mA} \qquad I_b = \frac{V_b - V_c}{R_3} = -558 \text{ mA}$$

$$I_c = \frac{V_c - V_d}{R_4} = 342 \text{ mA} \qquad I_d = \frac{V_e}{R_8} = 281 \text{ mA}$$

$$I_e = \frac{V_c - E_3}{R_6} = -900 \text{ mA} \qquad I_f = \frac{V_d}{R_7} = 619 \text{ mA}$$

Compare these answers with those of Example 8.50.

It is possible to analyse electrical networks containing more complex elements such as capacitors, inductors, active devices, etc., using the same approach. The equations are more complicated but the technique is the same. Often it is necessary to use iterative techniques in view of the size and complexity of the problem. These are examined in the following section.

8.13 Iterative techniques for the solution of simultaneous equations

The techniques met so far for the solution of simultaneous equations are known as **direct methods**, which generally lead to the solution after a finite number of stages in the calculation process have been carried out. An alternative collection of techniques is available and these are known as **iterative methods**. They generate a sequence of approximate solutions which may converge to the required solution, and are particularly advantageous when large systems of equations are to be solved by computer. We shall study two such techniques here: Jacobi's method and Gauss–Seidel iteration.

Example 8.51 Solve the equations

$$2x + y = 4$$
$$x - 3y = -5$$

using Jacobi's iterative method.

Solution We first rewrite the equations as

$$2x = -y + 4$$
$$-3y = -x - 5$$

and then as

$$x = -\tfrac{1}{2}y + 2$$
$$y = \tfrac{1}{3}x + \tfrac{5}{3}$$

(8.10)

Jacobi's method involves 'guessing' a solution and substituting the guess in the r.h.s. of the equations in (8.10). Suppose we guess $x = 0$, $y = 0$. Substitution then gives

$$x = 2$$
$$y = \tfrac{5}{3}$$

We now use these values as estimates of the solution and resubstitute into the r.h.s. of Equation (8.10). This time we find

$$x = -\tfrac{1}{2}\left(\tfrac{5}{3}\right) + 2 = 1.1667 \qquad \text{(to four decimal places)}$$

$$y = \tfrac{1}{3}(2) + \tfrac{5}{3} = 2.3333 \qquad \text{(to four decimal places)}$$

The whole process is repeated in the hope that each successive application or **iteration** will give an answer close to the required solution, that is successive **iterates** will converge. In order to keep track of the calculations, we label the initial guess $x^{(0)}$, $y^{(0)}$, the result of the first iteration $x^{(1)}$, $y^{(1)}$ and so on. Generally, we find

$$x^{(n+1)} = -\tfrac{1}{2}y^{(n)} + 2$$

$$y^{(n+1)} = \tfrac{1}{3}x^{(n)} + \tfrac{5}{3}$$

The results of successively applying these formulae are shown in Table 8.1. The sequence of values of $x^{(n)}$ seems to converge to 1 while that of $y^{(n)}$ seems to converge to 2.

Table 8.1
Iterates produced by
Jacobi's method.

Iteration no.(n)	$x^{(n)}$	$y^{(n)}$
0	0	0
1	2.0000	1.6667
2	1.1667	2.3333
3	0.8333	2.0556
4	0.9722	1.9444
5	1.0278	1.9907
6	1.0047	2.0093
7	0.9954	2.0016
8	0.9992	1.9985
9	1.0008	1.9997
10	1.0002	2.0003

Clearly this sort of approach is simple to program and iterative techniques such as Jacobi's method are best implemented on a computer. When writing the program a test should be incorporated so that after each iteration a check for convergence is made by comparing successive iterates. In many cases, even when convergence does occur, it is slow and so other techniques are used which converge more rapidly. The Gauss–Seidel method is attractive for this reason. It uses the most recent approximation to x when calculating y leading to improved rates of convergence as the following example shows.

Example 8.52   Use the Gauss–Seidel method to solve the equations of Example 8.51.

Solution   As before we write the equations in the form

$$x = -\tfrac{1}{2}y + 2$$

$$y = \tfrac{1}{3}x + \tfrac{5}{3}$$

With $x^{(0)} = 0$, $y^{(0)} = 0$ as our initial guess, we find

$$x^{(1)} = -\tfrac{1}{2}(0) + 2 = 2$$

To find $y^{(1)}$ we use the most recent approximation to x available, that is $x^{(1)}$:

$$y^{(1)} = \tfrac{1}{3}(2) + \tfrac{5}{3} = 2.3333$$

Generally, we find

$$x^{(n+1)} = -\tfrac{1}{2}y^{(n)} + 2$$

$$y^{(n+1)} = \tfrac{1}{3}x^{(n+1)} + \tfrac{5}{3}$$

and the results of successively applying these formulae are shown in Table 8.2. As before, we see that the sequence $x^{(n)}$ seems to converge to 1 and $y^{(n)}$ seems to converge to 2, although more rapidly than before.

Table 8.2
Iterates produced by
the Gauss–Seidel
method.

Iteration no.(n)	$x^{(n)}$	$y^{(n)}$
0	0	0
1	2.0000	2.3333
2	0.8334	1.9445
3	1.0278	2.0093
4	0.9954	1.9985
5	1.0008	2.0003
6	0.9999	2.0000

Both of these techniques generalize to larger systems of equations.

Example 8.53   Perform three iterations of Jacobi's method and three iterations of the Gauss–Seidel method to find an approximate solution of

$$-8x + y + z = 1$$
$$x - 5y + z = 16$$
$$x + y - 4z = 7$$

with an initial guess of $x = y = z = 0$.

Solution   We rewrite the system to make x, y and z the subject of the first, second and third equation, respectively:

$$x = \tfrac{1}{8}y + \tfrac{1}{8}z - \tfrac{1}{8}$$
$$y = \tfrac{1}{5}x + \tfrac{1}{5}z - \tfrac{16}{5} \tag{8.11}$$
$$z = \tfrac{1}{4}x + \tfrac{1}{4}y - \tfrac{7}{4}$$

To apply Jacobi's method we substitute the initial guess $x^{(0)} = y^{(0)} = z^{(0)} = 0$ into the r.h.s. of Equation (8.11) to obtain $x^{(1)}$, $y^{(1)}$ and $z^{(1)}$, and then repeat the process. In general,

$$x^{(n+1)} = \tfrac{1}{8}y^{(n)} + \tfrac{1}{8}z^{(n)} - \tfrac{1}{8}$$
$$y^{(n+1)} = \tfrac{1}{5}x^{(n)} + \tfrac{1}{5}z^{(n)} - \tfrac{16}{5}$$
$$z^{(n+1)} = \tfrac{1}{4}x^{(n)} + \tfrac{1}{4}y^{(n)} - \tfrac{7}{4}$$

We find

$$x^{(1)} = -\tfrac{1}{8} = -0.1250$$
$$y^{(1)} = -\tfrac{16}{5} = -3.2000$$
$$z^{(1)} = -\tfrac{7}{4} = -1.7500$$

Then,

$$x^{(2)} = \tfrac{1}{8}(-3.2000) + \tfrac{1}{8}(-1.7500) - \tfrac{1}{8} = -0.7438$$

$$y^{(2)} = \tfrac{1}{5}(-0.1250) + \tfrac{1}{5}(-1.7500) - \tfrac{16}{5} = -3.5750$$

$$z^{(2)} = \tfrac{1}{4}(-0.1250) + \tfrac{1}{4}(-3.2000) - \tfrac{7}{4} = -2.5813$$

Finally,

$$x^{(3)} = \tfrac{1}{8}(-3.5750) + \tfrac{1}{8}(-2.5813) - \tfrac{1}{8} = -0.8945$$

$$y^{(3)} = \tfrac{1}{5}(-0.7438) + \tfrac{1}{5}(-2.5813) - \tfrac{16}{5} = -3.8650$$

$$z^{(3)} = \tfrac{1}{4}(-0.7438) + \tfrac{1}{4}(-3.5750) - \tfrac{7}{4} = -2.8297$$

To apply the Gauss–Seidel iteration to Equation (8.11), the most recent approximation is used at each stage leading to

$$x^{(n+1)} = \tfrac{1}{8}y^{(n)} + \tfrac{1}{8}z^{(n)} - \tfrac{1}{8}$$

$$y^{(n+1)} = \tfrac{1}{5}x^{(n+1)} + \tfrac{1}{5}z^{(n)} - \tfrac{16}{5}$$

$$z^{(n+1)} = \tfrac{1}{4}x^{(n+1)} + \tfrac{1}{4}y^{(n+1)} - \tfrac{7}{4}$$

Starting from $x^{(0)} = y^{(0)} = z^{(0)} = 0$, we find

$$x^{(1)} = -\tfrac{1}{8} = -0.1250$$

$$y^{(1)} = \tfrac{1}{5}(-0.1250) + \tfrac{1}{5}(0) - \tfrac{16}{5} = -3.2250$$

$$z^{(1)} = \tfrac{1}{4}(-0.1250) + \tfrac{1}{4}(-3.2250) - \tfrac{7}{4} = -2.5875$$

Then,

$$x^{(2)} = \tfrac{1}{8}(-3.2250) + \tfrac{1}{8}(-2.5875) - \tfrac{1}{8} = -0.8516$$

$$y^{(2)} = \tfrac{1}{5}(-0.8516) + \tfrac{1}{5}(-2.5875) - \tfrac{16}{5} = -3.8878$$

$$z^{(2)} = \tfrac{1}{4}(-0.8516) + \tfrac{1}{4}(-3.8878) - \tfrac{7}{4} = -2.9348$$

Finally,

$$x^{(3)} = \tfrac{1}{8}(-3.8878) + \tfrac{1}{8}(-2.9348) - \tfrac{1}{8} = -0.9778$$

$$y^{(3)} = \tfrac{1}{5}(-0.9778) + \tfrac{1}{5}(-2.9348) - \tfrac{16}{5} = -3.9825$$

$$z^{(3)} = \tfrac{1}{4}(-0.9778) + \tfrac{1}{4}(-3.9825) - \tfrac{7}{4} = -2.9901$$

For completeness, further iterations are shown in Table 8.3.

As expected the Gauss–Seidel method converges more rapidly than Jacobi's. This is generally the case because it uses the most recently calculated values at each stage.

Table 8.3

Comparison of the Jacobi and Gauss–Seidel methods.

Iteration no.(n)	Jacobi's method $x^{(n)}$	$y^{(n)}$	$z^{(n)}$	Gauss–Seidel $x^{(n)}$	$y^{(n)}$	$z^{(n)}$
0	0.0000	0.0000	0.0000	0.0000	0.0000	0.0000
1	−0.1250	−3.2000	−1.7500	−0.1250	−3.2250	−2.5875
2	−0.7438	−3.5750	−2.5813	−0.8516	−3.8878	−2.9348
3	−0.8945	−3.8650	−2.8297	−0.9778	−3.9825	−2.9901
4	−0.9618	−3.9448	−2.9399	−0.9966	−3.9973	−2.9985
5	−0.9856	−3.9803	−2.9767	−0.9995	−3.9996	−2.9998
6	−0.9946	−3.9924	−2.9915	−0.9999	−3.9999	−3.0000
7	−0.9980	−3.9972	−2.9968			
8	−0.9992	−3.9990	−2.9988			
9	−0.9997	−3.9996	−2.9996			

Unfortunately, as with all iterative methods, convergence is not guaranteed. However, it can be shown that if the matrix of coefficients is **diagonally dominant**, that is each diagonal element is larger in modulus than the sum of the moduli of the other elements in its row, then the Gauss–Seidel method will converge.

Example 8.54   Use Jacobi's method and the Gauss–Seidel method to obtain approximate solutions for the node voltages of the electrical network examined in Example 8.50.

Solution   The node voltage equations are

$$6V_a - 4V_b - 2V_d = 12 \qquad\qquad 3V_a + 12V_c - 19V_d = 0$$
$$15V_a - 31V_b + 10V_c + 6V_e = 57 \qquad\qquad 4V_b - 9V_e = -8$$
$$2V_b - 11V_c + 6V_d = -12$$

These can be rearranged to give

$$V_a = \frac{2V_b + V_d + 6}{3} \qquad\qquad V_d = \frac{3V_a + 12V_c}{19}$$

$$V_b = \frac{15V_a + 10V_c + 6V_e - 57}{31} \qquad\qquad V_e = \frac{4V_b + 8}{9}$$

$$V_c = \frac{2V_b + 6V_d + 12}{11}$$

The results of applying Jacobi's method with an initial guess of

$$V_a^{(0)} = V_b^{(0)} = V_c^{(0)} = V_d^{(0)} = V_e^{(0)} = 0$$

are shown in Table 8.4. Convergence was achieved to within 0.001 after 44 iterations. The results of applying the Gauss–Seidel method are shown in Table 8.5. Convergence was achieved to within 0.001 after 21 iterations. Clearly the Gauss–Seidel method converges more rapidly than Jacobi's method.

Table 8.4
Node voltages derived from Jacobi's method.

Iteration no.(n)	$V_a^{(n)}$	$V_b^{(n)}$	$V_c^{(n)}$	$V_d^{(n)}$	$V_e^{(n)}$
0	0.0000	0.0000	0.0000	0.0000	0.0000
1	2.0000	−1.8387	1.0909	0.0000	0.8889
⋮					
20	2.8710	0.4802	2.1379	1.8265	1.0738
⋮					
44	2.9679	0.5243	2.1990	1.8578	1.1215

Table 8.5
Node voltages derived from the Gauss–Seidel method.

Iteration no.(n)	$V_a^{(n)}$	$V_b^{(n)}$	$V_c^{(n)}$	$V_d^{(n)}$	$V_e^{(n)}$
0	0.0000	0.0000	0.0000	0.0000	0.0000
1	2.0000	−0.8710	0.9326	0.9048	0.5018
⋮					
20	2.9665	0.5226	2.1985	1.8569	1.1212
21	2.9674	0.5233	2.1989	1.8573	1.1215

Exercises 8.13

1 Perform three iterations of the methods of Jacobi and Gauss–Seidel to obtain approximate solutions of the following. In each case, use an initial guess of
$$x^{(0)} = y^{(0)} = z^{(0)} = 0.$$

(a) $4x + y + z = -1$
$x + 6y + 2z = 0$
$x + 2y + 4z = 1$

(b) $5x + y - z = 4$
$x - 4y + z = -4$
$2x + 2y - 4z = -6$

(c) $4x + y + z = 17$
$x + 3y - z = 9$
$2x - y + 5z = 1$

Solutions

1 (a) Jacobi
$x_1 = -0.2500,\ y_1 = 0,\ z_1 = 0.2500$
$x_2 = -0.3125,\ y_2 = -0.0417,$
$z_2 = 0.3125$
$x_3 = -0.3177,\ y_3 = -0.0521,$
$z_3 = 0.3490$

Gauss–Seidel
$x_1 = -0.2500,\ y_1 = 0.0417,\ z_1 = 0.2917$
$x_2 = -0.3333,\ y_2 = -0.0417,$
$z_2 = 0.3542$

$x_3 = -0.3281,\ y_3 = -0.0634,$
$z_3 = 0.3637$

(b) Jacobi
$x_1 = 0.8000,\ y_1 = 1,\ z_1 = 1.5000$
$x_2 = 0.9000,\ y_2 = 1.5750,\ z_2 = 2.4000$
$x_3 = 0.9650,\ y_3 = 1.8250,\ z_3 = 2.7375$

Gauss–Seidel
$x_1 = 0.8000,\ y_1 = 1.2000,\ z_1 = 2.5000$
$x_2 = 1.0600,\ y_2 = 1.8900,\ z_2 = 2.9750$
$x_3 = 1.0170,\ y_3 = 1.9980,\ z_3 = 3.0075$

(c) Jacobi

$x_1 = 4.2500, y_1 = 3, z_1 = 0.2000$

$x_2 = 3.4500, y_2 = 1.6500, z_2 = -0.9000$

$x_3 = 4.0625, y_3 = 1.5500, z_3 = -0.8500$

Gauss–Seidel

$x_1 = 4.2500, y_1 = 1.5833, z_1 = -1.1833$

$x_2 = 4.1500, y_2 = 1.2222, z_2 = -1.2156$

$x_3 = 4.2484, y_3 = 1.1787, z_3 = -1.2636$

8.14 Computer solutions of matrix problems

A number of commercial software packages are available that can be used to solve engineering problems involving matrices. Often these packages have sophisticated facilities to enable the results to be plotted in a variety of graphical formats. These packages have transformed the design process for engineers. Gone are the days when engineers had to spend a long time designing and programming an algorithm in order to solve a numerical problem. Now it is possible to use one of these packages and specify a complex engineering problem relatively easily. This frees up time for an engineer to concentrate on the design of the engineering product itself.

One of the most popular of these packages is MATLAB. This is a general-purpose package that can be used to solve a variety of engineering problems. Consider again Example 8.32. The equations are of the form

$$AX = B$$

where

$$A = \begin{pmatrix} 3 & 2 & -1 \\ 2 & -1 & 2 \\ 1 & -3 & -4 \end{pmatrix} \qquad B = \begin{pmatrix} 4 \\ 10 \\ 5 \end{pmatrix} \qquad X = \begin{pmatrix} x \\ y \\ z \end{pmatrix}$$

In order to solve these equations it is first necessary to present the values of the matrices to the package. The code for this is

```
A= [3, 2, −1; 2, −1, 2; 1, −3, −4]
B= [4; 10; 5]
```

We note that commas are used to separate entries on the same row and semicolons are used to separate different rows.

The value of X can be obtained by the method of matrix inversion. The code for this is

```
X = inv(A) * B
```

Alternatively, X can be obtained by Gaussian elimination. The code for this is

```
X = A\B
```

Gaussian elimination is the usual method of solving systems of linear equations in MATLAB because it is computationally efficient. If we run this three-line program using

MATLAB then we obtain

$$A = [3, 2, -1; 2, -1, 2; 1, -3, -4]$$
$$B = [4; 10; 5]$$
$$X = A \backslash B$$

$$X = 3.0000$$
$$-2.0000$$
$$1.0000$$

and so $x = 3.0000$, $y = -2.0000$, $z = 1.0000$.

We see that MATLAB is a powerful tool for carrying out matrix calculations. Part of its power derives from the extremely high-level nature of its commands. A command such as inv(A) would require typically 50 lines if written in a normal high-level language such as C or FORTRAN.

Example 8.55   Solution of an electrical network using MATLAB

Consider again the electrical network of Example 8.50. Write the MATLAB code to solve this network.

Solution   The equations are of the form $V = RI'$ where V is the voltage vector of the network, R is the matrix of resistor values and I' is the current vector of the network. We know V and R and we wish to obtain I'. Using the values of Example 8.50 we can write

$$V = [3; -6; 4]$$
$$R = [10, -3, -1; -3, 14, -2; -1, -2, 6]$$
$$\text{IPRIME} = \text{inv(R)} * V$$

Running this program gives

$$\text{IPRIME} = 0.2778$$
$$-0.2806$$
$$0.6194$$

Review exercises 8

1   Evaluate the following products:

(a) $(-4 \ \ 1) \begin{pmatrix} 2 \\ 7 \end{pmatrix}$

(b) $(-4 \ \ 1) \begin{pmatrix} 3 \\ 6 \end{pmatrix}$

(c) $(-4 \ \ 1) \begin{pmatrix} 2 & 3 \\ 7 & 6 \end{pmatrix}$

(d) $\begin{pmatrix} 2 & -3 \\ 4 & 5 \end{pmatrix} \begin{pmatrix} -1 \\ 1 \end{pmatrix}$

(e) $(2 \ -1 \ \ 0) \begin{pmatrix} 1 & 3 & 1 \\ 2 & 4 & 0 \\ 1 & 0 & 7 \end{pmatrix}$

(f) $5 \begin{pmatrix} 2 & 1 \\ 3 & 6 \end{pmatrix}$

(g) $\dfrac{1}{2} \begin{pmatrix} 7 & 3 & 2 \\ 1 & 0 & 1 \end{pmatrix}$

2   Simplify $\begin{vmatrix} \cosh\theta & \sinh\theta \\ \sinh\theta & \cosh\theta \end{vmatrix}$.

3   Given that $A = \begin{pmatrix} 0 & 2 & 3 \\ 2 & 0 & 0 \\ 1 & -1 & 0 \end{pmatrix}$ find A^{-1} and A^2.

Show that $A^2 + 6A^{-1} - 7I = 0$, where I denotes the 3×3 identity matrix.

4   If $A = \begin{pmatrix} 2 & -1 & 4 \\ 1 & 0 & 0 \\ 1 & -2 & 0 \end{pmatrix}$ find

(a) $|A|$

(b) $\text{adj}(A)$

(c) A^{-1}

5 Find the inverse of the matrix

$$\begin{pmatrix} 1 & -2 & 0 \\ 3 & 1 & 5 \\ -1 & 2 & 3 \end{pmatrix}$$

Hence solve the equations

$$x - 2y = 3$$
$$3x + y + 5z = 12$$
$$-x + 2y + 3z = 3$$

6 Use Gaussian elimination to solve

$$x + 2y - 3z + 2w = 2$$
$$2x + 5y - 8z + 6w = 5$$
$$3x + 4y - 5z + 2w = 4$$

7 Use Jacobi's method to obtain a solution of $AX = B$ to three decimal places where

$$A = \begin{pmatrix} 10 & 1 & 0 \\ 1 & 10 & 1 \\ 0 & 1 & 10 \end{pmatrix} \quad \text{and} \quad B = \begin{pmatrix} 1 \\ 2 \\ 1 \end{pmatrix}$$

8 Use a matrix method to solve

$$2x + y - z = 3$$
$$x - y + 2z = 1$$
$$3x + 4y + 3z = 2$$

9 Consider the Vandermonde matrix

$$V = \begin{pmatrix} 1 & a & a^2 \\ 1 & b & b^2 \\ 1 & c & c^2 \end{pmatrix}.$$

(a) Find $\det V$ and show that it can be written as $(a - c)(a - b)(c - b)$.

(b) Show that if a, b and c are all different, then the Vandermonde matrix is non-singular.

10 (a) The signal $f(t) = \sin \dfrac{\pi t}{2}$ is to be approximated by a third-degree polynomial for values of t between -1 and 2. By forcing the original signal and its approximating polynomial to agree at $t = -1, t = 0, t = 1$ and $t = 2$, find this approximation. [*Hint*: see Example 8.39.]

(b) Use a graphics calculator or graph plotting package to compare the graphs of $f(t)$ and its approximating polynomial.

11 Suppose $A = \begin{pmatrix} 1 & -2 \\ 1 & 4 \end{pmatrix}$.

(a) Find $A\mathbf{v}$ when $\mathbf{v} = \begin{pmatrix} -2 \\ 2 \end{pmatrix}$.

(b) Find $3\mathbf{v}$ when $\mathbf{v} = \begin{pmatrix} -2 \\ 2 \end{pmatrix}$. Deduce that $A\mathbf{v} = 3\mathbf{v}$.

(c) Find $A\mathbf{v}$ when $\mathbf{v} = \begin{pmatrix} -\mu \\ \mu \end{pmatrix}$ for any constant μ. Deduce that $A\mathbf{v} = 3\mathbf{v}$.

12 Use the Gauss–Seidel method to find an approximate solution of

(a) $5x + 3y = -34$
$\quad 2x - 7y = 93$

(b) $3x + y + z = 6$
$\quad 2x + 5y - z = 5$
$\quad x - 3y + 8z = 14$

13 Determine which of the following systems have non-trivial solutions.

(a) $2x - y = 0$
$\quad 3x - 1.5y = 0$

(b) $6x + 5y = 0$
$\quad 5x + 6y = 0$

(c) $-x - 4y = 0$
$\quad 2x + 8y = 0$

(d) $7x - 3y = 0$
$\quad 1.4x - 0.6y = 0$

(e) $-4x + 5y = 0$
$\quad 3x - 4y = 0$

14 Determine which of the following systems have non-trivial solutions.

(a) $3x - 2y + 2z = 0$
$\quad x - y + z = 0$
$\quad 2x + 2y - z = 0$

(b) $x + 3y - z = 0$
$\quad 4x - y + 2z = 0$
$\quad 6x + 5y = 0$

(c) $x + 2y - z = 0$
$\quad x - 3z = 0$
$\quad 5x + 6y - 9z = 0$

15 The matrix A is defined by

$$A = \begin{pmatrix} 3 & 2 \\ -3 & -4 \end{pmatrix}$$

(a) Determine the characteristic equation of A.

(b) Determine the eigenvalues of A.

(c) Determine the eigenvectors of A.

(d) Form a new matrix M whose columns are the two eigenvectors of A. M is called a **modal matrix**.

(e) Show that $M^{-1}AM$ is a diagonal matrix, D, with the eigenvalues of A on its leading diagonal. D is called the **spectral matrix** corresponding to the modal matrix M.

16 (a) Show that the matrix

$$A = \begin{pmatrix} 5 & 2 \\ -2 & 1 \end{pmatrix}$$

has only one eigenvalue and determine it.

(b) Calculate the eigenvector of A.

17 The matrix H is given by

$$H = \begin{pmatrix} 4 & -1 & 1 \\ -2 & 4 & 0 \\ -4 & 3 & 1 \end{pmatrix}$$

(a) Find the eigenvalues of H.

(b) Determine the eigenvectors of H.

(c) Form a new matrix M whose columns are the three eigenvectors of H. M is called a **modal matrix**.

(d) Show that $M^{-1}HM$ is a diagonal matrix, D, with the eigenvalues of H on its leading diagonal. D is called the **spectral matrix** corresponding to the modal matrix M.

Solutions

1 (a) -1 (b) -6

(c) $(-1 \quad -6)$ (d) $\begin{pmatrix} -5 \\ 1 \end{pmatrix}$

(e) $(0 \quad 2 \quad 2)$ (f) $\begin{pmatrix} 10 & 5 \\ 15 & 30 \end{pmatrix}$

(g) $\begin{pmatrix} \frac{7}{2} & \frac{3}{2} & 1 \\ \frac{1}{2} & 0 & \frac{1}{2} \end{pmatrix}$

2 1

3 $A^{-1} = \dfrac{1}{6} \begin{pmatrix} 0 & 3 & 0 \\ 0 & 3 & -6 \\ 2 & -2 & 4 \end{pmatrix}$

$A^2 = \begin{pmatrix} 7 & -3 & 0 \\ 0 & 4 & 6 \\ -2 & 2 & 3 \end{pmatrix}$

4 (a) -8 (b) $\begin{pmatrix} 0 & -8 & 0 \\ 0 & -4 & 4 \\ -2 & 3 & 1 \end{pmatrix}$

(c) $\dfrac{1}{8} \begin{pmatrix} 0 & 8 & 0 \\ 0 & 4 & -4 \\ 2 & -3 & -1 \end{pmatrix}$

5 $\dfrac{1}{21} \begin{pmatrix} -7 & 6 & -10 \\ -14 & 3 & -5 \\ 7 & 0 & 7 \end{pmatrix}$

$x = 1, y = -1, z = 2$

6 $x = 2\mu - \lambda, y = 1 + 2\lambda - 2\mu, z = \lambda, w = \mu$

7 $x = 0.082, y = 0.184, z = 0.082$

8 $x = 1.462, y = -0.308, z = -0.385$

10 (a) $f(t) = \frac{4}{3}t - \frac{1}{3}t^3$

11 (a) $\begin{pmatrix} -6 \\ 6 \end{pmatrix}$ (b) $\begin{pmatrix} -6 \\ 6 \end{pmatrix}$ (c) $\begin{pmatrix} -3\mu \\ 3\mu \end{pmatrix}$

12 (a) $x = 1, y = -13$

(b) $x = 1, y = 1, z = 2$

13 (a), (c) and (d) have non-trivial solutions.

14 (b) and (c) have non-trivial solutions.

15 (a) $\lambda^2 + \lambda - 6 = 0$

(b) $\lambda = -3, 2$

(c) $\begin{pmatrix} 1 \\ -3 \end{pmatrix}, \begin{pmatrix} 1 \\ -0.5 \end{pmatrix}$

16 (a) $\lambda = 3$ (b) $\begin{pmatrix} 1 \\ -1 \end{pmatrix}$

17 (a) $\lambda = 2, 3, 4$ (b) $\begin{pmatrix} 1 \\ 1 \\ -1 \end{pmatrix}, \begin{pmatrix} 1 \\ 2 \\ 1 \end{pmatrix}, \begin{pmatrix} 0 \\ 1 \\ 1 \end{pmatrix}$

9 Complex numbers

Chapter 9	Contents	
9.1	Introduction	302
9.2	Complex numbers	302
9.3	Operations with complex numbers	306
9.4	Graphical representation of complex numbers	310
9.5	Polar form of a complex number	311
9.6	Vectors and complex numbers	315
9.7	The exponential form of a complex number	316
9.8	Phasors	318
9.9	De Moivre's theorem	322
9.10	Loci and regions of the complex plane	328
	Review exercises	332

9.1 Introduction

Complex numbers often seem strange when first encountered but it is worth persevering with them because they provide a powerful mathematical tool for solving several engineering problems. One of the main applications is to the analysis of alternating current (a.c.) circuits. Engineers are very interested in these because the mains supply is itself a.c., and electricity generation and transportation are dominated by a.c. voltages and currents.

A great deal of signal analysis and processing uses mathematical models based on complex numbers because they allow the manipulation of sinusoidal quantities to be undertaken more easily. Furthermore, the design of filters to be used in communications equipment relies heavily on their use.

One area of particular relevance is control engineering – so much so that control engineers often prefer to think of a control system in terms of a 'complex plane' representation rather than a 'time domain' representation. We will develop these concepts in this and subsequent chapters.

9.2 Complex numbers

We have already examined quadratic equations such as

$$x^2 - x - 6 = 0 \tag{9.1}$$

and have met techniques for finding the roots of such equations. The formula for obtaining the roots of a quadratic equation $ax^2 + bx + c = 0$ is

$$x = \frac{-b \pm \sqrt{b^2 - 4ac}}{2a} \tag{9.2}$$

Applying this formula to Equation (9.1), we find

$$x = \frac{+1 \pm \sqrt{(-1)^2 - 4(1)(-6)}}{2}$$

$$= \frac{1 \pm \sqrt{25}}{2}$$

$$= \frac{1 \pm 5}{2}$$

so that $x = 3$ and $x = -2$ are the two roots. However, if we try to apply the formula to the equation

$$2x^2 + 2x + 5 = 0$$

we find

$$x = \frac{-2 \pm \sqrt{-36}}{4}$$

A problem now arises in that we need to find the square root of a negative number. We know from experience that squaring both positive and negative numbers yields a positive result; thus,

$$6^2 = 36 \qquad \text{and} \qquad (-6)^2 = 36$$

so that there is no real number whose square is -36. In the general case, if $ax^2+bx+c = 0$, we see by examining the square root in Equation (9.2) that this problem will always arise whenever $b^2 - 4ac < 0$. Nevertheless, it turns out to be very useful to invent a technique for dealing with such situations, leading to the theory of complex numbers.

To make progress we introduce a number, denoted j, with the property that

$$j^2 = -1$$

We have already seen that using the real number system we cannot obtain a negative number by squaring a real number so the number j is not real – we say it is **imaginary**. This imaginary number has a very useful role to play in engineering mathematics. Using it we can now formally write down an expression for the square root of any negative number. Thus,

$$\sqrt{-36} = \sqrt{36 \times (-1)}$$
$$= \sqrt{36 \times j^2}$$
$$= 6j$$

Returning to the solution of the quadratic equation $2x^2 + 2x + 5 = 0$, we find

$$x = \frac{-2 \pm \sqrt{-36}}{4}$$
$$= \frac{-2 \pm 6j}{4}$$
$$= \frac{-1 \pm 3j}{2}$$

We have found two roots, namely $x = -\frac{1}{2} + \frac{3}{2}j$ and $x = -\frac{1}{2} - \frac{3}{2}j$. These numbers are called **complex numbers** and we see that they are made up of two parts – a **real part** and an **imaginary part**. For the first complex number the real part is $-\frac{1}{2}$ and the imaginary part is $\frac{3}{2}$. For the second complex number the real part is $-\frac{1}{2}$ and the imaginary part is $-\frac{3}{2}$. In a more general case we usually use the letter z to denote a complex number with real part a and imaginary part b, so $z = a + bj$. We write $a = \text{Re}(z)$ and $b = \text{Im}(z)$, and denote the set of all complex numbers by $\mathbb{C}$. Note that $a, b \in \mathbb{R}$ whereas $z \in \mathbb{C}$.

$z = a + bj$, z is a member of the set of complex numbers, that is $z \in \mathbb{C}$
$a = \text{Re}(z)$ $b = \text{Im}(z)$

Complex numbers which have a zero imaginary part are purely real and hence all real numbers are also complex numbers, that is $\mathbb{R} \subset \mathbb{C}$.

Example 9.1   Solve the quadratic equation $2s^2 - 3s + 7 = 0$.

Solution   Using the formula for solving a quadratic equation we find

$$s = \frac{-(-3) \pm \sqrt{(-3)^2 - 4(2)(7)}}{2(2)}$$

$$= \frac{3 \pm \sqrt{-47}}{4}$$

$$= \frac{3 \pm \sqrt{47}j}{4}$$

$$= 0.75 \pm 1.71j$$

Using the fact that $j^2 = -1$ we can develop other quantities.

Example 9.2   Simplify the expression j^3.

Solution   We have

$$j^3 = j^2 \times j$$

$$= (-1) \times j$$

$$= -j$$

9.2.1 The complex conjugate

If $z = a + bj$, we define its **complex conjugate** to be the number $\bar{z} = a - bj$; that is, we change the sign of the imaginary part.

Example 9.3   Write down the complex conjugates of

(a) $-7 + j$ (b) $6 - 5j$ (c) 6   (d) j

Solution   To find the complex conjugates of the given numbers we change the sign of the imaginary parts. A purely real number has an imaginary part 0. We find
(a) $-7 - j$ (b) $6 + 5j$ (c) 6, there is no imaginary part to alter   (d) $-j$

We recall that the solution of the quadratic equation $2x^2 + 2x + 5 = 0$ yielded the two complex numbers $-\frac{1}{2} + \frac{3}{2}j$ and $-\frac{1}{2} - \frac{3}{2}j$, and note that these form a complex conjugate pair. This illustrates a more general result:

When the polynomial equation $P(x) = 0$ has real coefficients, any complex roots will always occur in **complex conjugate pairs**.

Consider the following example.

Example 9.4 Show that the equation $x^3 - 7x^2 + 19x - 13 = 0$ has a root at $x = 1$ and find the other roots.

Solution If we let $P(x) = x^3 - 7x^2 + 19x - 13$, then $P(1) = 1 - 7 + 19 - 13 = 0$ so that $x = 1$ is a root. This means that $x - 1$ must be a factor of $P(x)$ and so we can express $P(x)$ in the form

$$P(x) = x^3 - 7x^2 + 19x - 13 = (x - 1)(\alpha x^2 + \beta x + \gamma)$$
$$= \alpha x^3 + (\beta - \alpha)x^2 + (\gamma - \beta)x - \gamma$$

where α, β and γ are coefficients to be determined. Comparing the coefficients of x^3 we find $\alpha = 1$. Comparing the constant coefficients we find $\gamma = 13$. Finally, comparing coefficients of x we find $\beta = -6$, and hence

$$P(x) = x^3 - 7x^2 + 19x - 13 = (x - 1)(x^2 - 6x + 13)$$

The other two roots of $P(x) = 0$ are found by solving the quadratic equation $x^2 - 6x + 13 = 0$, that is

$$x = \frac{6 \pm \sqrt{36 - 52}}{2} = \frac{6 \pm \sqrt{-16}}{2} = 3 \pm 2j$$

and again we note that the complex roots occur as a complex conjugate pair. This illustrates the general result given in Section 1.3 that an nth-degree polynomial has n roots.

Exercises 9.2

1 Solve the following equations:

(a) $x^2 + 1 = 0$

(b) $x^2 + 4 = 0$

(c) $3x^2 + 7 = 0$

(d) $x^2 + x + 1 = 0$

(e) $\dfrac{x^2}{2} - x + 2 = 0$

(f) $-x^2 - 3x - 4 = 0$

(g) $2x^2 + 3x + 3 = 0$

(h) $x^2 + 3x + 4 = 0$

2 Solve the cubic equation

$$3x^3 - 11x^2 + 16x - 12 = 0,$$

given that one of the roots is $x = 2$.

3 Write down the complex conjugates of the following complex numbers.

(a) $-11 - 8j$ (b) $5 + 3j$

(c) $\dfrac{1}{2}j$ (d) -17

(e) $\cos \omega t + j \sin \omega t$ (f) $\cos \omega t - j \sin \omega t$

(g) $-0.333j + 1$

4 Recall from Chapter 2 that the poles of a rational function $R(x) = P(x)/Q(x)$ are those values of x for which $Q(x) = 0$. Find any poles of

(a) $\dfrac{x}{x - 3}$

(b) $\dfrac{3x}{x^2 + 1}$

(c) $\dfrac{3}{x^2 + x + 1}$

5 Solve the equation $s^2 + 2s + 5 = 0$.

6 Express as a complex number
   (a) j^4 (b) j^5 (c) j^6

7 State $\text{Re}(z)$ and $\text{Im}(z)$ where

   (a) $z = 7 + 11j$

   (b) $z = -6 + j$

   (c) $z = 0$

   (d) $z = \dfrac{1+j}{2}$

   (e) $z = j$

   (f) $z = j^2$

Solutions

1 (a) $\pm j$ (b) $\pm 2j$
   (c) $\pm\sqrt{7/3}j$ (d) $-1/2 \pm (\sqrt{3}/2)j$
   (e) $1 \pm \sqrt{3}j$ (f) $-3/2 \pm (\sqrt{7}/2)j$
   (g) $-3/4 \pm (\sqrt{15}/4)j$ (h) $-3/2 \pm (\sqrt{7}/2)j$

2 $2, 5/6 \pm (\sqrt{47}/6)j$

3 (a) $-11 + 8j$ (b) $5 - 3j$
   (c) $-\frac{1}{2}j$ (d) -17
   (e) $\cos \omega t - j\sin \omega t$ (f) $\cos \omega t + j\sin \omega t$
   (g) $0.333j + 1$

4 (a) $x = 3$
   (b) $x = \pm j$
   (c) $x = -1/2 \pm (\sqrt{3}/2)j$

5 $s = -1 \pm 2j$

6 (a) 1 (b) j (c) -1

7 (a) $7, 11$ (b) $-6, 1$
   (c) $0, 0$ (d) $\frac{1}{2}, \frac{1}{2}$
   (e) $0, 1$ (f) $-1, 0$

9.3 Operations with complex numbers

Two complex numbers are equal if and only if their real parts are equal and their imaginary parts are equal.

Example 9.5 Find x and y so that $x + 6j$ and $3 - yj$ represent the same complex number.

Solution If both quantities represent the same complex number we have

$$x + 6j = 3 - yj$$

Since the real parts must be equal we can equate them, that is

$$x = 3$$

Similarly, we find, by equating imaginary parts

$$6 = -y$$

so that $y = -6$.

The operations of addition, subtraction, multiplication and division can all be performed on complex numbers.

9.3.1 Addition and subtraction

To add two complex numbers we simply add the real parts and add the imaginary parts; to subtract a complex number from another we subtract the corresponding real parts and subtract the corresponding imaginary parts as shown in Example 9.6.

Example 9.6 If $z_1 = 3 - 4j$ and $z_2 = 4 + 2j$ find $z_1 + z_2$ and $z_1 - z_2$.

Solution

$$
\begin{aligned}
z_1 + z_2 &= (3 - 4j) + (4 + 2j) \\
&= (3 + 4) + (-4 + 2)j \\
&= 7 - 2j \\
z_1 - z_2 &= (3 - 4j) - (4 + 2j) \\
&= (3 - 4) + (-4 - 2)j \\
&= -1 - 6j
\end{aligned}
$$

9.3.2 Multiplication

We can multiply a complex number by a real number. Both the real and imaginary parts of the complex number are multiplied by the real number. Thus $3(4 - 6j) = 12 - 18j$.
To multiply two complex numbers we use the fact that $j^2 = -1$.

Example 9.7 If $z_1 = 2 - 2j$ and $z_2 = 3 + 4j$, find $z_1 z_2$.

Solution

$$z_1 z_2 = (2 - 2j)(3 + 4j)$$

Removing brackets we find

$$
\begin{aligned}
z_1 z_2 &= 6 - 6j + 8j - 8j^2 \\
&= 6 - 6j + 8j + 8 \qquad \text{using } j^2 = -1 \\
&= 14 + 2j
\end{aligned}
$$

Example 9.8 If $z = 3 - 2j$ find $z\bar{z}$.

Solution If $z = 3 - 2j$ then its conjugate is $\bar{z} = 3 + 2j$. Therefore,

$$
\begin{aligned}
z\bar{z} &= (3 - 2j)(3 + 2j) \\
&= 9 - 6j + 6j - 4j^2 \\
&= 9 - 4j^2 \\
&= 13
\end{aligned}
$$

We see that the answer is a real number.

Whenever we multiply a complex number by its conjugate the answer is a real number. Thus if $z = a + bj$

$$z\bar{z} = (a + bj)(a - bj)$$
$$= a^2 + baj - abj - b^2j^2$$
$$= a^2 + b^2$$

If $z = a + bj$ then $z\bar{z} = a^2 + b^2$

9.3.3 Division

To divide two complex numbers it is necessary to make use of the complex conjugate. We multiply both the numerator and denominator by the conjugate of the denominator and then simplify the result.

Example 9.9 If $z_1 = 2 + 9j$ and $z_2 = 5 - 2j$ find $\dfrac{z_1}{z_2}$.

Solution We seek $\dfrac{2 + 9j}{5 - 2j}$. The complex conjugate of the denominator is $5 + 2j$, so we multiply both numerator and denominator by this quantity. The effect of this is to leave the value of $\dfrac{z_1}{z_2}$ unaltered since we have only multiplied by 1. Therefore,

$$\frac{z_1}{z_2} = \frac{2 + 9j}{5 - 2j} = \frac{(2 + 9j)}{(5 - 2j)}\frac{(5 + 2j)}{(5 + 2j)} = \frac{10 + 45j + 4j + 18j^2}{25 + 4} = \frac{-8 + 49j}{29}$$

$$= -\frac{8}{29} + \frac{49}{29}j$$

The multiplication of two conjugates in the denominator allows a useful simplification. We see that the effect of multiplying by the conjugate of the denominator is to make the denominator of the solution purely real.

If $z_1 = x_1 + jy_1$ and $z_2 = x_2 + jy_2$ then the quotient $\dfrac{z_1}{z_2}$ is found by multiplying both numerator and denominator by the conjugate of the denominator, that is

$$\frac{z_1}{z_2} = \frac{x_1 + jy_1}{x_2 + jy_2}$$

$$= \frac{x_1 + jy_1}{x_2 + jy_2} \times \frac{x_2 - jy_2}{x_2 - jy_2}$$

$$= \frac{x_1x_2 + y_1y_2 + j(x_2y_1 - x_1y_2)}{x_2^2 + y_2^2}$$

Exercises 9.3

1 If $z_1 = 3 + 2j$ and $z_2 = 4 - 8j$ find
(a) $z_1 + z_2$ (b) $z_1 - z_2$ (c) $z_2 - z_1$

2 Express the following in the form $a + bj$:

(a) $\dfrac{1}{1+j}$

(b) $\dfrac{-2}{j}$

(c) $\dfrac{1}{j} + \dfrac{1}{2-j}$

(d) $\dfrac{j}{1+j}$

(e) $\dfrac{3}{3+2j} + \dfrac{1}{5-j}$

3 Express the following in the form $a + bj$:

(a) $\dfrac{2}{1-j}$

(b) $\dfrac{-2+3j}{j}$

(c) $3j(4 - 2j)$

(d) $(7 - 2j)(5 + 6j)$

(e) $\dfrac{5+3j}{2+2j}$

4 Find a quadratic equation whose roots are $1 - 3j$ and $1 + 3j$.

5 If $(x + jy)^2 = 3 + 4j$, find x and y, where $x, y \in \mathbb{R}$.

6 Find the real and imaginary parts of

(a) $\dfrac{2}{4+j} - \dfrac{3}{2-j}$

(b) $j^4 - j^5$

(c) $\dfrac{1}{j} + j$

(d) $\dfrac{1}{j^3 - 3j}$

Solutions

1 (a) $7 - 6j$
(b) $-1 + 10j$
(c) $1 - 10j$

2 (a) $\frac{1}{2} - \frac{1}{2}j$
(b) $2j$
(c) $\frac{2}{5} - \frac{4}{5}j$
(d) $\frac{1}{2} + \frac{1}{2}j$
(e) $\dfrac{23 - 11j}{26}$

3 (a) $1 + j$
(b) $3 + 2j$

(c) $6 + 12j$
(d) $47 + 32j$
(e) $2 - \frac{1}{2}j$

4 $x^2 - 2x + 10 = 0$

5 $x = 2, y = 1; x = -2, y = -1$

6 (a) $-\frac{62}{85}, -\frac{61}{85}$
(b) $1, -1$
(c) $0, 0$
(d) $0, \frac{1}{4}$

Computer and calculator exercises 9.3

Computer algebra packages allow the user to input and manipulate complex numbers. Investigate how the complex number $a + bj$ is input to the package to which you have access.

1 Use a package to simplify the following complex numbers:

(a) $(1 + j)^5$

(b) $\dfrac{3j}{(1 - 2j)^7}$

(c) $\dfrac{4}{(3 + j)^3} - \dfrac{7}{(2 - 3j)^2}$

2 Solve the polynomial equations

   (a) $x^3 + 7x^2 + 9x + 63 = 0$
   (b) $x^4 + 15x^2 - 16 = 0$

3 Use a package to find the real and imaginary parts of $\dfrac{15 + j}{7 - 5j}$.

4 A common requirement in control theory is to find the poles of a rational function. Use a package to find the poles of the function

$$G(s) = \frac{0.5}{s^3 + 2s^2 + 0.2s + 0.0556}.$$

9.4 Graphical representation of complex numbers

Given a complex number $z = a + bj$ we can obtain a useful graphical interpretation of it by plotting the real part on the horizontal axis and the imaginary part on the vertical axis and obtain a unique point in the x–y plane (Figure 9.1). We call the x axis the **real axis** and the y axis the **imaginary axis**, and the whole picture an **Argand diagram**. In this context, the x–y plane is often referred to as the **complex plane**.

Example 9.10 Plot the complex numbers $z_1 = 7 + 2j$, $z_2 = -3 + 5j$, $z_3 = -1 - 2j$ and $z_4 = -4j$ on an Argand diagram.

Solution The Argand diagram is shown in Figure 9.2.

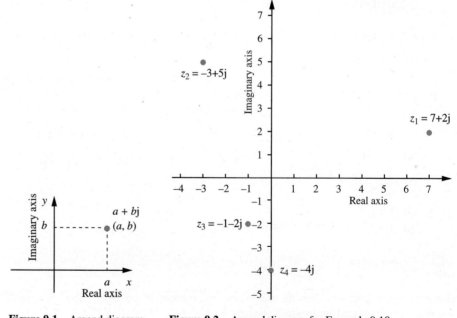

Figure 9.1 Argand diagram.   **Figure 9.2** Argand diagram for Example 9.10.

Exercises 9.4

1. Plot the following complex numbers on an Argand diagram:
   (a) $z_1 = -3 - 3j$ (b) $z_2 = 7 + 2j$
   (c) $z_3 = 3$ (d) $z_4 = -0.5j$
   (e) $z_5 = -2$

2. (a) Plot the complex number $z = 1 + j$ on an Argand diagram.

(b) Simplify the complex number $j(1 + j)$ and plot the result on your Argand diagram. Observe that the effect of multiplying the complex number by j is to rotate the complex number through an angle of $\pi/2$ radians anticlockwise about the origin.

Solutions

1. See Figure S.12.

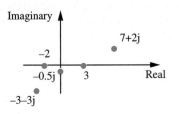

Figure S.12

2. (a) See Figure S.13.   (b) $j(1 + j) = -1 + j$

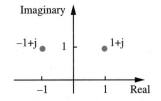

Figure S.13

9.5 Polar form of a complex number

It is often useful to exchange **Cartesian coordinates** (a, b) for **polar coordinates** r and θ as depicted in Figure 9.3.

From Figure 9.3 we note that

$$\cos \theta = \frac{a}{r} \qquad \sin \theta = \frac{b}{r}$$

and so,

$$a = r \cos \theta \qquad b = r \sin \theta$$

Furthermore,

$$\tan \theta = \frac{b}{a}$$

Using Pythagoras's theorem we obtain $r = \sqrt{a^2 + b^2}$. By finding r and θ we can express the complex number $z = a + bj$ in **polar form** as

$$z = r \cos \theta + jr \sin \theta = r(\cos \theta + j \sin \theta)$$

which we often abbreviate to $z = r \angle \theta$. Clearly, r is the 'distance' of the point (a, b) from the origin and is called the **modulus** of the complex number z. The modulus is always a non-negative number and is denoted $|z|$. The angle is conventionally measured

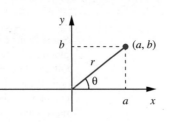

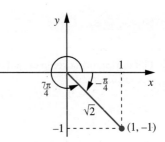

Figure 9.3 Polar and Cartesian forms of a complex number.

Figure 9.4 Argand diagram depicting $z = 1 - j$ in Example 9.11.

from the positive x axis. Angles measured in an anticlockwise sense are regarded as positive while those measured in a clockwise sense are regarded as negative. The angle θ is called the **argument** of z, denoted $\arg(z)$. Since adding or subtracting multiples of 2π from θ will result in the 'arm' in Figure 9.3 being in the same position, the argument can have many values. Usually we shall choose θ to satisfy $-\pi < \theta \leqslant \pi$.

Cartesian form: $z = a + bj$

Polar form: $z = r(\cos\theta + j\sin\theta) = r\angle\theta$

$|z| = r = \sqrt{a^2 + b^2}$

$a = r\cos\theta \qquad b = r\sin\theta \qquad \tan\theta = \dfrac{b}{a}$

Note that

$$r\angle(-\theta) = r(\cos(-\theta) + j\sin(-\theta))$$
$$= r(\cos\theta - j\sin\theta)$$
$$= \bar{z}$$

If $z = a + bj$ then $\bar{z} = a - bj$ and $\bar{z} = r\angle(-\theta)$.

Example 9.11

Depict the complex number $z = 1 - j$ on an Argand diagram and convert it into polar form.

Solution

The real part of z is 1 and the imaginary part is -1. We therefore plot a point in the x–y plane with $x = 1$ and $y = -1$ as shown in Figure 9.4.

From Figure 9.4 we see that $r = \sqrt{1^2 + (-1)^2} = \sqrt{2}$ and $\theta = -45°$ or $-\pi/4$ radians. Therefore $z = 1 - j = \sqrt{2}\angle(-\pi/4)$.

To express a complex number in polar form it is essential to draw an Argand diagram and not simply quote formulae, as the following example will show.

Figure 9.5
Argand diagram
depicting $z = -1 - j$
in Example 9.12.

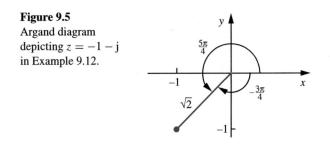

Example 9.12   Express $z = -1 - j$ in polar form.

Solution   If we use the formula $|z| = r = \sqrt{a^2 + b^2}$, we find that $r = \sqrt{2}$. Using $\tan\theta = b/a$, we find that $\tan\theta = -1/-1 = 1$ so that you may be tempted to take $\theta = \pi/4$. Figure 9.5 shows the Argand diagram and it is clear that $\theta = -3\pi/4$. Therefore, $z = -1 - j = \sqrt{2}\angle -3\pi/4$, and we see the importance of drawing an Argand diagram.

9.5.1 Multiplication and division in polar form

The polar form may seem more complicated than the Cartesian form but it is often more useful. For example, suppose we want to multiply the complex numbers

$$z_1 = r_1(\cos\theta_1 + j\sin\theta_1) \qquad \text{and} \qquad z_2 = r_2(\cos\theta_2 + j\sin\theta_2)$$

We find

$$z_1 z_2 = r_1(\cos\theta_1 + j\sin\theta_1)r_2(\cos\theta_2 + j\sin\theta_2)$$
$$= r_1 r_2\{(\cos\theta_1\cos\theta_2 - \sin\theta_1\sin\theta_2) + j(\sin\theta_1\cos\theta_2 + \sin\theta_2\cos\theta_1)\}$$

which can be written as

$$r_1 r_2\{\cos(\theta_1 + \theta_2) + j\sin(\theta_1 + \theta_2)\}$$

using the trigonometric identities of Section 3.5. This is a new complex number which, if we compare with the general form $r(\cos\theta + j\sin\theta)$, we see has a modulus of $r_1 r_2$ and an argument of $\theta_1 + \theta_2$. To summarize: to multiply two complex numbers we multiply their moduli and add their arguments, that is

$$z_1 z_2 = r_1 r_2 \angle(\theta_1 + \theta_2)$$

Example 9.13   If $z_1 = 3\angle\pi/3$ and $z_2 = 4\angle\pi/6$ find $z_1 z_2$.

Solution   Multiplying the moduli we find $r_1 r_2 = 12$, and adding the arguments we find $\theta_1 + \theta_2 = \pi/2$. Therefore $z_1 z_2 = 12\angle\pi/2$.

A similar development shows that to divide two complex numbers we divide their moduli and subtract their arguments, that is

$$\frac{z_1}{z_2} = \frac{r_1}{r_2} \angle(\theta_1 - \theta_2)$$

Example 9.14   If $z_1 = 3\angle\pi/3$ and $z_2 = 4\angle\pi/6$ find z_1/z_2.

Solution   Dividing the respective moduli, we find $r_1/r_2 = 3/4$ and subtracting the arguments, $\pi/3 - \pi/6 = \pi/6$. Hence $z_1/z_2 = 0.75\angle\pi/6$.

Exercises 9.5

1 Mark on an Argand diagram points representing $z_1 = 3 - 2j$, $z_2 = -j$, $z_3 = j^2$, $z_4 = -2 - 4j$ and $z_5 = 3$. Find the modulus and argument of each complex number.

2 Express the following complex numbers in polar form:

(a) $3 - j$

(b) 2

(c) $-j$

(d) $-5 + 12j$

3 Find the modulus and argument of
(a) $z_1 = -\sqrt{3} + j$ and (b) $z_2 = 4 + 4j$. Hence express $z_1 z_2$ and z_1/z_2 in polar form.

4 Express $\sqrt{2}\angle\pi/4$, $2\angle\pi/6$ and $2\angle-\pi/6$ in Cartesian form $a + bj$.

5 Prove the result $\dfrac{z_1}{z_2} = \dfrac{r_1}{r_2}\angle\theta_1 - \theta_2$.

6 Express $z = \dfrac{1}{j\omega C}$, where ω and $\dot{C}$ are real constants, in the form $a + bj$. Plot z on an Argand diagram.

7 If $z_1 = 4(\cos 40° + j\sin 40°)$ and $z_2 = 3(\cos 70° + j\sin 70°)$, express $z_1 z_2$ and z_1/z_2 in polar form.

8 Simplify

$$\frac{(\sqrt{2}\angle(5\pi/4))^2 (2\angle(-\pi/3))^2}{2\angle(-\pi/6)}$$

Solutions

1 $|z_1| = \sqrt{13}$, $\arg(z_1) = -0.5880$
$|z_2| = 1$, $\arg(z_2) = -\pi/2$
$|z_3| = 1$, $\arg(z_3) = \pi$
$|z_4| = \sqrt{20}$, $\arg(z_4) = -2.0344$
$|z_5| = 3$, $\arg(z_5) = 0$

2 (a) $\sqrt{10}\angle - 0.3218$

(b) $2\angle 0$

(c) $1\angle - \pi/2$

(d) $13\angle 1.9656$

3 (a) $2, 5\pi/6$

(b) $4\sqrt{2}, \pi/4$

$z_1 z_2 = 8\sqrt{2}\angle 13\pi/12$

$z_1/z_2 = \dfrac{\sqrt{2}}{4}\angle 7\pi/12$

4 $1 + j, \sqrt{3} + j, \sqrt{3} - j$

6 $-\dfrac{j}{\omega C}$

7 $z_1 z_2 = 12(\cos 110° + j\sin 110°)$

$z_1/z_2 = \frac{4}{3}(\cos 30° - j\sin 30°)$

8 4

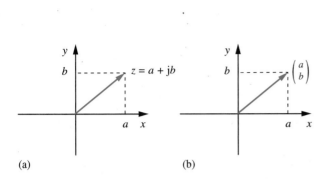

Figure 9.6 The complex number $z = a + jb$ and its equivalent vector.

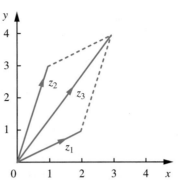

Figure 9.7 Vector addition in the complex plane.

9.6 Vectors and complex numbers

It is often convenient to represent complex numbers by vectors in the x–y plane. Figure 9.6(a) shows the complex number $z = a + jb$. Figure 9.6(b) shows the equivalent vector. Figure 9.7 shows the complex numbers $z_1 = 2 + j$ and $z_2 = 1 + 3j$.

If we now evaluate $z_3 = z_1 + z_2$ we find $z_3 = 3 + 4j$ which is also shown. If we form a parallelogram, two sides of which are the representations of z_1 and z_2, we find that z_3 is the diagonal of the parallelogram. If we regard z_1 and z_2 as vectors in the plane we see that there is a direct analogy between the triangle law of vector addition (see Section 7.2.3) and the addition of complex numbers.

More generally, if z_1 and z_2 are any complex numbers represented on an Argand diagram by the vectors $\vec{OA}$ and $\vec{OB}$ (Figure 9.8) then upon completing the parallelogram OBCA, the sum $z_1 + z_2$ is represented by the vector $\vec{OC}$. We can also obtain a representation of the difference of two complex numbers in the following way. If we write

$$z_3 = z_1 - z_2$$
$$= z_1 + (-z_2)$$

and note that if z_2 is represented by the vector $\vec{OB}$, then $-z_2$ is represented by the vector $-\vec{OB} = \vec{BO} = \vec{CA}$. The complex number z_1 is represented by $\vec{OA} = \vec{BC}$, so that $z_1 + (-z_2) = \vec{BC} + \vec{CA} = \vec{BA}$. Thus the difference $z_1 - z_2$ is represented by the diagonal BA. To summarize, the sum and difference of z_1 and z_2 are represented by the two diagonals of the parallelogram OBCA.

Example 9.15   Represent $z_1 = 6 + j$ and $z_2 = 3 + 4j$, and their sum and difference, on an Argand diagram.

Solution   We draw vectors $\vec{OA}$ and $\vec{OB}$ representing z_1 and z_2, respectively (Figure 9.9). Then we complete the parallelogram OACB as shown. The sum $z_1 + z_2$ is then represented by

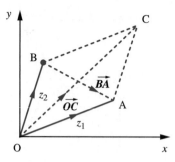

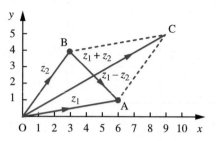

Figure 9.8   Vector addition and subtraction.   **Figure 9.9**   Diagram for Example 9.15.

$\overrightarrow{OC}$ and the difference $z_1 - z_2$ by $\overrightarrow{BA}$. It is easy to see that the vector $\overrightarrow{BA} = \begin{pmatrix} 3 \\ -3 \end{pmatrix}$, that is it represents the complex number $3 - 3j$, while $\overrightarrow{OC} = \begin{pmatrix} 9 \\ 5 \end{pmatrix}$, that is it represents $9 + 5j$, so that $z_1 + z_2 = 9 + 5j$ and $z_1 - z_2 = 3 - 3j$.

9.7   The exponential form of a complex number

You will recall from Chapter 6 that many functions possess a power series expansion, that is the function can be expressed as the sum of a sequence of terms involving integer powers of x. For example,

$$e^x = 1 + x + \frac{x^2}{2!} + \frac{x^3}{3!} + \cdots$$

and this representation is valid for any real value of x. The expression on the r.h.s. is, of course, an infinite sum but its terms get smaller and smaller, and as more are included, the sum we obtain approaches e^x. Other examples of power series include

$$\sin x = x - \frac{x^3}{3!} + \frac{x^5}{5!} - \cdots \tag{9.3}$$

and

$$\cos x = 1 - \frac{x^2}{2!} + \frac{x^4}{4!} - \cdots \tag{9.4}$$

which are also valid for any real value of x. It is useful to extend the range of applicability of these power series by allowing x to be a complex number. That is, we define the function e^z to be

$$e^z = 1 + z + \frac{z^2}{2!} + \frac{z^3}{3!} + \cdots$$

and theory beyond the scope of this book can be used to show that this representation is valid for all complex numbers z.

We have already seen that we can express a complex number in polar form:

$$z = r(\cos\theta + j\sin\theta)$$

Using Equations (9.3) and (9.4) we can write

$$z = r\left\{\left(1 - \frac{\theta^2}{2!} + \frac{\theta^4}{4!} - \cdots\right) + j\left(\theta - \frac{\theta^3}{3!} + \frac{\theta^5}{5!} - \cdots\right)\right\}$$
$$= r\left(1 + j\theta - \frac{\theta^2}{2!} - j\frac{\theta^3}{3!} + \frac{\theta^4}{4!} + j\frac{\theta^5}{5!}\cdots\right)$$

Furthermore, we note that $e^{j\theta}$ can be written as

$$e^{j\theta} = 1 + j\theta + \frac{j^2\theta^2}{2!} + \frac{j^3\theta^3}{3!} + \cdots$$
$$= 1 + j\theta - \frac{\theta^2}{2!} - j\frac{\theta^3}{3!} + \cdots$$

so that

$$z = r(\cos\theta + j\sin\theta) = re^{j\theta}$$

This is yet another form of the same complex number which we call the **exponential form**. We see that

$$e^{j\theta} = \cos\theta + j\sin\theta \qquad (9.5)$$

It is straightforward to show that

$$e^{-j\theta} = \cos\theta - j\sin\theta$$

Therefore, if $\overline{z} = r(\cos\theta - j\sin\theta)$ we can equivalently write $\overline{z} = re^{-j\theta}$. The two expressions for $e^{j\theta}$ and $e^{-j\theta}$ are known as Euler's relations. From these it is easy to obtain the following useful results:

$$\cos\theta = \frac{e^{j\theta} + e^{-j\theta}}{2} \qquad \sin\theta = \frac{e^{j\theta} - e^{-j\theta}}{2j}$$

Example 9.16

We saw in Section 3.6 that a waveform can be written in the form $f(t) = A\cos(\omega t + \phi)$. Consider the complex number $e^{j(\omega t + \phi)}$. We can use Euler's relations to write

$$e^{j(\omega t + \phi)} = \cos(\omega t + \phi) + j\sin(\omega t + \phi)$$

and hence,

$$f(t) = A\,\mathrm{Re}(e^{j(\omega t + \phi)})$$

Exercises 9.7

1. Find the modulus and argument of
   (a) $3e^{j\pi/4}$ (b) $2e^{-j\pi/6}$ (c) $7e^{j\pi/3}$

2. Find the real and imaginary parts of
   (a) $5e^{j\pi/3}$ (b) $e^{j2\pi/3}$
   (c) $11e^{j\pi}$ (d) $2e^{-j\pi}$

3. Express $z = 6(\cos 30° + j\sin 30°)$ in exponential form. Plot z on an Argand diagram and find its real and imaginary parts.

4. If $\sigma, \omega, T \in \mathbb{R}$, find the real and imaginary parts of $e^{(\sigma+j\omega)T}$.

5. Express $z = e^{1+j\pi/2}$ in the form $a + bj$.

6. Express $-1 - j$ in the form $re^{j\theta}$.

7. Express
   (a) $7 + 5j$ and
   (b) $\frac{1}{2} - \frac{1}{3}j$ in exponential form.

8. Express $z_1 = 1 - j$ and
   $$z_2 = \frac{1+j}{\sqrt{3}-j} \text{ in the form } re^{j\theta}.$$

Solutions

1. (a) $3, \pi/4$ (b) $2, -\pi/6$ (c) $7, \pi/3$

2. (a) $2.5, 4.3301$ (b) $-0.5, 0.8660$
   (c) $-11, 0$ (d) $-2, 0$

3. $6e^{(\pi/6)j}$, $\text{Re}(z) = 5.1962$, $\text{Im}(z) = 3$

4. Real part: $e^{\sigma T}\cos \omega T$, imaginary part: $e^{\sigma T}\sin \omega T$

5. ej

6. $\sqrt{2}e^{(-3\pi/4)j}$

7. (a) $\sqrt{74}e^{0.62j}$ (b) $0.60\,e^{-0.59j}$

8. $\sqrt{2}e^{(-\pi/4)j}$, $\frac{1}{\sqrt{2}}e^{(5\pi/12)j}$

9.8 Phasors

Electrical engineers are often interested in analysing circuits in which there is an a.c. power supply. Almost invariably the supply waveform is sinusoidal and the resulting currents and voltages within the circuit are also sinusoidal. For example, a typical voltage is of the form

$$v(t) = V\cos(\omega t + \phi) = V\cos(2\pi ft + \phi) \tag{9.6}$$

where V is the maximum or peak value, ω is the angular frequency, f is the frequency, and ϕ is the phase relative to some reference waveform. This is known as the **time domain representation**. Each of the voltages and currents in the circuit has the same frequency as the supply but differs in magnitude and phase.

In order to analyse such circuits it is necessary to add, subtract, multiply and divide these waveforms. If the time domain representation is used then the mathematics becomes extremely tedious. An alternative approach is to introduce a waveform representation known as a **phasor**. A phasor is an entity consisting of two distinct parts: a magnitude and an angle. It is possible to represent a phasor by a complex number in polar form. The fixed magnitude of this complex number corresponds to the magnitude of the phasor and hence the amplitude of the waveform. The argument of this complex number, ϕ, corresponds to the angle of the phasor and hence the phase angle of the waveform. Figure 9.10 shows a phasor for the sinusoidal waveform of Equation (9.6).

Figure 9.10
Illustration of the
phasor $\tilde{V} = V \angle \phi$
where ω = angular
frequency with which
the phasor rotates.

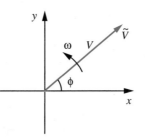

The time dependency of the waveform is catered for by rotating the phasor anti-clockwise at an angular frequency, ω. The projection of the phasor onto the real axis gives the instantaneous value of the waveform. However, the main interest of an engineer is in the phase relationships between the various sinusoids. Therefore the phasors are 'frozen' at a certain point in time. This may be chosen so that $t = 0$ or it may be chosen so that a convenient phasor, known as the **reference phasor**, aligns with the positive real axis. This approach is valid because the phase and magnitude relationships between the various phasors remain the same at all points in time once a circuit has recovered from any initial transients caused by switching.

Some textbooks refer to phasors as vectors. This can lead to confusion as it is possible to divide phasors whereas division of vectors by other vectors is not defined. In practice this is not a problem as phasors, although thought of as vectors, are manipulated as complex numbers, which can be divided. We will avoid these conceptual difficulties by introducing a different notation. We will denote a phasor by $\tilde{V}$, which corresponds to $V \angle \phi$ in complex number notation (see Figure 9.10). Thus, for example, a current $i(t) = I \cos(\omega t + \phi)$ would be written $\tilde{I}$ in phasor notation and $I \angle \phi$ in complex number notation.

Many engineers use the **root mean square** (r.m.s.) value of a sinusoid as the magnitude of a phasor. The justification for this is that it represents the value of a d.c. signal that would dissipate the same amount of power in a resistor as the sinusoid. For example, in the case of a current signal, $I_{rms}^2 R$ is the average power dissipated by the sinusoid $I \cos(\omega t + \phi)$ in a resistor R. For the case of a sinusoidal signal the r.m.s. value of the signal is $1/\sqrt{2}$ times the peak value of the signal (see Section 15.3, Example 15.6, for a proof of this). We will not adopt this approach but it is a common one.

We start by examining the phasor representation of individual circuit elements. In order to do this we need a phasor form of Ohm's law. This is

$$\tilde{V} = \tilde{I} Z \tag{9.7}$$

where $\tilde{V}$ is the voltage phasor, $\tilde{I}$ is the current phasor and Z is the impedance of an element or group of elements and may be a complex quantity. Note that phasors and complex numbers are mixed together in the same equation. This is a common practice because phasors are usually manipulated as complex numbers.

9.8.1 Resistor

Experimentally it can be shown that if an a.c. voltage is applied to a resistor then the current is in phase with the voltage. The ratio of the magnitude of the two waveforms is equal to the resistance, R. So, given $\tilde{I} = I \angle 0$, $Z = R \angle 0$, using Equation (9.7) we have $\tilde{V} = I R \angle 0$. This is illustrated in Figure 9.11.

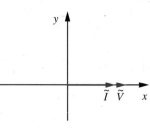

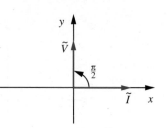

Figure 9.11   Phasor diagram for a resistor.   **Figure 9.12**   Phasor diagram for an inductor.

9.8.2   Inductor

For an inductor we know from experiment that the voltage leads the current by a phase of $\pi/2$, and so the phase angle of the impedance is $\pi/2$. We also know that the magnitude of the impedance is given by ωL. So, given $\tilde{I} = I\angle 0$, $Z = \omega L\angle \pi/2$, using Equation (9.7) we have $\tilde{V} = I\omega L\angle \pi/2$. An alternative way of representing Z for an inductor is to use the Cartesian form, that is

$$Z = \omega L e^{j\pi/2} = \omega L\left(\cos\frac{\pi}{2} + j\sin\frac{\pi}{2}\right)$$
$$= j\omega L$$

This is useful when phasors need to be added and subtracted. The phasor diagram for an inductor is illustrated in Figure 9.12.

9.8.3   Capacitor

For a capacitor it is known that the voltage lags the current by a phase of $\pi/2$ and the magnitude of the impedance is given by $\dfrac{1}{\omega C}$. So given $\tilde{I} = I\angle 0$, $Z = \dfrac{1}{\omega C}\angle -\pi/2$, we have, using Equation (9.7), $\tilde{V} = \dfrac{I}{\omega C}\angle -\pi/2$. Alternatively,

$$Z = \frac{e^{-j\pi/2}}{\omega C} = \frac{1}{\omega C}\left(\cos\frac{\pi}{2} - j\sin\frac{\pi}{2}\right)$$
$$= -\frac{j}{\omega C}$$

Engineers often prefer to rewrite this last expression as

$$\frac{1}{j\omega C}$$

The phasor diagram for the capacitor is illustrated in Figure 9.13.

We have shown how phasors can be multiplied by a complex number; division is very similar. Addition of phasors will now be illustrated; subtraction is similar. Consider the circuit shown in Figure 9.14 in which a resistor, capacitor and inductor are connected in series and fed by an a.c. source. As this is a series circuit, the current through each element, $\tilde{I}$, is the same by Kirchhoff's current law. By Kirchhoff's voltage law the voltage rise produced by the supply, $\tilde{V}_S$, must equal the sum of the voltage drops across the elements. Therefore,

$$\tilde{V}_S = \tilde{V}_R + \tilde{V}_C + \tilde{V}_L$$

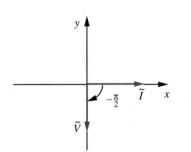

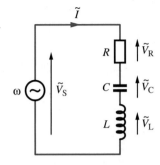

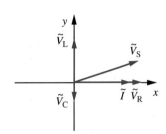

Figure 9.13 Phasor diagram for a capacitor.

Figure 9.14 *RLC* circuit.

Figure 9.15 Phasor diagram for the circuit in Figure 9.14.

Note that this is an addition of phasors so that the voltage drops across the elements do not necessarily have the same phase. The phasor diagram for the circuit is shown in Figure 9.15, in this case with $|\tilde{V}_L| > |\tilde{V}_C|$; $\tilde{I}$ is the reference phasor.

Note that the phasor addition of the element voltages gives the overall supply voltage for a particular supply current. If the magnitude of these element voltage phasors is known then it is possible to calculate the supply voltage graphically. In practice it is easier to convert the polar form of the phasors into Cartesian form and use algebra to analyse the circuit.

Now,

$$\tilde{V}_R = \tilde{I}R\angle 0 = \tilde{I}R$$
$$\tilde{V}_L = \tilde{I}\omega L\angle \pi/2 = \tilde{I}j\omega L$$
$$\tilde{V}_C = \frac{\tilde{I}}{\omega C}\angle - \pi/2 = \frac{\tilde{I}}{j\omega C}$$

Therefore,

$$\tilde{V}_S = \tilde{V}_R + \tilde{V}_C + \tilde{V}_L$$
$$= \tilde{I}R + \tilde{I}j\omega L + \frac{\tilde{I}}{j\omega C}$$
$$= \tilde{I}\left(R + j\omega L + \frac{1}{j\omega C}\right)$$

Therefore the impedance of the circuit is $Z = R + j\omega L + \dfrac{1}{j\omega C}$. We can calculate the frequency for which the impedance of the circuit has minimum magnitude:

$$Z = R + j\omega L + \frac{1}{j\omega C}$$
$$= R + j\omega L - \frac{j}{\omega C}$$
$$= R + j\left(\omega L - \frac{1}{\omega C}\right)$$

Now

$$|Z| = \sqrt{R^2 + \left(\omega L - \frac{1}{\omega C}\right)^2}$$

and so, as ω varies $|Z|$ is a minimum when

$$\omega L - \frac{1}{\omega C} = 0$$

$$\omega^2 = \frac{1}{LC}$$

$$\omega = \sqrt{\frac{1}{LC}}$$

This minimum value is $|Z| = R$. Examining Figure 9.15 it is clear that the minimum impedance occurs when $\tilde{V}_L$ and $\tilde{V}_C$ have the same magnitude, in which case $\tilde{V}_S$ has no imaginary component. The frequency at which this occurs is known as the **resonant frequency** of the circuit.

9.9 De Moivre's theorem

A very important result in complex number theory is De Moivre's theorem which states that if $n \in \mathbb{N}$,

$$(\cos\theta + j\sin\theta)^n = \cos n\theta + j\sin n\theta \qquad (9.8)$$

Example 9.17 Verify De Moivre's theorem when $n = 1$ and $n = 2$.

Solution When $n = 1$, the theorem states:

$$(\cos\theta + j\sin\theta)^1 = \cos 1\theta + j\sin 1\theta$$

which is clearly true, and the theorem holds. When $n = 2$, we find

$$(\cos\theta + j\sin\theta)^2 = (\cos\theta + j\sin\theta)(\cos\theta + j\sin\theta)$$
$$= \cos^2\theta + j\sin\theta\cos\theta + j\cos\theta\sin\theta + j^2\sin^2\theta$$
$$= \cos^2\theta - \sin^2\theta + j(2\sin\theta\cos\theta)$$

Recalling the trigonometric identities $\cos 2\theta = \cos^2\theta - \sin^2\theta$ and $\sin 2\theta = 2\sin\theta\cos\theta$, we can write the previous expression as

$$\cos 2\theta + j\sin 2\theta$$

Therefore,

$$(\cos\theta + j\sin\theta)^2 = \cos 2\theta + j\sin 2\theta$$

and De Moivre's theorem has been verified when $n = 2$.

The theorem also holds when n is a rational number, that is $n = p/q$ where p and q are integers. Thus we have

$$(\cos\theta + j\sin\theta)^{p/q} = \cos\frac{p}{q}\theta + j\sin\frac{p}{q}\theta$$

In this form it can be used to obtain roots of complex numbers. For example,

$$\sqrt[3]{\cos\theta + j\sin\theta} = (\cos\theta + j\sin\theta)^{1/3} = \cos\frac{1}{3}\theta + j\sin\frac{1}{3}\theta$$

In such a case the expression obtained is only one of the possible roots. Additional roots can be found as illustrated in Example 9.18.

De Moivre's theorem is particularly important for the solution of certain types of equation.

Example 9.18   Find all complex numbers z which satisfy

$$z^3 = 1 \qquad\qquad (9.9)$$

Solution   The solution of this equation is equivalent to finding the solutions of $z = 1^{1/3}$; that is, finding the cube roots of 1. Since we are allowing z to be complex, that is $z \in \mathbb{C}$, we can write

$$z = r(\cos\theta + j\sin\theta)$$

Then, using De Moivre's theorem,

$$z^3 = r^3(\cos\theta + j\sin\theta)^3$$
$$= r^3(\cos 3\theta + j\sin 3\theta)$$

We next convert the expression on the r.h.s. of Equation (9.9) into polar form. Figure 9.16 shows the number $1 = 1 + 0j$ on an Argand diagram.

From the Argand diagram we see that its modulus is 1 and its argument is 0, or possibly $\pm 2\pi$, $\pm 4\pi$, ..., that is $2n\pi$ where $n \in \mathbb{Z}$. Consequently, we can write

$$1 = 1(\cos 2n\pi + j\sin 2n\pi) \qquad n \in \mathbb{Z}$$

Using the polar form, Equation (9.9) becomes

$$r^3(\cos 3\theta + j\sin 3\theta) = 1(\cos 2n\pi + j\sin 2n\pi)$$

Comparing both sides of this equation we see that

$$r^3 = 1 \qquad \text{that is} \qquad r = 1 \text{ since } r \in \mathbb{R}$$

and

$$3\theta = 2n\pi \qquad \text{that is} \qquad \theta = 2n\pi/3 \qquad n \in \mathbb{Z}$$

Apparently θ can take infinitely many values, but, as we shall see, the corresponding complex numbers are simply repetitions. When $n = 0$, we find $\theta = 0$, so that

$$z = z_1 = 1(\cos 0 + j\sin 0) = 1$$

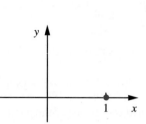

Figure 9.16 The complex number $z = 1 + 0j$.

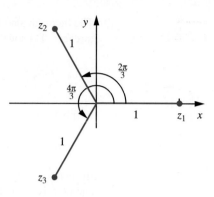

Figure 9.17 Solutions of $z^3 = 1$.

is the first solution. When $n = 1$ we find $\theta = 2\pi/3$, so that

$$z = z_2 = 1\left(\cos\frac{2\pi}{3} + j\sin\frac{2\pi}{3}\right) = -\frac{1}{2} + j\frac{\sqrt{3}}{2}$$

is the second solution. When $n = 2$ we find $\theta = 4\pi/3$, so that

$$z = z_3 = 1\left(\cos\frac{4\pi}{3} + j\sin\frac{4\pi}{3}\right) = -\frac{1}{2} - j\frac{\sqrt{3}}{2}$$

is the third solution. If we continue searching for solutions using larger values of n we find that we only repeat solutions already obtained. It is often useful to plot solutions on an Argand diagram and this is easily done directly from the polar form, as shown in Figure 9.17. We note that the solutions are equally spaced at angles of $2\pi/3$.

Example 9.19   Find the complex numbers z which satisfy $z^2 = 4j$.

Solution   Since $z \in \mathbb{C}$ we write $z = r(\cos\theta + j\sin\theta)$. Therefore,

$$z^2 = r^2(\cos\theta + j\sin\theta)^2$$
$$= r^2(\cos 2\theta + j\sin 2\theta)$$

by De Moivre's theorem. Furthermore, $4j$ has modulus 4 and argument $\pi/2 + 2n\pi$, $n \in \mathbb{Z}$, that is

$$4j = 4\{\cos(\pi/2 + 2n\pi) + j\sin(\pi/2 + 2n\pi)\} \qquad n \in \mathbb{Z}$$

Therefore,

$$r^2(\cos 2\theta + j\sin 2\theta) = 4\{\cos(\pi/2 + 2n\pi) + j\sin(\pi/2 + 2n\pi)\}$$

Comparing both sides of this equation, we see that

$$r^2 = 4 \qquad \text{and so} \qquad r = 2$$

Figure 9.18
Solution of $z^2 = 4j$.

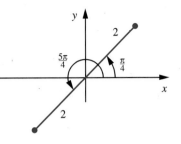

and

$$2\theta = \pi/2 + 2n\pi \qquad \text{and so} \qquad \theta = \pi/4 + n\pi$$

When $n = 0$ we find $\theta = \pi/4$, and when $n = 1$ we find $\theta = 5\pi/4$. Using larger values of n simply repeats solutions already obtained. These solutions are shown in Figure 9.18. We note that in this example the solutions are equally spaced at intervals of $2\pi/2 = \pi$. In Cartesian form,

$$z_1 = \frac{2}{\sqrt{2}} + j\frac{2}{\sqrt{2}} = \sqrt{2}(1+j) \qquad \text{and} \qquad z_2 = -\frac{2}{\sqrt{2}} - j\frac{2}{\sqrt{2}} = -\sqrt{2}(1+j)$$

In general, the n roots of $z^n = a + jb$ are equally spaced at angles $2\pi/n$.

Once the technique for solving equations like those in Examples 9.18 and 9.19 has been mastered, engineers find it simpler to work with the abbreviated form $r\angle\theta$. Example 9.19 reworked in this fashion becomes

$$\text{Let } z = r\angle\theta, \qquad \text{then} \qquad z^2 = r^2\angle 2\theta$$

Furthermore, $4j = 4\angle\pi/2 + 2n\pi$, and hence if $z^2 = 4j$, we have

$$r^2\angle 2\theta = 4\angle\left(\frac{\pi}{2} + 2n\pi\right)$$

from which

$$r^2 = 4 \qquad \text{and} \qquad 2\theta = \frac{\pi}{2} + 2n\pi$$

as before. Rework Example 9.18 for yourself using this approach.

Another application of De Moivre's theorem is the derivation of trigonometric identities.

Example 9.20 Use De Moivre's theorem to show that

$$\cos 3\theta = 4\cos^3\theta - 3\cos\theta$$

and

$$\sin 3\theta = 3\sin\theta - 4\sin^3\theta$$

Solution   We know that

$$(\cos\theta + j\sin\theta)^3 = \cos 3\theta + j\sin 3\theta$$

Expanding the l.h.s. we find

$$\cos^3\theta + 3j\cos^2\theta\sin\theta - 3\cos\theta\sin^2\theta - j\sin^3\theta = \cos 3\theta + j\sin 3\theta$$

Equating the real parts gives

$$\cos^3\theta - 3\cos\theta\sin^2\theta = \cos 3\theta \tag{9.10}$$

and equating the imaginary parts gives

$$3\cos^2\theta\sin\theta - \sin^3\theta = \sin 3\theta \tag{9.11}$$

Now, writing $\sin^2\theta = 1 - \cos^2\theta$ in Equation (9.10) and $\cos^2\theta = 1 - \sin^2\theta$ in Equation (9.11), we find

$$\cos 3\theta = \cos^3\theta - 3\cos\theta(1 - \cos^2\theta)$$
$$= \cos^3\theta + 3\cos^3\theta - 3\cos\theta$$
$$= 4\cos^3\theta - 3\cos\theta$$
$$\sin 3\theta = 3(1 - \sin^2\theta)\sin\theta - \sin^3\theta$$
$$= 3\sin\theta - 4\sin^3\theta$$

as required.

This technique allows trigonometric functions of multiples of angles to be expressed in terms of powers. Sometimes we want to carry out the reverse process and express a power in terms of multiple angles. Consider Example 9.21.

Example 9.21   If $z = \cos\theta + j\sin\theta$ show that

$$z + \frac{1}{z} = 2\cos\theta \qquad z - \frac{1}{z} = 2j\sin\theta$$

and find similar expressions for $z^n + \dfrac{1}{z^n}$ and $z^n - \dfrac{1}{z^n}$.

Solution   Consider the complex number

$$z = \cos\theta + j\sin\theta$$

Using De Moivre's theorem,

$$\frac{1}{z} = z^{-1} = (\cos\theta + j\sin\theta)^{-1} = \cos(-\theta) + j\sin(-\theta)$$

But $\cos(-\theta) = \cos\theta$ and $\sin(-\theta) = -\sin\theta$, so that if $z = \cos\theta + j\sin\theta$

$$\frac{1}{z} = \cos\theta - j\sin\theta$$

Consequently,

$$z + \frac{1}{z} = 2\cos\theta \qquad \text{and} \qquad z - \frac{1}{z} = 2j\sin\theta$$

Moreover,

$$z^n = \cos n\theta + j\sin n\theta \qquad \text{and} \qquad z^{-n} = \cos n\theta - j\sin n\theta$$

so that

$$z^n + \frac{1}{z^n} = 2\cos n\theta \qquad \text{and} \qquad z^n - \frac{1}{z^n} = 2j\sin n\theta$$

$$z^n + \frac{1}{z^n} = 2\cos n\theta \qquad \text{and} \qquad z^n - \frac{1}{z^n} = 2j\sin n\theta$$

Example 9.22 Show that $\cos^2\theta = \frac{1}{2}(\cos 2\theta + 1)$.

Solution The formulae obtained in Example 9.21 allow us to obtain expressions for powers of $\cos\theta$ and $\sin\theta$. Since $2\cos\theta = z + \frac{1}{z}$, squaring both sides we have

$$2^2\cos^2\theta = \left(z + \frac{1}{z}\right)^2 = z^2 + 2 + \frac{1}{z^2}$$

$$= \left(z^2 + \frac{1}{z^2}\right) + 2$$

But $z^2 + \frac{1}{z^2} = 2\cos 2\theta$, so

$$2^2\cos^2\theta = 2\cos 2\theta + 2$$

and therefore,

$$\cos^2\theta = \frac{1}{2}\cos 2\theta + \frac{1}{2}$$

$$= \frac{1}{2}(\cos 2\theta + 1)$$

as required.

Exercises 9.9

1 Express $(\cos\theta + j\sin\theta)^9$ and $(\cos\theta + j\sin\theta)^{1/2}$ in the form $\cos n\theta + j\sin n\theta$.

2 Use De Moivre's theorem to simplify

(a) $(\cos 3\theta + j\sin 3\theta)(\cos 4\theta + j\sin 4\theta)$

(b) $\dfrac{\cos 8\theta + j\sin 8\theta}{\cos 2\theta - j\sin 2\theta}$

3 Solve the equations

(a) $z^3 + 1 = 0$

(b) $z^4 = 1 + j$

4 Find $\sqrt[3]{2 + 2j}$ and display your solutions on an Argand diagram.

5 Prove the following trigonometric identities:

(a) $\cos 4\theta = 8\cos^4\theta - 8\cos^2\theta + 1$

(b) $32\sin^6\theta = 10 - 15\cos 2\theta + 6\cos 4\theta - \cos 6\theta$

6 Solve the equation $z^4 + 25 = 0$.

7 Find the fifth roots of j and depict your solutions on an Argand diagram.

8 Show that $\cos^3\theta = \frac{1}{4}(\cos 3\theta + 3\cos\theta)$.

9 Show that $\sin^4\theta = \frac{1}{8}(\cos 4\theta - 4\cos 2\theta + 3)$.

10 Express $\cos 5\theta$ in terms of powers of $\cos\theta$.

11 Express $\sin 5\theta$ in terms of powers of $\sin\theta$.

12 Given $e^{j\theta} = \cos\theta + j\sin\theta$, prove De Moivre's theorem in the form

$$(e^{j\theta})^n = \cos n\theta + j\sin n\theta$$

Solutions

1 $\cos 9\theta + j\sin 9\theta,\ \cos(\theta/2) + j\sin(\theta/2)$

2 (a) $\cos 7\theta + j\sin 7\theta$
 (b) $\cos 10\theta + j\sin 10\theta$

3 (a) $1\angle\pi/3 + 2n\pi/3$ $n = 0, 1, 2$
 (b) $2^{1/8}\angle\pi/16 + n\pi/2$ $n = 0, 1, 2, 3$

4 $8^{1/6}\angle\pi/12 + 2n\pi/3$ $n = 0, 1, 2$

6 $\sqrt{5}\angle\pi/4 + n\pi/2$ $n = 0, 1, 2, 3$

7 $1\angle\pi/10 + 2n\pi/5$ $n = 0, 1, 2, 3, 4$

10 $16\cos^5\theta - 20\cos^3\theta + 5\cos\theta$

11 $16\sin^5\theta - 20\sin^3\theta + 5\sin\theta$

9.10 Loci and regions of the complex plane

Regions of the complex plane can often be conveniently described by means of complex numbers. For example, the points that lie on a circle of radius 2 centred at the origin (Figure 9.19) represent complex numbers all of which have a modulus of 2. The arguments are any value of θ, $-\pi < \theta \leqslant \pi$. We can describe all the points on this circle by the simple expression

$$|z| = 2$$

that is, all complex numbers with modulus 2. We say that the locus (or path) of the point z is a circle, radius 2, centred at the origin. The interior of the circle is described by $|z| < 2$ while its exterior is described by $|z| > 2$.

Similarly all points lying in the first quadrant (shaded in Figure 9.20) have arguments between 0 and $\pi/2$. This quadrant is therefore described by the expression:

$$0 < \arg(z) < \pi/2$$

Example 9.23 Sketch the locus of the point satisfying $\arg(z) = \pi/4$.

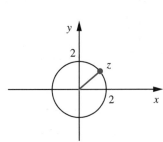

Figure 9.19 A circle, radius 2, centred at the origin.

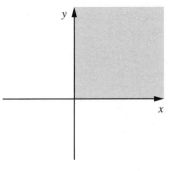

Figure 9.20 First quadrant of the x–y plane.

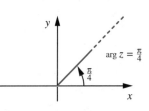

Figure 9.21 Locus of points satisfying $\arg(z) = \pi/4$.

Solution The set of points with $\arg(z) = \pi/4$ comprises complex numbers whose argument is $\pi/4$. All these complex numbers lie on the line shown in Figure 9.21.

Example 9.24 Sketch the locus of the point satisfying $|z - 2| = 3$.

Solution First mark the fixed point 2 on the Argand diagram labelling it 'A' (Figure 9.22). Consider the complex number z represented by the point P. From the vector triangle law of addition

$$\vec{OA} + \vec{AP} = \vec{OP}$$
$$\vec{AP} = \vec{OP} - \vec{OA}$$

Recall from Section 9.6 that the graphical representation of the sum and difference of vectors in the plane, and the sum and difference of complex numbers, are equivalent. Since vector $\vec{OP}$ represents the complex number z, and vector $\vec{OA}$ represents the complex number 2, $\vec{AP} = \vec{OP} - \vec{OA}$ will represent $z - 2$. Therefore $|z - 2|$ represents the distance between A and P. We are given that $|z - 2| = 3$, which therefore means that P can be any point such that its distance from A is 3. This means that P can be any point on a circle of radius 3 centred at A(2, 0). The locus is shown in Figure 9.23. $|z - 2| < 3$ represents the interior of the circle while $|z - 2| > 3$ represents the exterior.

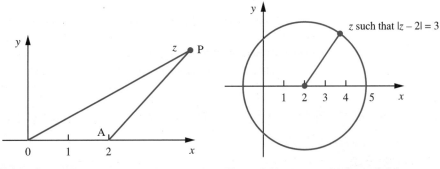

Figure 9.22 Points z and $2 + 0\mathrm{j}$.

Figure 9.23 Locus of points satisfying $|z - 2| = 3$.

Alternatively we can obtain the same result algebraically: given $|z - 2| = 3$ and also that $z = x + jy$, we can write

$$|z - 2| = |(x - 2) + jy| = 3$$

that is

$$\sqrt{(x - 2)^2 + y^2} = 3$$

or

$$(x - 2)^2 + y^2 = 9$$

Generally, the equation $(x - a)^2 + (y - b)^2 = r^2$ represents a circle of radius r centred at (a, b), so we see that $(x - 2)^2 + y^2 = 9$ represents a circle of radius 3 centred at $(2, 0)$, as before.

Example 9.25 Use the algebraic approach to find the locus of the point z which satisfies

$$|z - 1| = \tfrac{1}{2}|z - j|$$

Solution If $z = x + jy$, then we have

$$|(x - 1) + jy| = \tfrac{1}{2}|x + j(y - 1)|$$

Therefore,

$$(x - 1)^2 + y^2 = \tfrac{1}{4}\{x^2 + (y - 1)^2\}$$

and so

$$4(x - 1)^2 + 4y^2 = x^2 + (y - 1)^2$$

that is

$$3x^2 - 8x + 3y^2 + 2y + 3 = 0$$

By completing the square this may be written in the form

$$3\left(x - \tfrac{4}{3}\right)^2 + 3\left(y + \tfrac{1}{3}\right)^2 = \tfrac{8}{3}$$

that is

$$\left(x - \tfrac{4}{3}\right)^2 + \left(y + \tfrac{1}{3}\right)^2 = \tfrac{8}{9}$$

which represents a circle of radius $\sqrt{8}/3$ centred at $\left(\tfrac{4}{3}, -\tfrac{1}{3}\right)$.

Exercises 9.10

1 Sketch the loci defined by

(a) $\arg(z) = 0$

(b) $\arg(z) = \pi/2$

(c) $\arg(z - 4) = \pi/4$

(d) $|2z| = |z - 1|$

2 Sketch the regions defined by

   (a) $\operatorname{Re}(z) \geqslant 0$

   (b) $\operatorname{Im}(z) < 3$

   (c) $|z| > 3$

   (d) $0 \leqslant \arg(z) \leqslant \pi/2$

   (e) $|z + 2| \leqslant 3$

   (f) $|z + j| > 3$

   (g) $|z - 1| < |z - 2|$

3 If $s = \sigma + j\omega$ sketch the regions defined by

   (a) $\sigma \leqslant 0$

   (b) $\sigma \geqslant 0$

   (c) $-2 \leqslant \omega \leqslant 2$

Solutions

1 See Figure S.14.

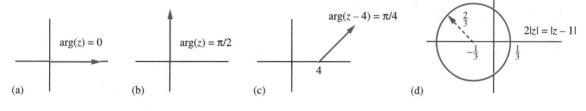

(a)   (b)   (c)   (d)

Figure S.14

2 See Figure S.15.

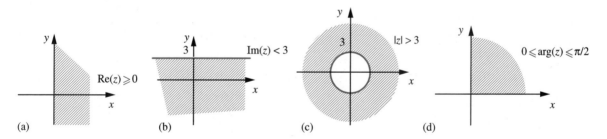

(a)   (b)   (c)   (d)

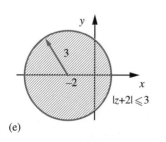 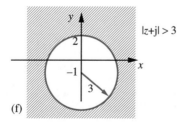 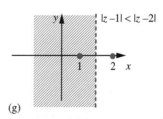

(e)   (f)   (g)

Figure S.15

3 See Figure S.16.

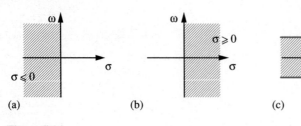

Figure S.16

Review exercises 9

1 Show that $\dfrac{1}{\cos\theta - j\sin\theta} = \cos\theta + j\sin\theta$.

2 Express in Cartesian form

(a) $\dfrac{5+4j}{5-4j}$

(b) $\dfrac{1}{2+3j}$

(c) $\dfrac{1}{2+3j} + \dfrac{1}{2-3j}$

(d) $\dfrac{1}{x-jy}$

3 Find the modulus and argument of $-j$, -3, $1+j$, $\cos\theta + j\sin\theta$.

4 Mark on an Argand diagram vectors corresponding to the following complex numbers: $-3+2j$, $-3-2j$, $\cos\pi + j\sin\pi$.

5 Express in the form $a + bj$:

(a) $(\cos\theta + j\sin\theta)^6$

(b) $\dfrac{1}{(\cos\theta + j\sin\theta)^3}$

(c) $\dfrac{\cos\theta + j\sin\theta}{\cos\phi + j\sin\phi}$

6 If $z \in \mathbb{C}$, show that

(a) $z + \bar{z} = 2\text{Re}(z)$

(b) $z - \bar{z} = 2j\,\text{Im}(z)$

(c) $z\bar{z} = |z|^2$

7 Show that $e^{j\omega t} + e^{-j\omega t} = 2\cos\omega t$ and find an expression for $e^{j\omega t} - e^{-j\omega t}$.

8 Express $1 + e^{2j\omega t}$ in the form $a + bj$.

9 Sketch the region in the complex plane described by $|z + 2j| < 1$.

10 Express $e^{(1/2-6j)}$ in the form $a + bj$.

11 Solve the equation $z^4 + 1 = j\sqrt{3}$.

12 Express $s^2 + 6s + 13$ in the form $(s-a)(s-b)$ where $a, b \in \mathbb{C}$.

13 Express $2s^2 + 8s + 11$ in the form $2(s-a)(s-b)$ where $a, b \in \mathbb{C}$.

Solutions

2 (a) $\frac{9}{41} + \frac{40}{41}j$ (b) $\frac{2}{13} - \frac{3}{13}j$ (c) $\frac{4}{13}$

(d) $\dfrac{x}{x^2+y^2} + \dfrac{y}{x^2+y^2}j$

3 $|-j| = 1$, $\arg(-j) = -\pi/2$; $|-3| = 3$, $\arg(-3) = \pi$; $|1+j| = \sqrt{2}$, $\arg(1+j) = \pi/4$, $|\cos\theta + j\sin\theta| = 1$, $\arg(\cos\theta + j\sin\theta) = \theta$

5 (a) $\cos 6\theta + j\sin 6\theta$ (b) $\cos 3\theta - j\sin 3\theta$
(c) $\cos(\theta - \phi) + j\sin(\theta - \phi)$

7 $e^{j\omega t} - e^{-j\omega t} = 2j\sin\omega t$

8 $1 + \cos 2\omega t + j\sin 2\omega t$

10 $1.5831 + 0.4607\,j$

11 $2^{1/4}\angle\pi/6 + n\pi/2$ $n = 0, 1, 2, 3$

12 $[s - (-3 + 2j)][s - (-3 - 2j)]$

13 $2\left[s - \left(-2 + \dfrac{\sqrt{6}}{2}j\right)\right]\left[s - \left(-2 - \dfrac{\sqrt{6}}{2}j\right)\right]$

10 Differentiation

Chapter 10 Contents

10.1	Introduction	334
10.2	Graphical approach to differentiation	334
10.3	Limits and continuity	336
10.4	Rate of change at a specific point	339
10.5	Rate of change at a general point	342
10.6	Existence of derivatives	348
10.7	Common derivatives	350
10.8	Differentiation as a linear operator	353
	Review exercises	362

10.1 Introduction

Differentiation is a mathematical technique for analysing the way in which functions change. In particular, it determines how rapidly a function is changing at any specific point. As the function in question may represent the magnetic field of a motor, the voltage across a capacitor, the temperature of a chemical mix, etc., it is often important to know how quickly these quantities change. For example, if the voltage on an electrical supply network is falling rapidly because of a short circuit, then it is necessary to detect this in order to switch out that part of the network where the fault has occurred. However, the system should not take action for normal voltage fluctuations and so it is important to distinguish different types and rates of change. Another example would be detecting a sudden rise in the pressure of a fermentation vessel and taking appropriate action to stabilize the pressure.

Differentiation will be introduced in this chapter. We shall derive a formula which can be used to find the rate of change of a function. To avoid always having to resort to the formula engineers often use a **table of derivatives**; such a table is given in Section 10.7. The chapter closes with a discussion of an important property of differentiation – that of linearity.

10.2 Graphical approach to differentiation

Differentiation is concerned with the rate at which a function is changing, rather than the actual change itself. We can explore the rate of change of a function by examining Figure 10.1. There are several regions to this curve corresponding to different intervals of t. In the interval [0, 5] the function does not change at all. The rate of change of y is zero. From $t = 5$ to $t = 7$ the function increases slightly. Thus the rate of change of y as t increases is small. Since y is increasing, the rate of change of y is positive. From $t = 7$ to $t = 8$ there is a rapid rise in the value of the function. The rate of change of y is large and positive. From $t = 8$ to $t = 9$ the value of y decreases very rapidly. The rate of change of y is large and negative. Finally from $t = 9$ to $t = 12$ the function decreases slightly. Thus the rate of change of y is small and negative.

The aim of **differential calculus** is to specify the rate of change of a function precisely. It is not sufficient to say 'the rate of change of a function is large'. We require an exact value or expression for the rate of change. Before being able to do this we need to introduce two concepts concerning the rate of change of a function.

Figure 10.1
The function $y(t)$ has different rates of change over different regions of t.

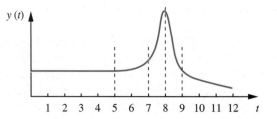

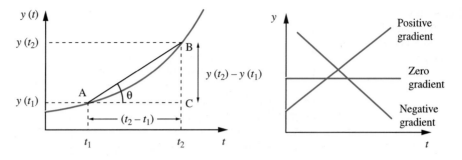

Figure 10.2 Average rate of change across an interval.

Figure 10.3 Lines can have different gradients.

10.2.1 Average rate of change of a function across an interval

Consider Figure 10.2. When $t = t_1$, the function has a value $y(t_1)$. This is denoted by A on the curve. When $t = t_2$, the function has a value of $y(t_2)$. This point is denoted by B on the curve. The function changes by an amount $y(t_2) - y(t_1)$ over the interval $[t_1, t_2]$. Thus the average rate of change of the function over the interval is

$$\frac{\text{change in } y}{\text{change in } t} = \frac{y(t_2) - y(t_1)}{t_2 - t_1}$$

The straight line joining A and B is known as a **chord**. Graphically, $y(t_2) - y(t_1)$ is the vertical distance and $t_2 - t_1$ the horizontal distance between A and B, so that the **gradient** of the chord AB is given by

$$\frac{\text{BC}}{\text{AC}} = \frac{y(t_2) - y(t_1)}{t_2 - t_1}$$

The gradient or **slope** of a line is a measure of its steepness and lines may have positive, negative or zero gradients as shown in Figure 10.3.

Thus the gradient of the chord AB corresponds to the average rate of change of the function between A and B. To summarize:

> The average rate of change of a function between two points A and B is the gradient of the chord AB.

10.2.2 Rate of change of a function at a point

Consider again Figure 10.2. Suppose we require the rate of change of the function at point A. We can use the gradient of the chord AB as an approximation to this value. If B is close to A then the approximation is better than if B is not so close to A. Therefore by moving B nearer to A it is possible to improve the accuracy of this approximation (see Figure 10.4).

Suppose the chord AB is extended as a straight line on both sides of AB, and B is moved closer and closer to A until both points eventually coincide. The straight line becomes a **tangent** to the curve at A. This is the straight line that just touches the curve at A. However, the rate of change of this tangent, that is its gradient, still corresponds to the rate of change of the function, but now it is the rate of change of the function at the point A. To summarize:

Figure 10.4
Point B is moved
nearer to A to improve
accuracy.

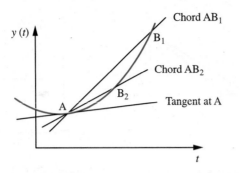

> The rate of change of a function at a point A on the curve is the gradient of the tangent to the curve at point A.

We have still to address the question of how the gradients of chords and tangents are found. This requires a knowledge of limits which is the topic of the next section.

10.3 Limits and continuity

The concept of a limit is crucial to the development of differentiation. We write $t \to c$ to denote that t approaches, or tends to, the value of c. Note carefully that this is distinct from stating $t = c$. As t tends to c we consider the value to which the function approaches and call this value the **limit** of the function as $t \to c$.

Example 10.1 If $t \to 2$, what value does

$$f(t) = t^2 + 2t - 3$$

approach?

Solution Figure 10.5 shows a graph of $f(t)$. Clearly, whether $t = 2$ is approached from the l.h.s. or the r.h.s. the function tends to 5. That is, if $t \to 2$, then $f(t) \to 5$. We note that this is the value of $f(2)$. Informally we are saying that as t gets nearer and nearer to the value 2, so $f(t)$ gets nearer and nearer to 5. This is usually written as

$$\lim_{t \to 2}(t^2 + 2t - 3) = 5$$

where 'lim' is an abbreviation of limit. In this example, the limit of $f(t)$ as $t \to 2$ is simply $f(2)$, but this is not true for all functions.

Example 10.2 Figure 10.6 illustrates $y(x)$ defined by

$$y(x) = \begin{cases} 1 - x & x < 0 \\ 3 & x = 0 \\ x + 1 & x > 0 \end{cases}$$

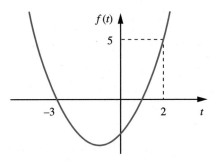

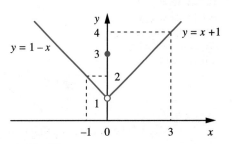

Figure 10.5   The curve $f(t) = t^2 + 2t - 3$.

Figure 10.6   As $x \to 0$, $y \to 1$, even though $y(0) = 3$.

Evaluate:

(a) $\lim_{x \to 3} y$ (b) $\lim_{x \to -1} y$ (c) $\lim_{x \to 0} y$

Solution   We note that this function is piecewise continuous. It has a discontinuity at $x = 0$.

(a) We seek the limit of y as x approaches 3. As x approaches 3, we will be on that part of the function defined by $x > 0$, that is $y(x) = x + 1$. As $x \to 3$, then $y \to 3 + 1$, that is $y \to 4$. So

$$\lim_{x \to 3} y = 4$$

(b) When x approaches -1, we will be on that part of the function defined by $x < 0$, that is $y(x) = 1 - x$. So as $x \to -1$, then $y \to 1 - (-1)$, that is $y \to 2$. Hence

$$\lim_{x \to -1} y = 2$$

(c) As x approaches 0 what value does y approach? Note that we are not evaluating $y(0)$ which actually has a value of 3. We simply ask the question 'What value is y near when x is near, but distinct from, 0?' From Figure 10.6 we see y is near to 1, that is

$$\lim_{x \to 0} y = 1$$

Example 10.3   The function $y(x)$ is defined by

$$y(x) = \begin{cases} 0 & x \leqslant 0 \\ x & 0 < x \leqslant 2 \\ x - 2 & x > 2 \end{cases}$$

(a) Sketch the function.

(b) State the limit of y as x approaches (i) 3, (ii) 2, (iii) 0.

Figure 10.7
The function y has
different limits as
$x \to 2$ from the left
and the right.

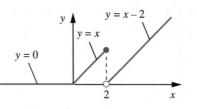

Solution

(a) The function is shown in Figure 10.7. Note that the figure has three parts; each part corresponds to a part in the algebraic definition.

(b) (i) As $x \to 3$, the relevant part of the function is $y(x) = x - 2$. Hence

$$\lim_{x \to 3} y = 1$$

(ii) Suppose $x < 2$ and gradually increases, approaching the value 2. Then, from the graph, we see that y approaches 2. Now, suppose $x > 2$ and gradually decreases, tending to 2. In this case y approaches 0. Hence, we cannot find the limit of y as x tends to 2. The $\lim_{x \to 2} y$ does not exist.

(iii) As x tends to 0, y tends to 0. This is true whether x approaches 0 from below, that is from the left, or from above, that is from the right. So,

$$\lim_{x \to 0} y = 0$$

It is appropriate at this stage to introduce the concept of **left-hand** and **right-hand** limits. Referring to Example 10.3, we see that as x approaches 2 from the left, that is from below, then y approaches 2. We say that the left-hand limit of y as x tends to 2 is 2. This is written as

$$\lim_{x \to 2^-} y = 2$$

Similarly, the right-hand limit of y is obtained by letting x tend to 2 from above. In this case, y approaches 0. This is written as

$$\lim_{x \to 2^+} y = 0$$

Consider a point at which the left-hand and right-hand limits are equal. At such a point we say 'the limit exists at that point'.

> The **limit** of a function, at a point $x = a$, exists only if the left-hand and right-hand limits are equal there.

10.3.1 Continuous and discontinuous functions

A function f is **continuous** at the point where $x = a$, if

$$\lim_{x \to a} f = f(a)$$

that is, the limit value matches the function value at a point of continuity. A function which is not continuous is **discontinuous**. In Example 10.3, the function is continuous at $x = 0$ because

$$\lim_{x \to 0} y = 0 = f(0)$$

but discontinuous at $x = 2$ because $\lim_{x \to 2} y$ does not exist. In Example 10.2, the function is discontinuous at $x = 0$ because $\lim_{x \to 0} y = 1$ but $y(0) = 3$. The concept of continuity corresponds to our natural understanding of a break in the graph of the function, as discussed in Chapter 2.

A function f is continuous at a point $x = a$ if and only if
$$\lim_{x \to a} f = f(a)$$
that is, the limit of f exists at $x = a$ and is equal to $f(a)$.

Exercises 10.3

1   The function, $f(t)$, is defined by

$$f(t) = \begin{cases} 1 & 0 \leqslant t \leqslant 2 \\ 2 & 2 < t \leqslant 3 \\ 3 & t > 3 \end{cases}$$

Sketch a graph of $f(t)$ and state the following limits if they exist.

(a) $\lim_{t \to 1.5} f$

(b) $\lim_{t \to 2^+} f$

(c) $\lim_{t \to 3} f$

(d) $\lim_{t \to 0^+} f$

(e) $\lim_{t \to 3^-} f$

2   The function $g(t)$ is defined by

$$g(t) = \begin{cases} 0 & t < 0 \\ t^2 & 0 \leqslant t \leqslant 3 \\ 2t + 3 & 3 < t \leqslant 4 \\ 12 & t > 4 \end{cases}$$

(a) Sketch g.

(b) State any points of discontinuity.

(c) Find, if they exist,

(i) $\lim_{t \to 3} g$

(ii) $\lim_{t \to 4} g$

(iii) $\lim_{t \to 4^-} g$

Solutions

1 (a) 1   (b) 2   (c) not defined
  (d) 1   (e) 2

2 (b) $t = 4$
  (c) (i) 9   (ii) not defined   (iii) 11

10.4 Rate of change at a specific point

We saw in Section 10.2 that the rate of change of a function at a point is the gradient of the tangent to the curve at that point. Also, we can think of a tangent at A as the limit of an extended chord AB as B $\to$ A. We now put these two ideas together to find the rate of change of a function at a point.

Figure 10.8
The function:
$y = 3x^2 + 2$.

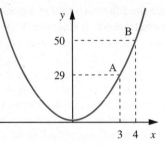

Example 10.4 Given $y = f(x) = 3x^2 + 2$, obtain estimates of the rate of change of y at $x = 3$ by considering the intervals

(a) [3, 4]   (b) [3, 3.1]   (c) [3, 3.01]

Solution (a) Consider Figure 10.8.

$$y(3) = 3(3)^2 + 2 = 29$$
$$y(4) = 3(4)^2 + 2 = 50$$

Let A be the point (3, 29) on the curve. Let B be the point (4, 50). Then

$$\text{average rate of change over the interval } [3, 4] = \frac{\text{change in } y}{\text{change in } x}$$

$$= \frac{y(4) - y(3)}{4 - 3}$$

$$= \frac{50 - 29}{4 - 3} = 21$$

This is the gradient of the chord AB and is an estimate of the gradient of the tangent at A. That is, the rate of change at A is approximately 21.

(b) $y(3.1) = 30.83$ and so,

$$\text{average rate of change over the interval } [3, 3.1] = \frac{30.83 - 29}{3.1 - 3} = 18.3$$

This is a more accurate estimate of the rate of change at A.

(c) $y(3.01) = 29.1803$ and so,

$$\text{average rate of change over the interval } [3, 3.01] = \frac{29.1803 - 29}{3.01 - 3}$$

$$= 18.03$$

This is an even better estimate of the rate of change at A. Hence at A, if x increases by 1 unit then y increases by approximately 18 units. This corresponds to a steep upward slope at A.

Example 10.4 illustrates the approach of estimating the rate of change at a point by using the 'shrinking interval' method. By taking smaller and smaller intervals, better and better estimates of the rate of change of the function at $x = 3$ can be obtained. However, we eventually want the interval to 'shrink' to the point $x = 3$. We introduce a small change or **increment** of x denoted by δx and consider the interval $[3, 3 + \delta x]$. By letting δx tend to zero, the interval $[3, 3 + \delta x]$ effectively shrinks to the point $x = 3$.

Example 10.5   Find the rate of change of $y = 3x^2 + 2$ at $x = 3$ by considering the interval $[3, 3 + \delta x]$ and letting δx tend to 0.

Solution   When $x = 3$, $y(3) = 29$. When $x = 3 + \delta x$ then

$$y(3 + \delta x) = 3(3 + \delta x)^2 + 2$$
$$= 3(9 + 6\delta x + (\delta x)^2) + 2$$
$$= 3(\delta x)^2 + 18\delta x + 29$$

So,

$$\text{average rate of change of } y \text{ across } [3, 3 + \delta x] = \frac{\text{change in } y}{\text{change in } x}$$

$$= \frac{(3(\delta x)^2 + 18\delta x + 29) - 29}{\delta x}$$

$$= \frac{3(\delta x)^2 + 18\delta x}{\delta x}$$

$$= \frac{\delta x (3\delta x + 18)}{\delta x}$$

$$= 3\delta x + 18$$

We now let δx tend to 0, so that the interval shrinks to a point:

$$\text{rate of change of } y \text{ when } x \text{ is } 3 = \lim_{\delta x \to 0} (3\delta x + 18) = 18$$

We have found the rate of change of y at a particular value of x, rather than across an interval. We usually write

$$\text{rate of change of } y \text{ when } x \text{ is } 3 = \lim_{\delta x \to 0} \left(\frac{y(3 + \delta x) - y(3)}{\delta x} \right)$$

$$= \lim_{\delta x \to 0} \left(\frac{3(\delta x)^2 + 18\delta x}{\delta x} \right) = \lim_{\delta x \to 0} (3\delta x + 18)$$

$$= 18$$

Exercises 10.4

1 Find the rate of change of $y = 3x^2 + 2$ at

(a) $x = 4$ by considering the interval $[4, 4 + \delta x]$

(b) $x = -2$ by considering the interval $[-2, -2 + \delta x]$

(c) $x = 1$ by considering the interval $[1 - \delta x, 1 + \delta x]$

2 Find the rate of change of $y = 1/x$ at $x = 2$.

3 To determine the rate of change of $y = x^2 - x$ at $x = 1$ the interval $[1, 1 + \delta x]$ could be used. Equally the intervals $[1 - \delta x, 1]$ or $[1 - \delta x, 1 + \delta x]$ could be used. Show that the

same answer results regardless of which interval is used.

4 Find the rate of change of $y(x) = 2 - x^2$ at

(a) $x = 3$, by considering the interval $[3, 3 + \delta x]$

(b) $x = -5$, by considering the interval $[-5, -5 + \delta x]$

(c) $x = 1$, by considering the interval $[1 - \delta x, 1 + \delta x]$.

5 Find the rate of change of $y(x) = \dfrac{x}{x + 3}$ at $x = 3$ by considering the interval $[3, 3 + \delta x]$.

Solutions

1 (a) 24   (b) -12 (c) 6

2 -0.25

3 1

4 (a) -6 (b) 10   (c) -2

5 $\frac{1}{12}$

10.5 Rate of change at a general point

Example 10.5 shows that the rate of change of a function at a particular point can be found. We will now develop a general terminology for the method. Suppose we have a function of x, $y(x)$. We wish to find the rate of change of y at a general value of x. We begin by finding the average rate of change of $y(x)$ across an interval and then allow the interval to shrink to a single point. Consider the interval $[x, x + \delta x]$. At the beginning of the interval y has a value of $y(x)$. At the end of the interval y has a value of $y(x + \delta x)$ so that the change in y is $y(x + \delta x) - y(x)$, which we denote by δy (see Figure 10.9). So,

$$\text{average rate of change of } y = \frac{\text{change in } y}{\text{change in } x}$$

$$= \frac{y(x + \delta x) - y(x)}{\delta x} = \frac{\delta y}{\delta x}$$

Now let δx tend to 0, so that the interval shrinks to a point. Then

$$\text{rate of change of } y = \lim_{\delta x \to 0}\left(\frac{y(x + \delta x) - y(x)}{\delta x}\right) = \lim_{\delta x \to 0}\left(\frac{\delta y}{\delta x}\right)$$

To see how we proceed to evaluate this limit consider Example 10.6.

Figure 10.9
The rate of change of y
at a point is found by
letting $\delta x \to 0$.

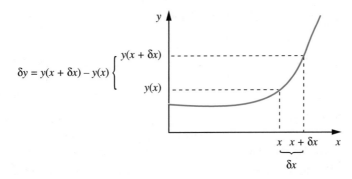

$$\delta y = y(x + \delta x) - y(x)$$

Example 10.6 Find the rate of change of $y(x) = 2x^2 + 3x$. Calculate the rate of change of y when $x = 2$ and when $x = -3$.

Solution Given $y(x) = 2x^2 + 3x$
then

$$y(x + \delta x) = 2(x + \delta x)^2 + 3(x + \delta x)$$
$$= 2x^2 + 4x\delta x + 2(\delta x)^2 + 3x + 3\delta x$$

Hence

$$y(x + \delta x) - y(x) = 2(\delta x)^2 + 4x\delta x + 3\delta x$$

So,

$$\text{rate of change of } y = \lim_{\delta x \to 0}\left(\frac{y(x + \delta x) - y(x)}{\delta x}\right)$$

$$= \lim_{\delta x \to 0}\left(\frac{2(\delta x)^2 + 4x\delta x + 3\delta x}{\delta x}\right)$$

$$= \lim_{\delta x \to 0}(2\delta x + 4x + 3) = 4x + 3$$

When $x = 2$, the rate of change of y is $4(2) + 3 = 11$. When $x = -3$, the rate of change of y is $4(-3) + 3 = -9$. A positive rate of change shows that the function is increasing at that particular point. A negative rate of change shows that the function is decreasing at that particular point.

The rate of change of y is called the **derivative** of y. We denote $\lim_{\delta x \to 0}\left(\frac{\delta y}{\delta x}\right)$ by $\frac{dy}{dx}$. This is pronounced 'dee y by dee x'.

$$\text{rate of change of } y(x) = \frac{dy}{dx} = \lim_{\delta x \to 0}\left(\frac{y(x + \delta x) - y(x)}{\delta x}\right)$$

Note that the notation $\frac{dy}{dx}$ means $\lim_{\delta x \to 0}\frac{\delta y}{\delta x}$.

Using the previous example, if

$$y(x) = 2x^2 + 3x$$

then

$$\frac{dy}{dx} = 4x + 3$$

$\frac{dy}{dx}$ is often abbreviated to y'

y' is pronounced 'y dash' or 'y prime'. To stress that y is the dependent variable and x the independent variable we often talk of 'the rate of change of y with respect to x', or more compactly, 'the rate of change of y w.r.t. x'. The process of finding y' from y is called **differentiation**. This shrinking interval method of finding the derivative is called **differentiation from first principles**. We know that the derivative $\frac{dy}{dx}$ is the gradient of the tangent to the function at a point. It is also the rate of change of the function. In many examples, the independent variable is t and we need to find the rate of change of y with respect to t; that is, find $\frac{dy}{dt}$. This is also often written as y' although $\dot{y}$, pronounced 'y dot', is also common. The reader should be aware of both notations. Finally, y' is used to denote the derivative of y whatever the independent variable may be. So $\frac{dy}{dz}$, $\frac{dy}{dr}$ and $\frac{dy}{dw}$ could all be represented by y'.

Example 10.7   Find the gradient of the tangent to $y = x^2$ at $A(1, 1)$, $B(-1, 1)$ and $C(2, 4)$.

Solution   We have $y = x^2$ and so

$$y(x + \delta x) = (x + \delta x)^2$$
$$= x^2 + 2x\delta x + (\delta x)^2$$

and hence

$$y(x + \delta x) - y(x) = x^2 + 2x\delta x + (\delta x)^2 - x^2$$
$$= 2x\delta x + (\delta x)^2$$

Then

$$\frac{dy}{dx} = \text{gradient of a tangent to curve}$$
$$= \lim_{\delta x \to 0} \left(\frac{y(x + \delta x) - y(x)}{\delta x} \right)$$
$$= \lim_{\delta x \to 0} \left(\frac{(x + \delta x)^2 - x^2}{\delta x} \right) = \lim_{\delta x \to 0} \left(\frac{2x\delta x + (\delta x)^2}{\delta x} \right)$$
$$= \lim_{\delta x \to 0} (2x + \delta x) = 2x$$

At (1, 1), $\dfrac{dy}{dx} = 2 =$ gradient of tangent at A. At $(-1, 1)$, $\dfrac{dy}{dx} = -2 =$ gradient of tangent at B. At (2, 4), $\dfrac{dy}{dx} = 4 =$ gradient of tangent at C.

Suppose we wish to evaluate the derivative, $\dfrac{dy}{dx}$, at a specific value of x, say x_0. This is denoted by

$$\dfrac{dy}{dx}(x = x_0) \qquad \text{or more compactly by} \quad \dfrac{dy}{dx}(x_0) \qquad \text{or } y'(x_0)$$

An alternative notation is

$$\left.\dfrac{dy}{dx}\right|_{x=x_0} \qquad \text{or} \qquad \left.\dfrac{dy}{dx}\right|_{x_0}$$

So, for Example 10.7 we could have written

$$\dfrac{dy}{dx}(1) = 2 \qquad \dfrac{dy}{dx}(x = -1) = -2 \qquad \left.\dfrac{dy}{dx}\right|_{x=2} = 4 \qquad y'(2) = 4$$

Example 10.8 Refer to Figure 10.10. By considering the gradient of the tangent at the points A, B, C, D and E state whether $\dfrac{dy}{dx}$ is positive, negative or zero at these points.

Solution At A and C the tangent is parallel to the x axis and so $\dfrac{dy}{dx}$ is zero. At B and E the tangent has a positive gradient and so $\dfrac{dy}{dx}$ is positive. At D the tangent has a negative gradient and thus $\dfrac{dy}{dx}$ is negative.

As we saw in Chapter 3, functions are used to represent physically important quantities such as voltage and current. When the current through certain devices changes, this can give rise to voltages, the magnitudes of which are proportional to the rate of change of the current. Consequently differentiation is needed to model these effects as illustrated in Examples 10.9 and 10.10.

Figure 10.10
Graph for
Example 10.8.

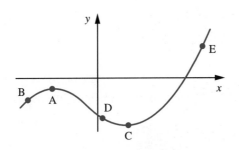

Example 10.9

Voltage across an inductor

The voltage, v, across an inductor with inductance, L, is related to the current, i, through the inductor by

$$v = L\frac{di}{dt}$$

This relationship is a quantification of Faraday's law which states that the voltage induced in a coil is proportional to the rate of change of magnetic flux through it. If the current in a coil is changing then this corresponds to a change in the magnetic flux through the coil. Note that if $\frac{di}{dt}$ is large then v is large.

Example 10.10

Current through a capacitor

The current, i, through a capacitor with capacitance, C, is related to the voltage, v, across the capacitor by

$$i = C\frac{dv}{dt}$$

It may appear confusing to talk of a current flow through a capacitor as no actual charge flows through the capacitor apart from that caused by any leakage current. Instead there is a build-up of charge on the plates of the capacitor. This in turn gives rise to a voltage across the capacitor. If the current flow is large then the rate of change of this voltage will be large. The current flow through the capacitor wires is termed a **conduction current** while that between the capacitor plates is called a **displacement current**.

We can relate the small changes δx and δy to the derivative $\frac{dy}{dx}$.

If δx is very small yet still finite we can state that

$$\frac{dy}{dx} \approx \frac{\delta y}{\delta x} \tag{10.1}$$

This result allows an important approximation to be made. From Equation (10.1) we see that if a small change, δx, is made to the independent variable, the corresponding change in the dependent variable is given by the following formula:

$$\delta y \approx \frac{dy}{dx}\delta x$$

Example 10.11

If $y = x^2$ estimate the change in y caused by changing x from 3 to 3.1.

Solution

If $y = x^2$ then $\frac{dy}{dx} = 2x$. The approximate change in the dependent variable is given by

$$\delta y \approx \frac{dy}{dx}\delta x = 2x\delta x$$

Taking $x = 3$ and $\delta x = 0.1$ we have

$$\delta y \approx (2)(3)(0.1) = 0.6$$

We conclude that at the point where $x = 3$ a change in x to 3.1 causes an approximate change of 0.6 in the value of y.

Exercises 10.5

1   Calculate the gradient of the functions at the specified points.

   (a) $y = 2x^2$ at (1, 2)

   (b) $y = 2x - x^2$ at (0, 0)

   (c) $y = 1 + x + x^2$ at (2, 7)

   (d) $y = 2x^2 + 1$ at (2, 9)

2   A function, y, is such that $\dfrac{dy}{dx}$ is constant. What can you say about the function, y?

3   For which graphs in Figure 10.11 is the derivative always (a) positive or (b) negative?

4   Find the derivative of $y(x)$ where y is

   (a) x^2

   (b) $-x^2 + 2x$

5   Differentiate $y = 2x^2 + 9$; that is, find $\dfrac{dy}{dx}$. What is the rate of change of y when $x = 3, -2, 1, 0$?

6   Find the rate of change of $y = 4t - t^2$. What is the value of $\dfrac{dy}{dt}$ when $t = 2$?

7   If $y = x^3 - 3x^2 + x$ then

$$\frac{dy}{dx} = 3x^2 - 6x + 1$$

Estimate the change in y as x changes from

   (a) 2 to 2.05

   (b) 0 to 0.025

   (c) -1 to -1.05

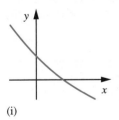 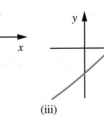

(i)   (ii)   (iii)   (iv)

Figure 10.11

Solutions

1   (a) 4   (b) 2   (c) 5   (d) 8

2   y is linear in x, that is $y = ax + b$

3   (i) always negative   (ii) always positive

   (iii) always positive   (iv) always negative

4   (a) $2x$ (b) $-2x + 2$

5   $4x$, 12, $-8, 4, 0$

6   $4 - 2t, 0$

7   (a) 0.05   (b) 0.025   (c) -0.5

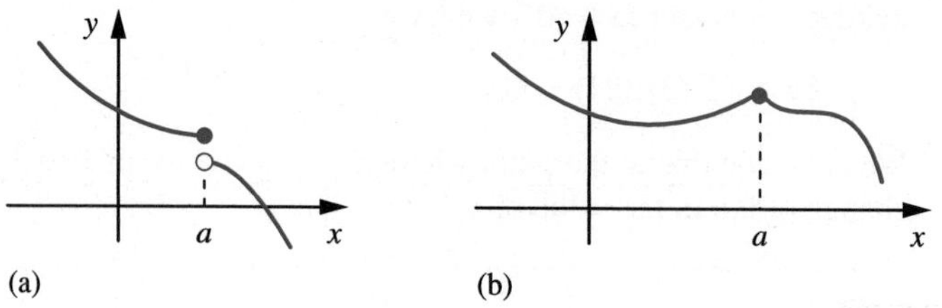

Figure 10.12
(a) The graph has a discontinuity at $x = a$.
(b) The graph has a cusp at $x = a$.

(a)   (b)

10.6 Existence of derivatives

So far we have seen that the derivative, $\dfrac{dy}{dx}$, of a function, $y(x)$, may be viewed either algebraically or geometrically.

$$\frac{dy}{dx} = \lim_{\delta x \to 0} \left(\frac{y(x + \delta x) - y(x)}{\delta x} \right)$$

$$\frac{dy}{dx} = \text{rate of change of } y$$

$$= \text{gradient of the graph of } y$$

We now discuss briefly the existence of $\dfrac{dy}{dx}$. For some functions the derivative does not exist at certain points and we need to be able to recognize such points. Consider the graphs shown in Figure 10.12. Figure 10.12(a) shows a function with a discontinuity at $x = a$. The function shown in Figure 10.12(b) is continuous but has a **cusp** or **corner** at $x = a$. In both cases it is impossible to draw a tangent at $x = a$, and so $\dfrac{dy}{dx}$ does not exist at $x = a$. It is impossible to draw a tangent to a curve at a point where the curve is not smooth. Note from Figure 10.12(b) that continuity is not sufficient to guarantee the existence of a derivative.

Example 10.12   Sketch the following functions. State the values of t for which the derivative does not exist.

(a) $y = |t|$ (b) $y = \tan t$ (c) $y = 1/t$

Solution   (a) The graph of $y = |t|$ is shown in Figure 10.13(a). A corner exists at $t = 0$ and so the derivative does not exist here.

(b) A graph of $y = \tan t$ is shown in Figure 10.13(b). There is a discontinuity in $\tan t$ when $t = \ldots - 3\pi/2, -\pi/2, \pi/2, 3\pi/2, \ldots$. No derivative exists at these points.

(c) Figure 10.13(c) shows a graph of $y = 1/t$. The function has one discontinuity at $t = 0$, and so the derivative does not exist here.

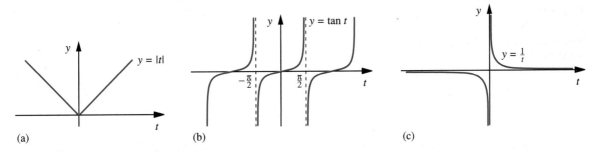

Figure 10.13 (a) There is a corner at $t = 0$; (b) $\tan t$ has discontinuities; (c) $y = 1/t$ has a discontinuity at $t = 0$.

Exercises 10.6

1 Sketch the functions and determine any points where a derivative does not exist.

(a) $y = \dfrac{1}{t-1}$

(b) $y = |\sin t|$

(c) $y = e^t$

(d) $y = |1/t|$

(e) The unit step function $u(t) = \begin{cases} 1 & t \geqslant 0 \\ 0 & t < 0 \end{cases}$

(f) The ramp function $f(t) = \begin{cases} ct & t \geqslant 0 \\ 0 & t < 0 \end{cases}$

Solutions

1 See Figure S.17.

(a) No derivative exists for $t = 1$

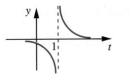

(b) No derivative exists for $t = n\pi$

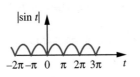

(c) Derivative exists for all values of t

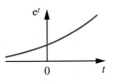

(d) No derivative exists for $t = 0$

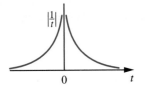

(e) No derivative exists for $t = 0$

(f) No derivative exists for $t = 0$, although the function is continuous here

Figure S.17

Table 10.1
Derivatives of
commonly used
functions.

Function, $y(x)$	Derivative, y'	Function, $y(x)$	Derivative, y'
constant	0	$\cos^{-1}(ax+b)$	$\dfrac{-a}{\sqrt{1-(ax+b)^2}}$
x^n	nx^{n-1}		
e^x	e^x	$\tan^{-1}(ax+b)$	$\dfrac{a}{1+(ax+b)^2}$
e^{-x}	$-e^{-x}$		
e^{ax}	ae^{ax}	$\sinh(ax+b)$	$a\cosh(ax+b)$
		$\cosh(ax+b)$	$a\sinh(ax+b)$
$\ln x$	$\dfrac{1}{x}$	$\tanh(ax+b)$	$a\,\text{sech}^2(ax+b)$
$\sin x$	$\cos x$	$\text{cosech}(ax+b)$	$-a\,\text{cosech}(ax+b)\times$
$\cos x$	$-\sin x$		$\coth(ax+b)$
$\sin(ax+b)$	$a\cos(ax+b)$	$\text{sech}(ax+b)$	$-a\,\text{sech}(ax+b)\times$
$\cos(ax+b)$	$-a\sin(ax+b)$		$\tanh(ax+b)$
$\tan(ax+b)$	$a\sec^2(ax+b)$	$\coth(ax+b)$	$-a\,\text{cosech}^2(ax+b)$
$\text{cosec}(ax+b)$	$-a\,\text{cosec}(ax+b)\cot(ax+b)$	$\sinh^{-1}(ax+b)$	$\dfrac{a}{\sqrt{(ax+b)^2+1}}$
$\sec(ax+b)$	$a\sec(ax+b)\tan(ax+b)$		
$\cot(ax+b)$	$-a\,\text{cosec}^2(ax+b)$	$\cosh^{-1}(ax+b)$	$\dfrac{a}{\sqrt{(ax+b)^2-1}}$
$\sin^{-1}(ax+b)$	$\dfrac{a}{\sqrt{1-(ax+b)^2}}$	$\tanh^{-1}(ax+b)$	$\dfrac{a}{1-(ax+b)^2}$

10.7 Common derivatives

It is time consuming to find the derivative of $y(x)$ using the 'shrinking interval' method (often referred to as **differentiation from first principles**). Consequently the derivatives of commonly used functions are listed for reference in Table 10.1. It will be helpful to memorize the most common derivatives. Note that a, b and n are constants. In the trigonometric functions, the quantity $ax+b$, being an angle, must be measured in radians.

A shorter table of the more common derivatives is given on the inside back cover of this book for easy reference.

Example 10.13 Use Table 10.1 to find y' when

(a) $y = e^{-7x}$

(b) $y = x^5$

(c) $y = \tan(3x-2)$

(d) $y = \sin(\omega x + \phi)$

(e) $y = \dfrac{1}{\sqrt{x}}$

(f) $y = \dfrac{1}{x^5}$

(g) $y = \cosh^{-1} 5x$

Solution (a) From Table 10.1, we find that if

$$y = e^{ax} \qquad \text{then} \qquad y' = a\,e^{ax}$$

In this case, $a = -7$ and so if

$$y = e^{-7x} \qquad \text{then} \qquad y' = -7\,e^{-7x}$$

(b) From Table 10.1, we find that if

$$y = x^n \qquad \text{then} \qquad y' = nx^{n-1}$$

In this case, $n = 5$ and so if

$$y = x^5 \qquad \text{then} \qquad y' = 5x^4$$

(c) If $y = \tan(ax + b)$ then $y' = a\sec^2(ax + b)$. In this case, $a = 3$ and $b = -2$. Hence if

$$y = \tan(3x - 2) \qquad \text{then} \qquad y' = 3\sec^2(3x - 2)$$

(d) If $y = \sin(ax + b)$ then $y' = a\cos(ax + b)$. Here $a = \omega$ and $b = \phi$, and so if

$$y = \sin(\omega x + \phi) \qquad \text{then} \qquad y' = \omega\cos(\omega x + \phi)$$

(e) Note that $\dfrac{1}{\sqrt{x}} = x^{-1/2}$. From Table 10.1 we find that if $y = x^n$ then $y' = nx^{n-1}$. In this case, $n = -1/2$ and so if

$$y = \dfrac{1}{\sqrt{x}} \qquad \text{then} \qquad y' = -\dfrac{1}{2}x^{-3/2}$$

(f) Note that $\dfrac{1}{x^5} = x^{-5}$. Using Table 10.1, we find that if $y = x^{-5}$ then $y' = -5x^{-6}$.

(g) From Table 10.1, if $y = \cosh^{-1}(ax + b)$ then

$$y' = \dfrac{a}{\sqrt{(ax + b)^2 - 1}}$$

In this case, $a = 5$ and $b = 0$. Hence, if

$$y = \cosh^{-1} 5x \qquad \text{then} \qquad y' = \dfrac{5}{\sqrt{25x^2 - 1}}$$

Example 10.14 Differentiate $y(t) = e^t$.

Solution We note that the independent variable is t. However, Table 10.1 can still be used. From Table 10.1, we find

$$\frac{dy}{dt} = e^t = y$$

We note that the derivative of e^t is again e^t. This is the only function which reproduces itself upon differentiation.

Exercises 10.7

1 Use Table 10.1 to find y' given:

(a) $y = t^2$

(b) $y = t^9$

(c) $y = t^{-3}$

(d) $y = t$

(e) $y = \dfrac{1}{t}$

(f) $y = \dfrac{1}{t^2}$

(g) $y = e^{3t}$

(h) $y = e^{-3t}$

(i) $y = \dfrac{1}{e^{5t}}$

(j) $y = t^{1/2}$

(k) $y = \sin(2t + 3)$

(l) $y = \cos(4 - t)$

(m) $y = \tan\left(\dfrac{t}{2} + 1\right)$

(n) $y = \mathrm{cosec}(3t + 7)$

(o) $y = \cot(1 - t)$

(p) $y = \sec(2t - \pi)$

(q) $y = \sin^{-1}(t + \pi)$

(r) $y = \pi$

(s) $y = \tan^{-1}(-2t - 1)$

(t) $y = \cos^{-1}(4t - 3)$

(u) $y = \tanh(6t)$

(v) $y = \cosh(2t + 5)$

(w) $y = \sinh\left(\dfrac{t + 3}{2}\right)$

(x) $y = \mathrm{sech}(-t)$

(y) $y = \coth\left(\dfrac{2t}{3} - \dfrac{1}{2}\right)$

(z) $y = \cosh^{-1}(t + 3)$

2 Find $\dfrac{dy}{dx}$ when

(a) $y = \dfrac{1}{\sqrt{x}}$

(b) $y = e^{2x/3}$

(c) $y = e^{-x/2}$

(d) $y = \ln x$

(e) $y = \mathrm{cosec}\left(\dfrac{2x - 1}{3}\right)$

(f) $y = \tan^{-1}(\pi x + 3)$

(g) $y = \tanh(2x + 1)$

(h) $y = \sinh^{-1}(-3x)$

(i) $y = \cot(\omega x + \pi)$ ω constant

(j) $y = \dfrac{1}{\sin(5x + 3)}$

(k) $y = \cos 3x$

(l) $y = \dfrac{1}{\cos 3x}$

(m) $y = \tan(2x + \pi)$

(n) $y = \mathrm{cosech}\left(\dfrac{x - 1}{2}\right)$

(o) $y = \tanh^{-1}\left(\dfrac{2x + 3}{7}\right)$

Solutions

1 (a) $2t$

(b) $9t^8$

(c) $-3t^{-4}$

(d) 1

(e) $-t^{-2}$

(f) $-2t^{-3}$

(g) $3e^{3t}$

(h) $-3e^{-3t}$

(i) $-5e^{-5t}$

(j) $0.5t^{-1/2}$

(k) $2\cos(2t+3)$

(l) $\sin(4-t)$

(m) $0.5\sec^2(t/2+1)$

(n) $-3\cosec(3t+7)\cot(3t+7)$

(o) $\cosec^2(1-t)$

(p) $2\sec(2t-\pi)\tan(2t-\pi)$

(q) $\dfrac{1}{\sqrt{1-(t+\pi)^2}}$

(r) 0

(s) $-\dfrac{2}{1+(-2t-1)^2}$

(t) $-\dfrac{4}{\sqrt{1-(4t-3)^2}}$

(u) $6\,\text{sech}^2\,6t$

(v) $2\sinh(2t+5)$

(w) $0.5\cosh\left(\dfrac{t+3}{2}\right)$

(x) $\text{sech}(-t)\tanh(-t)$

(y) $-\dfrac{2}{3}\text{cosech}^2\left(\dfrac{2t}{3}-\dfrac{1}{2}\right)$

(z) $\dfrac{1}{\sqrt{(t+3)^2-1}}$

2 (a) $-0.5x^{-3/2}$

(b) $\frac{2}{3}e^{2x/3}$

(c) $-0.5e^{-x/2}$

(d) $1/x$

(e) $-\dfrac{2}{3}\cosec\left(\dfrac{2x-1}{3}\right)\cot\left(\dfrac{2x-1}{3}\right)$

(f) $\dfrac{\pi}{1+(\pi x+3)^2}$

(g) $2\,\text{sech}^2(2x+1)$

(h) $-\dfrac{3}{\sqrt{9x^2+1}}$

(i) $-\omega\cosec^2(\omega x+\pi)$

(j) $-5\cosec(5x+3)\cot(5x+3)$

(k) $-3\sin 3x$

(l) $3\sec 3x\tan 3x$

(m) $2\sec^2(2x+\pi)$

(n) $-0.5\,\text{cosech}\left(\dfrac{x-1}{2}\right)\coth\left(\dfrac{x-1}{2}\right)$

(o) $\dfrac{2}{7\left[1-\left(\dfrac{2x+3}{7}\right)^2\right]}$

10.8 Differentiation as a linear operator

In mathematical language differentiation is a **linear operator**. This means that if we wish to differentiate the sum of two functions we can differentiate each function separately and then simply add the two derivatives, that is

derivative of $(f+g)$ = derivative of f + derivative of g

This is expressed mathematically as

$$\frac{\text{d}}{\text{d}x}(f+g) = \frac{\text{d}f}{\text{d}x} + \frac{\text{d}g}{\text{d}x}$$

We can regard $\dfrac{d}{dx}$ as the operation of differentiation being applied to the expression which follows it. The properties of a linear operator also make the handling of constant factors easy. To differentiate kf, where k is a constant, we take k times the derivative of f, that is

$$\text{derivative of } (kf) = k \times \text{derivative of } f$$

Mathematically, we would state:

$$\frac{d}{dx}(kf) = k\frac{df}{dx}$$

Table 10.1 together with these two linearity properties allows us to differentiate some quite complicated functions.

Example 10.15   Differentiate

(a) $3x^2$ (b) $9x$ (c) 7 (d) $3x^2 + 9x + 7$

Solution   (a) Let $y = 3x^2$, then

$$\frac{dy}{dx} = \frac{d}{dx}(3x^2)$$

$$= 3\frac{d}{dx}(x^2) \text{ using linearity}$$

$$= 3(2x) \text{ from the table}$$

$$= 6x$$

(b) Let $y = 9x$, then

$$\frac{dy}{dx} = \frac{d}{dx}(9x)$$

$$= 9\frac{d}{dx}(x) \text{ using linearity}$$

$$= 9$$

(c) Let $y = 7$, then $y' = 0$.

(d) Let $y = 3x^2 + 9x + 7$

$$\frac{dy}{dx} = \frac{d}{dx}(3x^2 + 9x + 7)$$

$$\frac{dy}{dx} = 3\frac{d}{dx}(x^2) + 9\frac{d}{dx}(x) + \frac{d}{dx}(7) \text{ using linearity}$$

$$= 6x + 9$$

Example 10.16

Fluid flow into a tank

If fluid is being poured into a tank at a rate of q m^3 s^{-1}, then this will result in an increase in volume, V, of fluid in the tank. The rate of increase in volume, $\dfrac{dV}{dt}$ m^3 s^{-1}, is given by

$$\frac{dV}{dt} = q$$

This relationship follows from the principle of conservation of mass. If q is large, then $\dfrac{dV}{dt}$ is large, which corresponds to the fluid volume in the tank increasing at a fast rate. Consequently, the height of the fluid, h, also increases at a fast rate. If the cross-sectional area of the tank, A, is constant, then $V = Ah$. Therefore,

$$\frac{dV}{dt} = \frac{d}{dt}(Ah) = A\frac{dh}{dt}$$

because differentiation is a linear operator. So,

$$A\frac{dh}{dt} = q$$

Example 10.17

Use Table 10.1 and the linearity properties of differentiation to find y' where

(a) $y = 3\,e^{2x}$

(b) $y = 1/x$

(c) $y = 3\sin 4x$

(d) $y = \sin 2x - \cos 5x$

(e) $y = 3\ln x$

(f) $y = \ln 2x$

(g) $y = 3x^2 + 7x - 5$

Solution

(a) If $y = 3\,e^{2x}$, then

$$\frac{dy}{dx} = \frac{d}{dx}(3e^{2x}) = 3\frac{d}{dx}(e^{2x}) \qquad \text{using linearity}$$

$$= 3(2e^{2x}) \qquad \text{using Table 10.1}$$

$$= 6\,e^{2x}$$

(b) If $y = x^{-1}$, then

$$y' = -1x^{-2} \qquad \text{from Table 10.1}$$

$$= -\frac{1}{x^2}$$

(c) If $y = 3 \sin 4x$, then

$$\frac{dy}{dx} = \frac{d}{dx}(3 \sin 4x) = 3\frac{d}{dx}(\sin 4x) \qquad \text{using linearity}$$

$$= 3(4 \cos 4x) \qquad \text{using Table 10.1}$$

$$= 12 \cos 4x$$

(d) The linearity properties allow us to differentiate each term individually. If,

$$y = \sin 2x - \cos 5x \qquad \text{then} \qquad \frac{dy}{dx} = \frac{d}{dx}(\sin 2x) - \frac{d}{dx}(\cos 5x)$$

$$= 2 \cos 2x + 5 \sin 5x$$

(e) If $y = 3 \ln x$, then

$$\frac{dy}{dx} = \frac{d}{dx}(3 \ln x) = 3\frac{d}{dx}(\ln x) \qquad \text{using linearity}$$

$$= \frac{3}{x} \qquad \text{using Table 10.1}$$

(f) If $y = \ln 2x$, then

$$y = \ln 2 + \ln x \qquad \text{using laws of logarithms}$$

and so

$$\frac{dy}{dx} = 0 + \frac{1}{x} = \frac{1}{x} \qquad \text{since } \ln 2 \text{ is constant}$$

(g) Each term is differentiated:

$$y' = 6x + 7 - 0 = 6x + 7$$

Example 10.18   **Small-signal resistance**

In Chapter 2, Example 2.18, we examined the mathematical model of a semiconductor diode. At room temperature this was

$$I = I_s(e^{40V} - 1)$$

where I is the diode current, V is the applied voltage and I_s is the constant reverse saturation current. Sometimes when a diode is used in a circuit it may be **biased** to operate in a certain region of its I–V characteristic. This means that its use is restricted to a certain voltage range. The point around which it operates is known as its **operating point**. This is illustrated in Figure 10.14.

Deviations from this operating point may be small in certain cases. If so, they are known as **small-signal** variations and are caused by small a.c. voltages being super-imposed on the main d.c. bias voltage. In calculating how the diode will react to such small-signal voltages, the slope of the diode characteristic around the operating point is

Figure 10.14
Diode characteristic
showing operating
point.

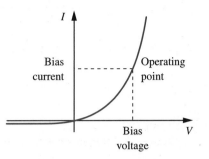

more relevant than the overall ratio of current to voltage. Provided the deviations from the operating point are not large, the tangent to the I–V curve at the operating point provides an adequate model for how the diode will behave. The slope of the curve can be obtained by differentiating the diode equation. If

$$I = I_s(e^{40V} - 1) = I_s e^{40V} - I_s$$

then

$$\frac{\mathrm{d}I}{\mathrm{d}V} = 40I_s\, e^{40V}$$

since I_s is constant.

It is usual to write small changes in current and voltage as δI and δV. Therefore, since

$$\frac{\delta I}{\delta V} \approx \frac{\mathrm{d}I}{\mathrm{d}V}$$

$$\delta I \approx 40I_s\, e^{40V}\, \delta V$$

This expression allows the change in diode current, δI, to be estimated given a change in diode voltage, δV, provided the operating point is known and the changes are small.

Example 10.19 Find the derivative of $y = e^{-t} + t^2$, when

(a) $t = 1$

(b) $t = 0$

Solution
$$y = e^{-t} + t^2$$
$$y' = -e^{-t} + 2t$$

(a) When $t = 1$, $y' = -e^{-1} + 2 = 1.632$, that is $y'(1) = 1.632$.

(b) When $t = 0$, $y' = -1$, that is $y'(0) = -1$.

Figure 10.15
A fluid system
comprising pump, tank
and valve.

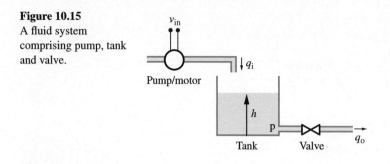

Example 10.20   Obtaining a linear model for a simple fluid system

Consider the fluid system illustrated in Figure 10.15. The pump is driven by a d.c. motor. The pump/motor can be modelled by a linear relationship in which the fluid flow rate, q_i, is proportional to the control voltage, v_{in}, that is

$$q_i = k_p v_{in}$$

where k_p = pump/motor constant, v_{in} = control voltage (V), q_i = flow rate into the tank (m³ s⁻¹). The valve has a non-linear characteristic given by the quadratic polynomial

$$p = 20\,000\, q_o^2$$

where p = pressure at the base of the tank (N m⁻²), q_o = flow out of the tank (m³ s⁻¹). The fluid being used is water which has a density $\rho = 998$ kg m⁻³. Assume $g = 9.81$ m s⁻² and that $k_p = 0.03$ m³ s⁻¹V⁻¹. Carry out the following:

(a) Calculate the flow rate out of the tank, q_o, and the control voltage, v_{in}, when the system is in equilibrium and the height of the water in the tank, h, is 0.25 m.

(b) Obtain a linear model for the system, valid for small changes about a water height of 0.25 m. Use this model to calculate the new water height and flow rate out of the tank when the control voltage is increased by 0.4 V.

Solution   (a) The pressure at the bottom of the tank is given by

$$p = \rho g h = 998 \times 9.81 \times 0.25 = 2448$$

The flow rate through the valve is given by

$$q_o^2 = \frac{p}{20\,000}$$

$$q_o = \sqrt{\frac{p}{20\,000}} = \sqrt{\frac{2448}{20\,000}} = 0.350 \text{ m}^3 \text{ s}^{-1}$$

Now if the system is in equilibrium, then the height of the water in the tank must have stabilized to a constant value. Therefore,

$$q_i = q_o = 0.350$$

and so

$$v_{in} = \frac{q_i}{k_p} = \frac{0.350}{0.03} = 11.7 \text{ V}$$

Figure 10.16
Relationship between
pressure across valve
(p) and flow through
valve (q_o).

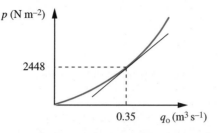

(b) Before answering this part it is worth examining what is meant by a **linear model**. Figure 10.16 shows the valve characteristic together with a linear approximation around an output flow rate of $q_o = 0.350$ m^3 s^{-1}. This corresponds to a water height of 0.25 m.

A linear model for the valve is one in which the relationship between p and q_o is approximated by the straight line which forms a tangent to the curve at the operating point. The operating point is the point around which the model is valid. It is clear that if the straight line approximation is used for points that are a large distance from the operating point, then the linear model will not be very accurate. However, for small changes around the operating point the approximation is reasonably accurate. Clearly a different operating point will require a different linear approximation. In order to obtain the gradient of this line it is necessary to differentiate the function relating valve pressure to valve flow. So,

$$p = 20\,000 q_o^2$$

$$\frac{dp}{dq_o} = 40\,000 q_o$$

At the operating point $q_o = 0.350$. Therefore,

$$\left. \frac{dp}{dq_o} \right|_{q_o = 0.350} = 40\,000 \times 0.350 = 14\,000$$

This value is the gradient of the tangent to the curve at the operating point. Small changes around an operating point are usually indicated by the notation δ. Therefore,

$$\frac{\delta p}{\delta q_o} \approx \left. \frac{dp}{dq_o} \right|_{q_o = 0.350} = 14\,000$$

$$\delta p = 14\,000 \delta q_o \tag{10.2}$$

Note that equality has been assumed for the purposes of the linear model. It is easy to relate a change in pump flow to a change in control voltage because the relationship is linear and so a linear approximation is not required. So,

$$q_i = k_p v_{in}$$

Differentiating this equation w.r.t. v_{in} yields

$$\frac{dq_i}{dv_{in}} = k_p$$

In this case

$$\frac{\delta q_i}{\delta v_{in}} = \frac{dq_i}{dv_{in}} = k_p$$

and has a constant value independent of the operating point:

$$\delta q_i = k_p \, \delta v_{in} \tag{10.3}$$

The relationship between pressure at the bottom of the tank and the water height is also linear.

Since $p = \rho g h$ we have $\dfrac{dp}{dh} = \rho g$. Because $\dfrac{dp}{dh}$ is a constant we can write

$$\frac{\delta p}{\delta h} = \frac{dp}{dh} = \rho g$$

$$\delta p = \rho g \, \delta h \tag{10.4}$$

The change in control voltage, δv_{in}, is given as 0.4. We also know that $k_p = 0.03$. Therefore, using Equation (10.3), we have

$$\delta q_i = 0.03 \times 0.4 = 0.012$$

Now if time is allowed for the system to reach equilibrium with this increased input flow, then $\delta q_o = \delta q_i$. In other words, the output flow increases by the same amount as the input flow and the water height once again stabilizes to a fixed value. Therefore,

$$\delta q_o = \delta q_i = 0.012$$

Using Equation (10.2), we find

$$\delta p = 14\,000 \, \delta q_o = 14\,000 \times 0.012 = 168$$

Using Equation (10.4), we get

$$\delta h = \frac{\delta p}{\rho g} = \frac{168}{998 \times 9.81} = 0.0172$$

Therefore the new water height is $0.25 + 0.0172 = 0.267$ m to three significant figures. The new water flow rate is $0.35 + 0.012 = 0.362$ m^3 s^{-1}.

To recap, all the elements of the fluid system were linear apart from the valve. By obtaining a linear model for the valve, valid for values close to the operating point, it was possible to calculate the effect of changing the control voltage to the motor. It is important to stress that the linear model for the valve is only good for small changes around the operating point. In this case the increase in control voltage was approximately 3%. The model would not have been very good for predicting the effect of a 50% increase in control voltage. Linear models of non-linear systems are particularly useful when several components are non-linear, as they are much easier to analyse. We examine these concepts in more detail in Chapter 18.

Exercises 10.8

1 Differentiate the following functions.

(a) $y = 4x^3 - 5x^2$

(b) $y = 3\sin(5t) + 2e^{4t}$

(c) $y = \sin(4t) + 3\cos(2t) - t$

(d) $y = \tan(3z)$

(e) $y = 2e^{3t} + 17 - 4\sin(2t)$

(f) $y = \dfrac{1}{t^3} + \dfrac{\cos 5t}{2}$

(g) $y = \dfrac{2w^3}{3} + \dfrac{e^{4w}}{2}$

(h) $y = \sqrt{x} + \ln(\sqrt{x})$. [*Hint:* $\sqrt{x} = x^{1/2}$, and use the laws of logarithms.]

2 Evaluate the derivatives of the functions at the given value.

(a) $y = 2t + 9 + e^{t/2}$ $t = 1$

(b) $y = \dfrac{t^2 - 4t + 6}{3}$ $t = 2$

(c) $y = \sin t + \cos t$ $t = 1$

(d) $y = 3e^{2t} - 2\sin\left(\dfrac{t}{2}\right)$ $t = 0$

(e) $y = 5\tan(2x) + \dfrac{1}{e^{2x}}$ $x = 0.5$

(f) $y = 3\ln t + \sin(3t)$ $t = 0.25$

3 Find $\dfrac{dx}{dt}$, if

(a) $x = e^{\omega t}$

(b) $x = e^{-\omega t}$

where ω is a constant.

4 Find the derivative of

(a) $y = 3\sin^{-1}(2t) - 5\cos^{-1}(3t)$

(b) $y = \frac{1}{2}\tan^{-1}(t + 2) + 4\cos^{-1}(2t - 1)$

(c) $y = 2\sinh(3t - 1) - 4\cosh\left(\dfrac{t - 3}{2}\right)$

(d) $y = \dfrac{\operatorname{cosech}(4t) + 3\operatorname{sech}(6t)}{2}$

(e) $y = 2\sinh^{-1}\left(\dfrac{t + 1}{2}\right) - 3\cosh^{-1}\left(\dfrac{1 - t}{2}\right)$

(f) $y = 3\tanh^{-1}(2t + 3) - 2\tanh^{-1}(3t + 2)$

5 A function, $y(t)$, is given by

$$y(t) = \frac{t^3}{3} - \frac{5t^2}{2} + 4t + 1$$

(a) Find $\dfrac{dy}{dt}$.

(b) For which values of t is the derivative zero?

6 Find the equation of the tangent to the curve

$$y(x) = x^3 + 7x^2 - 9$$

at the point $(2, 27)$.

7 Find values of t in the interval $[0, \pi]$ for which the tangent to $x(t) = \sin 2t$ has zero gradient.

8 Find the rate of change of

$$z(t) = 2e^{t/2} - t^2$$

when

(a) $t = 0$

(b) $t = 3$

Solutions

1 (a) $12x^2 - 10x$

(b) $15\cos 5t + 8e^{4t}$

(c) $4\cos 4t - 6\sin 2t - 1$

(d) $3\sec^2 3z$

(e) $6e^{3t} - 8\cos 2t$

(f) $-\dfrac{3}{t^4} - 2.5\sin 5t$

(g) $2w^2 + 2e^{4w}$

(h) $0.5x^{-1/2} + \dfrac{1}{2x}$

2 (a) 2.8244   (b) 0

(c) −0.3012   (d) 5

(e) 33.5194   (f) 14.195

3 (a) $\omega e^{\omega t}$ (b) $-\omega e^{-\omega t}$

4 (a) $\dfrac{6}{\sqrt{1-4t^2}} + \dfrac{15}{\sqrt{1-9t^2}}$

(b) $\dfrac{1}{2[1+(t+2)^2]} - \dfrac{4}{\sqrt{t(1-t)}}$

(c) $6\cosh(3t-1) - 2\sinh\dfrac{t-3}{2}$

(d) $-2\operatorname{cosech}4t \coth 4t - 9\operatorname{sech}6t \tanh 6t$

(e) $\dfrac{1}{\sqrt{\left(\frac{1}{2}(t+1)\right)^2+1}} + \dfrac{3}{2\sqrt{\left(\frac{1}{2}(1-t)\right)^2-1}}$

(f) $\dfrac{6}{1-(2t+3)^2} - \dfrac{6}{1-(3t+2)^2}$

5 (a) $t^2 - 5t + 4$ (b) $1, 4$

6 $y = 40x - 53$

7 $\pi/4,\ 3\pi/4$

8 (a) 1 (b) -1.5183

Review exercises 10

1 Find the rate of change of $f(x) = 5 + 3x^2$ at $x = 2$ by considering each of the intervals $[2-\delta x, 2], [2, 2+\delta x], [2-\delta x, 2+\delta x]$. Show that the same result is obtained in each case.

2 Use a table of derivatives and the linearity rules to differentiate

(a) $y = 4x^2 + 6x - 11$
(b) $y = -x^2 + 2x - 10$
(c) $y = x^{1/3} - x^{1/4}$
(d) $y = 5\cos 4x - 3\cos 2x$
(e) $y = \sin^{-1}(4x+3)$
(f) $y = \sqrt{2x^4} - \dfrac{5}{3x^2}$
(g) $y = t^{3/2} + \cos t$
(h) $y = t^2 - 14t + 8$
(i) $y = 5\ln t + \sin 4t$
(j) $y = \dfrac{1}{2}x - \dfrac{1}{3}x^2$
(k) $y = \dfrac{2t^2}{3} + e^{2t}$

3 Find the equation of the tangent to $y = x^2 + 7x - 4$ at the point on the graph where $x = 2$.

4 Find the rate of change of $f(t) = 2\cos t + 3\sin t$ at $t = 1$.

5 At any time t, the voltage, v, across an inductor of inductance L is related to the current, i, through the inductor by $v = L\dfrac{di}{dt}$.

(a) Find an expression for the voltage when $i = 5\cos\omega t$ where ω is the constant angular frequency.

(b) Find an expression for the voltage when the current takes the form of a sine wave with amplitude 10 and period 0.01 seconds.

6 Use the shrinking interval method to find the rate of change of $f(t) = \sin t$ at $t = 0$ by considering the interval $[0, \delta t]$. [*Hint*: use the trigonometric identities in Section 3.5 and the small-angle approximation in Section 6.5.] Use the shrinking interval method to find the rate of change of $f(t) = \sin t$ at a general point.

7 Given $y(t) = 3 + \sin 2t$, find the average rate of change of y as t varies from 0 to 2.

8 Explain the essential difference between $\dfrac{\delta y}{\delta x}$ and $\dfrac{dy}{dx}$.

9 Find y' for the following functions:

(a) $y = 2e^{-t} + 6\cos(t/2)$
(b) $y = (-t+2)^2$

10 Using derivatives, estimate the change in y as x changes from 1.5 to 1.55 where $y = 2e^{2x} + x^3$.

Solutions

1 12

2 (a) $8x + 6$

(b) $-2x + 2$

(c) $\frac{1}{3}x^{-2/3} - \frac{1}{4}x^{-3/4}$

(d) $-20\sin 4x + 6\sin 2x$

(e) $\dfrac{4}{\sqrt{1 - (4x + 3)^2}}$

(f) $2\sqrt{2}x + \dfrac{10}{3x^3}$

(g) $\frac{3}{2}t^{1/2} - \sin t$

(h) $2t - 14$

(i) $\dfrac{5}{t} + 4\cos 4t$

(j) $\frac{1}{2} - \frac{2}{3}x$

(k) $\frac{4}{3}t + 2e^{2t}$

3 $y = 11x - 8$

4 -0.062

5 (a) $-5\omega L \sin \omega t$ (b) $2000\pi L \cos 200\pi t$

7 -0.3784

9 (a) $-2e^{-t} - 3\sin\left(\dfrac{t}{2}\right)$ (b) $2t - 4$

10 4.355

11 Techniques of differentiation

Chapter 11	Contents	
11.1	Introduction	366
11.2	Rules of differentiation	366
11.3	Parametric, implicit and logarithmic differentiation	372
11.4	Higher derivatives	380
	Review exercises	384

11.1 Introduction

In this chapter we develop the techniques of differentiation introduced in Chapter 10 so that rates of change of more complicated functions can be found. We introduce rules for differentiating products and quotients of functions. The chain rule is used for differentiating functions of functions. We explain what is meant by defining functions implicitly and parametrically and show how these can be differentiated. The technique of logarithmic differentiation allows complicated products of functions to be simplified and then differentiated. Finally derivatives of functions can themselves be differentiated. This involves the use of higher derivatives which are explained towards the end of the chapter.

11.2 Rules of differentiation

There are three rules which enable us to differentiate more complicated functions. They are (a) the product rule, (b) the quotient rule, (c) the chain rule. Traditionally they are written with x as the independent variable but apply in an analogous way for other independent variables.

11.2.1 The product rule

As the name suggests, this rule allows us to differentiate a product of functions, such as $x \sin x$, $t^2 \cos 2t$ and $e^z \ln z$.

> The product rule states: if
>
> $$y(x) = u(x)\,v(x)$$
>
> then
>
> $$\frac{dy}{dx} = \frac{du}{dx}v + u\frac{dv}{dx} = u'v + uv'$$

To apply this rule one of the functions in the product must be chosen to be u, and the other, v. Before we can apply the rule we need to calculate u' and v'.

Example 11.1 Find y' given

(a) $y = x \sin x$

(b) $y = t^2 e^t$

(c) $y = e^{-2t} \cos 3t$

Solution (a) $y = x \sin x = uv$. Choose $u = x$ and $v = \sin x$. Then $u' = 1$, $v' = \cos x$. Applying the product rule to y yields

$$y' = \sin x + x \cos x$$

(b) $y = t^2 e^t = uv$. Choose $u = t^2$ and $v = e^t$. Then $u' = 2t$ and $v' = e^t$. Applying the product rule to y yields

$$y' = 2te^t + t^2 e^t$$

(c) $y = e^{-2t} \cos 3t = uv$. Choose $u = e^{-2t}$ and $v = \cos 3t$. Then $u' = -2e^{-2t}$ and $v' = -3 \sin 3t$. Applying the product rule yields

$$y' = -2e^{-2t} \cos 3t + e^{-2t}(-3 \sin 3t) = -e^{-2t}(2 \cos 3t + 3 \sin 3t)$$

11.2.2 The quotient rule

This rule allows us to differentiate a quotient of functions, such as $\dfrac{x}{\sin x}$, $\dfrac{t^2 - t + 3}{t + 2}$ and $\dfrac{e^{-3z}}{z^2 - 1}$.

The quotient rule states: when

$$y(x) = \frac{u(x)}{v(x)}$$

then

$$y' = \frac{v \left(\dfrac{du}{dx}\right) - u \left(\dfrac{dv}{dx}\right)}{v^2} = \frac{vu' - uv'}{v^2}$$

Example 11.2   Find y' given

(a) $y = \dfrac{\sin x}{x}$ (b) $y = \dfrac{t^2}{2t + 1}$ (c) $y = \dfrac{e^{2t}}{t^2 + 1}$

Solution   (a) $y = \dfrac{\sin x}{x} = \dfrac{u}{v}$. So $u = \sin x$, $v = x$ and $u' = \cos x$, $v' = 1$. Using the quotient rule the derivative of y is found:

$$y' = \frac{x \cos x - \sin x}{x^2}$$

(b) $y = \dfrac{t^2}{2t + 1} = \dfrac{u}{v}$. So $u = t^2$, $v = 2t + 1$ and $u' = 2t$, $v' = 2$. Hence,

$$y' = \frac{(2t + 1)2t - (t^2)(2)}{(2t + 1)^2} = \frac{2t(t + 1)}{(2t + 1)^2}$$

(c) $y = \dfrac{e^{2t}}{t^2 + 1}$. So $u = e^{2t}$, $v = t^2 + 1$ and $u' = 2e^{2t}$, $v' = 2t$. Application of the quotient rule yields

$$y' = \frac{(t^2 + 1)2e^{2t} - e^{2t}2t}{(t^2 + 1)^2} = \frac{2e^{2t}(t^2 - t + 1)}{(t^2 + 1)^2}$$

11.2.3 The chain rule

This rule helps us to differentiate complicated functions, where a substitution can be used to simplify the function. Suppose $y = y(z)$ and $z = z(x)$. Then y may be considered as a function of x. For example, if $y = z^3 - z$ and $z = \sin 3x$, then $y = (\sin 3x)^3 - \sin(3x)$. Suppose we seek the derivative, $\dfrac{dy}{dx}$. Note that the derivative w.r.t. x is sought.

The chain rule states:
$$\frac{dy}{dx} = \frac{dy}{dz} \times \frac{dz}{dx}$$

Example 11.3   Given $y = z^6$ where $z = x^2 + 1$ find $\dfrac{dy}{dx}$.

Solution   If $y = z^6$ and $z = x^2 + 1$, then $y = (x^2 + 1)^6$. We recognize this as the composition $y(z(x))$ (see Section 2.3.6). Now $y = z^6$ and so $\dfrac{dy}{dz} = 6z^5$. Also $z = x^2 + 1$ and so $\dfrac{dz}{dx} = 2x$. Using the chain rule,

$$\frac{dy}{dx} = \frac{dy}{dz} \times \frac{dz}{dx} = 6z^5 2x = 12x(x^2 + 1)^5$$

Example 11.4   If $y = \ln(3x^2 + 5x + 7)$, find $\dfrac{dy}{dx}$.

Solution   We use a substitution to simplify the given function: let $z = 3x^2 + 5x + 7$ so that $y = \ln z$. Since

$$y = \ln z \qquad \text{then} \qquad \frac{dy}{dz} = \frac{1}{z}$$

Also

$$z = 3x^2 + 5x + 7 \qquad \text{and so} \qquad \frac{dz}{dx} = 6x + 5$$

Using the chain rule we find

$$\frac{dy}{dx} = \frac{dy}{dz} \times \frac{dz}{dx}$$

$$= \frac{1}{z} \times (6x + 5)$$

$$= \frac{6x + 5}{3x^2 + 5x + 7}$$

Note that in the previous answer the numerator is the derivative of the denominator. This result is true more generally and can be applied when differentiating the natural logarithm of any function:

$$\text{When } y = \ln f(x) \text{ then } \frac{dy}{dx} = \frac{f'(x)}{f(x)}$$

Example 11.5   Find y' when

(a) $y = \ln(x^5 + 8)$ (b) $y = \ln(1 - t)$ (c) $y = 8 \ln(2 - 3t)$

(d) $y = \ln(1 + x)$ (e) $y = \ln(1 + \cos x)$

Solution   In each case we apply the previous rule.

(a) If $y = \ln(x^5 + 8)$, then $y' = \dfrac{5x^4}{x^5 + 8}$.

(b) If $y = \ln(1 - t)$, then $y' = \dfrac{-1}{1 - t} = -\dfrac{1}{1 - t} = \dfrac{1}{t - 1}$.

(c) If $y = 8 \ln(2 - 3t)$, then $y' = 8\dfrac{-3}{2 - 3t} = -\dfrac{24}{2 - 3t} = \dfrac{24}{3t - 2}$.

(d) If $y = \ln(1 + x)$ then $y' = \dfrac{1}{1 + x}$.

(e) If $y = \ln(1 + \cos x)$ then $y' = \dfrac{-\sin x}{1 + \cos x} = -\dfrac{\sin x}{1 + \cos x}$.

Example 11.6   Differentiate

(a) $y = 3e^{\sin x}$

(b) $y = (3t^2 + 2t - 9)^{10}$

(c) $y = \sqrt{1 + t^2}$

Solution   In these examples we must formulate the function z ourselves.

(a) Let $z(x) = \sin x$. Then $y(z) = 3e^z$ so $\dfrac{dy}{dz} = 3e^z$; $z(x) = \sin x$ and so $\dfrac{dz}{dx} = \cos x$.

The chain rule is used to find $\dfrac{dy}{dx}$.

$$\frac{dy}{dx} = \frac{dy}{dz} \times \frac{dz}{dx} = 3e^z \cos x = 3e^{\sin x} \cos x$$

(b) Let $z(t) = 3t^2 + 2t - 9$. Then $y(z) = z^{10}$, $\dfrac{dy}{dz} = 10z^9$, $\dfrac{dz}{dt} = 6t + 2$. Using the chain rule $\dfrac{dy}{dt}$ is found:

$$\frac{dy}{dt} = \frac{dy}{dz} \times \frac{dz}{dt} = 10z^9(6t + 2) = 20(3t + 1)(3t^2 + 2t - 9)^9$$

(c) Let $z(t) = 1 + t^2$. Then $y = \sqrt{z} = z^{1/2}$, $\dfrac{dy}{dz} = \tfrac{1}{2}z^{-1/2}$ and $\dfrac{dz}{dt} = 2t$. Using the chain rule, we obtain

$$\frac{dy}{dt} = \frac{dy}{dz} \times \frac{dz}{dt} = \frac{1}{2}z^{-1/2}2t = \frac{t}{\sqrt{z}} = \frac{t}{\sqrt{1 + t^2}}$$

Exercises 11.2

1 Use the product rule to differentiate the following functions.

(a) $y = \sin x \cos x$

(b) $y = \ln t \tan t$

(c) $y = (t^3 + 1)e^{2t}$

(d) $y = \sqrt{x}e^x$

(e) $y = e^t \sin t \cos t$

(f) $y = 3 \sinh 2t \cosh 3t$

(g) $y = (1 + \sin t) \tan t$

(h) $y = 4 \sinh(t + 1) \cosh(1 - t)$

2 Use the quotient rule to find the derivatives of the following:

(a) $\dfrac{\cos x}{\sin x}$

(b) $\dfrac{\tan t}{\ln t}$

(c) $\dfrac{e^{2t}}{t^3 + 1}$

(d) $\dfrac{3x^2 + 2x - 9}{x^3 + 1}$

(e) $\dfrac{x^2 + x + 1}{1 + e^x}$

(f) $\dfrac{\sinh 2t}{\cosh 3t}$

(g) $\dfrac{1 + e^t}{1 + e^{2t}}$

3 Use the chain rule to differentiate the following.

(a) $(t^3 + 1)^{100}$

(b) $\sin^3(3t + 2)$

(c) $\ln(x^2 + 1)$

(d) $(2t + 1)^{1/2}$

(e) $3\sqrt{\cos(2x - 1)}$

(f) $\dfrac{1}{t + 1}$

(g) $(at + b)^n$, a and b constants

4 Differentiate each of the following functions:

(a) $y = 5\sin x$

(b) $y = 5e^x \sin x$

(c) $y = 5e^{\sin x}$

(d) $y = \dfrac{5\sin x}{e^{-x}}$

(e) $y = (t^3 + 4t)^{15}$

(f) $y = 7e^{-3t^2}$

(g) $y = \dfrac{\sin x}{4\cos x + 1}$

5 For which values of t is the derivative of $y(t) = e^{-t}t^2$ zero?

6 Find the rate of change of y at the specified values of t.

(a) $y = \sin\dfrac{1}{t}$ $t = 1$

(b) $y = (t^2 - 1)^{17}$ $t = 1$

(c) $y = \sinh(t^2)$ $t = 2$

(d) $y = \dfrac{1+t+t^2}{1-t}$ $t = 2$

(e) $y = \dfrac{e^t}{t\sin t}$ $t = 1$

7 Find the equation of the tangent to
$$y(x) = e^{3x}(1-x) \quad \text{at the point } (0, 1)$$

8 Differentiate

(a) $y = \ln x$

(b) $y = \ln 2x$

(c) $y = \ln kx, k$ constant

(d) $y = \ln(1+t)$

(e) $y = \ln(3+4t)$

(f) $y = \ln(5 + 7\sin x)$

Solutions

1 (a) $\cos^2 x - \sin^2 x$

(b) $\dfrac{1}{t}\tan t + \ln t \sec^2 t$

(c) $e^{2t}(2t^3 + 3t^2 + 2)$

(d) $e^x\left(\sqrt{x} + \dfrac{1}{2\sqrt{x}}\right)$

(e) $e^t(2\cos^2 t + \sin t \cos t - 1)$

(f) $3[2\cosh 2t \cosh 3t + 3\sinh 2t \sinh 3t]$

(g) $(1+\sin t)\sec^2 t + \sin t$

(h) $4[\cosh(t+1)\cosh(1-t) - \sinh(t+1)\sinh(1-t)]$

2 (a) $-\csc^2 x$

(b) $\dfrac{\ln t \sec^2 t - (\tan t)/t}{(\ln t)^2}$

(c) $\dfrac{e^{2t}(2t^3 - 3t^2 + 2)}{(t^3 + 1)^2}$

(d) $\dfrac{-3x^4 - 4x^3 + 27x^2 + 6x + 2}{(x^3 + 1)^2}$

(e) $\dfrac{e^x(-x^2 + x) + 2x + 1}{(e^x + 1)^2}$

(f) $\dfrac{2\cosh 2t \cosh 3t - 3\sinh 2t \sinh 3t}{(\cosh 3t)^2}$

(g) $\dfrac{-e^{3t} - 2e^{2t} + e^t}{(e^{2t} + 1)^2}$

3 (a) $300t^2(t^3 + 1)^{99}$

(b) $9\sin^2(3t+2)\cos(3t+2)$

(c) $\dfrac{2x}{x^2 + 1}$

(d) $(2t+1)^{-1/2}$

(e) $\dfrac{-3\sin(2x-1)}{\sqrt{\cos(2x-1)}}$

(f) $-(t+1)^{-2}$

(g) $an(at+b)^{n-1}$

4 (a) $5\cos x$

(b) $5e^x(\cos x + \sin x)$

(c) $5e^{\sin x}\cos x$

(d) $5e^x(\cos x + \sin x)$

(e) $15(t^3 + 4t)^{14}(3t^2 + 4)$

(f) $-42te^{-3t^2}$

(g) $\dfrac{4 + \cos x}{(4\cos x + 1)^2}$

5   0, 2

7    $y = 2x + 1$

8   (a) $\dfrac{1}{x}$ (b) $\dfrac{1}{x}$ (c) $\dfrac{1}{x}$

6   (a) -0.5403 (b) 0   (c) 109.2

   (d) $\dfrac{1}{1+t}$ (e) $\dfrac{4}{3+4t}$ (f) $\dfrac{7\cos x}{5+7\sin x}$

   (d) 2   (e) -2.0742

11.3 Parametric, implicit and logarithmic differentiation

11.3.1 Parametric differentiation

In some circumstances both y and x depend upon a third variable, t. This third variable is often called a **parameter**. By eliminating t, y can be found as a function of x. For example, if $y = (1 + t)^2$ and $x = 2t$ then, eliminating t, we can write $y = (1 + x/2)^2$.

Hence, y may be considered as a function of x, and so the derivative $\dfrac{dy}{dx}$ can be found. However, sometimes the elimination of t is difficult or even impossible. Consider the example $y = \sin t + t$, $x = t^2 + e^t$. In this case, it is impossible to obtain y in terms of x. The derivative $\dfrac{dy}{dx}$ can still be found using the chain rule.

$$\frac{dy}{dx} = \frac{dy}{dt} \times \frac{dt}{dx} = \frac{dy}{dt} \bigg/ \frac{dx}{dt}$$

Finding $\dfrac{dy}{dx}$ by this method is known as **parametric differentiation**.

Example 11.7   Given $y = (1 + t)^2$, $x = 2t$ find $\dfrac{dy}{dx}$.

Solution   By eliminating t, we see

$$y = \left(1 + \frac{x}{2}\right)^2 = 1 + x + \frac{x^2}{4}$$

and so

$$\frac{dy}{dx} = 1 + \frac{x}{2}$$

Parametric differentiation is an alternative method of finding $\dfrac{dy}{dx}$ which does not require the elimination of t.

$$\frac{dy}{dt} = 2(1 + t) \qquad \frac{dx}{dt} = 2$$

Using the chain rule, we obtain

$$\frac{dy}{dx} = \frac{dy}{dt} \bigg/ \frac{dx}{dt} = \frac{2(1 + t)}{2} = 1 + t = 1 + \frac{x}{2}$$

Example 11.8   Given $y = e^t + t$, $x = t^2 + 1$, find $\dfrac{dy}{dx}$ using parametric differentiation.

Solution $$\frac{dy}{dt} = e^t + 1 \qquad \frac{dx}{dt} = 2t$$

Hence,

$$\frac{dy}{dx} = \frac{dy}{dt} \bigg/ \frac{dx}{dt} = \frac{e^t + 1}{2t}$$

In this example, the derivative is expressed in terms of t. This will always be the case when t has not been eliminated between x and y.

Example 11.9   If $x = \sin t + \cos t$ and $y = t^2 - t + 1$ find $\dfrac{dy}{dx}$ $(t = 0)$.

Solution $$\frac{dy}{dt} = 2t - 1 \qquad \frac{dx}{dt} = \cos t - \sin t$$

Hence,

$$\frac{dy}{dx} = \frac{2t - 1}{\cos t - \sin t}$$

When $t = 0$, $\dfrac{dy}{dx} = \dfrac{-1}{1} = -1$.

11.3.2 Implicit differentiation

Suppose we are told that

$$y^3 + x^3 = 5 \sin x + 10 \cos y$$

Although y depends upon x, it is impossible to write the equation in the form $y = f(x)$. We say y is expressed **implicitly** in terms of x. The form $y = f(x)$ is an **explicit** expression for y in terms of x. However, given an implicit expression for y it is still possible to find $\dfrac{dy}{dx}$. Usually $\dfrac{dy}{dx}$ will be expressed in terms of both x and y. Essentially, the chain rule is used when differentiating implicit expressions.

When calculating $\dfrac{dy}{dx}$ we need to differentiate a function of y, as opposed to a function of x. For example, we may need to find $\dfrac{d}{dx}(y^4)$.

Example 11.10   Find

(a) $\dfrac{d}{dx}(y^4)$ (b) $\dfrac{d}{dx}(y^{-3})$

Solution   (a) We make a substitution and let $z = y^4$ so that the problem becomes that of finding $\dfrac{dz}{dx}$. Now, using the chain rule,

$$\frac{dz}{dx} = \frac{dz}{dy} \times \frac{dy}{dx}$$

If $z = y^4$ then $\dfrac{dz}{dy} = 4y^3$ and so

$$\frac{dz}{dx} = 4y^3 \frac{dy}{dx}$$

We conclude that

$$\frac{d}{dx}(y^4) = 4y^3 \frac{dy}{dx}$$

(b) We make a substitution and let $z = y^{-3}$ so that the problem becomes that of finding $\dfrac{dz}{dx}$.

If $z = y^{-3}$ then $\dfrac{dz}{dy} = -3y^{-4}$ and so

$$\frac{d}{dx}(y^{-3}) = \frac{dz}{dx} = \frac{dz}{dy} \times \frac{dy}{dx} = -3y^{-4}\frac{dy}{dx}$$

Example 11.11 Find $\dfrac{d}{dt}(\ln y)$.

Solution We let $z = \ln y$ so that the problem becomes that of finding $\dfrac{dz}{dt}$. If $z = \ln y$ then $\dfrac{dz}{dy} = \dfrac{1}{y}$ and so using the chain rule

$$\frac{dz}{dt} = \frac{dz}{dy} \times \frac{dy}{dt} = \frac{1}{y}\frac{dy}{dt}$$

we conclude that

$$\frac{d}{dt}(\ln y) = \frac{1}{y}\frac{dy}{dt}$$

Examples 11.10 and 11.11 illustrate the general formula:

$$\frac{d}{dx}(f(y)) = \frac{df}{dy} \times \frac{dy}{dx}.$$

This is simply the chain rule expressed in a slightly different form.

Example 11.12 Find $\dfrac{d}{dx}(y)$.

Solution We have

$$\frac{d}{dx}(y) = \frac{dy}{dy} \times \frac{dy}{dx} = \frac{dy}{dx}$$

Example 11.13 Given

$$x^3 + y = 1 + y^3$$

find $\dfrac{dy}{dx}$.

Solution Consider differentiation of the l.h.s. w.r.t. x.

$$\frac{d}{dx}(x^3 + y) = \frac{d}{dx}(x^3) + \frac{dy}{dx} = 3x^2 + \frac{dy}{dx}$$

Now consider differentiation of the r.h.s. w.r.t. x.

$$\frac{d}{dx}(1 + y^3) = \frac{d}{dx}(1) + \frac{d}{dx}(y^3) = \frac{d}{dx}(y^3)$$

We note from the formula following Example 11.11 that $\dfrac{d}{dx}(y^3) = 3y^2\dfrac{dy}{dx}$. So finally,

$$3x^2 + \frac{dy}{dx} = 3y^2\frac{dy}{dx}$$

from which

$$\frac{dy}{dx} = \frac{3x^2}{3y^2 - 1}$$

Note that $\dfrac{dy}{dx}$ is expressed in terms of x and y.

Example 11.14 Find $\dfrac{dy}{dx}$ given

(a) $\ln y = y - x^2$

(b) $x^2y^3 - e^y = e^{2x}$

Solution (a) Differentiating the given equation w.r.t. x yields

$$\frac{1}{y}\frac{dy}{dx} = \frac{dy}{dx} - 2x$$

from which

$$\frac{dy}{dx} = \frac{2xy}{y - 1}$$

(b) Consider $\dfrac{d}{dx}(x^2y^3)$. Using the product rule we find

$$\frac{d}{dx}(x^2y^3) = \frac{d}{dx}(x^2)y^3 + x^2\frac{d}{dx}(y^3) = 2xy^3 + x^23y^2\frac{dy}{dx}$$

Consider $\dfrac{d}{dx}(e^y)$. Let $z = e^y$ so $\dfrac{dz}{dy} = e^y$. Hence,

$$\frac{d}{dx}(e^y) = \frac{dz}{dx} = \frac{dz}{dy}\frac{dy}{dx} = e^y\frac{dy}{dx}$$

So, upon differentiating, the equation becomes

$$2xy^3 + x^2 3y^2\frac{dy}{dx} - e^y\frac{dy}{dx} = 2e^{2x}$$

So,

$$\frac{dy}{dx}(3x^2y^2 - e^y) = 2e^{2x} - 2xy^3$$

from which

$$\frac{dy}{dx} = \frac{2e^{2x} - 2xy^3}{3x^2y^2 - e^y}$$

11.3.3 Logarithmic differentiation

The technique of **logarithmic differentiation** is useful when we need to differentiate a cumbersome product. The method involves taking the natural logarithm of the function to be differentiated. This is illustrated in the following examples.

Example 11.15 Given that $y = t^2(1 - t)^8$ find $\dfrac{dy}{dt}$.

Solution The product rule could be used but we will demonstrate an alternative technique. Taking the natural logarithm of both sides of the given equation yields

$$\ln y = \ln(t^2(1 - t)^8)$$

Using the laws of logarithms we can write this as

$$\ln y = \ln t^2 + \ln(1 - t)^8$$
$$= 2\ln t + 8\ln(1 - t)$$

Both sides of this equation are now differentiated w.r.t. t to give

$$\frac{d}{dt}(\ln y) = \frac{d}{dt}(2\ln t) + \frac{d}{dt}(8\ln(1 - t))$$

The evaluation of $\dfrac{d}{dt}(\ln y)$ has already been found in Example 11.11, and so

$$\frac{1}{y}\frac{dy}{dt} = \frac{2}{t} - \frac{8}{1 - t}$$

Hence

$$\frac{dy}{dt} = y\left(\frac{2}{t} - \frac{8}{1-t}\right)$$

Finally, replacing y by $t^2(1-t)^8$ we have

$$\frac{dy}{dt} = t^2(1-t)^8\left(\frac{2}{t} - \frac{8}{1-t}\right)$$

Example 11.16   Given

$$y = x^3(1+x)^9 e^{6x}$$

find $\dfrac{dy}{dx}$.

Solution   The product rule could be used. However, we will use logarithmic differentiation. Taking the natural logarithm of the equation and applying the laws of logarithms produces

$$\ln y = \ln(x^3(1+x)^9 e^{6x}) = \ln x^3 + \ln(1+x)^9 + \ln e^{6x}$$
$$\ln y = 3\ln x + 9\ln(1+x) + 6x$$

This equation is now differentiated.

$$\frac{1}{y}\frac{dy}{dx} = \frac{3}{x} + \frac{9}{1+x} + 6$$

and so

$$\frac{dy}{dx} = y\left(\frac{3}{x} + \frac{9}{1+x} + 6\right)$$

$$= 3x^2(1+x)^9 e^{6x} + 9x^3(1+x)^8 e^{6x} + 6x^3(1+x)^9 e^{6x}$$

Example 11.17   If $y = \sqrt{1+t^2}\,\sin^2 t$ find y'.

Solution   Taking logarithms we find

$$\ln y = \ln(\sqrt{1+t^2}\,\sin^2 t)$$
$$= \ln\sqrt{1+t^2} + \ln(\sin^2 t)$$
$$= \frac{1}{2}\ln(1+t^2) + 2\ln(\sin t)$$

Differentiation yields

$$\frac{1}{y}y' = \frac{1}{2}\frac{2t}{1+t^2} + 2\frac{\cos t}{\sin t}$$

$$y' = y\left(\frac{t}{1+t^2} + 2\cot t\right) = \sqrt{1+t^2}\sin^2 t\left(\frac{t}{1+t^2} + 2\cot t\right)$$

Exercises 11.3

1 Find each of the following:

(a) $\dfrac{d}{dx}(x^5)$

(b) $\dfrac{d}{dx}(y^5)$

(c) $\dfrac{d}{dt}(y^5)$

(d) $\dfrac{d}{dx}(y^2)$

(e) $\dfrac{d}{dx}(5y)$

(f) $\dfrac{d}{dx}(y)$

(g) $\dfrac{d}{dx}(y^2+y^3)$

2 Find each of the following:

(a) $\dfrac{d}{dx}(e^y)$

(b) $\dfrac{d}{dx}(\sin y)$

(c) $\dfrac{d}{dx}(\cos 2y)$

(d) $\dfrac{d}{dx}(e^{-3y})$

(e) $\dfrac{d}{dx}(\sqrt{y})$

(f) $\dfrac{d}{dx}(x+y)$

(g) $\dfrac{d}{dx}(\cos(x+y))$

(h) $\dfrac{d}{dx}(\ln y)$

(i) $\dfrac{d}{dx}(\ln 7y)$

3 Find $\dfrac{dy}{dx}$ given

(a) $2y^2 - 3x^3 = x + y$

(b) $\sqrt{y} + \sqrt{x} = x^2 + y^3$

(c) $\sqrt{2x+3y} = 1 + e^x$

(d) $y = \dfrac{e^x\sqrt{1+x}}{x^2}$

(e) $2xy^4 = x^3 + 3xy^2$

(f) $\sin(x+y) = 1 + y$

(g) $\ln(x^2+y^2) = 2x - 3y$

(h) $ye^{2y} = x^2e^{x/2}$

4 Find $\dfrac{dy}{dx}$, given

(a) $x = t^2 \qquad y = 1+t^3$

(b) $x = \sin t \qquad y = e^t$

(c) $x = (1+t)^3 \qquad y = 1+t^3$

(d) $x = \cos 2t \qquad y = 3t$

(e) $x = \dfrac{3}{t} \qquad y = e^{2t}$

(f) $x = e^t - e^{-t} \qquad y = e^t + e^{-t}$

5 Use logarithmic differentiation to find the derivatives of the following functions:

(a) $y = x^4e^x$

(b) $y = \dfrac{1}{x}e^{-x}$

(c) $z = t^3(1+t)^9$

(d) $y = e^x \sin x$

(e) $y = x^7 \sin^4 x$

6   Use logarithmic differentiation to find the derivatives of the following functions:

(a) $z = t^4(1-t)^6(2+t)^4$

(b) $y = \dfrac{(1+x^2)^3 e^{7x}}{(2+x)^6}$

(c) $x = (1+t)^3(2+t)^4(3+t)^5$

(d) $y = \dfrac{(\sin^4 t)(2-t^2)^4}{(1+e^t)^6}$

(e) $y = x^3 e^x \sin x$

7   If $x = t + t^2 + t^3$ and $y = \sin 2t$, find $\dfrac{dy}{dx}$ when $t = 1$.

8   Given $x = 1 + t^6$ and $y = 1 - t^2$, find:

(a)   the rate of change of x w.r.t. t when $t = 2$

(b)   the rate of change of y w.r.t. t when $t = 1$

(c)   the rate of change of y w.r.t. x when $t = 1$

(d)   the rate of change of x w.r.t. y when $t = 2$

9   Find the equations of the tangents to

$$y^2 = x^2 + 6y$$

when $x = 4$.

10   Given the implicit function $3x^2 + y^3 = y$ find an expression for $\dfrac{dy}{dx}$.

Solutions

1   (a) $5x^4$

(b) $5y^4 \dfrac{dy}{dx}$

(c) $5y^4 \dfrac{dy}{dt}$

(d) $2y \dfrac{dy}{dx}$

(e) $5 \dfrac{dy}{dx}$

(f) $\dfrac{dy}{dx}$

(g) $(2y + 3y^2) \dfrac{dy}{dx}$

2   (a) $e^y \dfrac{dy}{dx}$

(b) $\cos y \dfrac{dy}{dx}$

(c) $-2 \sin 2y \dfrac{dy}{dx}$

(d) $-3e^{-3y} \dfrac{dy}{dx}$

(e) $\frac{1}{2} y^{-1/2} \dfrac{dy}{dx}$

(f) $1 + \dfrac{dy}{dx}$

(g) $-\sin(x+y)\left(1 + \dfrac{dy}{dx}\right)$

(h) $\dfrac{1}{y} \dfrac{dy}{dx}$

(i) $\dfrac{1}{y} \dfrac{dy}{dx}$

3   (a) $\dfrac{1 + 9x^2}{4y - 1}$

(b) $\dfrac{(4x\sqrt{x} - 1)\sqrt{y}}{(1 - 6y^2\sqrt{y})\sqrt{x}}$

(c) $\frac{2}{3}(e^x \sqrt{2x + 3y} - 1)$

(d) $y\left(\dfrac{1}{2(1+x)} + 1 - \dfrac{2}{x}\right)$

(e) $\dfrac{3x^2 + 3y^2 - 2y^4}{2xy(4y^2 - 3)}$

(f) $\dfrac{\cos(x+y)}{1 - \cos(x+y)}$

(g) $\dfrac{2(x^2 + y^2 - x)}{3x^2 + 3y^2 + 2y}$

(h) $\dfrac{e^{(x/2 - 2y)} x(x+4)}{2(1 + 2y)}$

4   (a) $3t/2$ (b) $\dfrac{e^t}{\cos t}$

(c) $\left(\dfrac{t}{1+t}\right)^2$ (d) $\dfrac{-3}{2 \sin 2t}$

(e) $-2e^{2t}t^2/3$ (f) $\dfrac{e^t - e^{-t}}{e^t + e^{-t}}$

5   (a) $(4x^3 + x^4)e^x$

(b) $-e^{-x}\left(\dfrac{1}{x^2} + \dfrac{1}{x}\right)$

(c) $t^3(1+t)^9\left(\dfrac{3}{t} + \dfrac{9}{1+t}\right)$

(d) $e^x \sin x (1 + \cot x)$

(e) $x^7 \sin^4 x \left(\dfrac{7}{x} + 4 \cot x \right)$

6 (a) $z \left(\dfrac{4}{t} - \dfrac{.6}{1-t} + \dfrac{4}{2+t} \right)$

(b) $y \left(\dfrac{6x}{1+x^2} + 7 - \dfrac{6}{2+x} \right)$

(c) $x \left(\dfrac{3}{1+t} + \dfrac{4}{2+t} + \dfrac{5}{3+t} \right)$

(d) $y \left(4 \cot t - \dfrac{8t}{2-t^2} - \dfrac{6e^t}{1+e^t} \right)$

(e) $x^3 e^x \sin x \left(\dfrac{3}{x} + 1 + \cot x \right)$

7 -0.1387

8 (a) 192

(b) -2

(c) $-\dfrac{1}{3}$

(d) $\dfrac{dx}{dy} = -3t^4$; when $t = 2$, $\dfrac{dx}{dy} = -48$

9 $y = \dfrac{-4x + 6}{5}$, $y = \dfrac{4x + 24}{5}$

10 $y' = \dfrac{6x}{1 - 3y^2}$

11.4 Higher derivatives

The derivative, y', of a function $y(x)$ is more correctly called the **first derivative** of y w.r.t. x. Since y' itself is a function of x, then it is often possible to differentiate this too. The derivative of y' is called the **second derivative** of y.

$$\text{second derivative of } y = \frac{d}{dx} \left(\frac{dy}{dx} \right)$$

which is written as $\dfrac{d^2 y}{dx^2}$ or more compactly as y''.

Example 11.18 If $y(x) = 3x^2 + 8x + 9$, find y' and y''.

Solution $y' = 6x + 8 \qquad y'' = \dfrac{d}{dx}(6x + 8) = 6$

Example 11.19 If $y(t) = 2 \sin 3t$, find y' and y''.

Solution $y' = 6 \cos 3t \qquad y'' = -18 \sin 3t$

The first and second derivatives w.r.t. time, t, are also denoted by $\dot{y}$ and $\ddot{y}$.

Example 11.20 Find y'' given

$$1 + xy = x^2 + y^2$$

Solution The equation is differentiated implicitly to obtain $\dfrac{dy}{dx}$.

$$0 + y + xy' = 2x + 2yy'$$

$$y' = \frac{2x - y}{x - 2y}$$

The quotient rule is now used with $u = 2x - y$ and $v = x - 2y$. The derivatives of u and v are

$$\frac{du}{dx} = u' = 2 - y' \qquad \frac{dv}{dx} = v' = 1 - 2y'$$

Then,

$$y'' = \frac{(x - 2y)(2 - y') - (2x - y)(1 - 2y')}{(x - 2y)^2}$$

This is simplified to

$$y'' = \frac{3xy' - 3y}{(x - 2y)^2}$$

Replacing y' by $\dfrac{2x - y}{x - 2y}$ and simplifying yields

$$y'' = \frac{6(x^2 - xy + y^2)}{(x - 2y)^3}$$

Note that it is possible to simplify this further by observing that $x^2 + y^2 = 1 + xy$ as given. Therefore,

$$y'' = \frac{6(1 + xy - xy)}{(x - 2y)^3} = \frac{6}{(x - 2y)^3}$$

Just as the first derivative may be differentiated to obtain the second derivative, so the second derivative may be differentiated to find the third derivative and so on. A similar notation is used. The third derivative is written $\dfrac{d^3y}{dx^3}$ or y''' or $y^{(3)}$. The fourth derivative is written $\dfrac{d^4y}{dx^4}$ or y^{iv} or $y^{(4)}$. The fifth derivative is written $\dfrac{d^5y}{dx^5}$ or y^v or $y^{(5)}$.

Example 11.21 Find the first five derivatives of $z(t) = 2t^3 + \sin t$.

Solution

$$z' = 6t^2 + \cos t \qquad z^{iv} = \sin t$$
$$z'' = 12t - \sin t \qquad z^v = \cos t$$
$$z''' = 12 - \cos t$$

Example 11.22 Calculate the values of x for which $y'' = 0$, given $y = x^4 - x^3$.

Solution

$$y = x^4 - x^3 \qquad y' = 4x^3 - 3x^2 \qquad y'' = 12x^2 - 6x$$

Putting $y'' = 0$ gives

$$12x^2 - 6x = 0 \qquad \text{and so} \qquad 6x(2x - 1) = 0$$

Hence

$$x = 0, \tfrac{1}{2}$$

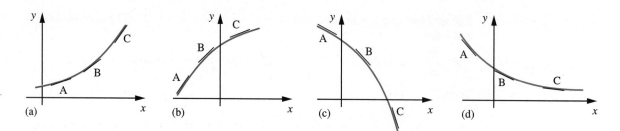

Figure 11.1 (a) y is concave up ($y' > 0$, $y'' > 0$); (b) y is concave down ($y' > 0$, $y'' < 0$); (c) y is concave down ($y' < 0$, $y'' < 0$); (d) y is concave up ($y' < 0$, $y'' > 0$).

The first and second derivatives can be used to describe the nature of increasing and decreasing functions. In Figure 11.1(a, b) the tangents to the curves have positive gradients, that is $y' > 0$. As can be seen, as x increases the value of the function increases. Conversely, in Figure 11.1(c, d) the tangents have negative gradients ($y' < 0$) and as x increases the value of the function decreases. The sign of the first derivative tells us whether y is increasing or decreasing. However, the curves in (a) and (b) both show y increasing but, clearly, there is a difference in the way y changes.

Consider again Figure 11.1(a). The tangents at A, B and C are shown. As x increases the gradient of the tangent increases, that is y' increases as x increases. Since y' increases as x increases then the derivative of y' is positive, that is $y'' > 0$. (Compare with: y increases when its derivative is positive.) So for the curve shown in Figure 11.1(a), $y' > 0$ and $y'' > 0$.

For that shown in Figure 11.1(b) the situation is different. The value of y' decreases as x increases, as can be seen by considering the gradients of the tangents at A, B and C, that is the derivative of y' must be negative. For this curve $y' > 0$ and $y'' < 0$.

A function is **concave down** when y' decreases and **concave up** when y' increases. Hence Figure 11.1(a) illustrates a concave up function; Figure 11.1(b) illustrates a concave down function. The sign of the second derivative can be used to distinguish between concave up and concave down functions.

Consider now the functions shown in Figure 11.1(c) and Figure 11.1(d). In both (c) and (d), y is decreasing and so $y' < 0$. In (c) the gradient of the tangent becomes increasingly negative; that is, it is decreasing. Hence, for the function in (c) $y'' < 0$. Conversely, for the function in (d) the gradient of the tangent is increasing as x increases, although it is always negative, that is $y'' > 0$. So for the function in (c) $y' < 0$ and $y'' < 0$; that is, the function is concave down. For the function in (d) $y' < 0$ and $y'' > 0$; that is, the function is concave up. In summary, we can state:

> When $y' > 0$, y is increasing. When $y' < 0$, y is decreasing.
> When y' is increasing the function is concave up. In this case $y'' > 0$.
> When y' is decreasing the function is concave down. In this case $y'' < 0$.

An easy way of determining the concavity of a curve is to note that as the curve is traced from left to right, an anticlockwise motion reveals that the curve is concave up. A clockwise motion means that the curve is concave down.

As will be seen in the next chapter, higher derivatives are used to determine the location and nature of important points called maximum points, minimum points and points of inflexion.

Exercises 11.4

1 Calculate $\dfrac{dy}{dt}$ and $\dfrac{d^2y}{dt^2}$ given

(a) $y = t^2 + t$

(b) $y = 2t^3 - t^2 + 1$

(c) $y = \sin 2t$

(d) $y = \sin kt \qquad k$ constant

(e) $y = 2e^{3t} - t^2 + 1$

(f) $y = \dfrac{t}{t+1}$

(g) $y = 4\cos\dfrac{t}{2}$

(h) $y = e^t t$

(i) $y = \sinh 4t$

(j) $y = \sin^2 t$

2 If

$$y = 2x^3 + 3x^2 - 12x + 1$$

find values of x for which $y'' = 0$.

3 If $\dfrac{dy}{dt} = 3t^2 + t$, find

(a) $\dfrac{d^2y}{dt^2}$ \qquad (b) $\dfrac{d^3y}{dt^3}$

4 Find values of t at which $y'' = 0$, where

$$y = \dfrac{t^3}{3} - \dfrac{7t^2}{2} + 12t - 1$$

5 Determine whether the following functions are concave up or concave down.

(a) $y = e^t$

(b) $y = t^2$

(c) $y = 1 + t - t^2$

6 Determine the interval on which $y = t^3$ is
(a) concave up,
(b) concave down.

7 Evaluate y'' at the specified value of t.

(a) $y = 2\cos t - t^2 \qquad t = 1$

(b) $y = \dfrac{\sin t + \cos t}{2} \qquad t = \pi/2$

(c) $y = (1+t)e^t \qquad t = 0$

8 Find $\dfrac{d^2y}{dx^2}$ given $xy + x^2 = y^2$.

9 Find $\dfrac{dx}{dt}$ when $x^3 + \dfrac{x}{t} = t^2 + x^2 t$.

Solutions

1 (a) $2t + 1, 2$

(b) $6t^2 - 2t, 12t - 2$

(c) $2\cos 2t, -4\sin 2t$

(d) $k\cos kt, -k^2 \sin kt$

(e) $6e^{3t} - 2t, 18e^{3t} - 2$

(f) $\dfrac{1}{(t+1)^2}, -\dfrac{2}{(t+1)^3}$

(g) $-2\sin(t/2), -\cos(t/2)$

(h) $e^t(t+1), e^t(t+2)$

(i) $4\cosh 4t, 16\sinh 4t$

(j) $2\sin t \cos t, 2\cos 2t$

2 $-\dfrac{1}{2}$

3 (a) $6t + 1$ \qquad (b) 6

4 $\dfrac{7}{2}$

5 (a) concave up

(b) concave up

(c) concave down

6 (a) concave up on $(0, \infty)$

(b) concave down on $(-\infty, 0)$

7 (a) -3.08 \qquad (b) $-\dfrac{1}{2}$ \qquad (c) 3

8 $\dfrac{10y^2 - 10x^2 - 10yx}{(2y - x)^3}$

9 $\dfrac{x + 2t^3 + x^2 t^2}{3x^2 t^2 + t - 2xt^3}$

Review exercises 11

1 Differentiate each of the following functions:

(a) $y = \sin(5 + x)^2$

(b) $y = e^{2\sin x}$

(c) $y = (4x + 7)^5$

(d) $y = x^4 \sin 3x$

(e) $y = \dfrac{e^{4x}}{x^3 + 11}$

(f) $y = x^2 \tan x$

(g) $y = \dfrac{\cos 3x}{x^2}$

(h) $y = e^{-x}\cos 5x$

(i) $y = \ln \cos 4x$

(j) $y = \sin 2t \cos 2t$

(k) $y = \dfrac{1}{x^2 + 1}$

2 Find $\dfrac{dy}{dx}$ in each of the following cases:

(a) $y = \dfrac{x^3 \sin 2x}{\cos x}$

(b) $y = x^3 e^{-x} \tan x$

(c) $y = \dfrac{xe^{5x}}{\sin x}$

(d) $x^2 + 3xy + y^2 = 5$

(e) $9 = 3x^3 + 2xy^2 - y$

3 If $x = \dfrac{5 + 3t}{1 - t}$ and $y = \dfrac{2 - t}{1 - t}$ find $\dfrac{dy}{dx}$ and $\dfrac{d^2y}{dx^2}$.

4 If $x = 4(1 + \cos\theta)$ and $y = 3(\theta - \sin\theta)$ find $\dfrac{dy}{dx}$.

5 If $x = 3\cos^2\theta$ and $y = 2\sin^2\theta$ find $\dfrac{dy}{dx}$ and $\dfrac{d^2y}{dx^2}$.

6 Show that $y = e^{-4x}\sin 8x$ satisfies the equation $y'' + 8y' + 80y = 0$.

7 Differentiate $y = x^x$.

8 Given $y = x^3 e^{2x}$ find

(a) $\dfrac{dy}{dx}$　(b) $\dfrac{d^2y}{dx^2}$　(c) $\dfrac{d^3y}{dx^3}$

9 Use logarithmic differentiation to find $\dfrac{dx}{dt}$ given

(a) $x = te^t \sin t$

(b) $x = t^2 e^{-t}\cos 3t$

(c) $x = t^2 e^{3t}\sin 4t \cos 3t$

10 Show that if $y(t) = A\sin\omega t + B\cos\omega t$, where ω is a constant, then

$$y'' + \omega^2 y = 0$$

Solutions

1 (a) $2(5 + x)\cos(5 + x)^2$

(b) $2\cos x e^{2\sin x}$

(c) $20(4x + 7)^4$

(d) $3x^4 \cos 3x + 4x^3 \sin 3x$

(e) $\dfrac{e^{4x}(4x^3 - 3x^2 + 44)}{(x^3 + 11)^2}$

(f) $x^2 \sec^2 x + 2x \tan x$

(g) $\dfrac{-3x\sin 3x - 2\cos 3x}{x^3}$

(h) $-e^{-x}(5\sin 5x + \cos 5x)$

(i) $-4\tan 4x$

(j) $2\cos 4t$

(k) $\dfrac{-2x}{(x^2 + 1)^2}$

2 (a) $\dfrac{\cos x(2x^3 \cos 2x + 3x^2 \sin 2x) + x^3 \sin 2x \sin x}{\cos^2 x}$

which simplifies to $2x^3 \cos x + 6x^2 \sin x$

(b) $e^{-x}(x^3 \sec^2 x - x^3 \tan x + 3x^2 \tan x)$

(c) $\dfrac{e^{5x}(5x\sin x + \sin x - x\cos x)}{\sin^2 x}$

(d) $-\dfrac{2x + 3y}{3x + 2y}$

(e) $\dfrac{9x^2 + 2y^2}{1 - 4xy}$

3 $\frac{1}{8}, 0$

4 $-\dfrac{3(1-\cos\theta)}{4\sin\theta}$

5 $-\dfrac{2}{3}, 0$

7 $x^x(\ln x + 1)$

8 (a) $e^{2x}(2x^3 + 3x^2)$

   (b) $2xe^{2x}(2x^2 + 6x + 3)$

(c) $2e^{2x}(4x^3 + 18x^2 + 18x + 3)$

9 (a) $e^t(t\cos t + (t+1)\sin t)$

   (b) $-e^{-t}((t^2 - 2t)\cos 3t + 3t^2 \sin 3t)$

   (c) $t^2 e^{3t} \sin 4t \cos 3t \left(\dfrac{2}{t} + 3 + \dfrac{4\cos 4t}{\sin 4t} - \dfrac{3\sin 3t}{\cos 3t} \right)$

12 Applications of differentiation

Chapter 12	Contents	

12.1	Introduction	388
12.2	Maximum points and minimum points	388
12.3	Points of inflexion	397
12.4	The Newton–Raphson method for solving equations	400
12.5	Differentiation of vectors	405
	Review exercises	409

12.1 Introduction

In this chapter the techniques of differentiation are used to solve a variety of problems. It is possible to use differentiation to find the maximum or minimum values of a function. For example, it is possible to find the maximum power transferred from a voltage source to a load resistor, as we shall show later in the chapter. Differentiation is also used in the Newton–Raphson method of solving non-linear equations. Such an equation needs to be solved to calculate the steady-state values of current and voltage in a series diode–resistor circuit.

Finally we show how vectors can be differentiated. This forms an introduction to the important topic of vector calculus which is discussed in Chapter 26.

12.2 Maximum points and minimum points

Consider Figure 12.1. A and B are important points on the curve. At A the function stops increasing and starts to decrease. At B it stops decreasing and starts to increase. A is a **local maximum**, B is a **local minimum**. Note that A is not the highest point on the curve, nor B the lowest point. However, for that part of the curve near to A, A is the highest point. The word 'local' is used to stress that A is maximum in its locality. Similarly, B is the lowest point in its locality.

In Figure 12.1(a) tangents drawn at A and B would be parallel to the x axis and so at these points $\dfrac{dy}{dx}$ is zero. However, in Figure 12.1(b) there are corners at A and B. It is impossible to draw tangents at these points and so $\dfrac{dy}{dx}$ does not exist at these points.

Hence, when searching for maximum and minimum points we need only examine those points at which $\dfrac{dy}{dx}$ is zero, or $\dfrac{dy}{dx}$ does not exist.

Points at which $\dfrac{dy}{dx}$ is zero are known as **turning points** or **stationary values** of the function.

At maximum and minimum points either:

(i) $\dfrac{dy}{dx}$ does not exist, or

(ii) $\dfrac{dy}{dx} = 0$

To distinguish between maximum and minimum points we can study the sign of $\dfrac{dy}{dx}$ on either side of the point. At maximum points such as A, y is increasing immediately to the left of the point, and decreasing immediately to the right. That is, $\dfrac{dy}{dx}$ is positive immediately to the left, and $\dfrac{dy}{dx}$ is negative immediately to the right. At minimum points

Figure 12.1
The function y has a local maximum at A and a local minimum at B.

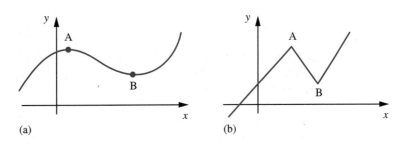

(a)　　　　　　　　(b)

such as B, y is decreasing immediately to the left of the point, and increasing immediately to the right. That is, $\dfrac{dy}{dx}$ is negative immediately to the left, and $\dfrac{dy}{dx}$ is positive immediately to the right. This so-called first-derivative test enables us to distinguish maxima from minima. This test can be used even when the derivative does not exist at the point in question.

> The **first-derivative test** to distinguish maxima from minima:
>
> To the left of a maximum point, $\dfrac{dy}{dx}$ is positive; to the right, $\dfrac{dy}{dx}$ is negative.
>
> To the left of a minimum point, $\dfrac{dy}{dx}$ is negative; to the right, $\dfrac{dy}{dx}$ is positive.

Example 12.1 Determine the position and nature of all maximum and minimum points of the following functions.

(a) $y = x^2$

(b) $y = -t^2 + t + 1$

(c) $y = \dfrac{x^3}{3} + \dfrac{x^2}{2} - 2x + 1$

(d) $y = |t|$

Solution (a) If $y = x^2$, then by differentiation $\dfrac{dy}{dx} = 2x$.

Recall that at maximum and minimum points either

(i) $\dfrac{dy}{dx}$ does not exist, or

(ii) $\dfrac{dy}{dx} = 0$. We must check both of these conditions.

The function $2x$ exists for all values of x, and so we move to examine any points where $\dfrac{dy}{dx} = 0$. So, we have

$$\frac{dy}{dx} = 2x = 0$$

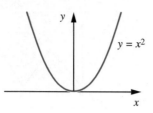

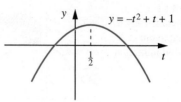

Figure 12.2 The function y has a minimum at $x = 0$.

Figure 12.3 The function y has a maximum at $t = \frac{1}{2}$.

The equation $2x = 0$ has one solution, $x = 0$. We conclude that a turning point exists at $x = 0$. Furthermore, from the given function $y = x^2$, we see that when $x = 0$ the value of y is also 0, so a turning point exists at the point with coordinates $(0, 0)$. To determine whether this point is a maximum or minimum we use the first-derivative test and examine the sign of $\dfrac{dy}{dx}$ on either side of $x = 0$. To the left of $x = 0$, x is clearly negative and so $2x$ is also negative. To the right of $x = 0$, x is positive and so $2x$ is also positive. Hence y has a minimum at $x = 0$. A graph of $y = x^2$ showing this minimum is given in Figure 12.2.

(b) If $y = -t^2 + t + 1$, then $y' = -2t + 1$ and this function exists for all values of t. Solving $y' = 0$ we have

$$-2t + 1 = 0 \qquad \text{and so } t = \frac{1}{2}$$

We conclude that there is a turning point at $t = \frac{1}{2}$. The y coordinate here is $-\left(\frac{1}{2}\right)^2 + \frac{1}{2} + 1 = 1\frac{1}{4}$. We now inspect the sign of y' to the left and to the right of $t = \frac{1}{2}$. A little to the left, say at $t = 0$, we see that $y' = -2(0) + 1 = 1$ which is positive. A little to the right, say at $t = 1$, we see that $y' = -2(1) + 1 = -1$ which is negative. Hence there is a maximum at the point $\left(\frac{1}{2}, 1\frac{1}{4}\right)$.

A graph of the function is shown in Figure 12.3.

(c) If $y = \dfrac{x^3}{3} + \dfrac{x^2}{2} - 2x + 1$, then $y' = x^2 + x - 2$ and this function exists for all values of x. Solving $y' = 0$ we find

$$x^2 + x - 2 = 0$$
$$(x - 1)(x + 2) = 0$$
$$x = 1, -2$$

There are therefore two turning points, one at $x = 1$ and one at $x = -2$. We consider each in turn.

At $x = 1$, we examine the sign of y' to the left and to the right of $x = 1$. A little way to the left, say at $x = 0$, we see that $y' = -2$ which is negative. A little to the right, say at $x = 2$, we see that $y' = 2^2 + 2 - 2 = 4$ which is positive. So the point where $x = 1$ is a minimum.

At $x = -2$, we examine the sign of y' to the left and to the right of $x = -2$. A little way to the left, say at $x = -3$, we see that $y' = (-3)^2 + (-3) - 2 = 4$ which is

Figure 12.4
The function y has a maximum at $x = -2$ and a minimum at $x = 1$.

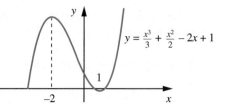

$$y = \frac{x^3}{3} + \frac{x^2}{2} - 2x + 1$$

positive. A little to the right, say at $x = -1$, we see that $y' = (-1)^2 + (-1) - 2 = -2$ which is negative. So the point where $x = -2$ is a maximum.

A graph of the function is shown in Figure 12.4.

(d) Recall that the modulus function $y = |t|$ is defined as follows:

$$y = |t| = \begin{cases} -t & t \leq 0 \\ t & t > 0 \end{cases}$$

A graph of this function was given in Figure 10.13(a) and this should be looked at before continuing. Note that $\frac{dy}{dt} = -1$ for t negative, and $\frac{dy}{dt} = +1$ for t positive. The derivative is not defined at $t = 0$ because of the corner there. There are no points when $\frac{dy}{dt} = 0$. Because the derivative is not defined at $t = 0$ this point requires further scrutiny. To the left of $t = 0$, $\frac{dy}{dt} < 0$; to the right $\frac{dy}{dt} > 0$ and so $t = 0$ is a minimum point.

Rather than examine the sign of y' on both sides of the point, a second-derivative test may be used. On passing through a maximum point y' changes from positive to 0 to negative, as shown in Figure 12.5. Hence, y' is decreasing. If y'' is negative then this indicates y' is decreasing and the point is therefore a maximum point. Conversely, on passing through a minimum point, y' increases, going from negative to 0 to positive (see Figure 12.6). If y'' is positive then y' is increasing and this indicates a minimum point.

So, having located the points where $y' = 0$, we look at the second derivative, y''. Thus $y'' > 0$ implies a minimum point; $y'' < 0$ implies a maximum point. If $y'' = 0$, then we must return to the earlier, more basic test of examining y' on both sides of the point. In summary:

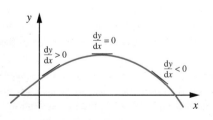

Figure 12.5 The derivative $\frac{dy}{dx}$ decreases on passing through a maximum point.

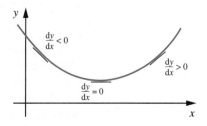

Figure 12.6 The derivative $\frac{dy}{dx}$ increases on passing through a minimum point.

The **second-derivative test** to distinguish maxima from minima:
If $y' = 0$ and $y'' < 0$ at a point, then this indicates that the point is a maximum turning point.
If $y' = 0$ and $y'' > 0$ at a point, then this indicates that the point is a minimum turning point.
If $y' = 0$ and $y'' = 0$ at a point, the second-derivative test fails and you must use the first-derivative test.

Example 12.2

Use the second-derivative test to find all maximum and minimum points of the functions in Example 12.1.

Solution

(a) Given $y = x^2$ then $y' = 2x$ and $y'' = 2$. We locate the position of maximum and minimum points by solving $y' = 0$ and so such a point exists at $x = 0$. Evaluating y'' at this point we see that $y''(0) = 2$ which is positive. Using the second-derivative test we conclude that the point is a minimum.

(b) Given $y = -t^2 + t + 1$ then $y' = -2t + 1$ and $y'' = -2$. Solving $y' = 0$ we find $t = \frac{1}{2}$. Evaluating y'' at this point we find $y''(\frac{1}{2}) = -2$ which is negative. Using the second-derivative test we conclude that $t = \frac{1}{2}$ is a maximum point.

(c) Given $y = \dfrac{x^3}{3} + \dfrac{x^2}{2} - 2x + 1$, then $y' = x^2 + x - 2$ and $y'' = 2x + 1$. $y' = 0$ at $x = 1$ and $x = -2$. At $x = 1$, $y'' = 3$ which is positive and so the point is a minimum. At $x = -2$, $y'' = -3$ which is negative and so the point is a maximum.

(d) $y' = \begin{cases} -1 & t < 0 \\ 1 & t > 0 \\ \text{undefined at } t = 0 \end{cases}$

Since $y'(0)$ is undefined, we use the first-derivative test. This was employed in Example 12.1.

Example 12.3

Risetime for a second-order electrical system

Consider the electrical system illustrated in Figure 12.7. The input voltage, v_i, is applied to terminals a–b. The output from the system is a voltage, v_o, measured across the terminals c–d. The easiest way to determine the time response of this system to a particular input is to use the technique of Laplace transforms (see Chapter 21).

When a step input is applied to the system, the general form of the response depends on whether a quantity called the damping ratio, ζ, is such that $\zeta > 1$, $\zeta = 1$ or $\zeta < 1$. The quantity ζ itself depends upon the values of L, C and R. This is illustrated in Figure 12.8. If the damping ratio, $\zeta < 1$, then v_o overshoots its final value and the system is said to be underdamped. For this case it can be shown that

$$ v_o = U - Ue^{-\alpha t}\left(\cos(\beta t) + \frac{\alpha \sin(\beta t)}{\beta}\right) \qquad \text{for} \qquad t > 0 \qquad (12.1) $$

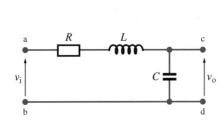

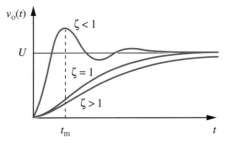

Figure 12.7 A second-order electrical system.

Figure 12.8 Response of a second-order system to a step input.

where U is the height of a step input applied at $t = 0$, and

$$\alpha = \frac{R}{2L} \tag{12.2}$$

$$\omega_r = \frac{1}{\sqrt{LC}} \qquad \text{resonant frequency} \tag{12.3}$$

$$\beta = \sqrt{\omega_r^2 - \alpha^2} \qquad \text{natural frequency} \tag{12.4}$$

Engineers are often interested in knowing how quickly a system will respond to a particular input. For many systems this is an important design criterion. One way of characterizing the speed of response of the system is the time taken for the output to reach a certain level in response to a step input. This is known as the **risetime** and is often defined as the time taken for the output to rise from 10% to 90% of its final value. However, by looking at the underdamped response illustrated in Figure 12.8 it is clear that the time, t_m, required for the output to reach its maximum value would also provide an indicator of system response time. As the derivative of a function is zero at a maximum point it is possible to calculate this time.

Differentiating Equation (12.1) and using the product rule,

$$\frac{dv_o}{dt} = \frac{d}{dt}\left(U - Ue^{-\alpha t}\left(\cos(\beta t) + \frac{\alpha \sin(\beta t)}{\beta}\right)\right) \qquad t > 0$$

$$= 0 - U\frac{d}{dt}(e^{-\alpha t}\cos(\beta t)) - U\frac{d}{dt}\left(\frac{e^{-\alpha t}\alpha \sin(\beta t)}{\beta}\right)$$

$$= -U(-\alpha e^{-\alpha t}\cos(\beta t) - e^{-\alpha t}\beta \sin(\beta t))$$

$$-U\left(\frac{-\alpha e^{-\alpha t}\alpha \sin(\beta t)}{\beta} + \frac{e^{-\alpha t}\alpha\beta \cos(\beta t)}{\beta}\right)$$

$$= -Ue^{-\alpha t}\left(-\alpha \cos(\beta t) - \beta \sin(\beta t) - \frac{\alpha^2 \sin(\beta t)}{\beta} + \alpha \cos(\beta t)\right)$$

$$= Ue^{-\alpha t}\left(\beta + \frac{\alpha^2}{\beta}\right)\sin(\beta t)$$

At a turning point $\dfrac{dv_\mathrm{o}}{dt} = 0$. Hence

$$U e^{-\alpha t} \left(\frac{\beta^2 + \alpha^2}{\beta} \right) \sin(\beta t) = 0$$

This occurs when $\sin(\beta t) = 0$, which corresponds to $t = k\pi/\beta$, $k = 0, 1, 2 \ldots$. It is now straightforward to calculate t_m, once β has been calculated, using Equations (12.2), (12.3) and (12.4) for particular values of R, L and C. You may like to show that the turning point corresponding to $k = 1$ is a maximum by calculating $\dfrac{d^2 v_\mathrm{o}}{dt^2}$ and carrying out the second-derivative test.

It is possible to check whether or not a system is underdamped using the following formulae:

$$\zeta = \frac{R}{R_\mathrm{c}} \qquad \text{damping ratio} \tag{12.5}$$

$$R_\mathrm{c} = 2\sqrt{\frac{L}{C}} \qquad \text{critical resistance} \tag{12.6}$$

Let us look at a specific case with typical values $L = 40$ mH, $C = 1\ \mu\mathrm{F}$, $R = 200\ \Omega$. Using Equations (12.5) and (12.6), we find

$$R_\mathrm{c} = 2\sqrt{\frac{L}{C}} = 2\sqrt{\frac{4 \times 10^{-2}}{1 \times 10^{-6}}} = 400$$

$$\zeta = \frac{R}{R_\mathrm{c}} = \frac{200}{400} = 0.5$$

and therefore the system is underdamped because $\zeta < 1$.
   Also,

$$\omega_\mathrm{r} = \frac{1}{\sqrt{LC}} = 5000$$

$$\alpha = \frac{R}{2L} = \frac{200}{2 \times 4 \times 10^{-2}} = 2500$$

$$\beta = \sqrt{\omega_\mathrm{r}^2 - \alpha^2} = \sqrt{5000^2 - 2500^2} = 4330$$

Finally,

$$t_\mathrm{m} = \frac{\pi}{4330} = 7.26 \times 10^{-4} = 726\ \mu\mathrm{s}$$

We conclude for this case that the risetime is 726 μs.

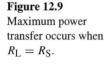
Figure 12.9
Maximum power
transfer occurs when
$R_L = R_S$.

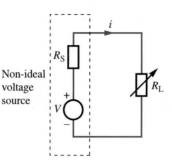

Non-ideal
voltage
source

R_S

i

R_L

V

Example 12.4 **Maximum power transfer**

Consider the circuit of Figure 12.9 in which a non-ideal voltage source is connected to a variable load resistor with resistance R_L. The source voltage is V and its internal resistance is R_S. Calculate the value of R_L which results in the maximum power being transferred from the voltage source to the load resistor.

Solution Let i be the current flowing in the circuit. Using Kirchhoff's voltage law and Ohm's law gives

$$V = i(R_S + R_L)$$

Let P be the power developed in the load resistor. Then,

$$P = i^2 R_L = \frac{V^2 R_L}{(R_S + R_L)^2}$$

Clearly P depends on the value of R_L. Differentiating w.r.t. R_L and using the quotient rule, we obtain

$$\frac{dP}{dR_L} = V^2 \frac{1(R_S + R_L)^2 - R_L 2(R_S + R_L)}{(R_S + R_L)^4}$$

$$= V^2 \frac{(R_S + R_L) - 2R_L}{(R_S + R_L)^3}$$

$$= V^2 \frac{R_S - R_L}{(R_S + R_L)^3}$$

Equating $\dfrac{dP}{dR_L}$ to zero to obtain the turning point gives

$$V^2 \frac{R_S - R_L}{(R_S + R_L)^3} = 0$$

that is,

$$R_L = R_S$$

So a turning point occurs when the load resistance equals the source resistance. We need to check if this is a maximum turning point, so

$$\frac{dP}{dR_L} = V^2 \frac{R_S - R_L}{(R_S + R_L)^3}$$

$$\frac{d^2P}{dR_L^2} = V^2 \frac{-1(R_S + R_L)^3 - (R_S - R_L)3(R_S + R_L)^2}{(R_S + R_L)^6}$$

$$= V^2 \frac{-(R_S + R_L) - 3(R_S - R_L)}{(R_S + R_L)^4}$$

$$= V^2 \frac{2R_L - 4R_S}{(R_S + R_L)^4}$$

$$= 2V^2 \frac{(R_L - 2R_S)}{(R_S + R_L)^4}$$

When $R_L = R_S$, this expression is negative and so the turning point is a maximum. Therefore, maximum power transfer occurs when the load resistance equals the source resistance.

Exercises 12.2

1 Locate the position of any turning points of the following functions and determine whether they are maxima or minima.

(a) $y = x^2 - x + 6$

(b) $y = 2x^2 + 3x + 1$

(c) $y = x - 1$

(d) $y = 1 + x - 2x^2$

(e) $y = x^3 - 12x$

(f) $y = 7 + 3x$

2 Locate and identify all turning points of

(a) $y = \frac{x^3}{3} - 3x^2 + 8x + 1$

(b) $y = te^{-t}$

(c) $y = x^4 - 2x^2$

Solutions

1 (a) $\left(\frac{1}{2}, 5\frac{3}{4}\right)$, minimum

(b) $(-0.75, -0.125)$, minimum

(c) none

(d) $(0.25, 1.125)$, maximum

(e) $(2, -16)$ minimum, $(-2, 16)$ maximum

(f) none

2 (a) $\left(2, \frac{23}{3}\right)$ maximum, $\left(4, \frac{19}{3}\right)$ minimum

(b) $(1, 0.368)$, maximum

(c) $(0, 0)$ maximum, $(1, -1)$ minimum, $(-1, -1)$ minimum

Computer and calculator exercises 12.2

Computer algebra packages are able to differentiate functions and to solve equations and so they can be used to find turning points.

1 (a) Use a package to find y' and y'' when
$$y = e^{-0.2t} \cos t.$$

(b) Solve $y' = 0$ and hence locate any turning points in the interval $[0, 6]$ and determine their type.

(c) Plot a graph of y and check the position of the turning points with the results obtained in part (b).

12.3 Points of inflexion

Recall from Section 11.4 that when the gradient of a curve, that is y', is increasing, the second derivative y'' is positive and the curve is said to be concave up. When the gradient is decreasing the second derivative y'' is negative and the curve is said to be concave down. A point at which the concavity of a curve changes from concave up to concave down or vice versa is called a **point of inflexion**.

A point of inflexion is a point on a curve where the concavity changes from concave up to concave down or vice versa. It follows that $y'' = 0$ at such a point or, in exceptional cases, y'' does not exist.

Figure 12.10(a) shows a graph for which a point of inflexion occurs at the point marked A. Note that at this point the gradient of the graph is zero. Figure 12.10(b) shows a graph with points of inflexion occurring at A and B. Note that at these points the gradient of the graph is not zero.

Figure 12.10
(a) There is a point of inflexion at A;
(b) there are points of inflexion at A and B.

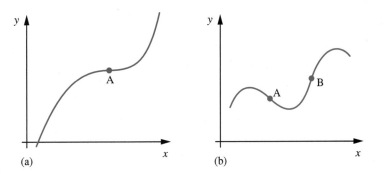

(a)   (b)

To locate a point of inflexion we must look for a point where $y'' = 0$ or does not exist. We must then examine the concavity of the curve on either side of such a point.

Example 12.5   Locate any points of inflexion of the curve $y = x^3$.

Solution   Given $y = x^3$, then $y' = 3x^2$ and $y'' = 6x$. Points of inflexion can only occur where $y'' = 0$ or does not exist. Clearly y'' exists for all x and is zero when $x = 0$. It is possible

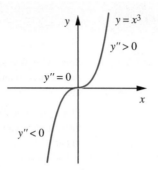

Figure 12.11 The second derivative, y'', changes sign at $x = 0$.

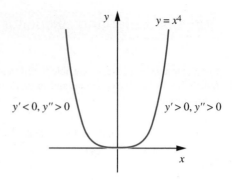

Figure 12.12 The derivative, y', changes sign at $x = 0$, but y'' remains positive.

that a point of inflexion occurs when $x = 0$ but we must examine the concavity of the curve on either side. To the left of $x = 0$, x is negative and so y'' is negative. Hence to the left, the curve is concave down. To the right of $x = 0$, x is positive and so y'' is positive. Hence to the right, the curve is concave up. Thus the concavity changes at $x = 0$. We conclude that $x = 0$ is a point of inflexion. A graph is shown in Figure 12.11. Note that at this point of inflexion $y' = 0$ too.

A common error is to state that if $y' = y'' = 0$ then there is a point of inflexion. This is not always true; consider the next example.

Example 12.6 Locate all maximum points, minimum points and points of inflexion of $y = x^4$.

Solution $$y' = 4x^3 \qquad y'' = 12x^2$$

$y' = 0$ at $x = 0$. Also $y'' = 0$ at $x = 0$ and so the second-derivative test is of no help in determining the position of maximum and minimum points. We return to examine y' on both sides of $x = 0$. To the left of $x = 0$, $y' < 0$; to the right $y' > 0$ and so $x = 0$ is a minimum point. Figure 12.12 illustrates this. Note that at the point $x = 0$, the second derivative y'' is zero. However, y'' is positive both to the left and to the right of $x = 0$; thus $x = 0$ is not a point of inflexion.

Example 12.7 Find any maximum points, minimum points and points of inflexion of $y = x^3 + 2x^2$.

Solution Given $y = x^3 + 2x^2$ then $y' = 3x^2 + 4x$ and $y'' = 6x + 4$. Let us first find any maximum and minimum points. The first derivative y' is zero when $3x^2 + 4x = x(3x + 4) = 0$, that is when $x = 0$ or $x = -\frac{4}{3}$. Using the second-derivative test we find $y''(0) = 4$ which corresponds to a minimum point. Similarly, $y''\left(-\frac{4}{3}\right) = -4$ which corresponds to a maximum point.

We seek points of inflexion by looking for points where $y'' = 0$ and then examining the concavity on either side. $y'' = 0$ when $x = -\frac{2}{3}$.

Figure 12.13
There is a maximum at
$x = -\frac{4}{3}$, a minimum
at $x = 0$ and a point of
inflexion at $x = -\frac{2}{3}$.

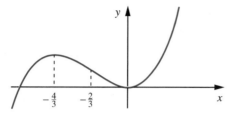

Since y'' is negative when $x < -\frac{2}{3}$, then y' is decreasing there, that is the function is concave down. Also, y'' is positive when $x > -\frac{2}{3}$ and so y' is then increasing, that is the function is concave up. Hence there is a point of inflexion when $x = -\frac{2}{3}$. The graph of $y = x^3 + 2x^2$ is shown in Figure 12.13.

From Examples 12.6 and 12.7 we note that

(1) The condition $y'' = 0$ is not sufficient to ensure a point is a point of inflexion. The concavity of the function on either side of the point where $y'' = 0$ must be considered.

(2) At a point of inflexion it is not necessary to have $y' = 0$.

(3) At a point of inflexion $y'' = 0$ or y'' does not exist.

Exercises 12.3

1 Locate the maximum points, minimum points and points of inflexion of

(a) $y = 3t^2 + 6t - 1$

(b) $y = 4 - t - t^2$

(c) $y = \frac{x^3}{3} - \frac{x^2}{2} + 10$

(d) $y = \frac{x^3}{3} + \frac{x^2}{2} - 20x + 7$

(e) $y = t^5$

(f) $y = t^6$

(g) $y = x^4 - 2x^2$

(h) $z = t + \frac{1}{t}$

(i) $y = x^5 - \frac{5x^3}{3}$

(j) $y = t^{1/3}$

Solutions

1 (a) $(-1, -4)$ minimum

(b) $(-0.5, 4.25)$ maximum

(c) $(0, 10)$ maximum, $\left(1, \frac{59}{6}\right)$ minimum,

$\left(\frac{1}{2}, \frac{119}{12}\right)$ point of inflexion

(d) $\left(4, -\frac{131}{3}\right)$ minimum, $(-5, 77.83)$

maximum, $\left(-\frac{1}{2}, 17.08\right)$ point of inflexion

(e) $(0, 0)$ point of inflexion

(f) $(0, 0)$ minimum

(g) (0, 0) maximum, (1, −1) minimum,

(−1, −1) minimum, $\left(\dfrac{1}{\sqrt{3}}, -\dfrac{5}{9}\right)$,

$\left(-\dfrac{1}{\sqrt{3}}, -\dfrac{5}{9}\right)$ points of inflexion

(h) (1, 2) minimum, (−1, −2) maximum

(i) $\left(1, -\dfrac{2}{3}\right)$ minimum, $\left(-1, \dfrac{2}{3}\right)$ maximum,

(0, 0), $\left(\dfrac{1}{\sqrt{2}}, -\dfrac{7}{12\sqrt{2}}\right)$, $\left(-\dfrac{1}{\sqrt{2}}, \dfrac{7}{12\sqrt{2}}\right)$

are also points of inflexion

(j) (0, 0) point of inflexion

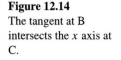

Computer and calculator exercises 12.3

1 (a) Use a graph plotting package to sketch a graph of $y = 3t^{1/5}$.

(b) From your graph find the position of any maxima, minima or points of inflexion.

12.4 The Newton–Raphson method for solving equations

We often need to solve equations such as

$$f(x) = 2x^4 - x^3 + x^2 - 10 = 0$$
$$f(t) = 2e^{-3t} - t^2 = 0$$
$$f(t) = t - \sin t = 0$$

The Newton–Raphson technique is a method of obtaining an approximate solution, or root, of such equations. It involves the use of differentiation.

Suppose we wish to find a root of $f(x) = 0$. Figure 12.14 illustrates the curve $y = f(x)$. Roots of the equation $f(x) = 0$ correspond to where the curve cuts the x axis. One such root is illustrated and is labelled $x = \hat{x}$. Suppose we know that $x = x_1$ is an approximate solution. Let A be the point on the x axis where $x = x_1$ and let B be the point on the curve where $x = x_1$. The tangent at B is drawn and cuts the x axis at C where $x = x_2$. Clearly $x = x_2$ is a better approximation to $\hat{x}$ than x_1. We now find x_2 in terms of the known value, x_1.

$$AB = \text{distance of B above the } x \text{ axis} = f(x_1)$$
$$CA = x_1 - x_2$$

Figure 12.14
The tangent at B intersects the x axis at C.

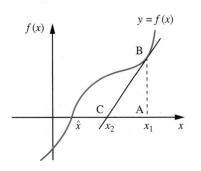

Hence,

$$\text{gradient of line CB} = \frac{AB}{CA} = \frac{f(x_1)}{x_1 - x_2}$$

But CB is a tangent to the curve at $x = x_1$ and so has gradient $f'(x_1)$. Hence,

$$f'(x_1) = \frac{f(x_1)}{x_1 - x_2}$$

$$x_1 - x_2 = \frac{f(x_1)}{f'(x_1)}$$

and therefore,

$$x_2 = x_1 - \frac{f(x_1)}{f'(x_1)} \tag{12.7}$$

Equation (12.7) is known as the Newton–Raphson formula. Knowing an approximate root of $f(x) = 0$, that is x_1, the Newton–Raphson formula enables us to calculate an improved approximate root, x_2.

Example 12.8   Given that $x_1 = 7.5$ is an approximate root of $e^x - 6x^3 = 0$, use the Newton–Raphson technique to find an improved value.

Solution

$$x_1 = 7.5$$
$$f(x) = e^x - 6x^3 \qquad f(x_1) = -723$$
$$f'(x) = e^x - 18x^2 \qquad f'(x_1) = 796$$

Using the Newton–Raphson technique the value of x_2 is found:

$$x_2 = x_1 - \frac{f(x_1)}{f'(x_1)} = 7.5 - \frac{(-723)}{796} = 8.41$$

An improved estimate of the root of $e^x - 6x^3 = 0$ is $x = 8.41$. To two decimal places the true answer is $x = 8.05$.

The Newton–Raphson technique can be used repeatedly as illustrated in Example 12.9. This generates a sequence of approximate solutions which may converge to the required root. Each application of the method is known as an **iteration**.

Example 12.9   A root of $3 \sin x = x$ is near to $x = 2.5$. Use two iterations of the Newton–Raphson technique to find a more accurate approximation.

Solution   The equation must first be written in the form $f(x) = 0$, that is

$$f(x) = 3 \sin x - x = 0$$

Then

$$x_1 = 2.5$$

$$f(x) = 3 \sin x - x \qquad f(x_1) = -0.705$$

$$f'(x) = 3 \cos x - 1 \qquad f'(x_1) = -3.403$$

Then

$$x_2 = 2.5 - \frac{(-0.705)}{(-3.403)} = 2.293$$

The process is repeated with $x_1 = 2.293$ as the initial approximation:

$$x_1 = 2.293 \qquad f(x_1) = -0.042 \qquad f'(x_1) = -2.983$$

Then

$$x_2 = 2.293 - \frac{(-0.042)}{(-2.983)} = 2.279$$

Using two iterations of the Newton–Raphson technique, we obtain $x = 2.28$ as an improved estimate of the root.

Example 12.10

An approximate root of

$$x^3 - 2x^2 - 5 = 0$$

is $x = 3$. By using the Newton–Raphson technique repeatedly, determine the value of the root correct to two decimal places.

Solution We have

$$x_1 = 3$$

$$f(x) = x^3 - 2x^2 - 5 \qquad f(x_1) = 4$$

$$f'(x) = 3x^2 - 4x \qquad f'(x_1) = 15$$

Hence

$$x_2 = 3 - \frac{4}{15} = 2.733$$

An improved estimate of the value of the root is 2.73 (2 d.p.). The method is used again, taking $x_1 = 2.73$ as the initial approximation.

$$x_1 = 2.73 \qquad f(x_1) = 0.441 \qquad f'(x_1) = 11.439$$

$$x_2 = 2.73 - \frac{0.441}{11.439} = 2.691$$

An improved estimate is $x = 2.69$ (2 d.p.). The method is used again:

$$x_1 = 2.69 \qquad f(x_1) = -0.007 \qquad f'(x_1) = 10.948$$

So

$$x_2 = 2.69 - \frac{(-0.007)}{10.948} = 2.691$$

There is no change in the value of the approximate root and so to two decimal places the root of $f(x) = 0$ is $x = 2.69$.

The previous examples illustrate the general Newton–Raphson formula.

If $x = x_n$ is an approximate root of $f(x) = 0$, then an improved estimate, x_{n+1}, is given by

$$x_{n+1} = x_n - \frac{f(x_n)}{f'(x_n)}$$

The Newton–Raphson formula is easy to program in a loop structure. Exit from the loop is usually conditional upon $|x_{n+1} - x_n|$ being smaller than some prescribed very small value. This condition shows that successive approximate roots are very close to each other.

Example 12.11   **Series diode–resistor circuit**

Consider the circuit of Figure 12.15(a). A diode is in series with a resistor with resistance, R. The voltage across the diode is denoted by v and the current through the diode is denoted by i. The i–v relationship for the diode is non-linear and is given by

$$i = I_s(e^{40v} - 1)$$

where I_s is the reverse saturation current of the diode. Given that the supply voltage, V_s, is 2 V, I_s is 10^{-14} A and R is 22 kΩ, calculate the steady-state values of i and v.

Solution   There are several ways to solve this problem. A difficulty exists because the diode i–v relationship is non-linear. One possibility is to draw a **load line** for the resistor superimposed on the diode i–v characteristic, as shown in Figure 12.15(b). The load line is an equation for the resistor characteristic written in terms of the voltage across

Figure 12.15
A simple non-linear
circuit: (a) series
diode–resistor circuit;
(b) resistor load line
superimposed on diode
characteristic.

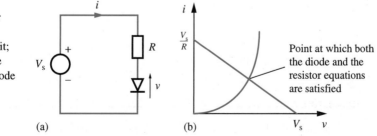

the diode, v, and the current through the diode, i. It is given by

$$V_s - v = iR$$

$$i = -\frac{1}{R}v + \frac{V_s}{R}$$

This is a straight line with slope $-\frac{1}{R}$ and vertical intercept $\frac{V_s}{R}$. When $v = 0$, $i = \frac{V_s}{R}$. This corresponds to all of the supply voltage being dropped across the resistor. When $v = V_s$, $i = 0$. This corresponds to all of the supply voltage being dropped across the diode. Therefore, these two limits correspond to the points within which the circuit must operate. The solution to the circuit can be obtained by determining the intercept of the diode characteristic and the load line. This is possible because both the resistor characteristic and diode characteristic are formulated in terms of v and i, and so any solution must have the same values of i and v for both components. If an accurate graph is used, it is possible to obtain a reasonably good solution. An alternative approach is to use the Newton–Raphson technique. Combining the two component equations gives

$$-v + V_s = RI_s(e^{40v} - 1)$$

Now $R = 2.2 \times 10^4$, $I_s = 10^{-14}$, $V_s = 2$ and so

$$-v + 2 = 2.2 \times 10^4 \times 10^{-14}(e^{40v} - 1)$$

Now, define $f(v)$ by

$$f(v) = 2.2 \times 10^{-10}(e^{40v} - 1) + v - 2$$

We wish to solve $f(v) = 0$. We have

$$f'(v) = 2.2 \times 10^{-10} \times 40e^{40v} + 1 = 8.8 \times 10^{-9}e^{40v} + 1$$

Choose an initial guess of $v_1 = 0.5$:

$$v_2 = v_1 - \frac{f(v_1)}{f'(v_1)} = 0.5 - \frac{2.2 \times 10^{-10}(e^{20} - 1) + 0.5 - 2}{8.8 \times 10^{-9}e^{20} + 1} = 0.7644$$

With an equation of this complexity, it is better to use a computer or a programmable calculator. Doing so gives

$$v_5 = 0.6895, \ldots, v_{10} = 0.5770, \ldots, v_{14} = 0.5650$$

which is accurate to four decimal places.

It is useful to check the solution by independently calculating the current through the diode using the two different expressions. So,

$$i = 10^{-14}(e^{40 \times 0.5650} - 1) = 6.53 \times 10^{-5} \text{ A}$$

$$i = -\frac{0.5650}{2.2 \times 10^4} + \frac{2}{2.2 \times 10^4} = 6.53 \times 10^{-5} \text{ A}$$

and therefore the solution is correct.

Exercises 12.4

1 Use the Newton–Raphson technique to find the value of a root of the following equations correct to two decimal places. An approximate root, x_1, is given in each case.

(a) $2\cos x = x^2$ $x_1 = 0.8$

(b) $3x^3 - 4x^2 + 2x - 9 = 0$ $x_1 = 2$

(c) $e^{x/2} - 5x = 0$ $x_1 = 6$

(d) $\ln x = \dfrac{1}{x}$ $x_1 = 1.6$

(e) $\sin x + \dfrac{2x}{\pi} = 1$ $x_1 = 0.6$

2 Explain circumstances in which the Newton–Raphson technique may fail to converge to a root of $f(x) = 0$.

Solutions

1 (a) 1.02   (b) 1.85   (c) 7.15   (d) 1.76   (e) 0.64

12.5 Differentiation of vectors

Consider Figure 12.16. If $\mathbf{r}$ represents the position vector of an object and that object moves along a curve C, then the position vector will be dependent upon the time, t. We write $\mathbf{r} = \mathbf{r}(t)$ to show the dependence upon time. Suppose that the object is at the point P with position vector $\mathbf{r}$ at time t and at the point Q with position vector $\mathbf{r}(t + \delta t)$ at the later time $t + \delta t$ as shown in Figure 12.17. Then $\overrightarrow{PQ}$ represents the displacement vector of the object during the interval of time δt. The length of the displacement vector represents the distance travelled while its direction gives the direction of motion. The average velocity during the time from t to $t + \delta t$ is the displacement vector divided by the time interval δt, that is

$$\text{average velocity} = \frac{\overrightarrow{PQ}}{\delta t} = \frac{\mathbf{r}(t + \delta t) - \mathbf{r}(t)}{\delta t}$$

The instantaneous velocity, $\mathbf{v}$, is given by

$$\mathbf{v} = \lim_{\delta t \to 0} \frac{\mathbf{r}(t + \delta t) - \mathbf{r}(t)}{\delta t} = \frac{d\mathbf{r}}{dt}$$

Now, since the x and y coordinates of the object depend upon the time, we can write the position vector $\mathbf{r}$ as

$$\mathbf{r}(t) = x(t)\mathbf{i} + y(t)\mathbf{j}$$

Therefore,

$$\mathbf{r}(t + \delta t) = x(t + \delta t)\mathbf{i} + y(t + \delta t)\mathbf{j}$$

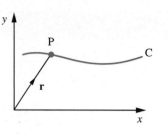

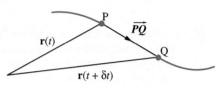

Figure 12.16 Position vector of a point P on a curve C.

Figure 12.17 Vector $\overrightarrow{PQ}$ represents the displacement of the object during the time interval δt.

so that

$$\mathbf{v}(t) = \lim_{\delta t \to 0} \frac{x(t+\delta t)\mathbf{i} + y(t+\delta t)\mathbf{j} - x(t)\mathbf{i} - y(t)\mathbf{j}}{\delta t}$$

$$= \lim_{\delta t \to 0} \left\{ \frac{x(t+\delta t) - x(t)}{\delta t}\mathbf{i} + \frac{y(t+\delta t) - y(t)}{\delta t}\mathbf{j} \right\}$$

$$= \frac{dx}{dt}\mathbf{i} + \frac{dy}{dt}\mathbf{j}$$

often abbreviated to $\mathbf{v} = \dot{\mathbf{r}} = \dot{x}\mathbf{i} + \dot{y}\mathbf{j}$. Recall the dot notation for derivatives w.r.t. time which is commonly used when differentiating vectors. So the velocity vector is the derivative of the position vector with respect to time. This result generalizes in an obvious way to three dimensions. If

$$\mathbf{r}(t) = x(t)\mathbf{i} + y(t)\mathbf{j} + z(t)\mathbf{k}$$

then

$$\dot{\mathbf{r}}(t) = \dot{x}(t)\mathbf{i} + \dot{y}(t)\mathbf{j} + \dot{z}(t)\mathbf{k}$$

The magnitude of the velocity vector gives the speed of the object. We can define the acceleration in a similar way:

$$\mathbf{a} = \frac{d\mathbf{v}}{dt} = \frac{d^2\mathbf{r}}{dt^2} = \ddot{\mathbf{r}} = \ddot{x}\mathbf{i} + \ddot{y}\mathbf{j} + \ddot{z}\mathbf{k}$$

In more general situations, we will not be dealing with position vectors but other physical quantities such as time-dependent electric or magnetic fields.

Example 12.12 If $\mathbf{a} = 3t^2\mathbf{i} + \cos 2t\mathbf{j}$, find

(a) $\dfrac{d\mathbf{a}}{dt}$ (b) $\left| \dfrac{d\mathbf{a}}{dt} \right|$ (c) $\dfrac{d^2\mathbf{a}}{dt^2}$

Solution (a) If $\mathbf{a} = 3t^2\mathbf{i} + \cos 2t\mathbf{j}$, then differentiation with respect to t yields

$$\frac{d\mathbf{a}}{dt} = 6t\mathbf{i} - 2\sin 2t\mathbf{j}$$

(b) $\left|\dfrac{d\mathbf{a}}{dt}\right| = \sqrt{(6t)^2 + (-2\sin 2t)^2} = \sqrt{36t^2 + 4\sin^2 2t}$

(c) $\dfrac{d^2\mathbf{a}}{dt^2} = 6\mathbf{i} - 4\cos 2t\,\mathbf{j}$

It is possible to differentiate more complicated expressions involving vectors provided certain rules are adhered to. If $\mathbf{a}$ and $\mathbf{b}$ are vectors and c is a scalar, all functions of time t, then

$$\frac{d}{dt}(c\mathbf{a}) = c\frac{d\mathbf{a}}{dt} + \frac{dc}{dt}\mathbf{a} \qquad \frac{d}{dt}(\mathbf{a}\cdot\mathbf{b}) = \mathbf{a}\cdot\frac{d\mathbf{b}}{dt} + \frac{d\mathbf{a}}{dt}\cdot\mathbf{b}$$

$$\frac{d}{dt}(\mathbf{a}+\mathbf{b}) = \frac{d\mathbf{a}}{dt} + \frac{d\mathbf{b}}{dt} \qquad \frac{d}{dt}(\mathbf{a}\times\mathbf{b}) = \mathbf{a}\times\frac{d\mathbf{b}}{dt} + \frac{d\mathbf{a}}{dt}\times\mathbf{b}$$

Example 12.13 If $\mathbf{a} = 3t\mathbf{i} - t^2\mathbf{j}$ and $\mathbf{b} = 2t^2\mathbf{i} + 3\mathbf{j}$, verify

(a) $\dfrac{d}{dt}(\mathbf{a}\cdot\mathbf{b}) = \mathbf{a}\cdot\dfrac{d\mathbf{b}}{dt} + \dfrac{d\mathbf{a}}{dt}\cdot\mathbf{b}$ (b) $\dfrac{d}{dt}(\mathbf{a}\times\mathbf{b}) = \mathbf{a}\times\dfrac{d\mathbf{b}}{dt} + \dfrac{d\mathbf{a}}{dt}\times\mathbf{b}$

Solution (a) $\mathbf{a}\cdot\mathbf{b} = (3t\mathbf{i} - t^2\mathbf{j})\cdot(2t^2\mathbf{i} + 3\mathbf{j}) = 6t^3 - 3t^2$

$$\frac{d}{dt}(\mathbf{a}\cdot\mathbf{b}) = 18t^2 - 6t$$

Also

$$\frac{d\mathbf{a}}{dt} = 3\mathbf{i} - 2t\mathbf{j} \qquad \frac{d\mathbf{b}}{dt} = 4t\mathbf{i}$$

So,

$$\mathbf{a}\cdot\frac{d\mathbf{b}}{dt} + \mathbf{b}\cdot\frac{d\mathbf{a}}{dt} = (3t\mathbf{i} - t^2\mathbf{j})\cdot(4t\mathbf{i}) + (2t^2\mathbf{i} + 3\mathbf{j})\cdot(3\mathbf{i} - 2t\mathbf{j})$$
$$= 12t^2 + 6t^2 - 6t = 18t^2 - 6t$$

We have verified $\dfrac{d}{dt}(\mathbf{a}\cdot\mathbf{b}) = \mathbf{a}\cdot\dfrac{d\mathbf{b}}{dt} + \dfrac{d\mathbf{a}}{dt}\cdot\mathbf{b}$.

(b) $\mathbf{a}\times\mathbf{b} = \begin{vmatrix} \mathbf{i} & \mathbf{j} & \mathbf{k} \\ 3t & -t^2 & 0 \\ 2t^2 & 3 & 0 \end{vmatrix}$
$= (9t + 2t^4)\mathbf{k}$

$$\frac{d}{dt}(\mathbf{a}\times\mathbf{b}) = (9 + 8t^3)\mathbf{k}$$

Also,

$$\mathbf{a} \times \frac{d\mathbf{b}}{dt} = \begin{vmatrix} \mathbf{i} & \mathbf{j} & \mathbf{k} \\ 3t & -t^2 & 0 \\ 4t & 0 & 0 \end{vmatrix}$$

$$= 4t^3\mathbf{k}$$

$$\frac{d\mathbf{a}}{dt} \times \mathbf{b} = \begin{vmatrix} \mathbf{i} & \mathbf{j} & \mathbf{k} \\ 3 & -2t & 0 \\ 2t^2 & 3 & 0 \end{vmatrix}$$

$$= (9 + 4t^3)\mathbf{k}$$

and so

$$\mathbf{a} \times \frac{d\mathbf{b}}{dt} + \frac{d\mathbf{a}}{dt} \times \mathbf{b} = 4t^3\mathbf{k} + (9 + 4t^3)\mathbf{k} = (9 + 8t^3)\mathbf{k} = \frac{d}{dt}(\mathbf{a} \times \mathbf{b})$$

as required.

Exercises 12.5

1 If $\mathbf{r} = 3t\mathbf{i} + 2t^2\mathbf{j} + t^3\mathbf{k}$, find

  (a) $\dfrac{d\mathbf{r}}{dt}$ (b) $\dfrac{d^2\mathbf{r}}{dt^2}$

2 Given $\mathbf{B} = te^{-t}\mathbf{i} + \cos t\mathbf{j}$ find

  (a) $\dfrac{d\mathbf{B}}{dt}$ (b) $\dfrac{d^2\mathbf{B}}{dt^2}$

3 If $\mathbf{r} = 4t^2\mathbf{i} + 2t\mathbf{j} - 7\mathbf{k}$ evaluate $\mathbf{r}$ and $\dfrac{d\mathbf{r}}{dt}$ when $t = 1$.

4 If $\mathbf{a} = t^3\mathbf{i} - 7t\mathbf{k}$, and $\mathbf{b} = (2 + t)\mathbf{i} + t^2\mathbf{j} - 2\mathbf{k}$,

  (a) find $\mathbf{a} \cdot \mathbf{b}$

  (b) find $\dfrac{d\mathbf{a}}{dt}$

  (c) find $\dfrac{d\mathbf{b}}{dt}$

  (d) show that $\dfrac{d}{dt}(\mathbf{a} \cdot \mathbf{b}) = \mathbf{a} \cdot \dfrac{d\mathbf{b}}{dt} + \dfrac{d\mathbf{a}}{dt} \cdot \mathbf{b}$.

5 Given $\mathbf{r} = \sin t\mathbf{i} + \cos t\mathbf{j}$, find

  (a) $\dot{\mathbf{r}}$ (b) $\ddot{\mathbf{r}}$ (c) $|\mathbf{r}|$

  Show that the position vector and velocity vector are perpendicular.

6 Show $\mathbf{r} = 3e^{-t}\mathbf{i} + (2 + t)\mathbf{j}$ satisfies

$$\ddot{\mathbf{r}} + \dot{\mathbf{r}} = \mathbf{j}$$

7 Given $\mathbf{a} = t^2\mathbf{i} - (4 - t)\mathbf{j}$, $\mathbf{b} = \mathbf{i} + t\mathbf{j}$ show

  (a) $\dfrac{d}{dt}(\mathbf{a} \times \mathbf{b}) = \left(\mathbf{a} \times \dfrac{d\mathbf{b}}{dt}\right) + \left(\dfrac{d\mathbf{a}}{dt} \times \mathbf{b}\right)$

  (b) $\dfrac{d}{dt}(\mathbf{a} \cdot \mathbf{b}) = \mathbf{a} \cdot \dfrac{d\mathbf{b}}{dt} + \mathbf{b} \cdot \dfrac{d\mathbf{a}}{dt}$

Solutions

1 (a) $3\mathbf{i} + 4t\mathbf{j} + 3t^2\mathbf{k}$

  (b) $4\mathbf{j} + 6t\mathbf{k}$

2 (a) $(-te^{-t} + e^{-t})\mathbf{i} - \sin t\mathbf{j}$

  (b) $e^{-t}(t - 2)\mathbf{i} - \cos t\mathbf{j}$

3 $4\mathbf{i} + 2\mathbf{j} - 7\mathbf{k}$, $8\mathbf{i} + 2\mathbf{j}$

4 (a) $t(t^3 + 2t^2 + 14)$

  (b) $3t^2\mathbf{i} - 7\mathbf{k}$

  (c) $\mathbf{i} + 2t\mathbf{j}$

5 (a) $\cos t\mathbf{i} - \sin t\mathbf{j}$

  (b) $-\sin t\mathbf{i} - \cos t\mathbf{j}$

  (c) 1

Review exercises 12

1 Determine the position of all maximum points, minimum points and points of inflexion of

(a) $y = 2t^3 - 21t^2 + 60t + 9$

(b) $y = t(t^2 - 1)$

2 In Section 9.8 we showed that the impedance of an LCR circuit can be written as

$$Z = R + j\left(\omega L - \frac{1}{\omega C}\right)$$

(a) Find $|Z|$.

(b) For a given circuit, R, L and C are constants, and ω can be varied. Find $\dfrac{d|Z|}{d\omega}$.

(c) For what value of ω will $|Z|$ have a maximum or minimum value? Does this value give a maximum or minimum value of $|Z|$?

3 Use two iterations of the Newton–Raphson technique to find an improved estimate of the root of

$$t^3 = e^t$$

given $t = 1.8$ is an approximate root.

4 Given
$$\mathbf{a} = (t^2 + 1)\mathbf{i} - \mathbf{j} + t\mathbf{k}$$
$$\mathbf{b} = 2t\mathbf{j} - \mathbf{k}$$
find

(a) $\dfrac{d\mathbf{a}}{dt}$ (b) $\dfrac{d\mathbf{b}}{dt}$

(c) $\dfrac{d}{dt}(\mathbf{a} \cdot \mathbf{b})$ (d) $\dfrac{d}{dt}(\mathbf{a} \times \mathbf{b})$

5 Use two iterations of the Newton–Raphson method to find an improved estimate of the root of $\sin t = 1 - \dfrac{t}{2}$, $0 \leqslant t \leqslant \pi$, given $t = 0.7$ is an approximate root.

6 Determine the position of all maximum points, minimum points and points of inflexion of

(a) $y = e^{-x^2}$

(b) $y = t^3 e^{-t}$

(c) $y = x^3 - 3x^2 + 3x - 1$

(d) $y = e^x + e^{-x}$

(e) $y = |t| - t^2$

Solutions

1 (a) $(2, 61)$ maximum, $(5, 34)$ minimum, $\left(\frac{7}{2}, \frac{95}{2}\right)$ point of inflexion

(b) $\left(\frac{1}{\sqrt{3}}, -\frac{2}{3\sqrt{3}}\right)$ minimum, $\left(-\frac{1}{\sqrt{3}}, \frac{2}{3\sqrt{3}}\right)$ maximum, $(0, 0)$ point of inflexion

2 (a) $\sqrt{R^2 + \omega^2 L^2 - \dfrac{2L}{C} + \dfrac{1}{\omega^2 C^2}}$

(b) $\dfrac{\omega L^2 - 1/\omega^3 C^2}{\sqrt{R^2 + \omega^2 L^2 - 2L/C + 1/(\omega^2 C^2)}}$

(c) $\omega = \dfrac{1}{\sqrt{LC}}$ produces a minimum value of Z

3 $1.859, 1.857$

4 (a) $2t\mathbf{i} + \mathbf{k}$

(b) $2\mathbf{j}$

(c) -3

(d) $-4t\mathbf{i} + 2t\mathbf{j} + (6t^2 + 2)\mathbf{k}$

5 $0.705, 0.705$

6 (a) $(0, 1)$ is a maximum

Points of inflexion when $x = \pm\dfrac{\sqrt{2}}{2}$

(b) $(0, 0)$ point of inflexion, $(3, 1.34)$ maximum. Further points of inflexion when $t = 4.73, 1.27$

(c) $(1, 0)$ point of inflexion

(d) $(0, 2)$ minimum

(e) $(0.5, 0.25)$ maximum, $(-0.5, 0.25)$ maximum, minimum at $(0, 0)$ (y' does not exist here)

13 Integration

Chapter 13	Contents	

13.1	Introduction	412
13.2	Elementary integration	412
13.3	Definite and indefinite integrals	425
	Review exercises	435

13.1 Introduction

When a function, $f(x)$, is known we can differentiate it to obtain the derivative, $\dfrac{df}{dx}$.
The reverse process is to obtain the function $f(x)$ from knowledge of its derivative. This process is called **integration**. Thus, integration is the reverse of differentiation.

A problem related to integration is to find the area between a curve and the x axis. At first sight it may not be clear that the calculation of area is connected to integration. This chapter aims to explain the connection. An area can have various interpretations. For example, the area under a graph of power used by a motor plotted against time represents the total energy used by the motor in a particular time period. The area under a graph of current flow into a capacitor against time represents the total charge stored by the capacitor.

Circuits to carry out integration are used extensively in electronics. For example, a circuit to display the total distance travelled by a car may have a speed signal as input and may integrate this signal to give the distance travelled as output. Integrator circuits are widely used in analog computers. These computers can be used to model a physical system and observe its response to a range of inputs. The advantage of this approach is that the system parameters can be varied in order to see what effect they have on system performance. This avoids the need to build the actual system and allows design ideas to be explored relatively quickly and cheaply by an engineer.

13.2 Elementary integration

Consider the following problem: given $\dfrac{dy}{dx} = 2x$, find $y(x)$. Differentiation of the function $y(x) = x^2 + c$, where c is a constant, yields $\dfrac{dy}{dx} = 2x$ for any c. Therefore $y(x) = x^2 + c$ is a solution to the problem. As c can be any constant, there are an infinite number of different solutions. The constant c is known as a **constant of integration**. In this example, the function y has been found from a knowledge of its derivative. We say $2x$ has been **integrated**, yielding $x^2 + c$. To indicate the process of integration the symbols $\int$ and dx are used. The $\int$ sign denotes that integration is to be performed and the dx indicates that x is the independent variable. Returning to the previous problem, we write

$$\frac{dy}{dx} = 2x$$

$$y = \int 2x \, dx = x^2 + c$$

$$\uparrow \qquad \uparrow \qquad\qquad \uparrow$$

symbols for   constant of integration
integration

In general, if

$$\frac{dy}{dx} = f(x)$$

then

$$y = \int f(x)\,dx$$

Consider a simple example.

Example 13.1 Given $\dfrac{dy}{dx} = \cos x - x$, find y.

Solution We need to find a function which, when differentiated, yields $\cos x - x$. Differentiating $\sin x$ yields $\cos x$, while differentiating $-x^2/2$ yields $-x$. Hence,

$$y = \int (\cos x - x)\,dx = \sin x - \frac{x^2}{2} + c$$

where c is the constant of integration. Usually brackets are not used and the integral is written simply as $\int \cos x - x\,dx$.

The function to be integrated is known as the **integrand**. In Example 13.1 the integrand is $\cos x - x$.

Example 13.2 Find $\dfrac{d}{dx}\left(\dfrac{x^{n+1}}{n+1} + c\right)$ and hence deduce that $\int x^n\,dx = \dfrac{x^{n+1}}{n+1} + c$.

Solution From Table 10.1 we find

$$\frac{d}{dx}\left(\frac{x^{n+1}}{n+1} + c\right) = \frac{d}{dx}\left(\frac{x^{n+1}}{n+1}\right) + \frac{d}{dx}(c) \qquad \begin{array}{l}\text{using the linearity}\\\text{of differentiation}\end{array}$$

$$= \frac{1}{n+1}\frac{d}{dx}(x^{n+1}) + \frac{d}{dx}(c) \qquad \begin{array}{l}\text{again using the}\\\text{linearity of differentiation}\end{array}$$

$$= \frac{1}{n+1}\{(n+1)x^n\} + 0 \qquad \text{using Table 10.1.}$$

$$= x^n$$

Consequently, reversing the process we find

$$\int x^n\,dx = \frac{x^{n+1}}{n+1} + c$$

as required. Note that this result is invalid if $n = -1$ and so this result could not be applied to the integral $\int (1/x)\,dx$.

Table 13.1
The integrals of some
common functions.

$f(x)$	$\int f(x)\,dx$	$f(x)$	$\int f(x)\,dx$
k, constant	$kx + c$	$\cos(ax + b)$	$\dfrac{\sin(ax + b)}{a} + c$
x^n	$\dfrac{x^{n+1}}{n+1} + c \quad n \neq -1$	$\tan x$	$\ln \lvert \sec x \rvert + c$
$x^{-1} = \dfrac{1}{x}$	$\ln \lvert x \rvert + c$	$\tan ax$	$\dfrac{\ln \lvert \sec ax \rvert}{a} + c$
e^x	$e^x + c$	$\tan(ax + b)$	$\dfrac{\ln \lvert \sec(ax + b) \rvert}{a} + c$
e^{-x}	$-e^{-x} + c$	$\csc(ax + b)$	$\dfrac{1}{a}\{\ln \lvert \csc(ax + b)$
e^{ax}	$\dfrac{e^{ax}}{a} + c$		$-\cot(ax + b)\rvert\} + c$
$\sin x$	$-\cos x + c$	$\sec(ax + b)$	$\dfrac{1}{a}\{\ln \lvert \sec(ax + b)$
$\sin ax$	$\dfrac{-\cos ax}{a} + c$		$+\tan(ax + b)\rvert\} + c$
$\sin(ax + b)$	$\dfrac{-\cos(ax + b)}{a} + c$	$\cot(ax + b)$	$\dfrac{1}{a}\{\ln \lvert \sin(ax + b)\rvert\} + c$
$\cos x$	$\sin x + c$	$\dfrac{1}{\sqrt{a^2 - x^2}}$	$\sin^{-1}\dfrac{x}{a} + c$
$\cos ax$	$\dfrac{\sin ax}{a} + c$	$\dfrac{1}{a^2 + x^2}$	$\dfrac{1}{a}\tan^{-1}\dfrac{x}{a} + c$

Note that a, b, n and c are constants. When integrating trigonometric functions, angles must be in radians.

Table 13.1 lists several common functions and their integrals. Although the variable x is used throughout Table 13.1, we can use this table to integrate functions of other variables, for example t and z.

Example 13.3   Use Table 13.1 to integrate the following functions:

(a) x^4

(b) $\cos kx$, where k is a constant

(c) $\sin(3x + 2)$

(d) 5.9

(e) $\tan(6t - 4)$

(f) e^{-3z}

(g) $\dfrac{1}{x^2}$

(h) $\cos 100 n \pi t$, where n is a constant

Solution   (a) From Table 13.1, we find $\int x^n \, dx = \dfrac{x^{n+1}}{n+1} + c, n \neq -1$. To find $\int x^4 \, dx$ let $n = 4$; we obtain

$$\int x^4 \, dx = \frac{x^5}{5} + c$$

(b) From Table 13.1, we find $\int \cos(ax) \, dx = \dfrac{\sin(ax)}{a} + c$. In this case $a = k$ and so

$$\int \cos kx \, dx = \frac{\sin kx}{k} + c$$

(c) From Table 13.1, we find $\int \sin(ax+b) \, dx = \dfrac{-\cos(ax+b)}{a} + c$. In this case $a = 3$ and $b = 2$, and so

$$\int \sin(3x + 2) \, dx = \frac{-\cos(3x + 2)}{3} + c$$

(d) From Table 13.1, we find that if k is a constant then $\int k \, dx = kx + c$. Hence,

$$\int 5.9 \, dx = 5.9x + c$$

(e) In this example, the independent variable is t but nevertheless from Table 13.1 we can deduce

$$\int \tan(at + b) \, dt = \frac{\ln |\sec(at + b)|}{a} + c$$

Hence with $a = 6$ and $b = -4$, we obtain

$$\int \tan(6t - 4) \, dt = \frac{\ln |\sec(6t - 4)|}{6} + c$$

(f) The independent variable is z but from Table 13.1 we can deduce $\int e^{az} \, dz = \dfrac{e^{az}}{a} + c$. Hence, taking $a = -3$ we obtain

$$\int e^{-3z} \, dz = \frac{e^{-3z}}{-3} + c = -\frac{e^{-3z}}{3} + c$$

(g) Since $\dfrac{1}{x^2} = x^{-2}$, we find

$$\int \frac{1}{x^2} \, dx = \int x^{-2} \, dx = \frac{x^{-1}}{-1} + c = -\frac{1}{x} + c$$

(h) When integrating $\cos 100n\pi t$ with respect to t, note that $100n\pi$ is a constant. Hence, using part (b) we find

$$\int \cos 100n\pi t \, dt = \frac{\sin 100n\pi t}{100n\pi} + c$$

13.2.1 Integration as a linear operator

Integration, like differentiation, is a linear operator. If f and g are two functions of x, then

$$\int f + g \, dx = \int f \, dx + \int g \, dx$$

This states that the integral of a sum of functions is the sum of the integrals of the individual functions. If A is a constant and f a function of x, then

$$\int Af \, dx = A \int f \, dx$$

Thus, constant factors can be taken through the integral sign.

If A and B are constants, and f and g are functions of x, then

$$\int Af + Bg \, dx = A \int f \, dx + B \int g \, dx$$

These three properties are all consequences of the fact that integration is a linear operator. Note that the first two are special cases of the third. The properties are used in Example 13.4.

Example 13.4   Use Table 13.1 and the properties of a linear operator to integrate the following expressions:

(a) $x^2 + 9$

(b) $3t^4 - \sqrt{t}$

(c) $\dfrac{1}{x}$

(d) $(t+2)^2$

(e) $\dfrac{1}{z} + z$

(f) $4e^{2z}$

(g) $3 \sin 4t$

(h) $4 \cos(9x + 2)$

(i) $3e^{2z}$

(j) $\dfrac{\sin x + \cos x}{2}$

(k) $2t - e^t$

(l) $\tan\left(\dfrac{z-1}{2}\right)$

(m) $e^t + e^{-t}$

(n) $3 \sec(4x - 1)$

(o) $2 \cot 9x$

(p) $7 \operatorname{cosec}(\pi/3)$

Solution   (a) $\displaystyle\int x^2 + 9 \, dx = \int x^2 \, dx + \int 9 \, dx$ using linearity

$$= \frac{x^3}{3} + 9x + c$$ using Table 13.1

Note that only a single constant of integration is required.

(b) $\displaystyle\int 3t^4 - \sqrt{t} \, dt = 3 \int t^4 \, dt - \int t^{1/2} \, dt$ using linearity

$$= 3\left(\frac{t^5}{5}\right) - \frac{t^{3/2}}{3/2} + c$$ using Table 13.1

$$= \frac{3t^5}{5} - \frac{2t^{3/2}}{3} + c$$

(c) $\displaystyle\int \frac{1}{x}\,dx = \ln|x| + c$ using Table 13.1.

Sometimes it is convenient to use the laws of logarithms to rewrite answers involving logarithms. For example, we can write $\ln|x| + c$ as $\ln|x| + \ln|A|$ where $c = \ln|A|$. This enables us to write the integral as

$$\int \frac{1}{x}\,dx = \ln|Ax|$$

(d) $\displaystyle\int (t+2)^2\,dt = \int t^2 + 4t + 4\,dt = \frac{t^3}{3} + 2t^2 + 4t + c$

(e) $\displaystyle\int \frac{1}{z} + z\,dz = \ln|z| + \frac{z^2}{2} + c$

(f) $\displaystyle\int 4e^{2z}\,dz = \frac{4e^{2z}}{2} + c = 2e^{2z} + c$

(g) $\displaystyle\int 3\sin(4t)\,dt = -\frac{3\cos 4t}{4} + c$

(h) $\displaystyle\int 4\cos(9x+2)\,dx = \frac{4\sin(9x+2)}{9} + c$

(i) $\displaystyle\int 3e^{2z}\,dz = \frac{3e^{2z}}{2} + c$

(j) $\displaystyle\int \frac{\sin x + \cos x}{2}\,dx = \frac{-\cos x + \sin x}{2} + c$

(k) $\displaystyle\int 2t - e^t\,dt = t^2 - e^t + c$

(l) $\displaystyle\int \tan\left(\frac{z-1}{2}\right)\,dz = 2\ln\left|\sec\left(\frac{z-1}{2}\right)\right| + c$

(m) $\displaystyle\int e^t + e^{-t}\,dt = e^t - e^{-t} + c$

(n) $\displaystyle\int 3\sec(4x-1)\,dx = \frac{3}{4}\ln|\sec(4x-1) + \tan(4x-1)| + c$

(o) $\displaystyle\int 2\cot 9x\,dx = \frac{2}{9}\ln|\sin 9x| + c$

(p) $\displaystyle\int 7\operatorname{cosec}(\pi/3)\,dx = \{7\operatorname{cosec}(\pi/3)\}x + c$ as $\operatorname{cosec}(\pi/3)$ is a constant

Example 13.5 | **Distance travelled by a particle**

The speed, v, of a particle is the rate of change of distance, s, with respect to time t, that is $v = \dfrac{ds}{dt}$. The speed at time t is given by $3 + 2t$. Find the distance in terms of t.

Solution We are given that

$$v = \frac{ds}{dt} = 3 + 2t$$

and are required to find s. Therefore,

$$s = \int 3 + 2t \ dt = 3t + t^2 + c$$

Example 13.6 | **Voltage across a capacitor**

The current, i, through a capacitor depends upon time, t, and is given by

$$i = C\frac{dv}{dt}$$

where v is the voltage across the capacitor and C is the capacitance of the capacitor. Derive an expression for v.

Solution If

$$i = C\frac{dv}{dt} \qquad \text{then} \qquad \frac{dv}{dt} = \frac{i}{C}$$

Therefore,

$$v = \int \frac{i}{C} \ dt = \frac{1}{C} \int i \ dt \qquad \text{using linearity}$$

Note that whereas the capacitance, C, is constant, the current, i, is not and so it cannot be taken through the integral sign. In order to perform the integration we need to know i as a function of t.

13.2.2 Electronic integrators

Often there is a requirement in engineering to integrate electronic signals. Various circuits are available to carry out this task. One of the simplest circuits is shown in Figure 13.1. The input voltage is v_i, the output voltage is v_o, the voltage drop across the resistor is v_R and the current flowing in the circuit is i. Applying Kirchhoff's voltage law yields

$$v_i = v_R + v_o \tag{13.1}$$

For the resistor with resistance, R,

$$v_R = iR \tag{13.2}$$

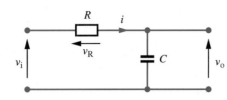

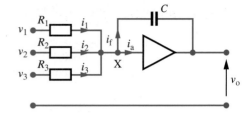

Figure 13.1   Simple integrator.   **Figure 13.2**   Electronic integrator.

For the capacitor with capacitance, C,

$$i = C\frac{dv_o}{dt} \tag{13.3}$$

Combining Equations (13.1) to (13.3) yields

$$v_i = RC\frac{dv_o}{dt} + v_o \tag{13.4}$$

In general, v_i will be an a.c. signal consisting of a range of frequencies. The a.c. resistance of a capacitor, known as the **capacitive reactance**, or **impedance**, X_c, is given by

$$X_c = \frac{1}{2\pi f C}$$

where f = frequency of the signal (Hz). It can be seen that X_c decreases with increasing frequency, f. For frequencies where X_c is small compared with R, most of the voltage drop takes place across the resistor. In other words, v_o is small compared with v_R. Examining Equation (13.1) for the case when X_c is very much less than R (written as $X_c \ll R$), and $v_o \ll v_R$, it can be seen that Equation (13.4) simplifies to

$$v_i = RC\frac{dv_o}{dt} \tag{13.5}$$

This equation is only valid for the range of frequencies for which $X_c \ll R$. Rearranging Equation (13.5) yields

$$\frac{dv_o}{dt} = \frac{v_i}{RC}$$

$$v_o = \frac{1}{RC}\int v_i \, dt$$

The output voltage from the circuit is an integrated version of the input voltage with a scaling factor $\frac{1}{RC}$.

A better electronic integrator, valid over a much greater range of frequencies, can be obtained using an operational amplifier circuit. Consider the circuit shown in Figure 13.2. One of the main characteristics of an operational amplifier is its extremely high voltage gain. This means that the input voltage must be much smaller than the output voltage if the amplifier is not to be driven into **saturation**. Saturation is a condition in which the output voltage reaches the supply voltage of the amplifier and cannot increase further. This means that point X in Figure 13.2 is virtually at a voltage of zero volts. For this reason it is known as a **virtual earth** point. For similar reasons the current drawn by the amplifier, i_a, is also very small. Using this information, it is now possible to analyse the circuit.

Assuming point X is at zero volts, and using Ohm's law, gives

$$i_1 = \frac{v_1}{R_1} \qquad i_2 = \frac{v_2}{R_2} \qquad i_3 = \frac{v_3}{R_3} \tag{13.6}$$

Assuming i_a is negligible, then

$$i_f = i_1 + i_2 + i_3 \tag{13.7}$$

For the capacitor,

$$i_f = -C\frac{dv_o}{dt} \tag{13.8}$$

The negative sign is a result of the direction chosen for i_f. Combining Equations (13.6)–(13.8) yields

$$\frac{v_1}{R_1} + \frac{v_2}{R_2} + \frac{v_3}{R_3} = -C\frac{dv_o}{dt}$$

$$v_o = -\int \frac{v_1}{R_1 C} + \frac{v_2}{R_2 C} + \frac{v_3}{R_3 C} \, dt$$

The circuit therefore acts as an integrator. An additional benefit is that it allows voltages to be summed before integration.

13.2.3 Integration of trigonometric functions

The trigonometric identities given in Table 3.1 together with Table 13.1 allow us to integrate a number of trigonometric functions.

Example 13.7 Evaluate

(a) $\int \cos^2 t \, dt$

(b) $\int \sin^2 t \, dt$

Solution Powers of trigonometric functions, for example $\sin^2 t$, do not appear in the table of standard integrals. What we must attempt to do is rewrite the integrand to obtain a standard form.

(a) From Table 3.1

$$\cos^2 t = \frac{1 + \cos 2t}{2}$$

and so

$$\int \cos^2 t \, dt = \int \frac{1 + \cos 2t}{2} \, dt$$

$$= \int \frac{1}{2} \, dt + \int \frac{\cos 2t}{2} \, dt$$

$$= \frac{t}{2} + \frac{\sin 2t}{4} + c$$

(b) $\quad \int \sin^2 t \, dt = \int 1 - \cos^2 t \, dt \qquad$ using the trigonometric identities

$$= \int 1 \, dt - \int \cos^2 t \, dt \qquad \text{using linearity}$$

$$= t - \left(\frac{t}{2} + \frac{\sin 2t}{4} + c \right) \qquad \text{using part (a)}$$

$$= \frac{t}{2} - \frac{\sin 2t}{4} + k$$

Example 13.8   Find

(a) $\int \sin 2t \cos t \, dt$

(b) $\int \sin mt \sin nt \, dt$, where m and n are constants with $m \neq n$

Solution   (a) Using the identities in Table 3.1 we find

$$2 \sin A \cos B = \sin(A + B) + \sin(A - B)$$

hence $\sin 2t \cos t$ can be written $\frac{1}{2}(\sin 3t + \sin t)$. Therefore,

$$\int \sin 2t \cos t \, dt = \int \frac{1}{2}(\sin 3t + \sin t) \, dt$$

$$= \frac{1}{2}\left(\frac{-\cos 3t}{3} - \cos t \right) + c$$

$$= -\frac{1}{6} \cos 3t - \frac{1}{2} \cos t + c$$

(b) Using the identity $2 \sin A \sin B = \cos(A - B) - \cos(A + B)$, we find

$$\sin mt \sin nt = \frac{1}{2}\{\cos(m - n)t - \cos(m + n)t\}$$

Therefore,

$$\int \sin mt \sin nt \, dt = \int \frac{1}{2}\{\cos(m-n)t - \cos(m+n)t\} \, dt$$

$$= \frac{1}{2}\left\{ \frac{\sin(m-n)t}{m-n} - \frac{\sin(m+n)t}{m+n} \right\} + c$$

Exercises 13.2

1 Integrate the following expressions using Table 13.1.

(a) x^{10} (b) 9 (c) $x^{1.5}$

(d) $\sqrt{t}$ (e) $\frac{1}{z}$ (f) -3.2

(g) $\frac{1}{x^3}$ (h) $\frac{1}{\sqrt{t}}$ (i) $(x^2)^3$

(j) x^{-2} (k) $t^{1/3}$

2 Integrate the following expressions using Table 13.1.

(a) e^{5x} (b) e^{6x} (c) e^{-3t}

(d) $\frac{1}{e^x}$ (e) $e^{0.5t}$ (f) $e^{z/3}$

(g) $\frac{1}{e^{4t}}$ (h) $e^{-2.5x}$

3 Integrate the following expressions using Table 13.1.

(a) $\sin 4x$ (b) $\sin 9t$

(c) $\sin\left(\frac{x}{2}\right)$ (d) $\sin\left(\frac{2t}{5}\right)$

(e) $\cos 7x$ (f) $\cos(-3x)$

(g) $\cos\left(\frac{5t}{3}\right)$ (h) $\tan 9x$

(i) $\csc 2x$ (j) $\sec 5t$

(k) $\cot 8y$ (l) $\cos(5t+1)$

(m) $\tan(3x+4)$ (n) $\sin(3t-\pi)$

(o) $\csc(5z+2)$ (p) $\sec\left(\frac{x}{2}+1\right)$

(q) $\sin\left(\frac{2t}{3}-1\right)$ (r) $\cot(5-x)$

(s) $\csc(\pi-2x)$

4 Use Table 13.1 to integrate the following expressions.

(a) $\dfrac{1}{1+x^2}$ (b) $\dfrac{1}{\sqrt{1-x^2}}$

(c) $\dfrac{1}{\sqrt{4-x^2}}$ (d) $\dfrac{1}{9+z^2}$

(e) $\dfrac{1}{\sqrt{0.25-x^2}}$ (f) $\dfrac{1}{0.01+v^2}$

(g) $\dfrac{1}{10^6+r^2}$ (h) $\dfrac{1}{10+t^2}$

(i) $\dfrac{1}{\sqrt{2-x^2}}$ (j) $\dfrac{1}{\frac{1}{9}+x^2}$

5 Integrate the following expressions.

(a) $3+x+\dfrac{1}{x}$

(b) $e^{2x}-e^{-2x}$

(c) $2\sin 3x + \cos 3x$

(d) $\sec(2t+\pi)+\cot\left(\dfrac{t}{2}-\pi\right)$

(e) $\tan\left(\dfrac{t}{2}\right)+\csc(3t-\pi)$

(f) $\sin x + \dfrac{x}{3}+\dfrac{1}{e^x}$

(g) $\dfrac{1}{\cos(3x)}$

(h) $\left(t+\dfrac{1}{t}\right)^2$

(i) $\dfrac{1}{3e^{2x}}$

(j) $\tan(4t - 3) + 2\sin(-t - 1)$

(k) $1 + 2\cot 3x$

(l) $\sin\left(\dfrac{t}{2}\right) - 3\cos\left(\dfrac{t}{2}\right)$

(m) $(t - 2)^2$

(n) $3e^{-t} - e^{-t/2}$

(o) $7 - 7x^6 + e^{-x}$

(p) $(k + t)^2$ k constant

(q) $k\sin t - \cos kt$ k constant

(r) $\dfrac{1}{25 + t^2}$

(s) $\dfrac{1}{\sqrt{25 - t^2}}$

(t) $\dfrac{6}{1 + x^2} + \dfrac{1 + x^2}{6}$

6 The acceleration, a, of a particle is the rate of change of speed, v, with respect to time t, that is $a = \dfrac{dv}{dt}$. The speed of the particle is the rate of change of distance, s, that is $v = \dfrac{ds}{dt}$. If the acceleration is given by $1 + \dfrac{t}{2}$, find expressions for speed and distance.

7 The speed, v, of a particle varies with time according to
$$v(t) = 2 - e^{-t}$$

(a) Obtain an expression for distance travelled by the particle.

(b) Calculate the distance travelled by the particle between $t = 0$ and $t = 3$.

8 By writing $\sinh ax$ and $\cosh ax$ in terms of the exponential function find

(a) $\int \sinh ax \, dx$

(b) $\int \cosh ax \, dx$

(c) Use your results from (a) and (b) to find $\int 3\sinh 2x + \cosh 4x \, dx$.

9 A capacitor of capacitance 10^{-2} F has a current $i(t)$ through it where
$$i(t) = 10 - e^{-t}$$

Find an expression for the voltage across the capacitor.

10 Integrate the following:

(a) $\dfrac{1}{x^2 + 4}$ (b) $\dfrac{1}{2x^2 + 4}$

(c) $\dfrac{3}{2x^2 + 1}$ (d) $\dfrac{1}{\sqrt{9 - x^2}}$

(e) $\dfrac{2}{\sqrt{4 - x^2}}$ (f) $\dfrac{-7}{\sqrt{2 - 3x^2}}$

(g) $\dfrac{1}{\sqrt{1 - (x^2/2)}}$

11 By writing $\dfrac{3 + x}{x}$ in the form $\dfrac{3}{x} + 1$, find
$$\int \dfrac{3 + x}{x} \, dx.$$

12 (a) Express
$$\dfrac{x^2 + 2x + 1}{x(x^2 + 1)}$$
as its partial fractions.

(b) Hence find $\displaystyle\int \dfrac{x^2 + 2x + 1}{x(x^2 + 1)} \, dx$

13 The velocity, v, of a particle is given by
$$v = 2 + e^{-t/2}$$

(a) Given distance, s, and v are related by $\dfrac{ds}{dt} = v$ find an expression for distance.

(b) Acceleration is the rate of change of velocity with respect to t. Determine the acceleration.

14 (a) Use the product rule of differentiation to verify
$$\dfrac{d}{dx}(x\,e^{2x}) = e^{2x} + 2xe^{2x}$$

(b) Hence show
$$\int xe^{2x} \, dx = \dfrac{xe^{2x}}{2} - \dfrac{e^{2x}}{4} + c$$

15 Integrate

(a) $\dfrac{2 - t^2}{t^3}$ (b) $\dfrac{4 + e^{2t}}{e^{3t}}$

(c) $\dfrac{\cos 4x}{\sin 4x}$ (d) $\dfrac{1}{2\sin 3x}$

(e) $\dfrac{2 + x^2}{1 + x^2}$ (f) $\sin^2 t + \cos^2 t$

Solutions

1 (a) $\dfrac{x^{11}}{11} + c$ (b) $9x + c$

(c) $\frac{2}{5}x^{2.5} + c$ (d) $\frac{2}{3}t^{1.5} + c$

(e) $\ln|z| + c$ (f) $-3.2x + c$

(g) $-\dfrac{1}{2x^2} + c$ (h) $2\sqrt{t} + c$

(i) $\dfrac{x^7}{7} + c$ (j) $-\dfrac{1}{x} + c$

(k) $\frac{3}{4}t^{4/3} + c$

2 (a) $\dfrac{e^{5x}}{5} + c$ (b) $\dfrac{e^{6x}}{6} + c$

(c) $-\dfrac{e^{-3t}}{3} + c$ (d) $-e^{-x} + c$

(e) $2e^{0.5t} + c$ (f) $3e^{z/3} + c$

(g) $-\dfrac{e^{-4t}}{4} + c$ (h) $-\dfrac{2e^{-2.5x}}{5} + c$

3 (a) $-\dfrac{\cos 4x}{4} + c$

(b) $-\dfrac{\cos 9t}{9} + c$

(c) $-2\cos\left(\dfrac{x}{2}\right) + c$

(d) $-\dfrac{5}{2}\cos\left(\dfrac{2t}{5}\right) + c$

(e) $\dfrac{\sin 7x}{7} + c$

(f) $-\frac{1}{3}\sin(-3x) + c$

(g) $\dfrac{3}{5}\sin\left(\dfrac{5t}{3}\right) + c$

(h) $\dfrac{\ln|\sec 9x|}{9} + c$

(i) $\frac{1}{2}(\ln|\cosec 2x - \cot 2x|) + c$

(j) $\frac{1}{5}(\ln|\sec 5t + \tan 5t|) + c$

(k) $\frac{1}{8}\ln|\sin 8y| + c$

(l) $\frac{1}{5}\sin(5t + 1) + c$

(m) $\frac{1}{3}\ln|\sec(3x + 4)| + c$

(n) $-\frac{1}{3}\cos(3t - \pi) + c$

(o) $\frac{1}{5}\ln|\cosec(5z + 2) - \cot(5z + 2)| + c$

(p) $2\ln\left|\sec\left(\dfrac{x}{2} + 1\right) + \tan\left(\dfrac{x}{2} + 1\right)\right| + c$

(q) $-\dfrac{3}{2}\cos\left(\dfrac{2t}{3} - 1\right) + c$

(r) $-\ln|\sin(5 - x)| + c$

(s) $-\frac{1}{2}\ln|\cosec(\pi - 2x) - \cot(\pi - 2x)| + c$

4 (a) $\tan^{-1}x + c$

(b) $\sin^{-1}x + c$

(c) $\sin^{-1}\left(\dfrac{x}{2}\right) + c$

(d) $\dfrac{1}{3}\tan^{-1}\left(\dfrac{z}{3}\right) + c$

(e) $\sin^{-1}(2x) + c$

(f) $10\tan^{-1}(10v) + c$

(g) $10^{-3}\tan^{-1}\left(\dfrac{x}{10^3}\right) + c$

(h) $\dfrac{1}{\sqrt{10}}\tan^{-1}\left(\dfrac{t}{\sqrt{10}}\right) + c$

(i) $\sin^{-1}\left(\dfrac{x}{\sqrt{2}}\right) + c$

(j) $3\tan^{-1}(3x) + c$

5 (a) $3x + \dfrac{x^2}{2} + \ln|x| + c$

(b) $\dfrac{e^{2x}}{2} + \dfrac{e^{-2x}}{2} + c$

(c) $-\dfrac{2}{3}\cos(3x) + \dfrac{\sin 3x}{3} + c$

(d) $0.5\ln|\sec(2t + \pi) + \tan(2t + \pi)|$

$\quad + 2\ln\left|\sin\left(\dfrac{t}{2} - \pi\right)\right| + c$

(e) $2\ln\left|\sec\left(\dfrac{t}{2}\right)\right| + \dfrac{1}{3}\ln|\cosec(3t - \pi)$

$\quad - \cot(3t - \pi)| + c$

(f) $-\cos x + \dfrac{x^2}{6} - e^{-x} + c$

(g) $\frac{1}{3} \ln | \sec 3x + \tan 3x | + c$

(h) $\frac{t^3}{3} + 2t - \frac{1}{t} + c$

(i) $-\frac{e^{-2x}}{6} + c$

(j) $\frac{1}{4} \ln | \sec(4t - 3)| + 2\cos(-t - 1) + c$

(k) $x + \frac{2}{3} \ln | \sin 3x | + c$

(l) $-2\cos\left(\frac{t}{2}\right) - 6\sin\left(\frac{t}{2}\right) + c$

(m) $\frac{t^3}{3} - 2t^2 + 4t + c$

(n) $-3e^{-t} + 2e^{-t/2} + c$

(o) $7x - x^7 - e^{-x} + c$

(p) $k^2 t + kt^2 + \frac{t^3}{3} + c$

(q) $-k\cos t - \frac{\sin kt}{k} + c$

(r) $\frac{1}{5} \tan^{-1}\left(\frac{t}{5}\right) + c$

(s) $\sin^{-1}\left(\frac{t}{5}\right) + c$

(t) $6\tan^{-1} x + \frac{x}{6} + \frac{x^3}{18} + c$

6 Speed: $t + \frac{t^2}{4} + c$, distance: $\frac{t^2}{2} + \frac{t^3}{12} + ct + d$

7 (a) $2t + e^{-t} + c$ · (b) 5.0498

8 (a) $\frac{\cosh ax}{a} + c$

(b) $\frac{\sinh ax}{a} + c$

(c) $\frac{3}{2} \cosh 2x + \frac{1}{4} \sinh 4x + c$

9 $100(10t + e^{-t}) + c$

10 (a) $\frac{1}{2} \tan^{-1}\left(\frac{x}{2}\right) + c$

(b) $\frac{1}{2\sqrt{2}} \tan^{-1}\left(\frac{x}{\sqrt{2}}\right) + c$

(c) $\frac{3}{\sqrt{2}} \tan^{-1}(\sqrt{2}x) + c$

(d) $\sin^{-1}\left(\frac{x}{3}\right) + c$

(e) $2\sin^{-1}\left(\frac{x}{2}\right) + c$

(f) $\frac{-7}{\sqrt{3}} \sin^{-1}\left(\frac{\sqrt{3}}{\sqrt{2}}x\right) + c$

(g) $\sqrt{2} \sin^{-1}\left(\frac{x}{\sqrt{2}}\right) + c$

11 $3\ln |x| + x + c$

12 (a) $\frac{1}{x} + \frac{2}{x^2 + 1}$ (b) $\ln |x| + 2\tan^{-1} x + c$

13 (a) $2t - 2e^{-t/2} + c$ (b) $-\frac{1}{2}e^{-t/2}$

15 (a) $-t^{-2} - \ln |t| + c$

(b) $-\frac{4}{3}e^{-3t} - e^{-t} + c$

(c) $\frac{1}{4} \ln | \sin 4x | + c$

(d) $\frac{1}{6} \ln | \csc 3x - \cot 3x | + c$

(e) $x + \tan^{-1} x + c$

(f) $t + c$

13.3 Definite and indefinite integrals

All the integration solutions so far encountered have contained a constant of integration. Such integrals are known as **indefinite integrals**. Integration can be used to determine the area under curves and this gives rise to **definite integrals**.

To estimate the area under $y(x)$, it is divided into thin rectangles. The sum of the rectangular areas is an approximation to the area under the curve. Several thin rectangles will give a better approximation than a few wide ones.

Consider Figure 13.3 where the area is approximated by a large number of rectangles. Suppose each rectangle has width δx. The area of rectangle 1 is $y(x_2)\delta x$, the area

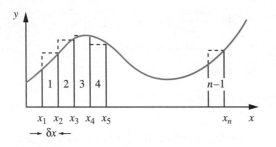

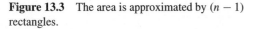

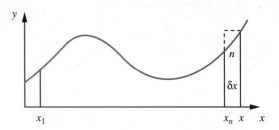

Figure 13.3   The area is approximated by $(n-1)$ rectangles.

Figure 13.4   The area is extended by adding an extra rectangle.

of rectangle 2 is $y(x_3)\delta x$ and so on. Let $A(x_n)$ denote the total area under the curve from x_1 to x_n. Then,

$$A(x_n) \approx \text{sum of the rectangular areas} = \sum_{i=2}^{n} y(x_i)\delta x$$

Let the area be increased by extending the base from x_n to x. Then $A(x)$ is the total area under the curve from x_1 to x (see Figure 13.4). Then,

$$\text{increase in area} = \delta A = A(x) - A(x_n) \approx y(x)\delta x$$

So,

$$\frac{\delta A}{\delta x} \approx y(x)$$

In the limit as $\delta x \to 0$, we get

$$\lim_{\delta x \to 0}\left(\frac{\delta A}{\delta x}\right) = \frac{\mathrm{d}A}{\mathrm{d}x} = y(x)$$

Since differentiation is the reverse of integration, we can write

$$A = \int y(x)\,\mathrm{d}x$$

To denote the limits of the area being considered we place values on the integral sign.

The area under the curve, $y(x)$, between $x = a$ and $x = b$ is denoted as

$$\int_{x=a}^{x=b} y\,\mathrm{d}x$$

or more compactly by

$$\int_{a}^{b} y\,\mathrm{d}x$$

The constants a and b are known as the **limits** of the integral: **lower** and **upper**, respectively. Since an area has a specific value, such an integral is called a definite integral. The area under the curve up to the vertical line $x = b$ is $A(b)$ (see Figure 13.5). Similarly $A(a)$ is the area up to the vertical line $x = a$. So the area between $x = a$ and $x = b$ is $A(b) - A(a)$, as shown in Figure 13.6.

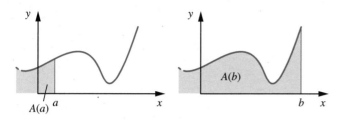

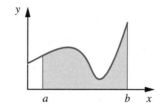

Figure 13.5   The area depends on the limits a and b.

Figure 13.6   The area between $x = a$ and $x = b$ is $A(b) - A(a)$.

The area between $x = a$ and $x = b$ is given by

$$\text{Area} = \int_a^b y \, dx = A(b) - A(a)$$

The integral is evaluated at the upper limit, b, and at the lower limit, a, and the difference between these gives the required area.

The expression $A(b) - A(a)$ is often written as $[A(x)]_a^b$. Similarly $[x^2 + 1]_2^3$ is the value of $x^2 + 1$ at $x = 3$ less the value of $x^2 + 1$ at $x = 2$. Thus

$$[x^2 + 1]_2^3 = (3^2 + 1) - (2^2 + 1) = 5$$

In general

$$[f(x)]_a^b = f(b) - f(a)$$

Note that since

$$\int_a^b y \, dx = A(b) - A(a)$$

then, interchanging upper and lower limits,

$$\int_b^a y \, dx = A(a) - A(b) = -\{A(b) - A(a)\}$$

that is,

$$\int_a^b y \, dx = -\int_b^a y \, dx$$

Interchanging the limits changes the sign of the integral.

The evaluation of definite integrals is illustrated in the following examples.

Example 13.9   Evaluate

(a) $\displaystyle\int_1^2 x^2 + 1 \, dx$ (b) $\displaystyle\int_2^1 x^2 + 1 \, dx$ (c) $\displaystyle\int_0^\pi \sin x \, dx$

Figure 13.7
The area is given by a
definite integral.

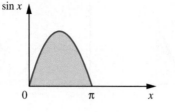

Solution   (a) Let I stand for $\int_1^2 x^2 + 1 \, dx$.

$$I = \int_1^2 x^2 + 1 \, dx = \left[\frac{x^3}{3} + x\right]_1^2$$

The integral is now evaluated at the upper and lower limits. The difference gives the value required.

$$I = \left(\frac{2^3}{3} + 2\right) - \left(\frac{1^3}{3} + 1\right) = \frac{8}{3} + 2 - \frac{4}{3} = \frac{10}{3}$$

(b) Because interchanging the limits of integration changes the sign of the integral, we find

$$\int_2^1 x^2 + 1 \, dx = -\int_1^2 x^2 + 1 \, dx = -\frac{10}{3}$$

(c) $\int_0^\pi \sin x \, dx = [-\cos x]_0^\pi = (-\cos \pi) - (-\cos 0) = 1 - (-1) = 2$

Figure 13.7 illustrates this area.

Note that:

(1) The integrated function is evaluated at the upper and lower limits, and the difference found.

(2) No constant of integration is needed.

(3) Any angles are measured in radians.

Example 13.10   Find the area under $z(t) = e^{2t}$ from $t = 1$ to $t = 3$.

Solution $\text{area} = \int_1^3 z \, dt = \int_1^3 e^{2t} \, dt = \left[\frac{e^{2t}}{2}\right]_1^3$

$$= \left[\frac{e^6}{2}\right] - \left[\frac{e^2}{2}\right] = 198$$

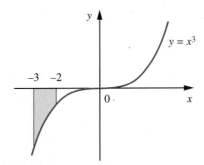

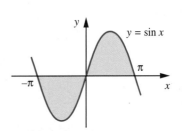

Figure 13.8 Areas below the x axis are classed as negative.

Figure 13.9 The positive and negative areas cancel each other out.

If the evaluation of an area by integration yields a negative quantity this means that some or all of the corresponding area is below the horizontal axis. This is illustrated in Example 13.11.

Example 13.11   Find the area bounded by $y = x^3$ and the x axis from $x = -3$ to $x = -2$.

Solution   Figure 13.8 illustrates the required area.

$$\int_{-3}^{-2} x^3 \, dx = \left[\frac{x^4}{4} \right]_{-3}^{-2}$$

$$= \left\{ \frac{(-2)^4}{4} \right\} - \left\{ \frac{(-3)^4}{4} \right\} = -\frac{65}{4}$$

The area is $65/4$ square units; the negative sign indicates that it is below the x axis.

Example 13.12   (a)   Sketch $y = \sin x$ for $x = -\pi$ to $x = \pi$.

(b)   Calculate $\displaystyle\int_{-\pi}^{\pi} \sin x \, dx$ and comment on your findings.

(c)   Calculate the area enclosed by $y = \sin x$ and the x axis between $x = -\pi$ and $x = \pi$.

Solution   (a)   A graph of $y = \sin x$ between $x = -\pi$ and $x = \pi$ is shown in Figure 13.9.

(b) $\displaystyle\int_{-\pi}^{\pi} \sin x \, dx = [-\cos x]_{-\pi}^{\pi} = -\cos(\pi) + \cos(-\pi) = 0$

Examining Figure 13.9 we see that the positive and negative contributions have cancelled each other out; that is, the area above the x axis is equal in size to the area below the x axis.

Figure 13.10
The positive and
negative areas are
calculated separately.

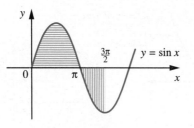

(c) From (b) the area above the x axis is equal in size to the area below the x axis. From Example 13.9(c) the area above the x axis is 2. Hence the total area enclosed by $y = \sin x$ and the x axis from $x = -\pi$ to $x = \pi$ is 4.

If an area contains parts both above and below the horizontal axis then calculating an integral will give the net area. If the total area is required, then the relevant limits must first be found. A sketch of the function often clarifies the situation.

Example 13.13   Find the area contained by $y = \sin x$ from $x = 0$ to $x = 3\pi/2$.

Solution   Figure 13.10 illustrates the required area. From this we see that there are parts both above and below the x axis and the crossover point occurs when $x = \pi$.

$$\int_0^\pi \sin x \; dx = [-\cos x]_0^\pi$$

$$= -\cos \pi + \cos 0 = 2$$

$$\int_\pi^{3\pi/2} \sin x \; dx = [-\cos x]_\pi^{3\pi/2}$$

$$= -\cos\left(\frac{3\pi}{2}\right) + \cos \pi = -1$$

The total area is 3 square units. Note, however, that the single integral over 0 to $3\pi/2$ evaluates to 1; that is, it gives the net value of 2 and -1.

$$\int_0^{3\pi/2} \sin x \; dx = [-\cos x]_0^{3\pi/2} = -\cos\left(\frac{3\pi}{2}\right) + \cos 0 = 1$$

The need to evaluate the area under a curve is a common requirement in engineering. Often the rate of change of an engineering variable with time is known and it is required to calculate the value of the engineering variable. This corresponds to calculating the area under a curve.

Example 13.14   **Energy used by an electric motor**

Consider a small d.c. electric motor being used to drive an electric screwdriver. The amount of power that is supplied to the motor by the batteries depends on the load on

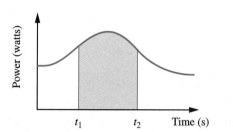

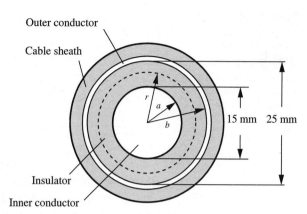

Figure 13.11 Shaded area represents the energy used to drive the motor during the time interval $t_1 \leqslant t \leqslant t_2$.

Figure 13.12 Cross-section of a concentric cable.

the screwdriver. Therefore the power supplied to the screwdriver is a function that varies with time. Figure 13.11 shows a typical curve of power versus time. Now,

$$P = \frac{\mathrm{d}E}{\mathrm{d}t}$$

where P = power (W), E = energy (J). Therefore, to calculate the energy used by the motor between times t_1 and t_2, we can write

$$E = \int_{t_1}^{t_2} P \, \mathrm{d}t$$

This is equivalent to evaluating the area under the curve, $P(t)$, between t_1 and t_2, which is shown as the shaded region in Figure 13.11.

Example 13.15	**Capacitance of a concentric cable**

A concentric cable has an inner conductor with a diameter of 15 mm and an outer conductor with an internal diameter of 25 mm, as shown in Figure 13.12. The insulator separating the two conductors has a relative permittivity of 2.5. Let us calculate the capacitance of the cable per metre length.

Before solving this problem it is instructive to derive the formula for the capacitance of a concentric cable. Imagine that the inner conductor has a charge of $+Q$ per metre length and that the outer conductor has a charge of $-Q$ per metre length. Further assume the cable is long and a central section is being analysed in order that end effects can be ignored.

Consider an imaginary cylindrical surface, radius r and length l, within the insulator (or dielectric). Gauss's theorem states that the electric flux out of any closed surface is equal to the charge enclosed by the surface. In this case, because of symmetry, the electric flux points radially outwards and so no flux is directed through the ends of the imaginary cylinder; that is, end effects can be neglected. The curved surface area of the cylinder is $2\pi rl$. Therefore, using Gauss's theorem

$$D \times 2\pi rl = Ql$$

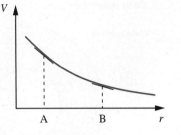

where D = electric flux density.

When an insulator or dielectric is present then $D = \varepsilon_r\varepsilon_0 E$, where E = electric field strength, ε_r = relative permittivity, ε_0 = permittivity of free space = 8.854×10^{-12} F m^{-1}. Therefore,

$$\varepsilon_r\varepsilon_0 E 2\pi r l = Ql$$

that is,

$$E = \frac{Q}{2\pi\varepsilon_r\varepsilon_0 r} \tag{13.9}$$

This equation gives a value for the electric field within the dielectric. In order to calculate the capacitance of the cable it is necessary to calculate the voltage difference between the two conductors. Let V_a represent the voltage of the inner conductor and V_b the voltage of the outer conductor.

The electric field is a measure of the rate of change of the voltage with position. In other words, if the voltage is changing rapidly with position then this corresponds to a large magnitude of the electric field. This is illustrated in Figure 13.13. The magnitude of the electric field at point A is larger than at point B. As a positive electric field, E, corresponds to a decrease in voltage, V, with position the relationship between E and V, in general, is

$$E = -\frac{dV}{dr} \tag{13.10}$$

This expression can be used to calculate the voltage difference arising as a result of an electric field. In practice, this is a simplified equation and is only valid provided r is in the same direction as the electric field. If this is not the case, then a modified vector form of Equation (13.10) is needed.

In the case of the concentric cable, E is in the same direction as r and so Equation (13.10) can be used to calculate the voltage difference between the two conductors. From Equation (13.10)

$$\frac{dV}{dr} = -E$$

Therefore the voltage at an arbitrary point, r, is given by

$$V = -\int E\, dr$$

Consequently, the voltage difference between points $r = b$ and $r = a$ is given by

$$V_b - V_a = -\int_a^b E \, dr$$

$$= -\frac{Q}{2\pi\varepsilon_r\varepsilon_0} \int_a^b \frac{1}{r} \, dr \qquad \text{using Equation (13.9)}$$

$$= -\frac{Q}{2\pi\varepsilon_r\varepsilon_0} [\ln r]_a^b$$

$$= -\frac{Q}{2\pi\varepsilon_r\varepsilon_0} \ln\left(\frac{b}{a}\right)$$

This gives the voltage of the outer conductor relative to the inner one. Thus the voltage of the inner conductor relative to the outer one is

$$V_a - V_b = \frac{Q}{2\pi\varepsilon_r\varepsilon_0} \ln\left(\frac{b}{a}\right)$$

More generally, capacitance is defined as $C = Q/V$, where V is the voltage difference. Therefore

$$C = \frac{Q}{V_a - V_b} = \frac{2\pi\varepsilon_r\varepsilon_0}{\ln\left(\dfrac{b}{a}\right)}$$

Note that this is the capacitance per unit length of cable. Using $\varepsilon_r = 2.5$, $a = 7.5 \times 10^{-3}$ m, $b = 12.5 \times 10^{-3}$ m, we get

$$C = \frac{2\pi \times 2.5 \times 8.854 \times 10^{-12}}{\ln\left(\dfrac{12.5 \times 10^{-3}}{7.5 \times 10^{-3}}\right)} = 2.72 \times 10^{-10} = 272 \text{ pF m}^{-1}$$

13.3.1 Use of a dummy variable

Consider the following integrals, I_1 and I_2:

$$I_1 = \int_0^1 t^2 \, dt \qquad I_2 = \int_0^1 x^2 \, dx$$

Then,

$$I_1 = \left[\frac{t^3}{3}\right]_0^1 = \left(\frac{1}{3}\right) - (0) = \frac{1}{3}$$

$$I_2 = \left[\frac{x^3}{3}\right]_0^1 = \left(\frac{1}{3}\right) - (0) = \frac{1}{3}$$

So clearly $I_1 = I_2$. The value of I_1 does not depend upon t, and the value of I_2 does not depend upon x. In general,

$$I = \int_a^b f(t) \, dt = \int_a^b f(x) \, dx$$

Because the value of I is the same, regardless of what the integrating variable may be, we say x and t are **dummy variables**. Indeed we could write

$$I = \int_a^b f(z)\,dz = \int_a^b f(r)\,dr = \int_a^b f(y)\,dy$$

Then z, r and y are dummy variables.

Exercises 13.3

1 Evaluate the following integrals.

(a) $\displaystyle\int_1^3 x^3\,dx$

(b) $\displaystyle\int_1^4 \frac{1}{x}\,dx$

(c) $\displaystyle\int_0^1 2\,dx$

(d) $\displaystyle\int_{-1}^1 e^x\,dx$

(e) $\displaystyle\int_0^{\pi/3} \sin t\,dt$

(f) $\displaystyle\int_0^\pi \sin(t+3)\,dt$

(g) $\displaystyle\int_0^{\pi/2} \cos 3t\,dt$

(h) $\displaystyle\int_1^2 \cos \pi t\,dt$

(i) $\displaystyle\int_1^{1.2} \tan x\,dx$

2 Evaluate the following integrals.

(a) $\displaystyle\int_0^1 t^2 + 1\,dt$

(b) $\displaystyle\int_0^1 \frac{1}{1+t^2}\,dt$

(c) $\displaystyle\int_1^2 3e^{2x} - 2e^{3x}\,dx$

(d) $\displaystyle\int_1^2 (x+1)(x+2)\,dx$

(e) $\displaystyle\int_0^2 2\sin 4t\,dt$

(f) $\displaystyle\int_0^\pi 4\cos\left(\frac{t}{2}\right)\,dt$

3 Evaluate the following integrals:

(a) $\displaystyle\int_0^1 t^2 + 0.5t - 6\,dt$

(b) $\displaystyle\int_2^3 \frac{3}{2x} + \frac{2x}{3}\,dx$

(c) $\displaystyle\int_1^2 e^{-2x} - 3e^{-x}\,dx$

(d) $\displaystyle\int_0^2 3\sin(4t-\pi) + 5\cos(3t+\pi/2)\,dt$

(e) $\displaystyle\int_0^1 2\tan t\,dt$

(f) $\displaystyle\int_0^{1.5} \frac{2}{1+x^2} - \frac{1}{\sqrt{4-x^2}}\,dx$

4 Calculate the area between $f(t) = \cos t$ and the t axis as t varies from

(a) 0 to $\dfrac{\pi}{4}$ (b) 0 to $\dfrac{\pi}{2}$

(c) $\dfrac{3\pi}{4}$ to π (d) 0 to π

5 Calculate the total area between $f(t) = \cos 2t$ and the t axis as t varies from

(a) 0 to $\dfrac{\pi}{4}$ (b) $\dfrac{\pi}{4}$ to $\dfrac{\pi}{2}$ (c) 0 to $\dfrac{\pi}{2}$

6 Calculate the area enclosed by the curves $y = x^2$ and $y = x$.

7 Calculate the area enclosed by the graphs of the functions $y = t^2 + 5$ and $y = 6$.

8 Evaluate the following definite integrals:

(a) $\displaystyle\int_1^{1.5} \frac{1}{t} + \frac{1}{e^t} + \frac{1}{\sin t}\,dt$

(b) $\displaystyle\int_1^4 \frac{5}{8+3x^2}\,dx$

(c) $\displaystyle\int_{-1}^{1} \sinh x \, dx$

(d) $\displaystyle\int_{-1}^{1} \cosh x \, dx$

9 Calculate the area between $y = 2\tan t$ and the t axis for $-1 \leqslant t \leqslant 1.4$.

10 Find the area between $y = \sin t$, $y = \cos t$ and the y axis, for $t \geqslant 0$.

11 The velocity, v, of a particle is given by

$$v = (1 + t)^2$$

Find the distance travelled by the particle from $t = 1$ to $t = 4$; that is, evaluate $\int_1^4 v \, dt$.

12 Evaluate the area under the function $x = 1/t$ for $1 \leqslant t \leqslant 10$.

13 Evaluate

(a) $\displaystyle\int_3^2 x^{1.4} \, dx$

(b) $\displaystyle\int_0^1 (e^t)^2 \, dt$

(c) $\displaystyle\int_0^\pi \sin x \cos x \, dx$

(d) $\displaystyle\int_1^2 \sinh^2 x \, dx$

Solutions

1 (a) 20 (b) 1.3863 (c) 2

(d) 2.3504 (e) 0.5 (f) −1.9800

(g) $-\frac{1}{3}$ (h) 0 (i) 0.3995

2 (a) $\frac{4}{3}$ (b) $\frac{\pi}{4}$ (c) −184.75

(d) $\frac{53}{6}$ (e) 0.5728 (f) 8

3 (a) $-\frac{65}{12}$ (b) 2.275 (c) −0.639

(d) −0.9255 (e) 1.2313 (f) 1.1175

4 (a) 0.7071 (b) 1

(c) 0.7071 (d) 2

5 (a) $\frac{1}{2}$ (b) $\frac{1}{2}$ (c) 1

6 $\frac{1}{6}$

7 $\frac{4}{3}$

8 (a) 1.0839 (b) 0.6468

(c) 0 (d) 2.3504

9 4.7756

10 0.4142

11 39

12 2.3026

13 (a) −3.6202 (b) 3.1945

(c) 0 (d) 5.4158

Review exercises 13

1 Find the following integrals:

(a) $\displaystyle\int 3x^2 + x \, dx$

(b) $\displaystyle\int \frac{2}{t} + 2t + 2 \, dt$

(c) $\displaystyle\int (1 + z)(1 - z) \, dz$

(d) $\displaystyle\int \sqrt{t} - \frac{1}{\sqrt{t}} \, dt$

(e) $\displaystyle\int x^{2/3} + 4x^3 \, dx$

2 Given

$$\frac{dy}{dx} = x^2 + \sin x + \cos 2x + 1$$

find an expression for $y(x)$.

3 Find the following integrals:

(a) $\displaystyle\int 3e^x + \frac{3}{e^x} \, dx$

(b) $\displaystyle\int (1 + e^x)(1 - e^{-x}) \, dx$

(c) $\displaystyle\int 2e^{4t} + 1 \, dt$

(d) $\displaystyle\int e^x (1 + e^x) \, dx$

(e) $\displaystyle\int 4e^{-t} - e^{-2t} \, dt$

4 Find the integrals

(a) $\displaystyle\int \sin 2x + \cos 2x \, dx$

(b) $\displaystyle\int 2\sin t - \cos t \, dt$

(c) $\displaystyle\int 4\tan\left(\frac{t}{2}\right) dt$

(d) $\displaystyle\int \sin(\pi - z) + \cos(\pi - 2z) \, dz$

(e) $\displaystyle\int \tan(t + \pi) \, dt$

(f) $\displaystyle\int 2\sin 3t + 2\sin\left(\frac{t}{3}\right) dt$

5 Find the following integrals:

(a) $\displaystyle\int \operatorname{cosec}(3t + \pi) \, dt$

(b) $\displaystyle\int \sec\left(\frac{x}{2} + 1\right) dx$

(c) $\displaystyle\int \cot\left(\frac{\pi + t}{2}\right) dt$

(d) $\displaystyle\int 3\operatorname{cosec}\left(\frac{y}{3} - 2\right) dy$

(e) $\displaystyle\int \frac{1}{2}\cot(\pi - 2z) \, dz$

(f) $\displaystyle\int \frac{2}{3}\sec(2t - \pi) \, dt$

6 Find the following integrals:

(a) $\displaystyle\int \frac{4}{\sqrt{1 - v^2}} \, dv$

(b) $\displaystyle\int \frac{1}{2\sqrt{1 - v^2}} \, dv$

(c) $\displaystyle\int \frac{1}{49 + t^2} \, dt$

(d) $\displaystyle\int \frac{1}{50 + 2t^2} \, dt$

(e) $\displaystyle\int \frac{2}{\sqrt{1 - 4t^2}} \, dt$

(f) $\displaystyle\int \frac{1}{\sqrt{36 - 9x^2}} \, dx$

(g) $\displaystyle\int \frac{3}{x^2 + 3} \, dx$

7 The speed, $v(t)$, of a particle is given by

$$v(t) = t + e^{-t}$$

(a) Find the distance travelled by the particle.

(b) Calculate the distance travelled between $t = 1$ and $t = 3$.

8 The capacitance of a capacitor is 0.1 F. The current, $i(t)$, through the capacitor is given by

$$i(t) = 50\sin \pi t$$

Derive an expression for the voltage across the capacitor.

9 By using suitable trigonometric identities find

(a) $\displaystyle\int \sin^2 2t + \cos^2 2t \, dt$

(b) $\displaystyle\int \sin 2t \cos 2t \, dt$

(c) $\displaystyle\int \frac{1}{\sin 2t} \, dt$

(d) $\displaystyle\int \frac{\cos 2t}{\sin 2t} \, dt$

(e) $\displaystyle\int \frac{\sin 2t}{\cos 2t} \, dt$

10 By expressing

$$\frac{2x^2 + x + 2}{x^3 + x}$$

as its partial fractions, find

$$\int \frac{2x^2 + x + 2}{x^3 + x} \, dx$$

11 Evaluate the following definite integrals:

(a) $\displaystyle\int_0^1 2t^2 + t^3 \, dt$

(b) $\displaystyle\int_1^3 \frac{2}{x} - \frac{x}{2} \, dx$

(c) $\displaystyle\int_0^1 7 - t + 7t^2 \, dt$

(d) $\displaystyle\int_0^2 (z + 1)(z + 2) \, dz$

(e) $\displaystyle\int_1^4 \sqrt{x} \, dx$

(f) $\displaystyle\int_{-2}^{-1} \frac{x - 2}{x} \, dx$

12 Evaluate the following definite integrals:

(a) $\int_0^1 e^{3x+1}\,dx$

(b) $\int_{-1}^1 e^{2t} - e^t + 1\,dt$

(c) $\int_1^2 (e^z - 1)^2\,dz$

(d) $\int_0^1 e^{-2x} + e^{2x}\,dx$

(e) $\int_{-1}^0 x + e^x\,dx$

13 Evaluate the following integrals:

(a) $\int_0^{\pi/2} 2\sin 3t\,dt$

(b) $\int_{\pi/2}^{\pi} \sin 2t - \cos 2t\,dt$

(c) $\int_0^{\pi/4} \tan t + t\,dt$

(d) $\int_0^{\pi/4} \sin\left(\frac{t}{2}\right) + \cos\left(\frac{t}{2}\right)\,dt$

(e) $\int_0^{0.1} \tan 3t\,dt$

14 Evaluate the following definite integrals:

(a) $\int_0^{2\pi/k} \sin kt\,dt$

(b) $\int_0^{2\pi/k} \cos kt\,dt$

where k is a constant.

15 Evaluate the following definite integrals:

(a) $\int_0^{0.5} \operatorname{cosec}(2x + 1)\,dx$

(b) $\int_0^{0.1} \sec 3t\,dt$

(c) $\int_{-\pi/4}^{\pi/4} \tan(x + \pi)\,dx$

16 Evaluate the following definite integrals:

(a) $\int_0^2 \frac{3}{\sqrt{9 - x^2}}\,dx$

(b) $\int_{-1}^1 \frac{2}{9 + x^2}\,dx$

(c) $\int_0^1 \frac{1}{\sqrt{8 - 2x^2}}\,dx$

(d) $\int_1^3 \frac{1}{10 + 4t^2}\,dt$

17 (a) Calculate the area enclosed by the curve $y = x^3$, the x axis and $x = 2$.

(b) Calculate the area enclosed by the curve $y = x^3$, the y axis and $y = 8$.

18 Find the total area between $f(t) = t^2 - 4$ and the t axis on the following intervals:

(a) $[-4, -3]$ (b) $[-3, -1]$
(c) $[0, 3]$ (d) $[-3, 3]$

19 Calculate the area enclosed by the curve $y = x^2 - x - 6$ and the x axis.

20 Calculate the total area between $y = x^2 - 3x - 4$ and the x axis on the following intervals:

(a) $[-2, -1]$ (b) $[-2, 1]$
(c) $[2, 4]$ (d) $[2, 5]$

21 Calculate the area enclosed by the curve $y = x^3$ and the line $y = x$.

22 Calculate the area enclosed by $y = x^2 + 4$ and $y = 12 - x^2$.

23 Calculate the area enclosed by $y = \sin x$ and $y = \frac{2x}{\pi}$.

Solutions

1 (a) $x^3 + \dfrac{x^2}{2} + c$

(b) $2\ln|t| + t^2 + 2t + c$

(c) $z - \dfrac{z^3}{3} + c$

(d) $\frac{2}{3}t^{3/2} - 2t^{1/2} + c$

(e) $\frac{3}{5}x^{5/3} + x^4 + c$

2 $\frac{x^3}{3} - \cos x + \frac{1}{2}\sin 2x + x + c$

3 (a) $3e^x - 3e^{-x} + c$

    (b) $e^x + e^{-x} + c$

    (c) $\frac{e^{4t}}{2} + t + c$

    (d) $e^x + \frac{e^{2x}}{2} + c$

    (e) $-4e^{-t} + \frac{e^{-2t}}{2} + c$

4 (a) $-\frac{1}{2}\cos 2x + \frac{1}{2}\sin 2x + c$

    (b) $-2\cos t - \sin t + c$

    (c) $8\ln\left|\sec\left(\frac{t}{2}\right)\right| + c$

    (d) $\cos(\pi - z) - \frac{1}{2}\sin(\pi - 2z) + c$

    (e) $\ln|\sec(t + \pi)| + c$

    (f) $-\frac{2}{3}\cos 3t - 6\cos\left(\frac{t}{3}\right) + c$

5 (a) $\frac{1}{3}\ln|\csc(3t + \pi) - \cot(3t + \pi)| + c$

    (b) $2\ln\left|\sec\left(\frac{x}{2} + 1\right) + \tan\left(\frac{x}{2} + 1\right)\right| + c$

    (c) $2\ln\left|\sin\left(\frac{\pi + t}{2}\right)\right| + c$

    (d) $9\ln\left|\csc\left(\frac{y}{3} - 2\right) - \cot\left(\frac{y}{3} - 2\right)\right| + c$

    (e) $-\frac{1}{4}\ln|\sin(\pi - 2z)| + c$

    (f) $\frac{1}{3}\ln|\sec(2t - \pi) + \tan(2t - \pi)| + c$

6 (a) $4\sin^{-1}v + c$

    (b) $\frac{1}{2}\sin^{-1}v + c$

    (c) $\frac{1}{7}\tan^{-1}\left(\frac{t}{7}\right) + c$

    (d) $\frac{1}{10}\tan^{-1}\left(\frac{t}{5}\right) + c$

    (e) $\sin^{-1}(2t) + c$

    (f) $\frac{1}{3}\sin^{-1}\left(\frac{x}{2}\right) + c$

    (g) $\sqrt{3}\tan^{-1}\left(\frac{x}{\sqrt{3}}\right) + c$

7 (a) $\frac{t^2}{2} - e^{-t} + c$ (b) 4.3181

8 $-\frac{500}{\pi}\cos \pi t + c$

9 (a) $t + c$

    (b) $-\frac{\cos 4t}{8} + c$

    (c) $\frac{1}{2}\ln|\csc 2t - \cot 2t| + c$

    (d) $\frac{1}{2}\ln|\sin 2t| + c$

    (e) $\frac{1}{2}\ln|\sec 2t| + c$

10 $2\ln|x| + \tan^{-1}x + c$

11 (a) $\frac{11}{12}$ (b) 0.1972   (c) $\frac{53}{6}$

     (d) $\frac{38}{3}$ (e) $\frac{14}{3}$ (f) 2.3863

12 (a) 17.2933   (b) 3.2765   (c) 15.2630

     (d) 3.6269   (e) 0.1321

13 (a) $\frac{2}{3}$ (b) -1 (c) 0.6550

     (d) 0.9176   (e) 0.0152

14 (a) 0   (b) 0

15 (a) 0.5238   (b) 0.1015   (c) 0

16 (a) 2.1892   (b) 0.4290

     (c) 0.3702   (d) 0.0825

17 (a) 4   (b) 12

18 (a) $\frac{25}{3}$ (b) 4   (c) $\frac{23}{3}$ (d) $\frac{46}{3}$

19 $\frac{125}{6}$

20 (a) $\frac{17}{6}$ (b) $\frac{61}{6}$ (c) $\frac{22}{3}$ (d) $\frac{61}{6}$

21 0.5

22 $\frac{64}{3}$

23 0.4292

14 Techniques of integration

Chapter 14	Contents	
14.1	Introduction	440
14.2	Integration by parts	440
14.3	Integration by substitution	446
14.4	Integration using partial fractions	449
	Review exercises	452

14.1 Introduction

The previous chapter showed us how to integrate functions which matched the list of standard integrals given in Table 13.1. Clearly, it is impossible to list all possible functions in the table and so some general techniques are required. Integration techniques may be classified as **analytical**, that is exact, or **numerical**, that is approximate. We will now study three analytical techniques:

(1) integration by parts;

(2) integration by substitution;

(3) integration using partial fractions.

14.2 Integration by parts

This technique is used to integrate a product, and is derived from the product rule for differentiation. Let u and v be functions of x. Then the product rule of differentiation states:

$$\frac{\mathrm{d}}{\mathrm{d}x}(uv) = \frac{\mathrm{d}u}{\mathrm{d}x}v + u\frac{\mathrm{d}v}{\mathrm{d}x}$$

Rearranging we have

$$u\frac{\mathrm{d}v}{\mathrm{d}x} = \frac{\mathrm{d}}{\mathrm{d}x}(uv) - v\frac{\mathrm{d}u}{\mathrm{d}x}$$

Integrating this equation yields

$$\int u\frac{\mathrm{d}v}{\mathrm{d}x}\,\mathrm{d}x = \int \frac{\mathrm{d}}{\mathrm{d}x}(uv)\,\mathrm{d}x - \int v\frac{\mathrm{d}u}{\mathrm{d}x}\,\mathrm{d}x$$

Recognizing that integration and differentiation are inverse processes allows

$$\int \frac{\mathrm{d}(uv)}{\mathrm{d}x}\,\mathrm{d}x$$

to be simplified to uv. Hence,

$$\int u\left(\frac{\mathrm{d}v}{\mathrm{d}x}\right)\mathrm{d}x = uv - \int v\left(\frac{\mathrm{d}u}{\mathrm{d}x}\right)\mathrm{d}x$$

This is the formula for integration by parts.

Example 14.1 Find $\int x \sin x \, \mathrm{d}x$.

Solution We recognize the integrand as a product of the functions x and $\sin x$. Let $u = x$, $\dfrac{dv}{dx} = \sin x$. Then $\dfrac{du}{dx} = 1$, $v = -\cos x$. Using the integration by parts formula we get

$$\int x \sin x \, dx = x(-\cos x) - \int (-\cos x) 1 \, dx$$

$$= -x \cos x + \sin x + c$$

When dealing with definite integrals the corresponding formula for integration by parts is

$$\int_a^b u\left(\frac{dv}{dx}\right) dx = [uv]_a^b - \int_a^b v\left(\frac{du}{dx}\right) dx$$

Example 14.2 Evaluate

$$\int_0^2 x e^x \, dx$$

Solution We let

$$u = x \qquad \text{and} \qquad \frac{dv}{dx} = e^x$$

Then

$$\frac{du}{dx} = 1 \qquad \text{and} \qquad v = e^x$$

Using the integration by parts formula for definite integrals we have

$$\int_0^2 x e^x \, dx = [x e^x]_0^2 - \int_0^2 e^x \cdot 1 \, dx$$

$$= 2e^2 - [e^x]_0^2$$

$$= 2e^2 - [e^2 - 1]$$

$$= e^2 + 1$$

Sometimes integration by parts needs to be used twice, as the next example illustrates.

Example 14.3 Evaluate

$$\int_0^2 x^2 e^x \, dx$$

Solution   We let

$$u = x^2 \quad \text{and} \quad \frac{dv}{dx} = e^x$$

Then

$$\frac{du}{dx} = 2x \quad \text{and} \quad v = e^x$$

Using the integration by parts formula we have

$$\int_0^2 x^2 e^x \, dx = [x^2 e^x]_0^2 - \int_0^2 2x e^x \, dx$$

$$= 4e^2 - 2 \int_0^2 x e^x \, dx$$

Now $\int_0^2 x e^x \, dx$ has been evaluated using integration by parts in Example 14.2. So

$$\int_0^2 x^2 e^x \, dx = 4e^2 - 2[e^2 + 1] = 2e^2 - 2 = 12.78$$

The next example illustrates a case in which the integral to be found reappears after repeated application of integration by parts.

Example 14.4   Find

$$\int e^t \sin t \, dt$$

Solution   We let

$$u = e^t \quad \text{and} \quad \frac{dv}{dt} = \sin t$$

and so

$$\frac{du}{dt} = e^t \quad \text{and} \quad v = -\cos t$$

Applying integration by parts yields

$$\int e^t \sin t \, dt = -e^t \cos t - \int (-\cos t) e^t \, dt + c$$

$$= -e^t \cos t + \int e^t \cos t \, dt + c \qquad (14.1)$$

We now apply integration by parts to $\int e^t \cos t \, dt$. We let

$$u = e^t \quad \text{and} \quad \frac{dv}{dt} = \cos t$$

Then

$$\frac{du}{dt} = e^t \qquad \text{and} \qquad v = \sin t$$

So

$$\int e^t \cos t \, dt = e^t \sin t - \int e^t \sin t \, dt \qquad (14.2)$$

Substituting Equation (14.2) into Equation (14.1) yields

$$\int e^t \sin t \, dt = -e^t \cos t + e^t \sin t - \int e^t \sin t \, dt + c$$

Rearranging the equation gives

$$2 \int e^t \sin t \, dt = -e^t \cos t + e^t \sin t + c$$

from which we see that

$$\int e^t \sin t \, dt = \frac{-e^t \cos t + e^t \sin t + c}{2}$$

Example 14.5   Evaluate

$$\int_0^2 x^n e^x \, dx$$

for $n = 3, 4, 5$.

Solution   The integral may be evaluated by using integration by parts repeatedly. However, this is slow and cumbersome. Instead it is useful to develop a **reduction formula** as is now illustrated.

Let $u = x^n$ and $\dfrac{dv}{dx} = e^x$. Then $\dfrac{du}{dx} = nx^{n-1}$ and $v = e^x$.

Using integration by parts we have

$$\int_0^2 x^n e^x \, dx = [x^n e^x]_0^2 - \int_0^2 nx^{n-1} e^x \, dx$$

$$= 2^n e^2 - n \int_0^2 x^{n-1} e^x \, dx$$

Writing

$$I_n = \int_0^2 x^n e^x \, dx$$

we see that

$$I_{n-1} = \int_0^2 x^{n-1} e^x \, dx$$

Hence

$$I_n = 2^n e^2 - n I_{n-1} \qquad (14.3)$$

Equation (14.3) is called a **reduction formula**.

We have already evaluated I_1, that is $\int_0^2 xe^x \, dx$ in Example 14.2, and found

$$I_1 = e^2 + 1$$

Using the reduction formula with $n = 2$ gives

$$\int_0^2 x^2 e^x \, dx = I_2 = 2^2 e^2 - 2I_1$$
$$= 4e^2 - 2(e^2 + 1)$$
$$= 2e^2 - 2$$

Note that this is in agreement with Example 14.3.
With $n = 3$ the reduction formula yields

$$\int_0^2 x^3 e^x \, dx = I_3 = 2^3 e^2 - 3I_2$$
$$= 8e^2 - 3(2e^2 - 2)$$
$$= 2e^2 + 6$$

With $n = 4$ we have

$$\int_0^2 x^4 e^x \, dx = I_4 = 2^4 e^2 - 4I_3$$
$$= 16e^2 - 4(2e^2 + 6)$$
$$= 8e^2 - 24$$

With $n = 5$ we have

$$\int_0^2 x^5 e^x \, dx = I_5 = 2^5 e^2 - 5I_4$$
$$= 32e^2 - 5(8e^2 - 24)$$
$$= 120 - 8e^2$$

Exercises 14.2

1 Use integration by parts to find the following:

(a) $\int x \sin(2x) \, dx$

(b) $\int te^{3t} \, dt$

(c) $\int x \cos x \, dx$

(d) $\int 2v \sin\left(\dfrac{v}{2}\right) dv$

(e) $\int \dfrac{x}{e^x} \, dx$

2   Use integration by parts to find

(a) $\displaystyle\int t \ln t \, dt$

(b) $\displaystyle\int \ln t \, dt$

(c) $\displaystyle\int t^n \ln t \, dt$ $(n \neq -1)$

(d) $\displaystyle\int t \sin(at + b) \, dt$ a, b constants

(e) $\displaystyle\int t e^{at+b} \, dt$ a, b constants

3   Evaluate the following definite integrals:

(a) $\displaystyle\int_0^1 x \cos 2x \, dx$

(b) $\displaystyle\int_0^{\pi/2} x \sin 2x \, dx$

(c) $\displaystyle\int_{-1}^1 t e^{2t} \, dt$

(d) $\displaystyle\int_1^3 t^2 \ln t \, dt$

(e) $\displaystyle\int_0^2 \frac{2x}{e^{2x}} \, dx$

4   Find

(a) $\displaystyle\int t^2 e^{2t} \, dt$

(b) $\displaystyle\int t^2 \cos 3t \, dt$

(c) $\displaystyle\int t^2 \sin\left(\frac{t}{2}\right) dt$

5   Evaluate the following definite integrals:

(a) $\displaystyle\int_0^2 t^2 e^t \, dt$

(b) $\displaystyle\int_{-1}^1 t^2 \sin t \, dt$

(c) $\displaystyle\int_0^1 t^2 \cos 3t \, dt$

6   Obtain a reduction formula for

$$I_n = \int t^n e^{kt} \, dt \qquad n, k \text{ constants}$$

Hence find $\displaystyle\int t^2 e^{3t} \, dt, \int t^3 e^{3t} \, dt$ and

$\displaystyle\int t^4 e^{3t} \, dt.$

7   Use integration by parts twice to obtain a reduction formula for

$$I_n = \int_0^{\pi/2} t^n \sin t \, dt$$

Hence find $\displaystyle\int_0^{\pi/2} t^3 \sin t \, dt, \int_0^{\pi/2} t^5 \sin t \, dt$

and $\displaystyle\int_0^{\pi/2} t^7 \sin t \, dt.$

8   Use integration by parts to find

$$\int_0^{\pi/2} e^{2x} \cos x \, dx$$

Solutions

1   (a) $\dfrac{\sin 2x}{4} - \dfrac{x \cos 2x}{2} + c$

(b) $e^{3t}\left(\dfrac{t}{3} - \dfrac{1}{9}\right) + c$

(c) $\cos x + x \sin x + c$

(d) $8 \sin\left(\dfrac{v}{2}\right) - 4v \cos\left(\dfrac{v}{2}\right) + c$

(e) $-e^{-x}(x + 1) + c$

2   (a) $\dfrac{t^2 \ln t}{2} - \dfrac{t^2}{4} + c$

(b) $t \ln t - t + c$

(c) $\dfrac{(\ln t) t^{n+1}}{n + 1} - \dfrac{t^{n+1}}{(n + 1)^2} + c$

(d) $\dfrac{\sin(at + b)}{a^2} - \dfrac{t \cos(at + b)}{a} + c$

(e) $e^{at+b}\left(\dfrac{t}{a} - \dfrac{1}{a^2}\right) + c$

3   (a) 0.1006   (b) 0.7854   (c) 1.9488

     (d) 6.9986   (e) 0.4542

4 (a) $\dfrac{e^{2t}(2t^2-2t+1)}{4}+c$

(b) $\dfrac{2}{9}t\cos 3t+\left(\dfrac{t^2}{3}-\dfrac{2}{27}\right)\sin 3t+c$

(c) $8t\sin\left(\dfrac{t}{2}\right)-2(t^2-8)\cos\left(\dfrac{t}{2}\right)+c$

5 (a) 12.7781   (b) 0   (c) −0.1834

6 $I_n=\dfrac{t^n e^{kt}}{k}-\dfrac{n}{k}I_{n-1},\ \dfrac{e^{3t}(9t^2-6t+2)}{27},$

$\dfrac{e^{3t}(9t^3-9t^2+6t-2)}{27},$

$\dfrac{e^{3t}(27t^4-36t^3+36t^2-24t+8)}{81}$

7 $I_n=n\left\{\left(\dfrac{\pi}{2}\right)^{n-1}-(n-1)I_{n-2}\right\}$

1.4022, 2.3963, 4.5084

8 4.2281

14.3 Integration by substitution

This technique is the integral equivalent of the chain rule. It is best illustrated by examples.

Example 14.6 Find $\displaystyle\int (3x+1)^{2.7}\,dx$.

Solution Let $z=3x+1$, so that $\dfrac{dz}{dx}=3$, that is $dx=\dfrac{dz}{3}$. Writing the integral in terms of z, it becomes

$$\int z^{2.7}\frac{1}{3}\,dz=\frac{1}{3}\int z^{2.7}dz=\frac{1}{3}\left(\frac{z^{3.7}}{3.7}\right)+c=\frac{1}{3}\frac{(3x+1)^{3.7}}{3.7}+c$$

Example 14.7 Evaluate $\displaystyle\int_2^3 t\sin(t^2)\,dt$.

Solution Let $v=t^2$ so $\dfrac{dv}{dt}=2t$, that is

$$dt=\frac{1}{2t}\,dv$$

When changing the integral from one in terms of t to one in terms of v, the limits must also be changed. When $t=2$, $v=4$; when $t=3$, $v=9$. Hence, the integral becomes

$$\int_4^9 \frac{\sin v}{2}\,dv=\frac{1}{2}[-\cos v]_4^9=\frac{1}{2}[-\cos 9+\cos 4]=0.129$$

Sometimes the substitution can involve a trigonometric function.

Example 14.8 Evaluate $\displaystyle\int_1^2 \sin t\,\cos^2 t\,dt$.

Solution Put $z = \cos t$ so that $\dfrac{dz}{dt} = -\sin t$, that is $\sin t \, dt = -dz$. When $t = 1$, $z = \cos 1$; when $t = 2$, $z = \cos 2$. Hence

$$\int_1^2 \sin t \, \cos^2 t \, dt = -\int_{\cos 1}^{\cos 2} z^2 \, dz = -\left[\frac{z^3}{3}\right]_{\cos 1}^{\cos 2}$$

$$= \frac{\cos^3 1 - \cos^3 2}{3} = 0.0766$$

Example 14.9 Find $\displaystyle\int \frac{e^{\tan x}}{\cos^2 x} \, dx$.

Solution Put $z = \tan x$. Then $\dfrac{dz}{dx} = \sec^2 x$, $dz = \dfrac{dx}{\cos^2 x}$. Hence,

$$\int \frac{e^{\tan x}}{\cos^2 x} \, dx = \int e^z \, dz = e^z + c = e^{\tan x} + c$$

Integration by substitution allows functions of the form $\dfrac{df/dx}{f}$ to be integrated.

Example 14.10 Find $\displaystyle\int \frac{3x^2 + 1}{x^3 + x + 2} \, dx$.

Solution Put $z = x^3 + x + 2$, then $\dfrac{dz}{dx} = 3x^2 + 1$, that is $dz = (3x^2 + 1) \, dx$. Hence,

$$\int \frac{3x^2 + 1}{x^3 + x + 2} \, dx = \int \frac{dz}{z} = \ln |z| + c = \ln |x^3 + x + 2| + c$$

Example 14.11 Find $\displaystyle\int \frac{df/dx}{f} \, dx$.

Solution Put $z = f$. Then $\dfrac{dz}{dx} = \dfrac{df}{dx}$, that is

$$dz = \frac{df}{dx} \, dx.$$

Hence,

$$\int \frac{df/dx}{f} \, dx = \int \frac{dz}{z} = \ln |z| + c = \ln |f| + c$$

and so

$$\int \frac{df/dx}{f} \, dx = \ln |f| + c$$

The result of Example 14.11 is particularly important.

$$\int \frac{df/dx}{f} \, dx = \ln|f| + c$$

Example 14.12   Evaluate $\displaystyle\int_2^4 \frac{3t^2 + 2t}{t^3 + t^2 + 1} \, dt$.

Solution   The numerator is the derivative of the denominator and so

$$\int_2^4 \frac{3t^2 + 2t}{t^3 + t^2 + 1} \, dt = [\ln|t^3 + t^2 + 1|]_2^4 = \ln 81 - \ln 13 = 1.83$$

Example 14.13   Find

(a) $\displaystyle\int \frac{4}{5x - 7} \, dx$

(b) $\displaystyle\int \frac{t}{t^2 + 1} \, dt$

(c) $\displaystyle\int \frac{e^{t/2}}{e^{t/2} + 1} \, dt$

Solution   The integrands are rewritten so that the numerator is the derivative of the denominator.

(a) $\displaystyle\int \frac{4}{5x - 7} \, dx = \frac{4}{5} \int \frac{5}{5x - 7} \, dx = \frac{4}{5} \ln|5x - 7| + c$

(b) $\displaystyle\int \frac{t}{t^2 + 1} \, dt = \frac{1}{2} \int \frac{2t}{t^2 + 1} \, dt$

$$= \frac{1}{2} \ln|t^2 + 1| + c$$

(c) $\displaystyle\int \frac{e^{t/2}}{e^{t/2} + 1} \, dt = 2 \int \frac{\frac{1}{2}e^{t/2}}{e^{t/2} + 1} \, dt = 2\ln|e^{t/2} + 1| + c$

Exercises 14.3

1   Use the given substitutions to find the following integrals:

(a) $\displaystyle\int (4x + 1)^7 \, dx$, $z = 4x + 1$

(b) $\displaystyle\int t^2 \sin(t^3 + 1) \, dt$, $z = t^3 + 1$

(c) $\displaystyle\int 4te^{-t^2} \, dt$, $z = t^2$

(d) $\displaystyle\int (1 - z)^{1/3} \, dz$, $t = 1 - z$

(e) $\displaystyle\int \cos t (\sin^5 t) \, dt$, $z = \sin t$

2 Evaluate the following definite integrals:

(a) $\displaystyle\int_1^2 (2t+3)^7 \, dt$

(b) $\displaystyle\int_0^{\pi/2} \sin 2t \cos^4 2t \, dt$

(c) $\displaystyle\int_0^1 3t^2 e^{t^3} \, dt$

(d) $\displaystyle\int_0^2 \sqrt{4+3x} \, dx$

(e) $\displaystyle\int_1^2 \frac{\sin(\sqrt{x})}{\sqrt{x}} \, dx$

3 Find the area between $y = x(3x^2+2)^4$ and the x axis from $x = 0$ to $x = 1$.

4 Find

(a) $\displaystyle\int \frac{4x+1}{2x^2+x+3} \, dx$

(b) $\displaystyle\int \frac{2\sin 2x}{\cos 2x + 7} \, dx$

(c) $\displaystyle\int \frac{3}{9-2x} \, dx$

(d) $\displaystyle\int \frac{t}{t^2+1} \, dt$

(e) $\displaystyle\int \frac{1}{t \ln t} \, dt$

5 Evaluate the following:

(a) $\displaystyle\int_0^1 \frac{2}{(1+3x)^2} \, dx$

(b) $\displaystyle\int_0^{\pi/2} \sin t \sqrt{\cos t} \, dt$

(c) $\displaystyle\int_1^2 \frac{3+x}{x^2+6x+1} \, dx$

(d) $\displaystyle\int_1^2 \frac{e^{\sqrt{t}}}{\sqrt{t}} \, dt$

(e) $\displaystyle\int_0^2 x \sin(\pi - x^2) \, dx$

Solutions

1 (a) $\dfrac{(4x+1)^8}{32} + c$

(b) $-\dfrac{\cos(t^3+1)}{3} + c$

(c) $-2e^{-t^2} + c$

(d) $-\frac{3}{4}(1-z)^{4/3} + c$

(e) $\frac{1}{6}\sin^6 t + c$

2 (a) 3.3588×10^5

(b) 0.2

(c) 1.7183

(d) 5.2495

(e) 0.7687

3 103.098

4 (a) $\ln(2x^2 + x + 3) + c$

(b) $-\ln(\cos 2x + 7) + c$

(c) $-\frac{3}{2}\ln(9 - 2x) + c$

(d) $\frac{1}{2}\ln(t^2 + 1) + c$

(e) $\ln(\ln t) + c$

5 (a) 0.5

(b) 0.6667

(c) 0.3769

(d) 2.7899

(e) 0.8268

14.4	Integration using partial fractions

The technique of expressing a rational function as the sum of its partial fractions has been covered in Section 1.6. Some expressions which at first sight look impossible to integrate may in fact be integrated when expressed as their partial fractions.

Example 14.14 Find

(a) $\displaystyle\int \frac{1}{x^3 + x}\, dx$

(b) $\displaystyle\int \frac{13x - 4}{6x^2 - x - 2}\, dx$

Solution (a) First express the integrand in partial fractions:

$$\frac{1}{x^3 + x} = \frac{1}{x(x^2 + 1)} = \frac{A}{x} + \frac{Bx + C}{x^2 + 1}$$

Then,

$$1 = A(x^2 + 1) + x(Bx + C)$$

Equating the constant terms: $1 = A$ so that $A = 1$.

Equating the coefficients of x: $0 = C$ so that $C = 0$.

Equating the coefficients of x^2: $0 = A + B$ and hence $B = -1$.

Then,

$$\int \frac{1}{x^3 + x}\, dx = \int \frac{1}{x} - \frac{x}{x^2 + 1}\, dx$$

$$= \ln|x| - \frac{1}{2}\ln|x^2 + 1| + c = \ln\left|\frac{x}{\sqrt{x^2 + 1}}\right| + c$$

(b) $\displaystyle\int \frac{13x - 4}{6x^2 - x - 2}\, dx = \int \frac{13x - 4}{(2x + 1)(3x - 2)}\, dx$

$$= \int \frac{3}{2x + 1} + \frac{2}{3x - 2}\, dx \qquad \text{using partial fractions}$$

$$= \frac{3}{2}\int \frac{2}{2x + 1}\, dx + \frac{2}{3}\int \frac{3}{3x - 2}\, dx$$

$$= \frac{3}{2}\ln|2x + 1| + \frac{2}{3}\ln|3x - 2| + c$$

Example 14.15 Evaluate $\displaystyle\int_0^1 \frac{4t^3 - 2t^2 + 3t - 1}{2t^2 + 1}\, dt$.

Solution Using partial fractions we may write

$$\frac{4t^3 - 2t^2 + 3t - 1}{2t^2 + 1} = 2t - 1 + \frac{t}{2t^2 + 1}$$

Hence,

$$\int_0^1 \frac{4t^3 - 2t^2 + 3t - 1}{2t^2 + 1}\,dt = \int_0^1 2t - 1 + \frac{t}{2t^2 + 1}\,dt = \left[t^2 - t + \frac{1}{4}\ln|2t^2 + 1|\right]_0^1$$

$$= \left[1 - 1 + \frac{1}{4}\ln 3\right] - \left[0 - 0 + \frac{1}{4}\ln 1\right] = 0.275$$

Exercises 14.4

1 By writing the integrand as its partial fractions find

(a) $\displaystyle\int \frac{x + 3}{x^2 + x}\,dx$

(b) $\displaystyle\int \frac{t - 3}{t^2 - 1}\,dt$

(c) $\displaystyle\int \frac{8x + 10}{4x^2 + 8x + 3}\,dx$

(d) $\displaystyle\int \frac{2t^2 + 3t + 3}{2(t + 1)}\,dt$

(e) $\displaystyle\int \frac{2x^2 + x + 1}{x^3 + x^2}\,dx$

2 Evaluate the following integrals:

(a) $\displaystyle\int_1^3 \frac{5x + 6}{2x^2 + 4x}\,dx$

(b) $\displaystyle\int_0^1 \frac{3x + 5}{(x + 1)(x + 2)}\,dx$

(c) $\displaystyle\int_1^2 \frac{3 - 3x}{2x^2 + 6x}\,dx$

(d) $\displaystyle\int_{-1}^0 \frac{4x + 1}{2x^2 + x - 6}\,dx$

(e) $\displaystyle\int_2^3 \frac{x^2 + 2x - 1}{(x^2 + 1)(x - 1)}\,dx$

3 Find the area between $y = \dfrac{4x + 7}{4x^2 + 8x + 3}$ and the x axis from $x = 0$ to $x = 1$.

4 Use partial fractions to find

(a) $\displaystyle\int_2^3 \frac{3x + 2}{x^2 - 1}\,dx$

(b) $\displaystyle\int \frac{t + 3}{t^2 + 2t + 1}\,dt$

(c) $\displaystyle\int \frac{2t^2 + 3t + 1}{t^3 + t}\,dt$

(d) $\displaystyle\int \frac{6t + 3}{2t^2 - 5t + 2}\,dt$

Solutions

1 (a) $3\ln x - 2\ln(x + 1) + c$

(b) $2\ln(t + 1) - \ln(t - 1) + c$

(c) $\frac{1}{2}\ln(2x + 3) + \frac{3}{2}\ln(2x + 1) + c$

(d) $\ln(t + 1) + \dfrac{t(t + 1)}{2} + c$

(e) $2\ln(x + 1) - \dfrac{1}{x} + c$

2 (a) 2.1587

(b) 1.7918

(c) −0.09971

(d) 0.1823

(e) 0.9769

3 1.2456

4 (a) 1.8767

(b) $\ln(t + 1) - \dfrac{2}{t + 1} + c$

(c) $3\tan^{-1} t + \frac{1}{2}\ln(t^2 + 1) + \ln t + c$

(d) $5\ln(t - 2) - 2\ln(2t - 1) + c$

Review exercises 14

1 Use the given substitution to find the following integrals:

(a) $\displaystyle\int_0^1 (9t+2)^{10}\,dt \qquad z = 9t+2$

(b) $\displaystyle\int_3^5 (-t+1)^6\,dt \qquad z = -t+1$

(c) $\displaystyle\int_6^3 (4x-1)^{27}\,dx \qquad z = 4x-1$

(d) $\displaystyle\int \sqrt{3t+1}\,dt \qquad z = 3t+1$

(e) $\displaystyle\int (9y-2)^{17}\,dy \qquad z = 9y-2$

(f) $\displaystyle\int_0^2 \frac{3}{(2z+5)^6}\,dz \qquad y = 2z+5$

(g) $\displaystyle\int t^2 \sin(t^3)\,dt \qquad z = t^3$

(h) $\displaystyle\int x^2 e^{x^3+1}\,dx \qquad z = x^3+1$

(i) $\displaystyle\int_0^{0.5} \sin(2t)e^{\cos(2t)}\,dt \qquad z = \cos(2t)$

(j) $\displaystyle\int_0^{\pi} \sin t \cos^2 t\,dt \qquad z = \cos t$

(k) $\displaystyle\int \cos t\sqrt{\sin t}\,dt \qquad z = \sin t$

2 Use integration by parts to find

(a) $\displaystyle\int_0^{\pi/2} e^{2x}\cos x\,dx$

(b) $\displaystyle\int_0^{\pi/2} e^{2x}\sin x\,dx$

3 Find

$$\int \frac{\ln t}{t}\,dt$$

using

(a) integration by parts

(b) the substitution $z = \ln t$.

4 The integral I_n is given by

$$I_n = \int_0^{\pi/2} \sin^n \theta\,d\theta$$

(a) State I_{n-2}.

(b) Show

$$I_n = \frac{n-1}{n}I_{n-2}$$

(c) Evaluate I_0, I_1, I_2 and I_3.

5 Evaluate

(a) $\displaystyle\int \frac{t^2}{t^3+1}\,dt$

(b) $\displaystyle\int_0^{\pi/3} \sin t \cos t\,dt$

(c) $\displaystyle\int_1^3 \frac{4}{e^{2t}}\,dt$

(d) $\displaystyle\int \frac{3x-7}{(x-2)(x-3)(x-4)}\,dx$

(e) $\displaystyle\int \frac{e^x}{e^x+1}\,dx$

6 Evaluate

(a) $\displaystyle\int_0^1 \frac{3}{(e^t)^2} + \sin t \cos^2 t\,dt$

(b) $\displaystyle\int_0^1 4t^2 e^{t^3} + t(1+t^2)^{12}\,dt$

(c) $\displaystyle\int_0^{\pi} \sin^2 \omega t + \cos^2 \omega t + \omega\,dt$
ω constant

(d) $\displaystyle\int_1^2 \frac{1+t+t^2}{t(1+t^2)}\,dt$

(e) $\displaystyle\int_0^1 (t+e^t)\sin t\,dt$

(f) $\displaystyle\int_1^3 \frac{1+4x}{2x+4x^2}\,dx$

7 Calculate the area under $y(x) = \dfrac{1+2e^{2x}}{x+e^{2x}}$ from $x = 1$ to $x = 3$.

8 Evaluate the following integrals:

(a) $\displaystyle\int (-2t+0.1)^4\,dt$

(b) $\displaystyle\int (1+x)\sin x\,dx$

(c) $\displaystyle\int_1^2 x\sin(1+x)\,dx$

(d) $\displaystyle\int_3^6 \frac{t}{\sqrt{t^2+1}}\,dt$

(e) $\displaystyle\int \frac{1}{t^3+2t^2+t}\,dt$

(f) $\displaystyle\int_1^5 \frac{1}{1+e^t}\,dt$

9 Find

(a) $\displaystyle\int \frac{\cos t}{10+\sin t}\,dt$

(b) $\displaystyle\int \frac{2\sin t \cos t}{1+\sin^2 t}\,dt$

(c) $\displaystyle\int \frac{1}{t(1+\ln t)}\,dt$

(d) $\displaystyle\int \frac{1}{e^t(1+e^{-t})}\,dt$

(e) $\displaystyle\int \frac{1+\ln x}{x\ln x}\,dx$

10 Find $\displaystyle\int x^3 e^{x^2}\,dx$.

Solutions

1 (a) 2.8819×10^9

(b) 2322

(c) -1.2×10^{36}

(d) $\frac{2}{9}(3t+1)^{3/2}+c$

(e) $\dfrac{(9y-2)^{18}}{162}+c$

(f) 9.092×10^{-5}

(g) $-\frac{1}{3}\cos(t^3)+c$

(h) $\dfrac{e^{x^3+1}}{3}+c$

(i) 0.5009

(j) $\frac{2}{3}$

(k) $\frac{2}{3}(\sin t)^{3/2}+c$

2 (a) 4.2281   (b) 9.4563

3 $\dfrac{(\ln t)^2}{2}+c$

4 (a) $I_{n-2}=\displaystyle\int_0^{\pi/2}\sin^{n-2}\theta\,d\theta$

(c) $\dfrac{\pi}{2}, 1, 0.7854, 0.6667$

5 (a) $\frac{1}{3}\ln|t^3+1|+c$

(b) $\frac{3}{8}$

(c) 0.2657

(d) $-\frac{1}{2}\ln|x-2|-2\ln|x-3|+\frac{5}{2}\ln|x-4|+c$

(e) $\ln|e^x+1|+c$

6 (a) 1.5778   (b) 317.3   (c) $\pi(1+\omega)$

(d) 1.0149   (e) 1.2105   (f) 0.9730

7 3.8805

8 (a) $-\dfrac{(-2t+0.1)^5}{10}+c$

(b) $-(1+x)\cos x+\sin x+c$

(c) 0.7957

(d) 2.9205

(e) $\ln|t|-\ln|t+1|+\dfrac{1}{t+1}+c$

(f) 0.3066

9 (a) $\ln(\sin t+10)+c$

(b) $\ln(\sin^2 t+1)+c$

(c) $\ln(1+\ln t)+c$

(d) $-\ln(1+e^{-t})+c$

(e) $\ln(x\ln x)+c$

10 $\dfrac{e^{x^2}(x^2-1)}{2}+c$

15 Applications of integration

Chapter 15 Contents

15.1	Introduction	456
15.2	Average value of a function	456
15.3	Root mean square value of a function	459
	Review exercises	463

15.1 Introduction

Currents and voltages often vary with time. Engineers may wish to know the average value of such a current or voltage over some particular time interval. The average value of a time-varying function is defined in terms of an integral. An associated quantity is the root mean square (r.m.s.) value of a function. The r.m.s. value of a current is used in the calculation of the power dissipated by a resistor.

15.2 Average value of a function

Suppose $f(t)$ is a function defined on $a \leqslant t \leqslant b$. The area, A, under f is given by

$$A = \int_a^b f \, dt$$

A rectangle with base spanning the interval $[a, b]$ and height h has an area of $h(b - a)$. Suppose the height, h, is chosen so that the area under f and the area of the rectangle are equal. This means

$$h(b - a) = \int_a^b f \, dt$$

$$h = \frac{\int_a^b f \, dt}{b - a}$$

Then h is called the **average value** of the function across the interval $[a, b]$ and is illustrated in Figure 15.1.

$$\text{average value} = \frac{\int_a^b f \, dt}{b - a}$$

Figure 15.1
The area under the curve from $t = a$ to $t = b$ and the area of the rectangle are equal.

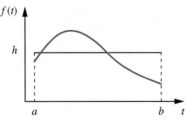

Example 15.1   Find the average value of $f(t) = t^2$ across

(a) $[1, 3]$

(b) $[2, 5]$

Solution (a) average value $= \dfrac{\int_1^3 t^2 \, dt}{3-1} = \dfrac{1}{2}\left[\dfrac{t^3}{3}\right]_1^3 = \dfrac{13}{3}$

(b) average value $= \dfrac{\int_2^5 t^2 \, dt}{5-2} = \dfrac{1}{3}\left[\dfrac{t^3}{3}\right]_2^5 = 13$

Example 15.1 shows that if the interval of integration changes then the average value of a function can change.

Example 15.2 **Sawtooth waveform**

Consider the sawtooth waveform shown in Figure 15.2.

Figure 15.2
A sawtooth waveform.

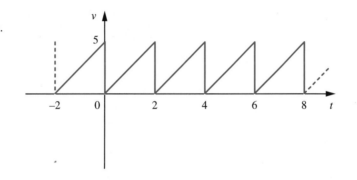

Calculate the average value of this waveform over a complete period.

Solution We first need to obtain an equation for the waveform. We choose the interval $0 \leqslant t < 2$. The general equation for a straight line is

$$v = mt + c$$

When $t = 0$ then $v = 0$. So

$$0 = 0 + c$$
$$c = 0$$

When $t = 2$ then $v = 5$. So

$$5 = m(2)$$
$$m = 2.5$$

Hence

$$v = 2.5t$$

The average value is given by

$$v_{av} = \frac{1}{2} \int_0^2 2.5t \, dt = \frac{1}{2} \left[\frac{2.5t^2}{2} \right]_0^2$$

$$v_{av} = \frac{1}{2} \left(\frac{2.5 \times 4}{2} - 0 \right) = \frac{10}{4} = 2.5 \text{ V}$$

Example 15.3   **A thyristor firing circuit**

Figure 15.3 shows a simple circuit to control the voltage across a load resistor, R_L. This circuit has many uses, one of which is to adjust the level of lighting in a room. The circuit has an a.c. power supply with peak voltage, V_S. The main control element is the thyristor. This device is similar in many ways to a diode. It has a very high resistance when it is reverse biased and a low resistance when it is forward biased. However, unlike a diode, this low resistance depends on the thyristor being 'switched on' by the application of a gate current. The point at which the thyristor is switched on can be varied by varying the resistor, R_G. Figure 15.4 shows a typical waveform of the voltage, v_L, across the load resistor.

The point at which the thyristor is turned on in each cycle is characterized by the quantity αT, where $0 \leqslant \alpha \leqslant 0.25$ and T is the period of the waveform. This restriction on α reflects the fact that if the thyristor has not turned on when the supply voltage has peaked in the forward direction then it will never turn on.

Calculate the average value of the waveform over a period and comment on the result.

Solution   The average value of load voltage is

$$\frac{1}{T} \int_0^T v_L \, dt = \frac{1}{T} \int_{\alpha T}^{T/2} V_S \sin\left(\frac{2\pi t}{T}\right) dt$$

$$= \frac{V_S}{T} \frac{T}{2\pi} \left[-\cos\left(\frac{2\pi t}{T}\right) \right]_{\alpha T}^{T/2} = \frac{V_S}{2\pi} (1 + \cos 2\pi\alpha)$$

If $\alpha = 0$, then the average value is V_S/π, the maximum value for this circuit. If $\alpha = 0.25$, then the average value is $V_S/2\pi$ which illustrates that delaying the turning on of the thyristor reduces the average value of the load voltage.

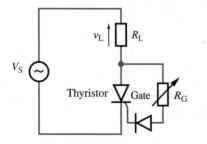

Figure 15.3   A thyristor firing circuit.

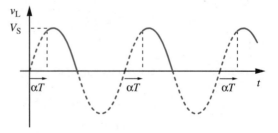

Figure 15.4   Load voltage waveform.

Exercises 15.2

1 Calculate the average value of the given functions across the specified interval.

(a) $f(t) = 1 + t$ across $[0, 2]$

(b) $f(x) = 2x - 1$ across $[-1, 1]$

(c) $f(t) = t^2$ across $[0, 1]$

(d) $f(t) = t^2$ across $[0, 2]$

(e) $f(z) = z^2 + z$ across $[1, 3]$

2 Calculate the average value of the given functions over the specified interval.

(a) $f(x) = x^3$ across $[1, 3]$

(b) $f(x) = \dfrac{1}{x}$ across $[1, 2]$

(c) $f(t) = \sqrt{t}$ across $[0, 2]$

(d) $f(z) = z^3 - 1$ across $[-1, 1]$

(e) $f(t) = \dfrac{1}{t^2}$ across $[-3, -2]$

3 Calculate the average value of the following:

(a) $f(t) = \sin t$ across $\left[0, \dfrac{\pi}{2}\right]$

(b) $f(t) = \sin t$ across $[0, \pi]$

(c) $f(t) = \sin \omega t$ across $[0, \pi]$

(d) $f(t) = \cos t$ across $\left[0, \dfrac{\pi}{2}\right]$

(e) $f(t) = \cos t$ across $[0, \pi]$

(f) $f(t) = \cos \omega t$ across $[0, \pi]$

(g) $f(t) = \sin \omega t + \cos \omega t$ across $[0, 1]$

4 Calculate the average value of the following functions.

(a) $f(t) = \sqrt{t + 1}$ across $[0, 3]$

(b) $f(t) = e^t$ across $[-1, 1]$

(c) $f(t) = 1 + e^t$ across $[-1, 1]$

Solutions

1 (a) 2   (b) −1   (c) $\frac{1}{3}$

    (d) $\frac{4}{3}$ (e) $\frac{19}{3}$

2 (a) 10   (b) 0.6931   (c) 0.9428

    (d) −1   (e) $\frac{1}{6}$

3 (a) $\dfrac{2}{\pi}$

    (b) $\dfrac{2}{\pi}$

    (c) $\dfrac{1}{\pi \omega}[1 - \cos(\pi \omega)]$

    (d) $\dfrac{2}{\pi}$

    (e) 0

    (f) $\dfrac{\sin(\pi \omega)}{\pi \omega}$

    (g) $\dfrac{1 + \sin \omega - \cos \omega}{\omega}$

4 (a) $\frac{14}{9}$ (b) 1.1752   (c) 2.1752

15.3 Root mean square value of a function

If $f(t)$ is defined on $[a, b]$, the **root mean square** (r.m.s.) value is

$$\text{r.m.s.} = \sqrt{\frac{\int_a^b (f(t))^2 \, dt}{b - a}}$$

Example 15.4   Find the r.m.s. value of $f(t) = t^2$ across $[1, 3]$.

Solution $\text{r.m.s.} = \sqrt{\dfrac{\int_1^3 (t^2)^2 \, dt}{3 - 1}} = \sqrt{\dfrac{\int_1^3 t^4 \, dt}{2}} = \sqrt{\dfrac{[t^5/5]_1^3}{2}} = \sqrt{\dfrac{242}{10}} = 4.92$

Example 15.5   Calculate the r.m.s. value of $f(t) = A \sin t$ across $[0, 2\pi]$.

Solution $\text{r.m.s.} = \sqrt{\dfrac{\int_0^{2\pi} A^2 \sin^2 t \, dt}{2\pi}}$

$= \sqrt{\dfrac{A^2 \int_0^{2\pi} (1 - \cos 2t)/2 \, dt}{2\pi}}$

$= \sqrt{\dfrac{A^2}{4\pi} \left[t - \dfrac{\sin 2t}{2} \right]_0^{2\pi}}$

$= \sqrt{\dfrac{A^2 2\pi}{4\pi}} = \dfrac{A}{\sqrt{2}} = 0.707 A$

Thus the r.m.s. value is $0.707 \times$ the amplitude.

Example 15.6   Calculate the r.m.s. value of $f(t) = A \sin(\omega t + \phi)$ across $[0, 2\pi/\omega]$.

Solution $\text{r.m.s.} = \sqrt{\dfrac{\int_0^{2\pi/\omega} A^2 \sin^2(\omega t + \phi) \, dt}{2\pi/\omega}}$

$= \sqrt{\dfrac{A^2 \omega}{4\pi} \int_0^{2\pi/\omega} 1 - \cos 2(\omega t + \phi) \, dt}$

$= \sqrt{\dfrac{A^2 \omega}{4\pi} \left[t - \dfrac{\sin 2(\omega t + \phi)}{2\omega} \right]_0^{2\pi/\omega}}$

$= \sqrt{\dfrac{A^2 \omega}{4\pi} \left(\dfrac{2\pi}{\omega} - \dfrac{\sin 2(2\pi + \phi)}{2\omega} + \dfrac{\sin 2\phi}{2\omega} \right)}$

Now $\sin 2(2\pi + \phi) = \sin(4\pi + 2\phi)$ and since $\sin(t + \phi)$ has period 2π we see that $\sin(4\pi + 2\phi) = \sin 2\phi$. Hence,

$\text{r.m.s.} = \sqrt{\dfrac{A^2 \omega}{4\pi} \dfrac{2\pi}{\omega}} = \sqrt{\dfrac{A^2}{2}} = \dfrac{A}{\sqrt{2}} = 0.707 A$

Note that $\sin(\omega t + \phi)$ has period $2\pi/\omega$. The result of Example 15.6 illustrates a general result:

> The r.m.s. value of any sinusoidal waveform taken across an interval of length one period is
>
> $0.707 \times$ amplitude of the waveform

Root mean square value is an effective measure of the energy transfer capability of a time-varying electrical current. To see why this is so, consider the following.

Consider a current $i(t)$ which develops a power $p(t)$ in a load resistor R. This current flows from time $t = t_1$ to time $t = t_2$. Let P_{av} be the average power developed across the resistor during the time interval $[t_1, t_2]$. We require that total energy transfer, E, be the same in both cases. So we have

$$E = P_{av}(t_2 - t_1) = \int_{t_1}^{t_2} p(t)\, dt$$

Now

$$p(t) = (i(t))^2 R$$

and so

$$P_{av}(t_2 - t_1) = \int_{t_1}^{t_2} i^2 R\, dt$$

If we now consider the average power across the resistor to be the result of an effective current I_{eff} then we have

$$I_{eff}^2 R(t_2 - t_1) = \int_{t_1}^{t_2} i^2 R\, dt$$

$$I_{eff}^2(t_2 - t_1) = \int_{t_1}^{t_2} i^2\, dt$$

$$I_{eff}^2 = \frac{\int_{t_1}^{t_2} i^2\, dt}{t_2 - t_1}$$

$$I_{eff} = \sqrt{\frac{\int_{t_1}^{t_2} i^2\, dt}{t_2 - t_1}}$$

We see that the equivalent d.c. current is the r.m.s. value of the time-varying current.

Example 15.7 Consider the periodic waveform shown in Figure 15.5.

The current $i(t)$ is

$$i(t) = 20\, e^{-t} \qquad 0 \leqslant t < 10, \qquad \text{period } T = 10$$

Figure 15.5
Waveform for
Example 15.7.

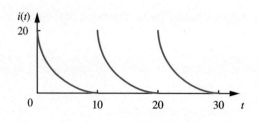

(a) Calculate the average value of the current over a complete period.

(b) Calculate the r.m.s. value of the current over a complete period.

Solution (a) As the waveform is periodic, we need only consider the interval $0 \leqslant t < 10$.

$$I_{av} = \frac{1}{T} \int_0^T i(t)\,dt = \frac{1}{10} \int_0^{10} 20\,e^{-t}\,dt$$

$$= \frac{1}{10}[-20\,e^{-t}]_0^{10}$$

$$= \frac{1}{10}(-20\,e^{-10} + 20\,e^0)$$

$$= \frac{20}{10}(1 - e^{-10}) = 2 \times 0.999\,95 = 2.000\,\text{A}$$

(b) $$I_{eff} = \sqrt{\frac{\int_{t_1}^{t_2} i^2\,dt}{t_2 - t_1}}$$

Here

$$t_1 = 0 \qquad t_2 = 10 \qquad i(t) = 20\,e^{-t}$$

First we evaluate

$$\int_{t_1}^{t_2} i^2\,dt = \int_0^{10} 400\,e^{-2t}\,dt$$

$$= 400\left[\frac{e^{-2t}}{-2}\right]_0^{10}$$

$$= \frac{400}{-2}(e^{-20} - e^0)$$

$$= 200(1 - e^{-20}) = 200.00$$

So

$$I_{eff} = \sqrt{\frac{200.00}{10 - 0}}$$

$$= 4.4721\,\text{A}$$

Exercises 15.3

1 Calculate the r.m.s. values of the functions in Question 1 in Exercises 15.2.

2 Calculate the r.m.s. values of the functions in Question 2 in Exercises 15.2.

3 Calculate the r.m.s. values of the functions in Question 3 in Exercises 15.2.

4 Calculate the r.m.s. values of the functions in Question 4 in Exercises 15.2.

Solutions

1 (a) 2.0817   (b) 1.5275   (c) 0.4472

   (d) 1.7889   (e) 6.9666

2 (a) 12.4957   (b) 0.7071   (c) 1

   (d) 1.0690   (e) 0.1712

3 (a) 0.7071

   (b) 0.7071

   (c) $\sqrt{\dfrac{1}{2} - \dfrac{\sin \pi \omega \cos \pi \omega}{2\pi \omega}}$

(d) 0.7071

(e) 0.7071

(f) $\sqrt{\dfrac{1}{2} + \dfrac{\sin \pi \omega \cos \pi \omega}{2\pi \omega}}$

(g) $\sqrt{1 + \dfrac{\sin^2 \omega}{\omega}}$

4 (a) 1.5811   (b) 1.3466   (c) 2.2724

Review exercises 15

1 Find the average value of the following functions across the specified interval.

(a) $f(t) = 3 - t$ across $[0, 4]$

(b) $f(t) = t^2 - 2$ across $[1, 3]$

(c) $f(t) = t + \dfrac{1}{t}$ across $[1, 4]$

(d) $f(t) = \sqrt{t} + 1$ across $[0, 4]$

(e) $f(t) = t^{2/3}$ across $[0, 1]$

2 Calculate the average value of the following:

(a) $f(t) = 2 \sin 2t$ across $\left[0, \dfrac{\pi}{2}\right]$

(b) $f(t) = A \sin 4t$ across $\left[0, \dfrac{\pi}{2}\right]$

(c) $f(t) = \sin t + \cos t$ across $[0, \pi]$

(d) $f(t) = \cos\left(\dfrac{t}{2}\right)$ across $\left[0, \dfrac{\pi}{2}\right]$

(e) $f(t) = \sin t \cos t$ across $[0, \pi]$

3 Calculate the average value of the following functions:

(a) $f(t) = A\,e^{kt}$ across $[0, 1]$

(b) $f(t) = \dfrac{1}{e^{3t}}$ across $[0, 2]$

(c) $f(t) = 3 - e^{-t}$ across $[1, 3]$

(d) $f(t) = e^t + e^{-t}$ across $[0, 2]$

(e) $f(t) = t + e^t$ across $[0, 2]$

4 Find the average and r.m.s. values of $A \cos t + B \sin t$ across

(a) $[0, 2\pi]$

(b) $[0, \pi]$

5 Find the r.m.s. values of the functions in Question 1.

6 Find the r.m.s. values of the functions in Question 2.

7 Find the r.m.s. values of the functions in Question 3.

Solutions

1 (a) 1

(b) $\frac{7}{3}$

(c) 2.9621

(d) $\frac{7}{3}$

(e) $\frac{3}{5}$

2 (a) $\dfrac{4}{\pi}$

(b) 0

(c) $\dfrac{2}{\pi}$

(d) 0.9003

(e) 0

3 (a) $A\left(\dfrac{e^k - 1}{k}\right)$

(b) 0.1663

(c) 2.8410

(d) 3.6269

(e) 4.1945

4 (a) average $= 0$, r.m.s. $= \sqrt{\dfrac{A^2 + B^2}{2}}$

(b) average $= \dfrac{2B}{\pi}$, r.m.s. $= \sqrt{\dfrac{A^2 + B^2}{2}}$

5 (a) 1.5275

(b) 3.2965

(c) 3.0414

(d) 2.3805

(e) 0.6547

6 (a) 1.4142

(b) $\dfrac{A}{\sqrt{2}}$

(c) 1

(d) 0.9046

(e) 0.3536

7 (a) $A\sqrt{\dfrac{e^{2k} - 1}{2k}}$

(b) 0.2887

(c) 2.8423

(d) 3.9554

(e) 4.8085

16 Further topics in integration

Chapter 16 Contents

16.1	Introduction	466
16.2	Orthogonal functions	466
16.3	Improper integrals	469
16.4	Integral properties of the delta function	474
16.5	Integration of piecewise continuous functions	477
16.6	Integration of vectors	478
	Review exercises	479

16.1 Introduction

This chapter examines some further topics in integration. Orthogonal functions are introduced in Section 16.2. These functions are used extensively in Fourier analysis (see Chapter 23). Some integrals have one or two infinite limits of integration, or have an integrand which becomes infinite at particular points in the interval of integration. Such integrals are termed 'improper' and require special treatment. They are used extensively in the theory of Laplace and Fourier transforms. The Dirac delta function, $\delta(t)$, has been introduced in Chapter 2. The integral properties are examined in Section 16.4. The chapter concludes with the integration of piecewise continuous functions and the integration of vectors.

16.2 Orthogonal functions

Two functions $f(x)$ and $g(x)$ are said to be orthogonal over the interval $[a, b]$ if

$$\int_a^b f(x)g(x)\,dx = 0$$

To show that two functions are orthogonal we must demonstrate that the integral of their product over the interval of interest is zero.

Example 16.1 Show that $f(x) = x$ and $g(x) = x - 1$ are orthogonal on $\left[0, \dfrac{3}{2}\right]$.

Solution

$$\int_0^{3/2} x(x-1)\,dx = \int_0^{3/2} x^2 - x\,dx = \left[\frac{x^3}{3} - \frac{x^2}{2}\right]_0^{3/2} = \frac{9}{8} - \frac{9}{8} = 0$$

Hence f and g are orthogonal over the interval $\left[0, \dfrac{3}{2}\right]$.

Clearly functions may be orthogonal over one interval but not orthogonal over others. For example,

$$\int_0^1 x(x-1)\,dx \neq 0$$

and so x and $x - 1$ are not orthogonal over $[0, 1]$.

Example 16.2 Show $f(t) = 1$, $g(t) = \sin t$ and $h(t) = \cos t$ are mutually orthogonal over $[-\pi, \pi]$.

Solution We are required to show that any pair of functions is orthogonal over $[-\pi, \pi]$.

$$\int_{-\pi}^{\pi} 1 \sin t \, dt = [-\cos t]_{-\pi}^{\pi} = -\cos \pi + \cos(-\pi)$$

$$= -(-1) + (-1) = 0$$

$$\int_{-\pi}^{\pi} 1 \cos t \, dt = [\sin t]_{-\pi}^{\pi} = \sin \pi - \sin(-\pi) = 0$$

Using the trigonometric identity $\sin 2A = 2 \sin A \cos A$, we can write

$$\int_{-\pi}^{\pi} \sin t \cos t \, dt = \int_{-\pi}^{\pi} \frac{1}{2} \sin(2t) \, dt = -\left[\frac{\cos(2t)}{4}\right]_{-\pi}^{\pi}$$

$$= -\frac{\cos(2\pi) - \cos(-2\pi)}{4} = 0$$

Hence the functions 1, $\sin t$, $\cos t$ form an orthogonal set over $[-\pi, \pi]$.

The set of Example 16.2 may be extended to

$$\{1, \sin t, \cos t, \sin(2t), \cos(2t), \sin(3t), \cos(3t), \ldots, \sin(nt), \cos(nt)\} \qquad n \in \mathbb{N}$$

Example 16.3 Verify that $\{1, \sin t, \cos t, \sin(2t), \cos(2t), \ldots\}$ forms an orthogonal set over $[-\pi, \pi]$.

Solution Suppose $n, m \in \mathbb{N}$. We must show that all combinations of 1, $\sin nt$, $\sin mt$, $\cos nt$ and $\cos mt$ are orthogonal.

$$\int_{-\pi}^{\pi} 1 \sin(nt) \, dt = \left[\frac{-\cos(nt)}{n}\right]_{-\pi}^{\pi} = \frac{-\cos(n\pi) + \cos(-n\pi)}{n} = 0$$

In a similar manner, it is easy to show

$$\int_{-\pi}^{\pi} 1 \cos(nt) \, dt = 0$$

Also, using the trigonometric identities in Section 3.5

$$\int_{-\pi}^{\pi} \cos(nt) \sin(mt) \, dt = \frac{1}{2} \int_{-\pi}^{\pi} \sin(n+m)t - \sin(n-m)t \, dt$$

We have seen that $\int_{-\pi}^{\pi} \sin nt \, dt = 0$ for any $n \in \mathbb{N}$. Noting that $(n+m) \in \mathbb{N}$ and $(n-m) \in \mathbb{N}$, we see that

$$\int_{-\pi}^{\pi} \sin(n+m)t - \sin(n-m)t \, dt = 0$$

It is left as an exercise for the reader to show that

$$\int_{-\pi}^{\pi} \sin nt \sin mt \, dt = 0 \qquad n \neq m$$

$$\int_{-\pi}^{\pi} \cos nt \cos mt \, dt = 0 \qquad n \neq m$$

The functions thus form an orthogonal set across $[-\pi, \pi]$.

The result of Example 16.3 can be extended:

{1, $\sin t$, $\cos t$, $\sin 2t$, $\cos 2t$, ...} is an orthogonal set over any interval of length 2π.

More generally:

$$\left\{ 1, \sin\left(\frac{2\pi t}{T}\right), \cos\left(\frac{2\pi t}{T}\right), \sin\left(\frac{4\pi t}{T}\right), \cos\left(\frac{4\pi t}{T}\right), \ldots \right\}$$

is an orthogonal set over any interval of length T. In particular, the set is orthogonal over $[0, T]$ and $\left[-\frac{T}{2}, \frac{T}{2} \right]$.

These results are used extensively in Fourier analysis.

Example 16.4   Find

(a) $\displaystyle\int_{-\pi}^{\pi} \sin^2(nt)\, dt$ $n \in \mathbb{Z}$ $n \neq 0$

(b) $\displaystyle\int_{-\pi}^{\pi} \cos^2(nt)\, dt$ $n \in \mathbb{Z}$ $n \neq 0$

Solution   (a) We use the trigonometric identity

$$\sin^2 nt = \frac{1 - \cos 2nt}{2}$$

to get

$$\int_{-\pi}^{\pi} \sin^2(nt)\, dt = \int_{-\pi}^{\pi} \frac{1 - \cos 2nt}{2}\, dt = \int_{-\pi}^{\pi} \frac{1}{2}\, dt = \pi$$

using the orthogonal properties of $\cos(nt)$.

(b) $\displaystyle\int_{-\pi}^{\pi} \cos^2(nt)\, dt = \int_{-\pi}^{\pi} 1 - \sin^2(nt)\, dt$

$$= 2\pi - \pi = \pi$$

It is a simple extension to show that integrating $\sin^2(nt)$ or $\cos^2(nt)$ over any interval of length 2π yields the same result, namely π. It is also possible to extend the result of Example 16.4 to show

$$\int_{-T/2}^{T/2} \sin^2\left(\frac{2n\pi t}{T}\right) dt = \int_{-T/2}^{T/2} \cos^2\left(\frac{2n\pi t}{T}\right) dt = \frac{T}{2} \qquad n \in \mathbb{Z} \qquad n \neq 0$$

Finally, integrating $\sin^2\left(\dfrac{2n\pi t}{T}\right)$ and $\cos^2\left(\dfrac{2n\pi t}{T}\right)$ over any interval of length T gives the same result, that is $\dfrac{T}{2}$.

Exercises 16.2

1 Show $f(x) = x^2$ and $g(x) = 1 - x$ are orthogonal across $\left[0, \dfrac{4}{3}\right]$.

2 Show $f(x) = \dfrac{1}{x}$ and $g(x) = x^2$ are orthogonal over $[-k, k]$.

3 (a) Show $f(t) = 1 - t$ and $g(t) = 1 + t$ are orthogonal over $[0, \sqrt{3}]$.

(b) Find another interval over which $f(t)$ and $g(t)$ are orthogonal.

4 Show $f(t) = e^t$ and $g(t) = 1 - e^{-2t}$ are orthogonal across $[-1, 1]$.

5 Show $f(x) = \sqrt{x}$ and $g(x) = 1 - \sqrt{x}$ are orthogonal on $\left[0, \dfrac{16}{9}\right]$.

Solutions

3 (b) $[-\sqrt{3}, 0]$

16.3 Improper integrals

There are two cases when evaluation of an integral needs special care:

(1) one, or both, of the limits of an integral are infinite;

(2) the integrand becomes infinite at one, or more, points of the interval of integration.

If either (1) or (2) is true the integral is called an **improper integral**. Evaluation of improper integrals involves the use of limits.

Example 16.5 Evaluate $\displaystyle\int_2^\infty \dfrac{1}{t^2}\, dt$.

Solution

$$\int_2^\infty \dfrac{1}{t^2}\, dt = \left[-\dfrac{1}{t}\right]_2^\infty$$

To evaluate $-\dfrac{1}{t}$ at the upper limit we consider $\displaystyle\lim_{t\to\infty} -\dfrac{1}{t}$. Clearly the limit is 0. Hence,

$$\int_2^\infty \dfrac{1}{t^2}\, dt = 0 - \left(-\dfrac{1}{2}\right) = \dfrac{1}{2}$$

Example 16.6   Evaluate $\displaystyle\int_{-\infty}^{1} e^{2x}\,dx$.

Solution
$$\int_{-\infty}^{1} e^{2x}\,dx = \left[\frac{e^{2x}}{2}\right]_{-\infty}^{1}$$

We need to evaluate $\displaystyle\lim_{x\to -\infty} \frac{e^{2x}}{2}$. This limit is 0. So,

$$\int_{-\infty}^{1} e^{2x}\,dx = \left[\frac{e^{2x}}{2}\right]_{-\infty}^{1} = \frac{e^2}{2} - 0 = 3.69$$

Example 16.7   **Capacitors in series**

Derive an expression for the equivalent capacitance of two capacitors connected together in series (see Figure 16.1).

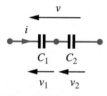

Figure 16.1   Two capacitors connected in series.

Solution
In Example 13.6 we obtained an expression for the voltage across a capacitor. This was

$$v = \frac{1}{C}\int i\,dt$$

This can be written as a definite integral to give the voltage expression across the capacitor at a general point in time, t. The expression is

$$v = \frac{1}{C}\int_{-\infty}^{t} i\,dt$$

Now consider the situation depicted in Figure 16.1. Writing an equation for each of the capacitors gives

$$v_1 = \frac{1}{C_1}\int_{-\infty}^{t} i\,dt \qquad v_2 = \frac{1}{C_2}\int_{-\infty}^{t} i\,dt$$

By Kirchhoff's voltage law, $v = v_1 + v_2$ and so

$$v = \frac{1}{C_1}\int_{-\infty}^{t} i\,dt + \frac{1}{C_2}\int_{-\infty}^{t} i\,dt = \left(\frac{1}{C_1} + \frac{1}{C_2}\right)\int_{-\infty}^{t} i\,dt$$

Therefore, the two capacitors can be replaced by an equivalent capacitance, C, given by

$$\frac{1}{C} = \frac{1}{C_1} + \frac{1}{C_2} = \frac{C_1 + C_2}{C_1 C_2}$$

so that

$$C = \frac{C_1 C_2}{C_1 + C_2}$$

Example 16.8   Evaluate $\displaystyle\int_3^\infty \frac{2}{2t+1} - \frac{1}{t}\,dt$.

Solution $\displaystyle\int_3^\infty \frac{2}{2t+1} - \frac{1}{t}\,dt = [\ln|2t+1| - \ln|t|]_3^\infty$

$$= \left[\ln\left|\frac{2t+1}{t}\right|\right]_3^\infty = \left[\ln\left|2 + \frac{1}{t}\right|\right]_3^\infty$$

$$= \lim_{t\to\infty}\left[\ln\left(2 + \frac{1}{t}\right)\right] - \ln\frac{7}{3}$$

$$= \ln 2 - \ln\frac{7}{3} = \ln\frac{6}{7} = -0.1542$$

Example 16.9   Evaluate $\displaystyle\int_1^\infty \sin t\,dt$.

Solution $\displaystyle\int_1^\infty \sin t\,dt = [-\cos t]_1^\infty$

Now $\lim_{t\to\infty}(-\cos t)$ does not exist, that is the function $\cos t$ does not approach a limit as $t \to \infty$, and so the integral cannot be evaluated. We say the integral **diverges**.

Example 16.10   Evaluate $\displaystyle\int_0^1 \frac{1}{\sqrt{x}}\,dx$.

Solution   The integrand, $\dfrac{1}{\sqrt{x}}$, becomes infinite when $x = 0$, which is in the interval of integration.

The point $x = 0$ is 'removed' from the interval. We consider $\displaystyle\int_b^1 \frac{1}{\sqrt{x}}\,dx$ where b is slightly greater than 0, and then let $b \to 0^+$. Now,

$$\int_b^1 \frac{1}{\sqrt{x}}\,dx = [2\sqrt{x}]_b^1 = 2 - 2\sqrt{b}$$

Then,

$$\int_0^1 \frac{1}{\sqrt{x}}\,dx = \lim_{b\to 0^+}\int_b^1 \frac{1}{\sqrt{x}}\,dx = \lim_{b\to 0^+}(2 - 2\sqrt{b}) = 2$$

The improper integral exists and has value 2.

Example 16.11   Determine whether the integral $\displaystyle\int_0^2 \frac{1}{x}\,dx$ exists or not.

Solution As in Example 16.10 the integrand is not defined at $x = 0$, so we consider $\int_b^2 \frac{1}{x} \, dx$ for $b > 0$ and then let $b \to 0^+$.

$$\int_b^2 \frac{1}{x} \, dx = [\ln |x|]_b^2 = \ln 2 - \ln b$$

So,

$$\lim_{b \to 0} \left(\int_b^2 \frac{1}{x} \, dx \right) = \lim_{b \to 0} (\ln 2 - \ln b)$$

Since $\lim_{b \to 0} \ln b$ does not exist the integral diverges.

Example 16.12 Evaluate $\int_{-1}^2 \frac{1}{x} \, dx$ if possible.

Solution We 'remove' the point $x = 0$ where the integrand becomes infinite and consider two integrals: $\int_{-1}^b \frac{1}{x} \, dx$ where b is slightly smaller than 0, and $\int_c^2 \frac{1}{x} \, dx$ where c is slightly larger than 0. If these integrals exist as $b \to 0^-$ and $c \to 0^+$ then $\int_{-1}^2 \frac{1}{x} \, dx$ converges. If either of the integrals fails to converge then $\int_{-1}^2 \frac{1}{x} \, dx$ diverges. Now,

$$\int_{-1}^b \frac{1}{x} \, dx = \ln |b| - \ln |-1| = \ln |b|$$

$$\lim_{b \to 0^-} \int_{-1}^b \frac{1}{x} \, dx = \lim_{b \to 0^-} (\ln |b|)$$

This limit fails to exist and so $\int_{-1}^2 \frac{1}{x} \, dx$ diverges.

Example 16.13 **Energy stored in a capacitor**

Consider the circuit in Figure 16.2.

A capacitor has a voltage, V, across it as a result of stored charge. We wish to calculate the amount of energy stored in the capacitor. The switch is closed at $t = 0$ and a current, i, flows in the circuit. We have already seen in Chapter 2 that for such a case the time-varying voltage across the capacitor decays exponentially and is given by

$$v = Ve^{-t/RC}$$

So, using Ohm's law

$$i = \frac{v}{R} = \frac{Ve^{-t/RC}}{R}$$

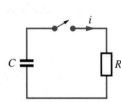

Figure 16.2 The capacitor is discharged by closing the switch.

Now the effect of closing the switch is to allow the energy stored in the capacitor to be dissipated in the resistor. Therefore, if the total energy dissipated in the resistor is calculated then this will allow the energy stored in the capacitor to be obtained. However, the energy dissipation rate, that is power dissipated, is not a constant for the resistor but depends on the current flowing through it. The total energy dissipated, E, is given by

$$E = \int_0^\infty P(t)\, dt$$

where $P(t)$ is the power dissipated in the resistor at time t. This equation has been discussed in Example 13.14. Now,

$$P = i^2 R = \frac{RV^2 e^{-2t/RC}}{R^2} = \frac{V^2 e^{-2t/RC}}{R}$$

$$E = \int_0^\infty \frac{V^2 e^{-2t/RC}}{R}\, dt = \frac{V^2}{R} \int_0^\infty e^{-2t/RC}\, dt$$

$$= \frac{V^2 RC}{-2R} \left[e^{-2t/RC} \right]_0^\infty$$

Now

$$\lim_{t \to \infty} e^{-2t/RC} = 0$$

and so the energy stored in the capacitor is given by

$$E = \frac{CV^2}{2}$$

Example 16.14 Find

$$\int_0^\infty e^{-st} \sin t\, dt \qquad s > 0$$

Solution Using integration by parts, with $u = e^{-st}$ and $\dfrac{dv}{dt} = \sin t$, we have

$$\int_0^\infty e^{-st} \sin t\, dt = \left[-e^{-st} \cos t \right]_0^\infty - s \int_0^\infty e^{-st} \cos t\, dt$$

Consider the first term on the r.h.s. We need to evaluate $\left[-e^{-st} \cos t \right]$ as $t \to \infty$ and when $t = 0$. Note that $-e^{-st} \cos t \to 0$ as $t \to \infty$ because we are given that s is positive. When $t = 0$, $-e^{-st} \cos t$ evaluates to -1, and so

$$\int_0^\infty e^{-st} \sin t\, dt = 1 - s \int_0^\infty e^{-st} \cos t\, dt$$

Integrating by parts for a second time yields

$$\int_0^\infty e^{-st} \sin t\, dt = 1 - s \left\{ \left[e^{-st} \sin t \right]_0^\infty + s \int_0^\infty e^{-st} \sin t\, dt \right\}$$

$$= 1 - s^2 \int_0^\infty e^{-st} \sin t\, dt$$

because $\left[e^{-st} \sin t\right]_0^\infty$ evaluates to zero at both limits. At this stage the reader might suspect that we have gone around in a circle and still need to evaluate the original integral. However, some algebraic manipulation yields the required result. We have

$$\int_0^\infty e^{-st} \sin t \, dt + s^2 \int_0^\infty e^{-st} \sin t \, dt = 1$$

$$(1 + s^2) \int_0^\infty e^{-st} \sin t \, dt = 1$$

$$\int_0^\infty e^{-st} \sin t \, dt = \frac{1}{1 + s^2}$$

Exercises 16.3

1   Evaluate, if possible,

(a) $\displaystyle\int_0^\infty e^{-t} \, dt$

(b) $\displaystyle\int_0^\infty e^{-kt} \, dt$ k is a constant, $k > 0$

(c) $\displaystyle\int_1^\infty \frac{1}{x} \, dx$

(d) $\displaystyle\int_1^\infty \frac{1}{x^2} \, dx$

(e) $\displaystyle\int_1^3 \frac{1}{x - 2} \, dx$

2   Evaluate the following integrals where possible:

(a) $\displaystyle\int_0^4 \frac{3}{x - 2} \, dx$

(b) $\displaystyle\int_0^3 \frac{1}{x - 1} + \frac{1}{x - 2} \, dx$

(c) $\displaystyle\int_0^2 \frac{1}{x^2 - 1} \, dx$

(d) $\displaystyle\int_0^\infty \sin 3t \, dt$

(e) $\displaystyle\int_{-\infty}^3 x e^x \, dx$

3   Find

$$\int_0^\infty e^{-st} \cos t \, dt \qquad s > 0$$

Solutions

1   (a) 1

(b) $\dfrac{1}{k}$

(c) does not exist

(d) 1

(e) does not exist

2   (a) does not exist

(b) does not exist

(c) does not exist

(d) does not exist

(e) $2e^3$

3   $\dfrac{s}{s^2 + 1}$

16.4   Integral properties of the delta function

The delta function, $\delta(t - d)$, was introduced in Chapter 2. The function is defined to be a rectangle whose area is 1 in the limit as the base length tends to 0 and as the height tends to infinity. Sometimes we need to integrate the delta function. In particular, we consider the improper integral

$$\int_{-\infty}^{\infty} \delta(t-d)\, dt$$

The integral gives the area under the function and this is defined to be 1. Hence,

$$\int_{-\infty}^{\infty} \delta(t-d)\, dt = 1$$

In Chapter 21 we need to consider the improper integral

$$\int_{-\infty}^{\infty} f(t)\delta(t-d)\, dt$$

where $f(t)$ is some known function of time. The delta function $\delta(t-d)$ is zero everywhere except at $t = d$. When $t = d$, then $f(t)$ has a value $f(d)$. Hence,

$$\int_{-\infty}^{\infty} f(t)\delta(t-d)\, dt = \int_{-\infty}^{\infty} f(d)\delta(t-d)\, dt = f(d)\int_{-\infty}^{\infty} \delta(t-d)\, dt$$

since $f(d)$ is a constant. But $\int_{-\infty}^{\infty} \delta(t-d)\, dt = 1$ and hence

$$\int_{-\infty}^{\infty} f(t)\delta(t-d)\, dt = f(d)$$

$$\int_{-\infty}^{\infty} \delta(t-d)\, dt = 1$$

$$\int_{-\infty}^{\infty} f(t)\delta(t-d)\, dt = f(d)$$

The result

$$\int_{-\infty}^{\infty} f(t)\delta(t-d)\, dt = f(d)$$

is known as the **sifting property** of the delta function. By multiplying a function, $f(t)$, by $\delta(t-d)$ and integrating from $-\infty$ to ∞ we sift from the function the value $f(d)$.

Example 16.15   Evaluate the following integrals.

(a) $\displaystyle\int_{-\infty}^{\infty} t^2 \delta(t-2)\, dt$ (b) $\displaystyle\int_{0}^{\infty} e^t \delta(t-1)\, dt$

Solution   (a)   We use

$$\int_{-\infty}^{\infty} f(t)\delta(t-d)\, dt = f(d)$$

with $f(t) = t^2$ and $d = 2$. Hence

$$\int_{-\infty}^{\infty} t^2 \delta(t - 2) \, dt = f(2) = 2^2 = 4$$

(b) We note that the expression $e^t \delta(t - 1)$ is 0 everywhere except at $t = 1$. Hence

$$\int_0^{\infty} e^t \delta(t - 1) \, dt = \int_{-\infty}^{\infty} e^t \delta(t - 1) \, dt$$

Using

$$\int_{-\infty}^{\infty} f(t) \delta(t - d) \, dt = f(d)$$

with $f(t) = e^t$ and $d = 1$ gives

$$\int_0^{\infty} e^t \delta(t - 1) \, dt = f(1) = e^1 = e$$

Exercises 16.4

1 Evaluate

(a) $\displaystyle\int_{-\infty}^{\infty} e^t \delta(t) \, dt$

(b) $\displaystyle\int_{-\infty}^{\infty} e^t \delta(t - 4) \, dt$

(c) $\displaystyle\int_{-\infty}^{\infty} e^t \delta(t + 3) \, dt$

(d) $\displaystyle 4 \int_{-\infty}^{\infty} t^2 \delta(t - 3) \, dt$

(e) $\displaystyle\int_{-\infty}^{\infty} \frac{(1 + t)\delta(t - 1)}{2} \, dt$

(f) $\displaystyle\int_{-\infty}^{\infty} e^{-kt} \delta(t) \, dt$

(g) $\displaystyle\int_{-\infty}^{\infty} e^{-kt} \delta(t - a) \, dt$

(h) $\displaystyle\int_{-\infty}^{\infty} e^{-k(t-a)} \delta(t - a) \, dt$

2 Evaluate the following integrals.

(a) $\displaystyle\int_{-\infty}^{\infty} (\sin t)\delta(t - 2) \, dt$

(b) $\displaystyle\int_{-\infty}^{\infty} e^{-t} \delta(t + 1) \, dt$

(c) $\displaystyle\int_{-\infty}^{0} e^{-t} \delta(t + 3) \, dt$

(d) $\displaystyle\int_0^{10} x^3 \delta(x - 2) \, dx$

(e) $\displaystyle\int_{-1}^{1} x^2 \delta(x + 2) \, dx$

3 Evaluate the following:

(a) $\displaystyle\int_{-\infty}^{\infty} t(\sin 2t)\delta(t - 3) \, dt$

(b) $\displaystyle\int_0^{\infty} \delta(t + 1) - \delta(t - 1) \, dt$

(c) $\displaystyle\int_0^{\infty} \delta(t - d) \, dt$

(d) $\displaystyle\int_{-a}^{a} \delta(t - d) \, dt$

Solutions

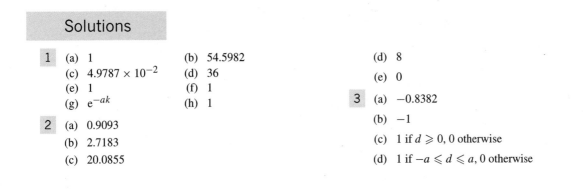

1 (a) 1
   (c) 4.9787×10^{-2}
   (e) 1
   (g) e^{-ak}

   (b) 54.5982
   (d) 36
   (f) 1
   (h) 1

   (d) 8
   (e) 0

2 (a) 0.9093
   (b) 2.7183
   (c) 20.0855

3 (a) -0.8382
   (b) -1
   (c) 1 if $d \geqslant 0$, 0 otherwise
   (d) 1 if $-a \leqslant d \leqslant a$, 0 otherwise

16.5 Integration of piecewise continuous functions

Integration of piecewise continuous functions is illustrated in Example 16.16. If a discontinuity occurs within the limits of integration then the interval is divided into sub-intervals so that the integrand is continuous on each sub-interval.

Example 16.16 Given

$$f(t) = \begin{cases} 2 & 0 \leqslant t < 1 \\ t^2 & 1 < t \leqslant 3 \end{cases}$$

evaluate $\int_0^3 f(t)\,dt$.

Solution The function, $f(t)$, is piecewise continuous with a discontinuity at $t = 1$. The function is illustrated in Figure 16.3. The discontinuity occurs within the limits of integration. We split the interval of integration at the discontinuity thus:

$$\int_0^3 f(t)\,dt = \int_0^1 f(t)\,dt + \int_1^3 f(t)\,dt$$

Figure 16.3
The function
$f(t) =$
$\begin{cases} 2 & 0 \leqslant t < 1 \\ t^2 & 1 < t \leqslant 3. \end{cases}$

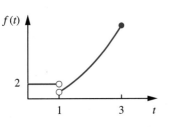

On the intervals $(0, 1)$ and $(1, 3)$, $f(t)$ is continuous, so

$$\int_0^3 f\,dt = \int_0^1 2\,dt + \int_1^3 t^2\,dt$$

$$= \left[2t\right]_0^1 + \left[\frac{t^3}{3}\right]_1^3 = 2 + \left[9 - \frac{1}{3}\right] = \frac{32}{3}$$

Exercises   16.5

1   Given

$$f(t) = \begin{cases} 3 & -1 \leqslant t < 1 \\ 2t & 1 \leqslant t \leqslant 2 \\ t^2 & 2 < t \leqslant 3 \end{cases}$$

evaluate

(a) $\int_{-1}^{1} f \, dt$

(b) $\int_{-0.5}^{1.5} f \, dt$

(c) $\int_{0}^{2.5} f \, dt$

(d) $\int_{-1}^{3} f \, dt$

2   Given

$$g(t) = \begin{cases} 3t & 0 \leqslant t < 3 \\ 15 - 2t & 3 \leqslant t < 4 \\ 6 & 4 \leqslant t \leqslant 6 \end{cases}$$

evaluate

(a) $\int_{0}^{2} g(t) \, dt$

(b) $\int_{2}^{4} g(t) \, dt$

(c) $\int_{3}^{5} g(t) \, dt$

(d) $\int_{0}^{6} g(t) \, dt$

(e) $\int_{3.5}^{4.5} g(t) \, dt$

3   Given $u(t)$ is the unit step function, evaluate

(a) $\int_{0}^{4} u(t) \, dt$

(b) $\int_{-3}^{2} u(t) \, dt$

(c) $\int_{-2}^{4} 2u(t + 1) \, dt$

(d) $\int_{-1}^{2} t \, u(t) \, dt$

(e) $\int_{0}^{4} e^{kt} u(t - 3) \, dt$ k constant

Solutions

1   (a) 6   (b) 5.75
    (c) 8.5417   (d) 15.3333

2   (a) 6   (b) 15.5
    (c) 14   (d) 33.5
    (e) 6.75

3   (a) 4   (b) 2
    (c) 10   (d) 2
    (e) $\dfrac{e^{4k} - e^{3k}}{k}$

16.6   Integration of vectors

If a vector depends upon time t, it is often necessary to integrate it with respect to time. Recall that $\mathbf{i}, \mathbf{j}$ and $\mathbf{k}$ are constant vectors and are treated thus in any integration. Hence the integral

$$\mathbf{I} = \int (f(t)\mathbf{i} + g(t)\mathbf{j} + h(t)\mathbf{k}) \, dt$$

is simply evaluated as three scalar integrals, and so

$$\mathbf{I} = \left(\int f(t) \, dt \right)\mathbf{i} + \left(\int g(t) \, dt \right)\mathbf{j} + \left(\int h(t) \, dt \right)\mathbf{k}$$

Example 16.17   If $\mathbf{r} = 3t\mathbf{i} + t^2\mathbf{j} + (1 + 2t)\mathbf{k}$, evaluate $\int_0^1 \mathbf{r} \, dt$.

Solution
$$\int_0^1 \mathbf{r} \, dt = \left(\int_0^1 3t \, dt \right) \mathbf{i} + \left(\int_0^1 t^2 \, dt \right) \mathbf{j} + \left(\int_0^1 1 + 2t \, dt \right) \mathbf{k}$$

$$= \left[\frac{3t^2}{2} \right]_0^1 \mathbf{i} + \left[\frac{t^3}{3} \right]_0^1 \mathbf{j} + \left[t + t^2 \right]_0^1 \mathbf{k} = \frac{3}{2}\mathbf{i} + \frac{1}{3}\mathbf{j} + 2\mathbf{k}$$

Exercises   16.6

1   Given $\mathbf{r} = 3 \sin t\mathbf{i} - \cos t\mathbf{j} + (2 - t)\mathbf{k}$, evaluate $\int_0^\pi \mathbf{r} \, dt$.

2   Given $\mathbf{v} = \mathbf{i} - 3\mathbf{j} + \mathbf{k}$, evaluate

(a) $\int_0^1 \mathbf{v} \, dt$

(b) $\int_0^2 \mathbf{v} \, dt$

3   The vector, $\mathbf{a}$, is defined by

$$\mathbf{a} = t^2\mathbf{i} + e^{-t}\mathbf{j} + t\mathbf{k}$$

Evaluate

(a) $\int_0^1 \mathbf{a} \, dt$

(b) $\int_2^3 \mathbf{a} \, dt$

(c) $\int_1^4 \mathbf{a} \, dt$

4   Let $\mathbf{a}$ and $\mathbf{b}$ be two three-dimensional vectors. Is the following true?

$$\int_{t_1}^{t_2} \mathbf{a} \, dt \times \int_{t_1}^{t_2} \mathbf{b} \, dt = \int_{t_1}^{t_2} \mathbf{a} \times \mathbf{b} \, dt$$

Recall that $\times$ denotes the vector product.

Solutions

1 $6\mathbf{i} + 1.348\mathbf{k}$

2   (a) $\mathbf{i} - 3\mathbf{j} + \mathbf{k}$ (b) $2\mathbf{i} - 6\mathbf{j} + 2\mathbf{k}$

3   (a) $0.333\mathbf{i} + 0.632\mathbf{j} + 0.5\mathbf{k}$

(b) $6.333\mathbf{i} + 0.0855\mathbf{j} + 2.5\mathbf{k}$

(c) $21\mathbf{i} + 0.3496\mathbf{j} + 7.5\mathbf{k}$

4   no

Review exercises 16

1   Show $f(x) = x^n$ and $g(x) = x^m$ are orthogonal on $[-k, k]$ if $n + m$ is an odd number.

2   Show $f(t) = \sin t$ and $g(t) = \cos t$ are orthogonal on $[a, a + n\pi]$.

3   Show $f(t) = \sinh t$ and $g(t) = \cosh t$ are orthogonal over $[-k, k]$.

4   Determine the values of k for which $\int_0^\infty t^k \, dt$ exists.

5   Evaluate if possible

(a) $\int_0^\infty u(t) \, dt$

(b) $\int_{-\infty}^\infty e^{-1000t} \, dt$

(c) $\int_{-2}^0 \frac{1}{x + 1} \, dx$

(d) $\displaystyle\int_{-\infty}^{\infty} u(t)e^{-t}\,dt$

(e) $\displaystyle\int_{-2}^{2} \frac{1}{x^2-1}\,dx$

(Note that $u(t)$ is the unit step function.)

6 Find the values of k for which $\int_0^{\infty} e^{kt}\,dt$ exists.

7 Evaluate

(a) $\displaystyle\int_{-\infty}^{\infty} (t^2+1)\delta(t-1)\,dt$

(b) $\displaystyle\int_{-\infty}^{\infty} te^t\delta(t-2)\,dt$

(c) $\displaystyle\int_{-\infty}^{\infty} (t^2+t+2)\delta(t-1)\,dt$

(d) $\displaystyle\int_{-\infty}^{\infty} \frac{\delta(t+2)}{t^2+1}\,dt$

(e) $\displaystyle\int_{-\infty}^{\infty} \delta(t+1)\delta(t+2)\,dt$

8 (a) Evaluate

$$\int_{-\infty}^{\infty} (t^2+1)\delta(2t)\,dt$$

[*Hint:* substitute $z=2t$.]

(b) Show

$$\int_{-\infty}^{\infty} f(t)\delta(nt)\,dt = \frac{1}{n}f(0), \qquad n>0$$

9 Evaluate

(a) $\displaystyle\int_0^{\infty} (1+t)\delta(t-2)\,dt$

(b) $\displaystyle\int_{-\infty}^{\infty} t\delta(1+t)\,dt$

(c) $\displaystyle\int_{-\infty}^{\infty} (1+t)\delta(-t)\,dt$

(d) $\displaystyle\int_{-\infty}^{0} \delta(t-6)+\delta(t+6)\,dt$

(e) $\displaystyle\int_{-2k}^{4k} \delta(t+k)+\delta(t+3k)+\delta(t+5k)\,dt$

$k>0$

10 The function $g(t)$ is piecewise continuous and defined by

$$g(t) = \begin{cases} 2t & 0 \leqslant t \leqslant 1 \\ 3 & 1 < t \leqslant 2 \end{cases}$$

Evaluate

(a) $\displaystyle\int_0^1 g(t)\,dt$

(b) $\displaystyle\int_0^{1.5} g(t)\,dt$

(c) $\displaystyle\int_{0.5}^{1.7} g(t)\,dt$

(d) $\displaystyle\int_1^2 g(t)\,dt$

(e) $\displaystyle\int_{1.3}^{1.5} g(t)\,dt$

11 Given

$$f(t) = \begin{cases} 1+t & -1 \leqslant t < 3 \\ t-1 & 3 \leqslant t \leqslant 4 \\ 0 & \text{otherwise} \end{cases}$$

evaluate

(a) $\displaystyle\int_{-1}^2 f(t)\,dt$

(b) $\displaystyle\int_{-1}^4 f(t)\,dt$

(c) $\displaystyle\int_0^5 f(t)\,dt$

(d) $\displaystyle\int_{-\infty}^{\infty} f(t)\delta(t-2)\,dt$

(e) $\displaystyle\int_{-\infty}^{\infty} f(t)u(t)\,dt$

12 Given

$$h(t) = \begin{cases} t^2 & -2 \leqslant t \leqslant 2 \\ t^3 & 2 < t \leqslant 3 \\ 4 & 3 < t \leqslant 5 \end{cases}$$

evaluate

(a) $\displaystyle\int_{-1}^2 h(t)\,dt$

(b) $\displaystyle\int_0^{2.5} h(t)\,dt$

(c) $\displaystyle\int_2^4 h(t)+1\,dt$

(d) $\int_0^4 h(t+1)\,dt$

(e) $\int_{-1}^2 h(2t)\,dt$

13 If $\mathbf{a} = t\mathbf{i} - 2t\mathbf{j} + 3t\mathbf{k}$, find $\int_0^1 \mathbf{a}\,dt$.

14 Given
$$\mathbf{v}(t) = 2t\mathbf{i} + (3 - t^2)\mathbf{j} + t^3\mathbf{k}$$
find

(a) $\int_0^1 \mathbf{v}\,dt$

(b) $\int_1^2 \mathbf{v}\,dt$

(c) $\int_0^2 \mathbf{v}\,dt$

15 Evaluate the following integrals:

(a) $\int_{-1}^3 |t|\,dt$

(b) $\int_{-3}^2 |t+2|\,dt$

(c) $\int_0^2 |3t-1|\,dt$

Solutions

4 $k < -1$

5 (a) does not exist
(b) does not exist
(c) does not exist
(d) 1
(e) does not exist

6 $k < 0$

7 (a) 2
(b) 14.7781
(c) 4
(d) 0.2
(e) 0

8 (a) $\frac{1}{2}$

9 (a) 3
(b) -1
(c) 1
(d) 1
(e) 1

10 (a) 1

(b) $\frac{5}{2}$
(c) 2.85
(d) 3
(e) 0.6

11 (a) 4.5
(b) 10.5
(c) 10
(d) 3
(e) 10

12 (a) 3
(b) 8.4323
(c) 22.25
(d) 26.5833
(e) 12.7917

13 $0.5\mathbf{i} - \mathbf{j} + 1.5\mathbf{k}$

14 (a) $\mathbf{i} + \frac{8}{3}\mathbf{j} + \frac{1}{4}\mathbf{k}$
(b) $3\mathbf{i} + \frac{2}{3}\mathbf{j} + \frac{15}{4}\mathbf{k}$
(c) $4\mathbf{i} + \frac{10}{3}\mathbf{j} + 4\mathbf{k}$

15 (a) 5 (b) 8.5 (c) $\frac{13}{3}$

17 Numerical integration

Chapter 17 Contents

17.1	Introduction	484
17.2	Trapezium rule	484
17.3	Simpson's rule	488
	Review exercises	493

17.1 Introduction

Many functions, for example $\sin x^2$ and $\dfrac{e^x}{x}$, cannot be integrated analytically. Integration of such functions must be performed numerically. This section outlines two simple numerical techniques – the trapezium rule and Simpson's rule. More sophisticated ones exist and there are many excellent software packages available which implement these methods.

17.2 Trapezium rule

We wish to find the area under $y(x)$, from $x = a$ to $x = b$, that is we wish to evaluate $\int_a^b y \, dx$. The required area is divided into n strips, each of width h. Note that the width, h, of each strip is given by $h = \dfrac{b - a}{n}$. Each strip is then approximated by a trapezium.

A typical trapezium is shown in Figure 17.1. The area of the trapezium is $\frac{1}{2}h[y_i + y_{i+1}]$. Summing the areas of all the trapezia will yield an approximation to the total area.

$$
\begin{aligned}
\text{area of trapezia} &= \frac{h}{2}(y_0 + y_1) + \frac{h}{2}(y_1 + y_2) + \cdots + \frac{h}{2}(y_{n-1} + y_n) \\
&= \frac{h}{2}(y_0 + 2y_1 + 2y_2 + 2y_3 + \cdots + 2y_{n-1} + y_n)
\end{aligned}
$$

If the number of strips is increased, that is h is decreased, then the accuracy of the approximation is increased.

Figure 17.1
Each strip is
approximated by a
trapezium.

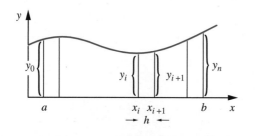

Example 17.1 Use the trapezium rule to estimate $\displaystyle\int_{0.5}^{1.3} e^{(x^2)} \, dx$ using

(a) a strip width of 0.2   (b) a strip width of 0.1.

Solution (a) Table 17.1 lists values of x and corresponding values of $e^{(x^2)}$.
We note that $h = 0.2$. Using the trapezium rule we find

$$
\begin{aligned}
\text{sum of areas of trapezia} &= \frac{0.2}{2}\{1.2840 + 2(1.6323) + 2(2.2479) \\
&\quad + 2(3.3535) + 5.4195\} \\
&= 2.117
\end{aligned}
$$

Table 17.1

x	$y = e^{(x^2)}$
0.5	$1.2840 = y_0$
0.7	$1.6323 = y_1$
0.9	$2.2479 = y_2$
1.1	$3.3535 = y_3$
1.3	$5.4195 = y_4$

Table 17.2

x	$y = e^{(x^2)}$
$x_0 = 0.5$	$1.2840 = y_0$
$x_1 = 0.6$	$1.4333 = y_1$
$x_2 = 0.7$	$1.6323 = y_2$
$x_3 = 0.8$	$1.8965 = y_3$
$x_4 = 0.9$	$2.2479 = y_4$
$x_5 = 1.0$	$2.7183 = y_5$
$x_6 = 1.1$	$3.3535 = y_6$
$x_7 = 1.2$	$4.2207 = y_7$
$x_8 = 1.3$	$5.4195 = y_8$

Table 17.3

Time (s)	Speed (m s^{-1})
0	10.1
1	17.2
2	24.4
3	29.2
4	34.6
5	41.2
6	50.9
7	57.8
8	60.3
9	61.2
10	62.1

Hence

$$\int_{0.5}^{1.3} e^{(x^2)} \, dx \approx 2.117$$

(b) Table 17.2 lists x values and corresponding values of $e^{(x^2)}$.
Using Table 17.2, we find

$$\text{sum of areas of trapezia} = \frac{0.1}{2}\{1.2840 + 2(1.4333) + 2(1.6323) + \cdots$$

$$+ 2(4.2207) + 5.4195\}$$

$$= 2.085$$

Hence $\int_{0.5}^{1.3} e^{(x^2)} \, dx \approx 2.085$.

Dividing the interval [0.5, 1.3] into strips of width 0.1 results in a more accurate estimate than using strips of width 0.2.

Example 17.2 **Distance travelled by a rocket**

A rocket is released and travels at a variable speed v. A motion sensor on the rocket measures this speed and the value is sampled by an onboard computer at 1 second intervals. The computer is required to calculate the distance travelled by the rocket and relay the value to a ground station at regular intervals. Table 17.3 records values of the measurements taken by the computer during the first 10 seconds of flight. Assuming that the computer uses the trapezium rule to estimate the distance travelled by the rocket, calculate the value that the computer will relay to the ground station after 10 seconds.

Solution We know that $v = \dfrac{ds}{dt}$ where $v = $ speed and $s = $ distance travelled in time t. So

$$s = \int_0^t v \, dt$$

We estimate the value of this integral using the trapezium rule. We choose a strip of width $h = 1$ as this is the time interval at which data is collected by the computer. Therefore

$$s = \int_0^{10} v \, dt \approx \tfrac{1}{2}\{10.1 + 2(17.2 + 24.4 + 29.2 + 34.6$$

$$+ \; 41.2 + 50.9 + 57.8 + 60.3 + 61.2) + 62.1\}$$

$$= \tfrac{1}{2}(825.8)$$

$$= 412.9$$

The distance travelled after 10 seconds is approximately 412.9 m.

17.2.1 Error due to the trapezium rule

Suppose we wish to estimate $\int_a^b f \, dx$ using the trapezium rule. The interval $[a, b]$ is divided into n equal strips, each of width $h = \dfrac{b - a}{n}$.

The difference between the estimated value of the integral and the true value of the integral is the **error**. So

$$\text{error} = \text{estimated value} - \text{true value}$$

We are able to find the maximum value of $|\text{error}|$. Firstly we calculate the second derivative of f, that is f''. Suppose that $|f''|$ is never greater than some value, M, throughout the interval $[a, b]$, that is

$$|f''| \leqslant M \qquad \text{for all } x \text{ values on } [a, b]$$

We say that M is an **upper bound** for $|f''|$ on $[a, b]$. Then the error due to the trapezium rule is such that

$$| \text{ error } | \leqslant \frac{(b - a)}{12} h^2 M$$

The expression $\dfrac{(b - a)}{12} h^2 M$ is an upper bound for the error. Note that the error depends upon h^2: if the strip width, h, is halved the error reduces by a factor of 4; if h is divided by 10 the error is divided by 100.

Example 17.3 Find an upper bound for the error in the estimates calculated in Example 17.1. Hence find upper and lower bounds for the true value of $\int_{0.5}^{1.3} e^{(x^2)} \, dx$.

Solution   We have $f = e^{(x^2)}$. Then

$$f' = 2xe^{(x^2)} \qquad \text{and} \qquad f'' = 2e^{(x^2)}(1 + 2x^2)$$

We note that f'' is increasing on $[0.5, 1.3]$ and so its maximum value is obtained at $x = 1.3$. Thus the maximum value of f'' on $[0.5, 1.3]$ is $2e^{(1.3)^2}[1 + 2(1.3)^2]$. Noting that $2e^{(1.3)^2}[1 + 2(1.3)^2] = 47.47$ we see that 48 is an upper bound for f'' on $[0.5, 1.3]$, that is $M = 48$.

We note that $a = 0.5$, $b = 1.3$. Thus

$$| \text{ error } | \leqslant \frac{(0.8)h^2(48)}{12} = 3.2h^2$$

(a) In Example 17.1(a), $h = 0.2$ and so

$$| \text{ error } | \leqslant 3.2(0.2)^2 = 0.128$$

Thus an upper bound for the error is 0.128. We have

$$-0.128 \leqslant \text{ error } \leqslant 0.128$$

The estimated value of the integral is 2.117 and so

$$2.117 - 0.128 \leqslant \text{ true value of integral } \leqslant 2.117 + 0.128$$

that is

$$1.989 \leqslant \int_{0.5}^{1.3} e^{(x^2)} \, dx \leqslant 2.245$$

An upper bound for $\int_{0.5}^{1.3} e^{(x^2)} \, dx$ is 2.245 and a lower bound is 1.989.

(b) In Example 17.1(b), $h = 0.1$ and so

$$| \text{ error } | \leqslant 3.2(0.1)^2 = 0.032$$

Hence an upper bound for the error is 0.032. Now

$$-0.032 \leqslant \text{ error } \leqslant 0.032$$

The estimated value of the integral is 2.085 and so

$$2.085 - 0.032 \leqslant \int_{0.5}^{1.3} e^{(x^2)} \, dx \leqslant 2.085 + 0.032$$

that is

$$2.053 \leqslant \int_{0.5}^{1.3} e^{(x^2)} \, dx \leqslant 2.117$$

Exercises 17.2

1 Estimate the following definite integrals using the trapezium rule.

(a) $\displaystyle\int_0^1 \sin(t^2)\, dt$ use $h = 0.2$

(b) $\displaystyle\int_1^{1.2} \frac{e^x}{x}\, dx$ use five strips

Solutions

1 (a) 0.3139   (b) 0.5467

🖥 Computer and calculator exercises 17.2

1 (a) Plot the second derivative of $f(t) = \sin(t^2)$ for $0 \leqslant t \leqslant 1$. Use your graph to find an upper bound for $f''(t)$ for $0 \leqslant t \leqslant 1$. Hence find an upper bound for the error in Question 1(a) in Exercises 17.2. State upper and lower bounds for the integral given in the question.

(b) Repeat (a) with $f(x) = \dfrac{e^x}{x}$ for $1 \leqslant x \leqslant 1.2$. Hence find an upper bound for the error in Question 1(b) in Exercises 17.2. State upper and lower bounds for the integral given in the question.

17.3 Simpson's rule

In the trapezium rule the curve $y(x)$ is approximated by a series of straight line segments. In Simpson's rule the curve is approximated by a series of quadratic curves as shown in Figure 17.2. The area is divided into an even number of strips of equal width. Consider the first pair of strips. A quadratic curve is fitted through the points A, B and C. Another quadratic curve is fitted through the points C, D and E. After some analysis an expression for approximating the area is found.

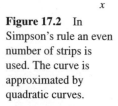

Figure 17.2 In Simpson's rule an even number of strips is used. The curve is approximated by quadratic curves.

Simpson's rule states:

$$\text{area} \approx \frac{h}{3}(y_0 + 4y_1 + 2y_2 + 4y_3 + 2y_4 + \cdots + 2y_{n-2} + 4y_{n-1} + y_n)$$

$$= \frac{h}{3}\{y_0 + 4(y_1 + y_3 + \cdots) + 2(y_2 + y_4 + \cdots) + y_n\}$$

where n is an even number.

Example 17.4 Estimate $\displaystyle\int_{0.5}^{1.3} e^{(x^2)}\, dx$ using Simpson's rule with (a) four strips, (b) eight strips.

Solution (a) We use Table 17.1 and note that $h = 0.2$. Using Simpson's rule we have

$$\text{estimated value} = \frac{0.2}{3}\{1.2840 + 4(1.6323 + 3.3535) + 2(2.2479) + 5.4195\}$$

$$= 2.0762$$

Using Simpson's rule we have found $\int_{0.5}^{1.3} e^{(x^2)} \, dx \approx 2.0762$.

(b) We use Table 17.2 and note that $h = 0.1$:

$$\text{estimated value} = \frac{0.1}{3}\{1.2840 + 4(1.4333 + 1.8965 + 2.7183 + 4.2207)$$

$$+ 2(1.6323 + 2.2479 + 3.3535) + 5.4195\}$$

$$= 2.0749$$

Using Simpson's rule we have found $\int_{0.5}^{1.3} e^{(x^2)} \, dx \approx 2.0749$.

Example 17.5 Estimate $\int_1^2 \sqrt{1 + x^3} \, dx$ using Simpson's rule with 10 strips.

Solution With 10 strips $h = 0.1$. Using Table 17.4, we find

$$\text{estimated value} \approx \frac{0.1}{3}\{1.4142 + 4(1.5268 + 1.7880 + 2.0917 + 2.4317 + 2.8034)$$

$$+ 2(1.6517 + 1.9349 + 2.2574 + 2.6138) + 3.000\}$$

$$= 2.130$$

In some cases the numerical values are not derived from a function but from actual measurements. Numerical methods can still be applied in an identical manner.

Example 17.6 Measurements of a variable, f, were made at 1 second intervals and are given in Table 17.5. Estimate $\int_0^6 f \, dt$ using

(a) the trapezium rule

(b) Simpson's rule.

Solution (a) The sum of the areas of the trapezia is

$$\tfrac{1}{2}[4 + 2(4.7 + 4.9 + 5.3 + 6.0 + 5.3) + 5.9] = 31.2$$

(b) The area has been divided into six strips and so Simpson's rule can be applied:

$$\text{approximate value of integral} = \tfrac{1}{3}[4 + 4(4.7 + 5.3 + 5.3)$$

$$+ 2(4.9 + 6.0) + 5.9] = 31.0.$$

Table 17.4 Using Simpson's rule to estimate $\int_1^2 \sqrt{1+x^3}\, dx$.	
x	$y = \sqrt{1+x^3}$
$x_0 = 1.0$	$1.4142 = y_0$
$x_1 = 1.1$	$1.5268 = y_1$
$x_2 = 1.2$	$1.6517 = y_2$
$x_3 = 1.3$	$1.7880 = y_3$
$x_4 = 1.4$	$1.9349 = y_4$
$x_5 = 1.5$	$2.0917 = y_5$
$x_6 = 1.6$	$2.2574 = y_6$
$x_7 = 1.7$	$2.4317 = y_7$
$x_8 = 1.8$	$2.6138 = y_8$
$x_9 = 1.9$	$2.8034 = y_9$
$x_{10} = 2.0$	$3.0000 = y_{10}$

Table 17.5 Measurements used to estimate the integral.

t	**Measurement (f)**
0	4
1	4.7
2	4.9
3	5.3
4	6.0
5	5.3
6	5.9

Example 17.7 Energy dissipation in a resistor

A resistor is being used to dissipate energy from a variable d.c. supply. A calculation is needed of how much energy has been dissipated over a period of time. Table 17.6 contains values of current, I, through the resistor, and voltage, V, across the resistor for the first 100 seconds since electrical power was first applied. Calculate the energy dissipation during this time period using Simpson's rule with a step interval of 10 seconds.

Solution The energy dissipated, E, is given by

$$E = \int_0^t P\, dt$$

where P is the power. Also $P = IV$, and so

$$E = \int_0^t IV\, dt$$

We first need to evaluate P as shown in Table 17.7.
Then using Simpson's rule with $h = 10$ we have

$$E = \int_0^{100} IV\, dt \approx \tfrac{10}{3}\{510.05 + 4(2040.20 + 1296.05 + 1843.20 + 1344.80$$

$$+ 2289.80) + 2(911.25 + 1692.80 + 1232.45 + 1638.05)$$

$$+ 1479.20\}$$

$$= 160\,648.5 \text{ J}$$

$$= 160.649 \text{ kJ}$$

The energy dissipated is therefore approximately 160.6 kJ.

Table 17.6

Time (s)	Voltage (V)	Current (A)
0	50.5	10.1
10	101.0	20.2
20	67.5	13.5
30	80.5	16.1
40	92.0	18.4
50	96.0	19.2
60	78.5	15.7
70	82.0	16.4
80	90.5	18.1
90	107.0	21.4
100	86.0	17.2

Table 17.7

Time (s)	Voltage (V)	Current (A)	Power (W)
0	50.5	10.1	510.05
10	101.0	20.2	2040.20
20	67.5	13.5	911.25
30	80.5	16.1	1296.05
40	92.0	18.4	1692.80
50	96.0	19.2	1843.20
60	78.5	15.7	1232.45
70	82.0	16.4	1344.80
80	90.5	18.1	1638.05
90	107.0	21.4	2289.80
100	86.0	17.2	1479.20

17.3.1 Error due to Simpson's rule

Simpson's rule provides an estimated value of a definite integral. The difference between the estimated value and the true (exact) value is the error. Just as with the trapezium rule, we can calculate an upper bound for this error.

We need to calculate the fourth derivative of f, that is $f^{(4)}$. Suppose $|f^{(4)}|$ is never greater than some value, M, throughout the interval $[a, b]$, that is

$$|f^{(4)}| \leqslant M \qquad \text{for all } x \text{ values on } [a, b]$$

Clearly M is an upper bound for $|f^{(4)}|$ on $[a, b]$. The error due to Simpson's rule is such that

$$|\text{error}| \leqslant \frac{(b-a)h^4 M}{180}$$

Note that the error is proportional to h^4.

Example 17.8 Find an upper bound for the error in the estimates calculated in Example 17.4. Hence find upper and lower bounds for $\int_{0.5}^{1.3} e^{(x^2)} \, dx$.

Solution Here we have $f = e^{(x^2)}$. Calculating the fourth derivative gives

$$f^{(4)} = 4e^{(x^2)}(4x^4 + 12x^2 + 3)$$

We seek an upper bound for $|f^{(4)}|$ on $[0.5, 1.3]$. We note that $f^{(4)}$ increases as x increases and so its maximum value in the interval occurs when $x = 1.3$.

$$f^{(4)}(1.3) = 752.319 < 753$$

Hence 753 is an upper bound for $|f^{(4)}|$.

In this example $a = 0.5$ and $b = 1.3$ and so

$$| \text{error} | \leqslant \frac{(0.8)h^4(753)}{180} = 3.347h^4$$

(a) Here $h = 0.2$ and so

$$| \text{error} | \leqslant 3.347(0.2)^4 = 0.0054$$

An upper bound for the error is 0.0054. Now

$$-0.0054 \leqslant \text{error} \leqslant 0.0054$$

The estimated value of the integral is 2.0762 and so

$$2.0762 - 0.0054 \leqslant \int_{0.5}^{1.3} e^{(x^2)} \, dx \leqslant 2.0762 + 0.0054$$

that is

$$2.0708 \leqslant \int_{0.5}^{1.3} e^{(x^2)} \, dx \leqslant 2.0816$$

(b) Here $h = 0.1$ and so

$$| \text{error} | \leqslant 3.347(0.1)^4 = 3.347 \times 10^{-4}$$

An upper bound for the error is 3.347×10^{-4}. Now

$$-3.347 \times 10^{-4} \leqslant \text{error} \leqslant 3.347 \times 10^{-4}$$

Noting that the estimated value of the integral is 2.0749 we have

$$2.0749 - 3.347 \times 10^{-4} \leqslant \int_{0.5}^{1.3} e^{(x^2)} \, dx \leqslant 2.0749 + 3.347 \times 10^{-4}$$

that is

$$2.0746 \leqslant \int_{0.5}^{1.3} e^{(x^2)} \, dx \leqslant 2.0752$$

Exercises 17.3

1 Estimate the values of the following integrals using Simpson's rule.

(a) $\int_{2}^{3} \ln(x^3 + 1) \, dx$ use 10 strips

(b) $\int_{1}^{2.6} \sqrt{t} e^t \, dt$ use eight strips

2 Evaluate, using the trapezium rule and
Simpson's rule,

(a) $\int_0^1 (x^2 + 1)^{3/2}\, dx$ use four strips

(b) $\int_1^{1.6} \frac{\sin 2t}{t}\, dt$ use six strips

Solutions

1 (a) 2.7955   (b) 15.1164

2 (a) trapezium rule: 1.5900, Simpson's rule:
1.5681

(b) trapezium rule: 0.2464, Simpson's rule:
0.2460

Computer and calculator exercises 17.3

1 (a) Plot the fourth derivative of
$f(x) = \ln(x^3 + 1)$ for $2 \leqslant x \leqslant 3$. Use
your graph to find an upper bound for
$f^{(4)}(x)$ for $2 \leqslant x \leqslant 3$. Hence find an
upper bound for the error in Question 1(a)
in Exercises 17.3. State upper and lower
bounds for the integral given in the
question.

(b) Repeat (a) with $f(t) = \sqrt{t}e^t$ for
$1 \leqslant t \leqslant 2.6$. Hence find an upper bound for
the error in Question 1(b) in Exercises 17.3.
State lower and upper bounds for the
integral given in the question.

2 Use a computer algebra package and graph
plotting package to find upper and lower bounds
for the integrals in Question 2 in Exercises 17.3.

Review exercises 17

1 If $f(t) = \sqrt{t^2 + 1}$ find $\int_1^2 f(t)\, dt$ using

(a) the trapezium rule with $h = 0.25$
(b) Simpson's rule using eight strips.

2 Estimate the following definite integrals using
the trapezium rule with six strips:

(a) $\int_1^4 \sqrt{x^3 + 1}\, dx$

(b) $\int_0^{0.6} \sin(t^2)\, dt$

(c) $\int_{0.2}^{0.8} e^{(t^2)}\, dt$

(d) $\int_0^{0.3} \frac{3}{x^3 + 2}\, dx$

(e) $\int_1^{2.5} \frac{e^t}{t}\, dt$

3 Estimate the definite integrals in Question 2
using Simpson's rule with six strips.

4 Estimate the following definite integrals using
the trapezium rule with eight strips:

(a) $\int_0^4 \cos(\sqrt{t})\, dt$

(b) $\int_{-2}^6 (t^2 + 1)^{3/2}\, dt$

(c) $\int_1^3 e^{\sqrt{x}}\, dx$

(d) $\int_0^{0.8} \tan(t^2)\, dt$

(e) $\int_3^5 \ln(x^2 + 1)\, dx$

Solutions

1 (a) 1.8111
   (b) 1.8101
2 (a) 12.9113
   (b) 0.072 27
   (c) 0.808 60
   (d) 0.448 45
   (e) 5.193 84
3 (a) 12.871 81
   (b) 0.071 334

(c) 0.806 43
(d) 0.448 49
(e) 5.178 79

4 (a) 0.810 58
   (b) 370.25
   (c) 8.276 86
   (d) 0.183 90
   (e) 5.630 32

Review computer exercise 17

1 Use a suitable computer algebra and graph plotting package to find upper bounds for the errors in Questions 1 to 4 in Review exercises 17. Hence find upper and lower bounds for the integrals given in these questions.

18 Taylor polynomials, Taylor series and Maclaurin series

Chapter 18	Contents	

18.1	Introduction	496
18.2	Linearization using first order Taylor polynomials	496
18.3	Second order Taylor polynomials	501
18.4	Taylor polynomials of the nth order	506
18.5	Taylor's formula and the remainder term	510
18.6	Taylor and Maclaurin series	513
	Review exercises	519

18.1 Introduction

Often the value of a function and the values of its derivatives are known at a particular point and from this information it is desired to obtain values of the function around that point. The Taylor polynomials and Taylor series allow engineers to make such estimates. One application of this is in obtaining linearized models of non-linear systems. The great advantage of a linear model is that it is much easier to analyse than a non-linear one. It is possible to make use of the principle of superposition: this allows the effects of multiple inputs to a system to be considered separately, and the resultant output to be obtained by summing the individual outputs.

Often a system may contain only a few components that are non-linear. By linearizing these it is then possible to produce a linear model for the system. We saw an example of this when we analysed a fluid system in Example 10.20. Although electrical systems are often linear, mechanical, thermal and fluid systems, or systems containing a mixture of these, are likely to contain some non-linear components. Unfortunately it may not be possible to obtain a sufficiently accurate linear model for every non-linear system as we shall see in this chapter.

Taylor polynomials of higher degree can be found which approximate to a given function. This is dealt with in Sections 18.3 and 18.4. The difference between a given function and the corresponding Taylor polynomial is covered in Section 18.5. The chapter closes with a treatment of Taylor and Maclaurin series.

18.2 Linearization using first order Taylor polynomials

Suppose we know that y is a function of x and we know the values of y and y' when $x = a$, that is $y(a)$ and $y'(a)$ are known. We can use $y(a)$ and $y'(a)$ to determine a linear polynomial which approximates to $y(x)$. Let this polynomial be

$$p_1(x) = c_0 + c_1 x$$

We choose the constants c_0 and c_1 so that

$$p_1(a) = y(a)$$
$$p_1'(a) = y'(a)$$

that is, the values of p_1 and its first derivative evaluated at $x = a$ match the values of y and its first derivative evaluated at $x = a$. Then,

$$p_1(a) = y(a) = c_0 + c_1 a$$
$$p_1'(a) = y'(a) = c_1$$

Solving for c_0 and c_1 yields

$$c_0 = y(a) - ay'(a) \qquad c_1 = y'(a)$$

Thus,

$$p_1(x) = y(a) - ay'(a) + y'(a)x$$

$$p_1(x) = y(a) + y'(a)(x - a)$$

$p_1(x)$ is the **first-order Taylor polynomial** generated by y at $x = a$.

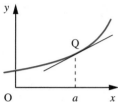

Figure 18.1
Graphical
representation of a
first-order Taylor
polynomial.

The function, $y(x)$, is often referred to as the **generating function**. Note that $p_1(x)$ and its first derivative evaluated at $x = a$ agree with $y(x)$ and its first derivative evaluated at $x = a$.

First-order Taylor polynomials can also be viewed from a graphical perspective. Figure 18.1 shows the function, $y(x)$, and a tangent at Q where $x = a$. Let the equation of the tangent at $x = a$ be

$$p(x) = mx + c$$

The gradient of the tangent is, by definition, the derivative of y at $x = a$, that is $y'(a)$. So,

$$p(x) = y'(a)x + c$$

The tangent passes through the point $(a, y(a))$, and so

$$y(a) = y'(a)a + c$$

that is $c = y(a) - y'(a)a$. The equation of the tangent is thus

$$p(x) = y'(a)x + y(a) - y'(a)a$$
$$p(x) = y(a) + y'(a)(x - a)$$

This is the first-order Taylor polynomial. We see that the first-order Taylor polynomial is simply the equation of the tangent to $y(x)$ where $x = a$.

Clearly, for values of x near to $x = a$ the value of $p_1(x)$ will be near to $y(x)$; $p_1(x)$ is a linear approximation to $y(x)$. In the neighbourhood of $x = a$, $p_1(x)$ closely approximates $y(x)$, but being linear is a much easier function to deal with.

Example 18.1

A function, y, and its first derivative are evaluated at $x = 2$.

$$y(2) = 1 \qquad y'(2) = 3$$

(a) State the first-order Taylor polynomial generated by y at $x = 2$.

(b) Estimate $y(2.5)$.

Solution

(a) $p_1(x) = y(2) + y'(2)(x - 2) = 1 + 3(x - 2) = -5 + 3x$

(b) We use the first-order Taylor polynomial to estimate $y(2.5)$:

$$p_1(2.5) = -5 + 3(2.5) = 2.5$$

Hence, $y(2.5) \approx 2.5$.

Example 18.2   Find a linear approximation to $y(t) = t^2$ near $t = 3$.

Solution   We require the equation of the tangent to $y = t^2$ at $t = 3$, that is the first-order Taylor polynomial about $t = 3$. Note that $y(3) = 9$ and $y'(3) = 6$.

$$
\begin{aligned}
p_1(t) &= y(a) + y'(a)(t - a) = y(3) + y'(3)(t - 3) \\
&= 9 + 6(t - 3) \\
&= 6t - 9
\end{aligned}
$$

At $t = 3$, $p_1(t)$ and $y(t)$ have an identical value. Near to $t = 3$, $p_1(t)$ and $y(t)$ have similar values, for example $p_1(2.8) = 7.8$, $y(2.8) = 7.84$.

18.2.1 Linearization

It is a frequent requirement in engineering to obtain a linear mathematical model of a system which is basically non-linear. Mathematically and computationally linear models are far easier to deal with than non-linear models. The main reason for this is that linear models obey the principle of superposition. It follows that if the application, separately, of inputs $u_1(t)$ and $u_2(t)$ to the system produces outputs $y_1(t)$ and $y_2(t)$, respectively, then the application of an input $u_1(t) + u_2(t)$ will produce an output $y_1(t) + y_2(t)$. This is only true for linear systems.

The value of this principle is that the effect of several inputs to a system can be calculated merely by adding together the effects of the individual inputs. This allows the effect of simple individual inputs to the system to be analysed and then combined to evaluate the effect of more complicated combinations of inputs. A few examples will help clarify these points.

Example 18.3   **A d.c. electrical network**

Consider the d.c. network of Figure 18.2. This network is a linear system. This is because the voltage/current characteristic of a resistor is linear provided a certain voltage is not exceeded. Recall Ohm's law which is given by

$$
V = IR
$$

where V is the voltage across the resistor, I is the current through the resistor and R is the resistance. This makes the analysis of the network relatively easy. The voltage sources, V_1, V_2, V_3, V_4, can be thought of as the inputs to the system. It is possible to analyse the effect of each of these sources separately, for example the voltage drop across the resistor, R_5, resulting from the voltage source V_1, and then combine these effects to obtain the total effect on the system. The voltage drop across R_5 when all sources are considered would be the sum of each of the voltage drops due to the individual sources V_1, V_2, V_3 and V_4.

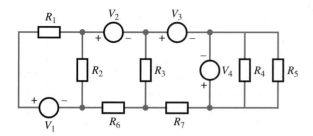

Figure 18.2 A d.c. electrical network.

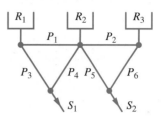

Figure 18.3 A water supply network.

Example 18.4 — A gravity feed water supply

Consider the water supply network of Figure 18.3. The network consists of three source reservoirs and a series of connecting pipes. Water is taken from the network at two points, S_1 and S_2. In a practical network, reservoirs are usually several kilometres away from the points at which water is taken from the network and so the effect of pressure drops along the pipes is significant. For this reason many networks require pumps to boost the pressure.

The main problem with analysing this network is that it is non-linear. This is because the relationship between pressure drop along a pipe and water flow through a pipe is not linear: a doubling of pressure does not lead to a doubling of flow. For this reason, it is not possible to use the principle of superposition when analysing the network. For example, if the effect of the pressure at S_1 for a given flow rate was calculated separately for each of the inputs to the system – the reservoirs R_1, R_2, R_3 – then the effect of all the reservoirs could not be obtained by adding the individual effects. It is not possible to obtain a linear model for this system except under very restrictive conditions and so the analysis of water networks is very complicated.

Having demonstrated the value of linear models it is worth analysing how and when a non-linear system can be linearized. The first thing to note is that many systems may contain a mixture of linear and non-linear components and so it is only necessary to linearize certain parts of the system. A system of this type has been studied in Example 10.20. Therefore linearization involves deciding which components of a system are non-linear, deciding whether it would be valid to linearize the components and, if so, then obtaining linearized models of the components.

Consider again Figure 18.1. Imagine it illustrates a component characteristic. The actual component characteristic is unimportant for the purposes of this discussion. For instance, it could be the pressure/flow relationship of a valve or the voltage/current relationship of an electronic device. The main factor in deciding whether a valid linear model can be obtained is the range of values over which the component is required to operate. If an operating point Q were chosen and deviations from this operating point were small then it is clear from Figure 18.1 that a linear model – corresponding to the tangent to the curve at point Q – would be an appropriate model.

Obtaining a linear model is relatively straightforward. It consists of calculating the first-order Taylor polynomial centred around the operating point Q. This is given by

$$p_1(x) = y(a) + y'(a)(x - a)$$

Then $p_1(x)$ is used as the linearized model of the component with characteristic $y(x)$. It is valid provided that it is only used for values of x such that $|x - a|$ is sufficiently small. As stated, $p_1(x)$ is also the equation of the tangent to the curve at point Q. The range of values for which the model is valid depends on the curvature of the characteristic and the accuracy required.

Example 18.5   **Power dissipation in a resistor**

The power dissipated in a resistor varies with the current. Derive a linear model for this power variation valid for an operating point of 0.5 A. The resistor has a resistance of 10 Ω.

Solution   For a resistor

$$P = I^2 R$$

where

$$P = \text{power dissipated (W)}$$

$$I = \text{current (A)}$$

$$R = \text{resistance } (\Omega).$$

The first-order polynomial, valid around an operating point $I = 0.5$, is

$$p_1(I) = P(0.5) + P'(0.5)(I - 0.5)$$

Now $P(0.5) = (0.5)^2 10 = 2.5$, $P'(0.5) = 2(0.5)(10) = 10$, and so

$$p_1(I) = 2.5 + 10(I - 0.5) = 10I - 2.5$$

It is interesting to compare this linear approximation with the true curve for values of I around the operating point. Table 18.1 shows some typical values. Notice that the linear approximation is quite good when close to the operating point but deteriorates further away.

Table 18.1
A comparison of linear approximations with true values.

I (A)	True value of P (W)	Approximate value of P (W)
0.5	2.5	2.5
0.499	2.490 01	2.49
0.501	2.510 01	2.51
0.49	2.401	2.4
0.51	2.601	2.6
0.4	1.6	1.5
0.6	3.6	3.5
1.0	10	7.5

Exercises 18.2

1 Calculate the first-order Taylor polynomial generated by $y(x) = e^x$ about

(a) $x = 0$

(b) $x = 2$

(c) $x = -3$

2 Calculate the first-order Taylor polynomial generated by $y(x) = \sin x$ about

(a) $x = 0$

(b) $x = 1$

(c) $x = -0.5$

3 Calculate the first-order Taylor polynomial generated by $y(x) = \cos x$ about

(a) $x = 0$

(b) $x = 1$

(c) $x = -0.5$

4 (a) Find a linear approximation, $p_1(t)$, to $h(t) = t^3$ about $t = 2$.

(b) Evaluate $h(2.3)$ and $p_1(2.3)$.

5 (a) Find a linear approximation, $p_1(t)$, to $R(t) = \dfrac{1}{t}$ about $t = 0.5$.

(b) Evaluate $R(0.7)$ and $p_1(0.7)$.

Solutions

1 (a) $p_1(x) = x + 1$

(b) $p_1(x) = e^2(x - 1)$

(c) $p_1(x) = e^{-3}(x + 4)$

2 (a) $p_1(x) = x$

(b) $p_1(x) = 0.5403x + 0.3012$

(c) $p_1(x) = 0.8776x - 0.0406$

3 (a) $p_1(x) = 1$

(b) $p_1(x) = -0.8415x + 1.3818$

(c) $p_1(x) = 0.4794x + 1.1173$

4 (a) $p_1(t) = 12t - 16$

(b) $h(2.3) = 12.167$, $p_1(2.3) = 11.6$

5 (a) $p_1(t) = -4t + 4$

(b) $R(0.7) = 1.4286$, $p_1(0.7) = 1.2$

18.3 Second order Taylor polynomials

Suppose that in addition to $y(a)$ and $y'(a)$, we also have a value of $y''(a)$. With this information a second-order Taylor polynomial can be found, which provides a quadratic approximation to $y(x)$. Let

$$p_2(x) = c_0 + c_1x + c_2x^2$$

We require

$$p_2(a) = y(a)$$
$$p_2'(a) = y'(a)$$
$$p_2''(a) = y''(a)$$

that is, the polynomial and its first two derivatives evaluated at $x = a$ match the function and its first two derivatives evaluated at $x = a$. Hence

$$p_2(a) = c_0 + c_1 a + c_2 a^2 = y(a) \tag{18.1}$$

$$p_2'(a) = c_1 + 2c_2 a = y'(a) \tag{18.2}$$

$$p_2''(a) = 2c_2 = y''(a) \tag{18.3}$$

Solving for c_0, c_1 and c_2 yields

$$c_2 = \frac{y''(a)}{2} \qquad \text{from Equation (18.3)}$$

$$c_1 = y'(a) - ay''(a) \qquad \text{from Equation (18.2)}$$

$$c_0 = y(a) - ay'(a) + \frac{a^2}{2} y''(a) \qquad \text{from Equation (18.1)}$$

Hence,

$$p_2(x) = y(a) - ay'(a) + \frac{a^2}{2} y''(a)$$

$$+ \{y'(a) - ay''(a)\}x + \frac{y''(a)}{2} x^2$$

Finally,

$$p_2(x) = y(a) + y'(a)(x - a) + y''(a)\frac{(x - a)^2}{2}$$

$p_2(x)$ is the **second-order Taylor polynomial** generated by y about $x = a$.

Example 18.6 Given $y(1) = 0$, $y'(1) = 1$, $y''(1) = -2$, estimate

(a) $y(1.5)$

(b) $y(2)$

(c) $y(0.5)$

using the second-order Taylor polynomial.

Solution The second-order Taylor polynomial is $p_2(x)$.

$$p_2(x) = y(1) + y'(1)(x - 1) + y''(1)\frac{(x - 1)^2}{2}$$

$$= x - 1 - 2\frac{(x - 1)^2}{2} = x - 1 - (x - 1)^2 = -x^2 + 3x - 2$$

We use $p_2(x)$ as an approximation to $y(x)$.

(a) The value of $y(1.5)$ is approximated by $p_2(1.5)$.

$$y(1.5) \approx p_2(1.5) = 0.25$$

(b) The value of $y(2)$ is approximated by $p_2(2)$.

$$y(2) \approx p_2(2) = 0$$

(c) The value of $y(0.5)$ is approximated by $p_2(0.5)$.

$$y(0.5) \approx p_2(0.5) = -0.75$$

Example 18.7 (a) Calculate the second-order Taylor polynomial, $p_2(x)$, generated by $y(x) = x^3 + x^2 - 6$ about $x = 2$.

(b) Verify that $y(2) = p_2(2)$, $y'(2) = p_2'(2)$ and $y''(2) = p_2''(2)$.

(c) Compare $y(2.1)$ and $p_2(2.1)$.

Solution (a) We need to calculate $y(2)$, $y'(2)$ and $y''(2)$. Now

$$y(x) = x^3 + x^2 - 6, \ y'(x) = 3x^2 + 2x, \ y''(x) = 6x + 2$$

and so

$$y(2) = 6, \ y'(2) = 16, \ y''(2) = 14$$

The required second-order Taylor polynomial, $p_2(x)$, is thus given by

$$p_2(x) = y(2) + y'(2)(x - 2) + y''(2)\frac{(x - 2)^2}{2}$$

$$= 6 + 16(x - 2) + 14\frac{(x - 2)^2}{2}$$

$$= 6 + 16x - 32 + 7(x^2 - 4x + 4)$$

$$= 7x^2 - 12x + 2$$

(b) Using (a) we can see that

$$p_2(x) = 7x^2 - 12x + 2, \ p_2'(x) = 14x - 12, \ p_2''(x) = 14$$

and so

$$p_2(2) = 6, \ p_2'(2) = 16, \ p_2''(2) = 14$$

Hence

$$y(2) = p_2(2), \ y'(2) = p_2'(2), \ y''(2) = p_2''(2)$$

(c) We have

$$y(2.1) = (2.1)^3 + (2.1)^2 - 6 = 7.671$$
$$p_2(2.1) = 7(2.1)^2 - 12(2.1) + 2 = 7.67$$

Clearly there is a very close agreement between values of $y(x)$ and $p_2(x)$ near to $x = 2$.

Example 18.8 **Quadratic approximation to a diode characteristic**

In Example 10.18 we derived a linear approximation to a diode characteristic suitable for small signal variations around an operating point. Sometimes it is not possible to use a linear approximation because the variations are too large to maintain sufficient accuracy. Even so, an approximate model may be desirable. In general, a higher order Taylor polynomial will give a more accurate model than that of a lower order polynomial. We will consider a quadratic model for a diode characteristic. Recall that for a diode at room temperature,

$$I = I(V) = I_s(e^{40V} - 1)$$

Given an operating point, V_a, the second-order Taylor polynomial is

$$p_2(V) = I(V_a) + I'(V_a)(V - V_a) + I''(V_a)\frac{(V - V_a)^2}{2}$$

Now

$$I'(V) = 40I_s\, e^{40V} \qquad I''(V) = 1600I_s\, e^{40V}$$

so

$$p_2(V) = I_s(e^{40V_a} - 1) + 40I_s\, e^{40V_a}(V - V_a) + 1600I_s\, e^{40V_a}\frac{(V - V_a)^2}{2}$$

The coefficients need to be calculated only once. After that the calculation of a current value only involves evaluating a quadratic.

Exercises 18.3

1 (a) Obtain the second-order Taylor polynomial, $p_2(x)$, generated by $y(x) = 3x^4 + 1$ about $x = 2$.

(b) Verify that $y(2) = p_2(2)$, $y'(2) = p_2'(2)$ and $y''(2) = p_2''(2)$.

(c) Evaluate $p_2(1.8)$ and $y(1.8)$.

2 (a) Calculate the second-order Taylor

polynomial, $p_2(x)$, generated by $y(x) = \sin x$ about $x = 0$.

(b) Calculate the second-order Taylor polynomial, $p_2(x)$, generated by $y(x) = \cos x$ about $x = 0$.

(c) Compare your results from (a) and (b) with the small-angle approximations given in Section 6.5.

3　A function, $y(x)$, is such that $y(-1) = 3$, $y'(-1) = 2$ and $y''(-1) = -2$.

(a)　State the second-order Taylor polynomial generated by y about $x = -1$.

(b)　Estimate $y(-0.9)$.

4　A function, $y(x)$, satisfies the equation

$$y' = y^2 + x \qquad y(1) = 2$$

(a)　Estimate $y(1.3)$ using a first-order Taylor polynomial.

(b)　By differentiating the equation with respect to x, obtain an expression for y''. Hence evaluate $y''(1)$.

(c)　Estimate $y(1.3)$ using a second-order Taylor polynomial.

5　A function, $x(t)$, satisfies the equation

$$\dot{x} = x + \sqrt{t+1} \qquad x(0) = 2$$

(a)　Estimate $x(0.2)$ using a first-order Taylor polynomial.

(b)　Differentiate the equation w.r.t. t and hence obtain an expression for $\ddot{x}$.

(c)　Estimate $x(0.2)$ using a second-order Taylor polynomial.

6　A function, $h(t)$, is defined by

$$h(t) = \sin 2t + \cos 3t$$

Obtain the second-order Taylor polynomial generated by $h(t)$ about $t = 0$.

7　The functions $y_1(x)$, $y_2(x)$ and $y_3(x)$ are defined by

$$y_1(x) = Ae^x, \, y_2(x) = Bx^3 + Cx,$$
$$y_3(x) = y_1(x) + y_2(x)$$

(a)　Obtain a second-order Taylor polynomial for $y_1(x)$ about $x = 0$.

(b)　Obtain a second-order Taylor polynomial for $y_2(x)$ about $x = 0$.

(c)　Obtain a second-order Taylor polynomial for $y_3(x)$ about $x = 0$.

(d)　Can you draw any conclusions from your answers to (a), (b) and (c)?

Solutions

1　(a)　$p_2(x) = 72x^2 - 192x + 145$

(c)　$p_2(1.8) = 32.68$, $y(1.8) = 32.4928$

2　(a)　$p_2(x) = x$　　(b)　$p_2(x) = 1 - \dfrac{x^2}{2}$

3　(a)　$p_2(x) = -x^2 + 4$

(b)　$p_2(-0.9) = 3.19$. This is an approximation to $y(-0.9)$

4　(a)　3.5

(b)　$y'' = 2yy' + 1$, $y''(1) = 21$

(c)　4.445

5　(a)　2.6

(b)　$\ddot{x} = \dot{x} + \dfrac{1}{2\sqrt{t+1}}$

(c)　2.67

6　$p_2(t) = 1 + 2t - 4.5t^2$

7　(a)　$A\left(1 + x + \dfrac{x^2}{2}\right)$

(b)　Cx

(c)　$A + (A + C)x + \dfrac{Ax^2}{2}$

Computer and calculator exercises 18.3

1　(a)　Calculate the second-order Taylor polynomial, $p_2(x)$, generated by $y(x) = x^3$ about $x = 0$.

(b)　Draw $y(x)$ and $p_2(x)$ for $-2 \leqslant x \leqslant 2$.

2　(a)　Calculate the second-order Taylor polynomial, $p_2(x)$, generated by $y(x) = \sin x$ about $x = 0$.

(b)　Draw $y(x)$ and $p_2(x)$ for $-2 \leqslant x \leqslant 2$.

3 (a) Calculate the second-order Taylor polynomial, $p_2(x)$, generated by
$$y(x) = \sin\left(\frac{1}{x}\right) \text{ about } x = 3.$$

(b) Draw $y(x)$ and $p_2(x)$ for $1 \leqslant x \leqslant 5$.

4 (a) Calculate the second-order Taylor polynomial, $p_2(x)$, generated by $y(x) = e^{\cos x}$ about $x = 0$.

(b) Draw $y(x)$ and $p_2(x)$ for $-2 \leqslant x \leqslant 2$.

18.4 Taylor polynomials of the nth order

If we know y and its first n derivatives evaluated at $x = a$, that is $y(a)$, $y'(a)$, $y''(a)$, ..., $y^{(n)}(a)$, then the **nth-order Taylor polynomial**, $p_n(x)$, may be written as

$$p_n(x) = y(a) + y'(a)(x - a) + y''(a)\frac{(x - a)^2}{2!} + y^{(3)}(a)\frac{(x - a)^3}{3!}$$
$$+ \cdots + y^{(n)}(a)\frac{(x - a)^n}{n!}$$

This provides an approximation to $y(x)$. The polynomial and its first n derivatives evaluated at $x = a$ match the values of $y(x)$ and its first n derivatives evaluated at $x = a$, that is

$$p_n(a) = y(a)$$
$$p'_n(a) = y'(a)$$
$$p''_n(a) = y''(a)$$
$$\vdots$$
$$p_n^{(n)}(a) = y^{(n)}(a)$$

Example 18.9 Given $y(0) = 1$, $y'(0) = 1$, $y''(0) = 1$, $y^{(3)}(0) = -1$, $y^{(4)}(0) = 2$, obtain a fourth-order Taylor polynomial generated by y about $x = 0$. Estimate $y(0.2)$.

Solution In this example $a = 0$ and hence

$$p_4(x) = y(0) + y'(0)x + y''(0)\frac{x^2}{2!} + y^{(3)}(0)\frac{x^3}{3!} + y^{(4)}(0)\frac{x^4}{4!}$$

$$= 1 + x + \frac{x^2}{2} - \frac{x^3}{6} + \frac{x^4}{12}$$

The Taylor polynomial can be used to estimate $y(0.2)$.

$$p_4(0.2) = 1 + 0.2 + \frac{(0.2)^2}{2} - \frac{(0.2)^3}{6} + \frac{(0.2)^4}{12} = 1.2188$$

$$y(0.2) \approx 1.2188$$

Figure 18.4
A graph of $y = e^x$ and four Taylor polynomials.

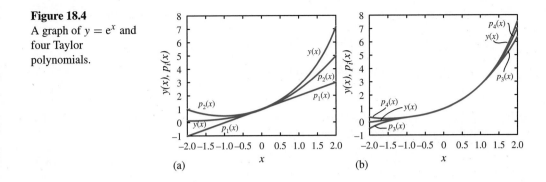

(a)

(b)

Example 18.10

(a) Calculate the first-, second-, third- and fourth-order Taylor polynomials generated by $y(x) = e^x$ about $x = 0$.

(b) Plot $y = e^x$ and the Taylor polynomials for $-2 \leqslant x \leqslant 2$.

Solution

(a) We have

$$y(x) = y'(x) = y''(x) = y^{(3)}(x) = y^{(4)}(x) = e^x$$

and

$$y(0) = y'(0) = y''(0) = y^{(3)}(0) = y^{(4)}(0) = 1$$

Thus the Taylor polynomials, $p_1(x)$, $p_2(x)$, $p_3(x)$ and $p_4(x)$, are given by

$$p_1(x) = y(0) + y'(0)x = 1 + x$$

$$p_2(x) = y(0) + y'(0)x + y''(0)\frac{x^2}{2} = 1 + x + \frac{x^2}{2}$$

$$p_3(x) = y(0) + y'(0)x + y''(0)\frac{x^2}{2} + y^{(3)}(0)\frac{x^3}{3!} = 1 + x + \frac{x^2}{2} + \frac{x^3}{6}$$

$$p_4(x) = y(0) + y'(0)x + y''(0)\frac{x^2}{2} + y^{(3)}(0)\frac{x^3}{3!} + y^{(4)}(0)\frac{x^4}{4!}$$

$$= 1 + x + \frac{x^2}{2} + \frac{x^3}{6} + \frac{x^4}{24}$$

(b) The graphs of $y = e^x$ and the Taylor polynomials are shown in Figure 18.4. Note that the Taylor polynomials become better and better approximations to e^x as the order of the polynomial increases.

Example 18.11

Given that y satisfies the equation

$$y'' - (y')^2 + 2y = x^2 \qquad (18.4)$$

and also the conditions

$$y(0) = 1 \qquad y'(0) = 2$$

use a third-order Taylor polynomial to estimate $y(0.5)$.

Solution To write down the third-order Taylor polynomial about $x = 0$ we require $y(0)$, $y'(0)$, $y''(0)$ and $y^{(3)}(0)$. From Equation (18.4),

$$y''(x) = x^2 + \{y'(x)\}^2 - 2y(x) \tag{18.5}$$

So,

$$y''(0) = 0 + \{y'(0)\}^2 - 2y(0) = 2$$

To find $y^{(3)}(0)$, Equation (18.5) is differentiated w.r.t. x.

$$y^{(3)}(x) = 2x + 2y'(x)y''(x) - 2y'(x)$$
$$y^{(3)}(0) = 2y'(0)y''(0) - 2y'(0) = 4$$

The Taylor polynomial may now be written as

$$p_3(x) = y(0) + y'(0)x + y''(0)\frac{x^2}{2} + y^{(3)}(0)\frac{x^3}{6}$$
$$= 1 + 2x + x^2 + \frac{2x^3}{3}$$

We use $p_3(x)$ as an approximation to $y(x)$.

$$p_3(0.5) = 1 + 1 + 0.25 + 0.0833 = 2.333$$

that is,

$$y(0.5) \approx 2.333$$

Exercises 18.4

1 A function, $y(x)$, has $y(0) = 3$, $y'(0) = 1$, $y''(0) = -1$ and $y^{(3)}(0) = 2$.

(a) Obtain a third-order Taylor polynomial, $p_3(x)$, generated by $y(x)$ about $x = 0$.

(b) Estimate $y(0.2)$.

2 A function, $h(t)$, has $h(2) = 1$, $h'(2) = 4$, $h''(2) = -2$, $h^{(3)}(2) = 1$ and $h^{(4)}(2) = 3$.

(a) Obtain a fourth-order Taylor polynomial, $p_4(t)$, generated by $h(t)$ about $t = 2$.

(b) Estimate $h(1.8)$.

3 Given $y(x) = \sin x$, obtain the third-, fourth- and fifth-order Taylor polynomials generated by $y(x)$ about $x = 0$,

4 Given $y(x) = \cos x$, obtain the third-, fourth- and fifth-order Taylor polynomials generated by $y(x)$ about $x = 0$.

5 (a) Given $y(x) = \sin(kx)$, k a constant, obtain the third-, fourth- and fifth-order Taylor polynomials generated by $y(x)$ about $x = 0$.

(b) Write down the third-, fourth- and fifth-order Taylor polynomials generated by $y = \sin(-x)$ about $x = 0$.

6 (a) Given $y(x) = \cos(kx)$, k a constant, obtain the third-, fourth- and fifth-order Taylor polynomials generated by $y(x)$ about $x = 0$.

(b) Write down the third-, fourth- and fifth-order Taylor polynomials generated by $y = \cos(2x)$ about $x = 0$.

7 If $p_n(x)$ is the nth-order Taylor polynomial generated by $y(x)$ about $x = 0$, show that $p_n(kx)$ is the nth-order Taylor polynomial generated by $y(kx)$ about $x = 0$.

8 The function, $y(x)$, satisfies the equation

$$y'' = y + 3x^2 \qquad y(1) = 1, \ y'(1) = 2$$

(a) Obtain a third-order Taylor polynomial generated by y about $x = 1$.

(b) Estimate $y(1.3)$ using (a).

(c) Obtain a fourth-order Taylor polynomial generated by y about $x = 1$.

(d) Estimate $y(1.3)$ using (c).

9 A function, $y(x)$, satisfies the equation

$$y'' + y^2 = x^3 \qquad y(0) = 1, \ y'(0) = -1$$

(a) Estimate $y(0.25)$ using a third-order Taylor polynomial.

(b) Estimate $y(0.25)$ using a fourth-order Taylor polynomial.

10 A function, $y(x)$, has $y(1) = 3$, $y'(1) = 6$, $y''(1) = 1$ and $y^{(3)}(1) = -1$.

(a) Estimate $y(1.2)$ using a third-order Taylor polynomial.

(b) Estimate $y'(1.2)$ using an appropriate second-order Taylor polynomial. [*Hint:* define a new variable, z, given by $z = y'$.]

Solutions

1 (a) $3 + x - \dfrac{x^2}{2} + \dfrac{x^3}{3}$

(b) 3.1827

2 (a) $\dfrac{t^4}{8} - \dfrac{5t^3}{6} + t^2 + 6t - \dfrac{31}{3}$

(b) 0.1589

3 $p_3(x) = x - \dfrac{x^3}{3!}$,

$p_4(x) = x - \dfrac{x^3}{3!}$,

$p_5(x) = x - \dfrac{x^3}{3!} + \dfrac{x^5}{5!}$

4 $p_3(x) = 1 - \dfrac{x^2}{2!}$,

$p_4(x) = 1 - \dfrac{x^2}{2!} + \dfrac{x^4}{4!}$,

$p_5(x) = 1 - \dfrac{x^2}{2!} + \dfrac{x^4}{4!}$

5 (a) $p_3(x) = kx - \dfrac{k^3 x^3}{3!}$,

$p_4(x) = kx - \dfrac{k^3 x^3}{3!}$,

$p_5(x) = kx - \dfrac{k^3 x^3}{3!} + \dfrac{k^5 x^5}{5!}$

(b) $p_3(x) = -x + \dfrac{x^3}{3!}$,

$p_4(x) = -x + \dfrac{x^3}{3!}$,

$p_5(x) = -x + \dfrac{x^3}{3!} - \dfrac{x^5}{5!}$

6 (a) $p_3(x) = 1 - \dfrac{k^2 x^2}{2!}$,

$p_4(x) = 1 - \dfrac{k^2 x^2}{2!} + \dfrac{k^4 x^4}{4!}$,

$p_5(x) = 1 - \dfrac{k^2 x^2}{2!} + \dfrac{k^4 x^4}{4!}$

(b) $p_3(x) = 1 - 2x^2$,

$p_4(x) = 1 - 2x^2 + \dfrac{2x^4}{3}$,

$p_5(x) = 1 - 2x^2 + \dfrac{2x^4}{3}$

8 (a) $\dfrac{4x^3}{3} - 2x^2 + 2x - \dfrac{1}{3}$

   (b) 1.816

   (c) $\dfrac{5x^4}{12} - \dfrac{x^3}{3} + \dfrac{x^2}{2} + \dfrac{x}{3} + \dfrac{1}{12}$

   (d) 1.8194

9 (a) 0.7240   (b) 0.7240

10 (a) 4.2187   (b) 6.18

🖳 Computer and calculator exercises 18.4

1 Draw $y(x) = \dfrac{1}{x}$ for $1 \leqslant x \leqslant 8$. On the same axes draw the fourth-order Taylor polynomial generated by $y(x)$ about $x = 3$.

2 Draw $y = \tan x$ for $-1 \leqslant x \leqslant 1$. Using the same axes, draw the fifth-order Taylor

polynomial generated by $y(x)$ about $x = 0$.

3 Draw $y(x) = \ln x$ for $0.5 \leqslant x \leqslant 10$. On the same axes, draw the third-, fourth- and fifth-order Taylor polynomials generated by $y(x)$ about $x = 1$.

18.5 Taylor's formula and the remainder term

So far we have found Taylor polynomials of orders 1, 2, 3, 4 and so on. Example 18.10 suggests that the generating function, $y(x)$, and the Taylor polynomials are in close agreement for values of x near to the point where $x = a$. It is reasonable to ask:

'How accurately do Taylor polynomials generated by $y(x)$ at $x = a$ approximate to y at values of x other than a?'
'If more and more terms are used in the Taylor polynomial will this produce a better and better approximation to y?'

To answer these questions we introduce Taylor's formula and the remainder term.
Suppose $p_n(x)$ is an nth-order Taylor polynomial generated by $y(x)$ about $x = a$. Then **Taylor's formula** states:

$$y(x) = p_n(x) + R_n(x)$$

where $R_n(x)$ is called the **remainder of order n** and is given by

$$\text{remainder of order } n = R_n(x) = \frac{y^{(n+1)}(c)(x-a)^{n+1}}{(n+1)!}$$

for some number c between a and x.

The remainder of order n is also called the **error term**. The error term in effect gives the difference between the function, $y(x)$, and the Taylor polynomial generated by $y(x)$. For a Taylor polynomial to be a close approximation to the generating function requires the error term to be small.

Example 18.12 Calculate the error term of order 5 due to $y(x) = e^x$ generating a Taylor polynomial about $x = 0$.

Solution Here $n = 5$ and so $n + 1 = 6$. In this example $a = 0$. We see that $y = e^x$ and so

$$y'(x) = y''(x) = \cdots = y^{(5)}(x) = y^{(6)}(x) = e^x$$

and so $y^{(6)}(c) = e^c$. The remainder term of order 5, $R_5(x)$, is given by

$$R_5(x) = \frac{e^c x^6}{6!} \qquad \text{for some number } c \text{ between } 0 \text{ and } x$$

Example 18.13 (a) Calculate the fourth-order Taylor polynomial, $p_4(x)$, generated by $y(x) = \sin 2x$ about $x = 0$.

(b) State the fourth-order error term, $R_4(x)$.

(c) Calculate an upper bound for this error term given $|x| < 1$.

(d) Compare $y(0.5)$ and $p_4(0.5)$.

Solution (a)

$$\begin{aligned}
y(x) &= \sin 2x, & y(0) &= 0 \\
y'(x) &= 2 \cos 2x, & y'(0) &= 2 \\
y''(x) &= -4 \sin 2x, & y''(0) &= 0 \\
y^{(3)}(x) &= -8 \cos 2x, & y^{(3)}(0) &= -8 \\
y^{(4)}(x) &= 16 \sin 2x, & y^{(4)}(0) &= 0
\end{aligned}$$

The fourth-order Taylor polynomial, $p_4(x)$, is

$$p_4(x) = y(0) + y'(0)x + y''(0)\frac{x^2}{2!} + y^{(3)}(0)\frac{x^3}{3!} + y^{(4)}(0)\frac{x^4}{4!}$$

$$= 0 + 2x + 0 - \frac{8x^3}{6} + 0$$

$$= 2x - \frac{4x^3}{3}$$

(b) We note that $y^{(5)}(x) = 32 \cos 2x$ and so $y^{(5)}(c) = 32 \cos(2c)$. The error term, $R_4(x)$, is given by

$$R_4(x) = y^{(5)}(c)\frac{x^5}{5!}$$

$$= \frac{32 \cos(2c)x^5}{120}$$

$$= \frac{4}{15} \cos(2c)x^5 \qquad \text{where } c \text{ is a number between } 0 \text{ and } x$$

(c) In order to calculate an upper bound for this error term we note that $|\cos(2c)| \leqslant 1$ for any value of c. Hence an upper bound for $R_4(x)$ is given by

$$|R_4(x)| \leqslant \left| \frac{4x^5}{15} \right|$$

We know $|x| < 1$, and so $\dfrac{4x^5}{15}$ is never greater than $\dfrac{4}{15}$. Hence an upper bound for the error term is $\dfrac{4}{15}$. If we use $p_4(x)$ to approximate $y = \sin 2x$ the error will be no greater than $\dfrac{4}{15}$ provided $|x| < 1$.

(d) We let $x = 0.5$.

$$y(0.5) = \sin 1 = 0.8415$$

$$p_4(0.5) = 2(0.5) - \frac{4}{3}(0.5)^3 = 0.8333$$

The difference between $y(0.5)$ and $p_4(0.5)$ can never be greater than an upper bound of the error term evaluated at $x = 0.5$. This is verified numerically.

$$y(0.5) - p_4(0.5) = 0.8415 - 0.8333 = 0.0082$$

and

$$|R_4(0.5)| \leqslant \frac{4}{15}(0.5)^5 = 0.0083$$

Exercises 18.5

1 The function, $y(x)$, is given by $y(x) = \sin x$.

(a) Calculate the fifth-order Taylor polynomial generated by y about $x = 0$.

(b) Find an expression for the remainder term of order 5.

(c) State an upper bound for your expression in (b).

2 Repeat Question 1 with $y(x) = \cos x$.

3 The function $y(x) = e^x$ may be approximated by the quadratic expression $1 + x + \dfrac{x^2}{2}$. Find an upper bound for the error term given $|x| < 0.5$.

4 (a) Find the third-order Taylor polynomial generated by $h(t) = \dfrac{1}{t}$ about $t = 2$.

(b) State the error term.

(c) Find an upper bound for the error term given $1 \leqslant t \leqslant 4$.

5 The function $y(x) = x^5 + x^6$ is approximated by a third-order Taylor polynomial about $x = 1$.

(a) Find an expression for the third-order error term.

(b) Find an upper bound for the error term given $0 \leqslant x \leqslant 2$.

Solutions

1 (a) $x - \dfrac{x^3}{3!} + \dfrac{x^5}{5!}$

(b) $R_5 = -\dfrac{(\sin c)x^6}{6!}$

where c lies between 0 and x

(c) $\left| \dfrac{x^6}{6!} \right|$

2 (a) $1 - \dfrac{x^2}{2!} + \dfrac{x^4}{4!}$

(b) $R_5 = -\dfrac{(\cos c)x^6}{6!}$

where c lies between 0 and x

(c) $\left| \dfrac{x^6}{6!} \right|$

3 3.435×10^{-2}

4 (a) $-\dfrac{t^3}{16} + \dfrac{t^2}{2} - \dfrac{3t}{2} + 2$

(b) $\dfrac{(t-2)^4}{c^5}$ where c lies between 2 and t

(c) 0.5

5 (a) $5c(1 + 3c)(x - 1)^4$ for c between 1 and x

(b) 70

18.6 Taylor and Maclaurin series

We have seen that y and its first n derivatives evaluated at $x = a$ match $p_n(x)$ and its first n derivatives evaluated at $x = a$. We have studied the difference between $y(x)$ and $p_n(x)$, that is the error term, $R_n(x)$.

As more and more terms are included in the Taylor polynomial, we obtain an infinite series, called a **Taylor series**. We denote this infinite series by $p(x)$.

Taylor series:

$$p(x) = y(a) + y'(a)(x - a) + y''(a)\frac{(x - a)^2}{2!} + y^{(3)}(a)\frac{(x - a)^3}{3!}$$
$$+ \cdots + y^{(n)}(a)\frac{(x - a)^n}{n!} + \cdots$$

For some Taylor series, the value of the series equals the value of the generating function for every value of x. For example, the Taylor series for e^x, $\sin x$ and $\cos x$ equal the values of e^x, $\sin x$ and $\cos x$ for every value of x. However, some functions have a Taylor series which equals the function only for a limited range of x values. Example 18.18 gives a case of a function which equals its Taylor series only when $-1 < x < 1$.

To determine whether a Taylor series, $p(x)$, is equal to its generating function, $y(x)$, we need to examine the error term of order n, that is $R_n(x)$. We examine this error term as more and more terms are included in the Taylor polynomial, that is as n tends to infinity. If this error term approaches 0 as n increases, then the Taylor series equates to the generating function, $y(x)$. Sometimes the error term approaches 0 as n increases for all values of x, sometimes it approaches 0 only when x lies in some specified interval, say, for example, $(-1, 1)$. Hence we have:

If $R_n(x) \to 0$ as $n \to \infty$ for all values of x, then the Taylor series, $p(x)$, and the generating function, $y(x)$, are equal for all values of x.

If $R_n(x) \to 0$ as $n \to \infty$ for values of x in the interval (α, β), then the Taylor series, $p(x)$, and the generating function, $y(x)$, are equal for x values on the interval (α, β). For values of x outside the interval (α, β), the values of $p(x)$ and $y(x)$ are different.

By examining the error terms associated with $y = e^x$, $y = \sin x$ and $y = \cos x$ it is possible to show that these errors all approach 0 as $n \to \infty$ for all values of x. Hence the functions $y = e^x$, $y = \sin x$ and $y = \cos x$ are all equal to their corresponding Taylor series for all values of x.

A special, commonly used, case of a Taylor series occurs when $a = 0$. This is known as the **Maclaurin series**.

Maclaurin series:

$$p(x) = y(0) + y'(0)x + y''(0)\frac{x^2}{2!} + y^{(3)}(0)\frac{x^3}{3!} + \cdots + y^{(n)}(0)\frac{x^n}{n!} + \cdots$$

Example 18.14 Determine the Maclaurin series for $y = e^x$.

Solution In this example $y(x) = e^x$ and clearly $y'(x) = e^x$ too. Similarly,

$$y''(x) = y^{(3)}(x) = \cdots = y^{(n)}(x) = e^x$$

for all values of n. Evaluating at $x = 0$ yields

$$y(0) = y'(0) = y''(0) = \cdots = y^{(n)}(0) = 1$$

and so

$$p(x) = 1 + x + \frac{x^2}{2!} + \frac{x^3}{3!} + \cdots + \frac{x^n}{n!} + \cdots$$

As mentioned earlier, the series and the generating function are equal for all values of x. Hence,

$$e^x = 1 + x + \frac{x^2}{2!} + \frac{x^3}{3!} + \cdots$$

for all values of x, that is

$$e^x = \sum_{n=0}^{\infty} \frac{x^n}{n!}$$

Example 18.15 Obtain the Maclaurin series for $y(x) = \sin x$.

Solution

$$y(x) = \sin x \qquad y(0) = 0$$
$$y'(x) = \cos x \qquad y'(0) = 1$$
$$y''(x) = -\sin x \qquad y''(0) = 0$$
$$y^{(3)}(x) = -\cos x \qquad y^{(3)}(0) = -1$$
$$y^{(4)}(x) = \sin x \qquad y^{(4)}(0) = 0$$

$$p(x) = y(0) + y'(0)x + \frac{y''(0)x^2}{2!} + \frac{y^{(3)}(0)x^3}{3!} + \cdots$$

$$= x - \frac{x^3}{3!} + \frac{x^5}{5!} - \frac{x^7}{7!} + \cdots$$

$$= \sum_{i=0}^{\infty} \frac{(-1)^i x^{2i+1}}{(2i+1)!}$$

Since the generating function and series are equal for all values of x we have

$$\sin x = \sum_{i=0}^{\infty} \frac{(-1)^i x^{2i+1}}{(2i+1)!} = x - \frac{x^3}{3!} + \frac{x^5}{5!} - \frac{x^7}{7!} + \cdots$$

Example 18.16 Obtain the Maclaurin series for $y(x) = \cos x$.

Solution

$$y(x) = \cos x, \qquad y(0) = 1$$
$$y'(x) = -\sin x, \qquad y'(0) = 0$$
$$y''(x) = -\cos x, \qquad y''(0) = -1$$
$$y^{(3)}(x) = \sin x, \qquad y^{(3)}(0) = 0$$
$$y^{(4)}(x) = \cos x, \qquad y^{(4)}(0) = 1$$

and so on. Therefore

$$p(x) = y(0) + y'(0)x + y''(0)\frac{x^2}{2!} + y^{(3)}(0)\frac{x^3}{3!} + y^{(4)}(0)\frac{x^4}{4!} + \cdots$$

$$= 1 - \frac{x^2}{2!} + \frac{x^4}{4!} - \cdots$$

$$= \sum_{i=0}^{\infty} \frac{(-1)^i x^{2i}}{(2i)!}$$

Since the series and the generating function are equal for all values of x then

$$\cos x = \sum_{i=0}^{\infty} \frac{(-1)^i x^{2i}}{(2i)!} = 1 - \frac{x^2}{2!} + \frac{x^4}{4!} - \frac{x^6}{6!} + \cdots$$

From Examples 18.14, 18.15 and 18.16 we note three important Maclaurin series:

$$e^x = 1 + x + \frac{x^2}{2!} + \frac{x^3}{3!} + \frac{x^4}{4!} + \cdots \qquad \text{for all values of } x$$

$$\sin x = x - \frac{x^3}{3!} + \frac{x^5}{5!} - \frac{x^7}{7!} + \cdots \qquad \text{for all values of } x$$

$$\cos x = 1 - \frac{x^2}{2!} + \frac{x^4}{4!} - \frac{x^6}{6!} + \cdots \qquad \text{for all values of } x$$

Example 18.17

Find the Maclaurin series for the following functions.

(a) $y = e^{2x}$ (b) $y = \sin 3x$ (c) $y = \cos\left(\dfrac{x}{2}\right)$

Solution

We use the previously stated series.

(a) We note that

$$e^z = 1 + z + \frac{z^2}{2!} + \frac{z^3}{3!} + \frac{z^4}{4!} + \cdots$$

Substituting $z = 2x$ we obtain

$$e^{2x} = 1 + 2x + \frac{(2x)^2}{2!} + \frac{(2x)^3}{3!} + \frac{(2x)^4}{4!} + \cdots$$

$$= 1 + 2x + 2x^2 + \frac{4x^3}{3} + \frac{2x^4}{3} + \cdots$$

(b) We note that

$$\sin z = z - \frac{z^3}{3!} + \frac{z^5}{5!} - \frac{z^7}{7!} + \cdots$$

By putting $z = 3x$ we obtain

$$\sin 3x = 3x - \frac{(3x)^3}{3!} + \frac{(3x)^5}{5!} - \frac{(3x)^7}{7!} + \cdots$$

$$= 3x - \frac{9}{2}x^3 + \frac{81}{40}x^5 - \frac{243}{560}x^7 + \cdots$$

(c) We note that

$$\cos z = 1 - \frac{z^2}{2!} + \frac{z^4}{4!} - \frac{z^6}{6!} + \cdots$$

Putting $z = \dfrac{x}{2}$ we obtain

$$\cos\left(\frac{x}{2}\right) = 1 - \frac{(x/2)^2}{2!} + \frac{(x/2)^4}{4!} - \frac{(x/2)^6}{6!} + \cdots$$

$$= 1 - \frac{x^2}{8} + \frac{x^4}{384} - \frac{x^6}{46\,080} + \cdots$$

Example 18.18   Determine the Maclaurin series for $y(x) = \dfrac{1}{1+x}$.

Solution   The value of y and its derivatives at $x = 0$ are found.

$$y(x) = \frac{1}{1+x} \qquad\qquad y(0) = 1$$

$$y'(x) = \frac{-1}{(1+x)^2} \qquad\qquad y'(0) = -1$$

$$y''(x) = \frac{2!}{(1+x)^3} \qquad\qquad y''(0) = 2!$$

$$y'''(x) = \frac{-3!}{(1+x)^4} \qquad\qquad y'''(0) = -3!$$

$$\vdots \qquad\qquad \vdots$$

$$y^{(n)}(x) = \frac{(-1)^n n!}{(1+x)^{n+1}} \qquad\qquad y^{(n)}(0) = (-1)^n n!$$

Hence using the formula for the Maclaurin series we find

$$p(x) = 1 - 1(x) + 2!\frac{x^2}{2!} - 3!\frac{x^3}{3!} + \cdots (-1)^n n!\frac{x^n}{n!} + \cdots$$

$$= 1 - x + x^2 - x^3 + x^4 - \cdots + (-1)^n x^n + \cdots$$

It can be shown that this series converges to $\dfrac{1}{1+x}$ for $|x| < 1$. Hence,

$$\frac{1}{1+x} = 1 - x + x^2 - x^3 + \cdots = \sum_0^\infty (-1)^n x^n \qquad \text{for } |x| < 1$$

For values of x outside $(-1, 1)$ the values of $\dfrac{1}{1+x}$ and $\sum (-1)^n x^n$ are simply not equal; try evaluating the l.h.s. and r.h.s. with, say, $x = -2$.

Example 18.19   Find the Taylor series for $y(x) = e^{-x}$ about $x = 1$.

Solution

$$y = e^{-x} \qquad y(1) = e^{-1}$$
$$y' = -e^{-x} \qquad y'(1) = -e^{-1}$$
$$y'' = e^{-x} \qquad y''(1) = e^{-1}$$

and so on. Hence,

$$e^{-x} = e^{-1} - (e^{-1})(x-1) + e^{-1}\frac{(x-1)^2}{2!} - e^{-1}\frac{(x-1)^3}{3!} + \cdots$$

$$= e^{-1}\left\{ 1 - (x-1) + \frac{(x-1)^2}{2!} - \frac{(x-1)^3}{3!} + \cdots \right\}$$

$$e^{-x} = e^{-1} \sum_0^\infty (-1)^n \frac{(x-1)^n}{n!}$$

Figure 18.5
The value $y(x_0 + h)$ can be estimated using values of y and its derivatives at $x = x_0$.

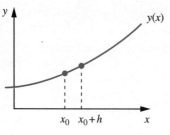

Example 18.20

Find the Maclaurin series for $y(x) = x \cos x$.

Solution   The Maclaurin series, $p(x)$, for $\cos x$ is

$$\cos x = p(x) = 1 - \frac{x^2}{2!} + \frac{x^4}{4!} - \frac{x^6}{6!} + \cdots$$

So the Maclaurin series for $x \cos x$ is $xp(x)$, that is

$$x \cos x = xp(x) = x - \frac{x^3}{2!} + \frac{x^5}{4!} - \frac{x^7}{6!} + \cdots$$

An alternative form of Taylor series is often used in numerical analysis. We know that the Taylor series for $y(x)$ generated about $x = a$ is given by

$$y(x) = y(a) + y'(a)(x - a) + y''(a)\frac{(x - a)^2}{2!} + y^{(3)}(a)\frac{(x - a)^3}{3!} + \cdots$$

Replacing a by x_0 we obtain

$$y(x) = y(x_0) + y'(x_0)(x - x_0) + y''(x_0)\frac{(x - x_0)^2}{2!} + y^{(3)}(x_0)\frac{(x - x_0)^3}{3!} + \cdots$$

If we now let $x - x_0 = h$, we see that

$$y(x_0 + h) = y(x_0) + y'(x_0)h + y''(x_0)\frac{h^2}{2!} + y^{(3)}(x_0)\frac{h^3}{3!} + \cdots$$

To interpret this form of Taylor series we refer to Figure 18.5.

If y and its derivatives are known when $x = x_0$, then the Taylor series can be used to find y at a nearby point, where $x = x_0 + h$. This form of Taylor series is used in numerical methods of solving differential equations.

Exercises 18.6

1   Use the Maclaurin series for $\sin x$ to write down the Maclaurin series for $\sin 5x$.

2   Use the Maclaurin series for $\cos x$ to write down the Maclaurin series for $\cos 3x$.

3   Use the Maclaurin series for e^x to write down the Maclaurin series for $\dfrac{1}{e^x}$.

4   Find the Taylor series for $y(x) = \sqrt{x}$ about $x = 1$.

5 (a) Find the Maclaurin series for
$y(x) = x^2 + \sin x$.

(b) Deduce the Maclaurin series for
$y(x) = x^n + \sin x$ for any positive integer
n.

6 (a) Obtain the Maclaurin series for
$y(x) = xe^x$.

(b) State the range of values of x for which
$y(x)$ equals its Maclaurin series.

7 Find the Taylor series for $y(x) = x + e^x$ about
$x = 1$.

8 Find the Maclaurin series for $y(x) = \ln(1 + x)$.

Solutions

1 $5x - \dfrac{(5x)^3}{3!} + \dfrac{(5x)^5}{5!} - \cdots$

2 $1 - \dfrac{(3x)^2}{2!} + \dfrac{(3x)^4}{4!} - \dfrac{(3x)^6}{6!} + \cdots$

3 $1 - x + \dfrac{x^2}{2!} - \dfrac{x^3}{3!} + \dfrac{x^4}{4!} - \cdots$

4 $1 + \dfrac{x-1}{2} - \dfrac{(x-1)^2}{8} + \dfrac{(x-1)^3}{16}$
$- \dfrac{5(x-1)^4}{128} + \cdots$

5 (a) $x + x^2 - \dfrac{x^3}{3!} + \dfrac{x^5}{5!} - \dfrac{x^7}{7!} + \cdots$

(b) $x^n + x - \dfrac{x^3}{3!} + \dfrac{x^5}{5!} - \dfrac{x^7}{7!} + \cdots$

6 (a) $x + x^2 + \dfrac{x^3}{2!} + \dfrac{x^4}{3!} + \dfrac{x^5}{4!} + \cdots$

(b) For all values of x

7 $p(x) = (1 + e)x$
$+ e\left\{ \dfrac{(x-1)^2}{2!} + \dfrac{(x-1)^3}{3!} + \dfrac{(x-1)^4}{4!} + \cdots \right\}$

8 $x - \dfrac{x^2}{2} + \dfrac{x^3}{3} - \dfrac{x^4}{4} + \dfrac{x^5}{5} - \cdots$

Review exercises 18

1 A function, $f(t)$, and its first and second
derivatives are evaluated at $t = 3$. Find the
second-order Taylor polynomial generated by f
about $t = 3$.

$$f(3) = 2 \qquad f'(3) = -1 \qquad f''(3) = 1$$

2 A function, $s(t)$, and its first derivative are
evaluated at $t = 3$; $s(3) = 4$, $s'(3) = -1$.

(a) Find the first-order Taylor polynomial
generated by s at $t = 3$.

(b) Estimate $s(2.9)$ and $s(3.2)$.

(c) If additionally we know $s''(3) = 1$, use a
second-order Taylor polynomial to estimate
$s(2.9)$ and $s(3.2)$.

3 Obtain a linear approximation to
$y(t) = at^4 + bt^3 + ct^2 + dt + e$ around $t = 1$.

4 Find a quadratic approximation to $y = x^3$ near
$x = 2$.

5 Find linear approximations to

(a) $z(t) = e^t$ near $t = 1$

(b) $w(t) = \sin 3t$ near $t = 1$

(c) $v(t) = e^t + \sin 3t$ near $t = 1$

6 The function, $y(x)$, satisfies the equation

$$y'' + xy' - 3y = x^2 + 1$$
$$y(0) = 1 \qquad y'(0) = 2$$

(a) Evaluate $y''(0)$.

(b) Differentiate the equation.

(c) Evaluate $y^{(3)}(0)$.

(d) Write down a cubic approximation for
$y(x)$.

(e) Estimate $y(0.5)$.

7 Given that y satisfies the equation

$$\frac{dy}{dx} + \frac{y^2}{2} = xy \qquad y(1) = 2$$

(a) Calculate $y'(1)$, $y''(1)$ and $y^{(3)}(1)$.

(b) State the third-order Taylor polynomial
generated by $y(x)$ about $x = 1$.

(c) Estimate $y(1.25)$.

8 (a) Find the third-order Taylor polynomial generated by $y(x) = e^{-x}$ about $x = 1$.

(b) State the third-order error term.

(c) Find an upper bound for the error term given $|x| < 1$.

9 (a) Find a quadratic approximation to $y(x) = \sin^2 x$ about $x = 0$.

(b) State the remainder term of order 2.

(c) State an upper bound for the remainder term given $|x| < 0.5$.

10 (a) Find a cubic approximation to $y(x) = x \cos x$ about $x = 0$.

(b) State the error term of order 3.

(c) State an upper bound for the error term given $|x| < 0.25$.

11 Given that $y(x) = x^2$,

(a) Calculate the Taylor series of $y(x)$ about $x = a$.

(b) Calculate the Maclaurin series of $y(x)$.

12 Find the Maclaurin expansion of $y(x) = \ln(2 + x)$ up to and including the term in x^4.

13 By considering the Maclaurin expansions of $\sin(kx)$ and $\cos(kx)$, k constant, evaluate if possible

(a) $\lim\limits_{x \to 0} \dfrac{\sin(kx)}{x}$

(b) $\lim\limits_{x \to 0} \dfrac{\cos(kx) - 1}{x}$

(c) $\lim\limits_{x \to 0} \dfrac{\sin(kx)}{1 - \cos(kx)}$

Solutions

1 $\dfrac{t^2}{2} - 4t + \dfrac{19}{2}$

2 (a) $-t + 7$ (b) $4.1, 3.8$ (c) $4.105, 3.82$

3 $(4a + 3b + 2c + d)t - 3a - 2b - c + e$

4 $6x^2 - 12x + 8$

5 (a) et
(b) $-2.97t + 3.11$
(c) $-0.25t + 3.11$

6 (a) 4
(b) $y''' + xy'' - 2y' = 2x$
(c) 4
(d) $1 + 2x + 2x^2 + \frac{2}{3}x^3$
(e) 2.5833

7 (a) $0, 2, -2$
(b) $-\dfrac{x^3}{3} + 2x^2 - 3x + \dfrac{10}{3}$
(c) 2.0573

8 (a) $e^{-1}\left\{ -\dfrac{x^3}{6} + x^2 - \dfrac{5x}{2} + \dfrac{8}{3} \right\}$
(b) $\dfrac{e^{-c}(x-1)^4}{4!}$ where c lies between 1 and x
(c) $\dfrac{2e}{3}$

9 (a) x^2
(b) $-\dfrac{2 \sin(2c)x^3}{3}$ for c between 0 and x
(c) 0.07

10 (a) $x - \dfrac{x^3}{2!}$
(b) $(4 \sin c + c \cos c)\dfrac{x^4}{4!}$ for c between 0 and x
(c) 2×10^{-4}

11 (a) x^2 (b) x^2

12 $\ln 2 + \dfrac{x}{2} - \dfrac{x^2}{8} + \dfrac{x^3}{24} - \dfrac{x^4}{64} + \cdots$

13 (a) k (b) 0 (c) not defined

19 Ordinary differential equations I

Contents

19.1	Introduction	522
19.2	Basic definitions	522
19.3	First order equations: simple equations and separation of variables	528
19.4	First order linear equations: use of an integrating factor	535
19.5	Second order linear equations	547
	Review exercises	568

19.1 Introduction

The solution of problems concerning the motion of objects, the flow of charged particles, heat transport, etc., often involves discussion of relations of the form

$$\frac{d^2x}{dt^2} + 6\frac{dx}{dt} + 2x = 3t \qquad \text{or} \qquad \frac{dq}{dt} + 8q = \sin t$$

In the first equation, x might represent distance. For this case $\dfrac{dx}{dt}$ is the rate of change of distance with respect to time t, that is speed, and $\dfrac{d^2x}{dt^2}$ represents acceleration. In the second equation, q might be charge and $\dfrac{dq}{dt}$ the rate of flow of charge, that is current. These are examples of **differential equations**, so called because they are equations involving the derivatives of various quantities. Such equations arise out of situations in which change is occurring. To solve such a differential equation means to find the function $x(t)$ or $q(t)$ when we are given the differential equation. Solutions to these equations may be **analytical** in that we can write down an answer in terms of common elementary functions such as e^t, $\sin t$ and so on. Alternatively, the problem may be so difficult that only **numerical methods** are available, which produce approximate solutions.

In engineering, differential equations are most commonly used to model **dynamic systems**. These are systems which change with time. Examples include an electronic circuit with time-dependent currents and voltages, a chemical production line in which pressures, tank levels, flow rates, etc., vary with time, and a semiconductor device in which hole and electron densities change with time.

19.2 Basic definitions

In order to solve a differential equation it is important to identify certain features. Recall from Chapter 2 that in a function such as $y = x^2 + 3x$ we say x is the independent variable and y is the dependent variable since the value of y depends upon the choice we have made for x.

In a differential equation such as

$$\frac{dy}{dx} - 2y = 3x^2$$

x is the independent variable, and y is the dependent variable.

Similarly, for the differential equation

$$\frac{dx}{dt} + 7x = e^t$$

t is the independent variable and x is the dependent variable.

We see that the variable being differentiated is the dependent variable.

Before classifying differential equations, we will derive one.

Figure 19.1
An *RC* charging circuit.

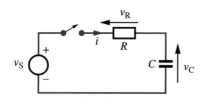

| Example 19.1 | **An *RC* charging circuit** |

Consider the *RC* circuit of Figure 19.1. Suppose we wish to derive a differential equation which models the circuit so that we can determine the voltage across the capacitor at any time, t. Clearly there are two different cases corresponding to the switch being open and the switch being closed. We will concentrate on the latter and for convenience assume that the switch is closed at $t = 0$. From Kirchhoff's voltage law we have

$$v_S = v_R + v_C \qquad \text{that is} \qquad v_R = v_S - v_C$$

where v_S is the voltage of the supply, v_C is the voltage across the capacitor, and v_R is the voltage across the resistor. Using Ohm's law for the resistor then gives

$$i = \frac{v_S - v_C}{R}$$

where i is the current flowing in the circuit after the switch is closed. For the capacitor

$$i = C\frac{dv_C}{dt}$$

Combining these equations gives

$$C\frac{dv_C}{dt} = \frac{v_S - v_C}{R}$$

and hence

$$RC\frac{dv_C}{dt} + v_C = v_S$$

This is the differential equation which models the variation in voltage across the capacitor with time. Here v_C is the dependent variable and t is the independent variable, and when we are required to solve this differential equation we must attempt to find v_C as a function of t.

Differential equations which have features in common are often grouped together and given certain classifications and it is usually the case that appropriate methods of solution depend upon the classifications. Some important terminology is now given.

19.2.1 Order

The **order** of a differential equation is the order of its highest derivative.

Example 19.2 State the order of

(a) $\dfrac{d^2 y}{dx^2} + \dfrac{dy}{dx} = x$ (b) $\dfrac{dx}{dt} = (xt)^5$

Solution (a) The highest derivative is $\dfrac{d^2 y}{dx^2}$, a second derivative. The order is therefore two.

(b) The only derivative appearing is $\dfrac{dx}{dt}$, a first derivative. The order is therefore one.

19.2.2 Linearity

Recall that in a differential equation such as $\dfrac{dy}{dx} + 3y = x^2$, the independent variable is x and the dependent variable is y.

A differential equation is said to be **linear** if:

(1) the dependent variable and its derivatives occur to the first power only,

(2) there are no products involving the dependent variable with its derivatives, and

(3) there are no non-linear functions of the dependent variable such as sine, exponential, etc.

If an equation is not linear, then it is said to be **non-linear**. Note from (2) that a product of terms involving the dependent variable such as $y\dfrac{dy}{dx}$ is non-linear. Note from (3) that the existence of terms such as y^2, $\sin y$ and e^y causes an equation to be non-linear.

Note also that the conditions for linearity are conditions on the dependent variable. The linearity of a differential equation is not determined or affected by the presence of non-linear terms involving the independent variable.

The distinction between a linear and a non-linear differential equation is important because the methods of solution depend upon whether an equation is linear or non-linear. Furthermore, it is usually the case that a linear differential equation is easier to solve.

Example 19.3 Decide whether or not the following equations are linear.

(a) $\sin x \dfrac{dy}{dx} + y = x$

(b) $\dfrac{dx}{dt} + x = t^3$

(c) $\dfrac{d^2 y}{dx^2} + y^2 = 0$

(d) $\dfrac{dy}{dx} + \sin y = 0$

Solution   In (a), (c) and (d) the dependent variable is y, and the independent variable is x. In (b) the dependent variable is x and the independent variable is t.

(a) This equation is linear.

(b) This equation is linear. It does not matter that the term in t, the independent variable, is raised to the power 3.

(c) This equation is non-linear, the non-linearity arising through the term y^2.

(d) This equation is non-linear, the non-linearity arising through the term $\sin y$.

19.2.3 The solution of a differential equation

The **solution** of a differential equation is a relationship between the dependent and independent variables such that the differential equation is satisfied for all values of the independent variable over a specified domain.

Example 19.4   Verify that $y = e^x$ is a solution of the differential equation

$$\frac{dy}{dx} = y$$

Solution   If $y = e^x$ then $\dfrac{dy}{dx} = e^x$. For all values of x, we see that $\dfrac{dy}{dx} = y$ and so $y = e^x$ is a solution. Note also that this equation is first order and linear.

There are frequently many different functions which satisfy a differential equation; that is, there are many solutions. The **general solution** embraces all of these and all possible solutions can be obtained from it.

Example 19.5   Verify that $y = C\,e^x$ is a solution of $\dfrac{dy}{dx} = y$, where C is any constant.

Solution   If $y = C\,e^x$, then $\dfrac{dy}{dx} = C\,e^x$. Therefore, for all values of x, $\dfrac{dy}{dx} = y$ and the equation is satisfied for any constant C; C is called an **arbitrary constant** and by varying it, all possible solutions can be obtained. For example, by choosing C to be 1, we obtain the solution of the previous example. In fact, $y = C\,e^x$ is the general solution of $\dfrac{dy}{dx} = y$.

More generally, to determine C we require more information given in the form of a **condition**. For example, if we are told that at $x = 0$, $y = 4$ then from $y = C\,e^x$ we have

$$4 = C\,e^0 = C$$

so that $C = 4$. Therefore $y = 4\,e^x$ is the solution of the differential equation which additionally satisfies the condition $y(0) = 4$. This is called a **particular solution**. In general, application of conditions to the general solution yields the particular solution. To obtain a particular solution, the number of given independent conditions must be the same as the number of constants.

Consider the following example.

Example 19.6   Consider the second-order differential equation

$$\frac{d^2y}{dx^2} + y = 0$$

The general solution of this equation can be shown to be

$$y = A \cos x + B \sin x$$

where A and B are arbitrary constants.

Find the particular solution which satisfies the conditions

(a) when $x = 0$, then $y = 0$, and

(b) when $x = \dfrac{3\pi}{2}$, then $y = 1$.

Solution   We note that because the general solution has two arbitrary constants, A and B, then two conditions are necessary to obtain a particular solution. Applying the first condition to the general solution gives

$$0 = A \cos 0 + B \sin 0$$
$$= A$$

Therefore $A = 0$, and the solution reduces to $y = B \sin x$. Applying the second condition we find

$$1 = B \sin \frac{3\pi}{2}$$

from which

$$1 = B(-1)$$
$$B = -1$$

The particular solution becomes $y = -\sin x$.

Sometimes the conditions involve derivatives.

Example 19.7 For the differential equation of Example 19.6 find the particular solution which satisfies the conditions

(a) when $x = 0$, then $y = 0$, and

(b) when $x = 0$, then $\dfrac{dy}{dx} = 5$.

Solution Application of the first condition to the general solution $y = A \cos x + B \sin x$ gives

$$0 = A \cos 0 + B \sin 0$$
$$= A$$

Therefore $A = 0$ and the solution becomes $y = B \sin x$. To apply the second condition we must differentiate y.

$$\frac{dy}{dx} = B \cos x$$

Then applying the second condition we get

$$5 = B \cos 0$$
$$= B$$

so that $B = 5$. Finally the required particular solution is $y = 5 \sin x$.

In this example both conditions have been specified at $x = 0$, and are often referred to as **initial conditions**.

Exercises 19.2

1 Verify that $y = 3 \sin 2x$ is a solution of
$$\frac{d^2 y}{dx^2} + 4y = 0.$$

2 Verify that $3 e^x$, $Ax e^x$, $Ax e^x + B e^x$, where A, B are constants, all satisfy the differential equation
$$\frac{d^2 y}{dx^2} - 2\frac{dy}{dx} + y = 0$$

3 Verify that $x = t^2 + A \ln t + B$ is a solution of
$$t\frac{d^2 x}{dt^2} + \frac{dx}{dt} = 4t$$

4 Verify that $y = A \cos x + B \sin x$ satisfies the differential equation
$$\frac{d^2 y}{dx^2} + y = 0$$
Verify also that $y = A \cos x$ and $y = B \sin x$ each individually satisfy the equation.

5 If $y = A e^{2x}$ is the general solution of
$$\frac{dy}{dx} = 2y,$$ find the particular solution satisfying $y(0) = 3$. What is the particular solution satisfying $\dfrac{dy}{dx} = 2$ when $x = 0$?

6 Identify the dependent and independent variables of the following differential equations. Give the order of the equations and state which are linear.

(a) $\dfrac{dy}{dx} + 9y = 0$

(b) $\left(\dfrac{dy}{dx}\right)\left(\dfrac{d^2y}{dx^2}\right) + 3\dfrac{dy}{dx} = 0$

(c) $\dfrac{d^3x}{dt^3} + 5\dfrac{dx}{dt} = \sin x$

7 Show that $x(t) = 7\cos 3t - 2\sin 2t$ is a solution of:

$$\dfrac{d^2x}{dt^2} + 2x = -49\cos 3t + 4\sin 2t$$

8 The general solution of the equation

$$\dfrac{d^2x}{dt^2} - 3\dfrac{dx}{dt} + 2x = 0 \text{ is given by}$$

$$x = A\,e^t + B\,e^{2t}$$

Find the particular solution which satisfies

$x = 3$ and $\dfrac{dx}{dt} = 5$ when $t = 0$.

9 The general solution of $\dfrac{d^2y}{dx^2} - 2\dfrac{dy}{dx} + y = 0$ is
$y = Ax\,e^x + B\,e^x$. Find the particular solution satisfying $y(0) = 0$, $\dfrac{dy}{dx}(0) = 1$.

10 The general solution of $\dfrac{d^2x}{dt^2} = -\omega^2 x$ is
$x = A\,e^{j\omega t} + B\,e^{-j\omega t}$, where $j^2 = -1$. Verify that this is indeed a solution. What is the particular solution satisfying $x(0) = 0$,
$\dfrac{dx}{dt}(0) = 1$? Express the general solution and the particular solution in terms of trigonometric functions.

Solutions

5 $y(x) = 3\,e^{2x}$, $y(x) = e^{2x}$

6 (a) y is the dependent variable; x is the independent variable; first order, linear

(b) y is the dependent variable; x is the independent variable; second order, non-linear

(c) x is the dependent variable; t is the

independent variable; third order, non-linear.

8 $x = e^t + 2\,e^{2t}$

9 $y = x\,e^x$

10 particular solution: $\sin \omega t/\omega$
general solution:
$(A + B)\cos \omega t + (A - B)j\sin \omega t$

19.3 First order equations: simple equations and separation of variables

19.3.1 Simple equations

The simplest first-order equations to deal with are those of the form

$$\dfrac{dy}{dx} = f(x)$$

where the r.h.s. is a function of the independent variable only. No special treatment is necessary and direct integration yields y as a function of x, that is

$$y = \int f(x)\,dx$$

Example 19.8 Find the general solution of $\dfrac{dy}{dx} = 3\cos 2x$.

Solution Given that $\dfrac{dy}{dx} = 3\cos 2x$, then $y = \int 3\cos 2x\,dx = \frac{3}{2}\sin 2x + C$. This is the required general solution.

$$\text{If } \frac{dy}{dx} = f(x) \text{ then } y = \int f(x)\,dx.$$

19.3.2 Separation of variables

When the function f on the r.h.s. of the equation depends upon both independent and dependent variables this approach is not possible. However, first-order equations which can be written in the form

$$\frac{dy}{dx} = f(x)g(y) \tag{19.1}$$

form an important class known as **separable equations**. For example,

$$\frac{dy}{dx} = 3x^2 e^{-4y}$$

is a separable equation for which

$$f(x) = 3x^2 \quad \text{and} \quad g(y) = e^{-4y}$$

To obtain a solution we first divide both sides of Equation (19.1) by $g(y)$ to give

$$\frac{1}{g(y)}\frac{dy}{dx} = f(x)$$

Integrating both sides with respect to x yields

$$\int \frac{1}{g(y)}\frac{dy}{dx}\,dx = \int \frac{1}{g(y)}\,dy = \int f(x)\,dx$$

The equation is then said to be separated. If the last two integrals can be found, we obtain a relationship between y and x, although it is not always possible to write y explicitly in terms of x as the following examples will show.

Separation of variables:

The solution of $\dfrac{dy}{dx} = f(x)g(y)$ is found from

$$\int \frac{1}{g(y)}\,dy = \int f(x)\,dx$$

Example 19.9 Solve $\dfrac{dy}{dx} = \dfrac{e^{-x}}{y}$.

Solution   Here $f(x) = e^{-x}$ and $g(y) = \dfrac{1}{y}$. Multiplication through by y yields

$$y\frac{dy}{dx} = e^{-x}$$

Integration of both sides with respect to x gives

$$\int y\,dy = \int e^{-x}\,dx$$

so that

$$\frac{y^2}{2} = -e^{-x} + C$$

Note that the constants arising from the two integrals have been combined to give a single constant, C. Finally we can rearrange this expression to give y in terms of x:

$$y^2 = -2\,e^{-x} + 2C$$

that is,

$$y = \pm\sqrt{D - 2\,e^{-x}}$$

where $D = 2C$.

It is important to stress that the constant of integration must be inserted at the stage at which the integration is actually carried out, and not simply added to the answer at the end.

Example 19.10   Solve $\dfrac{dy}{dx} = 3x^2\,e^{-y}$ subject to $y(0) = 1$.

Solution   Here $g(y) = e^{-y}$ and $f(x) = 3x^2$. Separating the variables and integrating we find

$$\int e^y\,dy = \int 3x^2\,dx$$

so that $e^y = x^3 + C$. Imposing the initial condition $y(0) = 1$ we find

$$e^1 = (0)^3 + C$$

so that $C = e$. Therefore,

$$e^y = x^3 + e$$

Note that since the exponential function is always positive, the solution will be valid only for $x^3 + e > 0$. Taking natural logarithms gives the particular solution explicitly:

$$y = \ln(x^3 + e)$$

Example 19.11   Solve

$$\frac{\mathrm{d}x}{\mathrm{d}t} = \frac{t^2 + 1}{x^2 + 1}$$

Solution   Separating the variables and integrating we find

$$\int x^2 + 1 \, \mathrm{d}x = \int t^2 + 1 \, \mathrm{d}t$$

Therefore,

$$\frac{x^3}{3} + x = \frac{t^3}{3} + t + C$$

which is the general solution. Here we note that x has not been obtained explicitly in terms of t, although we have found a relationship between x and t which satisfies the differential equation. To obtain the value of x at any given t it would be necessary to solve the cubic equation.

Sometimes, equations which are not immediately separable can be reduced to separable form by an appropriate substitution as the following example shows.

Example 19.12   By means of the substitution $z = \dfrac{y}{x}$, solve the equation

$$\frac{\mathrm{d}y}{\mathrm{d}x} = \frac{y^2}{x^2} + \frac{y}{x} + 1 \tag{19.2}$$

Solution   If $z = \dfrac{y}{x}$ then $y = zx$. Because the solution, y, is a function of x the variable z depends upon x also. The product rule gives $\dfrac{\mathrm{d}y}{\mathrm{d}x} = z + x\dfrac{\mathrm{d}z}{\mathrm{d}x}$, so that Equation (19.2) becomes

$$z + x\frac{\mathrm{d}z}{\mathrm{d}x} = z^2 + z + 1$$

that is,

$$x\frac{\mathrm{d}z}{\mathrm{d}x} = z^2 + 1$$

This new equation has independent variable x and dependent variable z, and is separable. We find

$$\int \frac{\mathrm{d}z}{z^2 + 1} = \int \frac{\mathrm{d}x}{x}$$

so that $\tan^{-1} z = \ln|x| + C$. Writing $C = \ln|D|$ we have

$$\tan^{-1} z = \ln|x| + \ln|D| = \ln|Dx|$$

so that $z = \tan(\ln|Dx|)$. Returning to the original variables we see that the general solution is

$$y = zx = x\tan(\ln|Dx|)$$

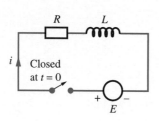

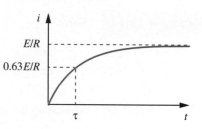

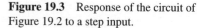

Figure 19.2 A step voltage is applied to the circuit at $t = 0$.

Figure 19.3 Response of the circuit of Figure 19.2 to a step input.

Example 19.13   *RL circuit with step input*

Write down the differential equation governing the current, i, flowing in the RL circuit shown in Figure 19.2 when a step voltage of magnitude E is applied to the circuit at $t = 0$. Solve this differential equation to obtain $i(t)$. Assume that when $t = 0$, $i = 0$.

Solution   Applying Kirchhoff's voltage law and Ohm's law to the circuit we find

$$iR + L\frac{di}{dt} = E \qquad \text{for} \qquad t \geqslant 0$$

that is,

$$L\frac{di}{dt} = E - iR$$

so that

$$\int \frac{L}{E - iR}\, di = \int dt$$

Note in particular that in this equation L, E and R are constants and so the variables i and t have been separated. If the applied voltage, E, varied with time this would not have been the case since the l.h.s. would contain terms dependent upon t. Integrating, we find

$$\int \frac{L}{E - iR}\, di = \frac{-L}{R} \int \frac{-R}{E - iR}\, di = -\frac{L}{R}\ln(E - iR) = t + C$$

To find the constant of integration, C, a condition is required. The physical condition $i = 0$ at $t = 0$ provides this. Applying $i = 0$ when $t = 0$ we find

$$C = -\frac{L}{R}\ln E$$

Substituting this value gives

$$-\frac{L}{R}\ln(E - iR) = t - \frac{L}{R}\ln E$$

Thus,

$$\frac{L}{R}[\ln E - \ln(E - iR)] = t$$

so that

$$\frac{L}{R} \ln \frac{E}{E - iR} = t$$

Then

$$\ln \frac{E}{E - iR} = \frac{Rt}{L}$$

hence

$$\frac{E}{E - iR} = e^{Rt/L}$$

Rearranging to obtain E gives

$$E = (E - iR)\, e^{Rt/L}$$

hence

$$E = Ee^{Rt/L} - i R e^{Rt/L}$$

and so

$$i R e^{Rt/L} = E(e^{Rt/L} - 1)$$

so

$$i R = E(1 - e^{-Rt/L})$$

Finally we have

$$i = \frac{E}{R}(1 - e^{-Rt/L})$$

The graph of this current against time is shown in Figure 19.3. We note that as $t \to \infty$, $i \to \dfrac{E}{R}$. The rate at which the current increases towards its final value depends upon the values of the components R and L. It is common to define a **time constant**, τ, for the circuit. In this case $\tau = \dfrac{L}{R}$ and the equation for the current can be written as

$$i = \frac{E}{R}(1 - e^{-t/\tau})$$

The smaller the value of τ, the more rapidly the current reaches its final value. It is possible to estimate a value of τ from a laboratory test curve by noting that after one time constant, that is $t = \tau$, i has reached $1 - e^{-1} \approx 0.63$ of its final value.

Exercises 19.3

1 Find the general solution of the following equations:

(a) $\dfrac{dy}{dx} = 3$

(b) $\dfrac{dx}{dt} = 5$

(c) $\dfrac{dy}{dx} = 2x$

(d) $\dfrac{dy}{dt} = 6t$

(e) $\dfrac{dy}{dx} = 8x^2$

(f) $\dfrac{dx}{dt} = 3t^3$

(g) $\dfrac{dy}{dx} = \dfrac{x^2}{y}$

(h) $\dfrac{dx}{dt} = \dfrac{t^3}{x^2}$

(i) $\dfrac{dx}{dt} = \dfrac{e^t}{x}$

(j) $\dfrac{dy}{dx} = \dfrac{e^{-2x}}{y^2}$

(k) $\dfrac{dy}{dx} = \dfrac{6 \sin x}{y}$

(l) $\dfrac{dx}{dt} = \dfrac{9 \cos 4t}{x^2}$

(m) $\dfrac{dx}{dt} = \dfrac{3 \cos 2t + 8 \sin 4t}{x^2 + x}$

2 Find the particular solution of the following equations:

(a) $\dfrac{dx}{dt} = 3t, \qquad x(0) = 1$

(b) $\dfrac{dy}{dx} = \dfrac{6x^2}{y}, \qquad y(0) = 1$

(c) $\dfrac{dy}{dt} = \dfrac{3 \sin t}{y}, \qquad y(0) = 2$

(d) $\dfrac{dy}{dx} = \dfrac{e^{-x}}{y}, \qquad y(0) = 3$

(e) $\dfrac{dx}{dt} = \dfrac{4 \sin t + 6 \cos 2t}{x}, \qquad x(0) = 2$

3 Find the general solution of $\dfrac{dx}{dt} = \ln t$. Find the particular solution satisfying $x(1) = 1$.

4 Find the general solutions of the following equations:

(a) $\dfrac{dy}{dx} = kx, \qquad k$ constant

(b) $\dfrac{dy}{dx} = -ky, \qquad k$ constant

(c) $\dfrac{dy}{dx} = y^2$

(d) $y\dfrac{dy}{dx} = \sin x$

(e) $y\dfrac{dy}{dx} = x + 2$

(f) $x^2\dfrac{dy}{dx} = 2y^2 + yx$

(g) $\dfrac{dx}{dt} = \dfrac{t^4}{x^5}$

5 Find the general solutions of the following equations:

(a) $\dfrac{dx}{dt} = xt$

(b) $\dfrac{dy}{dx} = \dfrac{x}{y}$

(c) $t\dfrac{dx}{dt} = \tan x$

(d) $\dfrac{dx}{dt} = \dfrac{x^2 - 1}{t}$

6 Find the general solution of the equation $\dfrac{dx}{dt} = t(x - 2)$. Find the particular solution which satisfies $x(0) = 5$.

Solutions

1 (a) $y = 3x + c$

(b) $x = 5t + c$

(c) $y = x^2 + c$

(d) $y = 3t^2 + c$

(e) $y = \frac{8}{3}x^3 + c$

(f) $x = \frac{3}{4}t^4 + c$

(g) $\dfrac{y^2}{2} = \dfrac{x^3}{3} + c$

(h) $\dfrac{x^3}{3} = \dfrac{t^4}{4} + c$

(i) $\dfrac{x^2}{2} = e^t + c$

(j) $\dfrac{y^3}{3} = c - \dfrac{e^{-2x}}{2}$

(k) $\dfrac{y^2}{2} = c - 6\cos x$

(l) $\dfrac{x^3}{3} = \dfrac{9}{4}\sin 4t + c$

(m) $\dfrac{x^3}{3} + \dfrac{x^2}{2} = \dfrac{3}{2}\sin 2t - 2\cos 4t + c$

2 (a) $x = \frac{3}{2}t^2 + 1$

(b) $y^2 = 4x^3 + 1$

(c) $\dfrac{y^2}{2} = 5 - 3\cos t$

(d) $y^2 = 11 - 2e^{-x}$

(e) $\dfrac{x^2}{2} = 3\sin 2t - 4\cos t + 6$

3 $t\ln|t| - t + c,\ t\ln|t| - t + 2$

4 (a) $\dfrac{kx^2}{2} + c$

(b) Ae^{-kx}

(c) $-\dfrac{1}{x+c}$

(d) $y^2 = 2(c - \cos x)$

(e) $y^2 = x^2 + 4x + c$

(f) $\dfrac{x}{A - 2\ln|x|}$

(g) $\dfrac{x^6}{6} = \dfrac{t^5}{5} + c$

5 (a) $x = Ae^{t^2/2}$

(b) $y^2 = x^2 + c$

(c) $x = \sin^{-1}(kt)$

(d) $x = \dfrac{1 + At^2}{1 - At^2}$

6 $2 + Ae^{t^2/2},\ 2 + 3e^{t^2/2}$

19.4   First order linear equations: use of an integrating factor

In this section we develop a method for solving first-order linear differential equations.

19.4.1   Exact equations

Consider the differential equation

$$\frac{dy}{dx} = 3x^2$$

This can be solved very easily by simply integrating both sides to give

$$y = \int 3x^2 dx$$
$$= x^3 + c$$

where c is the constant of integration. An equation which can be solved by integrating both sides is said to be an **exact** equation. A more complicated example which, nevertheless, can be solved in the same way is

$$\frac{d}{dx}(xy) = 3x^2$$

Integrating both sides we find

$$xy = \int 3x^2 dx$$
$$= x^3 + c$$

and dividing through by x gives the general solution

$$y = x^2 + \frac{c}{x}$$

The differential equation we have just solved is an exact equation.

Example 19.14 Solve the equation

$$\frac{d}{dx}\left(x^2 y\right) = \cos x$$

Solution Integrating both sides we find

$$x^2 y = \int \cos x \, dx$$

$$= \sin x + c$$

so that

$$y = \frac{\sin x}{x^2} + \frac{c}{x^2}$$

Consider again the differential equation of the previous example:

$$\frac{d}{dx}(x^2 y) = \cos x$$

Using the product rule for differentiation we can expand the l.h.s. as follows:

$$\frac{d}{dx}(x^2 y) = x^2 \frac{dy}{dx} + 2xy$$

Doing this, the differential equation can be written in the equivalent form

$$x^2 \frac{dy}{dx} + 2xy = \cos x$$

Suppose we had posed the question in this form. A method of solving this equation would be to recognize that the equation is exact and that the l.h.s. could be written as $\frac{d}{dx}(x^2 y)$.

It is easy to recognize an exact equation because it will always take the form

$$\mu \frac{dy}{dx} + \mu' y = f(x)$$

where μ is some function of x. That is, the coefficient of y is the derivative of the coefficient of $\frac{dy}{dx}$. When this is the case the l.h.s. can be written $\frac{d}{dx}(\mu y)$.

Example 19.15 The following equations are exact. Note in each case that the coefficient of y is the derivative of the coefficient of $\dfrac{dy}{dx}$. Solve them.

(a) $x^3\dfrac{dy}{dx} + 3x^2y = e^{2x}$

(b) $\cos x\dfrac{dy}{dx} - (\sin x)y = 1$

Solution (a) The equation can be written

$$\frac{d}{dx}(x^3y) = e^{2x}$$

and so, upon integrating,

$$x^3y = \int e^{2x}dx$$

$$= \frac{e^{2x}}{2} + c$$

so that

$$y = \frac{e^{2x}}{2x^3} + \frac{c}{x^3}$$

(b) The equation can be written

$$\frac{d}{dx}((\cos x)\,y) = 1$$

and so, upon integrating,

$$(\cos x)\,y = x + c$$

so that

$$y = \frac{x}{\cos x} + \frac{c}{\cos x}$$

Exercises 19.4.1

1 Each of the following equations is exact. Solve them.

(a) $x^2\dfrac{dy}{dx} + 2xy = x^3$

(b) $\dfrac{1}{x^2}\dfrac{dy}{dx} - \dfrac{2}{x^3}y = 5x^3$

(c) $e^x\left(y + \dfrac{dy}{dx}\right) = \cos x$

Solutions

1 (a) $y = \dfrac{x^2}{4} + \dfrac{C}{x^2}$.

(c) $y = e^{-x}\sin x + C e^{-x}$

(b) $y = \dfrac{5x^6}{4} + Cx^2$.

19.4.2 A preliminary result involving separation of variables

Consider the following differential equation for the dependent variable μ:

$$\frac{d\mu}{dx} = \mu P \tag{19.3}$$

where P is some function of x only. Using separation of variables we have

$$\frac{1}{\mu}\frac{d\mu}{dx} = P$$

and integrating both sides

$$\int \frac{1}{\mu}d\mu = \int P\,dx$$

$$\ln\mu = \int P\,dx$$

$$\mu = e^{\int P\,dx}$$

In this development the constant of integration has been omitted. The reason for this will be apparent in what follows. So the solution of Equation (19.3), for any function $P(x)$, is $\mu = e^{\int P\,dx}$.

For example, if $P(x) = \dfrac{1}{x}$, then Equation (19.3) is $\dfrac{d\mu}{dx} = \dfrac{\mu}{x}$ and its solution is $\mu = e^{\int(1/x)dx} = e^{\ln x} = x$.

19.4.3 First-order linear equations

First-order linear differential equations can always be written in the 'standard' form

$$\frac{dy}{dx} + P(x)y = Q(x) \tag{19.4}$$

where P and Q are both functions of the independent variable, x, only. In some cases, either of these may be simply constants.

An example of such an equation is

$$\frac{dy}{dx} + 3xy = 7x^2$$

Comparing this with the standard form in Equation (19.4), note that $P(x) = 3x$ and $Q(x) = 7x^2$. As a second example consider

$$\frac{dy}{dx} - \frac{2y}{x} = 4e^{-x}$$

Here $P(x) = -\dfrac{2}{x}$ (note in particular the minus sign) and $Q(x) = 4\,\mathrm{e}^{-x}$.

Finally, in the equation

$$\frac{dy}{dx} - 5y = \sin x$$

note that $P(x)$ is simply the constant -5.

Variables other than y and x may be used. So, for example,

$$\frac{dx}{dt} + 8t\,x = 3t^2 - 5t$$

is a first-order linear equation in the form of Equation (19.4) but with independent variable t and dependent variable x. Here $P(t) = 8t$ and $Q(t) = 3t^2 - 5t$.

In what follows it will be important that you can distinguish between the dependent and independent variables, and also that you are able to identify the functions P and Q.

Equations such as these arise naturally when modelling many engineering applications. For example, the equation which determines the current flow in a series RL circuit when the applied voltage takes the form of a ramp is given by

$$\frac{di}{dt} + \frac{R}{L}i = \frac{t}{L}$$

This is a first-order linear equation in which $P(t)$ is the constant $\dfrac{R}{L}$ and $Q(t) = \dfrac{t}{L}$. You will learn how to solve such equations in the following section.

19.4.4 The integrating factor method

All first-order linear equations, even when they are not exact, can be made exact by multiplying them through by a function known as an **integrating factor**. As we have seen, the solution then follows by performing an integration. For example, the linear equation

$$\frac{dy}{dx} + \frac{3}{x}y = \frac{\mathrm{e}^{2x}}{x^3}$$

is not exact, but multiplying it through by x^3 produces the differential equation in Example 19.15(a) which is exact.

Consider again a first-order linear equation in standard form:

$$\frac{dy}{dx} + Py = Q \tag{19.5}$$

where P and Q are functions of x only. We are aiming to solve this and express the dependent variable y in terms of the independent variable x. The aim is to multiply (19.5) through by a function μ to make the equation exact. That is, so that the l.h.s. can be written in the form

$$\frac{d}{dx}(\mu y)$$

At this stage the function μ is not known. Multiplying (19.5) through by μ yields

$$\mu\frac{dy}{dx} + \mu Py = \mu Q \tag{19.6}$$

If the l.h.s. is to equal $\dfrac{\mathrm{d}}{\mathrm{d}x}(\mu y)$ then we must have

$$\frac{\mathrm{d}}{\mathrm{d}x}(\mu y) = \mu\frac{\mathrm{d}y}{\mathrm{d}x} + \mu P y$$

Expanding the l.h.s. using the product rule gives

$$\mu\frac{\mathrm{d}y}{\mathrm{d}x} + y\frac{\mathrm{d}\mu}{\mathrm{d}x} = \mu\frac{\mathrm{d}y}{\mathrm{d}x} + \mu P y$$

which simplifies to

$$y\frac{\mathrm{d}\mu}{\mathrm{d}x} = \mu P y$$

and consequently

$$\frac{\mathrm{d}\mu}{\mathrm{d}x} = \mu P$$

Using the result in Section 19.4.2 we see that this equation has solution

$$\mu = e^{\int P\,\mathrm{d}x}$$

The function μ is called an **integrating factor** and is a function of x only. With this choice of μ, the l.h.s. of (19.6) is the same as $\dfrac{\mathrm{d}}{\mathrm{d}x}(\mu y)$ and hence (19.6) can be written

$$\frac{\mathrm{d}}{\mathrm{d}x}(\mu y) = \mu Q$$

This exact equation can be solved by integration to give

$$\mu y = \int \mu Q\,\mathrm{d}x$$

and consequently

$$y = \frac{1}{\mu}\int \mu Q\,\mathrm{d}x$$

In summary:

Given any first-order linear equation in standard form

$$\frac{\mathrm{d}y}{\mathrm{d}x} + Py = Q$$

where P and Q are functions of x, the integrating factor μ is given by

$$\mu = e^{\int P\,\mathrm{d}x}$$

and the solution of the equation is then obtained from

$$\mu y = \int \mu Q\,\mathrm{d}x$$

It is important when working on a particular differential equation to rewrite the standard formulae in the correct form before use. Essentially this means using the correct dependent and independent variables in the equations. For example, if x is the dependent variable and t is the independent variable then the equations are as follows:

The integrating factor for

$$\frac{dx}{dt} + Px = Q$$

where P and Q are functions of t, is given by

$$\mu = e^{\int P\, dt}$$

and the solution of the equation is obtained from

$$\mu x = \int \mu\, Q\, dt$$

These results are illustrated in the examples which follow.

Example 19.16 Solve the differential equation $\dfrac{dy}{dx} + \dfrac{y}{x} = 1$ using the integrating factor method.

Solution Referring to the standard first-order linear equation

$$\frac{dy}{dx} + P(x)y = Q(x)$$

we see that $P(x) = \dfrac{1}{x}$ and $Q(x) = 1$. Using the previous formula for $\mu(x)$, we find

$$\mu(x) = e^{\int (1/x)\, dx}$$
$$= e^{\ln x}$$
$$= x$$

Then from the key point on page 540 with $\mu = x$ and $Q = 1$ we have

$$xy = \int x\, dx = \frac{x^2}{2} + C$$

and finally $y = \dfrac{x}{2} + \dfrac{C}{x}$ is the required general solution.

Example 19.17 **RL circuit with ramp input**

The differential equation governing current flow, $i(t)$, in a series RL circuit, when a voltage $u(t)t$ is applied, is given by

$$iR + L\frac{di}{dt} = t \qquad \text{for} \qquad t \geqslant 0 \qquad i(0) = 0$$

Show that this equation can be written in the form of Equation (19.4). Hence use the integrating factor method to find $i(t)$.

Solution   This equation can be written as

$$\frac{di}{dt} + \frac{R}{L}i = \frac{t}{L} \qquad \text{for} \qquad t \geqslant 0$$

which is a first-order linear equation.

Note in this case that the independent variable is t and the dependent variable is i. In standard form, we have

$$\frac{di}{dt} + P(t)i = Q(t)$$

where $P(t) = \dfrac{R}{L}$ and $Q(t) = \dfrac{t}{L}$. The integrating factor, μ, is given by

$$\mu = e^{\int P(t)\,dt}$$
$$= e^{\int (R/L)\,dt}$$
$$= e^{Rt/L}$$

Then

$$ie^{Rt/L} = \frac{1}{L}\int te^{Rt/L}\,dt$$

$$= \frac{1}{L}\left(\frac{te^{Rt/L}}{R/L} - \int \frac{e^{Rt/L}}{R/L}\,dt\right)$$

$$= \frac{te^{Rt/L}}{R} - \frac{L}{R^2}e^{Rt/L} + K$$

where K is the constant of integration. The general solution is

$$i = \frac{t}{R} - \frac{L}{R^2} + Ke^{-Rt/L}$$

When $t = 0$, $i = 0$. This gives the initial condition required to find K. Applying $i(0) = 0$ gives $K = L/R^2$ so that the particular solution is

$$i = \frac{t}{R} + \frac{L}{R^2}(e^{-Rt/L} - 1)$$

In many engineering applications the terms transient response, steady-state response, zero-input response, and zero-state response arise through the solution of differential equations. These terms are explained in the following example.

Example 19.18   **RC circuit: zero-input response and zero-state response**

The differential equation which is used to model the variation in voltage across a capacitor, $v_C(t)$, in a series RC circuit was derived in Example 19.1:

$$RC\frac{dv_C}{dt} + v_C = v_S(t)$$

where $v_S(t)$ is the applied voltage. Suppose that this applied voltage takes the form $v_S(t) = V\cos\omega t$. Suppose also that when the switch is closed at $t = 0$, the initial voltage across the capacitor is V_0, that is $v_C(0) = V_0$.

(a) Show that this equation can be written in the form of Equation (19.4); that is, it is a first-order linear equation.

(b) Use the integrating factor method to obtain the particular solution of this equation which satisfies the given initial condition.

(c) Obtain the particular solution of the equation subject instead to the initial condition $v_C(0) = 0$. It corresponds to the response of the system when there is no initial energy in the circuit. This solution is referred to as the **zero-state response**.

(d) Obtain the solution of the equation in the case when the supply voltage is identically zero, $v_S(t) = 0$, subject to the given condition $v_C(0) = V_0$. This solution is often referred to as the **zero-input response**, and represents the response of the system when the input is zero.

(e) Show that the solution in (b) can be written as the sum of the zero-state response and the zero-input response.

(f) Identify the transient and steady-state terms in the solution to part (e).

Solution (a) The given differential equation can be rewritten as

$$\frac{dv_C}{dt} + \frac{1}{RC}v_C = \frac{1}{RC}v_S(t)$$

Comparing the form of this equation with (19.4) we see that it is a first-order linear equation, with independent variable t, and dependent variable v_C, in which

$$P(t) = \frac{1}{RC} \text{ and } Q(t) = \frac{1}{RC}v_S(t).$$

(b) The integrating factor is given by

$$\mu = e^{\int (1/RC)dt} = e^{t/(RC)}$$

It follows from the key point on page 541 that

$$e^{t/(RC)}v_C = \frac{V}{RC}\int e^{t/(RC)} \cos \omega t \, dt$$

This integral can be evaluated using integration by parts twice following the technique in Example 14.4. You should verify that

$$\int e^{t/(RC)} \cos \omega t \, dt = \frac{R^2 C^2 e^{t/(RC)}}{R^2 C^2 \omega^2 + 1} \left[\omega \sin \omega t + \frac{\cos \omega t}{RC} \right]$$

$$+ \text{ constant of integration}$$

Then

$$e^{t/(RC)}v_C = \frac{VRCe^{t/(RC)}}{R^2 C^2 \omega^2 + 1} \left[\omega \sin \omega t + \frac{\cos \omega t}{RC} \right] + K$$

from which

$$v_C = \frac{VRC}{R^2C^2\omega^2 + 1}\left[\omega\sin\omega t + \frac{\cos\omega t}{RC}\right] + K\,e^{-t/(RC)}$$

This is the general solution of the differential equation. Applying the initial condition gives us a value for K. When $t = 0$, $v_C = V_0$, so

$$V_0 = \frac{VRC}{R^2C^2\omega^2 + 1}\left[\frac{1}{RC}\right] + K$$

from which

$$K = V_0 - \frac{V}{R^2C^2\omega^2 + 1}$$

Finally,

$$v_C = \frac{VRC}{R^2C^2\omega^2 + 1}\left[\omega\sin\omega t + \frac{\cos\omega t}{RC}\right] + \left(V_0 - \frac{V}{R^2C^2\omega^2 + 1}\right)e^{-t/(RC)}$$

This is the particular solution which satisfies the given initial condition. It tells us the voltage across the capacitor as a function of time t.

(c) To find the particular solution subject to the condition $v_C(0) = 0$ we need only replace V_0 by 0 in the particular solution obtained in part (b). Hence the zero-state response is

$$v_C(t) = \frac{VRC}{R^2C^2\omega^2 + 1}\left[\omega\sin\omega t + \frac{\cos\omega t}{RC}\right] - \frac{V}{R^2C^2\omega^2 + 1}e^{-t/(RC)}$$

(d) In the case of zero input we have $v_S(t) = 0$. In part (b) we solved the equation with $v_S(t) = V\cos\omega t$. Hence, putting $V = 0$ in the solution to part (b) will yield the solution when $v_S(t) = 0$. So,

$$v_C(t) = V_0\,e^{-t/(RC)}$$

Alternatively we can note that when $v_S(t) = 0$ the original equation becomes

$$\frac{dv_C}{dt} + \frac{1}{RC}v_C = 0$$

subject to $v_C(0) = V_0$. This can be solved using separation of variables. So

$$\frac{1}{v_C}\frac{dv_C}{dt} = -\frac{1}{RC}$$

Integration yields

$$\int \frac{1}{v_C}dv_C = -\int \frac{1}{RC}dt$$

$$\ln v_C = -\frac{t}{RC} + k \qquad (k \text{ a constant})$$

$$v_C = e^{-t/(RC)+k}$$

$$= e^k e^{-t/(RC)}$$

$$= A e^{-t/(RC)}$$

where A is the constant e^k. Applying the initial condition $v_C(0) = V_0$ we find $V_0 = A$ and so finally

$$v_C(t) = V_0 e^{-t/(RC)}$$

as before.

(e) Inspection of part (b) shows that it is the sum of the zero-input response and the zero-state response.

$$\underbrace{v_C(t) = V_0 e^{-t/(RC)}}_{\substack{\text{zero-input} \\ \text{response}}} + \underbrace{\frac{V RC}{R^2C^2\omega^2+1}\left[\omega\sin\omega t + \frac{\cos\omega t}{RC}\right] - \frac{V}{R^2C^2\omega^2+1}e^{-t/(RC)}}_{\text{zero-state response}}$$

(f) In this example, the terms involving $e^{-t/(RC)}$ tend to zero as t increases, and are termed **transients**. Once the system has settled down their contribution will not be important. The remaining terms represent the longer term behaviour of the system or the so-called **steady state**.

Hence the transient terms are

$$V_0 e^{-t/(RC)} - \frac{V}{R^2C^2\omega^2 + 1}e^{-t/(RC)}$$

and the steady-state terms are

$$\frac{V RC}{R^2C^2\omega^2 + 1}\left[\omega\sin\omega t + \frac{\cos\omega t}{RC}\right]$$

Exercises 19.4.4

1 Find the general solution of the following equations:

(a) $\dfrac{dy}{dx} + y = 1$

(b) $\dfrac{dy}{dx} + 2y = 6$

(c) $\dfrac{dx}{dt} + 6x = 4$

(d) $\dfrac{dy}{dx} - 3y = 2$

(e) $\dfrac{dy}{dx} = 6y + 9$

(f) $\dfrac{dx}{dt} = 3x - 8$

2 Find the particular solution of the following equations:

(a) $\dfrac{dy}{dx} + 4y = 7,$ $\qquad y(0) = 1$

(b) $\dfrac{dx}{dt} - x = 4,$ $\qquad x(0) = 2$

(c) $\dfrac{dy}{dt} = 3y + 2,$ $\qquad y(0) = 2$

(d) $\dfrac{dy}{dx} = 4y - 8,$ $\qquad y(1) = 2$

3 Find the general solution of $\dfrac{dx}{dt} = 2x + 4t.$ What is the particular solution which satisfies $x(1) = 2$?

4 Find the general solution of $\dfrac{dy}{dx} + y = 2x + 5.$

5 Solve $\dfrac{dx}{dt} = t - tx, x(0) = 0.$

6 Use an integrating factor to obtain the general solution of $iR + L\dfrac{di}{dt} = \sin \omega t$ where R, L and ω are constants.

7 Solve $x\dfrac{dy}{dx} + y = x^4.$

8 Use an integrating factor to find the general solution of $t\dfrac{dx}{dt} + x = 3t.$

9 Find the general solution of $\dfrac{dx}{dt} + 2xt = t.$ Find the particular solution satisfying the condition $x(0) = -1.$

10 Find the general solution of

$$t\dot{x} + 3x = \frac{e^t}{t^2}.$$

Solutions

1 (a) $y = 1 + c\,e^{-x}$

(b) $y = 3 + c\,e^{-2x}$

(c) $x = \frac{2}{3} + c\,e^{-6t}$

(d) $y = c\,e^{3x} - \frac{2}{3}$

(e) $y = c\,e^{6x} - \frac{3}{2}$

(f) $x = \frac{8}{3} + c\,e^{3t}$

2 (a) $y = \frac{7}{4} - \frac{3}{4}e^{-4x}$

(b) $x = 6e^t - 4$

(c) $y = \frac{8}{3}e^{3t} - \frac{2}{3}$

(d) $y = 2$

3 $-2t - 1 + c\,e^{2t},\ -2t - 1 + 5\,e^{2(t-1)}$

4 $2x + 3 + c\,e^{-x}$

5 $1 - e^{-t^2/2}$

6 $\dfrac{L((R/L)\sin \omega t - \omega \cos \omega t)}{R^2 + L^2\omega^2} + c\,e^{-Rt/L}$

7 $\dfrac{x^4}{5} + \dfrac{c}{x}$

8 $\dfrac{3t}{2} + \dfrac{c}{t}$

9 $\frac{1}{2} - \frac{3}{2}e^{-t^2}$

10 $\dfrac{e^t + c}{t^3}$

19.5 Second order linear equations

The general form of a second-order linear ordinary differential equation is

$$p(x)\frac{d^2y}{dx^2} + q(x)\frac{dy}{dx} + r(x)y = f(x) \tag{19.7}$$

where $p(x), q(x), r(x)$ and $f(x)$ are functions of x only.

An important relative of this equation is

$$p(x)\frac{d^2y}{dx^2} + q(x)\frac{dy}{dx} + r(x)y = 0 \tag{19.8}$$

which is obtained from Equation (19.7) by ignoring the term which is independent of y. Equation (19.8) is said to be a **homogeneous** equation – all its terms contain y or its derivatives. Equation (19.7) is said to be **inhomogeneous**.

For example,

$$x^2\frac{d^2y}{dx^2} + x\frac{dy}{dx} + (x^2 - 1)y = e^{-x}$$

is an inhomogeneous second-order linear equation in which $p(x) = x^2$, $q(x) = x$, $r(x) = x^2 - 1$ and $f(x) = e^{-x}$. The associated homogeneous equation is

$$x\frac{d^2y}{dx^2} + x\frac{dy}{dx} + (x^2 - 1)y = 0$$

The following properties of linear equations are necessary for finding solutions of second-order linear equations.

19.5.1 Property 1

If $y_1(x)$ and $y_2(x)$ are any two linearly independent solutions of a second-order homogeneous equation then the general solution, $y_H(x)$, is

$$y_H(x) = Ay_1(x) + By_2(x)$$

where A, B are constants.

We see that the second-order linear ordinary differential equation has two arbitrary constants in its general solution. The functions $y_1(x)$ and $y_2(x)$ are **linearly independent** if one is not simply a multiple of the other.

19.5.2 Property 2

Let $y_p(x)$ be any solution of an inhomogeneous equation. Let $y_H(x)$ be the general solution of the associated homogeneous equation. The general solution of the inhomogeneous equation is then given by

$$y(x) = y_H(x) + y_P(x)$$

In other words, to find the general solution of an inhomogeneous equation we must first find the general solution of the corresponding homogeneous problem, and then add to it any solution of the inhomogeneous equation.

The function $y_H(x)$ is known as the **complementary function** and $y_P(x)$ is called the **particular integral**. Clearly the complementary function of a homogeneous problem is the same as its general solution; we shall often write $y(x)$ for both. If conditions are given they are applied to the general solution of the inhomogeneous equation to determine any unknown constants. This yields the particular solution satisfying the given conditions.

Example 19.19   Verify that $y_1(x) = x$ and $y_2(x) = 1$ both satisfy $\dfrac{d^2y}{dx^2} = 0$. Write down the general solution of this equation and verify that this indeed satisfies the equation.

Solution   If $y_1(x) = x$ then $\dfrac{dy_1}{dx} = 1$ and $\dfrac{d^2y_1}{dx^2} = 0$, so that y_1 satisfies $\dfrac{d^2y}{dx^2} = 0$. If $y_2(x) = 1$,

then $\dfrac{dy_2}{dx} = 0$ and $\dfrac{d^2y_2}{dx^2} = 0$, so that y_2 satisfies $\dfrac{d^2y}{dx^2} = 0$. From Property 1, the general

solution of $\dfrac{d^2y}{dx^2} = 0$ is

$$y_H(x) = Ax + B(1)$$
$$= Ax + B$$

To verify that this satisfies the equation proceed as follows:

$$\frac{dy_H}{dx} = A$$

$$\frac{d^2y_H}{dx^2} = 0$$

and so $y_H(x)$ satisfies $\dfrac{d^2y}{dx^2} = 0$.

Example 19.20   Given

$$\frac{d^2y}{dx^2} + y = x \tag{19.9}$$

(a) Show that $y_H = A\cos x + B\sin x$ is a solution of the corresponding homogeneous equation.

(b) Verify that $y_P = x$ is a particular integral.

(c) Verify that $y_H + y_P$ does indeed satisfy the inhomogeneous equation.

Solution   (a) If $y_H = A \cos x + B \sin x$, then

$$y'_H = -A \sin x + B \cos x \qquad y''_H = -A \cos x - B \sin x$$

We see immediately that $y_H + y''_H = 0$ so that y_H is a solution of the homogeneous equation.

(b) If $y_P = x$ then $y'_P = 1$ and $y''_P = 0$. Substitution into the inhomogeneous equation shows that y_P satisfies Equation (19.9), that is $y_P = x$ is a particular integral.

(c) Writing

$$y = A \cos x + B \sin x + x$$

we have

$$y' = -A \sin x + B \cos x + 1 \qquad y'' = -A \cos x - B \sin x$$

Substitution into the l.h.s. of Equation (19.9) gives

$$(-A \cos x - B \sin x) + (A \cos x + B \sin x + x)$$

which equals x, and so the complementary function plus the particular integral is indeed a solution of the inhomogeneous equation, as required by Property 2.

19.5.3 Constant coefficient equations

We now proceed to study in detail those second-order linear equations which have constant coefficients. The general form of such an equation is

$$a\frac{d^2 y}{dx^2} + b\frac{dy}{dx} + cy = f(x) \tag{19.10}$$

where a, b, c are constants. The homogeneous form of Equation (19.10) is

$$a\frac{d^2 y}{dx^2} + b\frac{dy}{dx} + cy = 0 \tag{19.11}$$

Equations of this form arise in the analysis of circuits. Consider the following example.

Example 19.21   The *LCR* circuit

Write down the differential equation governing the current flowing in the series *LCR* circuit shown in Figure 19.4.

Figure 19.4
An LCR circuit.

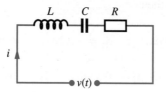

Solution   Using Kirchhoff's voltage law and the individual laws for each component we find

$$L\frac{di}{dt} + iR + \frac{1}{C}\int i \, dt = v(t)$$

If this equation is now differentiated w.r.t. t we find

$$L\frac{d^2i}{dt^2} + R\frac{di}{dt} + \frac{1}{C}i = \frac{dv(t)}{dt}$$

This is an inhomogeneous second-order differential equation, with the inhomogeneity arising from the term $\frac{dv}{dt}$. When the circuit components L, R and C are constants we have what is termed a **linear time-invariant system**, and the differential equation then has constant coefficients.

A linear time-invariant system has components whose properties do not vary with time and as such can be modelled by a linear constant coefficient differential equation.

19.5.4 Finding the complementary function

As stated in Property 2, finding the general solution of $ay'' + by' + cy = f$ is a two-stage process. The first task is to determine the complementary function. This is the general solution of the corresponding homogeneous equation, that is $ay'' + by' + cy = 0$. We now focus attention on the solution of such equations.

Example 19.22   Verify that $y_1 = e^{4x}$ and $y_2 = e^{2x}$ both satisfy the constant coefficient homogeneous equation

$$\frac{d^2y}{dx^2} - 6\frac{dy}{dx} + 8y = 0 \tag{19.12}$$

Write down the general solution of this equation.

Solution   If $y_1 = e^{4x}$, differentiation yields

$$\frac{dy_1}{dx} = 4e^{4x}$$

and similarly,

$$\frac{d^2 y_1}{dx^2} = 16 e^{4x}$$

Substitution into Equation (19.12) gives

$$16 e^{4x} - 6(4 e^{4x}) + 8 e^{4x} = 0$$

so that $y_1 = e^{4x}$ is indeed a solution. Similarly if $y_2 = e^{2x}$, then $\dfrac{dy_2}{dx} = 2 e^{2x}$ and $\dfrac{d^2 y_2}{dx^2} = 4 e^{2x}$. Substitution into Equation (19.12) gives

$$4 e^{2x} - 6(2 e^{2x}) + 8 e^{2x} = 0$$

so that $y_2 = e^{2x}$ is also a solution of Equation (19.12). Now e^{2x} and e^{4x} are linearly independent functions. So, from Property 1 we have

$$y_H(x) = A e^{4x} + B e^{2x}$$

as the general solution of Equation (19.12).

Example 19.23   Find values of k so that $y = e^{kx}$ is a solution of

$$\frac{d^2 y}{dx^2} - \frac{dy}{dx} - 6y = 0$$

Hence state the general solution.

Solution   As suggested we try a solution of the form $y = e^{kx}$. Differentiating we find $\dfrac{dy}{dx} = k e^{kx}$ and $\dfrac{d^2 y}{dx^2} = k^2 e^{kx}$. Substitution into the given equation yields

$$k^2 e^{kx} - k e^{kx} - 6 e^{kx} = 0$$

that is,

$$(k^2 - k - 6) e^{kx} = 0$$

The only way this equation can be satisfied for all values of x is if

$$k^2 - k - 6 = 0 \qquad\qquad (19.13)$$

that is,

$$(k - 3)(k + 2) = 0$$

so that $k = 3$ or $k = -2$. That is to say, if $y = e^{kx}$ is to be a solution of the differential equation k must be either 3 or -2. We therefore have found two solutions

$$y_1(x) = e^{3x} \qquad \text{and} \qquad y_2(x) = e^{-2x}$$

These two functions are linearly independent and we can therefore apply Property 1 to give the general solution:

$$y_H(x) = A e^{3x} + B e^{-2x}$$

Equation (19.13) for determining k is called the **auxiliary equation**.

Example 19.24   Find the auxiliary equation of the differential equation

$$a\frac{d^2 y}{dx^2} + b\frac{dy}{dx} + cy = 0$$

Solution   We try a solution of the form $y = e^{kx}$ so that $\dfrac{dy}{dx} = k e^{kx}$ and $\dfrac{d^2 y}{dx^2} = k^2 e^{kx}$. Substitution into the given differential equation yields

$$ak^2 e^{kx} + bk e^{kx} + c e^{kx} = 0$$

that is,

$$(ak^2 + bk + c) e^{kx} = 0$$

Since this equation is to be satisfied for all values of x, then

$$ak^2 + bk + c = 0$$

is the required auxiliary equation.

The auxiliary equation of $a\dfrac{d^2 y}{dx^2} + b\dfrac{dy}{dx} + cy = 0$ is

$$ak^2 + bk + c = 0$$

Solution of this quadratic equation gives the values of k which we seek. Clearly the nature of the roots will depend upon the values of a, b and c. If $b^2 > 4ac$ the roots will be real and distinct. The two values of k thus obtained, k_1 and k_2, will allow us to write down two independent solutions:

$$y_1(x) = e^{k_1 x} \qquad y_2(x) = e^{k_2 x}$$

and so the general solution of the differential equation will be

$$y(x) = A e^{k_1 x} + B e^{k_2 x}$$

> If the auxiliary equation has real, distinct roots k_1 and k_2, the complementary function will be
>
> $$y(x) = A e^{k_1 x} + B e^{k_2 x}$$

On the other hand, if $b^2 = 4ac$ the two roots of the auxiliary equation will be equal and this method will therefore only yield one independent solution. In this case, special treatment is required. If $b^2 < 4ac$ the two roots of the auxiliary equation will be complex, that is k_1 and k_2 will be complex numbers. The procedure for dealing with such cases will become apparent in the following examples.

Example 19.25   Find the general solution of

$$\frac{d^2 y}{dx^2} + 3\frac{dy}{dx} - 10y = 0$$

Find the particular solution which satisfies the conditions $y(0) = 1$ and $y'(0) = 1$.

Solution   By letting $y = e^{kx}$, so that $\dfrac{dy}{dx} = k e^{kx}$ and $\dfrac{d^2 y}{dx^2} = k^2 e^{kx}$, the auxiliary equation is found to be

$$k^2 + 3k - 10 = 0$$

Therefore,

$$(k - 2)(k + 5) = 0$$

so that $k = 2$ and $k = -5$. Thus there exist two solutions, $y_1 = e^{2x}$ and $y_2 = e^{-5x}$. From Property 1 we can write the general solution as

$$y = A e^{2x} + B e^{-5x}$$

To find the particular solution we must now impose the given conditions:

$$y(0) = 1 \qquad \text{gives} \qquad 1 = A + B$$
$$y'(0) = 1 \qquad \text{gives} \qquad 1 = 2A - 5B$$

from which $A = \frac{6}{7}$ and $B = \frac{1}{7}$. Finally, the required particular solution is $y = \frac{6}{7} e^{2x} + \frac{1}{7} e^{-5x}$.

Example 19.26   Find the general solution of

$$\frac{d^2 y}{dx^2} + 4y = 0$$

Solution　As before, let $y = e^{kx}$ so that $\dfrac{dy}{dx} = k\,e^{kx}$ and $\dfrac{d^2y}{dx^2} = k^2\,e^{kx}$. The auxiliary equation is easily found to be

$$k^2 + 4 = 0$$

that is

$$k^2 = -4$$

so that

$$k = \pm 2\mathrm{j}$$

that is, we have complex roots. The two independent solutions of the equation are thus

$$y_1(x) = e^{2\mathrm{j}x} \qquad \text{and} \qquad y_2(x) = e^{-2\mathrm{j}x}$$

so that the general solution can be written in the form

$$y(x) = A\,e^{2\mathrm{j}x} + B\,e^{-2\mathrm{j}x}$$

However, in cases such as this, it is usual to rewrite the solution in the following way. Recall from Chapter 9 that Euler's relations give

$$e^{2\mathrm{j}x} = \cos 2x + \mathrm{j}\sin 2x$$

and

$$e^{-2\mathrm{j}x} = \cos 2x - \mathrm{j}\sin 2x$$

so that

$$y(x) = A(\cos 2x + \mathrm{j}\sin 2x) + B(\cos 2x - \mathrm{j}\sin 2x)$$

If we now relabel the constants such that

$$A + B = C \qquad \text{and} \qquad A\mathrm{j} - B\mathrm{j} = D$$

we can write the general solution in the form

$$y(x) = C\cos 2x + D\sin 2x$$

Example 19.27　Given $ay'' + by' + cy = 0$, write down the auxiliary equation. If the roots of the auxiliary equation are complex and are denoted by

$$k_1 = \alpha + \beta\mathrm{j} \qquad k_2 = \alpha - \beta\mathrm{j}$$

show that the general solution is

$$y(x) = e^{\alpha x}(A\cos \beta x + B\sin \beta x)$$

Solution　Substitution of $y = e^{kx}$ into the differential equation yields

$$(ak^2 + bk + c)\,e^{kx} = 0$$

and so

$$ak^2 + bk + c = 0$$

This is the auxiliary equation. If $k_1 = \alpha + \beta j$, $k_2 = \alpha - \beta j$ then the general solution is

$$y = C e^{(\alpha + \beta j)x} + D e^{(\alpha - \beta j)x}$$

where C and D are arbitrary constants. Using the laws of indices this is rewritten as

$$y = C e^{\alpha x} e^{\beta j x} + D e^{\alpha x} e^{-\beta j x} = e^{\alpha x}(C e^{\beta j x} + D e^{-\beta j x})$$

Then, using Euler's relations, we obtain

$$y = e^{\alpha x}(C \cos \beta x + Cj \sin \beta x + D \cos \beta x - Dj \sin \beta x)$$
$$= e^{\alpha x}\{(C + D) \cos \beta x + (Cj - Dj) \sin \beta x\}$$

Writing $A = C + D$ and $B = Cj - Dj$, we find

$$y = e^{\alpha x}(A \cos \beta x + B \sin \beta x)$$

This is the required solution.

If the auxiliary equation has complex roots $\alpha + \beta j$ and $\alpha - \beta j$, then the complementary function is

$$y = e^{\alpha x}(A \cos \beta x + B \sin \beta x)$$

Note that Example 19.26 is a special case of Example 19.27 with $\alpha = 0$ and $\beta = 2$.

Example 19.28 Find the general solution of $y'' + 2y' + 4y = 0$.

Solution The auxiliary equation is $k^2 + 2k + 4 = 0$. This equation has complex roots given by

$$k = \frac{-2 \pm \sqrt{4 - 16}}{2}$$
$$= \frac{-2 \pm \sqrt{12}j}{2}$$
$$= -1 \pm \sqrt{3}j$$

Using the result of Example 19.27 with $\alpha = -1$ and $\beta = \sqrt{3}$ we find the general solution is

$$y = e^{-x}(A \cos \sqrt{3}x + B \sin \sqrt{3}x)$$

Example 19.29

The auxiliary equation of $ay'' + by' + cy = 0$ is $ak^2 + bk + c = 0$. Suppose this equation has equal roots $k = k_1$. Verify that $y = x\,e^{k_1 x}$ is a solution of the differential equation.

Solution

We have

$$y = x\,e^{k_1 x} \qquad y' = e^{k_1 x}(1 + k_1 x) \qquad y'' = e^{k_1 x}(k_1^2 x + 2k_1)$$

Substitution into the l.h.s. of the differential equation yields

$$e^{k_1 x}\{a(k_1^2 x + 2k_1) + b(1 + k_1 x) + cx\} = e^{k_1 x}\{(ak_1^2 + bk_1 + c)x + 2ak_1 + b\}$$

But $ak_1^2 + bk_1 + c = 0$ since k_1 satisfies the auxiliary equation. Also,

$$k_1 = \frac{-b \pm \sqrt{b^2 - 4ac}}{2a}$$

but since the roots are equal, then $b^2 - 4ac = 0$ and hence $k_1 = -\dfrac{b}{2a}$. So $2ak_1 + b = 0$. We conclude that $y = x\,e^{k_1 x}$ is a solution of $ay'' + by' + cy = 0$ when the roots of the auxiliary equation are equal.

If the auxiliary equation has two equal roots, k_1, the complementary function is

$$y = A\,e^{k_1 x} + Bx\,e^{k_1 x}$$

Example 19.30

Obtain the general solution of the equation

$$\frac{d^2 y}{dx^2} + 8\frac{dy}{dx} + 16y = 0$$

Solution

As before, a trial solution of the form $y = e^{kx}$ yields an auxiliary equation:

$$k^2 + 8k + 16 = 0$$

This equation factorizes so that

$$(k + 4)(k + 4) = 0$$

and we obtain equal roots, that is $k = -4$ (twice). If we proceed as before, writing $y_1(x) = e^{-4x}$, $y_2(x) = e^{-4x}$, it is clear that the two solutions are not independent. To apply Property 1 we need to find a second independent solution. Using the result of Example 19.29 we conclude that, because the roots of the auxiliary equation are equal, the second independent solution is $y_2 = x\,e^{-4x}$. The general solution is then

$$y(x) = A\,e^{-4x} + Bx\,e^{-4x}$$

Exercises 19.5.4

1 Obtain the general solutions, that is the complementary functions, of the following homogeneous equations:

(a) $\dfrac{d^2y}{dx^2} - 3\dfrac{dy}{dx} + 2y = 0$

(b) $\dfrac{d^2y}{dx^2} + 7\dfrac{dy}{dx} + 6y = 0$

(c) $\dfrac{d^2x}{dt^2} + 5\dfrac{dx}{dt} + 6x = 0$

(d) $\dfrac{d^2y}{dt^2} + 2\dfrac{dy}{dt} + y = 0$

(e) $\dfrac{d^2y}{dx^2} - 4\dfrac{dy}{dx} + 4y = 0$

(f) $\dfrac{d^2y}{dt^2} + \dfrac{dy}{dt} + 8y = 0$

(g) $\dfrac{d^2y}{dx^2} - 2\dfrac{dy}{dx} + y = 0$

(h) $\dfrac{d^2y}{dt^2} + \dfrac{dy}{dt} + 5y = 0$

(i) $\dfrac{d^2y}{dx^2} + \dfrac{dy}{dx} - 2y = 0$

(j) $\dfrac{d^2y}{dx^2} + 9y = 0$

(k) $\dfrac{d^2y}{dx^2} - 2\dfrac{dy}{dx} = 0$

(l) $\dfrac{d^2x}{dt^2} - 16x = 0$

2 Find the auxiliary equation for the differential equation

$$L\dfrac{d^2i}{dt^2} + R\dfrac{di}{dt} + \dfrac{1}{C}i = 0$$

Hence write down the complementary function.

3 Find the complementary function of the equation

$$\dfrac{d^2y}{dx^2} + \dfrac{dy}{dx} + y = 0$$

Solutions

1 (a) $y = A e^x + B e^{2x}$

(b) $y = A e^{-x} + B e^{-6x}$

(c) $x = A e^{-2t} + B e^{-3t}$

(d) $y = A e^{-t} + B t e^{-t}$

(e) $y = A e^{2x} + B x e^{2x}$

(f) $y = e^{-0.5t}(A \cos 2.78t + B \sin 2.78t)$

(g) $y = A e^x + B x e^x$

(h) $y = e^{-0.5t}(A \cos 2.18t + B \sin 2.18t)$

(i) $y = A e^{-2x} + B e^x$

(j) $y = A \cos 3x + B \sin 3x$

(k) $y = A + B e^{2x}$

(l) $x = A e^{4t} + B e^{-4t}$

2 $Lk^2 + Rk + \dfrac{1}{C} = 0$ $i(t) = A e^{k_1 t} + B e^{k_2 t}$

where

$$k_1, k_2 = \dfrac{-R \pm \sqrt{\dfrac{R^2 C - 4L}{C}}}{2L}$$

3 $e^{-x/2}\left(A \cos \dfrac{\sqrt{3}x}{2} + B \sin \dfrac{\sqrt{3}x}{2}\right)$

19.5.5   Finding a particular integral

We stated in Property 2 that the general solution of an inhomogeneous equation is the sum of the complementary function and a particular integral. We have seen how to find the complementary function in the case of a constant coefficient equation. We shall now deal with the problem of finding a particular integral. Recall that the particular integral is any solution of the inhomogeneous equation. There are a number of advanced techniques available for finding such solutions but these are beyond the scope of this book. We shall adopt a simpler strategy. Since any solution will do we shall try to find such a solution by a combination of educated guesswork and trial and error.

Example 19.31   Find the general solution of the equation

$$\frac{d^2y}{dx^2} - \frac{dy}{dx} - 6y = e^{2x} \tag{19.14}$$

Solution   The complementary function for this equation has already been shown in Example 19.23 to be

$$y_H = A\,e^{3x} + B\,e^{-2x}$$

We shall attempt to find a solution of the inhomogeneous problem by trying a function of the same form as that on the r.h.s. In particular, let us try $y_P(x) = \alpha\,e^{2x}$, where α is a constant that we shall now determine. If $y_P(x) = \alpha\,e^{2x}$ then $\dfrac{dy_P}{dx} = 2\alpha\,e^{2x}$ and $\dfrac{d^2y_P}{dx^2} = 4\alpha\,e^{2x}$. Substitution in Equation (19.14) gives

$$4\alpha\,e^{2x} - 2\alpha\,e^{2x} - 6\alpha\,e^{2x} = e^{2x}$$

that is,

$$-4\alpha\,e^{2x} = e^{2x}$$

so that y_P will be a solution if α is chosen so that $-4\alpha = 1$, that is $\alpha = -\frac{1}{4}$. Therefore the particular integral is $y_P(x) = -\dfrac{e^{2x}}{4}$. From Property 2 the general solution of the inhomogeneous equation is found by summing this particular integral and the complementary function

$$y(x) = A\,e^{3x} + B\,e^{-2x} - \tfrac{1}{4}e^{2x}$$

Example 19.32   Obtain a particular integral of the equation

$$\frac{d^2y}{dx^2} - 6\frac{dy}{dx} + 8y = x$$

Solution   In the last example, we found that a fruitful approach was to assume a solution in the same form as that on the r.h.s. Suppose we assume a solution $y_p(x) = \alpha x$ and proceed to determine α. This approach will actually fail, but let us see why. If $y_P(x) = \alpha x$ then $\dfrac{dy_P}{dx} = \alpha$ and $\dfrac{d^2y_P}{dx^2} = 0$. Substitution into the differential equation yields

$$0 - 6\alpha + 8\alpha x = x$$

and α ought now to be chosen so that this expression is true for all x. If we equate the coefficients of x we find $8\alpha = 1$ so that $\alpha = \frac{1}{8}$, but with this value of α the constant terms are inconsistent. Clearly a particular integral of the form αx is not possible. The problem arises because differentiation of the term αx produces constant terms which are unbalanced on the r.h.s. So, we try a solution of the form

$$y_P(x) = \alpha x + \beta$$

with α, β constants. Proceeding as before, $\dfrac{dy_P}{dx} = \alpha$, $\dfrac{d^2 y_P}{dx^2} = 0$. Substitution in the differential equation now gives

$$0 - 6\alpha + 8(\alpha x + \beta) = x$$

Equating coefficients of x we find

$$8\alpha = 1 \tag{19.15}$$

and equating constant terms we find

$$-6\alpha + 8\beta = 0 \tag{19.16}$$

From Equation (19.15), $\alpha = \frac{1}{8}$ and then from Equation (19.16)

$$-6\left(\tfrac{1}{8}\right) + 8\beta = 0$$

so that

$$8\beta = \tfrac{3}{4}$$

that is,

$$\beta = \tfrac{3}{32}$$

The required particular integral is $y_P(x) = \dfrac{x}{8} + \dfrac{3}{32}$.

Experience leads to the trial solutions suggested in Table 19.1.

Table 19.1
Trial solutions to find the particular integral.

$f(x)$	Trial solution
constant	constant
polynomial in x of degree r	polynomial in x of degree r
$\cos kx$	$a \cos kx + b \sin kx$
$\sin kx$	$a \cos kx + b \sin kx$
$a\,e^{kx}$	$\alpha\,e^{kx}$

Example 19.33   Find a particular integral for the equation

$$\frac{d^2 y}{dx^2} - 6\frac{dy}{dx} + 8y = 3\cos x$$

Solution We shall try a solution of the form

$$y_P(x) = \alpha \cos x + \beta \sin x$$

Differentiating, we find

$$\frac{dy_P}{dx} = -\alpha \sin x + \beta \cos x$$

$$\frac{d^2 y_P}{dx^2} = -\alpha \cos x - \beta \sin x$$

Substitution into the differential equation gives

$$(-\alpha \cos x - \beta \sin x) - 6(-\alpha \sin x + \beta \cos x) + 8(\alpha \cos x + \beta \sin x)$$
$$= 3 \cos x$$

Equating coefficients of $\cos x$ we find

$$-\alpha - 6\beta + 8\alpha = 3 \tag{19.17}$$

while those of $\sin x$ give

$$-\beta + 6\alpha + 8\beta = 0 \tag{19.18}$$

Solving Equations (19.17) and (19.18) simultaneously we find $\alpha = \frac{21}{85}$ and $\beta = -\frac{18}{85}$, so that the particular integral is

$$y_P(x) = \frac{21}{85} \cos x - \frac{18}{85} \sin x$$

Example 19.34 **An *LC* circuit with sinusoidal input**

The differential equation governing the flow of current in a series LC circuit when subject to an applied voltage $v(t) = V_0 \sin \omega t$ is

$$L \frac{d^2 i}{dt^2} + \frac{1}{C} i = \omega V_0 \cos \omega t$$

Derive this equation and then obtain its general solution.

Solution Kirchhoff's voltage law and the component laws give

$$L \frac{di}{dt} + \frac{1}{C} \int i \, dt = V_0 \sin \omega t$$

To avoid processes of differentiation and integration in the same equation let us differentiate this equation w.r.t. t. This yields

$$L \frac{d^2 i}{dt^2} + \frac{1}{C} i = \omega V_0 \cos \omega t$$

as required.

The homogeneous equation is $L\dfrac{d^2i}{dt^2} + \dfrac{i}{C} = 0$. Letting $i = e^{kt}$ we find the auxiliary equation is $Lk^2 + \dfrac{1}{C} = 0$ so that $k = \pm\dfrac{j}{\sqrt{LC}}$. Therefore, using the result of Example 19.27, with $\alpha = 0$ and $\beta = \dfrac{1}{\sqrt{LC}}$, the complementary function is

$$i = A\cos\frac{t}{\sqrt{LC}} + B\sin\frac{t}{\sqrt{LC}}$$

To find a particular integral, try $i = E\cos\omega t + F\sin\omega t$, where E and F are constants. We find

$$\frac{di}{dt} = -\omega E\sin\omega t + \omega F\cos\omega t$$

$$\frac{d^2i}{dt^2} = -\omega^2 E\cos\omega t - \omega^2 F\sin\omega t$$

Substitution into the inhomogeneous equation yields

$$L(-\omega^2 E\cos\omega t - \omega^2 F\sin\omega t) + \frac{1}{C}(E\cos\omega t + F\sin\omega t) = V_0\omega\cos\omega t$$

Equating coefficients of $\sin\omega t$ gives

$$-\omega^2 LF + \frac{F}{C} = 0$$

Equating coefficients of $\cos\omega t$ gives

$$-\omega^2 LE + \frac{E}{C} = V_0\omega$$

so that $F = 0$ and $E = \dfrac{CV_0\omega}{1 - \omega^2 LC}$. It follows that the particular integral is $i = \dfrac{CV_0\omega}{1 - \omega^2 LC}\cos\omega t$. Finally, the general solution is

$$i = A\cos\frac{t}{\sqrt{LC}} + B\sin\frac{t}{\sqrt{LC}} + \frac{CV_0\omega\cos\omega t}{1 - \omega^2 LC}$$

The terms zero-input response and zero-state response were introduced in Section 19.4 in connection with first-order equations. This terminology is identical when we deal with second-order equations as the following example illustrates.

Example 19.35

Parallel *RLC* circuit

Figure 19.5 shows a parallel RLC circuit which has a current source $i_S(t)$. The inductor current, i, can be found by solving the second-order differential equation

$$LC\frac{d^2i}{dt^2} + \frac{L}{R}\frac{di}{dt} + i = i_S(t) \qquad \text{for } t \geqslant 0$$

Figure 19.5
A parallel *RLC* circuit.

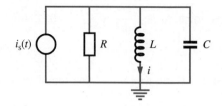

It would be a useful exercise for you to derive this equation. Note that this equation is second order, and inhomogeneous due to the source term $i_S(t)$.

Suppose $L = 10$ H, $R = 10\ \Omega$, $C = 0.1$ F and $i_S(t) = e^{-2t}$ and that the initial conditions are $i = 1$ and $\dfrac{di}{dt} = 2$ when $t = 0$.

(a) Obtain the solution of this equation subject to the given initial conditions and hence state the inductor current i.

(b) Obtain the zero-input response. This is the solution when $i_S(t) = 0$.

(c) Obtain the zero-state response. This is the solution of the inhomogeneous equation subject to the conditions $i = 0$ and $\dfrac{di}{dt} = 0$ at $t = 0$. It corresponds to there being no initial energy in the circuit.

(d) Show that the solution in (a) is the sum of the zero-input response and the zero-state response.

Solution   (a) With the given parameter values the differential equation becomes

$$\frac{d^2 i}{dt^2} + \frac{di}{dt} + i = e^{-2t}$$

It is first necessary to find the complementary function. Letting $i = e^{kt}$, the auxiliary equation is $k^2 + k + 1 = 0$ which has complex solutions

$$k = -\frac{1}{2} \pm \frac{\sqrt{3}}{2}j$$

The complementary function is therefore

$$i = e^{-t/2}\left(A \cos \frac{\sqrt{3}}{2}t + B \sin \frac{\sqrt{3}}{2}t\right)$$

For a particular integral we try a solution of the form $i = \alpha e^{-2t}$. Substitution into the differential equation gives

$$4\alpha\, e^{-2t} - 2\alpha\, e^{-2t} + \alpha\, e^{-2t} = e^{-2t}$$

so that

$$3\alpha = 1, \qquad \text{that is} \qquad \alpha = \frac{1}{3}$$

Hence a particular integral is $i = \frac{1}{3}e^{-2t}$. The general solution is the sum of the complementary function and the particular integral:

$$i = e^{-t/2}\left(A \cos \frac{\sqrt{3}}{2}t + B \sin \frac{\sqrt{3}}{2}t \right) + \frac{1}{3}e^{-2t}$$

We now apply the initial conditions to find the constants A and B. Given $i = 1$ when $t = 0$ means

$$1 = A + \frac{1}{3} \qquad \text{so that} \qquad A = \frac{2}{3}$$

To apply the second condition we need to find $\dfrac{di}{dt}$:

$$\frac{di}{dt} = e^{-t/2}\left(-\frac{\sqrt{3}}{2}A \sin \frac{\sqrt{3}}{2}t + \frac{\sqrt{3}}{2}B \cos \frac{\sqrt{3}}{2}t \right)$$

$$-\frac{1}{2}e^{-t/2}\left(A \cos \frac{\sqrt{3}}{2}t + B \sin \frac{\sqrt{3}}{2}t \right) - \frac{2}{3}e^{-2t}$$

Given $\dfrac{di}{dt} = 2$ when $t = 0$ means

$$2 = \frac{\sqrt{3}}{2}B - \frac{1}{2}(A) - \frac{2}{3}$$

$$2 = \frac{\sqrt{3}}{2}B - \frac{1}{2}\left(\frac{2}{3}\right) - \frac{2}{3}$$

$$2 = \frac{\sqrt{3}}{2}B - 1$$

$$3 = \frac{\sqrt{3}}{2}B$$

$$B = \frac{6}{\sqrt{3}}$$

$$= 2\sqrt{3}$$

Finally, the required particular solution which gives the current through the inductor at any time is

$$i = e^{-t/2}\left(\frac{2}{3} \cos \frac{\sqrt{3}}{2}t + 2\sqrt{3} \sin \frac{\sqrt{3}}{2}t \right) + \frac{1}{3}e^{-2t}$$

(b) The zero-input response is obtained by ignoring the source term $i_S(t)$. From (a) we see that this is just the complementary function:

$$i = e^{-t/2}\left(A \cos \frac{\sqrt{3}}{2}t + B \sin \frac{\sqrt{3}}{2}t \right)$$

Applying the given initial conditions to this solution gives $A = 1$ and $B = \dfrac{5}{\sqrt{3}}$ and so the zero-input response is

$$i = e^{-t/2}\left(\cos\frac{\sqrt{3}}{2}t + \frac{5}{\sqrt{3}}\sin\frac{\sqrt{3}}{2}t \right)$$

(c) The zero-state response of the inhomogeneous equation is found by applying the conditions $i = 0$ and $\dfrac{di}{dt} = 0$ at $t = 0$ to the general solution already obtained in (a). It is straightforward to show that $A = -\dfrac{1}{3}$ and $B = \dfrac{1}{\sqrt{3}}$. So the zero-state response is

$$i = e^{-t/2}\left(-\frac{1}{3}\cos\frac{\sqrt{3}}{2}t + \frac{1}{\sqrt{3}}\sin\frac{\sqrt{3}}{2}t \right) + \frac{1}{3}e^{-2t}$$

(d) Inspection of the previous working shows that the particular solution obtained in (a) is the sum of the zero-state response and zero-input response.

Example 19.36 **Transmission lines**

A transmission line is an arrangement of electrical conductors for transporting electromagnetic waves. Although this definition could be applied to most electrical cables, it is usually restricted to cables used to transport high-frequency electromagnetic waves. There are several different types of transmission lines. The most familiar one is the coaxial cable which is used to carry the signal from a television aerial to a television set (see Figure 19.6). When a high-frequency wave is being carried by a cable several effects become important which can usually be neglected when dealing with a low-frequency wave. These are

(1) the capacitance, C, between the two conductors,

(2) the series inductance, L, of the two conductors,

(3) the leakage current through the insulation layer that separates the two conductors.

The electrical parameters of a coaxial cable are evenly distributed along its length. This is true for transmission lines in general and so it is usual to specify per unit length values for the parameters. When constructing a mathematical model of a transmission line it is easier to think in terms of lumped components spanning a distance δz and then allow δz to tend to zero (see Figure 19.7). The leakage between the two conductors is conventionally modelled by a conductance, G, as this simplifies the mathematics and avoids confusion with the line resistance, R. Note that C, G, L and R are per unit length values for the transmission line.

For most transmission lines of interest the signal that is being carried varies sinusoidally with time. Therefore the voltage and current depend on both position along the line, z, and time, t. However, it is common to separate the time dependence from the voltage and current expressions in order to simplify the analysis. It must be remembered that any voltage and current variation with position has superimposed upon it a

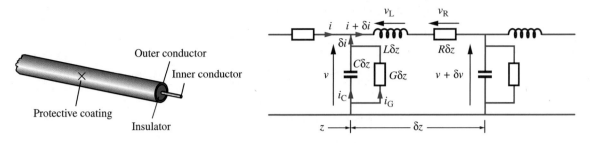

Figure 19.6 A coaxial cable.   **Figure 19.7** A section of a transmission line.

sinusoidal variation with time. Therefore, ignoring the time-dependent element we write the voltage as v and the current as i, knowing that they are functions of z.

Consider the circuit of Figure 19.7 which represents a section of the transmission line of length δz. Applying Kirchhoff's voltage law to the circuit yields

$$v + \delta v - v + v_L + v_R = 0$$
$$\delta v = -v_L - v_R$$

where v_L is the voltage across the inductor and v_R is the voltage across the resistor. Using the individual component laws for the inductor and resistor gives

$$\delta v = -ij\omega L\delta z - iR\delta z$$
$$= -i(R + j\omega L)\delta z$$

Note that δi has been ignored because it is small compared to i. Now consider the parallel combination of the capacitor and resistor (with units of conductance). Applying Kirchhoff's current law to this combination yields

$$\delta i = i_C + i_G$$

where i_C is the current through the capacitor and i_G is the current through the resistor. Using the individual component laws for the capacitor and resistor gives

$$\delta i = -vj\omega C\delta z - vG\delta z$$
$$= -v(G + j\omega C)\delta z$$

Dividing these two circuit equations by δz yields

$$\frac{\delta v}{\delta z} = -i(R + j\omega L)$$

$$\frac{\delta i}{\delta z} = -v(G + j\omega C)$$

In order to model a continuous transmission line with evenly distributed parameters, δz is allowed to tend to zero. In the limit the two circuit equations become

$$\frac{dv}{dz} = -i(R + j\omega L) \tag{19.19}$$

$$\frac{di}{dz} = -v(G + j\omega C) \tag{19.20}$$

Differentiating Equation (19.19) yields

$$\frac{d^2v}{dz^2} = -(R + j\omega L)\frac{di}{dz}$$

Substituting for $\dfrac{di}{dz}$ from Equation (19.20) yields

$$\frac{d^2v}{dz^2} = (R + j\omega L)(G + j\omega C)v$$

This is usually written as

$$\frac{d^2v}{dz^2} = \gamma^2 v \qquad \text{where} \qquad \gamma^2 = (R + j\omega L)(G + j\omega C) \tag{19.21}$$

This is the differential equation that describes the variation of the voltage, v, with position, z, along the transmission line. The general solution of this equation is easily shown to be

$$v = v_1 e^{-\gamma z} + v_2 e^{\gamma z} \tag{19.22}$$

where v_1 and v_2 are constants that depend on the initial conditions for the transmission line. It is useful to write $\gamma = \alpha + j\beta$ thus separating the real and imaginary parts of γ. Equation (19.22) can then be written as

$$v = v_1 e^{-\alpha z} e^{-j\beta z} + v_2 e^{\alpha z} e^{j\beta z} \tag{19.23}$$

The quantity $v_1 e^{-\alpha z} e^{-j\beta z}$ represents the forward wave on the transmission line. It consists of a decaying exponential multiplied by a sinusoidal term. The decaying exponential represents a gradual attenuation of the wave caused by losses as it travels along the transmission line. The quantity $v_2 e^{\alpha z} e^{j\beta z}$ represents the backward wave produced by reflection. Reflection occurs if the transmission line is not matched with its load. As the wave is travelling in the opposite direction to the forward wave, $e^{\alpha z}$ still represents an attenuation but in this case an attenuation as z decreases.

A **loss-less** line is one in which the attenuation is negligible. This case corresponds to $\alpha = 0$, and so $\gamma = j\beta$. If $\gamma = j\beta$ then $\gamma^2 = -\beta^2$ so that, from Equation (19.21), $(R + j\omega L)(G + j\omega C)$ must be real and negative. We see that this is the case when $R = 0$ and $G = 0$. This agrees with what would be expected in practice as it is the resistive and conductive terms that lead to energy dissipation.

19.5.6 Inhomogeneous term appears in the complementary function

In some examples, terms which form part of the complementary function also appear in the inhomogeneous term. This gives rise to an additional complication. Consider Example 19.37.

Example 19.37

Consider the equation $y'' - y' - 6y = e^{3x}$. It is straightforward to show that the complementary function is

$$y = A e^{3x} + B e^{-2x}$$

Find a particular integral and deduce the general solution.

Solution   Suppose we try to find a particular integral by using a trial solution of the form $y_P = \alpha\,e^{3x}$. Substitution into the l.h.s. of the inhomogeneous equation yields

$$9\alpha\,e^{3x} - 3\alpha\,e^{3x} - 6\alpha\,e^{3x} \text{ which simplifies to } 0$$

so that $\alpha\,e^{3x}$ is clearly not a solution of the inhomogeneous equation. The reason is that e^{3x} is part of the complementary function and so causes the l.h.s. to vanish. To obtain a particular integral in such a case, we carry out the procedure required when the auxiliary equation has equal roots. That is, we try $y_P = \alpha x\,e^{3x}$. We find

$$y' = \alpha\,e^{3x}(3x+1) \qquad y'' = \alpha\,e^{3x}(9x+6)$$

Substitution into the inhomogeneous equation yields

$$\alpha\,e^{3x}(9x+6) - \alpha\,e^{3x}(3x+1) - 6\alpha x\,e^{3x} = e^{3x}$$

Most terms cancel, leaving

$$5\alpha\,e^{3x} = e^{3x}$$

so that $\alpha = \frac{1}{5}$. Finally, the required particular integral is $y_P = \dfrac{x\,e^{3x}}{5}$. The general solution is then $y = A\,e^{3x} + B\,e^{-2x} + \dfrac{x\,e^{3x}}{5}$.

Exercises 19.5.6

1 Find the general solution of the following equations:

(a) $\dfrac{d^2x}{dt^2} - 2\dfrac{dx}{dt} - 3x = 6$

(b) $\dfrac{d^2y}{dx^2} + 5\dfrac{dy}{dx} + 4y = 8$

(c) $\dfrac{d^2y}{dt^2} + 5\dfrac{dy}{dt} + 6y = 2t$

(d) $\dfrac{d^2x}{dt^2} + 11\dfrac{dx}{dt} + 30x = 8t$

(e) $\dfrac{d^2y}{dx^2} + 2\dfrac{dy}{dx} + 3y = 2\sin 2x$

(f) $\dfrac{d^2y}{dt^2} + \dfrac{dy}{dt} + y = 4\cos 3t$

(g) $\dfrac{d^2y}{dx^2} + 9y = 4\,e^{8x}$

(h) $\dfrac{d^2x}{dt^2} - 16x = 9\,e^{6t}$

2 Find a particular integral for the equation

$$\dfrac{d^2x}{dt^2} - 3\dfrac{dx}{dt} + 2x = 5\,e^{3t}$$

3 Find a particular integral for the equation

$$\dfrac{d^2x}{dt^2} - x = 4\,e^{-2t}$$

4 Obtain the general solution of $y'' - y' - 2y = 6$.

5 Obtain the general solution of the equation

$$\dfrac{d^2y}{dx^2} + 3\dfrac{dy}{dx} + 2y = 10\cos 2x$$

Find the particular solution satisfying

$$y(0) = 1, \quad \dfrac{dy}{dx}(0) = 0.$$

6 Find a particular integral for the equation

$$\dfrac{d^2y}{dx^2} + \dfrac{dy}{dx} + y = 1 + x$$

7 Find the general solution of

(a) $\dfrac{d^2x}{dt^2} - 6\dfrac{dx}{dt} + 5x = 3$

(b) $\dfrac{d^2x}{dt^2} - 2\dfrac{dx}{dt} + x = e^t$

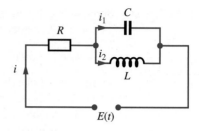

8 For the circuit shown in Figure 19.8 show that

$$RCL\dfrac{d^2i_2}{dt^2} + L\dfrac{di_2}{dt} + Ri_2 = E(t)$$

If $L = 1$ mH, $R = 10\ \Omega$, $C = 1\ \mu$F and
$E(t) = 2 \sin 100\pi t$, find the complementary
function.

9 Find the general solution of

$$\dfrac{d^2i}{dt^2} + 8\dfrac{di}{dt} + 25i = 48 \cos 3t - 16 \sin 3t$$

Figure 19.8

Solutions

1 (a) $x = A e^{-t} + B e^{3t} - 2$

(b) $y = A e^{-x} + B e^{-4x} + 2$

(c) $y = A e^{-2t} + B e^{-3t} + \dfrac{t}{3} - \dfrac{5}{18}$

(d) $x = A e^{-6t} + B e^{-5t} + 0.267t - 0.0978$

(e) $y = e^{-x}[A \sin \sqrt{2}x + B \cos \sqrt{2}x] - \dfrac{8}{17}\cos 2x - \dfrac{2}{17}\sin 2x$

(f) $y = e^{-0.5t}(A \cos 0.866t + B \sin 0.866t) - 0.438 \cos 3t + 0.164 \sin 3t$

(g) $y = A \cos 3x + B \sin 3x + 0.0548\, e^{8x}$

(h) $x = A e^{4t} + B e^{-4t} + \dfrac{9}{20} e^{6t}$

2 $x = 2.5\, e^{3t}$

3 $x = \frac{4}{3} e^{-2t}$

4 $A e^{2x} + B e^{-x} - 3$

5 $A e^{-2x} + B e^{-x} + \frac{3}{2} \sin 2x - \frac{1}{2} \cos 2x,$
   $\frac{3}{2} e^{-2x} + \frac{3}{2} \sin 2x - \frac{1}{2} \cos 2x$

6 x

7 (a) $A e^t + B e^{5t} + \frac{3}{5}$

(b) $A e^t + Bt\, e^t + \frac{1}{2}t^2\, e^t$

8 $A e^{-11270t} + B e^{-88730t}$

9 $e^{-4t}(A \sin 3t + B \cos 3t) + \dfrac{14 \sin 3t + 18 \cos 3t}{13}$

Review exercises 19

1 Find the general solution of the following
equations:

(a) $\dfrac{dx}{dt} = 2x$

(b) $(1 + t)\dfrac{dx}{dt} = 3$

(c) $\dfrac{dy}{dx} = y^2 \cos x$

2 Solve $\dfrac{dy}{dx} = 2$, subject to $y(0) = 3$.

3 Find the general solution of $t\dot{x} + x = 2t$.

4 Solve $\dfrac{dx}{dt} + 2x = e^{2t} \cos t$

(a) by using an integrating factor

(b) by finding its complementary function and
a particular integral.

5 Find the general solution of $y'' + 16y = x^2$.

6 Find the particular solution of
$y'' + 3y' - 4y = e^x$, $y(0) = 2$, $y'(0) = 0$.

7 A particle moves in a straight line such that its
displacement from the origin O is x, where x
satisfies the differential equation

$$\dfrac{d^2x}{dt^2} + 16x = 0$$

(a) Find the general solution of this equation.

(b) If $x\left(\dfrac{\pi}{4}\right) = -12$, and $\dot{x}\left(\dfrac{\pi}{4}\right) = 20$, find the displacement of the particle when $t = \dfrac{\pi}{2}$.

8 Use an integrating factor to solve the differential equation

$$\frac{dx}{dt} + x \cot t = \cos 3t$$

Solutions

1 (a) $x = A\,e^{2t}$

(b) $x = 3\ln|1+t| + c$

(c) $y = \dfrac{1}{A - \sin x}$

2 $y = 2x + 3$

3 $x = t + \dfrac{c}{t}$

4 $x = \dfrac{e^{2t}(4\cos t + \sin t)}{17} + c\,e^{-2t}$

5 $y = A\cos 4x + B\sin 4x + \dfrac{x^2}{16} - \dfrac{1}{128}$

6 $y = \dfrac{39\,e^x + 11\,e^{-4x}}{25} + \dfrac{x\,e^x}{5}$

7 (a) $A\sin 4t + B\cos 4t$ (b) 12

8 $\sin t; x(t) = \dfrac{\cos 2t - \frac{1}{2}\cos 4t + c}{4\sin t}$

20 Ordinary differential equations II

Chapter 20	Contents	
20.1	Introduction	572
20.2	Analog simulation	572
20.3	Higher order equations	574
20.4	State-space models	578
20.5	Numerical methods	584
20.6	Euler's method	584
20.7	Improved Euler method	589
20.8	Runge–Kutta method of order 4	592
	Review exercises	595

20.1 Introduction

Engineers sometimes find it convenient to represent a differential equation using an electronic circuit. This is known as analog simulation. Complicated engineering systems need to be modelled using a set of differential equations. This leads to the topic of state-space modelling. Such models find widespread use in the aerospace industries as well as in other areas that have complex systems. Numerical techniques are very important as they allow differential equations to be solved using computers. Often this is the only way to obtain a solution of a differential equation, owing to its complexity. State-space models are almost always solved using computers.

20.2 Analog simulation

It is possible to solve differential equations using electronic circuits based on operational amplifiers. The advantage of this approach is the ease with which the coefficients of the differential equation can be adjusted and the effect on the solution observed. The technique is known as **analog simulation**. This is a common approach in engineering design because an engineer is often required to analyse many different mathematical models. Special-purpose computers, known as analog computers, are available with the electronic circuits already incorporated, thus making it easier to simulate a particular differential equation.

Three basic types of circuit are required to enable ordinary differential equations with constant coefficients to be simulated. The first type is an integrator which has already been discussed in Section 13.2. The usual symbol for such a circuit is shown in Figure 20.1.

If an analog computer is used it is common for there to be a gain of only 1 or 10 on the input voltage. A gain above 10 is better achieved by linking together two circuits in series. In addition there is usually a facility to allow initial conditions to be set. The equation for the circuit of Figure 20.1 is

$$v_o = - \int_0^t (10v_1 + v_2 + v_3) \, dt - v_{ic} \tag{20.1}$$

where v_{ic} indicates the initial output voltage. Note that the gain is usually written on the input line.

The second type of circuit is the summer. It has the symbol shown in Figure 20.2.

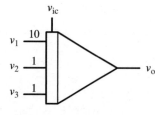

Figure 20.1 An integrator.

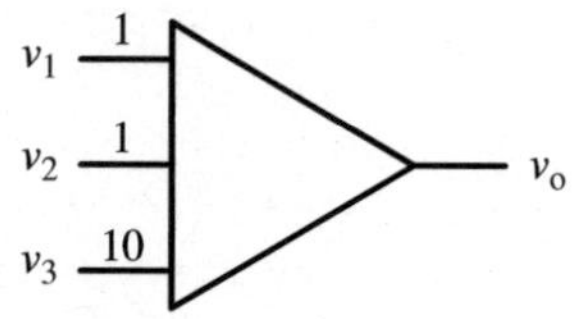

Figure 20.2 A summer.

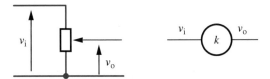

Figure 20.3   A potentiometer.

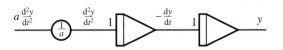

Figure 20.4   First stage in synthesizing Equation (20.4).

The equation for the circuit of Figure 20.2 is

$$v_o = -(v_1 + v_2 + 10v_3) \tag{20.2}$$

Finally, a circuit is required to allow gains to be varied. This is simply a potentiometer and is illustrated together with its symbol in Figure 20.3. The equation for the circuit of Figure 20.3 is simply

$$v_o = kv_i \qquad 0 \leqslant k \leqslant 1 \tag{20.3}$$

The potentiometer only allows the gain to be varied between 0 and 1. If a variable gain greater than 1 is required, the potentiometer must be placed in series with a circuit that increases gain, for example a one-input summer with a gain of 10.

These circuits can be combined to obtain the solutions of differential equations. This is best illustrated by means of an example. Consider the general form of a second-order differential equation with constant coefficients:

$$a\frac{d^2y}{dt^2} + b\frac{dy}{dt} + cy = f(t) \tag{20.4}$$

The general approach to obtaining the circuit for a particular differential equation is to assume a certain point in the circuit corresponds to a particular term and then arrange to connect that point to the correctly synthesized value. It is more straightforward if the assumed point corresponds to the highest derivative. Rearranging Equation (20.4) we find

$$a\frac{d^2y}{dt^2} = f(t) - b\frac{dy}{dt} - cy \tag{20.5}$$

Assuming $a\dfrac{d^2y}{dt^2}$ is already available, a potentiometer can be used to obtain $\dfrac{d^2y}{dt^2}$. Integrators can then be used to obtain the variables $\dfrac{dy}{dt}$ and y. This is shown in Figure 20.4.

The next stage is to obtain the expression corresponding to the r.h.s. of Equation (20.5). This requires a summer to add together the individual terms and potentiometers to allow individual coefficients to be obtained. An invertor is also required to obtain the correct sign for the variable $\dfrac{dy}{dt}$. This simply consists of a summer with one input and a gain of 1. The final circuit is shown in Figure 20.5. The three potentiometers allow different values of a, b and c to be obtained. If gains greater than 1 were required then extra summers would be needed, or alternatively the input gains of the existing summers could be adjusted. The input to the circuit, $f(t)$, can be simulated by applying a signal at the appropriate point in the circuit. The output of the circuit, $y(t)$, corresponds to the solution of the differential equation. It may be necessary to include initial conditions corresponding to $y(0)$ and $\dfrac{dy}{dt}(0)$.

Figure 20.5
The complete circuit to synthesize Equation (20.4).

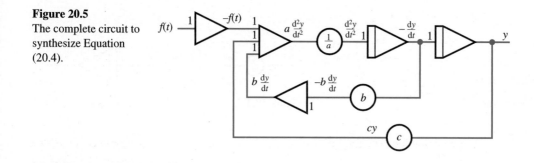

20.3 Higher order equations

In this section we shall consider second- and higher order equations and show how they can be represented as a set of simultaneous first-order equations. The main reason for doing this is that when a computer solution is required it is useful to express an equation in this form. Details of the analytical solution of such systems are not considered here although one technique is discussed in Section 21.10.

It is possible to express a second-order differential equation as two first-order equations. Thus if we have

$$\frac{d^2y}{dx^2} = f\left(\frac{dy}{dx}, y, x\right) \tag{20.6}$$

we can introduce the new dependent variables y_1 and y_2 such that $y_1 = y$ and $y_2 = \dfrac{dy}{dx}$.
Equation (20.6) then becomes

$$\frac{dy_1}{dx} = y_2 \qquad \frac{dy_2}{dx} = f(y_2, y_1, x) \tag{20.7}$$

These first-order simultaneous differential equations are often referred to as **coupled** equations.

Example 20.1   Express the equation

$$\frac{d^2y}{dx^2} - 7\frac{dy}{dx} + 3y = 0$$

as a set of first-order equations.

Solution   Letting $y_1 = y$, and $y_2 = \dfrac{dy}{dx}$, we find $\dfrac{dy_2}{dx} = \dfrac{d^2y}{dx^2}$. Therefore the differential equation becomes

$$\frac{dy_1}{dx} = y_2 \qquad \frac{dy_2}{dx} - 7y_2 + 3y_1 = 0$$

We note that these equations can also be written as

$$\frac{dy_1}{dx} = y_2$$

$$\frac{dy_2}{dx} = -3y_1 + 7y_2$$

or, in matrix form,

$$\begin{pmatrix} y_1' \\ y_2' \end{pmatrix} = \begin{pmatrix} 0 & 1 \\ -3 & 7 \end{pmatrix} \begin{pmatrix} y_1 \\ y_2 \end{pmatrix}$$

where $'$ denotes $\dfrac{d}{dx}$.

Higher order differential equations can be reduced to a set of first-order equations in a similar way:

Example 20.2   Express the equation

$$\frac{d^3 x}{dt^3} - 7\frac{d^2 x}{dt^2} + 3\frac{dx}{dt} + 2x = 0$$

as a set of first-order equations.

Solution   Letting $x_1 = x$, $x_2 = \dfrac{dx}{dt}$ and $x_3 = \dfrac{d^2 x}{dt^2}$ we find

$$\frac{dx_1}{dt} = x_2$$

$$\frac{dx_2}{dt} = x_3$$

$$\frac{dx_3}{dt} - 7x_3 + 3x_2 + 2x_1 = 0$$

is the set of first-order equations representing the given differential equation.

Example 20.3   (a) Express the coupled first-order equations

$$\frac{dy_1}{dx} = y_1 + y_2$$

$$\frac{dy_2}{dx} = 4y_1 - 2y_2$$

as a second-order ordinary differential equation, and obtain its general solution.

(b) Express the given equations in the form

$$\begin{pmatrix} y_1' \\ y_2' \end{pmatrix} = A \begin{pmatrix} y_1 \\ y_2 \end{pmatrix}$$

where A is a 2×2 matrix.

Solution   (a) Differentiating the second of the given equations we have

$$\frac{d^2 y_2}{dx^2} = 4\frac{dy_1}{dx} - 2\frac{dy_2}{dx}$$

and then, using the first, we find

$$\frac{d^2 y_2}{dx^2} = 4(y_1 + y_2) - 2\frac{dy_2}{dx}$$

But from the second given equation $4y_1 = \frac{dy_2}{dx} + 2y_2$, and therefore

$$\frac{d^2 y_2}{dx^2} = \frac{dy_2}{dx} + 2y_2 + 4y_2 - 2\frac{dy_2}{dx}$$

that is,

$$\frac{d^2 y_2}{dx^2} + \frac{dy_2}{dx} - 6y_2 = 0$$

Writing y for y_2 we find

$$\frac{d^2 y}{dx^2} + \frac{dy}{dx} - 6y = 0$$

To solve this we let $y = e^{kx}$ to obtain

$$k^2 + k - 6 = 0$$

$$(k - 2)(k + 3) = 0$$

Therefore,

$$k = 2, -3$$

The general solution is then $y = y_2 = Ae^{2x} + Be^{-3x}$. It is straightforward to show that y_1 satisfies the same second-order differential equation and hence has the same general solution, but with different arbitrary constants.

(b) The first-order equations can be written as

$$\begin{pmatrix} y_1' \\ y_2' \end{pmatrix} = \begin{pmatrix} 1 & 1 \\ 4 & -2 \end{pmatrix} \begin{pmatrix} y_1 \\ y_2 \end{pmatrix}$$

Therefore $A = \begin{pmatrix} 1 & 1 \\ 4 & -2 \end{pmatrix}$.

Exercises 20.3

1 Express the following equations as a set of first-order equations:

(a) $\dfrac{d^2y}{dx^2} + 2\dfrac{dy}{dx} + 3y = 0$

(b) $\dfrac{d^2y}{dx^2} + 8\dfrac{dy}{dx} + 9y = 0$

(c) $\dfrac{d^2x}{dt^2} + 4\dfrac{dx}{dt} + 6x = 0$

(d) $\dfrac{d^2y}{dt^2} + 6\dfrac{dy}{dt} + 7y = 0$

(e) $\dfrac{d^3y}{dx^3} + 6\dfrac{d^2y}{dx^2} + 2\dfrac{dy}{dx} + y = 0$

(f) $\dfrac{d^3x}{dt^3} + 2\dfrac{d^2x}{dt^2} + 4\dfrac{dx}{dt} + 2x = 0$

2 Express the following coupled first-order equations as a single second-order differential equation:

(a) $\dfrac{dy_1}{dx} = y_1 + y_2, \quad \dfrac{dy_2}{dx} = 2y_1 - 2y_2$

(b) $\dfrac{dy_1}{dx} = 2y_1 - y_2, \quad \dfrac{dy_2}{dx} = 4y_1 + y_2$

(c) $\dfrac{dx_1}{dt} = 3x_1 + x_2, \quad \dfrac{dx_2}{dt} = 2x_1 - 3x_2$

(d) $\dfrac{dy_1}{dt} = 2y_1 + 4y_2, \quad \dfrac{dy_2}{dt} = 6y_1 - 7y_2$

3 Express

$$\dfrac{dy_1}{dt} = 2y_1 + 6y_2 \quad \text{and}$$

$$\dfrac{dy_2}{dt} = -2y_1 - 5y_2$$

as a single second-order equation. Solve this equation and hence find y_1 and y_2. Express the equations in the form $y' = Ay$.

Solutions

1 (a) $\dfrac{dy_1}{dx} = y_2 \qquad \dfrac{dy_2}{dx} = -3y_1 - 2y_2$

(b) $\dfrac{dy_1}{dx} = y_2 \qquad \dfrac{dy_2}{dx} = -9y_1 - 8y_2$

(c) $\dfrac{dx_1}{dt} = x_2 \qquad \dfrac{dx_2}{dt} = -6x_1 - 4x_2$

(d) $\dfrac{dy_1}{dt} = y_2 \qquad \dfrac{dy_2}{dt} = -7y_1 - 6y_2$

(e) $\dfrac{dy_1}{dx} = y_2 \qquad \dfrac{dy_2}{dx} = y_3$

$\dfrac{dy_3}{dx} = -y_1 - 2y_2 - 6y_3$

(f) $\dfrac{dx_1}{dt} = x_2 \qquad \dfrac{dx_2}{dt} = x_3$

$\dfrac{dx_3}{dt} = -2x_1 - 4x_2 - 2x_3$

2 (a) $\dfrac{d^2y}{dx^2} + \dfrac{dy}{dx} - 4y = 0$

(b) $\dfrac{d^2y}{dx^2} - 3\dfrac{dy}{dx} + 6y = 0$

(c) $\dfrac{d^2x}{dt^2} - 11x = 0$

(d) $\dfrac{d^2y}{dt^2} + 5\dfrac{dy}{dt} - 38y = 0$

3 $y'' + 3y' + 2y = 0$

$y_1(t) = Ae^{-2t} + Be^{-t}$

$y_2(t) = -\dfrac{2}{3}Ae^{-2t} - \dfrac{1}{2}Be^{-t}$

$\begin{pmatrix} y_1' \\ y_2' \end{pmatrix} = \begin{pmatrix} 2 & 6 \\ -2 & -5 \end{pmatrix} \begin{pmatrix} y_1 \\ y_2 \end{pmatrix}$

20.4 State-space models

There are several ways to model linear time-invariant systems mathematically. One way, which we have already examined, is to use linear differential equations with constant coefficients. A second method is to use transfer functions which will be discussed in Chapter 21. A third type of model is the state-space model. The state-space technique is particularly useful for modelling complex engineering systems in which there are several inputs and outputs. It also has a convenient form for solution by means of a digital computer.

The basis of the state-space technique is the representation of a system by means of a set of first-order coupled differential equations, known as **state equations**. The number of first-order differential equations required to model a system defines the **order** of the system. For example, if three differential equations are required then the system is a third-order system. Associated with the first-order differential equations are a set of **state variables**, the same number as there are differential equations.

The concept of a state variable lies at the heart of the state-space technique. A system is defined by means of its state variables. Provided the initial values of these state variables are known, it is possible to predict the behaviour of the system with time by means of the first-order differential equations. One complication is that the choice of state variables to characterize a system is not unique. Many different choices of a set of state variables for a particular system are often possible. However, a system of order n only requires n state variables to specify it. Introducing more state variables than this only introduces redundancy.

The choice of state variables for a system is, to some extent, dependent on experience but there are certain guidelines that can be followed to obtain a valid choice of variables. One thing that is particularly important is that the state variables are independent of each other. For example, for the electrical system of Figure 20.6, the choice of v_C and $3v_C$ would lead to the two state variables being dependent on each other. A valid choice would be v_C and i which are not directly dependent on each other. This is a second-order system and so only requires two state variables to model its behaviour.

Many engineering systems may have a high order and so require several differential equations to model their behaviour. For this reason, a standard way of laying out these equations has evolved to reduce the chance of making errors. There is also an added advantage in that the standard layout makes it easier to present the equations to a digital computer for solution. Before introducing the standard form, an example will be presented to illustrate the state variable method.

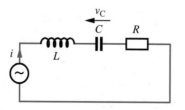

Figure 20.6 The circuit could be modelled using v_C and i as the state variables.

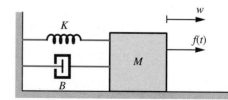

Figure 20.7 A second-order mechanical system.

Example 20.4 Consider the mechanical system illustrated in Figure 20.7. A mass rests on a frictionless surface and is connected to a fixed wall by means of an ideal spring and an ideal damper. A force, $f(t)$, is applied to the mass and the position of the mass is w.

By considering the forces acting on the mass, M, it is possible to devise a differential equation that models the behaviour of the system. The force produced by the spring is Kw (K is the spring stiffness) and opposes the forward motion. The force produced by the damper is $B\dfrac{dw}{dt}$ (B is the damping coefficient) and this also opposes the forward motion. Since the mass is constant, Newton's second law of motion states that the net force on the mass is equal to the product of the mass and its acceleration. Thus we find

$$f(t) - B\frac{dw}{dt} - Kw = M\frac{d^2w}{dt^2} \qquad (20.8)$$

Note that this is a second-order differential equation and so the system is a second-order system.

In order to obtain a state-space model the state variables have to be chosen. There are several possible choices. An obvious one is the position, w, of the mass. A second state variable is required as the system is second order. In this case the velocity of the mass will be chosen. The velocity of the mass is not directly dependent on its position and so the two variables are independent. Another possible choice would have been $\dfrac{dw}{dt} - w$. This may seem a clumsy choice but for certain problems such choices may lead to simplifications in the state variable equations.

It is customary to use the symbols $x_1, x_2, x_3, \ldots$ to represent variables for reasons that will become clear shortly. So,

$$x_1 = w \qquad (20.9a)$$

$$x_2 = \frac{dw}{dt} \qquad (20.9b)$$

Because of the particular choice of state variables, it is easy to obtain the first of the first-order differential equations – thus illustrating the need for experience when choosing state variables.

Differentiating Equation (20.9a) gives

$$\frac{dx_1}{dt} = \frac{dw}{dt} = x_2$$

This is the first state equation although it is usually written as

$$\dot{x}_1 = x_2$$

where $\dot{x}_1$ denotes $\dfrac{dx_1}{dt}$. The second of the first-order equations is obtained by rearranging Equation (20.8):

$$\frac{d^2w}{dt^2} = -\frac{K}{M}w - \frac{B}{M}\frac{dw}{dt} + \frac{1}{M}f(t) \qquad (20.10)$$

However, differentiating Equation (20.9b) we get

$$\frac{d^2w}{dt^2} = \dot{x}_2$$

Then, using Equation (20.10) we obtain

$$\dot{x}_2 = -\frac{K}{M}x_1 - \frac{B}{M}x_2 + \frac{1}{M}f(t)$$

Finally, it is usual to arrange the state equations in a particular way:

$$\dot{x}_1 = \qquad + \quad x_2$$

$$\dot{x}_2 = -\frac{K}{M}x_1 - \frac{B}{M}x_2 + \frac{1}{M}f(t)$$

$$w = x_1$$

Note that it is conventional to relate the output of the system to the state variables. Assume that for this system the required output variable is the position of the mass, that is w.

It is straightforward to rewrite these equations in matrix form:

$$\begin{pmatrix} \dot{x}_1 \\ \dot{x}_2 \end{pmatrix} = \begin{pmatrix} 0 & 1 \\ -K/M & -B/M \end{pmatrix} \begin{pmatrix} x_1 \\ x_2 \end{pmatrix} + \begin{pmatrix} 0 \\ 1/M \end{pmatrix} f(t)$$

$$w = \begin{pmatrix} 1 & 0 \end{pmatrix} \begin{pmatrix} x_1 \\ x_2 \end{pmatrix}$$

More generally, the standard form of the state equations for a linear system is given by

$$\dot{\mathbf{x}}(t) = A\mathbf{x}(t) + B\mathbf{u}(t)$$
$$\mathbf{y}(t) = C\mathbf{x}(t) + D\mathbf{u}(t)$$

For a system with n state variables, r inputs and p outputs:

$\mathbf{x}(t)$ is an n-component column vector representing the states of the nth-order system. It is usually called the **state vector**.

$\mathbf{u}(t)$ is an r-component column vector composed of the input functions to the system. It is usually called the **input vector**.

$\mathbf{y}(t)$ is a p-component column vector composed of the defined outputs of the system. It is referred to as the **output vector**.

$A = (n \times n)$ matrix, known as the **state matrix**.

$B = (n \times r)$ matrix, known as the **input matrix**.

$C = (p \times n)$ matrix, known as the **output matrix**.

$D = (p \times r)$ matrix, known as the **direct transmission matrix**.

A, B, C and D have constant elements if the system is time invariant. When presented in this form the equations appear to be extremely complicated. In fact, the problem is only one of notation. The general nature of the notation allows any linear system to be specified but in many cases the matrices are zero or have simple coefficient values. For example, the matrix D is often zero for a system as it is unusual to have direct coupling between the input and the output of a system. In this format it would be straightforward to present the equations to a digital computer for solution.

Figure 20.8
An armature-
controlled d.c. motor.

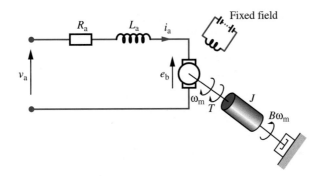

<table>
<tr><td>

Example 20.5

</td><td>

An armature-controlled d.c. motor

</td></tr>
</table>

Derive a state-space model for an armature-controlled d.c. motor connected to a mechanical load with combined moment of inertia J, and viscous friction coefficient B. The arrangement is shown in Figure 20.8.

v_a = applied armature voltage	e_b = back e.m.f. of the motor
i_a = armature current	ω_m = angular speed of the motor
R_a = armature resistance	T = torque generated by the motor.
L_a = armature inductance	

Solution   Let us assume that the system input is the armature voltage, v_a, and the system output is the angular speed of the motor, ω_m. This is a second-order system and so two state variables are required. We will choose the armature current and the angular speed of the motor. So,

$$x_1 = i_a \qquad x_2 = \omega_m$$

The next stage is to obtain a mathematical model for the system. Using Kirchhoff's voltage law and the component laws for the resistor and inductor we obtain, for the armature circuit,

$$v_a = i_a R_a + L_a \frac{di_a}{dt} + e_b$$

Now for a d.c. motor the back e.m.f. is proportional to the speed of the motor and is given by $e_b = K_e \omega_m$, K_e constant. So,

$$v_a = i_a R_a + L_a \frac{di_a}{dt} + K_e \omega_m$$

$$\frac{di_a}{dt} = -\frac{R_a}{L_a} i_a - \frac{K_e}{L_a} \omega_m + \frac{1}{L_a} v_a \qquad (20.11)$$

Let us now turn to the mechanical part of the system. If G is the net torque about the axis of rotation then the rotational form of Newton's second law of motion states $G = J \dfrac{d\omega}{dt}$, where J is the moment of inertia, and $\dfrac{d\omega}{dt}$ is the angular acceleration. In this example, the torques are that generated by the motor, T, and a frictional torque $B\omega_m$ which opposes the motion, so that

$$T - B\omega_m = J\frac{d\omega_m}{dt}$$

For a d.c. motor, the torque developed by the motor is proportional to the armature current and is given by $T = K_T i_a$, where K_T is a constant. So,

$$K_T i_a - B\omega_m = J\frac{d\omega_m}{dt}$$

$$\frac{d\omega_m}{dt} = \frac{K_T}{J}i_a - \frac{B}{J}\omega_m \tag{20.12}$$

Equations (20.11) and (20.12) are the state equations for the system. They can be arranged in matrix form to give

$$\begin{pmatrix} \dot{i}_a \\ \dot{\omega}_m \end{pmatrix} = \begin{pmatrix} -R_a/L_a & -K_e/L_a \\ K_T/J & -B/J \end{pmatrix} \begin{pmatrix} i_a \\ \omega_m \end{pmatrix} + \begin{pmatrix} 1/L_a \\ 0 \end{pmatrix} v_a$$

Alternatively the notation $\mathbf{x} = \begin{pmatrix} x_1 \\ x_2 \end{pmatrix} = \begin{pmatrix} i_a \\ \omega_m \end{pmatrix}$ and $u = v_a$ can be used. However, when there is no confusion it is better to retain the original symbols because it makes it easier to see at a glance what the state variables are.

Finally, an output equation is needed. In this case it is trivial as the output variable is the same as one of the state variables. So,

$$\omega_m = \begin{pmatrix} 0 & 1 \end{pmatrix} \begin{pmatrix} i_a \\ \omega_m \end{pmatrix}$$

Coupled tanks

Derive a state-space model for the coupled tank system shown in Figure 20.9. The tanks have cross-sectional areas A_1 and A_2, valve resistances R_1 and R_2, fluid heights h_1 and h_2, input flows q_1 and q_2. Additionally, there is a flow, q_o, out of tank 2. Assume that the valves can be modelled as linear elements and let the density of the fluid in the tanks be ρ. Let q_i be the intermediate flow between the two tanks.

Figure 20.9
Coupled tanks.

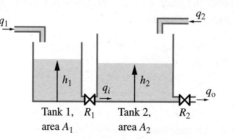

Solution A convenient choice of state variables is the height of the fluid in each of the tanks, although a perfectly acceptable choice would be the volume of fluid in each of the tanks. For tank 1, conservation of mass gives

$$q_1 - q_i = A_1 \frac{dh_1}{dt}$$

For the resistance element, R_1, the pressure difference across the valve is equal to the product of the flow through the valve and the valve resistance. This can be thought of as a fluid equivalent of Ohm's law. Note that atmospheric pressure has been ignored as it is the same on both sides of the valve. So,

$$\rho g h_1 - \rho g h_2 = q_i R_1$$

$$q_i = \frac{\rho g}{R_1}(h_1 - h_2) \qquad (20.13)$$

Combining these two equations gives

$$\frac{dh_1}{dt} = -\frac{\rho g}{R_1 A_1} h_1 + \frac{\rho g}{R_1 A_1} h_2 + \frac{1}{A_1} q_1 \qquad (20.14)$$

For tank 2,

$$q_i + q_2 - q_o = A_2 \frac{dh_2}{dt}$$

$$\rho g h_2 = R_2 q_o \qquad (20.15)$$

Combining these equations and using Equation (20.13) to eliminate q_i and q_o gives

$$\frac{dh_2}{dt} = \frac{\rho g}{R_1 A_2} h_1 - \left(\frac{\rho g}{R_1 A_2} + \frac{\rho g}{R_2 A_2} \right) h_2 + \frac{1}{A_2} q_2 \qquad (20.16)$$

Equations (20.14) and (20.16) are the state-space equations for the system and can be written in matrix form as

$$\begin{pmatrix} \dot{h}_1 \\ \dot{h}_2 \end{pmatrix} = \begin{pmatrix} \dfrac{-\rho g}{R_1 A_1} & \dfrac{\rho g}{R_1 A_1} \\ \dfrac{\rho g}{R_1 A_2} & -\dfrac{\rho g}{R_1 A_2} - \dfrac{\rho g}{R_2 A_2} \end{pmatrix} \begin{pmatrix} h_1 \\ h_2 \end{pmatrix} + \begin{pmatrix} \dfrac{1}{A_1} & 0 \\ 0 & \dfrac{1}{A_2} \end{pmatrix} \begin{pmatrix} q_1 \\ q_2 \end{pmatrix}$$

Note that in this case the input vector is two-dimensional as there are two inputs to the system. The output equation is given by

$$q_o = \begin{pmatrix} 0 & \rho g / R_2 \end{pmatrix} \begin{pmatrix} h_1 \\ h_2 \end{pmatrix}$$

and is obtained directly from Equation (20.15).

20.5 Numerical methods

All the techniques we have so far met for solving differential equations are known as analytical methods, and these methods give rise to a solution in terms of elementary functions such as $\sin x$, e^x, x^3, etc. In practice, most engineering problems involving differential equations are too complicated to be solved easily using analytical techniques. It is therefore frequently necessary to make use of computers. One such approach is to use analog simulation, which we discussed in Section 20.2. Another, more common, approach is to use digital computers.

There are a variety of computer packages available for solving differential equations. A popular package is MATLAB. This contains several different commands to enable differential equations to be solved. All of the packages are based around a common set of mathematical techniques known as numerical methods. We will examine some of the more simple of these techniques in this section.

When using numerical methods it is important to note that they result in approximate solutions to differential equations and solutions are only calculated at discrete intervals of the independent variable, typically x or t. We shall begin by examining the first-order differential equation

$$\frac{\mathrm{d}y}{\mathrm{d}x} = f(x, y)$$

subject to the initial condition $y(x_0) = y_0$. Usually the solution is obtained at equally spaced values of x, and we call this spacing the **step size**, denoted by h. By choosing a suitable value of h we can control the accuracy of the approximate solution obtained. We shall write y_n for this approximate solution at $x = x_n$, whereas we write $y(x_n)$ for the true solution at $x = x_n$. Generally these values will not be the same although we try to ensure the difference is small for obvious reasons.

The simplest numerical method for the solution of the differential equation

$$\frac{\mathrm{d}y}{\mathrm{d}x} = f(x, y)$$

with initial condition

$$y(x_0) = y_0$$

is Euler's method which we shall study in the next section.

20.6 Euler's method

You will recall, from Chapter 12, that given a function $y(x)$, the quantity $\dfrac{\mathrm{d}y}{\mathrm{d}x}$ represents the gradient of that function. So if $\dfrac{\mathrm{d}y}{\mathrm{d}x} = f(x, y)$ and we seek $y(x)$, we see that the differential equation tells us the gradient of the required function. Given the initial condition $y = y_0$ when $x = x_0$ we can picture this single point as shown in Figure 20.10.

Figure 20.10
Approximation used in
Euler's method.

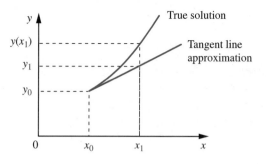

Moreover, we know the gradient of the solution here. Because $\dfrac{dy}{dx} = f(x, y)$ we see that

$$\left.\frac{dy}{dx}\right|_{x=x_0} = f(x_0, y_0)$$

which equals the gradient of the solution at $x = x_0$. Thus the exact solution passes through (x_0, y_0) and has gradient $f(x_0, y_0)$ there. We can draw a straight line through this point with the required gradient to approximate the solution as shown in Figure 20.10. This straight line approximates the true solution, but only near (x_0, y_0) because, in general, the gradient is not constant but changes. So, in practice we only extend it a short distance, h, along the x axis to where $x = x_1$. The y coordinate at this point is then taken as y_1. We now develop an expression for y_1. The straight line has gradient $f(x_0, y_0)$ and passes through (x_0, y_0). It can be shown that its equation is therefore

$$y = y_0 + (x - x_0) f(x_0, y_0)$$

When $x = x_1$ the y coordinate is then given by

$$y_1 = y_0 + (x_1 - x_0) f(x_0, y_0)$$

and since $x_1 - x_0 = h$ we find

$$y_1 = y_0 + hf(x_0, y_0)$$

This equation can be used to find y_1. We then regard (x_1, y_1) as known. From this known point the whole process is then repeated using the formula

$$y_{i+1} = y_i + hf(x_i, y_i)$$

and we can therefore generate a whole sequence of approximate values of y. Naturally, the accuracy of the solution will depend upon the step size, h. In fact, for Euler's method, the error incurred is roughly proportional to h, so that by halving the step size we roughly halve the error.

An alternative way of deriving Euler's method is to use a Taylor series expansion. Recall from Chapter 18 that

$$y(x_0 + h) = y(x_0) + hy'(x_0) + \frac{h^2}{2!} y''(x_0) + \cdots$$

If we truncate after the second term we find

$$y(x_0 + h) \approx y(x_0) + hy'(x_0)$$

that is,

$$y_1 = y_0 + hy'(x_0) = y_0 + hf(x_0, y_0)$$

so that Euler's method is equivalent to the Taylor series truncated after the second term.

Example 20.7

Use Euler's method with $h = 0.25$ to obtain a numerical solution of

$$\frac{dy}{dx} = -xy^2$$

subject to $y(0) = 2$, giving approximate values of y for $0 \leqslant x \leqslant 1$. Work throughout to three decimal places and determine the exact solution for comparison.

Solution

We need to calculate y_1, y_2, y_3 and y_4. The corresponding x values are $x_1 = 0.25$, $x_2 = 0.5$, $x_3 = 0.75$ and $x_4 = 1.0$. Euler's method becomes

$$y_{i+1} = y_i + 0.25(-x_i y_i^2) \qquad \text{with} \qquad x_0 = 0 \qquad y_0 = 2$$

We find

$$y_1 = 2 - 0.25(0)(2^2) = 2.000$$
$$y_2 = 2 - 0.25(0.25)(2^2) = 1.750$$
$$y_3 = 1.750 - 0.25(0.5)(1.750^2) = 1.367$$
$$y_4 = 1.367 - 0.25(0.75)(1.367^2) = 1.017$$

The exact solution can be found by separating the variables:

$$\int \frac{dy}{y^2} = -\int x \, dx$$

so that

$$-\frac{1}{y} = -\frac{x^2}{2} + C$$

Imposing $y(0) = 2$ gives $C = -\frac{1}{2}$ so that

$$-\frac{1}{y} = -\frac{x^2}{2} - \frac{1}{2}$$

Finally,

$$y = \frac{2}{x^2 + 1}$$

Table 20.1 summarizes the numerical and exact solutions. In this example only one correct significant figure is obtained. In practice, for most equations a very small step size is necessary which means that computation is extremely time consuming. An improvement to Euler's method, which usually yields more accurate solutions, is given in Section 20.7.

Table 20.1 Comparison of numerical solution by Euler's method with exact solution.

i	x_i	y_i numerical	$y(x_i)$ exact
0	0.000	2.000	2.000
1	0.250	2.000	1.882
2	0.500	1.750	1.600
3	0.750	1.367	1.280
4	1.000	1.017	1.000

Table 20.2 The solution to Example 20.8 by Euler's method.

i	x_i	y_i
0	1.00	1.00
1	1.20	1.20
2	1.40	1.40
3	1.60	1.60
4	1.80	1.80
5	2.00	2.00

Example 20.8   Obtain a solution for values of x between 1 and 2 of

$$\frac{dy}{dx} = \frac{y}{x}$$

subject to $y = 1$ when $x = 1$ using Euler's method. Use a step size of $h = 0.2$, working throughout to two decimal places of accuracy. Compare your answer with the analytical solution. Comment upon the approximate and exact solutions.

Solution   Here we have $f(x, y) = \frac{y}{x}$, $y_0 = 1$, $x_0 = 1$ and $h = 0.20$. With a step size of 0.2, $x_1 = 1.2, x_2 = 1.4, \ldots, x_5 = 2.0$. We need to calculate $y_1, y_2, \ldots, y_5$. Euler's method, $y_{i+1} = y_i + hf(x_i, y_i)$ reduces to

$$y_{i+1} = y_i + 0.2\left(\frac{y_i}{x_i}\right)$$

Therefore,

$$y_1 = y_0 + 0.2\left(\frac{y_0}{x_0}\right) = 1 + 0.2\left(\frac{1}{1}\right) = 1.20$$

Similarly,

$$y_2 = y_1 + 0.2\left(\frac{y_1}{x_1}\right) = 1.20 + 0.2\left(\frac{1.20}{1.20}\right) = 1.40$$

Continuing in a similar fashion we obtain the results shown in Table 20.2. To obtain the analytical solution we separate the variables to give

$$\int \frac{dy}{y} = \int \frac{dx}{x}$$

so that

$$\ln y = \ln x + \ln D = \ln Dx$$

Therefore,

$$y = Dx$$

When $x = 1$, $y = 1$ so that $D = 1$, and the analytical solution is therefore $y = x$. We see that in this example the numerical solution by Euler's method produces the exact solution. This will always be the case when the exact solution is a linear function and exact arithmetic is employed.

Exercises 20.6

1 Using Euler's method estimate $y(3)$ given

$$y' = \frac{x+y}{x} \qquad y(2) = 1$$

Use $h = 0.5$ and $h = 0.25$. Solve this equation analytically and compare your numerical solutions with the true solution.

2 Find $y(0.5)$ if $y' = x + y$, $y(0) = 0$. Use $h = 0.25$ and $h = 0.1$. Find the true solution for

comparison.

3 Use Euler's method to find $v(0.01)$ given

$$10^{-2}\frac{dv}{dt} + v = \sin 100\pi t \qquad v(0) = 0$$

Take $h = 0.005$ and $h = 0.002$. Find the analytical solution for comparison.

Solutions

1 Exact: $y = x \ln|x| - 0.1931x$

x_i	y_i (h = 0.5)	y_i (h = 0.25)	y (exact)
2.00	1.0000	1.0000	1.0000
2.25	–	1.3750	1.3901
2.50	1.7500	1.7778	1.8080
2.75	–	2.2056	2.2509
3.00	2.6000	2.6561	2.7165

2 Exact: $y = -x - 1 + e^x$

x_i	y_i (h = 0.25)	y (exact)
0	0.0000	0.0000
0.25	0.0000	0.0340
0.50	0.0625	0.1487

x_i	y_i (h = 0.1)	y (exact)
0	0.0000	0.0000
0.1	0.0000	0.0052
0.2	0.0100	0.0214
0.3	0.0310	0.0499
0.4	0.0641	0.0918
0.5	0.1105	0.1487

3 Exact:

$$v = \frac{\sin 100\pi t - \pi \cos 100\pi t + \pi e^{-100t}}{\pi^2 + 1}$$

t_i	v_i (h = 0.005)	v (exact)
0	0.0000	0.0000
0.005	0.0000	0.2673
0.010	0.5000	0.3954

t_i	v_i (h = 0.002)	v (exact)
0	0.0000	0.0000
0.002	0.0000	0.0569
0.004	0.1176	0.1919
0.006	0.2843	0.3354
0.008	0.4176	0.4178
0.010	0.4517	0.3954

20.7 Improved Euler method

You will recall that Euler's method is obtained by first finding the slope of the solution at (x_0, y_0) and imposing a straight line approximation (often called a tangent line approximation) there as indicated in Figure 20.10. If we knew the gradient of the solution at $x = x_1$ in addition to the gradient at $x = x_0$, a better approximation to the gradient over the whole interval might be the mean of the two. Unfortunately, the gradient at $x = x_1$ which is

$$\left. \frac{dy}{dx} \right|_{x=x_1} = f(x_1, y_1)$$

cannot be obtained until we know y_1. What we can do, however, is use the value of y_1 obtained by Euler's method in estimating the gradient at $x = x_1$. This gives rise to the improved Euler method.

$$y_1 = y_0 + h \times \text{(average of gradients at } x_0 \text{ and } x_1)$$

$$= y_0 + h \times \left\{ \frac{f(x_0, y_0) + f(x_1, y_1)}{2} \right\}$$

$$= y_0 + \frac{h}{2} \{ f(x_0, y_0) + f(x_1, y_0 + hf(x_0, y_0)) \}$$

Then, knowing y_1 the whole process is started again to find y_2, etc. Generally,

$$y_{i+1} = y_i + \frac{h}{2} \{ f(x_i, y_i) + f(x_{i+1}, y_i + hf(x_i, y_i)) \}$$

It can be shown that, like Euler's method, the improved Euler method is equivalent to truncating the Taylor series expansion, in this case after the third term.

Example 20.9 Use the improved Euler method to solve the differential equation $y' = -xy^2$, $y(0) = 2$, in Example 20.7. As before take $h = 0.25$, but work throughout to four decimal places.

Solution Here $f(x, y) = -xy^2$, $y_0 = 2$, $x_0 = 0$. We find $f(x_0, y_0) = f(0, 2) = -0(2^2) = 0$. The improved Euler method

$$y_1 = y_0 + \frac{h}{2} \{ f(x_0, y_0) + f(x_1, y_0 + hf(x_0, y_0)) \}$$

yields

$$y_1 = 2 + \frac{0.25}{2} \{ 0 + f(0.25, 2) \}$$

Now $f(0.25, 2) = -0.25(2^2) = -1$, so that

$$y_1 = 2 + 0.125(-1) = 1.875$$

We shall set out the calculations required in Table 20.3. You should work through the next few stages yourself. Comparing the values obtained in this way with the exact solution, we see that, over the interval of interest, our solution is usually correct to two decimal places (Table 20.4).

Table 20.3 Applying the improved Euler method to Example 20.9.

i	x_i	y_i	$f(x_i, y_i)$	$y_i + hf(x_i, y_i)$	$f(x_{i+1}, y_i + hf(x_i, y_i))$	y_{i+1}
0	0	2	0	2	-1	1.8750
1	0.25	1.8750	-0.8789	1.6553	-1.3700	1.5939
2	0.5	1.5939	-1.2703	1.2763	-1.2217	1.2824
3	0.75	1.2824	-1.2334	0.9741	-0.9489	1.0096

Table 20.4 Comparison of the improved Euler method with the exact solution.

i	x_i	y_i	$y(x_i)$
0	0.000	2.0000	2.0000
1	0.2500	1.8750	1.8824
2	0.5000	1.5939	1.6000
3	0.7500	1.2824	1.2800
4	1.0000	1.0096	1.0000

Example 20.10 Apply both Euler's method and the improved Euler method to the solution of

$$\frac{dy}{dx} = 2x \qquad y = 1 \text{ when } x = 0$$

for $0 \leqslant x \leqslant 0.5$ using $h = 0.1$. Compare your answers with the analytical solution. Work throughout to three decimal places.

Solution We have $\dfrac{dy}{dx} = 2x$, $x_0 = 0$, $y_0 = 1$. Therefore, using Euler's method we find

$$y_{i+1} = y_i + hf(x_i, y_i)$$
$$= y_i + 0.1(2x_i)$$
$$= y_i + 0.2x_i$$

Therefore,

$$y_1 = y_0 + 0.2x_0 = 1 + (0.2)(0) = 1$$
$$y_2 = y_1 + 0.2x_1 = 1 + (0.2)(0.1) = 1.02$$

The complete solution appears in Table 20.5. Check the values given in the table for yourself. Using the improved Euler method we have

$$y_{i+1} = y_i + \frac{h}{2}\{f(x_i, y_i) + f(x_{i+1}, y_i + hf(x_i, y_i))\}$$
$$= y_i + 0.05(2x_i + 2x_{i+1})$$
$$= y_i + 0.1(x_i + x_{i+1})$$

Therefore,

$$y_1 = y_0 + 0.1(x_0 + x_1) = 1 + 0.1(0 + 0.1) = 1.01$$
$$y_2 = y_1 + 0.1(x_1 + x_2) = 1.01 + 0.1(0.1 + 0.2) = 1.04$$

and so on. The complete solution appears in Table 20.5. Check this for yourself. The analytical solution is

$$y = \int 2x \, dx = x^2 + c$$

Table 20.5
The solution of
Example 20.10 using
Euler's method, the
improved Euler
method and the exact
solution.

x_i	y_i (Euler)	y_i (improved Euler)	$y(x_i)$ (exact)
0	1.000	1.000	1.000
0.1	1.000	1.010	1.010
0.2	1.020	1.040	1.040
0.3	1.060	1.090	1.090
0.4	1.120	1.160	1.160
0.5	1.200	1.250	1.250

Applying the condition $y(0) = 1$ gives $c = 1$, and so $y = x^2 + 1$. Values of this function are also shown in the table and we note the marked improvement given by the improved Euler method.

Exercises 20.7

1 Apply the improved Euler method to Question 1 in Exercises 20.6.

2 Apply the improved Euler method to Question 2 in Exercises 20.6.

3 Apply the improved Euler method to Question 3 in Exercises 20.6.

Solutions

1

x_i	y_i ($h = 0.5$)	y_i ($h = 0.25$)	y (exact)
2.00	1.0000	1.0000	1.0000
2.25	–	1.3889	1.3901
2.50	1.8000	1.8057	1.8080
2.75	–	2.2476	2.2509
3.00	2.7017	2.7123	2.7165

2

x_i	y_i ($h = 0.25$)	y (exact)
0	0.0000	0.0000
0.25	0.0313	0.0340
0.50	0.1416	0.1487

x_i	y_i ($h = 0.1$)	y (exact)
0	0.0000	0.0000
0.1	0.0050	0.0052
0.2	0.0210	0.0214
0.3	0.0492	0.0499
0.4	0.0909	0.0918
0.5	0.1474	0.1487

3

t_i	v_i ($h = 0.005$)	v (exact)
0	0.0000	0.0000
0.005	0.2500	0.2673
0.010	0.2813	0.3954

t_i	v_i ($h = 0.002$)	v (exact)
0	0.0000	0.0000
0.002	0.0588	0.0569
0.004	0.1903	0.1919
0.006	0.3273	0.3354
0.008	0.4032	0.4178
0.010	0.3777	0.3954

20.8 Runge–Kutta method of order 4

The 'Runge–Kutta' methods are a large family of methods used for solving differential equations. The Euler and improved Euler methods are special cases of this family. The order of the method refers to the highest power of h included in the Taylor series expansion. We shall now present the fourth-order Runge–Kutta method. The derivation of this is beyond the scope of this book.

To solve the equation $\dfrac{dy}{dx} = f(x, y)$ subject to $y = y_0$ when $x = x_0$ we generate the sequence of values, y_i, from the formula

$$y_{i+1} = y_i + \frac{h}{6}(k_1 + 2k_2 + 2k_3 + k_4) \tag{20.17}$$

where

$$k_1 = f(x_i, y_i)$$

$$k_2 = f\left(x_i + \frac{h}{2}, y_i + \frac{h}{2}k_1\right)$$

$$k_3 = f\left(x_i + \frac{h}{2}, y_i + \frac{h}{2}k_2\right)$$

$$k_4 = f(x_i + h, y_i + hk_3)$$

Example 20.11 Use the Runge–Kutta method to solve $\dfrac{dy}{dx} = -xy^2$, for $0 \leqslant x \leqslant 1$, subject to $y(0) = 2$. Use $h = 0.25$ and work to four decimal places.

Solution We shall show the calculations required to find y_1. You should follow this through and then verify the results in Table 20.6. The exact solution is shown for comparison.

$$f(x, y) = -xy^2 \qquad h = 0.25 \qquad x_0 = 0 \qquad y_0 = 2$$

Taking $i = 0$ in Equation (20.17), we have

$$k_1 = f(x_0, y_0) = -0(2)^2 = 0$$

$$k_2 = f(0.125, 2) = -0.125(2)^2 = -0.5$$

$$k_3 = f\left(0.125, 2 + \frac{0.25}{2}(-0.5)\right) = f(0.125, 1.9375)$$

$$= -0.125(1.9375)^2 = -0.4692$$

$$k_4 = f(0.25, 2 + 0.25(-0.4692)) = f(0.25, 1.8827)$$

$$= -0.25(1.8827)^2 = -0.8861$$

Therefore,

$$y_1 = 2 + \frac{0.25}{6}(0 + 2(-0.5) + 2(-0.4692) + (-0.8861)) = 1.8823$$

Table 20.6 Comparison of the Runge–Kutta method with exact solutions.

i	x_i	y_i	$y(x_i)$
0	0.0	2.0	2.0
1	0.25	1.8823	1.8824
2	0.5	1.5999	1.6000
3	0.75	1.2799	1.2800
4	1.0	1.0000	1.0000

Table 20.7 The solution to Example 20.12.

x_i	y_i
0.0	0.0
0.2	0.0213
0.4	0.0897
0.6	0.2112

Example 20.12 Use the fourth-order Runge–Kutta method to obtain a solution of

$$\frac{dy}{dx} = x^2 + x - y$$

subject to $y = 0$ when $x = 0$, for $0 \leqslant x \leqslant 0.6$ with $h = 0.2$. Work throughout to four decimal places.

Solution We have

$$y_{i+1} = y_i + \frac{h}{6}(k_1 + 2k_2 + 2k_3 + k_4)$$

where

$$k_1 = f(x_i, y_i)$$

$$k_2 = f\left(x_i + \frac{h}{2}, y_i + \frac{h}{2}k_1\right)$$

$$k_3 = f\left(x_i + \frac{h}{2}, y_i + \frac{h}{2}k_2\right)$$

$$k_4 = f(x_i + h, y_i + hk_3)$$

In this example, $f(x, y) = x^2 + x - y$ and $x_0 = 0$, $y_0 = 0$. The first stage in the solution is given by

$$k_1 = f(x_0, y_0) = 0$$

$$k_2 = f(0.1, 0) = 0.11$$

$$k_3 = f(0.1, 0 + (0.1)(0.11)) = f(0.1, 0.011) = 0.099$$

$$k_4 = f(0.2, 0 + (0.2)(0.099)) = f(0.2, 0.0198) = 0.2202$$

Therefore,

$$y_1 = 0 + \frac{0.2}{6}(0 + 2(0.11) + 2(0.099) + 0.2202) = 0.0213$$

which, in fact, is correct to four decimal places. Check the next stage for yourself. The complete solution is shown in Table 20.7.

20.8.1 Higher order equations

The techniques discussed for the solution of single first-order equations generalize readily to higher order equations such as those described in Section 20.3 and Section 20.4. It is obvious that a computer solution is essential and there are a wide variety of computer packages available to solve such equations.

Exercises 20.8

1 Find $y(0.4)$ if $y' = (x+y)^2$ and $y(0) = 1$ using the Runge–Kutta method of order 4. Take
(a) $h = 0.2$ and (b) $h = 0.1$.

2 Repeat Question 1 in Exercises 20.6 using the fourth-order Runge–Kutta method.

3 Repeat Question 2 in Exercises 20.6 using the fourth-order Runge–Kutta method.

4 Repeat Question 3 in Exercises 20.6 using the fourth-order Runge–Kutta method.

Solutions

1 (a)

x_i	y_i
0	1.0000
0.2	1.3085
0.4	2.0640

(b)

x_i	y_i
0	1.0000
0.1	1.1230
0.2	1.3085
0.3	1.5958
0.4	2.0649

2

x_i	y_i ($h = 0.5$)	y_i ($h = 0.25$)	y (exact)
2.00	1.0000	1.0000	1.0000
2.25	–	1.3900	1.3901
2.50	1.8078	1.8079	1.8080
2.75	–	2.2507	2.2509
3.00	2.7163	2.7164	2.7165

3

x_i	y_i ($h = 0.25$)	y (exact)
0.00	0.0000	0.0000
0.25	0.0340	0.0340
0.50	0.1487	0.1487

x_i	y_i ($h = 0.1$)	y (exact)
0.0	0.0000	0.0000
0.1	0.0052	0.0052
0.2	0.0214	0.0214
0.3	0.0499	0.0499
0.4	0.0918	0.0918
0.5	0.1487	0.1487

4

t_i	v_i ($h = 0.005$)	v (exact)
0	0.0000	0.0000
0.005	0.2675	0.2673
0.010	0.3959	0.3954

t_i	v_i ($h = 0.002$)	v (exact)
0	0.0000	0.0000
0.002	0.0569	0.0569
0.004	0.1919	0.1919
0.006	0.3352	0.3354
0.008	0.4178	0.4178
0.010	0.3954	0.3954

Review exercises 20

1 Use Euler's method with $h = 0.1$ to estimate $x(0.4)$ given $\dfrac{dx}{dt} = x^2 - 2xt$, $x(0) = 2$.

2 The generalization of Euler's method to the two coupled equations

$$\frac{dy_1}{dx} = f(x, y_1, y_2)$$

$$\frac{dy_2}{dx} = g(x, y_1, y_2)$$

is given by

$$y_{1_{(i+1)}} = y_{1_{(i)}} + hf(x_i, y_{1_{(i)}}, y_{2_{(i)}})$$

$$y_{2_{(i+1)}} = y_{2_{(i)}} + hg(x_i, y_{1_{(i)}}, y_{2_{(i)}})$$

Given the coupled equations

$$\frac{dy_1}{dx} = xy_1 + y_2 \qquad \frac{dy_2}{dx} = xy_2 + y_1$$

estimate $y_1(0.3)$ and $y_2(0.3)$, if $y_1(0) = 1$ and $y_2(0) = -1$. Take $h = 0.1$.

3 Express the following equations as a set of first-order equations:

(a) $\dfrac{d^2 y}{dt^2} + 6\dfrac{dy}{dt} + 8y = 0$

(b) $3\dfrac{d^2 x}{dt^2} + 5\dfrac{dx}{dt} + 4x = 0$

(c) $4\dfrac{d^3 x}{dt^3} + 8\dfrac{d^2 x}{dt^2} + 6\dfrac{dx}{dt} + 5x = 0$

4 Express the following coupled first-order equations as a single second-order differential equation:

(a) $\dfrac{dy_1}{dx} = 3y_1 + 4y_2,\ 2\dfrac{dy_2}{dx} = 6y_1 + 8y_2$

(b) $\dfrac{dx_1}{dt} = 6x_1 - 5x_2,\ 2\dfrac{dx_2}{dt} = 4x_1 - 3x_2$

(c) $\dfrac{dy_1}{dt} = 8y_1 + 4y_2,\ 2\dfrac{dy_2}{dt} = 4y_1 - 6y_2$

Solutions

1 4.7937

2 0.7535, −0.7535

3 (a) $\dfrac{dy_1}{dt} = y_2 \qquad \dfrac{dy_2}{dt} = -8y_1 - 6y_2$

(b) $\dfrac{dx_1}{dt} = x_2 \qquad 3\dfrac{dx_2}{dt} = -4x_1 - 5x_2$

(c) $\dfrac{dx_1}{dt} = x_2 \qquad \dfrac{dx_2}{dt} = x_3$

$\qquad 4\dfrac{dx_3}{dt} = -5x_1 - 6x_2 - 8x_3$

4 (a) $\dfrac{d^2 y}{dx^2} - 7\dfrac{dy}{dx} = 0$

(b) $\dfrac{d^2 x}{dt^2} - \dfrac{9}{2}\dfrac{dx}{dt} + x = 0$

(c) $\dfrac{d^2 y}{dt^2} - 5\dfrac{dy}{dt} - 32y = 0$

Chapter 21 Contents

21.1	Introduction	598
21.2	Definition of the Laplace transform	598
21.3	Laplace transforms of some common functions	599
21.4	Properties of the Laplace transform	601
21.5	Laplace transform of derivatives and integrals	606
21.6	Inverse Laplace transforms	608
21.7	Using partial fractions to find the inverse Laplace transform	612
21.8	Finding the inverse Laplace transform using complex numbers	614
21.9	The convolution theorem	618
21.10	Solving linear constant coefficient differential equations using the Laplace transform	621
21.11	Transfer functions	631
21.12	Poles, zeros and the s plane	640
21.13	Laplace transforms of some special functions	644
	Review exercises	648

21.1 Introduction

The Laplace transform is used to solve linear constant coefficient differential equations. This is achieved by transforming them to algebraic equations. The algebraic equations are solved, then the inverse Laplace transform is used to obtain a solution in terms of the original variables. This technique can be applied to both single and simultaneous differential equations and so is extremely useful given that differential equation models are common as we saw in Chapters 19 and 20.

The Laplace transform is also used to produce transfer functions for the elements of an engineering system. These are represented in diagrammatic form as blocks. The various blocks of the system, corresponding to the system elements, are connected together and the result is a block diagram for the whole system. By breaking down a system in this way it is much easier to visualize how the various parts of the system interact and so a transfer function model is complementary to a time domain model and is a valuable way of viewing an engineering system. Transfer functions are useful in many areas of engineering, but are particularly important in the design of control systems.

21.2 Definition of the Laplace transform

Let $f(t)$ be a function of time t. In many real problems only values of $t \geqslant 0$ are of interest. Hence $f(t)$ is given for $t \geqslant 0$, and for all $t < 0$, $f(t)$ is taken to be 0.

> The Laplace transform of $f(t)$ is $F(s)$, defined by
>
> $$F(s) = \int_0^\infty e^{-st} f(t) \, dt$$

Note that to find the Laplace transform of a function $f(t)$, we multiply it by e^{-st} and integrate between the limits 0 and ∞.

The Laplace transform changes, or transforms, the function $f(t)$ into a different function $F(s)$. Note also that whereas $f(t)$ is a function of t, $F(s)$ is a function of s. To denote the Laplace transform of $f(t)$ we write $\mathcal{L}\{f(t)\}$. We use a lower case letter to represent the time domain function and an upper case letter to represent the s domain function. The variable s may be real or complex. As the integral is improper restrictions may need to be placed on s to ensure that the integral does not diverge.

Example 21.1 Find the Laplace transforms of

(a) 1

(b) e^{-at}

Solution (a) $\mathcal{L}\{1\} = \int_0^\infty e^{-st} 1 \, dt = \left[\dfrac{e^{-st}}{-s} \right]_0^\infty = \dfrac{1}{s} = F(s)$

This transform exists provided the real part of s, $\mathrm{Re}(s)$, is positive.

(b) $\mathcal{L}\{e^{-at}\} = \int_0^\infty e^{-st}e^{-at}\,dt$

$$= \int_0^\infty e^{-(s+a)t}\,dt$$

$$= \left[\frac{e^{-(s+a)t}}{-(s+a)}\right]_0^\infty$$

$$= 0 - \left(\frac{1}{-(s+a)}\right)$$

$$= \frac{1}{s+a} = F(s)$$

This transform exists provided $s + a > 0$.

Throughout the chapter it is assumed that s has a value such that all integrals exist.

21.3 Laplace transforms of some common functions

Determining the Laplace transform of a given function, $f(t)$, is essentially an exercise in integration. In order to save effort a look-up table is often used. Table 21.1 lists some common functions and their corresponding Laplace transforms.

Example 21.2 Use Table 21.1 to determine the Laplace transform of each of the following functions.

(a) t^3

(b) t^7

(c) $\sin 4t$

(d) e^{-2t}

(e) $\cos\left(\dfrac{t}{2}\right)$

(f) $\sinh 3t$

(g) $\cosh 5t$

(h) $t \sin 4t$

(i) $e^{-t} \sin 2t$

(j) $e^{3t} \cos t$

Solution From Table 21.1 we find the results listed in Table 21.2.

Table 21.1
The Laplace transforms of some common functions.

Function, $f(t)$	Laplace transform, $F(s)$	Function, $f(t)$	Laplace transform, $F(s)$
1	$\dfrac{1}{s}$	$e^{-at}\cos bt$	$\dfrac{s+a}{(s+a)^2+b^2}$
t	$\dfrac{1}{s^2}$	$\sinh bt$	$\dfrac{b}{s^2-b^2}$
t^2	$\dfrac{2}{s^3}$	$\cosh bt$	$\dfrac{s}{s^2-b^2}$
t^n	$\dfrac{n!}{s^{n+1}}$	$e^{-at}\sinh bt$	$\dfrac{b}{(s+a)^2-b^2}$
e^{at}	$\dfrac{1}{s-a}$	$e^{-at}\cosh bt$	$\dfrac{s+a}{(s+a)^2-b^2}$
e^{-at}	$\dfrac{1}{s+a}$	$t\sin bt$	$\dfrac{2bs}{(s^2+b^2)^2}$
$t^n e^{-at}$	$\dfrac{n!}{(s+a)^{n+1}}$	$t\cos bt$	$\dfrac{s^2-b^2}{(s^2+b^2)^2}$
$\sin bt$	$\dfrac{b}{s^2+b^2}$	$u(t)$ unit step	$\dfrac{1}{s}$
$\cos bt$	$\dfrac{s}{s^2+b^2}$	$u(t-d)$	$\dfrac{e^{-sd}}{s}$
$e^{-at}\sin bt$	$\dfrac{b}{(s+a)^2+b^2}$	$\delta(t)$	1
		$\delta(t-d)$	e^{-sd}

shifters $\begin{cases} e^{at} \\ e^{-at} \end{cases}$

Table 21.2

$f(t)$	$F(s)$	$f(t)$	$F(s)$	$f(t)$	$F(s)$
(a) t^3	$\dfrac{6}{s^4}$	(e) $\cos(t/2)$	$\dfrac{s}{s^2+0.25}$	(h) $t\sin 4t$	$\dfrac{8s}{(s^2+16)^2}$
(b) t^7	$\dfrac{7!}{s^8}$	(f) $\sinh 3t$	$\dfrac{3}{s^2-9}$	(i) $e^{-t}\sin 2t$	$\dfrac{2}{(s+1)^2+4}$
(c) $\sin 4t$	$\dfrac{4}{s^2+16}$	(g) $\cosh 5t$	$\dfrac{s}{s^2-25}$	(j) $e^{3t}\cos t$	$\dfrac{s-3}{(s-3)^2+1}$
(d) e^{-2t}	$\dfrac{1}{s+2}$				

Exercises 21.3

1 Determine the Laplace transforms of the following functions.

(a) $\sin 6t$

(b) $\cos 4t$

(c) $\sin\left(\dfrac{2t}{3}\right)$

(d) $\cos\left(\dfrac{4t}{3}\right)$

(e) t^4

(f) $t^2 t^3$

(g) e^{-3t}

(h) e^{3t}

(i) $\dfrac{1}{e^{4t}}$

(j) $t\cos 3t$

(k) $t\sin t$

(l) $e^{-t}\sin 3t$

(m) $\dfrac{\cos 7t}{e^{5t}}$

(n) $\sinh 6t$

(o) $\cosh 5t$

(p) $e^{-3t}\sinh 4t$

(q) $e^{-2t}\cosh 7t$

(r) $e^{4t}\sinh 3t$

(s) $e^{7t}\cosh 9t$

2 Show from the definition of the Laplace transform that

$$\mathcal{L}\{u(t-d)\} = \frac{e^{-sd}}{s}, d>0$$

Solutions

1 (a) $\dfrac{6}{s^2+36}$

(b) $\dfrac{s}{s^2+16}$

(c) $\dfrac{6}{9s^2+4}$

(d) $\dfrac{9s}{9s^2+16}$

(e) $\dfrac{24}{s^5}$

(f) $\dfrac{120}{s^6}$

(g) $\dfrac{1}{s+3}$

(h) $\dfrac{1}{s-3}$

(i) $\dfrac{1}{s+4}$

(j) $\dfrac{s^2-9}{(s^2+9)^2}$

(k) $\dfrac{2s}{(s^2+1)^2}$

(l) $\dfrac{3}{(s+1)^2+9}$

(m) $\dfrac{s+5}{(s+5)^2+49}$

(n) $\dfrac{6}{s^2-36}$

(o) $\dfrac{s}{s^2-25}$

(p) $\dfrac{4}{(s+3)^2-16}$

(q) $\dfrac{s+2}{(s+2)^2-49}$

(r) $\dfrac{3}{(s-4)^2-9}$

(s) $\dfrac{s-7}{(s-7)^2-81}$

21.4 Properties of the Laplace transform

There are some useful properties of the Laplace transform that can be exploited. They allow us to find the Laplace transforms of more difficult functions. The properties we shall examine are:

(1) Linearity

(2) Shift theorems

(3) Final value theorem

21.4.1 Linearity

Let f and g be two functions of t and let k be a constant which may be negative. Then

$$\mathcal{L}\{f + g\} = \mathcal{L}\{f\} + \mathcal{L}\{g\}$$
$$\mathcal{L}\{kf\} = k\mathcal{L}\{f\}$$

The first property states that to find the Laplace transform of a sum of functions, we simply sum the Laplace transforms of the individual functions. The second property says that if we multiply a function by a constant k, then the corresponding transform is also multiplied by k. Both of these properties follow directly from the definition of the Laplace transform and linearity properties of integrals, and mean that the Laplace transform is a linear operator. Using the linearity properties and Table 21.1, we can find the Laplace transforms of more complicated functions.

Example 21.3 Find the Laplace transforms of the following functions:

(a) $3 + 2t$ (b) $5t^2 - 2e^t$

Solution (a) $\mathcal{L}\{3 + 2t\} = \mathcal{L}\{3\} + \mathcal{L}\{2t\}$

$$= 3\mathcal{L}\{1\} + 2\mathcal{L}\{t\}$$

$$= \frac{3}{s} + \frac{2}{s^2}$$

(b) $\mathcal{L}\{5t^2 - 2e^t\} = \mathcal{L}\{5t^2\} + \mathcal{L}\{-2e^t\}$

$$= 5\mathcal{L}\{t^2\} - 2\mathcal{L}\{e^t\}$$

$$= \frac{10}{s^3} - \frac{2}{s - 1}$$

With a little practice, some of the intermediate steps may be excluded.

Example 21.4 Find the Laplace transforms of the following:

(a) $5\cos 3t + 2\sin 5t - 6t^3$

(b) $-e^{-t} + \frac{1}{2}(\sin t + \cos t)$

Solution (a) $\mathcal{L}\{5\cos 3t + 2\sin 5t - 6t^3\} = \dfrac{5s}{s^2 + 9} + \dfrac{10}{s^2 + 25} - \dfrac{36}{s^4}$

(b) $\mathcal{L}\left\{-e^{-t} + \dfrac{\sin t + \cos t}{2}\right\} = \dfrac{-1}{s + 1} + \dfrac{1}{2(s^2 + 1)} + \dfrac{s}{2(s^2 + 1)}$

$$= \frac{-1}{s + 1} + \frac{1 + s}{2(s^2 + 1)}$$

21.4.2 First shift theorem

> If $\mathcal{L}\{f(t)\} = F(s)$ then
>
> $\mathcal{L}\{e^{-at} f(t)\} = F(s + a)$ a constant

We obtain $F(s + a)$ by replacing every 's' in $F(s)$ by '$s + a$'. The variable s has been shifted by an amount a.

Example 21.5   (a) Use Table 21.1 to find the Laplace transform of

$$f(t) = t \sin 5t$$

(b) Use the first shift theorem to write down

$$\mathcal{L}\{e^{-3t} t \sin 5t\}$$

Solution   (a) From Table 21.1 we have

$$\mathcal{L}\{f(t)\} = \mathcal{L}\{t \sin 5t\} = \frac{10s}{(s^2 + 25)^2} = F(s)$$

(b) From the first shift theorem with $a = 3$ we have

$$\mathcal{L}\{e^{-3t} f(t)\} = F(s + 3)$$

$$= \frac{10(s + 3)}{((s + 3)^2 + 25)^2}$$

$$= \frac{10(s + 3)}{(s^2 + 6s + 34)^2}$$

Example 21.6   The Laplace transform of a function, $f(t)$, is given by

$$F(s) = \frac{2s + 1}{s(s + 1)}$$

State the Laplace transform of
(a) $e^{-2t} f(t)$ (b) $e^{3t} f(t)$

Solution   (a) Use the first shift theorem with $a = 2$.

$$\mathcal{L}\{e^{-2t} f(t)\} = F(s + 2)$$

$$= \frac{2(s + 2) + 1}{(s + 2)(s + 2 + 1)}$$

$$= \frac{2s + 5}{(s + 2)(s + 3)}$$

(b) Use the first shift theorem with $a = -3$.

$$\mathcal{L}\{e^{3t} f(t)\} = F(s - 3)$$

$$= \frac{2(s - 3) + 1}{(s - 3)(s - 3 + 1)}$$

$$= \frac{2s - 5}{(s - 3)(s - 2)}$$

21.4.3 Second shift theorem

If $\mathcal{L}\{f(t)\} = F(s)$ then

$$\mathcal{L}\{u(t - d) f(t - d)\} = e^{-sd} F(s) \qquad d > 0$$

The function, $u(t-d) f(t-d)$, is obtained by moving $u(t) f(t)$ to the right by an amount d. This is illustrated in Figure 21.1. Note that because $f(t)$ is defined to be 0 for $t < 0$, then $f(t - d) = 0$ for $t < d$. It may appear that $u(t - d)$ is redundant. However, it is necessary for inversion of the Laplace transform, which will be covered in Section 21.6.

Example 21.7 Given $\mathcal{L}\{f(t)\} = \dfrac{2s}{s + 9}$, find $\mathcal{L}\{u(t - 2) f(t - 2)\}$.

Solution Use the second shift theorem with $d = 2$.

$$\mathcal{L}\{u(t - 2) f(t - 2)\} = \frac{2s\, e^{-2s}}{s + 9}$$

Example 21.8 The Laplace transform of a function is $\dfrac{e^{-3s}}{s^2}$. Find the function.

Solution The exponential term in the transform suggests that the second shift theorem is used. Let

$$e^{-sd} F(s) = \frac{e^{-3s}}{s^2}$$

so that $d = 3$ and $F(s) = \dfrac{1}{s^2}$. If we let

$$\mathcal{L}\{f(t)\} = F(s) = \frac{1}{s^2}$$

then $f(t) = t$ and so $f(t - 3) = t - 3$. Now, using the second shift theorem

$$\mathcal{L}\{u(t - 3) f(t - 3)\} = \mathcal{L}\{u(t - 3)(t - 3)\} = \frac{e^{-3s}}{s^2}$$

Hence the required function is $u(t - 3)(t - 3)$ as shown in Figure 21.2.

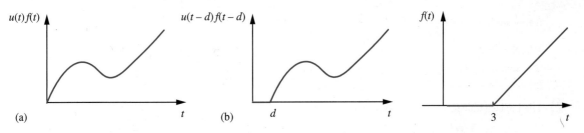

Figure 21.1 Shifting the function $u(t) f(t)$ to the right by an amount d yields the function $u(t - d) f(t - d)$.

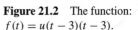

Figure 21.2 The function: $f(t) = u(t - 3)(t - 3)$.

21.4.4 Final value theorem

This theorem applies only to real values of s and for functions, $f(t)$, which possess a limit as $t \to \infty$.

> The final value theorem states:
> $$\lim_{s \to 0} s F(s) = \lim_{t \to \infty} f(t)$$

Some care is needed when applying the theorem. The Laplace transform of some functions exists only for $\text{Re}(s) > 0$ and for these functions taking the limit as $s \to 0$ is not sensible.

Example 21.9   Verify the final value theorem for $f(t) = e^{-2t}$.

Solution $\int_0^\infty e^{-st} e^{-2t} \, dt$ exists provided $\text{Re}(s) > -2$ and so

$$F(s) = \frac{1}{s + 2} \qquad \text{Re}(s) > -2$$

Since we only require $\text{Re}(s) > -2$, it is permissible to let $s \to 0$.

$$\lim_{s \to 0} s F(s) = \lim_{s \to 0} \frac{s}{s + 2} = 0$$

Furthermore

$$\lim_{t \to \infty} e^{-2t} = 0$$

So $\lim_{s \to 0} s F(s) = \lim_{t \to \infty} f(t)$ and the theorem is verified.

Exercises 21.4

1   Find the Laplace transforms of the following functions.

(a) $3t^2 - 4$

(b) $2 \sin 4t + 11 - t$

(c) $2 - t^2 + 2t^4$

(d) $3 e^{2t} + 4 \sin t$

(e) $\frac{1}{3}\sin 3t - 4\cos\left(\frac{t}{2}\right)$

(f) $3t^4 e^{5t} + t$

(g) $\sinh 2t + 3\cosh 2t$

(h) $e^{-t}\sin 3t + 4e^{-t}\cos 3t$

2 The Laplace transform of $f(t)$ is given as

$$F(s) = \frac{3s^2 - 1}{s^2 + s + 1}$$

Find the Laplace transform of

(a) $e^{-t} f(t)$

(b) $e^{3t} f(t)$

(c) $e^{-t/2} f(t)$

3 Given

$$\mathcal{L}\{f(t)\} = \frac{4s}{s^2 + 1}$$

find

(a) $\mathcal{L}\{u(t-1)f(t-1)\}$

(b) $\mathcal{L}\{3u(t-2)f(t-2)\}$

(c) $\mathcal{L}\left\{u(t-4)\dfrac{f(t-4)}{2}\right\}$

4 Find the final value of the following functions using the final value theorem:

(a) $f(t) = e^{-t}\sin t$

(b) $f(t) = e^{-t} + 1$

(c) $f(t) = e^{-3t}\cos t + 5$

Solutions

1 (a) $\dfrac{6}{s^3} - \dfrac{4}{s}$

(b) $\dfrac{8}{s^2 + 16} + \dfrac{11}{s} - \dfrac{1}{s^2}$

(c) $\dfrac{2}{s} - \dfrac{2}{s^3} + \dfrac{48}{s^5}$

(d) $\dfrac{3}{s-2} + \dfrac{4}{s^2 + 1}$

(e) $\dfrac{1}{s^2 + 9} - \dfrac{16s}{4s^2 + 1}$

(f) $\dfrac{72}{(s-5)^5} + \dfrac{1}{s^2}$

(g) $\dfrac{3s + 2}{s^2 - 4}$

(h) $\dfrac{4s + 7}{(s+1)^2 + 9}$

2 (a) $\dfrac{3s^2 + 6s + 2}{s^2 + 3s + 3}$

(b) $\dfrac{3s^2 - 18s + 26}{s^2 - 5s + 7}$

(c) $\dfrac{12s^2 + 12s - 1}{4s^2 + 8s + 7}$

3 (a) $\dfrac{4s\,e^{-s}}{s^2 + 1}$

(b) $\dfrac{12s\,e^{-2s}}{s^2 + 1}$

(c) $\dfrac{2s\,e^{-4s}}{s^2 + 1}$

4 (a) 0   (b) 1   (c) 5

21.5 Laplace transform of derivatives and integrals

In later sections we shall use the Laplace transform to solve differential equations. In order to do this we need to be able to find the Laplace transform of derivatives of functions. Let $f(t)$ be a function of t, and f' and f'' the first and second derivatives of f. The Laplace transform of $f(t)$ is $F(s)$. Then

$$\mathcal{L}\{f'\} = sF(s) - f(0)$$
$$\mathcal{L}\{f''\} = s^2F(s) - sf(0) - f'(0)$$

where $f(0)$ and $f'(0)$ are the initial values of f and f'. The general case for the Laplace transform of an nth derivative is

$$\mathcal{L}\{f^{(n)}\} = s^n F(s) - s^{n-1} f(0) - s^{n-2} f'(0) - \cdots - f^{(n-1)}(0)$$

Another useful result is

$$\mathcal{L}\left\{\int_0^t f(t)\, dt\right\} = \frac{1}{s}F(s)$$

Example 21.10

The Laplace transform of $x(t)$ is $X(s)$. Given $x(0) = 2$ and $x'(0) = -1$, write expressions for the Laplace transforms of

(a) $2x'' - 3x' + x$

(b) $-x'' + 2x' + x$

Solution

$$\mathcal{L}\{x'\} = sX(s) - x(0) = sX(s) - 2$$
$$\mathcal{L}\{x''\} = s^2X(s) - sx(0) - x'(0) = s^2X(s) - 2s + 1$$

(a) $\mathcal{L}\{2x'' - 3x' + x\} = 2(s^2X(s) - 2s + 1) - 3(sX(s) - 2) + X(s)$
$$= (2s^2 - 3s + 1)X(s) - 4s + 8$$

(b) $\mathcal{L}\{-x'' + 2x' + x\} = -(s^2X(s) - 2s + 1) + 2(sX(s) - 2) + X(s)$
$$= (-s^2 + 2s + 1)X(s) + 2s - 5$$

Example 21.11

Voltage across a capacitor

The voltage, $v(t)$, across a capacitor of capacitance C is given by

$$v(t) = \frac{1}{C}\int_0^t i(t)\, dt$$

Taking Laplace transforms yields

$$V(s) = \frac{1}{Cs}I(s)$$

where $V(s) = \mathcal{L}\{v(t)\}$ and $I(s) = \mathcal{L}\{i(t)\}$.

Exercises 21.5

1 The Laplace transform of $y(t)$ is $Y(s)$, $y(0) = 3$, $y'(0) = 1$. Find the Laplace transforms of the following expressions.

(a) y'

(b) y''

(c) $3y'' - y'$

(d) $y'' + 2y' + 3y$

(e) $3y'' - y' + 2y$

(f) $-4y'' + 5y' - 3y$

(g) $3\dfrac{d^2 y}{dt^2} + 6\dfrac{dy}{dt} + 8y$

(h) $4\dfrac{d^2 y}{dt^2} - 8\dfrac{dy}{dt} + 6y$

2 Given the Laplace transform of $f(t)$ is $F(s)$, $f(0) = 2$, $f'(0) = 3$ and $f''(0) = -1$, find the Laplace transforms of

(a) $3f' - 2f$

(b) $3f'' - f' + f$

(c) f'''

(d) $2f''' - f'' + 4f' - 2f$

3 (a) If $F(s) = \mathcal{L}\{f(t)\} = \int_0^\infty e^{-st} f(t)\, dt$, show using integration by parts that

    (i) $\mathcal{L}\{f'(t)\} = sF(s) - f(0)$

    (ii) $\mathcal{L}\{f''(t)\} = s^2 F(s) - sf(0) - f'(0)$

(b) If $F(s) = \mathcal{L}\{f(t)\}$ prove that

$$\mathcal{L}\{e^{-at} f(t)\} = F(s + a)$$

Deduce $\mathcal{L}\{te^{-t}\}$, given $\mathcal{L}\{t\} = \dfrac{1}{s^2}$.

Solutions

1 (a) $sY - 3$

(b) $s^2 Y - 3s - 1$

(c) $3s^2 Y - sY - 9s$

(d) $(s^2 + 2s + 3)Y - 3s - 7$

(e) $(3s^2 - s + 2)Y - 9s$

(f) $(-4s^2 + 5s - 3)Y + 12s - 11$

(g) $(3s^2 + 6s + 8)Y - 9s - 21$

(h) $(4s^2 - 8s + 6)Y - 12s + 20$

2 (a) $(3s - 2)F - 6$

(b) $(3s^2 - s + 1)F - 6s - 7$

(c) $s^3 F - 2s^2 - 3s + 1$

(d) $(2s^3 - s^2 + 4s - 2)F - 4s^2 - 4s - 3$

3 (b) $\dfrac{1}{(s + 1)^2}$

21.6   Inverse Laplace transforms

As mentioned in Section 21.5, the Laplace transform can be used to solve differential equations. However, before such an application can be put into practice, we must study the inverse Laplace transform. So far in this chapter we have been given functions of t and found their Laplace transforms. We now consider the problem of finding a function $f(t)$, having been given the Laplace transform, $F(s)$. Clearly Table 21.1 and the properties of Laplace transforms will help us to do this. If $\mathcal{L}\{f(t)\} = F(s)$ we write

$$f(t) = \mathcal{L}^{-1}\{F(s)\}$$

and call $\mathcal{L}^{-1}$ the inverse Laplace transform. Like $\mathcal{L}$, $\mathcal{L}^{-1}$ can be shown to be a linear operator.

Example 21.12 Find the inverse Laplace transforms of the following:

(a) $\dfrac{2}{s^3}$ (b) $\dfrac{16}{s^3}$ (c) $\dfrac{s}{s^2+1}$ (d) $\dfrac{1}{s^2+1}$ (e) $\dfrac{s+1}{s^2+1}$

Solution (a) We need to find a function of t which has a Laplace transform of $\dfrac{2}{s^3}$. Using Table 21.1 we see $\mathcal{L}^{-1}\left\{\dfrac{2}{s^3}\right\} = t^2$.

(b) $\mathcal{L}^{-1}\left\{\dfrac{16}{s^3}\right\} = 8\mathcal{L}^{-1}\left\{\dfrac{2}{s^3}\right\} = 8t^2$

(c) $\mathcal{L}^{-1}\left\{\dfrac{s}{s^2+1}\right\} = \cos t$

(d) $\mathcal{L}^{-1}\left\{\dfrac{1}{s^2+1}\right\} = \sin t$

(e) $\mathcal{L}^{-1}\left\{\dfrac{s+1}{s^2+1}\right\} = \mathcal{L}^{-1}\left\{\dfrac{s}{s^2+1}\right\} + \mathcal{L}^{-1}\left\{\dfrac{1}{s^2+1}\right\} = \cos t + \sin t$

In parts (a), (c) and (d) we obtained the inverse Laplace transform by referring directly to the table. In (b) and (e) we used the linearity properties of the inverse transform, and then referred to Table 21.1.

Example 21.13 Find the inverse Laplace transforms of the following functions:

(a) $\dfrac{10}{(s+2)^4}$ (b) $\dfrac{(s+1)}{(s+1)^2+4}$ (c) $\dfrac{15}{(s-1)^2-9}$

Solution (a) $\mathcal{L}^{-1}\left\{\dfrac{10}{(s+2)^4}\right\} = \dfrac{10}{6}\mathcal{L}^{-1}\left\{\dfrac{6}{(s+2)^4}\right\} = \dfrac{5t^3\,e^{-2t}}{3}$

(b) $\mathcal{L}^{-1}\left\{\dfrac{s+1}{(s+1)^2+4}\right\} = \mathcal{L}^{-1}\left\{\dfrac{s+1}{(s+1)^2+2^2}\right\} = e^{-t}\cos 2t$

(c) $\mathcal{L}^{-1}\left\{\dfrac{15}{(s-1)^2-9}\right\} = 5\mathcal{L}^{-1}\left\{\dfrac{3}{(s-1)^2-3^2}\right\} = 5\,e^t\sinh 3t$

The function is written to match exactly the standard forms given in Table 21.1, with possibly a constant factor being present. Often the denominator needs to be written in standard form as illustrated in the next example.

Example 21.14   Find the inverse Laplace transforms of the following functions.

(a) $\dfrac{s+3}{s^2+6s+13}$ (b) $\dfrac{2s+3}{s^2+6s+13}$ (c) $\dfrac{s-1}{2s^2+8s+11}$

Solution   (a) By completing the square we can write

$$s^2+6s+13=(s+3)^2+4=(s+3)^2+2^2$$

Hence we may write

$$\mathcal{L}^{-1}\left\{\frac{s+3}{s^2+6s+13}\right\}=\mathcal{L}^{-1}\left\{\frac{s+3}{(s+3)^2+2^2}\right\}=\mathrm{e}^{-3t}\cos 2t$$

(b) $\dfrac{2s+3}{s^2+6s+13}=\dfrac{2s+3}{(s+3)^2+2^2}=\dfrac{2s+6}{(s+3)^2+2^2}-\dfrac{3}{(s+3)^2+2^2}$

$$=2\left(\frac{s+3}{(s+3)^2+2^2}\right)-\frac{3}{2}\left(\frac{2}{(s+3)^2+2^2}\right)$$

The expressions in brackets are standard forms so their inverse Laplace transforms can be found from Table 21.1.

$$\mathcal{L}^{-1}\left\{\frac{2s+3}{s^2+6s+13}\right\}=2\,\mathrm{e}^{-3t}\cos 2t-\frac{3\,\mathrm{e}^{-3t}\sin 2t}{2}$$

(c) We write the expression using standard forms.

$$\frac{s-1}{2s^2+8s+11}=\frac{1}{2}\frac{s-1}{s^2+4s+5.5}=\frac{1}{2}\frac{s-1}{(s+2)^2+1.5}$$

$$=\frac{1}{2}\left(\frac{s+2}{(s+2)^2+1.5}-\frac{3}{(s+2)^2+1.5}\right)$$

$$=\frac{1}{2}\left(\frac{s+2}{(s+2)^2+1.5}-\frac{3}{\sqrt{1.5}}\frac{\sqrt{1.5}}{(s+2)^2+1.5}\right)$$

Having written the expression in terms of standard forms, the inverse Laplace transform can now be found.

$$\mathcal{L}^{-1}\left\{\frac{s-1}{2s^2+8s+11}\right\}=\frac{1}{2}\left(\mathrm{e}^{-2t}\cos\sqrt{1.5}t-\frac{3}{\sqrt{1.5}}\mathrm{e}^{-2t}\sin\sqrt{1.5}t\right)$$

In every case the given function of s is written as a linear combination of standard forms contained in Table 21.1.

Exercises 21.6

1 By using the standard forms in Table 21.1 find the inverse Laplace transforms of the following functions:

(a) $\dfrac{1}{s}$ (b) $\dfrac{2}{s^3}$

(c) $\dfrac{8}{s}$ (d) $\dfrac{1}{s+2}$

(e) $\dfrac{6}{s+4}$ (f) $\dfrac{5}{s-3}$

(g) $\dfrac{7}{s+8}$ (h) $\dfrac{2}{s^2+4}$

(i) $\dfrac{s}{s^2+9}$ (j) $\dfrac{6s}{s^2+4}$

(k) $\dfrac{20}{s^2+16}$ (l) $\dfrac{2}{(s+1)^2}$

(m) $\dfrac{8}{(s+2)^2}$ (n) $\dfrac{9}{(s+3)^3}$

(o) $\dfrac{e^{-3s}}{s}$ (p) $\dfrac{4e^{-6s}}{s}$

(q) e^{-9s} (r) $4e^{-8s}$

(s) $\dfrac{4}{s^2-16}$ (t) $\dfrac{s}{s^2-9}$

(u) $\dfrac{12}{s^2-9}$ (v) $\dfrac{6s}{s^2-8}$

(w) $\dfrac{2}{(s+1)^2-4}$ (x) $\dfrac{s+3}{(s+3)^2-4}$

(y) $\dfrac{2}{(s+3)^2-4}$ (z) $\dfrac{6s}{s^2-5}$

2 Find the inverse Laplace transforms of the following functions:

(a) $\dfrac{3}{2s}$ (b) $\dfrac{4}{s}-\dfrac{1}{s^3}$

(c) $\dfrac{30}{s^2}$ (d) $\dfrac{1}{3(s+2)}$

(e) $\dfrac{3s-7}{s^2+9}$ (f) $\dfrac{s-6}{s-4}$

(g) $\dfrac{s+4}{(s+4)^2+1}$ (h) $\dfrac{5}{(s+4)^2+1}$

(i) $\dfrac{6s+17}{(s+4)^2+1}$ (j) $\dfrac{s}{s^2+2s+7}$

(k) $\dfrac{0.5}{(s+0.5)^2}$ (l) $\dfrac{s+5}{s^2+8s+20}$

(m) $\dfrac{6s+9}{s^2+2s+10}$ (n) $\dfrac{7s+3}{s^2+4s+8}$

Solutions

1 (a) 1   (b) t^2

(c) 8   (d) e^{-2t}

(e) $6e^{-4t}$ (f) $5e^{3t}$

(g) $7e^{-8t}$ (h) $\sin 2t$

(i) $\cos 3t$ (j) $6\cos 2t$

(k) $5\sin 4t$ (l) $2te^{-t}$

(m) $8te^{-2t}$ (n) $\frac{9}{2}t^2 e^{-3t}$

(o) $u(t-3)$ (p) $4u(t-6)$

(q) $\delta(t-9)$ (r) $4\delta(t-8)$

(s) $\sinh 4t$ (t) $\cosh 3t$

(u) $4\sinh 3t$ (v) $6\cosh\sqrt{8}t$

(w) $e^{-t}\sinh 2t$ (x) $e^{-3t}\cosh 2t$

(y) $e^{-3t}\sinh 2t$ (z) $6\cosh\sqrt{5}t$

2 (a) $\frac{3}{2}$

(b) $4-\dfrac{t^2}{2}$

(c) $30t$

(d) $\dfrac{e^{-2t}}{3}$

(e) $3\cos 3t-\frac{7}{3}\sin 3t$

(f) $\delta(t)-2e^{4t}$

(g) $e^{-4t}\cos t$

(h) $5e^{-4t}\sin t$

(i) $6e^{-4t}\cos t-7e^{-4t}\sin t$

(j) $e^{-t}\cos\sqrt{6}t-\dfrac{1}{\sqrt{6}}e^{-t}\sin\sqrt{6}t$

(k) $\dfrac{te^{-t/2}}{2}$

(l) $e^{-4t}\cos 2t+\frac{1}{2}e^{-4t}\sin 2t$

(m) $6e^{-t}\cos 3t+e^{-t}\sin 3t$

(n) $7e^{-2t}\cos 2t-\frac{11}{2}e^{-2t}\sin 2t$

21.7 Using partial fractions to find the inverse Laplace transform

The inverse Laplace transform of a fraction is often best found by expressing it as its partial fractions, and finding the inverse transform of these. (See Section 1.6 for a treatment of partial fractions.)

Example 21.15 Find the inverse Laplace transform of

(a) $\dfrac{4s - 1}{s^2 - s}$ (b) $\dfrac{6s + 8}{s^2 + 3s + 2}$

Solution (a) We express $\dfrac{4s - 1}{s^2 - s}$ as its partial fractions:

$$\frac{4s - 1}{s^2 - s} = \frac{4s - 1}{s(s - 1)} = \frac{A}{s} + \frac{B}{s - 1}$$

Using the technique of Section 1.6 we find that $A = 1$, $B = 3$ and hence

$$\frac{4s - 1}{s^2 - s} = \frac{1}{s} + \frac{3}{s - 1}$$

The inverse Laplace transform of each partial fraction is found:

$$\mathcal{L}^{-1}\left(\frac{1}{s}\right) = 1, \qquad \mathcal{L}^{-1}\left(\frac{3}{s - 1}\right) = 3\,e^t$$

Hence

$$\mathcal{L}^{-1}\left(\frac{4s - 1}{s^2 - s}\right) = 1 + 3\,e^t$$

(b) The expression is expressed as its partial fractions. This was done in Section 1.6.

$$\frac{6s + 8}{s^2 + 3s + 2} = \frac{2}{s + 1} + \frac{4}{s + 2}$$

The inverse Laplace transform of each partial fraction is noted:

$$\mathcal{L}^{-1}\left(\frac{2}{s + 1}\right) = 2\,e^{-t} \qquad \mathcal{L}^{-1}\left(\frac{4}{s + 2}\right) = 4\,e^{-2t}$$

and so

$$\mathcal{L}^{-1}\left(\frac{6s + 8}{s^2 + 3s + 2}\right) = 2\,e^{-t} + 4\,e^{-2t}$$

Example 21.16   Find the inverse Laplace transform of $\dfrac{3s^2 + 6s + 2}{s^3 + 3s^2 + 2s}$.

Solution   Following from the work in Section 1.6.1, we have

$$\frac{3s^2 + 6s + 2}{s^3 + 3s^2 + 2s} = \frac{1}{s} + \frac{1}{s+1} + \frac{1}{s+2}$$

The inverse Laplace transform of the partial fractions is easily found.

$$\mathcal{L}^{-1}\left\{\frac{3s^2 + 6s + 2}{s^3 + 3s^2 + 2s}\right\} = 1 + e^{-t} + e^{-2t}$$

Example 21.17   Find the inverse Laplace transform of $\dfrac{3s^2 + 11s + 14}{s^3 + 2s^2 - 11s - 52}$.

Solution   From Example 1.33 we have

$$\frac{3s^2 + 11s + 14}{s^3 + 2s^2 - 11s - 52} = \frac{2}{s-4} + \frac{s+3}{s^2 + 6s + 13}$$

We find the inverse Laplace transforms of the partial fractions.

$$\mathcal{L}^{-1}\left\{\frac{2}{s-4}\right\} = 2\,e^{4t}$$

$$\mathcal{L}^{-1}\left\{\frac{s+3}{s^2 + 6s + 13}\right\} = e^{-3t}\cos 2t$$

So

$$\mathcal{L}^{-1}\left\{\frac{3s^2 + 11s + 14}{s^3 + 2s^2 - 11s - 52}\right\} = 2\,e^{4t} + e^{-3t}\cos 2t$$

Exercises 21.7

1 Express the following as partial fractions and hence find their inverse Laplace transforms:

(a) $\dfrac{5s + 2}{(s+1)(s+2)}$

(b) $\dfrac{3s + 4}{(s+2)(s+3)}$

(c) $\dfrac{4s + 1}{(s+3)(s+4)}$

(d) $\dfrac{6s - 5}{(s+5)(s+3)}$

(e) $\dfrac{4s + 1}{s(s+2)(s+3)}$

(f) $\dfrac{7s + 3}{s(s+3)(s+4)}$

(g) $\dfrac{6s + 7}{s(s+2)(s+4)}$

(h) $\dfrac{8s - 5}{(s+1)(s+2)(s+3)}$

(i) $\dfrac{3s+5}{(s+1)(s^2+3s+2)}$

(j) $\dfrac{2s-8}{(s+2)(s^2+7s+6)}$

2 Express the following fractions as partial fractions and hence find their inverse Laplace transforms:

(a) $\dfrac{3s+3}{(s-1)(s+2)}$

(b) $\dfrac{5s}{(s+1)(2s-3)}$

(c) $\dfrac{2s+5}{s+2}$

(d) $\dfrac{s^2+4s+4}{s^3+2s^2+5s}$

(e) $\dfrac{1-s}{(s+1)(s^2+2s+2)}$

(f) $\dfrac{s+4}{s^2+4s+4}$

(g) $\dfrac{2(s^3-3s^2+s-1)}{(s^2+4s+1)(s^2+1)}$

(h) $\dfrac{3s^2-s+8}{(s^2-2s+3)(s+2)}$

Solutions

1 (a) $8e^{-2t}-3e^{-t}$

(b) $5e^{-3t}-2e^{-2t}$

(c) $15e^{-4t}-11e^{-3t}$

(d) $\frac{35}{2}e^{-5t}-\frac{23}{2}e^{-3t}$

(e) $\frac{1}{6}+\frac{7}{2}e^{-2t}-\frac{11}{3}e^{-3t}$

(f) $\frac{1}{4}+6e^{-3t}-\frac{25}{4}e^{-4t}$

(g) $\frac{7}{8}+\frac{5}{4}e^{-2t}-\frac{17}{8}e^{-4t}$

(h) $21e^{-2t}-\frac{29}{2}e^{-3t}-\frac{13}{2}e^{-t}$

(i) $e^{-t}+2te^{-t}-e^{-2t}$

(j) $3e^{-2t}-e^{-6t}-2e^{-t}$

2 (a) $2e^t+e^{-2t}$

(b) $e^{-t}+\dfrac{3e^{3t/2}}{2}$

(c) $2\delta(t)+e^{-2t}$

(d) $\frac{1}{5}(4+e^{-t}\cos 2t+\frac{11}{2}e^{-t}\sin 2t)$

(e) $e^{-t}(2-2\cos t-\sin t)$

(f) $e^{-2t}(1+2t)$

(g) $e^{-2t}\left(3\cosh\sqrt{3}t-\dfrac{8}{\sqrt{3}}\sinh\sqrt{3}t\right)-\cos t$

(h) $e^t(\cos\sqrt{2}t+\sqrt{2}\sin\sqrt{2}t)+2e^{-2t}$

21.8 Finding the inverse Laplace transform using complex numbers

In Sections 21.6 and 21.7 we found the inverse Laplace transform using standard forms and partial fractions. We now look at a method of finding inverse Laplace transforms using complex numbers. Essentially the method is one using partial fractions, but where all the factors in the denominator are linear – that is, there are no quadratic factors. We illustrate the method using Example 21.14.

Example 21.18 Find the inverse Laplace transforms of the following functions.

(a) $\dfrac{s+3}{s^2+6s+13}$ (b) $\dfrac{2s+3}{s^2+6s+13}$ (c) $\dfrac{s-1}{2s^2+8s+11}$

Solution   (a)   We first factorize the denominator. To do this we solve $s^2 + 6s + 13 = 0$ using the formula:

$$s = \frac{-6 \pm \sqrt{36 - 4(13)}}{2}$$

$$= \frac{-6 \pm \sqrt{-16}}{2}$$

$$= \frac{-6 \pm 4j}{2}$$

$$= -3 \pm 2j$$

It then follows that the denominator can be factorized as $(s - a)(s - b)$ where $a = -3 + 2j$ and $b = -3 - 2j$. Then, using the partial fractions method

$$\frac{s + 3}{s^2 + 6s + 13} = \frac{s + 3}{(s - a)(s - b)} = \frac{A}{s - a} + \frac{B}{s - b}$$

The unknown constants A and B can now be found.

$$s + 3 = A(s - b) + B(s - a)$$

Put $s = a = -3 + 2j$

$$2j = A(-3 + 2j - b) = A(4j)$$

$$A = \frac{1}{2}$$

Equate the coefficients of s:

$$1 = A + B$$
$$B = \frac{1}{2}$$

So,

$$\frac{s + 3}{s^2 + 6s + 13} = \frac{1}{2}\left(\frac{1}{s - a} + \frac{1}{s - b}\right)$$

The inverse Laplace transform can now be found.

$$\mathcal{L}^{-1}\left\{\frac{s + 3}{s^2 + 6s + 13}\right\} = \frac{1}{2}\mathcal{L}^{-1}\left\{\frac{1}{s - a} + \frac{1}{s - b}\right\}$$

$$= \frac{1}{2}(e^{at} + e^{bt}) = \frac{1}{2}(e^{(-3+2j)t} + e^{(-3-2j)t})$$

$$= \frac{1}{2}e^{-3t}(e^{2jt} + e^{-2jt})$$

$$= \frac{1}{2}e^{-3t}(\cos 2t + j \sin 2t + \cos 2t - j \sin 2t)$$

$$= e^{-3t}\cos 2t$$

(b) $\dfrac{2s+3}{s^2+6s+13} = \dfrac{2s+3}{(s-a)(s-b)} = \dfrac{A}{s-a} + \dfrac{B}{s-b}$

where $a = -3 + 2j$ and $b = -3 - 2j$. Hence,

$$2s + 3 = A(s-b) + B(s-a)$$

Put $s = a = -3 + 2j$,

$$-3 + 4j = A(4j)$$
$$A = 1 + 0.75j$$

Equate the coefficients of s:

$$2 = A + B$$
$$B = 1 - 0.75j$$

Hence,

$$\dfrac{2s+3}{s^2+6s+13} = \dfrac{1+0.75j}{s-a} + \dfrac{1-0.75j}{s-b}$$

Taking the inverse Laplace transform yields

$$\mathcal{L}^{-1}\left\{\dfrac{2s+3}{s^2+6s+13}\right\} = (1+0.75j)e^{at} + (1-0.75j)\,e^{bt}$$

$$= (1+0.75j)\,e^{(-3+2j)t} + (1-0.75j)\,e^{(-3-2j)t}$$

$$= (1+0.75j)\,e^{-3t}(\cos 2t + j\sin 2t)$$

$$+ (1-0.75j)\,e^{-3t}(\cos 2t - j\sin 2t)$$

$$= e^{-3t}(2\cos 2t - 1.5\sin 2t)$$

(c) $\dfrac{s-1}{2s^2+8s+11} = \dfrac{1}{2}\left(\dfrac{s-1}{s^2+4s+5.5}\right) = \dfrac{1}{2}\left(\dfrac{s-1}{(s-a)(s-b)}\right)$

where $a = -2 + \sqrt{1.5}j$, $b = -2 - \sqrt{1.5}j$.

Applying the method of partial fractions produces

$$\dfrac{s-1}{(s-a)(s-b)} = \dfrac{A}{s-a} + \dfrac{B}{s-b}$$

Hence,

$$s - 1 = A(s-b) + B(s-a)$$

By letting $s = a$, then $s = b$ in turn, gives

$$A = 0.5 + \sqrt{1.5}j \qquad B = 0.5 - \sqrt{1.5}j$$

Hence we may write

$$\frac{s - 1}{(s - a)(s - b)} = \frac{0.5 + \sqrt{1.5}j}{s - a} + \frac{0.5 - \sqrt{1.5}j}{s - b}$$

Taking the inverse Laplace transform yields

$$\mathcal{L}^{-1}\left\{\frac{s - 1}{(s - a)(s - b)}\right\} = (0.5 + \sqrt{1.5}j)\, e^{at} + (0.5 - \sqrt{1.5}j)\, e^{bt}$$

$$= (0.5 + \sqrt{1.5}j)\, e^{(-2 + \sqrt{1.5}j)t}$$

$$+ (0.5 - \sqrt{1.5}j)\, e^{(-2 - \sqrt{1.5}j)t}$$

$$= e^{-2t}\{(0.5 + \sqrt{1.5}j)\, e^{\sqrt{1.5}jt}$$

$$+ (0.5 - \sqrt{1.5}j)\, e^{-\sqrt{1.5}jt}\}$$

$$= e^{-2t}\{(0.5 + \sqrt{1.5}j)(\cos\sqrt{1.5}t + j\sin\sqrt{1.5}t)$$

$$+ (0.5 - \sqrt{1.5}j)(\cos\sqrt{1.5}t - j\sin\sqrt{1.5}t)\}$$

$$= e^{-2t}(\cos\sqrt{1.5}t - 2\sqrt{1.5}\sin\sqrt{1.5}t)$$

Hence

$$\mathcal{L}^{-1}\left\{\frac{s - 1}{2s^2 + 8s + 11}\right\} = \frac{e^{-2t}}{2}(\cos\sqrt{1.5}t - 2\sqrt{1.5}\sin\sqrt{1.5}t)$$

As seen from Example 21.18, when complex numbers are allowed, all the factors in the denominator are linear. The unknown constants are evaluated using particular values of s or equating coefficients.

Exercises 21.8

1 Express the following expressions as partial fractions, using complex numbers if necessary. Hence find their inverse Laplace transforms.

(a) $\dfrac{3s - 2}{s^2 + 6s + 13}$

(b) $\dfrac{2s + 1}{s^2 - 2s + 2}$

(c) $\dfrac{s^2}{(s^2/2) - s + 5}$

(d) $\dfrac{s^2 + s + 1}{s^2 - 2s + 3}$

(e) $\dfrac{2s + 3}{-s^2 + 2s - 5}$

Solutions

1 (a) $\dfrac{\frac{3}{2}+11j/4}{s-a}+\dfrac{\frac{3}{2}-11j/4}{s-b}$

where $a=-3+2j$, $b=-3-2j$,

$e^{-3t}\left[3\cos 2t-\frac{11}{2}\sin 2t\right]$

(b) $\dfrac{1-3j/2}{s-a}+\dfrac{1+3j/2}{s-b}$

where $a=1+j$, $b=1-j$,

$e^t(2\cos t+3\sin t)$

(c) $\dfrac{2+8j/3}{s-a}+\dfrac{2-8j/3}{s-b}+2$

where $a=1+3j$, $b=1-3j$,

$e^t\left(4\cos 3t-\frac{16}{3}\sin 3t\right)+2\delta(t)$

(d) $1+\dfrac{\frac{3}{2}-j/(2\sqrt{2})}{s-a}+\dfrac{\frac{3}{2}+j/(2\sqrt{2})}{s-b}$

where $a=1+\sqrt{2}j$, $b=1-\sqrt{2}j$,

$\delta(t)+e^t\left(3\cos\sqrt{2}t+\dfrac{1}{\sqrt{2}}\sin\sqrt{2}t\right)$

(e) $\dfrac{-1+5j/4}{s-a}+\dfrac{-1-5j/4}{s-b}$

where $a=1+2j$, $b=1-2j$,

$e^t\left(-2\cos 2t-\frac{5}{2}\sin 2t\right)$

21.9 The convolution theorem

Let $f(t)$ and $g(t)$ be two piecewise continuous functions. The **convolution** of $f(t)$ and $g(t)$, denoted $(f*g)(t)$, is defined by

$$(f*g)(t)=\int_0^t f(t-v)g(v)\,dv$$

Example 21.19 Find the convolution of $2t$ and t^3.

Solution $f(t)=2t$, $g(t)=t^3$, $f(t-v)=2(t-v)$, $g(v)=v^3$.

$$2t*t^3=\int_0^t 2(t-v)v^3\,dv=2\int_0^t tv^3-v^4\,dv$$

$$=2\left[\frac{tv^4}{4}-\frac{v^5}{5}\right]_0^t=2\left[\frac{t^5}{4}-\frac{t^5}{5}\right]$$

$$=\frac{t^5}{10}$$

It can be shown that

$$f*g=g*f$$

but the proof is omitted. Instead, this property is illustrated by an example.

Example 21.20 Show that $f * g = g * f$ where $f(t) = 2t$ and $g(t) = t^3$.

Solution $f * g = 2t * t^3 = t^5/10$ by Example 21.19. From the definition of convolution

$$(g * f)(t) = \int_0^t g(t - v) f(v) \, dv$$

We have $g(t) = t^3$, so $g(t - v) = (t - v)^3$, and $f(v) = 2v$. Therefore

$$g * f = t^3 * 2t = \int_0^t (t - v)^3 2v \, dv$$

$$= \int_0^t (t^3 - 3t^2 v + 3t v^2 - v^3) 2v \, dv$$

$$= 2 \int_0^t t^3 v - 3t^2 v^2 + 3t v^3 - v^4 \, dv$$

$$= 2 \left[\frac{t^3 v^2}{2} - t^2 v^3 + \frac{3t v^4}{4} - \frac{v^5}{5} \right]_0^t = \frac{t^5}{10}$$

For any functions $f(t)$ and $g(t)$

$$f * g = g * f$$

21.9.1 The convolution theorem

Let $f(t)$ and $g(t)$ be piecewise continuous functions, with $\mathcal{L}\{f(t)\} = F(s)$ and $\mathcal{L}\{g(t)\} = G(s)$. The convolution theorem allows us to find the inverse Laplace transform of a product of transforms, $F(s)G(s)$.

$$\mathcal{L}^{-1}\{F(s)G(s)\} = (f * g)(t)$$

Example 21.21 Use the convolution theorem to find the inverse Laplace transforms of the following functions.

(a) $\dfrac{1}{(s + 2)(s + 3)}$ (b) $\dfrac{3}{s(s^2 + 4)}$

Solution (a) Let $F(s) = \dfrac{1}{s + 2}$, $G(s) = \dfrac{1}{s + 3}$.

Then $f(t) = \mathcal{L}^{-1}\{F(s)\} = e^{-2t}$, $g(t) = \mathcal{L}^{-1}\{G(s)\} = e^{-3t}$.

$$\mathcal{L}^{-1}\left\{\frac{1}{(s+2)(s+3)}\right\} = \mathcal{L}^{-1}\{F(s)G(s)\} = (f * g)(t)$$

$$= \int_0^t e^{-2(t-v)}e^{-3v}\,dv = \int_0^t e^{-2t}e^{2v}e^{-3v}\,dv$$

$$= \int_0^t e^{-2t}e^{-v}\,dv$$

$$= e^{-2t}[-e^{-v}]_0^t = e^{-2t}(-e^{-t}+1) = e^{-2t} - e^{-3t}$$

(b) Let $F(s) = \dfrac{3}{s}$, $G(s) = \dfrac{1}{s^2+4}$. Then $f(t) = 3$, $g(t) = \frac{1}{2}\sin 2t$. So,

$$\mathcal{L}^{-1}\left\{\frac{3}{s(s^2+4)}\right\} = \mathcal{L}^{-1}\{F(s)G(s)\}$$

$$= (f * g)(t)$$

$$= \int_0^t 3\frac{\sin 2v}{2}\,dv = \frac{3}{2}\int_0^t \sin 2v\,dv$$

$$= \frac{3}{2}\left[\frac{-\cos 2v}{2}\right]_0^t = \frac{3}{4}(1 - \cos 2t)$$

Exercises 21.9

1 Find

(a) $e^{-2t} * e^{-t}$

(b) $t^2 * e^{-3t}$

2 Find $f * g$ when

(a) $f = 1, g = t$

(b) $f = t^2, g = t$

(c) $f = e^t, g = t$

(d) $f = \sin t, g = t$

In each case verify that
$\mathcal{L}\{f\} \times \mathcal{L}\{g\} = \mathcal{L}\{f * g\}$.

3 If $F(s) = \dfrac{1}{s-1}$, $G(s) = \dfrac{1}{s}$ and

$H(s) = \dfrac{1}{2s+3}$ use the convolution theorem to find the inverse Laplace transforms of

(a) $F(s)G(s)$

(b) $F(s)H(s)$

(c) $G(s)H(s)$

4 Use the convolution theorem to determine the inverse Laplace transforms of

(a) $\dfrac{1}{s^2(s+1)}$

(b) $\dfrac{1}{(s+3)(s-2)}$

(c) $\dfrac{1}{(s^2+1)^2}$

Solutions

1 (a) $e^{-t} - e^{-2t}$

(b) $\dfrac{t^2}{3} - \dfrac{2t}{9} + \dfrac{2}{27} - \dfrac{2e^{-3t}}{27}$

2 (a) $\dfrac{t^2}{2}$

(b) $\dfrac{t^4}{12}$

(c) $-t - 1 + e^t$

(d) $t - \sin t$

3 (a) $e^t - 1$

(b) $\dfrac{e^t - e^{-3t/2}}{5}$

(c) $\dfrac{1 - e^{-3t/2}}{3}$

4 (a) $t - 1 + e^{-t}$

(b) $\dfrac{e^{2t} - e^{-3t}}{5}$

(c) $\dfrac{\sin t - t\cos t}{2}$

21.10 Solving linear constant coefficient differential equations using the Laplace transform

So far we have seen how to find the Laplace transform of a function of time and how to find the inverse Laplace transform. We now apply this to finding the particular solution of differential equations. The initial conditions are automatically satisfied when solving an equation using the Laplace transform. They are contained in the transform of the derivative terms.

The Laplace transform of the equation is found. This transforms the differential equation into an algebraic equation. The transform of the dependent variable is found and then the inverse transform is calculated to yield the required particular solution.

Example 21.22 Solve the differential equation

$$\frac{dx}{dt} + x = 0 \qquad x(0) = 3$$

using Laplace transforms.

Solution The Laplace transform of each term is found:

$$\mathcal{L}(x) = X(s), \qquad \mathcal{L}\left(\frac{dx}{dt}\right) = sX(s) - x(0) = sX(s) - 3$$

Note that we write $X(s)$ to draw attention to the fact that X is a function of s; $X(s)$ does not mean X multiplied by s. Taking the Laplace transform of the equation yields

$$sX(s) - 3 + X(s) = 0$$

The equation is rearranged for $X(s)$:

$$sX(s) + X(s) = 3$$
$$(s + 1)X(s) = 3$$
$$X(s) = \frac{3}{s + 1}$$

Taking the inverse Laplace transform of both sides of the equation gives

$$x(t) = 3\,e^{-t}$$

Example 21.23 Solve

$$\frac{dx}{dt} + x = 9\,e^{2t} \qquad x(0) = 3$$

using the Laplace transform.

Solution The Laplace transform of both sides of the equation is found.

$$sX(s) - x(0) + X(s) = \frac{9}{s - 2}$$

$$sX(s) - 3 + X(s) = \frac{9}{s - 2}$$

$$(s + 1)X(s) = \frac{9}{s - 2} + 3$$

$$(s + 1)X(s) = \frac{3(s + 1)}{s - 2}$$

$$X(s) = \frac{3}{s - 2}$$

Taking the inverse Laplace transform yields

$$x(t) = 3\,e^{2t}$$

Example 21.24 ***RL* circuit with ramp input**

Use the Laplace transform to solve

$$iR + L\frac{di}{dt} = t \qquad t \geqslant 0 \qquad i(0) = 0$$

This equation was introduced in Example 19.17.

Solution Let

$$\mathcal{L}(i(t)) = I(s)$$

Then

$$\mathcal{L}\left(\frac{di}{dt}\right) = sI(s) - i(0) = sI(s) - 0 = sI(s)$$

From Table 21.1 we see that

$$\mathcal{L}(t) = \frac{1}{s^2}$$

We note that R and L are constants. We can now take the Laplace transform of the given equation. This gives

$$I(s)R + LsI(s) = \frac{1}{s^2}$$

This equation is solved for $I(s)$.

$$I(s)(R + Ls) = \frac{1}{s^2}$$

$$I(s) = \frac{1}{s^2(R + Ls)}$$

In order to take the inverse Laplace transform and hence find $i(t)$ we express $I(s)$ as the sum of its partial fractions. The expression

$$\frac{1}{s^2(R + Ls)}$$

has a repeated linear factor, s^2 in the denominator, giving rise to partial fractions

$$\frac{A}{s} + \frac{B}{s^2}$$

The linear factor, $R + Ls$, gives rise to a partial fraction of the form

$$\frac{C}{R + Ls}$$

Hence

$$I(s) = \frac{1}{s^2(R + Ls)} = \frac{A}{s} + \frac{B}{s^2} + \frac{C}{R + Ls}$$

The unknown constants, A, B and C, need to be expressed in terms of the known constants R and L. Multiplying the above equation by $s^2(R + Ls)$ yields

$$1 = As(R + Ls) + B(R + Ls) + Cs^2 \tag{1}$$

Letting $s = 0$ in Equation (1) gives

$$1 = BR$$

and so $B = \dfrac{1}{R}$.

We note that when $s = -\dfrac{R}{L}$ then $R + Ls$ is 0. Hence letting $s = -\dfrac{R}{L}$ in Equation (1) gives

$$1 = C\left(-\frac{R}{L}\right)^2 \text{ from which } C = \frac{L^2}{R^2}$$

Comparing the coefficient of s on both sides of Equation (1) gives

$$0 = AR + BL$$

$$A = -\frac{BL}{R} = -\frac{L}{R^2}$$

Substituting the expressions for A, B and C into the expression for $I(s)$ gives

$$I(s) = -\frac{L}{R^2 s} + \frac{1}{R s^2} + \frac{L^2}{R^2(R + Ls)}$$

In readiness for taking inverse Laplace transforms we write the final term as follows:

$$\frac{L^2}{R^2(R + Ls)} = \frac{L^2}{R^2 L \left(\frac{R}{L} + s\right)} = \frac{L}{R^2 \left(\frac{R}{L} + s\right)}$$

Hence

$$I(s) = -\frac{L}{R^2 s} + \frac{1}{R s^2} + \frac{L}{R^2 \left(\frac{R}{L} + s\right)}$$

Taking the inverse Laplace transform yields

$$i(t) = -\frac{L}{R^2} + \frac{t}{R} + \frac{L}{R^2} e^{-(R/L)t} \qquad t \geqslant 0$$

This may be rearranged as

$$i(t) = \frac{t}{R} + \frac{L}{R^2}(e^{-(R/L)t} - 1) \qquad t \geqslant 0$$

Example 21.25   Solve

$$y'' - y = -t^2 \qquad y(0) = 2, \ y'(0) = 0$$

using the Laplace transform.

Solution   Let $\mathcal{L}(y) = Y(s)$. Then using the result stated in Section 21.5 we have

$$\mathcal{L}(y'') = s^2 Y(s) - sy(0) - y'(0) = s^2 Y(s) - 2s$$

We also note that

$$\mathcal{L}(-t^2) = -\frac{2}{s^3}$$

The Laplace transform of the differential equation is taken. This yields

$$s^2 Y(s) - 2s - Y(s) = -\frac{2}{s^3}$$

The equation is rearranged for $Y(s)$.

$$(s^2 - 1)Y(s) = -\frac{2}{s^3} + 2s$$

$$= \frac{2(s^4 - 1)}{s^3}$$

$$= \frac{2(s^2 - 1)(s^2 + 1)}{s^3}$$

By dividing the equation by $(s^2 - 1)$ we obtain

$$Y(s) = \frac{2(s^2 - 1)(s^2 + 1)}{s^3(s^2 - 1)} = \frac{2(s^2 + 1)}{s^3}$$

$$= \frac{2s^2}{s^3} + \frac{2}{s^3} = \frac{2}{s} + \frac{2}{s^3}$$

Taking the inverse Laplace transform gives

$$y(t) = 2 + t^2$$

Example 21.26   Solve

$$y'' + y' - 2y = -2 \qquad y(0) = 2, \ y'(0) = 1$$

Solution   Let $\mathcal{L}(y) = Y(s)$. Then

$$\mathcal{L}(y') = sY(s) - y(0) = sY(s) - 2$$
$$\mathcal{L}(y'') = s^2Y(s) - sy(0) - y'(0) = s^2Y(s) - 2s - 1$$

We also note that

$$\mathcal{L}(-2) = -\frac{2}{s}$$

We can now take the Laplace transform of the differential equation to get

$$s^2Y(s) - 2s - 1 + sY(s) - 2 - 2Y(s) = -\frac{2}{s}$$

and so

$$(s^2 + s - 2)Y(s) = -\frac{2}{s} + 2s + 3$$

$$(s - 1)(s + 2)Y(s) = \frac{2s^2 + 3s - 2}{s} = \frac{(2s - 1)(s + 2)}{s}$$

Dividing the equation by $(s - 1)(s + 2)$ gives

$$Y(s) = \frac{(2s - 1)(s + 2)}{s(s - 1)(s + 2)} = \frac{2s - 1}{s(s - 1)}$$

The expression, $\dfrac{2s - 1}{s(s - 1)}$, is written as its partial fractions:

$$Y(s) = \frac{1}{s} + \frac{1}{s - 1}$$

Taking the inverse Laplace transform yields

$$y(t) = 1 + e^t$$

Example 21.27   Solve

$$x'' + 2x' + 2x = e^{-t} \qquad x(0) = x'(0) = 0$$

using Laplace transforms.

Solution   Taking the Laplace transform of both sides:

$$s^2 X(s) - sx(0) - x'(0) + 2(sX(s) - x(0)) + 2X(s) = \frac{1}{s+1}$$

Therefore,

$$(s^2 + 2s + 2)X(s) = \frac{1}{s+1} \qquad \text{since } x(0) = x'(0) = 0$$

$$X(s) = \frac{1}{(s+1)(s^2 + 2s + 2)} = \frac{1}{(s+1)(s-a)(s-b)}$$

where $a = -1 + j$, $b = -1 - j$. Using partial fractions gives

$$X(s) = \frac{1}{s+1} - \frac{1}{2}\left(\frac{1}{s-a} + \frac{1}{s-b}\right)$$

Taking the inverse Laplace transform

$$x(t) = e^{-t} - \frac{1}{2}(e^{at} + e^{bt})$$

$$= e^{-t} - \frac{1}{2}(e^{(-1+j)t} + e^{(-1-j)t})$$

$$= e^{-t} - \frac{e^{-t}}{2}(e^{jt} + e^{-jt})$$

$$= e^{-t} - \frac{e^{-t}}{2}(\cos t + j\sin t + \cos t - j\sin t)$$

$$= e^{-t} - e^{-t}\cos t$$

Example 21.28   Solve

$$x'' - 5x' + 6x = 6t - 4 \qquad x(0) = 1, \ x'(0) = 2$$

Solution   The Laplace transform of both sides of the equation is found. Let $\mathcal{L}\{x\} = X(s)$.

$$s^2 X(s) - sx(0) - x'(0) - 5(sX(s) - x(0)) + 6X(s) = \frac{6}{s^2} - \frac{4}{s}$$

$$(s^2 - 5s + 6)X(s) = \frac{6}{s^2} - \frac{4}{s} + s - 3 = \frac{s^3 - 3s^2 - 4s + 6}{s^2}$$

$$X(s) = \frac{s^3 - 3s^2 - 4s + 6}{s^2(s^2 - 5s + 6)} = \frac{s^3 - 3s^2 - 4s + 6}{s^2(s - 2)(s - 3)}$$

$$= \frac{A}{s} + \frac{B}{s^2} + \frac{C}{s-2} + \frac{D}{s-3}$$

The constants A, B, C and D are evaluated in the usual way.

$$X(s) = \frac{1}{6s} + \frac{1}{s^2} + \frac{3}{2(s-2)} - \frac{2}{3(s-3)}$$

Taking the inverse Laplace transform yields

$$x(t) = \frac{1}{6} + t + \frac{3}{2}e^{2t} - \frac{2}{3}e^{3t}$$

Example 21.29   **Discharge of a capacitor**

In Example 2.17, we examined the variation in voltage across a capacitor, C, when it was switched in series with a resistor, R, at time $t = 0$. We stated a relationship for the time-varying voltage, v, across the capacitor. Prove this relationship. Refer to the example for details of the circuit.

Solution   First we must derive a differential equation for the circuit. Using Kirchhoff's voltage law and denoting the voltage across the resistor by v_R we obtain

$$v + v_R = 0$$

Using Ohm's law and denoting the current in the circuit by i we obtain

$$v + iR = 0$$

For the capacitor,

$$i = C\frac{dv}{dt}$$

Combining these equations gives

$$v + RC\frac{dv}{dt} = 0$$

We now take the Laplace transform of this equation. Using $\mathcal{L}\{v\} = V(s)$ we obtain

$$V(s) + RC(sV(s) - v(0)) = 0$$

$$V(s)(1 + RCs) = RCv(0)$$

$$V(s) = \frac{RCv(0)}{1 + RCs} = \frac{v(0)}{\dfrac{1}{RC} + s}$$

Taking the inverse Laplace transform of the equation yields

$$v = v(0)\,e^{-t/(RC)} \qquad t \geqslant 0$$

This is equivalent to the relationship stated in Example 2.17.

Example 21.30 **Electronic thermometer measuring oven temperature**

Many engineering systems can be modelled by a first-order differential equation. The time constant is a measure of the rapidity with which these systems respond to a change in input. Suppose an electronic thermometer is used to measure the temperature of an oven. The sensing element does not respond instantly to changes in the oven temperature because it takes time for the element to heat up or cool down. Provided the electronic circuitry does not introduce further time delays then the differential equation that models the thermometer is given by

$$\tau \frac{dv_m}{dt} + v_m = v_o$$

where v_m = measured temperature, v_o = oven temperature, τ = time constant of the sensor. For convenience the temperature is measured relative to the ambient room temperature, which forms a 'base line' for temperature measurement.

Suppose the sensing element of an electronic thermometer has a time constant of 2 seconds. If the temperature of the oven increases linearly at the rate of $3\,°C\ s^{-1}$ starting from an ambient room temperature of $20\,°C$ at $t = 0$, calculate the response of the thermometer to the changing oven temperature. State the maximum temperature error.

Solution Taking Laplace transforms of the equation gives

$$\tau(s V_m(s) - v_m(0)) + V_m(s) = V_o(s)$$

$v_m(0) = 0$ as the oven temperature and sensor temperature are identical at $t = 0$. Therefore,

$$\tau s V_m(s) + V_m(s) = V_o(s)$$

$$V_m(s) = \frac{V_o(s)}{1 + \tau s} \tag{21.1}$$

For this example, the input to the thermometer is a temperature ramp with a slope of $3\,°C\ s^{-1}$. Therefore, $v_o = 3t$ for $t \geqslant 0$:

$$V_o(s) = \mathcal{L}\{v_o(t)\} = \frac{3}{s^2} \tag{21.2}$$

Combining Equations (21.1) and (21.2) yields

$$V_m(s) = \frac{3}{s^2(1 + \tau s)} = \frac{3}{s^2(1 + 2s)} \qquad \text{since } \tau = 2$$

Then using partial fractions, we have

$$V_m(s) = \frac{3}{s^2} - \frac{6}{s} + \frac{12}{1 + 2s}$$

Taking the inverse Laplace transform yields

$$v_m = 3t - 6 + 6e^{-0.5t} \qquad t \geqslant 0$$

This response consists of three parts:

(1) a decaying transient, $6e^{-0.5t}$, which disappears with time;

(2) a ramp, $3t$, with the same slope as the oven temperature;

(3) a fixed negative temperature error, -6.

Therefore, after the transient has decayed the measured temperature follows the oven temperature with a fixed negative error. It is instructive to obtain the temperature error by an alternative method. Given that the temperature error is v_e, then

$$v_e = v_m - v_o$$

and

$$V_e(s) = V_m(s) - V_o(s) \tag{21.3}$$

Combining Equations (21.1) and (21.3) yields

$$V_e(s) = \frac{V_o(s)}{1 + \tau s} - V_o(s) = \frac{-\tau s V_o(s)}{1 + \tau s} \tag{21.4}$$

Combining Equations (21.2) and (21.4) yields

$$V_e(s) = \frac{-\tau s}{1 + \tau s} \frac{3}{s^2} = \frac{-3\tau}{s(1 + \tau s)}$$

The final value theorem can be used to find the steady-state error.

$$\lim_{t \to \infty} v_e(t) = \lim_{s \to 0} s V_e(s) = \lim_{s \to 0} \left[\frac{-3\tau s}{s(1 + \tau s)} \right] = -3\tau = -6$$

that is, the steady-state temperature error is $-6\,°C$. It is important to note that the final value theorem can only be used if it is known that the time function tends to a limit as $t \to \infty$. In many cases engineers know this is the case from experience.

The Laplace transform technique can also be used to solve simultaneous differential equations.

Example 21.31   Solve the simultaneous differential equations

$$x' + x + \frac{y'}{2} = 1 \qquad x(0) = y(0) = 0$$

$$\frac{x'}{2} + y' + y = 0$$

Solution   Take the Laplace transforms of both equations.

$$sX(s) - x(0) + X(s) + \frac{sY(s) - y(0)}{2} = \frac{1}{s}$$

$$\frac{sX(s) - x(0)}{2} + sY(s) - y(0) + Y(s) = 0$$

These are rearranged to give

$$(s+1)X(s) + \frac{sY(s)}{2} = \frac{1}{s}$$

$$\frac{sX(s)}{2} + (s+1)Y(s) = 0$$

These simultaneous algebraic equations need to be solved for $X(s)$ and $Y(s)$. By Cramer's rule (see Section 8.7.2)

$$Y(s) = \frac{\begin{vmatrix} s+1 & 1/s \\ s/2 & 0 \end{vmatrix}}{\begin{vmatrix} s+1 & s/2 \\ s/2 & s+1 \end{vmatrix}} = \frac{-1/2}{(s+1)^2 - s^2/4}$$

$$= -\frac{1}{2}\left\{\frac{1}{3s^2/4 + 2s + 1}\right\}$$

$$= -\frac{1}{2}\left\{\frac{4}{3s^2 + 8s + 4}\right\}$$

$$= -\frac{1}{2}\left\{\frac{4}{(3s+2)(s+2)}\right\}$$

Using partial fractions we find

$$Y(s) = -\frac{1}{2}\left\{\frac{3}{3s+2} - \frac{1}{s+2}\right\}$$

$$= -\frac{1}{2}\left\{\frac{1}{s+\frac{2}{3}} - \frac{1}{s+2}\right\}$$

and hence

$$y(t) = \frac{1}{2}(e^{-2t} - e^{-2t/3})$$

Similarly,

$$X(s) = \frac{4(s+1)}{s(3s+2)(s+2)} = \frac{1}{s} - \frac{1}{2(s+\frac{2}{3})} - \frac{1}{2(s+2)}$$

and so

$$x(t) = 1 - \tfrac{1}{2}(e^{-2t/3} + e^{-2t})$$

Exercises 21.10

1 Use Laplace transforms to solve

(a) $x' + x = 3$,
$x(0) = 1$

(b) $3\dfrac{dx}{dt} + 4x = 2$,
$x(0) = 2$

(c) $2\dfrac{dy}{dt} + 4y = 1$,
$y(0) = 4$

(d) $4\dfrac{dy}{dt} + 8y = 7$,
$y(0) = 6$

(e) $y'' + y' + y = 1$,
$y(0) = 1,\ y'(0) = 3$

2 Use Laplace transforms to solve

(a) $x'' + x = 2t$,
$x(0) = 0,\ x'(0) = 5$

(b) $2x'' + x' - x = 27\cos 2t + 6\sin 2t$,
$x(0) = -1,\ x'(0) = -2$

(c) $x'' + x' - 2x = 1 - 2t$,
$x(0) = 6,\ x'(0) = -11$

(d) $x'' - 4x = 4(\cos 2t - 1)$,
$x(0) = 1,\ x'(0) = 0$

(e) $x' - 2x - y' + 2y = -2t^2 + 7$,
$\dfrac{x'}{2} + x + 3y' + y = t^2 + 6$
$x(0) = 3,\ y(0) = 6$

(f) $x' + x + y' + y = 6e^t$,
$x' + 2x - y' - y = 2e^{-t}$
$x(0) = 2,\ y(0) = 1$

3 Using Laplace transforms find the particular solution of

$$\frac{d^2y}{dt^2} - 5\frac{dy}{dt} - 6y = 14e^{-t}$$

satisfying $y = 3$ and $\dfrac{dy}{dt} = 8$ when $t = 0$.

Solutions

1 (a) $x(t) = 3 - 2e^{-t}$

(b) $\frac{3}{2}e^{-4t/3} + \frac{1}{2}$

(c) $\frac{1}{4} + \frac{15}{4}e^{-2t}$

(d) $y(t) = \frac{7}{8} + \frac{41}{8}e^{-2t}$

(e) $y(t) = 1 + 3.464\,e^{-0.5t}\sin 0.866t$

2 (a) $3\sin t + 2t$

(b) $-3\cos 2t + 2e^{-t}$

(c) $t + 6e^{-2t}$

(d) $\dfrac{e^{-2t}}{4} + \dfrac{e^{2t}}{4} - \dfrac{1}{2}\cos 2t + 1$

(e) $x = t^2 + 3,\ y = 6 - t$

(f) $x(t) = \dfrac{6e^t}{5} + 2e^{-t} - \dfrac{6e^{-3t/2}}{5}$,
$y(t) = \dfrac{6e^{-3t/2}}{5} - 2e^{-t} + \dfrac{9e^t}{5}$

3 $-2te^{-t} + \dfrac{8e^{-t}}{7} + \dfrac{13e^{6t}}{7}$

21.11 Transfer functions

It is possible to obtain a mathematical model of an engineering system that consists of one or more differential equations. This approach was introduced in Section 20.4. We have already seen that the solution of differential equations can be found by using the

Laplace transform. This leads naturally to the concept of a transfer function which will be developed in this section. Consider the differential equation

$$\frac{dx(t)}{dt} + x(t) = f(t) \qquad x(0) = x_0 \qquad \qquad (21.5)$$

and assume that it models a simple engineering system. Then $f(t)$ represents the input to the system and $x(t)$ represents the output, or response of the system to the input $f(t)$. For reasons that will be explained below it is necessary to assume that the initial conditions associated with the differential equation are zero. In Equation (21.5) this means we take x_0 to be zero. Taking the Laplace transform of Equation (21.5) yields

$$sX(s) - x_0 + X(s) = F(s)$$
$$(1 + s)X(s) = F(s) \qquad \text{assuming } x_0 = 0$$

so that

$$\frac{X(s)}{F(s)} = \frac{1}{1 + s}$$

The function, $X(s)/F(s)$, is called a **transfer function**. It is the ratio of the Laplace transform of the output to the Laplace transform of the input. It is often denoted by $G(s)$. Therefore, for Equation (21.5),

$$G(s) = \frac{1}{1 + s}$$

The concept of a transfer function is very useful in engineering. It provides a simple algebraic relationship between the input and the output. In other words, it allows the analysis of dynamic systems based on the differential equation to proceed in a relatively straightforward manner. Earlier we noted that it was necessary to assume zero initial conditions in order to form the transfer function. Without such an assumption, the relationship between the input and the output would have been more complicated. What is more, the relationship would vary depending on how much energy is stored in the system at $t = 0$. By assuming zero initial conditions, the transfer function depends purely on the system characteristics. Such an approach, whilst very convenient, does have its limitations. The transfer function approach is useful for analysing the effect of an input to the system. However, if one requires the effect of the combination of a system input and initial conditions, then it is necessary to carry out a full solution of the differential equation as we did in Section 21.10. In practice there are many cases where the simplified treatment provided by the transfer function is perfectly acceptable. An alternative approach is provided by state-space models, which we examined in Section 20.4. These provide a natural way of handling initial conditions. In order to solve a state-space model where there are initial conditions, all that is necessary is to use a non-zero initial value of the state vector. Recall that in Section 20.4 we only set up the state-space models and did not solve them. However, the method for the standard solution of a state space model can be found in many textbooks on control and systems engineering (for example, Phillips, Charles L. and Harbor, Royce D., *Feedback Control Systems*, Fourth Edition, Prentice Hall, Harlow, 2000, pp. 80–88).

Example 21.32 Find the transfer functions of the following equations assuming that $f(t)$ represents the input and $x(t)$ represents the output.

(a) $\dfrac{dx(t)}{dt} - 4x(t) = 3f(t),$ $\qquad x(0) = 0$

(b) $\dfrac{d^2x(t)}{dt^2} + 3\dfrac{dx(t)}{dt} - x(t) = f(t),$ $\qquad \dfrac{dx(0)}{dt} = 0,$ $\qquad x(0) = 0$

Solution (a) Taking Laplace transforms of the differential equation gives

$$sX(s) - x(0) - 4X(s) = 3F(s)$$
$$(s - 4)X(s) = 3F(s) \qquad \text{as } x(0) = 0$$
$$\frac{X(s)}{F(s)} = G(s) = \frac{3}{s - 4}$$

(b) Taking Laplace transforms of the differential equation gives

$$s^2 X(s) - sx(0) - \frac{dx(0)}{dt} + 3(sX(s) - x(0)) - X(s) = F(s)$$
$$(s^2 + 3s - 1)X(s) = F(s) \qquad \text{as } \frac{dx(0)}{dt} = 0 \qquad \text{and} \qquad x(0) = 0$$
$$\frac{X(s)}{F(s)} = G(s) = \frac{1}{s^2 + 3s - 1}$$

When creating a mathematical model of an engineering system it is often convenient to think of the variables within the system as signals and elements of the system as means by which these signals are modified. The word signal is used in a very general sense and is not restricted to, say, voltage. On this basis each of the elements of the system can be modelled by a transfer function. A transfer function defines the relationship between an input signal and an output signal. The relationship is defined in terms of the Laplace transforms of the signals. The advantage of this is that the rules governing the manipulation of transfer functions are then of a purely algebraic nature. Consider Figure 21.3. If

$$R(s) = \mathcal{L}\{r(t)\} = \text{ Laplace transform of the input signal}$$
$$Y(s) = \mathcal{L}\{y(t)\} = \text{ Laplace transform of the output signal}$$
$$G(s) = \text{ transfer function}$$

then

$$Y(s) = G(s)R(s)$$

Transfer functions are represented schematically by rectangular blocks, while signals are represented as arrows. Engineers often speak of the **time domain** and the **s domain** in order to distinguish between the two mathematical representations of an engineering system. However, it is important to emphasize the equivalence between the two domains.

Often when constructing a mathematical model of a system using transfer functions, it is convenient first to obtain transfer functions of the elements of the system and then combine them. Before the overall transfer function is calculated a block diagram

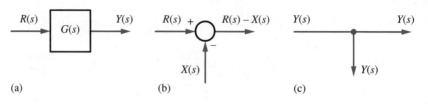

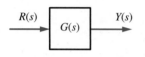

Figure 21.3 The relationship $Y(s) = G(s)R(s)$ holds for a single block.

Figure 21.4 The three components of block diagrams. (a) A basic block; the block contains a transfer function which relates the input and output signals. (b) A summing point. (c) A take-off point.

is drawn which shows the relationship between the various transfer functions. Block diagrams consist of three basic components. These are shown in Figure 21.4.

We have already examined the **basic block** which is governed by the relationship $Y(s) = G(s)R(s)$. A **summing point** adds together the incoming signals to the summing point and produces an outgoing signal. The polarity of the incoming signals is denoted by means of a positive or negative sign. There can be several incoming signals but only one outgoing signal. A **take-off point** is a point where a signal is tapped. This process of tapping the signal has no effect on the signal value; that is, the tap does not load the original signal. There are several rules governing the manipulation of block diagrams. Only two will be considered here.

21.11.1 Rule 1. Combining two transfer functions in series

Consider Figure 21.5. The following relationships hold:

$$X(s) = G_1(s)R(s) \qquad Y(s) = G_2(s)X(s)$$

Eliminating $X(s)$ from these equations yields

$$Y(s) = G_1(s)G_2(s)R(s)$$

$$\frac{Y(s)}{R(s)} = G_1(s)G_2(s)$$

Finally the overall transfer function, $G(s)$, is given by $G_1(s)G_2(s)$ as shown in Figure 21.6.

For two transfer functions in series the overall transfer function is given by

$$G(s) = G_1(s)G_2(s)$$

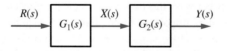

Figure 21.5 Two blocks in series.

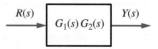

Figure 21.6 Figure 21.5 is simplified to a single block.

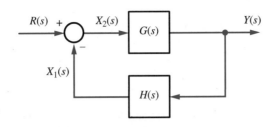

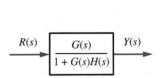

Figure 21.7 Block diagram for a negative feedback loop.

Figure 21.8 Simplified block diagram for a negative feedback loop.

21.11.2 Rule 2. Eliminating a negative feedback loop

Consider Figure 21.7 which shows a negative feedback loop. It is so called because the output signal is 'fed back' and subtracted from the input signal. Such loops are common in a variety of engineering systems. The quantities $X_1(s)$ and $X_2(s)$ represent intermediate signals in the system. We wish to obtain an overall transfer function for this system relating $Y(s)$ and $R(s)$. For the two transfer functions the following hold:

$$Y(s) = G(s)X_2(s) \qquad (21.6)$$

$$X_1(s) = H(s)Y(s) \qquad (21.7)$$

For the summing point

$$X_2(s) = R(s) - X_1(s) \qquad (21.8)$$

Combining Equations (21.7) and (21.8) gives

$$X_2(s) = R(s) - H(s)Y(s) \qquad (21.9)$$

Combining Equations (21.6) and (21.9) gives

$$Y(s) = G(s)(R(s) - H(s)Y(s)) = G(s)R(s) - G(s)H(s)Y(s)$$

$$Y(s)(1 + G(s)H(s)) = G(s)R(s)$$

$$Y(s) = \frac{G(s)R(s)}{1 + G(s)H(s)}$$

The overall transfer function for a negative feedback loop is given by

$$\frac{Y(s)}{R(s)} = \frac{G(s)}{1 + G(s)H(s)}$$

The simplified block diagram for a negative feedback loop is shown in Figure 21.8.

A complicated engineering system may be represented by many differential equations. The output from one part of the system may form the input to another part. Consider the following example.

Example 21.33   A system is modelled by the differential equations

$$x' + 2x = f(t) \tag{21.10}$$

$$2y' - y = x(t) \tag{21.11}$$

In Equation (21.10) the input is $f(t)$ and the output is $x(t)$. In Equation (21.11), $x(t)$ is the input and $y(t)$ is the final output of the system. Find the overall system transfer function assuming zero initial conditions.

Solution   The output from Equation (21.10) is $x(t)$; this forms the input to Equation (21.11). The block diagrams for Equations (21.10) and (21.11) are combined into a single block diagram as shown in Figure 21.9.

Using Rule 1, the overall system transfer function can then be found.

$$G(s) = \frac{Y(s)}{F(s)} = \frac{1}{(s+2)(2s-1)}$$

This transfer function relates $Y(s)$ and $F(s)$ (see Figure 21.10).

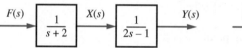

Figure 21.9 Combined block diagram for Equations (21.10) and (21.11).

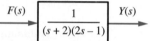

Figure 21.10 The overall system transfer function.

Example 21.34   A system is represented by the differential equations

$$2x' - x = f(t)$$

$$y' + 3y = x(t)$$

$$z' + z = y(t)$$

The initial input is $f(t)$ and the final output is $z(t)$. Find the overall system transfer function, assuming zero initial conditions.

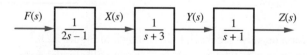

Figure 21.11 Block diagram for the system given in Example 21.34.

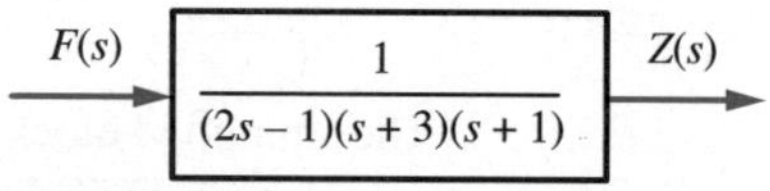

Figure 21.12 Simplified block diagram for Example 21.34.

Solution The transfer function for each equation is found and combined into one block diagram (see Figure 21.11). The three blocks are simplified to a single block as shown in Figure 21.12. The overall system transfer function is

$$G(s) = \frac{Z(s)}{F(s)} = \frac{1}{(2s-1)(s+3)(s+1)}.$$

Example 21.35 Transfer lag

Transport lag is a term used to describe the time delay that may be present in certain engineering systems. A typical example would be a conveyor belt feeding a furnace with coal supplied by a hopper (see Figure 21.13). The amount of fuel supplied to the furnace can be varied by varying the opening at the base of the hopper but there is a time delay before this changed quantity of fuel reaches the furnace. The time delay depends on the speed and length of the conveyor. Mathematically, the function describing the variation in the quantity of fuel entering the furnace is a time-shifted version of the function describing the variation in the quantity of fuel placed on the conveyor (see Figure 21.14).

Let

$$u(t)q(t) = \text{quantity of fuel placed on the conveyor,}$$
$$\text{where } u(t) \text{ is the unit step function,}$$
$$u(t-d)q(t-d) = \text{quantity of fuel entering the furnace,}$$
$$d = \text{time delay introduced by the conveyor,}$$
$$l = \text{length of conveyor (m),}$$
$$v = \text{speed of conveyor (m s}^{-1}).$$

The input to the conveyor is $u(t)q(t)$. The output from the conveyor is $u(t-d)q(t-d)$. If the conveyor is moving at a constant speed then $v = \dfrac{l}{d}$ and so $d = \dfrac{l}{v}$. The transfer function that models the conveyor belt can be obtained by using the second shift theorem.

$$Q_d(s) = \mathcal{L}\{u(t-d)q(t-d)\} = e^{-sd}\mathcal{L}\{q(t)\} = e^{-sd}Q(s)$$

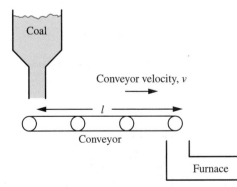

Figure 21.13 Coal is fed into the furnace via the conveyor belt.

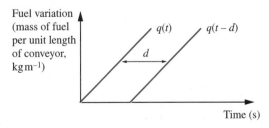

Figure 21.14 The time delay, d, is introduced by the conveyor belt.

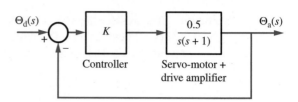

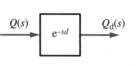

Figure 21.15 Block diagram
for the conveyor belt.

Figure 21.16 Position control system.

The transfer function for the conveyor is shown in Figure 21.15.

Transport lags can cause difficulty when trying to control a system because of
the delay between taking a control action and its effect being felt. In this example,
increasing the quantity of fuel on the conveyor does not lead to an immediate increase in
fuel entering the furnace. The difficulty of controlling the furnace temperature increases
as the transport lag introduced by the conveyor increases.

Example 21.36 **Position control system**

There are many examples of position control systems in engineering, for example control of the position of a plotter pen, and control of the position of a radio telescope. The
common term for these systems is **servo-systems.**

Consider the block diagram of Figure 21.16 which represents a simple servo-
system. The actual position of the motor is denoted by $\Theta_a(s)$ in the s domain and $\theta_a(t)$
in the time domain. The desired position is denoted by $\Theta_d(s)$ and $\theta_d(t)$, respectively.
The system is a closed loop with negative feedback. The difference between the desired
and the actual position generates an error signal which is fed to a controller with gain
K. The output signal from the controller is fed to a servo-motor and its associated drive
circuitry. The aim of the control system is to maintain the actual position of the motor
at a value corresponding to the desired position. In practice, if a new desired position is
requested then the system will take some time to attain this new position. The engineer
can choose a value of the controller gain to obtain the best type of response from the
control system. We will examine the effect of varying K on the response of the servo-
system.

We can use Rules 1 and 2 to obtain an overall transfer function for the system. The
forward transfer function is

$$G(s) = \frac{0.5K}{s(s+1)} \qquad \text{by Rule 1}$$

The overall transfer function $\dfrac{\Theta_a(s)}{\Theta_d(s)}$ is obtained by Rule 2 with $H(s) = 1$. So,

$$\frac{\Theta_a(s)}{\Theta_d(s)} = \frac{\dfrac{0.5K}{s(s+1)}}{1 + \dfrac{0.5K(1)}{s(s+1)}} = \frac{0.5K}{s(s+1)+0.5K} = \frac{0.5K}{s^2 + s + 0.5K}$$

Let us now examine the effect of varying K. We will consider three values, $K = 0.375$,
$K = 0.5$, $K = 5$, and examine the response of the system to a unit step input in each
case.

For $K = 0.375$

$$\frac{\Theta_a(s)}{\Theta_d(s)} = \frac{0.1875}{s^2 + s + 0.1875}$$

With $\Theta_d(s) = \dfrac{1}{s}$, then

$$\Theta_a(s) = \frac{0.1875}{(s^2 + s + 0.1875)s} = \frac{1}{s} + \frac{0.5}{s + 0.75} - \frac{1.5}{s + 0.25} \quad \text{using partial fractions}$$

So,

$$\theta_a(t) = 1 + 0.5\,e^{-0.75t} - 1.5\,e^{-0.25t} \qquad t \geqslant 0$$

This is shown in Figure 21.17. Engineers usually refer to this as an **overdamped** response. The response does not overshoot the final value.

For $K = 0.5$

$$\frac{\Theta_a(s)}{\Theta_d(s)} = \frac{0.25}{s^2 + s + 0.25}$$

$$\Theta_a(s) = \frac{0.25}{s(s^2 + s + 0.25)} = \frac{1}{s} - \frac{1}{s + 0.5} - \frac{0.5}{(s + 0.5)^2}$$

$$\theta_a(t) = 1 - e^{-0.5t} - 0.5te^{-0.5t} \qquad t \geqslant 0$$

This is shown in Figure 21.17 and is termed a **critically damped** response. It corresponds to the fastest rise time of the system without overshooting.

For $K = 5$

$$\frac{\Theta_a(s)}{\Theta_d(s)} = \frac{2.5}{s^2 + s + 2.5}$$

$$\Theta_a(s) = \frac{2.5}{s(s^2 + s + 2.5)}$$

Rearranging to enable standard forms to be inverted gives

$$\Theta_a(s) = \frac{1}{s} - \frac{s + 0.5}{(s + 0.5)^2 + 1.5^2} - \frac{0.5}{(s + 0.5^2) + 1.5^2}$$

$$\theta_a(t) = 1 - e^{-0.5t}\cos 1.5t - \tfrac{1}{3}e^{-0.5t}\sin 1.5t$$

The trigonometric terms can be expressed as a single sinusoid using the techniques given in Section 3.6. Thus,

$$\theta_a(t) = 1 - 1.054\,e^{-0.5t}\sin(1.5t + 1.249) \qquad \text{for} \qquad t \geqslant 0$$

This is shown in Figure 21.17 and is termed an **underdamped** response. The system overshoots its final value.

In a practical system it is common to design for some overshoot, provided it is not excessive, as this enables the desired value to be reached more quickly. It is interesting to compare the system response for the three cases with the nature of their respective

Figure 21.17
Time response for
various values of K.

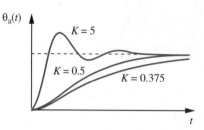

transfer function poles. For the overdamped case the poles are real and unequal, for the critically damped case the poles are real and equal, and for the underdamped case the poles are complex. Engineers rely heavily on pole positions when designing a system to have a particular response. By varying the value of K it is possible to obtain a range of system responses and corresponding pole positions.

Exercises 21.11

1 Find the transfer function for each of the following equations assuming zero initial conditions:

(a) $x'' + x = f(t)$

(b) $2\dfrac{d^2x}{dt^2} + \dfrac{dx}{dt} - x = f(t)$

(c) $2\dfrac{d^2y}{dt^2} + 3\dfrac{dy}{dt} + 6y = p(t)$

(d) $3\dfrac{d^3y}{dt^3} + 6\dfrac{d^2y}{dt^2} + 8\dfrac{dy}{dt} + 4y = g(t)$

(e) $6\dfrac{d^2y}{dt^2} + 8\dfrac{dy}{dt} + 4y = 3\dfrac{df}{dt} + 4f$,
    f is the system input.

(f) $6x''' + 2x'' - x' + 4x = 4f'' + 2f' + 6f$,
    f is the system input

Solutions

1 (a) $\dfrac{1}{s^2+1}$

(b) $\dfrac{1}{2s^2+s-1}$

(c) $\dfrac{1}{2s^2+3s+6}$

(d) $\dfrac{1}{3s^3+6s^2+8s+4}$

(e) $\dfrac{3s+4}{6s^2+8s+4}$

(f) $\dfrac{4s^2+2s+6}{6s^3+2s^2-s+4}$

21.12 Poles, zeros and the s plane

Most transfer functions for engineering systems can be written as rational functions: that is, as ratios of two polynomials in s, with a constant factor, K:

$$G(s) = K\frac{P(s)}{Q(s)}$$

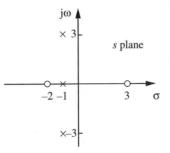

Figure 21.18 Poles and zeros plotted for the transfer function:
$$G(s) = \frac{3(s - 3)(s + 2)}{(s + 1)(s + 1 + 3j)(s + 1 - 3j)}.$$

$P(s)$ is of order m, and $Q(s)$ is of order n; for a physically realizable system $m < n$. Hence $G(s)$ may be written as

$$G(s) = \frac{K(s - z_1)(s - z_2)\ldots(s - z_m)}{(s - p_1)(s - p_2)\ldots(s - p_n)}$$

The values of s that make $G(s)$ zero are known as the **system zeros** and correspond to the roots of $P(s) = 0$, that is $s = z_1, z_2, \ldots, z_m$. The values of s that make $G(s)$ infinite are known as the **system poles** and correspond to the roots of $Q(s) = 0$, that is $s = p_1, p_2, \ldots, p_n$. As we have seen, poles may be real or complex. Complex poles always occur in complex conjugate pairs whenever the polynomial $Q(s)$ has real coefficients.

Engineers find it useful to plot these poles and zeros on an s plane diagram. A complex plane plot is used with, conventionally, a real axis label of σ and an imaginary axis label of $j\omega$. Poles are marked as crosses and zeros are marked as small circles. Figure 21.18 shows an s plane plot for the transfer function

$$G(s) = \frac{3(s - 3)(s + 2)}{(s + 1)(s + 1 + 3j)(s + 1 - 3j)}$$

The benefit of this approach is that it allows the character of a linear system to be determined by examining the s plane plot. In particular, the transient response of the system can easily be visualized by the number and positions of the system poles and zeros.

Example 21.37   Find the poles of $\dfrac{s - 2}{(s^2 + 2s + 5)(s + 1)}$.

Solution   The denominator is factorized into linear factors:

$$(s^2 + 2s + 5)(s + 1) = (s - p_1)(s - p_2)(s - p_3)$$

where $p_1 = -1 + 2j$, $p_2 = -1 - 2j$, $p_3 = -1$. The poles are $-1 + 2j$, $-1 - 2j$, -1.

If $X(s) = \dfrac{1}{s - p_1}$ where the pole p_1 is given by $a + bj$, then

$$x(t) = e^{p_1 t} = e^{at} e^{btj} = e^{at}(\cos bt + j \sin bt)$$

Hence the real part of the pole, a, gives rise to an exponential term and the imaginary part, b, gives rise to an oscillatory term. If $a < 0$ the response, $x(t)$, will decrease to zero as $t \to \infty$.

Consider the Laplace transform in Example 21.27. There are three poles: -1, $-1 + j$ and $-1 - j$. The real pole is negative, and the real parts of the complex poles are also negative. This ensures the response, $x(t)$, decreases with time. The imaginary part of the complex poles gives rise to the oscillatory term, $\cos t$. The characteristics of poles and the corresponding responses are now discussed.

Given a system with transfer function $G(s)$, input signal $R(s)$, and output signal $C(s)$, then

$$\frac{C(s)}{R(s)} = G(s)$$

that is,

$$C(s) = G(s)R(s)$$

and so

$$C(s) = \frac{K(s - z_1)(s - z_2) \ldots (s - z_m) R(s)}{(s - p_1)(s - p_2) \ldots (s - p_n)}$$

The poles and zeros of the system are independent of the input that is applied. All that $R(s)$ contributes to the expression for $C(s)$ is extra poles and zeros.

Consider the case where $R(s) = \dfrac{1}{s}$, corresponding to a unit step input.

$$C(s) = \frac{K(s - z_1)(s - z_2) \ldots (s - z_m)}{(s - p_1)(s - p_2) \ldots (s - p_n)s}$$

$$= \frac{A_1}{s - p_1} + \frac{A_2}{s - p_2} + \cdots + \frac{A_n}{s - p_n} + \frac{B_1}{s}$$

where $A_1, A_2, \ldots, A_n$ and B_1 are constants. Taking inverse Laplace transforms yields

$$c(t) = A_1 e^{p_1 t} + A_2 e^{p_2 t} + \cdots + A_n e^{p_n t} + B_1$$

If the system is stable then $p_1, p_2, \ldots, p_n$ will have negative real parts and their contribution to $c(t)$ will vanish as $t \to \infty$.

The response caused by the system poles is often called a **transient response** because it decreases with time for a stable system. The component of the transient response due to a particular pole is often termed its **transient**. Notice that the form of the transient response is independent of the system input and is determined by the nature of the system poles. It is now possible to derive a series of rules relating the transient response of the system to the positions of the system poles in the s plane.

Figure 21.19
A pole with a negative real part leads to a decaying transient while a pole with a zero real part leads to a transient that does not decay with time.

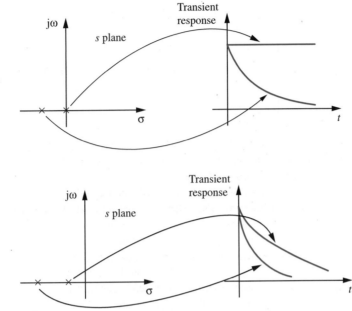

Figure 21.20
The further a pole is from the imaginary axis, the quicker the decay of its transient.

21.12.1 Rule 1

The poles may be either real or complex but for a particular pole it is necessary for the real part to be negative if the transient caused by that pole is to decay with time. Otherwise the transient response will increase with time and the system will be unstable, a condition engineers usually design to avoid. In simple terms this means that the poles of a linear system must all lie in the left half of the *s* plane for stability. Poles on the imaginary axis lead to marginal stability as the transients introduced by such poles do not grow or decay. This is illustrated in Figure 21.19.

21.12.2 Rule 2

The further a pole is to the left of the imaginary axis the faster its transient decays (see Figure 21.20). This is because its transient contains a larger negative exponential term. For example, e^{-5t} decays faster than e^{-2t}. The poles near to the imaginary axis are termed the **dominant poles** as their transients take the longest to decay. It is quite common for engineers to ignore the effect of poles that are more than five or six times further away from the imaginary axis than the dominant poles.

21.12.3 Rule 3

For a real system, poles with imaginary components occur as complex conjugate pairs. The transient resulting from this pair of poles has the form of a sinusoidal term multiplying an exponential term. For a pair of stable poles, that is negative real part, the transient can be sketched by drawing a sinusoid confined within a 'decaying exponential envelope' (see Figure 21.21). The reason for this is that when the sinusoidal term has a value of 1 the transient touches the decaying exponential. When the sinusoidal term has a value of -1 the transient touches the reflection in the *t* axis of the decaying

Figure 21.21
A pair of stable
complex poles gives
rise to a decaying
sinusoid transient.

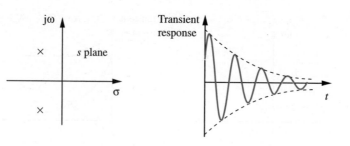

exponential. The larger the imaginary component of the pair of poles the higher the frequency of the sinusoidal term.

It should now be clear how useful a concept the s plane plot is when analysing the response of a linear system. A complex system may have many poles and zeros but by plotting them on the s plane the engineer begins to get a feel for the character of the system. The form of the transients relating to particular poles or pairs of poles can be obtained using the above rules. The magnitude of the transients, that is the values of the coefficients $A_1, A_2, \ldots, A_n$, depends on the system zeros.

It can be shown that having a zero near to a pole reduces the magnitude of the transient relating to that pole. Engineers often deliberately introduce zeros into a system to reduce the effect of unwanted poles. If a zero coincides with the pole, it cancels it and the transient corresponding to that pole is eliminated.

21.13 Laplace transforms of some special functions

In this section we apply the Laplace transform to the delta function and periodic functions. These functions were introduced in Chapter 2.

21.13.1 The delta function, $\delta(t - d)$

Recall the integral property of the delta function (see Section 16.4),

$$\int_{-\infty}^{\infty} f(t)\delta(t - d)\, \mathrm{d}t = f(d)$$

The Laplace transform follows from this integral property. Let $f(t) = \mathrm{e}^{-st}$ so that $f(d) = \mathrm{e}^{-sd}$. Then

$$\int_{-\infty}^{\infty} \mathrm{e}^{-st}\delta(t - d)\, \mathrm{d}t = \int_{0}^{\infty} \mathrm{e}^{-st}\delta(t - d)\, \mathrm{d}t = f(d) = \mathrm{e}^{-sd}$$

that is,

$$\mathcal{L}\{\delta(t - d)\} = \mathrm{e}^{-sd}$$

The Laplace transform of $\delta(t)$ follows by setting $d = 0$:

$$\mathcal{L}\{\delta(t)\} = 1$$

Example 21.38 For a particular circuit it can be shown that the transfer function, $G(s)$, is given by

$$G(s) = \frac{V_o(s)}{V_i(s)} = \frac{1}{s+2}$$

where $V_i(s)$ and $V_o(s)$ are the Laplace transforms of the input and output voltages respectively.

(a) Find $v_o(t)$ when $v_i(t) = \delta(t)$.

(b) Use the convolution theorem to find $v_o(t)$ when

$$v_i(t) = \begin{cases} e^{-t} & t \geqslant 0 \\ 0 & t < 0 \end{cases}$$

Solution (a) We are given the transfer function

$$G(s) = \frac{V_o(s)}{V_i(s)} = \frac{1}{s+2}$$

When $v_i(t) = \delta(t)$, $V_i(s) = 1$ and hence

$$V_o(s) = \frac{1}{s+2}$$

and

$$v_o(t) = \mathcal{L}^{-1}\left\{\frac{1}{s+2}\right\} = e^{-2t}$$

This is known as the **impulse response** of the system, $g(t)$. If the impulse response, $g(t)$, is known then the response, $v_o(t)$, to any other input, $v_i(t)$, can be obtained by convolution, that is $v_o(t) = g(t) * v_i(t)$.

(b) The response to an input, $v_i(t) = u(t)e^{-t}$, is given by

$$v_o(t) = g(t) * v_i(t) = \int_0^t g(\lambda)v_i(t-\lambda)\,d\lambda$$

$$= \int_0^t e^{-2\lambda}e^{-(t-\lambda)}\,d\lambda$$

$$= e^{-t}\int_0^t e^{-\lambda}\,d\lambda$$

$$= e^{-t}\left[\frac{e^{-\lambda}}{-1}\right]_0^t$$

$$= e^{-t}(1 - e^{-t})$$

$$= e^{-t} - e^{-2t}$$

21.13.2 Periodic functions

Recall the definition of a periodic function, $f(t)$. Given $T > 0$, $f(t)$ is periodic if $f(t) = f(t + T)$ for all t in the domain. If $f(t)$ is periodic and we know the values of $f(t)$ over a period, then we know the values of $f(t)$ over its entire domain. Hence, it seems reasonable that the Laplace transform of $f(t)$ can be found by studying an appropriate integral over an interval whose length is just one period. This is indeed the case and forms the basis of the following development.

Let $f(t)$ be periodic, with period T. The Laplace transform of $f(t)$ is

$$\mathcal{L}\{f(t)\} = F(s) = \int_0^\infty e^{-st} f(t)\, dt$$

$$= \int_0^T e^{-st} f(t)\, dt + \int_T^{2T} e^{-st} f(t)\, dt + \int_{2T}^{3T} e^{-st} f(t)\, dt + \cdots$$

Let $t = x$ in the first integral, $t = x + T$ in the second, $t = x + 2T$ in the third and so on.

$$F(s) = \int_0^T e^{-sx} f(x)\, dx + \int_0^T e^{-s(x+T)} f(x + T)\, dx$$

$$+ \int_0^T e^{-s(x+2T)} f(x + 2T)\, dx + \cdots$$

Since f is periodic with period T then

$$f(x) = f(x + T) = f(x + 2T) = \cdots$$

So,

$$F(s) = \int_0^T e^{-sx} f(x)\, dx + \int_0^T e^{-sT} e^{-sx} f(x)\, dx + \int_0^T e^{-2sT} e^{-sx} f(x)\, dx + \cdots$$

$$= (1 + e^{-sT} + e^{-2sT} + \cdots) \int_0^T e^{-sx} f(x)\, dx$$

We recognize the terms in brackets as a geometric series whose sum to infinity is $\dfrac{1}{1 - e^{-sT}}$. Hence,

$$F(s) = \frac{\int_0^T e^{-st} f(t)\, dt}{1 - e^{-sT}}$$

Example 21.39 A waveform, $f(t)$, is defined as follows:

$$f(t) = \begin{cases} 2 & 0 < t \leqslant 1.25 \\ 0 & 1.25 < t \leqslant 1.5 \end{cases}$$

and $f(t)$ is periodic with period of 1.5. Find the Laplace transform of the waveform.

Solution $\mathcal{L}\{f(t)\} = \dfrac{\int_0^{1.5} e^{-st} f(t)\, dt}{1 - e^{-1.5s}}$

$$= \dfrac{\int_0^{1.25} 2\,e^{-st}\, dt + \int_{1.25}^{1.5} 0 e^{-st}\, dt}{1 - e^{-1.5s}}$$

$$= \dfrac{2(1 - e^{-1.25s})}{s(1 - e^{-1.5s})}$$

Exercises 21.13

1 Find the Laplace transforms of

(a) $3u(t) + \delta(t)$

(b) $-6u(t) + 4\delta(t)$

(c) $3u(t - 2) + \delta(t - 2)$

(d) $u(t - 3) - \delta(t - 4)$

(e) $\frac{1}{2}u(t - 4) + 3\delta(t - 4)$

where $u(t)$ is the unit step function.

2 Find the inverse Laplace transforms of

(a) $\dfrac{2}{s} - 1$

(b) $\dfrac{2}{3s} + \dfrac{1}{2}$

(c) $\dfrac{3 - 2s}{s}$

(d) $\dfrac{4s - 3}{s}$

3 A periodic waveform is defined by

$$f(t) = \begin{cases} t & 0 \leqslant t \leqslant 1 \\ 2 - t & 1 < t \leqslant 2 \end{cases}$$

and has a period of 2.

(a) Sketch two cycles of $f(t)$.

(b) Find $\mathcal{L}\{f(t)\}$.

4 A waveform, $f(t)$, is defined by

$$f(t) = \begin{cases} 2 & 0 \leqslant t \leqslant 1.5 \\ -2t + 5 & 1.5 < t < 2.5 \end{cases}$$

and has a period of 2.5.

(a) Sketch $f(t)$ on $[0, 5]$.

(b) Find $\mathcal{L}\{f(t)\}$.

5 If the impulse response of a network is $g(t) = 10e^{-4t}$ find the output when the input is $f(t) = e^{-t} \cos 2t, \; t \geqslant 0.$

Solutions

1 (a) $\dfrac{3}{s} + 1$

(b) $-\dfrac{6}{s} + 4$

(c) $\dfrac{3e^{-2s}}{s} + e^{-2s}$

(d) $\dfrac{e^{-3s}}{s} - e^{-4s}$

(e) $\dfrac{e^{-4s}}{2s} + 3e^{-4s}$

2 (a) $2u(t) - \delta(t)$

(b) $\dfrac{2u(t)}{3} + \dfrac{\delta(t)}{2}$

(c) $3u(t) - 2\delta(t)$

(d) $4\delta(t) - 3u(t)$

3 (b) $\dfrac{1 - e^{-s}}{s^2(1 + e^{-s})}$

4 (b) $\dfrac{2(s + e^{-2.5s} - e^{-1.5s})}{s^2(1 - e^{-2.5s})}$

5 $\dfrac{(30\cos 2t + 20\sin 2t)\,e^{-t}}{13} - \dfrac{30e^{-4t}}{13}$

Review exercises 21

1 Given $F(s) = \dfrac{s+1}{s^2+2}$ is the Laplace transform of $f(t)$, find the Laplace transforms of the following:

(a) $\dfrac{f(t)}{e^{2t}}$

(b) $3e^{2t}f(t)$

(c) $2e^{-t}(f(t)+1)$

(d) $u(t-1)f(t-1)$

(e) $4u(t-3)f(t-3)$

(f) $e^{-2t}u(t-2)f(t-2)$

2 Find the Laplace transforms of the following:

(a) $2t\sin 3t$

(b) $\frac{1}{2}(-3t\cos 2t)$

(c) $e^{-t}u(t)$

(d) $e^{-t}u(t-1)$

(e) $3t^2u(t-1)$

(f) $e^{-t}\delta(t-2)$

3 Find the inverse Laplace transforms of

(a) $\dfrac{2s+3}{(s+1)(s+2)}$

(b) $\dfrac{4s}{s^2-9}$

(c) $\dfrac{2(s^3+4s^2+4s+64)}{(s^2+4)(s^2+16)}$

(d) $e^{-2s}\dfrac{6}{s^4}$

(e) $e^{-s}\dfrac{s+1}{s^2}$

4 Solve the following differential equations using the Laplace transform method.

(a) $x'' + 2x' - 3x = 2t$,
    $x(0) = 1 \qquad x'(0) = 2$

(b) $x'' - 2x' + 5x = \cos t$,
    $x(0) = 0 \qquad x'(0) = 1$

(c) $\dot{x} + \dot{y} + x + y = \frac{3}{2}(1+t)$
    $\dot{x} - 2\dot{y} + x + 2y = 2t$
    $x(0) = 0 \qquad y(0) = 0$

(d) $\dot{x} - \dot{y} + x = -1,\ x(0) = 0 \qquad y(0) = 2$
    $2\dot{x} - \dot{y} + \dfrac{y}{2} - x = 1$

5 The current, $i(t)$, in a series LC circuit is governed by

$$L\frac{di}{dt} + \frac{1}{C}\int_0^t i\,dt = v(t)$$

where $v(t)$ is the applied voltage.

(a) Assuming zero initial conditions show that

$$LsI + \frac{1}{Cs}I = V(s)$$

(b) If $v(t) = \delta(t)$ show that

$$i(t) = \frac{1}{L}\cos\frac{t}{\sqrt{LC}}$$

6 The input and output voltages, $v_i(t)$ and $v_o(t)$, of a series RC network are related by the differential equation

$$CR\frac{dv_o}{dt} + v_o = v_i$$

(a) If $V_o(s) = \mathcal{L}\{v_o(t)\}$ and $V_i(s) = \mathcal{L}\{v_i(t)\}$, show that the transfer function, $\dfrac{V_o(s)}{V_i(s)}$, is given by $\dfrac{1}{sCR+1}$.

(b) If $C = 0.1\ \mu F$, $R = 100\ k\Omega$ find, and sketch a graph of the response, $v_o(t)$, when

$$v_i(t) = \begin{cases} 5\text{ volts} & t \geqslant 0 \\ 0 & t < 0 \end{cases}$$

(c) Using the component values given in (b) find the response when the input is a unit impulse, $\delta(t)$.

(d) Using the component values given in (b) use the convolution theorem to determine the response when $v_i(t) = 5e^{-100t}$.

7 Express the square wave

$$f(t) = \begin{cases} 1 & 0 < t < a \\ -1 & a < t < 2a \end{cases} \qquad \text{period } 2a$$

in terms of unit step functions. Hence deduce its Laplace transform.

Consider the circuit shown in Figure 21.22.

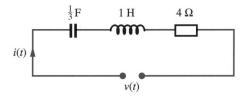

Figure 21.22

(a) Show that

$$\frac{di}{dt} + 4i + 3 \int_0^t i \, dt = v(t)$$

(b) Assuming zero initial conditions, show that

$$I(s) = \frac{s}{(s+1)(s+3)} V(s)$$

(c) Find $i(t)$ if $v(t) = \delta(t)$.

(d) Find $i(t)$ if

$$v(t) = \begin{cases} 2e^{-2t} & t \geq 0 \\ 0 & \text{otherwise} \end{cases}$$

Solutions

1 (a) $\dfrac{s+3}{s^2+4s+6}$

(b) $\dfrac{3(s-1)}{s^2-4s+6}$

(c) $\dfrac{2(2s^2+5s+5)}{(s+1)(s^2+2s+3)}$

(d) $\dfrac{e^{-s}(s+1)}{s^2+2}$

(e) $\dfrac{4e^{-3s}(s+1)}{s^2+2}$

(f) $\dfrac{e^{-2(s+2)}(s+3)}{s^2+4s+6}$

2 (a) $\dfrac{12s}{(s^2+9)^2}$

(b) $-\dfrac{3(s^2-4)}{2(s^2+4)^2}$

(c) $\dfrac{1}{s+1}$

(d) $\dfrac{e^{-(s+1)}}{s+1}$

(e) $3e^{-s}\left(\dfrac{2}{s^3} + \dfrac{2}{s^2} + \dfrac{1}{s}\right)$

(f) $e^{-2(s+1)}$

3 (a) $e^{-t} + e^{-2t}$

(b) $2e^{-3t} + 2e^{3t}$

(c) $2(2\sin 2t + \cos 4t)$

(d) $u(t-2)(t-2)^3$

(e) $u(t-1)t$

4 (a) $-\dfrac{11e^{-3t}}{36} + \dfrac{7e^t}{4} - \dfrac{2t}{3} - \dfrac{4}{9}$

(b) $e^t\left[-\dfrac{1}{5}\cos 2t + \dfrac{13}{20}\sin 2t\right]$
$\quad +\dfrac{1}{5}\cos t - \dfrac{1}{10}\sin t$

(c) $x = t, y = t/2$

(d) $x = e^t - 1, y = 2e^t$

6 (b) $v_0(t) = 5 - 5e^{-100t}$

(c) $100e^{-100t}$

(d) $500te^{-100t}$

7 $\dfrac{1 - e^{-as}}{s(1 + e^{-as})}$

8 (c) $\dfrac{3e^{-3t}}{2} - \dfrac{e^{-t}}{2}$

(d) $-e^{-t} + 4e^{-2t} - 3e^{-3t}$

22 Difference equations and the z transform

Chapter 22   Contents

22.1	Introduction	652
22.2	Basic definitions	652
22.3	Rewriting difference equations	657
22.4	Block diagram representation of difference equations	659
22.5	Design of a discrete-time controller	663
22.6	Numerical solution of difference equations	665
22.7	Definition of the z transform	668
22.8	Sampling a continuous signal	672
22.9	The relationship between the z transform and the Laplace transform	674
22.10	Properties of the z transform	680
22.11	Inversion of z transforms	686
22.12	The z transform and difference equations	690
	Review exercises	692

22.1 Introduction

Difference equations are the discrete equivalent of differential equations. The terminology is similar and the methods of solution have much in common with each other. Difference equations arise whenever an independent variable can have only discrete values. They are of growing importance in engineering in view of their association with discrete-time systems based on the microprocessor.

In Chapter 21 the Laplace transform was shown to be a useful tool for the solution of ordinary differential equations, and for the construction of transfer functions in circuit analysis, control theory, etc. Generally, Laplace transform methods apply when the variables being measured are continuous. The z transform plays a similar role for discrete systems to that played by the Laplace transform for continuous ones. In this chapter you will be introduced to the z transform and one of its applications – the solution of linear constant coefficient difference equations. The z transform is of increasing importance as more and more engineering systems now contain a microprocessor or computer and so have one or more discrete-time components. For example, most industrial controllers now have an embedded microprocessor, and overall control of a factory is often by means of a supervisory process control computer. Many factories also have a production control computer to schedule production.

22.2 Basic definitions

Before classifying difference equations we will first derive an example of one.

Suppose a microprocessor system is being used to capture and analyse images. The number of instruction cycles, i, of the microprocessor needed to process an image depends on the number of pixels, n, that the image is broken down into. Clearly n is a non-negative integer, that is $n \in N$. Since i depends upon n we write $i = i[n]$. The square brackets notation reflects the fact that n is a discrete variable (see Section 6.2). If there are n items of data, the number of instruction cycles used is $i[n]$.

Suppose that if there are $n + 1$ items of data, the number of instruction cycles used increases by $10n + 1$. Then,

$$i[n + 1] = i[n] + 10n + 1$$

This is an example of a **difference equation**. The dependent variable is i; the independent variable is n.

Putting $n = 0$ in the difference equation gives

$$i[1] = i[0] + 10(0) + 1 = 1$$

Similarly, $i[2] = 12, i[3] = 33, i[4] = 64$ and so on. We see that the difference equation gives rise to a sequence of values.

There are strong similarities between difference and differential equations. The important point to note is that with difference equations, the independent variable is discrete, not continuous. In the above example, n is the number of pixels; it can have only integer values. This discrete property of the independent variable is an essential and distinguishing feature of difference equations. Much of the terminology of differential equations is applied, with identical meaning, to difference equations.

22.2.1 Dependent and independent variables

Consider a simple difference equation:

$$x[n+1] - x[n] = 10$$

The dependent variable is x; the independent variable is n. In the difference equation

$$y[k+1] - y[k] = 3k + 5$$

the dependent variable is y and the independent variable is k.

22.2.2 The solution of a difference equation

A **solution** is obtained when the dependent variable is known for each value of interest of the independent variable. Thus the solution takes the form of a sequence. There are frequently many different sequences which satisfy a difference equation; that is, there are many solutions. The **general solution** embraces all of these and all possible solutions can be obtained from it.

Example 22.1 Show $x[n] = A2^n$, where A is a constant, is a solution of

$$x[n+1] - 2x[n] = 0$$

Solution $x[n] = A2^n \qquad x[n+1] = A2^{n+1} = 2A2^n$

Hence,

$$x[n+1] - 2x[n] = 2A2^n - 2A2^n = 0$$

Hence $x[n] = A2^n$ is a solution of the given difference equation. In fact $x[n]$ is the general solution.

If additionally we are given a condition, say $x[0] = 3$, the constant A can be found. If $x[n] = A2^n$, then $x[0] = A2^0 = A$ and hence

$$A = 3$$

The solution is thus $x[n] = 3(2^n)$. This is the **specific solution** and satisfies both the difference equation and the given condition.

22.2.3 Linear and non-linear equations

An equation is linear if the dependent variable occurs only to the first power. If an equation is not linear it is non-linear. For example,

$$3x[n+1] - x[n] = 10$$
$$y[n+1] - 2y[n-1] = n^2$$
$$kz[k+2] + z[k] = z[k-1]$$

are all linear equations. Note that the presence of the term n^2 does not make the equation non-linear, since n is the independent variable. However,

$$(x[n+1])^2 - x[n] = 10$$
$$y[k+1] = \sqrt{y[k]+1}$$

are both non-linear. Also,

$$z[n+1]z[n] = n^2 + 100$$
$$\sin x[n] = x[n-1]$$

are non-linear. The product term $z[n+1]z[n]$ and the term $\sin x[n]$ are the causes of the non-linearity.

22.2.4 Order

The **order** is the difference between the highest and lowest arguments of the dependent variable. The equation

$$3x[n+2] - x[n+1] - 7x[n] = n$$

is second order because the difference between $n+2$ and n is 2.

$$x[n+1]x[n-1] = 7x[n-2]$$

is third order because the difference between $n+1$ and $n-2$ is 3. In general, the higher the order of an equation, the more difficult it is to solve.

In some difference equations the dependent variable occurs only once. These are classified as zero order. Engineers refer to them as **non-recursive** difference equations because calculation of the value of the dependent variable does not require knowledge of the previous values. In contrast, difference equations of order 1 or greater are referred to as **recursive** difference equations because their solution requires knowledge of previous values of the dependent variable. The difference equation

$$x[n] = n^2 + n + 1$$

has zero order and so is a non-recursive difference equation.

22.2.5 Homogeneous and inhomogeneous equations

The meanings of homogeneous and inhomogeneous as applied to linear difference equations are analogous to those meanings when applied to differential equations. To decide whether a linear equation is homogeneous or inhomogeneous it is written in standard form, with all the dependent variable terms on the l.h.s. Any remaining independent variable terms are written on the r.h.s. For example,

$$3nx[n+1] - 2n^3 = x[n-1]$$

is written as

$$3nx[n+1] - x[n-1] = 2n^3 \tag{22.1}$$

If the r.h.s. is 0, the equation is homogeneous; otherwise it is inhomogeneous. Equation (22.1) is inhomogeneous but

$$3nx[n+1] - x[n-1] = 0$$

is homogeneous.

Example 22.2

Signal processing using a microprocessor

In engineering, an increasing number of products contain a microprocessor or computer which is solving a difference equation. The input to the microprocessor is a sequence of signal values, in many cases formed as a result of sampling a continuous input signal. The output from the microprocessor is a sequence of signal values which may be subsequently converted into a continuous signal. For example, an inhomogeneous difference equation could be of the form

$$y[n] - 2y[n - 1] = 0.1s[n] + 0.2s[n - 1] - 0.5s[n - 2]$$

where $y[n]$ is the **output sequence** or dependent variable and $s[n]$ is the **input sequence**. Note that the input sequence can still be thought of as the independent variable but instead of being expressed analytically in terms of n it arises as a result of sampling. The corresponding homogeneous equation is

$$y[n] - 2y[n - 1] = 0$$

22.2.6 Coefficient

The term **coefficient** refers to the coefficient of the dependent variable. In Equation (22.1) the coefficients are $3n$ and -1.

Example 22.3

(a) State the order of each of the following equations (i)–(vii).

(b) State whether each equation is linear or non-linear.

(c) For each linear equation, state whether it is homogeneous or inhomogeneous.

    (i) $2x[n] - 3nx[n - 1] + x[n - 2] + n^2 = 0$

    (ii) $\frac{1}{3}(x[n + 1] - x[n - 1]) = x[n]$

    (iii) $z[n + 2](2n - z[n - 1]) = n + 1$

    (iv) $\dfrac{7x[n - 1]}{x[n - 2]} = \dfrac{n + 1}{n - 1}$

    (v) $w[n + 3]w[n + 1] = n^3 - 1$

    (vi) $y[n + 2] + 2y[n + 1] = 6s[n + 2] - 2s[n + 1] + s[n]$ where y is the dependent variable

    (vii) $x[k + 3] - 2x[k + 2] + x[k] = e[k + 2] - e[k]$ where x is the dependent variable.

Solution   (a) (i)   Second order

        (ii)   Second order

        (iii)   Third order

(iv) First order

(v) Second order

(vi) First order

(vii) Third order

(b) (i) Linear

(ii) Linear

(iii) Non-linear

(iv) Linear

(v) Non-linear

(vi) Linear

(vii) Linear

(c) Equations (iii) and (v) are non-linear. The linear equations are written in standard form:

(i) $2x[n] - 3nx[n-1] + x[n-2] = -n^2$

(ii) $x[n+1] - 3x[n] - x[n-1] = 0$

(iv) $7(n-1)x[n-1] - (n+1)x[n-2] = 0$

(vi) and (vii) are already in standard form.

Hence we find the following:

(i) Inhomogeneous

(ii) Homogeneous

(iv) Homogeneous

(vi) Inhomogeneous

(vii) Inhomogeneous

Exercises 22.2

1 For each of the following equations (a)–(e):
(i) State the order of the equation. (ii) State whether each equation is linear or non-linear. (iii) For each linear equation, state whether it is homogeneous or inhomogeneous.

(a) $n(3n + x[n]) = x[n-1]$

(b) $\dfrac{2z[k-4]}{z[k-3]} = z[k-2]$

(c) $y[n-2] + y[n-1] + y[n] = n^2$

(d) $\sqrt{n + x[n]} = x[n-2] + e[n]$, where x is the dependent variable.

(e) $(2w[n-1] + 1)^2 = w[n-2] + s[n-1] - s[n-2]$, where w is the dependent variable.

Solutions

1 (a) First order; linear; inhomogeneous

  (b) Second order; non-linear

  (c) Second order; linear; inhomogeneous

  (d) Second order; non-linear

  (e) First order; non-linear

22.3 Rewriting difference equations

Sometimes an equation or expression can be written in different ways. At first sight, it may appear there are two independent equations when in fact there is only one. Thus we need to be able to rewrite equations so that comparisons can be made. When general solutions of equations are to be found, usually the equation is first written in a standard form. So once again there is a need to rewrite equations.

Example 22.4   Rewrite the equation so that the highest argument of the dependent variable is $n + 1$.

$$x[n + 3] - x[n + 2] = 2n \qquad x[2] = 7$$

Solution   The highest argument in the given equation is $n + 3$; this must be reduced by 2 to $n + 1$. To do this n is replaced by $n - 2$. The equation becomes

$$x[n + 1] - x[n] = 2(n - 2) \qquad x[2] = 7$$

Note, however, that the initial condition, $x[2] = 7$, is not changed. This is simply stating that x has a value of 7 when the independent variable has a value of 2.

Example 22.5   Write the following equations so that the highest argument of the dependent variable is $n + 2$.

  (a) $3x[n + 4] - 2nx[n + 2] = (n - 1)^2 \qquad x[3] = 6 \qquad x[4] = -7$

  (b) $z[n - 2] + z[n - 1] + z[n] = 1 + n \qquad z[0] = 1 \qquad z[1] = 0$

Solution   (a) The highest argument, $n + 4$, must be replaced by $n + 2$, that is n is replaced by $n - 2$ throughout the equation.

$$3x[n + 2] - 2(n - 2)x[n] = (n - 3)^2 \qquad x[3] = 6 \qquad x[4] = -7$$

  (b) The highest argument, n, is increased to $n + 2$, that is n is replaced by $n + 2$.

$$z[n] + z[n + 1] + z[n + 2] = n + 3 \qquad z[0] = 1 \qquad z[1] = 0$$

Example 22.6 Write the following equations so that the highest argument of the dependent variable is k.

(a) $a[k+2] = \dfrac{s[k+2] - 2s[k+1] + s[k]}{15}$

where a is the dependent variable.

(b) $a[k+3] = \dfrac{l[k+3] + l[k+2] + l[k+1] + l[k] + l[k-1]}{5}$

where a is the dependent variable.

Solution (a) The highest argument, $k+2$, must be replaced by k, that is k is replaced by $k-2$ throughout the equation.

$$a[k] = \frac{s[k] - 2s[k-1] + s[k-2]}{15}$$

(b) The highest argument, $k+3$, must be replaced by k, that is k is replaced by $k-3$ throughout the equation.

$$a[k] = \frac{l[k] + l[k-1] + l[k-2] + l[k-3] + l[k-4]}{5}$$

Exercises 22.3

1 Write each equation so that the highest argument of the dependent variable is as specified.

(a) $p[k] - 3p[k+1] = p[k-2]$, highest argument of the dependent variable is to be $k+2$.

(b) $R[n-1] - R[n-2] - R[n-3] = n$, $R[0] = 1$, $R[1] = -2$, highest argument of the dependent variable is to be n.

(c) $q[t] + tq[t-1] = 3q[t+1]$, $q[1] = 0$, $q[2] = -2$, highest argument of the dependent variable is to be $t-1$.

(d) $T[m] + (m-1)T[m-2] = m^2$, $T[0] = T[1] = 1$, highest argument of the dependent variable is to be $m+2$.

(e) $y[k+1] - y[k+3] = (s[k+2] - s[k+4])/2$, where y is the dependent variable and the highest argument of the dependent variable is to be k.

Solutions

1 (a) $p[k+1] - 3p[k+2] = p[k-1]$

(b) $R[n] - R[n-1] - R[n-2] = n+1$
$R[0] = 1$, $R[1] = -2$

(c) $q[t-2] + (t-2)q[t-3] = 3q[t-1]$
$q[1] = 0$, $q[2] = -2$

(d) $T[m+2] + (m+1)T[m] = (m+2)^2$
$T[0] = T[1] = 1$

(e) $y[k-2] - y[k] = \dfrac{s[k-1] - s[k+1]}{2}$

Figure 22.1
(a) Continuous signal;
(b) sequence produced
as a result of sampling.

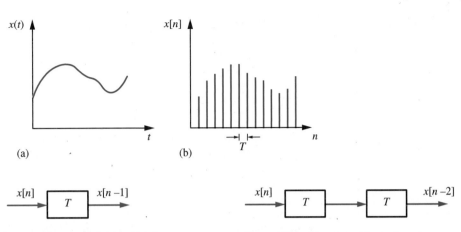

(a) (b)

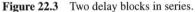

Figure 22.2 A delay block delays a sequence by a time interval, T.

Figure 22.3 Two delay blocks in series.

22.4 Block diagram representation of difference equations

Many engineering systems can be modelled by means of difference equations. It is possible to represent a difference equation pictorially by means of a block diagram. The use of a block diagram representation helps an engineer to visualize a system and may often be helpful in suggesting the required hardware or software to implement a particular difference equation. This is particularly important in areas such as digital signal processing and digital control engineering.

Before discussing block diagrams it is necessary to review the topic of sampling. Difference equations operate on discrete-time data and therefore a continuous signal needs to be sampled before use. In the most common form of sampling, a sample is taken at regular intervals, T. A continuous signal and the sequence produced by sampling it are shown in Figure 22.1. Some authors write the sequence as $x[nT]$ to indicate that the sequence has been obtained by sampling a continuous waveform at intervals T. We will not use this convention but simply refer to the sampled sequence as $x[n]$.

Several components are used in a block diagram. The **delay block** is shown in Figure 22.2. The effect of this element is to delay the sequence by one sampling interval, T. For example, if

$$x[n] = 6, 4, 3, -2, 0, 2, 5, 0, \ldots \qquad n = 0, 1, 2, \ldots$$

we can write this as $x[0] = 6$, $x[1] = 4$, $x[2] = 3$, $x[3] = -2, \ldots$, and then

$$x[n-1] = 0, 6, 4, 3, -2, 0, 2, 5, 0, \ldots \qquad n = 0, 1, 2, \ldots$$

Note that $x[n-1]$ is undefined when $n = 0$ and so this is assigned a value of 0. A delay of two sampling intervals results in the sequence $x[n-2]$ as shown in Figure 22.3.

Another block diagram element represents the addition of a constant to a sequence and is shown in Figure 22.4. A sequence can be scaled by a constant. This is shown in Figure 22.5. Finally, sequences can be added together using a **summer**. This is shown in Figure 22.6.

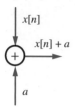

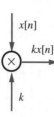

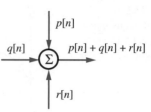

Figure 22.4 Adding a constant to a sequence.

Figure 22.5 Scaling a sequence by a constant.

Figure 22.6 Adding sequences together using a summer.

Example 22.7 Discrete-time filter

A simple example of a discrete-time filter is one described by the difference equation

$$y[n] - ay[n-1] = x[n]$$

where $x[n]$ is the input sequence, $y[n]$ is the output sequence and a is a constant. If a is positive then the filter behaves as a low-pass filter which rejects high frequencies but allows low frequencies to pass. If a is negative then the filter behaves as a high-pass filter. A block diagram for the filter is shown in Figure 22.7. Note that this is a recursive filter because calculation of $y[n]$ requires knowledge of previous values of the output sequence. Note also that the block diagram contains a feedback path. This is a feature of recursive difference equations.

Example 22.8

A computer is fed a signal representing the position of an object as a function of time. Prior to entering the computer the signal is sampled using an analog-to-digital converter. Derive a difference equation and associated block diagram to obtain the acceleration of the object as a function of time.

Solution Let $s =$ position, $v =$ speed and $a =$ acceleration.

$$v = \frac{ds}{dt} \qquad a = \frac{dv}{dt} = \frac{d^2s}{dt^2}$$

Therefore, in order to obtain an acceleration signal the position signal must be differentiated twice. For a small time interval T, the derivative, $y(t)$, of a signal $x(t)$ can be approximated by

$$y(t) \approx \frac{x(t) - x(t-T)}{T}$$

This follows directly from the definition of differentiation. If the signal $x(t)$ is sampled to give $x[n]$ then the process of differentiation is represented by the difference equation

$$y[n] = \frac{x[n] - x[n-1]}{T}$$

Figure 22.8 shows a block diagram for the differentiator. It is important to note that this difference equation is only an approximation to the process of differentiation. This could be implemented using special-purpose hardware or by software on a microprocessor. It follows that the speed of the object is given by

$$v[n] = \frac{s[n] - s[n-1]}{T}$$

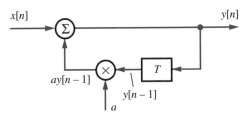

Figure 22.7 Discrete-time filter.

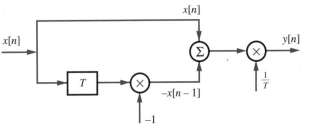

Figure 22.8 Block diagram of a differentiator.

Figure 22.9
Two differentiators in
series.

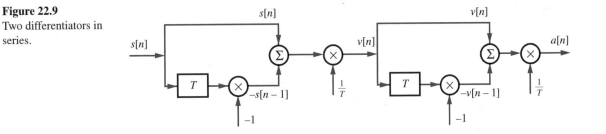

The problem of finding the acceleration, $a[n]$, can now be solved by coupling two
differentiators together as shown in Figure 22.9. An alternative approach to this problem
is to obtain a difference equation for the process of finding a second derivative. Given
that

$$v[n] = \frac{s[n] - s[n-1]}{T} \tag{22.2}$$

and

$$a[n] = \frac{v[n] - v[n-1]}{T} \tag{22.3}$$

then substituting Equation (22.2) into Equation (22.3) gives

$$a[n] = \frac{(s[n] - s[n-1]) - (s[n-1] - s[n-2])}{T^2}$$

$$a[n] = \frac{s[n] - 2s[n-1] + s[n-2]}{T^2}$$

The block diagram for this difference equation is shown in Figure 22.10. Note that the
difference equation is non-recursive and so there are no feedback paths in the block
diagram. The output sequence is $a[n]$ and the input sequence is $s[n]$. The independent
variable is n.

Example 22.9

A signal is received by a computer in a sampled form from a transducer measuring
the height of acetic acid in a large chemical tank. The measurements are known to
fluctuate as a result of the acid swilling about in the tank. It is therefore decided to
smooth out these fluctuations by averaging the five most recently measured values of

Figure 22.10
$a[n]$ is obtained by calculating the second derivative of $s[n]$.

Figure 22.11
Block diagram of a moving averager.

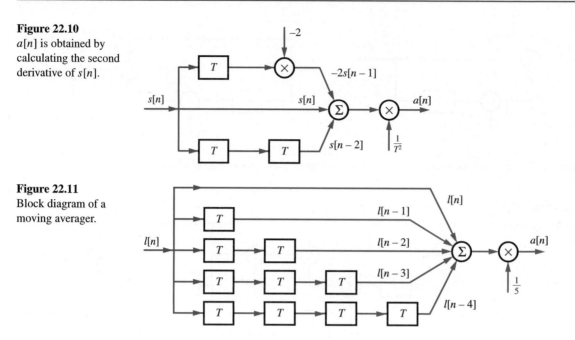

the level and to use this **moving average** as a measure of the height of the acid in the tank. Formulate a difference equation to carry out this averaging and draw a block diagram of the difference equation.

Solution   Let $a[n]$ represent the average level of the acid in the tank and let $l[n]$ represent the sampled values of the level measurements received from the transducer. Then,

$$a[n] = \frac{l[n] + l[n-1] + l[n-2] + l[n-3] + l[n-4]}{5}$$

The block diagram for this difference equation is shown in Figure 22.11. The action of taking a moving average of sampled values is equivalent to passing the sampled values through a low-pass filter because it filters out high-frequency variations in the sampled values. This process is termed **digital filtering** or **digital signal processing**.

Exercises 22.4

1   Design a digital filter based on taking a moving average of the last three values of a sampled signal.

2   A computer is fed a signal representing the velocity of an object as a function of time. Prior to entering the computer the signal is sampled using an analog-to-digital converter. Derive a difference equation and associated block diagram to obtain the acceleration of the object as a function of time.

Solutions

1 See Figure S.18.

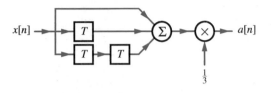

Figure S.18

2 $a[n] = \dfrac{v[n] - v[n-1]}{T}$. See Figure S.19.

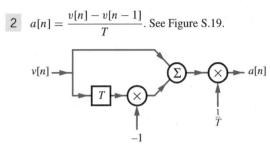

Figure S.19

22.5 Design of a discrete-time controller

Figure 22.12 shows a block diagram of a single loop industrial control system. The control system employs feedback to compare the desired value of a process variable with the actual value. Any difference between the two generates an error signal $e(t)$. This signal is processed by the controller to produce a controller signal $m(t)$. An amplifier is often present to magnify this signal to make it suitable for driving the plant that is being controlled.

The controller can be implemented by means of an analog electronic circuit. However, digital computers are being used increasingly as controllers. The signals $e(t)$ and $m(t)$ are both continuous in time and so it is necessary to sample $e(t)$ before it can be used by the computer and to reconstruct the signal generated by the computer to produce the controller output, $m(t)$. The arrangement for implementing a digital controller is shown in Figure 22.13.

The most common type of controller used in industry is the proportional/integral/derivative (p.i.d.) controller. It can be shown that the analog form of this controller is modelled by the equation

$$m(t) = K_p e(t) + K_i \int_0^t e(t)\,dt + K_d \frac{de(t)}{dt} \tag{22.4}$$

Figure 22.12
A single loop industrial control system.

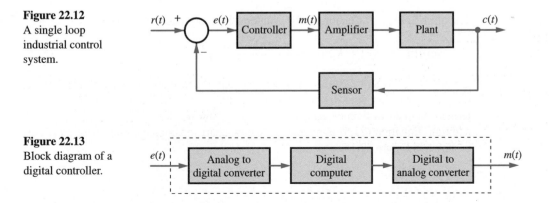

Figure 22.13
Block diagram of a digital controller.

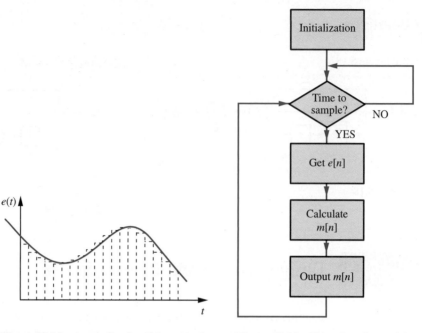

Figure 22.14 Approximating the area under the curve by a series of rectangles.

Figure 22.15 Flow chart for a p.i.d. controller.

where K_p, K_i and K_d are constants. In order to implement a discrete-time (digital) controller it is necessary to convert this equation into an equivalent difference equation. The approximation for the process of differentiation has already been examined in Example 22.8, and is given by

$$\frac{de(t)}{dt} \approx \frac{e[n] - e[n-1]}{T}$$

There are several possible ways of approximating the process of integration. One method is illustrated in Figure 22.14. Here the area under the curve is approximated by a series of rectangles, each of width T. If the approximate area under the curve from $t = 0$ to $t = nT$ is denoted by $x[n]$, then

$$x[n] = x[n-1] + T e[n] \tag{22.5}$$

The discrete form of Equation (22.4) can now be formulated. It is given by

$$m[n] = K_p e[n] + K_i x[n] + K_d \frac{e[n] - e[n-1]}{T} \tag{22.6}$$

Equations (22.5) and (22.6) form a set of equations to implement a discrete form of the p.i.d. controller on a digital computer or microprocessor. These two equations are termed coupled difference equations because both are needed to calculate $m[n]$. In addition, Equation (22.5) is recursive. A flow chart for implementing these equations is shown in Figure 22.15.

Exercises 22.5

1 A transducer is used to measure the speed of a motor car. Design a digital filter to calculate the distance travelled by the car.

2 Draw a block diagram for Equations (22.5) and (22.6).

Solutions

1 $s[n] = s[n-1] + Tv[n]$. See Figure S.20.

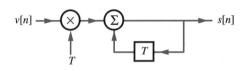

Figure S.20

22.6 Numerical solution of difference equations

Having seen how difference equations are formulated we now proceed to methods of solution. The numerical method illustrated may be applied to all classes of difference equation.

Example 22.10 Given

$$x[n+1] - x[n] = n \qquad x[0] = 1$$

determine $x[1]$, $x[2]$ and $x[3]$.

Solution The terms in the equation are evaluated for various values of n.

$n = 0$	$n = 1$	$n = 2$
$x[1] - x[0] = 0$	$x[2] - x[1] = 1$	$x[3] - x[2] = 2$
$x[1] = 1$	$x[2] = 2$	$x[3] = 4$

Example 22.11 Determine $x[4]$ given

$$2x[k+2] - x[k+1] + x[k] = -k^2 \qquad x[0] = 1 \qquad x[1] = 3$$

Solution $k = 0$ $k = 1$

$\qquad 2x[2] - x[1] + x[0] = 0 \qquad\qquad 2x[3] - x[2] + x[1] = -1$

$\qquad x[2] = 1 \qquad\qquad\qquad\qquad\qquad\qquad x[3] = -\frac{3}{2}$

$k = 2$

$\qquad 2x[4] - x[3] + x[2] = -4$

$\qquad x[4] = -\frac{13}{4}$

As the previous examples illustrate, to determine a unique solution to a first-order equation requires one initial condition; for a second-order equation, two initial values are required.

Example 22.12

Low-pass filter

Recall from Example 22.7 the formula for a simple discrete-time filter:

$$y[n] - ay[n-1] = x[n]$$

If a is positive then the filter is a low-pass filter. We will choose $a = 0.5$ and so

$$y[n] = 0.5y[n-1] + x[n]$$

Let us examine the response of this filter to a unit step input applied at $n = 0$, that is

$$x[n] = \begin{cases} 0 & n < 0 \\ 1 & \text{otherwise} \end{cases} \qquad n \in \mathbb{Z}$$

Assume the output of the filter is zero prior to the application of the step input, that is $y[n] = 0$ for $n \leqslant -1$. From the difference equation, we find

$$\begin{aligned} y[0] &= 0.5y[-1] + x[0] \\ &= 0.5(0) + 1 \\ &= 1 \end{aligned}$$

Similarly,

$$\begin{aligned} y[1] &= 0.5y[0] + x[1] \\ &= 0.5(1) + 1 \\ &= 1.5 \end{aligned}$$

Table 22.1 Numerical solution of a difference equation.

n	$x[n]$	$y[n-1]$	$y[n]$
-1	0	0	0
0	1	0	1
1	1	1	1.5
2	1	1.5	1.75
3	1	1.75	1.88
4	1	1.88	1.94
5	1	1.94	1.97
6	1	1.97	1.99
7	1	1.99	2.00
8	1	2.00	2.00
9	1	2.00	2.00
10	1	2.00	2.00

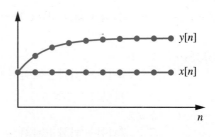

Figure 22.16 Input and output sequences for the low-pass filter.

and so on. When numerically solving a difference equation, it is often useful to form a table with intermediate results. Table 22.1 shows such a table.

Figure 22.16 shows the input and output sequences superimposed on the same graph. The sequence values have been joined to illustrate their trends. Note that the input signal reaches its final value immediately whereas the output signal takes several sample intervals to reach its final value. Engineers often refer to this process as 'smoothing' the input signal. We will see in Chapter 23 that rapidly changing signals tend to be richer in high frequencies than those that change more slowly. The effect of the low-pass filter is to filter out these high frequencies and so the output from the filter changes more slowly than the input. In Chapter 23 we will also examine a continuous low-pass filter which does the same job for continuous signals.

Numerical solution of difference equations is often the only feasible method of obtaining a solution for many practical engineering systems. This is because the input terms are usually obtained as a result of sampling an input signal and so cannot be expressed analytically. However, in some cases it is possible to express the input analytically and then an analytical solution to the difference equation may be feasible. While analytical methods analogous to those applied to differential equations are available, z transform techniques are more popular with engineers and so these are introduced in the following sections.

Exercises 22.6

1 Given

$$x[n+2] + x[n+1] - x[n] = 2$$
$$x[0] = 3 \qquad x[1] = 5$$

find $x[2]$, $x[3]$, $x[4]$ and $x[5]$.

2 If

$$z[n]z[n-1] = n^2 \qquad z[1] = 7$$

find $z[2]$, $z[3]$ and $z[4]$.

3 Determine $x[2]$ and $x[3]$ given

(a) $2x[n+2] - 5x[n+1] = 4n$, $x[1] = 2$

(b) $6x[n] - x[n-1] + 2x[n-2]$
$= n^2 - n$, $x[0] = 1$, $x[1] = 2$

(c) $3x[n-1] + x[n-2] - 9x[n-3]$
$= (n-1)^2$, $x[0] = 3$, $x[1] = 2$

4 Calculate the first five terms of the following difference equations with the given initial conditions:

(a) $x[n+1] - x[n] = 2$, $x[0] = 3$

(b) $x[n+2] + x[n+1] - x[n] = 4$,
$x[0] = 5$, $x[1] = 7$

(c) $x[p+2] - x[p+1] + 2x[p] = 2$,
$x[0] = 1$, $x[1] = 1$

Solutions

1 $0, 7, -5, 14$

2 $\frac{4}{7}, \frac{63}{4}, \frac{64}{63}$

3 (a) $5, \frac{29}{2}$ \qquad (b) $\frac{1}{3}, \frac{7}{18}$ \qquad (c) $\frac{29}{3}, \frac{52}{9}$

4 (a) $3, 5, 7, 9, 11$

(b) $5, 7, 2, 9, -3$

(c) $1, 1, 1, 1, 1$

22.7 Definition of the z transform

Suppose we have a sequence $f[k], k \in \mathbb{N}$. Such a sequence may have arisen by sampling a continuous signal. We define its z transform to be

$$F(z) = \mathcal{Z}\{f[k]\} = \sum_{k=0}^{\infty} f[k]z^{-k} \tag{22.7}$$

We see from the definition that the z transform is an infinite series formed from the terms of the sequence. Explicitly, we have

$$\mathcal{Z}\{f[k]\} = f[0] + \frac{f[1]}{z} + \frac{f[2]}{z^2} + \frac{f[3]}{z^3} + \cdots$$

In most engineering applications we do not actually need to work with the infinite series since it is often possible to express this in a closed form. The closed form is generally valid for values of z within a region known as the **radius of absolute convergence** as will become apparent from the following examples.

Example 22.13 Find the z transform of the sequence defined by

$$f[k] = \begin{cases} 1 & k = 0 \\ 0 & k \neq 0 \end{cases}$$

This sequence is sometimes called the **Kronecker delta sequence**, often denoted by $\delta[k]$.

Solution
$$\mathcal{Z}\{f[k]\} = \sum_{k=0}^{\infty} f[k]z^{-k}$$

$$= f[0] + \frac{f[1]}{z} + \frac{f[2]}{z^2} + \frac{f[3]}{z^3} + \cdots$$

$$= 1 + \frac{0}{z} + \frac{0}{z^2} + \frac{0}{z^3} + \cdots$$

$$= 1$$

Hence $F(z) = 1$.

Example 22.14 Find the z transform of the sequence defined by

$$f[k] = 1 \qquad k \in \mathbb{N}$$

This is the **unit step sequence**, often denoted by $u[k]$.

Solution
$$\mathcal{Z}\{f[k]\} = \sum_{k=0}^{\infty} f[k]z^{-k}$$

$$= 1 + \frac{1}{z} + \frac{1}{z^2} + \frac{1}{z^3} + \cdots$$

This is a geometric progression with first term 1 and common ratio $\frac{1}{z}$. The progression converges if $|z| > 1$ in which case the sum to infinity is

$$\frac{1}{1 - 1/z} = \frac{z}{z-1}$$

We see that $F(z)$ has the convenient closed-form

$$F(z) = \frac{z}{z-1}$$

for $|z| > 1$.

Note that the process of taking the z transform converts the sequence $f[k]$ into the continuous function $F(z)$.

Example 22.15   Find the z transform of the sequence defined by $f[k] = k$, $k \in \mathbb{N}$. This sequence is called the **unit ramp sequence**.

Solution
$$F(z) = \mathcal{Z}\{f[k]\} = \sum_{k=0}^{\infty} kz^{-k}$$

$$= \frac{1}{z} + \frac{2}{z^2} + \frac{3}{z^3} + \cdots$$

$$= \frac{1}{z}\left\{ 1 + \frac{2}{z} + \frac{3}{z^2} + \cdots \right\}$$

If we use the binomial theorem (Section 6.4) to express $\left(1 - \frac{1}{z}\right)^{-2}$ as an infinite series, we find that

$$\left(1 - \frac{1}{z}\right)^{-2} = 1 + \frac{2}{z} + \frac{3}{z^2} + \cdots \qquad \text{provided } \left|\frac{1}{z}\right| < 1, \text{ that is } |z| > 1$$

Using this result we see that $\mathcal{Z}\{f[k]\}$ can be written as

$$F(z) = \frac{1}{z}\left(1 - \frac{1}{z}\right)^{-2}$$

and so

$$F(z) = \frac{1}{z}\frac{1}{(1 - 1/z)^2} = \frac{z}{(z-1)^2} \quad \text{for } |z| > 1$$

Example 22.16 Find the z transform of the sequence defined by

$$f[k] = Ak \qquad A \text{ constant}$$

Solution We find

$$F(z) = \mathcal{Z}\{f[k]\} = \sum_{k=0}^{\infty} Akz^{-k}$$

$$= A\sum_{k=0}^{\infty} kz^{-k}$$

$$= \frac{Az}{(z-1)^2} \qquad \text{using Example 22.15}$$

In the same way as has been done for Laplace transforms, we can build up a library of sequences and their z transforms. Some common examples appear in Table 22.2. Note that in Table 22.2 a and b are constants.

Table 22.2
The z transforms of some common functions.

$f[k]$	$F(z)$	$f[k]$	$F(z)$
$\delta[k] = \begin{cases} 1 & k=0 \\ 0 & k \neq 0 \end{cases}$	1	k^2	$\dfrac{z(z+1)}{(z-1)^3}$
$u[k] = \begin{cases} 1 & k \geqslant 0 \\ 0 & k < 0 \end{cases}$	$\dfrac{z}{z-1}$	k^3	$\dfrac{z(z^2+4z+1)}{(z-1)^4}$
k	$\dfrac{z}{(z-1)^2}$	$\sin ak$	$\dfrac{z \sin a}{z^2 - 2z \cos a + 1}$
e^{-ak}	$\dfrac{z}{z-e^{-a}}$	$\cos ak$	$\dfrac{z(z - \cos a)}{z^2 - 2z \cos a + 1}$
a^k	$\dfrac{z}{z-a}$	$e^{-ak} \sin bk$	$\dfrac{ze^{-a} \sin b}{z^2 - 2ze^{-a} \cos b + e^{-2a}}$
ka^k	$\dfrac{az}{(z-a)^2}$	$e^{-ak} \cos bk$	$\dfrac{z^2 - ze^{-a} \cos b}{z^2 - 2ze^{-a} \cos b + e^{-2a}}$
$k^2 a^k$	$\dfrac{az(z+a)}{(z-a)^3}$		

Example 22.17 Use Table 22.2 to find the z transforms of

(a) $\sin \frac{1}{2}k$ (b) $e^{3k} \cos 2k$

Solution Directly from Table 22.2 we find

(a) $\mathcal{Z}\{\sin \frac{1}{2}k\} = \dfrac{z \sin \frac{1}{2}}{z^2 - 2z \cos \frac{1}{2} + 1}$

(b) $\mathcal{Z}\{e^{3k} \cos 2k\} = \dfrac{z^2 - ze^3 \cos 2}{z^2 - 2ze^3 \cos 2 + e^6}$

Exercises 22.7

1 Using the definition of the z transform, find closed-form expressions for the z transforms of the following sequences $f[k]$ where

(a) $f[0] = 0,\ f[1] = 0,\ f[k] = 1$ for $k \geqslant 2$

(b) $f[k] = \begin{cases} 0 & k = 0, 1, \ldots, 5 \\ 4 & k > 5 \end{cases}$

(c) $f[k] = 3k,\ k \geqslant 0$

(d) $f[k] = e^{-k},\ k = 0, 1, 2, \ldots$

(e) $f[0] = 1,\ f[1] = 2,\ f[2] = 3,$
$f[k] = 0,\ k \geqslant 3$

(f) $f[0] = 3,\ f[k] = 0,\ k \neq 0$

(g) $f[k] = \begin{cases} 2 & k \geqslant 0 \\ 0 & k < 0 \end{cases}$

2 Use Table 22.2 to find the z transforms of

(a) $\cos 3k$

(b) e^k

(c) $e^{-2k} \cos k$

(d) $e^{4k} \sin 2k$

(e) 4^k

(f) $(-3)^k$

(g) $\sin\left(\dfrac{k\pi}{2}\right)$

(h) $\cos\left(\dfrac{k\pi}{2}\right)$

3 Find, from Table 22.2, the sequences which have the following z transforms:

(a) $\dfrac{z}{z + 4}$

(b) $\dfrac{2z}{2z - 1}$

(c) $\dfrac{3z}{3z + 1}$

(d) $\dfrac{z}{z - e^3}$

(e) $\dfrac{z}{z^2 + 1}$

4 By considering the Taylor series expansion of $e^{1/z}$, find the z transform of the sequence

$$f[k] = \frac{1}{k!},\ k \geqslant 0.$$

Solutions

1 (a) $\dfrac{1}{z(z - 1)}$

(b) $\dfrac{4}{z^5(z - 1)}$

(c) $\dfrac{3z}{(z - 1)^2}$

(d) $\dfrac{ez}{ez - 1}$

(e) $\dfrac{z^2 + 2z + 3}{z^2}$

(f) 3

(g) $\dfrac{2z}{z - 1}$

2 (a) $\dfrac{z(z - \cos 3)}{z^2 - 2z \cos 3 + 1}$

(b) $\dfrac{z}{z - e}$

(c) $\dfrac{z^2 - ze^{-2} \cos 1}{z^2 - 2ze^{-2} \cos 1 + e^{-4}}$

(d) $\dfrac{ze^4 \sin 2}{z^2 - 2ze^4 \cos 2 + e^8}$

(e) $\dfrac{z}{z-4}$

(f) $\dfrac{z}{z+3}$

(g) $\dfrac{z}{z^2+1}$

(h) $\dfrac{z^2}{z^2+1}$

3   (a) $(-4)^k$ (b) $(1/2)^k$ (c) $(-1/3)^k$
    (d) e^{3k} (e) $\sin(\pi k/2)$

4   $e^{1/z}$

22.8 Sampling a continuous signal

We have already introduced sampling in Section 22.4. We now return to the topic. Most of the signals that are encountered in the physical world are **continuous** in time. This means that they have a signal level for every value of time over a particular time interval of interest. An example is the measured value of the temperature of an oven obtained using an electronic thermometer. This type of signal can be modelled using a continuous mathematical function in which for each value of t there is a continuous signal level, $f(t)$. Several engineering systems contain signals whose values are important only at particular points in time. These points are usually equally spaced and separated by a time interval, T. Such signals are referred to as discrete time, or more compactly, **discrete** signals. They are modelled by a mathematical function that is only defined at certain points in time. An example of a discrete system is a digital computer. It carries out calculations at fixed intervals governed by an electronic clock.

Suppose we have a continuous signal $f(t)$, defined for $t \geqslant 0$, which we **sample**, that is measure, at intervals of time, T. We obtain a sequence of sampled values of $f(t)$, that is $f[0], f[1], f[2], \ldots, f[k], \ldots$. Returning to the example of the oven temperature signal, a discrete signal with a time interval of 5 seconds can be obtained by noting the value of the electronic thermometer display every 5 seconds. Some textbooks use the notation $f[kT]$ as a reminder that the sequence has been obtained by sampling at an interval T. We will not use this notation as it can become clumsy. However, it is important to note that changing the value of T changes the z transform as we shall see in Example 22.18. It can be shown that sampling a continuous signal does not lose the essence of the signal provided the sampling rate is sufficiently high, and it is in fact possible to recreate the original continuous signal from the discrete signal, if required. It is often convenient to represent a discrete signal as a series of weighted impulses. The strength of each impulse is the level of the signal at the corresponding point in time. We write

$$f^*(t) = \sum_{k=0}^{\infty} f[k]\delta(t - kT) \tag{22.8}$$

the * indicating that $f(t)$ has been sampled. This representation is discussed in Appendix I. This is a useful mathematical way of representing a discrete signal as the properties of the impulse function lend themselves to a value that only exists for a short interval of time. In practice, no sampling method has zero sampling time but provided the sampling time is much smaller than the sampling interval, then this is a valid mathematical model of a discrete signal.

We can apply the z transform directly to a continuous function, $f(t)$, if we regard the function as having been sampled at discrete intervals of time. Consider the following example.

Example 22.18 (a) Find the z transform of $f(t) = e^{-t}$ sampled at $t = 0, 0.1, 0.2, \ldots$

(b) Find the z transform of $f(t) = e^{-t}$ sampled at $t = 0, 0.01, 0.02, \ldots$

(c) Express the sequences obtained in (a) and (b) as series of weighted impulses.

Solution (a) The sequence of sampled values is

$$1, e^{-0.1}, e^{-0.2}, \ldots$$

that is,

$$e^{-0.1k} \qquad k \in \mathbb{N} \text{ and } T = 0.1$$

From Table 22.2 we find the z transform of this sequence is $\dfrac{z}{z - e^{-0.1}}$.

(b) The sequence of sampled values is

$$1, e^{-0.01}, e^{-0.02}, \ldots$$

that is,

$$e^{-0.01k} \qquad k \in \mathbb{N} \qquad \text{and} \qquad T = 0.01$$

From Table 22.2 we find the z transform of this sequence is $\dfrac{z}{z - e^{-0.01}}$. We note that modifying the sampling interval, T, alters the z transform even though we are dealing with the same function $f(t)$.

(c) When $T = 0.1$ we have, from Equation (22.8),

$$f^*(t) = \sum_{k=0}^{\infty} e^{-0.1k} \delta(t - 0.1k)$$

$$= 1\delta(t) + e^{-0.1}\delta(t - 0.1) + e^{-0.2}\delta(t - 0.2) + \cdots$$

Note that an advantage of expressing the sequence as a series of weighted impulses is that information concerning the time of occurrence of a particular value is contained in the corresponding δ term.

When $T = 0.01$, we have

$$f^*(t) = \sum_{k=0}^{\infty} e^{-0.01k} \delta(t - 0.01k)$$

$$= 1\delta(t) + e^{-0.01}\delta(t - 0.01) + e^{-0.02}\delta(t - 0.02) + \cdots$$

Example 22.19 (a) Find the z transform of the continuous function $f(t) = \cos 3t$ sampled at $t = kT$, $k \in \mathbb{N}$.

(b) Write down the first four terms of the sampled sequence when $T = 0.2$, and express the sequence as a series of weighted impulses.

Solution (a) The sampled sequence is

$$f[k] = \cos 3kT = \cos((3T)k)$$

The z transform of this sequence can be obtained directly from Table 22.2 from which we have

$$\mathcal{Z}\{\cos ak\} = \frac{z(z - \cos a)}{z^2 - 2z \cos a + 1}$$

Writing $a = 3T$ we find

$$\mathcal{Z}\{\cos 3kT\} = \frac{z(z - \cos 3T)}{z^2 - 2z \cos 3T + 1}$$

(b) When $T = 0.2$, the first four terms are

$$1 \qquad \cos 0.6 \qquad \cos 1.2 \qquad \cos 1.8$$

From Equation (22.8), the sequence of sampled values can be represented as the following series of weighted impulses:

$$f^*(t) = \sum_{k=0}^{\infty} \cos 3kT \delta(t - kT)$$

$$= \sum_{k=0}^{\infty} \cos 0.6k \delta(t - 0.2k)$$

$$= \delta(t) + \cos 0.6 \delta(t - 0.2) + \cos 1.2 \delta(t - 0.4) + \cos 1.8 \delta(t - 0.6) + \cdots$$

22.9 The relationship between the z transform and the Laplace transform

We have defined the z transform quite independently of any other transform. However, there is a close relationship between the z transform and the Laplace transform, the z being regarded as the discrete equivalent of the Laplace. This can be seen from the following argument.

If the continuous signal $f(t)$ is sampled at intervals of time, T, we obtain a sequence of sampled values $f[k]$, $k \in \mathbb{N}$. From Section 22.8 we note that this sequence can be regarded as a train of impulses.

$$f^*(t) = \sum_{k=0}^{\infty} f[k] \delta(t - kT)$$

Taking the Laplace transform, we have

$$\mathcal{L}\{f^*(t)\} = \int_0^\infty e^{-st} \sum_{k=0}^\infty f[k]\delta(t - kT)\,dt$$

$$= \sum_{k=0}^\infty f[k] \int_0^\infty e^{-st}\delta(t - kT)\,dt$$

assuming that it is permissible to interchange the order of summation and integration. Noting from Table 21.1 that the Laplace transform of the function $\delta(t - kT)$ is e^{-skT}, we can write

$$\mathcal{L}\{f^*(t)\} = \sum_{k=0}^\infty f[k]e^{-skT} \tag{22.9}$$

Now, making the change of variable $z = e^{sT}$, we have

$$\mathcal{L}\{f^*(t)\} = \sum_{k=0}^\infty f[k]z^{-k}$$

which is the definition of the z transform. The expression $\mathcal{L}\{f^*(t)\}$ is commonly written as $F^*(s)$.

In Appendix I it is shown that the continuous function $f(t)$ can be approximated by multiplying the function $f^*(t)$ by the sampling interval T. Correspondingly, $TF^*(s)$ is an approximation to the Laplace transform of $f(t)$. This is illustrated in the following example.

Example 22.20

Consider the function $f(t) = u(t)e^{-t}$ which has Laplace transform $F(s) = \dfrac{1}{s+1}$. Suppose $f(t)$ is sampled at intervals T to give the sequence $f[k] = e^{-kT}$, for $k = 0, 1, 2\ldots$.

(a) Use Table 22.2 to find the z transform of $f[k]$.

(b) Make the change of variable $z = e^{sT}$ to obtain $F^*(s)$.

(c) Show that provided the sample interval T is sufficiently small, $TF^*(s)$ approximates the Laplace transform $F(s)$.

Solution

(a) From Table 22.2 we find $\mathcal{Z}\{f[k]\} = F(z) = \dfrac{z}{z - e^{-T}}$.

(b) Letting $z = e^{sT}$ gives $F^*(s) = \dfrac{e^{sT}}{e^{sT} - e^{-T}}$. Dividing numerator and denominator by e^{sT} gives $F^*(s) = \dfrac{1}{1 - e^{-T(1+s)}}$.

(c) Using the power series expansion for e^x we can write $e^x = 1 + x + \dfrac{x^2}{2!} + \cdots$. So we can approximate $e^{-T(1+s)}$ for sufficiently small T as $1 - T(1 + s)$. Hence

$$F^*(s) \approx \frac{1}{1 - (1 - T(1 + s))}$$

$$= \frac{1}{T(1 + s)}$$

and so $TF^*(s) \approx \dfrac{1}{1+s}$, that is the Laplace transform of $f(t)$.

We have illustrated the connection between the two transforms and shown how the z transform can be regarded as the discrete equivalent of the Laplace transform.

22.9.1 Mapping the s plane to the z plane

When designing an engineering system it is often useful to consider an s plane representation of the system. The characteristics of a system can be quickly identified by the positions of the poles and zeros as we saw in Chapter 21. Engineers will often modify the system characteristics by introducing new poles and zeros or by changing the positions of existing ones. Unfortunately, it is not convenient to use the s plane to analyse discrete systems. For a sampled signal Equation (22.9) yields

$$F^*(s) = \mathcal{L}\{f^*(t)\} = \sum_{k=0}^{\infty} f[k] e^{-skT}$$

The continuous signals and systems that were analysed in Chapter 21 had Laplace transforms that were simple ratios of polynomials in s. This was one of the main reasons for using Laplace transforms to solve differential equations; the problem was reduced to one of reasonably straightforward algebraic manipulation. Here we have a Laplace transform that is very complicated. In fact it can have an infinite number of poles and zeros. To see this consider the following example.

Example 22.21
The continuous signal $f(t) = \cos\left(\dfrac{\pi t}{2}\right)$ is sampled at 1 second intervals starting from $t = 0$.

(a) Find the Laplace transform of the sampled signal $f^*(t)$.

(b) Show that $F^*(s)$ has an infinity of poles.

(c) Find the z transform of the sampled signal and show that this has just two poles.

Solution
(a) The continuous signal $f(t) = \cos\left(\dfrac{\pi t}{2}\right)$ sampled at 1 second intervals gives rise to the sequence $1, 0, -1, 0, 1, 0, -1, \ldots$. Consequently, from Equation (22.9)

$$F^*(s) = \mathcal{L}\{f^*(t)\} = \sum_{k=0}^{\infty} f[k] e^{-skT} = \sum_{k=0}^{\infty} f[k] e^{-sk} \qquad \text{since } T = 1$$

that is,

$$F^*(s) = 1 + 0 - e^{-2s} + 0 + e^{-4s} + 0 - e^{-6s} + \cdots$$

This is a geometric progression with common ratio $-e^{-2s}$ and hence its sum to infinity is

$$\frac{1}{1 - (-e^{-2s})}$$

that is,

$$F^*(s) = \frac{1}{1 + e^{-2s}}$$

(b) Poles of $F^*(s)$ will occur when $1 + e^{-2s} = 0$. Writing $s = \sigma + j\omega$ we see that poles will occur when $e^{-2(\sigma + j\omega)} = -1$. Since -1 can be written as $e^{j(2n-1)\pi}$, $n \in \mathbb{Z}$ (see Chapter 9), we see that poles will occur when

$$e^{-2\sigma - 2j\omega} = e^{j(2n-1)\pi}$$

that is, when $\sigma = 0$ and $\omega = -(2n-1)\pi/2$. Thus there exist an infinite number of poles occurring when

$$s = -(2n-1)\frac{\pi}{2}j \qquad n \in \mathbb{Z}$$

Some of these are illustrated in Figure 22.17.

(c) The z transform of the sampled signal is

$$\mathcal{Z}\{f^*(t)\} = 1 + \frac{0}{z} - \frac{1}{z^2} + \frac{0}{z^3} + \frac{1}{z^4} + \cdots$$

$$= \frac{1}{1 - (-1/z^2)}$$

$$= \frac{z^2}{z^2 + 1}$$

which has just two poles at $z = \pm j$ as shown in Figure 22.18.

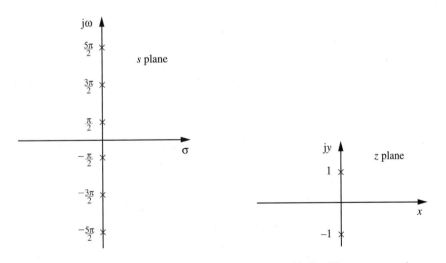

Figure 22.17   The sampled signal has an infinite number of poles.

Figure 22.18   There are two poles at $z = \pm j$.

It is possible to show in general that the result of sampling a continuous signal is to convert each simple pole of the Laplace transform into an infinite set of poles. Suppose that the Laplace transform of the signal $f(t)$ can be broken down by using partial fractions into a series of $n+1$ terms with simple poles $a_0, a_1, \ldots, a_n$. For simplicity, repeating poles will not be considered but the proof for such a case is similar. So,

$$F(s) = \frac{A_0}{s - a_0} + \frac{A_1}{s - a_1} + \frac{A_2}{s - a_2} + \cdots + \frac{A_n}{s - a_n}$$

In the time domain this corresponds to

$$f(t) = A_0 e^{a_0 t} + A_1 e^{a_1 t} + \cdots + A_n e^{a_n t}$$

Now we consider the Laplace transform of the sampled signal $f^*(t)$.

$$F^*(s) = \mathcal{L}\{f^*(t)\} = \sum_{k=0}^{\infty} f[k] e^{-skT}$$

$$= \sum_{k=0}^{\infty} (A_0 e^{a_0 kT} + A_1 e^{a_1 kT} + \cdots + A_n e^{a_n kT}) e^{-skT}$$

$$= A_0 \sum_{k=0}^{\infty} e^{-kT(s-a_0)} + A_1 \sum_{k=0}^{\infty} e^{-kT(s-a_1)} + \cdots$$

$$+ A_n \sum_{k=0}^{\infty} e^{-kT(s-a_n)}$$

Now each of the summations can be converted into a closed form. For example,

$$\sum_{k=0}^{\infty} e^{-kT(s-a_0)} = 1 + e^{-T(s-a_0)} + e^{-2T(s-a_0)} + e^{-3T(s-a_0)} + \cdots$$

$$= \frac{1}{1 - e^{-T(s-a_0)}}$$

Therefore,

$$F^*(s) = \frac{A_0}{1 - e^{-T(s-a_0)}} + \frac{A_1}{1 - e^{-T(s-a_1)}} + \cdots + \frac{A_n}{1 - e^{-T(s-a_n)}}$$

It is possible to show that for each simple pole in $F(s)$ there is now an infinite set of poles. Consider the pole at $s = a_0$. This contributes the term

$$\frac{A_0}{1 - e^{-T(s-a_0)}}$$

to $F^*(s)$. This term has poles whenever $1 - e^{-T(s-a_0)} = 0$, that is $e^{-T(s-a_0)} = 1$. This corresponds to $T(s - a_0) = 2\pi m j$, $m \in \mathbb{Z}$. Therefore,

$$T(s - a_0) = 2\pi m j$$

$$s - a_0 = \frac{2\pi m}{T} j$$

$$s = a_0 + \frac{2\pi m}{T} j \qquad m \in \mathbb{Z}$$

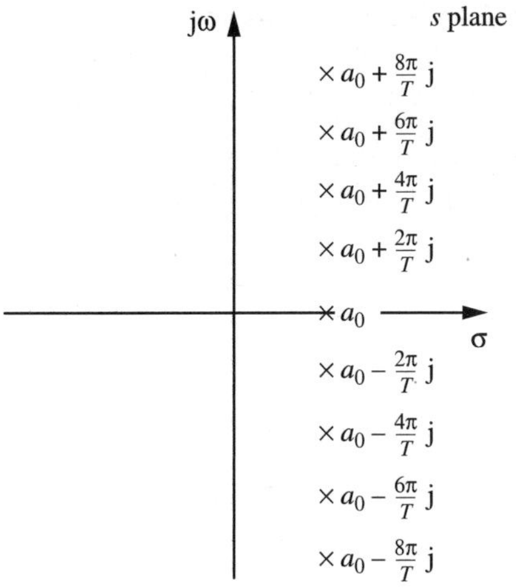

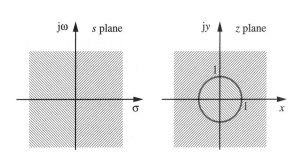

Figure 22.19 The effect of sampling is to introduce an infinite set of poles.

Figure 22.20 The left half of the s plane maps to the inside of the unit circle of the z plane.

The effect of sampling is to introduce an infinite set of poles. Each one is equal to the pole of the original continuous signal but displaced by an imaginary component. This is illustrated in Figure 22.19 for a real pole a_0. However, the proof is equally valid for a complex conjugate pair of poles but the diagram is more cluttered and has, therefore, not been shown.

Clearly discrete systems are not amenable to s plane design techniques. Fortunately, the z plane can be used for analysing discrete systems in the same way that the s plane can be used when analysing continuous systems. It is possible to map points from the s plane to the z plane using the relation $z = e^{sT}$ which gives rise to the definition of the z transform as described previously.

The great advantage of the z plane is that it eliminates the problem of infinitely repeating poles and zeros when analysing discrete systems. This can be illustrated by considering how the imaginary axis of the s plane maps to the z plane.

Referring to Figure 22.20, we see that $s = \sigma + j\omega$. On the imaginary axis $\sigma = 0$ and therefore $z = e^{sT} = e^{j\omega T}$. As ω varies between $-\dfrac{\pi}{T}$ and $\dfrac{\pi}{T}$, the locus of z is a circle of radius 1, centred at the origin (see Section 9.10). As ω is increased from 0 to $\dfrac{\pi}{T}$ the upper half of the unit circle is traced out, while as ω is decreased from 0 to $-\dfrac{\pi}{T}$, the lower half of the unit circle is traced out. Increasing ω above $\dfrac{\pi}{T}$ or decreasing it below $-\dfrac{\pi}{T}$ leads to a retracing of the unit circle. In other words, the repeated s plane points are superimposed on top of each other. This is the reason why the z plane approach is much simpler than the s plane approach when analysing discrete systems.

The z transforms of discrete signals and systems are, in many cases, simple ratios of polynomials. We shall see shortly that this means the process of analysing difference equations which model these signals and systems is reduced to relatively simple algebraic manipulations.

22.10 | Properties of the z transform

Because of the relationship between the two transforms we would expect that many of the properties of the Laplace transform would be mirrored by properties of the z transform. This is indeed the case and some of these properties are given now. These are:

(1) Linearity

(2) Shift theorems

(3) The complex translation theorem

22.10.1 Linearity

If $f[k]$ and $g[k]$ are two sequences then

$$\mathcal{Z}\{f[k] + g[k]\} = \mathcal{Z}\{f[k]\} + \mathcal{Z}\{g[k]\}$$

This statement simply says that to find the z transform of the sum of two sequences we can add the z transforms of the two sequences. If c is a constant, which may be negative, and $f[k]$ is a sequence, then

$$\mathcal{Z}\{cf[k]\} = c\mathcal{Z}\{f[k]\}$$

Together these two properties mean that the z transform is a linear operator.

Example 22.22   Find the z transform of $e^{-k} + k$.

Solution   From Table 22.2 we have

$$\mathcal{Z}\{e^{-k}\} = \frac{z}{z - e^{-1}}$$

and

$$\mathcal{Z}\{k\} = \frac{z}{(z - 1)^2}$$

Therefore,

$$\mathcal{Z}\{e^{-k} + k\} = \frac{z}{z - e^{-1}} + \frac{z}{(z - 1)^2}$$

Example 22.23   Find the z transform of $3k$.

Solution   From Table 22.2 we have

$$\mathcal{Z}\{k\} = \frac{z}{(z - 1)^2}$$

Therefore,

$$\mathcal{Z}\{3k\} = 3\mathcal{Z}\{k\} = 3 \times \frac{z}{(z - 1)^2} = \frac{3z}{(z - 1)^2}$$

Example 22.24 Find the *z* transform of the function $f(t) = 2t^2$ sampled at $t = kT$, $k \in \mathbb{N}$.

Solution The sequence of sampled values is

$$f[k] = 2(kT)^2 = 2T^2 k^2$$

The *z* transform of this sequence can be read directly from Table 22.2 using the linearity properties. We have

$$\mathcal{Z}\{2T^2 k^2\} = 2T^2 \mathcal{Z}\{k^2\} = \frac{2T^2 z(z+1)}{(z-1)^3}$$

22.10.2 First shift theorem

If $f[k]$ is a sequence and $F(z)$ is its *z* transform, then

$$\mathcal{Z}\{f[k+i]\} = z^i F(z) - (z^i f[0] + z^{i-1} f[1] + \cdots + zf[i-1]) \quad i \in \mathbb{N}^+ \text{(22.10)}$$

In particular, if $i = 1$ we have

$$\mathcal{Z}\{f[k+1]\} = zF(z) - zf[0] \tag{22.11}$$

If $i = 2$ we have

$$\mathcal{Z}\{f[k+2]\} = z^2 F(z) - z^2 f[0] - zf[1]$$

Example 22.25 The sequence $f[k]$ is defined by

$$f[k] = \begin{cases} 0 & k = 0, 1, 2, 3 \\ 1 & k = 4, 5, 6, \ldots \end{cases}$$

Write down the sequence $f[k+1]$ and verify that

$$\mathcal{Z}\{f[k+1]\} = zF(z) - zf[0]$$

where $F(z)$ is the *z* transform of $f[k]$.

Solution The graph of $f[k]$ is illustrated in Figure 22.21. The sequence $f[k+1]$ is defined as follows:

When $k = 0$, $f[k+1] = f[1]$ which is 0.

When $k = 1$, $f[k+1] = f[2]$ which is 0.

When $k = 2$, $f[k+1] = f[3]$ which is 0.

When $k = 3$, $f[k+1] = f[4]$ which is 1, and so on.

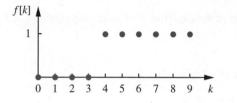

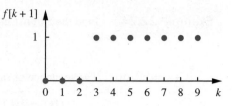

Figure 22.21 The sequence of Example 22.24.

Figure 22.22 A shifted version of the sequence of Figure 22.21.

Consequently,

$$f[k+1] = \begin{cases} 0 & k = 0, 1, 2 \\ 1 & k = 3, 4, 5, \ldots \end{cases}$$

as illustrated in Figure 22.22. We see that the graph of $f[k+1]$ is simply that of $f[k]$ shifted one place to the left. More generally, $f[k+i]$ is the sequence $f[k]$ shifted i places to the left. Now

$$F(z) = \mathcal{Z}\{f[k]\} = \sum_{k=0}^{\infty} f[k]z^{-k}$$

$$= \sum_{k=4}^{\infty} z^{-k}$$

$$= \frac{1}{z^4} + \frac{1}{z^5} + \frac{1}{z^6} + \cdots$$

$$= \frac{1}{z^4}\left(1 + \frac{1}{z} + \frac{1}{z^2} + \cdots\right)$$

$$= \frac{1}{z^4}\frac{1}{1 - 1/z}$$

$$= \frac{1}{z^4}\frac{z}{z - 1}$$

$$= \frac{1}{z^3}\frac{1}{z - 1}$$

The same argument shows that

$$\mathcal{Z}\{f[k+1]\} = \frac{1}{z^2}\frac{1}{z - 1}$$

It then follows that

$$\mathcal{Z}\{f[k+1]\} = \frac{1}{z^2}\frac{1}{z - 1} = zF(z) - zf[0]$$

since $f[0] = 0$. This illustrates the first shift theorem.

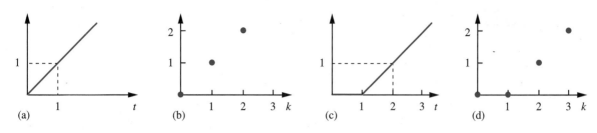

Figure 22.23 Graphs for Example 22.26: (a) $tu(t)$; (b) $ku[k]$; (c) $(t-1)u(t-1)$; (d) $(k-1)u[k-1]$.

22.10.3 Second shift theorem

The function $f(t)u(t)$ is defined by

$$f(t)u(t) = \begin{cases} f(t) & t \geq 0 \\ 0 & t < 0 \end{cases}$$

where $u(t)$ is the unit step function. The function $f(t-iT)u(t-iT)$, where i is a positive integer, represents a shift to the right of i sample intervals. Suppose this shifted function is sampled; then we obtain

$$f[k-i]u[k-i] \qquad k \in \mathbb{N}$$

The second shift theorem states:

$$\mathcal{Z}\{f[k-i]u[k-i]\} = z^{-i}F(z) \qquad i \in \mathbb{N}^+$$

where $F(z)$ is the z transform of $f[k]$.

Example 22.26

The function $t\,u(t)$ is sampled at intervals $T=1$ to give $k\,u[k]$. This sample is then shifted to the right by one sampling interval to give

$$(k-1)u[k-1]$$

Find its z transform.

Solution Figure 22.23(a) shows $t\,u(t)$ and Figure 22.23(b) shows the sampled function. Figures 22.23(c) and (d) show $(t-1)u(t-1)$ and $(k-1)u[k-1]$, respectively. From Table 22.2, we have

$$\mathcal{Z}\{k\} = \frac{z}{(z-1)^2}$$

and so, from the second shift theorem with $i=1$, we have

$$\mathcal{Z}\{(k-1)u[k-1]\} = z^{-1}\frac{z}{(z-1)^2} = \frac{1}{(z-1)^2}$$

Example 22.27   Find the z transform of the unit step function $u(t)$ and the shifted unit step $u(t-2T)$, sampled at intervals of T seconds.

Solution   If the function $u(t)$ is sampled at intervals T then we are concerned with finding the z transform of the sequence $u[k]$. This has been derived earlier: $\mathcal{Z}\{u[k]\} = \dfrac{z}{z-1}$. If $u(t-2T)$ is sampled, we have

$$u[k-2] = \begin{cases} 1 & k = 2, 3, 4, \ldots \\ 0 & \text{otherwise} \end{cases}$$

Therefore, by the second shift theorem,

$$\mathcal{Z}\{u[k-2]\} = z^{-2}\mathcal{Z}\{u[k]\}$$

$$= z^{-2}\frac{z}{z-1}$$

$$= \frac{1}{z(z-1)}$$

Example 22.28   Find the sequence whose z transform is $\dfrac{1}{z-1}$.

Solution $\dfrac{1}{z-1} = \dfrac{1}{z}\dfrac{z}{z-1} = z^{-1}\dfrac{z}{z-1}$

From Table 22.2 we have

$$\mathcal{Z}\{u[k]\} = \frac{z}{z-1}$$

So from the second shift property, we have

$$\mathcal{Z}\{u[k-1]\} = z^{-1}\frac{z}{z-1}$$

The required sequence is therefore $u[k-1]$.

Example 22.29   Find the sequence whose z transform is $\dfrac{1}{z^2(z-1)^2}$.

Solution   The expression $\dfrac{1}{z^2(z-1)^2}$ does not appear in the table of transforms, but we observe that

$$\frac{1}{z^2(z-1)^2} = \frac{1}{z^3}\frac{z}{(z-1)^2}$$

and $\dfrac{z}{(z-1)^2}$ does appear. It follows from Table 22.2 that

$$\mathcal{Z}\{k\} = \frac{z}{(z-1)^2}$$

From the second shift property, $z^{-3}\dfrac{z}{(z-1)^2}$ is the z transform of $(k-3)u[k-3]$.

22.10.4 The complex translation theorem

$$\mathcal{Z}\{e^{-bk} f[k]\} = F(e^b z) \text{ where } F(z) \text{ is the } z \text{ transform of } f[k].$$

Example 22.30 Given that the z transform of $\cos(ak)$ is

$$\frac{z(z - \cos a)}{z^2 - 2z \cos a + 1}$$

find the z transform of $e^{-2k} \cos(ak)$.

Solution Since $b = 2$, the complex translation theorem states that we replace z by $e^2 z$ in the z transform $F(z)$.

$$F(e^2 z) = \frac{e^2 z(e^2 z - \cos a)}{e^4 z^2 - 2e^2 z \cos a + 1}$$

is therefore the required transform.

Exercises 22.10

1 Use Table 22.2 to find the z transforms of

(a) $3(4)^k + 7k^2, k \geqslant 0$
(b) $3e^{-k} \sin 4k - k, k \geqslant 0$

2 Find the z transforms of the following continuous functions sampled at $t = kT, k \in \mathbb{N}$.

(a) t^2 (b) $4t$ (c) $\sin 2t$
(d) $u(t - 4T)$ (e) e^{3t}

3 Find the z transform of $(k - 3)u[k - 3]$ by direct use of the definition of the z transform. Hence verify the result of Example 22.29.

4 Prove that the z transform of $e^{-at} f(t)$ is $F(e^{aT} z)$.

5 Prove the first and second shift theorems.

6 Use the complex translation theorem to find the z transforms of

(a) ke^{-bk} (b) $e^{-k} \sin k$

7 If $f[k] = 4(3)^k$ find $\mathcal{Z}\{f[k]\}$. Use the first shift theorem to deduce $\mathcal{Z}\{f[k + 1]\}$. Show that $\mathcal{Z}\{f[k + 1]\} - 3\mathcal{Z}\{f[k]\} = 0$.

8 Write down the first five terms of the sequence defined by $f[k] = 4(2)^{k-1}u[k - 1], k \geqslant 0$. Find its z transform directly, and also by using the second shift theorem.

Solutions

1 (a) $\dfrac{3z}{z - 4} + \dfrac{7z(z + 1)}{(z - 1)^3}$

(b) $\dfrac{3ze^{-1} \sin 4}{z^2 - 2ze^{-1} \cos 4 + e^{-2}} - \dfrac{z}{(z - 1)^2}$

2 (a) $\dfrac{T^2 z(z + 1)}{(z - 1)^3}$

(b) $\dfrac{4Tz}{(z - 1)^2}$

(c) $\dfrac{z \sin 2T}{z^2 - 2z \cos 2T + 1}$

(d) $\dfrac{1}{z^3(z - 1)}$

(e) $\dfrac{z}{z - e^{3T}}$

3 $\dfrac{1}{z^2(z - 1)^2}$

6 (a) $\dfrac{ze^b}{(ze^b - 1)^2}$

   (b) $\dfrac{ez \sin 1}{e^2 z^2 - 2\,ez \cos 1 + 1}$

7 $\dfrac{4z}{z-3}, \dfrac{12z}{z-3}$

8 $0, 4, 8, 16, 32, \ldots \dfrac{4}{z-2}$

22.11 Inversion of *z* transforms

Just as it is necessary to invert Laplace transforms we need to be able to invert *z* transforms and as before we can make use of tables of transforms, partial fractions and the shift theorems. In very complicated cases more advanced techniques are required.

Example 22.31   If $F(z) = \dfrac{z+3}{z-2}$, find $f[k]$.

Solution   Note that we can write $F(z)$ as

$$\frac{z+3}{z-2} = \frac{z}{z-2} + \frac{3}{z-2}$$

The reason for this choice is that quantities like the first on the r.h.s. appear in Table 22.2. From this table we find

$$\mathcal{Z}\{2^k\} = \frac{z}{z-2}$$

and write

$$\mathcal{Z}^{-1}\left\{\frac{z}{z-2}\right\} = 2^k$$

where $\mathcal{Z}^{-1}$ denotes the inverse *z* transform. Also,

$$\frac{3}{z-2} = \frac{3}{z}\frac{z}{z-2}$$

$$= 3z^{-1}\frac{z}{z-2}$$

Using the second shift property we see that

$$\mathcal{Z}\{3(2)^{k-1}u[k-1]\} = \frac{3}{z}\frac{z}{z-2}$$

so that

$$\mathcal{Z}^{-1}\left\{\frac{z+3}{z-2}\right\} = \mathcal{Z}^{-1}\left\{\frac{z}{z-2}\right\} + \mathcal{Z}^{-1}\left\{3z^{-1}\frac{z}{z-2}\right\}$$

$$= 2^k + 3(2)^{k-1}u[k-1]$$

$$= \begin{cases} 1 & k = 0 \\ 2^k + 3(2)^{k-1} & k = 1, 2, \dots \end{cases}$$

$$= \begin{cases} 1 & k = 0 \\ 2(2)^{k-1} + 3(2)^{k-1} & k = 1, 2, \dots \end{cases}$$

$$= \begin{cases} 1 & k = 0 \\ 5(2)^{k-1} & k = 1, 2, \dots \end{cases}$$

Often it is necessary to split a complicated expression into several simpler ones, using partial fractions, before inversion can be carried out. Also, if we examine the z transform table, Table 22.2, we notice that nearly all of the entries have a z term in the numerator. For this reason it is convenient to divide a complicated expression by z before splitting it into partial fractions. We illustrate this technique by means of an example.

Example 22.32   Find the sequence whose z transform is

$$F(z) = \frac{2z^2 - z}{(z-5)(z+4)}$$

Solution   The first stage is to divide the expression for $F(z)$ by z. We have

$$F(z) = \frac{2z^2 - z}{(z-5)(z+4)}$$

$$F(z) = \frac{z(2z-1)}{(z-5)(z+4)}$$

$$\frac{F(z)}{z} = \frac{2z-1}{(z-5)(z+4)}$$

We now split the r.h.s. expression into partial fractions using the standard techniques discussed in Section 1.6. This gives

$$\frac{F(z)}{z} = \frac{1}{z-5} + \frac{1}{z+4}$$

Multiplying by z gives

$$F(z) = \frac{z}{z-5} + \frac{z}{z+4}$$

It is now possible to invert this expression for $F(z)$ using the z transform table, Table 22.2. This gives

$$f[k] = 5^k + (-4)^k$$

22.11.1 Direct inversion

Sometimes it is possible to invert a transform $F(z)$ directly by reading off the coefficients.

Example 22.33 Find $f[k]$ if

$$F(z) = 1 + z^{-1} + z^{-2} + z^{-3} + \cdots$$

Solution Using the definition of the z transform we see that

$$f[k] = 1, 1, 1, \ldots$$

Occasionally it is possible to rewrite $F(z)$ to obtain the required form.

Example 22.34 Use the binomial theorem to expand $\left(1 - \dfrac{1}{z}\right)^{-3}$ up to the term $\dfrac{1}{z^4}$. Hence find the sequence with z transform $F(z) = \dfrac{z^3}{(z-1)^3}$.

Solution Using the binomial theorem, we have

$$\left(1 - \frac{1}{z}\right)^{-3} = 1 + (-3)\left(-\frac{1}{z}\right) + \frac{(-3)(-4)}{2!}\left(-\frac{1}{z}\right)^2$$

$$+ \frac{(-3)(-4)(-5)}{3!}\left(-\frac{1}{z}\right)^3 + \frac{(-3)(-4)(-5)(-6)}{4!}\left(-\frac{1}{z}\right)^4 + \cdots$$

$$= 1 + \frac{3}{z} + \frac{6}{z^2} + \frac{10}{z^3} + \frac{15}{z^4} + \cdots$$

provided $|z| > 1$. Since

$$F(z) = \frac{z^3}{(z-1)^3} = \left(\frac{z-1}{z}\right)^{-3} = \left(1 - \frac{1}{z}\right)^{-3}$$

we have

$$F(z) = 1 + \frac{3}{z} + \frac{6}{z^2} + \frac{10}{z^3} + \frac{15}{z^4} + \cdots$$

Thus $F(z)$ can be inverted directly to give

$$f[k] = 1, 3, 6, 10, 15, \ldots \qquad \text{that is, } f[k] = \frac{(k+2)(k+1)}{2} \qquad k \geqslant 0$$

Exercises 22.11

1 Find the inverse z transforms of the following:

(a) $\dfrac{4z}{z-4}$

(b) $\dfrac{z^2+2z}{3z^2-4z-7}$

(c) $\dfrac{z+1}{(z-3)z^2}$

(d) $\dfrac{2z^3+z}{(z-3)^2(z-1)}$

2 Find the inverse z transforms of

(a) $\dfrac{2z}{(z-2)(z-3)}$

(b) $\dfrac{ez}{(ez-1)^2}$

(c) $1 - \dfrac{2}{z} + \dfrac{z}{(z-3)(z-4)}$

(d) $\dfrac{z^2}{(z^2 - \frac{1}{9})}$

(e) $\dfrac{2z^2}{(z-1)(z-0.905)}$

3 Express

$$F(z) = \frac{(z+1)(2z-3)(z-2)}{z^3}$$

in partial fractions and hence obtain its inverse z transform.

4 If

$$F(z) = \frac{10z}{(z-1)(z-2)}$$

find $f[k]$.

Solutions

1 (a) $4(4^k)$

(b) $\dfrac{13(7/3)^k}{30} - \dfrac{(-1)^k}{10}$

(c) $u[k-2]\dfrac{4(3)^{k-2} - \delta[k-2]}{3}$

May be written as:

$3^{k-2}u[k-2] + 3^{k-3}u[k-3]$

(d) $\dfrac{19k(3^k)}{6} + \dfrac{3u[k]}{4} + \dfrac{5(3^k)}{4}$

2 (a) $-2(2^k) + 2(3^k)$

(b) $e^{-k}k$

(c) $\delta[k] - 2\delta[k-1] + 4^k - 3^k$

(d) $\dfrac{(1/3)^k + (-1/3)^k}{2}$

(e) $21.05u[k] - 19.05(0.905)^k$

3 $2 - \dfrac{5}{z} - \dfrac{1}{z^2} + \dfrac{6}{z^3}$

$f[0] = 2, \ f[1] = -5, \ f[2] = -1,$

$f[3] = 6, \ f[k] = 0 \qquad k \geqslant 4$

4 $10(2^k - u[k])$

22.12 The z transform and difference equations

In Chapter 21 we saw how useful the Laplace transform can be in the solution of linear, constant coefficient, ordinary differential equations. Similarly the z transform has a role to play in the solution of difference equations.

Example 22.35   Solve the difference equation $y[k + 1] - 3y[k] = 0$, $y[0] = 4$.

Solution   Taking the z transform of both sides of the equation we have

$$\mathcal{Z}\{y[k + 1] - 3y[k]\} = \mathcal{Z}\{0\} = 0$$

since $\mathcal{Z}\{0\} = 0$. Using the properties of linearity we find

$$\mathcal{Z}\{y[k + 1]\} - 3\mathcal{Z}\{y[k]\} = 0$$

Using the first shift theorem on the first of the terms on the l.h.s. we obtain

$$z\mathcal{Z}\{y[k]\} - 4z - 3\mathcal{Z}\{y[k]\} = 0$$

Writing $\mathcal{Z}\{y[k]\} = Y(z)$, this becomes

$$(z - 3)Y(z) = 4z$$

so that

$$Y(z) = \frac{4z}{z - 3}$$

The function on the r.h.s is the z transform of the required solution. Inverting this, from Table 22.2 we find $y[k] = 4(3)^k$.

Higher order equations are treated in the same way:

Example 22.36   Solve the second-order difference equation

$$y[k + 2] - 5y[k + 1] + 6y[k] = 0 \qquad y[0] = 0 \qquad y[1] = 2$$

Solution   Taking the z transform of both sides of the equation and using the properties of linearity we have

$$\mathcal{Z}\{y[k + 2]\} - 5\mathcal{Z}\{y[k + 1]\} + 6\mathcal{Z}\{y[k]\} = 0$$

From the first shift theorem we have

$$z^2 Y(z) - z^2 y[0] - zy[1] - 5(zY(z) - zy[0]) + 6Y(z) = 0$$

where

$$Y(z) = \mathcal{Z}\{y[k]\}$$

Substituting values for the conditions gives

$$z^2Y(z) - 0z^2 - 2z - 5(zY(z) - 0z) + 6Y(z) = 0$$
$$z^2Y(z) - 5zY(z) + 6Y(z) = 2z$$

Hence

$$(z^2 - 5z + 6)Y(z) = 2z$$

so that

$$Y(z) = \mathcal{Z}\{y[k]\} = \frac{2z}{(z-2)(z-3)}$$

Dividing both sides by z gives

$$\frac{Y(z)}{z} = \frac{2}{(z-2)(z-3)}$$

Expressing the r.h.s. in partial fractions yields

$$\frac{Y(z)}{z} = \frac{2}{z-3} - \frac{2}{z-2}$$
$$Y(z) = \frac{2z}{z-3} - \frac{2z}{z-2}$$

Inverting gives the solution to the difference equation:

$$y[k] = 2(3^k) - 2(2^k)$$

Exercises 22.12

1 Use z transforms to solve the following difference equations.

(a) $x[k+1] - 3x[k] = -6$, $x[0] = 1$

(b) $2x[k+1] - x[k] = 2^k$, $x[0] = 2$

(c) $x[k+1] + x[k] = 2k + 1$, $x[0] = 0$

(d) $x[k+2] - 8x[k+1] + 16x[k] = 0$,
     $x[0] = 10$, $x[1] = 20$

(e) $x[k+2] - x[k] = 0$, $x[0] = 0$, $x[1] = 1$

2 Solve the difference equation

$$x[k+2] - 3x[k+1] + 2x[k] = \delta[k]$$

subject to the conditions $x[0] = x[1] = 0$.

3 Solve the difference equation

$$y[k+2] + 3y[k+1] + 2y[k] = 0$$

subject to the conditions $y[0] = 0$, $y[1] = 1$.

4 Solve the difference equation

$$x[k+2] - 7x[k+1] + 12x[k] = k$$

subject to the conditions $x[0] = 1$, $x[1] = 1$.

Solutions

1 (a) $x[k] = 3 - 2(3^k)$

(b) $\dfrac{2^k}{3} + \dfrac{5(1/2)^k}{3}$

(c) k

(d) $10(4^k) - 5(k4^k)$

(e) $\dfrac{u[k] - (-1)^k}{2}$

May be expressed as $x[k] = \begin{cases} 0 & k \text{ even} \\ 1 & k \text{ odd} \end{cases}$

2 $(2^{k-1} - 1)u[k - 1]$

3 $(-1)^k - (-2)^k$

4 $\dfrac{k}{6} - \dfrac{31}{36}u[k] + \dfrac{11}{3}(3)^k - \dfrac{17}{9}(4)^k$

Review exercises 22

1 State

(i) the order

(ii) the independent variable

(iii) the dependent variable

(iv) whether linear or non-linear

for each of the following equations:

(a) $x[n] + x[n - 2] = 6$

(b) $y[k + 1] + ky[k - 1] - k = 0$

(c) $(y[z] + 1)y[z + 1] = z^2$

(d) $z[n] - z[n - 1] = n^2 z[n - 2]$

(e) $q[k + 3] + \sqrt{q[k + 2]} = q[k] - 1$

For each linear equation state whether it is homogeneous or inhomogeneous.

2 Given

$$3(x[n + 1])^2 - 2x[n] = n^2 \qquad x[0] = 2$$

find $x[1]$, $x[2]$ and $x[3]$.

3 Rewrite each equation so that the highest argument of the dependent variable is as specified.

(a) $3ny[n + 1] - y[n - 1] = n^2$, highest argument of the dependent variable is to be n.

(b) $z[k + 2] + (3 + k/2)z[k] = \sqrt{k} \, z[k - 1]$, highest argument of the dependent variable is to be $k + 1$.

(c) $x[3]x[n] - x[2]x[n - 1] = (n + 1)^2$, highest argument of the dependent variable is to be $n + 1$.

4 Find $f[k]$ if

$$F(z) = \frac{z(1 - a)}{(z - 1)(z - a)}$$

5 Find the inverse z transform of

(a) $\dfrac{3z(z + 2)}{(z - 2)(z - 3)^2}$

(b) $\dfrac{z^2 + 3z}{3z^2 + 2z - 5}$

6 The sequence $\delta[k - i]$ is the Kronecker delta sequence shifted i units to the right. Find its z transform.

7 Show that $\sin ak$ can be written as

$$\frac{e^{akj} - e^{-akj}}{2j}$$

Given that

$$\mathcal{Z}\{e^{-ak}\} = \frac{z}{z - e^{-a}}$$

show that

$$\mathcal{Z}\{\sin ak\} = \frac{z \sin a}{z^2 - 2z \cos a + 1}$$

Solutions

1 (a) Second order, n, x, linear, inhomogeneous

(b) Second order, k, y, linear, inhomogeneous

(c) First order, z, y, non-linear

(d) Second order, n, z, linear, homogeneous

(e) Third order, k, q, non-linear

2 1.1547, 1.0503, 1.4260

3 (a) $3(n-1)y[n] - y[n-2] = (n-1)^2$

(b) $z[k+1] + \left(3 + \frac{1}{2}(k-1)\right) z[k-1]$
$= \sqrt{k-1}\,z[k-2]$

(c) $x[3]x[n+1] - x[2]x[n] = (n+2)^2$

4 $u[k] - a^k$

5 (a) $12(2^k) - 12(3^k) + 5k3^k$

(b) $\dfrac{u[k] - (-5/3)^k/3}{2}$

6 $\dfrac{1}{z^i}$

23 Fourier series

Chapter 23 Contents

23.1	Introduction	696
23.2	Periodic waveforms	696
23.3	Odd and even functions	700
23.4	Orthogonality relations and other useful identities	705
23.5	Fourier series	706
23.6	Half-range series	717
23.7	Parseval's theorem	721
23.8	Complex notation	721
23.9	Frequency response of a linear system	724
	Review exercises	728

23.1 Introduction

The ability to analyse waveforms of various types is an important engineering skill. Fourier analysis provides a set of mathematical tools which enable the engineer to break down a wave into its various frequency components. It is then possible to predict the effect a particular waveform may have from knowledge of the effects of its individual frequency components. Often an engineer finds it useful to think of a signal in terms of its frequency components rather than in terms of its time domain representation. This alternative view is called a frequency domain representation. It is particularly useful when trying to understand the effect of a filter on a signal. Filters are used extensively in many areas of engineering. In particular, communication engineers use them in signal reception equipment for filtering out unwanted frequencies in the received signal; that is, removing the transmission signal to leave the audio signal. We shall begin this chapter by reviewing the essential properties of waves before describing how breaking down into frequency components is achieved.

23.2 Periodic waveforms

In this chapter we shall be concerned with periodic functions, especially sine and cosine functions. Let us recall some important definitions and properties already discussed in Section 3.6. The function $f(t) = A \sin(\omega t + \phi) = A \sin \omega \left(t + \dfrac{\phi}{\omega} \right)$ is a sine wave of amplitude A, angular frequency ω, frequency $\dfrac{\omega}{2\pi}$, period $T = \dfrac{2\pi}{\omega}$ and phase angle ϕ.

The time displacement is defined to be $\dfrac{\phi}{\omega}$. These quantities are shown in Figure 23.1.

Similar remarks can be made about the function $A \cos(\omega t + \phi)$ and together the sine and cosine functions form a class of functions known as **sinusoids** or **harmonics**. It will be particularly important for what follows that you have mastered the skills of integrating these functions. The following results can be found in Table 13.1:

$$\int \sin n\omega t \, dt = -\frac{\cos n\omega t}{n\omega} + c \qquad \int \cos n\omega t \, dt = \frac{\sin n\omega t}{n\omega} + c$$

$$\text{for } n = \pm 1, \pm 2, \ldots$$

Figure 23.1
The function:
$f(t) = A \sin(\omega t + \phi)$.

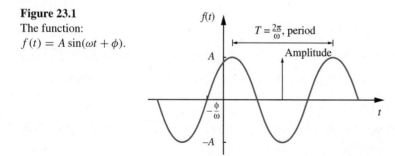

Sometimes a function occurs as the sum of a number of different sine or cosine components such as

$$f(t) = 2\sin\omega_1 t + 0.8\sin 2\omega_1 t + 0.7\sin 4\omega_1 t \tag{23.1}$$

The r.h.s. of Equation (23.1) is a **linear combination** of sinusoids.

Note in particular that the angular frequencies of all components in Equation (23.1) are integer multiples of the angular frequency ω_1. Functions like these can easily be plotted using a graphics calculator or computer graph plotting package. The component with the lowest frequency, or largest period, is $2\sin\omega_1 t$. The quantity ω_1 is called the **fundamental angular frequency** and this component is called the **fundamental** or **first harmonic**. The component with angular frequency $2\omega_1$ is called the second harmonic and so on. In what follows all angular frequencies are integer multiples of the fundamental angular frequency as in Equation (23.1). A consequence of this is that the resulting function, $f(t)$, is periodic and has the same frequency as the fundamental. Some harmonics may be missing. For example, in Equation (23.1) the third harmonic is missing. In some cases the first harmonic may be missing. For example, if

$$f(t) = \cos 2\omega_1 t + 0.5\cos 3\omega_1 t + 0.4\cos 4\omega_1 t + \cdots$$

all angular frequencies are integer multiples of the fundamental angular frequency ω_1, which is missing. Nevertheless, $f(t)$ has the same angular frequency as the fundamental. A common value for ω_1 is 100π as this corresponds to a frequency of 50 Hz, the frequency of the UK mains supply.

Example 23.1 Describe the frequency and amplitude characteristics of the different harmonic components of the function

$$f(t) = \cos 20\pi t + 0.6\cos 60\pi t - 0.2\sin 140\pi t$$

Solution The fundamental angular frequency is 20π arising through the term $\cos 20\pi t$. This corresponds to a frequency of 10 Hz. This term has amplitude 1. The second, fourth, fifth and sixth harmonics are missing, while the third and seventh have amplitudes 0.6 and 0.2, respectively.

Example 23.2 If $f(t) = 2\sin t + 3\cos t$, express $f(t)$ as a single sinusoid and hence determine its amplitude and phase.

Solution Both terms have angular frequency $\omega = 1$. Recalling the trigonometric identity (Section 3.5)

$$R\cos(\omega t - \theta) = a\cos\omega t + b\sin\omega t$$

where $R = \sqrt{a^2 + b^2}$, $\tan\theta = \dfrac{b}{a}$, we see that in this case $R = \sqrt{3^2 + 2^2} = \sqrt{13}$ and $\tan\theta = \frac{2}{3}$, that is $\theta = 0.59$ radians. Therefore we can express $f(t)$ in the form

$$f(t) = \sqrt{13}\cos(t - 0.59)$$

We see immediately that this is a sinusoid of amplitude $\sqrt{13}$ and phase angle -0.59 radians.

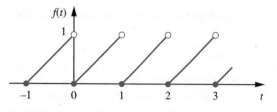

Figure 23.2   Graph for Example 23.4.

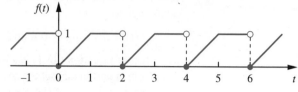

Figure 23.3   Graph for Example 23.5.

Example 23.3   Find the amplitude and phase of the fundamental component of the function

$$f(t) = 0.5 \sin \omega_1 t + 1.5 \cos \omega_1 t + 3.5 \sin 2\omega_1 t - 3 \cos 3\omega_1 t$$

Solution   Contributions to the fundamental component – that is, that with the lowest frequency – come from the terms $0.5 \sin \omega_1 t$ and $1.5 \cos \omega_1 t$ only. To find the amplitude and phase we must express these as a single component. Using the trigonometric identity

$$R \cos(\omega t - \theta) = a \cos \omega t + b \sin \omega t$$

where $R = \sqrt{a^2 + b^2}$, $\tan \theta = \dfrac{b}{a}$, we find

$$R = \sqrt{1.5^2 + 0.5^2} = 1.58$$

$$\tan \theta = \frac{0.5}{1.5} = \frac{1}{3} \qquad \text{that is, } \theta = 0.32 \text{ radians}$$

Therefore the fundamental can be written $1.58 \cos(\omega_1 t - 0.32)$ and has amplitude 1.58 and phase angle -0.32 radians.

Many other periodic functions arise in engineering applications as well as the more familiar harmonic waves. Remember, to be periodic the function values must repeat at regular intervals known as the period, T. The angular frequency ω is given by $\omega = \dfrac{2\pi}{T}$. To describe a periodic function mathematically it is sufficient to give its equation over one full period and state that period. From this information the complete graph can be drawn as Examples 23.4 and 23.5 show.

Example 23.4   Sketch the graph of the periodic function defined by

$$f(t) = t \qquad 0 \leqslant t < 1 \qquad \text{period 1}$$

Solution   To proceed we first sketch the graph on the given interval $0 \leqslant t < 1$ (Figure 23.2), and then use the fact that the function repeats regularly with period 1 to complete the picture.

Example 23.5 Write down a mathematical expression for the function whose graph is shown in Figure 23.3.

Solution We first note that the interval over which the function repeats itself is 2; that is, period = 2. It is then sufficient to describe the function over any interval of length 2. The simplest interval to take is $0 \leqslant t < 2$. We note in this example that a single formula is insufficient to describe the function for $0 \leqslant t < 2$ since different behaviour is exhibited in the two intervals $0 \leqslant t < 1$ and $1 \leqslant t < 2$. For $0 \leqslant t < 1$ the function is a ramp with slope 1 and passes through the origin, that is it has equation $f(t) = t$. For $1 \leqslant t < 2$ the function value remains constant at 1. Therefore this periodic function can be described by the expression

$$f(t) = \begin{cases} t & 0 \leqslant t < 1 \\ 1 & 1 \leqslant t < 2 \end{cases} \quad \text{period 2}$$

Exercises 23.2

1 Describe the frequency and amplitude characteristics of the different harmonic components of the following waveforms:

(a) $f(t) = 3 \sin 100\pi t - 4 \sin 200\pi t + 0.7 \sin 300\pi t$

(b) $f(t) = \sin 40t - 0.5 \cos 120t + 0.3 \cos 240t$

Use a graph plotting computer package or graphics calculator to graph these waveforms.

2 Express each of the following functions as a single sinusoid and hence find their amplitudes and phases.

(a) $f(t) = 2 \cos t - 3 \sin t$

(b) $f(t) = 0.5 \cos t + 3.2 \sin t$

(c) $f(t) = 3 \cos 3t$

(d) $f(t) = 2 \cos 2t + 3 \sin 2t$

3 Sketch the graphs of the following functions.

(a) $f(t) = t^2, -1 \leqslant t \leqslant 1$, period 2

(b) $f(t) = \begin{cases} 0 & 0 \leqslant t < \pi/2 \\ \sin t & \pi/2 \leqslant t \leqslant \pi \end{cases} \quad \text{period } \pi$

(c) $f(t) = \begin{cases} -t & -2 \leqslant t < 0 \\ t & 0 \leqslant t < 1 \end{cases} \quad \text{period 3}$

4 Write down mathematical expressions to describe the functions whose graphs are shown in Figure 23.4.

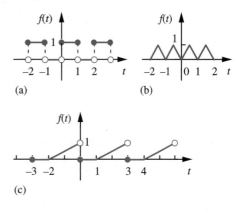

(a)

(b)

(c)

Figure 23.4

Solutions

1 (a) Fundamental frequency is 50 Hz, amplitude 3. Second harmonic has frequency of 100 Hz, amplitude 4. Third harmonic has frequency of 150 Hz, amplitude 0.7.

(b) Fundamental frequency is $\dfrac{20}{\pi}$ Hz, amplitude 1. Second harmonic is missing. Third harmonic has frequency of $\dfrac{60}{\pi}$ Hz, amplitude 0.5. Fourth and fifth harmonics are missing. Sixth harmonic has frequency of $\dfrac{120}{\pi}$ Hz, amplitude 0.3.

2 (a) $\sqrt{13}\cos(t + 0.983)$; amplitude $= \sqrt{13}$, phase $= 0.983$

(b) $3.24\cos(t + 4.867)$; amplitude $= 3.24$, phase $= 4.867$

(c) $3\cos 3t$; amplitude $= 3$, phase $= 0$

(d) $\sqrt{13}\cos(2t - 0.983)$; amplitude $= \sqrt{13}$, phase $= -0.983$

4 (a) $f(t) = \begin{cases} 1 & 0 \leqslant t \leqslant 1 \\ 0 & 1 < t < 2 \end{cases}$ period $= 2$

(b) $f(t) = \begin{cases} 2t & 0 \leqslant t \leqslant 1/2 \\ 2 - 2t & 1/2 < t < 1 \end{cases}$

period $= 1$

(c) $f(t) = \begin{cases} 0 & 0 \leqslant t \leqslant 1 \\ t/2 - 1/2 & 1 < t < 3 \end{cases}$

period $= 3$

23.3 Odd and even functions

The functions $\sin t$ and $\cos t$ each possess certain properties which can be generalized to other functions. Figure 23.5 shows the graph of $f(t) = \cos t$. It is obvious from the graph that the function value at a negative t value, say $-\dfrac{\pi}{4}$, will be the same as the function value at the corresponding positive t value, in this case $+\dfrac{\pi}{4}$. This is true because the graph is symmetrical about the vertical axis. We can therefore state that for any value of t, $\cos(-t) = \cos t$.

More generally, any function with the property that $f(t) = f(-t)$ for any value of its argument, t, is said to be an **even** function.

> If $f(t) = f(-t)$ then f is an even function.

In particular, the set of functions $\cos n\omega t$, for any integer n, is even. The graphs of all

Figure 23.5
The function:
$f(t) = \cos t$.

Figure 23.6
Examples of even functions:
(a) $f(t) = t^2$;
(b) $f(t) = 3$.

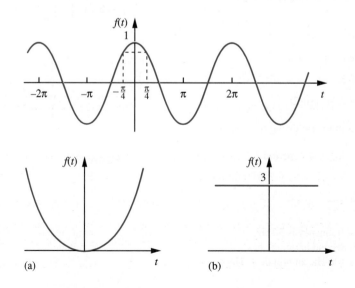

(a)

(b)

even functions are symmetrical about the vertical axis – or equivalently, the graph on the left of the origin can be obtained by reflecting in the vertical axis that on the right. Some other examples of even functions are shown in Figure 23.6.

Sketching a graph shows up the required symmetry immediately. However, even functions can be identified by an algebraic approach as shown in Example 23.6. Given any function $f(t)$, we examine $f(-t)$ to see if $f(t) = f(-t)$.

Example 23.6 Show that $f(t) = t^2$ is even.

Solution We can argue as follows. If

$$f(t) = t^2$$

then

$$f(-t) = (-t)^2$$
$$= t^2$$
$$= f(t)$$

so that $f(t)$ is even, by definition.

Example 23.7 Test whether or not the function $f(t) = 4t^3$ is even.

Solution If

$$f(t) = 4t^3$$

then

$$f(-t) = 4(-t)^3$$
$$= -4t^3$$
$$= -f(t)$$

so that $f(-t)$ is not equal to $f(t)$ and therefore the given function is not even.

Let us turn now to the graph of $f(t) = \sin t$ in Figure 23.7. It is obvious from the graph that the function value at a negative t value, say $-\dfrac{\pi}{4}$, will not be the same as the function value at the corresponding positive t value, in this case $+\dfrac{\pi}{4}$. This graph is not symmetrical about the vertical axis. However, we can state something else. The function value at a negative t value is minus the function value at the corresponding positive t value. For example, $\sin\left(-\dfrac{\pi}{4}\right) = -\sin\left(\dfrac{\pi}{4}\right)$. In fact, for all values of t we

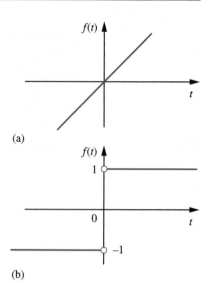

(a)

(b)

Figure 23.8 Examples of odd functions:
(a) $f(t) = t$; (b) $f(t) = \begin{cases} 1 & t > 0 \\ -1 & t < 0. \end{cases}$

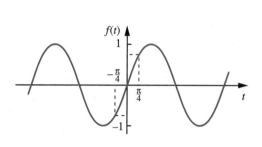

Figure 23.7 The function: $f(t) = \sin t$.

can state that $\sin(-t) = -\sin t$. More generally, any function with the property that $f(-t) = -f(t)$ for all values of its argument, t, is said to be an **odd** function.

> If $f(-t) = -f(t)$ then f is an odd function.

In particular, the set of functions $\sin n\omega t$, for any integer n, is odd. In Example 23.7, $f(t) = 4t^3$, we found that $f(-t) = -f(t)$ so this function is odd. The graph of an odd function can be obtained by reflection first in the horizontal axis and then in the vertical axis. Some more examples of odd functions are shown in Figure 23.8.

There are some functions that are neither odd nor even – for example, the exponential function (see Chapter 2).

Example 23.8

Show that any function, $f(t)$, can be expressed as the sum of an odd component and an even component.

Solution

We can write

$$f(t) = f(t) + \frac{f(-t)}{2} - \frac{f(-t)}{2}$$

$$= \frac{f(t)}{2} + \frac{f(t)}{2} + \frac{f(-t)}{2} - \frac{f(-t)}{2}$$

Rearranging gives

$$f(t) = \frac{f(t) + f(-t)}{2} + \frac{f(t) - f(-t)}{2}$$

Now it is easy to check that the first term on the r.h.s. is even and the second term is odd, so that we have expressed $f(t)$ as the sum of an even and an odd component as required.

Example 23.9 Show that the product of two even functions is itself an even function. Determine whether the product of two odd functions is even or odd. Is the product of an even function and an odd function even or odd?

Solution If $f(t)$ and $g(t)$ are even then $f(-t) = f(t)$ and $g(-t) = g(t)$. Let $P(t) = f(t)g(t)$ be the product of f and g. Then

$$P(-t) = f(-t)g(-t) \qquad \text{by definition}$$
$$= f(t)g(t) \qquad \text{since } f \text{ and } g \text{ are even}$$
$$= P(t)$$

Therefore, $P(-t) = P(t)$ and so the product $f(t)g(t)$ is itself an even function. On the other hand, if $f(t)$ and $g(t)$ are both odd we find

$$P(-t) = f(-t)g(-t)$$
$$= (-f(t))(-g(t))$$
$$= f(t)g(t)$$
$$= P(t)$$

so that the product $f(t)g(t)$ is even.
   If $f(t)$ is even and $g(t)$ is odd, we find

$$P(-t) = f(-t)g(-t)$$
$$= f(t)(-g(t))$$
$$= -f(t)g(t)$$
$$= -P(t)$$

so the product is an odd function. These rules are obviously analogous to the rules for multiplying positive and negative numbers.

The results of Example 23.9 are summarized thus:

$(\text{even}) \times (\text{even}) = \text{even}$
$(\text{odd}) \times (\text{odd}) = \text{even}$
$(\text{even}) \times (\text{odd}) = \text{odd}$

23.3.1 Integral properties of even and odd functions

Consider a typical odd function, $f(t)$, such as that shown in Figure 23.9. Suppose we wish to evaluate $\int_{-a}^{a} f(t)\,dt$ where the interval of integration $[-a, a]$ is symmetrical about the vertical axis. Recall from Chapter 13 that a definite integral can be regarded as the area bounded by the graph of the integrand and the horizontal axis. Areas above the

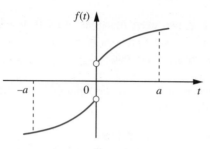

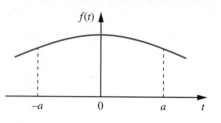

Figure 23.9   A typical odd function, $f(t)$.   **Figure 23.10**   A typical even function, $f(t)$.

horizontal axis are positive while those below are negative. We see that because positive and negative contributions cancel, the integral of an odd function over an interval which is symmetrical about the vertical axis will be 0.

Example 23.10   Evaluate $\int_{-\pi}^{\pi} t \cos n\omega t \, dt$.

Solution   The function t is odd. The function $\cos n\omega t$ is even and hence the product $t \cos n\omega t$ is odd. The interval $[-\pi, \pi]$ is symmetrical about the vertical axis and hence the required integral is zero.

Consider now a typical even function, $f(t)$, such as that shown in Figure 23.10. Suppose we wish to evaluate $\int_{-a}^{a} f(t) \, dt$. Clearly the area bounded by the graph and the t axis in the interval $[-a, 0]$ is the same as the corresponding area in the interval $[0, a]$. Hence we can write

$$\int_{-a}^{a} f(t) \, dt = 2 \int_{0}^{a} f(t) \, dt$$

Example 23.11   Evaluate $\int_{-\pi}^{\pi} t \sin t \, dt$.

Solution   The functions t and $\sin t$ are both odd, and hence their product is even. Therefore, using the fact that the integrand is even we can write

$$\int_{-\pi}^{\pi} t \sin t \, dt = 2 \int_{0}^{\pi} t \sin t \, dt$$

So, integrating by parts,

$$2 \int_{0}^{\pi} t \sin t \, dt = 2 \left([-t \cos t]_{0}^{\pi} + \int_{0}^{\pi} \cos t \, dt \right)$$
$$= 2((-\pi \cos \pi) - (0) + [\sin t]_{0}^{\pi})$$
$$= 2\pi$$

Exercises 23.3

1 Determine by inspection whether each of the functions in Figure 23.11 is odd, even or neither.

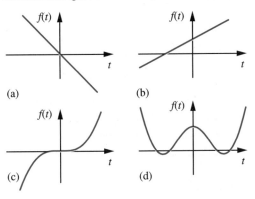

Figure 23.11 (a) The function: $f(t) = -t$;
(b) $f(t) = \dfrac{t}{2} + 1$; (c) $f(t) = t^3$;
(d) $f(t) = \cos t + 0.1t^2$.

2 By using the properties of odd and even functions developed in Example 23.9 state

whether the following are odd, even or neither.

(a) $t^3 \sin \omega t$

(b) $t \cos 2t$

(c) $\sin t \sin 4t$

(d) $\cos \omega t \sin 2\omega t$

(e) $e^t \sin t$

3 Evaluate the following integrals using the integral properties of odd and even functions where appropriate.

(a) $\int_{-5}^{5} t^3 \, dt$

(b) $\int_{-5}^{5} t^3 \cos 3t \, dt$

(c) $\int_{-\pi}^{\pi} t^2 \sin t \, dt$

(d) $\int_{-2}^{2} t \cosh 3t \, dt$

(e) $\int_{-1}^{1} |t| \, dt$

(f) $\int_{-1}^{1} t|t| \, dt$

Solutions

1 (a) odd   (b) neither
   (c) odd   (d) even

2 (a) even   (b) odd   (c) even
   (d) odd   (e) neither

3 (a) 0   (b) 0
   (c) 0   (d) 0
   (e) 1   (f) 0

23.4 Orthogonality relations and other useful identities

Recall from Chapter 16 that two functions $f(t)$ and $g(t)$ are said to be orthogonal on the interval $a \leqslant t \leqslant b$ if

$$\int_a^b f(t)g(t) \, dt = 0$$

Example 23.12 Show that the functions $\cos m\omega t$ and $\cos n\omega t$ with m, n positive integers and $m \neq n$ are orthogonal on the interval $-\dfrac{\pi}{\omega} \leqslant t \leqslant \dfrac{\pi}{\omega}$.

Solution We must evaluate

$$\int_{-\pi/\omega}^{\pi/\omega} \cos m\omega t \, \cos n\omega t \, dt$$

Using the trigonometric identity $2 \cos A \cos B = \cos(A + B) + \cos(A - B)$, we find the integral becomes

$$\frac{1}{2} \int_{-\pi/\omega}^{\pi/\omega} \cos(m + n)\omega t + \cos(m - n)\omega t \, dt$$

$$= \frac{1}{2} \left[\frac{\sin(m + n)\omega t}{(m + n)\omega} + \frac{\sin(m - n)\omega t}{(m - n)\omega} \right]_{-\pi/\omega}^{\pi/\omega}$$

$$= 0$$

since $\sin(m \pm n)\pi = 0$ for all integers m, n. It was necessary to require $m \neq n$ since otherwise the second quantity in brackets becomes undefined.

Hence $\cos m\omega t$ and $\cos n\omega t$ are orthogonal on the given interval.

A number of other functions regularly appearing in work connected with Fourier analysis are orthogonal. The main results together with some other useful integral identities are given in Table 23.1.

Table 23.1
Some useful integral identities.

$$\int_0^T \sin \frac{2n\pi t}{T} \, dt = 0 \qquad \text{for all integers } n$$

$$\int_0^T \cos \frac{2n\pi t}{T} \, dt = 0 \qquad n = 1, 2, 3, \ldots$$

$$\int_0^T \cos \frac{2n\pi t}{T} \, dt = T \qquad n = 0$$

$$\int_0^T \cos \frac{2m\pi t}{T} \cos \frac{2n\pi t}{T} \, dt = \begin{cases} 0 & m \neq n \\ T/2 & m = n \neq 0 \end{cases}$$

$$\int_0^T \sin \frac{2m\pi t}{T} \sin \frac{2n\pi t}{T} \, dt = \begin{cases} 0 & m \neq n \\ T/2 & m = n \neq 0 \end{cases}$$

$$\int_0^T \sin \frac{2m\pi t}{T} \cos \frac{2n\pi t}{T} \, dt = 0 \qquad \text{for all integers } m \text{ and } n$$

23.5 Fourier series

We have seen that the functions $\sin \omega t$, $\sin 2\omega t$, $\sin 3\omega t$, $\ldots$, $\cos \omega t$, $\cos 2\omega t$, $\ldots$ are periodic. Furthermore, linear combinations of them are also periodic. They are also convenient functions to deal with because they can be easily differentiated, integrated, etc. They also possess another very useful property – that of **completeness**. This means that almost any periodic function can be expressed as a linear combination of them and no additional functions are required to do this. In other words, they can be used as building blocks to construct periodic functions simply by adding particular multiples of them together.

Figure 23.12
Sawtooth waveform.

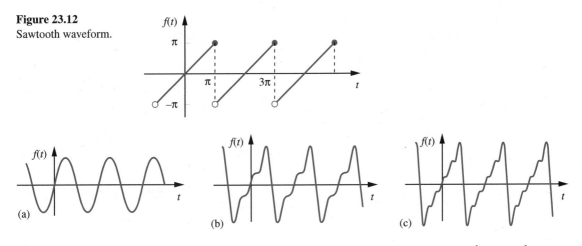

Figure 23.13 Fourier synthesis of a sawtooth waveform: (a) $f(t) = 2 \sin t$; (b) $f(t) = 2(\sin t - \frac{1}{2} \sin 2t + \frac{1}{3} \sin 3t)$; (c) $f(t) = 2(\sin t - \frac{1}{2} \sin 2t + \frac{1}{3} \sin 3t - \frac{1}{4} \sin 4t + \frac{1}{5} \sin 5t)$.

We shall see, for example, that the sawtooth waveform with period 2π, shown in Figure 23.12, is given by the particular combination

$$f(t) = 2\left(\sin t - \tfrac{1}{2} \sin 2t + \tfrac{1}{3} \sin 3t - \tfrac{1}{4} \sin 4t + \tfrac{1}{5} \sin 5t - \cdots\right)$$

This is an infinite series which can be shown to converge for almost all values of t to the function f. This means that if any value of t is substituted into the infinite series and the series is summed, the result will be the same as the value of the sawtooth function at that value of t. There is an exception: if t is one of the points of discontinuity the infinite series will converge to the mean of the values to its left and right, that is 0.

To obtain a feel for what is happening consider Figure 23.13. Graphs (a), (b) and (c) show the effect of including more and more terms in the series. As more terms are taken we see that the series approaches the desired sawtooth waveform. The process of adding together sinusoids to form a new periodic function is called **Fourier synthesis**. We see that the sawtooth waveform has been expressed as an infinite series of harmonic waves, $\sin t$ being the fundamental or first harmonic, and the rest being waves with frequencies that are integer multiples of the fundamental frequency. This infinite series is called the **Fourier series** representation of $f(t)$ and what we have succeeded in doing is to break down $f(t)$ into its component harmonic waveforms. In this example, only sine waves were required to construct the function. More generally we shall need both sine and cosine waves.

Suppose the function $f(t)$ is defined in the interval $0 < t < T$ and is periodic with period T. Then, under certain conditions, its Fourier series is given by

$$f(t) = \frac{a_0}{2} + \sum_{n=1}^{\infty}\left(a_n \cos \frac{2n\pi t}{T} + b_n \sin \frac{2n\pi t}{T}\right) \qquad (23.2)$$

or equivalently

$$f(t) = \frac{a_0}{2} + \sum_{n=1}^{\infty}(a_n \cos n\omega t + b_n \sin n\omega t)$$

where a_n and b_n are constants called the **Fourier coefficients**. These are given by the formulae

$$a_0 = \frac{2}{T} \int_0^T f(t)\, dt \qquad\qquad (23.3)$$

$$a_n = \frac{2}{T} \int_0^T f(t) \cos \frac{2n\pi t}{T}\, dt \qquad \text{for } n \text{ a positive integer} \qquad (23.4)$$

$$b_n = \frac{2}{T} \int_0^T f(t) \sin \frac{2n\pi t}{T}\, dt \qquad \text{for } n \text{ a positive integer} \qquad (23.5)$$

The term $\dfrac{a_0}{2}$ represents the mean value or d.c. component of the waveform (see Section 15.2). The derivation of these formulae appears in Example 23.16. It is important to point out that the integrals in Equations (23.3), (23.4) and (23.5) can be evaluated over any complete period, for example from $t = -\dfrac{T}{2}$ to $t = \dfrac{T}{2}$. Prudent choice of the interval of integration can often save effort. The expression appearing in the r.h.s. of the Fourier representation, Equation (23.2), is an infinite series. We list conditions, often called the Dirichlet conditions, sufficient for the series to converge to the value of the function $f(t)$. The integral $\int |f(t)|\, dt$ over a complete period must be finite, and $f(t)$ may have no more than a finite number of discontinuities in any finite interval. Fortunately, most signals of interest to engineers satisfy these conditions. At a point of discontinuity the Fourier series converges to the average of the two function values at either side of the discontinuity.

Example 23.13 Find the Fourier series representation of the function with period $T = \frac{1}{50}$ given by

$$f(t) = \begin{cases} 1 & 0 \leqslant t < 0.01 \\ 0 & 0.01 \leqslant t < 0.02 \end{cases}$$

Solution The function $f(t)$ is shown in Figure 23.14. Note that $f(t)$ is defined to be zero between $t = 0.01$ and $t = 0.02$. This means we need only consider $0 \leqslant t < 0.01$. Using

Figure 23.14
Graph for
Example 23.13.

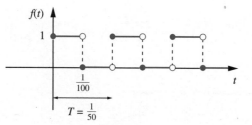

Equations (23.3)–(23.5) we find

$$a_0 = 100 \int_0^{0.02} f(t)\,dt = 100 \int_0^{0.01} 1\,dt + 100 \int_{0.01}^{0.02} 0\,dt$$

$$= 100[t]_0^{0.01} = 1$$

$$a_n = 100 \int_0^{0.01} \cos 100n\pi t\,dt = 100 \left[\frac{\sin 100n\pi t}{100n\pi} \right]_0^{0.01}$$

$$= 0$$

$$b_n = 100 \int_0^{0.01} \sin 100\,n\pi t\,dt = 100 \left[\frac{-\cos 100n\pi t}{100n\pi} \right]_0^{0.01}$$

$$= -\frac{1}{n\pi}(\cos n\pi - \cos 0)$$

Noting that $\cos n\pi = (-1)^n$ we find

$$b_n = \frac{1}{n\pi}(1 - (-1)^n)$$

If n is even $b_n = 0$. If n is odd $b_n = \frac{2}{n\pi}$. Therefore the Fourier series representation of $f(t)$ is

$$f(t) = \frac{1}{2} + \frac{2}{\pi}\left(\sin 100\pi t + \frac{\sin 300\pi t}{3} + \frac{\sin 500\pi t}{5} + \cdots \right)$$

The average value of the waveform is $\frac{1}{2}$. This is the zero frequency component or d.c. value. We note that in this example only odd harmonics are present.

Example 23.14 Find the Fourier series representation of $f(t) = 1 + t$, $-\pi < t \leqslant \pi$, period 2π.

Solution As usual we sketch $f(t)$ first as this often provides insight into what follows (see Figure 23.15). Here $T = 2\pi$, $\omega = 1$, and for convenience we shall consider the period

Figure 23.15
Graph for
Example 23.14.

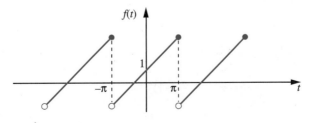

of integration to be $[-\pi, \pi]$. Using Equation (23.3) we find

$$a_0 = \frac{1}{\pi} \int_{-\pi}^{\pi} 1 + t \, dt = \frac{1}{\pi} \left[t + \frac{t^2}{2} \right]_{-\pi}^{\pi}$$

$$= \frac{1}{\pi} \left(\left(\pi + \frac{\pi^2}{2} \right) - \left(-\pi + \frac{\pi^2}{2} \right) \right)$$

$$= \frac{1}{\pi} (2\pi)$$

$$= 2$$

Similarly, using Equation (23.4) we find

$$a_n = \frac{1}{\pi} \int_{-\pi}^{\pi} (1 + t) \cos nt \, dt$$

Integrating by parts gives

$$a_n = \frac{1}{\pi} \left(\left[(1 + t) \frac{\sin nt}{n} \right]_{-\pi}^{\pi} - \int_{-\pi}^{\pi} \frac{\sin nt}{n} \, dt \right)$$

$$= \frac{1}{\pi} \left(0 + \left[\frac{\cos nt}{n^2} \right]_{-\pi}^{\pi} \right) \qquad \text{since } \sin \pm n\pi = 0$$

$$= \frac{1}{\pi n^2} (\cos n\pi - \cos(-n\pi))$$

but $\cos(-n\pi) = \cos n\pi$ and hence $a_n = 0$, for all positive integers n. Using Equation (23.5) we find

$$b_n = \frac{1}{\pi} \int_{-\pi}^{\pi} (1 + t) \sin nt \, dt$$

$$= \frac{1}{\pi} \left(\left[-(1 + t) \frac{\cos nt}{n} \right]_{-\pi}^{\pi} + \int_{-\pi}^{\pi} \frac{\cos nt}{n} \, dt \right)$$

$$= \frac{1}{\pi} \left(-(1 + \pi) \frac{\cos n\pi}{n} + (1 - \pi) \frac{\cos(-n\pi)}{n} + \left[\frac{\sin nt}{n^2} \right]_{-\pi}^{\pi} \right)$$

$$= \frac{1}{\pi n} (-2\pi \cos n\pi)$$

since $\sin \pm n\pi = 0$. Hence,

$$b_n = -\frac{2}{n} \cos n\pi = -\frac{2}{n} (-1)^n$$

We find $b_1 = 2$, $b_2 = -1$, $b_3 = \frac{2}{3}$, ... Thus the Fourier series representation is given from Equation (23.2) as

$$f(t) = 1 + 2 \sin t - \sin 2t + \tfrac{2}{3} \sin 3t + \cdots$$

which we can write concisely as

$$f(t) = 1 - \sum_{n=1}^{\infty} \frac{2}{n} (-1)^n \sin nt$$

Example 23.15   Find the Fourier series representation of the function with period 2π defined by $f(t) = t^2, 0 < t \leqslant 2\pi$.

Solution   As usual we sketch $f(t)$, as shown in Figure 23.16. Here $T = 2\pi$ and we shall integrate, for convenience, over the interval $[0, 2\pi]$. Using Equation (23.3) we find

$$a_0 = \frac{1}{\pi} \int_0^{2\pi} t^2 \, dt = \frac{1}{\pi} \left[\frac{t^3}{3} \right]_0^{2\pi} = \frac{8\pi^2}{3}$$

Using Equation (23.4) we have

$$a_n = \frac{1}{\pi} \int_0^{2\pi} t^2 \cos nt \, dt$$

Integrating by parts, we find

$$a_n = \frac{1}{\pi} \left(\left[t^2 \frac{\sin nt}{n} \right]_0^{2\pi} - \int_0^{2\pi} 2t \frac{\sin nt}{n} \, dt \right)$$

$$= -\frac{2}{n\pi} \int_0^{2\pi} t \sin nt \, dt$$

$$= -\frac{2}{n\pi} \left(\left[-t \frac{\cos nt}{n} \right]_0^{2\pi} + \int_0^{2\pi} \frac{\cos nt}{n} \, dt \right)$$

$$= -\frac{2}{n\pi} \left(\frac{-2\pi \cos 2n\pi}{n} + \left[\frac{\sin nt}{n^2} \right]_0^{2\pi} \right)$$

$$= \frac{4}{n^2}$$

Figure 23.16
Graph for
Example 23.15.

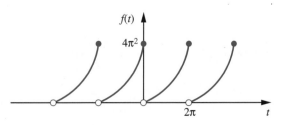

Hence $a_1 = 4$, $a_2 = 1$, $a_3 = \frac{4}{9}$, ... Similarly,

$$b_n = \frac{1}{\pi} \int_0^{2\pi} t^2 \sin nt \, dt$$

$$= \frac{1}{\pi} \left(\left[-t^2 \frac{\cos nt}{n} \right]_0^{2\pi} + \int_0^{2\pi} 2t \frac{\cos nt}{n} \, dt \right)$$

$$= \frac{1}{\pi} \left(-\frac{4\pi^2}{n} \cos 2n\pi + \frac{2}{n} \int_0^{2\pi} t \cos nt \, dt \right)$$

$$= \frac{1}{\pi} \left(-\frac{4\pi^2}{n} + \frac{2}{n} \left(\left[\frac{t \sin nt}{n} \right]_0^{2\pi} - \int_0^{2\pi} \frac{\sin nt}{n} \, dt \right) \right)$$

$$= \frac{1}{\pi} \left(-\frac{4\pi^2}{n} - \frac{2}{n^2} \left[-\frac{\cos nt}{n} \right]_0^{2\pi} \right)$$

$$= -\frac{4\pi}{n}$$

Thus $b_1 = -4\pi$, $b_2 = -2\pi$, ... Finally, the required Fourier series representation is given by

$$f(t) = \frac{4\pi^2}{3} + \left(4 \cos t + \cos 2t + \frac{4}{9} \cos 3t + \cdots \right)$$

$$- \pi \left(4 \sin t + 2 \sin 2t + \frac{4 \sin 3t}{3} + \cdots \right)$$

Example 23.16 Obtain the expressions for the Fourier coefficients a_0, a_n and b_n in Equations (23.3), (23.4) and (23.5).

Solution Assume that $f(t)$ can be expressed in the form

$$f(t) = \frac{a_0}{2} + \sum_{n=1}^{\infty} \left(a_n \cos \frac{2n\pi t}{T} + b_n \sin \frac{2n\pi t}{T} \right) \tag{23.6}$$

Multiplying Equation (23.6) through by $\cos \dfrac{2m\pi t}{T}$ and integrating from 0 to T we find

$$\int_0^T f(t) \cos \frac{2m\pi t}{T} \, dt = \int_0^T \frac{a_0}{2} \cos \frac{2m\pi t}{T} \, dt$$

$$+ \int_0^T \sum_{n=1}^{\infty} \left(a_n \cos \frac{2n\pi t}{T} + b_n \sin \frac{2n\pi t}{T} \right) \cos \frac{2m\pi t}{T} \, dt$$

If we now assume that it is legitimate to interchange the order of integration and summation we obtain

$$\int_0^T f(t) \cos \frac{2m\pi t}{T} \, dt = \int_0^T \frac{a_0}{2} \cos \frac{2m\pi t}{T} \, dt$$

$$+ \sum_{n=1}^{\infty} \int_0^T \left(a_n \cos \frac{2n\pi t}{T} + b_n \sin \frac{2n\pi t}{T} \right) \cos \frac{2m\pi t}{T} \, dt$$

The first integral on the r.h.s. is easily shown to be zero unless $m = 0$. Furthermore, we can use the previously found orthogonality properties (Table 23.1) to show that the rest of the integrals on the r.h.s. vanish except for the case when $n = m$, in which case the r.h.s. reduces to $\dfrac{a_m T}{2}$. Consequently,

$$a_m = \frac{2}{T} \int_0^T f(t) \cos \frac{2m\pi t}{T} \, dt \qquad \text{for all positive integers } m$$

as required. When $m = 0$ all terms on the r.h.s. except the first vanish and we obtain

$$\int_0^T f(t) \, dt = \int_0^T \frac{a_0}{2} \, dt$$

$$= \frac{a_0 T}{2}$$

so that

$$a_0 = \frac{2}{T} \int_0^T f(t) \, dt$$

To obtain the formula for the b_n multiply Equation (23.6) through by $\sin \dfrac{2m\pi t}{T}$ and integrate from 0 to T.

$$\int_0^T f(t) \sin \frac{2m\pi t}{T} \, dt = \int_0^T \frac{a_0}{2} \sin \frac{2m\pi t}{T} \, dt$$

$$+ \int_0^T \sum_{n=1}^{\infty} \left(a_n \cos \frac{2n\pi t}{T} + b_n \sin \frac{2n\pi t}{T} \right) \sin \frac{2m\pi t}{T} \, dt$$

Again assuming that it is legitimate to interchange the order of integration and summation, we obtain

$$\int_0^T f(t) \sin \frac{2m\pi t}{T} \, dt = \int_0^T \frac{a_0}{2} \sin \frac{2m\pi t}{T} \, dt$$

$$+ \sum_{n=1}^{\infty} \int_0^T \left(a_n \cos \frac{2n\pi t}{T} + b_n \sin \frac{2n\pi t}{T} \right) \sin \frac{2m\pi t}{T} \, dt$$

The first integral on the r.h.s. is easily shown to be zero. Furthermore, we can use the properties given in Table 23.1 to show that the rest of the integrals on the r.h.s. vanish except for the case when $n = m$, in which case the r.h.s. reduces to $\dfrac{b_m T}{2}$. Hence we find

$$b_m = \frac{2}{T} \int_0^T f(t) \sin \frac{2m\pi t}{T} \, dt$$

as required.

23.5.1 Fourier series of odd and even functions

Let us now consider what happens when we determine Fourier series of functions which are either odd or even.

Example 23.17   Find the Fourier series for the function with period 2π defined by

$$f(t) = \begin{cases} 0 & -\pi < t < -\pi/2 \\ 4 & -\pi/2 \leqslant t \leqslant \pi/2 \\ 0 & \pi/2 < t < \pi \end{cases}$$

Solution   As usual we sketch the function first (Figure 23.17). Inspection of Figure 23.17 shows that the Dirichlet conditions (page 708) are satisfied. We note from the graph that the function is symmetrical about the vertical axis; that is, it is an even function. We shall see shortly that this fact has important implications for the Fourier series representation. For convenience we consider the period of integration to be $\left[-\dfrac{T}{2}, \dfrac{T}{2}\right]$. Hence Equation (23.4) becomes

$$a_n = \frac{2}{T} \int_{-T/2}^{T/2} f(t) \cos \frac{2n\pi t}{T} \, dt \qquad \text{for all positive integers } n$$

In this example the period T equals 2π. The formula for a_n then simplifies to

$$a_n = \frac{1}{\pi} \int_{-\pi}^{\pi} f(t) \cos nt \, dt$$

The interval of integration is from $t = -\pi$ to $t = \pi$. However, a glance at the graph shows that the function is zero outside the interval $-\dfrac{\pi}{2} \leqslant t \leqslant \dfrac{\pi}{2}$, and takes the value 4 inside. The integral thus reduces to

$$a_n = \frac{1}{\pi} \int_{-\pi/2}^{\pi/2} 4 \cos nt \, dt$$

$$= \frac{4}{\pi} \int_{-\pi/2}^{\pi/2} \cos nt \, dt$$

$$= \frac{4}{\pi} \left[\frac{\sin nt}{n} \right]_{-\pi/2}^{\pi/2}$$

$$= \frac{4}{n\pi} \left[\sin \frac{n\pi}{2} - \sin\left(-\frac{n\pi}{2}\right) \right]$$

$$= \frac{8}{n\pi} \sin \frac{n\pi}{2}$$

We obtain $a_1 = \dfrac{8}{\pi}$, $a_2 = 0$, $a_3 = -\dfrac{8}{3\pi}$, etc. We find a_0 using Equation (23.3), again

Figure 23.17
Graph for
Example 23.17.

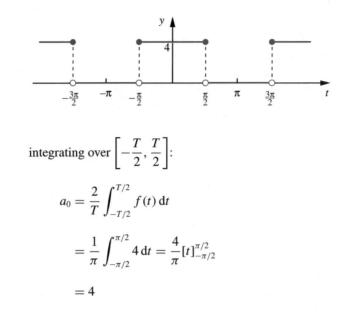

integrating over $\left[-\dfrac{T}{2}, \dfrac{T}{2}\right]$:

$$a_0 = \frac{2}{T} \int_{-T/2}^{T/2} f(t)\, dt$$

$$= \frac{1}{\pi} \int_{-\pi/2}^{\pi/2} 4\, dt = \frac{4}{\pi} [t]_{-\pi/2}^{\pi/2}$$

$$= 4$$

Similarly, to find the Fourier coefficients, b_n, we use Equation (23.5):

$$b_n = \frac{2}{T} \int_{-T/2}^{T/2} f(t) \sin \frac{2n\pi t}{T}\, dt$$

which reduces to

$$b_n = \frac{1}{\pi} \int_{-\pi/2}^{\pi/2} 4 \sin nt\, dt$$

$$= \frac{4}{\pi} \left[\frac{-\cos nt}{n} \right]_{-\pi/2}^{\pi/2}$$

$$= \frac{4}{n\pi} \left[-\cos \frac{n\pi}{2} + \cos \frac{n\pi}{2} \right]$$

$$= 0$$

that is, all the Fourier coefficients, b_n, are zero. Finally we can gather together all our results and write down the Fourier series representation of $f(t)$:

$$f(t) = 2 + \frac{8}{\pi} \cos t - \frac{8}{3\pi} \cos 3t + \frac{8}{5\pi} \cos 5t - \cdots$$

In this example we see that there are no sine terms at all. In fact, whenever a function is even its Fourier series will possess no sine terms. To see this we note that b_n can be found from

$$b_n = \frac{2}{T} \int_{-T/2}^{T/2} f(t) \sin \frac{2n\pi t}{T}\, dt$$

Since $f(t)$ is even and $\sin\dfrac{2n\pi t}{T}$ is odd, the product $f(t)\sin\dfrac{2n\pi t}{T}$ is odd also. Now the integral of an odd function on an interval which is symmetrical about the vertical axis was shown in Section 23.3 to be zero. Hence whenever $f(t)$ is even we can immediately assume $b_n = 0$ for all n.

Correspondingly, when a function is odd its Fourier series will contain no cosine or constant terms. This is because the product

$$f(t)\cos\frac{2n\pi t}{T}$$

is odd also and so the integral

$$a_n = \frac{2}{T}\int_{-T/2}^{T/2} f(t)\cos\frac{2n\pi t}{T}\,dt$$

will equal zero. We conclude that when $f(t)$ is odd, $a_n = 0$ for all n. These facts can often be used to save time and effort. Knowing the function in Example 23.17 was even before we started the Fourier analysis, we could have assumed that the b_n would all be zero.

Example 23.18   Find the Fourier series representation of the sawtooth waveform described at the beginning of this section (see Figure 23.12).

Solution   This function is defined by $f(t) = t$, $-\pi < t < \pi$, and has period $T = 2\pi$. It is an odd function and hence $a_n = 0$ for all n. To find the b_n we must evaluate

$$b_n = \frac{1}{\pi}\int_{-\pi}^{\pi} t\sin nt\,dt$$

$$= \frac{1}{\pi}\left\{\left[\frac{-t\cos nt}{n}\right]_{-\pi}^{\pi} + \int_{-\pi}^{\pi}\frac{\cos nt}{n}\,dt\right\}$$

$$= \frac{1}{n\pi}\{-\pi\cos n\pi - \pi\cos n\pi\}$$

since the last integral vanishes. Therefore,

$$b_n = -\frac{2}{n}\cos n\pi = -\frac{2}{n}(-1)^n$$

We conclude that $b_1 = 2$, $b_2 = -1$, $b_3 = \frac{2}{3}$, ... Therefore $f(t)$ has Fourier series

$$f(t) = 2\{\sin t - \tfrac{1}{2}\sin 2t + \tfrac{1}{3}\sin 3t - \tfrac{1}{4}\sin 4t + \tfrac{1}{5}\sin 5t - \cdots\}$$

Exercises 23.5

1 Find the Fourier series representation of the function

$$f(t) = \begin{cases} 0 & -5 < t < 0 \\ 1 & 0 < t < 5 \end{cases} \quad \text{period } 10$$

2 Find the Fourier series representation of the function

$$f(t) = \begin{cases} -t & -\pi < t < 0 \\ 0 & 0 < t < \pi \end{cases} \quad \text{period } 2\pi$$

3 Find the Fourier series representation of the function

$$f(t) = t^2 + \pi t \quad -\pi < t < \pi \quad \text{period } 2\pi$$

4 Find the Fourier series representation of the function

$$f(t) = \begin{cases} -4 & -\pi < t \leqslant 0 \\ 4 & 0 < t < \pi \end{cases} \quad \text{period } 2\pi$$

5 Find the Fourier series representation of the function

$$f(t) = \begin{cases} 2(1+t) & -1 < t \leqslant 0 \\ 0 & 0 < t < 1 \end{cases} \quad \text{period } 2$$

6 Find the Fourier series representation of the function with period 2π given by

$$f(t) = \begin{cases} t^2 & 0 \leqslant t < \pi \\ 0 & \pi \leqslant t < 2\pi \end{cases}$$

7 Find the Fourier series representation of the function

$$f(t) = 2\sin t \quad 0 < t < 2\pi \quad \text{period } 2\pi$$

Solutions

1 $\dfrac{1}{2} + \dfrac{2}{\pi}\sin\dfrac{\pi t}{5} + \dfrac{2}{3\pi}\sin\dfrac{3\pi t}{5} + \dfrac{2}{5\pi}\sin\dfrac{5\pi t}{5} + \dfrac{2}{7\pi}\sin\dfrac{7\pi t}{5}\cdots$

2 $\dfrac{\pi}{4} - \dfrac{2}{\pi}\cos t - \sin t + \dfrac{1}{2}\sin 2t - \dfrac{2}{9\pi}\cos 3t - \dfrac{1}{3}\sin 3t\ldots$

3 $\dfrac{\pi^2}{3} + 2\pi\sin t - 4\cos t - \pi\sin 2t + \cos 2t + \dfrac{2\pi}{3}\sin 3t - \dfrac{4}{9}\cos 3t\cdots$

4 $\dfrac{8\left(2\sin t + \frac{2}{3}\sin 3t + \frac{2}{5}\sin 5t + \cdots\right)}{\pi}$

5 $\dfrac{1}{2} + \dfrac{2\{(2/\pi)\cos \pi t - \sin \pi t - \frac{1}{2}\sin 2\pi t + (2/9\pi)\cos 3\pi t - \frac{1}{3}\sin 3\pi t + \cdots\}}{\pi}$

6 $\dfrac{\pi^2}{6} + \dfrac{\pi^2-4}{\pi}\sin t - 2\cos t - \dfrac{\pi}{2}\sin 2t + \dfrac{1}{2}\cos 2t + \dfrac{9\pi^2-4}{27\pi}\sin 3t - \dfrac{2}{9}\cos 3t + \cdots$

7 $2\sin t$

23.6 Half-range series

Sometimes an engineering function is not periodic but is only defined over a finite interval, $0 < t < \dfrac{T}{2}$ say, as shown in Figure 23.18. In cases like this Fourier analysis can still be useful. Because the region of interest is only that between $t = 0$ and $t = \dfrac{T}{2}$ we may choose to define the function arbitrarily outside the interval. In particular, we can make our choice so that the resulting function is periodic, with period T. There is more than one way to proceed. For example, we can reflect the above function in the vertical axis and then repeat it periodically so that the result is the periodic even function shown in Figure 23.19. We have performed what is called a **periodic extension** of the given function. Note that within the interval of interest nothing has altered but we have now achieved our objective of finding a periodic function. We can find the Fourier series of this periodic function and within the interval of interest this will converge to the required function. What happens outside this interval is not important. Moreover, since the periodic function is even the Fourier series will contain no sine terms.

An alternative periodic extension is that shown in Figure 23.20, which has been obtained by reflecting in both the vertical and t axes before repeating it periodically to give a periodic odd function. Its Fourier series will contain no cosine terms and within the interval of interest will converge to the function required.

A third alternative periodic extension is shown in Figure 23.21. However, this extension is neither odd nor even and so it has none of the desirable properties of the other two. Whichever extension we choose, the resulting Fourier series only gives a representation of the original function in the interval $0 < t < \dfrac{T}{2}$ and as such is termed a **half-range** Fourier series. Similarly we have the terminology **half-range sine series** for a series containing only sine terms and **half-range cosine series** for a series containing only cosine terms. The Fourier series formulae then simplify to give the following half-range formulae:

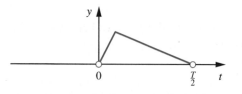

Figure 23.18   Function defined over interval $0 < t < \dfrac{T}{2}$.

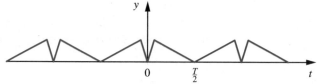

Figure 23.19   An even periodic extension.

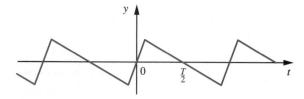

Figure 23.20   An odd periodic extension.

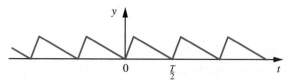

Figure 23.21   A periodic extension that is neither even nor odd.

Half-range sine series:

$$a_0 = 0, a_n = 0 \quad \text{for } n \text{ a positive integer}$$

$$b_n = \frac{4}{T} \int_0^{T/2} f(t) \sin \frac{2n\pi t}{T} \, dt \quad \text{for } n \text{ a positive integer} \tag{23.7}$$

and $f(t)$ is given by

$$f(t) = \sum_{n=1}^{\infty} b_n \sin \frac{2n\pi t}{T}$$

Half-range cosine series:

$$a_0 = \frac{4}{T} \int_0^{T/2} f(t) \, dt \tag{23.8}$$

$$a_n = \frac{4}{T} \int_0^{T/2} f(t) \cos \frac{2n\pi t}{T} \, dt \quad \text{for } n \text{ a positive integer} \tag{23.9}$$

$$b_n = 0 \quad \text{for } n \text{ a positive integer}$$

and then $f(t)$ is given by

$$f(t) = \frac{a_0}{2} + \sum_{n=1}^{\infty} a_n \cos \frac{2n\pi t}{T}$$

Example 23.19   By defining an appropriate periodic extension of the function illustrated in Figure 23.22, find the half-range cosine series representation.

Solution   The function illustrated in Figure 23.22 is given by the formula $f(t) = t$ for $0 < t < \pi$ and is undefined outside this interval. Since the cosine series is required an even periodic extension must be formed. This is illustrated in Figure 23.23. Taking $T = 2\pi$ in Equations (23.8) and (23.9), we find a_0 and a_n.

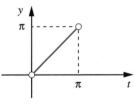

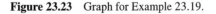

Figure 23.22   Graph for Example 23.19.

Figure 23.23   Graph for Example 23.19.

$$a_0 = \frac{2}{\pi} \int_0^\pi t \, dt$$

$$= \frac{2}{\pi} \left[\frac{t^2}{2} \right]_0^\pi$$

$$= \pi$$

$$a_n = \frac{2}{\pi} \int_0^\pi t \cos nt \, dt$$

$$= \frac{2}{\pi} \left\{ \left[\frac{t \sin nt}{n} \right]_0^\pi - \int_0^\pi \frac{\sin nt}{n} \, dt \right\}$$

$$= \frac{2}{\pi} \left[\frac{\cos nt}{n^2} \right]_0^\pi$$

Now $\cos n\pi = (-1)^n$, so that

$$a_n = \frac{2}{\pi} \left(\frac{(-1)^n}{n^2} - \frac{1}{n^2} \right) \qquad n = 1, 2, \ldots$$

Of course, all the b_n are zero. Therefore the half-range cosine series is

$$f(t) = \frac{\pi}{2} - \frac{4}{\pi} \cos t - \frac{4}{9\pi} \cos 3t \ldots$$

and this series converges to the given function within the interval $0 < t < \pi$.

Exercises 23.6

1 Graph an appropriate periodic extension of

$$f(t) = 3t \qquad 0 < t < \pi$$

and hence find its half-range cosine series representation.

2 Find the half-range sine series representation of the function given in Example 23.19.

3 Find the half-range cosine series representing

the function

$$f(t) = \sin t \qquad 0 < t < \pi$$

4 Graph an appropriate periodic extension of

$$f(t) = e^t \qquad 0 < t < 1$$

and find its half-range cosine series.

5 Find the half-range sine series representation of $f(t) = 2 - t, \, 0 \leqslant t \leqslant 2$.

Solutions

1 $\dfrac{3\pi}{2} + \dfrac{6}{\pi} \sum_1^\infty \left(\dfrac{\cos n\pi - 1}{n^2} \right) \cos nt$

2 $-2 \sum_1^\infty \left(\dfrac{\cos n\pi}{n} \right) \sin nt$

3 $\quad \dfrac{2}{\pi} - \dfrac{2}{\pi} \sum_{2}^{\infty} \left(\dfrac{\cos n\pi + 1}{n^2 - 1} \right) \cos nt$

5 $\quad \dfrac{4}{\pi} \sum_{1}^{\infty} \dfrac{\sin(n\pi t/2)}{n}$

4 $\quad e - 1 + 2 \sum_{1}^{\infty} \left(\dfrac{e \cos n\pi - 1}{n^2 \pi^2 + 1} \right) \cos n\pi t$

23.7 Parseval's theorem

If the function $f(t)$ is periodic with period T and has Fourier coefficients a_n and b_n, then Parseval's theorem states:

$$\frac{2}{T} \int_0^T (f(t))^2 \, dt = \tfrac{1}{2} a_0^2 + \sum_{n=1}^{\infty} (a_n^2 + b_n^2)$$

It is frequently useful in power calculations as the following example shows.

Example 23.20

Average power of a signal

Find the average power developed across a 1 Ω resistor by a voltage signal with period 2π given by

$$v(t) = \cos t - \frac{1}{3} \sin 2t + \frac{1}{2} \cos 3t$$

Solution

We note that $v(t)$ is periodic with period $T = 2\pi$; $v(t)$ is already expressed as a Fourier series with $a_1 = 1$, $a_3 = \frac{1}{2}$ and $b_2 = -\frac{1}{3}$. All other Fourier coefficients are 0. The instantaneous power is $(v(t))^2$ and hence the average power over one period is given by

$$P_{av} = \frac{1}{2\pi} \int_0^{2\pi} (v(t))^2 \, dt$$

Therefore, using Parseval's theorem we find

$$P_{av} = \frac{1}{2} \left(1^2 + \left(-\frac{1}{3} \right)^2 + \left(\frac{1}{2} \right)^2 \right) = 0.68 \text{ W}$$

23.8 Complex notation

An alternative notation for Fourier series involving complex numbers is available which leads naturally into the more general topic of Fourier transforms. Recall from Chapter 9 the Euler relations

$$e^{\pm j\theta} = \cos \theta \pm j \sin \theta$$

from which we can obtain expressions for $\cos\theta$ and $\sin\theta$:

$$\cos\theta = \frac{e^{j\theta} + e^{-j\theta}}{2} \qquad \sin\theta = \frac{e^{j\theta} - e^{-j\theta}}{2j}$$

which enable us to rewrite the Fourier representation

$$f(t) = \frac{a_0}{2} + \sum_{n=1}^{\infty}\left(a_n \cos\frac{2n\pi t}{T} + b_n \sin\frac{2n\pi t}{T}\right)$$

as

$$f(t) = \frac{a_0}{2} + \sum_{n=1}^{\infty}\left(a_n \frac{e^{j2n\pi t/T} + e^{-j2n\pi t/T}}{2} + b_n \frac{e^{j2n\pi t/T} - e^{-j2n\pi t/T}}{2j}\right)$$

$$= \frac{a_0}{2} + \sum_{n=1}^{\infty}\left(\frac{a_n - jb_n}{2} e^{j2n\pi t/T} + \frac{a_n + jb_n}{2} e^{-j2n\pi t/T}\right)$$

which we can write equivalently as

$$f(t) = \sum_{n=-\infty}^{\infty} c_n e^{j2n\pi t/T}$$

where

$$c_n = \frac{a_n - jb_n}{2} \qquad c_{-n} = \frac{a_n + jb_n}{2} \qquad n = 1, 2, \ldots$$

and $c_0 = a_0/2$. It can be shown that the Fourier coefficients, c_n, are then given by

$$c_n = \frac{1}{T}\int_{-T/2}^{T/2} f(t)\, e^{-j2n\pi t/T}\, dt$$

The integral can also be evaluated over any complete period as convenient. Further, if we write $T = \dfrac{2\pi}{\omega_1}$ then this complex form can be expressed as

$$f(t) = \sum_{n=-\infty}^{\infty} c_n e^{jn\omega_1 t}$$

where

$$c_n = \frac{\omega_1}{2\pi}\int_{-\pi/\omega_1}^{\pi/\omega_1} f(t)\, e^{-jn\omega_1 t}\, dt$$

Example 23.21 Find the complex Fourier series representation of the function with period T defined by

$$f(t) = \begin{cases} 1 & -T/4 < t < T/4 \\ 0 & \text{otherwise} \end{cases}$$

Solution We find

$$c_n = \frac{1}{T} \int_{-T/4}^{T/4} 1 e^{-j2n\pi t/T} \, dt$$

$$= \frac{1}{T} \left[\frac{e^{-j2n\pi t/T}}{-j2n\pi/T} \right]_{-T/4}^{T/4}$$

$$= \frac{-1}{2n\pi j} (e^{-jn\pi/2} - e^{jn\pi/2})$$

$$= \frac{1}{n\pi} \left(\frac{e^{jn\pi/2} - e^{-jn\pi/2}}{2j} \right)$$

$$= \frac{1}{n\pi} \sin \frac{n\pi}{2}$$

Therefore,

$$f(t) = \sum_{n=-\infty}^{\infty} \frac{1}{n\pi} \sin \frac{n\pi}{2} e^{j2n\pi t/T}$$

The observant reader will note that the expressions for c_n appear invalid when $n = 0$, since the denominator is then zero. We can compute c_0 in either of two ways. Using an integral expression we see that

$$c_0 = \frac{1}{T} \int_{-T/4}^{T/4} 1 \, dt = \frac{1}{2}$$

Also, using a Taylor series expansion it is possible to show

$$\lim_{n \to 0} \frac{1}{T} \left[\frac{e^{-j2n\pi t/T}}{-j2n\pi/T} \right]_{-T/4}^{T/4} = \frac{1}{2}$$

giving a consistent result.

Exercises 23.8

1 Find the complex Fourier series representation of

(a) $f(t) = \begin{cases} 1 & 0 < t < 2 \\ 0 & 2 < t < 4 \end{cases}$ period 4

(b) $f(t) = e^t$ $-1 < t < 1$ period 2

(c) $f(t) = \begin{cases} A \sin \omega t & 0 < t < \pi/\omega \\ 0 & \pi/\omega < t < 2\pi/\omega \end{cases}$
   period $2\pi/\omega$

2 If

$$f(t) = \sum_{-\infty}^{\infty} c_n e^{j2n\pi t/T},$$

show that the coefficients, c_n, are given by

$$c_n = \frac{1}{T} \int_0^T f(t) e^{-j2n\pi t/T} \, dt$$

[*Hint*: multiply both sides by $e^{-j2m\pi t/T}$ and integrate over $[0, T]$.]

Solutions

1 (a) $\displaystyle\sum_{-\infty}^{\infty} \frac{j}{2n\pi}(\cos n\pi - 1)\,e^{jn\pi t/2}$

(c) $\displaystyle\sum_{-\infty}^{\infty} \frac{A(1 + e^{-jn\pi})\,e^{jn\omega t}}{2\pi(1 - n^2)}$

(b) $\displaystyle\frac{1}{2}\sum_{-\infty}^{\infty}\left(\frac{e^{-jn\pi+1} - e^{-1+jn\pi}}{1 - jn\pi}\right)e^{jn\pi t}$

23.9 Frequency response of a linear system

We have already examined some of the basic features of linear systems in Section 18.2. Linear systems have the property that the response to several inputs being applied to the system can be obtained by adding the effects of the individual inputs. Another useful property of linear systems is that if a sinusoidal input is applied to the system then the output will also be a sinusoid of the same frequency but with modified amplitude and phase. This is illustrated in Figure 23.24.

In Section 9.7 we saw that sinusoidal signals can be represented by complex numbers and that an a.c. electrical circuit can be analysed using complex numbers. This is true for linear systems in general. It is possible to define a **complex frequency function**, $G(j\omega)$, where ω is the frequency of the input; G relates the output and the input of a linear system.

If a sine wave of amplitude A_i is applied to the system then the amplitude, A_o, of the output is given by

$$A_o = |G(j\omega)|A_i$$

The phase shift, ϕ, is given by

$$\phi = \angle G(j\omega)$$

Note that A_o and ϕ depend upon ω. It is important to note that $G(j\omega)$ is a frequency-dependent function. Although the notation for $G(j\omega)$ may seem slightly odd it arises because one method of obtaining the frequency function for a linear system is to substitute $s = j\omega$ in the Laplace transform transfer function, $G(s)$, of the system.

It is now possible to analyse the effect of applying a generalized periodic waveform to a linear system. The first stage is to calculate the Fourier components of the input waveform. The amplitude and phase shift of each of the output components is then calculated using $G(j\omega)$. Finally, the output components are added to obtain the output waveform. This is only possible because of the additive nature of linear systems. An example will help to clarify these points.

Figure 23.24
The response of a linear system to a sinusoidal input is also sinusoidal.

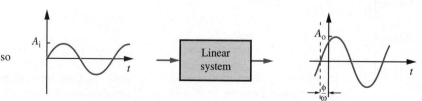

Example 23.22	**Low-pass filter**

Consider the circuit of Figure 23.25. Using Kirchhoff's voltage law and Ohm's law we obtain

$$v_i = iR + v_o$$

For the capacitor,

$$v_o = \frac{i}{j\omega C}$$

Eliminating i yields

$$v_i = v_o j\omega CR + v_o = v_o(1 + j\omega RC)$$

$$\frac{v_o}{v_i} = \frac{1}{1 + j\omega RC} \qquad (23.10)$$

Equation (23.10) relates the output of the system to the input of the system. Therefore,

$$G(j\omega) = \frac{1}{1 + j\omega RC}$$

It is convenient to convert $G(j\omega)$ into polar form:

$$G(j\omega) = \frac{1\angle 0}{\sqrt{1 + (\omega RC)^2}\angle \tan^{-1}\omega RC}$$

$$= \frac{1}{\sqrt{1 + (\omega RC)^2}}\angle - \tan^{-1}\omega RC$$

Therefore,

$$|G(j\omega)| = \frac{1}{\sqrt{1 + (\omega RC)^2}} \qquad (23.11)$$

$$\angle G(j\omega) = -\tan^{-1}\omega RC \qquad (23.12)$$

The amplitude and phase characteristics for the circuit of Figure 23.25 are shown in Figure 23.26. These show the variation of $|G(j\omega)|$ and $\angle G(j\omega)$ with angular frequency ω.

Note that the circuit is a low-pass filter; it allows low frequencies to pass easily and rejects high frequencies. The cut-off point of the filter, that is the point at which significant frequency attenuation begins to occur, can be varied by changing the values of R and C. The quantity RC is usually known as the time constant for the system. Consider the case when $RC = 0.3$. Equations (23.11) and (23.12) reduce to

$$|G(j\omega)| = \frac{1}{\sqrt{1 + 0.09\omega^2}} \qquad (23.13)$$

$$\angle G(j\omega) = -\tan^{-1}0.3\omega \qquad (23.14)$$

Let us examine the response of this system to a square wave input with fundamental angular frequency 1 and amplitude 1. This waveform is shown in Figure 23.27(a). We

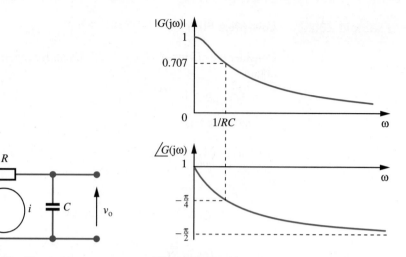

Figure 23.25 Circuit for
Example 23.22.

Figure 23.26 Amplitude and phase characteristics
for the circuit of Figure 23.25.

note that $T = 2\pi$. The waveform function is odd and so will not contain any cosine
Fourier components. It has an average value of 0 and so will not have a zero frequency
component; that is, there will be no d.c. component. Therefore calculating the Fourier
components reduces to evaluating

$$f(t) = \sum_{n=1}^{\infty} b_n \sin \frac{2\pi nt}{T}$$

$$b_n = \frac{2}{T} \int_{-T/2}^{T/2} f(t) \sin \frac{2\pi nt}{T} \, dt \qquad \text{for positive integers } n$$

Since $T = 2\pi$, we find

$$b_n = \frac{1}{\pi} \left(\int_{-\pi}^{0} -1 \sin nt \, dt + \int_{0}^{\pi} \sin nt \, dt \right)$$

$$= \frac{1}{\pi} \left(\left[\frac{\cos nt}{n} \right]_{-\pi}^{0} + \left[\frac{-\cos nt}{n} \right]_{0}^{\pi} \right)$$

$$= \frac{1}{n\pi} (\cos 0 - \cos \pi n - \cos \pi n + \cos 0)$$

$$= \frac{1}{n\pi} (2 - 2 \cos \pi n)$$

$$= \frac{2}{n\pi} (1 - \cos \pi n)$$

The values of the first few coefficients are

$$b_1 = \frac{2}{\pi}(1 - \cos \pi) = \frac{4}{\pi}$$

$$b_2 = \frac{2}{2\pi}(1 - \cos 2\pi) = 0$$

$$b_3 = \frac{2}{3\pi}(1 - \cos 3\pi) = \frac{4}{3\pi}$$

The next stage is to evaluate the gain and phase changes of the Fourier components. Using Equations (23.13) and (23.14):

<u>$n = 1$</u>

$$\omega_1 = 1$$

$$|G(j\omega_1)| = \frac{1}{\sqrt{1 + 0.09 \times 1}} = 0.96$$

$$\angle G(j\omega_1) = -\tan^{-1} 0.3 = -16.7°$$

<u>$n = 3$</u>

$$\omega_3 = 3$$

$$|G(j\omega_3)| = \frac{1}{\sqrt{1 + 0.09 \times 9}} = 0.74$$

$$\angle G(j\omega_3) = -\tan^{-1} 0.9 = -42.0°$$

<u>$n = 5$</u>

$$\omega_5 = 5$$

$$|G(j\omega_5)| = \frac{1}{\sqrt{1 + 0.09 \times 25}} = 0.55$$

$$\angle G(j\omega_5) = -\tan^{-1} 1.5 = -56.3°$$

It is clear that high-frequency Fourier components are attenuated and phase shifted more than low-frequency Fourier components. The effect is to produce a rounding of the rising and falling edges of the square wave input signal. This is illustrated in Figure 23.27(b). The output signal has been obtained by adding together the attenuated and phase-shifted output Fourier components. This is possible because the system is linear.

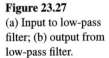

Figure 23.27
(a) Input to low-pass filter; (b) output from low-pass filter.

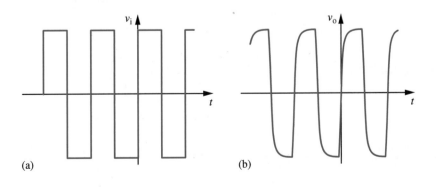

Review exercises 23

1. Find the half-range Fourier sine series representation of $f(t) = t \sin t, 0 \leqslant t \leqslant \pi$.

2. Find the half-range sine series representation of $f(t) = \cos 2t, 0 \leqslant t \leqslant \pi$.

3. Find (a) the half-range sine series, and (b) the half-range cosine series representation of the function defined in the interval $[0, \tau]$ by

$$f(t) = \begin{cases} \dfrac{4t}{\tau} & 0 \leqslant t \leqslant \dfrac{\tau}{4} \\ \dfrac{4}{3}\left(1 - \dfrac{t}{\tau}\right) & \dfrac{\tau}{4} \leqslant t \leqslant \tau \end{cases}$$

4. Find the Fourier series representation of the function with period T defined by

$$f(t) = \begin{cases} V \text{ (constant)} & |t| < T/6 \\ 0 & T/6 \leqslant |t| \leqslant T/2 \end{cases}$$

5. The output from a half-wave rectifier is given by

$$i(t) = \begin{cases} I \sin \omega t & 0 < t < T/2 \\ 0 & T/2 < t < T \end{cases}$$

and is periodic with period $T = \dfrac{2\pi}{\omega}$.

Find its Fourier series representation.

6. Find the complex Fourier series representation of the function with period $T = 0.02$ defined by

$$v(t) = \begin{cases} V \text{ (constant)} & 0 \leqslant t < 0.01 \\ 0 & 0.01 \leqslant t < 0.02 \end{cases}$$

7. Find the Fourier series representation of the function with period 8 given by

$$f(t) = \begin{cases} 2 - t & 0 < t < 4 \\ t - 6 & 4 < t < 8 \end{cases}$$

8. The r.m.s. voltage, $v_{\text{r.m.s.}}$, of a periodic waveform, $v(t)$, with period T, is given by

$$v_{\text{r.m.s.}} = \sqrt{\frac{1}{T} \int_0^T (v(t))^2 \, dt}$$

If $v(t)$ has Fourier coefficients a_n and b_n show, using Parseval's theorem, that

$$v_{\text{r.m.s.}} = \sqrt{\frac{1}{4}a_0^2 + \frac{1}{2}\sum_{n=1}^{\infty}(a_n^2 + b_n^2)}$$

9. If $f(t)$ has Fourier series

$$f(t) = \frac{a_0}{2} + \sum_{n=1}^{\infty}\left(a_n \cos \frac{2n\pi t}{T}\right.$$

$$\left. + b_n \sin \frac{2n\pi t}{T}\right)$$

prove Parseval's theorem.

[*Hint*: multiply both sides by $f(t)$ to obtain

$$(f(t))^2 = \frac{a_0 f(t)}{2} + \sum_{n=1}^{\infty}\left(a_n f(t) \cos \frac{2n\pi t}{T}\right.$$

$$\left. + b_n f(t) \sin \frac{2n\pi t}{T}\right)$$

and integrate both sides over the interval $[0, T]$ using Equations (23.3)–(23.5).]

10. Find the half-range cosine series and the half-range sine series for the function

$$f(t) = \sinh \pi t \qquad 0 < t < 1$$

Solutions

1. $\dfrac{\pi}{2} - \sum_{2}^{\infty} \dfrac{4n(1 + \cos n\pi)}{\pi(n+1)^2(n-1)^2} \sin(nt)$

2. $\dfrac{2}{\pi}\sum_{1}^{\infty} \dfrac{n(1 - \cos n\pi)}{(n^2 - 4)} \sin(nt)$

3. (a) $\dfrac{32}{3\pi^2}\sum_{1}^{\infty} \dfrac{\sin(n\pi/4)\sin(n\pi t/\tau)}{n^2}$

(b) $\dfrac{1}{2} + \dfrac{8}{\pi^2}$

$\times \sum_{1}^{\infty} \dfrac{4\cos(n\pi/4) - \cos n\pi - 3}{3n^2} \cos\left(\dfrac{n\pi t}{\tau}\right)$

4. $\dfrac{v}{3} + \dfrac{2v}{\pi}\sum_{1}^{\infty} \dfrac{\sin(n\pi/3)\cos(2n\pi t/T)}{n}$

5   $\dfrac{I}{\pi} + \dfrac{I}{2}\sin\omega t - \dfrac{I}{\pi}\displaystyle\sum_{2}^{\infty}\dfrac{\cos n\pi + 1}{n^2 - 1}\cos n\omega t$

6   $\dfrac{v}{2\pi}\displaystyle\sum_{-\infty}^{\infty}\mathrm{j}\dfrac{\cos n\pi - 1}{n}\,\mathrm{e}^{100n\pi \mathrm{j}t}$

7   $\dfrac{8}{\pi^2}\displaystyle\sum_{1}^{\infty}\dfrac{1 - \cos n\pi}{n^2}\cos\left(\dfrac{n\pi t}{4}\right)$

10   cosine series: $\dfrac{1}{\pi}(\cosh\pi - 1)$

$+ \displaystyle\sum_{n=1}^{\infty}\dfrac{2}{\pi(1+n^2)}((-1)^n\cosh\pi - 1)\cos n\pi t$

sine series:

$- \displaystyle\sum_{n=1}^{\infty}\dfrac{2n}{\pi(1+n^2)}(-1)^n\sinh\pi\sin n\pi t$

24 The Fourier transform

Chapter 24 Contents

24.1	Introduction	732
24.2	The Fourier transform – definitions	732
24.3	Some properties of the Fourier transform	736
24.4	Spectra	741
24.5	The t–ω duality principle	743
24.6	Fourier transforms of some special functions	744
24.7	The relationship between the Fourier transform and the Laplace transform	747
24.8	Convolution and correlation	749
24.9	The discrete Fourier transform	759
24.10	Derivation of the d.f.t.	762
24.11	Using the d.f.t. to estimate a Fourier transform	765
24.12	Matrix representation of the d.f.t.	767
24.13	Some properties of the d.f.t.	769
24.14	Discrete convolution and correlation	770
	Review exercises	785

24.1 Introduction

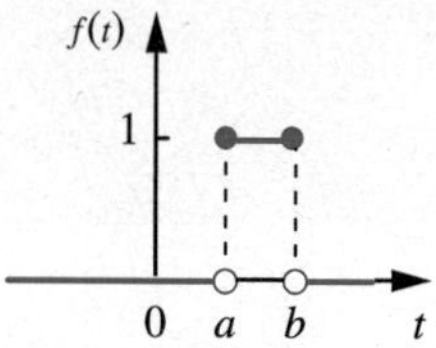

We have seen that almost any periodic signal can be represented as a linear combination of sine and cosine waves of various frequencies and amplitudes. All frequencies are integer multiples of the fundamental. However, many practical waveforms are not periodic. Examples are pulse signals and noise signals. The function shown in Figure 24.1 is an example of a non-periodic signal.

We shall now see how Fourier techniques can still be useful by introducing the Fourier transform which is used extensively in communications engineering and signal processing. For example, it can be used to analyse the processes of modulation, which involves superimposing an audio signal on to a carrier signal, and demodulation, which involves removing the carrier signal to leave the audio signal.

Figure 24.1 A non-periodic function.

24.2 The Fourier transform – definitions

Under certain conditions it can be shown that a non-periodic function, $f(t)$, can be expressed not as the sum of sine and cosine waves but as an integral. In particular,

$$f(t) = \int_0^\infty A(\omega)\cos \omega t + B(\omega)\sin \omega t \, d\omega \tag{24.1}$$

where

$$A(\omega) = \frac{1}{\pi}\int_{-\infty}^\infty f(t)\cos \omega t \, dt \quad \text{and} \quad B(\omega) = \frac{1}{\pi}\int_{-\infty}^\infty f(t)\sin \omega t \, dt \tag{24.2}$$

Provided

(1) $f(t)$ and $f'(t)$ are piecewise continuous in every finite interval, and

(2) $\int_{-\infty}^\infty |f(t)| \, dt$ exists

then the above Fourier integral representation of $f(t)$ holds. At a point of discontinuity of $f(t)$ the integral representation converges to the average value of the right- and left-hand limits. As with Fourier series, an equivalent complex representation exists which is, in fact, more commonly used:

Fourier integral representation of $f(t)$:

$$f(t) = \frac{1}{2\pi}\int_{-\infty}^\infty F(\omega)\, e^{j\omega t} \, d\omega \tag{24.3}$$

where

$$F(\omega) = \int_{-\infty}^\infty f(t)\, e^{-j\omega t} \, dt \tag{24.4}$$

There is no universal convention concerning the definition of these integrals and a number of variants are still correct. For instance, some authors write the factor $\frac{1}{2\pi}$ in the second integral rather than the first, while others place a factor $\dfrac{1}{\sqrt{2\pi}}$ in both, giving some symmetry to the equations. There is also variation in the location of the factors $e^{-j\omega t}$ and $e^{j\omega t}$. We shall use definitions (24.3) and (24.4) throughout but it is important to be aware of possible differences when consulting other texts.

Equations (24.3) and (24.4) form what is called a **Fourier transform pair**. The **Fourier transform** of $f(t)$ is $F(\omega)$ which is sometimes written $\mathcal{F}\{f(t)\}$. Similarly $f(t)$ in Equation (24.3) is the **inverse Fourier transform** of $F(\omega)$, usually denoted $\mathcal{F}^{-1}\{F(\omega)\}$.

The Fourier transform of $f(t)$ is defined to be

$$\mathcal{F}\{f(t)\} = F(\omega) = \int_{-\infty}^{\infty} f(t)e^{-j\omega t}\,dt$$

You will also note the similarity between Equation (24.4) and the definition of the Laplace transform of $f(t)$:

$$\mathcal{L}\{f(t)\} = \int_{0}^{\infty} f(t)\,e^{-st}\,dt \tag{24.5}$$

We see that, apart from the limits of integration, the substitution $j\omega = s$ in Equation (24.4) results in the Laplace transform in Equation (24.5). There is indeed an important relationship between the two transforms which we shall discuss in Section 24.7. We note that Equation (24.3) provides a formula for the inverse Fourier transform of $F(\omega)$, although the integral is frequently difficult to evaluate.

Example 24.1   Find the Fourier transform of the function $f(t) = u(t)\,e^{-t}$, where $u(t)$ is the unit step function.

Solution   The function $u(t)\,e^{-t}$ is shown in Figure 24.2. Using Equation (24.4), its Fourier transform is given by

$$F(\omega) = \int_{-\infty}^{\infty} f(t)\,e^{-j\omega t}\,dt$$

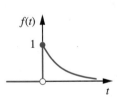

$$= \int_{0}^{\infty} e^{-t}\,e^{-j\omega t}\,dt \qquad \text{since } f(t) = 0 \text{ for } t < 0$$

$$= \int_{0}^{\infty} e^{-(1+j\omega)t}\,dt$$

Figure 24.2 Graph of $u(t)\,e^{-t}$.

$$= \left[\frac{e^{-(1+j\omega)t}}{-(1+j\omega)}\right]_{0}^{\infty}$$

$$= \frac{1}{1+j\omega} \qquad \text{since } e^{-(1+j\omega)t} \to 0 \text{ as } t \to \infty$$

that is,

$$F(\omega) = \frac{1}{1+j\omega}$$

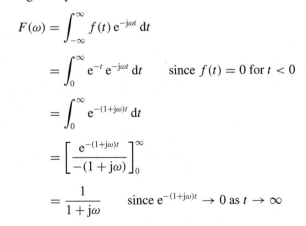

Example 24.2   Use Equation (24.3) to find the Fourier integral representation of the function defined by

$$f(t) = \begin{cases} 1 & -1 \leqslant t \leqslant 1 \\ 0 & |t| > 1 \end{cases}$$

Solution   Using Equation (24.3) we find

$$f(t) = \frac{1}{2\pi} \int_{-\infty}^{\infty} F(\omega)\, e^{j\omega t}\, d\omega$$

where

$$F(\omega) = \int_{-\infty}^{\infty} f(t)\, e^{-j\omega t}\, dt$$

$$= \int_{-1}^{1} 1 e^{-j\omega t}\, dt \qquad \text{since } f(t) \text{ is zero outside } [-1, 1]$$

$$= \left[\frac{e^{-j\omega t}}{-j\omega} \right]_{-1}^{1}$$

$$= \frac{e^{-j\omega} - e^{j\omega}}{-j\omega}$$

$$= \frac{e^{j\omega} - e^{-j\omega}}{j\omega}$$

Using Euler's relation (Section 9.6)

$$\sin\theta = \frac{e^{j\theta} - e^{-j\theta}}{2j}$$

we find

$$F(\omega) = \frac{2\sin\omega}{\omega}$$

so that

$$f(t) = \frac{1}{2\pi} \int_{-\infty}^{\infty} \frac{2\sin\omega}{\omega}\, e^{j\omega t}\, d\omega$$

is the required integral representation. Note that $F(\omega) = \dfrac{2\sin\omega}{\omega}$ is the Fourier transform of $f(t)$. The function $\dfrac{\sin\omega}{\omega}$ occurs frequently and is often referred to as the sinc function.

As with Laplace transforms, tables have been compiled for reference. Such a table of common transforms appears in Table 24.1.

Table 24.1
Common Fourier
transforms.

$f(t)$	$F(\omega)$
$f(t) = Au(t)\,\mathrm{e}^{-\alpha t}, \alpha > 0$	$\dfrac{A}{\alpha + \mathrm{j}\omega}$
$f(t) = \begin{cases} 1 & -\alpha \leqslant t \leqslant \alpha \\ 0 & \text{otherwise} \end{cases}$	$\dfrac{2\sin\omega\alpha}{\omega}$
$f(t) = A \quad\quad \text{constant}$	$2\pi A\delta(\omega)$
$f(t) = u(t)A$	$A\left(\pi\delta(\omega) - \dfrac{\mathrm{j}}{\omega}\right)$
$f(t) = \delta(t)$	1
$f(t) = \delta(t - a)$	$\mathrm{e}^{-\mathrm{j}\omega a}$
$f(t) = \cos at$	$\pi(\delta(\omega + a) + \delta(\omega - a))$
$f(t) = \sin at$	$\dfrac{\pi}{\mathrm{j}}(\delta(\omega - a) - \delta(\omega + a))$
$f(t) = \mathrm{e}^{-\alpha\lvert t\rvert}, \alpha > 0$	$\dfrac{2\alpha}{\alpha^2 + \omega^2}$
$f(t) = \mathrm{sgn}(t) = \begin{cases} 1 & t > 0 \\ -1 & t < 0 \end{cases}$	$\dfrac{2}{\mathrm{j}\omega}$
$f(t) = \dfrac{1}{t}$	$-\mathrm{j}\pi\,\mathrm{sgn}(\omega)$
$f(t) = \mathrm{e}^{-at^2}$	$\sqrt{\dfrac{\pi}{a}}\,\mathrm{e}^{-\omega^2/4a}$

Exercises 24.2

1 Find the Fourier transforms of

(a) $f(t) = \begin{cases} 1/4 & \lvert t\rvert \leqslant 3 \\ 0 & \lvert t\rvert > 3 \end{cases}$

(b) $f(t) = \begin{cases} 1 - \dfrac{t}{2} & 0 \leqslant t \leqslant 2 \\ 1 + \dfrac{t}{2} & -2 \leqslant t \leqslant 0 \\ 0 & \text{otherwise} \end{cases}$

(c) $f(t) = \begin{cases} \mathrm{e}^{-\alpha t} & t \geqslant 0 \\ \mathrm{e}^{\alpha t} & t < 0 \end{cases} \quad \alpha > 0$

(d) $f(t) = \begin{cases} \mathrm{e}^{-t}\cos t & t \geqslant 0 \\ 0 & t < 0 \end{cases}$

(e) $f(t) = u(t)\,\mathrm{e}^{-t/\tau}$ where τ is a constant

2 Find

(a) the Fourier transform, and

(b) the Laplace transform of

$$f(t) = u(t)\,\mathrm{e}^{-\alpha t} \quad\quad \alpha > 0$$

Show that making the substitution $s = \mathrm{j}\omega$ in the Laplace transform of f results in the Fourier transform.

3 If $f(t) = \begin{cases} 1 & \lvert t\rvert \leqslant 2 \\ 0 & \text{otherwise} \end{cases}$

and $g(t) = \mathrm{e}^{\mathrm{j}t}$, find $\mathcal{F}\{f(t)g(t)\}$.

Solutions

1 (a) $\dfrac{\sin 3\omega}{2\omega}$

   (b) $\dfrac{1 - \cos 2\omega}{\omega^2}$

   (c) $\dfrac{2\alpha}{\alpha^2 + \omega^2}$

   (d) $\dfrac{1 + j\omega}{(1 + j\omega)^2 + 1}$

   (e) $\dfrac{\tau}{1 + j\omega\tau}$

2 (a) $\dfrac{1}{\alpha + j\omega}$

   (b) $\dfrac{1}{s + \alpha}$

3 $\dfrac{2\sin 2(1 - \omega)}{1 - \omega}$

24.3	Some properties of the Fourier transform

A number of the properties of Laplace transforms that we have already discussed hold for Fourier transforms. We consider linearity and two shift theorems.

24.3.1 Linearity

If f and g are functions of t and k is a constant, then

$$\mathcal{F}\{f + g\} = \mathcal{F}\{f\} + \mathcal{F}\{g\}$$

$$\mathcal{F}\{kf\} = k\mathcal{F}\{f\}$$

Both of these properties follow directly from the definition and linearity properties of integrals, and mean that $\mathcal{F}$ is a linear operator.

Example 24.3   Find $\mathcal{F}\{u(t)\,\mathrm{e}^{-t} + u(t)\,\mathrm{e}^{-2t}\}$.

Solution   We saw in Example 24.1 that

$$\mathcal{F}\{u(t)\,\mathrm{e}^{-t}\} = \frac{1}{1 + j\omega}$$

Furthermore,

$$\mathcal{F}\{u(t)\,\mathrm{e}^{-2t}\} = \int_{-\infty}^{\infty} u(t)\,\mathrm{e}^{-2t}\,\mathrm{e}^{-j\omega t}\,\mathrm{d}t$$

$$= \int_{0}^{\infty} \mathrm{e}^{-(2 + j\omega)t}\,\mathrm{d}t$$

$$= \left[\frac{\mathrm{e}^{-(2 + j\omega)t}}{-(2 + j\omega)} \right]_{0}^{\infty}$$

$$= \frac{1}{2 + j\omega}$$

Therefore,

$$\mathcal{F}\{u(t)\,e^{-t} + u(t)\,e^{-2t}\} = \frac{1}{1+j\omega} + \frac{1}{2+j\omega} \qquad \text{by linearity}$$

$$= \frac{2+j\omega+1+j\omega}{(1+j\omega)(2+j\omega)}$$

$$= \frac{3+2j\omega}{2-\omega^2+3j\omega}$$

24.3.2 First shift theorem

If $F(\omega)$ is the Fourier transform of $f(t)$, then

$$\mathcal{F}\{e^{jat}\,f(t)\} = F(\omega - a) \qquad \text{where } a \text{ is a constant}$$

Example 24.4   (a) Show that the Fourier transform of

$$f(t) = \begin{cases} 3 & -2 \leqslant t \leqslant 2 \\ 0 & \text{otherwise} \end{cases}$$

is given by $F(\omega) = \dfrac{6\sin 2\omega}{\omega}$.

(b) Use the first shift theorem to find the Fourier transform of $e^{-jt}\,f(t)$.

(c) Verify the first shift theorem by obtaining the Fourier transform of $e^{-jt}\,f(t)$ directly.

Solution   (a) $F(\omega) = 3\displaystyle\int_{-2}^{2} e^{-j\omega t}\,dt = 3\left[\dfrac{e^{-j\omega t}}{-j\omega}\right]_{-2}^{2}$

$$= 3\left(\frac{e^{-2j\omega} - e^{2j\omega}}{-j\omega}\right)$$

$$= 6\left(\frac{e^{2j\omega} - e^{-2j\omega}}{2j\omega}\right)$$

$$= \frac{6}{\omega}\sin 2\omega$$

(b) We have $\mathcal{F}\{f(t)\} = F(\omega) = \dfrac{6\sin 2\omega}{\omega}$. Using the first shift theorem with $a = -1$ we have

$$\mathcal{F}\{e^{-jt}\,f(t)\} = F(\omega + 1) = \frac{6}{\omega+1}\sin 2(\omega + 1)$$

(c) $e^{-jt} f(t) = \begin{cases} 3e^{-jt} & -2 \leqslant t \leqslant 2 \\ 0 & \text{otherwise} \end{cases}$

So to evaluate its Fourier transform directly we must find

$$\mathcal{F}\{e^{-jt} f(t)\} = 3 \int_{-2}^{2} e^{-jt} e^{-j\omega t} \, dt$$

$$= 3 \int_{-2}^{2} e^{-(1+\omega)jt} \, dt$$

$$= 3 \left[\frac{e^{-(1+\omega)jt}}{-j(1+\omega)} \right]_{-2}^{2}$$

$$= \frac{6}{1+\omega} \left(\frac{e^{2(1+\omega)j} - e^{-2(1+\omega)j}}{2j} \right)$$

$$= \frac{6}{1+\omega} \sin 2(1+\omega)$$

as required.

Example 24.5   Use the first shift theorem to find the function whose Fourier transform is $\dfrac{1}{3 + j(\omega - 2)}$, given that $\mathcal{F}\{u(t) e^{-mt}\} = \dfrac{1}{m + j\omega}, m > 0.$

Solution   From the given result we have

$$\mathcal{F}\{u(t) e^{-3t}\} = \frac{1}{3 + j\omega} = F(\omega)$$

Now

$$\frac{1}{3 + j(\omega - 2)} = F(\omega - 2)$$

Therefore, from the first shift theorem with $a = 2$ we have

$$\mathcal{F}\{e^{2jt} u(t) e^{-3t}\} = \frac{1}{3 + j(\omega - 2)}$$

Consequently the function whose Fourier transform is $\dfrac{1}{3 + j(\omega - 2)}$ is $u(t) e^{-(3-2j)t}$.

Example 24.6   Find the Fourier transform of

$$f(t) = \begin{cases} e^{-3t} & t \geqslant 0 \\ e^{3t} & t < 0 \end{cases}$$

Deduce the function whose Fourier transform is $G(\omega) = \dfrac{6}{10 + 2\omega + \omega^2}$.

Solution $F(\omega) = \displaystyle\int_{-\infty}^{\infty} f(t)\,e^{-j\omega t}\,dt$

$$= \int_{-\infty}^{0} e^{3t}\,e^{-j\omega t}\,dt + \int_{0}^{\infty} e^{-3t}\,e^{-j\omega t}\,dt$$

$$= \int_{-\infty}^{0} e^{(3-j\omega)t}\,dt + \int_{0}^{\infty} e^{-(3+j\omega)t}\,dt$$

$$= \left[\frac{e^{(3-j\omega)t}}{3-j\omega}\right]_{-\infty}^{0} + \left[\frac{e^{-(3+j\omega)t}}{-(3+j\omega)}\right]_{0}^{\infty}$$

$$= \frac{1}{3-j\omega} + \frac{1}{3+j\omega}$$

$$= \frac{6}{9+\omega^2}$$

Now

$$G(\omega) = \frac{6}{10+2\omega+\omega^2} = \frac{6}{(\omega+1)^2+9} = F(\omega+1)$$

Then, using the first shift theorem $F(\omega+1)$ will be $\mathcal{F}\{e^{-jt} f(t)\}$; that is, the required function is

$$g(t) = \begin{cases} e^{(-3-j)t} & t \geqslant 0 \\ e^{(3-j)t} & t < 0 \end{cases}$$

24.3.3 Second shift theorem

If $F(\omega)$ is the Fourier transform of $f(t)$ then

$$\mathcal{F}\{f(t-\alpha)\} = e^{-j\alpha\omega} F(\omega)$$

Example 24.7   Given that when $f(t) = \begin{cases} 1 & |t| \leqslant 1 \\ 0 & |t| > 1 \end{cases}$, $F(\omega) = \dfrac{2\sin\omega}{\omega}$, apply the second shift theorem to find the Fourier transform of

$$g(t) = \begin{cases} 1 & 1 \leqslant t \leqslant 3 \\ 0 & \text{otherwise} \end{cases}$$

Verify your result directly.

Figure 24.3
The function
$$g(t) = \begin{cases} 1 & 1 \leqslant t \leqslant 3 \\ 0 & \text{otherwise.} \end{cases}$$

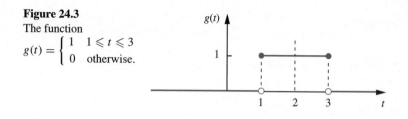

Solution The function $g(t)$ is depicted in Figure 24.3. Clearly $g(t)$ is the function $f(t)$ translated 2 units to the right, that is $g(t) = f(t-2)$. Now $F(\omega) = \dfrac{2\sin\omega}{\omega}$ is the Fourier transform of $f(t)$. Therefore, by the second shift theorem

$$\mathcal{F}\{g(t)\} = \mathcal{F}\{f(t-2)\} = e^{-2j\omega}F(\omega) = \frac{2e^{-2j\omega}\sin\omega}{\omega}$$

To verify this result directly we must evaluate

$$\mathcal{F}\{g(t)\} = \int_{-\infty}^{\infty} g(t)\,e^{-j\omega t}\,dt = \int_{1}^{3} e^{-j\omega t}\,dt = \left[\frac{e^{-j\omega t}}{-j\omega}\right]_{1}^{3}$$

$$= \frac{e^{-3j\omega} - e^{-j\omega}}{-j\omega} = e^{-2j\omega}\left(\frac{e^{-j\omega} - e^{j\omega}}{-j\omega}\right)$$

$$= \frac{2e^{-2j\omega}\sin\omega}{\omega}$$

as required.

Exercises 24.3

1 Prove the first shift theorem.

2 Find the Fourier transform of

$$f(t) = \begin{cases} 1 - t^2 & |t| \leqslant 1 \\ 0 & |t| > 1 \end{cases}$$

Use the first shift theorem to deduce the Fourier transforms of

(a) $g(t) = \begin{cases} e^{3jt}(1 - t^2) & |t| \leqslant 1 \\ 0 & |t| > 1 \end{cases}$

(b) $h(t) = \begin{cases} e^{-t}(1 - t^2) & |t| \leqslant 1 \\ 0 & |t| > 1 \end{cases}$

3 Find the inverse Fourier transforms of

(a) $\dfrac{1}{(\omega + 7)j + 1}$

(b) $\dfrac{2}{1 + 2(\omega - 1)j}$

4 Prove the second shift theorem.

5 Given $\mathcal{F}\{u(t)\,e^{-t}\} = \dfrac{1}{1 + j\omega}$, use the second shift theorem to find

$$\mathcal{F}\{u(t+4)\,e^{-(t+4)}\}$$

Verify your result by direct integration.

6 Find, using the second shift theorem,

$$\mathcal{F}^{-1}\left\{6e^{-4j\omega}\frac{\sin 2\omega}{\omega}\right\}$$

Solutions

2   $\dfrac{4\cos\omega}{-\omega^2} + \dfrac{4\sin\omega}{\omega^3}$

(a) $\dfrac{-4\cos(\omega-3)}{(\omega-3)^2} + \dfrac{4\sin(\omega-3)}{(\omega-3)^3}$

(b) $\dfrac{-4\cos(\omega-\mathrm{j})}{(\omega-\mathrm{j})^2} + \dfrac{4\sin(\omega-\mathrm{j})}{(\omega-\mathrm{j})^3}$

3   (a) $u(t)\,\mathrm{e}^{-t}\,\mathrm{e}^{-7\mathrm{j}t}$ (b) $\mathrm{e}^{\mathrm{j}t}u(t)\,\mathrm{e}^{-t/2}$

5   $\dfrac{\mathrm{e}^{4\mathrm{j}\omega}}{1+\mathrm{j}\omega}$

6   3 for $2 \leqslant t \leqslant 6$, 0 otherwise

24.4   Spectra

In the Fourier analysis of periodic waveforms we stated that although a waveform physi-cally exists in the time (or spatial) domain it can be regarded as comprising components with a variety of temporal (or spatial) frequencies. The amplitude and phase of these components are obtained from the Fourier coefficients a_n and b_n. This is known as a frequency domain description. Plots of amplitude versus frequency and phase versus frequency are together known as the **spectrum** of a waveform. Periodic functions have **discrete** or **line spectra**; that is, the spectra assume non-zero values only at certain frequencies. Only a discrete set of frequencies is required to synthesize a periodic waveform. On the other hand when analysing non-periodic phenomena via Fourier transform techniques we find that, in general, a continuous range of frequencies is required. Instead of discrete spectra we have **continuous spectra**. The modulus of the Fourier transform, $|F(\omega)|$, gives the spectrum amplitude while its argument $\arg(F(\omega))$ describes the spectrum phase.

Example 24.8

In Example 24.2 the Fourier transform of

$$f(t) = \begin{cases} 1 & |t| \leqslant 1 \\ 0 & |t| > 1 \end{cases}$$

was found to be $F(\omega) = \dfrac{2\sin\omega}{\omega}$. Sketch the spectrum of $f(t)$.

Solution $F(\omega)$ is purely real. The spectrum of $f(t)$ is depicted by plotting $|F(\omega)|$ against ω as il-lustrated in Figure 24.4. Note that $\displaystyle\lim_{\omega\to 0}\frac{\sin\omega}{\omega} = 1$. (See Review exercises in Chapter 18.)

Example 24.9   Amplitude modulation

Amplitude modulation is a technique that allows audio signals to be transmitted as electromagnetic radio waves. The maximum frequency of audio signals is typically 10 kHz. If these signals were to be transmitted directly then it would be necessary to use a very large antenna. This can be seen by calculating the wavelength of an electromagnetic wave of frequency 10 kHz using the formula

$$c = f\lambda$$

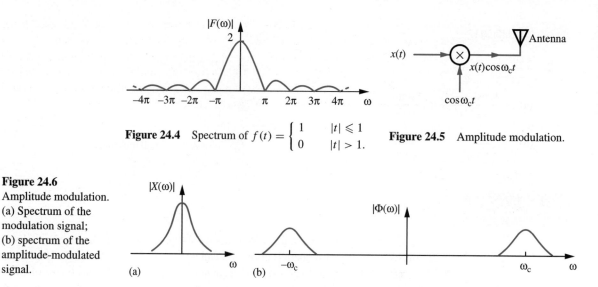

Figure 24.4 Spectrum of $f(t) = \begin{cases} 1 & |t| \leqslant 1 \\ 0 & |t| > 1. \end{cases}$

Figure 24.5 Amplitude modulation.

Figure 24.6
Amplitude modulation.
(a) Spectrum of the
modulation signal;
(b) spectrum of the
amplitude-modulated
signal.

Here c is the velocity of an electromagnetic wave in a vacuum (3×10^8 m s^{-1}), f is the frequency of the wave and λ is its wavelength, and hence $\lambda = \dfrac{c}{f} = 30\,000$ m.

It can be shown that an antenna must have dimensions of at least one-quarter of the wavelength of the signal being transmitted if it is to be reasonably efficient. Clearly a very large antenna would be needed to transmit a 10 kHz signal directly. The solution is to have a **carrier signal** of a much higher frequency than the audio signal which is usually termed the **modulation signal**. This allows the antenna to be a reasonable size as a higher frequency signal has a lower wavelength. The arrangement for mixing the two signals is shown in Figure 24.5.

Let us now derive an expression for the frequency spectrum of an amplitude-modulated signal given by

$$\phi(t) = x(t) \cos \omega_c t$$

where ω_c is the angular frequency of the carrier signal and $x(t)$ is the modulation signal. Now $\phi(t) = x(t) \cos \omega_c t$ can be written as

$$\phi(t) = x(t) \frac{e^{j\omega_c t} + e^{-j\omega_c t}}{2}$$

Taking the Fourier transform and using the first shift theorem yields

$$\mathcal{F}\{\phi(t)\} = \Phi(\omega) = \mathcal{F}\left\{ \frac{x(t)(e^{j\omega_c t} + e^{-j\omega_c t})}{2} \right\}$$

$$= \mathcal{F}\left\{ \frac{e^{j\omega_c t} x(t)}{2} \right\} + \mathcal{F}\left\{ \frac{e^{-j\omega_c t} x(t)}{2} \right\}$$

$$= \tfrac{1}{2}(X(\omega - \omega_c) + X(\omega + \omega_c))$$

where $X(\omega) = \mathcal{F}\{x(t)\}$, the frequency spectrum of the modulation signal.

Let us consider the case where the frequency spectrum, $|X(\omega)|$, has the profile shown in Figure 24.6(a). The frequency spectrum of the amplitude-modulated signal,

$|\Phi(\omega)|$, is shown in Figure 24.6(b). All of the frequencies of the amplitude-modulated signal are much higher than the frequencies of the modulation signal thus allowing a much smaller antenna to be used to transmit the signal. This method of amplitude modulation is known as **suppressed carrier amplitude modulation** because the carrier signal is modulated to its full depth and so the spectrum of the amplitude-modulated signal has no identifiable carrier component.

Exercises 24.4

1 Show that the Fourier transform of the pulse

$$f(t) = \begin{cases} t + 1 & -1 < t < 0 \\ 1 - t & 0 < t < 1 \end{cases}$$

can be written as

$$F(\omega) = \frac{2}{\omega^2}(1 - \cos \omega)$$

Plot a graph of the spectrum of $f(t)$ for $-2\pi \leqslant \omega \leqslant 2\pi$. Write down an integral expression for the pulse which would result if the signal $f(t)$ were passed through a filter which eliminates all angular frequencies greater than 2π.

Solutions

1 $\dfrac{1}{2\pi} \displaystyle\int_{-2\pi}^{2\pi} 2(1 - \cos \omega) \dfrac{e^{j\omega t}}{\omega^2}\, d\omega$

24.5 The *t–ω* duality principle

We have, from the definition of the Fourier integral,

$$f(t) = \frac{1}{2\pi} \int_{-\infty}^{\infty} F(\omega)\, e^{j\omega t}\, d\omega \qquad (24.6)$$

where

$$F(\omega) = \int_{-\infty}^{\infty} f(t)\, e^{-j\omega t}\, dt \qquad (24.7)$$

is the Fourier transform of $f(t)$. In Equation (24.6), ω is a dummy variable so, for example, Equation (24.6) could be equivalently written as

$$f(t) = \frac{1}{2\pi} \int_{-\infty}^{\infty} F(z)\, e^{jzt}\, dz \qquad (24.8)$$

Then, from Equation (24.8), replacing t by $-\omega$ we find

$$f(-\omega) = \frac{1}{2\pi} \int_{-\infty}^{\infty} F(z)\, e^{-j\omega z}\, dz = \frac{1}{2\pi} \int_{-\infty}^{\infty} F(t)\, e^{-j\omega t}\, dt$$

which we recognize as $\dfrac{1}{2\pi}$ times the Fourier transform of $F(t)$.

We have the following result:

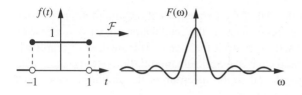

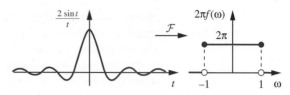

Figure 24.7   Illustrating the t–ω duality principle.   **Figure 24.8**   Illustrating the t–ω duality principle.

If $F(\omega)$ is the Fourier transform of $f(t)$ then

$$f(-\omega) \text{ is } \frac{1}{2\pi} \times \text{(the Fourier transform of } F(t)\text{)}.$$

which is known as the t–ω duality principle.
We have seen in Example 24.2 that if

$$f(t) = \begin{cases} 1 & |t| \leqslant 1 \\ 0 & |t| > 1 \end{cases}$$

then $F(\omega) = \dfrac{2\sin\omega}{\omega}$. This is depicted in Figure 24.7. From the duality principle we can immediately deduce that

$$\mathcal{F}\left\{\frac{2\sin t}{t}\right\} = 2\pi f(-\omega) = 2\pi f(\omega)$$

since f is an even function (Figure 24.8). Unfortunately it is very difficult to verify this result in most cases because while one of the integrals is relatively straightforward to evaluate, the other is usually very difficult. However, we can use the result to derive a number of new Fourier transforms.

Example 24.10   Given that the Fourier transform of $u(t)\,\mathrm{e}^{-t}$ is $\dfrac{1}{1+\mathrm{j}\omega}$ use the duality principle to deduce the transform of $\dfrac{1}{1+\mathrm{j}t}$.

Solution   We know $F(\omega) = \dfrac{1}{1+\mathrm{j}\omega}$ is the Fourier transform of $f(t) = u(t)\,\mathrm{e}^{-t}$. Therefore $2\pi\,(u(-\omega)\,\mathrm{e}^{\omega})$ is the Fourier transform of $\dfrac{1}{1+\mathrm{j}t}$.

24.6   Fourier transforms of some special functions

We saw in Section 24.4 that the Fourier transform tells us the frequency content of a signal. If we were to find the Fourier transform of a signal composed of only one frequency

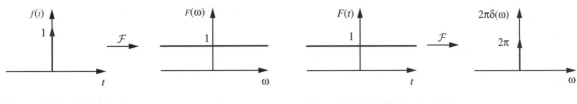

Figure 24.9 $\mathcal{F}\{\delta(t)\} = 1.$ **Figure 24.10** $\mathcal{F}\{1\} = 2\pi\,\delta(\omega).$

component, for example $f(t) = \sin t$, we would hope that the exercise of finding the Fourier transform would result in a spectrum containing that single frequency.

Unfortunately if we try to find the Fourier transform of, say, $f(t) = \sin t$ problems arise since the integral

$$\int_{-\infty}^{\infty} \sin t\, e^{-j\omega t}\, dt$$

cannot be evaluated in the usual sense because $\sin t$ oscillates indefinitely as $|t| \to \infty$. In particular, Condition (2) of Section 24.2 fails since $\int_{-\infty}^{\infty} |\sin t|\, dt$ diverges. There are many other functions which give rise to similar difficulties, for instance the unit step function, polynomials and so on. All these functions fail to have a Fourier transform in its usual sense. However, by making use of the delta function it is possible to make progress even with functions like these.

24.6.1   The Fourier transform of $\delta(t - a)$

Example 24.11   Use the properties of the delta function to deduce its Fourier transform.

Solution   By definition

$$\mathcal{F}\{\delta(t - a)\} = \int_{-\infty}^{\infty} \delta(t - a)\, e^{-j\omega t}\, dt$$

Next, recall the following property of the delta function:

$$\int_{-\infty}^{\infty} f(t)\delta(t - a)\, dt = f(a) \tag{24.9}$$

for any reasonably well-behaved function $f(t)$. Using Equation (24.9) with $f(t) = e^{-j\omega t}$ we have

$$\mathcal{F}\{\delta(t - a)\} = \int_{-\infty}^{\infty} e^{-j\omega t}\,\delta(t - a)\, dt = e^{-j\omega a}$$

In particular, if $a = 0$ we have $\mathcal{F}\{\delta(t)\} = 1$. This result is depicted in Figure 24.9.

Example 24.12   Apply the t–ω duality principle to the previous result. Interpret the result physically.

Solution   We have $f(t) = \delta(t)$ and $F(\omega) = 1$. The duality principle tells us that

$$f(-\omega) = \delta(-\omega) \qquad \text{which equals } \frac{1}{2\pi} \mathcal{F}\{1\}$$

that is,

$$\mathcal{F}\{1\} = 2\pi \delta(\omega)$$

(since $\delta(-\omega) = \delta(\omega)$). This is illustrated in Figure 24.10. Physically $F(t) = 1$ can be regarded as a d.c. waveform. This result confirms that a d.c. signal has only one frequency component, namely zero.

Example 24.13   Given that $\mathcal{F}\{\delta(t-a)\} = e^{-j\omega a}$ find $\mathcal{F}\{e^{-jta}\}$.

Solution   We have $f(t) = \delta(t-a)$, $F(\omega) = e^{-j\omega a}$. Applying the t–ω duality principle we find

$$f(-\omega) = \delta(-\omega - a) = \frac{1}{2\pi} \mathcal{F}\{e^{-jta}\}$$

Therefore

$$\begin{aligned}
\mathcal{F}\{e^{-jta}\} &= 2\pi \delta(-\omega - a) \\
&= 2\pi \delta(-(\omega + a)) \\
&= 2\pi \delta(\omega + a)
\end{aligned}$$

since $\delta(\omega)$ is an even function.

24.6.2   Fourier transforms of some periodic functions

From Example 24.13 we have $\mathcal{F}\{e^{-jta}\} = 2\pi \delta(\omega + a)$ and also, replacing a by $-a$, $\mathcal{F}\{e^{jta}\} = 2\pi \delta(\omega - a)$. Adding these two expressions we find

$$\mathcal{F}\{e^{-jta}\} + \mathcal{F}\{e^{jta}\} = 2\pi (\delta(\omega + a) + \delta(\omega - a))$$

Recalling the linearity properties of $\mathcal{F}$ we can write

$$\mathcal{F}\{e^{-jta} + e^{jta}\} = 2\pi (\delta(\omega + a) + \delta(\omega - a))$$

and using Euler's relations we find

$$\mathcal{F}\{\cos at\} = \pi (\delta(\omega + a) + \delta(\omega - a))$$

We see that the spectrum of $\cos at$ consists of single lines at $\omega = \pm a$ corresponding to a single frequency component (Figure 24.11).

Example 24.14   Find $\mathcal{F}\{\sin at\}$.

Figure 24.11
The spectrum of
$\cos at$.

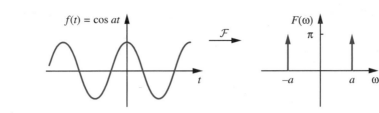

Solution Subtracting the previous expressions for $\mathcal{F}\{e^{jta}\}$ and $\mathcal{F}\{e^{-jta}\}$ and using Euler's relations we find

$$\mathcal{F}\{e^{jta}\} - \mathcal{F}\{e^{-jta}\} = 2\pi(\delta(\omega - a) - \delta(\omega + a))$$

that is,

$$\mathcal{F}\left\{\frac{e^{jta} - e^{-jta}}{2j}\right\} = \frac{\pi}{j}(\delta(\omega - a) - \delta(\omega + a))$$

so that

$$\mathcal{F}\{\sin at\} = \frac{\pi}{j}(\delta(\omega - a) - \delta(\omega + a))$$

24.7   The relationship between the Fourier transform and the Laplace transform

We have already noted (Section 24.2) the similarity between the Laplace transform and the Fourier transform. Let us now look at this a little more closely. We have

$$\mathcal{F}\{f(t)\} = \int_{-\infty}^{\infty} f(t)\, e^{-j\omega t}\, dt \qquad \text{and} \qquad \mathcal{L}\{f(t)\} = \int_{0}^{\infty} f(t)\, e^{-st}\, dt$$

In the definition of the Laplace transform, the parameter s is complex and we may write $s = \sigma + j\omega$, so that

$$\mathcal{L}\{f(t)\} = \int_{0}^{\infty} f(t)\, e^{-\sigma t}\, e^{-j\omega t}\, dt$$

Thus an additional factor, $e^{-\sigma t}$, appears in the integrand of the Laplace transform. For $\sigma > 0$ this represents an exponentially decaying factor, the presence of which means that the integral exists for a wider variety of functions than the corresponding Fourier integral.

Example 24.15 Find, if possible,

(a) the Laplace transform

(b) the Fourier transform

of $f(t) = u(t) e^{3t}$. Comment upon the result.

Solution (a) Either by integration, or from Table 21.1, we find

$$\mathcal{L}\{u(t) e^{3t}\} = \frac{1}{s-3} \qquad \text{provided } s > 3$$

(b) $\mathcal{F}\{u(t) e^{3t}\} = \displaystyle\int_0^\infty e^{3t} e^{-j\omega t}\, dt = \int_0^\infty e^{(3-j\omega)t}\, dt = \left[\frac{e^{(3-j\omega)t}}{3-j\omega}\right]_0^\infty .$

Now, as $t \to \infty$, $e^{3t} \to \infty$, so that the integral fails to exist. Clearly, $u(t) e^{3t}$ has a Laplace transform but no Fourier transform.

Suppose $f(t)$ is defined to be 0 for $t < 0$. Then its Fourier transform becomes

$$\mathcal{F}\{f(t)\} = \int_0^\infty f(t) e^{-j\omega t}\, dt$$

and its Laplace transform is

$$\mathcal{L}\{f(t)\} = \int_0^\infty f(t) e^{-st}\, dt$$

By replacing s by $j\omega$ in the Laplace transform we obtain the Fourier transform of $f(t)$ if it exists. Care must be taken here since we have seen that the Fourier transform may not exist for a function that nevertheless has a Laplace transform.

Example 24.16 Find the Laplace transforms of

(a) $u(t) e^{-2t}$

(b) $u(t) e^{2t}$

Let $s = j\omega$ and comment upon the result.

Solution (a) $\mathcal{L}\{u(t) e^{-2t}\} = \dfrac{1}{s+2}.$

(b) $\mathcal{L}\{u(t) e^{2t}\} = \dfrac{1}{s-2}.$

Replacing s by $j\omega$ in (a) gives $\dfrac{1}{j\omega+2}$. Similarly, replacing s by $j\omega$ in (b) gives $\dfrac{1}{j\omega-2}$. Now

$$\mathcal{F}\{u(t) e^{-2t}\} = \frac{1}{j\omega+2}$$

so that replacing s by $j\omega$ in the Laplace transform results in the Fourier transform. However, $\mathcal{F}\{u(t) e^{2t}\}$ does not exist and even though we can let $s = j\omega$ in the Laplace transform and obtain $\dfrac{1}{j\omega-2}$, we cannot interpret this as a Fourier transform.

The Fourier transform does possess certain advantages over the Laplace transform. While the Laplace transform can only be applied to functions which are zero for $t < 0$, the Fourier transform is applicable to functions with domain $-\infty < t < \infty$. In some applications where, for example, t represents not time but a spatial variable, it is often necessary to work with negative values.

The inverse Fourier transform is given by

$$\mathcal{F}^{-1}\{F(\omega)\} = \frac{1}{2\pi} \int_{-\infty}^{\infty} F(\omega)\, e^{j\omega t}\, d\omega \tag{24.10}$$

The corresponding inverse Laplace transform requires advanced techniques in the theory of complex variables which are beyond the scope of this book. The existence of Equation (24.10) is not quite as advantageous as it may seem because it is often difficult to perform the required integration analytically.

24.8   Convolution and correlation

Convolution is an important technique in signal and image processing. It provides a means of calculating the response or output of a system to an arbitrary input signal if the impulse response is known. The impulse response is the response of the system to an impulse function. Convolving the input signal and the impulse response results in the response to the arbitrary input. Correlation is a second important technique. It can be used to determine the time delay between a transmitted signal and a received signal as might occur in radar or sonar detection equipment.

24.8.1   Convolution and the convolution theorem

If $f(t)$ and $g(t)$ are two real piecewise continuous functions, their **convolution**, which we denote by $f * g$, is defined as follows:

> The convolution of $f(t)$ and $g(t)$:
>
> $$f * g = \int_{-\infty}^{\infty} f(\lambda) g(t - \lambda)\, d\lambda$$

$f * g$ is itself a function of t, and to show this explicitly we sometimes write $(f * g)(t)$. Note that convolution is an integral with respect to the dummy variable λ. In general, as can be seen from the limits of integration, λ varies from $-\infty$ to ∞, but in particular cases we will see that this interval of integration can be reduced. In the examples which follow the precise meaning of the terms $f(\lambda)$ and $g(t - \lambda)$ will become apparent.

Because convolution is commutative, that is $f * g = g * f$, the convolution can be defined equivalently as

$$\int_{-\infty}^{\infty} f(t - \lambda) g(\lambda)\, d\lambda$$

In cases when $f(t)$ and $g(t)$ are zero for $t < 0$ this expression reduces to that defined for the Laplace transform in Section 21.9.

The **convolution theorem** states that convolution in the time domain corresponds to multiplication in the frequency domain:

The convolution theorem:
If $\mathcal{F}\{f(t)\} = F(\omega)$ and $\mathcal{F}\{g(t)\} = G(\omega)$ then

$$\mathcal{F}\{f * g\} = F(\omega)G(\omega)$$

This theorem gives us a technique for calculating the convolution of two functions using the Fourier transform, since

$$f * g = \mathcal{F}^{-1}\{F(\omega)G(\omega)\}$$

So, it is possible to find the convolution of $f(t)$ and $g(t)$, by

(1) finding the corresponding Fourier transforms, $F(\omega)$ and $G(\omega)$,

(2) multiplying these together to form $F(\omega)G(\omega)$,

(3) finding the inverse Fourier transform which then yields $f * g$.

This is a process often used for finding convolutions using a computer as will be explained in Section 24.14.

A graphical representation of convolution is useful as it can throw light on the underlying process and help us to determine appropriate limits of integration. We will illustrate this in the following example.

Example 24.17 (a) Using the definition of convolution, calculate the convolution $f * g$ when

$$f(t) = u(t)\,e^{-t} \text{ and } g(t) = u(t)\,e^{-2t}, \text{ where } u(t) \text{ is the unit step function.}$$

(b) Verify the convolution theorem for these functions.

Solution (a) The convolution of f and g is given by

$$f * g = \int_{-\infty}^{\infty} f(\lambda)g(t - \lambda)\,d\lambda$$

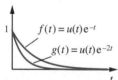

Figure 24.12 Graphs of $f(t) = u(t)\,e^{-t}$ and $g(t) = u(t)\,e^{-2t}$.

Graphs of $f(t)$ and $g(t)$ are shown in Figure 24.12.

Evaluating a convolution integral can be difficult, so we will develop the solution in stages. First of all it is necessary to be clear about the meaning of the different terms in the integrand. Note that if $f(t) = u(t)\,e^{-t}$ then $f(\lambda) = u(\lambda)\,e^{-\lambda}$. Similarly $g(\lambda) = u(\lambda)\,e^{-2\lambda}$. The function $g(-\lambda)$ is found by reflecting $g(\lambda)$ in the vertical axis as shown in Figure 24.13(a). In signal processing terminology this is also known as **folding**. The folded graph can be translated a distance t to the left or to the right by changing the argument of g to $g(t - \lambda)$. If t is negative the graph moves to the left as shown in Figure 24.13(b) whereas if t is positive it moves to the right as shown in Figure 24.13(c). In Figure 24.13 we have superimposed the graphs of $f(\lambda)$, shown dashed, and $g(t - \lambda)$, for t being negative, zero and positive. Where the graphs do not overlap, the product $f(\lambda)g(t - \lambda)$, and hence the convolution, must be zero. We examine separately the domains $t < 0$ and $t \geqslant 0$ corresponding to where the graphs do not overlap and where they do overlap respectively.

When $t < 0$

When $t < 0$ there is clearly no overlap and it follows that $f * g = 0$.

Figure 24.13
The function $g(t - \lambda)$
for various values of t.

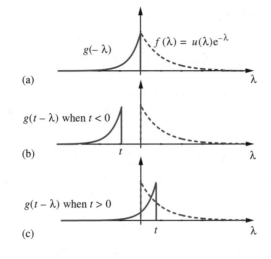

(a)

(b)

(c)

When $t \geqslant 0$

When $t \geqslant 0$ there is overlap for values of λ between 0 and t, that is when $0 \leqslant \lambda \leqslant t$, and hence

$$f * g = \int_0^t e^{-\lambda} e^{-2(t-\lambda)} \, d\lambda$$

$$= \int_0^t e^{-\lambda} e^{-2t} e^{2\lambda} \, d\lambda$$

$$= e^{-2t} \int_0^t e^{\lambda} d\lambda$$

$$= e^{-2t} [e^{\lambda}]_0^t$$

$$= e^{-2t} (e^t - 1)$$

$$= e^{-t} - e^{-2t}$$

Finally the complete expression for the convolution is

$$(f * g)(t) = \begin{cases} e^{-t} - e^{-2t} & \text{when } t \geqslant 0 \\ 0 & \text{when } t < 0 \end{cases}$$

This may also be written as

$$(f * g)(t) = u(t)(e^{-t} - e^{-2t})$$

(b) Using Table 24.1 the Fourier transforms of f and g are

$$F(\omega) = \frac{1}{1 + j\omega} \qquad G(\omega) = \frac{1}{2 + j\omega}$$

and their product is

$$F(\omega)G(\omega) = \frac{1}{(1+j\omega)(2+j\omega)} \tag{24.11}$$

The Fourier transform of the convolution is, using linearity and Table 24.1,

$$\mathcal{F}\{u(t)(e^{-t} - e^{-2t})\} = \frac{1}{1+j\omega} - \frac{1}{2+j\omega}$$

$$= \frac{(2+j\omega) - (1+j\omega)}{(1+j\omega)(2+j\omega)}$$

$$= \frac{1}{(1+j\omega)(2+j\omega)}$$

which is the same as Equation (24.11). We have shown that $\mathcal{F}\{f * g\} = F(\omega)G(\omega)$ and so the convolution theorem has been verified.

Example 24.18   (a) Using the definition of convolution find the convolution, $f * g$, of the 'top-hat' function

$$f(t) = \begin{cases} 1 & -1 \leqslant t \leqslant 1 \\ 0 & \text{otherwise} \end{cases}$$

and the function $g(t) = u(t) e^{-t}$, where $u(t)$ is the unit step function.

(b) Verify the convolution theorem for these functions.

Solution   (a) The functions $f(t)$ and $g(t)$ are shown in Figure 24.14.
The convolution of $f(t)$ and $g(t)$ is given by

$$f * g = \int_{-\infty}^{\infty} f(\lambda)g(t - \lambda) \, d\lambda$$

Note that since $g(t) = u(t) e^{-t}$, it follows that $g(\lambda) = u(\lambda) e^{-\lambda}$ as shown in Figure 24.15(a). The function $g(-\lambda)$ is found by reflecting, or folding, $g(\lambda)$ in the vertical axis. This folding is shown in Figure 24.15(b). The folded graph can be translated a distance t to the left or to the right by changing the argument of g to $g(t - \lambda)$. If t is negative the graph in Figure 24.15(b) moves to the left, whereas if t is positive it moves to the right. Study Figures 24.15(c–g) to observe this.

Figure 24.14
The 'top-hat' function
$f(t)$, and
$g(t) = u(t) e^{-t}$.

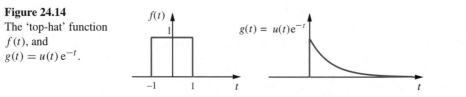

Figure 24.15
The function $g(t - \lambda)$
for various values of t.

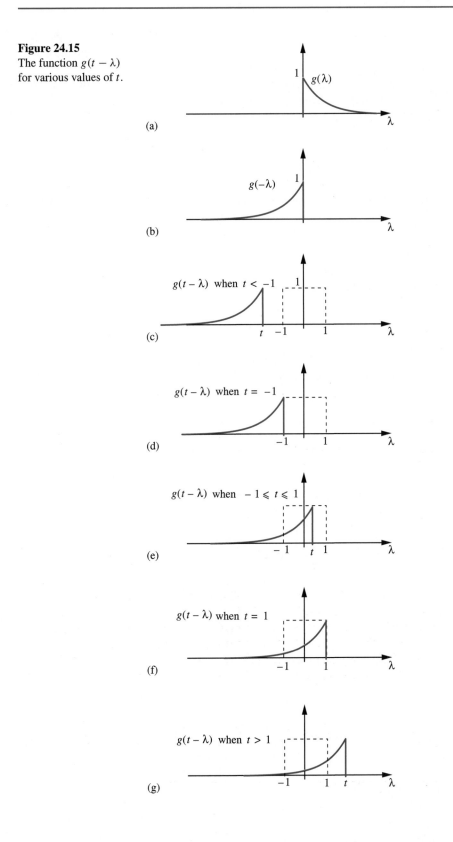

Convolution is the integral of the product of $f(\lambda)$ and $g(t - \lambda)$. We have superimposed $f(\lambda)$ on the graphs in Figure 24.15. For values of λ where the graphs do not overlap, this product must be zero.

Inspection of the graphs shows that when t is less than -1 (Figure 24.15(c)) there is no overlap and hence $f(\lambda)g(t - \lambda) = 0$. So:

if $t < -1$

$$f * g = 0$$

When t is greater than -1 but less than 1, as in Figure 24.15(e), there is an overlap, and hence a non-zero product. This occurs for values of λ between -1 and t, that is in the interval $-1 \leqslant \lambda \leqslant t$. Within this interval $f(\lambda) = 1$ and $g(t - \lambda) = e^{-(t-\lambda)}$. So:

if $-1 \leqslant t < 1$

$$f * g = \int_{-1}^{t} e^{-(t-\lambda)} \, d\lambda = e^{-t} \int_{-1}^{t} e^{\lambda} \, d\lambda = e^{-t}[e^{\lambda}]_{-1}^{t} = e^{-t}[e^{t} - e^{-1}] = 1 - e^{-1-t}$$

When t is greater than 1 the graphs overlap, but only for values of λ between -1 and 1, that is for $-1 \leqslant \lambda < 1$. So:

if $t > 1$

$$f * g = \int_{-1}^{1} e^{-(t-\lambda)} \, d\lambda = e^{-t}[e^{\lambda}]_{-1}^{1} = e^{-t}(e^{1} - e^{-1})$$

Putting all these results together

$$(f * g)(t) = \begin{cases} 0 & t < -1 \\ 1 - e^{-1-t} & -1 \leqslant t < 1 \\ e^{-t}(e^{1} - e^{-1}) & t \geqslant 1 \end{cases}$$

(b) Using Table 24.1 the Fourier transforms of f and g are

$$F(\omega) = \frac{2 \sin \omega}{\omega} \qquad G(\omega) = \frac{1}{1 + j\omega}$$

and their product is

$$F(\omega)G(\omega) = \frac{2 \sin \omega}{\omega(1 + j\omega)} \tag{24.12}$$

Since the convolution is defined differently on each part of the domain, then the Fourier transform of the convolution must be found by integrating over each part of the domain separately. You will also need to recall that

$$\sin \omega = \frac{e^{j\omega} - e^{-j\omega}}{2j}$$

So,

$$\mathcal{F}\{(f*g)(t)\} = \int_{-\infty}^{\infty} (f*g)(t)\,e^{-j\omega t}\,dt$$

$$= \int_{-\infty}^{-1} 0\cdot e^{-j\omega t}\,dt + \int_{-1}^{1} (1-e^{-1-t})\,e^{-j\omega t}\,dt$$

$$+ \int_{1}^{\infty} e^{-t}(e^{1}-e^{-1})\,e^{-j\omega t}\,dt$$

$$= \int_{-1}^{1} e^{-j\omega t} - e^{-1-t-j\omega t}\,dt + (e^{1}-e^{-1})\int_{1}^{\infty} e^{-t}\,e^{-j\omega t}\,dt$$

$$= \int_{-1}^{1} e^{-j\omega t} - e^{-1}\,e^{-t(1+j\omega)}\,dt + (e^{1}-e^{-1})\int_{1}^{\infty} e^{-t(1+j\omega)}\,dt$$

$$= \left[\frac{e^{-j\omega t}}{-j\omega}\right]_{-1}^{1} - e^{-1}\left[\frac{e^{-t(1+j\omega)}}{-(1+j\omega)}\right]_{-1}^{1} + (e^{1}-e^{-1})\left[\frac{e^{-t(1+j\omega)}}{-(1+j\omega)}\right]_{1}^{\infty}$$

$$= \frac{e^{-j\omega}}{-j\omega} + \frac{e^{j\omega}}{j\omega} - e^{-1}\left(\frac{e^{-(1+j\omega)}}{-(1+j\omega)}\right)$$

$$+ e^{-1}\left(\frac{e^{(1+j\omega)}}{-(1+j\omega)}\right) + (e^{1}-e^{-1})\left(\frac{e^{-(1+j\omega)}}{1+j\omega}\right)$$

The first two terms simplify to $\dfrac{2\sin\omega}{\omega}$. By simplifying and rearranging the remainder becomes $-\dfrac{e^{j\omega}-e^{-j\omega}}{1+j\omega}$. Putting all this together we find

$$\mathcal{F}\{(f*g)(t)\} = \frac{2\sin\omega}{\omega} - \frac{e^{j\omega}-e^{-j\omega}}{1+j\omega}$$

$$= \frac{2\sin\omega}{\omega} - \frac{2j\sin\omega}{1+j\omega}$$

$$= \frac{2\sin\omega}{\omega(1+j\omega)}$$

which is the same as Equation (24.12). We have shown that $\mathcal{F}\{f*g\} = F(\omega)G(\omega)$ and so the convolution theorem has been verified.

24.8.2 Correlation and the correlation theorem

If $f(t)$ and $g(t)$ are two piecewise continuous functions their **correlation** (also called their **cross-correlation**), which we denote by $f\star g$, is defined as follows:

The correlation of $f(t)$ and $g(t)$:

$$f\star g = \int_{-\infty}^{\infty} f(\lambda)g(\lambda-t)\,d\lambda$$

This formula is the same as that for convolution except for the important difference that the function g is not folded; that is, we have $g(\lambda - t)$ here rather than $g(t - \lambda)$.

It is possible to show that the correlation of $f(t)$ and $g(t)$ can be written in the alternative form

$$f \star g = \int_{-\infty}^{\infty} f(t + \lambda)g(\lambda)\,d\lambda$$

Some texts use this form, but note that it is the argument of f which is $t + \lambda$ (see Question 8 in Exercises 24.8).

We can now state the **correlation theorem**.

The correlation theorem:
If $\mathcal{F}\{f(t)\} = F(\omega)$ and $\mathcal{F}\{g(t)\} = G(\omega)$ then

$$\mathcal{F}\{f \star g\} = F(\omega)G(-\omega)$$

Example 24.19

(a) Using the definition of correlation, calculate the correlation of $f(t) = u(t)\,e^{-t}$ and $g(t) = u(t)\,e^{-2t}$, where $u(t)$ is the unit step function.

(b) Verify the correlation theorem for these functions.

Solution

(a) The correlation of f and g is given by

$$f \star g = \int_{-\infty}^{\infty} f(\lambda)g(\lambda - t)\,d\lambda$$

Graphs of $f(t)$ and $g(t)$ are shown in Figure 24.16.

In Figure 24.17 we have superimposed the graphs of $f(\lambda)$, shown dashed, and $g(\lambda - t)$, for t being negative, and then positive. Where the graphs do not overlap, the product $f(\lambda)g(\lambda - t)$, and hence the correlation, is zero.

Figure 24.16 Graphs of $f(t) = u(t)\,e^{-t}$ and $g(t) = u(t)\,e^{-2t}$.

When $t < 0$

When $t < 0$ the graphs overlap for $0 \leqslant \lambda < \infty$. Hence

$$f \star g = \int_0^{\infty} f(\lambda)g(\lambda - t)\,d\lambda$$

$$= \int_0^{\infty} e^{-\lambda}\,e^{-2(\lambda - t)}\,d\lambda$$

$$= e^{2t}\int_0^{\infty} e^{-3\lambda}\,d\lambda$$

$$= e^{2t}\left[\frac{e^{-3\lambda}}{-3}\right]_0^{\infty}$$

$$= \frac{1}{3}\,e^{2t}$$

Figure 24.17
Graphs of $f(\lambda)$, and
$g(\lambda - t)$ for (b) $t < 0$,
(c) $t > 0$.

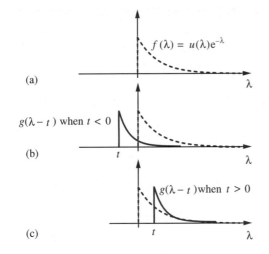

(a)

$g(\lambda - t)$ when $t < 0$

(b)

$g(\lambda - t)$ when $t > 0$

(c)

When $t \geqslant 0$

When $t \geqslant 0$ the graphs overlap for $t \leqslant \lambda < \infty$. Hence

$$f \star g = \int_t^\infty f(\lambda)g(\lambda - t)\, d\lambda$$

$$= \int_t^\infty e^{-\lambda}\, e^{-2(\lambda - t)}\, d\lambda$$

$$= e^{2t} \int_t^\infty e^{-3\lambda}\, d\lambda$$

$$= e^{2t} \left[\frac{e^{-3\lambda}}{-3} \right]_t^\infty$$

$$= e^{2t} \frac{e^{-3t}}{3}$$

$$= \frac{1}{3} e^{-t}$$

Finally the complete expression for the correlation is

$$(f \star g)(t) = \begin{cases} \frac{1}{3} e^{2t} & \text{when } t < 0 \\ \frac{1}{3} e^{-t} & \text{when } t \geqslant 0 \end{cases}$$

(b) Using Table 24.1 the Fourier transforms of f and g are

$$F(\omega) = \frac{1}{1 + j\omega} \qquad G(\omega) = \frac{1}{2 + j\omega}$$

and hence

$$F(\omega)G(-\omega) = \frac{1}{(1 + j\omega)(2 - j\omega)}$$

Furthermore, taking the Fourier transform of $f \star g$, obtained in part (a), we have

$$\mathcal{F}\{f \star g\} = \int_{-\infty}^{0} \tfrac{1}{3} e^{2t} e^{-j\omega t} \, dt + \int_{0}^{\infty} \tfrac{1}{3} e^{-t} e^{-j\omega t} \, dt$$

$$= \left[\frac{e^{t(2-j\omega)}}{3(2-j\omega)} \right]_{-\infty}^{0} + \left[\frac{e^{t(-1-j\omega)}}{3(-1-j\omega)} \right]_{0}^{\infty}$$

$$= \frac{1}{3(2-j\omega)} + \frac{1}{3(1+j\omega)}$$

$$= \frac{3 + 3j\omega + 6 - 3j\omega}{9(2-j\omega)(1+j\omega)}$$

$$= \frac{1}{(2-j\omega)(1+j\omega)}$$

We have shown that $\mathcal{F}\{f \star g\} = F(\omega)G(-\omega)$ and so the correlation theorem has been verified.

Exercises 24.8

1 Find the convolution of

$$f(t) = \begin{cases} \tfrac{2}{3}t & 0 \leqslant t \leqslant 3 \\ 0 & \text{otherwise} \end{cases}$$

and

$$g(t) = \begin{cases} 4 & -1 \leqslant t \leqslant 3 \\ 0 & \text{otherwise} \end{cases}$$

2 The convolution of a function with itself is known as **autoconvolution**. Find the autoconvolution $f * f$ when

$$f(t) = \begin{cases} 1 & -1 \leqslant t \leqslant 1 \\ 0 & \text{otherwise} \end{cases}$$

3 Find the correlation of $f(t) = 1$ for $-1 \leqslant t \leqslant 1$ and zero otherwise, and $g(t) = u(t) e^{-t}$. Verify the correlation theorem for these functions.

4 Prove that convolution is commutative, that is $f * g = g * f$. Note that correlation is not.

5 Show that if $f(t)$ and $g(t)$ are both zero, for $t < 0$ then $(f * g)(t) = \int_{0}^{t} f(\lambda)g(t - \lambda) \, d\lambda$.

6 Prove the convolution theorem.

7 Show that $f(t) \star g(t) = f(t) * g(-t)$. Deduce that a correlation can be expressed in terms of a convolution. Show also that $f(t) * g(t) = f(t) \star g(-t)$.

8 Prove that the correlation integral $f \star g = \int_{-\infty}^{\infty} f(\lambda)g(\lambda - t) \, d\lambda$ can also be written in the form $\int_{-\infty}^{\infty} g(\lambda)f(t + \lambda) \, d\lambda$.

9 Prove the correlation theorem.

Solutions

1 $f * g = \begin{cases} 0 & t \leqslant -1 \\ \tfrac{4}{3}(t+1)^2 & -1 < t \leqslant 2 \\ 12 & 2 < t \leqslant 3 \\ 12 - \tfrac{4}{3}(t-3)^2 & 3 < t \leqslant 6 \\ 0 & t > 6 \end{cases}$

2 $f * f = \begin{cases} t+2 & -2 \leqslant t \leqslant 0 \\ 2-t & 0 < t \leqslant 2 \\ 0 & \text{otherwise} \end{cases}$

3 $f \star g = \begin{cases} e^{t}(e^{1} - e^{-1}) & t < -1 \\ 1 - e^{t-1} & -1 \leqslant t \leqslant 1 \\ 0 & t > 1 \end{cases}$

24.9 The discrete Fourier transform

For most practical engineering problems requiring the evaluation of a Fourier transform it is necessary to use a computer and so some form of approximation is needed. In this section we show how a function $f(t)$, with Fourier transform $F(\omega)$, can be sampled at intervals of T to give a sequence of values $f(0), f(T), f(2T)\ldots$. The **discrete Fourier transform** (d.f.t.) takes such a sequence and processes it to produce a new sequence which can be thought of as a sampled version of $F(\omega)$. The d.f.t. is important as it is the basis of most signal and image processing methods. The use of a computer is essential because of the enormous number of calculations required.

We start by stating the transform and provide a simple example to show how it is calculated. The interested reader should refer to Section 24.10 for a derivation which shows the relationship between the Fourier transform and the d.f.t.

24.9.1 Definition of the d.f.t.

We consider a sequence of N terms, $f[0], f[1], f[2], \ldots, f[N-1]$.

> The d.f.t. of a sequence $f[n]$, $n = 0, 1, 2, \ldots, N-1$, is another sequence $F[k]$, also having N terms, defined by
>
> $$F[k] = \sum_{n=0}^{N-1} f[n]\, e^{-2jnk\pi/N} \qquad \text{for } k = 0, 1, 2, \ldots, N-1.$$

We write $F[k] = \mathcal{D}\{f[n]\}$ to denote the d.f.t. of the sequence $f[n]$.

There are a number of variations of this definition and you need to be aware that different authors may use slightly different formulae. This can cause confusion when the d.f.t. is first met. In particular, some authors include a factor $\dfrac{1}{N}$ in the definition, and others use a positive exponential term instead of the negative one given above. What is crucial is that you know which formula is being used and you apply it consistently.

We now give an example to show the application of the formula.

Example 24.20 Find the d.f.t. of the sequence $f[n] = 1, 2, -5, 3$.

Solution We use the formula

$$\mathcal{D}\{f[n]\} = F[k] = \sum_{n=0}^{N-1} f[n]\, e^{-2jnk\pi/N} \qquad \text{for } k = 0, 1, 2, \ldots, N-1$$

Here the number of terms, N, is four.

$$F[k] = \sum_{n=0}^{3} f[n]\, e^{-2jnk\pi/4} \qquad \text{for } k = 0, 1, 2, 3$$

So, when $k = 0$,

$$F[0] = \sum_{n=0}^{3} f[n] e^{0}$$
$$= 1 + 2 + (-5) + 3$$
$$= 1$$

When $k = 1$,

$$F[1] = \sum_{n=0}^{3} f[n] e^{-2jn\pi/4}$$
$$= 1 + 2e^{-2j\pi/4} + (-5) e^{-2j2\pi/4} + 3e^{-2j3\pi/4}$$
$$= 1 + 2e^{-\pi j/2} - 5e^{-\pi j} + 3e^{-3j\pi/2}$$
$$= 1 + 2(-j) - 5(-1) + 3j$$
$$= 6 + j$$

When $k = 2$,

$$F[2] = \sum_{n=0}^{3} f[n] e^{-2jn2\pi/4}$$
$$= \sum_{n=0}^{3} f[n] e^{-\pi jn}$$
$$= 1 + 2e^{-j\pi} + (-5) e^{-2j\pi} + 3e^{-3j\pi}$$
$$= 1 + 2(-1) - 5(1) + 3(-1)$$
$$= -9$$

Finally, when $k = 3$,

$$F[3] = \sum_{n=0}^{3} f[n] e^{-2jn3\pi/4}$$
$$= \sum_{n=0}^{3} f[n] e^{-3jn\pi/2}$$
$$= 1 + 2e^{-3j\pi/2} + (-5) e^{-3j\pi} + 3e^{-9j\pi/2}$$
$$= 1 + 2(j) - 5(-1) + 3(-j)$$
$$= 6 - j$$

So, the d.f.t. of the sequence $1, 2, -5, 3$ is the sequence $1, 6 + j, -9, 6 - j$.

You will note from this simple example that a significant amount of calculation is necessary even when there are just four points in the sampled sequence. This is why it is necessary to use a computer program to find the transform. Even then, the computation can be very time consuming. For this reason, much effort has gone into developing fast algorithms known as **fast Fourier transforms** (f.f.t.). For details of these algorithms you should refer to one of the many specialist texts on the subject. You should also investigate which packages are available to enable you to perform this sort of calculation. For example, the computer package MATLAB has built-in commands for finding a d.f.t. using an f.f.t. For example, the MATLAB command `fft(f)` calculates the d.f.t. of a sequence f as shown below:

```
>f=[1 2 -5 3];
>y=fft(f)

y =

    1.0000    6.0000+ 1.0000i   -9.0000    6.0000- 1.0000i
```

In MATLAB the symbol for $\sqrt{-1}$ is i rather than j. Other than this change of notation this is the result obtained in the previous example.

Exercises 24.9.1

1. Use the definition to find the d.f.t. of the sequences $f[n] = 1, 2, 0, -1$ and $g[n] = 3, 1, -1, 1$.

2. Calculate the d.f.t. of the sequence $f[n] = 5, -1, 2$.

3. Investigate whether you have access to a computer package which will calculate a d.f.t. Use the package to verify your answers to Questions 1 and 2.

4. From the definition of the d.f.t. show that if $f[n]$ is a sequence of real numbers with d.f.t. $F[k]$, then $\sum_{n=0}^{N-1} f[n] e^{2jnk\pi/N} = \overline{F[k]}$ where the overline denotes the complex conjugate of $F[k]$.

5. For a sequence of complex numbers $F[k]$, let $\overline{F[k]}$ represent the sequence obtained by taking the complex conjugate of each term in the sequence. Show that if $f[n]$ is a sequence of real numbers, then $F[N - k] = \overline{F[k]}$ for $k = 0, 1, 2, \dots, N/2$ if N is even, and for $k = 0, 1, 2, \dots, (N - 1)/2$ if N is odd. This can be seen in Example 24.20 where $N = 4$ and $F[3] = \overline{F[1]}$.

Solutions

1. $F[k] = 2, 1 - 3j, 0, 1 + 3j.$ $G[k] = 4, 4, 0, 4$

2. $6, 4.5 + 2.5981j, 4.5 - 2.5981j$

24.9.2 The inverse d.f.t.

Just as there is an inverse Fourier transform which transforms $F(\omega)$ back to $f(t)$, there is an inverse d.f.t. which converts $F[k]$ back to $f[n]$.

The inverse d.f.t. of the sequence $F[k]$, $k = 0, 1, 2, \dots, N - 1$, is the sequence $f[n]$, also having N terms, given by

$$\mathcal{D}^{-1}\{F[k]\} = f[n] = \frac{1}{N} \sum_{k=0}^{N-1} F[k] e^{2jkn\pi/N} \qquad n = 0, 1, 2, \dots, N - 1$$

Example 24.21 Using the definition, find the inverse d.f.t of the sequence $F[k]$, for $k = 0, 1, 2, 3$, given by

$$F[k] = -4, 1, 0, 1$$

Solution In this sequence there are four terms and so $N = 4$. From the definition

$$\mathcal{D}^{-1}\{F[k]\} = f[n] = \frac{1}{4}\sum_{k=0}^{3} F[k]\,e^{2jkn\pi/4} \qquad n = 0, 1, 2, 3$$

$$= \frac{1}{4}\sum_{k=0}^{3} F[k]\,e^{jkn\pi/2} \qquad n = 0, 1, 2, 3$$

$$= \frac{1}{4}(-4 + 1e^{jn\pi/2} + 0e^{jn\pi} + 1e^{3jn\pi/2})$$

Then, taking $n = 0, 1, 2, 3$ gives the sequence:

$$f[n] = -\frac{1}{2}, -1, -\frac{3}{2}, -1$$

Exercises   24.9.2

1 Use the definition to find the inverse d.f.t. of the sequence $F[k] = 6, -2, 2, -2$.

2 Investigate whether you have access to a computer package which will calculate an inverse d.f.t. Use the package to verify your answer to Question 1.

3 Prove that $f[n] = \frac{1}{N}\sum_{k=0}^{N-1} F[k]\,e^{2jkn\pi/N}$ is indeed the inverse of $F[k] = \sum_{m=0}^{N-1} f[m]\,e^{-2jkm\pi/N}$ by substituting the expression for $F[k]$ from the second formula into the first, interchanging the order of summation and simplifying the result.

Solutions

1 $f[n] = 1, 1, 3, 1$

24.10 Derivation of the d.f.t.

24.10.1 Some preliminary results

A number of results discussed earlier in this book will be required in the development which follows. To assist in this development we remind you of these now.

Euler's relations have been discussed in Section 9.7. Recall that

$$e^{-j\theta} = \cos\theta - j\sin\theta$$

and in particular that

$$e^{-2n\pi j} = \cos 2n\pi - j\sin 2n\pi$$

Furthermore, when n is an integer $\cos 2n\pi = 1$ and $\sin 2n\pi = 0$ and so $e^{-2n\pi j} = 1$.

The following integral property of the delta, or impulse, function will be needed:

$$\int_{-\infty}^{\infty} f(t)\delta(t-a)\,\mathrm{d}t = f(a)$$

So, multiplying any function, $f(t)$, by the delta function $\delta(t-a)$, representing an impulse occurring at $t = a$, and integrating, results in $f(a)$. This **sifting** property of the delta function, so called because it sifts out the value of $f(t)$ at the location of the impulse, has been discussed in Section 16.4. In particular, when $f(t) = e^{-j\omega t}$ we note

$$\int_{-\infty}^{\infty} e^{-j\omega t}\delta(t-a)\,\mathrm{d}t = e^{-j\omega a}$$

When a continuous function $f(t)$, which is defined for $t \geqslant 0$, is evaluated at times $t = 0, T, 2T, \ldots, nT, \ldots$ we obtain the sequence of values $f(0), f(T), f(2T), \ldots, f(nT), \ldots$, which we denote more concisely by the sequence $f[0], f[1], f[2], \ldots, f[n], \ldots$. This sequence can be expressed in the form of a continuous function, $\tilde{f}(t)$, in the following way:

$$\tilde{f}(t) = T \sum_{n=0}^{\infty} f[n]\delta(t-nT)$$

Note that whereas $f(t)$ is the original continuous function of t, $\tilde{f}(t)$ is an approximation obtained using only the sampled values. This representation is discussed in greater detail in Appendix I.

24.10.2 Derivation

This derivation is based upon the fact that a function $f(t)$, defined for $t \geqslant 0$, and having been sampled at intervals of T, can be represented by the function $\tilde{f}(t)$ where

$$\tilde{f}(t) = T \sum_{n=0}^{\infty} f[n]\delta(t-nT)$$

In any real problem it is only possible to sample a signal over a finite time interval. Suppose we obtain N samples of the signal at times $t = 0, T, 2T, \ldots, (N-1)T$. Then the sampled signal can be represented by amending the limits of summation and writing

$$\tilde{f}(t) = T \sum_{n=0}^{N-1} f[n]\delta(t-nT)$$

Taking the Fourier transform of both sides gives

$$\mathcal{F}\{\tilde{f}(t)\} = T \int_{-\infty}^{\infty} e^{-j\omega t} \sum_{n=0}^{N-1} f[n]\delta(t-nT)\,\mathrm{d}t$$

If we make the assumption that it is permissible to interchange the order of integration and summation we find

$$\mathcal{F}\{\tilde{f}(t)\} = T \sum_{n=0}^{N-1} f[n] \int_{-\infty}^{\infty} e^{-j\omega t}\delta(t-nT)\,\mathrm{d}t$$

$$= T \sum_{n=0}^{N-1} f[n]e^{-j\omega nT}$$

where we have used the sifting property of the delta function. The quantity on the r.h.s. is a continuous function of ω derived using the values in the sequence $f[n]$. Write this as $\tilde{F}(\omega)$ and note that $\tilde{F}(\omega)$ is an approximation to the Fourier transform $F(\omega) = \mathcal{F}\{f(t)\}$. It can also be thought of as a Fourier transform for sequences. An important point to note about this function of ω is that it is periodic with period $\dfrac{2\pi}{T}$. This is proved in the following example.

Example 24.22   Show that the function

$$\tilde{F}(\omega) = T \sum_{n=0}^{N-1} f[n] e^{-j\omega nT}$$

is periodic with period $\dfrac{2\pi}{T}$.

Solution   Consider $\tilde{F}\left(\omega + \dfrac{2\pi}{T}\right)$ for any ω.

$$\tilde{F}\left(\omega + \frac{2\pi}{T}\right) = T \sum_{n=0}^{N-1} f[n] e^{-j(\omega + 2\pi/T)nT}$$

$$= T \sum_{n=0}^{N-1} f[n] e^{-j\omega nT} e^{-j\frac{2\pi}{T}nT} \qquad \text{using the laws of indices}$$

$$= T \sum_{n=0}^{N-1} f[n] e^{-j\omega nT} e^{-2n\pi j}$$

Now we saw in Section 24.10.1 that

$$e^{-2n\pi j} = \cos 2n\pi - j \sin 2n\pi = 1$$

Finally we have

$$\tilde{F}\left(\omega + \frac{2\pi}{T}\right) = T \sum_{n=0}^{N-1} f[n] e^{-j\omega nT}$$

which equals $\tilde{F}(\omega)$.

We have shown that $\tilde{F}\left(\omega + \dfrac{2\pi}{T}\right) = \tilde{F}(\omega)$ for any ω. Hence $\tilde{F}(\omega)$ is periodic with period $\dfrac{2\pi}{T}$.

For computational purposes it is necessary to sample $\tilde{F}(\omega)$ at discrete values. Suppose we choose to sample at N points over the interval $0 \leqslant \omega < \dfrac{2\pi}{T}$. By choosing this interval we are sampling over a complete period in the frequency domain. So we choose the sample points given by $\omega = k\dfrac{2\pi}{NT}$ for $k = 0, 1, 2, \ldots, (N-1)$. Writing $\tilde{F}\left(k\dfrac{2\pi}{NT}\right)$ as $\tilde{F}(\omega_k)$ we have

$$\tilde{F}(\omega_k) = T\sum_{n=0}^{N-1} f[n]\,e^{-jk\frac{2\pi}{NT}nT}$$

$$= T\sum_{n=0}^{N-1} f[n]\,e^{-2jnk\pi/N} \tag{24.13}$$

This last sum, without the factor T, is usually taken as the definition of the d.f.t. of $f[n]$, written $F[k]$. To denote the d.f.t of the sequence $f[n]$ we will write $\mathcal{D}\{f[n]\}$.

> The d.f.t. of the sequence $f[n]$, $n = 0, 1, 2, \ldots, N-1$, is the sequence given by
>
> $$\mathcal{D}\{f[n]\} = F[k] = \sum_{n=0}^{N-1} f[n]\,e^{-2jnk\pi/N} \qquad \text{for } k = 0, 1, 2, \ldots, N-1$$

When we use this transform to approximate the Fourier transform of the function $f(t)$ sampled at intervals T, it follows from Equation (24.13) that we must multiply by the factor T to obtain our approximation. An example of this is given in the next section.

24.11 Using the d.f.t. to estimate a Fourier transform

One application of the d.f.t. is to estimate the continuous Fourier transform of a signal $f(t)$. The following example shows how this can be done.

Example 24.23

The signal $f(t) = u(t)\,e^{-2t}$, where $u(t)$ is the unit step function, is shown in Figure 24.18(a). Its Fourier transform, which can be found from Table 24.1, is $F(\omega) = \dfrac{1}{2+j\omega}$ and a graph of $|F(\omega)|$ is shown in Figure 24.18(b).

Suppose we obtain 16 sample values of $f(t)$ at intervals of $T = 0.1$ from $t = 0$ to $t = 1.5$.

Figure 24.18
The signal
$f(t) = u(t)\,e^{-2t}$
and its Fourier
transform.

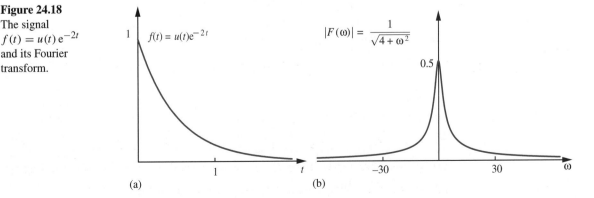

(a)   (b)

Table 24.2

n, k	$f[n] = \mathrm{e}^{-0.2n}$	$F[k]$	$F(\omega_k)$	$0.1F[k]$
0	1.0000	5.2918	0.5000	0.5292
1	0.8187	$1.4835 - 1.9082\mathrm{j}$	$0.1030 - 0.2022\mathrm{j}$	$0.1484 - 0.1908\mathrm{j}$
2	0.6703	$0.7882 - 1.0837\mathrm{j}$	$0.0304 - 0.1196\mathrm{j}$	$0.0788 - 0.1084\mathrm{j}$
3	0.5488	$0.6311 - 0.6952\mathrm{j}$	$0.0140 - 0.0825\mathrm{j}$	$0.0631 - 0.0695\mathrm{j}$
4	0.4493	$0.5743 - 0.4702\mathrm{j}$	$0.0080 - 0.0626\mathrm{j}$	$0.0574 - 0.0470\mathrm{j}$
5	0.3679	$0.5485 - 0.3159\mathrm{j}$	$0.0051 - 0.0504\mathrm{j}$	$0.0548 - 0.0316\mathrm{j}$
6	0.3012	$0.5355 - 0.1964\mathrm{j}$	$0.0036 - 0.0421\mathrm{j}$	$0.0536 - 0.0196\mathrm{j}$
7	0.2466	$0.5293 - 0.0944\mathrm{j}$	$0.0026 - 0.0362\mathrm{j}$	$0.0529 - 0.0094\mathrm{j}$
8	0.2019	0.5274	$0.0020 - 0.0317\mathrm{j}$	0.0527
9	0.1653	$0.5293 + 0.0944\mathrm{j}$	$0.0016 - 0.0282\mathrm{j}$	$0.0529 + 0.0094\mathrm{j}$
10	0.1353	$0.5355 + 0.1964\mathrm{j}$	$0.0013 - 0.0254\mathrm{j}$	$0.0536 + 0.0196\mathrm{j}$
11	0.1108	$0.5485 + 0.3159\mathrm{j}$	$0.0011 - 0.0231\mathrm{j}$	$0.0548 + 0.0316\mathrm{j}$
12	0.0907	$0.5743 + 0.4702\mathrm{j}$	$0.0009 - 0.0212\mathrm{j}$	$0.0574 + 0.0470\mathrm{j}$
13	0.0743	$0.6311 + 0.6952\mathrm{j}$	$0.0008 - 0.0196\mathrm{j}$	$0.0631 + 0.0695\mathrm{j}$
14	0.0608	$0.7882 + 1.0837\mathrm{j}$	$0.0007 - 0.0182\mathrm{j}$	$0.0788 + 0.1084\mathrm{j}$
15	0.0498	$1.4835 + 1.9082\mathrm{j}$	$0.0006 - 0.0170\mathrm{j}$	$0.1484 + 0.1908\mathrm{j}$

(a) Obtain the d.f.t. of the sampled sequence.

(b) Use the d.f.t. to estimate the true Fourier transform values.

(c) Plot a graph to compare values of $|F[k]|$ and $|F(\omega)|$.

Solution

(a) If $f(t) = u(t)\,\mathrm{e}^{-2t}$ is sampled at $t = nT$, that is $t = 0, 0.1, 0.2, \dots, 1.5$, we obtain the sequence $f[n] = \mathrm{e}^{-2nT} = \mathrm{e}^{-0.2n}$ for $n = 0, 1, 2, \dots, 15$. This is the sequence given in the second column of Table 24.2.

(b) The calculation of the d.f.t. is far too laborious to be done by hand. Instead we have used the MATLAB command `fft()` to do the calculation and the results, $F[k]$, have been placed in the third column.

(c) From Section 24.10 we know that the d.f.t. samples at intervals of $\dfrac{2\pi}{NT}$ in the frequency domain. So for comparison the fourth column shows the true values of $F(\omega)$ also sampled at intervals of $\dfrac{2\pi}{NT}$. Recall that to obtain an estimate of the Fourier transform of $f(t)$ we must multiply the d.f.t. values by $T = 0.1$. This is shown in the fifth column of the table.

Figure 24.19 shows graphs of $|0.1F[k]|$ and $|F(\omega)|$. Values of $|F[k]|$ obtained beyond $k = 8$ are mirror images of the earlier values. This is because $F[N - k] = \overline{F[k]}$ as proved in Question 5 in Exercises 24.9.1. This is a phenomenon of the d.f.t. and arises because of its periodicity and symmetry properties, further details of which are beyond the scope of this book. The interested reader is referred to a text on signal processing for further details (for example, Proakis, J. G. and Manolakis, D. G. *Digital Signal Processing: Principles, algorithms and applications*, Third Edition, Prentice Hall, Englewood Cliffs, NJ, 1995).

Figure 24.19
Comparison of true
values of a Fourier
transform and
approximate values
obtained using a d.f.t.

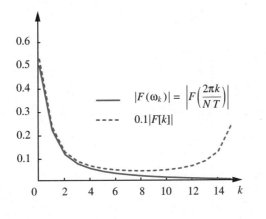

24.12 Matrix representation of the d.f.t.

When it is necessary to develop computer code for performing a d.f.t., an understanding
of the following matrix representation is useful.

We have seen that the d.f.t. of a sequence $f[n]$ is given by

$$F[k] = \sum_{n=0}^{N-1} f[n]\, e^{-2jnk\pi/N}$$

Consider the term $e^{-2jnk\pi/N}$ which can be written using the laws of indices as $(e^{-2j\pi/N})^{nk}$.
Define $W = e^{-2j\pi/N}$ so that

$$F[k] = \sum_{n=0}^{N-1} f[n]W^{nk}$$

Note that W does not depend upon n or k. For a fixed value of N we can calculate W
which is then a constant. Writing out this sum explicitly we find

$$F[k] = f[0]W^0 + f[1]W^k + f[2]W^{2k} + f[3]W^{3k} + \cdots$$
$$+ f[N-1]W^{(N-1)k} \qquad \text{for } k = 0, 1, 2, \ldots, N-1$$

Writing this out for each k we find

$$F[0] = f[0]W^0 + f[1]W^0 + f[2]W^0 + f[3]W^0 + \cdots + f[N-1]W^0$$
$$F[1] = f[0]W^0 + f[1]W^1 + f[2]W^2 + f[3]W^3 + \cdots + f[N-1]W^{N-1}$$
$$F[2] = f[0]W^0 + f[1]W^2 + f[2]W^4 + f[3]W^6 + \cdots + f[N-1]W^{2(N-1)}$$

$$\vdots = \vdots$$

$$F[N-1] = f[0]W^0 + f[1]W^{N-1} + f[2]W^{2(N-1)}$$
$$+ f[3]W^{3(N-1)} + \cdots + f[N-1]W^{(N-1)(N-1)}$$

These equations can be written in matrix form as follows:

$$
\begin{pmatrix} F[0] \\ F[1] \\ F[2] \\ \vdots \\ F[N-1] \end{pmatrix} = \begin{pmatrix} W^0 & W^0 & W^0 & \cdots & W^0 \\ W^0 & W^1 & W^2 & \cdots & W^{N-1} \\ W^0 & W^2 & W^4 & \cdots & W^{2(N-1)} \\ \vdots & \vdots & \vdots & \vdots & \vdots \\ W^0 & W^{N-1} & W^{2(N-1)} & \cdots & W^{(N-1)(N-1)} \end{pmatrix} \begin{pmatrix} f[0] \\ f[1] \\ f[2] \\ \vdots \\ f[N-1] \end{pmatrix}
$$

where $W = e^{-2j\pi/N}$.

Example 24.24 (a) Find the matrix representing a three-point d.f.t.

(b) Use the matrix to find the d.f.t. of the sequence $f[n] = 4, -7, 11$.

Solution (a) Here $N = 3$ and so $W = e^{-2\pi j/3}$. The required matrix is

$$
\begin{pmatrix} 1 & 1 & 1 \\ 1 & e^{-2\pi j/3} & e^{-4\pi j/3} \\ 1 & e^{-4\pi j/3} & e^{-8\pi j/3} \end{pmatrix}
$$

which using the Cartesian form can be written

$$
\begin{pmatrix} 1 & 1 & 1 \\ 1 & -\tfrac{1}{2} - j\tfrac{\sqrt{3}}{2} & -\tfrac{1}{2} + j\tfrac{\sqrt{3}}{2} \\ 1 & -\tfrac{1}{2} + j\tfrac{\sqrt{3}}{2} & -\tfrac{1}{2} - j\tfrac{\sqrt{3}}{2} \end{pmatrix}
$$

(b)
$$
\begin{pmatrix} F[0] \\ F[1] \\ F[2] \end{pmatrix} = \begin{pmatrix} 1 & 1 & 1 \\ 1 & -\tfrac{1}{2} - j\tfrac{\sqrt{3}}{2} & -\tfrac{1}{2} + j\tfrac{\sqrt{3}}{2} \\ 1 & -\tfrac{1}{2} + j\tfrac{\sqrt{3}}{2} & -\tfrac{1}{2} - j\tfrac{\sqrt{3}}{2} \end{pmatrix} \begin{pmatrix} 4 \\ -7 \\ 11 \end{pmatrix} = \begin{pmatrix} 8 \\ 2 + 15.5885j \\ 2 - 15.5885j \end{pmatrix}
$$

So, the required d.f.t. is the sequence

$$8, 2 + 15.5885j, 2 - 15.5885j$$

Exercises 24.12

1   Using the definition of the d.f.t. show that the matrix which can be used to implement the d.f.t. of a four-point signal is

$$
W = \begin{pmatrix} 1 & 1 & 1 & 1 \\ 1 & -j & -1 & j \\ 1 & -1 & 1 & -1 \\ 1 & j & -1 & -j \end{pmatrix}
$$

Use this matrix to find the d.f.t. of the sequences $f[n] = \{1, 2, 0, -1\}$ and $g[n] = \{3, 1, -1, 1\}$.

Solutions

1   $F[k] = 2, 1 - 3j, 0, 1 + 3j. \; G[k] = 4, 4, 0, 4$

24.13 | Some properties of the d.f.t.

24.13.1 Periodicity

The d.f.t. $F[k]$ is periodic with period N, that is

$$F[k + N] = F[k]$$

This is why we take only N terms in the frequency domain. Calculating further values will only reproduce the earlier ones. The inverse d.f.t. is also periodic with period N.

24.13.2 Linearity

The d.f.t. is a linear transform. This means that the d.f.t. of the sequence $af[n] + bg[n]$ where a and b are constants is $aF[k] + bG[k]$.

24.13.3 Parseval's theorem

If $\mathcal{D}\{f[n]\} = F[k]$ and $\mathcal{D}\{g[n]\} = G[k]$ then

$$\sum_{n=0}^{N-1} f[n]\overline{g[n]} = \frac{1}{N} \sum_{k=0}^{N-1} F[k]\overline{G[k]}$$

where the overline indicates the complex conjugate.

24.13.4 Rayleigh's theorem

This theorem is obtained from Parseval's theorem by letting $g[n] = f[n]$.

$$\sum_{n=0}^{N-1} |f[n]|^2 = \frac{1}{N} \sum_{k=0}^{N-1} |F[k]|^2$$

Example 24.25   Verify Rayleigh's theorem for the sequence $f[n] = 5, 4$.

Solution   Here $N = 2$. We first calculate $F[k]$.

$$F[k] = \sum_{n=0}^{1} f[n] e^{-jnk\pi}$$
$$= f[0] + f[1] e^{-jk\pi}$$
$$= 5 + 4e^{-jk\pi}$$

When $k = 0$, we have $F[0] = 5 + 4e^0 = 9$.

When $k = 1$, we have $F[1] = 5 + 4e^{-j\pi} = 5 - 4 = 1$.

For brevity we often write $F[k] = 9, 1$.

Then $\sum_{n=0}^{1} |f[n]|^2 = 5^2 + 4^2 = 41$.

Also, $\sum_{k=0}^{1} |F[k]|^2 = 9^2 + 1^2 = 82$.

We note that $41 = \frac{1}{2} \times 82$ and this verifies Rayleigh's theorem.

Exercises 24.13

1 (a) Obtain the d.f.t.s of $f[n] = 1, 2, 2, 1$ and $g[n] = 2, 1, 1, 2$.

   (b) Verify Rayleigh's theorem for each of these sequences.

2 Suppose $f[n] = 3, 1, 5, 4$ and $g[n] = 2, -1, 9, 5$.

   (a) Show that $\sum_{n=0}^{3} f[n]g[n] = 70$.

   (b) Obtain the d.f.t.s $F[k]$ and $G[k]$.

   (c) Calculate $F[k]\overline{G[k]}$.

   (d) Hence verify Parseval's theorem for these sequences.

3 Show that if the d.f.t. of $f[n]$ is $F[k]$ then the d.f.t. of $f[n - i]$ is $e^{-2\pi jki/N} F[k]$. This is known as the **shift theorem**.

4 Prove Parseval's theorem.

5 Prove Rayleigh's theorem.

Solutions

1 (a) $F[k] = 6, -1 - j, 0, -1 + j$.
   $G[k] = 6, 1 + j, 0, 1 - j$

   (b) $\sum |f[n]|^2 = 10, \sum |F[k]|^2 = 40$.
   $\sum |g[n]|^2 = 10, \sum |G[k]|^2 = 40$

2 (b) $F[k] = 13, -2 + 3j, 3, -2 - 3j$.
   $G[k] = 15, -7 + 6j, 7, -7 - 6j$

   (c) $195, 32 - 9j, 21, 32 + 9j$

24.14 Discrete convolution and correlation

As stated at the beginning of Section 24.8, convolution and correlation are important techniques in signal and image processing. In this section we will describe their discrete representations. Both of these can be implemented efficiently using the d.f.t.

24.14.1 Linear convolution

The **linear convolution** of two real sequences $f[n]$ and $g[n]$ is another sequence, $h[n]$ say, which we denote by $f * g$, which is defined as follows:

Linear convolution of $f[n]$ and $g[n]$:

$$h[n] = f * g = \sum_{m=-\infty}^{\infty} f[m]g[n - m] \quad \text{for } n = \ldots -3, -2, -1, 0, 1, 2, 3, \ldots$$

Notice the similarity between this definition and that of convolution defined in the context of the continuous Fourier transform in Section 24.8. Notice also that in this formula the sequence g is folded and shifted. This will be illustrated in the example which follows.

Frequently the sequences being considered will be finite.

Assume now that $f[n]$ is a finite sequence of N_1 terms, so that all terms other than $f[0], f[1], \ldots, f[N_1 - 1]$ are zero.

Suppose also that $g[n]$ is a finite sequence of N_2 terms, with all terms other than $g[0], g[1], \ldots, g[N_2 - 1]$ being zero.

It can be shown that the sequence $h[n]$ will have length $N_1 + N_2 - 1$, and the convolution sum simplifies to the following:

The linear convolution of the two finite sequences $f[n]$ and $g[n]$ is defined as

$$h[n] = f * g = \sum_{m=0}^{n} f[m]g[n - m] \quad \text{for } n = 0, 1, 2, 3, \ldots, (N_1 + N_2 - 2)$$

The terms of this sequence can be calculated by brute force as the following example will show, although in practice a convolution can be calculated much more efficiently using a d.f.t.

Example 24.26 Suppose $f[n]$ is the sequence $3, 9, 2, -1$, and $g[n]$ is the sequence $-4, 8, 5$.

(a) Find the linear convolution $h[n] = f * g$ using the previous formula.

(b) Develop a graphical interpretation of this process.

Solution (a) Note that both f and g are finite sequences of length 4 and 3 respectively. The convolution $f * g$ will be a sequence of length $4 + 3 - 1 = 6$. By definition,

$$h[n] = \sum_{m=0}^{n} f[m]g[n - m] \quad \text{for } n = 0, 1, 2, \ldots, 5.$$

The first term in $h[n]$ is obtained by letting $n = 0$:

$$h[0] = \sum_{m=0}^{0} f[m]g[0 - m]$$

$$= f[0]g[0]$$

$$= (3)(-4)$$

$$= -12$$

Figure 24.20
The sequences
$f[m] = 3, 9, 2, -1$
and $g[m] = -4, 8, 5$.

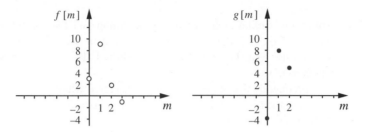

The second term is obtained by letting $n = 1$:

$$h[1] = \sum_{m=0}^{1} f[m]g[1 - m]$$

$$= f[0]g[1] + f[1]g[0]$$

$$= (3)(8) + (9)(-4)$$

$$= 24 - 36$$

$$= -12$$

Subsequent terms are calculated in a similar manner. You should obtain these for yourself to ensure that you understand the process. The complete sequence is

$$h[n] = f * g = -12, -12, 79, 65, 2, -5$$

(b) The graphical interpretation is developed along the same lines as was done for the continuous convolution in Section 24.8.

The sequences $f[m]$ and $g[m]$ are shown in Figure 24.20.
The sequence $g[-m]$ is found by reflection in the vertical axis, that is folding as shown in Figure 24.21(a). Then the folded graph can be translated n units to the left or the right by changing the argument of g from $g[m]$ to $g[n - m]$. If n is positive the graph moves to the right. Study Figures 24.21(b–g) to observe this. Convolution is the sum of products of $f[m]$ with $g[n - m]$. The graph of $f[m]$ is superimposed. We are only interested in values of n for which the graphs overlap – otherwise each product is zero. For each value of n the superimposed graphs make it easy to see which values must be multiplied together and added. If required, a table can be constructed which summarizes all the necessary information as shown below.

	m	-2	-1	0	1	2	3	4	5
	$f[m]$	–	–	3	9	2	-1	–	–
$n = 0$	$g[-m]$	5	8	-4	–	–	–	–	–
$n = 1$	$g[1 - m]$	–	5	8	-4	–	–	–	–
$n = 2$	$g[2 - m]$	–	–	5	8	-4	–	–	–
$n = 3$	$g[3 - m]$	–	–	–	5	8	-4	–	–
$n = 4$	$g[4 - m]$	–	–	–	–	5	8	-4	–
$n = 5$	$g[5 - m]$	–	–	–	–	–	5	8	-4

Figure 24.21
The effect of
translating $g[-m]$ by n
units, for
$n = 0, 1, \ldots, 5$.

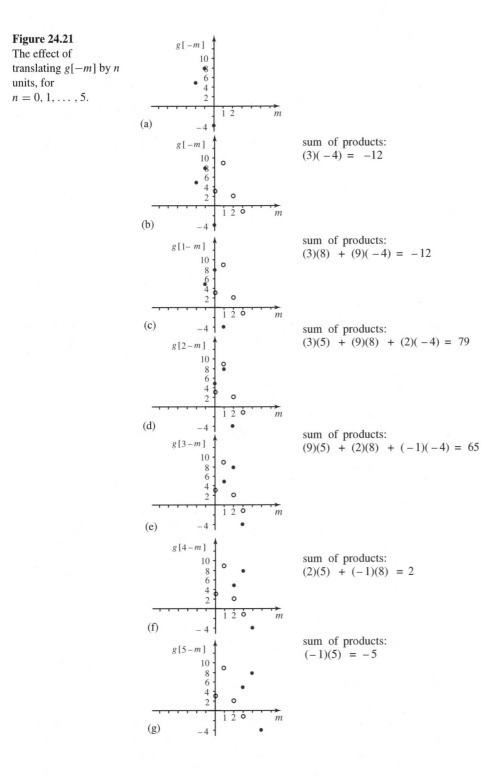

(a)

(b)

sum of products:
$(3)(-4) = -12$

(c)

sum of products:
$(3)(8) + (9)(-4) = -12$

(d)

sum of products:
$(3)(5) + (9)(8) + (2)(-4) = 79$

(e)

sum of products:
$(9)(5) + (2)(8) + (-1)(-4) = 65$

(f)

sum of products:
$(2)(5) + (-1)(8) = 2$

(g)

sum of products:
$(-1)(5) = -5$

Exercises 24.14.1

1 Given $f[n] = 1, 2, 2, 1$ and $g[n] = 2, 1, 1, 2$, find the linear convolution $f * g$.

2 (a) The linear convolution of the sequences $3, 9, 2, -1$ and $-4, 8, 5$ was obtained in Example 24.26. Show that this convolution is equivalent to multiplying the two polynomials $3 + 9x + 2x^2 - x^3$ and $-4 + 8x + 5x^2$.

(b) By using polynomial multiplication find the linear convolution of the sequences $f[n] = 9, -8$ and $g[n] = 1, 2, -4$.

3 Find the linear convolution of $f[n] = 1, -1, 1, 3$ and $g[n] = 7, 2, 0, 1$.

4 Prove from the definition that linear convolution is commutative, that is $f * g = g * f$.

Solutions

1 $2, 5, 7, 8, 7, 5, 2$

2 (b) $9, 10, -52, 32$

3 $7, -5, 5, 24, 5, 1, 3$

24.14.2 Circular convolution

In this section we consider periodic sequences having period N. We can select one period for examination by looking at the terms $f[0], f[1], f[2], \ldots, f[N-1]$, say. For example the sequence

$$f[n] = \ldots - 7, 11, 2, -7, 11, 2, -7, 11, 2 \ldots$$

is a periodic sequence with period $N = 3$. We can select the terms $f[0], f[1], f[2]$, that is terms $-7, 11, 2$, and use these to study the entire sequence.

Such a sequence can be represented graphically by listing its terms around a circle as shown in Figure 24.22. Doing this allows us to calculate further terms in the sequence as we require them. Rotation anticlockwise represents increasing n as in (a). Rotation clockwise represents decreasing n as in (b).

Figure 24.22
A periodic sequence can be visualized by listing its terms around a circle.

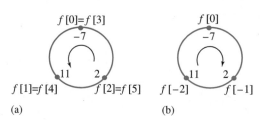

(a) (b)

Suppose $f[n]$ and $g[n]$ are two periodic sequences having period N. Their **circular convolution**, or **periodic convolution**, is the sequence $h[n]$, which we denote by $f \circledast g$ and which is defined as follows:

The circular convolution of two periodic sequences each of period N is defined as

$$h[n] = f \circledast g = \sum_{m=0}^{N-1} f[m]g[n-m] \quad \text{for } n = 0, 1, 2, \ldots, N-1$$

The sequence is periodic with period N and so we can state it for $n = 0, 1, 2, \ldots, N-1$.

Example 24.27

(a) Calculate the circular convolution, $h[n] = f \circledast g$, of the two periodic sequences $f[n] = 9, -1, 3$ and $g[n] = 7, 2, -4$.

(b) Develop a graphical representation of this process.

Solution

(a) The sequence $g[n]$ is depicted in Figure 24.23.
We use the formula given above. In this Example, $N = 3$. First let $n = 0$.

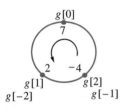

Figure 24.23 The periodic sequence $g[n] = 7, 2, -4$.

$$h[0] = \sum_{m=0}^{2} f[m]g[0-m]$$

$$= f[0]g[0] + f[1]g[-1] + f[2]g[-2]$$

$$= (9)(7) + (-1)(-4) + (3)(2)$$

$$= 73$$

Next let $n = 1$.

$$h[1] = \sum_{m=0}^{2} f[m]g[1-m]$$

$$= f[0]g[1] + f[1]g[0] + f[2]g[-1]$$

$$= (9)(2) + (-1)(7) + (3)(-4)$$

$$= -1$$

Finally, let $n = 2$.

$$h[2] = \sum_{m=0}^{2} f[m]g[2-m]$$

$$= f[0]g[2] + f[1]g[1] + f[2]g[0]$$

$$= (9)(-4) + (-1)(2) + (3)(7)$$

$$= -17$$

So the circular convolution $f \circledast g = 73, -1, -17$.

If required, a table can be constructed which summarizes all the necessary information as was shown in Example 24.26. The sequences must be extended to show their periodicity, and this time we are only interested in generating the convolution sequence over one period, namely that section of the table for $m = 0, 1, 2$.

	m	-2	-1	0	1	2	3	4	5
	$f[m]$	-1	3	9	-1	3	9	-1	3
$n = 0$	$g[-m]$	-4	2	7	-4	2	7	-4	2
$n = 1$	$g[1-m]$	7	-4	2	7	-4	2	7	-4
$n = 2$	$g[2-m]$	2	7	-4	2	7	-4	2	7

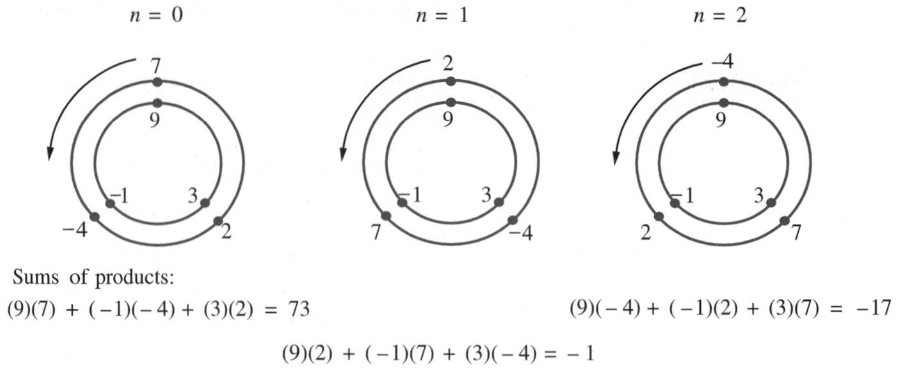

Figure 24.24
The sequences $f[m]$ drawn around the inner circle, and $g[n-m]$ drawn around the outer circle, for $n = 0, 1, 2.$

Sums of products:

$(9)(7) + (-1)(-4) + (3)(2) = 73$ $\qquad\qquad\qquad$ $(9)(-4) + (-1)(2) + (3)(7) = -17$

$(9)(2) + (-1)(7) + (3)(-4) = -1$

(b) A graphical representation can be developed by listing the fixed sequence $f[m]$, for $m = 0, 1, 2$, anticlockwise around an inner circle as shown in Figure 24.24. We list $g[-m]$ around an outer circle but do so clockwise to take account of the folding. By rotating the outer circle anticlockwise we obtain $g[1-m]$ and $g[2-m]$. By multiplying neighbouring terms and adding we obtain the required convolution. The result is $73, -1, -17$ as obtained in part (a).

In the following section you will see how circular convolution can be performed using the d.f.t.

Exercises 24.14.2

1   Calculate the circular convolution of $f[n] = 1, -1, 1, 3$ and $g[n] = 7, 2, 0, 1$.

Solutions

1   $12, -4, 8, 24$

24.14.3   The (circular) convolution theorem

Suppose $f[n]$ and $g[n]$ are periodic sequences of period N. Suppose further that the d.f.t.s of $f[n]$ and $g[n]$ for $n = 0, 1, 2, \ldots, N-1$ are calculated and are denoted by $F[k]$ and $G[k]$. The convolution theorem states that the d.f.t. of the circular convolution of $f[n]$ and $g[n]$ is equal to the product of the d.f.t.s of $f[n]$ and $g[n]$.

The convolution theorem:

$$\mathcal{D}\{f \circledast g\} = F[k]G[k]$$

This is important because it provides a technique for finding a circular convolution. It follows from the theorem that

$$f \circledast g = \mathcal{D}^{-1}\{F[k]G[k]\}$$

So, to find the circular convolution of $f[n]$ and $g[n]$ we proceed as follows:

(1) Find the corresponding d.f.t.s, $F[k]$ and $G[k]$.

(2) Multiply these together to obtain $F[k]G[k]$.

(3) Find the inverse d.f.t. to give $f \circledast g$.

Whilst this procedure may seem complicated, it is nevertheless an efficient way of calculating a convolution.

Example 24.28   Use the convolution theorem to find $f \circledast g$ when $f[n] = 5, 4$ and $g[n] = -1, 3$.

Solution   First we find the corresponding d.f.t.s, $F[k]$ and $G[k]$. Using

$$F[k] = \sum_{n=0}^{N-1} f[n] \, e^{-2jnk\pi/N}$$

with $N = 2$ gives

$$F[0] = \sum_{n=0}^{1} f[n] = 9, \qquad F[1] = \sum_{n=0}^{1} f[n] \, e^{-jn\pi} = 5 + 4e^{-j\pi} = 1$$

and similarly,

$$G[0] = \sum_{n=0}^{1} g[n] = 2, \qquad G[1] = \sum_{n=0}^{1} g[n] \, e^{-jn\pi} = -1 + 3e^{-j\pi} = -4$$

and so

$$F[k] = 9, 1 \qquad G[k] = 2, -4$$

These transforms are multiplied together, term by term, to give

$$H[k] = F[k]G[k] = (9)(2), (1)(-4) = 18, -4$$

Finally the inverse d.f.t. of the sequence $18, -4$, is found using

$$h[n] = \frac{1}{N} \sum_{k=0}^{N-1} H[k] \, e^{2jnk\pi/N}$$

to give

$$(f \circledast g)[0] = \frac{1}{2}(18 - 4) = 7$$

$$(f \circledast g)[1] = \frac{1}{2}(18) + \frac{1}{2}(-4e^{j\pi}) = 11$$

and so

$$f \circledast g = 7, 11$$

The convolution could also be evaluated directly using the technique of Section 24.14.2. You should try this to confirm the result obtained using the theorem.

Example 24.29   Use the convolution theorem and a computer package which calculates d.f.t.s to find the circular convolution of the sequences $f[n] = 1, 2, -1, 7$ and $g[n] = -1, 3, 2, -5$.

Solution   You will need access to a computer package such as MATLAB to work through this example. The d.f.t. of $f[n]$ can be calculated either directly, which is laborious, or using the MATLAB command `fft()`.

```
>F=fft([1 2 -1 7])

ans =
    9.0000     2.0000+ 5.0000i  -9.0000      2.0000- 5.0000i
```

Hence $F[k] = 9, 2 + 5j, -9, 2 - 5j$.
    Similarly,

```
>G=fft([-1 3 2 -5])

ans =
   -1.0000    -3.0000- 8.0000i   3.0000     -3.0000+ 8.0000i
```

Hence $G[k] = -1, -3 - 8j, 3, -3 + 8j$. Then, the product of these d.f.t.s is calculated by multiplying corresponding terms together:

$$F[k]G[k] = -9, 34 - 31j, -27, 34 + 31j$$

In MATLAB,

```
>product = F.*G

product =
   -9.0000    34.0000-31.0000i   -27.0000    34.0000+31.0000i
```

Finally, taking the inverse d.f.t., using the MATLAB command `ifft()`, gives

```
> ifft([-9 34-31i   -27 34+3i])
ans =
    8     20    -26    -11
```

This is the circular convolution of $f[n]$ and $g[n]$, that is

$$f[n] \circledast g[n] = 8, 20, -26, -11$$

This example has illustrated how circular convolution can be achieved through the use of the d.f.t.

The convolution theorem applies to circular convolution but not linear convolution. However, by modifying the procedure slightly, the linear convolution of two finite sequences can also be found.

If $f[n]$ is a finite sequence of length N_1 and $g[n]$ is a finite sequence of length N_2 we know from Section 24.14.1 that their linear convolution is a sequence of length $N_1 + N_2 - 1$.

First we extend both the sequences $f[n]$ and $g[n]$ to make each have length $N_1 + N_2 - 1$. This extension is done by adding zeros. This process is known as 'padding' with zeros. Then the d.f.t.s of the padded sequences are calculated to give $F[k]$ and $G[k]$. It can be shown that the linear convolution of the original sequences is equal to the circular convolution of the padded sequences. Hence the linear convolution $f * g$ is then found from

$$f * g = \mathcal{D}^{-1}\{F[k]G[k]\}$$

Consider the following example.

Example 24.30   If $f[n]$ is the finite sequence 7, -1 and $g[n]$ is the finite sequence 4, 2, -7 use circular convolution with padded zeros to obtain the linear convolution $f * g$.

Solution   Their linear convolution is a sequence of length $2 + 3 - 1 = 4$.
We pad f and g to give sequences of length 4.

$$f[n] = 7, -1, 0, 0 \text{ and } g[n] = 4, 2, -7, 0$$

Then, either by direct calculation or by using a computer package you can verify that

$$F[k] = 6, 7 + j, 8, 7 - j \qquad \text{and} \qquad G[k] = -1, 11 - 2j, -5, 11 + 2j$$

Then

$$F[k]G[k] = -6, 79 - 3j, -40, 79 + 3j$$

Then taking the inverse d.f.t. gives

$$\mathcal{D}^{-1}\{F[k]G[k]\} = 28, 10, -51, 7$$

which is the required linear convolution. You should verify this by calculating the linear convolution directly.

Exercises   24.14.3

1   The circular convolution of $f[n] = 1, -1, 1, 3$ and $g[n] = 7, 2, 0, 1$ was calculated in Question 1 in Exercises 24.14.2. Verify the convolution theorem for these sequences.

2   Use circular convolution and padding with zeros

to obtain the linear convolution of $f[n] = 9, 0, 1$ and $g[n] = 5, 4, 5, 2, 1$. Further, verify the convolution theorem for these sequences.

3   Prove the circular convolution theorem.

Solutions

1   $F[k] = 4, 4j, 0, -4j. \ G[k] = 10, 7 - j, 4, 7 + j$ 2   45, 36, 50, 22, 14, 2, 1

24.14.4   Linear cross-correlation

The **linear cross-correlation** of two real sequences $f[n]$ and $g[n]$ is another sequence, $c[n]$ say, which we denote by $f \star g$, which is defined as follows:

Linear cross-correlation of $f[n]$ and $g[n]$:

$$c[n] = f \star g = \sum_{m=-\infty}^{\infty} f[m]g[m-n] \qquad \text{for } n = \ldots -3, -2, -1, 0, 1, 2, 3 \ldots$$

Note the similarity between this definition and that of linear convolution defined in Section 24.14.1. In the formula for cross-correlation the sequence g is not folded. If the two sequences are finite and of length N, that is $f[n]$ and $g[n]$ are non-zero only when $0 \leqslant n \leqslant N - 1$, there are $2N - 1$ terms in the cross-correlation sequence and the formula can be written as follows:

Linear cross-correlation of two finite sequences $f[n]$ and $g[n]$:

$$c[n] = f \star g = \sum_{m=n}^{N-1} f[m]g[m-n] \qquad \text{for } n = 0, 1, 2, \ldots, N-1$$

and

$$c[n] = f \star g = \sum_{m=0}^{N+n-1} f[m]g[m-n] \qquad \text{for } n = 0, -1, -2, \ldots, -(N-1)$$

Example 24.31   Suppose $f[n] = 7, 2, -3$ and $g[n] = 1, 9, -1$. Assume both sequences f and g start at $n = 0$.

(a) Find the linear cross-correlation $c[n] = f \star g$ using the formulae above.

(b) Develop a graphical interpretation of this process.

Solution   (a) Both f and g are finite sequences of length $N = 3$. Their cross-correlation is a sequence $c[n]$, for $n = -2, -1, 0, 1, 2$, of length 5.
Using the formulae above with $n = -2$ gives

$$c[-2] = \sum_{m=0}^{0} f[m]g[m+2]$$
$$= f[0]g[2]$$
$$= (7)(-1)$$
$$= -7$$

Figure 24.25
The effect of
translating $g[m]$.

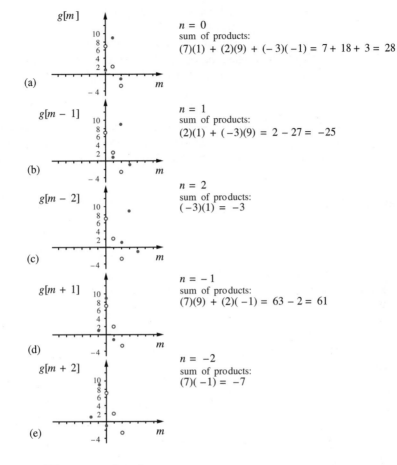

$g[m]$

(a)

$n = 0$
sum of products:
$(7)(1) + (2)(9) + (-3)(-1) = 7 + 18 + 3 = 28$

$g[m - 1]$

(b)

$n = 1$
sum of products:
$(2)(1) + (-3)(9) = 2 - 27 = -25$

$g[m - 2]$

(c)

$n = 2$
sum of products:
$(-3)(1) = -3$

$g[m + 1]$

(d)

$n = -1$
sum of products:
$(7)(9) + (2)(-1) = 63 - 2 = 61$

$g[m + 2]$

(e)

$n = -2$
sum of products:
$(7)(-1) = -7$

When $n = -1$ we have

$$c[-1] = \sum_{m=0}^{1} f[m]g[m + 1]$$
$$= f[0]g[1] + f[1]g[2]$$
$$= (7)(9) + (2)(-1)$$
$$= 61$$

The remaining terms are calculated in a similar fashion. You should calculate one
or two terms yourself to verify that the full sequence is

$$c[n] = -7, 61, 28, -25, -3 \qquad n = -2, -1, 0, 1, 2$$

(b) The graphical interpretation is developed along the same lines as for linear convolution in Example 24.26. Figure 24.25 shows the sequence $f[m]$, for $m = 0, 1, 2$,
denoted by the symbols ○. Also shown is the sequence $g[m]$ denoted by ●.

The graph of $g[m]$ can be translated n units to the left or right by changing the
argument of g from $g[m]$ to $g[m - n]$. If n is positive the graph moves to the right.
Study the figure to observe this. Correlation is the sum of products of $f[m]$ and

$g[m - n]$. For each value of n, the graph of $f[m]$ is superimposed. We are only interested in values of n for which the graphs overlap – otherwise each product is zero. For each value of n the superimposed graphs make it easy to see which values must be multiplied together and added. Placing these results in order confirms the result obtained in part (a), that is the correlation is $-7, 61, 28, -25, -3$.

When a sequence is cross-correlated with itself the process is known as **autocorrelation**. Autocorrelation is used to search for possible periodicities in signals, because if a signal is periodic with period N its autocorrelation sequence will show peaks at intervals of N.

Exercises 24.14.4

1. Find the linear cross-correlation of the sequences $f[n] = 4, 5, 9$, and $g[n] = 3, 1, 1$.

2. Show that the linear cross-correlation of $f[n]$ and $g[n]$ can be written in the alternative form $f \star g = \sum_{m=-\infty}^{\infty} f[m + n]g[m]$.

3. There are variants of the definition of correlation. Show that if $f \star g$ is redefined to be $\sum_{m=-\infty}^{\infty} f[m - n]g[m]$ then the corresponding correlation of the sequences in Question 1 is $27, 24, 26, 9, 4$.

4. Find the linear autocorrelation of the sequence $f[n] = 3, 2, 1$.

Solutions

1. $4, 9, 26, 24, 27$

4. $3, 8, 14, 8, 3$

24.14.5 Circular cross-correlation

The circular cross-correlation of two periodic sequences of period N is defined in a similar manner to their circular convolution. It is a sequence $c[n]$ of length N.

The circular cross-correlation of two periodic sequences, $f[n]$ and $g[n]$, each of period N is defined as

$$c[n] = f \circledast g = \sum_{m=0}^{N-1} f[m]g[m - n] \qquad \text{for } n = 0, 1, 2, \ldots, N - 1$$

When a sequence is cross-correlated with itself the process is known as autocorrelation.

Example 24.32

(a) Find the circular autocorrelation of the sequence $f[n] = 3, 2, 1$ using the formula.

(b) Develop a graphical method for performing this calculation.

Solution

(a) Here $N = 3$. From the definition

$$c[n] = f \circledast f = \sum_{m=0}^{2} f[m]f[m - n] \qquad \text{for } n = 0, 1, 2$$

Figure 24.26
Graphical calculation
of the autocorrelation
of $f[n] = 3, 2, 1$.

$n = 0$ 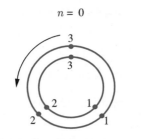 $n = 1$ 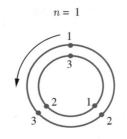 $n = 2$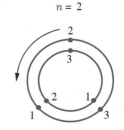

Sums of products:

$(3)(3) + (2)(2) + (1)(1) = 14$ $(3)(1) + (2)(3) + (1)(2) = 11$ $(3)(2) + (2)(1) + (1)(3) = 11$

$$c[0] = \sum_{m=0}^{2} f[m]f[m]$$
$$= (3)(3) + (2)(2) + (1)(1)$$
$$= 14$$

$$c[1] = \sum_{m=0}^{2} f[m]f[m-1]$$
$$= f[0]f[-1] + f[1]f[0] + f[2]f[1]$$
$$= (3)(1) + (2)(3) + (1)(2)$$
$$= 11$$

$$c[2] = \sum_{m=0}^{2} f[m]f[m-2]$$
$$= (3)(2) + (2)(1) + (1)(3)$$
$$= 11$$

Hence $c[n] = 14, 11, 11$.

(b) The graphical method involves listing the sequence $f[m]$, $m = 0, 1, 2$, around an inner circle. Around an outer circle we list it again. This method is identical to that used in Example 24.27 for circular convolution, but because now there is no folding, the sequence on the outer circle is not reversed. The calculation can be seen in Figure 24.26.

24.14.6 (Circular) correlation theorem

For real sequences $f[n]$ and $g[n]$ the correlation theorem states:

$$\mathcal{D}\{f \circledast g\} = F[k]\overline{G[k]}$$

where $\overline{G[k]}$ denotes the complex conjugate of $G[k]$.

This provides a technique for calculating a correlation using the d.f.t.

Example 24.33

Find the circular correlation $f \circledast g$ when $f[n] = 8, -9, 3, 2$ and $g[n] = 11, 4, -1, -5$.

Solution

Either directly from the definition of the d.f.t., or by using a computer package, we can show that

$$F[k] = 4, 5 + 11j, 18, 5 - 11j \qquad G[k] = 9, 12 - 9j, 11, 12 + 9j$$

The conjugate of $G[k]$ is $\overline{G[k]} = 9, 12 + 9j, 11, 12 - 9j$. Then

$$F[k]\overline{G[k]} = 36, -39 + 177j, 198, -39 - 177j$$

Either directly, or using a computer package, taking the inverse d.f.t. yields the sequence

$$39, -129, 78, 48$$

which is the required circular correlation. You may like to verify this by directly calculating $f \circledast g$.

It follows from the theorem that the circular autocorrelation sequence has the following property:

$$\mathcal{D}\{f \circledast f\} = F[k]\overline{F[k]}$$

Example 24.34

Use the d.f.t. to find the circular autocorrelation of the sequence $f[n] = 8, 3, -1, 2$.

Solution

It is straightforward but tedious to show that the d.f.t. of $f[n]$ is

$$F[k] = 12, 9 - j, 2, 9 + j$$

Then, the conjugate of $F[k]$ is $\overline{F[k]} = 12, 9 + j, 2, 9 - j$, and

$$F[k]\overline{F[k]} = 144, 82, 4, 82$$

Finally, taking the inverse d.f.t. gives the sequence $78, 35, -4, 35$ which you can verify is the circular autocorrelation of $f[n] = 8, 3, -1, 2$.

Exercises 24.14.6

1 Find the circular cross-correlation of $f[n] = 2, 3, -1$ and $g[n] = 8, 7, 1$. Verify the correlation theorem.

2 From the definition, prove the correlation theorem.

3 There are variants of the definition of correlation. Show that if $f \circledast g$ is redefined to be $\sum_{m=0}^{N-1} f[m - n]g[m]$ then the corresponding correlation theorem states $\mathcal{D}\{f \circledast g\} = \overline{F[k]}G[k]$.

Solutions

1 36, 19, 9

Review exercises 24

1 Find the Fourier transforms of

(a) $f(t) = \begin{cases} 1 - t^2 & |t| < 1 \\ 0 & \text{otherwise} \end{cases}$

(b) $f(t) = \begin{cases} \sin t & |t| < \pi \\ 0 & \text{otherwise} \end{cases}$

(c) $f(t) = \begin{cases} 1 & 0 < t < \tau \\ 0 & \text{otherwise} \end{cases}$

(d) $f(t) = \begin{cases} e^{-\alpha t} & t > 0 \\ -e^{\alpha t} & t < 0 \end{cases} \quad \alpha > 0$

2 Find the Fourier integral representations of

(a) $f(t) = \begin{cases} 3t & |t| < 2 \\ 0 & \text{otherwise} \end{cases}$

(b) $f(t) = \begin{cases} 0 & t < 0 \\ 6 & 0 < t < 2 \\ 0 & t > 2 \end{cases}$

3 (a) If $F(\omega) = \mathcal{F}\{f(t)\}$, show that
$\mathcal{F}\{f'(t)\} = j\omega F(\omega)$.

(b) If $F(\omega) = \mathcal{F}\{f(t)\}$, show that
$\mathcal{F}\{f^{(n)}(t)\} = (j\omega)^n F(\omega)$. These results
enable us to calculate the Fourier
transforms of derivatives of functions.

4 If $F(\omega) = \mathcal{F}\{f(t)\}$, show that
$\mathcal{F}\{f(at)\} = \dfrac{1}{a} F\left(\dfrac{\omega}{a}\right)$.

5 If $F(\omega)$ is the Fourier transform of $f(t)$ show
that

(a) $F(0) = \int_{-\infty}^{\infty} f(t)\,dt$.

(b) $f(0) = \dfrac{1}{2\pi} \int_{-\infty}^{\infty} F(\omega)\,d\omega$.

(c) Show that if $f(t)$ is an even function,
$F(\omega) = 2\int_0^{\infty} f(t) \cos \omega t\,dt$.

6 The convolution theorem given in
Section 24.8.1 represents convolution in the

time domain. Convolution can also be
performed in the frequency domain, in which
case the equivalent convolution theorem is

$$\mathcal{F}\{f(t)g(t)\} = \frac{1}{2\pi}[F(\omega) * G(\omega)]$$

Prove the convolution theorem in this form.

7 (a) Given that the Fourier transform of
$f(t) = e^{-\alpha|t|}$ is $\dfrac{2\alpha}{\alpha^2 + \omega^2}$ use the t–ω
duality principle to find the Fourier
transform of $\dfrac{1}{\alpha^2 + t^2}$.

(b) From a table of transforms write down the
Fourier transform of $\cos bt$.

(c) Use the convolution theorem obtained in
Question 6 to find the Fourier transform of
$\dfrac{\cos bt}{\alpha^2 + t^2}$, for $b > 0$.

(d) Using the result in part (c) evaluate the
integral
$$\int_{-\infty}^{\infty} \frac{\cos bt}{\alpha^2 + t^2}\,dt$$

8 Find the d.f.t. of the sequence
$f[n] = \{3, 3, 0, 3\}$. Verify Rayleigh's theorem
for this sequence.

9 Find the linear convolution of the two finite
sequences $f[n] = 3, -1, -7$, and
$g[n] = 4, 0, \frac{1}{2}$.

10 The signum function is defined to be

$$\text{sgn}(t) = \begin{cases} 1 & t > 0 \\ -1 & t < 0 \\ 0 & t = 0 \end{cases}$$

This function can be represented as the
exponential function $e^{-\epsilon t}$, if $t > 0$, and as
$-e^{\epsilon t}$, if $t < 0$, in the limit as $\epsilon \to 0$.

(a) Show that
$$\int_{-\infty}^{\infty} \text{sgn}(t)\,e^{-j\omega t}\,dt = \frac{2}{j\omega}$$

(b) Use the t–ω duality principle to show that

$$\int_{-\infty}^{\infty} \frac{1}{\pi t} e^{-j\omega t}\, dt = -j\,\mathrm{sgn}(\omega)$$

(c) Use the second result in part (b), the convolution theorem and the integral

properties of the delta function to show that

$$\frac{1}{\pi t} * \cos(\alpha t) = \sin(\alpha t)$$

11 Show that $f[n] \circledast g[n] = f[n] \circledast g[-n]$ and hence deduce that a correlation can be expressed in terms of a convolution.

Solutions

1 (a) $\dfrac{4(\sin\omega - \omega\cos\omega)}{\omega^3}$

(b) $-\dfrac{2j\sin\omega\pi}{1-\omega^2}$

(c) $\dfrac{\sin\omega\tau}{\omega} + \dfrac{j(\cos\omega\tau - 1)}{\omega}$

(d) $-\dfrac{2j\omega}{\alpha^2 + \omega^2}$

2 (a) $\dfrac{1}{2\pi}\displaystyle\int_{-\infty}^{\infty}\dfrac{6}{\omega^2}(2j\omega\cos 2\omega - j\sin 2\omega)\, e^{j\omega t}\, d\omega$

(b) $\dfrac{1}{2\pi}\displaystyle\int_{-\infty}^{\infty}\dfrac{6}{\omega}[\sin 2\omega + (\cos 2\omega - 1)j]\, e^{j\omega t}\, d\omega$

7 (a) $\dfrac{\pi}{\alpha} e^{-\alpha|\omega|}$

(c) $\dfrac{\pi}{2\alpha}[e^{-\alpha|\omega+b|} + e^{-\alpha|\omega-b|}]$

(d) $\dfrac{\pi e^{-\alpha b}}{\alpha}$

8 $F[k] = 9, 3, -3, 3$

9 $12, -4, -26.5, -0.5, -3.5$

25 Functions of several variables

Chapter 25   Contents

25.1	Introduction	788
25.2	Functions of more than one variable	788
25.3	Partial derivatives	789
25.4	Higher order derivatives	794
25.5	Partial differential equations	797
25.6	Taylor polynomials and Taylor series in two variables	800
25.7	Maximum and minimum points of a function of two variables	808
	Review exercises	813

25.1 Introduction

In engineering there are many functions which depend upon more than one variable. For example, the voltage on a transmission line depends upon position along the transmission line as well as time. The height of liquid in a tank depends upon the flow rates into and out of the tank. We shall examine some more examples in this chapter.

We have already discussed differentiation of functions of one variable. However, we also need to be able to differentiate functions of two or more variables. This is achieved by allowing one variable to change at a time, holding the others fixed. Differentiation under these conditions is called **partial differentiation**.

25.2 Functions of more than one variable

In Chapter 10 we saw how to differentiate a function $y(x)$ with respect to x. Many standard derivatives were listed and some techniques explained. Since y is a function of x we call y the dependent variable and x the independent variable. The function y depends upon the one variable x. Consider the following example.

The area, A, of a circle depends only upon the radius, r, and is given by

$$A(r) = \pi r^2$$

The rate of change of area w.r.t. the radius is $\dfrac{dA}{dr} = 2\pi r$. In practice functions often depend upon more than one variable. For example, the volume, V, of a cylinder depends upon the radius, r, and the height, h, and is given by

$$V = \pi r^2 h$$

where V is the dependent variable; r and h are independent variables. V is a function of the two independent variables, r and h. We write $V = V(r, h)$.

Example 25.1 Electrical potential inside a cathode ray tube

Within a cathode ray tube the electrical potential, V, will vary with spatial position and time. Given Cartesian coordinates x, y and z, we can write

$$V = V(x, y, z, t)$$

to show this dependence. Note that V is a function of four independent variables.

Example 25.2 Power dissipated in a variable resistor

The power, P, dissipated in a variable resistor depends upon the instantaneous voltage across the resistor, v, and the resistance, r. It is given by

$$P = \frac{v^2}{r}$$

Hence we may write $P = P(v, r)$ to show this dependence. The power is a function of two independent variables.

Figure 25.1
The height of the
surface above the x–y
plane is z.

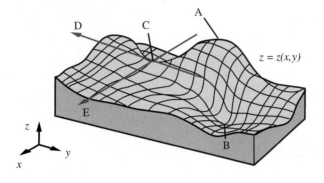

As another example of a function of more than one variable consider a three-dimensional surface as shown in Figure 25.1. The height, z, of the surface above the x–y plane depends upon the x and y coordinates, that is $z = z(x, y)$. If we are given values of x and y, then $z(x, y)$ can be evaluated. This value of z is the height of the surface above the point (x, y). We write, for example, $z(3, -1)$ for the value of z evaluated when $x = 3$ and $y = -1$. The dependent variable, z, is a function of the independent variables x and y.

Some important features are shown in Figure 25.1. The value of z at a **maximum point** is greater than the values of z at nearby points. Point A is such a point. As you move away from A the value of z decreases. A **minimum point** is similarly defined. At a minimum point, the value of z is smaller than the z value at nearby points. This is illustrated by point B. Point C illustrates a **saddle point**. At a saddle point, z increases in one direction, axis D on the figure, but decreases in the direction of axis E. These axes are at right angles to each other. The term 'saddle' is descriptive as a horse saddle has a similar shape. Maximum points, minimum points and saddle points are considered in greater depth in Section 25.7.

25.3 Partial derivatives

Consider

$$z = z(x, y)$$

that is, z is a function of the independent variables x and y. We can differentiate z either w.r.t x, or w.r.t. y. We need symbols to distinguish between these two cases. When finding the derivative w.r.t. x, the other independent variable, y, is held constant and only x changes. Similarly when differentiating w.r.t. y, the variable x is held constant. We write $\dfrac{\partial z}{\partial x}$ to denote differentiation of z w.r.t. x for a constant y. It is called the first partial derivative of z w.r.t. x. Similarly, the first partial derivative of z w.r.t. y is denoted $\dfrac{\partial z}{\partial y}$. Referring to the surface $z(x, y)$, $\dfrac{\partial z}{\partial x}$ gives the rate of change of z moving only in the x direction, and hence y is held fixed.

> If $z = z(x, y)$, then the **first partial derivatives** of z are
>
> $$\frac{\partial z}{\partial x} \quad \text{and} \quad \frac{\partial z}{\partial y}$$

If we wish to evaluate a partial derivative, say $\dfrac{\partial z}{\partial x}$, at a particular point (x_0, y_0), we indicate this by

$$\frac{\partial z}{\partial x}(x_0, y_0) \quad \text{or} \quad \left.\frac{\partial z}{\partial x}\right|_{(x_0, y_0)}$$

just as we did for functions of one variable.

Example 25.3 Given $z(x, y) = x^2 y + \sin x + x \cos y$ find $\dfrac{\partial z}{\partial x}$ and $\dfrac{\partial z}{\partial y}$.

Solution To find $\dfrac{\partial z}{\partial x}$ we differentiate z w.r.t. x, treating y as a constant. Note that since y is a constant then so is $\cos y$.

$$\frac{\partial z}{\partial x} = 2xy + \cos x + \cos y$$

In finding $\dfrac{\partial z}{\partial y}$, x and hence x^2 and $\sin x$ are held fixed, thus

$$\frac{\partial z}{\partial y} = x^2 - x \sin y$$

Example 25.4 Given $z(x, y) = 3\,e^x - 2\,e^y + x^2 y^3$

(a) find $z(1, 1)$

(b) find $\dfrac{\partial z}{\partial x}$ and $\dfrac{\partial z}{\partial y}$ when $x = y = 1$.

Solution (a) $z(1, 1) = 3\,e^1 - 2\,e^1 + 1 = 3.718$

(b)
$$\frac{\partial z}{\partial x} = 3\,e^x + 2xy^3$$

$$\frac{\partial z}{\partial y} = -2\,e^y + 3x^2 y^2$$

When $x = y = 1$, then

$$\frac{\partial z}{\partial x} = 3\,e + 2 = 10.155$$

$$\frac{\partial z}{\partial y} = -2\,e + 3 = -2.437$$

At the point $(1, 1, 3.718)$ on the surface defined by $z(x, y)$, the height of the surface above the x–y plane is increasing in the x direction, and decreasing in the y direction. Note that we could also write

$$\left.\frac{\partial z}{\partial x}\right|_{(1,1)} = 10.155 \quad \text{and} \quad \left.\frac{\partial z}{\partial y}\right|_{(1,1)} = -2.437$$

or

$$\frac{\partial z}{\partial x}(1, 1) = 10.155 \quad \text{and} \quad \frac{\partial z}{\partial y}(1, 1) = -2.437$$

Both notations are in common use.

Example 25.5   **Eddy current losses**

Eddy currents are circulating currents that arise in iron cores of electrical equipment as a result of an a.c. magnetic field. They lead to energy losses given by

$$P_e = k_e f^2 B_{max}^2$$

where

P_e = eddy current losses (W per unit mass),

B_{max} = maximum value of the magnetic field wave (T),

f = frequency of the magnetic field wave (Hz),

k_e = a constant that depends upon factors such as the lamination thickness of the iron core.

Calculate $\dfrac{\partial P_e}{\partial f}$, and $\dfrac{\partial P_e}{\partial B_{max}}$.

Solution $$\frac{\partial P_e}{\partial f} = 2k_e f B_{max}^2 \quad \text{and} \quad \frac{\partial P_e}{\partial B_{max}} = 2k_e f^2 B_{max}$$

Example 25.6   If $V(x, y) = \sin(xy)$, find $\dfrac{\partial V}{\partial x}$ and $\dfrac{\partial V}{\partial y}$.

Solution   To find $\dfrac{\partial V}{\partial x}$ we treat y as a constant. Recalling that $\dfrac{d}{dx}(\sin kx) = k \cos kx$ we find $\dfrac{\partial V}{\partial x} = y \cos(xy)$. To find $\dfrac{\partial V}{\partial y}$ we treat x as a constant. Thus $\dfrac{\partial V}{\partial y} = x \cos(xy)$.

Example 25.7   Find the first partial derivatives of z where

      (a) $z(x, y) = yx\,e^x$

      (b) $z(x, y) = x^2 \sin(xy)$

Solution   (a) To find $\dfrac{\partial z}{\partial x}$ we must treat y as a constant. However, the differentiation of the factor $x\,e^x$ will require use of the product rule. We find

$$\frac{\partial z}{\partial x} = y\frac{\partial}{\partial x}(x\,e^x)$$

$$= y((1)\,e^x + x\,e^x)$$

$$= y\,e^x(x + 1)$$

To find $\dfrac{\partial z}{\partial y}$ the variable x is held constant and so

$$\frac{\partial z}{\partial y} = x\,e^x$$

(b) Observe the product term in the variable x which means we shall need to use the product rule. We find

$$\frac{\partial z}{\partial x} = 2x \sin(xy) + x^2(y \cos(xy)) = 2x \sin(xy) + x^2 y \cos(xy)$$

To find $\dfrac{\partial z}{\partial y}$ we treat x as a constant and find

$$\frac{\partial z}{\partial y} = x^2(x \cos(xy)) = x^3 \cos(xy)$$

Exercises 25.3

1   Find the first partial derivatives of

    (a) $z = 2x + 3y$

    (b) $z = x - y + x^2$

    (c) $z = x^2 + y^2 + 3$

    (d) $z = xy - 1$

    (e) $z = x^2 y + xy^2$

    (f) $z = x^3 + 2x^2 y - 4xy^2 + 2y^3$

2   Find the first partial derivatives of

    (a) $z = \dfrac{x}{y}$

    (b) $z = \sqrt{x}\,y$

    (c) $z = \dfrac{y^2}{x^3} + 2$

    (d) $z = \dfrac{1}{xy}$

    (e) $z = \dfrac{3x^2}{y} - \dfrac{\sqrt{y}}{x}$

(f) $z = \sqrt{xy} - 3(x + y)$

3 Find the first partial derivatives of

(a) $z = 2\sin x + 3\cos y$

(b) $z = x\sin y$

(c) $z = x\tan y - y^2\sin x$

(d) $z = xy\sin y$

(e) $z = \sin(x + y)$

(f) $z = 4\cos(4x - 6y)$

(g) $z = \dfrac{\sin y}{x}$

4 Find the first partial derivatives of y. Note that y is a function of x and t.

(a) $y = t\,e^x$

(b) $y = x^2\,e^{-t}$

(c) $y = t\,e^t + x$

(d) $y = 3x^2\,e^{2t} + t^3\,e^{-x}$

(e) $y = e^{xt}$

(f) $y = e^{2x+3t}$

5 Find the first partial derivatives of z where

(a) $z = \sqrt{x^2 + y^2}$

(b) $z = \dfrac{x}{2x + 3y}$

(c) $z = \sin\left(\dfrac{x}{y}\right)$

(d) $z = e^{3xy}$

(e) $z = \ln(2x - 3y)$

(f) $z = \ln(xy)$

(g) $z = x\ln(xy)$

(h) $z = x\ln\left(\dfrac{y}{x}\right)$

6 Evaluate the first partial derivatives of f at $x = 1, y = 2$.

(a) $f = 3x^2y - 2xy$

(b) $f = \dfrac{x + y}{y}$

(c) $f = 2\sin(3x + 2y)$

(d) $f = 2e^{xy}$

(e) $f = y\ln x + \ln(xy)$

(f) $f = \sqrt{3x + y}$

7 Given

$$f(r, h) = 2r^2h - \sqrt{rh}$$

evaluate the first partial derivatives of f when $r = 2, h = 1$.

Solutions

1 (a) $\dfrac{\partial z}{\partial x} = 2,\ \dfrac{\partial z}{\partial y} = 3$

(b) $1 + 2x, -1$

(c) $2x, 2y$

(d) y, x

(e) $2xy + y^2, x^2 + 2xy$

(f) $3x^2 + 4xy - 4y^2, 2x^2 - 8xy + 6y^2$

2 (a) $\dfrac{\partial z}{\partial x} = \dfrac{1}{y}, \dfrac{\partial z}{\partial y} = -\dfrac{x}{y^2}$

(b) $\dfrac{y}{2\sqrt{x}}, \sqrt{x}$

(c) $-\dfrac{3y^2}{x^4}, \dfrac{2y}{x^3}$

(d) $-\dfrac{1}{x^2 y}, -\dfrac{1}{xy^2}$

(e) $\dfrac{6x}{y} + \dfrac{\sqrt{y}}{x^2}, -\dfrac{3x^2}{y^2} - \dfrac{1}{2x\sqrt{y}}$

(f) $\dfrac{1}{2}\sqrt{\dfrac{y}{x}} - 3, \dfrac{1}{2}\sqrt{\dfrac{x}{y}} - 3$

3 (a) $\dfrac{\partial z}{\partial x} = 2\cos x, \dfrac{\partial z}{\partial y} = -3\sin y$

(b) $\sin y, x\cos y$

(c) $\tan y - y^2\cos x, x\sec^2 y - 2y\sin x$

(d) $y\sin y, x\sin y + xy\cos y$

(e) $\cos(x + y), \cos(x + y)$

(f) $-16\sin(4x - 6y), 24\sin(4x - 6y)$

(g) $-\dfrac{\sin y}{x^2}, \dfrac{\cos y}{x}$

4 (a) $\dfrac{\partial y}{\partial x} = t\,e^x, \dfrac{\partial y}{\partial t} = e^x$

(b) $2x\,e^{-t}, -x^2\,e^{-t}$

(c) $1, e^t(1+t)$

(d) $6x\,e^{2t} - t^3\,e^{-x}, 6x^2\,e^{2t} + 3t^2\,e^{-x}$

(e) $t\,e^{xt}, x\,e^{xt}$

(f) $2\,e^{2x+3t}, 3\,e^{2x+3t}$

(f) $\dfrac{1}{x}, \dfrac{1}{y}$

(g) $1 + \ln(xy), \dfrac{x}{y}$

(h) $\ln\left(\dfrac{y}{x}\right) - 1, \dfrac{x}{y}$

5 (a) $\dfrac{\partial z}{\partial x} = \dfrac{x}{\sqrt{x^2 + y^2}}, \dfrac{\partial z}{\partial y} = \dfrac{y}{\sqrt{x^2 + y^2}}$

(b) $\dfrac{3y}{(2x+3y)^2}, -\dfrac{3x}{(2x+3y)^2}$

(c) $\dfrac{1}{y}\cos\left(\dfrac{x}{y}\right), -\dfrac{x}{y^2}\cos\left(\dfrac{x}{y}\right)$

(d) $3y\,e^{3xy}, 3x\,e^{3xy}$

(e) $\dfrac{2}{2x-3y}, -\dfrac{3}{2x-3y}$

6 (a) $\dfrac{\partial f}{\partial x}(1,2) = 8, \dfrac{\partial f}{\partial y}(1,2) = 1$

(b) $0.5, -0.25$

(c) $4.5234, 3.0156$

(d) $29.5562, 14.7781$

(e) $3, 0.5$

(f) $0.6708, 0.2236$

7 $\dfrac{\partial f}{\partial r}(2,1) = 7.6464, \dfrac{\partial f}{\partial h}(2,1) = 6.5858$

25.4 Higher order derivatives

Just as functions of one variable have second and higher derivatives, so do functions of several variables. Consider

$$z = z(x, y)$$

The first partial derivatives of z are $\dfrac{\partial z}{\partial x}$ and $\dfrac{\partial z}{\partial y}$. The second partial derivatives are found by differentiating the first derivatives. We can differentiate first partial derivatives either w.r.t. x or w.r.t. y to obtain various second partial derivatives:

$$\text{differentiating } \frac{\partial z}{\partial x} \text{ w.r.t. } x \text{ produces } \frac{\partial}{\partial x}\left(\frac{\partial z}{\partial x}\right) = \frac{\partial^2 z}{\partial x^2}$$

$$\text{differentiating } \frac{\partial z}{\partial x} \text{ w.r.t. } y \text{ produces } \frac{\partial}{\partial y}\left(\frac{\partial z}{\partial x}\right) = \frac{\partial^2 z}{\partial y \partial x}$$

$$\text{differentiating } \frac{\partial z}{\partial y} \text{ w.r.t. } x \text{ produces } \frac{\partial}{\partial x}\left(\frac{\partial z}{\partial y}\right) = \frac{\partial^2 z}{\partial x \partial y}$$

$$\text{differentiating } \frac{\partial z}{\partial y} \text{ w.r.t. } y \text{ produces } \frac{\partial}{\partial y}\left(\frac{\partial z}{\partial y}\right) = \frac{\partial^2 z}{\partial y^2}$$

For most common functions, the mixed derivatives $\dfrac{\partial^2 z}{\partial y \partial x}$ and $\dfrac{\partial^2 z}{\partial x \partial y}$ are equal.

Example 25.8 Given

$$z(x, y) = 3xy^3 - 2xy + \sin x$$

find all second partial derivatives of z.

Solution $\dfrac{\partial z}{\partial x} = 3y^3 - 2y + \cos x$ $\qquad$ $\dfrac{\partial z}{\partial y} = 9xy^2 - 2x$

$$\frac{\partial^2 z}{\partial x^2} = \frac{\partial}{\partial x}\left(\frac{\partial z}{\partial x}\right) = -\sin x \qquad \frac{\partial^2 z}{\partial y^2} = \frac{\partial}{\partial y}\left(\frac{\partial z}{\partial y}\right) = 18xy$$

$$\frac{\partial^2 z}{\partial x \partial y} = \frac{\partial}{\partial x}\left(\frac{\partial z}{\partial y}\right) = 9y^2 - 2 \qquad \frac{\partial^2 z}{\partial y \partial x} = \frac{\partial}{\partial y}\left(\frac{\partial z}{\partial x}\right) = 9y^2 - 2$$

Note that $\dfrac{\partial^2 z}{\partial x \partial y} = \dfrac{\partial^2 z}{\partial y \partial x}$.

Example 25.9 Given

$$H(x, t) = 3x^2 + t^2 + e^{xt}$$

verify that $\dfrac{\partial^2 H}{\partial x \partial t} = \dfrac{\partial^2 H}{\partial t \partial x}$.

Solution $\dfrac{\partial H}{\partial x} = 6x + t\,e^{xt}$ $\qquad$ $\dfrac{\partial H}{\partial t} = 2t + x\,e^{xt}$

$$\frac{\partial^2 H}{\partial t \partial x} = \frac{\partial}{\partial t}\left(\frac{\partial H}{\partial x}\right) = \frac{\partial}{\partial t}(6x + t\,e^{xt}) = e^{xt} + tx\,e^{xt}$$

$$\frac{\partial^2 H}{\partial x \partial t} = \frac{\partial}{\partial x}\left(\frac{\partial H}{\partial t}\right) = \frac{\partial}{\partial x}(2t + x\,e^{xt}) = e^{xt} + xt\,e^{xt}$$

Third, fourth and higher derivatives are found in a similar way to finding second derivatives. The third derivatives are found by differentiating the second derivatives and so on.

Example 25.10 Find all third derivatives of $f(r, s) = \sin(2r) - 3r^4 s^2$.

Solution $\dfrac{\partial f}{\partial r} = 2\cos(2r) - 12r^3 s^2$ $\qquad$ $\dfrac{\partial f}{\partial s} = -6r^4 s$

$$\frac{\partial^2 f}{\partial r^2} = -4\sin(2r) - 36r^2 s^2 \qquad \frac{\partial^2 f}{\partial s^2} = -6r^4$$

$$\frac{\partial^2 f}{\partial r \partial s} = -24r^3 s$$

The third derivatives are $\dfrac{\partial^3 f}{\partial r^3}$, $\dfrac{\partial^3 f}{\partial r^2 \partial s}$, $\dfrac{\partial^3 f}{\partial r \partial s^2}$ and $\dfrac{\partial^3 f}{\partial s^3}$, and these are found by differentiating the second derivatives.

$$\frac{\partial^3 f}{\partial r^3} = \frac{\partial}{\partial r}\left(\frac{\partial^2 f}{\partial r^2}\right) = -8\cos(2r) - 72rs^2$$

$$\frac{\partial^3 f}{\partial r^2 \partial s} = \frac{\partial}{\partial r}\left(\frac{\partial^2 f}{\partial r \partial s}\right) = -72r^2 s$$

$$\frac{\partial^3 f}{\partial r \partial s^2} = \frac{\partial}{\partial r}\left(\frac{\partial^2 f}{\partial s^2}\right) = -24r^3$$

$$\frac{\partial^3 f}{\partial s^3} = \frac{\partial}{\partial s}\left(\frac{\partial^2 f}{\partial s^2}\right) = 0$$

Note that the mixed derivatives can be calculated in a variety of ways.

$$\frac{\partial^3 f}{\partial r^2 \partial s} = \frac{\partial}{\partial r}\left(\frac{\partial^2 f}{\partial r \partial s}\right) = \frac{\partial}{\partial s}\left(\frac{\partial^2 f}{\partial r^2}\right)$$

$$\frac{\partial^3 f}{\partial r \partial s^2} = \frac{\partial}{\partial r}\left(\frac{\partial^2 f}{\partial s^2}\right) = \frac{\partial}{\partial s}\left(\frac{\partial^2 f}{\partial r \partial s}\right)$$

Exercises 25.4

1 Calculate all second derivatives of v where

$$v(h, r) = r^2\sqrt{h}$$

2 Find the second partial derivatives of f given

(a) $f = x^2 y + y^3$

(b) $f = 2x^4 y^3 - 3x^3 y^5$

(c) $f = 4\sqrt{x}y^2$

(d) $f = \dfrac{x^2 + 1}{y}$

(e) $f = \dfrac{3x^3}{\sqrt{y}}$

(f) $f = 4\sqrt{xy}$

3 Find all second partial derivatives of

(a) $z = x e^{2y}$

(b) $z = 2\sin(xy)$

(c) $z = x\cos(2x + 3y)$

(d) $z = y\sin(4xy)$

(e) $z = e^x \sin y$

(f) $z = e^{3x-y}$

(g) $z = e^{xy}$

4 Find all second partial derivatives of

(a) $z = (3x - 2y)^{20}$

(b) $z = \sqrt{2x + 5y}$

(c) $z = \sin(x^2 + y^2)$

(d) $z = \ln(2x + 5y)$

(e) $z = \dfrac{1}{3x - 2y}$

5 Find all third partial derivatives of z where

$$z(x, y) = \frac{x^2}{y + 1}$$

6 Evaluate all second partial derivatives of f at $x = 2, y = 1$.

(a) $f = y e^x$

(b) $f = \sin(2x - y)$

(c) $f = \ln\left(\dfrac{y}{x}\right)$

Solutions

1 $\dfrac{\partial^2 v}{\partial h^2} = -\dfrac{r^2}{4h^{3/2}}, \dfrac{\partial^2 v}{\partial h \partial r} = \dfrac{r}{\sqrt{h}}, \dfrac{\partial^2 v}{\partial r^2} = 2\sqrt{h}$

2 (a) $\dfrac{\partial^2 f}{\partial x^2} = 2y, \dfrac{\partial^2 f}{\partial x \partial y} = 2x, \dfrac{\partial^2 f}{\partial y^2} = 6y$

(b) $24x^2 y^3 - 18xy^5,$
$24x^3 y^2 - 45x^2 y^4,$
$12x^4 y - 60x^3 y^3$

(c) $-x^{-3/2} y^2, 4x^{-1/2} y, 8\sqrt{x}$

(d) $\dfrac{2}{y}, -\dfrac{2x}{y^2}, \dfrac{2(x^2 + 1)}{y^3}$

(e) $18xy^{-1/2}, -\tfrac{9}{2}x^2 y^{-3/2}, \tfrac{9}{4}x^3 y^{-5/2}$

(f) $-x^{-3/2} y^{1/2}, x^{-1/2} y^{-1/2}, -x^{1/2} y^{-3/2}$

3 (a) $\dfrac{\partial^2 z}{\partial x^2} = 0, \dfrac{\partial^2 z}{\partial x \partial y} = 2e^{2y}, \dfrac{\partial^2 z}{\partial y^2} = 4x e^{2y}$

(b) $-2y^2 \sin(xy),$
$2\cos(xy) - 2xy \sin(xy),$
$-2x^2 \sin(xy)$

(c) $-4\sin(2x + 3y) - 4x \cos(2x + 3y),$
$-3\sin(2x + 3y) - 6x \cos(2x + 3y),$
$-9x \cos(2x + 3y)$

(d) $-16y^3 \sin(4xy),$
$8y \cos(4xy) - 16xy^2 \sin(4xy),$
$8x \cos(4xy) - 16x^2 y \sin(4xy)$

(e) $e^x \sin y, e^x \cos y, -e^x \sin y$

(f) $9e^{3x-y}, -3e^{3x-y}, e^{3x-y}$

(g) $y^2 e^{xy}, e^{xy}(1 + xy), x^2 e^{xy}$

4 (a) $\dfrac{\partial^2 z}{\partial x^2} = 3420(3x - 2y)^{18},$

$\dfrac{\partial^2 z}{\partial x \partial y} = -2280(3x - 2y)^{18},$

$\dfrac{\partial^2 z}{\partial y^2} = 1520(3x - 2y)^{18}$

(b) $-(2x + 5y)^{-3/2},$
$-\tfrac{5}{2}(2x + 5y)^{-3/2},$
$-\tfrac{25}{4}(2x + 5y)^{-3/2}$

(c) $2\cos(x^2 + y^2) - 4x^2 \sin(x^2 + y^2),$
$-4xy \sin(x^2 + y^2),$
$2\cos(x^2 + y^2) - 4y^2 \sin(x^2 + y^2)$

(d) $-\dfrac{4}{(2x + 5y)^2},$

$-\dfrac{10}{(2x + 5y)^2},$

$-\dfrac{25}{(2x + 5y)^2}$

(e) $\dfrac{18}{(3x - 2y)^3}, -\dfrac{12}{(3x - 2y)^3}, \dfrac{8}{(3x - 2y)^3}$

5 $\dfrac{\partial^3 z}{\partial x^3} = 0, \dfrac{\partial^3 z}{\partial x^2 \partial y} = -\dfrac{2}{(y + 1)^2},$

$\dfrac{\partial^3 z}{\partial x \partial y^2} = \dfrac{4x}{(y + 1)^3}, \dfrac{\partial^3 z}{\partial y^3} = -\dfrac{6x^2}{(y + 1)^4}$

6 (a) $\dfrac{\partial^2 f}{\partial x^2}(2, 1) = 7.3891,$

$\dfrac{\partial^2 f}{\partial x \partial y}(2, 1) = 7.3891,$

$\dfrac{\partial^2 f}{\partial y^2}(2, 1) = 0$

(b) $-0.5645, 0.2822, -0.1411$

(c) $0.25, 0, -1$

25.5 Partial differential equations

Partial differential equations (p.d.e.s) occur in many areas of engineering. If a variable depends upon two or more independent variables, then it is likely this dependence can be described by a p.d.e. The independent variables are often time, t, and space coordinates x, y, z.

One example is the wave equation. The displacement, u, of the wave depends upon time and position. Under certain assumptions, the displacement of a wave travelling in one direction satisfies

$$\frac{\partial^2 u}{\partial t^2} = c^2 \frac{\partial^2 u}{\partial x^2}$$

where c is the speed of the wave. This p.d.e. is called the one-dimensional wave equation. Under prescribed conditions the subsequent displacement of the wave can be calculated as a function of position and time.

Example 25.11

Verify that

$$u(x, t) = \sin(x + 2t)$$

is a solution of the one-dimensional wave equation

$$\frac{\partial^2 u}{\partial t^2} = 4 \frac{\partial^2 u}{\partial x^2}$$

Solution

The first partial derivatives are calculated.

$$\frac{\partial u}{\partial x} = \cos(x + 2t) \qquad \frac{\partial u}{\partial t} = 2\cos(x + 2t)$$

The second derivatives, $\dfrac{\partial^2 u}{\partial x^2}$ and $\dfrac{\partial^2 u}{\partial t^2}$, are now found.

$$\frac{\partial^2 u}{\partial x^2} = -\sin(x + 2t) \qquad \frac{\partial^2 u}{\partial t^2} = -4\sin(x + 2t)$$

Now

$$\frac{\partial^2 u}{\partial t^2} = -4\sin(x + 2t) = 4[-\sin(x + 2t)] = 4\frac{\partial^2 u}{\partial x^2}$$

Hence $u(x, t) = \sin(x + 2t)$ is a solution of the given wave equation.

Another equally important p.d.e. is Laplace's equation. This equation is used extensively in electrostatics. Under certain conditions the electrostatic potential in a region is described by a function $\phi(x, y)$ which satisfies Laplace's equation in two dimensions.

$$\frac{\partial^2 \phi}{\partial x^2} + \frac{\partial^2 \phi}{\partial y^2} = 0$$

This equation is so important that a whole area of applied mathematics, called potential theory, is devoted to the study of its solution.

Example 25.12

Verify that

$$\phi(x, y, z) = \frac{1}{\sqrt{x^2 + y^2 + z^2}}$$

satisfies the three-dimensional Laplace's equation

$$\frac{\partial^2 \phi}{\partial x^2} + \frac{\partial^2 \phi}{\partial y^2} + \frac{\partial^2 \phi}{\partial z^2} = 0$$

Solution We begin by calculating the first partial derivative, $\dfrac{\partial \phi}{\partial x}$. We are given

$$\phi = (x^2 + y^2 + z^2)^{-1/2}$$

and so

$$\frac{\partial \phi}{\partial x} = -\frac{1}{2}(x^2 + y^2 + z^2)^{-3/2}(2x) = -x(x^2 + y^2 + z^2)^{-3/2}$$

We use the product rule to find $\dfrac{\partial^2 \phi}{\partial x^2}$.

$$\frac{\partial^2 \phi}{\partial x^2} = -1(x^2 + y^2 + z^2)^{-3/2} - x\left(-\tfrac{3}{2}\right)(x^2 + y^2 + z^2)^{-5/2}2x$$

$$= (x^2 + y^2 + z^2)^{-5/2}[-(x^2 + y^2 + z^2) + 3x^2]$$

By a similar analysis we have

$$\frac{\partial^2 \phi}{\partial y^2} = (x^2 + y^2 + z^2)^{-5/2}[-(x^2 + y^2 + z^2) + 3y^2]$$

$$\frac{\partial^2 \phi}{\partial z^2} = (x^2 + y^2 + z^2)^{-5/2}[-(x^2 + y^2 + z^2) + 3z^2]$$

So

$$\frac{\partial^2 \phi}{\partial x^2} + \frac{\partial^2 \phi}{\partial y^2} + \frac{\partial^2 \phi}{\partial z^2} = (x^2 + y^2 + z^2)^{-5/2}[-3(x^2 + y^2 + z^2) + 3x^2 + 3y^2 + 3z^2]$$

$$= 0$$

Hence $\phi = \dfrac{1}{\sqrt{x^2 + y^2 + z^2}}$ is a solution of the three-dimensional Laplace's equation.

The transmission equation is another important p.d.e. The potential, u, in a transmission cable with leakage satisfies a p.d.e. of the form

$$\frac{\partial^2 u}{\partial x^2} = A\frac{\partial^2 u}{\partial t^2} + B\frac{\partial u}{\partial t} + Cu$$

where A, B and C are constants relating to the physical properties of the cable.

The analytical and numerical solution of p.d.e.s is an important topic in engineering. Coverage is beyond the scope of this book.

Exercises 25.5

1 Verify that

$$u(x, y) = x^2 + xy$$

is a solution of the p.d.e.

$$\frac{\partial u}{\partial x} - 2\frac{\partial u}{\partial y} = y$$

2 Verify that

$$\phi = \sin(xy)$$

satisfies the equation

$$\frac{\partial^2 \phi}{\partial x^2} + \frac{\partial^2 \phi}{\partial y^2} + (x^2 + y^2)\phi = 0$$

3 Verify that

$$u(x, y) = x^3 y + xy^3$$

is a solution of the equation

$$xy\frac{\partial^2 u}{\partial x \partial y} + x\frac{\partial u}{\partial x} + y\frac{\partial u}{\partial y} = 7u$$

4 Verify that

$$u(x, y) = xy + \frac{x}{y}$$

is a solution of

$$y\frac{\partial^2 u}{\partial y^2} + 2x\frac{\partial^2 u}{\partial x \partial y} = 2x$$

5 Verify that

$$\phi(x, y) = x \sin y + e^x \cos y$$

satisfies

$$\frac{\partial^2 \phi}{\partial x^2} + \frac{\partial^2 \phi}{\partial y^2} = -x \sin y$$

6 Given

$$\phi = \sqrt{x^2 + y^2}$$

(a) Show

$$\frac{\partial^2 \phi}{\partial x^2} = y^2(x^2 + y^2)^{-3/2}$$

(b) Verify that ϕ is a solution of

$$\frac{\partial^2 \phi}{\partial x^2} + \frac{\partial^2 \phi}{\partial y^2} = (x^2 + y^2)^{-1/2}$$

25.6 Taylor polynomials and Taylor series in two variables

In Chapter 18 we introduced Taylor polynomials and Taylor series for functions of a single variable. We now extend this to include functions of two variables. Recall the main idea behind Taylor polynomials and series for a function of one variable. Knowing the values of a function, $f(x)$, and its derivatives at $x = a$ we can write down the Taylor polynomial generated by f about $x = a$. This polynomial approximates to the function f. The values of the Taylor polynomial and the function are usually in close agreement for values of x near to $x = a$. To put it another way, knowing the value of f and its derivatives at $x = a$ allows us to estimate the value of f near to $x = a$.

The same idea holds when f is a function of two variables, x and y. If we know the value of f and its partial derivatives at a point $x = a$, $y = b$, then the Taylor polynomials allow us to estimate f at points near to (a, b).

25.6.1 First-order Taylor polynomial in two variables

Suppose f is a function of two independent variables, x and y, and that the values of f, $\frac{\partial f}{\partial x}$ and $\frac{\partial f}{\partial y}$ are known at the point $x = a$, $y = b$, that is we know

$$f(a, b) \qquad \frac{\partial f}{\partial x}(a, b) \qquad \frac{\partial f}{\partial y}(a, b)$$

The first-order Taylor polynomial, $p_1(x, y)$, generated by f about (a, b) is given by

$$p_1(x, y) = f(a, b) + (x - a)\frac{\partial f}{\partial x}(a, b) + (y - b)\frac{\partial f}{\partial y}(a, b)$$

We note the following properties of a first-order Taylor polynomial:

(1) The values of the Taylor polynomial and the function are identical at the point (a, b).

(2) The values of the first partial derivatives of the Taylor polynomial and the function are identical at the point (a, b).

(3) The highest derivative needed to calculate the Taylor polynomial is the first derivative.

(4) The first-order Taylor polynomial contains only linear terms; that is, there are no powers of x or y higher than 1.

The first-order Taylor polynomial represents a plane which is tangent to the surface $f(x, y)$ at (a, b).
   We can use $p_1(x, y)$ to estimate the value of f near to (a, b).

Example 25.13   A function, f, is such that

$$f(3, 1) = 2 \qquad \frac{\partial f}{\partial x}(3, 1) = -1 \qquad \frac{\partial f}{\partial y}(3, 1) = 4$$

(a) State the first-order Taylor polynomial generated by f about $(3, 1)$.

(b) Estimate the values of $f(3.5, 1.2)$ and $f(3.2, 0.7)$.

(c) Verify that the Taylor polynomial and the function have identical values at $(3, 1)$.

(d) Verify that the first partial derivatives of the Taylor polynomial and the function are identical at $(3, 1)$.

Solution   (a) In this example $a = 3$ and $b = 1$. Hence

$$p_1(x, y) = f(3, 1) + (x - 3)\frac{\partial f}{\partial x}(3, 1) + (y - 1)\frac{\partial f}{\partial y}(3, 1)$$

$$= 2 + (x - 3)(-1) + (y - 1)4$$

$$= 4y - x + 1$$

The first-order Taylor polynomial generated by f about $(3, 1)$ is

$$p_1(x, y) = 4y - x + 1$$

(b) We use $p_1(x, y)$ to estimate $f(3.5, 1.2)$ and $f(3.2, 0.7)$.

$$p_1(3.5, 1.2) = 4(1.2) - 3.5 + 1 = 2.3$$
$$p_1(3.2, 0.7) = 4(0.7) - 3.2 + 1 = 0.6$$

Hence 2.3 is an estimate of $f(3.5, 1.2)$ and 0.6 is an estimate of $f(3.2, 0.7)$.

(c) We are given $f(3, 1) = 2$. Also

$$p_1(3, 1) = 4(1) - 3 + 1 = 2$$

and so $f(3, 1) = p_1(3, 1)$.

(d) We are given $\dfrac{\partial f}{\partial x}(3, 1) = -1$ and $\dfrac{\partial f}{\partial y}(3, 1) = 4$. Now

$$p_1(x, y) = 4y - x + 1$$

and so

$$\frac{\partial p_1}{\partial x} = -1 \qquad \frac{\partial p_1}{\partial y} = 4$$

Hence

$$\frac{\partial p_1}{\partial x}(3, 1) = \frac{\partial f}{\partial x}(3, 1) = -1 \qquad \frac{\partial p_1}{\partial y}(3, 1) = \frac{\partial f}{\partial y}(3, 1) = 4$$

Example 25.14 A function, $f(x, y)$, is defined by

$$f(x, y) = x^2 + xy - y^3$$

(a) State the first-order Taylor polynomial generated by f about $(1, 2)$.

(b) Verify that the Taylor polynomial in (a) and the function f have identical values at $(1, 2)$.

(c) Verify that the first partial derivatives of the Taylor polynomial and f have identical values at $(1, 2)$.

(d) Estimate $f(1.1, 1.9)$ using the Taylor polynomial. Compare this with the true value.

Solution (a) We are given $f = x^2 + xy - y^3$ and so

$$\frac{\partial f}{\partial x} = 2x + y \qquad \frac{\partial f}{\partial y} = x - 3y^2$$

Evaluating these at the point $(1, 2)$ gives

$$f(1, 2) = -5 \qquad \frac{\partial f}{\partial x}(1, 2) = 4 \qquad \frac{\partial f}{\partial y}(1, 2) = -11$$

Putting $a = 1$ and $b = 2$ in the formula for $p_1(x, y)$ we are able to write down the Taylor polynomial:

$$p_1(x, y) = f(1, 2) + (x - 1)\frac{\partial f}{\partial x}(1, 2) + (y - 2)\frac{\partial f}{\partial y}(1, 2)$$

$$= -5 + (x - 1)4 + (y - 2)(-11)$$

$$= 4x - 11y + 13$$

The first-order Taylor polynomial is $p_1(x, y) = 4x - 11y + 13$.

(b) We can evaluate the Taylor polynomial and the function at $(1, 2)$.

$$p_1(1, 2) = 4 - 22 + 13 = -5 \qquad f(1, 2) = -5$$

Hence $p_1(1, 2) = f(1, 2)$; that is, the Taylor polynomial and the function have identical values at $(1, 2)$.

(c) The first partial derivatives of $p_1(x, y)$ are found.

$$\frac{\partial p_1}{\partial x} = 4 \qquad \frac{\partial p_1}{\partial y} = -11 \qquad \frac{\partial f}{\partial x}(1, 2) = 4 \qquad \frac{\partial f}{\partial y}(1, 2) = -11$$

Hence the first partial derivatives of p_1 and f are identical at $(1, 2)$.

(d) $p_1(1.1, 1.9) = 4(1.1) - 11(1.9) + 13 = -3.5$

$f(1.1, 1.9) = (1.1)^2 + (1.1)(1.9) - (1.9)^3 = -3.559$

The values of the Taylor polynomial and the function are in close agreement near to the point $(1, 2)$.

25.6.2 Second-order Taylor polynomial in two variables

Given a function, f, and its first and second partial derivatives at (a, b) we can write down the second-order Taylor polynomial, $p_2(x, y)$.

$$p_2(x, y) = f(a, b) + (x - a)\frac{\partial f}{\partial x}(a, b) + (y - b)\frac{\partial f}{\partial y}(a, b)$$

$$+ \frac{1}{2!}\left((x-a)^2\frac{\partial^2 f}{\partial x^2}(a, b) + 2(x-a)(y-b)\frac{\partial^2 f}{\partial x \partial y}(a, b) + (y-b)^2\frac{\partial^2 f}{\partial y^2}(a, b)\right)$$

We note the following properties of the second-order Taylor polynomial:

(1) The values of the Taylor polynomial and the function are identical at (a, b).

(2) The values of the first partial derivatives of the Taylor polynomial and the function are identical at (a, b).

(3) The values of the second partial derivatives of the Taylor polynomial and the function are identical at (a, b).

(4) The second-order Taylor polynomial contains quadratic terms, that is terms involving x^2, y^2 and xy.

Example 25.15

A function, f, and its first and second partial derivatives are evaluated at $(2, -1)$. The values are

$$f = 3 \quad \frac{\partial f}{\partial x} = 4 \quad \frac{\partial f}{\partial y} = -3 \quad \frac{\partial^2 f}{\partial x^2} = 1 \quad \frac{\partial^2 f}{\partial x \partial y} = 2 \quad \frac{\partial^2 f}{\partial y^2} = -1$$

(a) State the second-order Taylor polynomial generated by f about $(2, -1)$.

(b) Estimate $f(1.8, -0.9)$.

(c) Verify that the Taylor polynomial and f have identical values at $(2, -1)$.

(d) Verify that the first partial derivatives of the Taylor polynomial and f are identical at $(2, -1)$.

(e) Verify that the second partial derivatives of the Taylor polynomial and f are identical at $(2, -1)$.

Solution

(a) We put $a = 2$ and $b = -1$ in the formula for $p_2(x, y)$.

$$p_2(x, y) = f + (x - 2)\frac{\partial f}{\partial x} + (y + 1)\frac{\partial f}{\partial y}$$

$$+ \frac{1}{2}\left((x - 2)^2\frac{\partial^2 f}{\partial x^2} + 2(x - 2)(y + 1)\frac{\partial^2 f}{\partial x \partial y} + (y + 1)^2\frac{\partial^2 f}{\partial y^2}\right)$$

where f and its derivatives are evaluated at $(2, -1)$. So

$$p_2(x, y) = 3 + (x - 2)4 + (y + 1)(-3) + \tfrac{1}{2}\{(x - 2)^2 + 2(x - 2)(y + 1)2$$

$$+ (y + 1)^2(-1)\} = \frac{x^2}{2} - \frac{y^2}{2} + 2xy + 4x - 8y - \frac{21}{2}$$

(b) The value of $p_2(1.8, -0.9)$ is an estimate of $f(1.8, -0.9)$.

$$p_2(1.8, -0.9) = \frac{(1.8)^2}{2} - \frac{(-0.9)^2}{2} + 2(1.8)(-0.9) + 4(1.8) - 8(-0.9) - \frac{21}{2}$$

$$= 1.875$$

(c) $p_2(2, -1) = \frac{2^2}{2} - \frac{(-1)^2}{2} + 2(2)(-1) + 4(2) - 8(-1) - \frac{21}{2} = 3$

$f(2, -1) = 3$

Hence $p_2(2, -1) = f(2, -1)$; that is, the Taylor polynomial and the function have identical values at $(2, -1)$.

(d) The first partial derivatives of p_2 are

$$\frac{\partial p_2}{\partial x} = x + 2y + 4 \qquad \frac{\partial p_2}{\partial y} = -y + 2x - 8$$

so

$$\frac{\partial p_2}{\partial x}(2, -1) = 2 + 2(-1) + 4 = 4 \qquad \frac{\partial p_2}{\partial y}(2, -1) = 1 + 4 - 8 = -3$$

Hence

$$\frac{\partial p_2}{\partial x}(2, -1) = \frac{\partial f}{\partial x}(2, -1) \qquad \frac{\partial p_2}{\partial y}(2, -1) = \frac{\partial f}{\partial y}(2, -1)$$

that is, the first partial derivatives of the Taylor polynomial and the function have identical values at $(2, -1)$.

(e) The second partial derivatives of p_2 are found.

$$\frac{\partial^2 p_2}{\partial x^2} = 1 \qquad \frac{\partial^2 p_2}{\partial x \partial y} = 2 \qquad \frac{\partial^2 p_2}{\partial y^2} = -1$$

These values are identical to the second partial derivatives of f at $(2, -1)$.

Example 25.16 A function f is given by

$$f(x, y) = x^3 + x^2 y + y^4$$

(a) State the second-order Taylor polynomial generated by f about $(1, 1)$.

(b) Use the polynomial to estimate $f(1.2, 0.9)$. Compare this value with the true value.

(c) Verify that the second partial derivatives of the function and the Taylor polynomial are identical at $(1, 1)$.

Solution (a) Here $a = 1$ and $b = 1$. We are given that $f = x^3 + x^2 y + y^4$ and so

$$\frac{\partial f}{\partial x} = 3x^2 + 2xy \qquad \frac{\partial f}{\partial y} = x^2 + 4y^3 \qquad \frac{\partial^2 f}{\partial x^2} = 6x + 2y$$

$$\frac{\partial^2 f}{\partial x \partial y} = 2x \qquad \frac{\partial^2 f}{\partial y^2} = 12y^2$$

Evaluation of f and its derivatives at $(1, 1)$ yields

$$f = 3 \qquad \frac{\partial f}{\partial x} = 5 \qquad \frac{\partial f}{\partial y} = 5 \qquad \frac{\partial^2 f}{\partial x^2} = 8 \qquad \frac{\partial^2 f}{\partial x \partial y} = 2 \qquad \frac{\partial^2 f}{\partial y^2} = 12$$

The second-order Taylor polynomial is $p_2(x, y)$:

$$p_2(x, y) = f + (x - 1)\frac{\partial f}{\partial x} + (y - 1)\frac{\partial f}{\partial y}$$

$$+ \frac{1}{2}\left((x - 1)^2\frac{\partial^2 f}{\partial x^2} + 2(x - 1)(y - 1)\frac{\partial^2 f}{\partial x \partial y} + (y - 1)^2\frac{\partial^2 f}{\partial y^2}\right)$$

$$= 3 + 5(x-1) + 5(y-1) + \frac{1}{2}(8(x-1)^2 + 4(x-1)(y-1) + 12(y-1)^2)$$

$$= 4x^2 + 6y^2 + 2xy - 5x - 9y + 5$$

(b) The value of $p_2(1.2, 0.9)$ is an estimate of $f(1.2, 0.9)$.

$$p_2(1.2, 0.9) = 4(1.2)^2 + 6(0.9)^2 + 2(1.2)(0.9) - 5(1.2) - 9(0.9) + 5 = 3.68$$

The actual value is

$$f(1.2, 0.9) = (1.2)^3 + (1.2)^2(0.9) + (0.9)^4 = 3.6801$$

(c) The partial derivatives of $p_2(x, y)$ are found.

$$\frac{\partial p_2}{\partial x} = 8x + 2y - 5 \qquad \frac{\partial p_2}{\partial y} = 12y + 2x - 9$$

$$\frac{\partial^2 p_2}{\partial x^2} = 8 \qquad \frac{\partial^2 p_2}{\partial x \partial y} = 2 \qquad \frac{\partial^2 p_2}{\partial y^2} = 12$$

The second partial derivatives of p_2 are identical to the second partial derivatives of f evaluated at $(1, 1)$.

25.6.3 Taylor series in two variables

The third-order Taylor polynomial involves all the third-order partial derivatives of f, the fourth-order Taylor polynomial involves all the fourth-order partial derivatives of f and so on. Taylor polynomials approximate more and more closely to the generating function as more and more terms are included. As more and more terms are included, we obtain an infinite series known as a Taylor series in two variables. The general form of this series is beyond the scope of this book.

Exercises 25.6

1 Use a first-order Taylor polynomial to estimate $f(2.1, 3.2)$ given

$$f(2, 3) = 4 \qquad \frac{\partial f}{\partial x}(2, 3) = -2$$

$$\frac{\partial f}{\partial y}(2, 3) = 3$$

2 Use a first-order Taylor polynomial to estimate $g(-1.1, 0.2)$ given

$$g(-1, 0) = 6 \qquad \frac{\partial g}{\partial x}(-1, 0) = 2$$

$$\frac{\partial g}{\partial y}(-1, 0) = -1$$

3 Use a first-order Taylor polynomial to estimate $h(-1.2, -0.7)$ given

$$h(-1.3, -0.6) = 4$$

$$\frac{\partial h}{\partial x}(-1.3, -0.6) = -1$$

$$\frac{\partial h}{\partial y}(-1.3, -0.6) = 1$$

4 Use a second-order Taylor polynomial to estimate $f(3.1, 4.2)$ given

$$f(3, 4) = 1 \qquad \frac{\partial f}{\partial x}(3, 4) = 0$$

$$\frac{\partial f}{\partial y}(3, 4) = 2 \qquad \frac{\partial^2 f}{\partial x^2}(3, 4) = -1$$

$$\frac{\partial^2 f}{\partial x \partial y}(3, 4) = 3 \qquad \frac{\partial^2 f}{\partial y^2}(3, 4) = 0.5$$

5 Use a second-order Taylor polynomial to estimate $g(-2.9, 3.1)$ given

$$g(-3, 3) = 1 \qquad \frac{\partial g}{\partial x}(-3, 3) = -1$$

$$\frac{\partial g}{\partial y}(-3, 3) = 4 \qquad \frac{\partial^2 g}{\partial x^2}(-3, 3) = 3$$

$$\frac{\partial^2 g}{\partial x \partial y}(-3, 3) = -2 \qquad \frac{\partial^2 g}{\partial y^2}(-3, 3) = 2$$

6 Use a second-order Taylor polynomial to estimate $h(0.1, 0.1)$ given

$$h(0, 0) = 4 \qquad \frac{\partial h}{\partial x}(0, 0) = -1$$

$$\frac{\partial h}{\partial y}(0, 0) = -3 \qquad \frac{\partial^2 h}{\partial x^2}(0, 0) = 2$$

$$\frac{\partial^2 h}{\partial x \partial y}(0, 0) = 2 \qquad \frac{\partial^2 h}{\partial y^2}(0, 0) = -1$$

7 A function, $f(x, y)$, is defined by

$$f(x, y) = x^3 y + xy^3$$

(a) Calculate the first-order Taylor polynomial generated by f about $(1, 1)$.

(b) Calculate the second-order Taylor polynomial generated by f about $(1, 1)$.

(c) Estimate $f(1.2, 1.2)$ using the first-order Taylor polynomial.

(d) Estimate $f(1.2, 1.2)$ using the second-order Taylor polynomial.

(e) Compare your answers in (c) and (d) with the true value of $f(1.2, 1.2)$.

8 A function $g(x, y)$ is defined by

$$g(x, y) = x \sin y + \frac{x}{y}$$

(a) Calculate the first-order Taylor polynomial generated by g about $(0, 1)$.

(b) Calculate the second-order Taylor polynomial generated by g about $(0, 1)$.

(c) Estimate $g(0.2, 0.9)$ using the polynomial in (a).

(d) Estimate $g(0.2, 0.9)$ using the polynomial in (b).

(e) Compare your estimates with the exact value of $g(0.2, 0.9)$.

9 A function $h(x, y)$ is defined by

$$h(x, y) = e^x y + x^2 e^y$$

(a) Calculate the first-order Taylor polynomial generated by h about $(0, 0)$.

(b) Calculate the second-order Taylor polynomial generated by h about $(0, 0)$.

(c) Estimate $h(0.2, 0.15)$ using the polynomial from (a).

(d) Estimate $h(0.2, 0.15)$ using the polynomial from (b).

(e) Compare your answers in (c) and (d) to the exact value of $h(0.2, 0.15)$.

10 A function, $f(x, y, z)$, is defined by

$$f(x, y, z) = x^2 + xyz + yz^2$$

(a) Write down the first-order Taylor polynomial generated by f about $(0, 1, 2)$.

(b) Use the polynomial from (a) to estimate $f(0.1, 1.2, 1.9)$.

(c) Compare your answer in (b) to the exact value of $f(0.1, 1.2, 1.9)$.

Solutions

1	4.4	(b)	$2.3012x - 0.4597xy$
2	5.6	(c)	0.3683
3	3.8	(d)	0.3775
4	1.465	(e)	0.3789
5	1.305	**9** (a)	y
6	3.625	(b)	$x^2 + xy + y$
7	(a) $4x + 4y - 6$	(c)	0.15
	(b) $3x^2 + 3y^2 + 6xy - 8x - 8y + 6$	(d)	0.22
	(c) 3.6	(e)	0.2297
	(d) 4.08	**10** (a)	$2x + 4y + 4z - 8$
	(e) 4.1472	(b)	4.6
8	(a) $1.8415x$	(c)	4.57

25.7 Maximum and minimum points of a function of two variables

We saw in Chapter 12 that to find the turning points of $y(x)$ we solve

$$\frac{dy}{dx} = 0$$

The sign of the second derivative, $\dfrac{d^2y}{dx^2}$, is then used to distinguish between a maximum point and a minimum point. The analysis is very similar for a function of two variables.

When considering a function of two variables, $f(x, y)$, we often seek maximum points, minimum points and saddle points. Collectively these are known as **stationary points**. Figure 25.1 illustrates a maximum point at A, a minimum point at B and a saddle point at C. When leaving a maximum point the value of the function decreases, when leaving a minimum point the value of the function increases. When leaving a saddle point, the function increases in one direction, axis D on the figure, and decreases in the other direction, axis E on the figure.

To locate stationary points we equate both first partial derivatives to zero, that is we solve

$$\frac{\partial f}{\partial x} = 0 \qquad \frac{\partial f}{\partial y} = 0$$

Stationary points are located by solving

$$\frac{\partial f}{\partial x} = 0 \qquad \frac{\partial f}{\partial y} = 0$$

Example 25.17 Locate the stationary points of

(a) $f(x, y) = 2x^2 - xy - 7y + y^2$

(b) $f(x, y) = x^2 - 6x + 4xy + y^2$

Solution (a) The first partial derivatives are found.

$$\frac{\partial f}{\partial x} = 4x - y \qquad \frac{\partial f}{\partial y} = -x - 7 + 2y$$

The stationary points are located by solving $\dfrac{\partial f}{\partial x} = 0$ and $\dfrac{\partial f}{\partial y} = 0$ simultaneously, that is

$$4x - y = 0$$
$$-x + 2y - 7 = 0$$

Solving these equations yields $x = 1$, $y = 4$. Hence the function $f(x, y)$ has one stationary point and it is located at $(1, 4)$.

(b) The first partial derivatives are found.

$$\frac{\partial f}{\partial x} = 2x - 6 + 4y \qquad \frac{\partial f}{\partial y} = 4x + 2y$$

The first partial derivatives are equated to zero.

$$2x + 4y - 6 = 0$$
$$4x + 2y = 0$$

Solving the equations simultaneously yields $x = -1$, $y = 2$. Thus the function has one stationary point located at $(-1, 2)$.

Example 25.18 Locate the stationary points of

$$f(x, y) = \frac{x^3}{3} + 3x^2 + xy + \frac{y^2}{2} + 6y$$

Solution The first partial derivatives are found.

$$\frac{\partial f}{\partial x} = x^2 + 6x + y \qquad \frac{\partial f}{\partial y} = x + y + 6$$

These derivatives are equated to zero.

$$x^2 + 6x + y = 0 \qquad (25.1)$$
$$x + y + 6 = 0 \qquad (25.2)$$

Equations (25.1) and (25.2) are solved simultaneously. From (25.2) $y = -x - 6$, and substituting this into Equation (25.1) yields $x^2 + 5x - 6 = 0$. Solving this quadratic equation gives $x = 1, -6$. When $x = 1$, $y = -7$, and when $x = -6$, $y = 0$. The function has stationary values at $(1, -7)$ and $(-6, 0)$.

Equating the first partial derivatives to zero locates the stationary points, but does not identify them as maximum points, minimum points or saddle points. To distinguish between these various points a test involving second partial derivatives must be made. Note that this is similar to locating and identifying turning points of a function of one variable.

To identify the stationary points we consider the expression

$$\frac{\partial^2 f}{\partial x^2} \frac{\partial^2 f}{\partial y^2} - \left(\frac{\partial^2 f}{\partial x \partial y} \right)^2$$

If the expression is negative at a stationary point, then that point is a saddle point.

If the expression is positive and in addition $\dfrac{\partial^2 f}{\partial x^2}$ is positive at a stationary point, then that point is a minimum point.

If the expression is positive and in addition $\dfrac{\partial^2 f}{\partial x^2}$ is negative at a stationary point, then that point is a maximum point.

If the expression is zero then further tests are required. These are beyond the scope of the book.

In summary:

$$\frac{\partial^2 f}{\partial x^2} \frac{\partial^2 f}{\partial y^2} - \left(\frac{\partial^2 f}{\partial x \partial y} \right)^2 < 0 \qquad \text{Saddle point}$$

$$\frac{\partial^2 f}{\partial x^2} \frac{\partial^2 f}{\partial y^2} - \left(\frac{\partial^2 f}{\partial x \partial y} \right)^2 > 0 \qquad \text{and} \qquad \frac{\partial^2 f}{\partial x^2} > 0 \qquad \text{Minimum point}$$

$$\frac{\partial^2 f}{\partial x^2} \frac{\partial^2 f}{\partial y^2} - \left(\frac{\partial^2 f}{\partial x \partial y} \right)^2 > 0 \qquad \text{and} \qquad \frac{\partial^2 f}{\partial x^2} < 0 \qquad \text{Maximum point}$$

Example 25.19   Locate and identify the stationary values of

$$f(x, y) = x^2 + xy + y$$

Solution   The first partial derivatives are found.

$$\frac{\partial f}{\partial x} = 2x + y \qquad \frac{\partial f}{\partial y} = x + 1$$

The first partial derivatives are equated to zero.

$$2x + y = 0$$
$$x + 1 = 0$$

This yields $x = -1$, $y = 2$. Thus there is one stationary point, positioned at $(-1, 2)$. The second partial derivatives are found.

$$\frac{\partial^2 f}{\partial x^2} = 2 \qquad \frac{\partial^2 f}{\partial x \partial y} = 1 \qquad \frac{\partial^2 f}{\partial y^2} = 0$$

Now

$$\frac{\partial^2 f}{\partial x^2}\frac{\partial^2 f}{\partial y^2} - \left(\frac{\partial^2 f}{\partial x \partial y}\right)^2 = 2(0) - (1)^2 = -1$$

Since the expression is negative, we conclude that $(-1, 2)$ is a saddle point.

Example 25.20 Locate and identify the stationary points of

$$f(x, y) = xy - x^2 - y^2$$

Solution The first partial derivatives are found.

$$\frac{\partial f}{\partial x} = y - 2x \qquad \frac{\partial f}{\partial y} = x - 2y$$

Solving $\dfrac{\partial f}{\partial x} = 0$, $\dfrac{\partial f}{\partial y} = 0$ yields $x = 0$, $y = 0$.

The second partial derivatives are found.

$$\frac{\partial^2 f}{\partial x^2} = -2 \qquad \frac{\partial^2 f}{\partial x \partial y} = 1 \qquad \frac{\partial^2 f}{\partial y^2} = -2$$

The second derivative test to identify the stationary point is used. Now

$$\frac{\partial^2 f}{\partial x^2}\frac{\partial^2 f}{\partial y^2} - \left(\frac{\partial^2 f}{\partial x \partial y}\right)^2 = (-2)(-2) - (1)^2 = 3$$

Since $\dfrac{\partial^2 f}{\partial x^2} < 0$ and $\dfrac{\partial^2 f}{\partial x^2}\dfrac{\partial^2 f}{\partial y^2} - \left(\dfrac{\partial^2 f}{\partial x \partial y}\right)^2 > 0$ then $(0, 0)$ is a maximum point.

Example 25.21 Locate and identify the stationary points of

$$f(x, y) = \frac{x^3}{3} - x + \frac{y^2}{2} + 2y$$

Solution The first partial derivatives are found.

$$\frac{\partial f}{\partial x} = x^2 - 1 \qquad \frac{\partial f}{\partial y} = y + 2$$

The first partial derivatives are equated to zero.

$$x^2 - 1 = 0$$
$$y + 2 = 0$$

These equations have two solutions: $x = 1$, $y = -2$ and $x = -1$, $y = -2$.

Figure 25.2
The function
$f(x, y) = \dfrac{x^3}{3} - x + \dfrac{y^2}{2} + 2y$ has a minimum at $(1, -2)$ and a saddle point at $(-1, -2)$.

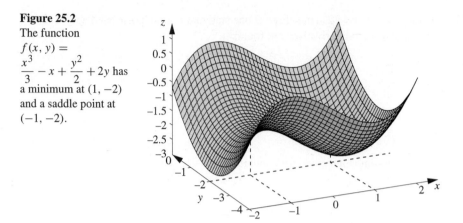

In order to identify the nature of each stationary point, the second derivatives are found.

$$\frac{\partial^2 f}{\partial x^2} = 2x \qquad \frac{\partial^2 f}{\partial x \partial y} = 0 \qquad \frac{\partial^2 f}{\partial y^2} = 1$$

Each stationary point is examined in turn.

At $(1, -2)$

$$\frac{\partial^2 f}{\partial x^2} \frac{\partial^2 f}{\partial y^2} - \left(\frac{\partial^2 f}{\partial x \partial y}\right)^2 = 2x(1) - 0^2 = 2x = 2 \text{ since } x = 1$$

$$\frac{\partial^2 f}{\partial x^2} = 2x = 2$$

Since both expressions are positive the point $(1, -2)$ is a minimum point.

At $(-1, -2)$

Here

$$\frac{\partial^2 f}{\partial x^2} \frac{\partial^2 f}{\partial y^2} - \left(\frac{\partial^2 f}{\partial x \partial y}\right)^2 = 2x = -2 \text{ since } x = -1$$

Since the expression is negative then $(-1, -2)$ is a saddle point.
Figure 25.2 illustrates a plot of the surface defined by $f(x, y)$.

Exercises 25.7

1 Determine the position and nature of the stationary points of the following functions.

(a) $f(x, y) = x + y + xy$

(b) $f(x, y) = x^2 + y^2 - 2y$

(c) $f(x, y) = x^2 + xy - y$

(d) $f(x, y) = x^2 + y^2 - xy$

(e) $f(x, y) = x^2 + 2y^2 - 3xy + x$

2 Determine the position and nature of the stationary points of the following functions.

(a) $z(x, y) = x^2 + y^2 - 3xy + 2x$

(b) $z(x, y) = x^3 + xy + y^2$

(c) $z(x, y) = \dfrac{y^3}{3} - x^2 - y$

(d) $z(x, y) = \dfrac{1}{x} + \dfrac{1}{y} - \dfrac{1}{xy}$

(e) $z(x, y) = 4x^2y - 6xy$

3 Locate and identify the stationary points of the following:

(a) $f(x, y) = x^2y - x^2 + y^2$

(b) $f(x, y) = \dfrac{x}{y} + x + y$

(c) $f(x, y) = x^4 + 16xy + y^4$

(d) $f(x, y) = y - y^2 - e^x x$

(e) $f(x, y) = \dfrac{e^x}{y^4} - xy$

Solutions

1 (a) $(-1, -1)$, saddle point

(b) $(0, 1)$, minimum

(c) $(1, -2)$, saddle point

(d) $(0, 0)$, minimum

(e) $(4, 3)$, saddle point

2 (a) $\left(\frac{4}{5}, \frac{6}{5}\right)$, saddle point

(b) $(0, 0)$, saddle point; $\left(\frac{1}{6}, -\frac{1}{12}\right)$, minimum

(c) $(0, 1)$, saddle point; $(0, -1)$, maximum

(d) $(1, 1)$, saddle point

(e) $(0, 0)$, $(1.5, 0)$, saddle points

3 (a) $(0, 0)$, saddle point

(b) $(1, -1)$, saddle point

(c) $(0, 0)$, saddle point; $(2, -2)$, minimum; $(-2, 2)$, minimum

(d) $(-1, 0.5)$, maximum

(e) $(-4, 0.4493)$, saddle point

Review exercises 25

1 Find all first partial derivatives of the following functions:

(a) $z(x, y) = 9x^2 + 2y^2$

(b) $z(x, y) = 3x^3y^6$

(c) $z(x, y) = 4x^3 - 5y^3$

(d) $z(x, y) = xy + x^2y^2$

(e) $z(x, y) = \sin(2xy)$

(f) $z(x, y) = 2e^{3xy}$

2 Evaluate the first partial derivatives of f at $x = -1, y = 2$.

(a) $f(x, y) = 3x^3 - y^3 + x^2y^2$

(b) $f(x, y) = \dfrac{4x}{y}$

(c) $f(x, y) = \sin x + 2\cos y$

(d) $f(x, y) = (xy)^3 + x$

(e) $f(x, y) = \dfrac{x + y}{x - y}$

(f) $f(x, y) = 2e^x e^y$

3 Find all second partial derivatives of z where

(a) $z(x, y) = 3x^4 - 9y^4 + x^3y^3$

(b) $z(x, y) = (x^2 + y^2)^2$

(c) $z(x, y) = 2e^{4x-3y}$

(d) $z(x, y) = \dfrac{2}{x + y}$

(e) $z(x, y) = 2\sqrt{x + y}$

(f) $z(x, y) = (\sin x)(\cos y)$

4 Find all first and second partial derivatives of

$$f(x, y) = (ax + by)^n$$

where a, b and n are constants.

5 Find the first partial derivatives of

$$f(x, y) = (ax^2 + by^2 + cxy)^n$$

where a, b, c and n are constants.

6 Verify that

$$z(x, y) = 3x + 2y + 1$$

is a solution of

$$\frac{\partial z}{\partial x} - \frac{\partial z}{\partial y} = 1$$

7 Verify that

$$z(x, y) = 2xy - x + y$$

is a solution of

$$\frac{\partial z}{\partial x} + \frac{\partial z}{\partial y} = 2(x + y)$$

8 Verify that

$$f(x, y) = x^2 + y^2 - 2xy$$

is a solution of

$$\frac{\partial f}{\partial x} + \frac{\partial f}{\partial y} = 0$$

9 Verify that

$$z(x, y) = \sin x + \cos y$$

is a solution of

$$\frac{\partial^2 z}{\partial x^2} + \frac{\partial^2 z}{\partial y^2} + z = 0$$

10 Verify that

$$z(x, y) = xy\,e^x$$

is a solution of

$$\frac{\partial^2 z}{\partial x^2} + \frac{\partial^2 z}{\partial y^2} - y\frac{\partial^2 z}{\partial x \partial y} = y\,e^x$$

11 (a) Write down the second-order Taylor polynomial generated by $f(x, y)$ about $x = 2, y = 3$ given

$$f(x, y) = 3x^3y - x^2y^3$$

(b) Estimate $f(2.1, 2.9)$ using your polynomial from (a) and compare this with the exact answer.

12 Write down the second-order Taylor polynomial generated by $z(x, y)$ about $x = 1, y = 1$ given

$$z(x, y) = \frac{x + y}{x}$$

13 Calculate the second-order Taylor polynomial generated by

$$f(x, y) = \sqrt{x^2 + y^2}$$

about $x = 1, y = 0$.

14 Locate and identify all the stationary points of the following functions:

(a) $f(x, y) = x^2 + y^3 - 3y$

(b) $f(x, y) = 4xy - x^2y$

(c) $f(x, y) = x^3 + 2y^2 - 12x$

(d) $f(x, y) = xy - y^2 - x^3$

15 Locate and identify the stationary points of

$$f(x, y) = \frac{y}{x} - x^2 + y^2$$

Solutions

1 (a) $\frac{\partial z}{\partial x} = 18x, \frac{\partial z}{\partial y} = 4y$

(b) $9x^2y^6, 18x^3y^5$

(c) $12x^2, -15y^2$

(d) $y + 2xy^2, x + 2x^2y$

(e) $2y\cos(2xy), 2x\cos(2xy)$

(f) $6y\,e^{3xy}, 6x\,e^{3xy}$

2 (a) $\frac{\partial f}{\partial x}(-1, 2) = 1, \frac{\partial f}{\partial y}(-1, 2) = -8$

(b) 2, 1

(c) 0.5403, −1.8186

(d) 25, −12

(e) $-\frac{4}{9}, -\frac{2}{9}$

(f) 5.4366, 5.4366

3 (a) $\frac{\partial^2 z}{\partial x^2} = 36x^2 + 6xy^3,$

$\frac{\partial^2 z}{\partial x \partial y} = 9x^2y^2,$

$\frac{\partial^2 z}{\partial y^2} = -108y^2 + 6x^3y$

(b) $12x^2 + 4y^2, 8xy, 4x^2 + 12y^2$

(c) $32\,e^{4x-3y}, -24\,e^{4x-3y}, 18\,e^{4x-3y}$

(d) $\frac{4}{(x+y)^3}, \frac{4}{(x+y)^3}, \frac{4}{(x+y)^3}$

(e) $-\frac{1}{2}(x+y)^{-3/2}$,

$-\frac{1}{2}(x+y)^{-3/2}$,

$-\frac{1}{2}(x+y)^{-3/2}$

(f) $-(\sin x)(\cos y)$,

$-(\cos x)(\sin y)$,

$-(\sin x)(\cos y)$

4 $\dfrac{\partial f}{\partial x} = an(ax+by)^{n-1}$,

$\dfrac{\partial f}{\partial y} = bn(ax+by)^{n-1}$,

$\dfrac{\partial^2 f}{\partial x^2} = a^2 n(n-1)(ax+by)^{n-2}$,

$\dfrac{\partial^2 f}{\partial x \partial y} = abn(n-1)(ax+by)^{n-2}$,

$\dfrac{\partial^2 f}{\partial y^2} = b^2 n(n-1)(ax+by)^{n-2}$

5 $\dfrac{\partial f}{\partial x} = (2ax+cy)n(ax^2+by^2+cxy)^{n-1}$,

$\dfrac{\partial f}{\partial y} = (2by+cx)n(ax^2+by^2+cxy)^{n-1}$

11 (a) $27x^2 - 36y^2 - 72xy + 108x + 276y - 432$

(b) $p_2(2.1, 2.9) = -26.97$,

$f(2.1, 2.9) = -26.985$

12 $x^2 - xy - 2x + 2y + 2$

13 $\dfrac{y^2}{2} + x$

14 (a) $(0, 1)$ minimum; $(0, -1)$ saddle point

(b) $(0, 0)$, $(4, 0)$ saddle points

(c) $(2, 0)$ minimum; $(-2, 0)$ saddle point

(d) $(0, 0)$ saddle point; $\left(\frac{1}{6}, \frac{1}{12}\right)$ maximum

15 $\left(\dfrac{1}{\sqrt{2}}, -\dfrac{1}{2\sqrt{2}}\right), \left(-\dfrac{1}{\sqrt{2}}, \dfrac{1}{2\sqrt{2}}\right)$; saddle points

26 Vector calculus

Chapter 26   Contents

26.1   Introduction   818

26.2   Partial differentiation of vectors   818

26.3   The gradient of a scalar field   820

26.4   The divergence of a vector field   824

26.5   The curl of a vector field   828

26.6   Combining the operators grad, div and curl   830

26.7   Vector calculus and electromagnetism   833

        Review exercises   834

26.1 Introduction

This chapter draws together several threads from previous chapters. It builds upon differential and integral calculus, functions of several variables and the study of vectors. These topics together form a branch of engineering mathematics known as **vector calculus**. Vector calculus is used to model a vast range of engineering phenomena including electrostatic charges, electromagnetic fields, air flow around aircraft, cars and other solid objects, fluid flow around ships and heat flow in nuclear reactors. The chapter starts by explaining what is meant by the operators grad, div and curl. These are used to carry out various differentiation operations on the fields.

26.2 Partial differentiation of vectors

Consider the vector field $\mathbf{v} = v_x\mathbf{i} + v_y\mathbf{j} + v_z\mathbf{k}$, where each component v_x, v_y and v_z is a function of x, y and z. We can partially differentiate the vector w.r.t. x as follows:

$$\frac{\partial \mathbf{v}}{\partial x} = \frac{\partial v_x}{\partial x}\mathbf{i} + \frac{\partial v_y}{\partial x}\mathbf{j} + \frac{\partial v_z}{\partial x}\mathbf{k}$$

This is a new vector with a magnitude and direction different from those of $\mathbf{v}$.

Partial differentiation w.r.t. y and z is defined in a similar way, as are higher derivatives. For example,

$$\frac{\partial^2 \mathbf{v}}{\partial x^2} = \frac{\partial^2 v_x}{\partial x^2}\mathbf{i} + \frac{\partial^2 v_y}{\partial x^2}\mathbf{j} + \frac{\partial^2 v_z}{\partial x^2}\mathbf{k}$$

Example 26.1   If $\mathbf{v} = 3x^2y\mathbf{i} + 2xyz\mathbf{j} - 3x^4y^2\mathbf{k}$, find $\dfrac{\partial \mathbf{v}}{\partial x}, \dfrac{\partial \mathbf{v}}{\partial y}, \dfrac{\partial \mathbf{v}}{\partial z}$. Further, find $\dfrac{\partial^2 \mathbf{v}}{\partial x^2}$ and $\dfrac{\partial^2 \mathbf{v}}{\partial x \partial z}$.

Solution   We find

$$\frac{\partial \mathbf{v}}{\partial x} = 6xy\mathbf{i} + 2yz\mathbf{j} - 12x^3y^2\mathbf{k}$$

$$\frac{\partial \mathbf{v}}{\partial y} = 3x^2\mathbf{i} + 2xz\mathbf{j} - 6x^4y\mathbf{k}$$

$$\frac{\partial \mathbf{v}}{\partial z} = 2xy\mathbf{j}$$

$$\frac{\partial^2 \mathbf{v}}{\partial x^2} = 6y\mathbf{i} - 36x^2y^2\mathbf{k}$$

$$\frac{\partial^2 \mathbf{v}}{\partial x \partial z} = 2y\mathbf{j}$$

Exercises 26.2

1 Given $\mathbf{v} = 2x\mathbf{i} + 3yz\mathbf{j} + 5xz^2\mathbf{k}$ find

(a) $\dfrac{\partial \mathbf{v}}{\partial x}$ (b) $\dfrac{\partial \mathbf{v}}{\partial y}$ (c) $\dfrac{\partial \mathbf{v}}{\partial z}$

2 If $\mathbf{f} = 2\mathbf{i} - xyz\mathbf{j} + 3x^2z\mathbf{k}$ find

(a) $\dfrac{\partial \mathbf{f}}{\partial x}$ (b) $\dfrac{\partial \mathbf{f}}{\partial y}$ (c) $\dfrac{\partial \mathbf{f}}{\partial z}$

(d) $\dfrac{\partial^2 \mathbf{f}}{\partial x^2}$ (e) $\dfrac{\partial^2 \mathbf{f}}{\partial y^2}$ (f) $\dfrac{\partial^2 \mathbf{f}}{\partial z^2}$

3 Given $\mathbf{E} = (x^2 + y)\mathbf{i} + (1 - z)\mathbf{j} + (x + 2z)\mathbf{k}$ find

(a) $\dfrac{\partial \mathbf{E}}{\partial x}$ (b) $\dfrac{\partial \mathbf{E}}{\partial y}$ (c) $\dfrac{\partial \mathbf{E}}{\partial z}$

(d) $\dfrac{\partial^2 \mathbf{E}}{\partial x^2}$ (e) $\dfrac{\partial^2 \mathbf{E}}{\partial y^2}$ (f) $\dfrac{\partial^2 \mathbf{E}}{\partial z^2}$

4 If $\mathbf{v} = 3xyz\mathbf{i} + (x^2 - y^2 + z^2)\mathbf{j} + (x + y^2)\mathbf{k}$

find $\dfrac{\partial \mathbf{v}}{\partial x}, \dfrac{\partial \mathbf{v}}{\partial y}, \dfrac{\partial \mathbf{v}}{\partial z}, \dfrac{\partial^2 \mathbf{v}}{\partial x^2}, \dfrac{\partial^2 \mathbf{v}}{\partial y^2}$, and $\dfrac{\partial^2 \mathbf{v}}{\partial z^2}$.

5 If $\mathbf{v} = \sin(xyz)\mathbf{i} + z\,e^{xy}\mathbf{j} - 2xy\mathbf{k}$ find
$\dfrac{\partial \mathbf{v}}{\partial x}, \dfrac{\partial \mathbf{v}}{\partial y}, \dfrac{\partial \mathbf{v}}{\partial z}$.

6 If $\mathbf{v} = x\mathbf{i} + x^2y\mathbf{j} - 3x^3\mathbf{k}$, and $\phi = xyz$ find
$\phi\mathbf{v}, \dfrac{\partial}{\partial x}(\phi\mathbf{v}), \dfrac{\partial \phi}{\partial x}, \dfrac{\partial \mathbf{v}}{\partial x}$. Deduce that

$$\frac{\partial}{\partial x}(\phi\mathbf{v}) = \phi\frac{\partial \mathbf{v}}{\partial x} + \frac{\partial \phi}{\partial x}\mathbf{v}$$

7 If $\mathbf{v} = \ln(xy)\mathbf{i} + 2xy\cos z\mathbf{j} - x^4yz\mathbf{k}$, find
$\dfrac{\partial \mathbf{v}}{\partial x}, \dfrac{\partial \mathbf{v}}{\partial y}, \dfrac{\partial \mathbf{v}}{\partial z}, \dfrac{\partial^2 \mathbf{v}}{\partial x^2}, \dfrac{\partial^2 \mathbf{v}}{\partial y^2}$, and $\dfrac{\partial^2 \mathbf{v}}{\partial z^2}$.

Solutions

1 (a) $2\mathbf{i} + 5z^2\mathbf{k}$ (b) $3z\mathbf{j}$
(c) $3y\mathbf{j} + 10xz\mathbf{k}$

2 (a) $-yz\mathbf{j} + 6xz\mathbf{k}$ (b) $-xz\mathbf{j}$
(c) $-xy\mathbf{j} + 3x^2\mathbf{k}$ (d) $6z\mathbf{k}$
(e) $\mathbf{0}$ (f) $\mathbf{0}$

3 (a) $2x\mathbf{i} + \mathbf{k}$ (b) $\mathbf{i}$
(c) $-\mathbf{j} + 2\mathbf{k}$ (d) $2\mathbf{i}$
(e) $\mathbf{0}$ (f) $\mathbf{0}$

4 $\dfrac{\partial \mathbf{v}}{\partial x} = 3yz\mathbf{i} + 2x\mathbf{j} + \mathbf{k}$

$\dfrac{\partial \mathbf{v}}{\partial y} = 3xz\mathbf{i} - 2y\mathbf{j} + 2y\mathbf{k}$

$\dfrac{\partial \mathbf{v}}{\partial z} = 3xy\mathbf{i} + 2z\mathbf{j}$

$\dfrac{\partial^2 \mathbf{v}}{\partial x^2} = 2\mathbf{j}$

$\dfrac{\partial^2 \mathbf{v}}{\partial y^2} = -2\mathbf{j} + 2\mathbf{k}$

$\dfrac{\partial^2 \mathbf{v}}{\partial z^2} = 2\mathbf{j}$

5 $\dfrac{\partial \mathbf{v}}{\partial x} = yz\cos(xyz)\mathbf{i} + yz\,e^{xy}\mathbf{j} - 2y\mathbf{k}$

$\dfrac{\partial \mathbf{v}}{\partial y} = xz\cos(xyz)\mathbf{i} + xz\,e^{xy}\mathbf{j} - 2x\mathbf{k}$

$\dfrac{\partial \mathbf{v}}{\partial z} = xy\cos(xyz)\mathbf{i} + e^{xy}\mathbf{j}$

6 $\phi\mathbf{v} = x^2yz\mathbf{i} + x^3y^2z\mathbf{j} - 3x^4yz\mathbf{k}$

$\dfrac{\partial(\phi\mathbf{v})}{\partial x} = 2xyz\mathbf{i} + 3x^2y^2z\mathbf{j} - 12x^3yz\mathbf{k}$

$\dfrac{\partial \phi}{\partial x} = yz$

$\dfrac{\partial \mathbf{v}}{\partial x} = \mathbf{i} + 2xy\mathbf{j} - 9x^2\mathbf{k}$

7 $\dfrac{\partial \mathbf{v}}{\partial x} = \dfrac{\mathbf{i}}{x} + 2y\cos z\mathbf{j} - 4x^3yz\mathbf{k}$

$\dfrac{\partial \mathbf{v}}{\partial y} = \dfrac{\mathbf{i}}{y} + 2x\cos z\mathbf{j} - x^4z\mathbf{k}$

$\dfrac{\partial \mathbf{v}}{\partial z} = -2xy\sin z\mathbf{j} - x^4y\mathbf{k}$

$\dfrac{\partial^2 \mathbf{v}}{\partial x^2} = -\dfrac{\mathbf{i}}{x^2} - 12x^2yz\mathbf{k}$

$\dfrac{\partial^2 \mathbf{v}}{\partial y^2} = -\dfrac{\mathbf{i}}{y^2}$

$\dfrac{\partial^2 \mathbf{v}}{\partial z^2} = -2xy\cos z\mathbf{j}$

26.3 | The gradient of a scalar field

Given a scalar function of x, y, z

$$\phi = \phi(x, y, z)$$

we can differentiate it partially w.r.t. each of its independent variables to find $\dfrac{\partial \phi}{\partial x}$, $\dfrac{\partial \phi}{\partial y}$ and $\dfrac{\partial \phi}{\partial z}$. If we do this, the vector

$$\frac{\partial \phi}{\partial x}\mathbf{i} + \frac{\partial \phi}{\partial y}\mathbf{j} + \frac{\partial \phi}{\partial z}\mathbf{k}$$

turns out to be particularly important. We call this vector the **gradient** of ϕ and denote it by

$$\nabla \phi \qquad \text{or} \qquad \text{grad } \phi$$

An alternative form of writing $\nabla \phi$ is as three components

$$\left(\frac{\partial \phi}{\partial x}, \frac{\partial \phi}{\partial y}, \frac{\partial \phi}{\partial z} \right)$$

$$\text{grad } \phi = \nabla \phi = \frac{\partial \phi}{\partial x}\mathbf{i} + \frac{\partial \phi}{\partial y}\mathbf{j} + \frac{\partial \phi}{\partial z}\mathbf{k}$$

The process of forming a gradient applies only to a scalar field and the result is always a vector field.

It is often useful to write $\nabla \phi$ in the form

$$\left(\frac{\partial}{\partial x}, \frac{\partial}{\partial y}, \frac{\partial}{\partial z} \right) \phi$$

where the quantity in brackets is called a **vector operator** and is regarded as operating on the scalar ϕ. Thus the vector operator, ∇, is given by

$$\left(\frac{\partial}{\partial x}, \frac{\partial}{\partial y}, \frac{\partial}{\partial z} \right)$$

Example 26.2   If $\phi = \phi(x, y, z) = 4x^3 y \sin z$, find $\nabla \phi$.

Solution $$\phi(x, y, z) = 4x^3 y \sin z$$

so that by partial differentiation we obtain

$$\frac{\partial \phi}{\partial x} = 12x^2 y \sin z$$

$$\frac{\partial \phi}{\partial y} = 4x^3 \sin z$$

$$\frac{\partial \phi}{\partial z} = 4x^3 y \cos z$$

Therefore

$$\nabla\phi = 12x^2y\sin z\mathbf{i} + 4x^3\sin z\mathbf{j} + 4x^3y\cos z\mathbf{k}$$

We often need to evaluate $\nabla\phi$ at a particular point, say, for example, at $(4, 2, 3)$. We write $\nabla\phi|_{(4,2,3)}$ to denote the value of $\nabla\phi$ at the point $(4, 2, 3)$.

Example 26.3   If $\phi = x^3y + xy^2 + 3y$ find

(a) $\nabla\phi$

(b) $\nabla\phi|_{(0,0,0)}$

(c) $|\nabla\phi|$ at $(1, 1, 1)$

Solution   (a) If $\phi = x^3y + xy^2 + 3y$ then

$$\frac{\partial\phi}{\partial x} = 3x^2y + y^2$$

$$\frac{\partial\phi}{\partial y} = x^3 + 2xy + 3$$

$$\frac{\partial\phi}{\partial z} = 0$$

so that

$$\nabla\phi = (3x^2y + y^2)\mathbf{i} + (x^3 + 2xy + 3)\mathbf{j} + 0\mathbf{k}$$

(b) At $(0, 0, 0)$, $\nabla\phi = 0\mathbf{i} + 3\mathbf{j} + 0\mathbf{k} = 3\mathbf{j}$.

(c) At $(1, 1, 1)$, $\nabla\phi = (3 \times 1^2 \times 1 + 1)\mathbf{i} + (1^3 + 2 \times 1 \times 1 + 3)\mathbf{j} + 0\mathbf{k} = 4\mathbf{i} + 6\mathbf{j} + 0\mathbf{k}$
so that $|\nabla\phi|$ at $(1, 1, 1)$ is equal to $\sqrt{4^2 + 6^2} = \sqrt{52}$.

So far we have been given ϕ and have calculated $\nabla\phi$. Sometimes we will be given $\nabla\phi$ and will need to find ϕ. Consider Example 26.4.

Example 26.4   If $\mathbf{F} = \nabla\phi$ find ϕ when $\mathbf{F} = (3x^2 + y^2)\mathbf{i} + (2xy + 5)\mathbf{j}$.

Solution   Note that in this example $\mathbf{F}$ has only two components. Consequently $\nabla\phi$ will have two components, that is $\mathbf{F} = \nabla\phi = \dfrac{\partial\phi}{\partial x}\mathbf{i} + \dfrac{\partial\phi}{\partial y}\mathbf{j}$. Therefore

$$(3x^2 + y^2)\mathbf{i} + (2xy + 5)\mathbf{j} = \frac{\partial\phi}{\partial x}\mathbf{i} + \frac{\partial\phi}{\partial y}\mathbf{j}$$

Equating the **i** components we have

$$\frac{\partial \phi}{\partial x} = 3x^2 + y^2 \tag{26.1}$$

Equating the **j** components we have

$$\frac{\partial \phi}{\partial y} = 2xy + 5 \tag{26.2}$$

Integrating Equation (26.1) w.r.t. x and treating y as a constant we find

$$\phi = x^3 + xy^2 + f(y) \tag{26.3}$$

where $f(y)$ is an arbitrary function of y which plays the same role as the constant of integration does when there is only one independent variable. Note in particular that $\frac{\partial}{\partial x} f(y) = 0$. Check by partial differentiation that $\frac{\partial \phi}{\partial x} = 3x^2 + y^2$.

Integrating Equation (26.2) w.r.t. y and treating x as a constant we find

$$\phi = xy^2 + 5y + g(x) \tag{26.4}$$

where $g(x)$ is an arbitrary function of x. Note that $\frac{\partial}{\partial y} g(x) = 0$. Check by partial differentiation that $\frac{\partial \phi}{\partial y} = 2xy + 5$. Comparing both forms for ϕ given in Equations (26.3) and (26.4) we see that by choosing $g(x) = x^3$ and $f(y) = 5y$ we have

$$\phi = x^3 + xy^2 + 5y$$

Check that **F** is indeed equal to $\nabla \phi$. Also check that by adding any constant to ϕ the same property holds, that is **F** is still equal to $\nabla \phi$.

26.3.1 Physical interpretation of $\nabla \phi$

Suppose we think of the scalar field $\phi(x, y, z)$ as describing the temperature throughout a region. This temperature will vary from point to point. At a particular point it can be shown that $\nabla \phi$ is a vector pointing in the direction in which the rate of temperature increase is greatest. $|\nabla \phi|$ is the magnitude of the rate of increase in that direction. Similarly, the rate of temperature decrease is greatest in the direction of $-\nabla \phi$. Analogous interpretations are possible for other scalar fields such as pressure and electrostatic potential.

Example 26.5 **Electrostatic potential**

The electrostatic potential, V, in a region is given by

$$V = \frac{y}{(x^2 + y^2 + z^2)^{3/2}}$$

Suppose a unit charge is located in the region at the point with coordinates $(2, 1, 0)$. Find the direction at this point, in which the rate of decrease in potential is greatest.

Solution   The rate of decrease is greatest in the direction of $-\nabla V$.
We first calculate the first partial derivatives of V. Writing

$$V = y(x^2 + y^2 + z^2)^{-3/2}$$

we find

$$\frac{\partial V}{\partial x} = \left(-\frac{3}{2}\right)y(x^2 + y^2 + z^2)^{-5/2}(2x) = -3xy(x^2 + y^2 + z^2)^{-5/2}$$

$$\frac{\partial V}{\partial y} = \left(-\frac{3}{2}\right)y(x^2 + y^2 + z^2)^{-5/2}(2y) + (x^2 + y^2 + z^2)^{-3/2}$$

$$= -3y^2(x^2 + y^2 + z^2)^{-5/2} + (x^2 + y^2 + z^2)^{-3/2}$$

$$\frac{\partial V}{\partial z} = \left(-\frac{3}{2}\right)y(x^2 + y^2 + z^2)^{-5/2}(2z) = -3yz(x^2 + y^2 + z^2)^{-5/2}$$

These partial derivatives can each be evaluated at the point (2, 1, 0). That is,

$$\left.\frac{\partial V}{\partial x}\right|_{(2,1,0)} = -0.107 \qquad \left.\frac{\partial V}{\partial y}\right|_{(2,1,0)} = 0.036 \qquad \left.\frac{\partial V}{\partial z}\right|_{(2,1,0)} = 0$$

and so

$$\nabla V|_{(2,1,0)} = -0.107\mathbf{i} + 0.036\mathbf{j} + 0\mathbf{k}$$

Finally,

$$-\nabla V|_{(2,1,0)} = 0.107\mathbf{i} - 0.036\mathbf{j} - 0\mathbf{k}$$

At the point (2, 1, 0) this vector points in the direction of greatest rate of decrease in potential. This is also the direction of the electrostatic force experienced by the unit charge at that point.

Exercises 26.3

1 If $\phi = x^2 - y^2 - 3xyz$, (a) find $\nabla\phi$,
(b) evaluate $\nabla\phi$ at the point (0, 0, 0).

2 If $\phi = x^2yz^3$, find (a) $\nabla\phi$, (b) $\nabla\phi$ at (1, 2, 1),
(c) $|\nabla\phi|$ at (1, 2, 1).

3 If $\mathbf{v} = \nabla\phi$, find ϕ when
$\mathbf{v} = (2x - 4y^2)\mathbf{i} - 8xy\mathbf{j}$.

4 Given $\phi = xyz$ find (a) $\nabla\phi$, (b) $-\nabla\phi$, (c) $\nabla\phi$
evaluated at (3, 0, −1).

5 Find ∇V when

(a) $V = x^2 + y^2 + z^2$

(b) $V = z\sin^{-1}\left(\dfrac{y}{x}\right)$

(c) $V = e^{x+y+z}$.

6 An electrostatic potential is given by
$V = xe^{-\sqrt{y}}$. Find ∇V and deduce the direction
in which the decrease of potential is greatest at
the point with coordinates (1, 1, 1).

7 In the theory of fluid mechanics the scalar field
ϕ is known as the **velocity potential** of a fluid
flow. The fluid velocity vector, $\mathbf{v}$, at a point can
be found from the equation $\mathbf{v} = \nabla\phi$. For a

particular type of flow $\phi = Ux$, where U is a constant. Show that the corresponding fluid motion is entirely parallel to the x axis, and at any point the fluid speed is U. Find a velocity potential for a similar flow which is entirely parallel to the y axis.

8 Is $-\nabla\phi$ the same as $\nabla(-\phi)$? Explain your answer.

9 Given $\phi = 3x^2y + xz$,

(a) determine $\nabla\phi$

(b) determine $\nabla(7\phi)$

(c) determine $7\nabla\phi$

(d) Is $\nabla(7\phi)$ the same as $7\nabla\phi$?

10 For any scalar field ϕ and any constant k, is $\nabla(k\phi)$ the same as $k\nabla\phi$?

Solutions

1 (a) $(2x - 3yz)\mathbf{i} - (2y + 3xz)\mathbf{j} - 3xy\mathbf{k}$
   (b) $\mathbf{0}$

2 (a) $2xyz^3\mathbf{i} + x^2z^3\mathbf{j} + 3x^2yz^2\mathbf{k}$
   (b) $4\mathbf{i} + \mathbf{j} + 6\mathbf{k}$
   (c) $\sqrt{53}$

3 $\phi = x^2 - 4xy^2 + c$

4 (a) $yz\mathbf{i} + xz\mathbf{j} + xy\mathbf{k}$
   (b) $-yz\mathbf{i} - xz\mathbf{j} - xy\mathbf{k}$
   (c) $-3\mathbf{j}$

5 (a) $2x\mathbf{i} + 2y\mathbf{j} + 2z\mathbf{k}$
   (b) $\dfrac{-zy}{x^2\sqrt{1-y^2/x^2}}\mathbf{i} + \dfrac{z}{x\sqrt{1-y^2/x^2}}\mathbf{j} + \sin^{-1}\left(\dfrac{y}{x}\right)\mathbf{k}$

(c) $e^{x+y+z}(\mathbf{i}+\mathbf{j}+\mathbf{k})$

6 $e^{-\sqrt{y}}\mathbf{i} - \dfrac{x\,e^{-\sqrt{y}}}{2\sqrt{y}}\mathbf{j}$, $-0.368\mathbf{i} + 0.184\mathbf{j}$

7 $\phi = Uy$

8 yes

9 (a) $(6xy + z)\mathbf{i} + 3x^2\mathbf{j} + x\mathbf{k}$
   (b) $(42xy + 7z)\mathbf{i} + 21x^2\mathbf{j} + 7x\mathbf{k}$
   (c) $(42xy + 7z)\mathbf{i} + 21x^2\mathbf{j} + 7x\mathbf{k}$
   (d) yes

10 yes

26.4 The divergence of a vector field

Given a vector field $\mathbf{v} = \mathbf{v}(x, y, z)$ let us consider what happens when we differentiate its individual components. If

$$\mathbf{v} = v_x\mathbf{i} + v_y\mathbf{j} + v_z\mathbf{k}$$

we can take each component in turn and differentiate it partially w.r.t. x, y and z, respectively; that is, we can evaluate

$$\frac{\partial v_x}{\partial x} \qquad \frac{\partial v_y}{\partial y} \qquad \frac{\partial v_z}{\partial z}$$

If we add the calculated quantities the result turns out to be a very useful scalar quantity known as the **divergence** of $\mathbf{v}$, that is

$$\text{divergence of } \mathbf{v} = \frac{\partial v_x}{\partial x} + \frac{\partial v_y}{\partial y} + \frac{\partial v_z}{\partial z}$$

This is usually abbreviated to div $\mathbf{v}$. Alternatively, the notation $\nabla \cdot \mathbf{v}$ is often used. If we use the vector operator notation introduced in the previous section we have

$$\nabla \cdot \mathbf{v} = \left(\frac{\partial}{\partial x}, \frac{\partial}{\partial y}, \frac{\partial}{\partial z} \right) \cdot \mathbf{v}$$

$$= \left(\frac{\partial}{\partial x}, \frac{\partial}{\partial y}, \frac{\partial}{\partial z} \right) \cdot (v_x, v_y, v_z)$$

Interpreting the $\cdot$ as a scalar product we find

$$\nabla \cdot \mathbf{v} = \frac{\partial v_x}{\partial x} + \frac{\partial v_y}{\partial y} + \frac{\partial v_z}{\partial z}$$

as before, although this is not a scalar product in the usual sense because $\left(\frac{\partial}{\partial x}, \frac{\partial}{\partial y}, \frac{\partial}{\partial z} \right)$ is a vector operator. We note that the process of finding the divergence is always performed on a vector field and the result is always a scalar field.

$$\text{div } \mathbf{v} = \nabla \cdot \mathbf{v} = \frac{\partial v_x}{\partial x} + \frac{\partial v_y}{\partial y} + \frac{\partial v_z}{\partial z}$$

Example 26.6   If $\mathbf{v} = x^2 z \mathbf{i} + 2y^3 z^2 \mathbf{j} + xyz^2 \mathbf{k}$ find div $\mathbf{v}$.

Solution   Partially differentiating the first component of $\mathbf{v}$ w.r.t. x we find

$$\frac{\partial v_x}{\partial x} = 2xz$$

Similarly,

$$\frac{\partial v_y}{\partial y} = 6y^2 z^2 \qquad \text{and} \qquad \frac{\partial v_z}{\partial z} = 2xyz$$

Adding these results we find

$$\text{div } \mathbf{v} = \nabla \cdot \mathbf{v} = 2xz + 6y^2 z^2 + 2xyz$$

26.4.1 Physical interpretation of $\nabla \cdot \mathbf{v}$

If the vector field $\mathbf{v}$ represents a fluid velocity field, then, loosely speaking, the divergence of $\mathbf{v}$ evaluated at a point represents the rate at which fluid is flowing away from or towards that point. If fluid is flowing away from a point then either the fluid density must be decreasing there or there must be some source providing a supply of new fluid.

If the divergence of a flow is zero at all points then outflow from any point must be matched by an equal inflow to balance this. Such a vector field is said to be **solenoidal**.

Example 26.7

Show that the vector field

$$\mathbf{v} = x \sin y \mathbf{i} + y \sin x \mathbf{j} - z(\sin x + \sin y)\mathbf{k}$$

is solenoidal.

Solution

We have

$$v_x = x \sin y \qquad \text{so that} \qquad \frac{\partial v_x}{\partial x} = \sin y$$

Also,

$$v_y = y \sin x \qquad \text{so that} \qquad \frac{\partial v_y}{\partial y} = \sin x$$

Finally,

$$v_z = -z(\sin x + \sin y) \qquad \text{so that} \qquad \frac{\partial v_z}{\partial z} = -(\sin x + \sin y)$$

Therefore,

$$\nabla \cdot \mathbf{v} = \sin y + \sin x - (\sin x + \sin y) = 0$$

and hence $\mathbf{v}$ is solenoidal.

Example 26.8

Electric flux and Gauss's law

We saw in Example 7.16 that electric charges produce an electric field, $\mathbf{E}$, around them which can be visualized by drawing lines of force. Suppose we surround a region containing charges with a surface S. If a small portion of this surface, δS, is chosen we can draw the field lines which pass through this portion as shown in Figure 26.1.

Figure 26.1
The flux of $\mathbf{E}$ through δS is a measure of the number of lines of force passing through δS.

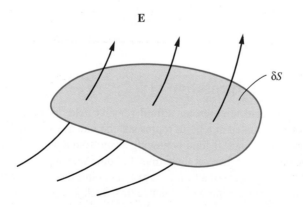

The **flux** of **E** through δS is a measure of the number of lines of force passing through δS. Gauss's law states that the total flux out of any closed surface S is proportional to the total charge enclosed. It is possible to show that this law can be expressed mathematically as

$$\nabla \cdot \mathbf{E} = \frac{\rho}{\varepsilon_0}$$

where ρ is the charge density and ε_0 is a constant called the **permittivity of free space**. Note that in a charge-free region, $\rho = 0$, and so $\nabla \cdot \mathbf{E} = 0$. This means there is no net flux of **E**.

Exercises 26.4

1 A vector field **v** is given by

$$\mathbf{v} = 3x^2 y\mathbf{i} + 2y^3 z\mathbf{j} + xz^3\mathbf{k}$$

Find

(a) v_x, v_y, v_z

(b) $\dfrac{\partial v_x}{\partial x}, \dfrac{\partial v_y}{\partial y}, \dfrac{\partial v_z}{\partial z}$

(c) $\nabla \cdot \mathbf{v}$

2 A vector field **F** is defined by

$$\mathbf{F} = (x + y^2)\mathbf{i} + (y^2 - z)\mathbf{j} + (y + z^2)\mathbf{k}$$

(a) Find $\nabla \cdot \mathbf{F}$.

(b) Calculate $\nabla \cdot \mathbf{F}$ at the point $(3, 2, -1)$.

3 If $\mathbf{A} = 3yz\mathbf{i} + 2xy\mathbf{j} + xyz\mathbf{k}$ find $\nabla \cdot \mathbf{A}$.

4 Find the divergence of each of the following vector fields.

(a) $\mathbf{v} = x^2\mathbf{i} + y^2\mathbf{j} + z^2\mathbf{k}$

(b) $\mathbf{v} = e^{xy}\mathbf{i} + 2z\sin(xy)\mathbf{j} + x^3 z\mathbf{k}$

(c) $\mathbf{v} = xy\mathbf{i} - 2yz\mathbf{j} + \mathbf{k}$

(d) $\mathbf{v} = x^2 y^2\mathbf{i} - y^2\mathbf{j} - xyz\mathbf{k}$

5 If $\mathbf{E} = x\mathbf{i} + z^2\mathbf{j} - yz\mathbf{k}$ find

(a) $\mathbf{E} \cdot \mathbf{i}$

(b) $\mathbf{E} \cdot \mathbf{j}$

(c) $\mathbf{E} \cdot \mathbf{k}$

(d) $\nabla \cdot \mathbf{E}$

6 A vector field is given by

$$\mathbf{F} = (3x^2 - z)\mathbf{i} + (2x + y)\mathbf{j}$$
$$+ (x + 3yz)\mathbf{k}$$

Find $\nabla \cdot \mathbf{F}$ at the point $(1, 2, 3)$.

7 Given the scalar field $\phi = x^2 + y^2 - 2z^2$, find $\nabla\phi$ and show that $\nabla \cdot (\nabla\phi) = 0$.

8 For any vector field **F** is $\nabla \cdot (-\mathbf{F})$ the same as $-(\nabla \cdot \mathbf{F})$?

9 The vector field **F** is given by

$$\mathbf{F} = xz^2\mathbf{i} + 2xy^2 z\mathbf{j} + xz^3\mathbf{k}$$

(a) Find $\nabla \cdot \mathbf{F}$.

(b) State $4\mathbf{F}$.

(c) Find $\nabla \cdot (4\mathbf{F})$.

(d) Is $4(\nabla \cdot \mathbf{F})$ the same as $\nabla \cdot (4\mathbf{F})$?

10 For any vector field **F** and any scalar constant k is $\nabla \cdot (k\mathbf{F})$ the same as $k\nabla \cdot \mathbf{F}$?

11 Give an example of a vector field $\mathbf{v} = v_x\mathbf{i} + v_y\mathbf{j} + v_z\mathbf{k}$ such that $\dfrac{\partial v_x}{\partial x} \neq 0, \dfrac{\partial v_y}{\partial y} \neq 0, \dfrac{\partial v_z}{\partial z} \neq 0$, but $\nabla \cdot \mathbf{v} = 0$.

Solutions

1 (a) $3x^2 y, 2y^3 z, xz^3$ (b) $6xy, 6y^2 z, 3xz^2$ (c) $6xy + 6y^2 z + 3xz^2$ T

2 (a) $1 + 2y + 2z$

   (b) 3

3 $\nabla \cdot \mathbf{A} = 2x + xy$

4 (a) $2x + 2y + 2z$

   (b) $y\,e^{xy} + 2xz\cos(xy) + x^3$

   (c) $y - 2z$

   (d) $2xy^2 - 2y - xy$

5 (a) x

   (b) z^2

   (c) $-yz$

   (d) $1 - y$

6 13

7 $\nabla\phi = 2x\mathbf{i} + 2y\mathbf{j} - 4z\mathbf{k}$

8 yes

9 (a) $z^2 + 4xyz + 3xz^2$

   (b) $4xz^2\mathbf{i} + 8xy^2z\mathbf{j} + 4xz^3\mathbf{k}$

   (c) $4z^2 + 16xyz + 12xz^2$

   (d) yes

10 yes

11 $\mathbf{v} = 2xy\mathbf{i} + y^2\mathbf{j} - 4yz\mathbf{k}$ for example

26.5   The curl of a vector field

A third differential operator is known as **curl**. It is defined rather like a vector product.

$$\operatorname{curl}\mathbf{v} = \nabla \times \mathbf{v}$$

$$= \left(\frac{\partial}{\partial x}, \frac{\partial}{\partial y}, \frac{\partial}{\partial z} \right) \times (v_x, v_y, v_z)$$

$$= \begin{vmatrix} \mathbf{i} & \mathbf{j} & \mathbf{k} \\ \dfrac{\partial}{\partial x} & \dfrac{\partial}{\partial y} & \dfrac{\partial}{\partial z} \\ v_x & v_y & v_z \end{vmatrix}$$

This determinant is evaluated in the usual way except that we must regard $\dfrac{\partial}{\partial x}, \dfrac{\partial}{\partial y}$ and $\dfrac{\partial}{\partial z}$ as operators, not multipliers. Thus, for example,

$$\begin{vmatrix} \dfrac{\partial}{\partial x} & \dfrac{\partial}{\partial y} \\ v_x & v_y \end{vmatrix} \qquad \text{means} \qquad \frac{\partial v_y}{\partial x} - \frac{\partial v_x}{\partial y}$$

Explicitly we have

$$\operatorname{curl}\mathbf{v} = \left(\frac{\partial v_z}{\partial y} - \frac{\partial v_y}{\partial z} \right)\mathbf{i} + \left(\frac{\partial v_x}{\partial z} - \frac{\partial v_z}{\partial x} \right)\mathbf{j} + \left(\frac{\partial v_y}{\partial x} - \frac{\partial v_x}{\partial y} \right)\mathbf{k}$$

Example 26.9   If $\mathbf{v} = x^2yz\mathbf{i} - 2xy\mathbf{j} + yz\mathbf{k}$ find $\nabla \times \mathbf{v}$.

Solution $\nabla \times \mathbf{v} = \begin{vmatrix} \mathbf{i} & \mathbf{j} & \mathbf{k} \\ \dfrac{\partial}{\partial x} & \dfrac{\partial}{\partial y} & \dfrac{\partial}{\partial z} \\ x^2 yz & -2xy & yz \end{vmatrix}$

$$= \left[\frac{\partial(yz)}{\partial y} - \frac{\partial(-2xy)}{\partial z} \right]\mathbf{i} - \left[\frac{\partial(yz)}{\partial x} - \frac{\partial(x^2 yz)}{\partial z} \right]\mathbf{j} + \left[\frac{\partial(-2xy)}{\partial x} - \frac{\partial(x^2 yz)}{\partial y} \right]\mathbf{k}$$

$$= z\mathbf{i} + x^2 y\mathbf{j} - (2y + x^2 z)\mathbf{k}$$

Note that the curl operation is only performed on a vector field and the result is another vector field.

A detailed discussion of the physical interpretation of the curl of a vector field is beyond the scope of this book. However, if the vector field $\mathbf{v}$ under consideration represents a fluid flow then it may be shown that curl $\mathbf{v}$ is a vector which measures the extent to which individual particles of the fluid are spinning or rotating. For this reason, a vector field whose curl is zero for all values of x, y and z is said to be **irrotational**.

Example 26.10 Show that the vector field

$$\mathbf{F} = y\,e^{xy}\mathbf{i} + x\,e^{xy}\mathbf{j} + 0\mathbf{k}$$

is irrotational.

Solution $\nabla \times \mathbf{F} = \begin{vmatrix} \mathbf{i} & \mathbf{j} & \mathbf{k} \\ \dfrac{\partial}{\partial x} & \dfrac{\partial}{\partial y} & \dfrac{\partial}{\partial z} \\ y\,e^{yx} & x\,e^{xy} & 0 \end{vmatrix}$

$$= \left(\frac{\partial}{\partial y}0 - \frac{\partial}{\partial z}x\,e^{xy} \right)\mathbf{i} - \left(\frac{\partial}{\partial x}0 - \frac{\partial}{\partial z}y\,e^{xy} \right)\mathbf{j} + \left(\frac{\partial}{\partial x}x\,e^{xy} - \frac{\partial}{\partial y}y\,e^{xy} \right)\mathbf{k}$$

$$= 0\mathbf{i} + 0\mathbf{j} + ((xy\,e^{xy} + e^{xy}) - (yx\,e^{xy} + e^{xy}))\mathbf{k}$$

$$= 0 \qquad \text{for all } x, y \text{ and } z$$

The field is therefore irrotational.

Exercises 26.5

1. Find the curl of the vector field
$\mathbf{v} = x\mathbf{i} - 3xy\mathbf{j} + 4z\mathbf{k}$.

2. If $\mathbf{v} = 3x\mathbf{i} - 2y^2 z\mathbf{j} + 3xyz\mathbf{k}$ find $\nabla \times \mathbf{v}$.

3. Suppose $\mathbf{F} = P(x, y)\mathbf{i} + Q(x, y)\mathbf{j}$ is a two-dimensional vector field. Show that $\mathbf{F}$ is

irrotational if $\dfrac{\partial P}{\partial y} = \dfrac{\partial Q}{\partial x}$.

4. Find the divergence and curl of the vector field
$\mathbf{E} = \cos x\mathbf{i} + \sin x\mathbf{j}$.

5. Find the curl of each of the following vector

fields:

(a) $E = x^2yi + 7xyzj + 3x^2k$

(b) $v = y^2xi + 4xzj + y^2xk$

(c) $F = \sin xi + \cos xj + 3xyzk$

6 A vector field F is given by

$$F = x^3yi + 2y^2j + (x + z^2)k$$

(a) Find $\nabla \times F$.

(b) State $3F$.

(c) Find $\nabla \times (3F)$.

(d) Is $3(\nabla \times F)$ the same as $\nabla \times (3F)$?

7 F is a vector field and k is a constant. Is $\nabla \times (kF)$ the same as $k(\nabla \times F)$?

Solutions

1 $-3yk$

2 $(3xz + 2y^2)i - 3yzj$

4 $-\sin x, \cos xk$

5 (a) $-7xyi - 6xj + (7yz - x^2)k$

   (b) $x(2y - 4)i - y^2j + (4z - 2xy)k$

(c) $3xzi - 3yzj - \sin xk$

6 (a) $-j - x^3k$

   (b) $3x^3yi + 6y^2j + 3(x + z^2)k$

   (c) $-3j - 3x^3k$ (d) yes

7 yes

26.6 Combining the operators grad, div and curl

We have now met three vector operators; these are summarized in Table 26.1.

It is important to be able to combine the three operators grad, div and curl in sensible ways. For instance, because the gradient of a scalar is a vector we can consider evaluating its divergence, that is

$$\nabla \cdot (\nabla \phi) = \nabla \cdot \left(\frac{\partial \phi}{\partial x}, \frac{\partial \phi}{\partial y}, \frac{\partial \phi}{\partial z} \right)$$

$$= \left(\frac{\partial}{\partial x}, \frac{\partial}{\partial y}, \frac{\partial}{\partial z} \right) \cdot \left(\frac{\partial \phi}{\partial x}, \frac{\partial \phi}{\partial y}, \frac{\partial \phi}{\partial z} \right)$$

$$= \frac{\partial^2 \phi}{\partial x^2} + \frac{\partial^2 \phi}{\partial y^2} + \frac{\partial^2 \phi}{\partial z^2}$$

Table 26.1
The three vector operators.

Operator	Acts on	Result is a	Definition
grad	scalar field	vector field	$\nabla \phi = \text{grad } \phi = \dfrac{\partial \phi}{\partial x}i + \dfrac{\partial \phi}{\partial y}j + \dfrac{\partial \phi}{\partial z}k$
div	vector field	scalar field	$\nabla \cdot v = \text{div } v = \dfrac{\partial v_x}{\partial x} + \dfrac{\partial v_y}{\partial y} + \dfrac{\partial v_z}{\partial z}$
curl	vector field	vector field	$\nabla \times v = \text{curl } v = \begin{vmatrix} i & j & k \\ \dfrac{\partial}{\partial x} & \dfrac{\partial}{\partial y} & \dfrac{\partial}{\partial z} \\ v_x & v_y & v_z \end{vmatrix}$

This last expression is very important and is often abbreviated to simply

$$\nabla^2 \phi$$

pronounced 'del-squared ϕ', and occurs in Laplace's equation $\nabla^2 \phi = 0$ and other partial differential equations.

Example 26.11   If $\phi = 2x^2 - y^2 - z^2$, find $\nabla\phi$, $\nabla \cdot (\nabla\phi)$ and deduce that ϕ satisfies Laplace's equation.

Solution $\nabla\phi = 4x\mathbf{i} - 2y\mathbf{j} - 2z\mathbf{k}$
$\nabla \cdot (\nabla\phi) = 4 - 2 - 2 = 0$

that is,

$$\nabla^2 \phi = 0$$

Hence ϕ satisfies Laplace's equation.

Example 26.12   If $\phi(x, y, z)$ is an arbitrary differentiable scalar field, show that $\mathrm{curl}(\mathrm{grad}\phi) = \nabla \times (\nabla\phi)$ is always zero.

Solution   Given $\phi = \phi(x, y, z)$ we have, by definition,

$$\nabla\phi = \frac{\partial\phi}{\partial x}\mathbf{i} + \frac{\partial\phi}{\partial y}\mathbf{j} + \frac{\partial\phi}{\partial z}\mathbf{k}$$

Then

$$\mathrm{curl}(\mathrm{grad}\phi) = \nabla \times (\nabla\phi)$$

$$= \begin{vmatrix} \mathbf{i} & \mathbf{j} & \mathbf{k} \\ \dfrac{\partial}{\partial x} & \dfrac{\partial}{\partial y} & \dfrac{\partial}{\partial z} \\ \dfrac{\partial\phi}{\partial x} & \dfrac{\partial\phi}{\partial y} & \dfrac{\partial\phi}{\partial z} \end{vmatrix}$$

$$= \left(\frac{\partial}{\partial y}\left(\frac{\partial\phi}{\partial z}\right) - \frac{\partial}{\partial z}\left(\frac{\partial\phi}{\partial y}\right) \right)\mathbf{i} - \left(\frac{\partial}{\partial x}\left(\frac{\partial\phi}{\partial z}\right) - \frac{\partial}{\partial z}\left(\frac{\partial\phi}{\partial x}\right) \right)\mathbf{j}$$

$$+ \left(\frac{\partial}{\partial x}\left(\frac{\partial\phi}{\partial y}\right) - \frac{\partial}{\partial y}\left(\frac{\partial\phi}{\partial x}\right) \right)\mathbf{k}$$

Now, since $\dfrac{\partial}{\partial x}\left(\dfrac{\partial\phi}{\partial y}\right) = \dfrac{\partial}{\partial y}\left(\dfrac{\partial\phi}{\partial x}\right)$ with similar results for the other mixed partial derivatives, it follows that

$$\nabla \times (\nabla\phi) = \mathbf{0}$$

for any scalar field ϕ whatsoever.

For an arbitrary differentiable scalar field ϕ

$$\nabla \times (\nabla\phi) = \mathbf{0}$$

Example 26.13   Poisson's equation

If $\mathbf{E}$ is an electric field and V an electrostatic potential, then the two fields are related by

$$\mathbf{E} = -\nabla V$$

From Example 26.8 we know Gauss's law: $\nabla \cdot \mathbf{E} = \dfrac{\rho}{\varepsilon_0}$. Combining these two equations we can write

$$\nabla \cdot (-\nabla V) = \frac{\rho}{\varepsilon_0}$$

that is

$$\nabla^2 V = -\frac{\rho}{\varepsilon_0}$$

This partial differential equation is known as Poisson's equation and by solving it we could determine the electrostatic potential in a region occupied by charges. Note that in a charge-free region, $\rho = 0$ and Poisson's equation reduces to Laplace's equation $\nabla^2 V = 0$.

Exercises   26.6

1 A scalar field ϕ is given by
$\phi = 3x + y - y^2z^2$. Show that ϕ satisfies
$\nabla^2\phi = -2(y^2 + z^2)$.

2 If $\phi = 2x^2y - xz^3$ show that $\nabla^2\phi = 4y - 6xz$.

3 If $\mathbf{v} = xy\mathbf{i} - yz\mathbf{j} + (y + 2z)\mathbf{k}$ find curl (curl (**v**)).

4 If $\phi = xyz$ and $\mathbf{v} = 3x^2\mathbf{i} + 2y^3\mathbf{j} + xy\mathbf{k}$ find
$\nabla\phi$, $\nabla \cdot \mathbf{v}$, and $\nabla \cdot (\phi\mathbf{v})$. Show that
$\nabla \cdot (\phi\mathbf{v}) = (\nabla\phi) \cdot \mathbf{v} + \phi\nabla \cdot \mathbf{v}$.

5 Verify that $\phi = x^2y + y^2z + z^2x$ satisfies
$\nabla \cdot (\nabla\phi) = 2(x + y + z)$.

6 If $\mathbf{A}$ is an arbitrary differentiable vector field show that the divergence of the curl of $\mathbf{A}$ is always 0.

7 Express each of the following in operator notation using '∇', '$\nabla\cdot$' and '$\nabla\times$'.

(a) grad (div **F**)

(b) curl (grad ϕ)

(c) curl (curl **F**)

(d) div (curl **F**)

(e) div (grad ϕ)

8 Scalar fields ϕ_1 and ϕ_2 are given by

$$\phi_1 = 2xy + y^2z \qquad \phi_2 = x^2z$$

(a) Find $\nabla\phi_1$.

(b) Find $\nabla\phi_2$.

(c) State $\phi_1\phi_2$.

(d) Find $\nabla(\phi_1\phi_2)$.

(e) Find $\phi_1\nabla\phi_2 + \phi_2\nabla\phi_1$.

(f) What do you conclude from (d) and (e)?

9 A scalar field ϕ and a vector field $\mathbf{F}$ are given by

$$\phi = xyz^2 \qquad \mathbf{F} = x^2\mathbf{i} + 2\mathbf{j} + z\mathbf{k}$$

(a) Find $\nabla\phi$.

(b) Find $\nabla \cdot \mathbf{F}$.

(c) Calculate $\phi(\nabla \cdot \mathbf{F}) + \mathbf{F} \cdot (\nabla\phi)$. [*Hint:* recall the dot product of two vectors.]

(d) State $\phi\mathbf{F}$.

(e) Calculate $\nabla \cdot (\phi\mathbf{F})$.

(f) What do you conclude from (c) and (e)?

Solutions

3 $\mathbf{j} - \mathbf{k}$

4 $\nabla\phi = yz\mathbf{i} + xz\mathbf{j} + xy\mathbf{k}$

$\nabla \cdot \mathbf{v} = 6x + 6y^2$

$\nabla \cdot (\phi\mathbf{v}) = 9x^2yz + 8xy^3z + x^2y^2$

7 (a) $\nabla(\nabla \cdot \mathbf{F})$

(b) $\nabla \times (\nabla\phi)$

(c) $\nabla \times (\nabla \times \mathbf{F})$

(d) $\nabla \cdot (\nabla \times \mathbf{F})$

(e) $\nabla \cdot (\nabla\phi)$

8 (a) $2y\mathbf{i} + (2x + 2yz)\mathbf{j} + y^2\mathbf{k}$

(b) $2xz\mathbf{i} + x^2\mathbf{k}$

(c) $2x^3yz + y^2x^2z^2$

(d) $(6x^2yz + 2xy^2z^2)\mathbf{i} + (2x^3z + 2yx^2z^2)\mathbf{j}$
$\quad + (2x^3y + 2y^2x^2z)\mathbf{k}$

(e) same as (d)

(f) $\nabla(\phi_1\phi_2) = \phi_1\nabla\phi_2 + \phi_2\nabla\phi_1$

9 (a) $yz^2\mathbf{i} + xz^2\mathbf{j} + 2xyz\mathbf{k}$

(b) $2x + 1$

(c) $3x^2yz^2 + 2xz^2 + 3xyz^2$

(d) $x^3yz^2\mathbf{i} + 2xyz^2\mathbf{j} + xyz^3\mathbf{k}$

(e) same as (c)

(f) $\nabla \cdot (\phi\mathbf{F}) = \phi(\nabla \cdot \mathbf{F}) + \mathbf{F} \cdot (\nabla\phi)$

26.7   Vector calculus and electromagnetism

Vector calculus provides a useful mechanism for expressing the fundamental laws of electromagnetism in a concise manner. These laws can be summarized by means of four equations, known as Maxwell's equations. Much of electromagnetism is concerned with solving Maxwell's equations for different boundary conditions.

Equation 1

$$\text{div } \mathbf{D} = \rho$$

where $\mathbf{D}$ = electric flux density, and ρ = charge density. This equation is a general form of Gauss's theorem which states that the total electric flux flowing out of a closed surface is proportional to the electric charge enclosed by that surface.

Equation 2

$$\text{div } \mathbf{B} = 0$$

where $\mathbf{B}$ is the magnetic flux density.

This equation arises from the observation that all magnetic poles occur in pairs and therefore magnetic field lines are continuous; that is, there are no isolated magnetic poles. In contrast, electric field lines originate on positive charges and terminate on negative charges and so a net positive charge in a region leads to an outflow of electric flux.

Equation 3

$$\text{curl } \mathbf{E} = -\frac{\partial \mathbf{B}}{\partial t}$$

where $\mathbf{E}$ is the electric field strength. This equation is a statement of Faraday's law. A time-varying magnetic field produces a space-varying electric field.

Equation 4

$$\text{curl } \mathbf{H} = \mathbf{J} + \frac{\partial \mathbf{D}}{\partial t}$$

where $\mathbf{H}$ is the magnetic field strength and $\mathbf{J}$ is the free current density. This equation states that a time-varying electric field gives rise to a space-varying magnetic field.

The derivation of these equations is beyond the scope of this text but can be found in many books on electromagnetism. The power of these equations lies in their generality. The brevity with which the main laws of electromagnetism can be expressed is a tribute to the utility of vector calculus.

Review exercises 26

1 Find $\nabla\phi$ if

   (a) $\phi = 3xyz$

   (b) $\phi = x^2yz + xy^2z + xyz^2$

   (c) $\phi = xy^2z^2 + x^2yz^2 + x^2y^2z$

2 If $\phi = 1/\sqrt{x^2 + y^2 + z^2}$, show that

$$\frac{\partial^2\phi}{\partial x^2} + \frac{\partial^2\phi}{\partial y^2} + \frac{\partial^2\phi}{\partial z^2} = 0$$

3 Functions satisfying Laplace's equation are called **harmonic functions**. Show that the following functions are harmonic.

   (a) $z = x^4 - 6x^2y^2 + y^4$

   (b) $z = 4x^3y - 4xy^3$

4 If $\mathbf{A} = x\mathbf{i} + y\mathbf{j} + z\mathbf{k}$ and $\mathbf{B} = \cos x\mathbf{i} - \sin x\mathbf{j}$, find

   (a) $\mathbf{A} \times \mathbf{B}$

   (b) $\nabla \cdot (\mathbf{A} \times \mathbf{B})$

   (c) $\nabla \times \mathbf{A}$

   (d) $\nabla \times \mathbf{B}$

Verify that
$$\nabla \cdot (\mathbf{A} \times \mathbf{B}) = \mathbf{B} \cdot (\nabla \times \mathbf{A}) - \mathbf{A} \cdot (\nabla \times \mathbf{B}).$$

5 For arbitrary differentiable scalar fields ϕ and ψ show that $\nabla(\phi\psi) = \psi\nabla\phi + \phi\nabla\psi$.

6 If $\psi = x^2y$ and $\mathbf{a} = x\mathbf{i} + y\mathbf{j} + z\mathbf{k}$, find $\nabla\psi$, $\nabla \times \mathbf{a}$, $\nabla \times (\psi\mathbf{a})$. Show that
$$\nabla \times (\psi\mathbf{a}) = \psi\nabla \times \mathbf{a} + (\nabla\psi) \times \mathbf{a}.$$

7 A scalar field ϕ is a function of x, z and t only. Vectors $\mathbf{E}$ and $\mathbf{H}$ are defined by

$$\mathbf{E} = \frac{1}{\varepsilon}\left(\frac{\partial\phi}{\partial z}\mathbf{i} - \frac{\partial\phi}{\partial x}\mathbf{k}\right) \qquad \mathbf{H} = -\frac{\partial\phi}{\partial t}\mathbf{j}$$

where ε is a constant.

   (a)   Show that $\nabla \cdot \mathbf{E} = 0$.

   (b)   Show that $\nabla \cdot \mathbf{H} = 0$.

Given that $\nabla \times \mathbf{E} = -\mu\dfrac{\partial \mathbf{H}}{\partial t}$, where μ is a constant, show that ϕ satisfies the partial differential equation

$$\frac{\partial^2\phi}{\partial x^2} + \frac{\partial^2\phi}{\partial z^2} = \mu\varepsilon\frac{\partial^2\phi}{\partial t^2}$$

8 If $\mathbf{v} = (2x^2y + 3x^5)\mathbf{i} + e^{xy}\mathbf{j} + xyz\mathbf{k}$ find $\dfrac{\partial\mathbf{v}}{\partial x}$ and $\dfrac{\partial^2\mathbf{v}}{\partial x^2}$.

9 An electrostatic potential is given by $V = 5xyz$. Find

(a) the associated electric field **E**,

(b) $|\mathbf{E}|$ at the point $(1, 1, 1)$.

10 An electrostatic field is given by
$\mathbf{E} = 3(x + y)\mathbf{i} + 2xy\mathbf{j}$. Find the direction of this field at

(a) the point $(2, 2)$

(b) the point $(3, 4)$.

11 Find the curl of $\mathbf{A} = y\mathbf{i} + 2xy\mathbf{j} + 3z\mathbf{k}$.

12 Find the curl of the vector field
$\mathbf{F} = (x^2 - y)\mathbf{i} + (xy - 4y^2)\mathbf{j}$.

13 If $\phi = 5\,e^{x+2y} \cos z$ find $\nabla\phi$ at the point $(0, 0, 0)$.

14 The vector fields **A** and **B** are given by

$$\mathbf{A} = x^2 y\mathbf{i} + 2xz\mathbf{j} + x\mathbf{k}$$
$$\mathbf{B} = yz\mathbf{i} + x^2 y\mathbf{j} + 3\mathbf{k}$$

(a) Calculate the vector product $\mathbf{A} \times \mathbf{B}$.

(b) Calculate $\nabla \cdot (\mathbf{A} \times \mathbf{B})$.

(c) Calculate $\mathbf{B} \cdot (\nabla \times \mathbf{A}) - \mathbf{A} \cdot (\nabla \times \mathbf{B})$.

(d) What do you conclude from (b) and (c)?

(e) Can you prove this result is true for any two vector fields?

15 Given

$$\mathbf{F} = (3x, 2y, 4z) \qquad \mathbf{G} = (1, -1, 3)$$
$$\phi = x^2 yz$$

find

(a) $\nabla \cdot \mathbf{F}$

(b) $\nabla\phi$

(c) $\nabla \times \mathbf{F}$

(d) $\nabla \cdot (\phi\mathbf{F})$

(e) $\nabla \times (\phi\mathbf{G})$

(f) $\nabla(\mathbf{F} \cdot \mathbf{G})$

(g) $\nabla \times (\mathbf{F} \times \mathbf{G})$

(h) $\nabla \cdot (\mathbf{F} + \mathbf{G})$

(i) $\nabla \times (3\mathbf{F} + 4\mathbf{G})$

Solutions

1 (a) $3yz\mathbf{i} + 3xz\mathbf{j} + 3xy\mathbf{k}$

(b) $(2xyz + y^2 z + yz^2)\mathbf{i}$
$+ (x^2 z + 2xyz + xz^2)\mathbf{j}$
$+ (x^2 y + xy^2 + 2xyz)\mathbf{k}$

(c) $(y^2 z^2 + 2xyz^2 + 2xy^2 z)\mathbf{i}$
$+ (2xyz^2 + x^2 z^2 + 2x^2 yz)\mathbf{j}$
$+ (2xy^2 z + 2x^2 yz + x^2 y^2)\mathbf{k}$

4 (a) $z \sin x\mathbf{i} + z \cos x\mathbf{j} + (-y \cos x - x \sin x)\mathbf{k}$

(b) $z \cos x$

(c) **0**

(d) $-\cos x\mathbf{k}$

6 $\nabla\psi = 2xy\mathbf{i} + x^2\mathbf{j}$

$\nabla \times \mathbf{a} = \mathbf{0}$

$\nabla \times (\psi\mathbf{a}) = x^2 z\mathbf{i} - 2xyz\mathbf{j} + (2xy^2 - x^3)\mathbf{k}$

8 $(4xy + 15x^4)\mathbf{i} + y\,e^{xy}\mathbf{j} + yz\mathbf{k}$,

$(4y + 60x^3)\mathbf{i} + y^2\,e^{xy}\mathbf{j}$

9 (a) $\mathbf{E} = -\nabla V = -5yz\mathbf{i} - 5xz\mathbf{j} - 5xy\mathbf{k}$

(b) $\sqrt{75}$

10 (a) $12\mathbf{i} + 8\mathbf{j}$

(b) $21\mathbf{i} + 24\mathbf{j}$

11 $(2y - 1)\mathbf{k}$

12 $(y + 1)\mathbf{k}$

13 $5\mathbf{i} + 10\mathbf{j}$

14 (a) $(6xz - x^3 y)\mathbf{i} + (xyz - 3x^2 y)\mathbf{j}$
$+ (x^4 y^2 - 2xyz^2)\mathbf{k}$

(b) $-3x^2(y + 1) - xz(4y - 1) + 6z$

(c) $-3x^2(y + 1) - xz(4y - 1) + 6z$

(d) $\nabla \cdot (\mathbf{A} \times \mathbf{B}) = \mathbf{B} \cdot (\nabla \times \mathbf{A}) - \mathbf{A} \cdot (\nabla \times \mathbf{B})$

15 (a) 9

(b) $2xyz\mathbf{i} + x^2 z\mathbf{j} + x^2 y\mathbf{k}$

(c) **0**

(d) $21x^2 yz$

(e) $x^2(y + 3z)\mathbf{i} + (x^2 y - 6xyz)\mathbf{j}$
$- (x^2 z + 2xyz)\mathbf{k}$

(f) $3\mathbf{i} - 2\mathbf{j} + 12\mathbf{k}$

(g) $-6\mathbf{i} + 7\mathbf{j} - 15\mathbf{k}$

(h) 9

(i) **0**

27 Line integrals and multiple integrals

Chapter 27 Contents

27.1	Introduction	838
27.2	Line integrals	838
27.3	Evaluation of line integrals in two dimensions	841
27.4	Evaluation of line integrals in three dimensions	844
27.5	Conservative fields and potential functions	845
27.6	Double and triple integrals	851
27.7	Some simple volume and surface integrals	860
27.8	The divergence theorem and Stokes' theorem	866
27.9	Maxwell's equations in integral form	871
	Review exercises	872

27.1

Introduction

In this chapter a number of new sorts of integral are introduced. These are intimately connected with the developments of the previous chapter on differential vector calculus. The chapter starts by explaining the physical significance of line integrals and how these are evaluated. This leads naturally into the topics of conservative vector fields and potential functions. These are important in the study of electrostatics. Double and triple integrals are then introduced; these generalize the earlier work on integration to integrands which contain two and three independent variables.

Finally some simple volume and surface integrals are introduced, together with the divergence theorem and Stokes' theorem. These enable Maxwell's equations to be expressed in integral form.

27.2

Line integrals

Consider an object of mass m placed in a gravitational field. Because the force of gravity is a vector the gravitational field is an example of a **vector field**. The gravitational force on the mass is known as its weight and is given by $m\mathbf{g}$ where $\mathbf{g}$ is a constant vector called **the acceleration due to gravity**. Suppose we release the mass and allow it to fall from point A in Figure 27.1. The vertical displacement measured downwards from A is s.

Work is being done by the gravitational force in order to make the mass accelerate. We wish to calculate the work done by the field in moving the mass from A to B. Suppose we consider the amount of work done as the mass moves from point M to point N, a distance δs. Elementary physics tells us that the work done is equal to the product of the magnitude of the force and the distance moved in the direction of the force. In this case the magnitude of the force is mg, and so the small amount of work done, δW, in moving from M to N, is

$$\delta W = mg \, \delta s$$

from which we have $\dfrac{\delta W}{\delta s} = mg$. As $\delta s \to 0$ we obtain

$$\lim_{\delta s \to 0} \frac{\delta W}{\delta s} = \frac{\mathrm{d}W}{\mathrm{d}s} = mg$$

To find the total work done as the mass falls from A to B we must add up, or integrate, the contributions over the whole interval of interest, that is

$$\text{total work done} = W = \int_A^B mg \, \mathrm{d}s$$

This is an elementary example of a **line integral**, so called because we are integrating along the line from A to B. In this case it is straightforward to evaluate. Since both g and m are constants the integral becomes

$$W = mg \int_A^B \mathrm{d}s$$

which equals $mg \times$ (distance from A to B).

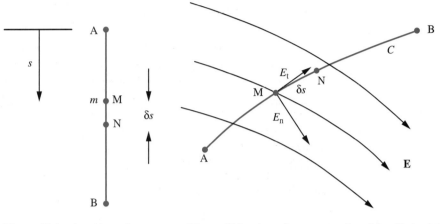

Figure 27.1 An object of mass *m* falls from A to B.

Figure 27.2 As a charge moves from M to N, the field **E** does work $E_t \delta s$.

Example 27.1 The work done by the gravitational field

An object of mass *m* falls vertically from A to B. If A is the point where $s = 0$ and B where $s = 10$ find the total work done by gravity as the mass falls from A to B.

Solution The work done by gravity is found by evaluating the line integral

$$W = mg \int_{s=0}^{s=10} \mathrm{d}s = mg[s]_0^{10} = 10mg$$

Note that this is also the potential energy lost by *m* in falling a distance of 10 units.

In the previous example the path along which we integrated was a straight line, but this need not always be the case. Consider the following example.

Example 27.2 The work done by an electric field

Figure 27.2 shows a unit charge moving along a curve *C* from point A to point B in an electric field **E**.

At the particular point of interest, M, we have resolved the electric field vector into two components. Resolving a vector into perpendicular components has been described in Example 7.3. One component is tangent to *C*, namely E_t, and one is normal to *C*, namely E_n. As a unit charge moves from M to N, a distance δs along the curve, the work done by the electric field is $E_t \delta s$. The component E_n does no work since there is no motion perpendicular to the curve *C*. To find the total work done we must add up all contributions, resulting in the integral

$$\text{total work done} = \int_A^B E_t \, \mathrm{d}s$$

This is a second example of a line integral, the line being the curve, *C*, joining A and B.

It is usual to denote this by

$$\text{total work done} = \int_C E_t \, ds$$

where the symbol $\int_C$ tells us to integrate along the curve C.

If the coordinates of the end-points of the curve C are known, say (x_1, y_1) and (x_2, y_2), we often write $\int_{(x_1,y_1)}^{(x_2,y_2)}$ to show this, but care must then be taken to define the intended route from A to B.

We now explain how to integrate a function along a curve. Consider a vector field, **F**, through which runs a curve, C, as shown in Figure 27.3.

Suppose we restrict ourselves to two-dimensional situations. In the general case the vector field will vary as x and y vary, that is $\mathbf{F} = \mathbf{F}(x, y)$. Consider the small element of C joining points M and N. Let θ be the angle between the tangent to the curve at M and the direction of the field there. We shall denote the vector joining M and N (i.e. $\overrightarrow{MN}$) by $\delta\mathbf{s}$. Consider the quantity

$$\mathbf{F} \cdot \delta\mathbf{s}$$

where $\cdot$ represents the scalar product. When **F** represents a gravitational force field, $\mathbf{F} \cdot \delta\mathbf{s}$ represents the small amount of work done by the field in moving a particle of unit mass from M to N. The appropriate integral along the whole curve represents the total work done. From the definition of the scalar product we note that

$$\mathbf{F} \cdot \delta\mathbf{s} = |\mathbf{F}||\delta\mathbf{s}| \cos\theta$$

Writing the modulus of **F** as simply F, and the modulus of $\delta\mathbf{s}$, as δs, we have

$$\mathbf{F} \cdot \delta\mathbf{s} = F\delta s \cos\theta$$
$$= (F\cos\theta)\delta s$$
$$= F_t\delta s$$

where F_t is the component of **F** tangential to C. This result is of the same form as the expressions for work done obtained previously. We are therefore interested in integrals of the form

$$\int_C \mathbf{F}(x, y) \cdot d\mathbf{s}$$

Since **F** is a vector function of x and y it will have Cartesian components $P(x, y)$ and $Q(x, y)$ and so we can write **F** in the form

$$\mathbf{F}(x, y) = P(x, y)\mathbf{i} + Q(x, y)\mathbf{j}$$

Similarly, referring to Figure 27.4, we can write the vector d**s** as $d\mathbf{s} = dx\mathbf{i} + dy\mathbf{j}$. Hence

$$\int_C \mathbf{F}(x, y) \cdot d\mathbf{s} = \int_C (P(x, y)\mathbf{i} + Q(x, y)\mathbf{j}) \cdot (dx\mathbf{i} + dy\mathbf{j})$$

Taking the scalar product gives

$$\int_C P(x, y) \, dx + Q(x, y) \, dy$$

and this is the line integral in Cartesian form.

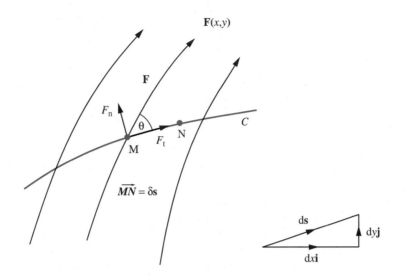

Figure 27.3 The integral $\displaystyle\int_C \mathbf{F} \cdot \mathrm{d}\mathbf{s}$ is equal to the work done by $\mathbf{F}$ as the particle moves along C.

Figure 27.4 The vector ds can be written as $\mathrm{d}x\mathbf{i} + \mathrm{d}y\mathbf{j}$.

If $\mathbf{F}(x, y) = P(x, y)\mathbf{i} + Q(x, y)\mathbf{j}$ then

$$\int_C \mathbf{F}(x, y) \cdot \mathrm{d}\mathbf{s} = \int_C (P(x, y)\mathbf{i} + Q(x, y)\mathbf{j}) \cdot (\mathrm{d}x\mathbf{i} + \mathrm{d}y\mathbf{j})$$

$$= \int_C P(x, y)\, \mathrm{d}x + Q(x, y)\, \mathrm{d}y$$

In order to proceed further we now need to explore how such integrals are evaluated in practice. This is the topic of the next section.

27.3 Evaluation of line integrals in two dimensions

Example 27.3   Evaluate

$$\int_C \mathbf{F} \cdot \mathrm{d}\mathbf{s}$$

where $\mathbf{F} = 5y^2\mathbf{i} + 2xy\mathbf{j}$ and C is the straight line joining the origin and the point $(1, 1)$.

Solution   We compare the integrand with the standard form and recognize that in this case $P(x, y) = 5y^2$ and $Q(x, y) = 2xy$. The integral becomes

$$\int_C 5y^2\, \mathrm{d}x + 2xy\, \mathrm{d}y$$

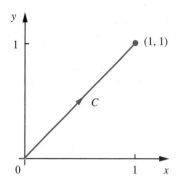

Figure 27.5 The path of integration joins $(0, 0)$ and $(1, 1)$ and has equation $y = x$.

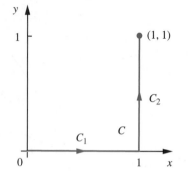

Figure 27.6 The path C is made up of two distinct parts. Integration is performed separately on each part.

The curve of interest, in this case a straight line, is shown in Figure 27.5. Along this curve it is clear that $y = x$ at all points. We use this fact to simplify the integral by writing everything in terms of x. We could equally well choose to write everything in terms of y. If $y = x$ then $\dfrac{dy}{dx} = 1$, that is $dy = dx$. As we move along the curve C, x ranges from 0 to 1, and the integral reduces to

$$\int_C 5x^2\,dx + 2x^2\,dx = \int_C 7x^2\,dx = \int_{x=0}^{x=1} 7x^2\,dx = \left[\frac{7x^3}{3}\right]_0^1 = \frac{7}{3}$$

Let us now see what happens when we choose to evaluate the integral of Example 27.3 along a different path joining $(0, 0)$ and $(1, 1)$.

Example 27.4 Evaluate the integral $\int_C 5y^2\,dx + 2xy\,dy$ along the curve, C, consisting of the x axis between $x = 0$ and $x = 1$ and the line $x = 1$ as shown in Figure 27.6.

Solution We evaluate this integral in two parts because the curve C is made up of two pieces. The first piece C_1 is horizontal, and the second C_2 is vertical. The required integral is the sum of the two separate ones. Along the x axis, $y = 0$ and $dy = 0$. This means that both the terms $5y^2\,dx$ and $2xy\,dy$ are zero, and so the integral reduces to

$$\int_{x=0}^{x=1} 0\,dx = 0$$

and so there is zero contribution to the final answer from this part of the curve C. Along the line $x = 1$, the quantity dx equals zero. Hence $5y^2\,dx$ also equals zero, and $2xy\,dy$ equals $2y\,dy$. Because y ranges from 0 to 1 the integral becomes

$$\int_{y=0}^{y=1} 2y\,dy = [y^2]_0^1 = 1$$

Note that this is a different answer from that obtained in Example 27.3.

As we have seen from Examples 27.3 and 27.4 the value of a line integral can depend upon the path taken. It is therefore essential to specify this path clearly.

Example 27.5 Evaluate the integral $\int_C \mathbf{F}(x, y) \cdot d\mathbf{s}$ where $\mathbf{F}(x, y) = (3x^2 + y)\mathbf{i} + (5x - y)\mathbf{j}$ and C is the portion of the curve $y = 2x^2$ between A(2, 8) and B(3, 18).

Solution
$$\int_C \mathbf{F}(x, y) \cdot d\mathbf{s} = \int_C (3x^2 + y)\, dx + (5x - y)\, dy$$

The curve C has equation $y = 2x^2$ for $2 \leqslant x \leqslant 3$. Along this curve we can replace y by $2x^2$. Note also that $\dfrac{dy}{dx} = 4x$ and so we can replace dy with $4x\, dx$. This will produce an integral entirely in terms of the variable x which is then integrated between $x = 2$ and $x = 3$. Thus

$$\int_C (3x^2 + y)\, dx + (5x - y)\, dy = \int_2^3 (3x^2 + 2x^2)\, dx + (5x - 2x^2)(4x\, dx)$$

$$= \int_2^3 25x^2 - 8x^3\, dx$$

$$= \left[\frac{25x^3}{3} - 2x^4 \right]_2^3$$

$$= 28.333$$

Exercises 27.3

1 Evaluate $\int_C 3y\, dx + 2x\, dy$ along the straight line C between (1, 1) and (3, 3).

2 Evaluate $\int_C 2yx\, dx + x^2\, dy$ along the straight line $y = 4x$ from (0, 0) to (3, 12).

3 Evaluate $\int_C (7x + 3y)\, dx + 2y\, dy$ along the curve $y = x^2$ between (0, 0) and (2, 4).

4 If $\mathbf{E} = (x + 2y)\mathbf{i} + (x - 3y)\mathbf{j}$, A is the point (0, 0) and B is the point (3, 2), evaluate

$$\int_A^B \mathbf{E} \cdot d\mathbf{s}$$

(a) along the straight line joining A and B,

(b) horizontally along the x axis from $x = 0$ to $x = 3$ and then vertically from $y = 0$ to $y = 2$.

5 If $\mathbf{F} = (2xy - y^4 + 3)\mathbf{i} + (x^2 - 4xy^3)\mathbf{j}$ evaluate $\int_C \mathbf{F} \cdot d\mathbf{s}$ where C is the straight line joining A(1, 3) and B(2, 5).

6 Evaluate the integral

$$\int_C (3x^2 + 2y)\, dx + (7x + y^2)\, dy$$

from A(0, 1) to B(2, 5) along the curve C defined by $y = 2x + 1$.

Solutions

1 20

2 108

3 38

4 (a) $\frac{15}{2}$ (b) $\frac{9}{2}$

5 −1149

6 $\frac{268}{3}$

27.4 Evaluation of line integrals in three dimensions

Evaluation of line integrals along curves lying in three-dimensional space is performed in a similar way. It is often helpful in this case to express the independent variables x, y and z in terms of a single parameter. Consider the following example.

Example 27.6

A curve, C, is defined parametrically by

$$x = 4 \qquad y = t^3 \qquad z = 5 + t$$

and is located within a vector field $\mathbf{F} = y\mathbf{i} + x^2\mathbf{j} + (z + x)\mathbf{k}$.

(a) Find the coordinates of the point P on the curve where the parameter t takes the value 1.

(b) Find the coordinates of the point Q where the parameter t takes the value 3.

(c) By expressing the line integral $\int_C \mathbf{F} \cdot \mathrm{d}\mathbf{s}$ entirely in terms of t find the value of the line integral from P to Q. Note that $\mathrm{d}\mathbf{s} = \mathrm{d}x\mathbf{i} + \mathrm{d}y\mathbf{j} + \mathrm{d}z\mathbf{k}$.

Solution

(a) When $t = 1$, $x = 4$, $y = 1$, and $z = 6$, and so P has coordinates (4, 1, 6).

(b) When $t = 3$, $x = 4$, $y = 27$ and $z = 8$, and so Q has coordinates (4, 27, 8).

(c) To express the line integral entirely in terms of t we note that if $x = 4$, $\dfrac{\mathrm{d}x}{\mathrm{d}t} = 0$ so that $\mathrm{d}x$ is also zero. If $y = t^3$ then $\dfrac{\mathrm{d}y}{\mathrm{d}t} = 3t^2$ so that $\mathrm{d}y = 3t^2\,\mathrm{d}t$. Similarly since $z = 5 + t$, $\dfrac{\mathrm{d}z}{\mathrm{d}t} = 1$ so that $\mathrm{d}z = \mathrm{d}t$. The line integral becomes

$$\int_C \mathbf{F} \cdot \mathrm{d}\mathbf{s} = \int_C (y\mathbf{i} + x^2\mathbf{j} + (z + x)\mathbf{k}) \cdot (\mathrm{d}x\mathbf{i} + \mathrm{d}y\mathbf{j} + \mathrm{d}z\mathbf{k})$$

$$= \int_C y\,\mathrm{d}x + x^2\mathrm{d}y + (z + x)\,\mathrm{d}z$$

$$= \int_{t=1}^{t=3} 0 + 16(3t^2)\,\mathrm{d}t + (9 + t)\,\mathrm{d}t$$

$$= \int_1^3 48t^2 + 9 + t\,\mathrm{d}t$$

$$= \left[\frac{48t^3}{3} + 9t + \frac{t^2}{2}\right]_1^3$$

$$= \left(\frac{48(3^3)}{3} + (9)(3) + \frac{3^2}{2}\right) - \left(\frac{48}{3} + 9 + \frac{1}{2}\right)$$

$$= 438$$

Exercises 27.4

1 You are required to evaluate the line integral $\int_C \mathbf{F} \cdot d\mathbf{s}$ where $\mathbf{F}$ is the vector field $\mathbf{F} = (2y + 3x)\mathbf{i} + (yz + x)\mathbf{j} + 3xy\mathbf{k}$ and $d\mathbf{s} = dx\mathbf{i} + dy\mathbf{j} + dz\mathbf{k}$. The curve C is defined parametrically by $x = t^2$, $y = 3t$ and $z = 2t$ for values of t between 0 and 1.

(a) Find the coordinates of the point A, where $t = 0$.

(b) Find the coordinates of the point B, where $t = 1$.

(c) By expressing the line integral entirely in terms of t, evaluate the line integral from A to B along the curve C.

Solutions

1 (a) $(0, 0, 0)$ (b) $(1, 3, 2)$ (c) 17

27.5 Conservative fields and potential functions

We have seen that, in general, the value of a line integral depends upon the particular path chosen. However, in special cases, the integral of a given vector field $\mathbf{F}$ turns out to be the same on any path with the same end-points; that is, it is independent of the path chosen. In these cases the vector field $\mathbf{F}$ is said to be **conservative**. There is a simple test which tells us whether or not $\mathbf{F}$ is conservative:

> $\mathbf{F}$ is a conservative vector field if
>
> $\quad$ curl $\mathbf{F} = \mathbf{0}$ $\quad$ everywhere

If we are dealing with a two-dimensional vector field $\mathbf{F}(x, y) = P(x, y)\mathbf{i} + Q(x, y)\mathbf{j}$ then this test becomes: $\mathbf{F}$ is conservative if $\dfrac{\partial P}{\partial y} = \dfrac{\partial Q}{\partial x}$. (See Question 7 in Exercises 27.5).

Example 27.7 Show that the vector field

$$\mathbf{F} = ze^x \sin y\,\mathbf{i} + ze^x \cos y\,\mathbf{j} + e^x \sin y\,\mathbf{k}$$

is a conservative field.

Solution We find curl $\mathbf{F}$.

$$\nabla \times \mathbf{F} = \begin{vmatrix} \mathbf{i} & \mathbf{j} & \mathbf{k} \\ \dfrac{\partial}{\partial x} & \dfrac{\partial}{\partial y} & \dfrac{\partial}{\partial z} \\ ze^x \sin y & ze^x \cos y & e^x \sin y \end{vmatrix}$$

$$= (e^x \cos y - e^x \cos y)\mathbf{i} - (e^x \sin y - e^x \sin y)\mathbf{j} + (ze^x \cos y - ze^x \cos y)\mathbf{k}$$

$$= \mathbf{0}$$

We have shown that $\nabla \times \mathbf{F} = \mathbf{0}$ and so the field is conservative. Note from Section 26.5 that such a field is also said to be irrotational.

There are two important properties of conservative vector fields which we now discuss.

27.5.1 The potential function

It can be shown that any conservative vector field, $\mathbf{F}$, can be expressed as the gradient of some scalar field ϕ. That is, we can find a scalar field ϕ such that $\mathbf{F} = \nabla \phi$. The scalar field ϕ is said to be a **potential function** and $\mathbf{F}$ is said to be **derivable from a potential**. In three dimensions, if

$$\mathbf{F} = P(x, y, z)\mathbf{i} + Q(x, y, z)\mathbf{j} + R(x, y, z)\mathbf{k}$$

is conservative, we can write

$$\mathbf{F} = \nabla \phi$$
$$= \frac{\partial \phi}{\partial x}\mathbf{i} + \frac{\partial \phi}{\partial y}\mathbf{j} + \frac{\partial \phi}{\partial z}\mathbf{k}$$

So

$$P = \frac{\partial \phi}{\partial x} \qquad Q = \frac{\partial \phi}{\partial y} \qquad R = \frac{\partial \phi}{\partial z}$$

You should refer back to Example 26.4 where this idea was introduced.

Example 27.8 The vector field $\mathbf{v}$ is derivable from the potential $\phi = 2xy + zx$. Find $\mathbf{v}$.

Solution If $\mathbf{v}$ is derivable from the potential ϕ, then $\mathbf{v} = \nabla \phi$ and so

$$\mathbf{v} = \nabla \phi = (2y + z)\mathbf{i} + 2x\mathbf{j} + x\mathbf{k}$$

This vector field is conservative as is easily verified by finding curl $\mathbf{v}$. In fact,

$$\nabla \times \mathbf{v} = \begin{vmatrix} \mathbf{i} & \mathbf{j} & \mathbf{k} \\ \dfrac{\partial}{\partial x} & \dfrac{\partial}{\partial y} & \dfrac{\partial}{\partial z} \\ 2y + z & 2x & x \end{vmatrix}$$

$$= 0\mathbf{i} - (1 - 1)\mathbf{j} + (2 - 2)\mathbf{k}$$

$$= \mathbf{0}$$

Indeed, recall from Example 26.12 that curl(grad ϕ) is identically zero for any ϕ.

When the vector field $\mathbf{F}$ is conservative there is an alternative method of evaluating the line integral $\int_C \mathbf{F} \cdot d\mathbf{s}$ which involves the use of the potential function ϕ. Consider the following example.

Example 27.9   The two-dimensional vector field $\mathbf{F} = \mathbf{i} + 2\mathbf{j}$ is conservative.

(a) Find a suitable potential function ϕ such that $\mathbf{F} = \nabla\phi = \dfrac{\partial \phi}{\partial x}\mathbf{i} + \dfrac{\partial \phi}{\partial y}\mathbf{j}$.

(b) Evaluate $\int_{(0,0)}^{(3,2)} \mathbf{F} \cdot d\mathbf{s}$ along any convenient path.

(c) Find the value of ϕ at B(3, 2), and the value of ϕ at A(0, 0), and show that the difference between these is equal to the value of the line integral obtained in part (b).

Solution   (a) We are given that $\dfrac{\partial \phi}{\partial x} = 1$ so that $\phi = x + f(y)$ where f is an arbitrary function of y. We are also given that $\dfrac{\partial \phi}{\partial y} = 2$ so that $\phi = 2y + g(x)$ where g is an arbitrary function of x. It is easy to verify that $\phi = x + 2y$ is a suitable potential function.

(b) To find the line integral we shall choose the straight line path, C, joining (0, 0) and (3, 2). This has equation $y = \frac{2}{3}x$. The line integral becomes

$$\int_{(0,0)}^{(3,2)} \mathbf{F} \cdot d\mathbf{s} = \int_{(0,0)}^{(3,2)} (\mathbf{i} + 2\mathbf{j}) \cdot (dx\mathbf{i} + dy\mathbf{j})$$

$$= \int_{(0,0)}^{(3,2)} dx + 2\,dy$$

$$= \int_{(0,0)}^{(3,2)} dx + \frac{4}{3}\,dx \qquad \text{since } dy = \frac{2}{3}dx \text{ on } C$$

$$= \int_{x=0}^{x=3} \frac{7}{3}\,dx$$

$$= \left[\frac{7}{3}x\right]_0^3$$

$$= 7$$

(c) The value of ϕ at B(3, 2) is $3 + 2(2) = 7$. The value of ϕ at A(0, 0) is 0. Clearly the difference between these values is 7, the same as the value of the line integral obtained in part (b).

The result obtained in the previous example is important:

> If $\mathbf{F}$ is a conservative vector field such that $\mathbf{F} = \nabla\phi$ then, for any points A and B,
>
> $$\int_A^B \mathbf{F} \cdot d\mathbf{s} = \phi(B) - \phi(A)$$

27.5.2 The line integral around a closed loop

A second important property of conservative fields arises when the curve C of integration forms a closed loop. Suppose we evaluate a line integral from A to B firstly along the curve C_1 and secondly along C_2 as shown in Figure 27.7.

If the field, $\mathbf{F}$, is conservative both integrals will yield the same answer, that is

$$\int_{C_1} \mathbf{F} \cdot d\mathbf{s} = \int_{C_2} \mathbf{F} \cdot d\mathbf{s}$$

But

$$\int \mathbf{F} \cdot d\mathbf{s} \text{ from A to B } = -\int \mathbf{F} \cdot d\mathbf{s} \text{ from B to A}$$

Consequently, the line integral around the closed curve A to B and back to A must equal zero. When the path of integration is a closed curve we use the symbol

$$\oint$$

to represent the integral. So, for a conservative field we have the result

$$\oint_C \mathbf{F} \cdot d\mathbf{s} = 0$$

for any closed curve C.

In summary we have the following results:

> For a conservative field, $\mathbf{F}$, all the following statements are equivalent:
>
> $$\nabla \times \mathbf{F} = \mathbf{0}$$
>
> $$\oint \mathbf{F} \cdot d\mathbf{s} = 0$$
>
> $$\int_A^B \mathbf{F} \cdot d\mathbf{s} \text{ is independent of the path between A and B}$$
>
> $\mathbf{F}$ is derivable from a scalar potential, that is $\mathbf{F} = \nabla\phi$

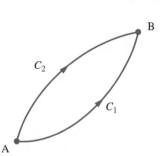

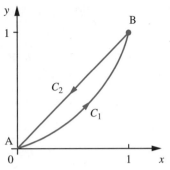

Figure 27.7 The line integral $\int \mathbf{F} \cdot d\mathbf{s}$ can be evaluated along different paths between A and B.

Figure 27.8 The path of integration is the curve C_1 followed by the line C_2.

Example 27.10 Evaluate

$$\int_C \mathbf{F} \cdot d\mathbf{s}$$

where $\mathbf{F}$ is the vector field $y^2\mathbf{i} + 2xy\mathbf{j}$ and where

(a) $C = C_1$ is the curve $y = x^2$ going from A(0, 0) to B(1, 1).

(b) $C = C_2$ is the straight line going from B(1, 1) to A(0, 0).

(c) Deduce that $\oint \mathbf{F} \cdot d\mathbf{s} = 0$ where the closed line integral is taken around the path C_1 and then C_2.

Solution The situation is depicted in Figure 27.8.

(a) C_1 has equation $y = x^2$ and so $dy = 2x\,dx$. Note that we are integrating from A to B.

Therefore

$$\int_{C_1} \mathbf{F} \cdot d\mathbf{s} = \int_{C_1} (y^2\mathbf{i} + 2xy\mathbf{j}) \cdot (dx\mathbf{i} + dy\mathbf{j}) = \int_{C_1} y^2\,dx + 2xy\,dy$$

Substituting $y = x^2$ and $dy = 2x\,dx$ we have

$$\int_{C_1} \mathbf{F} \cdot d\mathbf{s} = \int_{C_1} x^4 dx + (2x)x^2(2x\,dx)$$

$$= \int_{x=0}^{x=1} 5x^4\,dx = [x^5]_0^1 = 1$$

(b) C_2 has equation $y = x$ and so $dy = dx$. Note that this time we are integrating from B to A. Therefore

$$\int_{C_2} \mathbf{F} \cdot d\mathbf{s} = \int_{C_2} (y^2\mathbf{i} + 2xy\mathbf{j}) \cdot (dx\mathbf{i} + dy\mathbf{j}) = \int_{C_2} y^2 \, dx + 2xy \, dy$$

Substituting $y = x$ and $dy = dx$ we have

$$\int_{C_2} \mathbf{F} \cdot d\mathbf{s} = \int_{x=1}^{x=0} x^2 \, dx + 2x^2 \, dx = \int_1^0 3x^2 \, dx = [x^3]_1^0 = -1$$

(c) Now

$$\oint \mathbf{F} \cdot d\mathbf{s} = \int_{C_1} \mathbf{F} \cdot d\mathbf{s} + \int_{C_2} \mathbf{F} \cdot d\mathbf{s} = 1 - 1 = 0$$

The line integral around the closed path is zero because the field is conservative. You should check that $\nabla \times \mathbf{F} = \mathbf{0}$ and that a suitable potential function is $\phi = y^2x$.

Exercises 27.5

1. Verify that the vector field
$\mathbf{F} = (4x^3 + y)\mathbf{i} + x\mathbf{j}$ is conservative.

2. For the vector field
$\mathbf{F} = y \cos xy\mathbf{i} + x \cos xy\mathbf{j} + 2z\mathbf{k}$ find $\nabla \times \mathbf{F}$ and verify that the field is conservative.

3. Consider the field $\mathbf{F} = y\mathbf{i} + x\mathbf{j}$.

   (a) Show that $\mathbf{F}$ is a conservative field.

   (b) Find a function ϕ such that $\dfrac{\partial \phi}{\partial x} = y$ and
   $\dfrac{\partial \phi}{\partial y} = x$.

   (c) Find a suitable potential function ϕ for $\mathbf{F}$.

   (d) If A is the point $(2, 1)$ and B is the point $(5, 8)$ evaluate $\int_A^B \mathbf{F} \cdot d\mathbf{s}$.

   (e) Find ϕ at B and ϕ at A and show that the value of the line integral calculated in part (d) is equal to the difference between the values of ϕ at B and A.

4. Show that the vector field,
$\mathbf{F} = (2xy - y^4 + 3)\mathbf{i} + (x^2 - 4xy^3)\mathbf{j}$, of Question 5 in Exercises 27.3, is conservative and find a suitable potential function ϕ from which $\mathbf{F}$ can be derived. Show that the

difference between ϕ evaluated at B$(2, 1)$ and at A$(1, 0)$ is equal to the value of the line integral $\int_A^B \mathbf{F} \cdot d\mathbf{s}$.

5. Show that

$$I = \int_{(-1,-1)}^{(1,1)} 3x^2y^2 \, dx + 2x^3y \, dy$$

is independent of the path of integration, and evaluate the integral.

6. The function $\phi = 4xy$ is a potential function for which $\mathbf{F} = \nabla\phi$.

   (a) Find $\mathbf{F}$.

   (b) Evaluate $\int \mathbf{F} \cdot d\mathbf{s}$ along the curve $y = x^3$ from A$(0, 0)$ to B$(2, 8)$.

   (c) Evaluate ϕ at B and at A and show that the difference between these values is equal to the value of the line integral obtained in part (b).

7. If $\mathbf{F} = P(x, y)\mathbf{i} + Q(x, y)\mathbf{j} + 0\mathbf{k}$, show that
$\nabla \times \mathbf{F} = \left(\dfrac{\partial Q}{\partial x} - \dfrac{\partial P}{\partial y}\right)\mathbf{k}$. Deduce that if $\mathbf{F}$ is conservative then $\dfrac{\partial Q}{\partial x} = \dfrac{\partial P}{\partial y}$.

Solutions

3 (b) $\phi = xy + c$ (c) $xy + c$ (d) 38   5 2

4 $\phi = x^2 y - y^4 x + 3x + c, 5$ 6 (a) $\mathbf{F} = 4y\mathbf{i} + 4x\mathbf{j}$ (b) 64   (c) 64

27.6 Double and triple integrals

27.6.1 Double integrals

Expressions such as

$$\int_{y=y_1}^{y=y_2} \int_{x=x_1}^{x=x_2} f(x, y) \, dx \, dy$$

are known as **double integrals**. What is meant by the above is

$$\int_{y=y_1}^{y=y_2} \left(\int_{x=x_1}^{x=x_2} f(x, y) \, dx \right) dy$$

where firstly the inner integral is performed by integrating f with respect to x, treating y as if it were a constant. The limits of integration are inserted as usual and then the whole expression is integrated with respect to y between the limits y_1 and y_2.

It is important that you can distinguish between double integrals and line integrals. Physically they mean quite different things, and they are evaluated in different ways. Whilst both types of integral contain terms involving x, y, dx and dy, in a double integral dx and dy always occur as a product, that is as $dx \, dy$. In a line integral they occur separately. When evaluating a line integral we integrate along a curve. When evaluating a double integral we integrate over a two-dimensional region.

Double integrals may also be written in the form

$$\iint_R f(x, y) \, dx \, dy$$

where R is called the **region of integration**. The region R must be described mathematically. In the integral

$$\int_{y=y_1}^{y=y_2} \int_{x=x_1}^{x=x_2} f(x, y) \, dx \, dy$$

R is the rectangular region defined by $x_1 \leqslant x \leqslant x_2, y_1 \leqslant y \leqslant y_2$. Non-rectangular regions are also common.

Example 27.11   Sketch the region R defined by $1 \leqslant x \leqslant 4$ and $0 \leqslant y \leqslant 2$.

Solution   The region is shown in Figure 27.9. We see that x lies between 1 and 4, and y lies between 0 and 2. Consequently the region is rectangular.

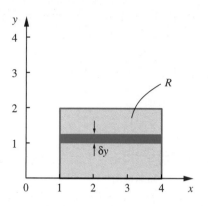

Figure 27.9 The rectangular region over which the integration in Example 27.12 is performed.

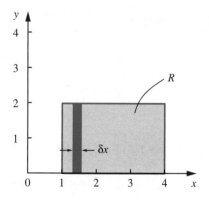

Figure 27.10 The integral could have been found by first integrating over a vertical strip such as that shown.

Example 27.12   Evaluate

$$\int_{y=0}^{y=2} \int_{x=1}^{x=4} x + 2y \, \mathrm{d}x \, \mathrm{d}y$$

over the region, R, given in Example 27.11 and defined by $1 \leqslant x \leqslant 4$ and $0 \leqslant y \leqslant 2$.

Solution   The inner integral is found first by integrating with respect to x, keeping y fixed, that is constant.

$$\int_{x=1}^{x=4} x + 2y \, \mathrm{d}x = \left[\frac{x^2}{2} + 2xy \right]_{x=1}^{x=4} = 8 + 8y - \frac{1}{2} - 2y = \frac{15}{2} + 6y$$

Then the outer integral is found by integrating the result with respect to y:

$$\int_{y=0}^{y=2} \frac{15}{2} + 6y \, \mathrm{d}y = \left[\frac{15}{2}y + 3y^2 \right]_0^2 = 15 + 12 = 27$$

Now consider again Example 27.12. By performing the inner integral first,

$$\int_{x=1}^{x=4} x + 2y \, \mathrm{d}x$$

we are effectively singling out a horizontal strip, such as that shown in Figure 27.9, and integrating along it from $x = 1$ to $x = 4$. When we then integrate the result from $y = 0$ to $y = 2$ we are effectively adding up contributions from all such horizontal strips.

The integral over the same region could also have been performed by integrating first over vertical strips for $0 \leqslant y \leqslant 2$ (Figure 27.10) yielding

$$\int_{y=0}^{y=2} x + 2y \, \mathrm{d}y = [xy + y^2]_{y=0}^{y=2} = 2x + 4$$

The result is then integrated from $x = 1$ to $x = 4$ effectively adding up contributions from each vertical strip:

$$\int_{x=1}^{x=4} 2x + 4 \, dx = [x^2 + 4x]_1^4 = 32 - 5 = 27$$

as expected. We note that

$$\int_{y=0}^{y=2} \int_{x=1}^{x=4} x + 2y \, dx \, dy = \int_{x=1}^{x=4} \int_{y=0}^{y=2} x + 2y \, dy \, dx \qquad (27.1)$$

In particular, note the order of dx and dy in Equation (27.1). The simple interchange of limits is only possible because in this example the region R is a rectangle.

> When evaluating a double integral over a *rectangular* region R, the integration may be carried out in any order, that is
>
> $$\iint_R f(x, y) \, dx \, dy = \iint_R f(x, y) \, dy \, dx$$

The double integral in Example 27.12 could have the following interpretation. Consider the surface $z = x + 2y$, for $0 \leqslant y \leqslant 2$, $1 \leqslant x \leqslant 4$, as shown in Figure 27.11. In this example the surface is a plane but the theory applies to more general surfaces. The variable z represents the height of the surface above the point (x, y) in the x–y plane. For example, consider a point in the x–y plane, say $(2, 3)$, that is $x = 2$, $y = 3$. Then at $(2, 3)$, $z = x + 2y = 2 + 2(3) = 8$. Thus the point on the surface directly above $(2, 3)$ is 8 units from $(2, 3)$.

Let us now consider $dx \, dy$. We call $dx \, dy$ an **element of area**. It is a rectangle with dimensions dx and dy and area $dx \, dy$. Hence $z \, dx \, dy$ represents the volume of a rectangular column of base $dx \, dy$. As we integrate with respect to x for $1 \leqslant x \leqslant 4$ and integrate with respect to y for $0 \leqslant y \leqslant 2$ we are effectively summing all such volumes. Thus

$$\int_{y=0}^{y=2} \int_{x=1}^{x=4} x + 2y \, dx \, dy$$

represents the volume bounded by the surface $z = x + 2y$ and the region R in the x–y plane.

Example 27.13   Sketch the region R over which we would evaluate the integral

$$\int_{y=0}^{y=1} \int_{x=0}^{x=2-2y} f(x, y) \, dx \, dy$$

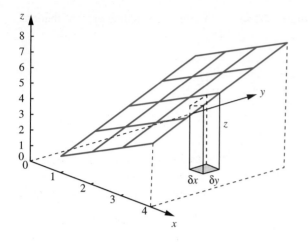

Figure 27.11 The surface $z = x + 2y$, $0 \leqslant y \leqslant 2$, $1 \leqslant x \leqslant 4$; the quantity $z \, dx \, dy$ is the volume of the rectangular column with base area $dx \, dy$.

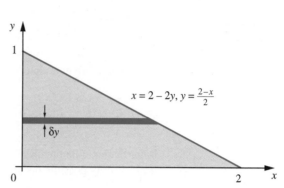

Figure 27.12 The region over which the integration in Example 27.14 is performed.

Solution   First consider the outer integral. The restriction on y means that interest can be confined to the horizontal strip $0 \leqslant y \leqslant 1$. Then examine the inner integral. The lower limit on x means that we need only consider values of x greater than or equal to 0. The upper x limit depends upon the value of y. If $y = 0$ this upper limit is $x = 2 - 2y = 2$. If $y = 1$ the upper limit is $x = 2 - 2y = 0$. At any other intermediate value of y we can calculate the corresponding upper x limit. This upper limit will lie on the straight line $x = 2 - 2y$. With this information the region of integration can be sketched. The region is shown in Figure 27.12 and is seen to be triangular.

Example 27.14   Evaluate

$$\int_{y=0}^{y=1} \int_{x=0}^{x=2-2y} 4x + 5 \, dx \, dy$$

over the region described in Example 27.13.

Solution   We first perform the inner integral

$$\int_{x=0}^{x=2-2y} 4x + 5 \, dx$$

integrating with respect to x. This gives

$$[2x^2 + 5x]_{x=0}^{x=2-2y} = 2(2 - 2y)^2 + 5(2 - 2y) - 0$$
$$= 8y^2 - 26y + 18$$

Next we perform the outer integral

$$\int_{y=0}^{y=1} 8y^2 - 26y + 18\, dy = \left[\frac{8y^3}{3} - \frac{26y^2}{2} + 18y\right]_0^1$$

$$= \frac{8}{3} - \frac{26}{2} + 18$$

$$= 7.667$$

The region of integration is shown in Figure 27.12. The first integral, with respect to x, corresponds to integrating along the horizontal strip from $x = 0$ to $x = 2 - 2y$. Then as y varies from 0 to 1 in the second integral, the horizontal strips will cover the entire region.

If we wish to change the order in which the integration is carried out, care must be taken with the limits of a non-rectangular region. Consider again Figure 27.12. The line $x = 2 - 2y$ can be written as $y = \dfrac{2 - x}{2}$. We can describe the region R by restricting attention to the vertical strip $0 \leqslant x \leqslant 2$, and then letting y vary from 0 up to $\dfrac{2 - x}{2}$, that is

$$\int_{x=0}^{x=2} \int_{y=0}^{y=(2-x)/2} 4x + 5\, dy\, dx$$

You should check by evaluating this integral that the same result is obtained as in Example 27.14.

Example 27.15 Evaluate the double integral of $f(x, y) = x^2 + 3xy$ over the region R indicated in Figure 27.13 by

(a) integrating first with respect to x, and then with respect to y,

(b) integrating first with respect to y, and then with respect to x.

Solution (a) If we integrate first with respect to x we must select an arbitrary horizontal strip as shown in Figure 27.13 and integrate in the x direction. On OB $y = x$ so that the lower limit of the x integration is $x = y$. On AB, $x = 1$ so the upper limit is $x = 1$. Therefore

$$\int_{x=y}^{x=1} x^2 + 3xy\, dx = \left[\frac{x^3}{3} + \frac{3x^2y}{2}\right]_y^1$$

$$= \left(\frac{1}{3} + \frac{3y}{2}\right) - \left(\frac{y^3}{3} + \frac{3y^3}{2}\right)$$

$$= \frac{1}{3} + \frac{3y}{2} - \frac{11y^3}{6}$$

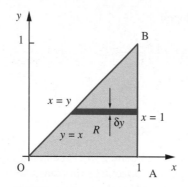

Figure 27.13 The integral with respect to x has limits $x = y$ and $x = 1$.

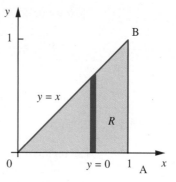

Figure 27.14 We integrate along a vertical strip from $y = 0$ to $y = x$.

As y varies from 0 to 1 the horizontal strips will cover the entire region. Hence the limits of integration of the y integral are 0 and 1. So

$$\int_{y=0}^{y=1} \frac{1}{3} + \frac{3y}{2} - \frac{11}{6}y^3 \, dy = \left[\frac{1}{3}y + \frac{3}{4}y^2 - \frac{11y^4}{24} \right]_0^1$$

$$= \frac{1}{3} + \frac{3}{4} - \frac{11}{24}$$

$$= \frac{15}{24}$$

$$= \frac{5}{8}$$

that is,

$$\int_{y=0}^{y=1} \int_{x=y}^{x=1} x^2 + 3xy \, dx \, dy = \frac{5}{8}$$

(b) If we choose to integrate with respect to y first we must select an arbitrary vertical strip as shown in Figure 27.14. At the lower end of the strip $y = 0$. At the upper end $y = x$.

To integrate along the strip we evaluate

$$\int_{y=0}^{y=x} x^2 + 3xy \, dy = \left[x^2 y + \frac{3xy^2}{2} \right]_0^x = x^3 + \frac{3x^3}{2} = \frac{5x^3}{2}$$

We add contributions of all such vertical strips by integrating with respect to x from $x = 0$ to $x = 1$:

$$\int_0^1 \frac{5x^3}{2} \, dx = \left[\frac{5x^4}{8} \right]_0^1 = \frac{5}{8}$$

We see that the prudent selection of the order of integration can yield substantial savings in the effort required.

27.6.2 Triple integrals

The techniques we have used for evaluating double integrals can be generalized naturally to **triple integrals**. Whereas double integrals are evaluated over two-dimensional regions, triple integrals are evaluated over volumes.

Example 27.16 Evaluate

$$I = \int_{x=0}^{x=1} \int_{y=0}^{y=1} \int_{z=0}^{z=1} x + y + z \, dz \, dy \, dx$$

Solution What is meant by this expression is

$$I = \int_{x=0}^{x=1} \left(\int_{y=0}^{y=1} \left(\int_{z=0}^{z=1} x + y + z \, dz \right) dy \right) dx$$

where, as before, the inner integral is performed first, integrating with respect to z, with x and y being treated as constants. So

$$I = \int_{x=0}^{x=1} \left(\int_{y=0}^{y=1} \left[xz + yz + \frac{z^2}{2} \right]_0^1 dy \right) dx$$

$$= \int_{x=0}^{x=1} \left(\int_{y=0}^{y=1} x + y + \frac{1}{2} \, dy \right) dx$$

$$= \int_{x=0}^{x=1} \left[xy + \frac{y^2}{2} + \frac{1}{2}y \right]_0^1 dx$$

$$= \int_{x=0}^{x=1} x + \frac{1}{2} + \frac{1}{2} \, dx$$

$$= \left[\frac{x^2}{2} + x \right]_0^1$$

$$= \frac{3}{2}$$

Consideration of the limits of integration shows that the integral is evaluated over a unit cube.

27.6.3 Green's theorem

There is an important relationship between line and double integrals expressed in **Green's theorem in the plane**:

If the functions $P(x, y)$ and $Q(x, y)$ are finite and continuous in a region of the x–y plane, R, and on its boundary, the closed curve C, provided the relevant partial derivatives exist and are continuous in and on C, then

$$\oint_C P \, dx + Q \, dy = \iint_R \left(\frac{\partial Q}{\partial x} - \frac{\partial P}{\partial y} \right) dx \, dy$$

where the direction of integration along C is such that the region R is always to the left.

The conditions given in the theorem are present for mathematical completeness. Most of the functions that engineers deal with satisfy these conditions, and so we will not consider these further. The important thing to note is that this relationship states that a line integral around a closed curve can be expressed in terms of a double integral over the region, R, enclosed by C.

Example 27.17 (a) Evaluate $\oint_C xy \, dx + x^2 \, dy$ around the sides of the square with vertices D(0, 0), E(1, 0), F(1, 1) and G(0, 1).

(b) Convert the line integral to a double integral and verify Green's theorem.

Solution (a) The path of integration is shown in Figure 27.15. To apply Green's theorem the path of integration should be followed in such a way that the region of integration is always to its left. We must therefore travel anticlockwise around C.

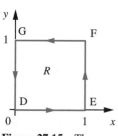

Figure 27.15 The path C is chosen so that the region R is always to its left.

On DE, $y = 0$, $dy = 0$ and $0 \leqslant x \leqslant 1$.
On EF, $x = 1$, $dx = 0$ and $0 \leqslant y \leqslant 1$.
On FG, $y = 1$, $dy = 0$ and x decreases from 1 to 0.
On GD, $x = 0$, $dx = 0$ and y decreases from 1 to 0.

The integral around the curve C can then be written as

$$\oint_C = \int_D^E + \int_E^F + \int_F^G + \int_G^D$$

Therefore

$$\oint_C xy \, dx + x^2 \, dy = 0 + \int_0^1 1 \, dy + \int_1^0 x \, dx + 0$$

$$= [y]_0^1 + \left[\frac{x^2}{2} \right]_1^0$$

$$= 1 - \frac{1}{2}$$

$$= \frac{1}{2}$$

(b) Applying Green's theorem with $P(x, y) = xy$ and $Q(x, y) = x^2$ we can convert the line integral into a double integral. Note that $\dfrac{\partial Q}{\partial x} = 2x$ and $\dfrac{\partial P}{\partial y} = x$. Clearly the region of integration is the square R. We find

$$\oint_C xy \, dx + x^2 \, dy = \iint_R (2x - x) \, dx \, dy$$

$$= \int_0^1 \int_0^1 x \, dx \, dy$$

$$= \int_0^1 \left[\frac{x^2}{2} \right]_0^1 dy$$

$$= \int_0^1 \frac{1}{2} \, dy$$

$$= \left[\frac{1}{2} y \right]_0^1$$

$$= \frac{1}{2}$$

We see that the same result as that in part (a) is obtained and so Green's theorem has been verified.

Exercises 27.6

1 Evaluate

(a) $\displaystyle\int_0^1 \int_0^3 z^2 \, dx \, dz$

(b) $\displaystyle\int_0^4 \int_0^2 x \, dy \, dz$

(c) $\displaystyle\int_1^2 \int_2^3 x^2 y + 1 \, dx \, dy$

(d) $\displaystyle\int_{-1}^1 \int_2^3 \frac{y}{x} \, dx \, dy$

2 R is the shaded region shown in Figure 27.16.

Evaluate $\iint_R x + \sqrt{y} \, dx \, dy$

(a) performing the integration with respect to x first,

(b) performing the integration with respect to y first.

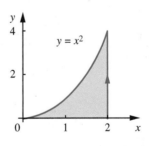

Figure 27.16 The region of integration for Question 2.

3 Evaluate $\iint_R (5x^2 + 2y^2) \, dx \, dy$ where R is the interior of the triangular region bounded by A(1, 1), B(2, 0) and C(2, 2).

4 (a) Sketch the region of integration of the double integral

$$\int_1^3 \int_1^{\sqrt{4-y}} y \, dx \, dy$$

(b) Evaluate the integral by first reversing the order of integration.

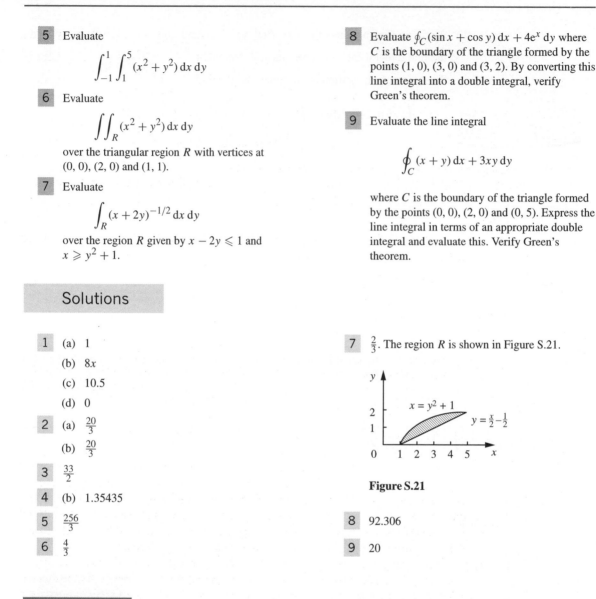

5 Evaluate

$$\int_{-1}^{1}\int_{1}^{5}(x^2+y^2)\,dx\,dy$$

6 Evaluate

$$\iint_{R}(x^2+y^2)\,dx\,dy$$

over the triangular region R with vertices at $(0, 0)$, $(2, 0)$ and $(1, 1)$.

7 Evaluate

$$\int_{R}(x+2y)^{-1/2}\,dx\,dy$$

over the region R given by $x - 2y \leqslant 1$ and $x \geqslant y^2 + 1$.

8 Evaluate $\oint_{C}(\sin x + \cos y)\,dx + 4e^x\,dy$ where C is the boundary of the triangle formed by the points $(1, 0)$, $(3, 0)$ and $(3, 2)$. By converting this line integral into a double integral, verify Green's theorem.

9 Evaluate the line integral

$$\oint_{C}(x+y)\,dx + 3xy\,dy$$

where C is the boundary of the triangle formed by the points $(0, 0)$, $(2, 0)$ and $(0, 5)$. Express the line integral in terms of an appropriate double integral and evaluate this. Verify Green's theorem.

Solutions

1 (a) 1

(b) $8x$

(c) 10.5

(d) 0

2 (a) $\frac{20}{3}$

(b) $\frac{20}{3}$

3 $\frac{33}{2}$

4 (b) 1.35435

5 $\frac{256}{3}$

6 $\frac{4}{3}$

7 $\frac{2}{3}$. The region R is shown in Figure S.21.

Figure S.21

8 92.306

9 20

Some simple volume and surface integrals

Volume and surface integrals arise frequently in electromagnetism and fluid mechanics. We will illustrate these concepts through some simple examples. For a thorough treatment of more general cases you will need to refer to a more advanced text.

Example 27.18 **The mass of a solid object**

Consider a solid object such as that shown in Figure 27.17. The density, ρ, of this object may vary from point to point. So, at any point P with coordinates (x, y, z), the density is a function of position, that is $\rho = \rho(x, y, z)$. Since density is a scalar, this is an example of a scalar field, like those discussed in Section 7.4.

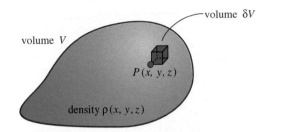

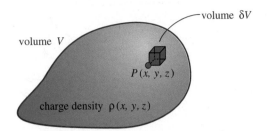

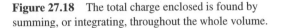

Figure 27.17   The total mass of a body is found by summing, or integrating, throughout the whole volume.

Figure 27.18   The total charge enclosed is found by summing, or integrating, throughout the whole volume.

Suppose we select a very small piece of this object having volume δV and located at $P(x, y, z)$. Recall from elementary physics that

$$\text{density} = \frac{\text{mass}}{\text{volume}}$$

Then the mass of this small piece, δm, is given by

$$\delta m = \rho \, \delta V$$

If we wish to calculate the total mass, M, of the object we must sum all such contributions from the entire volume. This is found by integrating throughout the volume. We write this as

$$\text{total mass, } M = \int_V \rho \, dV$$

This is an example of a **volume integral**, so called because the integration is performed throughout the volume. It will usually take the form of a triple integral such as those discussed in Section 27.6.2. Technically, there are three integral signs, but for brevity these have been replaced by the single $\int_V$ where it is to be understood that the integral is to be performed over a volume. In any specific problem care must be taken to ensure that the entire volume is included when the integration is performed.

For example, consider the case of a solid cube with sides of length 1 unit. Let one corner be positioned at the origin and let the edges coincide with the positive x, y and z axes. Suppose the density of the cube varies from point to point, and is given by $\rho(x, y, z) = x + y + z$. Then the integral which gives the mass of the cube is $\int_V (x + y + z) \, dV$, where the volume V is the region occupied by the cube. This integral has been evaluated in Example 27.16 and found to be $\frac{3}{2}$, representing the mass of the cube.

Example 27.19	**The electric charge enclosed in a region**

Suppose electric charge is distributed throughout a volume, V, and at any point has charge density $\rho(x, y, z)$. Charge density is a scalar field.

Suppose we select a very small portion having volume δV and located at $P(x, y, z)$ as shown in Figure 27.18. The charge in this portion, δQ, is given by

$$\delta Q = \rho \, \delta V$$

Figure 27.19
The vector field **v** represents fluid velocity and S is an imaginary surface through which the fluid flows.

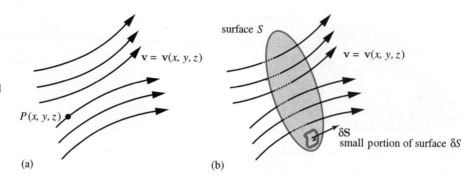

$P(x, y, z)$

$\mathbf{v} = \mathbf{v}(x, y, z)$

surface S

$\mathbf{v} = \mathbf{v}(x, y, z)$

$\delta \mathbf{S}$
small portion of surface δS

(a)   (b)

If we wish to calculate the total charge enclosed within the volume, we must sum all such contributions from the entire volume. This is found by integrating throughout the volume. We write this as

$$\text{total charge, } Q = \int_V \rho \, dV$$

This is another example of a volume integral.

Example 27.20   **Fluid flow across a surface**

Figure 27.19(a) represents the motion of a body of fluid throughout a region. At any point $P(x, y, z)$ fluid will be moving with a certain speed in a certain direction. So, each small fluid element has a particular velocity **v**, which varies with position, that is $\mathbf{v} = \mathbf{v}(x, y, z)$. This is an example of a vector field, as discussed in Section 7.4.

In Figure 27.19(b) we have placed an imaginary surface, S, within the flow and it is reasonable to ask 'what is the volume of fluid which crosses this surface in any given time?' Suppose we select a very small portion of the surface having area δS. Note that δS is a scalar. We can also define an associated vector $\delta \mathbf{S}$, which has magnitude δS and whose direction is normal to this portion of the surface. The component of fluid velocity in the direction of $\delta \mathbf{S}$ is given by the scalar product $\mathbf{v} \cdot \widehat{\delta \mathbf{S}}$ where $\widehat{\delta \mathbf{S}}$ is a unit vector in the direction of $\delta \mathbf{S}$. The volume of fluid crossing this portion each second is $\mathbf{v} \cdot \delta \mathbf{S}$. This is also known as the **flux** of **v**. If we wish to calculate the total flux through the surface S we must sum all such contributions over the entire surface. This is found by integrating over the surface. We write this as

$$\text{volume flow per second} = \text{total flux} = \int_S \mathbf{v} \cdot d\mathbf{S}$$

This is an example of a **surface integral**, so called because we must integrate over a surface. It will usually take the form of a double integral such as those discussed in Section 27.6.1. Technically, there are two integral signs, but for brevity these have been replaced by the single $\int_S$ where it is to be understood that the integral is to be performed over the surface S. In any specific problem care must be taken to ensure that the entire surface is included when the integration is performed. The double integrals evaluated in Section 27.6 are special cases of surface integrals, in which the surface is a plane region (the x–y plane).

For example, suppose the velocity field is given by $\mathbf{v} = (x + 2y)\mathbf{k}$. This represents a flow in the z direction whose magnitude varies with x and y. Suppose S is the plane

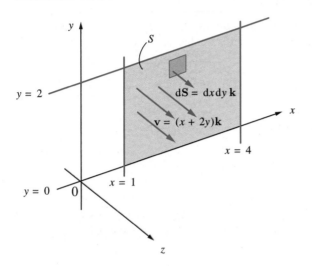

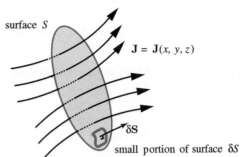

Figure 27.20 The vector field **v** represents fluid flowing across the surface S. The integral over the surface of $\mathbf{v} \cdot d\mathbf{S}$ gives the volume flow per second across S.

Figure 27.21 The electric current through a surface is obtained using a surface integral.

surface defined by $1 \leqslant x \leqslant 4$, $0 \leqslant y \leqslant 2$, $z = 0$. This surface is shown in Figure 27.20. Note that the normal to this surface is parallel to the z axis and so we can write $d\mathbf{S} = dx\,dy\,\mathbf{k}$. Then

$$\mathbf{v} \cdot d\mathbf{S} = (x + 2y)\mathbf{k} \cdot dx\,dy\,\mathbf{k}$$
$$= (x + 2y)\,dx\,dy$$

The surface integral which gives the flux of **v** through S is

$$\int_{y=0}^{y=2} \int_{x=1}^{x=4} (x + 2y)\,dx\,dy$$

Note how the limits of integration are chosen so that contributions from the whole surface are included. This integral has already been evaluated in Example 27.12 and found to be 27. This represents the volume flow per second through S.

Example 27.21 Electric current density

Electric current is the flow of electric charges. Figure 27.21 represents an electric current flowing across a surface S.

If $\rho(x, y, z)$ is the charge density at a point, and $\mathbf{v}(x, y, z)$ is the velocity of the charges, then the quantity **J** defined as

$$\mathbf{J} = \rho \mathbf{v}$$

is called the current density. Suppose we select a very small portion of the surface having area δS. Note that δS is a scalar. Suppose we define a vector, $\delta\mathbf{S}$, which has magnitude δS and which is normal to this portion of surface. The component of current density in the direction of $\delta\mathbf{S}$ is given by the scalar product $\mathbf{J} \cdot \delta\mathbf{S}$. The current crossing this portion is $\mathbf{J} \cdot \delta\mathbf{S}$. If we wish to calculate the total current, I, through the surface S we must sum all such contributions over the entire surface. This is found by integrating over the surface. We write this as

$$\text{current, } I = \int_S \mathbf{J} \cdot d\mathbf{S}$$

This is an example of a **surface integral**.

Example 27.22   Electric flux and Gauss's law

Electric charges produce an electric field, $\mathbf{E}$, which can be visualized by drawing lines of force. Suppose we surround a region containing charges with a surface S. The flux of $\mathbf{E}$ through S is a measure of the number of lines of force passing through it. The flux is given by

$$\text{flux} = \int_S \mathbf{E} \cdot d\mathbf{S}$$

Gauss's law states that the total flux out of any closed surface is proportional to the total charge enclosed. So consider a closed surface in free space, enclosing a volume V. The total charge enclosed in V is given by the volume integral

$$\text{total charge} = \int_V \rho \, dV$$

Gauss's law then states:

$$\oint_S \mathbf{E} \cdot d\mathbf{S} = \frac{1}{\varepsilon_0} \int_V \rho \, dV$$

where ε_0 is the permittivity of free space. The notation $\oint$ indicates that the surface is a closed surface. Note how a surface integral can be expressed as a volume integral. This relationship is generalized in the divergence theorem in the following section.

Example 27.23   A vector field is given by $\mathbf{v} = x^2\mathbf{i} + \frac{1}{2}y^2\mathbf{j} + \frac{1}{2}z^2\mathbf{k}$.

(a) Find div $\mathbf{v}$.

(b) Evaluate $\int_V \text{div } \mathbf{v} \, dV$ where V is the unit cube $0 \leqslant x \leqslant 1, 0 \leqslant y \leqslant 1, 0 \leqslant z \leqslant 1$.

Solution   (a) div $\mathbf{v} = 2x + y + z$.

(b) We seek $\int_V (2x + y + z) \, dV$ where V is the given unit cube. The small element of volume dV is equal to $dz \, dy \, dx$. With appropriate limits of integration the integral becomes

$$\int_{x=0}^{x=1} \int_{y=0}^{y=1} \int_{z=0}^{z=1} (2x + y + z) \, dz \, dy \, dx$$

This is a triple integral of the kind evaluated in Section 27.6.2.

$$\int_{x=0}^{x=1} \int_{y=0}^{y=1} \int_{z=0}^{z=1} (2x+y+z) \, dz \, dy \, dx = \int_{x=0}^{x=1} \int_{y=0}^{y=1} \left[2xz + yz + \frac{z^2}{2} \right]_0^1 dy \, dx$$

$$= \int_{x=0}^{x=1} \int_{y=0}^{y=1} \left(2x + y + \tfrac{1}{2} \right) dy \, dx$$

$$= \int_{x=0}^{x=1} \left[2xy + \frac{y^2}{2} + \frac{y}{2} \right]_0^1 dx$$

$$= \int_{x=0}^{x=1} 2x + 1 \, dx$$

$$= [x^2 + x]_0^1$$

$$= 2$$

Example 27.24

Evaluate $\oint_S \mathbf{v} \cdot d\mathbf{S}$ where $\mathbf{v} = x^2\mathbf{i} + \tfrac{1}{2}y^2\mathbf{j} + \tfrac{1}{2}z^2\mathbf{k}$ and where S is the surface of the unit cube $0 \leqslant x \leqslant 1, 0 \leqslant y \leqslant 1, 0 \leqslant z \leqslant 1$. The vector $d\mathbf{S}$ should be drawn on each of the six faces in an outward sense.

Figure 27.22
The integral is
evaluated over all six
surfaces.

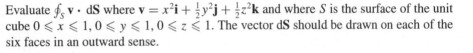

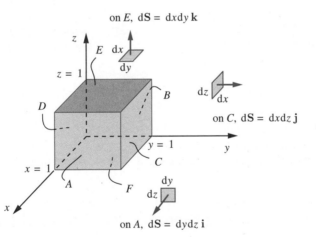

Solution

The cube is shown in Figure 27.22. We evaluate the surface integral over each of the six faces separately and then add the results.

On surface A, $x = 1$ and $0 \leqslant y \leqslant 1, 0 \leqslant z \leqslant 1$. $d\mathbf{S}$ is a vector normal to this surface, drawn in an outward sense, and so we can write it as $dy \, dz \, \mathbf{i}$. Then

$$\mathbf{v} \cdot d\mathbf{S} = \left(x^2\mathbf{i} + \tfrac{1}{2}y^2\mathbf{j} + \tfrac{1}{2}z^2\mathbf{k}\right) \cdot dy \, dz \, \mathbf{i}$$

$$= x^2 \, dy \, dz$$

$$= dy \, dz \qquad \text{since on } A, \, x = 1$$

The required surface integral over A is then

$$\int_{z=0}^{z=1}\int_{y=0}^{y=1} 1\, dy\, dz = \int_{z=0}^{z=1} [y]_0^1\, dz$$

$$= 1$$

On surface B, $x = 0$ and $0 \leqslant y \leqslant 1$, $0 \leqslant z \leqslant 1$. dS is a vector normal to this surface and so we can write it as $-dy\, dz\, \mathbf{i}$. Then $\mathbf{v} \cdot dS$ becomes $-x^2\, dy\, dz = 0$ since $x = 0$. Over this surface, the integral is zero.

You should verify in a similar manner that over each of C and E the integral is $\frac{1}{2}$, whilst integrals over D and F are zero. The total surface integral is then 2.

Exercises 27.7

1 Given $\mathbf{F} = -y\mathbf{i} - x\mathbf{k}$ evaluate $\oint_S \mathbf{F} \cdot dS$ where S is the surface of a unit cube $0 \leqslant x \leqslant 1$, $0 \leqslant y \leqslant 1$, $0 \leqslant z \leqslant 1$.

2 Given $\mathbf{F} = 6xy^2z^2\mathbf{k}$ evaluate $\int_S \mathbf{F} \cdot dS$ where S is the plane surface $z = 2$, $0 \leqslant x \leqslant 2$, $0 \leqslant y \leqslant 2$. Take the direction of the vector

element of area to be $\mathbf{k}$.

3 Evaluate the volume integral $\int_V 6x\, dV$ where V is the parallelepiped $0 \leqslant z \leqslant 2$, $0 \leqslant x \leqslant 1$, $0 \leqslant y \leqslant 3$.

4 Evaluate $\int_V 1 + z\, dV$ where V is a unit cube $0 \leqslant x \leqslant 1$, $0 \leqslant y \leqslant 1$, $0 \leqslant z \leqslant 1$.

Solutions

1 0

2 128

3 18

4 $\frac{3}{2}$

27.8 The divergence theorem and Stokes' theorem

There are a number of theorems in vector calculus which allow line, surface and volume integrals to be expressed in alternative forms. One of these, Green's theorem, has been described in Section 27.6.3. This allows a line integral to be written in terms of a double integral. Now we give details of the divergence theorem and Stokes' theorem.

27.8.1 The divergence theorem

The divergence theorem relates the integral over a volume, V, to an integral over the closed surface, S, which surrounds that volume, as illustrated in Figure 27.23.

When calculating such surface integrals vectors drawn normal to the surface should always be drawn in an outward sense, that is away from the enclosed volume. Recall that when a surface is closed the symbol for a surface integral is $\oint_S$.

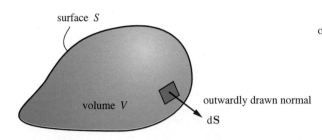

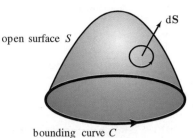

Figure 27.23 The divergence theorem relates a volume integral to a surface integral.

Figure 27.24 An open surface S with bounding curve C.

The **divergence theorem**:

$$\oint_S \mathbf{v} \cdot d\mathbf{S} = \int_V \operatorname{div} \mathbf{v} \, dV$$

Example 27.25

Verify the divergence theorem for the vector field $\mathbf{v} = x^2\mathbf{i} + \frac{1}{2}y^2\mathbf{j} + \frac{1}{2}z^2\mathbf{k}$ over the unit cube $0 \leqslant x \leqslant 1, 0 \leqslant y \leqslant 1, 0 \leqslant z \leqslant 1$.

Solution

Firstly we need to evaluate $\oint_S \mathbf{v} \cdot d\mathbf{S}$ where S is the surface of the cube. This integral has been calculated in Example 27.24 and shown to be 2.

Secondly we need to calculate $\int_V \operatorname{div} \mathbf{v} \, dV$ over the volume of the cube. This has been done in Example 27.23 and again the result is 2.

We have verified the divergence theorem that $\oint_S \mathbf{v} \cdot d\mathbf{S} = \int_V \operatorname{div} \mathbf{v} \, dV$.

27.8.2 Stokes' theorem

Stokes' theorem relates the integral over an open surface, S, to a line integral around a closed curve, C, which bounds that surface such as that shown in Figure 27.24.

When a surface is open we adopt the following convention when drawing vectors normal to the surface. When the direction of the normal vector has been specified, use the right-hand screw rule to obtain a sense of turning around the normal vector, as shown in Figure 27.24. Imagine now moving the circle which surrounds the normal vector along the surface until it just meets the curve C. Transfer its sense of turning to the curve C. When calculating the line integral around the curve C, it should be traversed in the same sense.

Specifically consider the two open surfaces shown in Figure 27.25. In both cases we are considering cubes. In the first case the cube has no top face. In the second case the cube has no bottom face. Drawing vector $dx\,dz\,\mathbf{j}$ note that the sense of turning required by the right-hand screw rule is that shown. The curve C must be traversed in the directions shown.

Recall that when a curve is closed the symbol for a line integral is $\oint_C$.

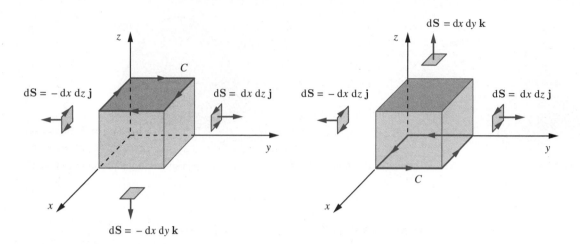

Figure 27.25 The right-hand screw rule gives the direction in which C must be traversed.

Figure 27.26
A cubical box with
open top bounded by
curve C.

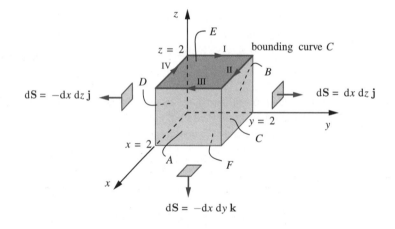

Stokes' theorem:

$$\oint_C \mathbf{v} \cdot d\mathbf{r} = \int_S \text{curl } \mathbf{v} \cdot d\mathbf{S}$$

Here $d\mathbf{r}$ is an element of length along the curve C. Recall that $d\mathbf{r} = dx\mathbf{i} + dy\mathbf{j} + dz\mathbf{k}$. We have used the symbol $d\mathbf{r}$ rather than $d\mathbf{s}$ as we did in Section 27.2 to avoid confusion with the element of area $d\mathbf{S}$.

Example 27.26

A cube of side 2 units is constructed with five solid faces and one open face. It is located in the region defined by $0 \leqslant x \leqslant 2, 0 \leqslant y \leqslant 2, 0 \leqslant z \leqslant 2$ and its open face is its top face, bounded by the curve C, lying in the plane $z = 2$, as shown in Figure 27.26.

Throughout this region a vector field is given by

$$\mathbf{v} = (x + y)\mathbf{i} + (y + z)\mathbf{j} + (x + z)\mathbf{k}$$

(a) Evaluate $\oint_C \mathbf{v} \cdot d\mathbf{r}$.

(b) Evaluate curl $\mathbf{v}$.

(c) Evaluate $\int_S$ curl $\mathbf{v} \, d\mathbf{S}$, and verify Stokes' theorem.

Solution   (a) The open face is highlighted in Figure 27.26. It is bounded by the curve C around which the line integral $\oint_C \mathbf{v} \cdot d\mathbf{r}$ must be performed in the sense shown. In this plane $z = 2$ and $dz = 0$, and hence

$$\mathbf{v} \cdot d\mathbf{r} = (x + y)\, dx + (y + 2)\, dy$$

We perform the line integral around C in four stages.

On I, $x = 0$, $dx = 0$ and hence $\mathbf{v} \cdot d\mathbf{r} = (y + 2)\, dy$. Noting that y varies from 0 to 2, the contribution to the line integral is

$$\int_0^2 y + 2 \, dy = \left[\frac{y^2}{2} + 2y \right]_0^2 = 6$$

On II, $y = 2$, $dy = 0$ and hence $\mathbf{v} \cdot d\mathbf{r} = (x + 2)\, dx$. Noting that x varies from 0 to 2, the contribution to the line integral is

$$\int_0^2 x + 2 \, dx = \left[\frac{x^2}{2} + 2x \right]_0^2 = 6$$

On III, $x = 2$, $dx = 0$ and hence $\mathbf{v} \cdot d\mathbf{r} = (y + 2)\, dy$. Here y varies from 2 to 0. This contribution to the line integral is

$$\int_2^0 y + 2 \, dy = \left[\frac{y^2}{2} + 2y \right]_2^0 = -6$$

On IV, $y = 0$, $dy = 0$ and hence $\mathbf{v} \cdot d\mathbf{r} = x \, dx$. Here x varies from 2 to 0. The contribution to the line integral is

$$\int_2^0 x \, dx = \left[\frac{x^2}{2} \right]_2^0 = -2$$

Putting all these results together we find

$$\oint_C \mathbf{v} \cdot d\mathbf{r} = 6 + 6 - 6 - 2 = 4$$

(b) $$\text{curl } \mathbf{v} = \begin{vmatrix} \mathbf{i} & \mathbf{j} & \mathbf{k} \\ \dfrac{\partial}{\partial x} & \dfrac{\partial}{\partial y} & \dfrac{\partial}{\partial z} \\ x+y & y+z & x+z \end{vmatrix} = -\mathbf{i} - \mathbf{j} - \mathbf{k}$$

(c) Now we calculate the surface integral which must be performed over the five solid surfaces separately. Refer to Figure 27.26. On surface A, the front face lying in the plane $x = 2$, $d\mathbf{S} = dy\,dz\,\mathbf{i}$. Hence curl $\mathbf{v} \cdot d\mathbf{S} = -dy\,dz$. Then

$$\int_A \text{curl } \mathbf{v} \cdot d\mathbf{S} = \int_{z=0}^{z=2} \int_{y=0}^{y=2} -dy\,dz$$

$$= \int_{z=0}^{z=2} [-y]_0^2 \, dz$$

$$= \int_{z=0}^{z=2} -2\,dz$$

$$= [-2z]_0^2$$

$$= -4$$

On B, the back face lying in the plane $x = 0$, $d\mathbf{S} = -dy\,dz\,\mathbf{i}$. It follows that curl $\mathbf{v} \cdot d\mathbf{S} = dy\,dz$. The required integral over B is

$$\int_{z=0}^{z=2} \int_{y=0}^{y=2} dy\,dz = 4$$

On C, the right-hand face, $d\mathbf{S} = dx\,dz\,\mathbf{j}$. Hence curl $\mathbf{v} \cdot d\mathbf{S} = -dx\,dz$. The required integral over C is

$$\int_{z=0}^{z=2} \int_{x=0}^{x=2} -dx\,dz = -4$$

Similarly, on D, the left-hand face, $d\mathbf{S} = -dx\,dz\,\mathbf{j}$. Hence curl $\mathbf{v} \cdot d\mathbf{S} = dx\,dz$. The required integral over D is

$$\int_{z=0}^{z=2} \int_{x=0}^{x=2} dx\,dz = 4$$

On surface F, the base, $z = 0$ and $d\mathbf{S} = -dx\,dy\,\mathbf{k}$. Hence curl $\mathbf{v} \cdot d\mathbf{S} = dx\,dy$. The required integral over F is

$$\int_{y=0}^{y=2} \int_{x=0}^{x=2} dx\,dy = 4$$

Recall that the top surface E is open, and so we have completed the surface integrals. Finally, putting these results together,

$$\int_S \text{curl } \mathbf{v} \cdot d\mathbf{S} = -4 + 4 - 4 + 4 + 4 = 4$$

Note from part (a) that this equals $\oint \mathbf{v} \cdot d\mathbf{r}$ and so we have verified Stokes' theorem.

Exercises   27.8

1   Verify Stokes' theorem for the field
$\mathbf{v} = xy\mathbf{i} + yz\mathbf{j}$ where S is the surface of the cube
$0 \leqslant x \leqslant 1, 0 \leqslant y \leqslant 1, 0 \leqslant z \leqslant 1$ and the face
$z = 0$ is open.

2   If $\mathbf{v} = 3x^2\mathbf{i} + xyz\mathbf{j} - 5z\mathbf{k}$ verify Stokes'
theorem where S is the surface of the cube
$0 \leqslant x \leqslant 1, 0 \leqslant y \leqslant 1, 0 \leqslant z \leqslant 1$ and the face
$z = 0$ is open.

3   Suppose $\mathbf{v} = x^3\mathbf{i} - 3x^2y^2z^2\mathbf{j} + (7x + z)\mathbf{k}$ and
S is the surface of a cube of side 2 units lying in
the region $0 \leqslant x \leqslant 2, 0 \leqslant y \leqslant 2, 0 \leqslant z \leqslant 2$
with an open top in the plane $z = 2$. Verify
Stokes' theorem for this field.

4   Consider a cube given by $0 \leqslant x \leqslant 1$,

$0 \leqslant y \leqslant 1, 1 \leqslant z \leqslant 2$, above the surface $z = 1$.
Suppose the surface $z = 1$ is the only open face.
Let S be the surface of this cube. Verify Stokes'
theorem for the field $\mathbf{v} = y\mathbf{i} + (x - 2xz)\mathbf{j} - xy\mathbf{k}$.
Take C as the square with corners $(0, 0, 1)$,
$(1, 0, 1)$, $(1, 1, 1)$, $(0, 1, 1)$ in the plane $z = 1$.

5   Consider that part of the positive octant, that is
where x, y and z are all positive, bounded by the
planes $x = 0$, $y = 0$, $z = 0$ and $x + y + 2z = 2$.
Assume that the tetrahedron so formed has three
solid faces, and one open face on the plane
$x + y + 2z = 2$. Verify Stokes' theorem for the
field $\mathbf{v} = x^2\mathbf{i} - 2xz\mathbf{k}$. Take C as the triangle
$(2, 0, 0)$, $(0, 2, 0)$, and $(0, 0, 1)$.

Solutions

When calculating the relevant line and surface integrals
the sign of the result depends upon the orientation of the
curve C.

1   $\oint \mathbf{v} \cdot d\mathbf{r} = \pm\frac{1}{2}$

2   $\oint \mathbf{v} \cdot d\mathbf{r} = 0$

3   $\oint \mathbf{v} \cdot d\mathbf{r} = \pm 128$

4   ± 2

5   $\pm\frac{2}{3}$

27.9 # Maxwell's equations in integral form

In Section 26.7 Maxwell's equations were stated as examples of the application of vector
calculus. In fact, alternative integral forms of these equations are often more useful and
these are given here for completeness.

Equation 1

$$\oint_S \mathbf{D} \cdot d\mathbf{S} = \int_V \rho \, dV$$

where $\mathbf{D}$ = electric flux density, and ρ is electric charge density. Note that the r.h.s. is the
total charge enclosed by the volume V. This equation states that the total flux crossing
a closed surface S which encloses a volume V is equal to the total charge enclosed by
the surface. This is also the integral form of Gauss's law. (See Example 27.22 which is
obtained by letting $\mathbf{D} = \varepsilon_0\mathbf{E}$.)

Equation 2

$$\oint_S \mathbf{B} \cdot d\mathbf{S} = 0$$

where $\mathbf{B}$ = magnetic flux density. This law states that the net magnetic flux crossing any closed surface is zero. So whilst charges can be thought of as sources or sinks of electric flux, there are no equivalent sources or sinks of magnetic flux.

Equation 3

$$\oint_C \mathbf{E} \cdot d\mathbf{r} = -\frac{\partial}{\partial t} \int_S \mathbf{B} \cdot d\mathbf{S}$$

Note that in the theory of electrostatics, differentiating partially with respect to time always yields zero, and so this equation reduces to $\oint_C \mathbf{E} \cdot d\mathbf{r} = 0$. This is a condition discussed in Section 27.5 and confirms that an electrostatic field is a conservative field.

Equation 4

$$\oint_C \mathbf{H} \cdot d\mathbf{r} = \frac{\partial}{\partial t} \int_S \mathbf{D} \cdot d\mathbf{S} + \int_S \mathbf{J} \cdot d\mathbf{S}$$

This is the integral form of Ampère's circuital law. The closed curve C bounds an open surface S. A current with density $\dfrac{\partial \mathbf{D}}{\partial t} + \mathbf{J}$ flows through the surface S.

Exercises 27.9

1 Starting with Maxwell's equation $\nabla \cdot \mathbf{D} = \rho$, by integrating both sides over an arbitrary volume V and using the divergence theorem obtain Equation 1 above.

2 Starting with Maxwell's equation $\nabla \cdot \mathbf{B} = 0$, by integrating both sides over an arbitrary volume V and using the divergence theorem obtain Equation 2 above.

3 Starting with the equation $\nabla \times \mathbf{E} = \mathbf{0}$ for static electric fields, use Stokes' theorem to show that $\oint \mathbf{E} \cdot d\mathbf{r} = 0$.

4 Starting from $\nabla \times \mathbf{H} = \dfrac{\partial \mathbf{D}}{\partial t} + \mathbf{J}$ and using Stokes' theorem obtain Equation 4.

5 In magnetostatics $\left(\dfrac{\partial}{\partial t} = 0\right)$, Ampère's law (or the magnetic circuit law) states:

$$\oint_C \mathbf{H} \cdot d\mathbf{r} = I$$

where I is the current enclosed by the closed path C. Obtain this law from Equation 4 and using $\int_S \mathbf{J} \cdot d\mathbf{S} = I$.

Review exercises 27

1 Find $\int_C (2x - y)\,dx + xy\,dy$ along the straight line joining $(-1, -1)$ and $(1, 1)$.

2 Find $\int_C (2x + y)\,dx + y^3\,dy$

   (a) along the curve $y = x^3$ between $(1, 1)$ and $(2, 8)$, and

   (b) along the straight line joining these points.

3 If $\mathbf{F} = 3xy\mathbf{i} + 2e^x y\mathbf{j}$ find $\int_C \mathbf{F} \cdot d\mathbf{s}$ where C is

the straight line $y = 2x + 1$ between $(1, 3)$ and $(4, 9)$.

4 Show that the field $\mathbf{F} = (2x + 1)y\mathbf{i} + (x^2 + x + 1)\mathbf{j}$ is conservative and find a suitable potential function ϕ.

5 Find $\oint_C (x^2\mathbf{i} + 4xy\mathbf{j}) \cdot d\mathbf{s}$ where C is a closed path in the form of a triangle with vertices at $(0, 0)$, $(3, 0)$ and $(3, 5)$.

6 Find $\int_{y=0}^{y=3} \int_{x=1}^{x=2} (3x - 5y) \, dx \, dy$.

7 Find $\int_{y=0}^{y=2} \int_{x=0}^{x=1+y} (2y + 5x) \, dx \, dy$.

8 Find

$\int_{x=0}^{x=2} \int_{y=0}^{y=1} \int_{z=0}^{z=3} (x^2 + y^2 + z^2) \, dz \, dy \, dx$.

9 Evaluate $\iint_R (4y + x^2) \, dx \, dy$ where R is the interior of the square with vertices at $(0, 0)$, $(4, 4)$, $(0, 4)$ and $(4, 0)$.

10 Evaluate $\oint_C e^y \, dx + e^x \, dy$ where C is the boundary of the triangle formed by the lines $y = x$, $y = 5$ and $x = 0$. By converting this line integral into a double integral verify Green's theorem in the plane.

11 The region R is bounded by the y axis and the lines $y = x$ and $y = 3 - 2x$.

   (a) Sketch the region R.

   (b) Find the volume between the surface $z = xy + 1$ and the region R.

12 The region R is shown in Figure 27.27. The vector field $\mathbf{F}$ is given by

$$\mathbf{F} = y^2 \mathbf{i} + 3xy \mathbf{j}$$

   (a) Evaluate $\oint_C \mathbf{F} \cdot d\mathbf{s}$ where C is the curve enclosing the region R.

   (b) Verify Green's theorem in the plane.

   (c) The surface, $z(x, y)$, is given by $z = 1 + x + xy$. Calculate the volume under the surface and above the region R.

13 The region R is bounded by the x axis and the curve $y = 8 + 2x - x^2$.

14 Evaluate

   (a) $\int_{-1}^{0} \int_{3}^{4} 3xy \, dx \, dy$

   (b) $\int_{2}^{3} \int_{0}^{2} 4 + x - y \, dy \, dx$

   (c) $\int_{0}^{1} \int_{2y}^{4} x^2 + y^2 \, dx \, dy$

   (d) $\int_{-2}^{-1} \int_{0}^{x^3} 1 \, dy \, dx$

15 Sketch the regions of integration of the double integrals in Question 14.

16 If a, b, c and d are constants show that

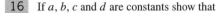

$$\int_{c}^{d} \int_{a}^{b} f(x)g(y) \, dx \, dy$$

is identical to

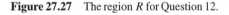

$$\left[\int_{a}^{b} f(x) \, dx \right] \left[\int_{c}^{d} g(y) \, dy \right]$$

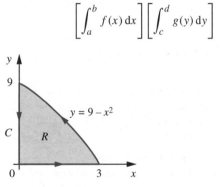

Figure 27.27 The region R for Question 12.

(a) Sketch R.

(b) Evaluate $\iint_R 3x + 2y \, dx \, dy$

Solutions

1 $\frac{2}{3}$

2 (a) 1030.5   (b) 1031.25

3 1666.37

4 $\phi = x^2y + yx + y + c$

5 50

6 -9

7 31

8 28

9 $\frac{640}{3}$

10 -452.239

11 (b) $\frac{17}{8}$

12 (a) 64.8   (c) 99

13 (b) 367.2

14 (a) $-\frac{21}{4}$ (b) 11   (c) 21.5

(d) $-\frac{15}{4}$

28 Probability

Chapter 28	Contents	
28.1	Introduction	876
28.2	Introducing probability	876
28.3	Mutually exclusive events: the addition law of probability	882
28.4	Complementary events	886
28.5	Concepts from communication theory	887
28.6	Conditional probability: the multiplication law	892
28.7	Independent events	897
	Review exercises	902

28.1 Introduction

Probability theory is applicable to several areas of engineering. One example is reliability engineering which is concerned with analysing the likelihood that an engineering system will fail. For most systems calculating the exact time of failure is not feasible but it is often possible to obtain a good estimate of whether or not a system will fail in a certain time interval. This is useful information to have for any engineering system, but it is vital if the failure of the system results in the possibility of injury or loss of life. Examples include the failure of high-voltage switchgear so that the casing becomes live, or electrical equipment producing a spark while being used underground in a mine.

Probability theory is also used extensively in production engineering, particularly in the field of quality control. No manufacturing process produces components of exactly the same quality each time. There is always some variation in quality and probability theory allows this variation to be quantified. This enables some predictability to be introduced into the activity of manufacturing and gives an engineer the confidence to say components of a certain quality can be supplied to a customer.

A final example is in the field of communication engineering. Communication channels are subject to noise which is random in nature and so is most successfully modelled using probability theory. We will examine some of these concepts in more detail in this chapter.

28.2 Introducing probability

Consider a machine which manufactures electronic components. These must meet a certain specification. The quality control department regularly samples the components. Suppose, on average, 92 out of 100 components meet the specification. Imagine that a component is selected at random and let A be the outcome that a component meets the specification; let B be the outcome that a component does not meet the specification. Then we say the **probability** of A occurring is $\dfrac{92}{100} = 0.92$ and the probability of B occurring is $\dfrac{8}{100} = 0.08$. The probability is thus a measure of the likelihood of the occurrence of a particular outcome. We write

$$P(A) = \text{probability of } A \text{ occurring } = 0.92$$
$$P(B) = \text{probability of } B \text{ occurring } = 0.08$$

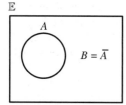

Figure 28.1 A: a component meets the specification. $B = \overline{A}$: a component fails to meet the specification.

We note that the sum of the probabilities of all possible outcomes is 1. The process of selecting a component is called a **trial**. The possible outcomes are also called **events**. In this example there are only two possible events, A and B. We can depict this situation using a Venn diagram as shown in Figure 28.1. Recall from Section 5.2 that Venn diagrams are used to depict sets. In this diagram we are depicting the events A and B as sets. The set of all possible outcomes is called the **sample space** and is represented by the universal set $\mathbb{E}$. The set A represents the event that a component meets the specification. The set B represents the event that a component fails to meet the specification. In this instance, when a trial takes place there are only two possible outcomes, either a component meets the specification or it does not; that is, either event A occurs or event

B occurs. An alternative notation is to write

$$B = \overline{A}$$

where $\overline{A}$ is said to be the **complement** of A. We could also write

$$A = \overline{B}$$

When a bar appears over a set then we say, for example, 'not A', or 'not B'.

We now seek to define probability in a more formal way. Let E be an event. We wish to obtain the probability that E will occur, that is $P(E)$, when a trial takes place. In order to do so we repeat the trial a large number of times, n. We count the number of times that event E occurs, denoted by m. We then conclude that

$$P(E) = \frac{m}{n} \qquad (28.1)$$

The larger the number of trials that take place, the more confident we are of our estimate of the probability of E occurring. For example, consider the trial of tossing a coin. If we wish to calculate the probability of a head occurring then measuring the results of 1000 tosses of the coin is likely to yield a more accurate estimate than measuring the results of 10 tosses of the coin. Various consequences flow from Equation (28.1). The number of times E occurs must be non-negative and less than or equal to the number of trials, that is $0 \leqslant m \leqslant n$. So,

$$0 \leqslant P(E) \leqslant 1$$

If $m = 0$, corresponding to event E never occurring in n trials, then

$$P(E) = \frac{0}{n} = 0$$

We conclude that E is an impossible event.

If $m = n$, corresponding to event E always occuring in n trials, then

$$P(E) = \frac{n}{n} = 1$$

We deduce that E is a certain event.

If $P(E) > 0.5$ then we conclude that E is more likely to occur than not.

The approach to defining probability that we have adopted so far is essentially experimental. We carry out a series of trials and measure the probability of an event occurring. Sometimes it is possible to deduce the probability of an event purely from theoretical considerations. Consider again the trial of tossing a coin. If the coin is fair then defining H to be the event that the coin lands with the head facing up we can easily deduce that

$$P(H) = 0.5$$

because we intuitively recognize that a head has the same likelihood of occurring as a tail. Similarly, if we roll a fair die – die is the singular of dice – and E is the event that a 6 is obtained, then $P(E) = \frac{1}{6}$.

Suppose there are two possible outcomes, E_1 and E_2, of a trial. Then

$$P(E_1) + P(E_2) = 1$$

If a trial has n possible outcomes, $E_1, E_2, \ldots, E_n$, then

$$P(E_1) + P(E_2) + \cdots + P(E_n) = 1$$

The sum of the probabilities of all possible outcomes is 1, representing the total probability.

28.2.1 Compound event

Consider the situation of rolling a fair die. It is possible to define a variety of events or outcomes associated with this trial. We choose to define two events, E_1 and E_2, as follows:

E_1 : a 1, 2, 3 or 4 is obtained

E_2 : an even number is obtained

So,

$$E_1 = \{1, 2, 3, 4\}$$
$$E_2 = \{2, 4, 6\}$$

Now the universal set is

$$\mathbb{E} = \{1, 2, 3, 4, 5, 6\}$$

which embraces all possible outcomes.

Suppose we now define the event E_3 as

E_3 : E_1 occurs and E_2 occurs

The event E_3 is known as a **compound event** and only occurs when both E_1 and E_2 occur at the same time. Using set notation we can write

$$E_3 = E_1 \cap E_2$$
$$= \{1, 2, 3, 4\} \cap \{2, 4, 6\}$$
$$= \{2, 4\}$$

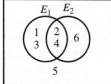

Figure 28.2 $E_1 \cap E_2$ corresponds to the compound event E_1 occurs and E_2 occurs.

So E_3 occurs when a 2 or a 4 is rolled. Hence $E_1 \cap E_2$ can occur in two out of six equally likely ways. Therefore,

$$P(E_3) = P(E_1 \cap E_2) = \frac{2}{6} = \frac{1}{3}$$

Figure 28.2 shows a Venn diagram for this example.

We could also define the compound event E_4 as

E_4 : E_1 occurs or E_2 occurs

The event E_4 occurs when either E_1 occurs or E_2 occurs, or both. We can write

$$E_4 = E_1 \cup E_2$$
$$= \{1, 2, 3, 4\} \cup \{2, 4, 6\}$$
$$= \{1, 2, 3, 4, 6\}$$

So,

$$P(E_4) = P(E_1 \cup E_2) = \frac{5}{6}$$

> If events A and B both occur then this compound event is denoted $A \cap B$.
> If either event A or event B occurs then this compound event is denoted $A \cup B$.

Example 28.1

Power supply to a computer

Computers used in the control of life-critical systems often have two separate power supplies. If one power supply fails then the other takes over. Let E_1 be the event that power supply 1 fails, and let E_2 be the event that power supply 2 fails. For the power supply to the computer to fail completely the compound event E_1 and E_2 must occur, that is $E_1 \cap E_2$ occurs.

Example 28.2

Machines A and B make components, which are then placed on a conveyor belt. Of those made by machine A, 93% are acceptable. Of those made by machine B, 95% are acceptable. Machine A makes 60% of the components and machine B makes the rest. Find the probability that a component selected at random from the conveyor belt is

(a) made by machine A

(b) made by machine A and acceptable

(c) made by machine B and acceptable

(d) made by machine B and unacceptable

Solution

(a) We are given that 60% of the components are made by machine A. Converting this percentage to a decimal number gives

$$P(\text{component is made by machine A}) = 0.6$$

(b) We know that 60% of the components are made by machine A and 93% of these are acceptable. Converting these percentages to decimal numbers we have

$$P(\text{component is made by machine A and is acceptable}) = \frac{60}{100} \times \frac{93}{100}$$
$$= 0.60 \times 0.93 = 0.558$$

(c) We know that 40% of the components are made by machine B and 95% of these are acceptable. So,

$$P(\text{component is made by machine B and is acceptable}) = \frac{40}{100} \times \frac{95}{100}$$
$$= 0.40 \times 0.95 = 0.38$$

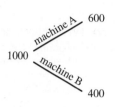

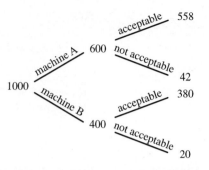

Figure 28.3 Partial tree diagram for Example 28.2.

Figure 28.4 Full tree diagram for Example 28.2.

(d) We know that 40% of the components are made by machine B and 5% of these are unacceptable. So,

$$P(\text{component is made by machine B and is unacceptable}) = \frac{40}{100} \times \frac{5}{100}$$

$$= 0.40 \times 0.05 = 0.02$$

An alternative way to solve this problem is by constructing a **tree diagram**. To do so, consider the case when 1000 components are picked from the conveyor belt. We know that machine A makes 60% of the components and so 600 of these components, on average, will be made by machine A and the other 400 must therefore be made by machine B. This is shown in Figure 28.3.

Of the 600 components made by machine A, we know that 93% of these are acceptable, that is 93% of $600 = 558$. So $600 - 558 = 42$ are unacceptable.

Of the 400 components made by machine B, we know that 95% of these are acceptable, that is 95% of $400 = 380$. So $400 - 380 = 20$ are unacceptable.

We can now complete a full tree diagram for this problem, which is shown in Figure 28.4.

Using the tree diagram it is straightforward to calculate the required probabilities.

(a) The probability a component is made by machine A is found by noting that 600 of the 1000 components are made by machine A, that is

$$P(\text{component is made by machine A}) = \frac{600}{1000} = 0.6$$

(b) The probability a component is made by machine A and is acceptable is found by noting that 558 of the 1000 components are made by machine A and acceptable, that is

$$P(\text{component is made by machine A and acceptable}) = \frac{558}{1000} = 0.558$$

(c) $$P(\text{component is made by machine B and acceptable}) = \frac{380}{1000} = 0.38$$

(d) $$P(\text{component is made by machine B and unacceptable}) = \frac{20}{1000} = 0.02$$

Exercises 28.2

1 A fair die is rolled. The events $E_1, \ldots, E_5$ are defined as follows:

E_1: an even number is obtained

E_2: an odd number is obtained

E_3: a score of less than 2 is obtained

E_4: a 3 is obtained

E_5: a score of more than 3 is obtained

Find

(a) $P(E_1), P(E_2), P(E_3), P(E_4), P(E_5)$

(b) $P(E_1 \cap E_3)$

(c) $P(E_2 \cap E_5)$

(d) $P(E_2 \cap E_3)$

(e) $P(E_3 \cap E_5)$

2 A trial can have three outcomes, E_1, E_2 and E_3. E_1 and E_2 are equally likely to occur. E_3 is three times more likely to occur than E_1. Find $P(E_1)$, $P(E_2)$ and $P(E_3)$.

3 A component is made by machines A and B. Machine A makes 70% of the components and machine B makes the rest. For both machines, the proportion of acceptable components is 90%. Find the probability that a component selected at random is

(a) unacceptable

(b) acceptable and is made by machine A

(c) unacceptable and is made by machine B

4 Machines A, B and C make components. Machine A makes 20% of the components, machine B makes 30% of the components and machine C makes the rest. The probability that a component is faulty is 0.07 when made by machine A, 0.06 when made by machine B and 0.05 when made by machine C. A component is picked at random. Calculate the probability that the component is

(a) made by machine C

(b) made by machine A and is faulty

(c) made by machine B and is not faulty

(d) made by machine C and is faulty

(e) made by machine A and is not faulty

(f) faulty and is not made by machine B

5 Circuit boards are made by machines A, B, C and D. Machine A makes 15% of the components, machine B makes 30%, machine C makes 35% and machine D makes the remainder. The probability that a board is acceptable is 0.93 when made by machine A, 0.96 when made by machine B, 0.95 when made by machine C and 0.93 when made by machine D. A board is picked at random. Calculate the probability that is

(a) made by machine D

(b) made by machine A and is acceptable

(c) made by machine B and is unacceptable

(d) made by machine C and is acceptable

(e) made by machine D and is unacceptable

(f) unacceptable and made by machine C

(g) In a batch of 1000 boards, how many would be expected to be acceptable and made by machine D?

Solutions

1 (a) $\frac{1}{2}, \frac{1}{2}, \frac{1}{6}, \frac{1}{6}, \frac{1}{2}$ (b) 0 (c) $\frac{1}{6}$

  (d) $\frac{1}{6}$ (e) 0

2 0.2, 0.2, 0.6

3 (a) 0.1 (b) 0.63 (c) 0.03

4 (a) 0.5 (b) 0.014 (c) 0.282

  (d) 0.025 (e) 0.186 (f) 0.039

5 (a) 0.2 (b) 0.1395 (c) 0.012

  (d) 0.3325 (e) 0.014 (f) 0.0175

  (g) 186

28.3 Mutually exclusive events: the addition law of probability

Consider a machine which manufactures car components. Suppose each component falls into one of four categories:

top quality

standard

substandard

reject

After many samples have been taken and tested, it is found that under certain specific conditions the probability that a component falls into a category is as shown in Table 28.1. The four categories cover all possibilities and so the probabilities must sum to 1. If 100 samples are taken, then on average 18 will be top quality, 65 of standard quality, 12 substandard and 5 will be rejected.

Example 28.3 Using the data in Table 28.1 calculate the probability that a component selected at random is either standard or top quality.

Solution On average 18 out of 100 components are top quality and 65 out of 100 are standard quality. So 83 out of 100 are either top quality or standard quality. Hence the probability that a component is either top quality or standard quality is 0.83. The solution may be expressed more formally as follows. Let A be the event that a component is top quality. Let B be the event that a component is standard quality.

$$P(A) = 0.18 \qquad P(B) = 0.65$$

Then,

$$P(A \cup B) = 0.18 + 0.65 = 0.83$$

Note that in this example

$$P(A \cup B) = P(A) + P(B)$$

In Example 28.3 the events A and B could not possibly occur together. A component is either top quality or standard quality but cannot be both. We say A and B are **mutually exclusive** because the occurrence of one excludes the occurrence of the other. The result applies more generally.

> If the occurrence of either of events E_i or E_j excludes the occurrence of the other, then E_i and E_j are said to be mutually exclusive events.

If E_i and E_j are mutually exclusive we denote this by

$$E_i \cap E_j = \varnothing$$

We use $\varnothing$ to denote the **empty set**, that is a set with no elements. In effect we are stating that the compound event $E_i \cap E_j$ is an **impossible event** and so will never occur. On a

Table 28.1 The probability of a car component falling into one of four categories.

Category	Probability
top quality	0.18
standard	0.65
substandard	0.12
reject	0.05

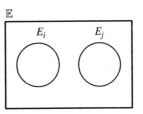

Figure 28.5 E_i and E_j are mutually exclusive events and so are depicted as disjoint sets.

Table 28.2
The lifespans of 5000 electrical components.

Lifespan of component (yrs)	Number
$L > 5$	500
$4 < L \leqslant 5$	2250
$3 < L \leqslant 4$	1850
$L \leqslant 3$	400

Venn diagram E_i and E_j are shown as disjoint sets (see Figure 28.5). Suppose that E_1, $E_2, \ldots, E_n$ are n events and that in a single trial only one of these events can occur. The occurrence of any event, E_i, excludes the occurrence of all other events. Such events are mutually exclusive.

For mutually exclusive events the addition law of probability applies:

$$P(E_1 \text{ or } E_2 \text{ or } \ldots \text{ or } E_n) = P(E_1 \cup E_2 \cup \cdots \cup E_n)$$
$$= P(E_1) + P(E_2) + \cdots + P(E_n)$$

Example 28.4

The lifespans of 5000 electrical components are measured to assess their reliability. The lifespan (L) is recorded and the results are shown in Table 28.2. Find the probability that a randomly selected component will last

(a) more than 3 years

(b) between 3 and 5 years

(c) less than 4 years

Solution We define events A, B, C and D.

A: the component lasts more than 5 years

B: the component lasts between 4 and 5 years

C: the component lasts between 3 and 4 years

D: the component lasts 3 years or less

$$P(A) = \frac{500}{5000} = 0.1, \; P(B) = \frac{2250}{5000} = 0.45, \; P(C) = \frac{1850}{5000} = 0.37,$$

$P(D) = \dfrac{400}{5000} = 0.08.$ The events A, B, C and D are clearly mutually exclusive and so the addition law may be applied.

(a) $P(\text{component lasts more than 3 years}) = P(A \cup B \cup C)$
$$= P(A) + P(B) + P(C)$$
$$= 0.1 + 0.45 + 0.37$$
$$= 0.92$$

There is a 92% chance a component will last for more than 3 years.

(b) $P(\text{component lasts between 3 and 5 years}) = P(B \cup C)$
$$= P(B) + P(C)$$
$$= 0.45 + 0.37$$
$$= 0.82$$

(c) $P(\text{component lasts less than 4 years}) = P(C \cup D)$
$$= P(C) + P(D)$$
$$= 0.37 + 0.08$$
$$= 0.45$$

Example 28.5 Machines A and B make components. Machine A makes 60% of the components. The probability that a component is acceptable is 0.93 when made by machine A and 0.95 when made by machine B. A component is picked at random. Calculate the probability that it is

(a) made by machine A and is acceptable

(b) made by machine B and is acceptable

(c) acceptable

Solution We have already looked at this problem in Example 28.2. Figure 28.4 shows the tree diagram for the problem.

(a) P (component is made by machine A and is acceptable) $= \dfrac{558}{1000} = 0.558.$

(b) P (component is made by machine B and is acceptable) $= \dfrac{380}{1000} = 0.38.$

(c) Note that the events described in (a) and (b) are mutually exclusive and so the addition law can be applied.

$$P(\text{component is acceptable}) = P(\text{component is made by machine A and is acceptable})$$
$$+ P(\text{component is made by machine B and is acceptable})$$
$$= 0.558 + 0.38$$
$$= 0.938$$

We can now obtain this probability directly from the tree diagram. We see that $558 + 380 = 938$ components are acceptable and so

$$P(\text{component is acceptable}) \;=\; \frac{938}{1000} = 0.938$$

Exercises 28.3

1   A component is classified as one of top quality, standard quality or substandard, with respective probabilities of 0.07, 0.85 and 0.08. Find the probability that a component is

(a) either top quality or standard quality

(b) not top quality

2   The lifespan (L) of each of 2000 valves is measured and given in Table 28.3.

Table 28.3   The lifespans of 2000 valves.

Lifespan (hours)	Number
$L \geqslant 1000$	119
$800 \leqslant L < 1000$	520
$600 \leqslant L < 800$	931
$400 \leqslant L < 600$	230
$L < 400$	200

Calculate the probability that the lifespan of a valve is

(a) more than 800 hours

(b) less than 600 hours

(c) between 400 and 800 hours

3   Chips are manufactured by machines A and B. Machine A makes 65% of the chips and machine B makes the remainder. The probability that a chip is faulty is 0.03 when made by machine A and 0.05 when made by machine B. A chip is selected at random. Calculate the probability that it is

(a) faulty and made by machine A

(b) faulty or made by machine A

(c) faulty or made by machine B

(d) faulty and made by machine B

(e) faulty

4   Components are made by machines A, B, C and D. Machine A makes 25% of the components, machine B makes 16% of the components, machine C makes 21% of the components and machine D makes the remainder. The probability that a component is acceptable is 0.92 when made by machine A, 0.90 when made by machine B, 0.96 when made by machine C and 0.93 when made by machine D. A component is picked at random. Calculate the probability that it is

(a) made by machine A or machine C

(b) made by machines A, B or D

(c) acceptable and made by machine B

(d) acceptable and made by machine C

(e) acceptable and made by machine B or acceptable and made by machine C

(f) acceptable or made by machine A

(g) acceptable

Solutions

1 (a) 0.92   (b) 0.93

2 (a) 0.3195   (b) 0.215   (c) 0.5805

3 (a) 0.0195   (b) 0.6675   (c) 0.3695
    (d) 0.0175   (e) 0.037

4 (a) 0.46   (b) 0.79   (c) 0.144
    (d) 0.2016   (e) 0.3456   (f) 0.949
    (g) 0.929

28.4   Complementary events

Consider an electronic circuit. Clearly, either the circuit works correctly or it does not work correctly. Let A be the event that the circuit works correctly, and let B be the event that the circuit does not work correctly. Either A or B must happen when the circuit is tested, and one excludes the other. The events A and B are said to be **complementary**. The Venn diagram corresponding to this situation is identical to that in Figure 28.1 where the set A corresponds to the event A, and the event B is represented by $\overline{A}$.

> Two events, A and B, are complementary if they are mutually exclusive and in a single trial either A or B must happen.

Hence, if A and B are complementary then

$$P(A) + P(B) = 1$$

and

$$P(A \cap B) = 0$$

It is usual to denote complementary events as A and $\overline{A}$. For example,

A : the component is top quality

$\overline{A}$: the component is not top quality

$B : n > 6$

$\overline{B} : n \leqslant 6$

C : the circuit has failed to meet the specification

$\overline{C}$: the circuit has met the specification

Recall from Example 28.4 that D was the event the component lasts 3 years or less, and this had probability $P(D) = 0.08$. We could say

D : the component lasts 3 years or less

$\overline{D}$: the component lasts more than 3 years

D and $\overline{D}$ are complementary events and so

$$P(D) + P(\overline{D}) = 1$$
$$P(\overline{D}) = 1 - P(D) = 1 - 0.08 = 0.92$$

Example 28.6	Three transistors are tested. The probability that none of them works is 0.03. What is the probability that at least one transistor works?

Solution   We define the events A and $\overline{A}$:

$$A : \text{all three transistors fail}$$

$$\overline{A} : \text{not all three transistors fail}$$

A and $\overline{A}$ are complementary events and so

$$P(A) = 0.03 \qquad P(\overline{A}) = 1 - P(A) = 0.97$$

To say that not all three transistors fail is the same as saying that one or more transistors work. So we could say

$$\overline{A} : \text{ at least one transistor works}$$

Hence the probability that at least one transistor works is 0.97.

Exercises 28.4

1 Which pairs of events are complementary?

      A: the component is reliable

      B: there is only one component

      C: there are less than two components

      D: more than two components are
            reliable

      E: the component is unreliable

      F: there is more than one component

      G: most of the components are
            unreliable

2 Events A, $\overline{B}$, C and D are defined.

      A: the lifespan is 90 days or less

      $\overline{B}$: the machine is reliable

      C: all components have been tested

      D: at least three components from
            the sample are unreliable

  State the events $\overline{A}$, B, $\overline{C}$ and $\overline{D}$.

Solutions

1 A and E; C and F

2 $\overline{A}$: the lifespan is more than 90 days
     B: the machine is unreliable

     $\overline{C}$: some components have not been tested
     $\overline{D}$: two or fewer components are unreliable

28.5	# Concepts from communication theory

Communication engineers find it useful to quantify information for the purposes of analysis. In order to do so a very restricted view of information is used. Information is seen in terms of knowledge of an event occurring. A highly improbable event occurring constitutes more information than an almost certain event occurring. This correlates to some extent with human experience as people tend to be much more interested in hearing about unlikely events. The **information**, I, associated with an event, is defined by

$$I = -\log p \qquad 0 < p \leqslant 1$$

where p = probability of an event occurring. Notice that $p = 0$ is excluded from the domain of the function as the logarithm is not defined at 0. In practice this is not a problem because an event with zero probability never occurs. Often logarithms to the base 2 are used when calculating information as in many cases information arrives in the form of a 'bit stream' consisting of a series of binary numbers. For this case I has units of bits and is given by

$$I = -\log_2 p$$

A formula for evaluating logarithms to the base 2 is given in Chapter 2.

Example 28.7

Suppose that a computer generates a binary stream of data and that 1s and 0s occur with equal probability, that is $P(0) = P(1) = 0.5$. Calculate the information per binary digit generated.

Solution

Here, $p = 0.5$ whether the binary digit is 0 or 1, so

$$I = -\log_2(0.5) = \frac{-\log_{10}(0.5)}{\log_{10} 2} = 1 \text{ bit}$$

Example 28.8

Suppose that a system generates a stream of upper case alphabetic characters and that the probability of a character occurring is the same for all characters. Calculate

(a) the information associated with the character G occurring

(b) the information associated with any single character.

Solution

(a) $P(\text{G occurring}) = \dfrac{1}{26}$, $\quad I = -\log_2\left(\dfrac{1}{26}\right) = \dfrac{-\log_{10}(1/26)}{\log_{10} 2} = 4.70 \text{ bits}$

(b) All characters are equally likely to occur and so

$$I = -\log_2\left(\frac{1}{26}\right) = \frac{-\log_{10}(1/26)}{\log_{10} 2} = 4.70 \text{ bits}$$

Often a series of events may occur that do not have the same probability. For example, if a stream of alphabetic characters is being generated then it is likely that some characters will occur more frequently than others and so have a higher probability associated with them. For this situation it becomes convenient to introduce the concept of average information. Given a source producing a set of events

$$E_1, E_2, E_3, \ldots , E_n$$

with probabilities

$$p_1, p_2, p_3, \ldots , p_n$$

then for a long series of events the **average information** per event is given by

$$H = -\sum_{i=1}^{i=n} p_i \log_2 p_i \text{ bits}$$

H is also termed the **entropy**.

Example 28.9   A source produces messages consisting of three characters, A, B and C. The probabilities of each of these characters occurring is $P(A) = 0.2$, $P(B) = 0.5$, $P(C) = 0.3$. Calculate the entropy of the signal.

Solution $H = -0.2 \log_2(0.2) - 0.5 \log_2(0.5) - 0.3 \log_2(0.3) = 1.49$ bits

Example 28.10   A source generates binary digits 0, 1, with probabilities $P(0) = 0.3$ and $P(1) = 0.7$. Calculate the entropy of the signal.

Solution $H = -0.3 \log_2(0.3) - 0.7 \log_2(0.7) = 0.881$ bits

Note that in Example 28.10, on average, each binary digit only carries 0.881 bits of information. In fact the maximum average amount of information that can be carried by a binary digit occurs when $P(0) = P(1) = 0.5$, as seen in Example 28.7. For this case $H = 1$.

For any data stream, the maximum average amount of information that can be carried by a digit occurs when all digits have equal probability, that is H is maximized when $p_1 = p_2 = p_3 = \cdots = p_n$.

H is maximized when $p_1 = p_2 = p_3 = \cdots = p_n$. The maximum value of H is denoted H_{max}.

When the probabilities are not the same then one way of viewing the reduction in H is to think of the likely event being given too much of the signalling time given its lower information content. It is interesting to explore the two limiting cases, that is (a) $P(0) = 0$, $P(1) = 1$; (b) $P(0) = 1$, $P(1) = 0$. In both cases it can be shown that $H = 0$. However, on examination this is reasonable because a continuous stream of

1s does not relay any useful information to the recipient and neither does a continuous stream of 0s.

The fact that some streams of symbols do not contain as much information as other streams of the same symbols leads to the concept of **redundancy**. This allows the efficiency with which information is being sent to be quantified and is defined as

$$\text{redundancy} = \frac{\text{maximum entropy} - \text{actual entropy}}{\text{maximum entropy}}$$

A low value of redundancy corresponds to efficient transmission of information.

Example 28.11

Consider the source of binary digits examined in Examples 28.7 and 28.10. The maximum entropy for a binary stream is 1 bit per binary digit. Calculate the redundancy in each case.

Solution

For Example 28.7

$$\text{redundancy} = \frac{1 - 1}{1} = 0$$

For Example 28.10

$$\text{redundancy} = \frac{1 - 0.881}{1} = 0.119$$

Example 28.12

A stream of data consists of four characters A, B, C, D with probabilities 0.1, 0.3, 0.2, 0.4, respectively. Calculate the redundancy.

Solution

It can be shown that the maximum entropy, H_{max}, corresponds to the situation in which the probability of each symbol is the same, that is 0.25.

$$H_{max} = 4 \times (-0.25 \log_2(0.25)) = 2 \text{ bits}$$

The actual entropy, H_{act}, is given by

$$H_{act} = -(0.1 \log_2(0.1) + 0.3 \log_2(0.3) + 0.2 \log_2(0.2) + 0.4 \log_2(0.4))$$
$$= 1.846 \text{ bits}$$

$$\text{redundancy} = \frac{2 - 1.846}{2} = 0.0770$$

In the examples we have examined so far we have used the bit as the unit of information because the most common form of digital signalling uses binary digits. When there are only two possible events it is possible to represent an event by a single binary digit. However, if there is a larger number of possible events then several binary digits are needed to represent a single event. When calculating values for information and entropy in these examples an assumption was made that each event was represented by binary sequences or **codes** of the same length. It is only possible to do this efficiently if the number of events is a power of 2, that is 2, 4, 8, 16, ... In practice this problem does not arise because it is more common to produce codes that have a small number of binary digits for likely events and a long number of binary digits for unlikely events. This allows the redundancy of a data stream to be reduced. The design of such codes is known as **coding theory**. One complication is that most streams of data are not transmitted with 100% accuracy as a result of the presence of noise within the communication channel. It is often necessary to build extra redundancy into a code in order to recover these errors.

Exercises 28.5

1 A source generates six characters, A, B, C, D, E, F with respective probabilities 0.05, 0.1, 0.25, 0.3, 0.15, 0.15. Calculate the average information per character and the redundancy.

2 A visual display unit has a resolution of 600 rows by 800 columns. Ten different grey levels are associated with each pixel and their probabilities are 0.05, 0.07, 0.09, 0.10, 0.11, 0.13, 0.12, 0.12, 0.11, 0.10. Calculate the average information content in each picture frame.

3 A source generates five characters A, B, C, D and E with respective probabilities of 0.1, 0.15, 0.2, 0.25, and 0.3.

  (a) Calculate the information associated with the character B.

  (b) Calculate the entropy.

  (c) Calculate the redundancy.

4 A data stream comprises the characters A, B, C, D and E with respective probabilities of 0.23,

0.16, 0.11, 0.37 and 0.13.

  (a) Calculate the information associated with the character B.

  (b) Calculate the information associated with the character D.

  (c) Calculate the entropy.

  (d) Calculate the redundancy.

5 A data stream comprises the characters A, B, C, D and E, with respective probabilities of 0.12, 0.21, 0.07, 0.31 and 0.29.

  (a) Which character carries the greatest information content?

  (b) Which character carries the least information content?

  (c) Calculate the information associated with the letter D.

  (d) Calculate the entropy.

  (e) Calculate the redundancy.

Solutions

1 2.3905, 0.0752

2 3.2790

3 (a) 2.7370   (b) 2.2282   (c) 0.0404

4 (a) 2.6439   (b) 1.4344   (c) 2.1743
    (d) 0.0636

5 (a) C   (b) D   (c) 1.6897
    (d) 2.1501   (e) 0.0740

Conditional probability: the multiplication law

Suppose two machines, M and N, both manufacture components. Of the components made by machine M, 92% are of an acceptable standard and 8% are rejected. For machine N, only 80% are of an acceptable standard and 20% are rejected. Consider now the event E:

E: a component is of an acceptable standard

If all the components are manufactured by machine M then $P(E) = 0.92$. However, if all the components are manufactured by machine N then $P(E) = 0.8$. If half the components are manufactured by machine M and half by machine N then $P(E) = 0.86$. To see why this is so consider 1000 components. Of the half made by machine M, $92\% \times 500 = 460$ will be of an acceptable standard. Of the half made by machine N, $80\% \times 500 = 400$ will be acceptable. Hence 860 of the 1000 components will be acceptable and so $P(E) = \dfrac{860}{1000} = 0.86$. Clearly, there are distinct probabilities of the same event; the probability changes as the conditions change. This is intuitive and leads to the idea of **conditional probability**.

We introduce a notation for conditional probability. Define events A and B by

A: the component is manufactured by machine M

B: the component is manufactured by machine N

Then the probability that a component is of an acceptable standard, given it is manufactured by machine M, is written as $P(E|A)$. We read this as the conditional probability of E given A. Similarly $P(E|B)$ is the probability of E happening, given B has already happened.

$$P(E|A) = 0.92 \qquad P(E|B) = 0.8$$

To be pedantic, all probabilities are conditional since the conditions surrounding any event can change. However, for many situations there is tacitly assumed a definite set of conditions which is always satisfied. The probability of an event calculated under only these conditions is known as the **unconditional probability**. If further well-defined conditions are attached, the probability is conditional.

Example 28.13 Machines M and N manufacture a component. The probability that the component is of an acceptable standard is 0.95 when manufactured by machine M and 0.83 when manufactured by machine N. Machine M supplies 65% of components; machine N supplies 35%. A component is picked at random.

(a) What is the probability that the component is of an acceptable standard?

(b) What is the probability that a component is of an acceptable standard and is made by machine M?

(c) What is the probability that the component is of an acceptable standard given it is made by machine M?

(d) What is the probability that the component was made by machine M?

(e) What is the probability that the component was made by machine M given it is of an acceptable standard?

(f) The component is not of an acceptable standard. What is the probability that it was made by machine N?

Solution We define the events:

A: the component is manufactured by machine M

B: the component is manufactured by machine N

C: the component is of an acceptable standard

(a) Consider 1000 components. Then 650 are manufactured by machine M, 350 by machine N. Of the 650 manufactured by machine M, 95% will be acceptable, that is $650 \times \dfrac{95}{100} = 617.5$. Of the 350 manufactured by machine N, 83% will be acceptable, that is $350 \times \dfrac{83}{100} = 290.5$. So on average in 1000 components, $617.5 + 290.5 = 908$ will be acceptable, that is $P(C) = 0.908$.

(b) From part (a) we know that out of 1000 components 617.5 will be made by machine M and be of an acceptable standard. Hence $P(A \cap C) = \dfrac{617.5}{1000} = 0.6175$.

(c) We require $P(C|A)$. The probability a component is acceptable given it is manufactured by machine M is

$$P(C|A) = 0.95$$

(d) Machine M makes 65% of components, that is $P(A) = 0.65$.

(e) We require $P(A|C)$. Consider again the 1000 components. On average 908 are acceptable. Of these 908 acceptable components, 617.5 are manufactured by machine M and 290.5 by machine N. We are told the component is acceptable and so we must restrict attention to the 908 acceptable components. So, out of 908 acceptable components, 617.5 are made by machine M, that is $P(A|C) = \dfrac{617.5}{908} = 0.68$.

(f) We require $P(B|\overline{C})$. Consider 1000 components. Machine M manufactures 650 components of which 617.5 are acceptable and hence 32.5 are unacceptable. Machine N manufactures 350 components of which 290.5 are acceptable and 59.5 are unacceptable. There are 92 unacceptable components of which 59.5 were made by machine N. The probability of the component being made by machine N given it is unacceptable is

$$P(B|\overline{C}) = \frac{59.5}{92} = 0.647$$

that is, almost 65% of unacceptable components are manufactured by machine N.

Figure 28.6
Tree diagram for
Example 28.13.

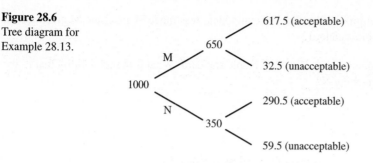

As an alternative method of solution, we can represent the information via a tree diagram. This is shown in Figure 28.6.

(a) There are $617.5 + 290.5 = 908$ acceptable components, so

$$P(\text{component is acceptable}) = 0.908$$

(b) There are 617.5 components which are acceptable and made by machine M. So

$$P(\text{component is acceptable and made by machine M}) = P(C \cap A) = 0.6175$$

(c) Of the 650 components made by machine M, 617.5 are acceptable, and so

$$P(\text{component is acceptable given it is made by machine M}) = P(C|A)$$
$$= \frac{617.5}{650} = 0.95$$

(d) Of the 1000 components, 650 are made by machine M, so

$$P(\text{component is made by machine M}) = P(A) = 0.65$$

(e) There are 908 acceptable components. Of these, 617.5 are made by machine M. Hence

$$P(\text{component is made by machine M given it is acceptable}) = P(A|C)$$
$$= \frac{617.5}{908} = 0.68$$

(f) There are $32.5 + 59.5 = 92$ unacceptable components. Of these 92, 59.5 are made by machine N. Thus

$$P(\text{component is made by machine N given it is not acceptable}) = P(B|\overline{C})$$
$$= \frac{59.5}{92} = 0.647$$

28.6.1 The multiplication law

Consider events A and B for which $A \cap B \neq \varnothing$ as shown in Figure 28.7. Suppose we know that event A has occurred and we seek the probability that B occurs, that is $P(B|A)$. Knowing event A has occurred we can restrict our attention to the set A. Event B will occur if any outcome is in $A \cap B$. Hence,

$$P(B|A) = \frac{P(A \cap B)}{P(A)}$$

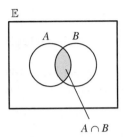

$A \cap B$

Figure 28.7 A and B are not mutually exclusive.

The multiplication law of probability states:

$$P(A \cap B) = P(A)P(B|A)$$

Since the compound event 'A and B' is identical to 'B and A' we may also say

$$P(A \cap B) = P(B \cap A) = P(B)P(A|B)$$

Consider Example 28.13(e). We require the probability that the component was manufactured by machine M, given it is acceptable. This is $P(A|C)$. Now

$$P(A \cap C) = P(C \cap A) = P(C)P(A|C)$$

$$P(A|C) = \frac{P(A \cap C)}{P(C)}$$

Now $P(A \cap C)$ is the probability that the component is manufactured by machine M and is acceptable. This is known to be 0.6175, using Example 28.13(b). Also from Example 28.13(a) we see $P(C) = 0.908$. Hence,

$$P(A|C) = \frac{0.6175}{0.908} = 0.68$$

Example 28.14

A manufacturer studies the reliability of a certain component so that suitable guarantees can be given: 83% of components remain reliable for at least 5 years; 92% remain reliable for at least 3 years. What is the probability that a component which has remained reliable for 3 years will remain reliable for 5 years?

Solution

We define the events:

A: a component remains reliable for at least 3 years

B: a component remains reliable for at least 5 years

Then $P(A) = 0.92$, $P(B) = 0.83$. Note that these are unconditional probabilities. We require $P(B|A)$, a conditional probability.

$$P(A \cap B) = P(A)P(B|A)$$

$A \cap B$ is the compound event a component remains reliable for at least 3 years and it remains reliable for at least 5 years. Clearly this is the same as the event B. So

$$P(A \cap B) = P(B)$$

Hence

$$P(B) = P(A)P(B|A)$$

$$P(B|A) = \frac{P(B)}{P(A)} = \frac{0.83}{0.92} = 0.90$$

that is, 90% of the components which remain reliable for 3 years will remain reliable for at least 5 years.

Alternatively, a tree diagram is shown in Figure 28.8. Starting with 100 components, 92 remain reliable 3 years later. Of these 92, 2 years later, 83 are still reliable. So

$$P(\text{component is reliable after 5 years, given it is reliable after 3 years}) = \frac{83}{92}$$

$$= 0.90$$

Figure 28.8
Tree diagram for
Example 28.14.

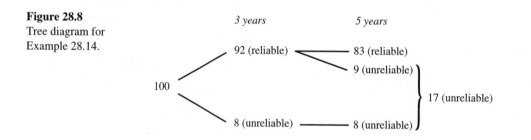

Exercises 28.6

1 A component is manufactured by machines 1 and 2. Machine 1 manufactures 72% of total production of the component. The percentage of components which are acceptable varies, depending upon which machine is used. For machine 1, 97% of components are acceptable and for machine 2, 92% are acceptable. A component is picked at random.

(a) What is the probability it was manufactured by machine 1?

(b) What is the probability it is not acceptable?

(c) What is the probability that it is acceptable and made by machine 2?

(d) If the component is acceptable what is the probability it was manufactured by machine 2?

(e) If the component is not acceptable what is the probability it was manufactured by machine 1?

2 The measured lifespans (L) of 1500 components are recorded in Table 28.4.

Table 28.4 Lifespans of 1500 components.

Lifespan (hours)	Number of components
$L \geqslant 1000$	210
$900 \leqslant L < 1000$	820
$800 \leqslant L < 900$	240
$700 \leqslant L < 800$	200
$L < 700$	30

(a) What is the probability that a component which is still working after 800 hours will last for at least 900 hours?

(b) What is the probability that a component which is still working after 900 hours will continue to last for at least 1000 hours?

3 The lifespan, L, of 1000 components is measured and detailed in Table 28.5.

(a) Calculate the probability that the lifespan of a component is more than 1000 hours.

(b) Calculate the probability that the lifespan of a component is less than 750 hours.

Table 28.5 Lifespans of 1000 components.

Lifespan (hours)	Number of components
$L \geqslant 1750$	70
$1500 \leqslant L < 1750$	110
$1250 \leqslant L < 1500$	150
$1000 \leqslant L < 1250$	200
$750 \leqslant L < 1000$	317
$500 \leqslant L < 750$	96
$250 \leqslant L < 500$	42
$L < 250$	15

(c) Calculate the probability that a component which is still working after 500 hours will continue to last for at least 1500 hours.

4 Machines A, B and C manufacture components. Machine A makes 50% of the components, machine B makes 30% of the components and machine C makes the rest. The probability that a component is reliable is 0.93 when made by machine A, 0.90 when made by machine B and 0.95 when made by machine C. A component is picked at random.

(a) Calculate the probability that it is reliable.

(b) Calculate the probability that it is made by machine B given it is unreliable.

5 Components are made by machines A, B, C and D. Machine A makes 17% of the components, machine B makes 21% of the components, machine C makes 20% of the components and machine D makes the remainder. For machine A 96% of the components are reliable, for machine B, 89% are reliable, for machine C, 92% are reliable and for machine D, 97% are reliable. A component is picked at random. Calculate the probability that it is

(a) reliable

(b) not reliable

(c) reliable, given it is made by machine B

(d) not reliable, given it is made by machine D

(e) made by machine A given it is reliable

(f) made by machine C given it is unreliable

Solutions

1 (a) 0.72   (b) 0.044   (c) 0.2576
   (d) 0.2695   (e) 0.4909

2 (a) 0.8110   (b) 0.2039

3 (a) 0.53   (b) 0.153   (c) 0.1909

4 (a) 0.925   (b) 0.4

5 (a) 0.9415   (b) 0.0585   (c) 0.89
   (d) 0.03   (e) 0.1733   (f) 0.2735

28.7 Independent events

Two events are independent if the occurrence of either event does not influence the probability of the other event occurring.

Example 28.15

Machine 1 manufactures an electronic chip, A, of which 90% are acceptable. Machine 2 manufactures an electronic chip, B, of which 83% are acceptable. Two chips are picked at random, one of each kind. Find the probability that they are both acceptable.

Solution

The events E_1 and E_2 are defined.

E_1: chip A is acceptable

E_2: chip B is acceptable

$$P(E_1) = 0.9 \qquad P(E_2) = 0.83$$

A single trial consists of choosing two chips at random. We require the probability that the compound event, $E_1 \cap E_2$, is true. Using the multiplication law we have

$$P(E_1 \cap E_2) = P(E_1)P(E_2|E_1) = 0.9P(E_2|E_1)$$

$P(E_2|E_1)$ is the probability of E_2 happening given E_1 has happened. However, machine 1 and machine 2 are independent, so the probability of chip B being acceptable is in no way influenced by the acceptability of chip A. The events E_1 and E_2 are independent.

$$P(E_2|E_1) = P(E_2) = 0.83$$

Therefore

$$P(E_1 \cap E_2) = P(E_1)P(E_2) = (0.9)(0.83) = 0.75$$

For independent events E_1 and E_2:

    (1) $P(E_1|E_2) = P(E_1), \qquad P(E_2|E_1) = P(E_2)$

    (2) $P(E_1 \cap E_2) = P(E_1)P(E_2)$

The concept of independence may be applied to more than two events. Three or more events are independent if every pair of events is independent. If $E_1, E_2, \ldots, E_n$ are n independent events then

$$P(E_i|E_j) = P(E_i) \qquad \text{for any } i \text{ and } j, i \neq j$$

and

$$P(E_i \cap E_j) = P(E_i)P(E_j) \qquad i \neq j$$

A compound event may comprise several independent events. The multiplication law is extended in an obvious way:

$$P(E_1 \cap E_2 \cap E_3) = P(E_1)P(E_2)P(E_3)$$
$$P(E_1 \cap E_2 \cap E_3 \cap E_4) = P(E_1)P(E_2)P(E_3)P(E_4)$$

and so on.

Example 28.16   The probability that a component is faulty is 0.04. Two components are picked at random. Calculate the probability that

(a) both components are faulty

(b) both components are not faulty

(c) one of the components is faulty

(d) one of the components is not faulty

(e) at least one of the components is faulty

(f) at least one of the components is not faulty

Solution   We define events F_1 and F_2 to be

> F_1: the first component is faulty
> F_2: the second component is faulty

Then events $\overline{F}_1$ and $\overline{F}_2$ are

> $\overline{F}_1$: the first component is not faulty
> $\overline{F}_2$: the second component is not faulty

Then

$$P(F_1) = P(F_2) = 0.04 \qquad P(\overline{F}_1) = P(\overline{F}_2) = 1 - 0.04 = 0.96$$

(a) We require both components to be faulty.

$$\begin{aligned} P(F_1 \cap F_2) &= P(F_1)P(F_2) \qquad \text{since events are independent} \\ &= (0.04)^2 \\ &= 0.0016 \end{aligned}$$

(b) We require both components to be not faulty.

$$\begin{aligned} P(\overline{F}_1 \cap \overline{F}_2) &= P(\overline{F}_1)P(\overline{F}_2) \\ &= (0.96)^2 \\ &= 0.9216 \end{aligned}$$

(c) Consider the two components. Then either both components are faulty or one component is faulty or neither of the components is faulty. So,

$$\begin{aligned} P(\text{one component is faulty}) &= 1 - P(\text{both components are faulty}) \\ &\quad - P(\text{neither of the components is faulty}) \\ &= 1 - 0.0016 - 0.9216 \\ &= 0.0768 \end{aligned}$$

An alternative approach is as follows. Either the first component is faulty and the second one is not faulty, or the first component is not faulty and the second one is faulty. These two cases are represented by $F_1 \cap \overline{F}_2$ and $\overline{F}_1 \cap F_2$. So,

$$
\begin{aligned}
P(\text{one component is faulty}) &= P(F_1 \cap \overline{F}_2) + P(\overline{F}_1 \cap F_2) \\
&= P(F_1)P(\overline{F}_2) + P(\overline{F}_1)P(F_2) \\
&= (0.04)(0.96) + (0.96)(0.04) \\
&= 0.0768
\end{aligned}
$$

(d) We require one component to be not faulty. Since there are two components then requiring one to be not faulty is equivalent to requiring one to be faulty. Hence the calculation is the same as that in (c).

$$
P(\text{one component is not faulty}) = 0.0768
$$

(e) At least one of the components is faulty means that one or both of the components is faulty.

$$
\begin{aligned}
P(\text{at least one component is faulty}) &= P(\text{exactly one component is faulty}) \\
&\quad + P(\text{both components are faulty}) \\
&= 0.0768 + 0.0016 \\
&= 0.0784
\end{aligned}
$$

As an alternative we can note that the complement of 'at least one of the components is faulty' is 'none of the components is faulty'. The probability that neither of the components is faulty is given in (b). Hence

$$
\begin{aligned}
P(\text{at least one component is faulty}) \\
= 1 - P(\text{none of the components is faulty}) \\
= 1 - 0.9216 \\
= 0.0784
\end{aligned}
$$

(f) At least one of the components is not faulty means that one or both of the components is not faulty. So

$$
\begin{aligned}
P(\text{at least one component is not faulty}) \\
= P(\text{exactly one component is not faulty}) \\
+ P(\text{both components are not faulty}) \\
= 0.0768 + 0.9216 \\
= 0.9984
\end{aligned}
$$

As an alternative we note that the complement of 'at least one of the components is not faulty' is 'none of the components are not faulty'. The last statement is equivalent to 'both the components are faulty'. Hence

$$
\begin{aligned}
P(\text{at least one component is not faulty}) &= 1 - P(\text{both components are faulty}) \\
&= 1 - 0.0016 \\
&= 0.9984
\end{aligned}
$$

Example 28.17 Machines 1, 2 and 3 manufacture resistors A, B and C, respectively. The probabilities of their respective acceptabilities are 0.9, 0.93 and 0.81. One of each resistor is selected at random.

(a) Find the probability that they are all acceptable.

(b) Find the probability that at least one resistor is acceptable.

Solution Define events E_1, E_2 and E_3 by

$$E_1: \text{resistor A is acceptable} \qquad P(E_1) = 0.9$$
$$E_2: \text{resistor B is acceptable} \qquad P(E_2) = 0.93$$
$$E_3: \text{resistor C is acceptable} \qquad P(E_3) = 0.81$$

E_1, E_2 and E_3 are independent events.

(a) $P(E_1 \cap E_2 \cap E_3) = P(E_1)P(E_2)P(E_3) = (0.9)(0.93)(0.81) = 0.68$

(b) Let E_4 and E_5 be the events:

$E_4:$ at least one resistor is acceptable

$E_5:$ no resistor is acceptable

E_4 and E_5 are complementary events and so

$$P(E_4) + P(E_5) = 1$$

E_5 may be expressed as:

$E_5:$ resistor A is not acceptable and resistor B is not acceptable and resistor C is not acceptable

that is, $\overline{E_1} \cap \overline{E_2} \cap \overline{E_3}$

$$
\begin{aligned}
P(E_5) &= P(\overline{E_1} \cap \overline{E_2} \cap \overline{E_3}) = P(\overline{E_1})P(\overline{E_2})P(\overline{E_3}) \\
&= (1 - 0.9)(1 - 0.93)(1 - 0.81) \\
&= (0.1)(0.07)(0.19) \\
&= 0.001\,33 \\
P(E_4) &= 1 - P(E_5) = 1 - 0.001\,33 = 0.998\,67
\end{aligned}
$$

Exercises 28.7

1 A and B are two independent events with $P(A) = 0.7$ and $P(B) = 0.4$. The compound event A occurs, then A occurs, then B occurs, is denoted AAB, and other compound events are denoted in a similar way. Calculate the probability of the following compound events.

(a) *AAB*

(b) *BAB*

(c) *AAAA*

2 The probability a component is faulty is 0.07. Two components are picked at random. Calculate the probability that

(a) both are faulty

(b) both are not faulty

(c) the first one picked is faulty and the second one picked is not faulty

(d) at least one is not faulty

3 The probability a component is acceptable is 0.92. Three components are picked at random. Calculate the probability that

(a) all three are acceptable

(b) none are acceptable

(c) exactly two are acceptable

(d) at least two are acceptable

4 Components are made by machines A, B and C. Machine A makes 30% of the components, machine B makes 25% of the components and machine C makes the rest. Two components are picked at random. Calculate the probability that

(a) they are both made by machine C

(b) one is made by machine A and one is made by machine B

(c) exactly one of the components is made by machine B

(d) at least one of the components is made by machine B

(e) both components are made by the same machine

5 Capacitors are manufactured by four machines, 1, 2, 3 and 4. The probability a capacitor is manufactured acceptably varies according to the machine. The probabilities are 0.94, 0.91, 0.97 and 0.94, respectively, for machines 1, 2, 3 and 4.

(a) A capacitor is taken from each machine. What is the probability all four capacitors are acceptable?

(b) Two capacitors are taken from machine 1 and two from machine 2. What is the probability all four capacitors are acceptable?

(c) A capacitor is taken from each machine. Calculate the probability that at least three capacitors are acceptable.

(d) A capacitor is taken from each machine. From this sample of four capacitors, one is taken at random.

   (i) What is the probability it is acceptable and made by machine 1?

   (ii) What is the probability it is acceptable and made by machine 2?

(e) A capacitor is taken from each machine. From this sample of four capacitors, one is taken at random. What is the probability it is acceptable? [*Hint:* use the results in (d).]

Solutions

1 (a) 0.196   (b) 0.112   (c) 0.2401

2 (a) 0.0049   (b) 0.8649   (c) 0.0651
   (d) 0.9951

3 (a) 0.7787   (b) 5.12×10^{-4}
   (c) 0.2031   (d) 0.9818

4 (a) 0.2025   (b) 0.15   (c) 0.375
   (d) 0.4375   (e) 0.355

5 (a) 0.7800   (b) 0.7317   (c) 0.9808
   (d) (i) 0.235 (ii) 0.2275 (e) 0.94

Review exercises 28

1 Components are made by machines A, B and C. Machine A makes 30% of the components, Machine B makes 50% of the components and machine C makes the rest. The probability that a component is acceptable when made by machine A is 0.96, when made by machine B

the probability is 0.91 and when made by machine C the probability is 0.93.

(a) A component is picked at random. Calculate the probability that it is made by machine C.

(b) A component is picked at random. Calculate the probability that it is made by either machine A or machine C.

(c) A component is picked at random. Calculate the probability that it is made by machine B and is acceptable.

(d) A component is picked at random. Calculate the probability that it is not acceptable.

(e) A component picked at random is not acceptable. Calculate the probability that it is made by machine A.

(f) A component picked at random is acceptable. Calculate the probability that it is made by either machine A or machine B.

(g) Two components are picked at random. Calculate the probability that they are both acceptable.

(h) Two components are picked at random. Calculate the probability that one is acceptable and one is unacceptable.

2 Three machines, A, B and C, manufacture a component. Machine A manufactures 35% of the components, machine B manufactures 40% of the components and machine C makes the rest. A component is either acceptable or not acceptable: 7% of components made by machine A are not acceptable, 12% of components made by machine B are not acceptable and 2% of those made by machine C are also not acceptable.

(a) Find the probability that a component is made by either machine A or machine B.

(b) Two components are picked at random. What is the probability that they are both made by machine B?

(c) Three components are picked at random. What is the probability they are each made by a different machine?

(d) A component is picked at random. What is the probability it is not acceptable?

(e) A component is picked at random. It is not acceptable. What is the probability it was made by machine B?

(f) A component is picked at random and is acceptable. What is the probability it was made by either machine A or machine B?

3 Machines M and N manufacture components. The probability that a component is of an acceptable standard is 0.93 when manufactured by machine M and 0.86 when manufactured by machine N. Machine M supplies 70% of the components and machine N supplies the rest.

(a) Calculate the probability that a component picked at random is of an acceptable standard.

(b) A component is not of an acceptable standard. Calculate the probability that it is made by machine N.

(c) Two components are picked at random. Calculate the probability that they are made by different machines.

4 E_1 is the event the component is reliable. E_2 is the event the component is made by machine A. State

(a) $\overline{E}_1$

(b) $\overline{E}_2$

(c) $E_1 \cap E_2$

(d) $E_1 \cup E_2$

(e) $E_2 \cap \overline{E}_1$

5 The lifespans, L, of 2500 components were measured and the results were recorded in Table 28.6.

Table 28.6

Lifespan (hours)	Number of components
$0 \leqslant L < 200$	76
$200 \leqslant L < 300$	293
$300 \leqslant L < 400$	574
$400 \leqslant L < 500$	1211
$500 \leqslant L < 600$	346

(a) Calculate the probability that a component has a lifespan of over 400 hours.

(b) Calculate the probability that a component has a lifespan of less than 300 hours.

(c) Calculate the probability that a component that lasts for 300 hours will continue to last for at least 500 hours.

6 Given the events E_1, E_2 and E_3 are
E_1: the circuit is functioning
E_2: the circuit is made by machine A
E_3: the circuit will last for at least 600 hours
state

(a) $\overline{E}_2$

(b) $\overline{E}_3$

(c) $E_1 \cup E_2$

(d) $E_1 \cap E_3$

(e) $E_2 \cap E_3$

7 A data stream consists of the characters A, B, C, D and E, with respective probabilities of 0.16, 0.23, 0.31, 0.12 and 0.18.

(a) Calculate the information associated with the character B.

(b) Calculate the entropy.

(c) Calculate the redundancy.

8 The probability a component is reliable is 0.93. Three components are picked at random. Calculate the probability that

(a) all components are unreliable

(b) exactly one component is reliable

(c) at least one component is reliable

(d) exactly two components are reliable

9 A circuit is as shown in Figure 28.9. The circuit is operational if current can flow from P to Q along any route. The probability that resistor type A is faulty is 0.09, and for resistor type B the probability of a fault is 0.14. Calculate the probability that the circuit is operational.

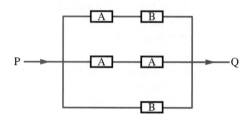

Figure 28.9

10 The probability a component is reliable is 0.96. Five components are picked at random. Calculate the probability that

(a) all five components are reliable

(b) none are reliable

(c) at least one is reliable

Solutions

1 (a) 0.2 (b) 0.5 (c) 0.455
   (d) 0.071 (e) 0.1690 (f) 0.7998
   (g) 0.8630 (h) 0.1319

2 (a) 0.75 (b) 0.16 (c) 0.21
   (d) 0.0775 (e) 0.619 (f) 0.734

3 (a) 0.909 (b) 0.4615 (c) 0.42

4 (a) The component is not reliable.
   (b) The component is not made by machine A.
   (c) The component is reliable and made by machine A.
   (d) The component is reliable or it is made by machine A.
   (e) The component is made by machine A and it is not reliable.

5 (a) 0.6228 (b) 0.1476 (c) 0.1624

6 (a) The circuit is not made by machine A.
   (b) The circuit will last for less than 600 hours.
   (c) The circuit is functioning or it is made by machine A.
   (d) The circuit is functioning and will last for at least 600 hours.
   (e) The circuit is made by machine A and will last for at least 600 hours.

7 (a) 2.1203 (b) 2.2469 (c) 0.0323

8 (a) 3.43×10^{-4} (b) 0.0137
   (c) 0.9997 (d) 0.1816

9 0.9948

10 (a) 0.8154 (b) 1.024×10^{-7}
    (c) 0.999 999 8

29 Statistics and probability distributions

	Chapter 29	Contents	

	29.1	Introduction	906
	29.2	Random variables	906
	29.3	Probability distributions – discrete variable	907
	29.4	Probability density functions – continuous variable	908
	29.5	Mean value	911
	29.6	Standard deviation	913
	29.7	Expected value of a random variable	916
	29.8	Standard deviation of a random variable	919
	29.9	Permutations and combinations	921
	29.10	The binomial distribution	927
	29.11	The Poisson distribution	931
	29.12	The uniform distribution	934
	29.13	The exponential distribution	935
	29.14	The normal distribution	937
	29.15	Reliability engineering	944
		Review exercises	951

29.1 Introduction

Engineers often need to measure many different variables, for example the output voltage of a system, the strength of a beam or the cost of a project. Variables are classified into one of two types, discrete or continuous. These are discussed in Section 29.2.

It is of interest to know the probability that a variable has of falling within a given range. There is a high probability that a given variable will fall within some ranges, and a small probability for other ranges of values. The way in which the probability is distributed across various ranges of values gives rise to the idea of a probability distribution. The study of probability distributions forms the major part of this chapter. The most important distributions, the binomial, the Poisson, the uniform, the exponential and the normal, are all included. The chapter concludes with a study of reliability engineering.

29.2 Random variables

Engineering quantities whose variation contains an element of chance are called **random variables**. Some examples are listed below:

(1) the diameter of a motor shaft of nominal size 0.2 m;

(2) the weight of a steel box used to contain an electronic circuit board;

(3) the number of components passing a point on a factory production line in 1 minute;

(4) the nominal resistance value of resistors;

(5) the length of time a machine works without failing.

All of these quantities vary. In (1), (2) and (5) the quantities vary continuously; that is, they can assume any value in some range. For example, a motor shaft may have any diameter between 0.197 m and 0.203 m; a steel box could have any weight between, say, 0.345 kg and 0.352 kg. These are examples of **continuous variables**. The value itself will only be recorded to a certain accuracy, which depends on the measuring device and the use to which the data will be put. For example, the shaft diameter may only be measured to the nearest tenth of a millimetre. Although such a measurement is only integer in multiples of a tenth of a millimetre, the variable being measured is continuous.

In (3) and (4) the variables can assume only a limited number of values. The number of components passing a point in a minute will be a non-negative integer $0, 1, 2, 3 \ldots$. The nominal resistance value of resistors has a limited number of values which is specified by manufacturers in their catalogues. Variables such as these, which can assume only a limited set of values, are called **discrete variables**.

Exercises 29.2

1 Is the length of time a machine works without failing a continuous or a discrete variable?

2 State whether the following variables are continuous or discrete.

(a) the length of a bridge

(b) the number of electrical sockets in a house

(c) the length of cable used to wire a house

(d) the weight of solder used to build a circuit board

3 State whether the following variables are discrete or continuous.

(a) the force required to stretch a spring by a specified length

(b) the output voltage of a system

(c) the height of a column of liquid

(d) the number of resistors in a circuit

(e) the number of bits of memory of a computer

Solutions

1 continuous

2 (a) continuous   (b) discrete
    (c) continuous   (d) continuous

3 (a) continuous   (b) continuous
    (c) continuous   (d) discrete
    (e) discrete

29.3 Probability distributions – discrete variable

The range of values that a variable can take does not give sufficient information about the variable. We need to know which values are likely to occur often and which values will occur only infrequently. For example, suppose x is a discrete random variable which can take values 0, 1, 2, 3, 4, 5 and 6. We may ask questions such as 'Which value is most likely to occur?', 'Is a 6 more likely to occur than a 5?', and so on. We need information on the probability of each value occurring. Suppose that information is provided and is given in Table 29.1. If x is sampled 100 times then on average 0 will occur 10 times, 1 will occur 10 times, 2 will occur 15 times and so on. Table 29.1 is called a **probability distribution** for the random variable x. Note that the probabilities sum to 1; the table tells us how the total probability is distributed among the various possible values of the random variable. Table 29.1 may be represented in graphical form (see Figure 29.1).

Table 29.1 The probability of a discrete value occurring.

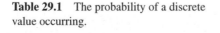

x	0	1	2	3	4	5	6
$P(x)$	0.1	0.1	0.15	0.3	0.2	0.1	0.05

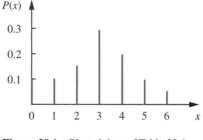

Figure 29.1 Plotted data of Table 29.1.

Exercises 29.3

1 The probability distribution for the random variable, x, is

x	2	2.5	3.0	3.5	4.0	4.5
$P(x)$	0.07	0.36	0.21	0.19	0.10	0.07

(a) State $P(x = 3.5)$
(b) Calculate $P(x \geqslant 3.0)$
(c) Calculate $P(x < 4.0)$
(d) Calculate $P(x > 3.5)$
(e) Calculate $P(x \leqslant 3.9)$
(f) The variable, x, is sampled 50 000 times. How many times would you expect x to have a value of 2.5?

2 The probability distribution of the random variable, y, is given as

y	−3	−2	−1	0	1	2	3
$P(y)$	0.63	0.20	0.09	0.04	0.02	0.01	0.01

Calculate

(a) $P(y \geqslant 0)$
(b) $P(y \leqslant 1)$
(c) $P(|y| \leqslant 1)$
(d) $P(y^2 > 3)$
(e) $P(y^2 < 6)$

Solutions

1 (a) 0.19 (b) 0.57 (c) 0.83
  (d) 0.17 (e) 0.83 (f) 18000

2 (a) 0.08 (b) 0.98 (c) 0.15
  (d) 0.85 (e) 0.36

29.4 Probability density functions – continuous variable

Suppose x is a continuous random variable which can take any value on [0, 1]. It is impossible to list all possible values because of the continuous nature of the variable. There are infinitely many values on [0, 1] so the probability of any one particular value occurring is zero. It is meaningful, however, to ask 'What is the probability of x falling in a sub-interval, $[a, b]$?' Dividing [0, 1] into sub-intervals and attaching probabilities to each sub-interval will result in a probability distribution. Table 29.2 gives an example. The probability that x will lie between 0.4 and 0.6 is 0.35, that is $P(0.4 \leqslant x < 0.6) = 0.35$. Similarly,

$$P(0.2 \leqslant x < 0.4) = 0.25$$

Figure 29.2 shows the table in a graphical form. By making the sub-intervals smaller a more refined distribution is obtained. Table 29.3 and Figure 29.3 illustrate this.

The probability that x lies in a particular interval is given by the sum of the heights of the rectangles on that interval. For example, the probability that x lies in [0.5, 0.8] is $0.2 + 0.1 + 0.1 = 0.4$; that is, there is a probability of 0.4 that x lies somewhere between 0.5 and 0.8. Note that the sum of all the heights is 1, representing total probability.

Consider the sub-interval $[a, b]$. We require the probability that x lies in this interval. The way this is answered is by means of a **probability density function** (p.d.f.), $f(x)$. Such a p.d.f. is shown in Figure 29.4, where it is the area under the graph between a and b that gives $P(a \leqslant x \leqslant b)$.

$$P(a \leqslant x \leqslant b) = \text{area above } [a, b] = \int_a^b f(x)\, dx$$

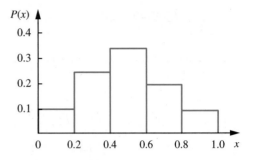

Table 29.2 Probability that x lies in a given sub-interval.

x	[0, 0.2)	[0.2, 0.4)	[0.4, 0.6)	[0.6, 0.8)	[0.8,1.0]
$P(x)$	0.1	0.25	0.35	0.2	0.1

Figure 29.2 Plotted data of Table 29.2.

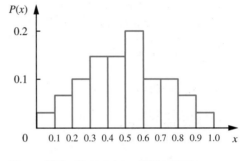

Table 29.3 Refining the sub-intervals in Table 29.2.

x	[0, 0.1)	[0.1, 0.2)	[0.2, 0.3)	[0.3, 0.4)	[0.4, 0.5)
$P(x)$	0.03	0.07	0.1	0.15	0.15

x	[0.5, 0.6)	[0.6, 0.7)	[0.7, 0.8)	[0.8, 0.9)	[0.9, 1.0]
$P(x)$	0.2	0.1	0.1	0.07	0.03

Figure 29.3 Plotted data of Table 29.3.

Figure 29.4
Shaded area represents
$P(a \leqslant x \leqslant b)$.

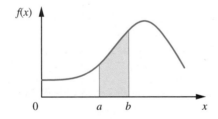

The total area under a p.d.f. is always 1.

Example 29.1 Suppose x is a continuous random variable taking any value on [1, 4]. Its p.d.f., $f(x)$, is given by

$$f(x) = \frac{1}{2\sqrt{x}} \qquad 1 \leqslant x \leqslant 4$$

(a) Check that $f(x)$ is a suitable function for a p.d.f.

(b) What is the probability that (i) x lies on [2, 3.5], (ii) $x \geqslant 2$, (iii) $x < 3$?

Solution (a) x can have any value on $[1, 4]$. For $f(x)$ to be a p.d.f., then the total area under it should equal 1, that is

$$\int_1^4 f(x)\,dx = 1$$

$$\int_1^4 f(x)\,dx = \int_1^4 \frac{1}{2\sqrt{x}}\,dx = [\sqrt{x}]_1^4 = 1$$

Hence $f(x)$ is a suitable function for a p.d.f.

(b) (i) $P(2 \leqslant x \leqslant 3.5) = \int_2^{3.5} f(x)\,dx = [\sqrt{x}]_2^{3.5} = 0.457$

(ii) $P(x \geqslant 2) = \int_2^4 f(x)\,dx = [\sqrt{x}]_2^4 = 0.586$

(iii) $P(x < 3) = \int_1^3 f(x)\,dx = [\sqrt{x}]_1^3 = 0.732$

Example 29.2 A random variable, z, has a p.d.f. $f(z)$ where

$$f(z) = e^{-z} \qquad 0 \leqslant z < \infty$$

Calculate the probability that

(a) $0 \leqslant z \leqslant 2$

(b) z is more than 1

(c) z is less than 0.5

Solution Note that $\int_0^\infty e^{-z}\,dz = 1$ so that $f(z) = e^{-z}$ is suitable as a p.d.f.

(a) $P(0 \leqslant z \leqslant 2) = \int_0^2 e^{-z}\,dz = [-e^{-z}]_0^2 = 0.865$

(b) $P(z > 1) = \int_1^\infty e^{-z}\,dz = [-e^{-z}]_1^\infty = 0.368$

(c) $P(z < 0.5) = [-e^{-z}]_0^{0.5} = 0.393$

Exercises 29.4

1 $f(x) = kx^2$, k constant, $-1 \leqslant x \leqslant 1$. $f(x)$ is a p.d.f.

(a) What is the value of k?

(b) Calculate the probability that $x > 0.5$.

(c) If $P(x > c) = 0.6$ then what is the value of c?

2 $f(x)$ is a p.d.f. for the random variable x, which can vary from 0 to 10. It is illustrated in

Figure 29.5. What is the probability that x lies in [2, 4]?

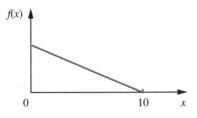

Figure 29.5 Probability density function for Question 2.

3 A p.d.f. is given by

$$f(z) = 2e^{-2z} \qquad 0 \leqslant z < \infty$$

(a) If 200 measurements of z are made, how many, on average, will be greater than 1?

(b) If 50% of measurements are less than k, find k.

4 A p.d.f., $h(x)$, is defined by

$$h(x) = \frac{3}{4}(1 - x^2) \qquad -1 \leqslant x \leqslant 1$$

Calculate

(a) $P(0 \leqslant x \leqslant 0.5)$

(b) $P(-0.3 \leqslant x \leqslant 0.7)$

(c) $P(|x| < 0.5)$

(d) $P(x > 0.5)$

(e) $P(x \leqslant 0.7)$

5 (a) Verify that

$$f(t) = \lambda e^{-\lambda t} \qquad t \geqslant 0$$

is suitable as a p.d.f.

(b) Calculate $P(t \geqslant 2)$ if $\lambda = 3$.

Solutions

1 (a) 1.5   (b) 0.4375   (c) -0.5848

2 0.28

3 (a) 27   (b) 0.3466

4 (a) 0.3438   (b) 0.6575   (c) 0.6875
    (d) 0.1563   (e) 0.9393

5 (b) 2.479×10^{-3}

29.5 Mean value

If $\{x_1, x_2, x_3, \ldots, x_n\}$ is a set of n numbers, then the **mean value** of these numbers, denoted by $\overline{x}$, is

$$\overline{x} = \frac{\text{sum of the numbers}}{n} = \frac{\sum x_i}{n}$$

$\overline{x}$ is sometimes called the **arithmetic mean**.

Example 29.3 Find the mean of $-2.3, 0, 1, 0.7$.

Solution $\overline{x} = \dfrac{-2.3 + 0 + 1 + 0.7}{4} = \dfrac{-0.6}{4} = -0.15$

The mean value is a single number which characterizes the set of numbers. It is useful in helping to make comparisons.

Example 29.4

A component is made by two machines, A and B. The lifespans of six components made by each machine are recorded in Table 29.4. Which is the preferred machine?

Table 29.4
The lifespans of six components made by machines A and B.

Lifespan (hours)					
Machine A	92	86	61	70	58	65
Machine B	64	75	84	80	63	70

Solution

For components manufactured by machine A

$$\text{average lifespan} = \frac{432}{6} = 72$$

For components manufactured by machine B

$$\text{average lifespan} = \frac{436}{6} = 72.7$$

Machine B produces components with a higher average lifespan and so is the preferred machine.

Example 29.5

A variable, x, can have values 2, 3, 4, 5 and 6. Many observations of x are made and denoted by x_i. They have corresponding frequencies, f_i. The results are as follows:

value (x_i)	2	3	4	5	6
frequency (f_i)	6	9	3	7	4

Calculate the mean of x.

Solution

The sum of all the measurements must be found. The value 2 occurs six times, contributing 12 to the total. Similarly, 3 occurs nine times contributing 27 to the total. Thus

$$\text{total} = 2(6) + 3(9) + 4(3) + 5(7) + 6(4) = 110$$

The number of measurements made is $6 + 9 + 3 + 7 + 4 = 29$. So,

$$\text{mean} = \bar{x} = \frac{110}{29} = 3.79$$

Example 29.5 illustrates a general principle.

If values $x_1, x_2, \ldots, x_n$ occur with frequencies $f_1, f_2, \ldots, f_n$ then

$$\bar{x} = \frac{\sum x_i f_i}{\sum f_i}$$

Exercises 29.5

1   Engineers in a design department are assessed by their leader. A '0' is 'Terrible' and a '5' is 'Outstanding'. The 29 members of the department are evaluated and their scores recorded as follows:

score	0	1	2	3	4	5
number of staff	2	5	6	9	4	3

What is the mean score for the whole department?

2   Two samples of nails are taken. The first sample has 12 nails with a mean length of 2.7 cm, the second sample has 20 nails with a mean length of 2.61 cm. What is the mean length of all 32 nails?

3   The output, in volts, from a system is measured 40 times. The results are recorded as follows:

voltage (volts)	9.5	10.0	10.5	11.0	11.5
number of measurements	6	14	8	7	5

Calculate the mean output voltage.

4   The current, in amps, through a resistor is measured 140 times. The results are:

current (amps)	2.25	2.50	2.75	3.00	3.25
number of measurements	32	27	39	22	20

Calculate the mean current through the resistor.

5   In a communication network, packets of information travel along lines. The number of lines used by each packet varies according to the following table:

number of lines used	1	2	3	4	5
number of packets		17	54	32	6	1

Calculate the mean number of lines used per packet.

Solutions

1   2.586

2   2.64

3   10.39

4   2.70

5   2.27

29.6   Standard deviation

Although the mean indicates where the centre of a set of numbers lies, it gives no measure of the spread of the numbers. For example, $-1, 0, 1$ and $-10, 0, 10$ both have a mean of 0 but clearly the numbers in the second set are much more widely dispersed than those in the first. A commonly used measure of dispersion is the **standard deviation**.

Let $x_1, x_2, \ldots, x_n$ be n measurements with a mean $\bar{x}$. Then $x_i - \bar{x}$ is the amount by which x_i differs from the mean. The quantity $x_i - \bar{x}$ is called the **deviation** of x_i from the mean. Some of these deviations will be positive, some negative. The mean of these deviations is always zero (see Question 3 in Exercises 29.6) and so this is not helpful in measuring the dispersion of the numbers. To avoid positive and negative deviations summing to zero the squared deviation is taken, $(x_i - \bar{x})^2$. The **variance** is the mean of the squared deviations.

$$\text{variance} = \frac{\sum(x_i - \bar{x})^2}{n}$$

and

$$\text{standard deviation} = \sqrt{\text{variance}}$$

Standard deviation has the same units as the x_i.

Example 29.6

Calculate the standard deviation of

(a) $-1, 0, 1$

(b) $-10, 0, 10$

Solution

(a) $x_1 = -1, x_2 = 0, x_3 = 1$. Clearly $\bar{x} = 0$.

$$x_1 - \bar{x} = -1 \qquad x_2 - \bar{x} = 0 \qquad x_3 - \bar{x} = 1$$

$$\text{variance} = \frac{(-1)^2 + 0^2 + 1^2}{3} = \frac{2}{3}$$

$$\text{standard deviation} = \sqrt{\frac{2}{3}} = 0.816$$

(b) $x_1 = -10, x_2 = 0, x_3 = 10$. Again $\bar{x} = 0$ and so $x_i - \bar{x} = x_i$, for $i = 1, 2, 3$.

$$\text{variance} = \frac{(-10)^2 + 0^2 + 10^2}{3} = \frac{200}{3}$$

$$\text{standard deviation} = \sqrt{\frac{200}{3}} = 8.165$$

As expected, the second set has a much higher standard deviation than the first.

Example 29.7

Find the standard deviation of $-2, 7.2, 6.9, -10.4, 5.3$.

Solution
$x_1 = -2, x_2 = 7.2, x_3 = 6.9, x_4 = -10.4, x_5 = 5.3, \bar{x} = 1.4$

$x_1 - \bar{x} = -3.4$

$x_2 - \bar{x} = 5.8$

$x_3 - \bar{x} = 5.5$

$x_4 - \bar{x} = -11.8$

$x_5 - \bar{x} = 3.9$

$$\text{variance} = \frac{(-3.4)^2 + (5.8)^2 + (5.5)^2 + (-11.8)^2 + (3.9)^2}{5} = \frac{229.9}{5}$$

$$\text{standard deviation} = \sqrt{\frac{229.9}{5}} = 6.78$$

Calculating $x_i - \bar{x}$, $i = 1, 2, \ldots, n$, is tedious for large n and so a more tractable form of the standard deviation is sought. Firstly observe that $\sum x_i = n\bar{x}$ and $\sum \bar{x}^2 = n\bar{x}^2$, since $\bar{x}^2$ is a constant. Now

$$\sum (x_i - \bar{x})^2 = \sum x_i^2 - \sum 2x_i\bar{x} + \sum \bar{x}^2$$

$$= \sum x_i^2 - 2\bar{x} \sum x_i + n\bar{x}^2$$

$$= \sum x_i^2 - 2\bar{x}(n\bar{x}) + n\bar{x}^2$$

$$= \sum x_i^2 - n\bar{x}^2$$

Hence,

$$\text{variance} = \frac{\sum x_i^2 - n\bar{x}^2}{n}$$

and

$$\text{standard deviation} = \sqrt{\frac{\sum x_i^2 - n\bar{x}^2}{n}}$$

Using these formulae it is not necessary to calculate $x_i - \bar{x}$.

Example 29.8
Repeat Example 29.7 using the newly derived formulae.

Solution
$\sum x_i^2 = (-2)^2 + (7.2)^2 + (6.9)^2 + (-10.4)^2 + (5.3)^2 = 239.7$

$$\text{standard deviation} = \sqrt{\frac{239.7 - 5(1.4)^2}{5}} = 6.78$$

Exercises 29.6

1 Calculate the means and standard deviations of:

(a) 1, 2, 3, 4, 5

(b) 2.1, 2.3, 2.7, 2.6

(c) 37, 26, 19, 21, 19, 25, 17

(d) 6, 6, 6, 6, 6, 6

(e) −1, 2, −3, 4, −5, 6

2 A set of measurements $\{x_1, x_2, x_3, \ldots, x_n\}$ has a mean of $\bar{x}$ and a standard deviation of s. What are the mean and standard deviation of the set $\{kx_1, kx_2, kx_3, \ldots, kx_n\}$ where k is a constant?

3 The mean of the numbers $\{x_1, x_2, x_3, \ldots, x_n\}$ is $\bar{x}$. Show that the sum of the deviations about the mean is 0; that is, show $\sum_{i=1}^{n}(x_i - \bar{x}) = 0$.

Solutions

1 (a) mean = 3; st. dev. = 1.414

(b) 2.425, 0.238

(c) 23.4, 6.321

(d) 6, 0

(e) 0.5, 3.862

2 mean = $k\bar{x}$, st. dev. = ks

29.7 Expected value of a random variable

In Sections 29.5 and 29.6 we showed how to calculate the mean and standard deviation of a given set of numbers. No reference was made to probability distributions or p.d.f.s. Suppose now that we have knowledge of the probability distribution of a discrete random variable or the p.d.f. of a continuous random variable. The mean value of the random variable can still be found. Under these circumstances the mean value is known as the **expected value** or **expectation**.

29.7.1 Expected value of a discrete random variable

Suppose for definiteness that x is a discrete random variable with probability distribution as given in Table 29.5.

Table 29.5
Probability distribution for a discrete random variable x.

x	0	1	2	3	4
$P(x)$	0.1	0.2	0.4	0.15	0.15

In 100 trials x will have a value of zero 10 times on average, a value of one 20 times on average and so on. The mean value, that is the expected value, is therefore

$$\text{expected value} = \frac{0(10) + 1(20) + 2(40) + 3(15) + 4(15)}{100} = 2.05$$

We could have arranged the calculation as follows:

$$\text{expected value} = 0\left(\frac{10}{100}\right) + 1\left(\frac{20}{100}\right) + 2\left(\frac{40}{100}\right) + 3\left(\frac{15}{100}\right) + 4\left(\frac{15}{100}\right)$$

$$= 0(0.1) + 1(0.2) + 2(0.4) + 3(0.15) + 4(0.15)$$

Each term is of the form (value) × (probability). Thus,

$$\text{expected value} = \sum_{i=1}^{i=5} x_i P(x_i)$$

The symbol, μ, is used to denote the expected value of a random variable.

If a discrete random variable can take values

$$x_1, x_2, \ldots, x_n$$

with probabilities $P(x_1), P(x_2), \ldots, P(x_n)$, then

$$\text{expected value of } x = \mu = \sum_{i=1}^{i=n} x_i P(x_i)$$

Example 29.9 A random variable, y, has a known probability distribution given by

y	2	4	6	8	10
$P(y)$	0.17	0.23	0.2	0.3	0.1

Find the expected value of y.

Solution We have
$$\mu = \text{expected value} = 2(0.17) + 4(0.23) + 6(0.2) + 8(0.3) + 10(0.1) = 5.86$$

29.7.2 Expected value of a continuous random variable

Suppose a continuous random variable, x, has p.d.f. $f(x)$, $a \leqslant x \leqslant b$. The probability that x lies in a very small interval, $[x, x + \delta x]$, is

$$\int_{x}^{x+\delta x} f(t)\, dt$$

Since the interval is very small, f will vary only slightly across the interval. Hence the probability is approximately $f(x)\delta x$: see Figure 29.6. The contribution to the expected value as a result of this interval is

(value) × (probability)

that is, $xf(x)\delta x$. Summing all such terms yields

$$\text{expected value} = \mu = \int_{a}^{b} xf(x)\, dx$$

Figure 29.6
The shaded area represents the probability that x lies in the small interval $[x, x + \delta x]$.

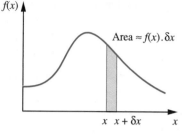

Example 29.10

A random variable has p.d.f. given by

$$f(x) = \frac{1}{2\sqrt{x}} \qquad 1 \leqslant x \leqslant 4$$

Calculate the expected value of x.

Solution

$$\mu = \int_1^4 x \frac{1}{2\sqrt{x}} \, dx = \int_1^4 \frac{\sqrt{x}}{2} \, dx$$

$$= \left[\frac{x^{3/2}}{3}\right]_1^4 = \frac{7}{3}$$

So, if several values of x are measured, the mean of these values will be near to $\frac{7}{3}$. As more and more values are measured the mean will get nearer and nearer to $\frac{7}{3}$.

Exercises 29.7

1 Calculate the expected value of the discrete random variable, h, whose probability distribution is

h	1	1.5	1.7	2.1	3.2
$P(h)$	0.32	0.24	0.17	0.15	0.12

2 Calculate the expected value of the random variable, x, whose probability distribution is

x	2	2.5	3.0	3.5	4.0	4.5
$P(x)$	0.07	0.36	0.21	0.19	0.10	0.07

3 A random variable, z, has p.d.f. $f(z) = e^{-z}$, $0 \leqslant z < \infty$. Calculate the expected value of z.

4 A random variable, x, has p.d.f. $f(x)$ given by

$$f(x) = \frac{5}{4x^2} \qquad 1 \leqslant x \leqslant 5$$

(a) Calculate the expected value of x.

(b) Ten values of x are measured. They are 1.9, 2.9, 2.8, 2.1, 3.2, 3.4, 2.7, 2.3, 2.8, 2.7 Calculate the mean of the observations and comment on your findings.

5 A p.d.f. $h(x)$ is defined by

$$h(x) = \tfrac{3}{4}(1 - x^2) \qquad -1 \leqslant x \leqslant 1$$

Calculate the expected value of x.

6 Is the expected value of a discrete random variable necessarily one of its possible values?

Solutions

1	1.668
2	3.05
3	1

4	(a) 2.012	(b) 2.68
5	0	
6	no	

29.8 Standard deviation of a random variable

29.8.1 Standard deviation of a discrete random variable

Recall from Section 29.6 that the standard deviation of a set of numbers, $\{x_1, x_2, \ldots, x_n\}$, is given by

$$\text{standard deviation} = \sqrt{\frac{\sum(x_i - \bar{x})^2}{n}}$$

Now suppose that x is a discrete random variable which can have values $x_1, x_2, x_3, \ldots, x_n$ with respective probabilities of $p_1, p_2, p_3, \ldots, p_n$; that is, we have

x	x_1	x_2	x_3	$\ldots$	x_n
$P(x)$	p_1	p_2	p_3	$\ldots$	p_n

Let the expected value of x be μ. Then the square of the deviation from the expected value has an identical probability distribution.

value	$(x_1 - \mu)^2$	$(x_2 - \mu)^2$	$\ldots$	$(x_n - \mu)^2$
probability	p_1	p_2	$\ldots$	p_n

The expected value of the mean squared deviation is the variance. The symbol σ^2 is used to denote the variance of a random variable.

$$\text{variance} = \sigma^2 = \sum_1^n p_i(x_i - \mu)^2$$

As before the standard deviation is the square root of the variance.

$$\text{standard deviation} = \sigma = \sqrt{\sum p_i(x_i - \mu)^2}$$

Example 29.11   A discrete random variable has probability distribution

x	1	2	3	4	5
$P(x)$	0.12	0.15	0.23	0.3	0.2

Calculate

(a) the expected value

(b) the standard deviation

Solution (a) $\mu = \sum x_i p_i = 1(0.12) + 2(0.15) + 3(0.23) + 4(0.3) + 5(0.2) = 3.31$

(b) $\sigma^2 = \sum p_i(x_i - \mu)^2$

$= 0.12(1 - 3.31)^2 + 0.15(2 - 3.31)^2 + 0.23(3 - 3.31)^2$

$\qquad + 0.3(4 - 3.31)^2 + 0.2(5 - 3.31)^2$

$= 1.6339$

standard deviation $= \sigma = \sqrt{1.6339} = 1.278$

29.8.2 Standard deviation of a continuous random variable

We simply state the formula for the standard deviation of a continuous random variable. It is analogous to the formula for the standard deviation of a discrete variable. Let x be a continuous random variable with p.d.f. $f(x)$, $a \leqslant x \leqslant b$. Then

$$\sigma = \sqrt{\int_a^b (x - \mu)^2 f(x)\, dx}$$

Example 29.12 A random variable, x, has p.d.f. $f(x)$ given by

$$f(x) = 1 \qquad 0 \leqslant x \leqslant 1$$

Calculate the standard deviation of x.

Solution The expected value, μ, is found.

$$\mu = \int_0^1 xf(x)\, dx = \left[\frac{x^2}{2}\right]_0^1 = \frac{1}{2}$$

The variance can now be found.

$$\text{variance} = \sigma^2 = \int_0^1 \left(x - \tfrac{1}{2}\right)^2 1\, dx$$

$$= \int_0^1 x^2 - x + \tfrac{1}{4}\, dx$$

$$= \left[\frac{x^3}{3} - \frac{x^2}{2} + \frac{x}{4}\right]_0^1 = \frac{1}{3} - \frac{1}{2} + \frac{1}{4} = \frac{1}{12}$$

Hence

$$\sigma = \sqrt{\tfrac{1}{12}} = 0.29$$

The standard deviation of x is 0.29.

Exercises 29.8

1 A p.d.f. $h(x)$ of the random variable x is defined by

$$h(x) = \frac{3}{4}(1 - x^2) \qquad -1 \leqslant x \leqslant 1$$

(a) Calculate the expected value of x.

(b) Calculate the standard deviation of x.

2 A random variable, t, has p.d.f. $H(t)$ given by

$$H(t) = 3\,e^{-3t} \qquad t \geqslant 0$$

(a) Calculate the expected value of t.

(b) Calculate the standard deviation of t.

3 A discrete random variable, w, has a known probability distribution.

w	-1	-0.5	0	0.5	1
$P(w)$	0.1	0.17	0.4	0.21	0.12

Calculate the standard deviation of w.

4 A discrete random variable, y, has a probability distribution

y	6	7	8	9	10	11
$P(y)$	0.13	0.26	0.14	0.09	0.11	0.27

Calculate the standard deviation of y.

5 A continuous random variable has p.d.f.

$$f(x) = \begin{cases} x + 1 & -1 \leqslant x \leqslant 0 \\ -x + 1 & 0 < x \leqslant 1 \end{cases}$$

(a) Calculate the expected value of x.

(b) Calculate the standard deviation of x.

Solutions

1 (a) 0 (b) 0.4472

2 (a) $\frac{1}{3}$ (b) $\frac{1}{3}$

3 0.5598

4 1.84

5 (a) 0 (b) 0.4082

29.9 Permutations and combinations

Both permutations and combinations are used extensively in the calculation of probabilities.

29.9.1 Permutations

The following problem introduces permutations.

Example 29.13

Linking process control computers

A primary and a secondary route must be chosen from available routes A, B and C, for the linking of two process control computers in order to provide redundancy in case one fails. In how many ways can the choices be made?

Solution

The various possibilities are listed.

Primary route	Secondary route
A	B
B	A
A	C
C	A
B	C
C	B

There are six ways in which the choices can be made. Alternatively we could argue as follows. Suppose the primary route is chosen first. There are three choices: any one of A, B or C. The secondary route is then chosen from the two remaining routes, giving two possible choices. Together there are $3 \times 2 = 6$ ways of choosing a primary route and a secondary route.

In Example 29.13 the choice AB is distinct from the choice BA, that is the order is important. Choosing two routes from three and arranging them in order is an example of a **permutation**. More generally,

A permutation of n distinct objects taken r at a time is an arrangement of r of the n objects.

In forming permutations, the order of the objects is important. If three letters are chosen from the alphabet the permutation XYZ is distinct from the permutation ZXY. We pose the question 'How many permutations are there of n objects taken r at a time?' The following example will help to establish a formula for the number of permutations.

Example 29.14

Calculate the number of permutations there are of

(a) four distinct objects taken two at a time

(b) five distinct objects taken three at a time

(c) seven distinct objects taken four at a time

Solution (a) Listing all possible permutations is not feasible when the numbers involved are large. In choosing the first object, four choices are possible. In choosing the second object, three choices are possible. There are thus $4 \times 3 = 12$ permutations of four objects taken two at a time. Note that 12 may be written as

$$12 = 4 \times 3 = \frac{4!}{2!} = \frac{4!}{(4-2)!}$$

(b) There are five objects available for the first choice, four for the second choice and three for the third choice. Hence there are $5 \times 4 \times 3 = 60$ permutations. Again note that

$$60 = \frac{5!}{2!} = \frac{5!}{(5-3)!}$$

(c) There are seven objects available for the first choice, six for the second, five for the third and four for the fourth. The number of permutations is $7 \times 6 \times 5 \times 4 = 840$. This may be written as $\dfrac{7!}{(7-4)!}$.

The example illustrates the following general rule.

The number of permutations of n distinct objects taken r at a time, written $P(n, r)$, is

$$P(n, r) = \frac{n!}{(n-r)!}$$

Example 29.15 Find the number of permutations of

(a) 10 distinct objects taken six at a time

(b) 15 distinct objects taken two at a time

(c) six distinct objects taken six at a time.

Solution (a) $P(10, 6) = \dfrac{10!}{(10-6)!} = \dfrac{10!}{4!} = 151\,200$

(b) $P(15, 2) = \dfrac{15!}{(15-2)!} = \dfrac{15!}{13!} = 210$

(c) $P(6, 6) = \dfrac{6!}{(6-6)!} = \dfrac{6!}{0!} = 720$ (Note that $0! = 1$)

$P(6, 6)$ is simply the number of ways of arranging all six of the objects.

Note that

$$P(n, n) = n!$$

This is the number of ways of arranging n given objects.

29.9.2 Combinations

Closely related to, but nevertheless distinct from, permutations are **combinations**.

> A combination is a selection of r distinct objects from n objects.

In making a selection the order is unimportant. For example, given the letters A, B and C, AB and BA are the same combination but different permutations. As with permutations we develop an expression for the number of combinations of n objects taken r at a time. Examples 29.16 and 29.17 help with this development.

Example 29.16   There are three routes, A, B and C, joining two computers. In how many ways can two routes be chosen from A, B and C?

Solution   The possible combinations (selections) can be listed as

AB, BC, AC

that is, there are three possible ways of making the selection. We can also use our knowledge of permutations to calculate the number of combinations. There are $P(3, 2)$ ways of arranging the three routes taken two at a time.

$$P(3, 2) = \frac{3!}{(3-2)!} = 6$$

Each combination of two routes can be arranged in $P(2, 2)$ ways; that is, each combination gives rise to two permutations. For example, the combination AB could be arranged as AB or BA, giving two permutations. Thus, the number of combinations is half the number of permutations. There are $6/2 = 3$ combinations.

Example 29.17   Calculate the number of combinations of

(a) six distinct objects taken four at a time

(b) 10 distinct objects taken six at a time

Solution   (a) Consider one combination of four objects. These four objects can be arranged in 4! ways; that is, each combination gives rise to 4! permutations. The number of permutations of six objects taken four at a time is

$$P(6, 4) = \frac{6!}{2!}$$

Hence the number of combinations is

$$\frac{P(6,4)}{4!} = \frac{6!}{2!4!} = 15$$

There are 15 combinations of six objects taken four at a time.

(b) Each combination, comprising six objects, gives rise to 6! permutations. The number of permutations of 10 objects taken six at a time is

$$P(10,6) = \frac{10!}{4!}$$

Hence the number of combinations $= \frac{P(10,6)}{6!} = \frac{10!}{4!6!} = 210.$

We write $\binom{n}{r}$ to denote the number of combinations of n objects taken r at a time. A formula for $\binom{n}{r}$ is now developed.

Each combination of r objects gives rise to $r!$ permutations, but

$$P(n,r) = \frac{n!}{(n-r)!}$$

The number of combinations of n distinct objects taken r at a time is

$$\binom{n}{r} = \frac{P(n,r)}{r!} = \frac{n!}{(n-r)!r!}$$

Example 29.18 Calculate the number of combinations of

(a) six distinct objects taken five at a time

(b) nine distinct objects taken nine at a time

(c) 25 distinct objects taken five at a time.

Solution (a) $\binom{6}{5} = \frac{6!}{1!5!} = 6$ (b) $\binom{9}{9} = \frac{9!}{0!9!} = 1$ (c) $\binom{25}{5} = \frac{25!}{5!20!} = 53\,130$

We can generalize the result of Example 29.18(b) and state that $\binom{n}{n} = 1$.

Example 29.19 There are k identical objects and n compartments ($n \geqslant k$). Each compartment can hold only one object. In how many different ways can the k objects be placed in the n compartments?

Solution The order in which the objects are placed is unimportant since all the objects are identical. Placing the k objects is identical to selecting k of the n compartments (see Figure 29.7). But the number of ways of selecting k compartments from n is precisely $\binom{n}{k}$. Hence the k objects can be placed in the n compartments in $\binom{n}{k}$ different ways.

Figure 29.7
Placing k objects in n compartments.

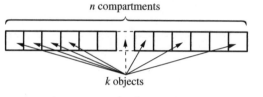

n compartments

k objects

Exercises 29.9

1 Evaluate
 (a) $P(8, 6)$ (b) $P(11, 7)$
 (c) $\binom{12}{9}$ (d) $\binom{15}{12}$ (e) $\binom{15}{3}$

2 Write out explicitly
 (a) $\binom{n}{0}$ (b) $\binom{n}{1}$ (c) $\binom{n}{2}$

3 The expansion of $(a + b)^n$ where n is a positive integer may be written with the help of combination notation.

$$(a + b)^n = a^n + \binom{n}{1} a^{n-1} b$$

$$+ \binom{n}{2} a^{n-2} b^2 + \cdots$$

$$+ \binom{n}{n-1} ab^{n-1} + \binom{n}{n} b^n$$

$$= \sum_{k=0}^{n} \binom{n}{k} a^{n-k} b^k$$

Expand
 (a) $(a + b)^4$ (b) $(1 + x)^6$ (c) $(p + q)^5$

4 Primary and secondary routes connecting two computers need to be chosen. Two primary routes are needed from eight which are suitable and three secondary routes must be chosen from four available. In how many ways can the routes be chosen?

5 A combination lock can be opened by dialling three correct letters followed by three correct digits. How many different possibilities are there for arranging the letters and digits? Is this more secure than a lock which has seven digits? Is the word 'combination' being used correctly?

6 A nuclear power station is to be built on one of 20 possible sites. A team of engineers is commissioned to examine the sites and rank the three most favourable in order. In how many ways can this be done?

Solutions

1 (a) 20 160   (b) 1 663 200   (c) 220
    (d) 455   (e) 455

2 (a) 1   (b) n

   (c) $\dfrac{n(n-1)}{2}$

3 (a) $a^4 + 4a^3b + 6a^2b^2 + 4ab^3 + b^4$

   (b) $1 + 6x + 15x^2 + 20x^3 + 15x^4 + 6x^5 + x^6$

   (c) $p^5 + 5p^4q + 10p^3q^2 + 10p^2q^3 + 5pq^4 + q^5$

4 112

5 17 576 000. Yes, it is more secure. Combination is not being used correctly: permutation lock would be better.

6 6840

29.10

The binomial distribution

In a single trial or experiment a particular result may or may not be obtained. For example, in an examination, a student may pass or fail; when testing a component it may work or not work. The important point is that the two outcomes are complementary. Assuming that the probability of an outcome is fixed, such a trial is called a **Bernoulli trial** in honour of the mathematician, J. Bernoulli.

We address the following problem. In a single trial the outcome is either A or B, that is $\overline{A}$. We refer to A as a **success** and B as a **failure**. If we know $P(A) = p$ then $P(B) = 1 - p$. If n independent trials are observed, what is the probability that A occurs k times, and B occurs $n - k$ times? The number of successful trials in n such experiments is a discrete random variable; such a variable is said to have a **binomial distribution**. Let us consider a particular problem.

Example 29.20

A machine makes components. The probability that a component is acceptable is 0.9.

(a) If three components are sampled find the probability that the first is acceptable, the second is acceptable and the third is not acceptable.

(b) If three components are sampled what is the probability that exactly two are acceptable?

Solution

Let the events A and B be defined thus:

A: the component is acceptable, $P(A) = 0.9$
B: the component is not acceptable, $P(B) = 0.1$

(a) We denote by AAB the compound event that the first is acceptable, the second is acceptable, the third is not acceptable. Since the three events are independent the multiplication law in Section 28.7 gives

$$P(AAB) = P(A)P(A)P(B) = (0.9)(0.9)(0.1) = (0.9)^2(0.1) = 0.081$$

(b) We are interested in the compound event in which two components are acceptable and one is not acceptable. We denote by AAB the compound event that the first is acceptable, the second is acceptable, the third is not acceptable. Compound events ABA and BAA have obvious interpretations.

If exactly two components are acceptable then either AAB or ABA or BAA occurs. These compound events are mutually exclusive and we can therefore use the addition law (see Section 28.3). Hence

$$P(\text{exactly two acceptable components}) = P(AAB) + P(ABA) + P(BAA)$$

From (a) $P(AAB) = 0.081$ and by similar reasoning $P(ABA) = P(BAA) = 0.081$. Hence,

$$P(\text{exactly two acceptable components}) = 3(0.081) = 0.243$$

29.10.1 Probability of k successes from n trials

Let us now return to the general problem posed earlier. We define the compound event C.

C: A occurs k times and B occurs $n - k$ times

The k occurrences of event A can be distributed amongst the n trials in $\binom{n}{k}$ different ways (see Example 29.19). The probability of a particular distribution of k occurrences of A and $n - k$ occurrences of B is $p^k(1 - p)^{n-k}$. Since there are $\binom{n}{k}$ distinct distributions possible then

$$P(C) = \binom{n}{k} p^k (1 - p)^{n-k} \qquad k = 0, 1, 2, \dots, n$$

Example 29.21 The probability that a component is acceptable is 0.93. Ten components are picked at random. What is the probability that

(a) at least nine are acceptable

(b) at most three are acceptable?

Solution (a) $P(\text{exactly 9 components are acceptable}) = \binom{10}{9} (0.93)^9 (0.07) = 0.364$

$$P(\text{exactly 10 components are acceptable}) = \binom{10}{10} (0.93)^{10} = 0.484$$

Hence,

$$P(\text{at least 9 components are acceptable}) = 0.364 + 0.484 = 0.848$$

(b) We require the probability that none are acceptable, one is acceptable, two are acceptable and three are acceptable.

$$P(0 \text{ are acceptable}) = \binom{10}{0} (0.93)^0 (0.07)^{10} = 2.825 \times 10^{-12}$$

$$P(1 \text{ is acceptable}) = \binom{10}{1} (0.93)^1 (0.07)^9 = 3.753 \times 10^{-10}$$

$$P(2 \text{ are acceptable}) = \binom{10}{2} (0.93)^2 (0.07)^8 = 2.244 \times 10^{-8}$$

$$P(3 \text{ are acceptable}) = \binom{10}{3} (0.93)^3 (0.07)^7 = 7.949 \times 10^{-7}$$

Hence,

$$P(\text{at most 3 are acceptable}) = 2.825 \times 10^{-12} + 3.753 \times 10^{-10}$$
$$+ 2.244 \times 10^{-8} + 7.949 \times 10^{-7}$$
$$= 8.18 \times 10^{-7}$$

that is, the probability that at most three components are acceptable is almost zero; it is virtually impossible.

29.10.2 Mean and standard deviation of a binomial distribution

Let the probability of success in a single trial be p and let the number of trials be n. The number of successes in n trials is a discrete random variable, x, with a binomial distribution. Then x can have any value from $\{0, 1, 2, 3, \dots, n\}$, although clearly some values are more likely to occur than others. The expected value of x can be shown to be np. Thus, if many values of x are recorded, the mean of these will approach np.

Expected value of the binomial distribution $= np$

The standard deviation of the binomial distribution can also be found. This is given by

standard deviation of the binomial distribution $= \sqrt{np(1-p)}$

29.10.3 Most likely number of successes

When conducting a series of trials it is sometimes desirable to know the most likely outcome. For example, what is the most likely number of acceptable components in a sample of five tested?

Example 29.22 The probability a component is acceptable is 0.8. Five components are picked at random. What is the most likely number of acceptable components?

Solution $P(\text{no acceptable components}) = \binom{5}{0}(0.8)^0(0.2)^5 = 3.2 \times 10^{-4}$

$P(1 \text{ acceptable component}) = \binom{5}{1}(0.8)^1(0.2)^4 = 6.4 \times 10^{-3}$

$P(2 \text{ acceptable components}) = \binom{5}{2}(0.8)^2(0.2)^3 = 0.0512$

$P(3 \text{ acceptable components}) = \binom{5}{3}(0.8)^3(0.2)^2 = 0.2048$

$P(4 \text{ acceptable components}) = \binom{5}{4}(0.8)^4(0.2)^1 = 0.4096$

$P(5 \text{ acceptable components}) = \binom{5}{5}(0.8)^5(0.2)^0 = 0.3277$

The most likely number of acceptable components is four.

Example 29.22 illustrates an important general result. Suppose we conduct n Bernoulli trials and wish to find the most likely number of successes. If p = probability of success on a single trial, and i = most likely number of successes in n trials, then

$$p(n+1) - 1 < i < p(n+1)$$

In Example 29.22, $p = 0.8$, $n = 5$ and so

$$(0.8)(6) - 1 < i < (0.8)(6)$$
$$3.8 < i < 4.8$$

Since i is an integer, then $i = 4$.

Exercises 29.10

1 The probability a component is acceptable is 0.8. Four components are sampled. What is the probability that

(a) exactly one is acceptable
(b) exactly two are acceptable?

2 A machine requires all seven of its micro-chips to operate correctly in order to be acceptable. The probability a micro-chip is operating correctly is 0.99.

(a) What is the probability the machine is acceptable?
(b) What is the probability that six of the seven chips are operating correctly?

(c) The machine is redesigned so that the original seven chips are replaced by four new chips. The probability a new chip operates correctly is 0.98. Is the new design more or less reliable than the original?

3 The probability a machine has a lifespan of more than 5 years is 0.8. Ten machines are chosen at random. What is the probability that

(a) eight machines have a lifespan of more than 5 years
(b) all machines have a lifespan of more than 5 years

(c) at least eight machines have a lifespan of more than 5 years

(d) no more than two machines have a lifespan of less than 5 years?

4 The probability a valve remains reliable for more than 10 years is 0.75. Eight valves are sampled. What is the most likely number of valves to remain reliable for more than 10 years?

5 The probability a chip is manufactured to an acceptable standard is 0.87. A sample of six chips is picked at random from a large batch.

(a) Calculate the probability all six chips are acceptable.

(b) Calculate the probability none of the chips is acceptable.

(c) Calculate the probability that fewer than five chips in the sample are acceptable.

(d) Calculate the most likely number of acceptable chips in the sample.

(e) Calculate the probability that more than two chips are unacceptable.

Solutions

1 (a) 0.0256 (b) 0.1536

2 (a) 0.9321 (b) 0.0659 (c) 0.9224.
New design is less reliable

3 (a) 0.3020 (b) 0.1074 (c) 0.678
(d) 0.678

4 6

5 (a) 0.4336

(b) 4.826×10^{-6}

(c) 0.1776

(d) 6

(e) 0.0324

29.11 The Poisson distribution

The Poisson distribution models the number of occurrences of an event in a given interval. Consider the number of emergency calls received by a service engineer in one day. We may know from experience that the number of calls is usually three or four per day, but occasionally it will be only one or two, or even none, and on some days it may be six or seven, or even more. This example suggests a need for assigning a probability to the number of occurrences of an event during a given time period. The Poisson distribution serves this purpose.

The number of occurrences of an event, E, in a given time period is a discrete random variable which we denote by X. We wish to find the probability that $X = 0$, $X = 1$, $X = 2$, $X = 3$, and so on. Suppose the occurrence of E in any time interval is not affected by its occurrence in any preceding time interval. For example, a car is not more, or less, likely to pass a given spot in the next 10 seconds because a car passed (or did not pass) the spot in the previous 10 seconds, that is the occurrences are independent.

Let λ be the expected (mean) value of X, the number of occurrences during the time period. If X is measured for many time periods the average value of X will be λ. Under the given conditions X follows a Poisson distribution. The probability that X has a value r is given by

$$P(X = r) = \frac{e^{-\lambda}\lambda^r}{r!} \qquad r = 0, 1, 2, \ldots$$

> The expected value and variance of the Poisson distribution are both equal to λ.

Example 29.23

Records show that on average three emergency calls per day are received by a service engineer. What is the probability that on a particular day
(a) three   (b) two   (c) four
calls will be received?

Solution

The number of calls received follows a Poisson distribution. The average number of calls is three per day, that is $\lambda = 3$.

(a) $P(X = 3) = \dfrac{e^{-3}3^3}{3!} = 0.224$ (b) $P(X = 2) = \dfrac{e^{-3}3^2}{2!} = 0.224$

(c) $P(X = 4) = \dfrac{e^{-3}3^4}{4!} = 0.168$

The engineer will receive three calls on approximately 22 days in 100, two calls on approximately 22 days in 100 and four calls on approximately 17 days in 100.

Example 29.24

A workshop has several machines. During a typical month two machines will break down. What are the probabilities that in a month
(a) none   (b) one   (c) more than two
will break down?

Solution

λ = average number of machines that break down = 2
X = number of machines broken down

(a) $P(X = 0) = \dfrac{e^{-2}2^0}{0!} = 0.135$

(b) $P(X = 1) = \dfrac{e^{-2}2^1}{1!} = 0.271$

(c) $P(X > 2) = 1 - P(X = 0) - P(X = 1) - P(X = 2)$
$\qquad\qquad = 1 - e^{-2} - 2e^{-2} - 2e^{-2} = 0.323$

29.11.1 Poisson approximation to the binomial

The Poisson and binomial distributions are related. Consider a binomial distribution, in which n trials take place and the probabiliity of success is p. If n increases and p decreases such that np is constant, the resulting binomial distribution can be approximated by a Poisson distribution with $\lambda = np$. Recall that np is the expected value of the binomial distribution, and λ is the expected value of the Poisson distribution.

To illustrate the above point, Table 29.6 lists the probabilities for binomial and Poisson distributions with $n = 15$, $p = 0.05$ and hence $\lambda = 15(0.05) = 0.75$. The remaining probabilities are all almost 0.

As n increases and p decreases with np remaining constant, agreement between the two distributions becomes closer.

Table 29.6
The probabilities for
binomial and Poisson
distributions.

	Binomial (n, p)	Poisson (λ)
	$P(X = r); n = 15, p = 0.05$	$P(X = r); \lambda = 0.75$
$r = 0$	0.463 39	0.472 37
$r = 1$	0.365 76	0.354 27
$r = 2$	0.134 75	0.132 85
$r = 3$	0.030 73	0.033 21
$r = 4$	0.004 85	0.006 23
$r = 5$	0.000 56	0.000 90
$r = 6$	0.000 05	0.000 07
$r = 7$	0.000 00	0.000 01

Example 29.25

A workforce comprises 250 people. The probability a person is absent on any one day is 0.02. Find the probability that on a day
(a) three   (b) seven
people are absent.

Solution

This problem may be treated either as a sequence of Bernoulli trials or as a Poisson process.

Bernoulli trials

The probabilities follow a binomial distribution.

E: a person is absent
n = number of trials = 250
p = probability that E occurs in a single trial = 0.02
X = number of occurrences of event E

(a) $P(X = 3) = \binom{250}{3} (0.02)^3 (0.98)^{247} = 0.140$

(b) $P(X = 7) = \binom{250}{7} (0.02)^7 (0.98)^{243} = 0.105$

Poisson process

Since n is large and p is small the Poisson distribution will be a good approximation to the binomial distribution

$\lambda = np = 5$

(a) $P(X = 3) = \dfrac{e^{-5}(5)^3}{3!} = 0.140$ (b) $P(X = 7) = \dfrac{e^{-5}(5)^7}{7!} = 0.104$

Exercises 29.11

1 A computer network has several hundred computers. During an 8 hour period, there are on average seven computers not functioning. Find the probability that during an 8 hour period
(a) nine (b) five
do not function.

2 A workforce has on average two people absent through illness on any given day. Find the probability that on a typical day

(a) two

(b) at least three

(c) less than four

people are absent.

3 A machine manufactures 300 micro-chips per hour. The probability an individual chip is faulty is 0.01. Calculate the probability that

(a) two

(b) four

(c) more than three

faulty chips are manufactured in a particular hour. Use both the binomial and Poisson approximations and compare the resulting probabilities.

4 The probability of a disk drive failure in any week is 0.007. A computer service company maintains 900 disk drives. Use the Poisson distribution to calculate the probability of
(a) seven (b) more than seven
disk drive failures in a week.

5 The probability an employee fails to come to work is 0.017. A large engineering firm employs 650 people. What is the probability that on a particular day
(a) nine (b) 10
people are away from work?

6 A machine manufactures electrical components for the car industry at the rate of 750 per hour. The probability a component is faulty is 0.013. Use both the binomial distribution and the corresponding Poisson approximation to find the probability that in a sample of 200 components

(a) none are faulty

(b) one is faulty

(c) two are faulty

(d) three are faulty

(e) more than three are faulty

Solutions

1 (a) 0.1014 (b) 0.1277

2 (a) 0.2707 (b) 0.3233 (c) 0.8571

3 (a) Binomial 0.2244; Poisson 0.2240
(b) 0.1689, 0.1680 (c) 0.353, 0.353

4 (a) 0.1435 (b) 0.2983

5 (a) 0.1075 (b) 0.1188

6 (a) Binomial 0.0730; Poisson 0.0743

(b) 0.1923, 0.1931

(c) 0.2521, 0.2510

(d) 0.2191, 0.2176

(e) 0.2634, 0.2640

29.12 The uniform distribution

We now consider a continuous distribution – the uniform distribution. Suppose the probability of an event occurring remains constant across a given time interval. The p.d.f., $f(t)$, of such a distribution takes the form shown in Figure 29.8.

The area under $f(t)$ must equal 1 and so if the interval is of length T, the height of the rectangle is $\dfrac{1}{T}$.

Figure 29.8
The uniform p.d.f.

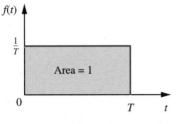

The p.d.f. for the uniform distribution is given by

$$f(t) = \begin{cases} \dfrac{1}{T} & 0 < t < T \\ 0 & \text{otherwise} \end{cases}$$

The probability an event occurs in an interval $[a, b]$ is $\int_a^b f(t)\,dt$. If $0 \leqslant a \leqslant b \leqslant T$ this probability is simply $\dfrac{b-a}{T}$. We shall make use of this distribution in Section 29.15 when we deal with reliability engineering.

Exercises 29.12

1 A random variable, x, has a uniform p.d.f. with $T = 10$. Calculate the probability that

(a) $1 \leqslant x \leqslant 3$

(b) $1.6 \leqslant x \leqslant 9.3$

(c) $x \geqslant 2.9$

(d) $x < 7.2$

(e) $-1 < x < 2$

(f) $9.1 < x < 12.3$

2 A random variable t has a uniform p.d.f. with $T = 1.5$. Calculate the probability that

(a) $0.7 \leqslant t \leqslant 1.3$

(b) $1 < t < 2$

(c) $|t| < 0.5$

(d) $|t| > 1$

Solutions

1 (a) 0.2   (b) 0.77   (c) 0.71
   (d) 0.72   (e) 0.2   (f) 0.09

2 (a) 0.4   (b) 0.3333   (c) 0.3333
   (d) 0.3333

29.13 The exponential distribution

Suppose a random variable has a Poisson distribution; for example, the random variable could be the number of customers arriving at a service point, the number of telephone calls received at a switchboard, the number of machines breaking down in a week. Then the time between events happening is a random variable which follows an **exponential distribution**. Note that whereas the number of events is a discrete variable, the time between events is a continuous variable.

Figure 29.9
The exponential p.d.f.
for various values of α.

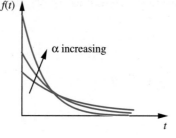

$f(t)$

α increasing

t

Let t be the time between events happening.

The exponential p.d.f. $f(t)$ is given by

$$f(t) = \begin{cases} \alpha e^{-\alpha t} & t \geqslant 0 \\ 0 & \text{otherwise} \end{cases}$$

where $\alpha > 0$.

The probability of an event occurring in a time interval, T, is given by $\int_0^T f(t)\,dt$. Figure 29.9 shows $f(t)$ for various values of α. The expected value of the distribution is given, by definition, as

$$\text{expected value} = \mu = \int_0^\infty t\alpha e^{-\alpha t}\,dt = \frac{1}{\alpha}$$

For example, if

$$f(t) = 3\,e^{-3t} \qquad t \text{ in seconds} \qquad t \geqslant 0$$

then the mean time between events is $\frac{1}{3}$ s; that is, on average there are three events happening per second.

Example 29.26
The time between breakdowns of a particular machine follows an exponential distribution, with a mean of 17 days. Calculate the probability that a machine breaks down in a 15 day period.

Solution
The mean time between breakdowns $= 17 = \dfrac{1}{\alpha}$, so $\alpha = \dfrac{1}{17}$. Thus the p.d.f., $f(t)$, is given by

$$f(t) = \frac{1}{17}\,e^{-t/17} \qquad t \geqslant 0$$

We require the probability that the machine breaks down in a 15 day period.

$$P(0 \leqslant t \leqslant 15) = \int_0^{15} f(t)\, \mathrm{d}t$$

$$= \int_0^{15} \frac{1}{17}\, \mathrm{e}^{-t/17}\, \mathrm{d}t$$

$$= \left[-\mathrm{e}^{-t/17} \right]_0^{15}$$

$$= -\mathrm{e}^{-15/17} + 1$$

$$= 0.5862$$

There is a 58.62% chance that the machine will break down in a 15 day period.

Exercises 29.13

1 A service engineer receives on average an emergency call every 3 hours. If the time between calls follows an exponential distribution, calculate the probability that the time from one emergency call to the next is

    (a) greater than 3 hours
    (b) less than 4.5 hours

2 The mean time between breakdowns for a certain type of machine is 400 hours. Calculate

the probability that the time between breakdowns for a particular machine is

    (a) greater than 450 hours
    (b) less than 350 hours

3 The mean time taken by an engineer to repair an electrical fault in a system is 2.7 hours. Calculate the probability that the engineer will repair a fault in less than the mean time.

Solutions

1 (a) 0.3679   (b) 0.7769

2 (a) 0.3247   (b) 0.5831

3 0.6321

29.14 The normal distribution

The normal probability density function, commonly called the **normal distribution**, is one of the most important and widely used. It is used to calculate the probable values of continuous variables, for example weight, length, density, error measurement. Probabilities calculated using the normal distribution have been shown to reflect accurately those which would be found using actual data.

Let x be a continuous random variable with a normal distribution, $N(x)$. Then

$$N(x) = \frac{1}{\sigma \sqrt{2\pi}}\, \mathrm{e}^{-(x-\mu)^2/2\sigma^2} \qquad -\infty < x < \infty$$

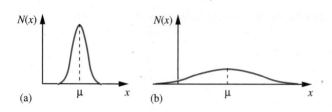

Figure 29.10 Two typical normal curves.

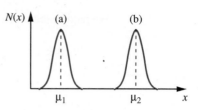

Figure 29.11 Two normal curves with the same standard deviation but different means.

where μ = expected (mean) value of x, σ = standard deviation of x. Figure 29.10 shows two typical normal curves. All normal distributions are bell shaped and symmetrical about μ.

In Figure 29.10(a) the values of x are grouped very closely to the mean. Such a distribution has a low standard deviation. Conversely, in Figure 29.10(b) the values of the variable are spread widely about the mean and so the distribution has a high standard deviation.

Figure 29.11 shows two normal distributions. They have the same standard deviation but different means. The mean of the distribution in Figure 29.11(a) is μ_1 while the mean of that in Figure 29.11(b) is μ_2. Note that the domain of $N(x)$ is $(-\infty, \infty)$; that is, the domain is all real numbers. As for all distribution curves the total area under the curve is 1.

29.14.1 The standard normal

A normal distribution is determined uniquely by specifying the mean and standard deviation. The probability that x lies in the interval $[a, b]$ is

$$P(a \leqslant x \leqslant b) = \int_a^b N(x)\,\mathrm{d}x$$

The mathematical form of the normal distribution makes analytic integration impossible, so all probabilities must be computed numerically. As these numerical values would change every time the value of μ or σ was altered some standardization is required. To this end we introduce the **standard normal**. The standard normal has a mean of 0 and a standard deviation of 1.

Consider the probability that the random variable, x, has a value less than z. For convenience we call this $A(z)$.

$$A(z) = P(x < z) = \int_{-\infty}^z N(x)\,\mathrm{d}x$$

Figure 29.12 illustrates $A(z)$. Values of $A(z)$ have been computed numerically and tabulated. They are given in Table 29.7. Using the table and the symmetrical property of the distribution, probabilities can be calculated.

Example 29.27

The continuous random variable x has a standard normal distribution. Calculate the probability that

(a) $x < 1.2$ (b) $x > 1.2$ (c) $x > -1.2$ (d) $x < -1.2$

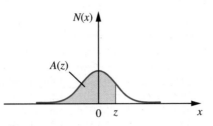

Figure 29.12
$A(z) = P(x < z) = \int_{-\infty}^{z} N(x)\,dx.$

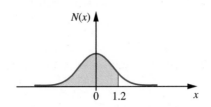

Figure 29.13 $P(x < 1.2) = 0.8849.$

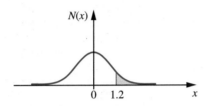

Figure 29.14 $P(x > 1.2) = 0.1151.$

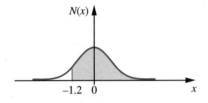

Figure 29.15 $P(x > -1.2) = 0.8849.$

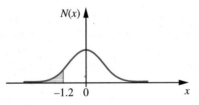

Figure 29.16 $P(x < -1.2) = 0.1151.$

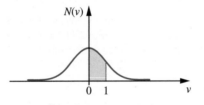

Figure 29.17 $P(0 < v < 1) = 0.3413.$

Solution (a) From Table 29.7

$$P(x < 1.2) = 0.8849$$

This is depicted in Figure 29.13.

(b) $P(x > 1.2) = 1 - 0.8849 = 0.1151$
This is shown in Figure 29.14.

(c) By symmetry $P(x > -1.2)$ is identical to $P(x < 1.2)$ (see Figure 29.15). So,

$$P(x > -1.2) = 0.8849$$

(d) Using part (c) we find

$$P(x < -1.2) = 1 - P(x > -1.2) = 0.1151$$

(see Figure 29.16).

Table 29.7 Cumulative normal probabilities.

z	$A(z)$	z	$A(z)$	z	$A(z)$	z	$A(z)$	z	$A(z)$	z	$A(z)$
0.00	0.500 000 0	0.40	0.655 421 7	0.80	0.788 144 6	1.20	0.884 930 3	1.60	0.945 200 7	2.00	0.977 249 9
0.01	0.503 989 4	0.41	0.659 097 0	0.81	0.791 029 9	1.21	0.886 860 6	1.61	0.946 301 1	2.01	0.977 784 4
0.02	0.507 978 3	0.42	0.662 757 3	0.82	0.793 891 9	1.22	0.888 767 6	1.62	0.947 383 9	2.02	0.978 308 3
0.03	0.511 966 5	0.43	0.666 402 2	0.83	0.796 730 6	1.23	0.890 651 4	1.63	0.948 449 3	2.03	0.978 821 7
0.04	0.515 953 4	0.44	0.670 031 4	0.84	0.799 545 8	1.24	0.892 512 3	1.64	0.949 497 4	2.04	0.979 324 8
0.05	0.519 938 8	0.45	0.673 644 8	0.85	0.802 337 5	1.25	0.894 350 2	1.65	0.950 528 5	2.05	0.979 817 8
0.06	0.523 922 2	0.46	0.677 241 9	0.86	0.805 105 5	1.26	0.896 165 3	1.66	0.951 542 8	2.06	0.980 300 7
0.07	0.527 903 2	0.47	0.680 822 5	0.87	0.807 849 8	1.27	0.897 957 7	1.67	0.952 540 3	2.07	0.980 773 8
0.08	0.531 881 4	0.48	0.684 386 3	0.88	0.810 570 3	1.28	0.899 727 4	1.68	0.953 521 3	2.08	0.981 237 2
0.09	0.535 856 4	0.49	0.687 933 1	0.89	0.813 267 1	1.29	0.901 474 7	1.69	0.954 486 0	2.09	0.981 691 1
0.10	0.539 827 8	0.50	0.691 462 5	0.90	0.815 939 9	1.30	0.903 199 5	1.70	0.955 434 5	2.10	0.982 135 6
0.11	0.543 795 3	0.51	0.694 974 3	0.91	0.818 588 7	1.31	0.904 902 1	1.71	0.956 367 1	2.11	0.982 570 8
0.12	0.547 758 4	0.52	0.698 468 2	0.92	0.821 213 6	1.32	0.906 582 5	1.72	0.957 283 8	2.12	0.982 997 0
0.13	0.551 716 8	0.53	0.701 944 0	0.93	0.823 814 5	1.33	0.908 240 9	1.73	0.958 184 9	2.13	0.983 414 2
0.14	0.555 670 0	0.54	0.705 401 5	0.94	0.826 391 2	1.34	0.909 877 3	1.74	0.959 070 5	2.14	0.983 822 6
0.15	0.559 617 7	0.55	0.708 840 3	0.95	0.828 943 9	1.35	0.911 492 0	1.75	0.959 940 8	2.15	0.984 222 4
0.16	0.563 559 5	0.56	0.712 260 3	0.96	0.831 472 4	1.36	0.913 085 0	1.76	0.960 796 1	2.16	0.984 613 7
0.17	0.567 494 9	0.57	0.715 661 2	0.97	0.833 976 8	1.37	0.914 656 5	1.77	0.961 636 4	2.17	0.984 996 6
0.18	0.571 423 7	0.58	0.719 042 7	0.98	0.836 456 9	1.38	0.916 206 7	1.78	0.962 462 0	2.18	0.985 371 3
0.19	0.575 345 4	0.59	0.722 404 7	0.99	0.838 912 9	1.39	0.917 735 6	1.79	0.963 273 0	2.19	0.985 737 9
0.20	0.579 259 7	0.60	0.725 746 9	1.00	0.841 344 7	1.40	0.919 243 3	1.80	0.964 069 7	2.20	0.986 096 6
0.21	0.583 166 2	0.61	0.729 069 1	1.01	0.843 752 4	1.41	0.920 730 2	1.81	0.964 852 1	2.21	0.986 447 4
0.22	0.587 060 4	0.62	0.732 371 1	1.02	0.846 135 8	1.42	0.922 196 2	1.82	0.965 620 5	2.22	0.986 790 6
0.23	0.590 954 1	0.63	0.735 652 7	1.03	0.848 495 0	1.43	0.923 641 5	1.83	0.966 375 0	2.23	0.987 126 3
0.24	0.594 834 9	0.64	0.738 913 7	1.04	0.850 830 0	1.44	0.925 066 3	1.84	0.967 115 9	2.24	0.987 454 5
0.25	0.598 706 3	0.65	0.742 153 9	1.05	0.853 140 9	1.45	0.926 470 7	1.85	0.967 843 2	2.25	0.987 775 5
0.26	0.602 568 1	0.66	0.745 373 1	1.06	0.855 427 7	1.46	0.927 855 0	1.86	0.968 557 2	2.26	0.988 089 4
0.27	0.606 419 9	0.67	0.748 571 1	1.07	0.857 690 3	1.47	0.929 219 1	1.87	0.969 258 1	2.27	0.988 396 2
0.28	0.610 261 2	0.68	0.751 747 8	1.08	0.859 928 9	1.48	0.930 563 4	1.88	0.969 946 0	2.28	0.988 696 2
0.29	0.614 009 1	0.69	0.754 902 9	1.09	0.862 143 4	1.49	0.931 887 9	1.89	0.970 621 0	2.29	0.988 998 3
0.30	0.617 911 4	0.70	0.758 036 3	1.10	0.864 333 9	1.50	0.933 192 8	1.90	0.971 283 4	2.30	0.989 275 9
0.31	0.621 719 5	0.71	0.761 147 9	1.11	0.866 500 5	1.51	0.934 478 3	1.91	0.971 933 4	2.31	0.989 555 9
0.32	0.625 515 8	0.72	0.764 237 5	1.12	0.868 643 1	1.52	0.935 744 5	1.92	0.972 571 1	2.32	0.989 829 6
0.33	0.629 300 0	0.73	0.767 304 9	1.13	0.870 761 9	1.53	0.936 991 6	1.93	0.973 196 6	2.33	0.990 096 9
0.34	0.633 071 7	0.74	0.770 350 0	1.14	0.872 856 8	1.54	0.938 219 8	1.94	0.973 810 2	2.34	0.990 358 1
0.35	0.636 830 7	0.75	0.773 372 6	1.15	0.874 928 1	1.55	0.939 429 2	1.95	0.974 411 9	2.35	0.990 613 3
0.36	0.640 576 4	0.76	0.776 372 7	1.16	0.876 975 6	1.56	0.940 620 1	1.96	0.975 002 1	2.36	0.990 862 5
0.37	0.644 308 8	0.77	0.779 350 1	1.17	0.878 999 5	1.57	0.941 792 4	1.97	0.975 580 8	2.37	0.991 106 0
0.38	0.648 027 3	0.78	0.782 304 6	1.18	0.880 999 9	1.58	0.942 946 6	1.98	0.976 148 2	2.38	0.991 343 7
0.39	0.651 731 7	0.79	0.785 236 1	1.19	0.882 976 8	1.59	0.944 082 6	1.99	0.976 704 5	2.39	0.991 575 8

(continued)

Table 29.7 Cumulative normal probabilities (*continued*).

z	$A(z)$	z	$A(z)$	z	$A(z)$	z	$A(z)$	z	$A(z)$	z	$A(z)$
2.40	0.991 802 5	2.45	0.992 857 2	2.50	0.993 790 3	2.55	0.994 613 9	2.60	0.995 338 3	3.20	0.999 312 9
2.41	0.992 023 7	2.46	0.993 053 1	2.51	0.993 963 4	2.56	0.994 766 4	2.70	0.996 533 0	3.40	0.999 663 1
2.42	0.992 239 7	2.47	0.993 244 3	2.52	0.994 132 3	2.57	0.994 915 1	2.80	0.997 444 9	3.60	0.999 840 9
2.43	0.992 450 6	2.48	0.993 430 9	2.53	0.994 296 6	2.58	0.995 060 0	2.90	0.998 134 2	3.80	0.999 927 7
2.44	0.992 656 4	2.49	0.993 612 8	2.54	0.994 457 4	2.59	0.995 201 2	3.00	0.998 650 1	4.00	0.999 968 3
										4.50	0.999 996 6
										5.00	0.999 999 7
										5.50	0.999 999 9

Example 29.28 The continuous random variable v has a standard normal distribution. Calculate the probability that

(a) $0 < v < 1$ (b) $-1 < v < 1$ (c) $-0.5 \leqslant v \leqslant 2$

Solution (a) Figure 29.17 shows the area (probability) required.

$$P(v < 1) = 0.8413 \qquad \text{using Table 29.7}$$
$$P(v < 0) = 0.5 \qquad \text{using symmetry}$$
$$P(0 < v < 1) = 0.8413 - 0.5 = 0.3413$$

(b) Figure 29.18 shows the area (probability) required.

$$P(-1 < v < 1) = 2 \times P(0 < v < 1) \qquad \text{using symmetry}$$
$$= 2 \times 0.3413 = 0.6826$$

This tells us that 68.3% of the values of v are within one standard deviation of the mean.

(c) Figure 29.19 shows the area (probability) required.

$$P(v \leqslant 2) = 0.9772$$
$$P(v \leqslant -0.5) = P(v > 0.5) = 1 - P(v < 0.5)$$
$$= 1 - 0.6915 = 0.3085$$
$$P(-0.5 \leqslant v \leqslant 2) = 0.9772 - 0.3085 = 0.6687$$

Note that whether or not inequalities defining v are strict is of no consequence in calculating the probabilities.

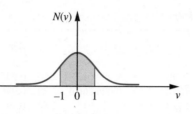

Figure 29.18 $P(-1 < v < 1) = 0.6826.$

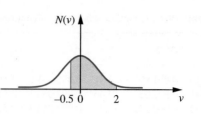

Figure 29.19 $P(-0.5 \leqslant v \leqslant 2) = 0.6687.$

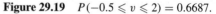

29.14.2   Non-standard normal

Table 29.7 allows us to calculate probabilities for a random variable with a standard normal distribution. This section show us how to use the same table when the variable has a non-standard distribution. A non-standard normal has a mean value other than 0 and/or a standard deviation other than 1. The non-standard normal is changed into a standard normal by application of a simple rule. Suppose the non-standard distribution has a mean μ and a standard deviation σ. Then all non-standard values are transformed to standard values using

non-standard $\rightarrow$ standard

$$X \rightarrow \frac{X - \mu}{\sigma}$$

Example 29.29   A random variable, h, has a normal distribution with mean 7 and standard deviation 2. Calculate the probability that

(a) $h > 9$ (b) $h < 6$ (c) $5 < h < 8$

Solution   (a) Applying the transformation gives

$$9 \rightarrow \frac{9 - 7}{2} = 1$$

So $h > 9$ has the same probability as $x > 1$, where x is a random variable with a standard normal distribution

$$P(h > 9) = P(x > 1) = 1 - P(x < 1) = 1 - 0.8413 = 0.1587$$

(b) Applying the transformation gives

$$6 \rightarrow \frac{6 - 7}{2} = -0.5$$

So $h < 6$ has the same probability as $x < -0.5$.

$$P(x < -0.5) = P(x > 0.5) = 1 - P(x < 0.5) = 0.3085$$

(c) Applying the transformation to 5 and 8 gives

$$5 \rightarrow \frac{5 - 7}{2} = -1 \qquad 8 \rightarrow \frac{8 - 7}{2} = 0.5$$

and so we require $P(-1 < x < 0.5)$. Therefore

$$P(x < 0.5) = 0.6915 \qquad P(x < -1) = 0.1587$$

and then

$$P(-1 < x < 0.5) = 0.6915 - 0.1587 = 0.5328$$

Exercises 29.14

1 A random variable, x, has a standard normal distribution. Calculate the probability that x lies in the following intervals.

(a) $(0.25, 0.75)$

(b) $(-0.3, 0.1)$

(c) within 1.5 standard deviations of the mean

(d) more than two standard deviations from the mean

(e) $(-1.7, -0.2)$

2 A random variable, x, has a normal distribution with mean 4 and standard deviation 0.8. Calculate the probability that

(a) $3.0 \leqslant x \leqslant 4.4$

(b) $2.5 < x < 3.9$

(c) $x > 4.6$

(d) $x < 4.2$

(e) x is within 0.6 of the mean

3 A random variable, t, has a normal distribution with mean 1 and standard deviation 2.5. Calculate the probability that
(a) $-1 \leqslant t \leqslant 2$ (b) $t > 0$
(c) $|t| \leqslant 0.9$ (d) $|t| > 1.6$

4 The scores from IQ tests have a mean of 100 and a standard deviation of 15. What should a person score in order to be described as in the top 10% of the population?

5 A machine produces car pistons. The diameter of the pistons follows a normal distribution, mean 6.04 cm with a standard deviation of 0.02 cm. The piston is acceptable if its diameter is in the range 6.010 cm to 6.055 cm. What percentage of pistons is acceptable?

6 The random variable, x, has a normal distribution. How many standard deviations above the mean must the point P be placed if the tail-end is to represent

(a) 10%   (b) 5%   (c) 1%

of the total area? (See Figure 29.20.)

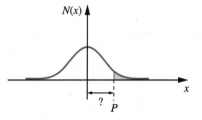

Figure 29.20   Graph for Question 6.

7 Consider Figure 29.21. The two tail-ends have equal area. How many standard deviations from the mean must A and B be placed if the tail-ends are

(a) 10%   (b) 5%   (c) 1%

of the total area?

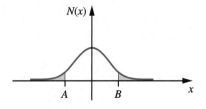

Figure 29.21   Graph for Question 7.

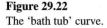
Solutions

1   (a) 0.1747   (b) 0.1577   (c) 0.8664   4   119
    (d) 0.0455   (e) 0.3762

                                            5   71%

2   (a) 0.5858   (b) 0.4199   (c) 0.2266
    (d) 0.5987   (e) 0.5467   6   (a) 1.28   (b) 1.645   (c) 2.33

3   (a) 0.4436   (b) 0.6554   (c) 0.2604
    (d) 0.5544   7   (a) 1.64   (b) 1.96   (c) 2.57

29.15   Reliability engineering

Reliability engineering is an important area of study. Unreliable products lead to human frustration, financial loss and in the case of life-critical systems can lead to death. As the complexity of engineering systems has increased, mathematical methods of assessing reliability have grown in importance. Probability theory forms a central part of the design of highly reliable systems. For most items the failure rate changes with time. A common pattern is exhibited by the appropriately named 'bath tub' curve, illustrated in Figure 29.22.

Figure 29.22
The 'bath tub' curve.

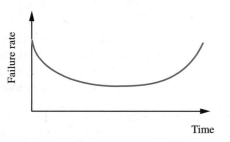

Car part failures are quite well modelled by this distribution. For example, a crankshaft may fail quite quickly as a result of a manufacturing defect. If it does not, then there is usually a long period during which the likelihood of failure is low. After many years the probability of failure increases.

Consider the probability of an item failing over a total time period T. This period, T, is the time during which the item is functioning. The time taken to repair the item is not considered in this calculation but is considered a little later on. Suppose the probability of failure is evenly distributed over this period; that is, the probability of failure is modelled by the uniform distribution (see Section 29.12). It is important to note that this is a fairly simplistic assumption. If N = number of failures of the item over a time period T, it is possible to define a mean failure rate, k, by

$$k = \frac{N}{T}$$

For example, if an item fails 10 times in a period of 5 years we define the mean failure rate to be $k = 10/5 = 2$, that is two failures per year. Because of the uniform distribution of the failures across the time period, the quantity k is constant. To illustrate this consider the previous example with a period of 10 years. During this time the item will fail 20 times and so

$$k = \tfrac{20}{10} = 2 \text{ failures per year}$$

as found earlier.

Another useful term is the **mean time between failures** *(MTBF)*, which is given by

$$MTBF = \frac{1}{k}$$

The term *MTBF* is only used for items that are repairable.

Let the interval T be divided into n small sub-intervals each of length δT, that is $n\delta T = T$. Suppose each sub-interval is so small that only one failure can occur during it. Note that since repair time has been neglected it is always possible to have a failure in a sub-interval. So the N failures which occur during time T occur in N distinct sub-intervals. The probability of failure occurring in a particular sub-interval, P_{f}, is then given by

$$P_{\text{f}} = \frac{\text{number of sub-intervals in which failure occurs}}{\text{total number of sub-intervals}}$$

$$= \frac{N}{n}$$

In each sub-interval, δT, the probability of an item not failing, P_{nf}, is

$$P_{\text{nf}} = 1 - P_{\text{f}} = 1 - \frac{N}{n} = \frac{n - N}{n}$$

As the item progresses through each of the successive sub-intervals δT it can be thought of as undergoing a series of trials, the result of which is failure or non-failure. Therefore, the probability of the item not failing as it passes through all of the n sub-intervals can be obtained by multiplying each of the sub-interval probabilities of not failing, that is

$$\text{probability of not failing in time } T = \left(\frac{n - N}{n}\right)^{n}$$

As the sub-interval δT becomes small, that is $\delta T \to 0$, the number of sub-intervals, n, becomes large, that is $n \to \infty$. Hence we need to consider the quantity

$$\lim_{n \to \infty} \left(\frac{n - N}{n}\right)^{n}$$

This limit can be shown to be e^{-N} (see Appendix IV). Hence

$$\text{probability of not failing in time } T = \mathrm{e}^{-N}$$

Finally, the probability of an item failing one or more times – items can be repaired and fail again – in the time interval T is given by

$$P(T) = 1 - \mathrm{e}^{-N} = 1 - \mathrm{e}^{-kT}$$

$P(T)$ is the probability of at least one failure in the time period T. As a consequence of the constancy of k, this formula can be used to calculate the probability of an item failing one or more times in an arbitrary time period, t, in which case

$$P(t) = 1 - \mathrm{e}^{-kt} \tag{29.1}$$

It is important to stress that this formula only applies if the probability of failure is evenly distributed.

Example 29.30

A factory process line makes use of 12 controllers to maintain process variables at their correct values; all 12 controllers need to be working in order for the process line to be operational. Records show that each controller fails, on average, once every six months. Calculate the probability of the process line being stopped as a result of a controller failure within a time period of one month.

Solution

The mean failure rate of each controller is 1/6 breakdowns per month. Given that there are 12 controllers the overall failure rate for controllers is $12/6 = 2$ breakdowns per month. Using Equation (29.1) with $k = 2$ and $t = 1$ gives the probability, $P(t)$, of the process line being stopped because of a controller failure within a period of one month as

$$P(t) = 1 - e^{-kt} = 1 - e^{-2} = 0.865$$

So far we have ignored the 'downtime' associated with an item waiting to be repaired after it has failed. This can be a significant factor with many engineering systems. The simplest possibility is that an item is out of action for a fixed period of time T_r while it is being repaired. If there are N failures during a period T then the total downtime is NT_r. The time the item is available, T_a, is given by

$$T_a = T - NT_r$$

A useful quantity is the **fractional dead time**, D, which is the ratio of the mean time the item is in the dead state to the total time. In this case

$$D = \frac{NT_r}{T} \tag{29.2}$$

Another useful quantity is the **availability**, A, which is the ratio of the mean time in the working state to the total time. For the present model

$$A = \frac{T - NT_r}{T} = 1 - D$$

The failure rate model developed previously was based on the time the item was working rather than the total time. When the repair time is included k becomes

$$k = \frac{N}{T_a}$$

and so

$$N = kT_a = k(T - NT_r)$$
$$N + kNT_r = kT$$

and therefore

$$N = \frac{kT}{1 + kT_r}$$

So using Equation (29.2)

$$D = \frac{kT}{1 + kT_r}\frac{T_r}{T} = \frac{kT_r}{1 + kT_r}$$

Also

$$A = 1 - D = 1 - \frac{kT_r}{1 + kT_r} = \frac{1}{1 + kT_r} \tag{29.3}$$

For more complicated repair characteristics the equations for D and A are correspondingly more complicated.

Example 29.31

The electrical supply to a large factory has a mean time between failures of 350 hours. When the supply fails it takes 3 hours to repair the failure and restore the supply. Calculate the average availability of the electrical supply to the factory.

Solution

Failure rate of the supply is k where $k = 1/350$ failures per hour. Using Equation (29.3) with $T_r = 3$ hours gives

$$A = \frac{1}{1 + 3/350} = 0.992 \qquad \text{that is, } 99.2\%$$

The supply is up and running for 99.2% of the time.

So far we have only examined systems in which failure was caused by one or more components each with the same failure rate or *MTBF*. A more common situation is one in which the different components of a system have different degrees of reliability. It is still useful to be able to calculate the overall reliability of the system although the analysis is more complicated. In order to do so it is necessary to define the term reliability. From Equation (29.1) we know that $P(t)$ defines the probability of one or more failures during a time period, t. Therefore the probability of no failures is given by $1 - P(t)$. The quantity $1 - P(t)$ is called the **reliability** of the system during a time period t, and is denoted $R(t)$, that is

$$R(t) = 1 - P(t) = e^{-kt} \tag{29.4}$$

$R(t)$ can be interpreted as the probability a component works properly during a period t. We now examine the reliability of two simple system configurations.

29.15.1 Series system

A **series system** is one in which all the components of a system must operate satisfactorily if the system is to function correctly. Consider a system consisting of three components, shown in Figure 29.23. The reliability of the system is the product of the reliabilities of the individual components, that is

$$R = R_A R_B R_C \tag{29.5}$$

This formula is a direct consequence of the fact that the failure of any one of the components is an independent event. So the probability of the system not failing, that is its reliability, is the product of the probabilities of each of the components not failing. (See Section 28.7 for independent events.)

Figure 29.23
Series system.

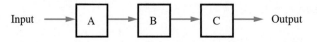

Input → A → B → C → Output

Example 29.32

A radio system consists of a power supply, a transmitter/amplifier and an antenna. During a 1000 hour period the reliability of the various components is as follows:

$$R_{ps} = 0.95$$
$$R_{ta} = 0.93$$
$$R_a = 0.99$$

Calculate the overall reliability of the radio system.

Solution

$$R = R_{ps} R_{ta} R_a = 0.95 \times 0.93 \times 0.99 = 0.87$$

that is, there is an 87% chance that the radio will not fail during a 1000 hour period.

Using Equations (29.4) and (29.5) it is possible to generate a formula for the reliability of a system consisting of n series components.

$$R = e^{-k_1 t} e^{-k_2 t} \ldots e^{-k_n t} = e^{-(k_1 + k_2 + \cdots + k_n)t}$$

where $k_1, k_2, \ldots, k_n$ are the mean failure rates of the n components.

Example 29.33

A satellite link is being used to transmit television pictures from America to England. The components of this system are the television studio in New York, the transmitter ground station, the satellite and the receiver ground station in London. The *MTBF* of each of the components is as follows:

$$MTBF_{ts} = 1000 \text{ hours}$$
$$MTBF_{tgs} = 2000 \text{ hours}$$
$$MTBF_s = 500\,000 \text{ hours}$$
$$MTBF_{rgs} = 5000 \text{ hours}$$

Calculate the overall reliability of the system during a 28 day period and a yearly period of 365 days.

Solution

First we calculate the mean failure rate of each of the components.

$$k_{ts} = \frac{1}{1000} = 1 \times 10^{-3} \text{ failures per hour}$$

$$k_{tgs} = \frac{1}{2000} = 5 \times 10^{-4} \text{ failures per hour}$$

$$k_s = \frac{1}{500\,000} = 2 \times 10^{-6} \text{ failures per hour}$$

$$k_{rgs} = \frac{1}{5000} = 2 \times 10^{-4} \text{ failures per hour}$$

So the overall reliability of the system is

$$R = e^{-(k_{ts}+k_{tgs}+k_s+k_{rgs})t} = e^{-(1\times10^{-3}+5\times10^{-4}+2\times10^{-6}+2\times10^{-4})t}$$

$$= e^{-1.702\times10^{-3}t}$$

For $t = 28 \times 24$ hours, $R = 0.319$.
For $t = 365 \times 24$ hours, $R = 3.35 \times 10^{-7}$. Clearly during a yearly period the system is almost certain to fail at least once.

29.15.2 Parallel system

A **parallel system** is one in which several components are in parallel and all of them must fail for the system to fail. The case of three components is shown in Figure 29.24. The probability of all three components failing in a time period, t, is the product of the individual probabilities of each component failing, that is $(1 - R_A)(1 - R_B)(1 - R_C)$. So the overall system reliability is

$$R = 1 - (1 - R_A)(1 - R_B)(1 - R_C)$$

This formula can be generalized to the case of n components in parallel quite easily.

Figure 29.24
Parallel system.

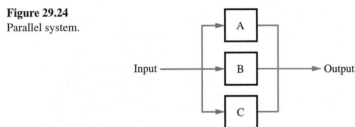

Example 29.34

A process control computer is supplied by two identical power supplies. If one fails then the other takes over. The *MTBF* of the power supplies is 1000 hours. Calculate the reliability of the power supply to the computer during a 28 day period. Compare this with the reliability if there is no standby power supply.

Solution

$$k = \frac{1}{1000} = 0.001 \text{ failures per hour}$$

$$R_{ps} = e^{-kt} = e^{-0.001\times24\times28} = 0.511$$

Therefore the overall reliability of the power supply to the computer is

$$R = 1 - (1 - 0.511)(1 - 0.511) = 0.761$$

Clearly the existence of a standby power supply does improve the reliability of the power supply to the computer. In practice, the figure would be much higher than this because once a power supply failed the standby would take over and maintenance engineers would quickly repair the failed power supply. Therefore the period of time in which the computer was relying on one power supply would be very small.

We have only examined the simplest possible reliability models. In practice, reliability engineering can often be very complicated. Some models can cater for maintenance strategies of the sort we touched on in the previous example. The effect of non-uniform failure rates can also be catered for. Also, many systems consist of a mixture of series and parallel subsystems of the type we have discussed as well as more complicated failure modes than we have examined.

Exercises 29.15

1   A computer contains 20 circuit boards each with an *MTBF* of 3 months. Calculate the probability that the computer will suffer a circuit board failure during a monthly period.

2   Three pumps are required to feed water to a boiler in a power station in order for it to be fully operational. The *MTBF* of each of the pumps is 10 days. Calculate the probability that the boiler will not be fully operational during a monthly period if there are only three pumps available.

3   A process control computer has a power supply with an *MTBF* of 600 hours. If the power supply fails then it takes 2 hours to replace it. Calculate the average availability of the computer power supply.

4   A radar station has an *MTBF* of 1000 hours. The average repair time is 10 hours. Calculate the average availability of the radar station.

5   A process line to manufacture bread consists of four main stages: mixing of ingredients, cooking, separation and finishing, packaging.

Each of the stages has an *MTBF* of

$$MTBF_m = 30 \text{ hours}$$
$$MTBF_c = 10 \text{ hours}$$
$$MTBF_{sf} = 20 \text{ hours}$$
$$MTBF_p = 15 \text{ hours}$$

Calculate the probability that the process line will be stopped during an 8 hour shift.

6   A remote water pumping station has two pumps. Only one pump is needed in normal operation; the other acts as a standby. Access to this station is difficult and so if a pump fails it is not easy to repair it immediately. Given that the *MTBF* of the pumps is 3000 hours, calculate the overall reliability of the pumping station during a 28 day period in which the maintenance engineers are unable to repair a pump which fails. Calculate the improvement in reliability that would be obtained if a second standby pump was installed in the pumping station.

7   Repeat the calculation carried out in Question 6 with the following information. The pumps, which are different from those in Question 6, can be considered to consist of two components: a motor and the pump itself. The *MTBF* of the motors is 4000 hours and that of the pumps is 6000 hours.

Solutions

1   0.999

2   0.9998

3   0.9967

4   0.9901

5   0.865

6   0.960, 0.992

7   0.940, 0.985

Review exercises 29

1 Find the mean and standard deviation of

$$8, 6.9, 7.2, 8.4, 9.6, 10.3, 7.4, 9.0$$

2 A discrete random variable, v, has a probability distribution given by

v	-2	-1.5	-1	-0.5	0	0.5	1.0
$P(v)$	0.23	0.17	0.06	0.03	0.17	0.31	0.03

Calculate
(a) $P(v = -1)$ (b) $P(v = -2 \text{ or } v = 0)$
(c) $P(v \geqslant 0)$ (d) $P(v < -0.5)$

3 A continuous random variable, x, has a p.d.f., $f(x)$, given by

$$f(x) = 3x^2 \qquad 0 \leqslant x \leqslant 1$$

(a) Find $P(0 \leqslant x \leqslant 0.5)$.
(b) Find $P(x > 0.3)$.
(c) Find $P(x < 0.6)$.
(d) Find the expected value of x.
(e) Find the standard deviation of x.

4 A discrete random variable, y, has a probability distribution given by

y	-0.25	0.25	0.75	1.25	1.75
$P(y)$	0.25	0.20	0.10	0.15	0.30

(a) Find the expected value of y.
(b) Find the standard deviation of y.

5 The random variable, t, has a p.d.f., $H(t)$, given by

$$H(t) = \lambda e^{-\lambda t} \qquad t \geqslant 0$$

(a) Calculate the expected value of t.
(b) Calculate the standard deviation of t.

6 Calculate the number of permutations of

(a) five distinct objects, taken two at a time
(b) eight distinct objects, taken four at a time

7 Calculate the number of combinations of

(a) seven distinct objects, taken four at a time

(b) 200 distinct objects, taken 198 at a time

8 The probability a component is manufactured to an acceptable standard is 0.92. Twelve components are picked at random. Calculate the probability that

(a) six are acceptable
(b) 10 are acceptable
(c) more than 10 are acceptable
(d) at least two are not acceptable

9 The number of breakdowns of a computer system in a month is a random variable with a Poisson distribution. The mean number of breakdowns per month is two. Calculate the probability that the number of breakdowns of the system in a month is

(a) two
(b) three
(c) one
(d) more than two

10 The probability of a computer failing in a system in a given week is 0.03. In a system there are 150 computers.

(a) Use the binomial distribution to calculate the probability that in a given week five computers fail.
(b) Use the binomial distribution to calculate the probability that in a given week more than two computers fail.
(c) Use the Poisson approximation to calculate the probability that in a given week four computers fail.
(d) Use the Poisson approximation to calculate the probability that in a given week more than three computers fail.

11 A random variable, t, has a uniform distribution, $f(t)$, given by

$$f(t) = \begin{cases} \frac{1}{4} & 0 < t < 4 \\ 0 & \text{otherwise} \end{cases}$$

Calculate the probability that
(a) $1 \leqslant t \leqslant 3$ (b) $0.2 \leqslant t \leqslant 2.7$
(c) $|t| > 1$ (d) $|t| \leqslant 1.5$

12 The time, t, between failures for a particular type of electrical component follows an exponential distribution with a mean value of 24 weeks. Calculate the probability that

(a) $t > 24$ (b) $t < 22$

13 The resistance of resistors is a random variable with a normal distribution with a mean of 3 ohms and a standard deviation of 0.1 ohm. Calculate the probability that a resistor has a resistance of

(a) between 2.9 and 3.05 ohms

(b) more than 2.95 ohms

(c) less than 2.83 ohms

14 The capacitance of capacitors is a random variable with a normal distribution, with a mean of 12 farads and a standard deviation of 0.6 farads. In a batch of 300 capacitors how many would you expect to have with capacitance

(a) between 11 and 12.3 farads

(b) more than 11.6 farads

(c) less than 12.8 farads?

15 A computer fails, on average, once every 4 months. An engineering system uses nine computers, all of which need to be working for the system to operate. Calculate the probability that the system will fail sometime during

(a) a 1 month period

(b) a 2 week period (i.e. half a month)

16 The *MTBF* for a motor is 270 hours. When the motor fails it takes 7 hours to repair. Calculate the availability of the motor.

17 A system comprises four components in series. The *MTBF* for each component is 170 hours, 200 hours, 250 hours and 210 hours. Calculate the reliability of the system over a 100 hour period.

18 A system comprises two components in parallel. The components have an *MTBF* of 150 hours and 170 hours. Calculate the probability the system will fail in a 200 hour period.

Solutions

1 mean $= 8.35$; st. dev. $= 1.1314$

2 (a) 0.06   (b) 0.4   (c) 0.51
(d) 0.46

3 (a) 0.125   (b) 0.973   (c) 0.216
(d) 0.75   (e) 0.194

4 (a) 0.775   (b) 0.799

5 (a) $\dfrac{1}{\lambda}$ (b) $\dfrac{1}{\lambda}$

6 (a) 20   (b) 1680

7 (a) 35   (b) 19 900

8 (a) 1.4687×10^{-4}

(b) 0.1835

(c) 0.7513

(d) 0.2487

9 (a) 0.2707   (b) 0.1804   (c) 0.2707
(d) 0.3233

10 (a) 0.1736   (b) 0.8307   (c) 0.1898
(d) 0.6577

11 (a) 0.5   (b) 0.625   (c) 0.75
(d) 0.375

12 (a) 0.3679   (b) 0.6002

13 (a) 0.5328   (b) 0.6915   (c) 0.0446

14 (a) 193   (b) 225   (c) 272

15 (a) 0.8946   (b) 0.6753

16 0.9747

17 0.1402

18 0.5093

Appendices

Appendix | Contents

Appendix	Contents	
Appendix I	Representing a continuous function and a sequence as a sum of weighted impulses	954
Appendix II	The Greek alphabet	956
Appendix I	SI units and prefixes	956
Appendix I	The binomial expansion of $\left(\frac{n-N}{n}\right)^n$	954

Figure AI.1
The limit of the
rectangle function is
the delta function.

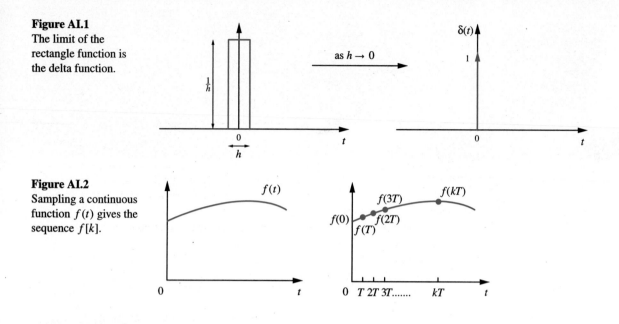

Figure AI.2
Sampling a continuous
function $f(t)$ gives the
sequence $f[k]$.

Representing a continuous function and a sequence as a sum of weighted impulses

In this appendix we show how a continuous function, $f(t)$, or a discrete sequence, $f[k]$, obtained by sampling this function, can be represented as a sum of weighted impulses. Such a representation is important in the study of the z transform and the discrete Fourier transform.

The delta function

The delta function is introduced in Chapter 2. For ease of reference we restate its development here. The delta function $\delta(t)$, or unit impulse function, is the limit of a rectangle function bounding an area of 1 unit, and located at the origin, as its width approaches zero, and its height increases accordingly to ensure that the area remains 1. The enclosed area is known as the strength, or the weight, of the impulse. This is illustrated in Figure AI.1. Note that the impulse is represented by an arrow and the height of the arrow gives the strength of the impulse. If the impulse occurs at the point $t = d$, then this is written $\delta(t - d)$. Further, by multiplying the delta function by a number A, to give $A\delta(t)$, we obtain the limit of a rectangle function bounding an area of A. This is an impulse of strength A.

Sampling a continuous function

Now consider a function $f(t)$ defined for $t \geqslant 0$ as shown in Figure AI.2. Suppose this function is sampled at times $t = 0, T, 2T, 3T, \ldots, kT, \ldots$, to generate a sequence of values $f(0), f(T), f(2T), f(3T), \ldots, f(kT), \ldots$, which we shall write as $f[0]$, $f[1]$, $f[2]$, $f[3], \ldots, f[k], \ldots$.

Note from the discussion above that the quantity $f[0]\delta(t)$ is the limit of a rectangle

Figure AI.3
The area under $f(t)$ can be approximated by a series of rectangular areas.

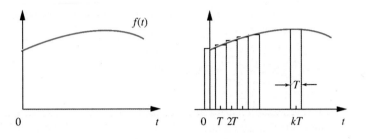

function located at the origin and bounding an area equal to $f[0]$.

Similarly, $f[1]\delta(t - T)$ is the limit of a rectangle function bounding an area equal to $f[1]$ and located at $t = T$.

In general $f[k]\delta(t - kT)$ is the limit of a rectangle function bounding an area equal to $f[k]$ and located at $t = kT$.

The quantity

$$\sum_{k=0}^{\infty} f[k]\delta(t - kT)$$

is a series of delta functions. The area bounded by these is given by

$$\text{area} = f[0] + f[1] + f[2] + \cdots + f[k] + \cdots, \qquad \text{that is } \sum_{k=0}^{\infty} f[k] \quad (AI.1)$$

Approximating the area under a curve

Now consider approximating the area under the continuous function $f(t)$ by a series of rectangular areas as shown in Figure AI.3. The first rectangle has width T and height $f(0)$ and so its area is $Tf(0)$. Using our sampling notation this may be written $Tf[0]$. Similarly, the second rectangle has width T and height $f(T)$ and so its area is $Tf(T)$. Using the sampling notation this is written $Tf[1]$. The third rectangle has area $Tf[2]$ and so on. The total area is thus given by

$$\text{area} = Tf[0] + Tf[1] + Tf[2] + \cdots + Tf[k] + \cdots = T\sum_{k=0}^{\infty} f[k] \quad (AI.2)$$

Now compare Equations (AI.1) and (AI.2). If we multiply the series of delta functions by T we see that

$$T\sum_{k=0}^{\infty} f[k]\delta(t - kT)$$

will bound the same area as our approximation to the area under the graph of $f(t)$. In this sense we can regard

$$T\sum_{k=0}^{\infty} f[k]\delta(t - kT)$$

as an approximation to the function $f(t)$. We will denote this approximation by $\tilde{f}(t)$.

In summary, a continuous function $f(t)$ can be represented as a sum of weighted impulses each of strength $f[k]$ occurring at $t = kT$.

$$\tilde{f}(t) = T \sum_{k=0}^{\infty} f[k]\delta(t - kT)$$

This representation can also be thought of as a way of expressing a discrete sequence of values, $f[k]$, as a continuous function $\tilde{f}(t)$. This is useful when studying the z transform and the discrete Fourier transform. Sometimes it will be convenient to work without the factor T, in which case we define

$$f^*(t) = \sum_{k=0}^{\infty} f[k]\delta(t - kT)$$

It should be remembered that when using this form, f^* needs to be multiplied by the factor T in order to approximate the function $f(t)$.

Appendix II The Greek alphabet

A	α	alpha	I	ι	iota	P	ρ	rho
B	β	beta	K	κ	kappa	Σ	σ	sigma
Γ	γ	gamma	Λ	λ	lambda	T	τ	tau
Δ	δ	delta	M	μ	mu	Y	υ	upsilon
E	ε	epsilon	N	ν	nu	Φ	ϕ	phi
Z	ζ	zeta	Ξ	ξ	xi	X	χ	chi
H	η	eta	O	o	omicron	Ψ	ψ	psi
Θ	θ	theta	Π	π	pi	Ω	ω	omega

Appendix III SI units and prefixes

Throughout this book SI units have been used. Below is a list of these units together with their symbols.

Quantity	SI unit	Symbol		Prefix	Symbol
length	metre	m	10^{12}	tera	T
mass	kilogram	kg	10^{9}	giga	G
time	second	s	10^{6}	mega	M
frequency	hertz	Hz	10^{3}	kilo	k
electric current	ampere	A	10^{2}	hecto	h
temperature	kelvin	K	10^{1}	deca	da
energy	joule	J	10^{-1}	deci	d
force	newton	N	10^{-2}	centi	c
power	watt	W	10^{-3}	milli	m
electric charge	coulomb	C	10^{-6}	micro	μ
potential difference	volt	V	10^{-9}	nano	n
resistance	ohm	Ω	10^{-12}	pico	p
capacitance	farad	F			
inductance	henry	H			

Appendix IV The binomial expansion of $\left(\frac{n-N}{n}\right)^n$

Consider the binomial expansion of $\left(\dfrac{n-N}{n}\right)^n$.

$$\left(\frac{n-N}{n}\right)^n = \left(1 - \frac{N}{n}\right)^n$$

$$= 1 + n\left(-\frac{N}{n}\right) + \frac{n(n-1)}{2!}\left(-\frac{N}{n}\right)^2$$

$$+ \frac{n(n-1)(n-2)}{3!}\left(-\frac{N}{n}\right)^3 + \cdots$$

$$= 1 - N + \left(\frac{n-1}{n}\right)\frac{N^2}{2!} - \left(\frac{n-1}{n}\right)\left(\frac{n-2}{n}\right)\frac{N^3}{3!} + \cdots$$

$$= 1 - N + \left(1 - \frac{1}{n}\right)\frac{N^2}{2!} - \left(1 - \frac{1}{n}\right)\left(1 - \frac{2}{n}\right)\frac{N^3}{3!} + \cdots$$

Suppose now we let $n \to \infty$. We find

$$\lim_{n\to\infty}\left(\frac{n-N}{n}\right)^n = 1 - N + \frac{N^2}{2!} - \frac{N^3}{3!} + \cdots$$

But this is the power series expansion of e^{-N} (see Section 6.5). We conclude that

$$\lim_{n\to\infty}\left(\frac{n-N}{n}\right)^n = e^{-N}$$

In particular, note that if $N = -1$

$$\lim_{n\to\infty}\left(\frac{n+1}{n}\right)^n = e$$

Index

A

absorption laws in Boolean algebra 161
addition
    of algebraic fractions 18–20
    of complex numbers 307
    in inequalities 21–5
    in probability 882–6
    of vectors 203–6
adjoint matrix 259
algebraic fractions 14–21
    addition of 18–20
    division of 17–18
    equivalent 15–16
    multiplication of 17–18
    proper and improper 15
    in simplest form 16–17
    subtraction of 18–20
algebraic techniques 1–38
alternating current waveforms 113
amplitude modulation 741–3
amplitude of wave 110
analog simulation of differential equations 572–4
AND gate 159
angular frequency of wave 110
arbitray constant in differential equations 525
area under a curve, approximating 955–6
arithmetic mean 911
arithmetic progressions 179–80
arithmetic series, finite, sum of 185–7

armature-controlled d.c. motor 581–2
associative law
    in Boolean algebra 161
    in matrix algebra 238
    in set theory 154
    of vectors 203
asymptotes 58
attenuation in transmission lines 566
augmented matrix in simultaneous equations 265
automated vehicle, routing 204
auxillary equation in second order linear equations 552–6
availability in reliability engineering 946
average power of a signal 721
average value of function 456–9

B

back substitution in simultaneous equations 265
base
    of exponential functions 63
    of indices 2
    of logarithms 68
Bernoulli trials 927, 933
binary full-adder circuit 166
binomial distribution 927–31
    mean and standard deviation 929
    most likely number of successes 929–30

and Poisson distribution 932–3
    probability of successes from trials 928–9
binomial expansion 957
binomial theorem 190–4
bode plot of linear circuit 76–8
Boolean algebra 160–71
    laws of 161–2
    logical equivalence in 162–8
bounded sequences 181
branch currents in electrical networks 286

C

capacitance of concentric cable 431–3
capacitive reactance 419
capacitors
    and complex numbers 320–2
    current through 346
    discharge of 65–6, 627
    energy stored in 472–3
    in series, integration for 470
carrier signal 742
Cartesian components of vectors
Cartesian coordinate system
    and polar coordinates 138
    three dimensions 134–6
    two dimensions 132–4
cathode ray tube, electrical potential inside 788
chain rule in differentiation 368–70, 446

characteristic equation in
eigenvectors 276
charged particle, movement in
electric field 222
chord 335
circular convolution and Fourier
transform 774–80
circular correlation and Fourier
transform 782–5
closed interval 41
coding theory 891
codomain of sets 154
coefficients
in difference equations 655–6
matrix of simultaneous
equations 262–3
of polynomial equations 8
cofactor in matrices 256, 259
column vector 211
combinations 924–7
common difference in arithmetic
progressions 179
common ratio in geometric
progressions 180
communication theory and
probability 887–91
commutative law
in Boolean algebra 161, 167
in matrix algebra 238
in scalar product 219
in set theory 154
of vectors 203, 206, 207
complement laws in Boolean
algebra 161, 167
complementary events 886–7
complementary function in
differential equations
548, 550–7
inhomogeneous term in 566–8
complements in set theory 153–4
completeness in Fourier series 706
completing squares in quadratic
equations 10–11
complex frequency function 724
complex notation 721–4
complex numbers 301–32
addition 307
complex conjugate 304–5

complex plane, loci and regions
328–30
and De Moivre's theorem
322–8
division 308–9
exponential form of 316–18
graphical representation
310–11
and inverse Laplace transform
614–18
multiplication 307–8
operations with 306–10
phasors 318–22
capacitor 320–2
inductor 320
resistor 319–20
polar form 311–15
subtraction 307
and vectors 315–16
complex roots of polynomial
equations 12
complex translation theorem in z
transform 685–6
compound events in probability
878–80
concentric cable, capacitance of
431–3
conditional probability 892–7
conduction current 346
conservative fields in line
integrals 845–51
constant coefficient equations
549–50
continuous functions 49–50
area under a curve 955–6
in differentiation 338–9
integration of 477–8
sampling 954–5
as sum of weighted impulses
954–6
continuous random variables
expected value 917–18
probability density functions
908–11
standard deviation of 920–1
continuous signal, sampling by
difference equations
672–4
continuous spectra 741

convergences
of sequences 181
of series 188, 189
convolution
and Fourier transform
circular 774–80
discrete 770–80
linear 770–4
theorem
and Fourier transforms
749–55
in Laplace transform 618–21
coordinate frames 244–7
correlation and Fourier transform
755–8
discrete 780–5
cosecant 100
cosine 97–100
functions 101–3
odd and even 700–5
modelling waves using 110–20
cotangent 100
coupled equations 574
first order 575–6
coupled tanks 582–3
Cramer's rule 257–8
cross-correlation 755
curl of vector field 828–30
current through capacitor 346
cylindrical polar coordinates
142–5

D

De Moivre's theorem 322–8
De Morgan's laws in Boolean
algebra 161, 167
decibels and signal ratios 69–70
definite integrals 425–35
degree
of equations 9
of improper fractions 32
of polynomial functions 55
degrees 96–7
delay blocks in difference
equations 659
delta (unit impulse) function 90–2
Fourier transform of 745–6
integration in 474–7

Laplace transform of 644–5
sifting property of 475
as sum of weighted impulses
    954
denominator
in algebraic fractions 14, 15, 16
in improper fractions 32
in partial fractions 27–8, 30
of polynomial functions 58
dependent variables 44
in difference equations 653
derivation of discrete Fourier
    transform 763–5
derivatives
in differentiation 343, 348–50
    common forms 350–3
    higher 380–3
higher order 794–7
Laplace transform of 606–8
partial 789–94
see also partial derivatives
determinants
in evaluation of vector products
    226–7
in finding vector products
    256–7
in matrix algebra 253, 255–9
deviation 914
diagonal matrices 248
diagonally dominant coefficients
    in iteration 295
difference equations 179, 651–93
block diagram representation
    659–63
continuous signal, sampling
    672–4
definitions 652–7
    coefficient 655–6
    dependent and independent
        variables 653
    homogeneous and
        inhomogeneous 654–5
    linear and non-linear 653–4
    order 654
    solution of 653
and discrete-time controller
    663–5
numerical solutions of 665–7
rewriting 657–9

z transform 690–2
complex translation theorem
    685–6
definition 668–72
direct inversion of 688–9
first shift theorem 681–3
inversion of 686–9
and Laplace transform 674–9
linearity 680–1
mapping s plane 676–9
properties 680–6
second shift theorem 683–4
differential calculus 334
differential equations 521–95
analog simulation 572–4
definitions 522–8
    linearity 524–5
    order 523–4
Euler's method 584–8
    improved method 588–91
exact equations 535–8
first order linear 538–9
    integrating factor method
        539–46
higher order equations 574–8
numerical methods in 522, 584
partial 797–800
Runge-Kutta method of order 4
    592–4
second order linear 547–68
    complementary function
        550–7
        inhomogeneous term in
            566–8
    constant coefficient
        equations 549–50
    particular integral 557–66
separation of variables 529–33
    results involving 538
simple equations 528–9
solution of 525–7
state-space models 578–83
differentiation 333–63
average rate of change across
    interval 335
continuous and discontinuous
    functions 338–9
derivatives in 343
    higher 380–3

first principles 344–5, 350
graphical approach to 334–6
implicit 373–6
limits and continuity 336–9
as linear operator 353–60
logarithmic 376–8
maximum and minimum points
    388–97
Newton-Raphson method
    400–5
parametric 372–3
points of inflexion 397–400
rate of change at a point 335–6
    at general point 342–8
    at specific point 339–42
rules 366–72
    chain rule 368–70
    product rule 366–7
    quotient rule 367–8
of vectors 405–8
digital filtering 662
digital signal processing 662
diode characteristic, quadratic
    approximation 504
diode equation 66
diode-resistor circuit, in series
    403–4
direct current electrical network
    498–9
direct current motor,
    armature-controlled
    581–2
direct inversion of z transform
    688–9
direct transmission matrix 580
Dirichlet conditions 708
discontinuous functions 49–50
    in differentiation 338–9
discrete convolution and Fourier
    transform 770–80
discrete correlation and Fourier
    transform 780–5
discrete Fourier transform 759–62
    definition 759
    derivation of 762–5
    estimation with 765–7
    inverse transform 761–2
    matrix representation of 767–9
    properties 769–70

linearity 769
periodicity 769
Rayleigh's theorem 769
discrete random variables
    expected value 916–17
    in probability distributions
        907–8
    standard deviation of 919–20
discrete spectra 741
discrete-time controller 663–5
discrete-time filter 660
disjoint sets 152
disjunctive normal form (d.n.f.) in
        Boolean algebra 164,
        167
displacement current 346
distributions
    binomial 927–31
        mean and standard deviation
            929
        most likely number of
            successes 929–30
        and Poisson distribution
            932–3
        probability of successes from
            trials 928–9
    exponential 935–7
    normal 937–44
        non-standard normal 942–3
        standard normal 938–42
    Poisson 931–4
        and binomial distribution
            932–3
distributive law
    in Boolean algebra 161, 167
    in scalar product 219
    in set theory 154
divergence of vector field 824–8
    physical interpretation of
        gradient 825–7
divergence theorem in volume and
        surface integrals 866–7
division
    of algebraic fractions 17–18
    of complex numbers 308–9
        in polar form 313–14
    in indices 4
    in inequalities 21–5
domain

of functions 44
of sets 154
dominant poles in Laplace
        transform 643
double integrals 851–6
dynamic systems, differential
        equations in 522

E

e (irrational constant) 64, 68
echelon form in simultaneous
        equations 268
eddy current losses 791
eigenvalues 275–80
    solutions to linear
        homogeneous equations
        271–5
eigenvectors 281–5
electric charge, enclosed 861–2
electric current density 863–4
electric displacement 218
electric field
    strength 218
    work done by 839–40
electric flux and Gauss's law
        826–7
    surface integrals in 864
electric motor, energy used by
        430–1
electrical networks
    analysis 285–90
        using MATLAB 298
    direct current 498–9
electrical potential inside cathode
        ray tube 788
electrical system, second-order,
        risetime for 392–5
electrode coordinates 133–4
electromagnetism and vector
        calculus 833–4
electronic integrators 418–20, 572
electronic thermometer
        measurements 628–9
electrostatic potential 218
    vector fields in 822–3
elements in set theory 150
elements of area in differentiation
        954

empty sets 152
    in probability 882–3
end point of interval 41
energy
    dissipated in a resistor 490–1
    stored in capacitor 472–3
    used by electric motor 430–1
engineering functions 40–94
entropy 889
equal sets 151–2
equal vectors 203
equating coefficients of partial
        fractions 28–9
equations, degree of 9
equivalent fractions 15–16
error term in Taylor polynomials
        510
Euler's method in differential
        equations 584–8
    improved method 588–91
evaluation of partial fractions
        using specific values 28
even functions 700–5
    Fourier series of 714–16
events, in probability 876
exact differential equations 535–8
exclusive OR gate 164
expansion of matrix along first
        row 255
expected value
    in Poisson distribution 932
    of random variable 916–19
exponential decay 64–5
exponential distribution 935–7
exponential form of complex
        numbers 316–18
exponential functions 63–7
    and logarithm functions 71
exponential growth 64–5

F

factorial notation 41
factorization
    of partial fractions 27–8
    of quadratic equations 9–10
fast Fourier transforms 760–1
Fibonacci sequence 179

finite arithmetic series, sum of 185–7
finite geometric series, sum of 187–8
finite series 185
first harmonic 697
first law of indices 3
first order coupled equations 575–6
first order linear equations 535–47
  exact equations 535–8
  integrating factor method in 539–46
  separation of variables in 538
first order Taylor polynomials 800–3
fluid flow
  across surface 862–3
  along a pipe 143
  into a tank 355
fluid system, linear model for 358–60
flux, and surface integrals 862
folding in signal processing 750
force, resoving into two perpendicular directions 205
forces (two) acting on a body 204
Fourier coefficients 708, 712
Fourier series 706–17
  odd and even functions 714–16
Fourier synthesis 707
Fourier transform 731–86
  common transforms 735
  convolution 749–55
    circular 774–80
    discrete 770–80
    linear 770–4
  correlation 755–8
    circular 782–5
    discrete 780–5
    linear 780–2
  definitions 732–6
  discrete transform 759–62
  fast transforms 760–1
  and Laplace transform 747–9
  properties 736–41
    first shift theorem 737–9
    ,linearity 736–7

second shift theorem 739–40
  of special functions 744–7
    delta function 745–6
    periodic functions 746–7
  on spectra 741–3
  on $t-w$ duality principle 743–4
fractional dead time 946
fractional indices 7
fractions, partial see partial fractions
free variables in simultaneous equations 266
free vectors 203
functions
  argument of 43
  composition of 46–7
  concepts 42–54
  continuous and piecewise 49–50
  delta (unit impulse) 90–2
  exponential 63–7
  graph of 44–5
  hyperbolic 80–4
  inverse of 47–9
  logarithm 67–70
  many-to-one rule 45–6
  modulus 84–7
  of multiple variables see variables, multiple
  one-to-many rule 45
  one-to-one rule 45–6
  parametric definition 46
  periodic 50–1
  polynomial 54–8
  ramp 87–8
  rational 58–63
  and sets 154–6
  unit step 88–90
fundamental angular frequency 697
fundamental harmonic 697

G

Gaussian elimination in simultaneous equations 264–9
  back substitution in 265
Gauss's law 826–7

surface integrals in 864
Gauss-Seidel method of iteration 291, 292–3, 294, 295–6
general solution
  of difference equations 653
  to differential equations 525
generating function in Taylor polynomials 497
geometric progressions 180
geometric series, finite, sum of 187–8
gradient of vector field 819–24
  physical interpretation of 822–3
graphs
  of complex numbers 310–11
  of functions 44–5
  in log-log and log-linear scales 72–6
  of polynomial functions 55, 59
gravitational field, work done by 839
gravity feed water supply 499
Greek alphabet 956
Green's theorem on line and double integrals 857–9

H

half-range cosine series 718
half-range series 717–21
half-range sine series 718
Hall effect in semiconductor 228–9
harmonics 696
higher order derivatives 794–7
homogeneous difference equations 654–5
homogeneous second order linear equations 547
hyperbolic functions 80–4
hyperbolic identities 82

I

identity laws in Boolean algebra 161, 167
identity matrices 248–9
impedance 419
implicit differentiation 373–6

impossible events 882–3
improper fractions 15
    in partial fractions 32–3
improper integrals 469–74
impulse response of system 91–2
inclusive OR gate 164–5
indefinite integrals 425–35
independent variables 44, 59
    in difference equations 653
indices 2–8
    division in 4
    fractional 7
    multiple 6
    multiplication in 3
    negative 5–6
inductor
    and complex numbers 320
    voltage across 346
inequalities, solution of 21–6
infinite sequences 181
infinite series 185
    sum of 188–9
information in communication
        theory 888
inhomogeneous equations
    difference equations 654–5
    second order linear 547
        and complementary function
            566–8
initial conditions in differential
        equations 527
input matrix 580
input vectors 580
integers 40
integral properties of odd and
        even functions 703–5
integrals
    double 851–6
        and Green's theorem 857–9
    Laplace transform of 606–8
    line
        evaluation of
            in two dimensions 841–3
    line 838–51
        around closed loop 848–50
        conservative fields 845–51
        evaluation of
            in three dimensions
                844–5

potential function 846–8
    and Maxwell's equations 871–2
    triple 857
    volume and surface 860–6
        and divergence theorem
            866–7
        and Stoke's theorem 867–70
integrating factor method in first
        order linear equations
        539–46
integration 411–38
    average value of function 456–9
    common functions 414
    constant of 411
    definite and indefinite integrals
        425–35
    delta function 474–7
    dummy variables in 433–4
    electronic 418–20
    improper integrals 469–74
    as linear operator 416–18
    numerical 483–94
    on orthogonal functions 466–9
    using partial fractions 449–51
    by parts 440–6
    of piecewise continuous
            functions 477–8
    region of 851
    root mean square of function
        459–63
    Simpson's rule 488–93
        error due to 491–2
    by substitution 446–9
    techniques 439–53
    trapezium rule 484–8
        error due to 486–7
    of trigomometric functions
        420–2
    of vectors 478–9
intersection in set theory 152
interval of convergence of power
        series 195
intervals 40–2
inverse discrete Fourier transform
        761–2
inverse hyperbolic functions 82–3
inverse Laplace transform 608–11
    and complex numbers 614–18
    partial fractions in 612–14

inverse of functions 47–9
inverse trigomometric functions
        102–3
inversion of z transform 686–9
irrational numbers 41
iterative techniques 196–8
    in differentiation 401
    on simultaneous equations
        291–7

J

Jacobi's method of iteration
        291–2, 293–4, 295–6

K

Kirchoff's voltage law 56, 286,
        288, 395, 550, 565, 725
Kronecker delta sequence 178,
        668

L

Laplace transform 597–649
    of common functions 599–601
    convolution theorem 618–21
    definition 598–9
    of delta function 644–5
    of derivatives and integrals
        606–8
    and Fourier transform 747–9
    inverse transforms 608–11
        and complex numbers
            614–18
        partial fractions in 612–14
    on linear constant coefficient
            differential equations
            621–31
    of periodic function 646–7
    poles 640–3
    properties 601–6
        final value theorem 605
        first shift theorem 603–4
        linearity 602
        second shift theorem 604–5
    s plane 641, 644
    transfer functions 631–40
        negative feedback loop,
            eliminating 635–40

in series 634–5
and z transform 674–9
zeros 640–3
Laplace's equation 798–9
LCR circuits 549–50
  with sinusoidal input 560–1
limits
  in differentiation 336–9
    left and right hand 338
  in integration 426–7
line integrals
  evaluation of
    in two dimensions 841–3
line integrals 838–51
  around closed loop 848–50
  conservative fields 845–51
  evaluation of
    in three dimensions 844–5
  and Green's theorem 857–9
  potential function 846–8
linear circuit, bode plot of 76–8
linear constant coefficient
        differential equations,
        Laplace transform on
        621–31
linear convolution and Fourier
        transform 770–4
linear correlation and Fourier
        transform 780–2
linear dependence of vectors
        215–16
linear difference equations 653–4
linear equations 196
linear factors of partial fractions
        27–9
linear independence of vectors
        216
linear operator
  differentiation as 353–60
  integration as 416–18
linear system, frequency response
        of 724–7
linear time-invariant systems 550
linearity
  in differential equations 524–5
  of discrete Fourier transform
        769
  in Fourier transforms 736–7
  of Laplace transform 602

of z transform 680–1
linearization using first-order
        Taylor polynomials
        496–501
load line in diode-resistor circuit
        403–4
logarithm functions 67–70
  and exponential functions 71
  log-log and log-linear scales
        72–6
logarithmic differentiation 376–8
logic 158–60
logical equivalence in Boolean
        algebra 162–8
log-linear scales 72–6
log-log scales 72–6
loss-less transmission lines 566
lower bound of set 42
lowest common denominator
        (l.c.d.) 18
low-pass filter 666–7
  Fourier series on 725–7

M

Maclaurin series 513–18
magnetic field due to moving
        charge 227–8
magnetic flux density and field
        strength 227
magnitude of vectors 202
many-to-one functions 45–6, 102
mapping in set theory 154
mass of solid object 860–1
MATLAB 297–8, 584, 761, 766
matrix algebra 235–300
  addition 237–8
  computer solutions 297–8
  Cramer's rule 257–8
  definitions 236–7
  inverse of
    2×2 matrix 251–5
    3×3 matrix 259–60
    finding 252–3
    row operations in 269–70
  multiplication 239–42
  in simultaneous equations
        261–4
  subtraction 237–8

maximum points 789
  in differentiation 388–97
  in two variables 808–13
Maxwell's equations 833–4
  volume and surface integrals
        871–2
mean time between failures 945,
        949
mean value 911–13
  of binomial distribution 929
mesh current vector 231
mesh in electrical networks 286
minimization laws in Boolean
        algebra 161
minimum points 789
  in differentiation 388–97
  in two variables 808–13
modulation signal 742
modulus
  of complex numbers 311–12
  functions 84–7
  of vectors 202
moving averages 662
multiple indices 6
multiplication
  of algebraic fractions 17–18
  of complex numbers 307–8
    in polar form 313–14
  in indices 3
  in inequalities 21–5
  in probability 892–7
  of vectors 208–9
mutually exclusive events in
        probability 882–6

N

NAND gate 160
natural logarithms 68
natural numbers 41
negative feedback loop,
        eliminating 635–40
negative indices 5–6
negative vectors 202–3
Newton-Raphson method
  in differentiation 400–5
  of iteration 198
node voltage method in electrical
        networks 288, 295–6

non-linear equations
  difference equations 653–4
  differential equations 524
  iterative solution of 196–8
non-recursive difference equations
    654
non-singular matrices 253
non-standard normal normal
    distribution 942–3
non-trivial solutions to linear
    homogeneous equations
    272, 276, 281
NOR gate 160
normal distribution 937–44
  non-standard normal 942–3
  standard normal 938–42
normal probabilities, cumulative
    940–1
NOT gate 159–60
numbers 40–2
numerator
  in algebraic fractions 14, 15, 16
  in improper fractions 32
  of polynomial functions 58
numerical methods in differential
    equations 522, 584
numerical solutions of difference
    equations 665–7

O

oblique asymptotes 59
odd functions 700–5
  Fourier series of 714–16
Ohm's law 56, 395, 498, 725
one-to-many functions 45, 102
one-to-one functions 45–6
open interval 41
OR gate 158–9
order
  in difference equations 654
  in differential equations 523–4,
    578
origin in coordinate systems 132
orthogonal functions, integration
    of 466–9
orthogonal matrices 253–4
orthogonal vectors 209
orthogonality relations 705–6

oscilating sequences 181
output matrix 580
output vectors 580

P

parametric differentiation 372–3
Parseval's theorem 721, 769
partial derivatives 789–94
partial differential equations
    797–800
partial differentiation in vector
    calculus 818–19
partial fractions 27–34
  improper fractions in 32–3
  integration using 449–51
  in inverse Laplace transform
    612–14
  linear factors of 27–9
  quadratic factors of 31
  repeated linear factors of 29–30
partial sums, sequence of 188
particle, distance travelled 418
particular integral in differential
    equations 548, 557–66
particular solution in differential
    equations 526
parts, integration by 440–6
Pascal's triangle 190–1
periodic convolution and Fourier
    transform 774–5
periodic extension in half-range
    series 718
periodic functions 50–1
  Fourier transform of 746–7
  Laplace transform of 646–7
  sine and cosine as 110–11
periodic waveforms 696–700
periodicity in discrete Fourier
    transform 769
permittivity of free space 827
permutations 921–4, 926–7
phase angle of wave 112
phasors 318–22
  capacitor 320–2
  inductor 320
  resistor 319–20
piecewise continuous functions
    49–50

integration of 477–8
place signs in matrices 256
points of inflexion in
    differentiation 397–400
Poisson distribution 931–4
  and binomial distribution 932–3
Poisson process 933
Poisson's equation 832
polar coordinates 136–40
  and complex numbers 311–15
polar curves 140–2
  equation of a circle 141–2
  equation of a line 140–1
poles
  of function 59
  in Laplace transform 640–3
polynomial equations 8–14
  coefficients of 8
  complex roots of 12
  higher degree 12–13
  real roots of 12
  roots of 8
polynomial expressions in
    algebraic fractions 14
polynomial functions 54–8
  degree of 55
position control system,
    transverse functions on
    638–40
positive integers 41
postmultiplication in matrix
    algebra 242
potential function in line integrals
    846–8
potential theory 798–9
power dissipated in a resistor
    500–1
  in variable resistor 788–9
power series 194–6
power supply, to computer 879
power transfer, maximum 395–6
powers *see* indices
premultiplication in matrix
    algebra 242
probability 875–904
  and communication theory
    887–91
  complementary events 886–7
  complements 877–8

compound events 878–80
conditional 892–7
   multiplication law 895–6
density functions - continuous
   variable 908–11
distributions - discrete variable
   907–8
independent events 897–902
mutually exclusive events
   882–6
see also statistics
process control computers, linking
   922
product rule in differentiation
   366–7
proper algebraic fractions 15
Pythagoras's theorem 138

Q

quadratic equations 9–11
   completing squares 10–11
   formula for 10
quadratic factors of partial
   fractions 31
quotient rule in differentiation
   367–8

R

radians 96–7
radius of absolute convergence, in
   z transforms 668
radius of convergence of power
   series 195
ramp function 87–8
random variables 906–7
   expected value 916–19
      continuous variable 917–18
      discrete variable 916–17
   standard deviation of 919–21
range
   in sets 154
   of variables 44
rational functions 58–63
rational numbers 41
Rayleigh's theorem 769
RC circuits
   charging 523

zero-input and zero-state
   responses 542–5
real line 41
real numbers 41
real roots of polynomial equations
   12
rectifier, full-wave 86–7
recurrence relation 179
recursive difference equations 654
recursive sequences 179
reduction formula in integration
   443–4
redundancy 890
relations in set theory 154
reliability engineering 944–51
   parallel system 949–50
   series system 947–9
remainder term in Taylor
   polynomials 510–13
repeated linear factors of partial
   fractions 29–30
resistance, equivalent 60–1
resistors
   and complex numbers 319–20
   energy dissipated in 490–1
   power dissipated in 45, 500–1
risetime in waveforms 51
   in second-order electrical
      system 392–5
RL circuit
   with ramp input 541–2, 622–4
   with step input 532–3
RLC circuit 89
   parallel circuit 561–4
robots
   coordinate frames 244–7
   pick and place 136–7
   positions 214–15
rocket, distance travelled by
   485–6
root mean square
   of function 459–63
   of waveform 319
roots
   of non-linear equations 196
   of polynomial equations 8
      complex 12
      real 12
rotation of vectors 245–7

row operations in simultaneous
   equations 265
row vector 211
Runge-Kutta method of order 4
   differential equations
   592–4

S

s domain 633
s plane in Laplace transform 641,
   644
   mapping to z plane 676–9
saddle points 789
sample space, in probability 876
sawtooth waveform, average value
   457
scalar fields 217–18, 825
   gradient of 820–4
      physical interpretation 822–3
scalar product 219–24
scalars
   concepts 202–10
   multiplication of 238–9
secant 100
second law of indices 4
second order linear differential
   equations 547–68
   complementary function 550–7
   constant coefficient equations
      549–50
   inhomogeneous term in 547,
      566–8
   particular integral 557–66
second order Taylor polynomials
   803–6
semiconductor, Hall effect in
   228–9
semi-open interval 41
separation of variables in
   differential equations
   529–33
   results involving 538
sequences 176–85
   arithmetic progressions 179–80
   geometric progressions 180
   infinite sequences 181
   iterative solution of non-linear
      equations 196–8

as sum of weighted impulses 954–6
series 185–90
 transfer functions in 634–5
set theory 150–8
 algebra of, laws 154
 complements 153–4
 equal sets 151–2
 and functions 154–6
 intersection 152
 special symbols in 151
 subsets 153
 union 152–3
 Venn diagrams 152
sets 40
SI units and prefixes 956
sifting property of delta function 763
signal, average power of 721
signal analysis and Vandermonde matrix 269
signal processing
 Fourier transforms on 750
 on microprocessor 655, 660–2
signal ratios and decibels 69–70
simple differential equations 528–9
simple iteration 197
Simpson's rule in integration 488–93
 error due to 491–2
simultaneous equations
 back substitution in 265
 Gaussian elimination in 264–9
 inconsistent 266
 iterative techniques on 291–7
 solution of, matrix algebra on 261–4
sine 97–100
 functions 101–3
  odd and even 700–5
 modelling waves using 110–20
singular matrices 253
sinusoids 696
 linear combination of 697
skew symmetric matrices 249–50
small-angle approximations 195
small-signal resistance 356–7

solid object, mass of 860–1
spectra 741–3
spherical polar coordinates 145–7
square matrices 248
square waveforms 51
standard deviation 913–16
 of binomial distribution 929
 of continuous random variable 920–1
 of discrete random variable 919–20
standard normal normal distribution 938–42
state equations 578
state matrix 580
state vectors 231, 580
state-space models in differential equations 578–83
stationary points 808
statistics 905–52
 mean values 911–13
 random variables 906–7
  expected value 916–19
   continuous variable 917–18
   discrete variable 916–17
  standard deviation of 919–21
 standard deviation 913–16
 see also distributions; reliability engineering
steady state in RC circuits 545
Stoke's theorem in volume and surface integrals 867–70
substitution, integration by 446–9
subtraction
 of algebraic fractions 18–20
 of complex numbers 307
 in inequalities 21–5
 of vectors 206–8
summer circuit 572, 659
summing point in transfer functions 634
suppressed carrier amplitude modulation 743
surface integrals 860–6
symmetric matrices 249

take-off point in transfer functions 634
tangent 97–100, 335
 functions 101–3
Taylor polynomials
 linearization using first-order 496–501
 and more than one variables 800–8
  first order 800–3
  second order 803–6
 of nth order 506–10
 and remainder term 510–13
 second-order 501–6
Taylor series 513–18
 in two variables 806
telescope drive signal 88
third law of indices 6
thyristor firing circuit 458
time displacement of wave 112
time domain
 representation of waveforms 318–19
 and transfer functions 633–4
transfer functions 631–40
 negative feedback loop, eliminating 635–40
 in series 634–5
transients
 in RC circuits 545
 response 642
translation of vectors 245–7
transmission lines, differential equations on 564–6
transport lag, transverse functions on 637–8
transpose of matrix 249
trapezium rule in integration 484–8
 error due to 486–7
tree diagrams 880, 894
trial, in probability 876
triangle law of vectors 203
triangular waveforms 51
trigomometric equations 120–5

trigonometric functions 95–129
  integration of 420–2
trigonometric identities 104–10
trigonometric ratios 97–101
triple integrals 857
trivial solution to linear
      homogeneous equations
      272
truth tables 159, 162–3
turning points in differentiation
      388
t-w duality principle 743–4

U

unbounded sequences 181
unconditional probability 892
uniform distribution 934–5
union in set theory 152–3
unit impulse function *see* delta
      (unit impulse) function
unit ramp sequence 669–70
unit step function 88–90
unit step sequence 177, 668
unit vectors 209
universal set 152
upper bound
  of set 42
  in trapesium rule 486

V

Vandermonde matrix 269
variables 44
  in Boolean algebra 160
  multiple (more than one),
      functions of 787–815
  higher order derivatives
      794–7
  maximum and minimum
      points 808–13
  partial derivatives 789–94
  partial differential equations
      797–800

Taylor polynomials 800–8
  first order 800–3
  second order 803–6
  Taylor series 806
separation of in differential
      equations 529–33
  results involving 538
variance 914
  in Poisson distribution 932
vector fields 217–18
  calculus of 817–36
    combining operators 830–3
    and electromagnetism 833–4
  curl of 828–30
    combining operators 830–3
  divergence of field 824–8
    combining operators 830–3
    physical interpretation of
        gradient 825–7
  gradient of scalar field 819–24
    combining operators 830–3
    physical interpretation of
        822–3
  and line integrals 838
  partial differentiation of 818–19
vector products 224–30
  applications of 227–30
  determinants in finding 256–7
  evaluation of 226–7
vectors 201–33
  addition of 203–6
  Cartesian components of
      210–17
  and complex numbers 315–16
  concepts 202–10
  differentiation of 405–8
  equal 203
  integration of 478–9
  multiplication of 208–9
  n dimensions 230–1
  negative 202–3
  orthogonal 209
  subtraction of 206–8

translation and rotation of
      245–7
  unit 209
  zero 214–15
Venn diagrams 152
  in probability 878
virtual earth in electrical circuits
      420
voltage
  across capacitor 418
    Laplace transform of 607
  across inductor 346
  source, non-ideal 56
volume integrals 860–6

W

waves
  combining 113–17
  modelling using sine and cosine
      110–20
work done
  by electric field 839–40
  by a force 221–2
  by gravitational field 839
world coordinate frame 245

Z

z transform in difference
      equations 690–2
  complex translation theorem
      685–6
  definition 668–72
  direct inversion of 688–9
  first shift theorem 681–3
  inversion of 686–9
  and Laplace transform 674–9
  linearity 680–1
  mapping s plane 676–9
  properties 680–6
  second shift theorem 683–4
zero vectors 214–15
zeros in Laplace transform 640–3